The Series in Marketing

Assael, *Consumer Behavior and Marketing Action, Fourth Edition*
Davis/Cosenza, *Business Research for Decision Making, Third Edition*
Dommermuth, *Promotion: Analysis, Strategy, and Creativity, Second Edition*
Haas, *Business Marketing Management Text and Cases: An Organizational Approach, Fifth Edition*
Jain, *International Marketing Management, Fourth Edition*
Kashani, *Global Marketing Management: Cases and Text*
Wotruba/Simpson, *Sales Management: Text and Cases, Second Edition*

FOURTH • EDITION

International Marketing Management

Subhash C. Jain
The University of Connecticut

Wadsworth Publishing Company
Belmont, California
A Division of Wadsworth, Inc.

To *Aarti* and *Amit*

Production Editor: Susan M. C. Caffey
Manufacturing Coordinator: Marcia A. Locke
Interior/Cover Designer: Susan M. C. Caffey
Cover Art: Comstock, Inc.
Typesetter: Pine Tree Composition, Inc.
Cover Printer: John P. Pow Company, Inc.
Text Printer/Binder: Arcata Graphics/Martinsburg

This book is printed on acid-free recycled paper.

2 3 4 5 6 7 8 9 10—97 96 95 94 93

Library of Congress Cataloging-in-Publication Data

Jain, Subhash C.
International marketing management / Subhash C. Jain. — 4th ed.
p. cm.
Includes index.
ISBN 0-534-93288-6
1. Export marketing—Management. I. Title.
HF1416.J35 1993
658.8′ 48—dc20 92-31978
CIP

Brief Contents

Contents

Preface

The United States plays a leading role in world trade. In recent years, however, the international business environment has been marked by far-reaching changes that have challenged U.S. business. In the context of these changes, international marketing as a discipline of study achieves greater significance than ever before.

After decades of resting comfortably at the top, American business has awakened to a fiercely competitive world. As more countries become industrial powerhouses and their companies seek larger marketplaces, the United States will meet more and stronger competitors. Japan, the most potent of them all, is pushing into such American strongholds as biotechnology and supercomputers. Western Europe is coming up fast in aeronautics and office equipment. The newly industrialized countries—Taiwan, South Korea, Malaysia, Singapore, India, Brazil—are establishing themselves as low-cost producers of everything from steel to television sets. In addition, the United States may face new competition in Canada and Mexico as a result of the free-trade agreement the three countries are working on.

After many years, U.S. export performance is finally improving. With the domestic U.S. market stagnant and competition from foreign companies intense, it's the only way to stay in business. Many wonder, however, if it will last. Americans have a record of exporting when it is easy then retreating when conditions shift.

On the other hand, a variety of forces are establishing an export culture among U.S. export companies that should endure. Americans are now low-cost manufacturers after a long decline in both labor costs and the dollar and a rise in productivity. They also find themselves with a wealth of high-quality products that are often known around the world. English has spread as the *lingua franca* of global business, which lowers language barriers. Yet it is safe to say that America's leadership in some industries is probably gone for good. The United States may never be able to make a significant comeback in mass-manufactured commodities; among them, textiles, shoes, consumer electronics, and machine tools. But the more complex the product, the more likely America can hold its edge. The United States is still strong in such products as semiconductors (world market share: 40 percent), personal computers (70 percent) and jet engines (90 percent). Moreover, the United States remains the leading force in health care, entertainment, and financial services. To take on the world, however, U.S. industry must continue to fight hard to regain its prowess in the marketplace.

As the President's Task Force on International Private Enterprise notes: "Competition in the U.S. marketplace is no longer national, but international. American businesses that adapt to changing circumstances and recognize opportunities will prosper; those that do not will, at best, survive temporarily. . . ."

At the same time that American supremacy is being challenged, the powerful force of technology is driving the world toward a converging commonality: the emergence of global markets. Millions worldwide want all the things they have heard about, seen, or experienced via new communication technologies. To capitalize on this trend, American companies must learn to operate and compete globally, as if the world were one large market, ignoring superficial regional and national differences. Global markets offer unlimited opportunities. Corporations geared to this new reality can benefit from enormous economies of scale in production, distribution, marketing, and management. By translating these benefits into reduced world prices, they can dislodge competitors who still operate with the perspectives of the 1970s and 1980s. Today, only companies capable of changing their perspective and becoming global will achieve long-term success.

As more business battles cross borders, managers must broaden their view of markets and competition. Doing business in a global economy requires a lot of new learning—including how to find the right country in which to build a plant, how to coordinate production schedules across borders, and how to absorb research wherever it occurs. They must learn what sort of people to hire, how to inculcate a global mentality in the ranks, and when to sell standardized products instead of customizing them for local markets.

Only a few managers are capable of handling the competitive rigors of the new global marketplace. Companies, even those long-accustomed to doing business overseas, find it difficult to make their managers look beyond their own domain to consider the capabilities and needs of the company as a whole to serve the global marketplace. They struggle to reorient their managers to be global strategists.

Business schools across the country face a similar problem. They must focus on the development of business education programs that produce graduates able to understand and function effectively in today's global business environment.

For over a decade, the American Assembly of Collegiate Schools of Business (AACSB) has been offering seminars emphasizing how business schools may internationalize their curriculum. The U.S. Department of Education continues to provide funding for enhancing international business education. These kinds of support have helped many schools in adding international components to their existing courses, and in developing new international courses. Despite these efforts, in most business education programs insufficient attention is paid to the international dimension of business. A recent study[1] commissioned by AACSB on the future of management education and development summarizes the problem:

> International business is an area of the curriculum where we found a considerable amount of, at worst, lip service, and, at best, serious concern on the part of

[1]Lyman W. Porter and Lawrence E. McKibbin, *Management Education and Development: Drift or Thrust into the 21st Century?* (New York: McGraw-Hill Book Co., 1988), p. 85.

> deans and faculty (but, we should point out, *not* on the part of most corporate-sector respondents). It was one of the four specific areas most often mentioned in both interviews and on the surveys as needing more emphasis in the curriculum. The problem, as most acknowledged, is how to implement this—whether to do it through adding more specific courses on international business, international finance, international marketing, and the like, or by putting more emphasis on international issues in courses already in the curriculum. This whole area has been the object of much discussion within the business school community, and we probably cannot shed much additional light on the curriculum aspects of the matter except to say this: Although there seems to be an increasing awareness among business school deans and faculty that more ought to be done to emphasize this area, this awareness or sensitivity so far does not appear to us to have been translated into a great deal of action. More is being done now than ten years ago, and this seems clearly demonstrable by an examination of curricula and in interviews with knowledgeable observers, but much more needs to be done.

As business schools globalize their curriculum, a variety of specific international courses are being added to give students a worldwide perspective. Because of the deep impact of local customs and business practices on marketing, marketing requires separate exposure in the international context, more so than any other area of business. Many business schools now have international marketing courses at the undergraduate level, and some even at the graduate level. Many more schools are rapidly adding such courses.

This book is designed to enable readers to develop skills to make marketing decisions in the global context: how to find new markets to replace saturated markets, how to customize products for the demands of new markets, which products world customers want, how to best reach the customers, what pricing strategies are most appropriate, what distribution channels are adequate to serve the world customers, how to overcome barriers that hinder implementation of marketing programs, and so on. National marketing boundaries are gradually dissolving. Marketers must monitor and evaluate emerging developments in a holistic and systematic way to define the oppotunity for globalized marketing. Successful monitoring requires close communication and cooperation within and between organizations. The successful marketer should "think globally, act locally."

In addition to covering all important frameworks of marketing, the book briefly touches upon those concepts from other disciplines (for example, finance and accounting) that must be grasped to understand fully the perspective of conducting marketing across national boundaries. Throughout the book, a variety of examples are used to illustrate the points made. Important frameworks and theories are explained with quotes from original sources. The learning objectives are summarized at the beginning of each chapter. Included at the end of each part are cases that describe unique decision-making situations in international marketing. The cases provide adequate information for an intelligent and lively discussion, and should enhance the learning experience.

The following objectives guided preparation of the fourth edition: (a) to incorporate material on new developments (e.g., the status of the Uruguay Round and the North American Free-Trade Agreement); (b) to rearrange the material within the chapters for a better flow of ideas; (c) to include new cases reflecting a variety of international marketing situations; (d) to completely revise Chapter 11 to examine major global markets; (e) to strengthen the discussion on such topics as entry stategies, international trade, U.S. exports, and marketing planning and strategy; and (f) to update concepts, illustrations, and statistics. Accomplishment of the above objectives leads to the following distinguishing features of the fourth edition: (a) new and expanded material on various concepts, theories, and frameworks; (b) an in-depth look at the rôle played by international agreements and institutions in formulating global marketing strategies, including discussion of the progress of the Europe 1992 program; (c) a chapter on the global marketplace; (d) new and interesting examples, both from industrialized and developing nations, to illustrate the underlying concepts; (e) a stand-alone book suitable for students with relatively little background in marketing; (f) discussion of the latest round of GATT talks (i.e., the Uruguay Round) and of emerging issues (e.g., the fall of communism); (g) substantial revision of chapters on economic analysis of multinational trade and business, multinational sales management and foreign sales promotion, export management, and marketing planning and strategy for international business; (h) updating of statistics, illustrations, and references to provide the most current perspectives on the subject; (i) increase in the number of cases from twenty-two to thirty, three of which are comprehensive; (j) an *Instructor's Manual* with a variety of pedagogical aids: answers to the end-of-chapter discussion questions, true-false and multiple choice examination questions, a computerized test bank, transparency masters, solutions to cases, suggestions for further reading, and a listing of additional cases.

A new feature of the fourth edition is the inclusion of International Marketing Highlights. Spread throughout the book, the highlights describe interesting ideas, stories, and factual information relevant to marketing decisions.

The book has been developed based on the methodological and theoretical underpinnings developed in various social sciences. It also attempts to integrate major marketing paradigms and frameworks. In each case, the cultural, legal, political, and institutional implications of international operations are properly analyzed. The book successfully makes the reader an "informed observer" of the global marketplace.

A project like this cannot be completed without help and advice from different sources. I have been fortunate in having the counsel of many scholars who have contributed comments and criticism on previous editions. While it may not be feasible to recognize them all here, I would like to thank

Alan R. Andreasen, *University of Connecticut;* Catherine N. Axinn, *Syracuse University;* Claude Cellich, *International Trade Center (UNCTAD/GATT), Geneva;* Rajan Chandran, *Temple University;* John R. Darling, *Louisiana State University at Shreveport;* Gary N. Dicer, *University of Tennessee;* Louis V. Dominguez, *University of Miami;* Roberto Friedman, *University of Georgia;* Thomas Greer, *University of Maryland;* Sandra M. Huszagh, *University of Georgia;* Hugh E. Kramer, *University of Hawaii at Manoa;* Ravi Parameswaran, *Oakland*

University; Samuel Rabino, *Northeastern University;* Ram Rao, *Cleveland State University;* John K. Ryans, Jr., *Kent State University;* and Attila Yaprak, *Wayne State University.*

My special thanks are due to

Robert P. Allerheiligen, *Colorado State University;* S. Tamer Cavusgil, *Michigan State University;* Andrew Forman, *Hofstra University;* William Lesch, *Illinois State University;* Marilyn Liebrenz-Himes, *George Washington University;* Gerald Parkhouse, *Elmira College;* and Surendra Singh, *University of Kansas*

for meticulously reviewing the third edition and the revised manuscript and making useful comments. The fourth edition has been much improved because of their input.

I owe a great debt to my students at the University of Connecticut and the Graduate School of Business Administration, Zurich, for their patience and enthusiasm in working with the ideas and helping me clarify my thinking in innumerable ways.

I also want to thank the following individuals for their permission to include cases written by them:

Mohammed Ali Alireza, *University of San Diego;* Lyn S. Amine, *St. Louis University;* Vinod Bavishi, *The University of Connecticut;* Grady D. Bruce, *California State University, Fullerton;* Mary R. Brooks, *Dalhousie University;* Farok J. Contractor, *Rutgers University;* Ellen Cook, *University of San Diego;* James DeConinck, *University of Arkansas;* Hazel Ezell, *University of Alabama;* Pervez N. Ghauri, *Oslo Business School;* Philip Hunsaker, *University of San Diego;* Erdener Kaynak, *Pennsylvania State University at Harrisburg;* Mohammed Khan, *St. Louis University;* Kwangsu Kim, *The University of Connecticut;* Barry Masor, *University of Alabama;* Morris Mayer, *University of Alabama;* Gordon H. G. McDougall, *Wilfrid Laurier University;* C. P. Rao, *University of Arkansas;* Hany A. Shawky, *State University of New York at Albany;* and David K. Smith, Jr., *Michigan State University.*

I am indebted to Stephen M. Walsh, State University of New York College at Oneonta, for contributing 125 objective questions to the *Instructor's Manual.*

A special mention of appreciation must go to my doctoral student Kiran Ahluwalia, and especially to my graduate assistant, Teresa Grusauskas, for coordinating various revision chores and for typing portions of the manuscript. I would like to thank my secretary, Mary Palmer, and student helper, Kathy Vitale, for their administrative support. I also acknowledge the assistance of Norma Holmquist at the University of Connecticut's Trecker Library in Hartford. I am thankful to many writers and publishers for granting me the permission to include excerpts from their works. Acknowledgement is due to John O'Connor, State Director, and Joan Bowley, Administrative Assistant, of the Connecticut Small Business Development Center, for their support and administrative help.

The talented staff at PWS-KENT Publishing Company deserves praise for their role in shaping the fourth edition. My editor, Al Bruckner, offered excellent advice and direction on the structure of the fourth edition, and his editorial assistant, Rosella Romagnoli, did a superb job of coordination. My production editor, Sue Caffey, did an excellent job of managing the manuscript to completion.

I want to thank my former dean, Ronald J. Patten, now at DePaul University, who initially encouraged me to write this book, and my former professor, Stuart U. Rich of the University of Oregon, who continues to influence my thinking through his writings.

Finally, my thanks go to my wife and our children, Aarti and Amit, who have put up with me through the hectic times of book revision. They provided the time, support, and inspiration so necessary to complete a project of this nature.

Subhash C. Jain
Storrs, Connecticut

PART • I

Framework of International Marketing

CHAPTER • 1

Aspects of International Marketing

CHAPTER FOCUS

After studying this chapter, you should be able to:

- Explain the growing importance of international business
- Describe how international marketing differs from domestic marketing
- Discuss the significant role of multinational corporations in the expansion of business on an international scale
- Compare alternative entry routes into foreign markets

One of the most significant economic developments since World War II is the increasing internationalization of business. Although business has been conducted across national boundaries for centuries, during the last four decades business dealings have escalated on a global scale. Leading corporations around the world have increasingly turned their attention to international business in order to maintain a competitive edge in today's dynamic economic scene.[1]

This global increase of international business affects the world economic order profoundly. It is a change with an impact comparable to that of the Industrial Revolution. In fact, today's global activity has been described as the second Industrial Revolution. Today's market provides not only a multiplicity of goods, but goods from many places. It is not surprising if your shirt comes from Taiwan, your jeans from Mexico, and your shoes from Italy. You may drive a Japanese car equipped with tires manufactured in France, nuts and bolts manufactured in India, and paint from a U.S. manufacturer (see International Marketing Highlight 1.1).

Gucci bags, Sony Walkmans, and McDonald's golden arches are seen on the streets of Tokyo, London, Paris, and New York. Thai goods wind up on U.S. grocery shelves as Dole canned pineapple and on French farms as livestock feed.

International Marketing Highlight 1.1

Do You Know Where Your Ford Was Made?

The 1992 Ford cars get controllers for their antilock brakes from Germany, engine computers from Spain, shock absorbers from Japan, and key axle parts from England. Windshields, instrument panels, seats, and fuel tanks are made in Mexico.

Source: Fortune, June 17, 1992, p. 53.

Briefly, worldwide consumers, particularly those in the developed countries, live in a global village. For example, young Europeans, Americans, and Japanese alike sport Benetton sweaters made in Italy, covet Japanese compact disk players, and haunt similar hangouts (see International Marketing Highlight 1.2).

Increasing competition and cost pressures are expected to further accelerate globalization in a variety of industries. As more business battles cross borders, companies must broaden their views of markets and competition and should develop global strategies to compete successfully in global markets.

America is irrevocably enmeshed in global business. We export some 20 percent of our industrial production, and we sell two out of five acres of our farm produce abroad. One out of every six jobs in U.S. manufacturing comes from exports. Almost one-third of U.S. corporate profits derives from international trade and foreign investment. The share of trade in the gross national product has more than doubled in the past decade. Considering our potential exposure to import penetration, more than three-fourths of U.S. goods are now effectively in international competition and more than half the supplies of twenty-four im-

International Marketing Highlight 1.2

Americanization of the World

Fifteen years ago, Japanese slept on mats in cotton quilts, shopped daily, grabbed a quick meal at a noodle shop, and drank green tea at breaks. Now they sleep in beds under sheets, shop once a week to fill their freezers, hit McDonald's for fast food, and have coffee and doughnuts at teatime.

Source: Kenichi Omhae, *Beyond National Borders* (Homewood, IL: Dow Jones–Irwin, 1987).

portant raw materials, ranging from petroleum to cobalt, come from foreign sources.

Briefly, a world view based on outmoded concepts of nationality and traditional antagonisms between nations and ethnic groups is not useful in today's environment. In fact, to dismiss such a view outright and consider the inhabitants of such countries as Japan, the European nations, and the United States as a single race of consumers with shared needs and aspirations is the first conceptual leap toward a pragmatic and productive businessperson's world view. This is critical, because recognition of new opportunities requires an awareness of new realities.

Doing business is a creative enterprise. Doing business outside one's own country is a much more demanding, complicated enterprise. Setting aside other difficulties, consider briefly the simple fact that business environments of countries are different. Consider advertising. In the United States, television advertising of consumer products is taken for granted. But in many countries, in the Netherlands, for example, commercials are not permitted on television. In some countries television advertising is permitted, but only on a limited scale. In Switzerland, commercials are broadcast between 6:30 A.M. and 8 A.M. on weekdays. Just from this limited consideration of one aspect of marketing, advertising, it is clear that international business necessitates an awareness of the clash of cultural standards among countries. These differences require international marketers to have good analytical abilities and sound business acumen in order to make viable decisions and operate successfully.

The Study of International Marketing

In this chapter we will examine what international marketing is, how it differs from domestic marketing, and why international marketing must be studied as a separate subject. Chapter 2 analyzes the rationale behind worldwide economic activity.

Chapters 3 through 5 in Part Two review the international institutions and agreements that continually create the conditions of the worldwide economic scene in which international marketing is conducted. Part Three, Chapters 6 through 9, explores the economic, cultural, political, and legal environments that affect business decisions. Chapters 10 and 11 provide the perspectives of the international marketplace. Chapters 12 through 16 are devoted to marketing decisions about products and their price, distribution, and promotion. Chapter 17 examines exporting.

The two final chapters deal with marketing planning and control. Chapter 18 discusses corporate organizational arrangements for international marketing management. Chapter 19 introduces the formulation of marketing strategy within the context of international business and provides a foundation for the advanced study of international marketing.

First, however, we must have an understanding of the state of the art of international business. Then we will discuss the crucial role of the marketing function in conducting business across national boundaries, a framework for making international marketing decisions, the reasons firms engage in foreign business, and the various modes of entry. Finally, we will consider the pivotal importance of the multinational corporation in global business.

International Business

The term ***international business*** refers to a wide range of activities involved in conducting business transactions across national boundaries. International business suggests a comprehensive approach to operations of both large and small firms engaged in business overseas. It is from this perspective that we will consider international marketing as it has developed and as it must, in the author's opinion, change and grow in the future.

Perspectives of U.S. Business Overseas

Although many United States firms had long engaged in international business ventures, greater impetus to overseas expansion came after World War II. While the United States government helped to reconstruct war-torn economies through the Marshall Plan by providing financial assistance to European countries, the postwar American economy emerged as the strongest in the world. America's economic assistance programs, in the absence of competition, stimulated extensive U.S. corporate interest overseas.

In recent years, overseas business has become a matter of necessity from the viewpoint of both U.S. corporations and the U.S. government. Increasing foreign competition faces many U.S. industries. Take the shoe industry, for example. The share of U.S. producers plunged from 50 percent in 1981 to 28 percent in 1985 to 21 percent in 1990.[2] The United States imports shoes from numerous countries, but the performance of Brazilian manufacturers is really impressive. Brazil has come from nowhere in the past decade or so to capture a big chunk of the U.S. shoe market. During the 1980s, its shoe exports to the United States zoomed by 500 percent.[3] The bicycle industry provides another example: the import share of bike sales jumped to 60 percent in 1990 from 42 percent in 1984.[4]

Faced with saturated markets at home, U.S. corporations have been forced to look for new markets. The flat growth rate of the beer industry in the early 1980s necessitated Anheuser-Busch's exploration of the huge overseas beer market. The company estimates that, by the year 2000, foreign operations will account for almost one-fourth of its earnings.[5]

In brief, the current unfavorable balance of trade, aggravated by U.S. dependence on energy imports, has made the need to expand exports a matter of vital national interest. Whereas in the 1950s and 1960s international business was a means of capitalizing on new opportunity, today's changing economic environment has made international business dealings vital for survival.

Essentially, there are two aspects of international business: direct investment and trade. At the end of 1990, according to a U.S. Department of Commerce report, the U.S. direct investment abroad stood at $403 billion, up from $314.3 billion in 1987 (see Table 1.1).[6]

Over 75 percent of U.S. investments overseas have traditionally been in developed countries. However, as many ***less-developed countries (LDCs)*** gained political freedom after the war, their governments also sought United States help to modernize their economies and improve their living standards. Thus, LDCs provided additional investment opportunities for U.S. corporations, especially in the more politically stable countries where United States foreign aid programs were in progress. However, it is interesting that, while for cultural, political, and economic reasons the more viable opportunities were found in Western Europe, Canada, and to a lesser extent, Japan, many developing countries provided a better return on direct U.S. investments.[7]

Foreigners have also made substantial direct investments in the United States. Direct foreign investment in the United States has come traditionally from Europe and Canada. Almost $328.5 billion of the $410 billion in book value of direct foreign investment in the United States at the end of 1990 came from the Netherlands, the United Kingdom, Canada, Germany, Japan, and Switzerland. By contrast, direct investment in the United States by the thirteen nations of the Organization of Petroleum Exporting Countries (OPEC) in 1990 was about $1.8 billion.[8]

Foreign investments in the United States have taken the form of both wholly owned subsidiaries and stock ownership. For example, Bic Pen Corporation (a French company), Lever Brothers (an English company), and Nestlé S.A. (a Swiss company) operate U.S. subsidiaries as part of their worldwide operations; that is, they are owned by the parent corporations. Other foreign investments are in the form of stock ownership in U.S. corporations. In 1981, for example, a Japanese trading company bought a 34 percent interest in Munsingwear Inc., a Minneapolis-based apparel manufacturer. Likewise, a German group maintains about one-third ownership in A & P (Great Atlantic and Pacific Tea Co.), a large food chain. In 1984, Nestlé S.A. acquired the Carnation Co. of Los Angeles for $3 billion. In 1987, Hoechst, a German chemical company, spent $2.8 billion for Celanese Corporation. In 1990, Matsushita Electric Industrial Co. of Japan, the world's largest maker of television sets and twelfth-largest corporation, bought MCA Inc. (the entertainment giant) for around $6.8 billion. As of late, the Japanese have substantially increased the tempo of their investments in the United States. Between 1987 and 1990 the Japanese investment in U.S. manufacturing facilities almost doubled, from $35.2 billion to $69.7 billion.[9]

TABLE 1.1 U.S. Direct Investment Position Abroad by Country, 1980–1989*

Country	DIRECT INVESTMENT POSITION (AT YEAR END)					
	1980	1985	1986	1987	1988	1989
All Countries	**215,375**	**230,250**	**259,800**	**314,307**	**333,501**	**373,436**
Developed countries	**158,214**	**172,158**	**194,280**	**237,508**	**252,757**	**279,310**
Canada	45,119	46,909	50,629	57,783	62,610	66,856
Europe	96,287	105,171	120,724	150,439	156,932	176,736
Austria	524	493	715	691	688	688
Belgium	6,259	5,038	5,006	7,267	7,448	8,290
Denmark	1,266	1,281	1,085	1,070	1,163	1,246
France	9,347	7,643	8,952	11,868	13,150	14,747
Greece	347	210	87	132	195	265
Ireland	2,319	3,693	4,308	5,425	6,212	6,237
Italy	5,397	5,906	7,426	9,264	9,540	10,634
Luxembourg	652	690	802	660	850	904
Netherlands	8,039	7,129	11,643	14,842	16,017	17,168
Norway	1,679	3,215	3,216	3,843	4,371	3,640
Portugal	257	237	288	495	546	612
Spain	2,678	2,281	2,707	4,076	4,979	6,002
Sweden	1,474	933	918	1,139	1,119	1,102
Switzerland	11,280	15,766	16,441	19,665	18,357	19,952
Turkey	207	234	215	207	246	312
United Kingdom	28,460	33,024	35,389	44,512	49,274	60,810
West Germany	15,415	16,764	20,932	24,388	21,742	23,059
Japan	6,225	9,235	11,472	15,684	17,927	19,341
Australia	7,654	8,772	9,340	11,363	13,186	14,495
New Zealand	579	576	598	743	833	1,167
South Africa	2,350	1,394	1,517	1,497	1,269	714
Developing countries	**53,206**	**52,764**	**61,072**	**73,017**	**77,560**	**90,552**
Latin America	38,761	28,261	36,851	47,551	51,041	61,364
South America	16,342	17,623	19,813	21,227	21,690	23,557
Argentina	2,540	2,705	2,913	2,744	2,597	2,624
Brazil	7,704	8,893	9,268	10,951	12,460	14,687
Chile	536	88	265	348	691	1,081
Colombia	1,012	2,148	3,291	3,104	2,248	1,900
Ecuador	322	361	413	466	431	395
Peru	1,665	1,243	1,103	1,022	986	912
Venezuela	1,908	1,588	1,987	2,095	1,897	1,537
Central America	10,193	9,658	10,698	12,218	13,119	15,880
Mexico	5,986	5,088	4,623	4,913	5,694	7,079
Panama	3,170	3,959	5,525	6,622	6,632	7,906
Other	1,037	611	549	683	793	895
Costa Rica	303	113	113	141	169	163
El Salvador	105	73	50	51	56	62
Guatemala	229	213	181	174	200	221
Honduras	288	171	167	185	240	318
Other W. Hemisphere	12,226	980	6,341	14,106	16,232	21,928
Bahamas, The	2,712	3,795	2,991	3,814	4,010	4,463
Bermuda	11,045	13,116	15,373	19,215	19,040	17,849
Dominican Republic	316	212	199	156	138	162
Jamaica	407	122	106	103	134	167
Netherlands Antilles	−4,336	−20,499	−16,969	−14,235	−11,633	−6,286
Trinidad and Tobago	951	484	424	400	447	530

(continued)

TABLE 1.1 *(Continued)*

Country	DIRECT INVESTMENT POSITION (AT YEAR END) 1980	1985	1986	1987	1988	1989
Other Africa	3,778	4,497	3,999	4,372	4,199	4,310
Egypt	1,038	1,926	1,807	1,669	1,670	1,802
Libya	575	325	241	310	315	311
Nigeria	18	44	781	894	660	461
Middle East	2,163	4,606	4,891	4,084	3,806	3,886
Israel	379	717	427	635	700	770
Saudi Arabia	1,037	2,442	2,460	2,092	1,782	1,812
United Arab Emirates	384	792	840	694	672	674
Bahrain	−16	440	320	−340	−311	−176
Other Asia and Pacific	8,505	15,400	15,332	17,010	18,515	20,991
China: Taiwan	498	750	869	1,372	1,622	1,949
Hong Kong	2,078	3,295	3,912	4,389	5,244	5,853
India	398	383	421	439	436	549
Indonesia	1,314	4,475	3,217	3,070	2,925	3,696
Malaysia	632	1,140	1,021	952	1,135	1,098
Philippines	1,259	1,032	1,299	1,396	1,511	1,682
Singapore	1,204	1,874	2,256	2,384	2,290	2,213
South Korea	575	743	782	1,178	1,501	1,889
Thailand	361	1,074	1,078	1,274	1,132	1,279
Other	186	635	476	556	719	782
China: Mainland	−6	311	167	207	307	370
International	**3,955**	**5,428**	**4,448**	**3,782**	**3,184**	**3,574**
Addendum-OPEC	*6,090*	*10,383*	*10,235*	*9,899*	*8,825*	*8,977*

*Figures in millions of dollars

Source: Statistical Abstract of the United States: 1991, Washington, D.C.: U.S. Department of Commerce, p. 797.

The other aspect of international business is trade. In 1991, the United States exported an estimated $421.6 billion of goods and services. Imports during the same year amounted to $488.1 billion, resulting in a balance-of-trade deficit of $66.5 billion.[10] While the subject of trade will be explored in detail in Chapter 17, it is important to note that the U.S. share of the world exports in 1990 for manufactured goods—measured by value—comes to about 13 percent, slightly higher than it was in the 1980s. It is also important to realize that this increase in U.S. market share can partly be attributed to the lower value of the U.S. dollar in the late 1980s.

The traditional view of foreign trade as an exchange of tangible goods is increasingly giving way to the more balanced view that trade encompasses both goods and services. As the economies of more and more countries have become service oriented, foreign sales of engineering, consulting, banking, transportation, motion pictures, insurance, tourism, franchising, construction, advertising, and computer services are gaining recognition as significant factors in the foreign trade position of many nations.[11] The importance of such exported U.S. services is borne out by the fact that United States deficits in merchandise trade have been partially balanced by growing services and investment income from abroad. Services exports and their income from overseas U.S. affiliates reached an estimated $119.8 billion in 1990, compared with $79.5 billion in 1987. Services imports in 1990 were estimated at $80.9 billion, giving a favorable balance of $38.9 billion.

Why Go International?

There are several reasons for U.S. firms to seek business opportunities elsewhere in the world. Traditionally the major focus of U.S. business has been on its large and expanding domestic market. There was little need in the past to look beyond United States borders for customers. In recent years, however, new factors have made international business the more desirable alternative for growth. These factors are expected to persist and to have even greater impact throughout the 1990s.

Even if a company does not conduct any international business, its competitors are likely to hail from all over and challenge its position in its own home market. For example, foreign manufacturers, including many from the so-called Third World, created problems for such established U.S. firms as USX, LTV, and other stay-at-home steelmakers.

Market Saturation Markets for a variety of goods in the United States are becoming saturated far faster than new markets are being found. Staple consumer goods such as cars, radios, and TVs already outnumber U.S. households, and other products are fast approaching the same level. The slowing growth of the U.S. population means that the number of households is likely to grow at less than 1.8 percent per year in the 1990s, and demand for consumer goods is unlikely to grow any faster.[12]

Thus companies in many industries must develop new markets to continue to operate successfully. International markets, especially those where market saturation is a distant threat, provide an attractive alternative. Take the case of the cigarette industry. While sales have stagnated in the United States, the Third World countries offer rich markets. In Indonesia, per capita cigarette consumption quadrupled from 1978 to 1985. Kenya's consumption has been rising 10 percent annually. Further, the Third World markets are unburdened by many of the restraints imposed in the United States and other industrialized nations. Firms generally can advertise freely on radio and television and packages don't have to carry health warnings.[13]

To transform global challenges into new opportunities, smart companies seek markets across national borders (see International Marketing Highlight 1.3). For example, Disney's theme park in France, following its great success in Japan, shows how important it is for a company to expand overseas in the wake of market saturation at home. Some U.S. hospitals, facing tighter health care budgets and dwindling occupancy rates, have started seeking foreign patients.[14]

United States Trade Deficit American industry grew up accustomed to a climate of private enterprise—nationwide markets without trade barriers to hamper the full development of economic efficiency. Most decisions could be made with-

International Marketing Highlight 1.3

Coors Brews Big Plans for Korea

Coors is going where the growth is. With Korean beer sales expanding 15 percent a year, compared with a puny 2 percent in the United States, Coors Brewing Co. is forming a joint venture with Jinro, Korea's largest producer of alcoholic beverages, to build a 1.8 million-barrel brewery in Seoul to produce Coors beer. Coors is aiming to capture 20 percent of the Korean market before long.

The plant is scheduled to come on line in 1995. It will be Coors's first outside the United States and is part of an international expansion program for America's third-largest brewer, which wants to be in twenty markets outside the U.S. by 1995. Coors beer is now for sale in seven countries outside the United States.

Source: Business Week, December 9, 1991, p. 44.

out considering what their effect would be on world market position. This is no longer true. United States business faces a declining share of world manufactured exports and a continuing balance-of-payments problem. In 1971 the United States experienced its first trade deficit since 1888. Preceding the drastic fall in the value of the United States dollar in 1978, U.S. producers were steadily losing world market share in several key industries—steel, textiles, shoes, and shipbuilding, among others. The United States share of world trade as a whole has also declined sharply, from 15.4 percent in 1970 to 13.6 in 1975 to 12.3 in 1988 and 12.2 in 1991. As cited above, in 1991 the United States incurred an estimated trade deficit of $66.5 billion.

Trade deficit means living beyond one's means. Just as an individual family should not, and cannot in the long run, live beyond its means, neither should a nation do so on a continuing basis. Therefore, the staggering U.S. trade deficit has to be balanced—the United States must make all attempts to increase exports.

Deficits have spread beyond the nation's "rust belt" industries to agricultural products and telecommunications equipment, long among America's most robust exports, as shown below:[15]

TRADE DEFICITS	1990 (IN BILLIONS OF U.S. DOLLARS)	% CHANGE 1985–90
Motor vehicles	$42.9	+158%
Apparel, accessories	17.4	+175
Telecommunications, sound equipment	16.4	+250
Miscellaneous consumer goods	12.8	+480
Iron, steel	10.4	+102

Today's big exporters—industries such as aircraft and plastics—have seen their surpluses erode.

TRADE SURPLUSES	1990 (IN BILLIONS OF U.S. DOLLARS)	% CHANGE 1985–90
Aircraft, transportation equipment	13.5	− 3.1%
Office machines, computers	4.9	−65
Professional, scientific instruments	4.1	−19
Specialized industrial machinery	3.2	−18.5
Synthetic resins, plastics	2.9	−60

In agriculture, global wheat production increased 16 percent during 1985–90. Rice harvests set world records for five consecutive years (1985–90). After four years of bumper crops, world sugar stocks exceeded demand by 40 percent in 1990. Countries that once were good customers of American farmers—India and China, for example—have become self-sufficient in food, and some even export grain themselves. Brazil turned into a major exporter of corn, wheat, and soybeans after increasing land under cultivation from 50 million acres to 135 million since 1970.[16] Saudi Arabia exports wheat to Middle Eastern neighbors and stores its surpluses in idle oil tankers.[17]

Foreign Competition In many industries, U.S. firms face fierce and intense competition from foreign manufacturers. Consider, for example, the copying machine business. Currently, foreign competitors are offering low-priced, high-quality machines and are invading what was once Xerox Corporation's undisputed turf. Xerox no longer can take industry leadership for granted. In a crowded field with some fourteen competitors from Japan alone, the battle resembles the one being fought—and lost—by U.S. automakers against foreign importers. At stake is a burgeoning, $37 billion-a-year copier market. In 1990, the Japanese dominated sales of inexpensive and middle range copiers, and were beginning to move toward entering the higher end, where Xerox still dominates. Kodak is another U.S. corporation that is losing its edge in an industry it created and long controlled. Although Americans are shooting more pictures each year, Kodak's domestic market share of color film has slipped to 82 percent from its virtual monopoly just fifteen years ago. A still greater problem is in the area of technology. Kodak, which was once the leader in technology development, now increasingly chases Fuji, whether in introducing faster-speed film or in marketing 35-millimeter disposable cameras.[18]

Another example is the $70 billion textile industry. Garment imports increased three-fold between 1980 and 1990 to $30 billion a year. Some 300 textile mills have been closed since 1980, and over 200,000 jobs have vanished. Industry experts think that textile apparel imports will continue to grow 15 percent annually. At this pace, imports will have 80 percent of the U.S. market by the year 2000.[19] The lure of imported fabrics is quality, often superior to that of the U.S. products at prices held down by low Asian pay scales. In addition to Japan, Taiwan, Hong Kong, and South Korea, even such countries as Bangladesh, Mauritius, and Indonesia find it relatively easy to produce apparel that appeals to the U.S. market.

During the 1970s the U.S. auto industry became susceptible to foreign competition with the entry into the American marketplace of aggressive, opportunistic foreign car importers. Because of this change, the U.S. auto market is far more competitive today. It is no longer the Big Three—General Motors Corporation, Ford Motor Company, and Chrysler Corporation—running the industry, but the Big Seven, including Toyota Motor, Volkswagen, Nissan Motor, and Honda Motor Company. The Japanese companies compete aggressively, influencing price setting tremendously. A 1980 study by the U.S. Department of Transportation reports that Japanese producers at that time had a per-unit cost advantage of about $2,000 over U.S. automakers because of Japan's lower wage rates, tax concessions, and less regulation.[20] The Japanese automakers lost their cost advantage, however, due to the decline in the value of the dollar against the yen, and they adopted new strategies to compete. For example, Honda has expanded its Ohio factory, opened in 1982, and now sells more cars than any other foreign company. The plant has also perfected a strategy that can be called the Americanization of Honda. Fully 43 percent of the cars the company sells worldwide are sold to Americans, and the proportion is likely to grow[21] (see International

International Marketing Highlight 1.4

How Japanese Automakers Invaded the U.S. Market

During the late 1960s, Japanese car manufacturers wanting to enter the U.S. market looked for a niche and found one at the low end of the market: students and other consumers who wanted no-frills transportation. The small-and-cheap car market, as it so happened, was a niche that did not interest the Detroit auto companies. (Even relatively small American-made cars, such as Ford's Falcon and Fairlane, were essentially family cars.) The only formidable presence in this market was Volkswagen. Even so, VW could not fill the wide-open small-car market fast enough. The Japanese companies responded by following a time-tested military strategy: taking uncontested ground first.

Datsun and Honda first began to introduce their cars into the United States around 1967. U.S. automakers paid little attention to the newcomers; they derided the Japanese cars as cheap models suitable only for a market that did not interest them in the first place. Essentially, the American automakers' attitude was to let Volkswagen fight it out with Datsun and Honda. Meanwhile, the Japanese focused on providing low-cost products, built up a following (and, more important still, a low-cost, high-quality manufacturing base), then gradually introduced larger, better, higher-priced models.

Now Toyota, Datsun, Honda, Mitsubishi, and the other major Japanese manufacturers have established themselves as a permanent, formidable presence in the U.S. automobile market. These companies have moved beyond their initial niche to satisfy America's demands for a wide variety of high-quality cars. The Detroit automakers have had an increasingly difficult time competing effectively against them.

TABLE 1.2 **U.S. International Market Position of Selected Products**

PRODUCT	U.S. SHARE OF WORLD MARKETS 1978	1988
Cars	29.0%	18.2%
Machine tools	14.0	6.9
Hard disks	84.0	75.0
Floppy disks	66.0	4.0
Drams	72.8	16.9
ASICs (customized chips)	90.0	53.0

Source: U.S. Department of Commerce.

Marketing Highlight 1.4). Unless the growing protectionist sentiment in Congress prevails, a development no one expects, foreign cars could reach 5.5 million units a year by the year 2000, or about 45 percent of the U.S. auto market.

The truth of the matter is that the United States' ability to compete in the world market has eroded significantly during the past two decades.[22] Most of this decline has occurred in such traditional industries as steel, automobiles, consumer electronics, apparel, and machine tools. Recently, even high-tech industries have become susceptible. Competition has forced some companies to shift their consumer electronics manufacturing to the Far East, which explains why the high-tech industry is losing its edge.[23] Even this measure did not succeed for General Electric, which in 1986 sold 80 percent of its consumer electronics business (including the RCA brand acquired in late 1985) to Thomson, France's state-owned leading electronics manufacturer. Thus in the color television business the United States becomes a minor player, yielding the market to Japanese and European companies. Japan leads with over 18 million units, while Europe accounts for 15 million units. The U.S. share is limited to 2 million sets.[24]

The declining international position of the United States in the high-tech area is a matter of serious concern. The U.S. has been losing market position in a number of product areas, as shown in Table 1.2. For example, the U.S. share of the world floppy disk market shrank from 66 percent in 1978 to an insignificant 4 percent in 1988. All the more troubling is the fact that many of these high-tech products derive from technology developed in the United States (see Table 1.3). Phonographs, color TVs, audiotape recorders, and videotape recorders were all invented in the United States, yet U.S. companies have practically no business left in these products (see International Marketing Highlight 1.5).

One way to meet the challenge from foreign companies is for U.S. companies to enter the home markets of their foreign competitors. While Japanese automakers had a leeway with American consumers in the early 1980s, there may be Japanese car buyers interested in U.S. cars now and in the future, but not if these cars have their steering wheels on the wrong side.

Emergence of New Markets The world is changing fast resulting in the emergence of new markets. In the 1990s, new business opportunities will flow from the European Community, enhanced by the reunification of Germany, the

TABLE 1.3 **Invented Here, Made Elsewhere**

U.S. INVENTED TECHNOLOGY	1987 MARKET SIZE (MILLIONS $)	U.S. PRODUCERS' SHARE OF DOMESTIC MARKET			
		1970	1975	1980	1987
Phonographs	$ 630	90%	40%	30%	1%
Color TVs	14,050	90	80	60	10
Audiotape recorders	500	40	10	10	0
Videotape recorders	2,895	10	10	1	1
Machine tool centers	485	99	97	79	35
Telephones	2,000	99	95	88	25
Semiconductors	19,100	89	71	65	64
Computers	53,500	n.a.	97	96	74

Source: Council on Competitiveness, U.S. Department of Commerce.

International Marketing Highlight 1.5

There Goes Another One

In recent years, U.S. companies have conceded one homegrown industry after another to more aggressive and competitive foreign rivals. First came cameras, then televisions, tape recorders, stereo equipment, and semiconductors. In September 1990, Cincinnati Milacron, the last independent U.S. producer of heavy industrial robots, agreed to sell the business to a subsidiary of Switzerland's Asea Brown Boveri.

Milacron retreated from the $4 billion market after thirteen years because its share of the business had dwindled from a commanding 75 percent to just 10 percent, and its losses from robotics had been mounting since the mid-1980s. The company will concentrate on its traditional lines of machine tools and other industrial products.

Source: Business Week, September 24, 1990, p. 71.

thriving economies in the Pacific Rim countries, efforts to curb inflation in Latin America, and the emerging market-based economies in Eastern Europe. Elsewhere in developing countries momentum toward privatization (i.e., transfer of business ownership from government to private citizens and/or institutions) and liberal policies promise new opportunities (see International Marketing Highlight 1.6).

Although an individual developing country may not provide adequate potential for U.S. corporations, developing countries as a group constitute a major market. In 1990, over one-fourth of our trade was with LDCs. In future years, the flow of U.S. trade with developing countries should increase. An Organization of Economic Cooperation and Development (OECD) study shows that in 1970, the OECD countries with just 20 percent of the world's people had 83

International Marketing Highlight 1.6

Gerber Locates a Niche in India

Gerber Products Company has undertaken extensive market research in India. Despite India's predominantly poor population, the country has a prosperous middle class and a small but wealthy upper class that Gerber considers a promising market.

Until recently, most Indians have been unlikely to show any interest in Western-style baby foods. Lately, though, the convenience of such products, plus their status appeal, has heightened consumers' curiosity and openness. Initial focus groups show that baby foods have high potential for success in certain areas of the subcontinent.

---

percent of the world's trade in manufactures, while the developing countries with 70 percent of the world's people had 11 percent of the trade. In the year 2000, however, it is estimated that the OECD countries with 15 percent of the population will have 63 percent of the world's trade in manufactures while the developing countries, with 78 percent of the population, will account for 28 percent of the trade.[25]

Most developing countries, particularly those referred to as newly industrialized countries (NICs), are achieving higher and higher economic growth rates every year. For example, during the decade of the 1980s the five fastest growing economies of the world were South Korea, Brazil, Singapore, Malaysia, and Thailand. These countries provide unprecedented opportunities. The point can be illustrated with reference to the Pacific basin countries. Over the last quarter century, the streams of food, fuels, textiles, cameras, cars, and VCRs flowing from countries all across Asia exerted heavy pressure on Western economies. Since 1962 this outpouring of exports has increased the Asian/Pacific share of world trade from 11 percent to 21 percent and pushed one Asian economy after another out of the Dark Ages and into the global marketplace.

For U.S. marketers, rising Pacific power holds great promise. There is the emergence of a market of more than two billion potential consumers. In the last twenty-five years, as the Pacific region began its time-bending leap into the 20th century, millions of Asians began an equally rapid transition from rural to urban, from agrarian to industrial, from feudal to contemporary society. With more of the Pacific region's rural population traveling to the cities to shop every day, the demand for goods and services—from the most basic household commodities to sophisticated technical devices—is soaring (see International Marketing Highlight 1.7). In coming years, as rising incomes continue to bolster the spending power of Asia's new consumer population, the opportunities for shrewd marketers will be unparalleled.[26]

Barriers to conducting business in the region are beginning to fall, too. Increasingly, throughout the region English is the language of commerce, and an

International Marketing Highlight 1.7

McDonald's in Moscow

McDonald's opened its first restaurant in Moscow in 1990. With indoor seating for 700, it is the biggest McDonald's in the world. Opened in a blaze of publicity, the Moscow McDonald's is fast becoming more than just a fast-food outlet. For Russian consumers used to chronic food shortages, slow-moving lines, and scowling or nonexistent service, it is like something out of another world. For both McDonald's Corp. and Russia, the experience seems as much cultural as culinary.

Prices are relatively high by Russian standards, with a Big Mac, french fries, and soft drink selling for 5.65 rubles ($9.32 at the official exchange rate), or the equivalent of the average pay for four hours of work. By contrast, lunch at a state-run cafe in Moscow can be had for about one ruble, while a sandwich at a private-sector Russian cafe costs about 1.50 rubles.

Nonetheless, many of the people flocking to the opening of the McDonald's on Pushkin Square, the first of twenty stores planned for the Russian capital, didn't seem put off by the prices. For one thing, the quality was far above that provided by ordinary Russian restaurants, and the McDonald's has many things that ordinary people here can't find elsewhere. There is soft toilet paper, a fast-moving queue, mayonnaise, plenty of edible meat, and, above all, cashiers who smile and say *priyatnovo appetita,* the Russian equivalent of "enjoy your meal."

The restaurant, part of a joint venture between McDonald's Restaurants of Canada Ltd. and Moscow city authorities, is almost completely dependent on Russian supplies of ingredients. In order to succeed where seventy-two years of socialist agriculture have failed, the venture built a $40 million food-processing plant on the outskirts of the city. Here, several hundred foreigners and Russians test, clean, chop, and freeze all the staples of fast-food fare: potatoes, meat, buns, onions, pickles, and lettuce. McDonald's agronomists even brought over the right type of seeds and helped plant them on local farms.

Apart from the food itself, McDonald's has had to overcome many other unusual problems. Known for its aversion to labor unions, it helped organize a work collective for its Russian staff to comply with the nation's labor laws. The restaurant has even built a small laundry room, where uniforms of the 630-member staff are washed in three German machines and ironed by hand.

It remains to be seen whether McDonald's can live up to its promises. Many joint catering ventures in the former Soviet Union were plagued by problems such as falling standards of cleanliness and large-scale theft, problems described by one European executive as "creeping Sovietization."

McDonald's managers, not surprisingly, are confident they can avoid such troubles. Nonetheless, the restaurant has taken some precautions against potential black marketeering: customers are limited to ten Big Macs to stop them from buying in bulk and reselling at a premium to the hungry crowds queuing outside.

Apart from the $40 million invested in the food-processing center, the joint venture has also spent $10 million on the first restaurant and extensive staff training. Behind the rhetoric, McDonald's does have arrangements that will enable it to earn at least some dollars from the venture. The first restaurant takes rubles only, which can't be freely converted into hard currency. But McDonald's hopes to sell some of the frozen produce processed at the venture's plant for dollars, and a second store, catering to tourists, near the Kremlin accepts only hard currency.

In addition, McDonald's will receive a small hard-currency royalty payment from its Russian partner for every ruble that it earns. But for the store's first paying customers, such intricacies seem far less important than the culture.

Source: Peter Gumbel, "Muscovites Queue Up at American Icon," *The Wall Street Journal,* February 1, 1990, p. A6.

allegiance to free-market economics is widespread. And, as companies such as McDonald's, General Foods, Unilever, and Coca-Cola have already discovered, from Penang to Taipei, this is a region where well-made and well-marketed products and services are generating increasing acceptance.

As modern influences exert greater pressure on traditional Asian cultures, two trends with important implications for marketers are starting to take shape:

- While each Asian nation is culturally distinct, consumers throughout the Pacific region are gradually sharing more of the same wants and needs. As Asian homogenization progresses, the sophisticated strategies and considerable economies of regional and global marketing and advertising will become increasingly relevant.[27]
- Many Western marketers misinterpret the nature of the current changes in the Pacific region. Despite the Big Macs, the Levis, the Nikes, and all the other familiar trappings, Asia is not Westernizing—it's modernizing. Asian consumers are buying Western goods and services, not Western values and cultures.

Elsewhere in the East, India and China, two large markets, should provide unprecedented opportunities in the 1990s as their economies become market-oriented. A growing number of U.S. consumer goods companies have begun to make inroads in China. In November 1987, Kentucky Fried Chicken Corp. opened the first Western fast-food restaurant in China. Coca-Cola Co. and PepsiCo. Inc. are aggressively expanding distribution. Kodak and other foreign film suppliers have attained a 70 percent share of the color film market. Nescafé and Maxwell House are waging coffee combat in a land of tea.[28] Thus, the LDCs provide new opportunities for U.S. corporations to expand business overseas—as their wealth grows, U.S. marketing possibilities expand (see International Marketing Highlight 1.8).

It has been observed that during the 1990s Latin American countries, too, will emerge as modern, Northern-styled marketplaces with improved transportation systems, subsidized credit to native businesses, and marketing education programs. All of these changes should result in more efficient channels of distribution, more local marketing support services, and fewer bottlenecks that hamper

International Marketing Highlight 1.8

Quick Shave

A few years ago, Gillette Co. discovered that only 8 percent of Mexican men who shave use shaving cream. Sensing an opportunity, Gillette in 1975 introduced plastic tubes of shaving cream in Guadalajara, Mexico, that sold for half the price of its aerosol. In a year's time 13 percent of Guadalajaran men began to use shaving cream. Gillette is planning to sell its new product, Prestobarba (Spanish for "quick shave"), in the rest of Mexico, Colombia, and Brazil.

Source: David Wessel, "Gillette Keys Sales to Third World Tastes," *The Wall Street Journal,* January 23, 1986, p. 35.

exchanges. All these indications point toward a variety of emerging opportunities for U.S. corporations in Latin America.

These emerging markets in LDCs can help many U.S. corporations to counter the results of demographic changes in the Western nations.[29] In most advanced nations of the world, birth rates are declining while population in the Third World countries is growing. The largest population growth rates in the 1990s will occur in Africa and Latin America.

Globalization of Markets Theodore Levitt asserts that technology has homogenized worldwide markets; therefore, companies should produce globally standardized products and market them in the same way to people everywhere.[30] All the principal barriers to the growth of such markets have weakened in the last decade. Tariffs have been reduced by the General Agreement on Tariffs and Trade (GATT). Transportation costs have declined with the use of containerization and larger-capacity ships. Many products have emerged that pack very high value into very small packages. Consumer needs in the industrialized nations have become increasingly similar, and purchasing power in certain Third World and OPEC countries has increased sharply. In consequence, a multitude of distinct national markets is beginning to coalesce into a true world market. This development can be a source of competitive advantage for companies that plan their strategies accordingly.[31]

A few examples will suggest how extensive the global product phenomenon has already become. Kids everywhere are playing on Nintendo and bounding along the streets to the sound of a Sony Walkman. The videocassette recorder market took off simultaneously in Japan, Europe, and the United States, but the most extensive use of videocassette recorders today is probably in places like Riyadh and Caracas. Shopping centers from Dusseldorf to Rio sell Gucci shoes, Yves St. Laurent suits, and Gloria Vanderbilt jeans. Siemens and International Telephone & Telegraph (ITT) telephones can be found almost everywhere in the world. Mercedes-Benz and the Toyota Corolla are as much objects of passion in Manila as in California.

Just about every gas turbine sold in the world has some General Electric technology or component in it, and what country doesn't need gas turbines? How many airlines around the world could survive without Boeing or McDonnell Douglas equipment? Third World markets for high-voltage transmission equipment and diesel-electric locomotives are bigger than those in the developed countries. And today's new industries—robotics, videodisks, fiber optics, satellite networks, high-technology plastics, artificial diamonds—seem to be global at birth.

Opportunities via Foreign Aid Programs Although in recent years the United States foreign aid programs for developing countries have declined gradually, in the 1950s and 1960s the United States government provided billions of dollars to developing countries to undertake programs of economic buildup. Most of these programs required that aid recipients spend U.S. money on goods and services from U.S. corporations, except in cases where the desired goods were available only from non-U.S. sources. In either circumstance, the aid money created new markets in developing countries. Even more recent aid programs, small as they were ($16.9 billion in 1990, $11.3 billion in economic support and $5.6 billion for military hardware), provided opportunities for some businesses to go abroad. For example, Bechtel Corporation, a San Francisco construction company, in 1985 had ninety-five $25-million-plus projects in seventeen countries. A large majority of these projects were in developing countries. The funding came from such diverse sources as the Export-Import Bank of the United States (Eximbank), the United States government Agency for International Development (AID), the Export Development Corporation of Canada, and the World Bank.[32]

Other Reasons A variety of other reasons make engagement in business across national boundaries profitable and attractive.

In industries where economies of scale are feasible, a large market is essential. But if the home market is not large enough to absorb the entire output of an industry, entry into foreign markets may be an attractive alternative. Polaroid Corporation, a dominant force in the U.S. photographic industry, claims to have achieved economies of scale by entering foreign markets.[33]

International business provides a safety net during business downturns. Usually a recession starts in one country and takes several quarters to move into other countries. It is said that European economies are affected by a United States recessionary trend after about six months. Thus, firms that do business internationally can shift their emphasis from U.S. to foreign markets during the recession. For example, during the United States recession of 1991, multinational companies were able to shift their marketing focus to Europe and the Middle East, where an economic boom was in progress.[34]

In many industries, labor constitutes a major proportion of costs, and since labor cost in Third World countries is much lower than in the United States, it is economically attractive for the companies to expand foreign operations. For example, electronics companies depend on hundreds, sometimes thousands, of young women to do the painstaking job of assembling tiny parts that are shipped to the United States for use in computers and other products. Labor sometimes represents as much as half of the cost of these parts, so the cheaper the labor, the higher the profit. Thus, a number of U.S. companies—Hewlett-Packard, Intel, National Semiconductor, and ITT, among a dozen others—have gone as far as Malaysia to save on labor cost.

Some nations offer tax incentives to attract foreign businesses to their countries. An important motive for extending such tax incentives is to increase scarce foreign exchange and create jobs at home. Typically a company finding such tax concessions viable will establish a plant in the low-tax country and then sell the manufactured goods locally, as well as export from there to its primary markets.

Many companies find it more desirable to develop and/or test new products outside the United States. This avoids exposure to competitors and, to some extent, keeps new development information secret until the product is ready for full introduction. Ford Motor Company, for example, did much of its world-car development in Germany.

Many international markets are less competitive than the U.S. market; several are still in an embryonic stage. Further, in some instances, governments will give companies a monopoly or quasi-monopoly position if they assemble and produce their products there.

Finally, international presence provides expanded access to advances in technology, worldwide raw materials, and diverse international economic groups. For example, European auto manufacturers led the way in fuel injection technology. Active U.S. auto company presence in Europe would have provided earlier insights into this technology. Some countries have easier access to certain markets that are difficult for U.S. companies to enter because of United States political postures. For example, Xerox Corporation found it easier to enter the Eastern European market by establishing an operation in India via its English subsidiary, Rank Xerox. India has bilateral agreements with Eastern European countries to trade in local currencies. This permits them to acquire Western products via India without dealing in U.S. dollars.[35]

International Marketing and Its Growing Importance

The term ***international marketing*** refers to exchanges across national boundaries for the satisfaction of human needs and wants. The extent of a firm's involvement abroad is a function of its commitment to the pursuit of foreign markets. A firm's overseas involvement may fall into one of several categories:

1. *Domestic:* Operate exclusively within a single country.
2. *Regional exporter:* Operate within a geographically defined region that crosses national boundaries. Markets served are economically and cul-

turally homogeneous. If activity occurs outside the home region, it is opportunistic.

3. *Exporter:* Run operations from a central office in the home region, exporting finished goods to a variety of countries; some marketing, sales, and distribution outside the home region.
4. *International:* Regional operations are somewhat autonomous, but key decisions are made/coordinated from the central office in the home region. Manufacturing and assembly, marketing, and sales are decentralized beyond the home region. Both finished goods and intermediate products are exported outside the home region.
5. *International to global:* Run independent and mainly self-sufficient subsidiaries in a range of countries. While some key functions (R&D, sourcing, financing) are decentralized, the home region is still the primary base for many functions.
6. *Global:* Highly decentralized organization operating across a broad range of countries. No geographic area (including the home region) is assumed a priori to be the primary base for any functional area, and each function, including R&D, sourcing, manufacturing, and marketing/sales, is performed in the location(s) around the world most suitable for that function.

Typically, the journey begins at home. Companies operating exclusively within a single country reach the limits to growth in their home market and face the need to expand in order to achieve further growth. The time that it takes to reach this outer growth limit depends almost entirely on the size of the home market; thus, North American companies will take longer to reach the outer limit than will companies in Singapore, South Korea, Taiwan, and Japan, whose home markets are substantially smaller and provide less room to grow. Once the domestic barrier is reached, companies evolve into an export modality, either on a limited, regional basis where markets are still economically and culturally homogeneous, or on a broader basis where finished goods are exported to a variety of countries. Regional exporters and export companies continue to run operations from a central office in the home market, though some marketing, sales, and distribution functions begin to crop up elsewhere.

As companies become more successful in their export operations, they reach that critical point where the need to achieve greater proximity to overseas markets becomes paramount. At this point, such companies begin to replicate their business systems in new markets through the creation of relatively autonomous regional operations. Manufacturing and assembly, marketing, and sales are decentralized and both finished goods and intermediate products are exported outside the home region, but key decisions are made, or at least coordinated, by a head office in the home region. Companies that have reached this stage of evolution may be characterized as international companies. The replication of a company's business system in various locations around the world does not, however, represent a long-term formula for profitable growth and, ultimately, international companies face the need to optimize their businesses globally by adopting a global model of operation. For global companies, no one geographic area is assumed to be the primary base for any function—research and development, sourcing, and manufacturing are situated in the most suitable locations worldwide.

Despite apparent opportunities and governmental incentives to engage in overseas marketing, a surprising 90 percent of U.S. firms confine themselves to domestic markets. Typically, it is only through infrequent or occasional efforts to capitalize on an isolated opportunity that firms become involved in foreign markets. For example, an overseas customer may approach a U.S. firm to buy its product without ever having been solicited by the latter. Some firms may, during recessionary periods at home, look to overseas markets to liquidate current inventories. Usually, large firms have worldwide marketing operations. They exhibit the strongest commitment to international business and supplement export activity with assembly and/or manufacturing operations on foreign soil.

As it becomes more commonplace for U.S. businesses to consider international markets, and as the number of U.S. businesses operating on an international and global scale increases, *all* business executives should be keenly aware of what transpires worldwide. Business decision makers, whether working for small companies or multinational corporations, should know how to scan and monitor global events and incorporate them into their corporate strategy. A global orientation is rapidly becoming essential even for businesses not directly involved in international business.

> The internationalization of business has expanded international influences even on domestic business so that all students of management should have a greater knowledge of these influences and how they affect business and management.[36]

Take the case of currency fluctuations. Of course, multinational concerns engaged in exports and imports have to be sensitive to exchange rates, but the purely domestic manufacturer is also exposed to currency risk. For instance, in 1989 the value of the dollar declined, thus opening the door to foreign markets. This offered an effective opportunity for firms of all sizes at a time when business conditions at home were less than optimum.

A recent empirical study on the subject demonstrated that international influences significantly affect domestic market performance. Internationalization of business provides growth opportunities well beyond those available in home markets. The smaller the home market, the more compelling the argument to internationalize. Thus, European, Japanese, and Pacific Rim companies have tended to push harder and faster to move beyond an export stage in order to fully realize growth potential and compete globally. Further, there is a correlation between increased market share abroad and increased market share at home. In addition, international companies also enjoy higher profit margins and greater return on assets than those that are strictly domestic.[37]

In the 1990s, international business increasingly will be treated not simply as an additional route to growth, but rather as shaping business strategy for all businesses, even those with strictly domestic markets. As Gluck notes:

> But while the reasons for globalization have been different in different industries, its implications have been the same for all. Most important, companies in global industries have had to reshape their strategies in fundamental ways. In order to compete profitably, they have been obliged to redesign their whole system of doing business to take advantage of the fact of global markets.
>
> In choosing technological processes, they follow the example of the Japanese in plain paper copiers and search the world for the technology offering greatest promise for most markets.
>
> In planning a new product, they design it to be marketable in the maximum number of countries (as Caterpillar has done with its heavy equipment), to serve an identifiable world market segment (as Toyota did with the Corolla), or to be easily adaptable to slightly different markets (as Ericsson has done in telecommunications equipment).
>
> In working out a manufacturing strategy, they pick the lowest-cost source—Malaysia for simple electronics, perhaps; Sri Lanka for textiles; Tokyo for advanced semiconductors; the United States for personal computers; Europe for precision machinery—and design a manufacturing system geared to the scale requirement of the world market.
>
> If scale is important to product economics, they design a marketing system that gives them the broadest coverage and quickest penetration of world markets—even if it means signing cross-marketing agreements with their competitors, selling under other manufacturers' names, or marketing through distributors and dealers they cannot really control.
>
> In short, they have thought hard about what global operations mean to the economics of their businesses, about where the economic leverage points in the business will be, and about how they must shape their own business systems to take advantage of leverage points. And they have acted accordingly.[38]

There was a time when the United States played a dominant role in shaping world economic events: even a business with a fully domestic orientation might have had to deal with international forces. But the decline in America's competitive clout makes specific international orientation extremely important. Further, in years ahead, businesses will confront changes quite different from the kinds most familiar to them. These new kinds of changes in the world environment are taking place at a fast pace. Now a business cannot hope to survive simply by examining changes as discrete occurrences. Rather, a well-organized system is needed to deal with world events.

Why Study International Marketing?

We already have examined the factors that make international business an important field of endeavor from the viewpoint of a businessperson. But how does this importance extend to marketing? Marketing is more significant, both for doing business abroad and for analyzing the impact of international happenings on business in the United States, than other functions of a business—such as manufacturing, finance, and research and development—because marketing responds to the local culture and businesses' multiple interrelationships with the local environment.[39] Growing internationalization of business brings about changes in the positioning of competitors and the appropriate competitive strategies. You can't sell what people won't buy is a truism. Consumers overseas have different needs and expectations than they do in America.[40]

The only way to guarantee long-term competitive success is by providing better value to customers. Let us consider an example. It is estimated that from 1978 to 1987, when the U.S. worldwide trade deficit deepened from $20.2 billion to $171.2 billion, the Japanese surplus swelled from $19.9 billion to $59.9 billion. American companies and U.S. government agencies began to worry and complained that restrictions, in the form of tariffs and visible (and invisible) nontariff barriers and constraints, tended to exclude much U.S. business from Japanese markets. However, an unbiased analysis showed that American business had not made a great effort to enter the Japanese market. As was remarked at the time:

> Americans still are going to have to practice the marketing methods they preach if they are going to exploit the opportunities that are opening up in Japanese markets. In short, U.S. businesses still must find out what the Japanese consumers want, tailor products to fit the Japanese market, and put these products into suitable distribution channels.[41]

A U.S. Chamber of Commerce report indicated that U.S. business had fallen short of success in Japan because it failed to keep track of changes in Japan's marketing environment. Certain U.S. consumer goods—such as automobiles, watches, cigarette lighters, and whiskey—had been regarded in Japan as status symbols and consumed by a limited number of wealthy buyers. Distribution of such products had been organized emphasizing the exclusiveness of the products and brand prestige. This traditional mode of marketing luxury items was inadequate to substantially increase exports to Japan or to develop a mass market. In brief, if imports were to become a part of Japanese daily life, rather than just status symbols, U.S. manufacturers had to reexamine pricing policies and distribution channels and then develop products that better fit Japanese consumers' needs.[42]

Briefly, U.S. companies frequently fumble overseas because they fail to respond to the peculiarities of the markets. Apple Computer, Inc., had the market to itself when it became the first company to sell a personal computer in Japan. But the company began to lose ground for failing to do the right things. Apple didn't provide Japanese manuals. The computers arrived with keyboards that didn't work, and the packaging was shoddy.[43] Like the English, the Japanese drive on the left. American automakers would like the Japanese to buy their cars, but they do not manufacture cars with steering on the right side.

In the developing world also, U.S. corporations have not been on target in marketing. Most firms pursue short-term strategies on the international scene by attempting to sell luxury goods to the affluent classes. Instead, an orientation toward developing and securing mass markets would provide lasting, long-term benefits. For example, malnutrition is a common problem in LDCs. Therefore, vitamin pills are important. But U.S. firms sell the same vitamin at about the same price in poor countries as they do in the United States. Obviously, the two markets cannot afford the same pills.

As a study conducted by the U.S. Embassy in Jeddah indicates, weaknesses in U.S. marketing strategy significantly contribute to poor U.S. performance in Saudi Arabia.[44] For example:

1. U.S. spare parts inventories are often in short supply.
2. U.S. agreements made locally even by senior negotiators can be overturned by their boards or lawyers back home.
3. U.S. firms are slow to comment on quotations.
4. U.S. businesspeople do not mingle with the general population. They stick to three market centers (Jeddah, Riyadh, and Dhahran), and never travel to secondary towns.
5. Many U.S. firms use export management companies that bring little except higher margins.
6. Many U.S. companies appoint two or more agents who compete against each other.
7. Many U.S. firms do not answer telexed inquiries.
8. Few U.S. firms adapt products to the local market.
9. The U.S. dollar value is high.
10. The reputation of all U.S. firms has been tarnished by exporters who substitute second-rate products for those originally offered.

Of course, such shortcomings of U.S. companies translate into strengths for the Japanese, the market challenger.

Mass markets are ready for U.S. products, but American business has not responded to the opportunities with responsible marketing. To cash in effectively on the opportunities these markets represent, in LDCs and elsewhere, U.S. corporations must become more sophisticated marketers.

It has been determined that the number of American managers stationed abroad most likely will not diminish during the current decade. At the same time it has been found that very high percentages of individuals who become presidents of multinational corporations do so without ever having had any international work experience. It has also been shown that many managers with international responsibilities have had no training in international studies prior to employment and have not participated in management development programs with international content while employed. In other words, they lack preparation for their international responsibilities.[45] These findings emphasize the importance of formal training in international business, with particular emphasis on training in marketing because marketing problems in overseas business surpass in complexity those in other areas. A recent study showed that marketing blunders in international business outweighed those in other areas by an overwhelmingly wide margin.[46]

Domestic Versus International Marketing

The basic nature of marketing does not change from domestic to international marketing, but marketing outside national boundaries does pose special problems. International marketing, unlike domestic marketing, requires operating simultaneously in more than one kind of environment, coordinating these operations, and using the experience gained in one country for making decisions in another country. The demands are tough and the stakes are high. International marketers not only must be sensitive to different marketing environments internationally but also must be able to balance marketing moves worldwide in order to seek optimum results for the company.

The impact of environment on international business can be illustrated by the watch industry. New technology, falling trade barriers, and changing cost relationships have affected the competitive patterns of the industry worldwide. Only companies with global perspective are operating successfully. A few *world companies* sell *world products* to increasingly brand-conscious consumers. This multinationalization of the watch industry has made four producers—Switzerland, Japan, Hong Kong, and the United States—dominate the scene by emphasizing brand names. Manufacturing operations are specialized by country according to costs of specific processes, components, and subassemblies.

To successfully compete globally, rather than simply operate domestically, companies should emphasize: (1) Global *configuration* of marketing activities (i.e., where activities such as new product development, advertising, sales promotion, channel selection, marketing research, and other functions should be performed), (2) global *coordination* of marketing activities (i.e., how global marketing activities performed in different countries should be coordinated); and (3) *linkage* of marketing activities (i.e., how marketing activities should be linked with other activities of the firm).[47]

Many marketing activities, unlike those in other functional areas, must be dispersed in each host country to make an adequate response to the local environment. Not all marketing activities need to be performed on a dispersed basis, however. In many cases, competitive advantage is gained, in the form of lower cost or enhanced differentiation, if selected activities are performed centrally as a result of technological changes, buyer shifts, and evolution of marketing media. These activities include production of promotional materials, sales force and service support organization training, and advertising. Further, international marketing activities dispersed in different countries should be properly coordinated to gain competitive advantage. Such coordination can be achieved in the following ways:

1. performing marketing activities using similar methods across countries;
2. transferring marketing know-how and skills from country to country;
3. sequencing marketing programs across countries; and
4. integrating the efforts of various marketing groups in different countries.

Finally, a global view of international marketing permits linking marketing to upstream and support activities of the firm, which could lead to advantages in various ways. For example, marketing can unlock economies of scale and learning in production and/or R&D by (1) supporting the development of universal products by providing the information necessary to develop a physical product design that can be sold worldwide; (2) creating demand for more universal products even if historical demand has been for more varied products in different countries; (3) identifying and penetrating segments in many countries to allow the sale of universal products; and (4) providing services and/or local accessories that effectively tailor the standard physical product to the local needs.

Framework of International Marketing

Marketing decisions relative to product, price, promotion, and distribution must be made whether business is conducted in the United States, France, Japan, or Mexico. But the environment within which these decisions are made is unique to each country. This differential of environment distinguishes international marketing from domestic marketing.

Typically, a firm should make domestic marketing decisions having given due consideration to internal and external environments. ***Internal environment factors*** primarily refers to corporate objectives, corporate organization, and resource availability. ***External environment factors*** include competition, technological change, the economic climate, political influences, social and cultural changes, pertinent legal requirements, current ethical business standards, consumerism, and changes among marketing channels.

A U.S. firm interested in doing business in a foreign country would face the same internal and external factors but from an entirely different environmental perspective. Economic conditions vary from one country to another. The antitrust laws in the United States are much tougher than those in Japan. The United States has a two-party political system, Mexico does not. Women have an important decision-making role as consumers in the United States and in other Western countries, but this is not the situation among the Muslims. As a matter of fact, business environments vary tremendously even among countries that are geographically in the same region, or that have the same cultural heritage. For instance, it would be wrong to assume that the United States and England have common marketing environments. There may be some similarities, but overall the two are very different.

Figure 1.1 depicts the marketing decisions and environments of international marketing. The nature of decision making in international business is essentially the same as in domestic business. Consideration of environment, however, is more philosophically abstract. In addition to the internal and external environmental aspects listed previously, the environment of each individual country has a combined environmental reality that the international marketer must perceive. The international marketer can sort out and combine these realities using four large general categories: economic, cultural, political, and legal environments. In addition, an understanding of international economic institutions (for example, the International Monetary Fund) and an understanding of agreements (for example, the General Agreement on Tariffs and Trade) among nations are essential, even though it may not be strictly correct to label these as a part of the country's marketing environment.

Further, an international marketer must be sensitive to certain aspects of

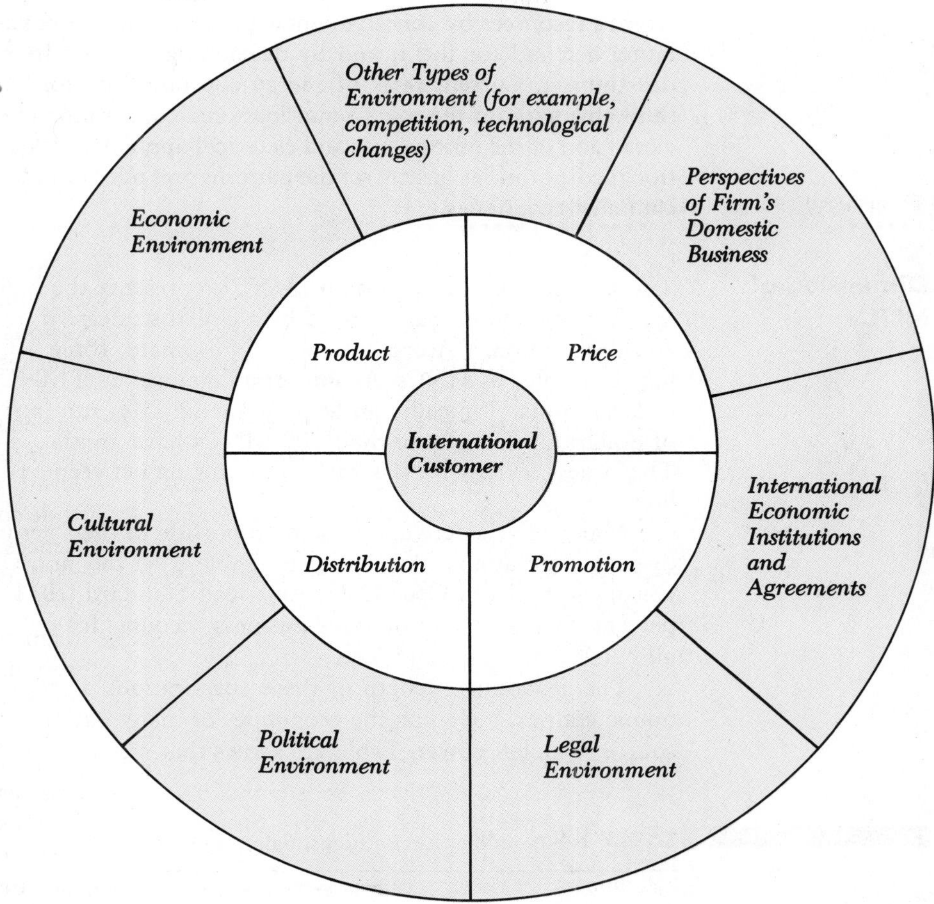

FIGURE 1.1 Decisions and Environments of International Marketing

the domestic U.S. environment, such as competition and technological changes, included in Figure 1.1 under other types of environments. Marketing decisions to serve the international customer also require consideration of the firm's domestic business—its objectives and strategies, commitments and resources, and organization structure.

Multinational Corporations

The multinational corporation is the principal instrument in the expansion of business on an international scale. In barely four decades, it has become, by all accounts, the most formidable single factor in world trade and investment. The multinational corporation plays a decisive role in the allocation and use of the world's resources by conceiving new products and services, by creating or stimulating demand for them, and by developing new modes of manufacturing and distribution. Current rates of energy consumption, for example, would be unthinkable without the role of multinational corporations in the development and expansion of the automobile and electrical appliance industries. Indeed, multinational corporations largely set the patterns and pace of industrialization in today's capitalist economies.

Dimension of MNCs

The ***multinational corporation*** *(MNC)* represents the highest level of overseas involvement and is characterized by a global strategy of investment, production, and distribution.[48] According to a UN estimate, some 10,000 firms worldwide may be labeled as MNCs. An important dimension of MNCs is the predominance of large firms. Typically, an MNC's annual sales run into hundreds of millions of dollars. In fact, more than 500 MNCs have annual sales of over $1 billion. The largest seventy MNCs have sales ranging between $10 billion and $120 billion.

Many MNCs derive a substantial portion of their net income and sales from overseas operations. As shown in Table 1.4, the non-U.S. earnings of Dow Chemical, Gillette, Coca-Cola, American Standard, IBM, and Avon exceed 50 percent. Similarly, international business accounts for over 40 percent of sales of all but W. R. Grace and Xerox.

The economic strength of these corporations as compared with other economic entities, including the economies of many nations, suggests an important source of global power. Table 1.5 shows that many MNCs have a higher annual

TABLE 1.4 Nondomestic Earnings, Sales, and Assets of Selected U.S. Firms (1991)

	PERCENT OF NET EARNINGS	PERCENT OF SALES	PERCENT OF ASSETS
American Standard	64	50	18
Avon	52	45	34
Black & Decker	49	51	56
Coca-Cola	56	46	34
Dow Chemical	53	59	52
Gillette	68	68	70
H.J. Heinz	43	44	46
IBM	65	58	56
ITT	48	47	48
Johnson & Johnson	42	43	41
W.R. Grace	50	36	35
Xerox	35	39	27
Colgate-Palmolive	55	62	34
Hewlett-Packard	52	58	27
Caterpillar	58	59	31

Source: Compiled by the author from the various companies' annual reports

TABLE 1.5 GNP of Various Countries Ranked with Sales of Selected Corporations—1990*

Switzerland	$188.9
Sweden	175.3
General Motors	124.7
Austria	123.7
Exxon	115.8
Ford Motor	97.7
Argentina	97.3
Denmark	82.4
IBM	69.0
Mobil	64.5
Sears Roebuck	56.0
General Electric	52.3
Greece	41.8
Texaco	36.5
DuPont	36.2
Colombia	36.1
Chevron	34.4
Singapore	23.5
New Zealand	22.1

*Figures in billions of U.S. dollars.

Source: GNP—The World Bank, 1991. Sales figures of corporations taken from the various companies' annual reports.

revenue than the GNP of various countries. For example, General Motors generates more revenue annually than the GNP of Denmark, Argentina, or Austria. Similarly, IBM's annual sales exceed the GNP of Colombia, Greece, or New Zealand.

Another important feature of MNCs is their predominantly oligopolistic character; that is, they operate in markets that are dominated by a few sellers. Further, their technological leads, their special skills, and their ability to differentiate their products through advertising are all factors that help to sustain or reinforce their oligopolistic nature. Most MNCs have a sizeable number of foreign branches and affiliates. Two hundred MNCs, among the largest in the world, have affiliates in twenty-five or more countries.

Multinational corporations are mainly the product of developed countries. However, the relative importance of MNCs from different home countries has changed in the last fifteen years—that of Japanese and Western European companies has increased and that of United States companies has declined. The available evidence suggests that these shifts are due primarily to changes in the international competitiveness of companies based in different home countries:

- Japanese MNCs sought to position themselves as producers in the huge United States market and also in Western Europe—markets in which they had negligible investments prior to 1975.

- Western European companies also made large investments in the United States during the 1980s.
- The foreign investments of MNCs based in the United States, on the other hand, expanded at a considerably weaker pace than in the past; those companies concentrated on improving their competitiveness at home.

Adding their home-country output and their production abroad, MNCs account for a significant proportion of total world output. It is estimated that the largest 600 industrial companies account for over one-fourth of value added in the production of goods in the world's market economies. Their importance as exporters and importers is probably even greater. For example, between 80 and 90 percent of the exports of both the United States and the United Kingdom are associated with MNCs. MNCs also loom large in international capital flows. Multinational banks (MNBs) and nonbank financial companies account for the bulk of international lending. Moreover, owing to the transnational character of their operations, nonfinancial MNCs hold liquid assets in several currencies and have in recent years become important participants in world financial markets. And, of course, MNCs are responsible for the vast majority of foreign direct investment (FDI) and production abroad.

Historically, the activity of MNCs developed first in extractive operations in natural resources and public utility areas, such as minerals and petroleum. The MNCs' manufacturing activities abroad started later, both in respect to the processing of raw materials and the production of consumer goods. Currently, manufacturing represents 60 percent of the total estimated stock of foreign direct investment of MNCs; petroleum accounts for 20 percent; mining and smelting, 5 percent; and other industries, 15 percent. In recent years MNCs have become active in services also, especially in banking, tourism, and various kinds of consulting. Banking, in particular, has grown spectacularly.[49] Between 1977 and 1987, U.S. banks almost doubled their foreign locations from 1,080 to 2,030.[50] In 1988, of the top ten banks in the world, seven were Japanese.

In the past, MNCs have made important contributions to developing countries in two critical and related areas: the transfer of technology and the transformation of many countries from exporters of primary commodities into exporters of manufactures. Indeed, this direct contribution to structural change in developing countries appears to be far more important than the transfer of financial resources associated with foreign direct investment by MNCs.

There is, of course, a wide range of issues that MNCs and host developing countries must jointly address. The characteristic features of MNCs are changing rapidly. New production technologies have reduced direct labor costs, while the shift to just-in-time inventory systems has frequently made location more important. Those changes appear to reduce the comparative advantage of developing countries in many assembly operations. The exceptions are countries with large internal markets or those in close proximity to developed-country markets. It might be necessary for developing countries to seek industries with less pronounced labor savings from new technologies. For their part, MNCs may utilize such institutional arrangements as long-term subcontracts to allow developing-countries producers to perfect the low-cost production methods that will be needed in the future. MNCs can also have an impact on social institutions and cultural values in host countries. This has frequently been a concern in developing countries, where the impact of "modernization" can come in conflict with traditional values.

But such issues may be more universal, as evidenced by concerns over the impact of United States–based MNCs in Canada and Western Europe, and the recent growing concern over the role of Japanese MNCs in the United States. Similarly, the role of MNCs in providing employment in developing countries, while at the same time reinforcing existing patterns of discrimination, is an area of mutual concern affecting host countries, and MNCs.

Perhaps the most important issue is the expansion of capital flow to developing countries. As the trade and fiscal imbalances characterizing the world economy diminish, it is hoped that a rising proportion of those funds will flow into developing countries; this would conform to the reasonable expectation that the international private-capital market should allocate funds from high-thrift countries to high-capital-productivity countries. The expansion of capital flow to developing countries, however, should not just be tied to the recycling of trade surpluses. Instead, an important principle is to tie such flow to economic growth.

Until lately, because of restrictions on equity participation, the role of MNCs in the former centrally planned economies has been limited to cooperative arrangements in production, the development and transfer of technology, and marketing. But the pace of political transformations in Eastern Europe and the former Soviet states open unprecedented opportunities. These nations are eagerly seeking Western capital and technology to improve their domestic economies. The eventual hope is that quality improvements and increased competitiveness provided by Western management techniques and resources will enhance the ability of these nations to attract investment capital and export manufactured goods in world markets.

MNCs are sensitive to opportunities in Eastern Europe and many companies have already sought entry. For example, General Electric Company has completed a $150 million contract for 5 percent of Tungsram, Hungary's state-owned maker of light bulbs. It was estimated that by the end of 1990, 9,700 joint ventures have been established in Poland, Hungary, and Czechoslovakia.[51]

Multinationals from the Third World

Multinational corporations belonging to the developing countries are a new source of competition in the world markets. The Birla Group of India, United Laboratories from the Philippines, and Autlan of Mexico are among the several hundred multinationals from the Third World whose overseas subsidiaries have increased from dozens around 1960 to a few thousand today. They are successfully competing for a share of world markets.

These multinationals have gone abroad following the international product life cycle concept (see Chapter 2). They began by seeking export markets. When tariffs, quotas, or other barriers threatened overseas markets, these companies started assembling abroad. Their initial move, and greatest impact so far, has been in neighboring developing countries.

The strength of Third World MNCs comes from their special experience with manufacturing for small home markets. Using low technology and local raw material, running job-shop kinds of plants, and making effective use of semiskilled labor, they are able to custom-design products best suited to host countries. For example, a Philippines paper company has managed projects in countries ranging from Indonesia to Nigeria. Its managers have drawn on their ability to make paper from inexpensive, locally available materials. In addition, they run a very efficient job-shop operation with printing, folding, and cutting machinery selected or built in-house to make very short runs of a wide range of cigarette, candy, and other packages. These are skills that the Western multinationals have usually forgotten.[52]

While small-scale manufacturing remains their unique strength, these companies also are moving in other areas that are particularly suited to local conditions. For example, a Thai company uses rice stalks for paper and plantain products for glue. A Brazilian company has developed sunfast dyes and household appliances that resist high humidity and can survive the fluctuating voltages common in the developing world.

The rapid growth of Third World multinationals provides both a threat and an opportunity to the multinationals from the advanced countries. The Third World MNCs can be tough competitors in seeking contract work in building plants that do not require high technology, such as steel plants and chemical complexes. But these MNCs also offer profitable opportunities to Western companies for joint operations. Lacking in marketing skills, for example, they may share their special know-how with traditional multinationals in exchange for brand names and skills in promoting new lines. Further, as Third World MNCs become visible and viable economic entities, their governments may well become more sympathetic to the needs of MNCs from the developed world.

MNCs and the Nation States

The expansion of MNCs proceeded on a relatively quiet basis during the 1950s and 1960s. The whole idea of producing as well as selling abroad was welcomed by most countries whether they were involved as investors or hosts. The international transfer of capital, management, and technology created new jobs and helped to develop natural resources. Within the prevailing world economic order, a favorable business environment grew in scores of countries. The system of fixed exchange rates, a downward trend in tariff barriers, and an expansive world economy encouraged companies—large and small—to join in and do business globally.

However, as the upsurge in international business gained strength during this period, questions began to be raised regarding the economic, political, and social significance of the change, first in Europe and elsewhere in the world. The idea was advanced in France that the spread of American business throughout Western Europe was generating a basic challenge to European societies as well as to European corporations.[53] A second wave of concern, which gained momentum in the developing countries during the 1960s, arose within the United Nations Conference on Trade and Development (UNCTAD). A new world bloc emerged, urging improved terms of trade between developed and developing regions of the world and a redistribution of labor and wealth on an international scale. Its members—sometimes referred to as the "Group of 77"—began to view the rising strength of the MNCs as a threat, rather than as a benefit, to their newly proposed world economic order.

This organized questioning of the concept of multinational business led, in the early 1970s, to passage of the United Nations Charter on Economic Rights and Duties of States. The charter was, and still is, viewed by business as an attempt at a basic reordering of the international economic environment. The impetus behind the charter soon led to the creation of the United Nations Commission on Transnational Corporations and the beginnings of a code of conduct for international business dealings and multinational enterprises.

These and other movements around the world—fueled by revelations of questionable practices of some multinational corporations—focused new attention on the fundamental concepts of multinational enterprises. In many respects, the rising storm of criticism centers on basic social considerations even more than on the economics of MNCs. The fundamental question is the extent to which these enterprises are either contributing to or threatening national economic and social development programs.

The criticism of MNCs is not limited to host developing countries. For example, domestic labor unions in the United States have decried the MNCs for transferring jobs overseas and for entering into shady deals through bribery and politicking.

Contributions and Criticisms of MNCs

There are as many arguments that favor MNCs as those that oppose them. Multinational corporations, on the whole, have made significant positive contributions to economic and social progress throughout the world. Through their technological and managerial capabilities, MNCs have helped to develop the material and productive resources of many nations and have worked to meet the world's growing needs for goods and services. Their investments have stimulated the diversification of local national economies. Their capital input has helped host governments to fulfill nationally defined economic development goals. They have provided jobs and helped to raise living standards in many areas.

Today's global corporations are entirely different from the East India companies of the past. They are nationality-less and do not bear any special allegiance to a country per se, even to the country of their origin. Today's consumers have become less nationalistic, and companies have become more responsive. True global corporations serve the interests of customers, not governments. They do not exploit local situations and then repatriate all the profits back home, leaving each host country poorer for having been there. They invest, they train, they pay taxes, they build up infrastructure, and they provide good value to customers in all countries where they do business. This is not altruism on their part, nor is it a calculated effort to win good press that will stop as soon as attention moves elsewhere. This is simply good—in fact, essential—for business, their mainstay.

If governments need not be so fearful of these foreign-based companies and erect barriers against them, neither have their obligations to their people ended. Governments still have the responsibility, now more important than ever, to educate their citizens and to provide first-class infrastructure for the businesses that will employ those citizens and provide them with goods and services. They must adopt policies that will attract global companies and induce them to do business and invest and pay taxes in their countries. Even better, they should nurture their local companies and help them expand into the global arena.

By and large, modern multinational corporations do not seek to exploit local resources or to strike private deals with governments for licenses to operate within their borders. What they come looking for now are good markets and good workers, and they bring in exchange, not private deals for officials, but the promise of a better life for the people. These are worthwhile potentialities to which governments must be ready to respond.

Nevertheless, in the 1970s, in response to the various criticisms of MNCs, significant changes did occur that affected the world environment in which MNCs must operate. Many MNCs responded appropriately by adopting new perspectives for doing business overseas. A number of MNCs issued codes of ethical conduct for transacting business abroad. The United States government took measures to regulate United States–based MNCs. For example, the Foreign Corrupt Practices Act was passed in 1977 to prohibit the MNCs from making questionable payments.

Corporate Responses

Until recently most United States–based multinational enterprises have had little need to focus rigorously on their objectives, strategies, or managerial mechanisms for handling international operations. For the most part, they have continued in old patterns and:

- Viewed their international markets as secondary to, and merely an extension of, the U.S. market.
- Assumed that the management tools utilized to run their domestic operations could be used to run their international operations or have been unable to develop new management tools to deal with the more complex problems of international management.
- Concentrated on the design of new organizational charts to be utilized in the management of their international operations, rather than on how best to reallocate resources to businesses instead of to products or geographic markets.
- Maintained a U.S.–based ethnocentric mentality.

The United States has now entered a phase, however, in which the use of these old perceptions and management tools will prove increasingly inadequate for dealing with the dynamic forces at work. Consequently, the following responses seem mandated for acknowledgment and action:

1. *Greater articulation of corporate objectives internationally.* Corporations should seriously question why they are operating internationally.
2. *Clearer articulation of competitive advantages and bargaining power.* Many United States–based multinational enterprises are in unique com-

petitive positions but are not taking full advantage of them. The increasing competition and the nationalistic pressures faced from abroad should force corporations to focus more sharply on the nature of their advantages and bargaining powers. For example, these may include unique capability because of multiple locations abroad and sophisticated information systems; unique technological capabilities; well-known trade names; economies of scale; unique capital position or access to capital markets; unique managerial competence; and the portfolio effect—that is, the capacity, resulting from multimarkets or multiple sources, to withstand negative cycles that stem from nationalistic, economic, or competitive pressures and the flexibility to respond more readily to opportunities and threats as they arise.

3. *Shift to more defensive strategies.* After several decades of rapid world growth, many United States–based multinational enterprises may give high priority to the preservation of the global systems already in place. Although the strategy is defensive, it does not necessarily suggest a mere maintenance of the status quo, but rather the importance of preserving and maximizing the efficiency of the systems already in place.
4. *Withdrawal to the U.S. domestic market.* Given the complexities of the international environment and increasing foreign competition, some United States–based multinationals may choose to withdraw from the international scene. Some may do so because of shaky shareholder support for foreign operations. Others may not be prepared to make the investment in people and management systems that is required to deal effectively with the inherent subtleties and complexities.
5. *The development of sophisticated monitoring systems.* Increased awareness of the importance of anticipating changes in the international environment will impel United States–based multinationals to develop more sophisticated mechanisms for scanning the international environment to better identify emerging opportunities and threats.
6. *More sophisticated techniques for managing risk.* Few firms have established effective systems for managing the many types of risks inherent in the international environment. As time progresses, they will be forced to do so more and more.

Strategic Implications

Now that the historical, present, and future changes in the international environment of the multinational corporations have been touched on, the question arises as to what strategies should be adopted to chart the waters of an uncertain future.

The most important strategy is to formulate programs with greater flexibility. The days of the multinationals dictating terms, running the operation, and taking out exorbitant returns on their investments with little concern for the impact on the host nation are gone forever. All countries, regardless of their stage of development, have become keenly aware of the economic world around them and are not likely to accept the arrangements characteristic of the past. Multinational corporations must be prepared for long, hard negotiations, often under disadvantageous conditions, and must be ready to make numerous concessions if they expect to gain access to foreign opportunities.

PepsiCo's deal in India illustrates the point. In 1988, the company, in a race to expand its world market share, accepted tough conditions from the Indian government to make and sell Pepsi-Cola. The company contracted to make a soft-drink concentrate, a fruit drink concentrate, and snack foods from locally acquired produce. In return for entry into the country, PepsiCo agreed that the venture would export five times the value of its imported components. If that condition is not met, PepsiCo cannot repatriate royalties and profits. Nor will PepsiCo hold a majority share: it owns 39.9 percent of the venture, and a government corporation has a 36.1 percent stake. The Tata Group, India's largest industrial corporation, owns 24 percent. PepsiCo acknowledged that, in comparison with similar accords PepsiCo signed with the former Soviet Union and China, the agreement's terms were harsh but necessary for early entry into India's developing market.[54] Beyond gaining access, the multinational corporations must also be prepared to contribute actively in ways never before imagined to the growth and prosperity of the people of the host nations.

In addition, the multinational should be tolerant of, and sensitive to, the policies and desires of its own country. The home government can offer a great deal of aid to the multinationals in the form of technical and research data, as well as protection against the dangers of expropriation. The knowledge that a home government is supportive and protective of its MNCs will further enhance their position in dealing with other foreign governments. To attain this end, the MNC should also attempt to enhance its image at home and abroad by educating the public on the positive aspects of its activities.

Finally, MNCs must continue to grow and expand in the world and keep themselves competitive with multinationals of other nations. Because resource scarcities are here to stay, it will be the responsibility of the multinationals to use their financial strength and technical ability to undertake the search for new ways to meet the needs of the world. At the same time, they must follow a growth and development strategy that includes locating and extracting resources cheaply in order to meet worldwide consumer and industrial demands.

In conclusion, the multinationals must develop strategies that stimulate their growth and competitiveness while at the same time stemming public apprehension about the misuse of MNC power. This is no easy task, but it must be done. Governments worldwide will force MNCs to temper their strategies for the public good. Obviously MNC and public objectives often will conflict, but the ultimate search should be for the optimal strategic blend. Flexibility and constant change of individual strategies will achieve more than will unwavering commitment to any one long-term strategy.

Entry Strategies

Four different modes of business offer a company entry into foreign markets: (1) exporting (2) contractual agreement, (3) joint venture, and (4) manufacturing.[55]

Exporting

A company may minimize the risk of dealing internationally by exporting domestically manufactured products either by minimal response to inquiries or by systematic development of demand in foreign markets. Exporting requires minimal capital and is easy to initiate. Exporting is also a good way to gain international experience. A major part of the overseas involvement of large U.S. firms is through export trade.

Contractual Agreement

There are several types of contractual agreements:

Patent Licensing Agreements These are based on either a fixed-fee or a royalty basis and include managerial training.

Turnkey Operations These are based on a fixed-fee or cost-plus arrangement and include plant construction, personnel training, and initial production runs.

Coproduction Agreements These are most common in the socialist countries, where plants are built and then paid for with part of the output.

Management Contracts Currently widely used in the Middle East, these require that a multinational corporation provide key personnel to operate the foreign enterprise for a fee until local people acquire the ability to manage the business independently. For example, Whittaker Corp. of Los Angeles operates government-owned hospitals in several cities in Saudi Arabia.

Licensing This works as a viable alternative in some contractual agreement situations where risk of expropriation and resistance to foreign investments create uncertainty. *Licensing* encompasses a variety of contractual agreements whereby a multinational marketer makes available intangible assets—such as patents, trade secrets, know-how, trademarks, and company name—to foreign companies in return for royalties or other forms of payment. Transfer of these assets usually is accompanied by technical services to ensure proper use. Licensing, however, has some advantages and disadvantages as summarized below.[56]

Some of the advantages of licensing are:

1. Licensing requires little capital and serves as a quick and easy entry to foreign markets.
2. In some countries, notably the developed communist countries, licensing is the only way to tap the market.
3. Licensing provides life extension for products in the maturity stage of their life cycles.
4. Licensing is a good alternative to foreign production and marketing in an environment where there is worldwide inflation, skilled-labor shortages, increasing domestic and foreign governmental regulation and restriction, and tough international competition.
5. Licensing royalties are guaranteed and periodic, whereas shared income from investment fluctuates and is risky.

6. Domestically based firms can benefit from product development abroad without research expense through technical feedback arrangements.
7. When exports no longer are profitable because of intense competition, licensing provides an alternative.
8. Licensing can overcome high transportation costs, which make some exports noncompetitive in the target markets.
9. Licensing is also immune to expropriation.
10. In some countries, manufacturers of military equipment or any product deemed critical to the national interest (including communication equipment) may be compelled to enter licensing agreements.

Some disadvantages of licensing are:

1. To attract licensees, a firm must possess distinctive technology, a trademark, and a company or brand name that is attractive to potential foreign users.
2. The licensor has no control over production and marketing by the licensee.
3. Licensing royalties are negligible compared with equity investment potential. Royalty rates seldom exceed 5 percent of gross sales because of host government restrictions.
4. The licensee may lose interest in renewing the contract unless the licensor holds interest through innovation and new technology.
5. There is a danger of creating competition in third, or even home, markets if the licensee violates territorial agreements. Going to court in these situations is expensive and time consuming and no international adjudicatory body exists.

Joint Venture

Joint venture represents a higher-risk alternative because it requires various levels of direct investment. A joint venture between a U.S. firm and a native operation abroad involves sharing risks to accomplish mutual enterprise. Joint ventures, incidentally, are the next most common form of entry once a firm moves beyond the exporting stage to a more regular overseas involvement. One example of a joint venture is General Motors Corporation's partnership with Egypt's state-owned Nasar Car Company to establish a plant to assemble trucks and diesel engines. Another example of a joint venture is between Matsushita of Japan and IBM to manufacture small computers. The alliance between Coca-Cola Co. and Nestlé S.A. to develop and sell ready-to-drink coffees and teas is still another example of a joint venture. Joint ventures normally are designed to take advantage of the strong functions of the partners and supplement their weak functions, be they management, research, or marketing.

Joint ventures provide a mutually beneficial opportunity for domestic and foreign businesses to join forces.[57] For both parties, the ventures are a means to share both capital and risk and make use of each other's technical strength. Japanese companies, for example, prefer entering into joint ventures with U.S. firms because such arrangements help ensure against possible American trade barriers. American firms, on the other hand, like the opportunity to enter a previously forbidden market, to utilize established channels, to link American product innovation with low-cost Japanese manufacturing technology, and to curb a potentially tough competitor.

As a case in point, General Foods Corporation tried for more than a decade to succeed in Japan on its own and watched the market share of its instant coffee (Maxwell House) drop from 20 to 14 percent. Then, in 1975 the firm established a joint venture with Ajinomoto, a food manufacturer, to use the full power of the Japanese partner's product distribution system and personnel and managerial capabilities. Within two years, Maxwell House's share of the Japanese instant coffee market had recovered and in 1982 was close to 25 percent.[58]

Joint ventures, however, are not an unmixed blessing. The major problem in managing joint ventures stems from one cause: there is more than one partner and one of the partners must play the key, dominant role to steer the business to success.

Joint ventures should be designed to supplement each partner's shortcomings, and not to exploit each other's strengths and weaknesses. It takes as much effort to make a joint venture a success as to start a grass-roots operation and eventually bring it up to a successful level. In both cases, each partner must be fully prepared to expend the effort necessary to understand customers, competitors, and himself. A joint venture is a means of resource appropriation and of easing a foreign business's entry into a new terrain. It should not be viewed as a handy vehicle to reap money without effort, interest, and/or additional resources.

Joint ventures are a wave of the future. There is hardly a Fortune 1000 company, active overseas, that does not have at least one joint venture. Widespread interest in joint ventures is related to:

1. *Seeking market opportunities.* Companies in mature industries in the United States find joint venture a desirable entry mode to enter attractive new markets overseas.
2. *Dealing with rising economic nationalism.* Often host governments are more receptive to or require joint ventures.
3. *Preempting raw materials.* Countries with raw materials, such as petroleum or extractable material, usually do not allow foreign firms to be active there other than through joint venture.
4. *Sharing risk.* Rather than taking the entire risk, a joint venture allows the risk to be shared with a partner, which can be especially important in politically sensitive areas.
5. *Developing an export base.* In areas where economic blocs play a significant role, joint venture with a local firm smooths the entry into the entire region, such as entry into the EC market through a joint venture with an English company.

6. *Selling technology.* Selling technology to developing countries becomes easier through a joint venture.

Even a joint venture with a well-qualified majority foreign partner may provide significant advantages, such as:

1. *Participation in income and growth.* The minority partner shares in the earnings and growth of the venture even if its own technology becomes obsolete.
2. *Low cash requirements.* Know-how or patents, or both, can be considered as partial capital contribution.
3. *Preferred treatment.* Since it is locally controlled, the venture is treated with preference by the government.
4. *Easier access to a market and to market information.* A locally controlled firm can seek market access and information much more easily than can a firm controlled by foreigners.
5. *Less drain on managerial resources.* The local partner takes care of most managerial responsibilities.
6. *United States income tax deferral.* Income to the U.S. minority partner is not subject to U.S. taxation until distribution.[59]

Although joint venture is an attractive entry mode, firms considering such an arrangement should be realistic about the potential failure of the joint venture. The underlying causes of joint venture failures include:[60]

1. *Product failure.* The joint venture fails to meet output objectives.
2. *Shared weaknesses.* Weaknesses of the joint venture partners frequently result in the project's failure.
3. *Unsatisfactory distribution of costs and benefits.* No joint venture would be established unless both parties believed that the benefits to be achieved would be commensurate with the costs, and that both partners would act in good faith to balance benefits. Either one or both of these assumptions may prove to be ill-founded. Violations of good faith are common, and problems often arise regarding information and intellectual property.
4. *Conflicts between partners.* A common conflict is over time frames—one partner is satisfied with slower progress, while the other may need shorter-term results. Conflicts also arise when the partners are competitors in other areas, or if the joint venture competes with one or both of the partners.
5. *Political or cultural conflicts.* Such conflicts can arise between partners within the joint venture organization or between the joint venture and external agencies or governments.
6. *Internal cultural conflicts.* Usually, these conflicts occur over work

styles. They are frequently exacerbated by unionization issues and legal restrictions.

When either partner in a joint venture concludes that the venture is a failure, there are five alternatives to resolve the problem. First, the joint venture may be continued even if it is seen as a failure if the circumstances force the partners to do so. Both partners may be temporarily dependent on the venture for some critical resource, or one party may have legal basis for forcing continuation. Second, one partner may be much more dependent on the joint venture than the other and want to continue the business. Third, another entity may acquire all or a major portion of the joint venture. Fourth, a new organization independent of the original partners is created to run the business. This option is usually relevant for joint ventures that have achieved some measure of success but that are no longer useful to the founding partners. Finally, the joint venture may be liquidated.

The choice of which termination strategy to use depends on a number of factors. If either partner is dependent on the joint venture for some critical resource, the preservation of that resource will be a critical consideration in selecting a strategy. Another factor is whether the joint venture could survive as an independent entity. If the joint venture is not dependent specifically on the founding partners, it may be able to shift its association to some other business organization.

If the owners decide not to continue a joint venture, the outcome will depend on whether the venture is worth more as a going concern than its liquidation value. New joint ventures will be less visible and less attractive to potential buyers than old ones. Small joint ventures are unlikely to have the necessary resources to survive as independent organizations. All of these factors suggest that new and small ventures will be liquidated. Larger and longer-established ventures have a greater opportunity for survival.

Manufacturing

A multinational corporation may also establish itself in an overseas market by direct investment in a manufacturing and/or assembly subsidiary. Because of the volatility of worldwide economic, social, and political conditions, this form of involvement is most risky. An example of a direct investment situation is Chesebrough-Pond's operation of overseas manufacturing plants in Japan, England, and Monte Carlo.

Manufacturing around the world is riskier, as illustrated by India's Bhopal disaster, in which a poisonous gas leak in a Union Carbide Corp. plant killed over 2,000 people and permanently disabled thousands (in the worst industrial accident that has ever occurred). It is suggested that MNCs should not manufacture overseas where the risk of a mishap may jeopardize the survival of the whole company. As a matter of fact, in the wake of the Bhopal accident, many host countries tightened safety and environmental regulations. For example, Brazil, the world's fourth-largest user of agricultural chemicals, restricted the use of the deadly methyl isocyanate.[61]

Conclusion

A firm interested in entering the international market must evaluate the risk and commitment involved with each entry and choose the entry mode that best fits the company's objectives and resources.[62] Entry risk and commitment can be examined by considering five factors:

1. Characteristics of the product.
2. The market's external macroenvironment—particularly economic and political factors, and the demand and buying pattern characteristics of potential customers.
3. The firm's competitive position—especially, the product's life cycle stage, as well as various corporate strengths and weaknesses.
4. Capital budgeting considerations including resource costs and availabilities.
5. Internal corporate perceptions, which affect corporate selection of information and the psychic distance between a firm's decision makers and its target customers, as well as control and risk-taking preferences.

These five factors combined indicate the risk to be reviewed vis-à-vis a company's resources before determining a mode of entry.

Computerized simulation models can be employed to determine the desired entry route by simultaneously evaluating such factors as environmental opportunity, risk index, competitive risk index, corporate strength index, product channel direction index, comparative cost index, and corporate policy and perception index.[63]

It is useful to remember that a company may use different modes of entry in different countries. For example, McDonald's Corporation deemed it sufficient to license three restaurants on the small Caribbean island of Aruba, but in Japan it has had a joint venture since 1971. The local partner helped McDonald's blanket the Japanese market to such an extent that there are now over 600 outlets across the country, the largest number of McDonald's restaurants in any country outside the United States.

Summary

In today's environment even firms that do not seek to do business outside their national boundaries have no choice but to be aware of the international business scene. The U.S. economy in particular is so intricately linked to international economics that even strictly domestic business is affected by what takes place in other countries. The far-reaching impact of international business necessitates that students of business be thoroughly informed about the perspectives of international business.

International marketing instruction in particular is required because, of all the functional areas of a business, marketing problems are the most fundamental and the most frequent. While basic marketing decisions do not change as marketers expand their business from the domestic field to the international field, the environments they must consider while making those decisions can be profoundly different. The major aspects of the international marketing environment include the economic, the cultural, and the legal and political environments.

International marketing is also affected by international institutional arrangements, such as the international monetary system vis-à-vis the International Monetary Fund, and multinational agreements, such as the European Community (EC).

A firm aspiring to enter the international scene may choose from the various entry modes—exporting, contractual agreement, joint venture, and manufacturing. Each entry mode provides different opportunities and risks.

Today's thrust for growth in international business comes from the MNCs (multinational corporations). In recent years, the tactics of the MNCs, however, have become a subject of intense discussion, particularly with reference to their operations in LDCs (less-developed countries). While the multinational corporation will continue to be an institution of great significance, the environment in the 1990s and beyond will require a greater awareness of the needs of host countries.

Review Questions

1. Why should a business operating entirely in the U.S. domestic market be concerned with happenings in the international business environment?
2. Why should international marketing be considered as a separate field of study even though marketing decisions in both domestic and international markets are basically the same?
3. What do you recommend that the multinational corporations do to become more acceptable in LDCs?
4. What are the different modes of entry into the international market? What are the relative advantages and disadvantages of each mode?
5. How can a firm's overseas involvement be categorized?
6. Why do a very large proportion of U.S. firms confine themselves to domestic markets?
7. Why should a firm enter international business? Explain the reasons with illustrations.

Endnotes

1. *See* Andrew Kupfer, "How to Be a Global Manager," *Fortune,* March 14, 1988, p. 52.
2. U.S. Department of Commerce.
3. Lynda Schuster, "Brazil Captures a Big Share of the U.S. Shoe Market," *The Wall Street Journal,* August 27, 1985.
4. U.S. Department of Commerce.
5. 1990 Annual Report of the Anheuser-Busch Companies.
6. The direct investment position is the net book value of U.S. companies and other investors' equity in and outstanding loans to foreign affiliates.
7. *The Global Century: A Source Book on U.S.*

Business and the Third World (Washington, D.C.: National Cooperative Business Association, 1989).

8. *Business America* April 22, 1991, pp. 2–7; and U.S. Department of Commerce.
9. Ibid.
10. "The U.S. Trade Outlook in 1992," *Business America,* April 5, 1992, pp. 2–4.
11. Sylvia Nasar, "America Still Reigns in Services," *Fortune,* June 5, 1989, p. 64.
12. Ken Dychtwald and Grey Gable, "American Diversity," *American Demographics,* July 1991, pp. 75–77.
13. *See* "No Smoking Sweeps America," *Business Week,* July 27, 1987, p. 40. *Also see* James S. Hirsch, "U.S. Liquor Makers Seek Tonic in Foreign Markets," *The Wall Street Journal,* October 24, 1989, p. B1.
14. *See Business Week,* February 29, 1988, p. 74.
15. Based on various editions of the *Statistical Abstract of the United States* (Washington, D.C.: U.S. Department of Commerce). *Also see* Edmund Faltermayer, "Is 'Made in U.S.A.' Fading Away," *Fortune,* September 24, 1990, p. 62; and Barbara Rosewicz, "Gulf Oil Spill Shows Iraq's Resolve to Wage War on Its Own Terms," *The Wall Street Journal,* January 18, 1991, p. 1.
16. U.S. Department of Agriculture.
17. *See* Wendy L. Wall, "World's Grain Output Surges as Nations Seek Food Self-Sufficiency," *The Wall Street Journal,* April 6, 1987, p. 1.
18. Clare Ansberry, "Eastman Kodak Co. Has Arduous Struggle to Regain Lost Edge," *The Wall Street Journal,* April 2, 1987, p. 1.
19. *See* Edmund Faltermayer, "Is 'Made in U.S.A.' Fading Away," *Fortune,* September 24, 1990, p. 62.
20. "Just What Detroit Needs: 200,000 More Toyotas a Year," *Business Week,* December 10, 1990, p. 29. *Also see* Alex Taylor III, "Can GM Remodel," *Fortune,* January 13, 1992, p. 26.
21. "The Americanization of Honda," *Business Week,* April 25, 1988, p. 90. *Also see* "The Potholes in Detroit's Path." *Business Week,* October 3, 1988, p. 3.
22. Robert Guenther and Michael R. Sesit, "U.S. Banks are Losing Business to Japanese at Home and Abroad," *The Wall Street Journal,* October 12, 1989, p. 1.
23. "America's High-Tech Crisis," *Business Week,* March 11, 1985, p. 56. *Also see* Bernard Wysocki, Jr., "American Firms Send Office Work Abroad to Use Cheaper Labor," *The Wall Street Journal,* August 14, 1991, p. 1.
24. *Business Week,* August 10, 1987, p. 54. *Also see* Robert L. Rose, "Zenith Sells a 5% Stake to Goldstar," *The Wall Street Journal,* February 26, 1991, p. A3.
25. "Leap Forward or Sink Back," *Development Forum,* March 1982, p. 3.
26. Ford S. Worthy, "A New Mass Market Emerges," *Fortune,* Pacific Rim 1990, p. 51.
27. *See* Richard N. Farmer, "Would You Want Your Granddaughter to Marry a Taiwanese Marketing Man?" *Journal of Marketing,* October 1987, pp. 111–116.
28. "Laying Foundation for the Great Mall of China," *Business Week,* January 25, 1988, p. 68.
29. *See* Anthony J. O'Reilly. "Establishing Successful Joint Ventures in Developing Nations: A CEO's Perspective," *Columbia Journal of World Business,* Spring 1988, pp. 3–9.
30. Theodore Levitt, "The Globalization of Markets," *Harvard Business Review,* May–June 1983, pp. 92–102.
31. *See* Vern Terpstra, "The Changing Environment of International Marketing," *International Marketing Review,* Autumn 1985, pp. 7–16.
32. "Solving the Third World's Growth Crisis," *Business Week,* August 12, 1985, p. 36. *Also see Foreign Assistance Program: FY 1986 Budget and 1985 Supplement Request* (Washington, D.C.: U.S. Department of State, May 1985), p. 2.
33. Adapted from Douglass C. Norvell and Sion Raveed, "Eleven Reasons for Firms to Go International," *Marketing News,* October 17, 1980, p. 1.
34. Neal Templin, "Beleaguered at Home, U.S. Car Makers Get a Boost From New Customers Abroad," *The Wall Street Journal,* November 8, 1991, p. B1.
35. Matt Miller, "Soviets, India Trade Without Hard Cash," *The Wall Street Journal,* July 24, 1987, p. 18.
36. *The International Dimension of Management Education,* a report by a Special Brookings Panel (Washington, D.C.: The Brookings Institution, 1975), p. 10.
37. *A Special Report on Globalization* (New

York: Booz, Allen & Hamilton, 1991), pp. 10–11.

38. Frederick W. Gluck, "Meeting the Challenge of Global Competition," *The McKinsey Quarterly,* Autumn 1982, p. 10.
39. *See* John Marcom, Jr., "British Industry Suffers from Failure to Heed Basics of Marketing," *The Wall Street Journal,* January 15, 1987, p. 1. *Also see* Tamer Cavusgil and John R. Nevin, "The State of the Art in International Marketing: An Assessment," in Subash C. Jain and Lewis R. Tucker, Jr., eds., *International Marketing: Managerial Perspectives* (Boston: Kent Publishing Co., 1986), pp. 27–59.
40. *See* Vern Terpstra, "The Evolution of International Marketing," *International Marketing Review,* Summer 1987, pp. 47–59.
41. Frank Meissner, "Americans Must Practice the Marketing They Preach to Succeed in Japan's Mass Markets," *Marketing News,* October 17, 1980, p. 5.
42. *See* Kenichi Ohmae, *Beyond National Borders* (Homewood, IL: Dow Jones–Irwin, 1987), Chapter 3.
43. Stephen K. Yoder, "Apple, Loser in Japan Computer Market, Tries to Recoup by Redesigning its Models," *The Wall Street Journal,* June 21, 1985, p. 30.
44. Secil Tuncalp, "U.S. Needs More Marketing in Saudi Arabian Market," *Marketing News,* June 19, 1987, p. 10. Published by and reprinted with permission from the American Marketing Association.
45. *Business and International Education,* a report of the Task Force on Business and International Education (Washington, D.C.: American Council on Education, 1977), p. 3.
46. David A. Ricks, *Big Business Blunders* (Homewood, IL: Dow Jones–Irwin, 1983).
47. Hirotaka Takeuchi and Michael E. Porter, "Three Roles of International Marketing in Global Strategy," in Michael Porter, ed., *Competition in Global Industries,* (Boston: Harvard Business School Press, 1986), pp. 111–146.
48. Factual information in this section is mainly from "Dimensions of Multinational Corporations," in Subhash C. Jain and Lewis R. Tucker, Jr., *International Marketing: Managerial Perspectives,* 2nd ed. (Boston: Kent Publishing Company, 1986), pp. 1–23; and *Transnational Corporations in World Development: Trends and Prospects* (New York: United Nations, 1988). Factual information was updated with the help of the UN Center for Transnational Corporations.
49. *See* J. J. Boddewyn, Marsha B. Halbrich, and A. C. Perry, Service Multinationals: Conceptualization, Measurement and Theory," *Journal of International Business Studies,* Fall 1986, pp. 41–57.
50. "The World's Top 50 Banks: It's Official—Japan Is Way Out Front," *Business Week,* June 27, 1988, p. 76.
51. Lewis R. Tucker and Subhash C. Jain, "MNC Market Opportunity Analysis of Eastern Europe: An Innovation Perspective," unpublished paper.
52. *See* Heidi Vernon-Wortzel and Lawrence H. Wortzel, "Globalizing Strategies for Multinationals from Developing Countries," *Columbia Journal of World Business,* Spring 1988, pp. 27–36.
53. *See* J. J. Servan-Schreiber, *The American Challenge* (New York: Atheneum, 1968).
54. Anthony Spaeth and Amal Kumar Naj, "PepsiCo Accepts Tough Conditions for the Right to Sell Cola in India," *The Wall Street Journal,* September 20, 1988, p. 44.
55. *See* Franklin R. Root, *Entry Strategies for the Foreign Markets: From Domestic to International Business* (New York: AMACOM, 1977). *Also see* James D. Goodnow, "Developments in International Mode of Entry Analysis," *International Marketing Review,* Autumn, 1985, pp. 17–30.
56. Allan C. Reddy, "International Licensing May Be Best Bet for Companies Seeking Foreign Markets," *Marketing News,* November 12, 1982, p. 6. *Also see* Farok J. Contractor, "Technology Licensing Practice in U.S. Companies: Corporate & Public Policy Implications," *Columbia Journal of World Business,* Fall 1983, pp. 80–88.
57. *See* Peter Lorange and Gilbert Probst, "Joint Ventures as Self-organizing Systems: A Key to Successful Joint Venture Design and Implementation," *Columbia Journal of World Business,* Summer 1987, pp. 71–78.
58. Kenichi Ohmae, *Triad Power* (New York: The Free Press, 1985), p. 116.
59. F. Kingston Berlew, "The Joint Venture: A Way into Foreign Markets." *Harvard Business Review,* July–August 1984, p. 48. *Also see* Farok Contractor, "A Generalized Theorem of Joint-Venture and Licensing Negotia-

tions," *Journal of International Business Studies,* Summer 1985, pp. 23–49.

60. Wilbur Moulton, "International Joint Ventures: What to Do When Things Go Wrong," *Global Perspective,* Fall 1990, p. 1.
61. "For Multinationals it Will Never Be the Same," *Business Week,* December 24, 1984, p. 57.
62. *See* M. Krishna Erramilli and C. P. Rao, "Choice of Foreign Market Entry Modes by Service Firms," 1988 Educators' Conference Proceedings (Chicago: American Marketing Association, 1988), p. 20.
63. James D. Goodnow, "Individual Product/Market Transnational Mode of Entry Strategies—Some Eclectic Decision-Making Formats," Working Papers Series 1980, No. 1, Walter E. Heller College of Business Administration, Roosevelt University, p. 6. *Also see* William H. Davidson, *Global Strategic Management* (New York: John Wiley & Sons, 1982); James D. Goodnow, "Development of Personal Computer Software for International Mode of Entry Decisions," a paper presented at the 1985 Annual Meeting of the Academy of International Business, New York, October 1985; and C. K. Prahalad and Yves L. Doz, *The Multinational Mission,* (New York: The Free Press, 1987), Chapter 3 and Chapter 4.

CHAPTER • 2

Economic Analysis of Multinational Trade and Business

CHAPTER FOCUS

After studying this chapter, you should be able to:

- Discuss the rationale for multinational trade and business
- Describe the barriers that nations impose to restrict free trade
- Examine the role of the General Agreement on Tariffs and Trade (GATT) in liberalizing world trade
- Describe the U.S. trade liberalization endeavors
- Discuss how a multinational corporation participates in global markets

Commerce is older than recorded history. Archaeological discoveries provide us with evidence of the antiquity of trade. Thousands of ancient commercial documents indicate that a considerable commercial class existed many centuries before any European or Mediterranean city attained a high degree of civilization. In the ancient world, there had even developed a system of payment of precious objects for traded goods—a forerunner of the modern system.

Trading has evolved through the ages in response to altering needs spurred by changes in technology and philosophy. Growth in trade was particularly stimulated by the discovery and use of metals and by the global horizons provided by advances first in transportation and later in communication. Trade has evolved from exchanges between isolated peoples, to trade through conquest, to trade among friendly neighbors, to a system of silent barter among both adversaries and friends. In brief, world trade as we know it today is not a new phenomenon. Groups of people have always traded.

As civilization progressed around the world, however, trading became more organized and productive. For example, ancient seaborne commerce was inefficient and, proportionately, insignificant. Piracy and raiding of ships were commonplace. Such hazards discouraged trade expansion and required that harbors be fortified for protection. In modern times, although nations still go to war, piracy and raiding have been virtually eliminated by a variety of treaties, arrangements, and other international laws.

World trade requires that nations be willing to cooperate with each other. Countries naturally trade with those nations with whom they are on friendly terms. But trading often goes on among nations even when political relations are not amicable. For example, the United States and China are politically opposed, yet the two nations trade with each other. The mutual benefits, or economic advantages, of U.S.–China trade outweigh political differences. Economic advantage has historically been the most important consideration that trading nations share. This chapter examines and discusses the nature of this advantage and also deals with the political and economic hindrances that produce economic disadvantage and tend to discourage trade, particularly among developed and developing countries.

In the post–World War II period, world trade has multiplied tremendously and has added new dimensions to global economic activity. An example is presented here to depict the emergence of the multinational corporation as the basic institution of present international economic activity. Current international economic activity is much wider in both scope and activity than the traditional importing and exporting trade described by classical economists.

Theory of Comparative Advantage

The classical economists—Adam Smith, David Ricardo, and John Stuart Mill—are credited with providing the theoretical economic justification for international trade.

In simple terms, modern trade takes place because a foreign country is able to provide a material or product more cheaply than native industry can. For example, if the landed cost of a Japanese TV is less than the cost of an American-made TV, it makes economic sense to import TVs from Japan. Likewise, if U.S. computers can be sold more cheaply in Japan than computers manufactured in Japan, Japanese businesses would find it economically desirable to import U.S. computers.

Ricardo advanced the concept of *relative or comparative costs* as the basis of international trade. Ricardo emphasized labor costs more than other aspects of production. He thought such aspects as land and capital either were of no significance or were so evenly distributed overall that they always operated in a fixed proportion, whereas labor did not. In sum the ***theory of comparative advantage*** states that even if a country is able to produce all its goods at lower costs than another country can, trade still benefits both countries, based on comparative, not absolute, costs. In other words, countries should concentrate efforts on producing goods that have a *comparative* advantage compared to other countries, and then export those goods in exchange for goods that command advantage in their native countries (see International Marketing Highlight 2.1).

To illustrate this point, let us assume the following information about the United States and Italy:

	LABOR COSTS PER UNIT (IN HOURS)	
COUNTRY	**Hand Calculators**	**Bottles of Wine**
United States	6	8
Italy	30	15

Suppose the cost of both manufacturing hand calculators and producing wine is lower in the United States than in Italy. Despite that, according to the theory of comparative advantage, the United States will be better off by specializing in hand calculators and exchanging them for Italian wine. In this way, the United States will be able to obtain from Italy a bottle of wine, which requires eight hours of effort at home, in exchange for a hand calculator, requiring only six hours for its manufacture. In other words, the wine is obtained for six hours of labor instead of the eight hours it would have required if it were produced in the United States. Italy would also gain from the exchange by concentrating on producing wine and exchanging it for hand calculators at the cost of fifteen instead of thirty hours of labor.

> One country may be absolutely more efficient in the production of every good than is the other country; and this means the other country has an *absolute* disadvantage in the production of every good. But so long as there are differences in the *relative* efficiencies of producing the different goods in the two countries, we can always be sure that even the poor country has a *comparative* advantage in the production of those commodities in which it is *relatively* most efficient; this same poor country will have a *comparative* disadvantage in those other commodities in which its inefficiency is more than average. Similarly, the rich, efficient

International Marketing Highlight 2.1

How the U.S. Pressed Managed Trade on the Japanese

On his January 1992 trip to Japan, U.S. President George Bush chose to match Japan's producer lobbies with a set of his own, led by the heads of General Motors, Ford, and Chrysler. These industrial leaders complained that the Japanese do not buy enough of their cars. Japanese carmakers obligingly promised to help out by buying American car parts and displaying American cars in their dealerships. This arrangement, however, does nothing but create an expectation among Americans that U.S. car sales to Japan will rise and that America's trade deficit will fall. Since neither is likely, Americans will be annoyed, not only with President Bush, but probably also with Japan.

The American approach can hardly be called trade. After all, it is an odd sort of trade in which a firm asks its competitors to sell its goods for it. It is also odd to claim that because Japan does not import large quantities of the same things as it exports, such trade is "adversarial," a term generally contrasted to the sort of trade that is "mutually beneficial." This is to misunderstand what trade is all about.

The point of trade is to allow an economy to specialize. If a country is better at making ships than sealing wax, it makes sense to put more resources into shipbuilding and to export some of the ships to pay for imports of sealing wax. This is true even if it is the world's best maker of sealing wax, for it will still prosper by making ships instead—which, in turn, is why countries can trade successfully even if they are not the best at anything. This is what David Ricardo, a British economist in the early nineteenth century, meant when he coined the term *comparative advantage*. That phrase is now one of the most misused of economic ideas, since it is often wrongly assumed to mean an advantage compared with other countries, as in, "Soon America will not have a comparative advantage in anything." This matters for more than merely semantic reasons, for Ricardo's insight was a powerful one.

Source: The Economist, January 11, 1992, p. 11.

country will find that it should specialize in those fields of production where it has a comparative advantage, planning to import those commodities in which it has a comparative disadvantage.

A traditional example used to illustrate this paradox of comparative advantage is the case of the best lawyer in town who is also the best typist in town. Will she not specialize in law and leave typing to a secretary? How can she afford to give up precious time from the legal field, where her comparative advantage is very great, to perform typing activities in which she is efficient but in which she lacks comparative advantage? Or look at it from the secretary's point of view. She is less efficient than the lawyer in both activities; but her relative disadvantage compared with the lawyer's is least in typing. Relatively speaking, the secretary has a comparative advantage in typing.

So with countries. Suppose America produces food with one third the labor that Europe does, and clothing with one half the labor. Then we shall see that

America has comparative advantage in food and comparative disadvantage in clothing—this, despite the fact that America is absolutely most efficient in everything. By the same token, Europe has comparative advantage in clothing.

The key to the concept is in the word "comparative"—which implies that each and every country has both definite "advantage" in some goods and definite "disadvantage" in other goods.[1]

The following example quantitatively demonstrates the benefits derived from free trade. Consider two countries, Japonia and Latinia. Japonia has a clear competitive advantage over Latinia in producing both radios and televisions, as follows:

	WORKER HOURS REQUIRED FOR ONE UNIT	
	Japonia	Latinia
RADIO	1	4
TV	4	8

It follows that forty-eight worker hours of production results in twenty-four radios and six televisions in Japonia. The same number of worker hours produces six radios and three TVs in Latinia. Therefore, the two countries can produce a total of thirty radios and nine TVs with ninety-six worker hours of effort.

Suddenly, Japonia and Latinia choose free trade and tear down the barriers they had erected against each other's products. With the same worker hour requirement per unit and the same number of worker hours devoted to production, their combined output now changes to thirty-two radios and ten TVs.

This is not really a miracle; it simply is division of labor based on comparative advantage. Under free trade, Latinia is induced to withdraw resources it had devoted to radio production and concentrate entirely on TVs. Now Latinia produces six TVs and no radios in forty-eight hours.

Japonia is induced to reallocate some resources. It devotes thirty-two worker hours to radios, where its comparative advantage is greatest, and the remaining sixteen hours to TVs, enabling it to turn out thirty-two radios and four TVs with every forty-eight worker hours of effort.

The world has more product, but are Japonia and Latinia better off individually? To find out, we have to introduce the price system. In doing that, one thing needs emphasis: it isn't prices per se that count, but price relationships. Differences in price relationships are what people act on.

Here is the lineup of prices (we'll use the same prices both before and after free trade):

	JAPONIA	LATINIA
RADIO	24,000 yen	600 pesos
TV	96,000 yen	1,200 pesos

After free trade, the Japonian retailer can choose a TV at 96,000 yen or 1,200 pesos, corresponding to an exchange ratio of 80:1. The retailer will want to buy pesos whenever they can be obtained for less than 80 yen apiece. The Latinian retailer can choose a radio at 24,000 yen or 600 pesos, corresponding to a ratio of 40:1. This retailer will be in the market for yen whenever more than 40 yen can be exchanged for a peso.

The differential in price relationships between TVs and radios in the two countries has created an entrepreneurial opportunity: buying and selling currencies. Price differentials on many products in addition to radios and TVs, and many other factors including people's expectations concerning the relative economic outlook of the countries involved, play a part in establishing exchange rates. But the Japonian and Latinian radio and TV marketers should be satisfied if the yen/peso rate falls somewhere between 40:1 and 80:1.

We could choose any number, but let us say that the exchange rate becomes 60:1—right in the middle. Before free trade, a Japonian retailer could buy a shipment of twenty radios and five TVs for 960,000 yen. A Latinian retailer could buy the same shipment for 18,000 pesos. After free trade, the Japonian and Latinian retailers, each acting in his or her own self-interest, do their buying. Here is the result:

JAPONIAN RETAILER:		
20 radios × 24,000 yen	=	480,000 yen
5 TVs × 1,200 pesos × 60 yen	=	360,000 yen
Shipment		840,000 yen
Saving: 120,000 yen		
LATINIAN RETAILER:		
20 radios × 24,000 yen ÷ 60 pesos	=	8,000 pesos
4 TVs × 1,200 pesos	=	6,000 pesos
Shipment		14,000 pesos
Saving: 4,000 pesos		

In both countries, purchasing power has been increased. Both can afford to buy more of the same things or to buy new things they could not afford before. Both are wealthier.

Possibly you aren't convinced until you can see it "in dollars and cents." So why not create a world price in dollars for radios and TVs and redo the arithmetic? At a 60:1 yen/peso exchange rate, the dollar price of a TV is $240, since 300 yen equals 5 pesos equals $1. You will find that Japonia will have enough extra radios to sell at $80 each to buy from Latinia the TVs it stopped producing, and it will still have some dollars to spare. Latinia will have dollars left over after selling extra TVs to buy all of the radios it no longer makes.

Rationale for Seeking Comparative Advantage

Every nation seeks to increase the material standard of living of its people; living standards increase as a function of productivity. With greater productivity, the same amount of labor yields more goods and services. As productivity increases, greater material wealth results.

Different countries enjoy productivity gains in different ways. Sweden has made a choice of longer vacations; the United States prefers increased material possessions. Whatever the eventual choice, increased productivity affords a wider range of choice.

Another ingredient of productivity is the specialization of production, whereby countries do not try to produce all the goods they require. Specialization is more efficient and, in effect, raises the standard of living by providing certain goods through import while providing certain goods and services nationally. These *sheltered* businesses include the provision of services such as health care, government administration, and goods distribution, as well as the production of special goods such as pharmaceuticals and essential military goods.

Businesses included in the sheltered category are influenced by consideration of economic feasibility, national security, and self-sufficiency. Sheltered manufacturing businesses include those in which increased production scale is not great enough to offset the costs of distributing the product to a larger geographic area. This category includes products that, for one reason or another, are expensive to transport, such as milk or sulfuric acid.

For a nation to have a high standard of living, it must export enough goods to balance the import of the goods it cannot efficiently produce itself. Exports are especially important for maintaining the living standard in a country whose resources are limited and whose imports, on balance, are relatively high. Consider Japan, which built a viable export market and in return developed an invulnerable position in many industries. South Korea, Taiwan, and Brazil appear to be following Japan's example by developing export markets.

In sheltered sectors, absolute productivity improvements can increase living standards; in internationally traded sectors, absolute productivity improvements may not be sufficient to improve living standards. Productivity improvement must be measured relative to others' production of the same goods. This is the basis of the theory of comparative advantage.

The standard of living of a nation heavily involved in world trade is essentially determined by that nation's international purchasing power per hour of labor—that is, the higher the standard of living, the greater the value of the foreign goods that can be purchased in exchange for each hour of work invested in producing the native country's exported goods. Most goods are produced and exported by more than one country, and the number of labor hours required to produce the goods tends to differ among producers. The price or value of these goods, on the other hand, usually varies little and is determined in the long run by the labor hours of the least efficient producer whose output is readily marketable.[2]

Table 2.1 presents a hypothetical comparison of two countries whose only export is oil. If the market absorbs the production of both countries, the price is usually set according to the cost of the labor hours required by the least efficient producer, in this case Country B. Country A may set a price slightly lower in order to guarantee the sale of all its output. Regardless, Country A's per-hour income will be much higher than that of Country B. This greater income can be used for higher wages, for reinvestment, to support a free health care system for

TABLE 2.1 **Relative Productivity: A Hypothetical Example**

	LABOR HOURS PER BARREL	
	Country A	Country B
Operating	1	3
Capital cost amortization	1	2
Total	2	5
World price (in labor-hour equivalents)	5.0	5.5
Income (per labor hour)	2.5	1.1

everyone in the country, or for whatever the country desires. In brief, specialization profits Country A and leads it to a higher standard of living than that of Country B.

Business Specialization and Trade

The ***economic law of comparative advantage*** states that every nation benefits when specialization and trade take place. Even when one nation cannot produce any good more efficiently than another can, it is still in the economic interest of both nations for each to specialize. Regardless of its productivity relative to other suppliers, every nation has comparative advantages in producing certain goods rather than others. The specialization and the advantage are achieved on the basis of one or more production factors—natural resources, technology, capital, managerial know-how, and/or labor.

Classical economists considered labor as the chief delineating factor of comparative advantage between two trading nations. In modern days, however, other factors besides labor may be more important in equipping a country for specialization. As a matter of fact, wage levels for blue-collar workers are becoming increasingly irrelevant in world competition. This is because blue-collar labor no longer accounts for enough of total costs to give low wages much competitive advantage. For example, blue-collar costs in U.S. manufacturing account for 18 percent of total costs, but they are down from 23 percent only a few years ago, and they are dropping fast.[3]

In addition to being influenced by the preceding production factors, a country's leverage may change with time and changes in the political, social, cultural, and economic environment. For example, Japan has a comparative advantage relative to the United States in producing steel. Japan's leverage in steel is based on managerial ability and technology. Even though Japan has to import the raw material of iron ore, other factors provide enough leeway to ensure comparative advantage. This does not mean that its current comparative advantage in steel is everlasting. The supplier of Japan's iron ore could stop supplying for political reasons, or another country could develop a technology superior to Japan's and supersede its advantage. Thus, leverage must be not only developed but also maintained for long-term gains.

Natural Resources

Nature randomly endowed different regions of the world with natural resources. The natural riches of a place bestow upon it unique economic advantages. But nations are groups of communities arbitrarily organized, usually without regard to such economic considerations as the abundance or lack of natural resources.

The most outstanding example of the possession of a resource providing economic leverage is the abundance of oil in the Middle East. In raw material exchanges based on natural resources, even if both nations have the same natural resource, one country may be better off than the other because of various physical characteristics of the resource. For example, certain economic considerations—such as seam thickness, depth, and purity of ore bodies or the number of hours required to pump a barrel of oil—come into play. Saudi Arabian oil from a shallow well is a richer resource than Iranian oil from a deep well.

Mineral trade is based on the natural availability of minerals in different countries. The aircraft industry is crucially dependent on cobalt, which is used in jet engine blades. Zambia and Zaire produce two-thirds of the world's cobalt and thus have a natural advantage in this area. Since the metal is important for an essential industry, the random distribution of the natural resource leads to world trade.

Incidentally, imports meet more than 50 percent of U.S. needs for twenty important minerals. These come mainly from the Republic of South Africa and its neighbors, and the former Soviet states.[4] The United States is quite concerned about its dependence on these countries. South Africa, for example, could resort to economic blackmail by threatening to withhold certain key minerals unless the United States abandons its anti-apartheid pressures. Third World countries rich in certain minerals could form cartels and exert economic pressure as OPEC has. Russia could cut off certain essential minerals to the West. The important point here is that the natural resources of a country can permit it to engage in international trade from an advantageous position.

Technology

Manufacturers in different countries have different production costs as a result of the unevenness of technological advances. Differences in production scale, run lengths, distribution structure, product mix, and technological development capability, among other things, often determine productivity differences among producers. For example, some Japanese companies can assemble a TV in one-third the time required by their European or American competitors. This advantage is derived from product designs that use fewer components, machines that automate some of the board assembly, and equipment that reduces labor in the handling of materials. Japan's technological advantage in manufacturing steel leads it to surpass India in the world markets. This happens despite the fact that Japan imports iron ore from India and Indian labor is much less expensive than Japanese labor.

Managerial Know-How

People who bring capital, labor, and resources together to fashion them into a productive organization that must face the risks of an uncertain world occupy strategic positions. Thus, given the same inputs, presumably a country with superior management will do better than one with weak management. The importance of managerial know-how can be illustrated by the airlines industry. Most airlines of the Free World use the same planes and offer essentially the same services while charging common prices. Yet some carriers outperform others. For example, Singapore Airlines does better than any other airline, partly because of its lower labor costs, but mainly because of superior management.[5]

Obviously an explanation of world business involves many elements. But with a basic understanding of the few elements covered so far—comparative advantage and specialization—we can now consider other reasons for nations to engage in international business.

Product Life Cycle and International Trade

The theory of comparative advantage is a classic explanation of world trade. In the late 1960s, researchers at the Harvard Business School provided a new explanation of international trade and investment patterns.[6] The new approach uses the concept of product life cycle in marketing and gives a significant insight into how multinational corporations evolve.

The ***product life cycle model*** states that products go through the following four stages:[7]

- Phase I U.S. export strength builds
- Phase II Foreign production starts
- Phase III Foreign production becomes competitive in export markets
- Phase IV Import competition begins in domestic U.S. markets

During Phase I, the product is manufactured in the United States for a high-income market and afterward introduced into foreign markets through exports. At that point, the United States usually holds a monopoly position as the only country able to supply the product. The product continues to be manufactured only in the United States since business acumen suggests locating operations close to markets where the demand exists. Overseas customers, however, import the U.S. product in response to their own market demands and thus create a program of export for the U.S. product.

During Phase II, as the product becomes popular, entrepreneurs in other advanced countries, perhaps in Western Europe, venture into producing the same product. The technology involved is by then fairly routine and easily transferred from the United States. Subsequently, the overseas manufactured product begins to outsell the U.S. export in selected markets because the overseas product benefits from lower labor costs and savings in transportation. The stage where overseas manufacturers are able to compete effectively against U.S. exports has been reached.

In the third phase, the foreign producers begin to compete against the U.S. exports in Third World countries. This further adds to the declining market for the U.S. exports. Between Phases II and III the U.S. firms begin to consider making direct investments abroad to sustain or regain their original market position.

The fourth phase occurs when the foreign firms, strong in their home and export markets, achieve economies of scale and then begin to invade the U.S. home markets. Presumably, the foreign firms have lower costs so that, despite ocean freight and U.S. customs costs, they are able to compete effectively against the domestically produced U.S. products.

These four phases complete the product life cycle and describe how American firms that once commanded a monopoly position in a product find themselves being pushed out of their home market.

The product life cycle theory of world trade holds that advanced countries, like the United States, play the innovative role in product development. Later on, other relatively advanced countries, like Japan or Western European countries, take over the market position held by the innovative country. The second-stage countries would go through the same cycle as did the innovative country and, in turn, would lose their markets to the next group of countries, say Third World countries. In other words, a product initially produced in the United States could eventually be produced only in LDCs (less-developed countries), with the result that the United States, Western Europe, and Japan would meet their needs for that product through import from LDCs.

The product life cycle model has been helpful in explaining the history of a number of products, particularly textiles, shoes, bicycles, radios, televisions, industrial fasteners, and standardized components for different uses. These products, available in the United States, Western Europe, and Japan, are being imported from Korea, Taiwan, Hong Kong, India, and other Third World countries. For example, South Korea has made enormous strides out-competing Japan in a number of consumer products (Table 2.2). Thus, abandoning years of prejudice against imports, Japanese are snatching up low-priced goods from newly industrialized countries. For example, an imported 20-in color TV is available for $375 while a similar Japanese-made TV is priced at $617.[8]

Despite its apparent validity in the manufacturing field, the product life cycle model does not provide a complete answer to the growth activities of multinational enterprises. Although the model

> may be an efficient way to look at enterprises in the U.S. economy that are on the threshold of developing a foreign business, [it] is losing some of its relevance for those enterprises that have long since acquired a global scanning capacity and a global habit of mind.[9]

Empirical studies show that the product life cycle theory is partially useful in explaining the behavior of world trade and business practice. Lutz and Green found that the theory has at least some explanatory relevance for the first three countries of the four (i.e., United States, Japan, United Kingdom, and West Germany) that were studied. For example, the United States has retained a comparative advantage in high-technology manufactures that were relatively new to the international market, while overall it had a declining share of world manufacturing exports.[10] Mullor-Sebastian's study supported the hypothesis that industrial

TABLE 2.2 South Korea's Price Edge Over Japan

KOREAN BRAND (MANUFACTURER)	EQUIVALENT JAPANESE BRAND (MANUFACTURER)
Subcompact autos	
Excel (Hyundai)	Sentra (Nissan)
\$5,500 to \$6,000	\$7,600
Personal computers	
Leading Edge (Daewoo)	Advanced-3 (NEC)
\$1,495	\$1,695
Videocassette recorders	
Samsung	Toshiba
\$270	\$350
Compact refrigerators	
Lucky-Goldstar	Sanyo
\$149	\$265
13-inch color TVs	
Samsung	Hitachi
\$148	\$189
Microwave owens	
Lucky-Goldstar	Toshiba
\$149	\$180
Videocassettes	
SKC (Sunkyong)	TDK
\$6	\$7
Floppy disks	
SKC (Sunkyong)	Fuji
\$2.70	\$2.60 to \$2.90

Source: Information collected from different stories on international marketing.

product groups behave in the manner predicted by the product life cycle theory on world markets. However, in the case of individual products, the results provided less support for the product life cycle thesis.[11]

Production Sharing

In the late 1970s Peter Drucker introduced a new concept of international business and trade. He labeled this concept ***production sharing*** and described it as

> the newest world economic trend. Although production sharing is neither "export" nor "import" in the traditional sense, this is how it is still shown in our trade figures and treated in economic and political discussions. Yet it is actually economic integration by stages of the productive process.[12]

The production-sharing concept describes an economic reality existing in developed countries where higher levels of education create higher levels of personal expectation. There then follows a gradual disappearance of semiskilled and unskilled labor, so necessary to labor-intensive manufacturing. Production sharing suggests that developed countries will turn to developing countries where the availability of labor is a major asset. This concept also covers the U.S. tariff-schedule advantage to U.S. companies whereby American components made by American labor can be further processed or assembled abroad and then returned to the U.S. market for further work or sale with duty paid only on the value added.

Production sharing enables firms in developed countries, possessing sophisticated management skills and high technology, to successfully combat profit-threatening foreign imports. For example, a U.S. firm may utilize its skilled labor and technology to process a product partially and then have the manufacturing stage requiring more labor performed elsewhere, say in Mexico, the Dominican Republic, or Costa Rica. This enables a firm to remain competitive with overseas imports. In essence, production sharing is an alternative to completely foreign imports.

Production sharing, however, also benefits developing countries, since they must find work for their surplus labor, which is qualified only for unskilled jobs. With only limited technology, capital, and management available to develop their own integrated industries, developing countries have difficulties absorbing unskilled and semiskilled people into the labor force. As a matter of fact, even if integrated industries could be established in developing countries, they would probably not have sufficient demand for the resultant products. Via production sharing, the developing nations find a mutually beneficial arrangement for solving their employment problem.

Drucker describes the whole process as follows:

> Men's shoes sold in the United States usually start out as the hide on the American cow. As a rule the hide is not tanned, however, in the United States, but shipped to a place like Brazil for tanning—highly labor-intensive work. The leather is then shipped—perhaps through the intermediary of a Japanese trading company—to the Caribbean. Part of it may be worked up into uppers in the British Virgin Islands, part into soles in Haiti. And then uppers and soles are shipped to islands like Barbados or Jamaica, the products of which have access to Britain, to the European Common Market, and to Puerto Rico, where they are worked up into shoes that enter the United States under the American tariff umbrella.
>
> Surely these are truly transnational shoes. The hide, though it's the largest single-cost element, still constitutes no more than one quarter of the manufacturer's cost of the shoe. By labor content these are "imported shoes." By skill content they are "American-made." Raising the cow, which is capital-intensive, heavily automated, and requires the greatest skill and advanced management, is done in a developed country, which has the skill, the knowledge and the equipment. The management of the entire process, the design of the shoes, their quality control and their marketing are also done entirely in developed countries where the manpower and the skills needed for these tasks are available.
>
> Another example of production-sharing is the hand-held electronic calculator. It may carry the nameplate of a Japanese company—but this is the only thing on it that is "Made in Japan." The electronic chips came from the United States.

> They were assembled in Singapore, in Malaya, in Indonesia, perhaps in Nigeria. The steel for the housing may be the product of an Indian steel mill. And then, in some free-port zone in Kobe or Yokohama, the label "Made in Japan" was put on. The calculator is then sold all over the world—the bulk, of course, in developed countries. The design, the quality control, and the marketing of the calculator were handled by a Japanese company located in a highly developed country. The stages of production that require high technology, tight quality control, high capital investment—that is the design and manufacture of the chips—were also handled in a developed country, the United States. But the labor-intensive work was done in developing countries.[13]

Currently, production sharing seems to be quite prevalent, and growing at a rapid pace. It is a new phenomenon for which there are no classic or neoclassic explanatory theories. Strictly speaking, production sharing is different from the traditional idea of international trade. It is a transnational business integration—a new relationship made possible by technological and business forces. Production sharing offers both the developed and developing countries of the world a chance to share their resources and strengths for their mutual benefit.

Internalization Theory

A multinational firm can serve a market across national boundaries either by exporting from a production facility located in the country of the parent company, or from a third country subsidiary, or it can set up production facilities in the market itself. The sourcing policy of the firm is the result of the firm's decisions as to which of its production facilities will service its various final markets. Thus, the firm establishes an international network linking production to markets. Such a network enables the firm to grow by eliminating external markets in intermediate goods and subsequently by *internalizing* those markets within the firm. When international markets are internalized, the internal transfers of goods and services are exports and/or imports for the nation states between which the goods and services are transferred. The incentives to internalize intermediate-goods markets are strongest in areas where research inputs and proprietary technology are an important part of the manufacturing process.[14]

Many intermediate-product markets, particularly for types of knowledge and expertise embodied in patents and human capital, are difficult to organize and costly to use. In such cases, the firm has an incentive to create internal markets whenever transactions can be carried out at a lower cost within the firm than through external markets. This internalization involves extending the direct operations of the firm and bringing under common ownership and control the activities by the market.

The creation of an internal market permits the firm to transform an intangible piece of research into a valuable property specific to the firm. The firm can exploit its advantage in all available markets and still keep the use of the information internal to the firm in order to recoup its initial expenditures on research and knowledge generation.[15]

The internalization theory assumes that the firm has a global horizon, and it recognizes that the enterprise needs a competitive advantage or a unique asset to expand. However, the underlying thesis of internalization is the firm's desire to extend its own direct operations rather than use external markets. The internalization approach rests on two general axioms: (a) firms choose the least-cost location for each activity they perform; and (b) firms grow by internalizing markets up to the point where the benefits of further internalization are outweighed by the costs.[16]

The internalization theory provides an economic rationale for the existence of MNCs. The sourcing decision rests on the costs and benefits to the firm, taking into consideration industry-specific factors (e.g., nature of the product) region-specific factors (e.g., geographic location), nation-specific factors (e.g., political climate), and firm-specific factors (e.g., managerial ability to internalize).

The internalization theory primarily focuses on the motives and decision processes within the multinational firm but pays little attention to the host country policies and other external factors that may affect internalization cost/benefit.

Trade Barriers and Trade Liberation

We have discussed different theories and frameworks that describe the economic rationale for international trade and business. No matter how we look at it, the internationalization of business and trade appears to perpetuate worldwide prosperity. Despite that fact, no one country permits international business dealings at will. Governments impose all sorts of barriers to restrict trade and business across national boundaries. But there are reasons for trade barriers and for the efforts that have been made internationally to liberate trade. The U.S. effort to promote free trade is particularly interesting.

Trade Barriers

There are two types of trade barriers: tariff and nontariff barriers.

Tariff Barriers ***Tariffs*** refer to taxes levied on goods moved between nations. The most important of these is the tax usually called the *customs duty,* which is levied by the importing nation. But a tax may also be imposed by the exporting nation, and that is called an *export tax*. Even a country through which goods pass on their way to their destination may impose a *transit tariff*. The real purpose behind trade barriers is to protect national interest. Exhibit 2.1 lists the major reasons that countries advance for such protection.

Different nations handle tariff barriers differently. A country may have a single tariff system for all goods from all sources. This is called a *unilinear or single-column tariff*. Another type of tariff is the *general-conventional tariff*. This tariff applies to all nations except those that have tariff treaties (or a convention to that effect) with a particular country. A tariff may be worked out on the basis of a tax permit, called *specific duty,* or as a percentage of the value of the item, which is referred to as *ad valorem* duty. Sometimes both specific and ad valorem duty may be levied on the same item as a combined duty.

EXHIBIT 2.1 Arguments for Protection

Keep-money-at-home argument: To prevent national wealth from being transferred in exchange with another nation for goods.
Home-market argument: To encourage home industry to perpetuate.
Equalization-of-costs-of-production argument: To make local goods compete fairly against imports, which otherwise may be cheaper because of technological advantages or other similar reasons.
Low-wage argument: To protect home industry from imports from low-wage countries.
Prevention-of-injury argument: To safeguard against potential trade concessions that may have to be made in response to multinational trade agreements.
Employment argument: To prevent level of home employment.
Antidumping argument: To prevent dumping of foreign products.
Bargaining-and-retaliation argument: To seek reduction of tariffs by other countries or to retaliate against another country.
National security argument: To be on one's own for national security reasons such as war or natural calamities.
Infant-industry argument: To encourage new industry in the country.
Diversification argument: To promote a broad spectrum of industries in the country.
Terms-of-trade argument and the optimum tariff: To compensate the country for loss in revenue when price elasticity of import demand is greater than zero.
The theory of the second-best: This argument is based on the fact that free trade, while the best alternative, cannot be pursued optimally due to a variety of distortions. As an alternative, new distortions or tariffs may be utilized to neutralize the existing distortions.

Source: Franklin R. Root, *International Trade & Investment,* 3rd ed. (Cincinnati, OH: South-Western Publishing Co., 1983), pp. 306–322.

Nontariff Barriers ***Nontariff barriers*** include quotas, import equalization taxes, road taxes, laws giving preferential treatment to domestic suppliers, administration of antidumping measures, exchange controls, and a variety of "invisible" tariffs that impede trade. Cao has summarized the principal nontariff barriers in the following categories:[17]

1. *Specific limitation on trade.* Included in this category are the measures that limit the allowable amount of imports, such as *quotas,* referring to quantity or value allowed for specific imported products during a specific period; *licensing requirements,* which obligate exporters and/or importers of specific products to obtain licenses before trading; *proportion restrictions of foreign to domestic goods,* which limit the quantity of imports to a specified proportion of domestic production; *minimum import price limits,* requiring adjustment of import prices to equal or surpass domestic prices; and *embargoes,* prohibiting import of specific products from specific origins.
2. *Customs and administrative entry procedures.* This category includes procedural requirements comprising *valuation of imports* (i.e., enforc-

ing a varying valuation process on imported goods that is often left at the discretion of customs officials and is highly arbitrary and discriminatory); *antidumping practices* (i.e., measures against imported goods sold at prices below those in the home market of the exporting country to injure the importing country industry); *tariff classifications* (i.e., arbitrary classification of imported products into a high-tariff category); *documentation requirements* (i.e., enforcing unnecessary and time-consuming bureaucratic requirements); and *fees* (i.e., imposing fees for different services to boost the price of imported goods).

3. *Standards.* This category includes unduly discriminatory health, safety, and quality standards, such as *standard disparities* (i.e., imposing higher standards on imported goods than on domestic products); *intergovernmental acceptance of testing methods* (i.e., using tougher testing methods than those used for domestic products to determine the wholesomeness of products); and applying *packaging, labeling, and marketing standards* of the country to imported goods in an unduly stringent and discriminatory way.

4. *Government participation in trade.* This category includes government involvement in trade through *procurement policies* favoring domestic products over the imported ones; *export subsidies* (i.e., providing tax incentives, export credit terms, or direct subsidies to domestic firms); *countervailing duties* (i.e., taxes levied to protect domestic products from the imported products that had been given export subsidy by the exporting country's government); and *domestic assistance programs* (i.e., other forms of assistance given to domestic products to strengthen their position against the imports).

5. *Charges on imports.* The category consists of various types of charges levied on imports to make them less competitive against the domestic goods, including *prior import deposit requirements* (i.e., requiring domestic importers to deposit a percentage of import value with the government before importing); *border tax adjustment* (i.e., levying various taxes on imported products that have been charged to domestic products); *administrative fees* (i.e., making an extra charge for processing import-related requirements); *special supplementary duties* (i.e., unusual charges levied on imports); *import credit discriminations* (i.e., providing credit accommodation to domestic producers); and *variable levies* (i.e., taxing imports at a higher rate than domestic goods).

6. *Other categories.* These categories include recent measures employed by importing countries to discourage imports, such as *voluntary export restraints,* whereby an exporting country, often at the request of the importing country, agrees to limit its exports of a specific product to a particular level, and *orderly marketing agreements,* which refers to explicit and formal agreements negotiated between exporting and importing countries to restrict imports.

Among the nontariff barriers, subsidies, quotas, and monetary barriers are the most common. Many nations provide direct payments to select industries to enable them to compete effectively against the imports. For example, since 1980 the United States government has been providing a kind of *subsidy* for the steel industry to strengthen its position against Japanese imports. *Quotas* impose a limit on the quantity of one kind of good that a country permits to be imported. A quota may be applied on a specific country basis or on a global basis without reference to exporting countries.[18] The United States, for example, has established quotas for textile imports from particular countries.

Monetary barriers are exchange controls of which there are three widespread types: blocked currency, differential exchange rate, and government approval to secure foreign exchange. Blockage of currency totally cuts importing by completely restricting the availability of foreign exchange. This barrier is often used politically against one or more nations. For example, in 1979, Iran used blockage of currency to avoid trading with the United States. The differential exchange-rate barrier describes setting different rates for converting local currencies into the foreign currency needed to import goods from overseas. A government can set higher conversion rates for items whose import it wishes to restrict, and vice versa. Finally, a country may require specific government approval before allowing the import of any goods. Most developing countries working toward maintaining a secure foreign exchange position not only strictly enforce, but also grudgingly grant, specific approval accompanied by a variety of hindrances and bureaucratic headaches. Additionally, many nations define their nontariff barriers in broad terms, leaving much to the interpretation and discretion of government officials. This makes assessment of certain countries difficult (see International Marketing Highlight 2.2).

In free trade practice, efficiently produced U.S. agricultural products should flow in great quantities to Japan. But they do not. In testimony before the Committee on Foreign Relations of the United States Senate on September 14, 1982, Ambassador David R. Macdonald, Deputy United States Trade Representative, points out that "Japan maintains quotas on 22 agricultural and marine item categories which cover over 100 products." Quotas, however, constitute only a part of the wall that has been built to prevent U.S. agricultural products from entering Japan.

For instance, the Japanese consume cigarettes at a per capita rate that is roughly equal to the American consumption rate. Cigarette sales in Japan represent a $10 billion business. However, largely because U.S. cigarettes must be distributed by the Japan Tobacco and Salt Corporation, a government-approved monopoly, U.S. cigarettes have only slightly over one percent of the Japanese market.

Japan has roughly 250,000 stores and 270,000 machines where consumers can purchase cigarettes. But only 20,000 of those outlets can sell American tobacco products. American cigarettes are subject to a 35 percent tariff in Japan and sell at prices set by the monopoly that are about 60 percent above the price of Japanese cigarettes. If U.S. marketers wish to promote their cigarettes with samples in Japan, they have to buy cigarettes for the promotion from a Japanese shopkeeper at retail prices.

International Marketing Highlight 2.2

Nontariff Barriers in Japan

Japanese standards are said to be written in a way that often excludes foreign products from the Japanese market. The Japanese standards-setting process is not easily understood, making participation—and even access to information—by foreigners difficult. Other problems include nonacceptance of foreign test data, lack of approval for product ingredients generally recognized as safe worldwide, and the nontransferability of product approval.

America's food processing industry, for example, maintains that these standards are deliberately discriminatory. Unlike the United States and most other countries whose governments issue lists of additives generally safe for human consumption and a comparable list of substances banned, the Japanese have only one list. A specific additive can only be used for a specific purpose and only in a prescribed amount. Foods containing additives not on the so-called "positive" list may not be imported into Japan, even if those additives are not considered unsafe. The explicit policy of the Ministry of Health and Welfare is not to add ingredients to the positive list.

Regarded as an even more exasperating problem is the fact that Japan does not accept the results of certain testing and certification procedures conducted outside Japan for certain products, such as drugs. The United States, on the other hand, generally accepts foreign data from testing done in accordance with appropriate U.S. standards and test procedures.

Furthermore, foreign manufacturers cannot apply directly to Japanese ministries for product approval. Only an approved Japanese entity can hold approval rights. Until recently, if foreign exporters wanted to change agents, their new agents had to reapply for product approval unless their formerly "approved" agents were willing to give up their rights. Of course American firms could circumvent this constraint by establishing a subsidiary in Japan, but this option is not necessarily open to all manufacturers.

Even the victories Americans have claimed in their highly publicized efforts to open the Japanese market to agricultural products have been hollow. In 1979, Japan was importing 16,800 tons of prime and choice beef from the United States. After a long series of discussions, the Japanese agreed to accept 14,000 more tons annually by 1983. That "breakthrough" was put in perspective by Senator Lloyd Bentsen of Texas when he noted that the increment was the equivalent of one McDonald's "Quarter Pounder" for each Japanese citizen per year.

American manufactured products also face formidable Japanese trade barriers. Under existing procedures each automobile imported into Japan has to be driven to the local department of motor vehicles for an inspection that typically requires a three- or four-hour wait before aggressive, hawkeyed inspectors finally descend upon the car. Imported cosmetic products missing even one single ingredient from the Japanese government's approved list must be held back for a safety test. It can take as long as two years to arrange such a test. While Japanese cosmetic

> manufacturers apparently have access to the top official list of 2500 ingredients approved by the Japanese government, foreigners don't.[19]

Nontariff barriers may also be classified, as shown in Table 2.3, according to their intent and manner of operation.

Tariff Reduction Programs

Internationally, systematic tariff reduction programs started after World War II. In 1947, the United States and twenty-two other major trading countries got together in Geneva to find ways to reduce tariffs and remove trade barriers. The ***General Agreement on Tariffs and Trade (GATT)*** resulted.[20] Since then, eight major efforts to reduce trade barriers have been undertaken under GATT's auspices (see Table 2.4).

The first two rounds, Geneva 1947 and Annecy (France) 1949, are considered significant, both for tariff reduction and for structuring GATT's organization. The Torquay (England) 1951 and Geneva 1956 rounds are regarded as less significant. Insurmountable differences arose among nations over the issue of tariff disparities, that is, the difference between the high tariff of one country and the low tariff of another. Next, the Dillon Round in 1962 resulted in further reduction of average world tariff rates. But it fell short of its goals: an across-the-board 20 percent reduction of tariffs and the settlement of problems unresolved since the 1956 meeting, especially those involving trade agreements with less-developed countries.

The Kennedy Round, sixth in the negotiation series, was the most comprehensive round of negotiations in terms of the number of participating countries, the value of the world trade involved, and the size of tariff reductions. The negotiations were concluded in 1972 with tariffs reduced on some 60,000 commodities valued at $40 billion in world trade. Despite its success, the Kennedy Round did not quite meet all the ambitious goals set for it. A major goal of the Kennedy Round was a 50 percent across-the-board reduction in tariffs on industrial products. However, overriding national interests forced exceptions to such a reduction for such commodities as chemicals, steel, aluminum, pulp, and paper. The question of tariff disparities, linked with the 50 percent goal, also yielded to exceptions because many Western European countries raised objections. Overall, the Kennedy Round negotiators agreed to tariff cuts on industrial products that averaged about 35 percent. The round was also meant to resolve the problem of nontariff barriers, but the results were rather modest except for the adoption of an antidumping code.

The principal objective of the Tokyo Round in 1973, seventh in the negotiation series, was "the expansion and ever-greater liberalization of world trade." The Tokyo Round recognized that the scope of exceptions should be limited and supported the general feeling that the special interests of the developing countries should be borne in mind in the tariff negotiations. The Tokyo Round, concluding in 1978, was the most complex and comprehensive trade negotiating effort attempted to date. It tried to develop a substantially freer world trading system with balanced opportunities for countries with different economic and political

TABLE 2.3 Classification of Nontariff Measures According to Intent and Manner of Operation

TYPE I MEASURES (PRIMARY DISTORTIVE INTENT)	TYPE II MEASURES (SECONDARY RESTRICTIVE INTENT)	TYPE III MEASURES (NO APPARENT TRADE-DISTORTIVE INTENT)
A. Import-Directed Measures 1. Quantitatively operating a. Import quotas, globally administered b. Import quotas, selectively administered c. Licensing, discretionary/restrictive d. Licensing, liberal e. "Voluntary" export restrictions f. Embargoes g. Domestic-procurement practices by national governments or other public units h. State-trading practices i. domestic-content and mixing regulations 2. Operating through costs and prices a. Variable levies and supplementary import charges b. Advance-deposit requirements c. Antidumping and countervailing charges d. Direct subsidies to import competitors e. Credit restrictions on importers	1. Quantitatively operating a. Communications-media restrictions b. Quantitative advertising and marketing restrictions 2. Operating through costs and prices a. Packaging/labeling regulations b. Health, sanitary, and quality standards c. Safety and industrial standards and regulations d. Border-tax adjustments e. Use taxes and excises f. Customs clearance procedures, consular formalities, and related practices g. Customs classification procedures and related practices h. Customs valuation procedures and related practices i. Exchange restrictions j. Disclosure regulations and "administrative guidance" k. Government-provided entrepreneurship, research and development financing, and related aids for the import-competing and export sectors	a. Government manufacturing, sales, and distribution monopolies covering individual products or groups of products b. Government structural and regional development policies affecting trade. c. Ad hoc government balance-of-payments policy measures d. Differences in tax systems e. Differences in national social-insurance systems f. Differences in allowable depreciation systems g. Spillovers from government-financed defense, aerospace, and nonmilitary procurement h. Scale effects induced by government procurement i. Variations in national standards, regulations, and practices j. External transport charges and government-sanctioned international transport agreements k. Port transfer costs

(continued)

TABLE 2.3 *(Continued)*

TYPE I MEASURES (PRIMARY DISTORTIVE INTENT)	TYPE II MEASURES (SECONDARY RESTRICTIVE INTENT)	TYPE III MEASURES (NO APPARENT TRADE-DISTORTIVE INTENT)
f. Tax benefits and other indirect subsidies to import competitors, including credit concessions		
g. Discriminatory internal transport charges		
h. International commodity agreements and orderly marketing arrangements		
B. Export-Directed Measures		
1. Quantitatively operating		
a. State trading practices		
b. Export quotas and licensing		
2. Operating through costs and prices		
a. Direct subsidies to exporters		
b. Indirect subsidies to exporters, including tax and credit measures		
c. Government-supported dumping practices		
d. Export charges		
e. International commodity agreements and orderly marketing arrangements		

TABLE 2.4 Dimensions of Agreements Under GATT

MAJOR AGREEMENTS	NUMBER OF CONTRACTING PARTIES	VALUE OF WORLD TRADE INVOLVED (BILLIONS OF DOLLARS)	PERCENT OF AVERAGE TARIFF REDUCTION
1947 Geneva	23	$10.0	n.a.*
1949 Annecy, France	33	n.a.*	n.a.*
1951 Torquay, England	37	n.a.*	n.a.*
1956 Geneva	35	2.5	4
1962 Geneva (Dillon Round)	40	4.9	7
1967 Geneva (Kennedy Round)	70	40.0	35
1973 Tokyo (Tokyo Round)	85	115.0	50
1986 Punta del Este (Uruguay Round)	107	n.a.*	n.a.*

*n.a.: not available.

systems and needs. While the actual achievements fell short of the goals, the overall results of the Tokyo Round were very encouraging.

In November 1985, ninety countries unanimously agreed to a U.S. proposal to launch a new round of global trade talks, eighth in the negotiation series, in September 1986 in Punta del Este, Uruguay, named the Uruguay Round. The focus of this round is on agricultural exports, services, intellectual properties, and voluntary trade limits.

The timing for another round of trade talks could not be more appropriate. Protectionist forces have been gaining momentum, particularly in the United States. In Europe, where half of all economic activity relates to trade, America's protectionist sentiments have created uneasiness. The Europeans have warned that they will retaliate if the United States adopts protective measures.[21] The developing economies do not know what to do, since the Western nations constitute a big market for their limited exportable products. Individual efforts of different nations to meet the protectionist threat have not succeeded. One of the achievements of fifty years of trade liberalization has been the expansion of world trade, which was being challenged in the 1980s. What countries cannot accomplish unilaterally, however, they may be able to accomplish under the GATT umbrella.

In the forty years of its existence, GATT can claim some successes: average tariffs in industrial countries have tumbled to around 5 percent today from an average of 40 percent in 1947. The volume of trade in manufactured goods has multiplied twentyfold. GATT's membership has quadrupled. But the growing protectionism nurtured by the economic difficulties that beset the world in the 1970s has served to undermine the credibility of GATT and threaten the open trading system it upholds.

Cars, steel, videos, semiconductors, and shoes have followed textiles and clothing into "managed trade." In agriculture, where the United States, the EC, and Japan are spending a total of $70 billion a year on subsidies, GATT rules have proved unworkable. GATT has never covered services (nearly 30 percent of all world trade) or investment abroad or intellectual property (patents, copyrights, and so on), which are of growing importance to the rich countries as the centers of manufacturing increasingly shift to the Third World.[22]

The Uruguay Round has generally been acknowledged to be a make-or-break affair for GATT. The intention is to strengthen GATT rules in its traditional areas, especially in agriculture where the rules are ambiguous; improve its enforcement powers; and extend its scope of neglected areas such as services. But after four years of talks, the Uruguay Round was suspended in December 1990 without an agreement. The global talks among 107 nations that were intended to guide the world into a new era of trade and prosperity all but collapsed. The talks stumbled over the refusal of different nations to make concessions demanded by others.[23]

Basically, the agenda was simple. The developing nations had two principal demands: fair markets for the exports of agricultural goods and for exports of textiles and apparel. The developed nations had two as well: freedom for service industries to operate anywhere and respect for intellectual property. Yet the nations found it difficult to agree for their own economic and political reasons as discussed below.[24]

Textiles and Apparel The U.S. has been the major obstruction to free trade in fabrics. Although the American textile industry has been mechanized in recent years and can sell denim, carpets, and yarns in many markets without government help, it still demands the protection of tariffs and quotas.

Aligned with the apparel industry, labor-intensive, and no match for the garment makers of low-wage countries, the textile industry is a formidable power. Textile's 900,000 workers and apparel's 1.1 million make up 10 percent of America's manufacturing work force, enough to demand Congress's attention.

The result is an intricate weave of tariffs and quotas. A typical arrangement limits the number of synthetic-fiber sweaters that can enter the United States from Taiwan to 48 million and puts a tariff of 34.2 percent on those that do. Taipei auctions off the quota to its manufacturers. Adding together all such auction prices and tariffs, protectionism adds 50 percent to wholesale clothing costs.

The burden could get heavier in the future. Imports are growing about 7 percent a year, but the U.S. Senate recently passed a bill that would restrict the annual increase to 1 percent. That could mean an additional cost to consumers over ten years of $220 billion, an amount comparable to the savings and loan bailout, if President Bush goes along with it.

Services The industrialized nations, particularly the United States, want their banks, insurance companies, construction firms, and other service providers to be allowed to move people, capital, and technology around the globe unimpeded. Instead they face a bewildering complexity of national regulations, most of them designed to guarantee jobs for local competitors. A new Turkish law, for example, forbids international accounting firms to bring in outside capital to set up offices and requires them to use the names of the local partners, rather than the prestigious international ones, in their marketing. To audit the books of a multinational company's branch in Buenos Aires, an accountant must have the equivalent of a high school education in Argentinean geography and history.

India is perhaps the most parochial big economy in the world these days; in many important respects, it is more difficult to enter than China. For example, it prevents international insurance companies from selling property and casualty policies to the country's swelling business community, or life insurance to its huge middle class.

Agriculture Nearly all industrial nations subsidize farmers, but the most lavishly protected farmers are European. The European Community not only guarantees its farmers' home markets but also underwrites their exports at the rate of $10 billion a year. The system works thus: If the world price of wheat is $100 a ton, say, a European grower can sell his crop to a foreign buyer at that price and collect an additional $100 or so a ton from the EC. With incentives like that, it is no wonder that Europe has more than 10 million farmers (versus 2.5 million in the United States).

That infuriates countries like Argentina, Brazil, Canada, the United States, Australia, and Thailand, where land and labor forces are more naturally suited to big-time farming. They and others refused any negotiations unless the EC agreed to cut the subsidies. But for EC leaders, such a move was not politically feasible. Helmut Kohl, for example, was not willing to undertake such a difficult sales job while campaigning to become the first chancellor of a reunited Germany.

Intellectual Property Many countries have weak laws or none at all protecting creativity. The major offenders are Brazil, Egypt, India, Korea, Malaysia, Nigeria, China, the Philippines, Saudi Arabia, and Taiwan. There and elsewhere, counterfeiters freely imitate patented drugs, chemicals, and other industrial products, and copy goods from computer software to movies and records.

Consider Pfizer, for example. It invests an average of $230 million and ten years to develop a drug, but a journeyman chemist can crush a new pill and figure out what's in it with surprising ease. In Argentina, Pfizer's antiarthritic Feldene faces twenty-four local competitors, none of which pays royalties. U.S. companies are estimated to lose more than $30 billion a year through theft of all kinds of intellectual property.

In December 1990, the outlook for reviving the stalled talks looked poor, primarily because the world was preoccupied. President Bush was busy with his battle in the Middle East; Chancellor Helmut Kohl of Germany was focusing on the unification of Germany; French President François Mitterrand was concerned with student riots, social unrest, and a weakening economy; and British newcomer, Prime Minister John Major, was coping with a deepening recession and a fractured political base. The one thing that was clear to all concerned was that the ultimate success of the Uruguay Round would depend on how much progress could be made in revamping agricultural trade, which was the most distorted sector of world trade. For example, Thailand refused to sign off on an agreement covering such areas as services and intellectual property unless it received a substantial revision in farm trade.

After almost a year, in the fall of 1991, President Bush and European leaders reached a compromise at The Hague in the Netherlands over the issue of agricultural subsidies, which opened the way for the revival of the Uruguay Round talks in the middle of 1992.[25] Under the compromise, the EC dropped its outright refusal to reduce subsidies to farmers while the United States changed the level of subsidies it would consider acceptable. It is likely the talks will be revived at their full scale in 1992, and a major overhaul of worldwide rules governing trade should result sometime in 1993.

U.S. Trade Liberalization

Liberalization of U.S. foreign trade began with the enactment of the Reciprocal Trade Agreement Act of 1934. With that act, the Congress authorized the president to reduce then-existing tariff duties by 50 percent. A noteworthy aspect of the act was the inclusion of the *most-favored-nation clause,* which limited discrimination in trade by extending to third parties the same terms provided to contracting parties. This clause has become a fundamental principle of U.S. trade policy.

The Reciprocal Trade Agreement Act of 1934 encouraged bilateral agreements that would increase U.S. exports, so long as the exports did not adversely affect domestic industry. In effect, the injury to domestic industry could not take place because of highly protective tariff rates and an item-by-item approach to negotiations, which allowed certain commodities to be excluded if a decrease in rates would result in an increase in imports.

The act was extended every three years, and by 1945 the United States had concluded negotiations with twenty-nine countries. Overall, the act helped in reducing the average rate of tariffs on taxable imports into the United States from 47 percent in 1934 to 28 percent in 1945. In 1945, the Congress authorized the president to cut rates by an additional 50 percent. While the act has been successful in reducing tariff barriers, it did little to reduce such nontariff barriers as quotas and internal taxes.

The second phase in U.S. trade liberalization efforts came in 1947. At that time the United States and twenty-two other major trading nations negotiated simultaneously for both reduction of tariffs and removal of trade barriers. These efforts, as previously discussed, resulted in the establishment of GATT.

The Trade Expansion Act of 1962 marks another phase in U.S. foreign trade policy. This act authorized the president to (1) reduce tariffs up to 50 percent of the rates existing as of July 1, 1962; (2) eliminate tariffs on products in which the United States and Common Market countries together accounted for at least 50 percent of world trade; and (3) eliminate rates that did not exceed 5 percent.[26]

The act empowered the president to negotiate across-the-board tariff reductions (rather than item-by-item reductions) and modify the safeguard provisions of the old trade agreements program. As a matter of fact, this act was designed to stimulate not only U.S. exports, but also world trade in general, so that benefits would accrue to all nations as a result of international specialization and trade. When the United States entered trade negotiations for the Kennedy Round, the authority of the Trade Expansion Act of 1962 was in effect.

In the 1970s, despite the urgency for a new international trade perspective, no effective trade legislation was passed by Congress. During the Nixon administration, however, DISC (Domestic International Sales Corporation) was authorized under the Revenue Act of 1971 as a part of President Nixon's economic policy. Essentially, DISC was set up to

1. Stimulate export sales of goods manufactured in the United States and improve the U.S. balance of payments position.
2. Offset the tax advantage enjoyed by U.S. corporations that manufacture abroad through the use of foreign subsidiaries.
3. Offset the tax advantages provided by the governments of major trading nations to their domestic producers to encourage exports.[27]

The DISC program soon became controversial. A special GATT panel found it to be in conflict with a GATT rule about unfair trade practices. Besides, the tax benefits under the DISC program appeared to accrue to large MNCs only. Effective December 31, 1984, the United States government replaced DISC with the Foreign Sales Corporation (see Chapter 17).

As a matter of fact, in the 1970s a variety of U.S. government measures hindered rather than helped trade. The Trade Act of 1974 barred export-import credit via the Export-Import Bank, which was established to finance "big-ticket" item exports like aircraft or nuclear power technology. The Foreign Corrupt Practices Act of 1977 imposed jail terms and fines for overseas payoffs by U.S. companies. The Carter administration's human rights legislation denied export-import credit to rights violators. Loans were withheld from South Africa, Uruguay, and Chile. United States trade embargoes banned exports to Cuba, Vietnam, Rhodesia, and other countries.

In the 1980s, the Reagan administration took a variety of ad hoc measures in response to emerging problems and crises. In 1982, President Reagan signed the Export Trading Company Act, which was designed to attract manufacturers, export-management companies, banks, freight forwarders, and other export services into joint efforts to gain foreign markets (see Chapter 17). In the fall of 1985, to avert a possible trade war stemming from mounting protectionist pressures in the Congress and the nation, the Reagan administration committed itself to join England, France, Germany, and Japan in intervening heavily on the world's financial markets to lower the dollar's value. This was planned to help the United States reduce its trade deficit. The U.S. government also unveiled a "fair trade" program built around the threat of retaliation against nations that refused to chop barriers to U.S. goods.

A hallmark of the Reagan era was the passage of the 1988 trade bill. To seek a long-term solution to the problem of the United States' trade deficit, the U.S. government enacted the Omnibus Trade and Competitiveness Act of 1988. This act was the product of a three-year effort involving Congress, the administration, and the business community. The act maintained the U.S. commitment to free trade. It did, however, provide better trade-remedy tools for judicious use in opening foreign markets.

The following are the principal features of the Omnibus Trade and Competitiveness Act of 1988.[28]

Trade Negotiating Authority—Enables trade agreements negotiated by the President to be considered by the Congress on an expedited, non-amendable basis. Other provisions will facilitate successful conclusion of the Uruguay Round of multilateral trade negotiations.

Windfall Profits Tax—Repeals the Windfall Profits Tax, a counterproductive tax that imposed substantial and unnecessary administrative costs on our energy industry while raising little revenue.

Worker Readjustment Program (WRAP)—Creates a considerably expanded and newly-designed program and authorizes $980 million for retraining of workers who must shift jobs as the economy adjusts to competitive challenges. An estimated 700,000 dislocated workers will be served by the new program when fully implemented. WRAP greatly expands services to dislocated workers, emphasizes early intervention, and incorporates a number of innovative approaches for serving these workers. These include rapid response teams to assist communities impacted by major layoffs and labor-management committees to coordinate assistance to workers, and emphasize high quality training to assist workers in the transition to emerging opportunities in the labor market.

Unfair Trade—Authorizes the U.S. Trade Representative to determine whether a foreign government's trade practice is unfair. Subject to specific direction of the President, allows the U.S. Trade Representative to decide what retaliatory action to take. Requires action in response to violations by foreign governments of trade agreements but provides exceptions, such as if the foreign government ends the practice. Provides new definitions of unfair trade practices and sets new deadlines for action. Under the so-called "Super 301," requires the U.S. Trade Representative in 1989 and 1990 to identify "priority countries" and to investigate those countries.

Intellectual Property—Requires the U.S. Trade Representative to identify priority countries that deny protection for U.S. patents and copyrights. Provides for expedited decisions.

Telecommunications—Provides for trade liberalizing negotiations. If the negotiations do not produce a satisfactory agreement, the President is required to take whatever action is appropriate and most likely to achieve the negotiating objectives.

Harmonized System—Implements the Harmonized System of tariff nomenclature, which creates a common tariff code system for all member nations.

Export Controls—Liberalizes the ability of U.S. exporters to obtain export licenses for products on the export control list.

Controlled Technology—Imposes sanctions against foreign firms that sell controlled technology in a manner that violates internationally agreed upon export controls and damages U.S. national security.

Anti-Dumping and Countervailing Duty—Enhances the authority of the Commerce Department to prevent circumvention through the practice of minor alteration of the merchandise covered by anti-dumping and countervailing duty orders or by additional minor assembly in the U.S. and third countries.

Foreign Corrupt Practices Act—Amends the Foreign Corrupt Practices Act so that only those businesses and persons who know of bribes and other illegal payments to foreign officials can be subject to civil and criminal liability.

Foreign Investment—Authorizes the President to halt the sale, merger or takeover of U.S. firms by foreign entities if such proposed transactions threaten the national security.

Government Procurement—Bans U.S. Government procurement of any or all goods/services from countries that have a significant and persistent pattern or practice of discriminating against U.S. products and services and whose products/services are acquired in significant amounts by the U.S. Government.

Agricultural Trade—Creates a marketing loan program for the 1990 crop of wheat, feed grains and soybeans, subject to Presidential waiver. Extends Export Assistance Program through FY 1990 and raises program ceiling to $2.5 billion. Increases funding for Targeted Export Enhancement Program to $215 million.

Trade Agreements—Implements recent trade agreements including the citrus and pasta agreement with the European Community and extends authority for U.S. participation in the international coffee agreement.

Nairobi Protocol—Implements Nairobi Protocol, which provides for duty-free imports of educational, scientific and cultural materials and articles for the handicapped.

Because of the extended controversy about the trade bill between the executive branch, the House, and the Senate, the trade bill finally enacted did not address many issues that were perceived as protectionist because they would have

- Established quotas on imports of lamb and steel products,
- Unilaterally revoked most-favored-nation treatment for Romania and Angola,
- Created a private right of action in U.S. courts for customs fraud, in addition to current administrative remedies,
- Provided a draconian remedy—exclusion from the U.S. market—for "scoff-law" (i.e., repeat) offenders of U.S. customs laws,
- Included requirements for the carriage of automobiles on U.S. vessels,
- Required the president to provide relief automatically in safeguard actions in which the U.S. International Trade Commission found injury to U.S. producers,
- Broadly mandated retaliation where unfair trade practices were established and required the "self-initiation" annually of such investigations (even when U.S. industry did not seek such an action),
- Redefined the term "subsidy" in the countervailing duty law to expand its application,
- Provided a private right of action in U.S. courts for dumping in addition to the antidumping law,

- Provided relief against diversionary ("upstream" or "downstream") dumping, in violation of existing international rules,
- Required application of the countervailing duty law to nonmarket economies,
- Amended the dumping law to increase the likelihood of the Commerce Department's discovering dumping by foreign producers and exporters selling in the United States through a related company, or in any case involving imports from a nonmarket economy, and
- Required the imposition of sweeping trade sanctions against "terrorist" nations. In response to strong objections from the administration, echoed by many trading partners, Congress simply dropped these and many other provisions characterized as protectionist.

During the Bush administration, the major emphasis has been on extending the U.S.–Canada Free Trade Agreement into a truly North American Free Trade Agreement, and on helping Eastern Europe, the former Soviet States, and Latin America toward greater reliance on market forces. Progress continued to be made in implementing the U.S.–Canada Free Trade Agreement that went into force in 1989, and the Congress authorized the president to pursue a similar agreement with Mexico. At the same time, negotiations had been in progress among the three governments to conclude a North American Free Trade Agreement. President Bush supports continental free trade that will enable all three countries to meet the economic challenges of the decades to come.

In both Eastern Europe and Latin America, the administration has provided strong support for the transitions to democratic societies and free-market economies. This support has been backed up by humanitarian, technical, and financial assistance and endorsement of measures to open markets and expand trade.

MNCs and World Markets

Multinational corporations are among the most, if not the most, influential factors in global economic life today. Within the last thirty years they have become the most formidable single factor in world trade and investment. MNCs play a decisive role in the allocation and use of the world's resources.[29] They conceive new products and services, create and stimulate demand for them, and develop new modes of manufacture and distribution (see International Marketing Highlight 2.3). Consider the example of Gillette and how it participates in world markets as a multinational corporation.

The Gillette Company

Gillette is the leading manufacturer of blades and safety razors in the world. Gillette's products are sold in more than 200 countries and territories throughout the world. While the company's market position varies from country to country, Gillette plays an important role in most blade/razor markets. As a matter of fact, the company holds a dominant position in many markets. In select markets, this dominance extends to its other product lines as well, such as grooming aids,

International Marketing Highlight 2.3

How to Become a Global Company

There is no handy formula for going global, but any company serious about joining the race will have to do most or all of the following:

- Make yourself at home in all three of the world's most important markets—North America, Europe, and Asia.
- Develop new products for the whole world.
- Replace profit centers based on countries or regions with ones based on product lines.
- "Glocalize," as the Japanese call it: Make global decisions on strategic questions about products, capital, and research, but let local units decide tactical questions about packaging, marketing, and advertising.
- Overcome parochial attitudes, such as the "not-invented-here" syndrome. Train people to think internationally, send them off on frequent trips, and give them the latest communications technology, such as teleconferencing.
- Open the senior ranks to foreign employees.
- Do whatever seems best wherever it seems best, even if people at home lose jobs or responsibilities.
- In markets that you cannot penetrate on your own, find allies.

Source: Jeremy Main, "How to Go Global and Why," *Fortune,* August 28, 1989, p. 76.

toiletries, and writing instruments. According to company management, its success in international markets is based on continual efforts at product innovation and improvement, strict quality control, aggressive marketing, and able management worldwide. Table 2.5 shows Gillette's financial results for 1988, 1989, and 1990.

TABLE 2.5 The Gillette Company Sales & Income (in Millions of U.S. Dollars)

DESCRIPTION	1988	1989	1990
Net Sales	Amount (percent)	Amount (percent)	Amount (percent)
U.S.	$1,251.3 (35)	$1,348.0 (35)	$1,433.4 (33)
Foreign	2,329.9 (65)	2,470.5 (65)	2,911.2 (67)
Total	3,581.2 (100)	3,818.5 (100)	4,344.6 (100)
Income (before taxes)	Amount (percent)	Amount (percent)	Amount (percent)
U.S.	$228.2 (37)	$218.7 (33)	$262.4 (34)
Foreign	413.7 (63)	476.7 (67)	528.9 (66)
Total	641.9 (100)	695.4 (100)	791.3 (100)

Source: Gillette Company Annual Report, 1991.

In addition to U.S. and Canadian plants, Gillette has manufacturing plants in a number of countries abroad. Shaving products plants are located in Isleworth (U.K.), Berlin, Annecy (France), Rio de Janeiro, Buenos Aires, Cali (Colombia), Mexico City, Melbourne, and Seville. These plants serve the host country as well as other countries in the region.

During 1990, Gillette Company derived over 67 percent of its sales and 66 percent of its income from markets outside the United States (excluding Canada). This statistic reveals the importance of its international operations. As a part of its global strategy, in 1967 Gillette acquired Braun AG, a market leader in electric shavers in Europe.

Organization Tradionally Gillette International, a division of Gillette Company, was responsible for overseas manufacturing and marketing, which affects almost all Gillette products including blades and razors, toiletries and grooming aids, and writing instruments.[30] In 1986, the company restructured its international operations. As shown in Figure 2.1, the Gillette Company is divided into two groups: Gillette North Atlantic and Gillette International. Gillette North Atlantic integrates the U.S., Canadian, and most of the European operations (Figure 2.2). Gillette International is responsible for the rest of the world.

Gillette North Atlantic's organization structure, depicted in Figure 2.2 integrates European and U.S. operations by different product groups: blade and razor group, personal care group, and stationery products group. Each group has a North American Division and a European Division, the latter organized into five areas each under the leadership of a general manager as follows: Northern Europe, Western Europe, Southeast Europe, Central Europe, and Iberia.

The integration of European operations within the U.S. organization indicates Gillette's move toward becoming a true global company. This should also help the company to take advantage of the European Market integration program.

As shown in Figure 2.3, Gillette International, located at company headquarters in Boston, has been organized into three groups: (1) Latin American, (2) Asian-Pacific, and (3) African, Middle Eastern, and Eastern European. Each of the three groups is headed by a group general manager. In addition, there is a

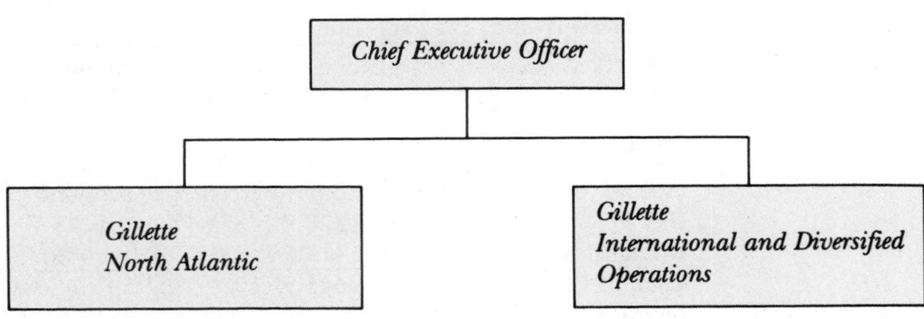

FIGURE 2.1 **The Gillette Company Organizational Chart**

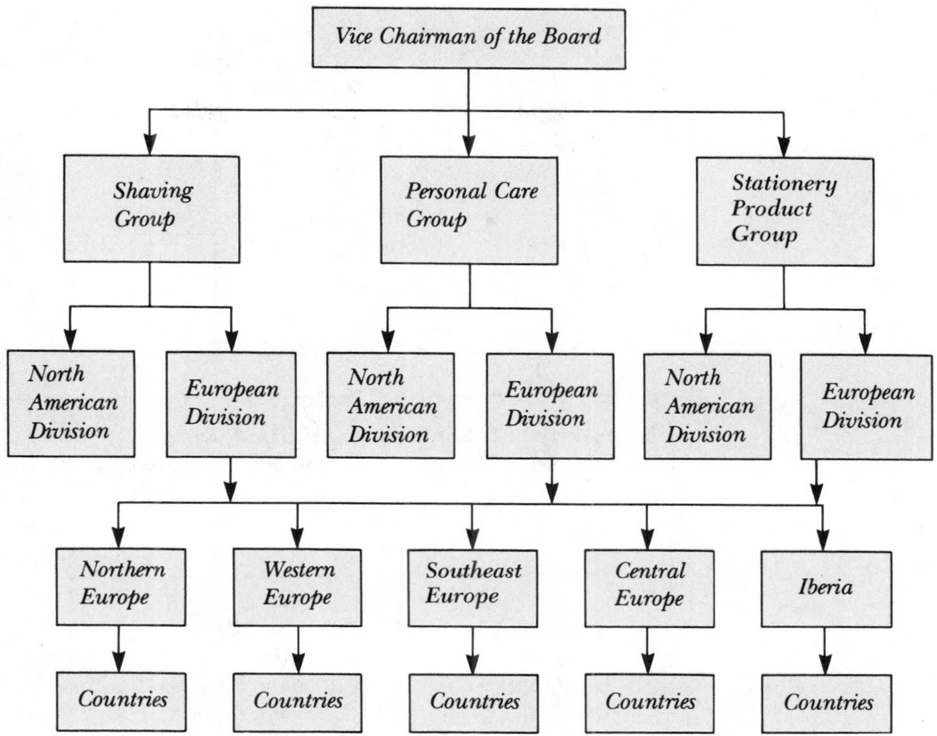

FIGURE 2.2 Gillette North Atlantic: Organization Chart

staff group called the Gillette International Marketing Department (GIMD), located in Boston, led by a marketing director, assisted by individual specialists in each product field and international coordinators in market research and advertising. These specialists give advice to marketing personnel worldwide. The organization in each country consists of a general manager to whom heads of manufacturing, marketing, personnel, and accounting report. The marketing organization, as shown in Figure 2.4, employs people in sales, market research, sales promotion, and brand management. The Gillette salesforce in each country handles a wide range of Gillette products, including shaving products, toiletries, and writing instruments. It is organized along the same line in each country and follows essentially the same selling technique.

Decision Making Gillette's global decision-making system is mostly centralized. The recommendations of executives based overseas are sought and considered, but major marketing decisions, including those that concern strategic goals, the price structure, and global advertising, are made in Boston. However, both Gillette International and Gillette North Atlantic are responsible for operational decision making in their own regions.

Within Gillette International, key marketing decisions are generally made at

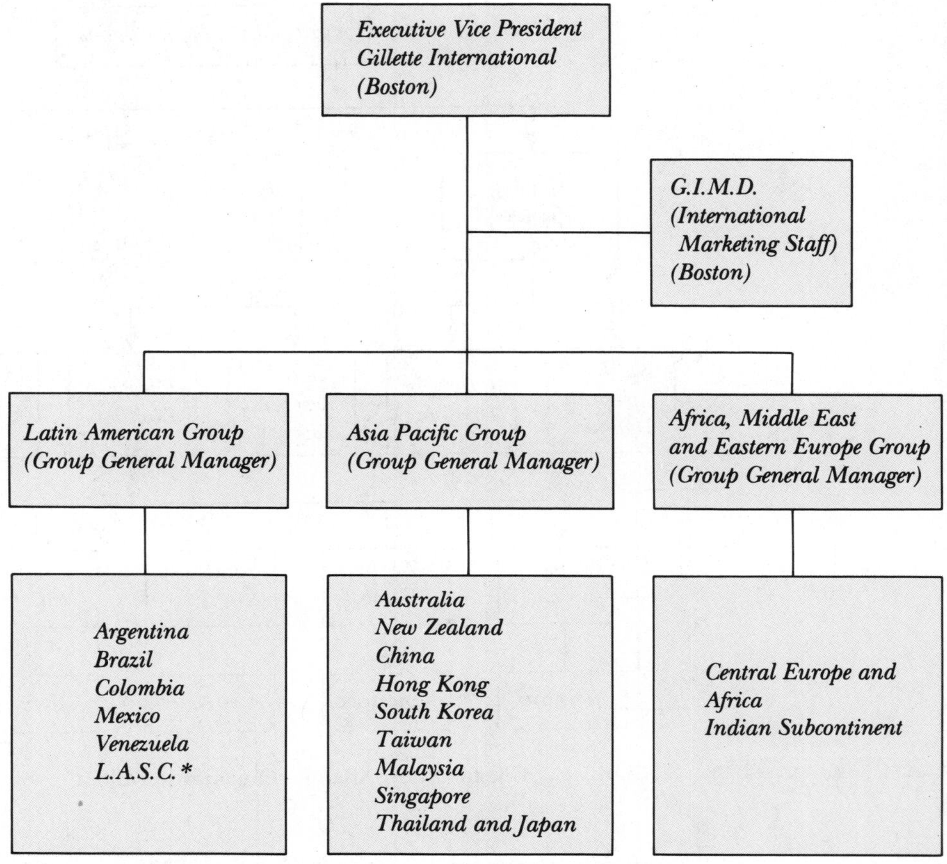

**Latin American Sales Companies:* Chile, Peru, Puerto Rico, plus: CAFTA (Guatemala, Honduras, Costa Rica, Salvador, and Nicaragua) and CIGSA (Panama, Ecuador, Bolivia, Paraguay, Dominican Republic, Aruba, Curaçao, Guyana, Surinam, Barbados, and the Bahamas).

FIGURE 2.3 An Organizational Chart for Gillette International—A Division of the Gillette Company

the headquarters level in Boston, where management of the three component regions is also based. Implementation decisions, such as advertising placement and local distribution, are made at the country level.

Subsidiary executives have the authority to set their own prices as long as they stay within the centrally planned positioning strategy. Distribution strategy is similarly planned centrally and adjusted, when necessary, by the subsidiaries.

Advertising campaigns are sometimes fine-tuned at the local level. Promotion campaigns, although developed locally, must also support marketing goals established by headquarters.

Most of Gillette North Atlantic's significant marketing decisions are made

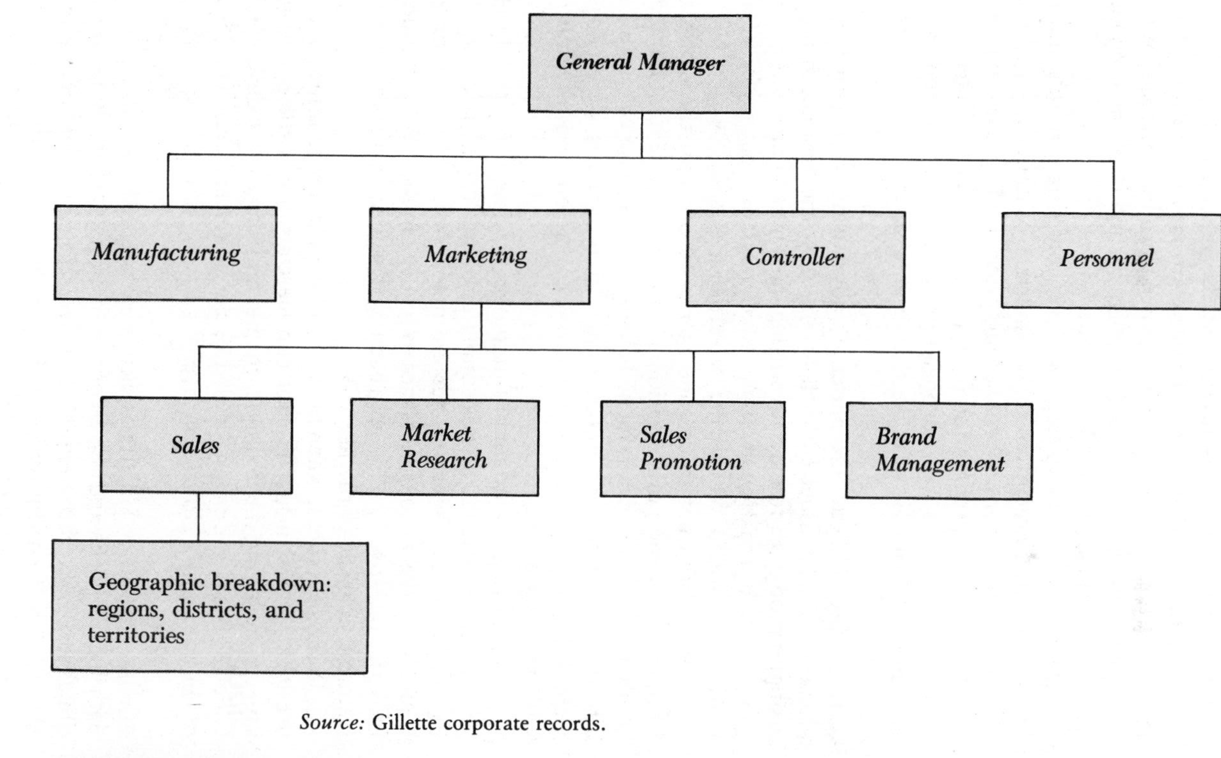

Source: Gillette corporate records.

FIGURE 2.4 Gillette International—Schematic Country Organization Chart

in Boston by the product division at the general manager's level. Like Gillette International, most strategic decisions are also centralized in Boston. Overseas executives are mainly involved in moving products through the distribution system to the final consumer, and in designing and implementing local store promotions, coupon campaigns, and so on.

Desired price relationships vis-à-vis competing brands and products are defined by product executives at headquarters. Within these parameters, subsidiary executives are responsible for setting prices in their own markets.

As part of its preparation for the post–1992 EC, Gillette North Atlantic recently switched to a pan-European packaging strategy, that relies less on words and more on symbols to make the same packaging usable in many countries.

Advertising Gillette International's advertising strategy is formulated at the regional level, and Gillette North Atlantic's at the product group level. Each uses a single, though different, advertising agency to create and coordinate its global campaigns. International retains McCann Erickson, while North Atlantic primarily uses BBDO Worldwide Advertising Agency.

The decision not to use one agency throughout the world follows logically from the two-region organizational structure Gillette has adopted. Moreover, the company's senior management believes it is unwise to put all its international advertising eggs in one basket. These two agencies were chosen because they were deemed to be particularly strong in the operating region of the respective Gillette entity each is to serve.

Both North Atlantic and International centralize virtually all aspects of advertising. This usually means simply dubbing foreign languages into ads created by headquarters. Typically, ads are made with only music on the basic soundtrack. Then the various messages to be used in the different countries are dubbed in with voice-overs. This approach is designed to make ads easily transferable from one market to the next.

In rare instances, when mandated by official regulation, overseas subsidiaries use local actors in locally shot commercials. Even then, however, the creative aspects, including the dialogue, theme, and slogan, are developed in Boston. The Gillette Sensor campaign, "Gillette, the best a man can get," is a good example of the company's global approach.

Foreign Staffing Gillette is firmly committed to staffing foreign subsidiaries with local citizens and third-country nationals. It attributes much of its international success to the strength of its overseas companies and management organizations. The company strives to be perceived as a local company in foreign markets rather than a locally established global company. For this reason, Gillette avoids filling executive openings at its subsidiaries, including those in marketing, with American expatriates.

Within Gillette International, no Americans hold group vice president positions. Latin America is headed by an Argentinean, the Africa/Middle East/Eastern Europe region by a Spaniard, and Asia/Pacific by a Briton. Most general managers are also local nationals or third-country nationals. Within Latin America, six of the seven key general managers are local nationals. Moreover, none of the eight general managers in the Asia/Pacific region is an American.

Gillette North Atlantic is similarly ethnically diverse: The general managers of the company's subsidiaries in Italy, Spain/Portugal, and Northern Europe are Italian, South African, and British, respectively.

Growth Strategy Tailoring its marketing to Third World budgets and tastes—from packaging blades so they can be sold one at a time, to educating the unshaven about the joys of a smooth face—has become an important part of Gillette's growth strategy.[31] The company sells its pens, toiletries, toothbrushes, and other products in developing countries.

The market for blades in developed countries is stagnant. In the Third World, there is a very high proportion of people under 15 years old who will be in the shaving population in a very short time.

Few U.S. consumer-products companies that compete in the Third World expended as much energy or made as many inroads as Gillette, which draws more than 60 percent of its sales from abroad. Since the company targeted the developing world in 1969, the proportion of its sales that come from Latin America, Asia, Africa, and the Middle East has doubled to 25 percent and the dollar volume has risen eightfold.

Gillette has had a strong business in Latin America since it began building plants there in the 1940s. Fidel Castro once told television interviewer Barbara Walters that he grew a beard during the Cuban revolution because he could not get Gillette blades while fighting in the mountains.

The company's push into Asia, Africa, and the Middle East dates to 1969, when Gillette dropped a policy of investing only where it could have wholly owned subsidiaries. That year, it formed a joint venture in Malaysia, which was threatening to bar imports of Gillette products. The company has added one foreign plant nearly every year in such countries as China, Egypt, Thailand, and India.

The company always starts with a factory that makes double-edged blades—still popular in the Third World—and, if all goes well, expands later into production of pens, deodorants, shampoo, or toothbrushes. Only a few ventures have failed: A Yugoslav project never got off the ground, and Gillette had to sell its interests in Iran to its local partners.

In a few markets, Gillette has developed products exclusively for Third World buyers. The low-cost shaving cream is one. Another is Black Silk, a hair relaxer developed for sale to blacks in South Africa and now being sold in Kenya, Nigeria, and other African countries.

More often, Gillette sells familiar products in different packages or smaller sizes. Because many Latin American consumers cannot afford a seven-ounce bottle of Silkience shampoo, for instance, Gillette sells it in half-ounce plastic bubbles. In Brazil, Gillette sells Right Guard deodorant in plastic squeeze bottles instead of metal cans (see International Marketing Highlight 2.4).

As is evident in the Gillette case, multinational corporations capitalize on opportunities far and wide the world over. In strictly theoretical terms, MNCs

International Marketing Highlight 2.4

How to Convince People to Shave

The hardest task for Gillette is convincing Third World men to shave. The company recently began dispatching portable theaters to remote villages to show movies and commercials that tout daily shaving.

In South African and Indonesian versions, a bewildered bearded man enters a locker room where clean-shaven friends show him how to shave. In the Mexican version, a handsome sheriff, tracking bandits who have kidnapped a woman, pauses on the trail to shave every morning. The camera lingers as he snaps a double-edged blade into his razor. In the end, of course, the smooth-faced sheriff gets the woman.

In other places, Gillette agents with an oversized shaving brush and a mug of shaving cream lather up and shave a villager while others watch. Plastic razors are then distributed free and blades—which, of course, must be bought—are left with the local storekeeper. Such campaigns have a lasting impact.

Source: David Wessel, "Gillette Keys Sales to Third Word Tastes," *The Wall Street Journal,* January 23, 1986, p. 35.

acquire raw materials and capital where they are most abundant, manufacture products where wages and other costs are lowest, and sell in the most profitable markets. In other words, MNCs seek to follow the economic law of comparative advantage—everyone benefits if each does its best work, *no matter where* the work is performed.

Summary

We have examined the rationale for world trade and business activity. The classic explanation of world trade is provided by the theory of comparative advantage. When one country has an advantage over another, not only in the production of one product but of all products, and its advantage in the production of the one product is greater than its advantage in the production of the other products, that country, according to the theory, has a comparative advantage in the production of the first product. To follow the theory of comparative advantage, each country should figure out which products have a comparative advantage and concentrate its productive efforts on those; other products should be imported in exchange.

Significant world trade and investment patterns in recent years have been examined in various other ways. We have also discussed three particular approaches to international business and trade activity. Using the concept of product life cycle, Harvard researchers Raymond Vernon and Louis Wells have hypothesized that products are first manufactured in the most developed countries like the United States and exported to other advanced countries like Japan and those of Western Europe. The advanced countries soon adapt the product and begin to manufacture it in their own countries. Then, the first manufacturer faces tough competition from the advanced countries not only in its home market but also in the Third World countries as well, where cheaper labor is available. This leads the first country to make direct investments in manufacturing in the second countries and thus counter their advantage. Despite this defensive measure, however, the first country may find it difficult to compete. This cycle continues with the result that the developing countries may eventually command the market everywhere.

In response to the limitations of the product life cycle theory, other concepts have been formulated. Peter Drucker has advanced the concept of production sharing. Production sharing postulates splitting manufacturing into stages undertaken in different countries.

Finally, according to the internalization theory, a firm establishes an international network linking production to its various markets. Such a network enables the firm to grow by eliminating external markets in intermediate goods and thus internalizing those markets within the firm.

We have also examined trade barriers and the international efforts that have been made to liberalize trade. Two types of barriers were mentioned: tariff and nontariff barriers. Efforts at liberalization of international trade in a systematic fashion began after World War II with the establishment of GATT. In all, eight rounds of multilateral negotiations have been held under GATT toward this end. The United States has made legislative efforts that have both encouraged and hindered liberal trade with other nations.

Unquestionably, the multinational corporation is the agent of modern day international business. The global business practices of the Gillette Company are illustrative of multinational trade and business in the 1990s.

Review Questions

1. Differentiate between absolute and relative advantage. Illustrate, with the help of an example, how comparative (relative) advantage encourages trade.
2. Despite the comparative advantage argument, nations continue to opt for self-sufficiency. How would you explain this behavior?
3. What are the limitations of the product life cycle theory of international trade?
4. Use an example to explain the concept of production sharing.
5. What factors lead countries to seek protection against imports?
6. What are the major types of tariffs that nations use against imports?
7. Discuss major types of nontariff barriers.
8. What role have GATT agreements played in reducing trade barriers?
9. How did the Kennedy Round negotiations differ from the Tokyo Round negotiations?

Endnotes

1. Paul Samuelson, *Economics* (New York: McGraw-Hill Book Company, 1981), p. 669. *Also see* David H. Blake. *The Politics of Global Economic Relations* (Englewood Cliffs, NJ: Prentice-Hall, 1983); Ian M. D. Little, *Economic Development: Theory, Policy and International Relations* (New York: Basic Books, 1982).
2. *Value* can sometimes be uncoupled from production hours, but typically only in cases of long-term scarcity (as with some precious metals) or when the quality of one producer's manufactured products is not matched by other suppliers. In these circumstances, virtual monopolies can develop.
3. Peter F. Drucker, "Low Wages No Longer Give Competitive Edge" *The Wall Street Journal,* March 16, 1988, p. 23.
4. Herbert E. Meyer, "How We're Fixed for Strategic Minerals," *Fortune,* February 9, 1981, pp. 68–71. *Also see* Peter Nulty, "How to Pay a Lot for Cobalt," *Fortune,* April 4, 1983, pp. 150–155.
5. G. Todd Russell, "Business Travelers Rate Asia's Airlines as the World's Best," *The Asian Wall Street Journal Weekly,* November 18, 1985, p. 1. *Also see* Louis Kraar, "Flying High with the Singapore Girls," *Fortune,* June 18, 1979, pp. 132–139.
6. Raymond Vernon, "International Investment and International Trade in the Product Cycle," *Quarterly Journal of Economics,* May 1966, pp. 190–207. *Also see* Raymond Vernon, *Sovereignty at Bay* (New York: Basic Books, 1971), pp. 65–112; Louis T. Wells, Jr., "Test of a Product Cycle Model of International Trade," *Quarterly Journal of Economics,* February 1969, pp. 152–162.
7. Louis T. Wells, Jr., "A Product Life Cycle for International Trade?" *Journal of Marketing,* July 1968, pp. 1–6. *Also see* J. F. Hennart, *A Theory of Multinational Enterprise* (Ann Arbor: University of Michigan Press, 1982).
8. Damon Darlin, "Japanese Learn Thrills of Bargain Shopping from Mentors Abroad," *The Wall Street Journal,* March 11, 1988, p. 1.
9. Raymond Vernon, *Sovereignty at Bay* (New York: Basic Books, 1971), p. 107.
10. James M. Lutz and Robert T. Green. "The Product Life Cycle and the Export Position of the United States," *Journal of International Business Studies,* Winter 1983, pp. 77–94. *Also see* Sak Onkvisit and John J. Shaw, "An Examination of the International Product Life Cycle and Its Application Within Marketing," *Columbia Journal of World Business,* Fall 1983, pp. 73–78.
11. Alicia Mullor-Sebastian, "The Product Life Cycle Theory: Empirical Evidence," *Journal of International Business Studies,* Winter 1983, pp. 95–106.
12. Peter F. Drucker, "The Rise of Production Sharing," *The Wall Street Journal,* March 15, 1977, p. 24. *Also see* Martin K. Starr, "Global Production and Operations Strategy," *Columbia Journal of World Business,* Winter 1984, pp. 17–22.
13. Peter F. Drucker, "Economics Erases National Boundaries," excerpt ad from *Managing in Turbulent Times* by Peter F. Drucker (New York: Harper & Row, 1979), in *Industry Week,* April 28, 1980, pp. 63–64.
14. Peter J. Buckley and Mark Casson, *The Future of the Multinational Enterprise* (New York: Holmes & Meier, 1976), p. 33. *Also see* Peter J. Buckley, "The Limits of Explanation: Testing the Internalization Theory of the Multinational," *Journal of International Business Studies,* Summer 1988, pp. 181–193.
15. Peter J. Buckley, *Multinational Enterprises and Economic Analysis* (Cambridge, England: Cambridge University Press, 1982). *Also see* Paul W. Beamish and John C. Banks, "Equity Joint Ventures and the Theory of the Multinational Enterprise," *Journal of International Business Studies,* Summer 1987, pp. 1–16.
16. Peter J. Buckley and R. D. Pierce, "Overseas Production and Exporting by the World's Largest Enterprises: A Study in Sourcing Policy," *Journal of International Business Studies,* Spring/Summer 1979, pp. 9–20. *Also see* Peter J. Buckley, "The Optional Timing of a Foreign Direct Investment," *Economic Journal,* March 1981, pp. 3–17.
17. A. D. Cao, "Non-tariff Barriers to U.S. Manufactured Exports," *Columbia Journal of World Business,* Summer 1980, pp. 93–102. *Also see* Alan Bauerschmidt, Daniel Sullivan, and Kate Gillespie, "Common Fac-

tors Underlying Barriers to Export: Studies in the U.S. Paper Industry," *Journal of International Business Studies,* Fall 1985, pp. 111–124.

18. See Tacho Bark and Jaime de Melo, "Export Quota Allocations, Export Earnings, and Market Diversification," *The World Bank Economic Review,* vol. 2, no. 3, pp. 341–348.
19. John J. Nevin, "Doorstop for Free Trade," *Harvard Business Review,* March–April 1983, p. 91.
20. At the time of the GATT negotiations, nations were also working toward setting up an international trade organization (ITO), but the matter was dropped since the participating nations failed to come to an agreement.
21. *See* Sylvia Nasar, "The New Case for Protectionism," *Fortune,* September 16, 1985, pp. 33–38.
22. *See* Jagdish N. Bhagwati, "Trade in Services and the Multilateral Trade Negotiations," *The World Bank Economic Review,* September 1987, pp. 549–570.
23. Peter Truell, "GATT Talks Break Down and Outlook for Reviving Negotiations Seems Bleak," *The Wall Street Journal,* December 10, 1990, p. A6.
24. Lee Smith, "What's At Stake in the Trade Talks," *Fortune,* August 27, 1990, p. 76.
25. "Compromise Reported in Trade Talks," *Washington Post,* October 25, p. D1.
26. *Future United States Foreign Trade Policy,* report to the President, submitted by the Special Representative for Trade Negotiations (Washington, D.C.: U.S. Government Printing Office, 1969). *Also see* Gordon L. Weil, *Trade Policy in the 70s* (New York: The Twentieth Century Fund, 1969).
27. Samuel Rabino, "An Attitudinal Evaluation of an Export Incentive Program: The Case of DISC," *Columbia Journal of World Trade,* Spring 1980, p. 61.
28. "Principal Features of the 'Trade Act' of 1988," *Business America,* September 26, 1988, p. 6. *Also see* "The New Trade Act," *Business America,* October 24, 1988, pp. 2–6.
29. Shawn Tully, "Nestlé Shows How to Gobble Markets," *Fortune,* January 16, 1989, p. 74.
30. Information on Gillette Company was obtained through a personal interview with a company executive and from the Company's Annual Report for 1987.
31. David Wessel, "Gillette Keys Sales to Third World Tastes," *The Wall Street Journal,* January 23, 1986, p. 35. *Also see* "Gillette Inches Closer to the Razor's Edge," *Business Week,* February 19, 1988, p. 36.

PART • I Cases

Case I: Marks and Spencer

J. Edward Sieff, president of Marks and Spencer, Ltd., sat in his office after a weekly meeting with his staff. He pondered about the future of his company and more specifically how it could maintain its growth and dominate the retail industry. During the staff meeting the major topic of discussion was the expansion of M & S to foreign markets. The United States retail market looked most favorable to many of the staff but Sieff had his reservations. During the mid-1970s the company had a lackluster experience in the Canadian retail market compared to the home market and this was still fresh on his mind.

Sieff was also aware of the French Printemps corporation's attempt to franchise into the U.S. market. Printemps had opened a store in Denver and had been struggling. The dominant French retailer was seeing powerful U.S. retailers opening stores in better locations near its fledgling, which squeezed the already weak operation.

M & S learned from these attempts by other companies, and from its own experience, that the U.S. market is tough to break into. On April 12, 1987, M & S sent a team to the U.S. to study the different entry possibilities open to the company. It is now July 10, 1987, and the pressing problem on Edward Sieff's mind is how to be competitive in this new foreign market. Will the company's current marketing strategy and other policies be effective in the U.S. or should they be altered? Should M & S try, as they did in Canada, to expand the current M & S company under a different name (D'Allaird's, Peoples) directly to the U.S., should they franchise as Printemps tried, or should they just acquire their way into the U.S. markets?

Company Background

In 1884, a Polish immigrant named Michael Marks began visiting town markets in northern England. There he set up stalls that featured a sign that read, "Don't ask the price—it's a penny." This slogan became so popular he began to open more shops that featured goods that cost a penny. High turnover overcame the low margins, and the business began to flourish. In 1894 Marks took Thomas Spencer as a partner. By 1903 the company had forty branches, and it was in this year that Marks and Spencer, Ltd. was formed with headquarters in Manchester.

By 1908, both Marks and his partner Spencer had passed away and the business temporarily left the family control. In 1914, the founder's son Simon Marks regained control of the company with its then-140 branches. After that time the family maintained a tight lock on the company control. In fact, in 1974 there were no outside members on the board of directors. Currently three of seventeen board members are from the family.

M & S was founded and run with the strong personal values of its founders. There was a strong commitment to the customer and to the employees of the company. There was also a deep concern for the society in general that had made the company very popular. In 1924 Simon Marks visited the U.S. and saw the "super stores" that were prevalent here. He returned to England committed to making M & S a chain of super stores with continuous merchandise flow and a central organization sensitive to customer needs. In 1926, M & S went public, and by 1936 it was present in every major town in England.

In 1933 a welfare department was established to look after the employees' needs. In 1936 a pension fund was initiated for employees. Benefits of employment included dental and medical coverage as well as special treatment for chiropody (prevalent among people who stand a lot). The stores had special rooms for the staff to eat and relax.

In 1928 M & S had its own brand name (St. Michael) and was committed to selling only brand name products at moderate prices. Quality was also critical to the M & S way. To help maintain quality, M & S began to work very closely with its suppliers. Since the suppliers were generally small firms they were anxious to cooperate, M & S made sure that suppliers used the newest technology and continually managed to keep their costs down. This created quality products at the best margins possible. M & S has worked with some of its suppliers for over thirty years.

After WW II, M & S experienced phenomenal growth. The St. Michael brand name became synonymous with quality and value. M & S became the dominant force in its market and began a modernization and expansion strategy. In 1956 there was large concern over the increase of overhead as the company grew. This concern resulted in a plan to reduce the bureaucracy and paperwork at the company. This plan was called "Operation Simplification." The emphasis for all management was to increase sales while not increasing overhead. M & S began to look everywhere to improve the efficiency of operation. The company eliminated 120 tons of paperwork each year. The number of company staff declined from 32,000 to 22,000. Managers were freed to personally get involved with their departments. Since that time, the company has been leery of statistics and has counted on the "seeing eyes" and "critical minds" to make correct decisions.

The efficiency emphasis has become a part of the corporate culture. Through the 1970s, the officers literally ate, slept, and dressed M & S. All executives wore only M & S clothing and worked about sixty hours a week. On their way home and on Saturdays they would drop in on stores to see how things had been going. This attitude was prevalent not only for management but also for all employees.

The employees of M & S were deeply committed to their jobs because the company was committed to them. M & S paid good wages and provided good benefits to its employees. The company sponsored social and recreational clubs for employees and the higher-level needs of the employees were met by listening to suggestions and providing challenging responsibilities. The company provided lunch rooms and meals for workers even during retirement. Some other important factors that promoted employee performance were teamwork and cross training.

The marketing at M & S was all based on the customer. Israel Sieff said: "The future of the business depends on quick imaginative study of what the people need, not on what the public can be persuaded to buy." M & S was committed to supplying the customers' needs for the long term. M & S offered a selective and streamlined range of products that turned over inventory very quickly. The company used the 80/20 rule that states 80 percent of revenue comes from 20 percent of their products. They prioritized their stock to the fastest-moving items. The company sold about 3,000 textile items and 700 food-related items. High quality at moderate prices was considered by customers to be "value for money." M & S originated with just one mark-up percentage for all items but has since allowed several different mark-up percentages depending on the items. M & S never held sales and only reduced slow-selling items for clearance. M & S also did very little advertising. They averaged about 0.3 percent of dollar sales spent on advertising as compared to 2–3 percent in the U.S. Advertising was limited to information on new product lines and other changes made to a store. The executives at M & S believed that the items sold themselves and most publicity for the stores was passed by word of mouth. M & S did not in the past sponsor credit cards for purchases. It is only recently that credit cards can be used at M & S stores. One other M & S strength was the optimum locations they had for each of their stores.

M & S also had to work within strict government regulations and tax structures in England. Many officers at M & S spoke out against the government's "misguided interference."

M & S had a good financial position. They paid high dividends and had low equity. They also had low debt. M & S was the only retail store in the world that had a triple A Standard and Poors bond rating.

Company Statistics

M & S has been called by many the most successful retail chain in the world, with 269 stores in the U.K., nine others in Europe, and 230 stores in Canada. In the U.K., M & S controls a hefty 16 percent of the clothing market. The profit margins that M & S enjoys are some 20 percent higher than the U.S. industry average. For the year ending March 31, 1987, M & S earned $812 million before taxes on sales of $7.9 billion. This was a 16 percent increase from the previous year. Food by now represented 37 percent of sales but expansion in this area was slowing.

The Canadian Experience

M & S has not always enjoyed good planning, as their Canadian expansion proved. They have stores under the names Peoples, D'Allaird's, and M & S. The Canadian operation lost money for ten of its first fourteen years. Analysts say that M & S was slow to read the Canadian customer and this resulted in most of the problems. For example, the stores in the U.K. do not have dressing rooms to try on clothing before purchasing it. This policy was a security measure adopted due to the shoplifting that was prevalent. In Canada, however, not having dressing rooms was a major deterrent to the customer.

Competition

The competition for M & S has always been stiff but they have been able to be dominant in all of their markets. In the U.K. they have intense customer loyalty and their competitors have difficulty creating this same commitment in their customers. The U.S. market is one of the most brutal retail markets in the world. The competition is powerful and difficult to dominate. U.S. competitors are very much in tune with their customers and are not afraid to spend ten times the amount M & S currently spends on advertising as a percentage of sales.

Case Considerations

The main consideration of the case is choosing the best way for M & S to enter the U.S. retail market. How should their current policies be adjusted, if at all, so they can be successful in this foreign market? Thought should be given to the best route to take for entering the market: franchise, acquisition, or building stores from scratch? What name should be used in the U.S. market? The reaction of powerful competitors in the U.S. must be examined if M & S is to make the U.S. a new growth market. How do U.S. customers and their preferences compare to U.K. customers?

Case 2: Hatfield Graphics, Inc.

In the spring of 1990, Mark Hunt, senior vice president of marketing at Hatfield Graphics, Inc. (HGI), was preparing an evaluation of the corporation's progress in penetrating overseas markets. While Hatfield's sales had been very respectable in their well-established European subsidiaries, Hunt was anxious to see the firm evaluate, penetrate, and develop some of the previously ignored markets in other parts of the world. He was particularly interested in China and the Eastern European countries, because he believed that these countries represented potentially large untapped markets for Hatfield products, especially in light of the lack of competition there. Hunt began to review the possible strategies the company could adopt to capture these markets.

Company Background

Hatfield Graphics, Inc., was organized in 1945. Headquartered in New Haven, Connecticut, it conducted its business through two principal subsidiaries: (1) the Hatfield Scientific Instrument Company, a manufacturer of computer-controlled drafting and plotting systems and turnkey interactive computer graphic design (IDS) and data management systems (DMS), and (2) Hatfield Garment Technology, Inc., a manufacturer of computer-controlled fabric cutting systems. In addition, the company owned about 54 percent interest in Ashi Engineering Development, Ltd., of Beersheba, Israel, whose principal products were electronic medical and dental instruments. The company's total sales in 1989 amounted to $148 million.

HGI's Businesses

Hatfield designed, manufactured, marketed, and serviced different computer-controlled drafting and cutting systems and provided software for its systems. Its principal businesses fell into three categories: drafting systems, cutting systems, and IDS and DMS. Following is the sales history of the company for five years.

Drafting Systems Hatfield's computer-controlled drafting systems were used primarily to produce finished engineering drawings and graphic artwork many times faster and more accurately than a draftsman could do the same work. A drafting system was composed of a control unit and a plotter. The control unit was computer programmed to receive instructions from an input device, such as a magnetic tape reader, and to process the information and issue commands to drive the plotter. The plotter was an electromechanical device that moved the drafting tool over the drafting medium. Hatfield produced a variety of plotters of different sizes, speeds, and accuracy. Computer-controlled drafting systems were used to produce engineering drawings in an array of industries including the automotive, aerospace, shipbuilding, mapmaking, garment, and electronic industries. The price of such drafting systems, including control software and various accessories, ranged from $50,000 to $500,000. Hatfield had been engaged in the production of computer-controlled drafting systems for fifteen years.

Cutting Systems Hatfield produced computer-controlled cutting systems that provided quick and accurate cutting of a wide variety of fabrics for different industries. Multiple layers of material spread on a long table and compressed by a patented vacuum system were cut to the desired shape by a computer-controlled cutterhead containing a reciprocating knife. Depending on the particular application, the user realized significant savings in materials and cutting and sewing operations, and there was a significant improvement in productivity. A typical cutter system was priced anywhere from $325,000 to $550,000.

Interactive Design and Data Management Systems A typical IDS consisted of a minicomputer, a keyboard, a cathode ray tube dis-

	1985	1986	1987	1988	1989
Drafting systems	58%	55%	59%	54%	42%
Cutting systems	30	22	30	25	32
IDS and DMS	8	18	7	17	23
Other	4	5	4	4	3
Total	100%	100%	100%	100%	100%

play, and other devices such as a plotter and applications software. A primary function of an IDS was the preparation and recording of data involved in the design process. In manufacturing industries, a design begins with the creation of a mathematical model of a tangible item, such as a mechanical part. The IDS provided the means for a design engineer to construct a mathematical model of the part easily and quickly, to view the part in the form of a graphic display, and to make engineering changes. From this design data, an IDS could produce documents, such as engineering drawings and layouts, on microfilm, paper, or vellum, as well as generate bills for materials. Using the final design data, manufacturing engineers could use the IDS to generate numerical control tapes for automatic operation of the machine tools used to produce the part.

The IDS could be used by all industries and businesses requiring graphic design. In addition to designing mechanical products such as those found in the aerospace and automotive industries, IDS could be used in architectural design, mapmaking, design of printed circuit boards, electrical schematics, tooling design, plant layout, and various other applications.

Hatfield's DMS provided flexibility by linking several IDS into a single "distributed" interactive graphics system. This networking, which used the DMS computer, permitted different engineering and manufacturing groups to share a common design data base as well as the computing and data storage resources. The DMS also could be linked together and to large mainframe computers, thus providing very large storage and data management capacity and computer power to run complex analysis programs for an IDS. The software of Hatfield's DMS provided full security of the design data, so that only persons with appropriate clearance had access to the data.

Hatfield's IDS and DMS were available in a large number of configurations, permitting each system to be tailored to a customer's particular requirements.

Research and Development

Hatfield had major research and development programs in effect, in both hardware and software. The objective of these programs was to create new products and improve, as well as modify, existing products for Hatfield's present customers. Research and development expenditures amounted to $3,270,000 in 1989. The company held more than 200 U.S. and more than 150 foreign patents.

Marketing

Hatfield's products were sold to end-users primarily through Hatfield's direct salesforce in the United States, through wholly owned subsidiaries in Western Europe, and through independent sales representatives in other areas. The Western European subsidiaries were headquartered in Belgium, Germany, and the United Kingdom, with sales personnel in other significant European countries. The subsidiaries served as sales representatives on a commission basis. Hatfield also had 54 percent interest in an Israeli company. In 1988, the company entered into agreements with Yokogawa Electric Works Ltd., Tokyo, which gave Yokogawa the exclusive right to manufacture and sell Hatfield's IDS and DMS in Japan, Korea, and Singapore.

Hatfield first began foreign sales and support activities through a combination of foreign sales agents and sales representatives. This gave Hatfield fast inroads into foreign markets because of its agents' and representatives' familiarity with the language, local industry, and business customs. Technical support and service for each sale, however, were handled by domestic personnel until local people could be trained as service personnel, usually employees of a subsidiary.

The first overseas offices, located in the United Kingdom and Brussels, were designed along the lines of the domestic sales organization. Each office operated independently and had both sales and service responsibility for its respective territory. Office staff were primarily composed of home nationals. Unfortunately, it was not long before serious personnel problems developed. Many employees complained of ambiguity in the channels of command and were unclear as to whether their loyalties were to the home office or the parent.

In view of these problems, Hatfield established wholly owned subsidiaries totally staffed by locals. The nationals naturally spoke the local language and were thought to be much more skilled in local sales techniques. They were also expected to have a competitive advantage over other foreign manufacturers because of their ability to deal on a local manufacturer to local customer basis.

Each overseas subsidiary was designed to support full sales, service, and manufacturing activities. Despite these capabilities, Hatfield conducted all manufacturing in the United States. Hunt explained:

> Back when we set up our subsidiaries, the cost of manufacturing overseas was lower due to a rather depressed wage scale. In addition, the U.S. dollar was overvalued relative to other currencies. However, the forecasts were for overseas wage rates to eventually climb beyond those in the United States and for the dollar to realign itself at a much lower level. For example, the average hourly wage rates in the United States were currently $7 to $8 with associated fringe benefits of 30 to 40 percent of total salary. Average hourly wages in Germany, by comparison, were $9 to $9.50 with fringe benefits amounting to 50 to 60 percent of salary.

Competition

Hatfield competed with a variety of companies, some of which were larger and had greater monetary resources. In the computer-controlled drafting systems, however, Hatfield was the major supplier in the United States, and one of the major suppliers in the Western European market. In other businesses, the company's position was among the major competitors. Approximately twelve companies offered turnkey interactive computer graphic design systems. Of those, Applicon, Inc., Autotrol Technology Corporation, Calma Company, and ComputerVision Corporation were the formidable competitors.

Expansion into International Markets

According to Hunt, three ingredients are essential in marketing products overseas:

1. The entire corporation must make a commitment to export the product overseas. Exports of your product must be recognized as a vital part of your business and as a major growth area in the future. Anything less than a full, long-term emotional commitment to overseas markets will not be profitable for the company.
2. The product must offer something useful to the market you are entering. It must either be seriously looking for the product you are offering or be developed by proving to the end-user the benefits of the product.
3. The product must be adapted to its target market. Environmental differences, such as the different power requirements in Europe, require that the product be modified in order to be accepted by the user.

Hatfield first became involved in foreign markets through unsolicited orders from large European electronics firms looking to acquire the high-technology products that Hatfield manufactured and that were not available in their own countries. As these orders became a more significant part of Hatfield's total sales revenue, the company began to develop aggressively a sales and service organization to address the needs of these foreign customers.

The prospect of an established overseas market for Hatfield's products had many attractive characteristics. One of the most appealing of these was the potential for effectively lowering its per-unit research and development costs through increased unit sales. Since Hatfield's products were highly specialized and required the most exact engineering, development costs were high and represented a substantial initial investment. An overseas market would allow the company to increase substantially their return on this investment.

The overseas market also offered an avenue by which they could increase the sales life expectancy of their products. "Many countries have not experienced the rapid advances in technology that we have in the United States," Hunt commented. "Some products considered nearly obsolete by our standards are thought to be state-of-the-art in foreign markets."

Finally, many industries that were prime users of Hatfield products were growing at a much faster rate overseas than in the United States. The European market for so-called systems products, for example, was estimated to be growing at 20 percent per year.

Future International Markets for Hatfield Products

Hunt discussed the possibilities for future expansion of Hatfield's sales overseas. Continued growth could be expected in the well-established European market, although at a declining rate. With this forecast, Hatfield was considering the possibilities for development of a number of new markets, particularly those in China and the Eastern European countries.

Chinese Market China, as described by Hunt, would provide Hatfield with an outlet for his company's software and marketing systems within the nation's large garment industry. The Chinese garment industry, unlike its European counterparts, did not have a need for Hatfield's fast, accurate garment cutters because of China's abundant, cheap labor resources. Materials, however, were in constantly short supply and very expensive, accounting for 85 percent of the total cost of each garment. The China market, therefore, seemed a likely candidate for Hatfield's AM-1 marker grading systems, which automatically arranged and marked materials for manual cutting operations. In addition, Mr. Hunt felt that the market offered great potential when viewed against several other criteria.

A primary consideration was the overall size of the Chinese marketplace. The country, with a population of approximately one billion people (the largest in the world), had a workforce that increased by 20 million annually. The Chinese government was also supporting a national modernization program for specific industries. The garment industry, while not an immediate high priority in that program, hoped to gain increased government support over the next three to ten years. Hunt, therefore, foresaw an overall increase in demand for Hatfield products in China over the long term.

Eastern European Countries The Eastern European countries offered rich potential markets for Hatfield's products. Romania, in particular, had expressed interest in Hatfield equipment. United States and Romanian government regulations and red tape, however, caused extremely long and frustrating sales transactions. In a previous sale in 1981, the Romanian and United States governments delayed a signed order for three years. When the order was finally approved, Hatfield was obligated to manufacture a then-obsolete piece of equipment at great expense and little profit. Despite these admitted difficulties, Hunt felt that Hatfield was in a strong financial position to explore possibilities in the post-communist Eastern European countries, which promised a vast potential in the coming years.

How to Proceed

While the China and Eastern European markets appeared attractive, Hunt was not sure what entry strategy would be most desirable to make inroads into these markets. In addition, he wondered what information should be gathered to determine entry routes.

Case 3: United Parcel Service

In August 1990, executives at United Parcel Service (UPS) met to discuss the new U.S.-Japan all-cargo route it had just been awarded. Executives were concerned that even though they had had a successful joint venture with Yamato K.K., now might be the time to dissolve the joint venture and create a wholly owned subsidiary. The responsibility fell squarely on John Larden, UPS International Operations Group Manager, to develop a viable plan that would fill a 747 aircraft.

Company Background

UPS is a privately held package distribution company founded in 1907 in Seattle, Washington, by Jim Casey, who had in mind the idea to provide the best delivery service at the lowest cost. Originally known as the American Messenger Service, UPS began as a messenger service with five or six boys, ready for business at any hour of the day. As the messenger service began to slow, Casey decided to specialize in deliveries to retail stores. This led to the development of the consolidated delivery system that UPS uses today, a system that eliminates duplication of travel and lowers costs. With one Ford car and a few motorcycles, regularly scheduled service was inaugurated in 1913 and the company name was changed to Merchants Parcel Delivery. Several years later, the name was changed to United Parcel Service. In 1990, UPS maintained a fleet of 119,000 vehicles and 162 jet aircrafts that delivered 11.5 million parcels and documents daily. UPS is the world's largest package distribution company (see Exhibit 1).

Characteristics of UPS Air Cargo

UPS offered a variety of options for shipping packages, documents, and air freight. The two largest options were next day air service and second day air service. The next day air service guaranteed delivery before 10:30 A.M. the next business day, while the second day air option guaranteed delivery in two business days. In 1989, the combined volume of the two services was 750,000 pieces daily. In addition, UPS Air Cargo service totaled 90 million pounds filling 27,000 container positions on what would have been empty space on regular UPS flights.

UPS operated 942 daily domestic flight segments and 415 international flight segments. These flight segments served 389 domestic airports and 208 international airports. UPS operated one main air hub located in Louisville, Kentucky, and three regional air hubs located in Philadelphia, Dallas, and Ontario, California. The European hub was located in Cologne/Bonn, West Germany, and the Pacific Rim hubs were located in Hong Kong, Singapore, and the newly operational Tokyo air hub. Serving the South American/Caribbean market was the Miami air hub.

The UPS jet aircraft fleet included fifty-five 737 PFs, forty-seven 727s, forty-nine DC-8s, and eleven 747s. This fleet served 180 countries and territories, covering eighty percent of the world's population.

EXHIBIT 1 United Parcel Service: Consolidated Income Account, years ended December 31

	1989	1988	1987
Revenues	$12,358	$11,032	$9,682
Wages and employment benefits	7,392	6,728	5,874
Other operating expenses	3,750	3,229	2,837
Operating income	1,216	1,075	971
Other income	15	5	4
Other expenses	23	33	23
Income before taxes	1,208	1,047	952
Taxes	510	288	168
Net income	698	759	784

Source: Moody's Transportation 1991.

International Air Service

UPS had a significant presence worldwide. In 1989, UPS acquired nine European-based transportation companies and an Asian delivery company that served parts of the continent along the Pacific Rim and down to Australia. One of the acquired companies, British-based IML Air Services Group Ltd., served over one hundred countries worldwide. The other eight European acquisitions were companies that had formerly been operating as service partners. At the end of 1989, UPS extended its International Air Service to four countries in Eastern Europe serving Moscow, Budapest, East Berlin, and Krakow. UPS was managing the entire delivery process inside Eastern Europe with UPS vehicles and nationals trained to UPS standards. International Air Cargo Service covered all points in Canada. Further, UPS was one of the three carriers to receive authority to fly scheduled all-cargo aircraft to Mexico.

Finally, after many years of difficult negotiations, an agreement was reached in the fall of 1989 between the U.S. and Japanese governments for a U.S.-Japan all-cargo route to be awarded to a U.S. carrier. The U.S. Department of Transportation held hearings in April 1990; in August 1990, UPS was awarded the coveted route (see Exhibits 2 and 3).

Japan and International Air Service

Since 1986, UPS had been seeking authority from the U.S. and Japanese governments to fly directly to Japan. Before being awarded the U.S.-Japan all-cargo route, UPS used Flying Tigers and Northwest Airlines to transport packages, documents, and air freight to Japan. In Japan, UPS used Yamato K.K. as a service partner to deliver packages, documents, and air freight. With the award of the new route, UPS planned to operate six days a week using a 747 flight originating in Louisville, stopping in Anchorage, and continuing to Tokyo's Narita Airport. The plane would be refueled and loaded at Narita and depart for the U.S. the same day. Japan was the U.S.'s largest foreign market for all-cargo air needs.

Competition and Japan Air Cargo

Because Japan was the largest market for air cargo, there were many competitors, but most of the competition came from passenger airlines. Japan Air Lines (JAL) and Northwest Airlines had a significant share of the market. In addition, DHL and Federal Express/Flying Tigers were formidable competitors.

How to Proceed?

UPS had been transporting both small packages and air freight between the U.S. and Japan utilizing other carriers, freight forwarders, and Yamato K.K. The problem John Larden faced was complex. Yamato K.K. was a direct competitor of the freight forwarders that used UPS for their air cargo needs. In the majority of the countries where UPS operated, the entire distribution of packages and air freight was performed entirely by UPS personnel. Should UPS sever ties with Yamato and form a wholly owned subsidiary to oversee the new operation? Or should UPS maintain its joint venture status and continue using Yamato K.K. as well as other freight forwarders?

EXHIBIT 2 United Parcel Service: International Operations of Certified Carriers, years ended December 31

	REVENUE MILES FLOWN (IN MILLIONS)	AVAILABLE TON MILES (IN MILLIONS)	REVENUE TOTAL (IN MILLIONS OF U.S. DOLLARS)
1986	401.9	20,479	64,456
1987	459.1	23,411	79,834
1988	537.9	27,068	93,992
1989	602.0	30,438	102,739

Source: Moody's Transportation 1991.

EXHIBIT 3 United Parcel Service: Traffic Statistics and Unit Revenues, years ended December 31

	REVENUE TON MILES (IN MILLIONS)		REVENUE PER TON MILE (IN MILLIONS OF U.S. DOLLARS)	
	Total	Freight	Total	Freight
1986	11,736	3,354.0	$70.53	$39.03
1987	14,408	3,920.7	72.73	40.55
1988	16,799	4,789.2	76.72	39.68
1989	18,617	5,358.8	77.41	46.94

Source: Moody's Transportation 1991.

Case 4: Metro Corporation

In the fall of 1979, Metro Corporation entered into a licensing agreement with Impecina, a Peruvian company. The negotiations went smoothly. In the aftermath, however, the management wondered what lessons the Peruvian deal offered for future technology transfer opportunities to other developing countries.

The Licensor Firm

Metro Corporation is a diversified steel rolling, fabricating, and construction company based in the Midwest and considers itself to be in a mature industry. Innovations are few and far between. With transport and tariff barriers, and the support given by many governments to their own companies, exporting as a means of doing foreign business is rather limited. Similarly, given the large investment, modest return, and political sensitivity of the industry, direct foreign investment is all but a closed option. In a global strategic sense then, Metro Corporation has far more frequently focused on licensing as a market entry method, with technologies confined to (1) processes and engineering peripheral to the basic steel making process, e.g., mining methods, coke oven door designs, galvanizing, etc., and (2) applications of steel in construction and other industries, e.g., petroleum tank design, welding methods, thermo-adhesion, etc.

All Metro's licensing is handled by its international division, International Construction and Engineering (ICE), which is beginning to develop a reputation in Western Europe and Latin America as a good source for specialized construction technology.

The Proposed Licensee

Impecina, a private firm, is the largest construction company in Peru and operates throughout Latin America. Impecina has a broad range of interests including residential and commercial buildings, hydraulic works, transportation, and maritime works. Employing several thousand personnel, engineers, and technicians, its sales had doubled in the last five years. It was still primarily a Peruvian business with most turnover in Peru but was in the process of expanding into Colombia, the North African Mediterranean countries, and Argentina, Brazil, and Venezuela. Impecina has advanced computer capacity with a large IBM and other computers at its branches. In oil storage tanks, Impecina's experience was limited to the smaller fixed-cone roof designs under 150 feet in diameter.

The Technology

National Tank Inc., a fabrication division of Metro, had designed a computerized design procedure for floating-roof oil storage tanks that minimized the use of steel within American Petroleum Institute or any other oil industry standards. Particularly for the larger tanks, for instance 150 feet in diameter and above, this design procedure would give the bidding contractor a significant cost advantage. National Tank had spent one man-year, at a direct cost of $225,000, to write the computer program alone. Patents were involved in an incidental manner, only for the seals of the floating roof. Metro had only filed for this patent in the U.S.

The Market

Peru's indigenous oil output is very low, but it imports and refines annually 50 million tons, mostly for domestic demand. Following the escalation of oil prices and tightening of supplies in 1973, the Peruvian government determinedly set about to formulate a program to augment Peru's oil storage capacity. Impecina's representatives,

This case is printed here with the permission of the author, Farok J. Contractor, of the State University of New Jersey, Rutgers.

at a preliminary meeting with ICE in the U.S. headquarters, said their government planned $200 million in expenditures on oil storage facilities over the next three years (mostly in large tanks). Of this, Impecina's "ambition" was to capture a one-third market share. That this appeared to be a credible target was illustrated by their existing 30 percent share of the "fixed-cone type under 150 feet in diameter." Additionally, they estimated private–sector construction value over the next three years to total $40 million.

Approximately half of a storage system's construction cost goes for the tank alone; the remainder for excavation, foundation, piping, instrumentation, and other ancillary equipment, all of which Impecina's engineers were very familiar with.

Neighboring Colombia was building a 12 million ton refinery but, according to the Impecina representative, the tank installation plans of other Latin American nations were not known.

Each of Impecina's competitors in Peru was affiliated with a prominent company: Umbertomas with Jefferson Inc. in the United States, Zapa with Philadelphia Iron & Steel, Cosmas with Peoria–Duluth Construction Inc., and so on. Thus association with Metro would help Impecina in bidding.

The First Meeting

National Tank division had in the past year bid jointly with Impecina on a project in southern Peru. Though that bid was unsuccessful, Impecina had learned about Metro's computerized design capabilities and initiated a formal first round of negotiations that were to lead to a licensing agreement. The meeting took place in the United States. Two Impecina executives of subdirector rank were accompanied by an American consultant. Metro was represented by the vice president of ICE, the ICE attorney, and an executive from National Tank Division.

Minutes of this meeting show it was exploratory; both genuine and rhetorical questions were asked. Important information and perceptions were exchanged, and the groundwork laid for concluding negotiations. Following is a bare summary of important issues gleaned from the somewhat circular discussion.

a. *License Market Coverage:* Impecina tried to represent itself as an essentially Peruvian firm. They reviewed their government's expenditure plans and their hoped-for market share. Yet throughout the meeting, the issue of the license also covering Libya, Algeria, Morocco, Columbia, Argentina, Brazil, and Venezuela kept cropping up.
b. *Exclusivity:* For Peru, Metro negotiators had no difficulty conceding exclusivity. They mentioned that granting exclusivity to a licensee for any territory was agreeable in principle, provided a minimum performance guarantee was given. At this, the question was deferred for future discussion. At one point a Metro executive remarked, "We could give Impecina a nonexclusive—and say, for example, we wouldn't give another [licensee] a license for one year [in those nations]" proposing the idea of a trial period for Impecina to generate business in a territory.
c. *Agreement Life:* Impecina very quickly agreed to a ten-year term, payment in U.S. dollars, and other minor issues.
d. *Trade Name:* The Impecina negotiators placed great emphasis on their ability to use Metro's name in bidding, explaining how their competition in Peru had technical collaboration with three U.S. companies (see above). "Did that mean Metro's National Tank Division could compete with Impecina in Peru?" they were asked rhetorically. (Actually, both sides seem to have tacitly agreed that it was not possible for Metro to do business directly in Peru.)
e. *Licensee Market Size:* Attention turned to the dollar value of the future large (floating-roof) tank market in Peru. Impecina threw

out an estimate of $200 million government expenditures and $40 million private-sector spending, over the coming three years, of which they targeted a one-third share. Later, a lower market size estimate of $150 million (government *and* private), with a share of $50 million received by Impecina over three years, was arrived at (memories are not clear on how the estimates were revised). The question "Will Impecina guarantee us they will obtain one-third of the market?" brought the response "That's an optimistic figure but we hope we can realize [it]." Impecina offered as evidence their existing one-third share of the "fixed-roof under 150 feet" market, an impressive achievement.

f. *Product Mix Covered by Licensee:* It became clear that Impecina wanted floating-roof technology for *all* sizes, *and* fixed-roof over 100 feet diameter. They suggested the agreement cover tanks over 100 feet in size. "Would Impecina pay on all tanks [of any size]?" to simplify royalty calculation and monitoring? After considerable discussion, Metro seems to have acceded to Impecina's proposal (to cover both types, only over 100 feet) based on consensus over three points.
   1. The competition probably does not pay (their licensors) on small tanks, and therefore Impecina would be at a disadvantage if they had to pay on small tanks also.
   2. The market in floating-roof tanks was over 100 feet anyway, usually.
   3. Impecina claimed that customers normally dictate the dimensions of the tanks, so Impecina cannot vary them in order to avoid paying a royalty to Metro.

g. *Compensation Formula.* Metro proposed an initial lump-sum payment (in two installments, one when the agreement is signed, the second on delivery of the computer program and designs), *plus* engineers and executives for bid assistance on a per-diem rate, *plus* a royalty on successful bids based on the barrel capacity installed by Impecina. Impecina's American consultant countered with the idea of royalties on a sliding scale, lower with larger capacity tanks, indicating talk about "one million barrel capacity tanks." The (rhetorical?) question "What is Peru's oil capacity?" seems to have brought the discussion down to earth and veered it off on a tangent, while both sides mentally regrouped.

   On returning to this topic, Impecina executives ventured that as a rule of thumb, their profit markup on a turnkey job was 6 percent. (However, on excluding the more price-sensitive portions such as excavation, piping, and ancillary equipment, which typically constitute half the value, Impecina conceded that on the tank alone they might mark up as much as 12 percent, although they kept insisting 5 to 6 percent was enough.)

   Impecina executives later offered only royalties (preferably sliding) *and* per-diem fees for bid assistance from Metro executives and engineers. Metro countered by pointing out that per-diem fees of, say, $225 plus travel costs amounted at best to recovering costs, not profit.

   At this stage, the compensation design question was deferred for later negotiation, the broad outlines having been laid. Metro's starting formal offer, which would mention specific numbers, was to be telexed to Lima in a week.

h. *The Royalty Basis:* Metro considered the fact that Impecina engineers were very familiar with excavation, piping wiring, and other ancillary equipment. Metro was transferring technology *for the tank alone,* which typically composed half of overall installed value.

i. *Government Intervention.* Toward the end of the discussions, Impecina brought up the question of the Peruvian government having to approve of the agreement. This led to their retreat from the idea of a ten-year term, agreed to earlier, and Impecina then mentioned five years. No agreement was reached. (Incidentally, Peru had in the last two years passed legislation indicating a "guideline" of five years for foreign licenses.)

Internal Discussion in Metro Leading to the Formal Offer

The advantages derived by the licensee would be acquisition of floating-roof technology, time and money saved in attempting to generate the computerized design procedure in-house, somewhat of a cost and efficiency advantage in bidding on larger tanks, and finally, the use of Metro's name.

a. It was estimated that National Tank division had spent $225,000 (one man-year = two executives for six months, plus other costs) in developing the computer program. Additionally, it may cost $40,000 (three-quarters of a man-year) to convert the program into Spanish and the metric system, and to adapt it to the material availability and labor cost factors peculiar to Peru. Simultaneously, there would be semiformal instruction of Impecina engineers in the use of the program, petroleum industry codes, and Metro fabrication methods. All this had to be done before the licensee would be ready for a single bid.

b. It was visualized that Metro would then assist Impecina for two man-weeks for each bid preparation and four man-weeks on successful receipt of a contract award. Additionally, if Metro's specialized construction equipment were used, three man-months of on-site training would be needed.

As the licensee's personnel moved along their learning curve, assistance of the type described in paragraph b would diminish until it was no longer needed after a few successful bids.

Additional considerations that went into a determination of the initial offer:

1. Metro obligations (and sunk costs) under paragraph a were fairly determinate, whereas their obligations under b depended on the technical sophistication and absorptive capacity of the licensee's engineers, their success rate in bidding, and so on.
2. If Impecina's market estimates were used, they would generate large tank orders worth $50 million, on which they would make a profit of $3 million (at 6 percent on $50 million or 12 percent on half the amount) over the next three years.
3. The market beyond three years was an unknown.
4. Exclusive rights might be given to Impecina in Peru and Colombia, with perhaps ICE reserving the right of conversion to nonexclusive if minimum market share was not captured.
5. While Impecina's multinational expansion plans were unknown, their business in other nations was too small to justify granting them exclusivity. They may be satisfied with a vague promise of future consideration as exclusive licensees in those territories.
6. Metro would try for an agreement term of ten years. It was felt that Impecina computer and engineering capability was strong enough so they would not need Metro assistance after a few bids.

Surprisingly, the discussions reveal no explicit consideration given to the idea that Impecina may emerge someday as a multinational competitor.

In view of the uncertainty about how successful the licensee would actually be in securing orders and the uncertainty surrounding the Peruvian government's attitude, a safe strategy seemed to be to try and get as large a front-end fee as possible. Almost arbitrarily, a figure of $400,000 was proposed. (This was roughly 150 percent of the development costs plus the initial cost of transferring the technology to the licensee.) There would be sufficient margin for negotiations and to cover uncertainties. In order that the licensee's competitiveness not be diminished by the large lump-sum fee, a formula may be devised whereby the first five years' royalties could be reduced (see the following material).

The Formal Offer

The formal offer communicated in a telex a week later called for the following payment terms:

- A $400,000 lump-sum fee payable in two installments.
- A 2 percent royalty on any tanks constructed of a size over 100 feet in diameter, with up to one half of royalties owed in each of the first five years reduced by an amount up to $40,000 each year, without carryovers from year to year. The royalty percentage would apply to the total contract value less excavation, foundation, dikes, piping, instrumentation, and pumps.
- Agreement life of ten years.
- Metro to provide services to Impecina described in paragraph a (page 103) in consideration of the lump-sum and royalty fees.
- For additional services, described in paragraph b (page 103), Metro would provide personnel at up to $225 per day on request, plus travel and living costs while away from their place of business. The per-diem rates would be subject to escalation based on a representative cost index. There would be a ceiling placed on the number of man-days Impecina could request in any year.
- All payments to be made in U.S. dollars, net after all local, withholding, and other taxes.
- Impecina would receive exclusive rights for Peru and Colombia only, and nonexclusive rights for Morocco, Libya, Algeria, Argentina, Venezuela, Brazil, and Colombia. These could be converted to an exclusive basis on demonstration of sufficient business, in the future. For Peru and Colombia, Metro reserves the right to treat the agreement as nonexclusive if Impecina fails to get at least 30 percent of installed capacity of a type covered by the agreement.
- Impecina would have the right to sublicense only to any of its controlled subsidiaries.
- Impecina would supply free of charge to ICE all improvements made by it on the technology during the term of the agreement.
- Impecina would be entitled to advertise its association with metro in assigned territories, on prior approval of ICE as to wording, form, and content.

The Final Agreement

ICE executives report that the Peruvians "did not bat an eyelash" at their demands and that an agreement was soon reached in a matter of weeks. The only significant change was Metro agreeing to take a lump sum of $300,000 (still a large margin over costs.) Other changes were minor: Impecina to continue to receive benefit of further R&D; ICE to provide, at cost, a construction engineer if specialized welding equipment was used; the per-diem fee fixed at $200 per day (indexed by an average hourly wage escalation factor used by the U.S. Department of Labor); and the $300,000 lump-sum fee to be paid in installments over the first year.

In other respects, such as territory, royalty rate, exclusivity, travel allowances, etc., the agreement conformed with Metro's initial offer.

An Upset

The Peruvian government disallowed a ten-year agreement life. By then, both parties had gone too far to want to reopen the entire negotiations and Metro appears to have resigned itself to an agreement life of five years, with a further extension of another five years subject to mutual consent. Given Impecina's in-house engineering and computer capability, extension of the agreement life was a very open question.

PART • 2

The Field of International Business

CHAPTER • 3

International Monetary System

CHAPTER FOCUS

After studying this chapter, you should be able to:

- Describe the development of today's international monetary system
- Explain how foreign exchange transactions are conducted
- Identify the problems associated with exchange rate fluctuations
- Discuss the balance of payments perspectives of the United States
- Explain the creation of Eurodollars and petrodollars and their monetary effect

This chapter examines the subject of international trade in monetary terms. Trade settlements involve topics such as determination of foreign exchange rates, balance of payments, foreign exchange transactions, international financial flows, and international financial and trade institutions.

Each country has its own currency through which it expresses the value of its goods. For international trade settlements, however, the various currencies of the world must be transformed from one into the other. This task is accomplished through foreign exchange markets.

Periodically, a country must review the status of its economic relations with the rest of the world in terms of its exports and imports, its exchange of various kinds of services, and its purchase and sale of different types of assets and other international payments or receipts and transfers. Such an overall review is necessary to ascertain if the country has a favorable or unfavorable monetary balance in relation to the rest of the world. In the post–World War II period, a number of institutions came into existence to monitor and assist countries, as necessary, in keeping their international financial commitments in order. As a result of the establishment of these institutions, a new system of international monetary relations emerged in the late 1950s. This institutional framework went a long way toward increasing international trade in the 1950s and 1960s. In the early 1970s, however, the weakening of the U.S. dollar caused the system to falter. The all-important commitment of the United States deserves mention here. In order to encourage worldwide monetary stability, the United States government agreed to exchange the dollar at the fixed price of $35 for an ounce of gold. With the value of the dollar stabilized, countries could deal in dollars without being constrained by currency fluctuations. Thus, the dollar became the common denominator in world trade. Because of the weakening of the dollar and other related issues, the monetary stability of the world was disturbed and remained unsettled into the 1970s and early 1980s. As the 1980s advanced, the U.S. economy stabilized and the value of the dollar, against other currencies, climbed to an all-time high, adversely affecting the U.S. trade balance. In the fall of 1985, leading industrialized countries joined in the U.S. effort to intervene in the foreign exchange markets to decrease the value of the dollar. The dollar continued to stay weak in the remaining years of the 1980s and in the early 1990s. It appears that the value of the dollar is unlikely to appreciate much in the 1990s.

The Development of Today's International Monetary System

Post–World War II financial developments had long-range effects on international financial arrangements, the role of gold, and the problems of adjustment of balance of payments disequilibria. Following World War II, a keen awareness of the need to achieve economic prosperity grew among nations. The war years had shattered Europe and Japan. They needed reconstruction. A number of countries were wresting political freedom from colonial rulers, particularly from Britain. It did not take long for these countries to realize that political freedom alone was not sufficient. Economic prosperity was not only necessary for existence but mandatory for long-term survival and growth. Countries realized that planned international cooperation fostered economic development and prosperity. Thus, immediately after the war, nations agreed to a framework of international rules—a code of behavior—to maintain monetary discipline and to ensure that dissenting nations did not frustrate economic development efforts through counteractions.

The Bretton Woods Conference

The negotiations to establish the postwar international monetary system took place at Bretton Woods, New Hampshire, in 1944. There was a general feeling at that time that the economically disastrous interwar period and, to an extent, the precipitation of World War II resulted from the failure to include economic factors as a major consideration in post–World War I planning. Thus, there was a strong determination to avoid the mistakes of the past and to adhere to goals that would bring economic prosperity.

The negotiators at Bretton Woods made certain recommendations in 1944:

- Each nation should be at liberty to use macroeconomic policies for full employment. (This tenet ruled out a return to the gold standard.)
- Free-floating exchange rates could not work. Their ineffectiveness had been demonstrated during the 1920s and 1930s. But the extremes of both permanently fixed and free-floating rates should be avoided.
- A monetary system was needed that would recognize that exchange rates were both a national and an international concern.[1]

The International Monetary Fund

After long and careful deliberations, a monetary system was agreed upon at Bretton Woods. Member countries agreed to control the limits of their exchange rates in a predetermined way. Under the original agreement, exchange rates were permitted to vary by 1 percent above or below par. As a country's rate of exchange attained or approached either limit, called "arbitrage support points," its central bank intervened in the market to prevent the rate from passing the limit. Market intervention required a nation to accumulate international reserves, composed of gold and foreign currencies, above normal trading requirements. An institution called the ***International Monetary Fund (IMF)*** was established at Bretton Woods to oversee the newly agreed upon monetary system. (See the appendix to this chapter for a more detailed discussion of the IMF.)

More and more nations joined the original fifty-five IMF signatories, so that today there are over 150 members. With the passage of time, various changes were made in the IMF system to ameliorate the difficulties that nations faced. For example, if a nation's fixed parity ceases to be realistic, it may therefore either overvalue or devalue its currency. In such cases, the IMF agreed on orderly and reasonable changes in parity based upon the initiative of the country concerned. Such a system of alterable pass is often termed "the adjustable peg."

There are several major accomplishments to the credit of the International Monetary System. For example, it

- Sustained a rapidly increasing volume of trade and investment.
- Displayed flexibility in adapting to changes in international commerce.
- Proved to be efficient (even when there were decreasing percentages of reserves to trade).
- Proved to be hardy (it survived a number of pre-1971 crises, speculative and otherwise, and the down-and-up swings of several business cycles).
- Allowed a growing degree of international cooperation.
- Established a capacity to accommodate reforms and improvements.[2]

To an extent the fund served as an international central bank to help countries during periods of temporary balance-of-payments difficulties, by protecting their rates of exchange. Because of that, countries did not need to resort to exchange controls and other barriers to restrict world trade.[3]

As time passed, it became evident that the fund's resources for providing short-term accommodation to countries in monetary difficulties were not sufficient. To resolve the situation, the fund, after much debate and long deliberations, created special drawing rights in 1969. ***Special drawing rights (SDRs),*** sometimes called *paper gold,* are special account entries on the IMF books designed to provide additional liquidity to support growing world commerce. Although SDRs are a form of fiat money not convertible to gold, their gold value is guaranteed, which helps to ensure their acceptability. Initially SDRs worth $9.5 billion were created.

Participant nations may use SDRs in a variety of ways: as a source of currency in a spot transaction, as a loan for clearing a financial obligation, as security for a loan, as a swap against currency, or in a forward exchange operation. A nation with a balance-of-payments need may use its SDRs to obtain usable currency from another nation designated by the fund. A participant also may use SDRs to make payments to the fund, such as repurchases. The fund itself may transfer SDRs to a participant for various purposes, including the transfer of SDRs instead of currency to a member using the fund's resources.

By providing a mechanism for international monetary cooperation, working to reduce restrictions to trade and capital flows, and helping members with their short-term balance-of-payments difficulties, the IMF makes a significant and unique contribution to human welfare and improved living standards throughout the world.

The IMF and the Debt Crisis

In the 1970s, developing nations all over the world found their efforts to manage their economic affairs swamped by a unique combination of adverse circumstances—dramatically increased oil prices followed by worldwide inflation, a collapse in commodity prices, the worst world recession since the 1930s, and historically high interest rates. When oil prices shot up, these countries borrowed heavily at high interest rates to stave off economic dislocation.

Between 1974 and 1982 the two oil price shocks created a temporary savings surplus in high-income oil-exporting countries. Their surplus funds were recycled to developing countries. This process is now well understood. In addition to increasing their development aid, high-income oil-exporting countries placed much of their surplus oil revenue with international commercial banks in the form of short-term Eurodollar deposits. This contributed to raising liquidity in the international banking system because credit demand in the industrial countries had been depressed by the oil price shocks. Liquidity and monetary expansion in the industrial countries drove real interest rates down. It also prompted banks to compensate for the slack in their traditional markets by lending more to developing countries.

Commercial lending to developing countries—along with official lending and aid—grew very rapidly during this period. As a result the total medium- and long-term debt of developing countries rose fourfold in nominal terms, from about $140 billion at the end of 1974 to about $560 billion in 1982. By the end of 1990, their indebtedness had reached $1.48 trillion.[4] Developing countries were happy to take advantage of this unaccustomed access to cheap loans with few strings attached. They stepped up their commercial borrowing. This enabled them to maintain domestic growth and to finance major public investment programs, especially in the energy sector. With hindsight it is clear that lending and borrowing decisions were often imprudent and resulted in excessive indebtedness in a number of countries. New funds were often channeled into low-yielding investments. And, in a number of countries, borrowings fueled a flight of capital that drained the pool of resources for investment even as the burden of foreign debt mounted.

The early 1980s were a turning point. The shift toward anti-inflationary macroeconomic policies in industrial countries led to a rapid rise in nominal interest rates. Developing countries with large foreign debts were hit hard. The combination of higher interest rates and lower export prices for non-oil commodities led to soaring real costs for all forms of new and existing debt. Finally, from 1982 onward, the rapid deterioration of the U.S. saving-investment balance caused the United States to stake a bigger claim on the world's savings at a time when the savings surplus of the high-income oil exporters was falling along with the price of oil.

Rising debt service and the cut in lending led to a reversal of net resource transfers to developing countries. In the five years prior to 1982, developing countries received positive net resource transfers of $147 billion through long-term lending (including concessional loads). Since 1982, resource transfers have become negative, totaling $132 billion.

The drain of resources forced many countries to undertake rigorous domestic adjustments. Limited access to foreign financing meant that current account deficits had to be cut back. This, in turn, meant that trade balances had to move strongly into surplus. For the seventeen highly indebted countries, for example, an aggregate trade surplus of only $2 billion in 1982 had to be turned into an average annual trade surplus of $32 billion during 1983–1987. This could be achieved only through import compression, lower investment, and reductions in per capita consumption; between 1980 and 1987 the imports of the highly indebted countries declined at an average annual rate of 6.3 percent, investment at 5.3 percent, and per capita consumption at 1.6 percent. The debt crisis of the

1980s thus dealt a double blow to the more vulnerable developing countries. Reductions in per capita consumption lowered economic welfare immediately, while large cuts in investment threatened the potential for future growth.

Besides trade, the cost and availability of international finance are the other main external determinants of the economic performance of developing countries. The debt crisis has had a profound impact. One of the most urgent tasks facing the international community is to find ways of reducing the drag exerted by the continuing debt overhang on economic growth in the developing world.

There can be no simple, single solution to the debt problem; a comprehensive framework is needed. Its main objectives should be, first, to enable debtor countries to allocate more resources to investment and consumption and, second, to strengthen their creditworthiness, thus eventually permitting a resumption of voluntary commercial lending. Debtors and creditors alike stand to gain from such an approach.[5] As creditworthiness is restored, the secondary-market discounts on outstanding debt—which exceed 50 percent for many of the highly indebted countries—would drop. Moreover, the debtors' improving growth prospects would enable them to import more from the industrial countries. That would assist in the global correction of external imbalances.

A framework to reduce the burden of debt must have two elements.[6] First, the debtors need to grow faster and export more. Second, the cost of debt service must fall. With the right policies in both industrial and developing countries, these elements can go hand in hand.

While long-term solutions to the debt crisis are being examined, most countries have sought IMF assistance for debt relief. In the debt crisis, the fund assumed a new role as financial organizer for the troubled debtor nations. For example, the fund worked out a two-year program of austerity, currency devaluations, and domestic economic restructuring designed to produce sustained economic health for Brazil in 1982. It helped Brazil emerge from a $16 billion balance-of-payments deficit in 1982 to a $530 million surplus in 1984. The devaluations stopped capital flight and spurred exports, mainly of steel, shoes, textiles, and alcohol. In addition, steps to conserve energy slashed oil imports. Since then Brazil has been able to service its over $100 billion debt.

International Monetary Crisis in the 1970s

Toward the end of the 1960s, the American economy began to deteriorate. Between 1950 and 1970, the net deficits of the United States totaled more than $34 billion. Inflation continued to increase, and unemployment became widespread. Subsequently, President Nixon announced on August 15, 1971, that the United States would not redeem dollars officially held in gold. In addition, the dollar was devalued in 1971 and again in 1973. Thus, starting with 1971, the dollar's link with gold was broken. The U.S. dollar began to float without any attachment to gold. The United States hoped this would force its trading partners to revalue their currencies. It was commonly held that many strong foreign currencies were undervalued, which gave them a substantial advantage against the dollar. Revaluation would have the effect of making the exports of revaluing countries, like Japan and West Germany, more expensive and their imports less expensive, thus working to reduce the U.S. balance-of-payments deficits.

Fixed Versus Floating Rates

In the 1960s, most monetarists considered so-called fixed exchange rates to be the backbone of international financial cooperation and the stability of the international monetary system. Floating, or "flexible," exchange rates were considered impractical. Today, however, all major nations have floating currencies.

In 1976, at an IMF meeting in Kingston, Jamaica, over 100 member nations reached consensus on amendments to the IMF Articles of Agreement that in effect accepted floating rates as the basis for the international monetary system.[7]

The amended agreement, while reaffirming the importance of international cooperation and exchange rate stability, recognized that such rate stability can only be achieved as the result of the stability in underlying economic and financial conditions. Exchange rate stability of any lasting duration cannot be imposed externally by adoption of the pegged exchange rates and heavy official intervention in the foreign exchange market.[8]

However, the merits attributed to floating exchange rates were not borne out. For example:

- When the floating exchange rates were introduced, it was said that balance-of-payments adjustments would be facilitated, but not only have imbalances not disappeared, they have become worse.
- It was thought that speculation would be curtailed. On the contrary, never has it assumed such proportions nor had such destabilizing effects.
- It was believed that market forces, left at last to their own devices, would determine the correct exchange-rate balance. But never have imbalances been so great, nor fluctuations so wide and erratic and so little justified by economic fundamentals.
- It was hoped that autonomy in economic and monetary policy would be preserved, allowing each country free choice of its monetary policy and rate of inflation. Facts have completely belied this illusion.

In the mid-1980s, the countries with primary responsibility for the world economy recognized the need for renewed international cooperation on monetary matters. Subsequently, in early 1987, the U.S., Japan, France, Britain, West Germany, Canada, and Italy concluded an accord, called the Louvre Agreements, on two complementary aspects: coordination of economic policy and more stable exchange rates. The seven signatories agreed to policies aimed at reducing their internal and external imbalances. For example, they agreed to intervene on exchange markets, if necessary.

Since then, the Louvre Agreements have been reconfirmed and adjusted as required by economic and market developments. Economic policy commitments have been adapted and strengthened, including those of central banks. Thus, a first milestone has been reached on the road to rebuilding an international monetary order, though it rests on the will and ability of governments to impose self-discipline. Beyond this stage, how might one envisage a true international monetary system with a standard unit of value, automatic mechanisms, and sanctions that would be beyond the control of the countries involved? The time is ripe for dispassionate consideration of this issue, since inflation has receded and the Louvre Agreements are at present working well.[9]

A new international monetary system, based on the spirit of the Louvre Agreements, may emerge in the 1990s. In their 1991 annual meeting in Bangkok, the IMF members reaffirmed their commitment to exchange rate stability. The members called for the creation of a representative committee of ministers from developing and industrial countries to consider the reform and improvement of the international monetary system.

The world is undergoing tremendous changes in its economic and political spheres. In the midst of such changes, further adjustments and amendments will be necessary to reform the international monetary system in future years (see International Marketing Highlight 3.1).

Foreign Exchange

An international marketer needs to transact financial transfers across national lines in order to close deals. The financial transfers from one country to another are made through the medium of foreign exchange. This section examines the framework for dealing in foreign exchange and reviews problems and complexities associated with the foreign exchange system.

The Meaning of Foreign Exchange

Foreign exchange is the monetary mechanism by which transactions involving two or more currencies take place. Assume a Mexican representative imports a machine from Cincinnati Milacron, a U.S. manufacturer. The machine costs 1.2 million U.S. dollars. Commercial exchanges take place in the United States in dollars, in Mexico in pesos. But Cincinnati Milacron wants to be paid in U.S. dollars, not pesos. The Mexican importer, therefore, must buy U.S. dollars against pesos, that is, obtain foreign exchange or, more specifically, dollar exchange to pay Milacron. Thus, ***foreign exchange*** refers to the exchange of one country's money for another country's money.

Related Terms

Transacting foreign exchange deals presents two problems. First, each country has its own methods and procedures for effecting foreign exchanges—usually developed by its central bank. The transactions themselves, however, take place through the banking system. Thus, both the methods and procedures of the central bank and commercial banking constraints must be thoroughly understood and followed to complete a foreign exchange transaction.

The second problem involves the fluctuation of the rates of exchange. Fluctuations in exchange rates are based on the supply and demand of different currencies. For example, back in the 1960s a U.S. dollar could be exchanged for about 5 Swiss francs. In the early 1990s, this rate of exchange went down to as low as 1.3 Swiss francs for a U.S. dollar. Thus, a U.S. businessperson interested in Swiss currency has to pay much more today than in the 1960s. As a matter of fact, the rate of exchange between two countries can fluctuate from day to day. This pro-

International Marketing Highlight 3.1

Cooperation Remains the Watchword

The Louvre Accord may constitute the most important watershed in the post–Bretton Woods era. The major industrialized countries agreed not only to cooperate closely in foreign exchange markets but also to coordinate their macroeconomic policies toward commonly agreed goals—sustainable noninflationary growth and the elimination of external imbalances.

Monetary policy has been managed broadly within the framework of such international policy coordination. Fiscal policy, however, has been managed more independently, owing partly to domestic political constraints. As a result, monetary policy has been overburdened and its independence called into question.

We are confronted with a most difficult policy problem: how to incorporate fiscal policy discipline within the framework of international macroeconomic policy coordination. We have not solved this problem under either the Bretton Woods regime or the managed floating system.

Here, we should consider the issue of structural adjustment. It is, of course, important to promote more efficient resource allocation through structural reform, which may in turn contribute to achieving the aims of macroeconomic policy. At the same time, however, we should keep in mind that structural reforms are basically support measures, and not a substitute, for demand management policy. It is also important to understand that such reforms take time. This is what Japan has told the United States repeatedly in recent meetings and on other occasions. There may be no policymakers nowadays who have not become keen advocates of international policy coordination. We should be prepared to subordinate national interests to international objectives when necessary.

Source: Takeshi Ohta, "Beyond Bretton Woods," *Speaking of Japan,* March 1990, p. 18.

duces a great deal of uncertainty since a businessperson cannot know the exact value of foreign obligations and claims.

To appreciate fully the complexities of foreign exchange, a few terms must be understood. Their understanding also will provide a historical perspective on the making of payments across national boundaries. The terms are gold standard, gold exchange standard, gold bullion standard, inconvertible currencies, and hard and soft currencies.

Gold standard refers to using gold as the medium of exchange for effecting foreign commercial transactions. Before World War I, most countries followed the gold standard. Private citizens were permitted to own gold, and it could be shipped in and out of the country by individuals or banks without government interference. After World War I, the gold standard was abandoned because gold holdings were concentrated in a few countries and that made international trade difficult to manage.

After the gold standard, many countries adopted the ***gold exchange standard,*** which means that the foreign exchange rate of a currency is set in relation to that country's gold holdings. The country on the gold exchange standard is able to buy in the free market its own currency when it falls in value and to sell it when it increases beyond a predetermined point. This mechanism facilitates minimizing fluctuations in foreign exchange value. Another way of maintaining a parity with gold is to be on the ***gold bullion standard,*** which amounts to holding an adequate quantity of gold in reserve in bar or bullion form to settle international transactions at the level of government. Under the gold bullion standard, private individuals are prohibited from possessing gold and it is no longer in coinage, but a government may deal in gold by buying and selling it. After World War II, most nations prohibited conversion of currency into gold. The phrase ***inconvertible currencies*** also refers to currencies that cannot be conveniently exchanged for other currencies. For example, many East European currencies are inconvertible to U.S. dollars. Currencies may also be labeled as ***hard and soft currencies:*** *hard* are those in great demand; *soft* are relatively easily available. The currencies of the majority of developing countries are described as soft currencies as far as international transactions are concerned, while those of developed nations are hard currencies.

Exchange Rates

When countries were on the gold standard, the value of two currencies was determined on the basis of the gold content of each currency. (The technical term used to describe this procedure of determining relationship between two currencies is *par of exchange.*) For example, in the 1920s a U.S. dollar had 23.22 grains of pure gold, while the British pound sterling had 113.0016 grains. Since the latter currency had 4.8665 times more fine gold than the American dollar, it was worth $4.8665.

For those countries off the gold standard, exchange rates are regulated by the central banks. Most countries, however, attempt to maintain a steady exchange rate. This is necessary to promote foreign trade. The base price of a currency is determined by the supply and demand of a currency.

The supply and demand of a currency is influenced by a variety of factors. For example, if a country continues to buy, year after year, more from other nations than it exports, the supply of its currency increases. Likewise, if a country spends overseas—say, to fight a war—its currency supply increases. Such increases adversely affect currency value, the base or market price.[10] (Table 3.1 lists the factors affecting the supply and demand of the U.S. dollar.)

The base or market price, however, may not be the real value of a currency since the central bank may set a different price in order to realize a stated set of objectives. For example, the value of the U.S. dollar was slowly deteriorating in the market in the 1960s, but President Johnson refused to devalue it.

Many countries set a lower value on their currency to encourage exports and/or to seek balance-of-payment adjustments. In other words, long-term objectives may lead a country to set a different value on its currency than the current market value. Incidentally, the International Monetary Fund assists nations in arriving at a realistic value for their currency in relation to long- and short-term goals. Frequently, the fund pressures a country to value its currency at what

TABLE 3.1 Factors Affecting the Supply and Demand of U.S. Dollars

THE FOLLOWING FACTORS INCREASE THE SUPPLY OF U.S. DOLLARS IN WORLD MARKETS	THE FOLLOWING FACTORS INCREASE THE DEMAND FOR U.S. DOLLARS IN WORLD MARKETS
1. Imports of merchandise	1. Exports of merchandise
2. Imports of gold and silver	2. Exports of gold and silver
3. Payments to foreign ships for freight and passenger service	3. Foreign payments to U.S. shippers
4. American tourist expenditures abroad	4. Foreign tourist expenditures in the United States
5. Banking and all other financial charges payable to foreigners	5. Banking and other financial charges receivable from foreigners
6. Interest and dividends due on American securities held abroad	6. Interest and dividends due on foreign securities held here
7. New purchases of foreign securities	7. New sale of American securities abroad
8. Repurchase and redemption of American securities held abroad	8. Repurchase and redemption of foreign securities held here
9. Transfer of American balances to foreign banks	9. Transfer of foreign balances to American banks
10. United States government grants and loans	

seems to be an unacceptable level. For example, the IMF persuaded the Philippines to devalue its currency, the peso, in 1986, and India to devalue its rupee in 1991.

Conducting Foreign Exchange Transactions

Foreign exchange transactions may be conducted by governments via their central bank, brokers, commercial banks, or business corporations. Described here is the process that corporations follow to conduct foreign exchange dealings. Let us assume Boeing wishes to buy $300 million worth of Rolls Royce (British) jet engines for use in its new series of airplanes. Boeing needs to buy the equivalent of $300 million in British pound sterling to pay Rolls Royce for the engines. Boeing may buy the British currency either on the spot or in a forward market. In the spot transaction, the purchase is effected right away; forward buying is finalized at a predetermined future date. If the payment is to be made right away, Boeing will have no choice but to buy British pound sterling on the spot. But if payment is to be made at a future date, Boeing may transact a forward deal. A forward deal will be preferable if British currency is currently available at a rate that is expected to increase by the time the payment is due. The forward deal will enable Boeing to buy British pound sterling at a future date at a currently agreed upon price.[11]

Whether the purchase is to be made on the spot or in the future, Boeing Company will contact a number of commercial banks to seek price quotations for British pound sterling in terms of the U.S. dollar. Usually, different banks will quote different prices. For example, a multinational bank like Citicorp might have acquired British pound sterling balances when British currency was priced very low. That bank would be able to offer a better price to Boeing than, say, Bank of America, which might not have British pound sterling on hand and would then have to buy it on the open market to satisfy Boeing's needs. The market might contain customers interested in exchanging British pound sterling for another currency, or a British bank might be willing to lend the local currency. Even when the British pound sterling must be bought from the market, one bank might quote a better price than the other. It all depends on the size of the transaction, the importance of the customer to the bank, the direction of the currency market, future prospects of the currency, and the bank's present financial position.[12] Other things being equal, Boeing would choose the bank providing the best price.

Many multinational corporations pointedly seek the foreign currencies of the countries in which they are active by making deals at advantageous times.[13] For example, if a currency is declining, a corporation would buy for future use.[14] A U.S. corporation with excess cash on hand might buy a currency whose price is low in expectation of the price going up when the corporation would need U.S. dollars again. In this way, a corporation, through astute money management, can make money dealing in foreign exchange transactions (see International Marketing Highlight 3.2).

Balance of Payments

The ***balance of payments*** of a country summarizes all the transactions that have taken place between its residents and foreigners in a given period, usually a year. The word *transactions* refers to exports and imports of goods and services, lending and borrowing of funds, remittances, and government aid and military expenditures. The term *residents* includes all individuals and business enterprises, including financial institutions, that are permanently residing within a country's borders, as well as government agencies at all levels. In other words, the balance of payments reflects the totality of a country's economic relations with the rest of the world: its trade in goods, its exchange of services, its purchase and sale of financial assets, and such important governmental transactions as foreign aid, military expenditures abroad, and the payment of reparation. Certain forces determine the volume of these transactions, how they are brought into balance, what problems arise when they fail to balance, and what policies are available to deal with those problems.

Recording Balance-of-Payments Transactions

Table 3.2 highlights the United States balance-of-payments position for the year 1991. The transactions are recorded in three categories: current account, capital account, and addendum. The balance-of-payments record is made on the basis of rules of debit and credit, similar to those in business accounting. For example, receipts are entered as credits, and payments as debits. Thus, exports, like sales, are entered as credits; imports, like purchases, are debits. All transactions affect-

International Marketing Highlight 3.2

Shock from the Rise in Yen's Value

Sony's annual report for 1986 published an enviable listing of business achievements—new products, sales gains in major ranges, production and distribution rationalization, and strong performances by overseas subsidiaries. Yet the same report broke the bad news that net sales were down 7 percent, operating income had plummeted 75 percent, and net income had fallen 43 percent.

Where did the shock come from? Why the miserable results? Sony was the victim of a 40 percent rise in the yen's value against the dollar. Business excellence—doing all the right things, including protecting the value of revenues through forward currency contracts—had failed to shield the company from the ravages of foreign exchange rate turbulence.

Sony is not alone in having to inform its shareholders of disastrous results following adverse movements in exchange rates. Many other companies that are heavily dependent on international markets are also at the mercy of exchange rates. The auto industry is an obvious example. In 1987, Honda reported that "the strong yen . . . [made] it impossible to raise prices sufficiently to keep pace with currency movements . . . leading to significant declines in earnings." In 1986, Swedish forest products group MoDo cited the falling dollar's lead role in inducing a severe displacement of competitiveness in North American pulp markets. Volvo, Sanyo, Nissan, Matsushita, Philips, and Porsche have all suffered. Losses can come quickly and be painful.

Source: Staffan Hertzell and Christian Caspar, "Coping with Unpredictable Currencies," *The McKinsey Quarterly,* Summer 1988, p. 12.

ing increases in assets, like direct investment abroad, or decreases in indebtedness, like the repayment of external debts, are recorded as credits. However, decreases in assets, like liquidation of foreign securities, and increases in liabilities, like borrowing abroad, are treated as debits.

The *current account* section shows U.S. trade in currently produced goods and services. The positive or negative sign preceding each figure indicates whether the transaction represents a gain (+) or a loss (−) of foreign currency. In merchandise transactions, there was a negative balance (of trade) in 1990, meaning the import of goods exceeded the export of goods by $108.7 billion. Line 4 shows the net effect of expenditures incurred by U.S. military installations abroad and the amount of foreign currency earned by selling armaments. Line 5 shows that in 1990 America spent $29.3 billion less on services (tourism, shipping, other) than foreigners spent in the United States. Line 6 focuses on another major source of our foreign earnings, return on U.S. investments abroad.

The net result of all trading in goods and services is shown on Line 7. Lines 8–10 describe *unilateral transfers,* comprising private gifts to foreigners and official foreign aid. The current account balance ($99.4 billion in 1990) is shown on Line 11.

TABLE 3.2 United States Balance of Payments Accounts, 1990*

CURRENT ACCOUNT		
(1) Balance of trade		−$108.7
(2) Merchandise exports	+$389.3	
(3) Merchandise imports	$−498.0	
(4) Net military transactions		−6.4
(5) Net services		+29.3
(6) Net income from investments		+7.5
(7) Balance on goods and services (Lines 1 plus 4 plus 5 plus 6)		−78.3
(8) Unilateral transfers		−21.1
(9) Private	−4.1	
(10) U.S. government (nonmilitary)	−17.0	
(11) Balance on current account (Lines 7 plus 8)		−99.4
CAPITAL ACCOUNT		
(12) Net private capital flows		−5.3
(13) Change in U.S. assets abroad	−62.1	
(14) Change in foreign assets in the U.S.	+56.8	
(15) Net governmental capital flows		+31.6
(16) Change in U.S. government assets	+0.8	
(17) Change in foreign official assets in the U.S.	+30.8	
(18) Balance on capital account (Lines 12 plus 15)		+26.3
ADDENDUM		
(19) Sum of Lines (11) and (18)		−73.1
(20) Statistical discrepancy		+73.1

*Figures in billions of dollars

Source: Statistical Abstract of the United States: 1991 (Washington, D.C.: U.S. Department of Commerce), pp. 790–791.

Lines 12–18 summarize the *capital* transactions. Line 12 shows that, on balance, Americans bought $5.3 billion less in assets abroad than private foreign investors bought in the United States (see the difference of Lines 13 and 14).

The whopping current account deficit combined with the surplus in the capital account left the United States with a yawning balance-of-payments deficit (see Line 19).

Since the two accounts together should balance as a simple matter of arithmetic, the difference is considered a *statistical discrepancy* (Line 20). While part of this discrepancy is attributable to errors in data collection and computation, the major portion reflects the United States balance-of-payments deficit.

The balance-of-payments record may not strictly follow double-entry bookkeeping in that not every transaction gives rise to equal and offsetting debit and credit entries. Discrepancies will occur when particular balance-of-payments entries do not represent the movement of funds, but rather the movement of a document or other proof of obligation. Further, some international payments are unilateral or one-sided, such as gifts, grants, and transfer payments. Payments of this type are entered as debits, and receipts as credits. Finally, instead of using the "T" account, the U.S. Department of Commerce posts all balance-of-payments transactions in a single column with debits preceded by minus signs and credits by no sign at all.

"Surplus" or "Deficit" Balance-of-Payments

In Exhibit 3.2, with the help of the statistical discrepancy item, the entries added up to zero. This is the usual way of striking the balance. But if the balance adds up to zero, what determines whether a country has a payments deficit or payments surplus? The answer is somewhat complex: the "deficit" or "surplus" is worked out based not on the aggregate of all transactions in the balance-of-payments accounts, but on the net balance in certain selected categories.[15]

Here is another way of explaining the determination of balance-of-payments status:

> The identification of a "surplus" or "deficit" therefore involves the segregation of certain items from the main body of the balance of payments as being different in some significant respect from the rest. The question of presenting and measuring the balance of payments can, thus, be posed in terms of the search for a suitable distinguishing principle or organizing concept for determining which items are to be placed in the main body of the balance of payments (above the line) and which are to be placed outside (below the line). Account being taken of errors and omissions . . . , both groups of items will net out to the same figure with opposite signs.
>
> Under such an "organizing concept," a negative balance (or an excess of debits over credits) for the transactions grouped above the line represents a balance-of-payments deficit, while a positive for the same group of transactions constitutes a balance-of-payments surplus.[16]

The fact that select transactions are included for determining the balance of payments raises the issue of which of the transactions should be considered. The IMF recommends that transactions be divided between regular and settlement (below-the-line) transactions. The regular transactions represent overseas involvement on a perpetual basis, such as trade and service transactions. The settlement transactions are meant to settle the deficit or surplus that may be said to have been caused or produced by the above-the-line items—that is, transactions directed toward bringing about a balance.

In the case of the United States, however, the distinction between the "regular" and the "settlement" items is quite difficult to make, for two reasons. First, the U.S. dollar plays a key role in international trade and finance even after its devaluation. For this reason, a number of transactions take place in U.S. dollars between other nations exclusive of the United States. Second, foreign central banks, as well as the IMF, hold U.S. dollars as investments and as working balances to finance international trade and payments. With the complexities produced by these numbers, no single number can adequately describe the international position of the United States during any given period.

To illustrate the difficulty involved in compiling the "true" balance-of-payments figure for the United States, consider the following case. Based on the balance-of-payments data, the dollar commonly was held to be overvalued in the 1980s. Rational analysis, however, shows that these data are suspect.[17] Official government statistics reveal that the United States has had continuous trade deficits since 1977. The trade deficit for 1985, for example, reached $150 billion. Further, with the exception of a very small surplus in 1980, the current account, a broader measure, has also been in deficit since 1977. Traditionally, nations with continuing balance-of-trade and current account deficits experience a drop in the international value of their currencies. Indeed, this is the basic adjustment mechanism in a floating exchange rate system. Yet, the United States until 1985 enjoyed a "strong" dollar. (In 1985, the United States' major trading partners agreed to bring the value of the dollar down.)

Balance-of-payments data are drawn from diverse sources, and serious gaps exist. Since debit and credit totals do not balance, statistical discrepancy is used as a residual, a balancing entry. If the account almost always had the same sign, and the dollar values were fairly consistent and relatively small, one could embrace the data with a strong degree of confidence. During the 1950s and most of the 1960s the statistical discrepancy was very small. From 1951 to 1959, the account bore a positive sign every year and the high/low values spanned roughly $1 billion. From 1960 to 1969, the entries all had negative signs and sparred some $2 billion.

During the 1970s, however, there were six years with negative signs and four with positive signs. Further, very large numbers began to appear. For example, the trade deficit of $25.5 billion in 1980 was accompanied by a statistical discrepancy entry of $29.5 billion. The $36 billion deficit in 1982 was accompanied by an error factor of $41.3 billion. Statistical discrepancy as a percentage of the trade balance ranged from 6.5 percent to 115.7 percent over the 1977–1983 period. Absolute annual swings in this account have been as high as $32 billion. These are huge sums, and the fluctuations are erratic. If, for example, one divides the statistical discrepancy figure by the current account balance, the results range from lows of 14 percent (1977) and 22 percent (1983) to less modest figures of 81 percent (1978) and 369 percent (1982) to a staggering 2,635 percent (1979). Consider how you might react to an accountant's report warranting a company's income statement as "accurate within 702 percent" (the ration for 1980).

When statistical discrepancy fell by $32 billion during 1982–1983, some economists heaved a sigh of relief, maintaining that the $9.3 billion entry for 1983 was a much more "manageable" figure. Actually, such a fluctuation is hardly comforting, but instead reinforces the unreliability of the data. The U.S. deficits, for instance, could be far worse than they reportedly are or perhaps not as bad as they seem to be. We really do not know. To be sure, we need a better handle on the facts before initiating policy changes.

The United States Balance-of-Payments Position

Since World War II, the international transactions of the United States have shown enormous growth. In 1950 total receipts came to $10,203 million. Such transactions in 1960 amounted to $19,650 million; in 1970 to $42,969 million; and in 1990 to an estimated $126,000 million. Even after adjusting for inflation, this reflects a vast growth in international dealings by the United States with the rest of the world. This phenomenon is reflected in the upsurge in U.S. private foreign investment, the rise in U.S. government expenditures abroad, and the emergence of the U.S. dollar as the world's principal reserve and trading currency.

Another interesting development is the gradually growing deficit in the international accounts of the United States. Historically, the United States has run a deficit in the international accounts in every year but two, 1957 and 1968. But in the 1950s the deficits aroused no concern. As a matter of fact, these deficits (averaging about $1.3 billion annually) during 1950–1957 were characterized as "purposeful," for those were the days of dollar shortages. In 1958, the situation changed. That year, the deficit amounted to $3.4 billion and the United States had to provide gold worth $2.3 billion to offset part of the deficit. During 1957–1967, the deficits averaged $2.7 billion a year and the gold outflow averaged $1.1 billion a year. The 1970s saw a drastic worsening of the situation. The deficit on merchandise trade alone shot up from $2.3 billion in 1971 to about $144.3 billion in 1985. Since then the situation has significantly improved. The deficit in 1991 was $66.5 billion (for further discussion on this topic, see Chapter 17).

In the closing years of the 1980s, the United States government began to adopt a variety of measures to improve the United States balance-of-payments position. For example, U.S. exports have been encouraged at all levels. Further, as the United States economy is restructured via new investments and technology, the productivity should rise to make U.S. products competitive abroad. Similarly, efforts have been made through persuasion and negotiations to limit Japanese exports to the United States. Finally, the efforts to bring the value of the U.S. dollar down by intervening in the financial markets should make U.S. products competitive in the export markets.

Eurodollars

The term ***Eurodollars*** refers to U.S. dollars accumulated over the years by European banks and other banks outside the United States. Since these dollars are outside the jurisdiction of the United States government, the European banks are free to deal in them without any restriction.

In addition to the U.S. dollars acquired by banks with their own or foreign currency, Eurodollars also come into existence when a domestic or foreign holder of dollar demand deposits in the United States places them on deposit in a bank outside the United States.

Usually banks are supposed to maintain certain reserves in some proportion to their deposits to protect their depositors. But dollar borrowing and lending can be done anywhere in the world without being subject to certain costly regulations imposed by the U.S. authorities on banks at home, particularly reserve requirements.[18]

The Eurodollars reached a substantial amount in early 1970. The total deposits were greater than the total gold reserves held by governments. It is estimated that in 1995, Eurodollars, or "stateless money" as they are sometimes called, will increase from $1.2 trillion to $1.5 trillion. The size of this amount can only be considered by relating it to the fact that total gold reserves held by governments are about $40 billion.

While the "offshore market" initially was created in U.S. dollars, today a number of other European currencies are freely deposited and borrowed outside their home bases. These are the German mark, the Swiss franc, the British pound sterling, and the French franc. As time passes, monetary authorities see the problem related not to the Eurodollar alone, but to the *Eurocurrencies*.

The prefix "Euro," incidentally, does not limit the dealings in Eurodollars (or Eurocurrencies) to Europe alone. It just happens that the market for the expatriate U.S. dollar grew up in Europe and that most of the dealing in Eurodollars was done by banks in London or in other European financial centers. Thus, the term *Eurodollar* has been loosely applied to deposits in Toronto, Rio de Janeiro, Hong Kong, Singapore, and Kuala Lumpur.

The market in "Asian dollars" is really only an offshoot of the Eurodollar market. The Asian market deals in U.S. dollars (and other leading currencies) deposited in local banks, and then lends them to Asian borrowers. Pioneered by the Bank of America in Singapore in 1968, the Asian market has since grown rapidly because of the deliberate relaxation of banking regulation and reserve requirements by the governments of Singapore and Malaysia.

Eurodollar Market

The Eurodollar market consists of a network of banks that accept deposits, grant loans, and make use of interbank structures to place excess reserves. The Eurodollar deposits bear interest and usually mature in ninety days or less. All Eurodollar transactions involve a change in ownership of U.S. bank dollar demand deposits, which are being used to pay off foreign debt. To illustrate the point, assume a businessperson has a demand deposit of $1 million in a New York bank. She might transfer the demand deposit to a Eurodollar bank that also has a demand account at the same New York bank. In this way, the New York bank's deposit level and structure is unchanged, while the Eurodollar bank incurs a $1 million increase in its time deposit liabilities and a $1 million increase in demand deposit assets in New York. The Eurobank could then lend the deposit through the interbank organization, either in U.S. dollars or after converting it to another currency. As long as the ultimate recipients of the Eurodollar loan funds decide to hold Eurodollar deposits, rather than U.S. bank deposits, Eurobanks are capable of multiple expansion of U.S. dollar-denominated deposits.

Monetary Effect of Eurodollars

Eurodollars often have been blamed for U.S. inflation and in part for the decline in the value of the U.S. dollar. Further, the Eurodollar has been thought to represent "loose" money that could lead to the collapse of worldwide money markets.[19]

While opinions differ, the problems attributed to Eurodollars are not fully documented. From the vantage point of the United States, however, the Eurodollar affects domestic monetary arrangements in two ways. First, the Eurodollar leads to a shift in the U.S. deposit structure. To resolve this problem the United States government in 1969 regulated reserve requirements on U.S. demand deposits held by both foreign branches of domestic banks and foreign banks. Thus, the first effect has been partially mitigated. Second, competition between U.S. banks can cause one bank to lose reserves to another as the result of Eurodollar activity. Since regulated interest ceilings prevent direct competition, a bank must compete aggressively through the provision of monetary services. This tends to increase the cost of funds for U.S. banks.

Overall, the Eurodollar market augments the world money supply, which increases the price of traded goods. It is difficult, however, to estimate the net addition of Eurodollars to the world money supply. Portions of the reserve balances of foreign countries, as well as that of the United States, support the operations of Eurodollar banks. Although the Eurodollar market lowers the effective ratio of reserves to deposits, the base assets support a substantial volume of conventional bank liabilities—which would cause difficulty were the Eurodollar market to vanish. The implication is that inflationary forces emanate not from institutional weakness in the Eurodollar market but from the combined policies of central banks worldwide.

Petrodollars

The term ***petrodollars*** refers to earnings from oil exports by the oil-producing countries, often referred to as OPEC countries. These countries are Saudi Arabia, Kuwait, Iran, Iraq, Libya, the United Arab Emirates, Nigeria, Venezuela, Indonesia, Algeria, Qatar, and Ecuador. The fourfold increase in the price of oil in 1973 and semiannual increases for many years thereafter have led to the biggest shift of financial resources from one group of nations to another in the economic and financial history of the world.

For the world's business and trade to run smoothly in the midst of such a resource shift, it is important that oil earnings be recycled into international capital markets. This is feasible in two ways: (1) through the importation of goods from non-oil-producing countries and (2) through depositing the surplus funds with multinational banks. Through this recycling process, the overall financial impact of petrodollars is reduced. Yet the existence and growth of petrodollars is a big issue confronting international economic policymakers for two reasons. First, the oil exporters' long-term investments, purchases of imports, and short-term placements of funds do not match the current account deficits of individual oil-importing countries. Thus, the surplus earnings of oil exporters have to be transferred, or "recycled," to the oil-importing countries with inadequate foreign exchange to pay for their petroleum imports. Second, the size of the financial holdings of oil exporters has altered the political-economic relationship between a sizable part of the developing world and industrialized nations.[20]

The United States has so far received a large proportion of petrodollars in the form of export earnings, via different kinds of goods and services, and through foreign investments in U.S. corporations, real estate, and direct deposits in U.S. banks. However, the United States economy is deeply interrelated with other nations of the world. Thus, the impact of events elsewhere, such as recessions in other industrialized countries as well as in Africa, Asia, and Latin America, is keenly felt by the United States economy. Failure to reallocate financial resources to enable individual nations to meet their oil import requirements leads to restrictions on their non-oil imports. The developing countries could even resort to foreign exchange restrictions and exchange-rate changes, as well as seeking renegotiation of overseas debt.

The OPEC nations are fully aware of their new power and have exploited the situation to their best advantage. At the same time, considering the susceptibility of their own fortunes to international disorder and their need to become fully acceptable members in world and Western-nation financial circles, they have gone along with a variety of measures to "recycle" petrodollars to the benefit of both developed and developing countries.

The rise of OPEC nations as new financial powers has to be accepted, as Japan had to be accepted in the 1960s as the emerging industrial power. For long-term stability in world financial circles, regional and bilateral deals are insufficient. Multilateral arrangements with the involvement of the IMF and the World Bank would go a long way toward providing the guarantees that developed countries seek and in meeting the financial problems of the poor nations.

Current and Emerging Issues

This section briefly examines the current strains on the world monetary system and attempts to project forthcoming events in the 1990s and beyond.[21] Although the world has overcome the crisis created by the 1973–1974 oil price increase, new trends seem pertinent to the future.[22]

In recent years OPEC has shown a decline in its surplus. OPEC may take measures in the 1990s to prevent a recurrence of the erosion. This may lead to a further increase in the price of oil and a continuing need to recycle funds from oil exporters to the rest of the world. On the other hand, if the price of oil continues to decline, many oil-producing countries, Nigeria and Mexico, for example, may face new difficulties.

A large number of countries lived through the 1970s by means of heavy borrowing. At the same time, their ability to repay debt declined. International bankers in the last few years were stunned by the inability of these countries to service and repay their debts. Although IMF assistance has helped many nations in meeting the immediate crisis, the debt problem is likely to linger on for many years.

The private international bankers are already overcommitted, especially in developing countries. These institutions may be unwilling to go much further in accommodating the growing needs of the LDCs in the 1990s.

Persistently high U.S. trade and budget deficits, and the growing concern about them at both governmental and public levels, could lead to moderate growth in the economies of LDCs in the 1990s. This eventually would result in less-buoyant export markets for the developing countries.

The Vulnerability of the International Financial System

Since the first oil crisis in 1973, international banking has become a dominant force in the international monetary and financial structure. This evolution has occurred in the following manner. The unspent surplus balances of the oil producers were mainly deposited in U.S. and European banks, while the banks played a crucial role in meeting the increasing financial needs of non-oil developing countries. The volume of international bank loans increased from $320 billion at the end of 1973 to $1,070 billion at the end of 1979, and to $1,995 billion at the end of 1990.

The vital role that private banks played in salvaging the developing countries in the 1970s has had the following consequences.[23]

1. The banks find it difficult to meet their normal obligations with short-term maturity funds.
2. Inflation has caused their capital ratios to decline.
3. They are rapidly running up against countries' borrowing limits, which were legally imposed or internally set for the containment of risks.
4. A large proportion of the loans are concentrated in potentially vulnerable countries like Zaire and Peru.
5. The profitability of international lending is declining.

The people involved with international banking are aware of the problems of the international financial system, and discussions have taken place in recent years about how to reduce international lending and liquidity risk. For example, it has been proposed that a *private safety net* be organized for individual banks to resort to in case of an emergency in terms of liquidity.[24] Such an arrangement would ensure the stability of the system by an injection of liquidity, if, for some reason, the deposits were to dry up. The idea of a safety net, however, has been opposed by representatives of Third World countries. They fear such a measure would scare private banks that deal with the developing countries. In the future, however, under the umbrella of IMF, some sort of multilateral agreement—a standby swap agreement between the IMF and each of the twenty or so major international banks—could be effected. Since a liquidity crisis very probably would be accompanied by an exchange crisis in which many banks of different nationalities might be involved, an international swap network would offer an adequate degree of security.

Summary

After World War II, an important realization about the future occurred among nations. For a secure future, national economies would have to be rebuilt and/or developed, and such a feat could only be accomplished through worldwide cooperation. Subsequently, a historic meeting of fifty-five nations took place at Bretton Woods, New Hampshire, to develop a monetary system that would ensure stable conditions for a healthy growth of the world economy. The International Monetary Fund (IMF) was originated to oversee the system. Essentially, the system controls the limits on exchange rate movements in its member countries in a predetermined way. The exchange rates are permitted to vary by 1 percent above and below par. As a country's rate of exchange attains or approaches either limit, the country's central bank intervenes in the market to prevent the rate from passing the limits. The IMF not only reviews the status of different economies but also gives advice on how a nation can achieve monetary stability.

In times of temporary balance-of-payments deficits, countries can approach the IMF for short-term loans to weather the difficult period. The IMF's short-term accommodation, however, proved insufficient, and, therefore, special drawing rights (SDRs) have been created to provide additional liquidity.

Along with the IMF system, the United States used to guarantee to convert the U.S. dollar into gold at a fixed rate of $35 per ounce of gold. This guarantee helped countries to trade. As a matter of fact, many countries linked their national currencies to the U.S. dollar. In the early 1970s, however, the value of the U.S. dollar began to decline. Finally, the United States devalued its dollar twice and abandoned the fixed parity between its dollar and gold. Since then, all currencies have floated free, and their values fluctuate on the basis of supply and demand.

This chapter also examined the framework for transacting payments in foreign trade. When people import something, they must make payment to the exporter for it. Since the exporting country ordinarily has a different currency than the one used in the importing country, the importer must obtain the exporter's currency in order to pay for the imported good. The importer obtains the exporter's currency from a central bank. The central bank of the country sets an exchange value on its currency for the other currency. In this way, it is possible to determine how much the importer needs, in local currency, to pay the bank in order to receive the requisite amount of the exporter's currency.

Also discussed was the balance-of-payments concept. This term refers to a systematic record of the economic transactions of a nation during a given period between its residents and the rest of the world. In general, if a nation exports more than it imports, it will have a favorable balance of payment; if the reverse is true, the nation will have an unfavorable balance of payment.

This chapter also examined the accumulation of U.S. dollars in two other forms outside the United States: Eurodollars and petrodollars. Eurodollars are U.S. dollars accumulated in Europe and in other parts of the world that are outside the regulatory jurisdiction of the United States government. Thus, their circulation becomes a matter of concern, since unlimited dealings in Eurodollars can lead to inflation. Petrodollars are accumulations of U.S. dollars among the OPEC nations. This problem is one of recycling the huge receipts of the oil-producing countries into the world monetary system. The petrodollar problem is more acute for developing countries because they are unable to export enough goods and services to the OPEC nations to meet their other import needs after spending so much on oil.

Review Questions

1. What reasons led nations to seek international monetary stability? How does such stability help promote world trade?
2. How did the Bretton Woods agreement provide a stable monetary environment?

3. What are special drawing rights? Why were they created?
4. What led the United States to devalue its dollar?
5. Why is it desirable for a country to maintain a stable foreign exchange rate for its currency?
6. Define *balance of payment.* How does it differ from balance of trade? How accurate are the U.S. balance-of-payment records?
7. What difficulties do Eurodollars present? What steps have been taken by the United States to restrict the free flow of Eurodollars?
8. What problems do petrodollars present?

Endnotes

1. Susan Strange, *International Economic Relations of the Western World: 1959–71* (New York: Oxford University Press, 1970). *Also see* Brian Tew, *International Monetary Cooperation, 1945–70.* 10th ed. (London: Hutchinson & Co., Publishers, Ltd., 1970); Delbert A. Snider, *Introduction to International Economics,* 5th ed. (Homewood, IL: Richard D. Irwin, 1981).
2. *The Role and Function of the International Monetary Fund* (Washington, D.C.: International Monetary Fund, 1985), p. 2.
3. Harry G. Johnson, "Political Economy Aspects of International Monetary Reform," *Journal of International Economics,* September 1972, pp. 403–411. *Also see* Jack Barnouin, "Trade and Economic Cooperation Among Developing Countries," *Finance & Development,* June 1982, pp. 24–27.
4. *World Development Report 1991* (New York: Oxford University Press, 1991). *Also see* "Third-World Debt," *Business Week,* January 23, 1988, p. 57.
5. John A. C. Congbeare, "On the Repudiation of Sovereign Debt: Sources of Stability and Risk," *Columbia Journal of World Business,* Summer/Spring 1990, pp. 46–52.
6. *See World Development Report 1991* (Washington, D.C.: The World Bank, 1991).
7. Thomas D. Willett, *Floating Exchange Rates and International Monetary Reform* (Washington, D.C.: American Enterprise Institute for Public Policy Research, 1977).
8. R. Bryant, *Money and Monetary Policy in Independent Nations* (Washington, D.C.: Brookings Institution, 1980).
9. *See* "Friends of the Dollar," *The Economist,* December 5, 1987, p. 14. *Also see* Edward Balladur, "Rebuilding an International Monetary System," *The Economist,* February 23, 1988, p. 28.
10. Robert G. Ruland and Timothy S. Doupink, "Foreign Currency Translation and the Behavior of Exchange Rates," *Journal of International Business Studies,* Fall 1988, pp. 461–476.
11. Raj Aggarwal and Luc A. Soenen, "Managing Persistent Real Changes in Currency Values: The Role of Multinational Operating Strategies," *Columbia Journal of World Business,* Fall 1989, pp. 60–67.
12. Arvind D. Jain and Douglas Nigh, "Politics and the International Lending Decisions of Banks," *Journal of International Business Studies,* Summer 1989, pp. 349–359.
13. Timothy A. Luehrman, "Exchange Rate Changes and the Distribution of Industry Value," *Journal of International Business Studies,* Fourth Quarter 1991, pp. 619–649.
14. Walter Kiechel III, "Playing the Global Game," *Fortune,* November 16, 1981, pp. 111–126. *Also see* Michael R. Sesit, "Funds Blocked Abroad by Exchange Controls Plague Big Companies," *The Wall Street Journal,* December 3, 1984, p. 1.
15. John Hein, *Understanding the Balance of Payments* (New York: The Conference Board, 1970), p. 10.
16. Andrew Crockett, "Issues in the Use of Fund Resources," *Finance & Development,* June 1982, pp. 24–27.
17. See various issues of *Survey of Current Business.*

18. Jürg Niehans and John Hewson, "The Eurodollar Market and Monetary Theory," *Journal of Money, Credit and Banking,* February 1976, p. 127.
19. Ian H. Griddy, "Why Eurodollars Grow," *Columbia Journal of World Business,* Fall 1979, pp. 54–60.
20. Guy F. Erb, "Petrodollars and Multilateral Development," in James W. Howe, ed., *The U.S. and World Development* (New York: Praeger, 1975), pp. 105–117.
21. *See World Development Report 1991* (New York: Oxford University Press, 1991).
22. Richard N. Cooper, "World Monetary System in the 1980s," *Current Policy No. 239,* United States Department of State, 1980. *Also see* David B. Zenoff and Geoffrey S. Howard, "SMR Forum: LDC Debt—Is the Sky Going to Fall?" *Sloan Management Review,* Fall 1980, pp. 55–62.
23. Rainaldo Ossola, "The Vulnerability of the International Financial System: International Lending and Liquidity Risk," *Review of International Economics,* January 1980, pp. 292–305.
24. Ibid.

APPENDIX

Select International Financial, Trade, and Business Institutions

In the post–World War II period a variety of institutions came into existence to strengthen global trade and business and to promote economic development. This section briefly examines some of these institutions, especially those that directly or indirectly affect international marketing decision making.

The International Monetary Fund (IMF)

The International Monetary Fund was founded, along with the World Bank, in 1944 at a conference held in Bretton Woods, New Hampshire. The IMF is a specialized agency within the United Nations system, cooperating with the UN on matters of mutual interest. Membership in the fund is requisite to membership in the World Bank, and a close working relationship exists between the two organizations, as well as between the fund and the General Agreement on Tariffs and Trade (GATT).

The fund was established to promote international monetary cooperation and to facilitate the expansion of trade, and in turn to contribute to increased employment and improved economic conditions in all member countries. Its purposes are defined in the following terms:

1. To promote international monetary cooperation through a permanent institution that provides the machinery for consultations and collaboration on international monetary problems.
2. To facilitate the expansion and balanced growth of international trade, and to contribute thereby to the promotion and maintenance of high levels of employment and real income and to the development of the productive resources of all members as primary objectives of economic policy.
3. To promote exchange stability, to maintain orderly exchange arrange-

ments among members, and to avoid competitive exchange depreciation.

4. To assist in the establishment of a multilateral system of payments in respect to current transactions between members and in the elimination of foreign exchange restrictions that hamper the growth of world trade.
5. To give confidence to members by making the general resources of the fund temporarily available to them under adequate safeguards, thus providing them with the opportunity to correct maladjustments in their balance of payments without resorting to measures destructive of national or international prosperity.
6. In accordance with the above, to shorten the duration and lessen the degree of disequilibrium in the international balance of payments to members.

To achieve its purposes, the fund has a code of economic behavior for its members. It makes financing available to members in balance-of-payments difficulties and provides them with technical assistance to improve their economic management. At present, the fund has 150 member countries, accounting for about four-fifths of total world production and 90 percent of world trade.

Member countries undertake to collaborate with the fund and with each other to ensure orderly exchange arrangements and a stable system of exchange rates. A multilateral system of payments is fostered that is free from restrictions and thus promotes balance in the payments among countries.

The fund maintains a large pool of financial resources that it makes available—temporarily, and subject to conditions—to member countries to enable them to carry out programs to remedy their payments deficits without resorting to restrictive measures that would adversely affect national or international prosperity. Members make repayments to the fund, so that its resources are used on a revolving basis and are continuously available to countries facing payment difficulties.

To enable the fund to carry out its policies, member countries continuously supply a broad range of economic and financial information and the fund consults regularly with each member country on its economic situation. The fund is, therefore, in a position to assist members in devising corrective steps when, or preferably before, problems arise in their balance of payments.

Because of its responsibility for the international payments system, the fund is particularly concerned with global liquidity, that is, the level and composition of the reserves that members have available for meeting their trade and payments requirements. In 1969, the fund was given the responsibility for creating and allocating special drawing rights (SDRs), the only worldwide reserve asset established by international agreement.

The fund helps members to coordinate their national economic policies internationally. In effect it provides a permanent international monetary forum. The focus of the fund is not only on the problems of individual countries, but also on the structure of the international monetary system and on the development of policies and strategies through which its members can work together to ensure a stable world financial system and continuing economic growth.

In order to carry out its responsibility, the fund exercises surveillance over the exchange rate policies of members. For this purpose, the fund has adopted principles for the guidance of members' exchange policies and has established procedures by which it exercises surveillance. These principles and procedures are designed to identify, and encourage the correction of, inappropriate exchange rate policies.

The General Agreement on Tariffs and Trade (GATT)

During World War II, the world economy was badly shattered. Immediately after the war ended, the reconstruction of the world economy and the restoration of trade, which had virtually stopped during the war, became a paramount global concern. The many import restrictions instituted during the Great Depression of the 1930s continued to be a major stumbling block in promoting trade. GATT was founded to alleviate this problem.

GATT was negotiated in 1947 and went into effect in January 1948. The twenty-three countries that originally signed it were engaged at the time in drawing up the charter for a proposed International Trade Organization (ITO), which would have been a United Nations special agency. GATT, based largely on select parts of the draft ITO charter, was concluded quickly in order to speed trade liberalization. It was expected that ITO would soon assume responsibility. However, plans for ITO were abandoned when it became clear that its charter would never be ratified, and GATT became the only international instrument of trade rules accepted by the world's major trade nations.

Today, GATT is a multilateral treaty, subscribed to by ninety governments, which together account for more than four-fifths of world trade. GATT's rules govern the trade of its member countries and the conduct of their trade relations with one another. The contractual rights and obligations that it embodies have been accepted voluntarily in the mutual interest of its member countries. Overseeing the application of these rules is an important and continuing part of GATT's activities. GATT is also a means whereby countries negotiate and work together for the reduction of trade barriers in pursuit of the constant and fundamental aim of further liberalization of world trade. In successive multilateral negotiations through GATT, obstacles to trade have been progressively reduced.

Since GATT has been in force, its activities have evolved in response to major changes in the world economic scene. These changes have included shifts in the relative economic strength of important countries or groups of countries, the emergence of the developing Third World as a major factor in international affairs, the trend toward regional or preferential economic groups, new monetary and payments difficulties, and the growing participation of Eastern European countries in GATT. These changes have emphasized GATT's role as a forum where such developments can be discussed and disputes resolved so that their undesirable effects can be countered through continuing efforts toward further liberalization of world trade.

The Organization for Economic Cooperation and Development (OECD)

After World War II, the United States agreed to offer Marshall Plan aid to European countries for reconstruction, provided that these countries worked together to seek recovery. To achieve mutual cooperation, therefore, the European countries formed the Organization for European Economic Cooperation (OEEC) in 1948.

By the 1960s the European economies had been restored. At that time, on both sides of the Atlantic, the interdependence of the industrialized countries of the Western world was recognized. In response to that recognition, Canada and the United States joined with the European countries of OEEC in a new organizaiton. On December 14, 1960, the twenty member countries signed the convention of the Organization for Economic Cooperation and Development (OECD) to:

- Promote economic growth of its member countries.
- Help the less-developed countries both within and outside of its membership.
- Seek trade expansion all over the world.

In 1964 Japan became a full member of the OECD. Finland became a full member in 1969, Australia in 1971, and New Zealand in 1973.

Currently, the membership of OECD consists of Australia, Austria, Belgium, Canada, Denmark, Finland, France, Germany, Greece, Iceland, Ireland, Italy, Japan, Luxembourg, the Netherlands, New Zealand, Norway, Portugal, Spain, Sweden, Switzerland, Turkey, the United Kingdom, and the United States. The following are aspects of OECD's work: economic policy and cooperation; energy; development; trade; financial and fiscal affairs; social affairs; manpower and education; the ecological environment; the world's cities; science, technology, and industry; and agriculture and fisheries.

Multilateral Development Banks

The U.S. participates in four multilateral development banks and funds (MDBs): the World Bank family, which consists of the International Bank for Reconstruction and Development (IBRD), its concessional window, the International Development Association (IDA), and the International Finance Corporation (IFC); the Inter-American Development Bank and its Fund for Special Operations (IDB/FSO); the Asian Development Bank and Fund (ADB/F); and the African Development Bank and Fund (AFDB/F). The World Bank makes loans to assist the growth of less-developed countries around the globe, while the regional banks focus on the development needs in their geographic areas. Each MDB can provide concessional ("soft") loans and ordinary ("hard" or near market rate) loans to their borrowing members. In addition, the IFC, the ADB, and the proposed Inter-American Investment Corporation (IIC) can take equity (partial ownership) positions. Concessional loans are reserved for the poorest countries.

MDBs are the largest source of sound economic policy advice and official development assistance available to the developing nations. In fiscal year 1987, the MDBs lent about $34.6 billion—$23.2 billion from the World Bank group, $5.8 billion from the IDB/FSO, $4.3 billion from the ADB/F, and $1.3 billion from the AFDB/F.

The World Bank, officially called the International Bank for Reconstruction and Development, was founded along with the International Monetary Fund in 1944 at a United Nations Monetary and Financial Conference of fifty-five governments at Bretton Woods, New Hampshire. The World Bank began operations in June 1946. Membership in the bank is open to all members of the IMF. Currently, 129 countries are members of the bank. The bank is owned and controlled by its member governments. Each member country subscribes to shares for an amount reflective of its relative economic strength. The United States is the bank's largest shareholder, providing 25.3 percent of the subscription capital.

The primary purpose of the bank is to provide financial and technical help for the development of poor countries. Currently, it lends about $8 billion a year to help raise the standard of living in poor countries. The bank provides support for a wide variety of projects related to agriculture, rural development, education, electric power, industry, population planning, tourism, transportation, telecommunications, urban development, and water supply. The bank lends money for productive purposes and seriously considers prospects of repayment before granting a loan.

While member countries subscribe to its share capital, the bank relies mainly (to the extent of almost 90 percent) on private investors for its financial resources through borrowing in various capital markets. In this way, private investors become involved in the development efforts of developing countries. Since the bank obtains most of its funds on commercial terms, it charges its borrowers a commensurate rate of interest. Loans usually are repayable over a twenty-year period.

Mention must be made of an affiliate of the bank, the International Development Association (IDA). In the 1950s it became evident that many poor countries needed loans on much easier terms than the bank could provide under its charter. IDA was established in 1960 to help meet this need. It was made an affiliate of the bank was to be administered in accordance with the bank's established methods.

Almost all IDA loans (usually called "credits" to distinguish them from the bank's loans) are granted for a period of fifty years without interest except for a small charge to cover administrative overhead. Repayment of loans does not start until after a ten-year grace period. The major portion of IDA's resources comes from three sources: transfers from the bank's net earnings, capital subscribed in convertible currencies by IDA members, and contributions from the association's richer members.

In the post–World War II period a number of regional financial institutions were established to provide assistance to developing countries in their economic development endeavors. The Inter-American Development Bank, the Asian Development Bank, and the African Development Bank are examples of such institutions. To illustrate the role of a regional bank, the Inter-American Development Bank is examined here.

The bank is owned by forty-three member countries. Twenty-seven of these countries—known as the regional members—are located in the Western hemisphere, and sixteen—known as the nonregional members—are in Europe, Asia, and the Middle East. The latter group was admitted to membership beginning in July 1976.

The bank is the principal source of external public financing for most of the countries of the Latin American region. Its cumulative lending and technical cooperation for development projects and programs exceeded $32 billion at the end of 1990.

The bank also serves as a catalyst for mobilizing external private capital for Latin America's development through borrowings in the international financial markets and by promoting cofinancing arrangements with other financial institutions for development projects in the region.

The bank's purposes are:

- To promote the investment of public and private capital in Latin America for development purposes.
- To use its own capital, funds raised in financial markets, and other available resources for financing high-priority economic and social projects in the region.
- To encourage private investment in projects, enterprises, and activities contributing to economic development and to supplement private investment when private capital is not available on reasonable terms and conditions.
- To cooperate with the member countries in orienting their development policies toward a better use of their resources while fostering greater mutuality in their economies and the orderly growth of their foreign trade.

CHAPTER • 4

International Finance and Accounting

CHAPTER FOCUS

After studying this chapter, you should be able to:

Explain the implications of financial decisions on international marketing strategy

Describe the perspectives of international money management

Discuss how international investment decisions are made

Compare U.S. accounting practices with those followed in other nations

Today's multinational enterprises must deal with an international monetary system that is full of complexities, challenges, and risks. Finance managers and treasurers in particular play a key role in managing worldwide money matters. It is important for future marketing managers to possess insight into multinational finance and accounting functions. An international marketer must have an understanding and appreciation of the financial side of international business in order to make wise marketing-related decisions. For example, without such understanding, a marketing manager for an airplane manufacturer that is supplying ten planes to a Mexican airline might accept routine negotiation for payment over three years in Mexican pesos. But a manager with international financial insight might foresee the depreciation of Mexican currency and opt for payment in U.S. dollars. The impact of the finance function on international marketing decisions can spell success or failure with each decision.

The financial objectives of a corporation typically constrain the latitude of a marketing person. Marketers are affected by their companies' money management—the raising of money, the investing of money, the maintenance of liquidity, even lesser factors like the repatriation of funds from subsidiaries to parent corporations. The decisions of marketing managers also are affected by accounting considerations.

Implications of Financial Decisions on Marketing

A discussion of the financial aspects of multinational business in a marketing text may appear odd. But the fact is, an enterprise ultimately ventures across national boundaries for the enhancement of its long-term profitability. Therefore, financial commitments and their results deeply affect the marketing perspective of a business. While the relationship between finance and marketing functions is nothing new, in the realm of international business, financial considerations can bear more heavily on marketing decisions.

Marketing is affected both directly and indirectly by the international financial policies of the parent corporation. Transfer pricing policy, for example, has a significant, direct impact on marketing. While ***transfer pricing*** will be discussed thoroughly in Chapter 13, it means, in brief, setting prices for the transfer of goods, services, and technology between related affiliates in different countries. Such intrafirm transfer pricing is affected by many considerations, such as fund positioning, income taxes, tariffs, and quotas; managerial incentives and evaluation; antitrust prosecution; the interest of joint-venture partners; and corporate bargaining power with suppliers and/or financial institutions.[1] Many of these conflicting considerations have financial underpinnings.

Eventually, all marketing decisions that involve capital investment and/or other types of long-term financial commitment on the part of the parent corporation must be reviewed in the context of corporate international financial policy. For example, marketing wisdom might suggest improving the provision of after-sale services, which might entail manufacturing parts locally. But the latter could require substantial investment and transfer of technology. Considered in the context of overall financial goals, the parent may find it undesirable to invest in manufacturing spare parts and supplies in a host country. Or the parent may learn that another affiliate recently expanded capacity to manufacture the same parts, or that the political situation in the host country is discouraging to additional investments, and so on. In the end, the decision, which appeared potentially desirable based on marketing considerations, may be postponed or dropped when reviewed from the financial angle.

The financial strength of a company deeply affects marketing, particularly in the company's ability to maintain inventories. Making timely deliveries to customers could provide important competitive leverage in international business, particularly if inventory replenishment involves great distances and time. Similarly, marketing is affected by the company's ability to make economical bulk purchases of merchandise. The company's capacity to undertake promotion in the mass media to strengthen the brand, to commit resources to research and development for the timely introduction of new and improved products, or to make investment in developing cordial relationships with channels of distribution are all influenced by financial decisions. This intimate relationship between the two functions of finance and marketing requires basic knowledge of financial matters to conduct international marketing with expertise (see International Marketing Highlight 4.1).

Few large companies today can afford to disregard the growing importance of overseas markets as a source of corporate growth. Increasingly interdependent trade flows and growing government involvement in economic affairs make financial management a difficult function. The volatility of exchange rates further adds to the difficulty. Quite clearly, given these difficulties and the turbulent world environment of the 1990s, setting marketing strategies for a global corporation without the benefit of financial inputs is like looking through a pair of binoculars with one eye closed.

Multinational Financial Management

The finance function has two principal aspects: (1) to provide the monetary wherewithal to do business and (2) to ensure an adequate financial return on the assets of the company commensurate with its objectives. Even in a strictly domestic business, the able management of funds and investment poses all sorts of problems. The problems relate to issues such as: What financial return is adequate? How should the return be defined? What sources of funds should be tapped? When should funds be raised? Where should funds be used? In the international arena, the problems multiply. Finance management must not only deal with different currencies and their fluctuating rates, but also allow for the vagaries of the economic and political environments of nations with varying perspectives. This section briefly examines various facets of the finance function and relates them to conducting business across national boundaries.

International Marketing Highlight 4.1

How Volkswagen Lost It All

To illustrate the impact of exchange rate changes, a financial perspective on marketing, consider the case of Volkswagen. In the 1960s, VW experienced phenomenal growth. During 1960–1970, its annual sales increased from DM (deutsche mark) 4 billion to DM 15 billion and its exports increased manyfold. In the early 1960s, exports represented half of total sales; toward the end of the decade, exports had become two-thirds of its total sales. VW emerged as the largest automobile exporter in the world.

Volkswagen's success in the U.S. market was highly remarkable. Since their introduction into the U.S. market in the early 1950s, VW's vehicles (particularly the Beetle) had filled an important market niche, catering to price-sensitive consumers. To many Americans, the Beetle was the ideal economy vehicle.

Volkswagen's commitment to the U.S. market was never in doubt. With service support and corporate commitment, annual sales increased from 200,000 vehicles in 1960 to 600,000 vehicles by the end of the decade. In the early 1960s, the United States was VW's largest foreign customer—accounting for 30 percent of VW's exports—the U.S. market for imported cars was increasing, and VW was getting an increasing share of a growing market. By 1970, when imported cars constituted 14 percent of the U.S. car market, VW's market share in the United States was 6 percent, compared with 3 percent in 1960.

Then came the decline, and by 1973 the losses were huge. In October 1969 the DM was revalued, and its full effect was felt in 1970. The revaluation of the DM weakened the competitive position of VW in all the export markets. Volkswagen's net earnings dropped from DM 330 million in 1969 to DM 190 million in 1970. In some European countries, considerable losses in market share were experienced. The DM was again revalued in 1971 and 1972, and by 1972 the DM's revaluation amounted to 40 percent over the 1969 figure. To partially offset currency change effects, VW prices were increased in the United States, and as a result VW lost its market share. In 1971 alone, the losses in the United States due to currency changes were estimated to be DM 200 million.

The early 1970s saw the gradual and regular strengthening of the DM and, with it, the weakening of VW's position. VW's fortunes were inextricably linked with those of the DM: as the DM rose, VW's profits fell. A strong currency clearly weakens the position of the country's exporters; this is particularly true if they are catering to price-sensitive markets. As its annual report of 1972 poignantly recorded, "Exports account for more than two-thirds of the Volkswagen AG's total sales. Of all the world's leading automobile manufacturers, VW is therefore the one most affected by variations in exchange rates."

Stuart Perkins, the chief executive of VW's American subsidiary, was so frustrated and exasperated by the havoc currency changes were playing on his sales that he exploded: "I used to call the sales people and ask how sales were doing. Last quarter, my first move was to call the financial people and ask how the D-mark-to-dollar exchange rate was doing."

The final collapse came in 1973, when VW incurred a loss of DM 807 million. Cash flow plunged from DM 1,671 million in 1972 to DM 618 million in 1973. Equity dropped to 24 percent of assets, from 31 percent the previous year. There was a steady decline in sales in the U.S. market, from a high of 570,000 vehicles in 1968 to 200,000 vehicles in 1976. VW ended 1975 in the red, with losses of DM 160 million.

Currency changes affected VW in three ways. First, the DM revaluation vis-à-vis the dollar made VW's position very uncompetitive in the United States, its biggest market. Second, the DM's revaluation in relation to other Western European currencies such as the pound sterling, the lira, and the French franc resulted in similar effects in those markets. VW found it increasingly difficult to compete in the U.K., France, and Italy. Third, within the [former] West German market, VW had to face increasing import competition, especially from Renault and Fiat. Because of the weakening of the French and Italian currencies, these automobiles became very competitive on the German market.

Source: Based on S. L. Srinivasulu, "Strategic Response to Foreign Exchange Risks," *Columbia Journal of World Business,* Spring 1981, pp. 13–24.

Financial Objectives

Consider the financial objectives of a multinational corporation that manufactures different types of parts and accessories for the automotive industry and related markets.

Financial Goals

The corporation's measure of performance is the return on capital employed. Capital employed is the sum of all assets plus the accumulated reserves for depreciation

It is recognized that not all operations are directly comparable, and targets for individual profit centers and operations will be set taking into account the nature of the operation, its performance plans, and its record of achievement against them.

Target profit performance shall consist of:

1. A competitive return on capital employed with a basic minimum pretax return of 15 percent, which shall be inflation adjusted from time to time.
2. An annual growth rate of pretax profits of at least 12 percent.

New projects and further capital commitments shall be subject to a minimum hurdle rate of 25 percent return on capital unless deemed otherwise necessary or desirable by the corporation in view of legal requirements or in the corporate best long-term interest.

Emphasis on asset management at all levels will include annual targets for cash generation, capital expenditures, and balance sheet items, including inventory and receivables management.

Particular attention is drawn to the differences between actual cash-generating capacity and book results. Each group and profit center is expected to develop not only net cash-generating capacity for its own requirements, but also sufficient funds for the corporation to meet its high-priority investment commitments and opportunities.

In the corporation's international borders, differing tax treatments and currency-exchange matters make cash self-sufficiency even more important.

It is intended to repatriate surplus funds for redeployment by the corporation as required. As a guideline the corporation intends each of its non-U.S.-dollar organizations to remit as dividends, or otherwise, an amount of its annual after-tax earnings equal to the same percentage that the corporation is currently paying from its consolidated after-tax income to its stockholders. Deviations from this policy may be expected when international restrictions exist or when it is in the corporation's best long-term interest.

Financial Limitations

1. Investment in net working capital of less than 35 percent of annual sales; investment in net fixed assets of less than 25 percent of annual sales.
2. Dividend payments of approximately 40 percent of earnings.
3. No significant dilution of shareholders' ownership.

This company has nicely blended the financial objectives for both domestic and international business. From every business deal it expects a minimum inflation-adjusted pretax return of 15 percent, a minimum annual growth of 12 percent in pretax profits, and a 25 percent return on capital from new projects—the hurdle rate. The company intends to regularly repatriate profits and duly provide for exchange rate fluctuations. The objectives clearly recognize the legal/political constraints that may be imposed by host governments, and the company is willing to accept deviations from its objectives to comply with the local environment.

The financial limitations, stated as a part of the objectives, provide guides for sources and uses of funds. The company wants to make rather substantial, regular dividend payments of approximately 40 percent. This means internal funds in the form of retained earnings will be limited for investment in growth. Also the company wants no significant dilution of shareholder's equity. It is possible then that equity capital will have to be considered as a last resort for raising money.

The objectives, as stated above, constitute the foundation for making financial decisions for that company. For example, in order to protect itself against exchange rate fluctuations, it might require managers in overseas subsidiaries to forecast regularly the exchange rates month-by-month for the upcoming six months. On the basis of those forecasts, corporate funds in a currency likely to be substantially depreciated would be utilized before funds in stronger currencies. To illustrate the point, in early 1990 the U.S. dollar continued to decline, and all indications pointed toward a further depreciation of the U.S. currency. At the same time the Japanese yen continued to strengthen. Thus, in 1991 international financial managers had good reason to spend their dollar accumulations and save yen.

Likewise, the goal to repatriate profits suggests that a financial manager in a foreign subsidiary can only plan in part on meeting future investment needs from retained earnings. According to the financial objectives, a new project proposed in a subsidiary outside the United States need not be put through the channels for final approval by the corporate management if it does not expect to meet the hurdle rate. Thus, financial objectives affect investment decisions as well.[2]

Money Management

Money management deals with sources and uses of funds. Money management involves such considerations as how funds should be obtained (equity versus debt); in which currency a corporation or subsidiary should be responsible for raising funds; how the transfer of funds from one subsidiary to another or between a subsidiary and corporation should be handled; and in which financial instrument the funds should be invested and in which market. Prudent international money management requires minimizing the cost of funds and maximizing the return on investment over time by means of the best combination of currency of denomination and maturity characteristics of financial assets and liabilities.[3] Such money management requirements are very complex in the international context. They require the formulation and revision of capital structure decisions for different entities, and budgets for intracompany funds transfer.

Typically, a multinational enterprise is susceptible to three risks related to money management: (1) the political risk of assets being taken over by the host country; (2) the exchange risk whereby the value of the U.S. dollar changes with reference to the host-country currency; and (3) the translation risk whereby the corporate financial statements are required by SEC (United States Securities and Exchange Commission) regulations to be based on historical costs rather than current value.[4]

The task of the international money manager becomes all the more difficult because of higher interest costs and exchange rate fluctuations (see International Marketing Highlight 4.2).

Financial management has always been a complex affair because of problems of communications, time differences, and distance. The vagaries of exchange markets and credit restrictions have exacerbated these traditional problems. The situation has been further complicated by the constant state of change in which companies must do business.

> The president of a large multinational corporation feels that "today we're paying for our past neglect of possible shifts in exchange rates. These changes have inflated our profits in some countries and caused us big losses in others. They've obsoleted all our resource, production, and logistic strategies and thrown a tremendous risk-management responsibility on the finance function— which unfortunately doesn't seem quite able to cope."
>
> With different rates of inflation in different countries, exports increasing faster than production, corporate overseas investment increasing faster than total capital investment, and no end in sight to the pattern of essential unpredictable exchange rate adjustments, the problem—and the penalty for those who fail to solve it—is rapidly gaining in gravity. Increasingly, foreign exchange movements pose a serious threat to the earning power of many corporations. It has become clear that a better approach to identifying foreign exchange risks and finding effective ways to deal with them is needed.[5]

International Marketing Highlight 4.2

Managing Money Across Nations

Assume that a United States–based corporation with $5 million equity has subsidiaries in Mexico, France, and Italy; in each case the assets are valued at $100,000. In establishing these foreign operations, the United States parent corporation contributed $25,000 in equity to each subsidiary and loaned each subsidiary an additional $60,000. The management philosophy of this firm requires that these subsidiaries buy from, and sell to, each other as well as to the parent corporation; that is, each unit of the corporation has a set of intracompany accounts in which are kept the accounts receivable/payable credit extensions within the firm.

In this example, the parent firm desires to reinvest 75 percent of locally earned profits while returning (repatriating) 25 percent to the parent firm as dividends. To add yet another element of realism to the example, assume that each subsidiary will be required to pay to the parent corporation $15,000 annually in royalties and $5,000 annually in management fees.

Before beginning a detailed discussion regarding this example, some of the potential impacts should be noted. First, if the United States dollar increases in value as against the peso, franc, and/or lira, there will be an immediate impact on the subsidiaries. Each payment in dollars from each of the subsidiaries to the parent corporation (interest, dividends, purchases) is now more expensive, while each receipt in dollars from the parent (intracompany sales) is now more valuable. To the parent, however, the impact point is largely deferred until the end of the accounting cycle. If the parent requires that all intracompany transactions between itself and its subsidiaries be denominated in dollars, the effect of the increased dollar value will be noted as a loss of value of the assets held by each of the foreign subsidiaries. This result is then noted on the parent firm's profit-and-loss statement as a "Foreign Exchange Loss."

These observations can be shown dramatically by interjecting into the example some real exchange prices. By selecting two real dates as an example (December 9, 1985, and January 10, 1986) one can note the effects of exchange prices. During this one-month interval, the United States dollar value of the peso rose from $.04382 to $.04386; the franc increased in value from $.2456 to $.2484; and the lira increased from $.001233 to $.001244. With all other factors equal, the Mexican subsidiary would receive 0.09 percent less for the goods it sold to the parent corporation for dollars, while the French and Italian subsidiaries would receive 1.14 percent and 0.89 percent less respectively for their intracompany sales to the parent.

Two other effects must be shown from the example. First, during this one-month period, the value of the peso fell against both the franc and lira thereby making any intracompany purchases of the Mexican subsidiary from either the French or Italian subsidiary more expensive (assuming that those purchases were made in those local currencies). If the Mexican subsidiary were directed to buy from the French subsidiary and pay for this purchase in pesos, the effect of change in currency value would shift to the French subsidiary, which would now receive lesser-valued pesos in payment for the goods sold by them to the Mexican firm.

Second, the impact of these exchange price changes on the parent firm's accounting statements is important. Current accounting conventions have a less than symmetrical (and, some would say, logical) impact. In an overview of this situation the parent firm's consolidated statements would reflect the increased value (due to the change in the value of currencies) of all cash, accounts receivable, and short- and long-term liabilities, while the historical exchange rates (i.e., the rates that prevailed when the firm acquired them) would be used to value all fixed assets. Inventories held by the subsidiaries would be valued on the parent's books at the lower of either the foreign inventory cost times the historical exchange rate (i.e., the United States dollar value of the foreign inventory at cost), or the foreign inventory at market prices times the current exchange rate (i.e., the United States dollar value of foreign inventory at current market value). All revenues and operating expenses of these subsidiaries would be translated to the parent's books at current exchange rates while their cost-of-goods-sold and depreciation would be translated at historical exchange rates.

Source: L. William Murray, "Guidelines for International Financial Management," *Arizona Business,* August–September 1980, pp. 8–9. (Updated by the author.)

The goal of an international money manager is to obtain finances for foreign projects in a way that minimizes after-tax interest costs and foreign exchange losses. The exchange rate parity theory suggests that international differentials in interest costs are offset by changes in foreign exchange rates; that is, the expected value for net financing costs will be equal for all currencies over any given time period, provided foreign exchange markets are efficient.[6] Thus, it makes no difference which currency is used to finance a foreign project.

Assuming the exchange rate parity theory holds, a number of considerations such as tax policies favor the use of host-country financing. Many countries—Australia, Indonesia, South Africa, and Germany, for example—have no taxes on gains or losses arising from most long-term exchange transactions.[7] In some countries, gains and losses from long-term exchange transactions are subject to preferential capital gains tax rates or reserves treatment.[8] Furthermore, most countries apply some kind of surtax on foreign interest payments. These taxes are generally of the withholding sort and are usually available for rebate. A few countries, Argentina for example, even impose a separate tax on foreign interest payments. These taxes increase the cost of borrowing in U.S. dollars or other foreign currency.[9] Such policies encourage MNCs to prefer the use of host-country financing. As a matter of fact, many firms require that all foreign projects be financed in the currency of the host country.

The use of host-country currency for financing limits the foreign exchange exposure and, hence, the risk.[10] Experience in India is relevant here.[11] Traditionally, foreign investors did not think that India provided an opportunity for raising capital locally. Back in 1985, however, Honda Motor Company's issue was oversubscribed 165 times within a span of seventy-two hours. Similarly, Burroughs Corporation's stock and debenture issue was oversubscribed thirty times. In brief, even in many developing countries there is no shortage of local capital.

Translation risk still arises from foreign financing decisions. On the whole, however, such translation risk is less severe because, while exchange risk leads to a realizable gain or loss, translation risk is a paper gain or loss. Besides, the former is taxable, while the effects of translation risk are rarely taxable. Thus, an effective argument can be made for host-country financing. The argument, however, is based on a variety of assumptions, both economic and noneconomic. In many less-developed countries, for example, the government may make it virtually impossible to raise money locally. In other situations, the local currency may be unusable. Thus, despite all the arguments advanced in favor of host-country financing, a company may be forced to seek funds in other markets.[12]

Although money management involves many facets, our discussion has been limited mainly to the question of host-country financing. For our purposes, however, such limited treatment of the subject is sufficient as all that is intended is to provide a bird's-eye view of money management.

To conclude the section, the following guidelines are offered for sound money management. Money management along these lines should provide a structured approach for optimal results.

- Make financial management anticipatory, based on a perception of future risks and opportunities.
- Review and strengthen reporting systems, particularly forecasting elements, to allow anticipatory management.
- Centralize control over exposure risk and liquidity utilization as far as possible.
- Cover economic transactional exposure generally and translation risk when the maximum potential losses are considered to be unacceptable by defined corporation criteria.
- Analyze and make financial decisions on an after-tax basis.
- Ensure availability of credit in uncertain markets on an individual subsidiary basis, even if this involves certain additional costs.
- Look skeptically at exchange rate forecasting that provides one point or very narrow-band estimates of future spot rates, and look just as skeptically at massive computer simulation programs that claim to simplify the decision-making process. The future rate uncertainty level is such that both seemingly facile approaches are of little value, although computer programs for efficient identification of risks and simple sensitivity analysis may be useful.
- Coordinate exchange-risk management closely with liquidity management,

since both have common goals and are equally affected by environmental and structural constraints.

Be aware of the nonfinancial implications of financial strategy, particularly the personnel effects of centralization and the necessity of dealing with an array of governmental and institutional contacts.[13]

Repatriation of Funds

In domestic business an important financial decision made by a corporation is the establishment of dividend policy; that is, the amount of earnings to be distributed to the owners, the stockholders. Likewise, a multinational firm needs to formulate a strategy on remission of dividends from overseas affiliates to headquarters. According to Eiteman and Stonehill, the international dividend policy is determined by the following six factors:

1. Tax implications
2. Political risk
3. Foreign exchange risk
4. Age and size of affiliate
5. Availability of funds
6. Presence of joint venture partners[14]

Many countries—Germany, for example—tax retained earnings, which would yield higher dividend payouts. Countries that levy withholding taxes on dividends paid to a foreign parent, on the other hand, discourage distribution of earnings in the form of dividends. Taxes aside, in the case of countries exhibiting higher political risk, the parent might require the remission of all earnings minus funds needed for working capital and approved capital projects planned for the next few months. Such a perspective would more often apply to developing countries. Where political risk may not be an important factor to reckon with, the dividend policy will be based on availability and use of funds. For example, if funds are needed in the United Kingdom, headquarters might decide to transfer its retained earnings from a German subsidiary to the United Kingdom rather than transferring funds from the United States. An alternative to this would be the investment of funds in German marks.

Another factor that affects international dividend payment is foreign exchange risk. If the value of the host-country currency is expected to decline substantially, other things being equal, common business wisdom will direct conversion of funds into a strong currency. Age and size of affiliates also influence the dividend policy. Research on the subject showed that older affiliates provide a larger proportion of their earnings to the parent since their reinvestment needs decline with time. By the same token, recently established affiliates provide only marginal dividends. As far as size is concerned, larger firms usually have a formal policy for dividend payout, but small firms depend on ad hoc decisions. Finally, if a foreign affiliate is formed as a joint venture, the interests of local stockholders force the company to follow a more stable dividend policy because the worldwide corporate perspective cannot be pursued at the cost of valid claims by local investors who do not necessarily benefit from the global dividend strategy of the parent.

On the basis of the six factors listed and discussed, a multinational firm may follow either a *pooled strategy* or a *flexible strategy* for distribution of earnings generated by foreign affiliates.[15] The pooled strategy refers to a stated policy of remittance of profits to the parent on a regular basis. The flexible strategy, on the other hand, leaves the decision on dividends to factors operating at the time. The flexible strategy permits the parent to make the most viable use of funds vis-à-vis its long-term corporate objectives. Overall, the flexible approach in foreign earnings permits a better utilization of the total financial resources available and eventually leads to a higher level of inflow of funds to the parent company in all forms—dividends, royalties, and various fees.

Making International Investments

Successful international companies continue to be interested in growth prospects. They receive a variety of proposals from different sources that potentially could lead to investments abroad. These sources include company employees, unknown host-country firms, licensees, distributors, and joint-venture partners. Essentially, two processes of an investment proposal determine its fate: the selling of the proposal and its review.[16] Proposal selling and reviewing go through a variety of formal and informal human interactions. The processes are significantly affected by the firm's internal politics—that is, factors such as who is backing the proposal, what the company's organization is, how company personalities interact—and by factors outside the firm.[17] Ultimately, the winning strength of a proposal depends on the diligent work of those who prepare it (see Exhibit 4.1).

Selling an Investment Proposal

Depending on the organizational arrangements of the company, the selling job begins at the middle-management level in the international division or department. When an opportunity arises that seems worthwhile, the manager involved, usually the manager of international development, begins checking with colleagues in manufacturing, marketing, and legal departments in a very informal fashion on such matters as sales projections, manufacturing estimates, patents, and taxes. The manager would also apprise superiors of the forthcoming proposal.

Throughout the early investigatory period that leads up to a formal presentation of the proposal to an international executive, it is important to concentrate on the really critical matters involved. Although these vary somewhat from industry to industry, the overriding emphasis should be put on marketing, because it is in this area that major problems occur. Once the investigation has been completed, a formal proposal is developed and submitted to the head of the international section.

The international head will make a more detailed study of the proposed project with the objective of strengthening the proposal. The location of the invest-

EXHIBIT 4.1 A Checklist for Getting an International Investment Proposal Approved

1. Check with all the people whose approval is needed.
2. Check with all the people *they* will call on for advice.
3. If possible, determine who is most important for which aspects of the proposal (but be careful not to categorize people too narrowly).
4. Sell at the highest possible level—there's nothing like having the president's office behind you from the opening whistle.
5. Establish "people priorities"—who, in descending order, is most important for passing on the project. (This will by no means necessarily be in order of rank.)
6. Set up a flexible "people timetable"—who should be won over in what order.
7. Think ahead as to what each person is going to want to know about the project, and program that into the project analysis. (As one executive put it, you should "do *their* homework" *for them.*)
8. Measure your proposal against *all* stated corporate policy objectives; although sales and profit objectives are the easy ones, don't forget others.
9. Identify any potential enemies to your project and any points of potential resistance, and then establish strategies, or at least mental contigency plans, for dealing with them.
10. Make sure that the investment proposal format corresponds exactly to that used for domestic proposals so as to avoid having it appear to be exotic and thereby attract special detailed scrutiny regarding risk.
11. Give careful thought to any objections that may be raised against your proposal.
12. Be sure you know where your allies stand at all times.
13. In terms of the proposal itself, check carefully that you have not overlooked any obviously important details. And then check for more subtle omissions, and be particularly aware of problem areas and weak points. Have a good idea of the margin of error in the estimates.
14. Anticipate as many objections as possible, but don't be defensive and show your refutations of the objections too hastily.
15. At all times, carefully monitor the pulse of the project's momentum. Momentum can change abruptly. Be ready to facilitate steady progress and to forestall hitches.
16. Be particularly wary of dangerous "parabusiness" environmental criticism of overseas projects, that is, qualitative or essentially subjective, negative social and political judgments. (A domestic officer wishing to shoot down an international proposal may revert to the very thing that is seldom, or rarely, considered for domestic investment proposals, namely, a careful analysis of the political and social climate.)
17. Try to keep the project moving forward at a deliberate speed. Don't let it get stalled in excessive reviewing.

ment, market estimates and sales forecasts, equipment costs, total capital required, sources of funding, raw materials availability, and human resources will be examined.[18] On the basis of this examination, the proposal is completed for submission to the corporate headquarters. Accompanied by a letter, the final proposal will include an appropriation request, an engineering report, the project proposal, and financial analysis. The letter activates the formal review procedure, first through the finance committee, and then through the board of directors.

Reviewing the Investment Proposal

The nature of the review process is intimately related to the perspectives of a company's top management. Often the process and philosophy behind the review of investment opportunities change dramatically with a new person at the helm.[19] In any event, most companies have a comprehensive system for reviewing investment proposals. To illustrate the point, we have included a discussion of a cosmetics firm and its review procedure.

> The firm expands abroad to a large extent through acquisitions. Its acquisition group is headed by an executive vice president (EVP) of the company. He has no staff as such but calls on whomever he needs. Internationally the company has organized its international division into five regions, each headed by a vice president.
>
> When an acquisition proposal penetrates the corporate skin, the acquisitions vice president makes an exploratory trip. If it results in a preliminary agreement that both [sides] should pursue the potential acquisition further, the company begins a thorough analysis of the overseas firm.
>
> In one recent case in Europe, a thorough examination was initiated by the European region's financial group to determine (a) what the company was worth financially, and (b) what the price might be. The European regional management's preliminary proposal was then broken down to essential parts and approved by the financial staff in the international division.
>
> The EVP then brought the proposal to the Executive Committee (consisting of the president, the EVP himself, the president of international, the marketing vice president, the company secretary and the company treasurer), which decided to go ahead with an in-depth analysis, conducted by field management under guidelines set by the Executive Committee. The field group conducting the study advises the EVP of their findings, and he in turn keeps other key executives up-to-date (in particular, those on the Executive Committee). If all goes well the study results in an agreement in principle with the potential acquiree that the company will buy [his company], subject to external audit and to verification of all representations on both sides.
>
> At that point, the company calls in outside accountants for a formal acquisition audit, following which the EVP takes the proposal through the Executive Committee to the board of directors for authorization. What he seeks from the board at this time is the authority to negotiate, rather than the final approval to commit funds. Hence his presentation is not definitive (he does give a rough estimate of the price at this time).
>
> With this authorization, he negotiates a final agreement with the acquiree, subject to final legal clearance and to definitive board approval. In the final request for acquisition authorization to the board, he includes a proposal as to how to pay for the acquisition.[20]

While the review procedure may vary, all corporations strive to determine whether the investment will be sound and provide a long-term, lasting benefit for the owners. It is important that the chief executive or another top officer participate actively in the review process of individual major investment decisions from the viewpoint of the long-term strategic posture of the company.

The checklist in Exhibit 4.2 indicates the type of information needed for review in order to approve an international investment project. With the use of this information, a framework for evaluating foreign investment projects can be laid out. In the final analysis, the evaluation should provide the cost-benefit effects of the project for the host country, parent corporation, and foreign subsidiary.[21]

EXHIBIT 4.2 A Checklist for Reviewing an International Investment Proposal

1. Carefully examine the record and predilections of the individual most directly responsible for the proposal. Is he or she chronically optimistic? Does he or she usually underestimate costs or overestimate future sales?
2. Who has been won over to her or his side? Why do certain managers support the proposals? Why do others oppose it?
3. Determine as best you can the politics of the situation and try to discount each aspect in your analysis.
4. Systematically review all the estimates and projections of the proposal.
5. Look at the details, but also sit back and broadly scurtinize the project. Does it hang together, not only in its details but also as a whole? Does it fit in with the company's long-term objectives?
6. Give particularly close attention to the most crucial elements in your industry—marketing, pricing, technical know-how, or financing.
7. Look for holes. Errors of omission are sometimes harder to spot than outright mistakes.
8. Probe the weak or questionable assumptions that lie behind the figures.
9. Make sure you don't overlook anybody on the corporate staff, or elsewhere in the company, whose advice would be useful and who should see the proposal.
10. Don't let the proposal get rapidly "railroaded" through the process without sufficiently careful analysis.
11. Make sure that the difficulties—present and future—of doing business in the country and region in question are not minimized. What about the future effects of nascent regional trade groups? Any serious chance of low-price competition from new sources, for example, in Japan or Eastern Europe?
12. Take a hard look at the broad political, social, and financial prospects of the country involved. Can you foresee the possibility of anything like a Libyan revolution, an Aquino election, or a French franc devaluation?
13. Look at the overall conditions of doing business in the country involved. What are the chances of price controls, nationalization of retail outlets (such as pharmacies are in Sweden), greater mandatory fringe benefits, new labor legislation, work permit problems (as exist in Switzerland)?
14. Test the key assumptions of the proposal by subjecting them to a test of their elasticity, and test the overall flexibility of the project by projecting the effects of changes on the project. Suppose, for example, that the sales forecast is off by 10 percent. What will that do to profitability?

International Accounting

Global economic interdependence and the existence of large, multinational enterprises create needs for measurement, information transfer, and evaluation of microinformation and macroinformation on an unprecedented scale. International accounting addresses these issues. Traditionally, the flow of information between the parent and its subsidiaries was limited. In the last twenty years or so, however, the communication of accounting data across national boundaries has increased enormously. The rapid development of computer capability, as well as achievements in the field of air travel and telecommunications, has made it possible for an MNC to assemble detailed data from its worldwide operations on short notice. But this raises the question of what information a parent corporation should request to serve both internal and external needs.

An international accounting system serves the same two basic purposes as domestic accounting. It provides information on the business conducted during a certain period and the results obtained. The first purpose is achieved through the income statement. The second purpose is accomplished through the balance sheet, which shows the position of a business, its assets, and its liabilities at a particular time. Accounting information is needed for the internal workings of the organization and to satisfy the requirements and expectations of the external community. But the internal contexts of an international corporation are obviously more complex and larger in scope. For internal purposes, accounting information must adhere to the needs of *both* the parent company and its foreign subsidiary. The internal use of information is related to decision making and control. This raises the question of how much of what information a corporation should compile in its internal accounting system. The external interest of corporate publics (e.g., stockholders, governments, financial communities, labor, customers, creditors, employees) in *both* the parent and host country should be served adequately through accounting information. The external use of information creates the company image of an economic institution of significance for current and potential investors.[22]

International Accounting Reports

The income statement and the balance sheet mainly constitute accounting reports all over the world. The emphasis placed on these statements, however, varies from country to country. In the United States, for example, the income statement is of primary interest. This is so because most large U.S. corporations are publicly owned and stockholders' wealth depends primarily on stock market prices, which, in turn, are greatly affected by earnings per share. In Europe, however, as well as in Latin America and Asia, the major concerns are the ownership of wealth (rather than the generation of income) and the position of the firm vis-à-vis its assets and the claims against them. This view makes the balance sheet of primary importance among Europeans, Latin Americans, and Asians.

The format of an income statement and a balance sheet also varies among countries.[23] In the United States balance sheet liabilities appear on the right and assets on the left. But in most European countries, the order is reversed, liabilities appearing on the left and assets on the right. Along the same lines, non-U.S.

International Marketing Highlight 4.3

Let the Investor Beware

So you want to invest overseas? That makes sense. After all, foreign stock markets often outperform the U.S. market. Now all you have to do is figure out what you're investing in.

It won't be easy. Disclosure and accounting rules overseas differ sharply from those in the U.S.—and also differ significantly among the foreign countries.

Only companies in the U.S. and Canada, for example, issue reports quarterly on profits and other key financial data. And most companies in Japan and Germany don't consolidate the financial data of majority-owned subsidiaries.

In some nations, the lack of a strong enforcement body like the Securities and Exchange Commission permits overseas companies to be more footloose and fancy-free with disclosures. And insider trading is often greeted with a wink by government regulators. In Holland, Spain, and France, where stock exchanges are relatively small, government regulation and oversight of company disclosures are very relaxed.

Source: The Wall Street Journal, September 22, 1989, p. R30.

balance sheets usually show fixed assets and stockholders' equity sections at the top, and current assets and current liabilities near the bottom. Such variations in format do not make a substantial difference in the information but simply indicate the styles and traditions adhered to in different parts of the world.

Another interesting facet of international accounting reports pertains to the information disclosed in them. By and large, in the United States much more information is disclosed than in accounting statements elsewhere. This is largely due to the requirements of the U.S. Securities and Exchange Commission, as well as the stock exchanges' listing requirements, particularly those of the New York Stock Exchange (see International Marketing Highlight 4.3). Among non-U.S. corporations, practices vary from country to country. Overall, European firms tend to maintain secrecy and disclose less than U.S. firms. A recent study on the subject concluded:

> To summarize, multinational companies based in Europe are generally forthright when it comes to disclosing foreign revenues in the aggregate or by geographic area. Revenue disclosure patterns evidenced in Europe were also characteristic of the U.S. and Canada and, to a lesser extent, Japan.
>
> In contrast to revenue data, profitability disclosure, either in the aggregate or by geographic area, was not prevalent in Europe excluding the U.K. and France. Within Europe, Germany and Switzerland were least forthcoming with regard to foreign income. Outside Europe, Japanese multinationals were the most reluctant group. The apparent fear among the Japanese executives, based on personal interviews, is the perceived impairment of long-standing commercial relationships with commercial customers who would be able to reduce relative profit margins from segmental income data. Even lower levels of disclosure by both European and Japan-based MNCs were discerned for foreign assets.

> European multinationals fared better in the areas of exports and capital expenditures and, notwithstanding intra-group differences (e.g., France, the Netherlands, and Switzerland), disclosure of exports from the home country averaged 42% in Europe as a whole versus 25% and 27% for the U.S. and Canada, respectively. Whereas Japanese multinationals revealed more about their exports than those from North America, their capital expenditure disclosure patterns were no better.[24]

Harmonization of International Accounting

In recent years there has been growing interest in making it more feasible to compare accounting information provided by multinational firms. Authorities on the subject, while discounting complete standardization and rejecting uniform accounting, recommend harmonization, which implies a reconciliation of different points of view. It is argued that harmonization of accounting would permit better communication of information in a form that could be interpreted and understood internationally.[25]

Multinational firms raise capital in different countries. It is desirable, therefore, that investors and creditors be provided common information in order to shape their investment decisions. Thus, a set of international accounting standards would facilitate the generation of common information. The principal force behind the accounting profession's attempt at harmonization has been the International Congress of Accountants (ICA). ICA in its tenth meeting in Sidney in 1972 established the International Coordination Committee for the Accounting Profession (ICCAP) to provide leadership in the harmonization effort. One of the outcomes of ICCAP's efforts was the 1973 formation of the International Accounting Standards Committee (IASC), which was formed to (1) develop basic standards to be observed in presenting audited financial statements and (2) promote worldwide acceptance and observance of these standards.[26]

Very much in the manner of the Financial Accounting Standards Board (FASB) in the United States, the IASC issues international accounting standards. By 1990 IASC had issued thirty-three standards.

The IASC has had only an indirect effect on the external financial reporting practices of U.S. multinational enterprises. The American Institute of CPAs (AICPA), for example, has pledged its best efforts to gain acceptance of IASC standards. Yet the FASB, not the AICPA, presently sets U.S. accounting standards and has done little to harmonize their standards with those of the IASC, nor has the IASC attempted to harmonize its pronouncements with the FASB. Thus, U.S. firms are bound by FASB, not IASC, standards and are not presently required to disclose whatever differences exist between these two sets of standards.

The IASC appears to have more influence with financial institutions in other countries. For example, the World Federation of Stock Exchanges has asked member exchanges to require compliance with IASC standards. In addition, the London Stock Exchange requires that listed companies conform with IASC standards.

The ultimate success of the IASC and its eventual effect on multinational enterprises depend primarily on the kinds of standards it issues. To be successful, the IASC must issue statements that either develop broad accounting principles acceptable to most countries or require disclosures that would enable users to compare more easily multinational enterprises.

Consolidation of Accounts

Most multinational corporations consolidate the accounting information from their different entities to present a single income statement and balance sheet for both parent and affiliates. The consolidation process is based on legal requirements of the parent company, information available from subsidiaries, and the practice established over time within the corporation. In the United States, multinational corporations are generally required by law to consolidate the accounts of a subsidiary if the parent owns 50 percent or more of the affiliate. In order to publish consolidated financial statements within a reasonable time after the end of the parent corporation's financial year, the U.S. multinationals usually require the affiliates to prepare their accounts earlier. For example, if the parent's financial year ends on December 31, the subsidiaries may end their financial year on October 31. This way subsidiaries' financial accounts will be available to the parent by December 31 for consolidation with its own.

Most corporations have standard procedures for the subsidiaries to report their accounting information. Thus, the management of subsidiaries not only have to satisfy the legal accounting requirements of their host countries, but also have to make the information available in the required format demanded by their corporate headquarters.[27] Usually U.S. multinationals require their subsidiaries to submit quarterly accounts, comparing actual results against the standards. But some corporations request monthly accounts. Review meetings are held to examine the future outlook of the business, on the basis of such periodic information. The recent trend has been to seek as much detailed information on the subsidiaries' activities as feasible including, in addition to accounting information, data on markets, industry, climate, and economic environment.

National differences and delayed international standardization make it necessary for each multinational enterprise to deal individually with the issue of adequate reporting (see International Marketing Highlight 4.4). Unfortunately, varying national approaches to inflation accounting, new regional requirements for consolidation, demands for social accounting data, and uncoordinated actions by international "standardizing" organizations create additional problems. Consequently, there is a great need for new developments in accounting theory and practice to provide adequate multinational information.

Summary

International marketing decisions are deeply affected by the finance and accounting function; therefore, a brief review of their conduct in the international business field is in order. Essentially, international finance deals with the management of financial resources, such as the sources and uses of funds and the remission of profits from subsidiaries. The underlying force behind finance decisions is a corporation's financial objectives. These objectives usually are defined in terms such as desired return on investment or assets, desired profit growth, hurdle rate

International Marketing Highlight 4.4

A Computer Comparison

To illustrate how tough it is to compare profit performance in different nations, three accounting professors at Rider College in Lawrenceville, New Jersey, set up a computer model of an imaginary company's financial reports in four countries. Starting with the same gross operating profit of $1.5 million, the company had net profit of $34,600 in the United States, $260,600 in the United Kingdom, $240,600 in Australia, and $10,402 in Germany—all because of varying accounting rules in each country.

Although many companies have worldwide operations, their financial results in different countries aren't comparable. This is a serious problem for accountants who may be called upon to analyze a foreign company's financial statements.

The results of companies in Japan, Germany, Switzerland, and Spain are among the most difficult to compare with those of their U.S. counterparts. In Japan and Germany, many corporations don't consolidate results of their majority-owned subsidiaries; in Switzerland and Spain, some concerns set up hidden reserves, which result in lower reported profits.

Investing in Korean companies can also be tricky. Some Korean companies create "special gains and losses" that sometimes don't relate to company successes or failures.

Source: The Wall Street Journal, September 22, 1989, p. R30.

(for accepting new projects), proportion of earnings desired to be paid in the form of dividends, and others.

With certain objectives given, a corporation can then decide how to raise funds—whether to borrow money or to make a stock offering; where to raise money—in the United States or in another capital market; and who should trigger certain actions—the parent or a subsidiary. Among other things, two important factors influence international finance decisions: (1) the varying and fluctuating exchange rates of different currencies and (2) the restrictions imposed by host countries on the transfer of funds. Thus, before the source of funds can be settled, the exchange rates of the countries where the funds are to be raised must be predicted. Then funds can be raised to avoid exchange losses on the one hand and to minimize the cost of capital on the other. Another factor that must be dealt with in money management is the political climate of the host country involved. If problems that may jeopardize the ownership of corporate funds can be foreseen, it might be desirable to transfer funds out of the country while there is still time, even at the cost of substantial exchange loss.

Remission of profits from one country to another is determined by such factors as tax implications, political risk, foreign exchange risk, age and size of affiliate, availability of funds, and presence of joint-venture partners. Multinational corporations pursue either a pooled or flexible strategy in the matter of profit transfer from a subsidiary to the parent and/or to another subsidiary. The pooled strategy spells out profit to the parent by each subsidiary on a predetermined basis. The flexible strategy leaves the decision on remission of profits to the circumstances of the critical moment.

Marketing is affected by financial decisions in many ways. Among these, two deserve mention. One is the area of transfer pricing— the price that a subsidiary charges to another subsidiary belonging to the same parent for its goods, services, and technology. The second is that the approval of projects that seem crucial from a marketing standpoint may be denied because overall corporate financial objectives do not support the project.

The chapter described the process that companies follow in making international investment decisions. Most multinationals have a systematic procedure to receive, evaluate, and approve projects requiring capital expenditures. The presentation for approval of such projects is approached in two ways: the selling of an investment project and the review of an investment proposal.

The section on international accounting described the varying importance placed on the income statement and the balance sheet in different countries. For example, in the United States the income statement is considered of prime importance. In Europe, Asia, and Latin America, the balance sheet has a greater significance.

Accounting systems and procedures, although essentially following the double entry system, differ worldwide. Therefore, it is difficult to draw comparisons from the information provided in accounting reports. Efforts at harmonization of international accounting are being spearheaded by the International Accounting Standards Committee (IASC).

Review Questions

1. Describe the meaning of money management in the international context.
2. What risks does a multinational enterprise sometimes face in international money management?
3. What are the arguments for and against raising capital in host-country currency?
4. What factors determine international dividend policy?
5. Explain the meaning of transfer pricing. What factors affect transfer pricing?
6. What sorts of reports usually are included with a project proposal?
7. Explain why the income statement is considered important in the United States while the balance sheet is more crucial in Europe.
8. Why is more information usually disclosed by U.S. firms in their financial accounts than by their counterparts in Europe?

Endnotes

1. William D. Turner and Stephen K. Green, "Global Challenge to Corporate Treasuries," *Euromoney*, July 1981, pp. 9–18. *Also see* Gerald M. Meier, *Problems of a World Monetary Order*, 2nd ed. (New York: Oxford University Press, 1982), pp. 180–185.

2. *See* Steven J. Cochran and Igbal Mansur, "The Interrelationships Between U.S. and Foreign Equity Market Yields: Tests of Granger Causality," *Journal of International Business Studies,* Fourth Quarter 1991, pp. 723–736.
3. Juan M. Rivera, "Prediction Performance of Earnings Forecasts: The Case of U.S. Multinationals," *Journal of International Business Studies,* Second Quarter 1991, pp. 265–288.
4. Reed Moyer, *International Business* (New York: John Wiley & Sons, 1984), pp. 275–279. *Also see* Stephen Korbin, "When Does Political Instability Result in Increased Investment Risk?" *Columbia Journal of World Business,* Fall 1978, pp. 54–62; Somerset Waters, "Exposure Management Is a Job for All Departments," *Euromoney,* December 1979, pp. 6–11. *Also see* Thomas H. Bates, "Foreign Exchange Risk Exposure Management: A Comparison of Japanese and U.S. Practices," *San Francisco State University School of Business Journal,* vol. 3 (1985), pp. 28–38.
5. Helmut Hagemann, "Anticipate Your Long-Term Foreign Exchange Risks," *Harvard Business Review,* March–April 1977, p. 82.
6. Alan Teck, "Control Your Exposure to Foreign Exchange," *Harvard Business Review,* January–February 1974, pp. 66–75. *Also see* Alan C. Shapiro, "Evaluating Financing Costs for Multinational Subsidiaries," *Journal of International Business Studies,* Fall 1975, pp. 25–32; Ike Mathur, "Managing Foreign Exchange Risk Profitably," *Columbia Journal of World Business,* Winter 1982, pp. 23–30.
7. *Investment, Licensing and Trading Conditions Abroad* (New York: Business International Corporation, 1979).
8. *See* Alan C. Shapiro, *Multinational Financial Management,* 3rd ed. (Boston: Allyn & Bacon, 1988), Chapter 13.
9. *See* Elwood L. Miller, *Accounting Problems of Multinational Enterprises* (Lexington, MA: Lexington Books, 1979), Chapter 14.
10. Jongmoo Jay Choi, "Diversification, Exchange Risk, and Corporate International Investment," *Journal of International Business Studies,* Spring 1989, pp. 145–156.
11. Matt Miller, "India's Stock Market Is Soaring as Investors Snap up Spate of Issues by Foreign Firms," *The Asian Wall Street Journal Weekly,* September 9, 1985, p. 1.
12. *See* William S. Sekely and J. Markham Collins, "Cultural Influences on International Capital Structure," *Journal of International Business Studies,* Spring 1988, pp. 87–100. *Also see* Kwang Chul Lee and Cluik C. Y. Kwok, "Multinational Corporations vs. Domestic Corporations: International Environmental Factors and Determinants of Capital Structure," *Journal of International Business Studies,* Summer 1988, pp. 195–218.
13. Andreas R. Prindl, "Guidelines for MNC Money Managers," *Harvard Business Review.* January–February 1976, pp. 79–80. *Also see* Lamberth H. Spronck, *The Financial Executive's Handbook for Managing Multinational Corporations* (New York: Wiley, 1980), Chapter 7.
14. David K. Eiteman and Arthur I. Stonehill, *Multinational Business Finance,* 4th ed. (Reading, MA: Addison-Wesley, 1987), pp. 410–412. *Also see* Michael Gendron, "Simple Approach to International Business," *Managerial Planning,* May/June 1985, pp. 56–60.
15. Alan C. Shapiro, *Multinational Financial Management* (Boston: Allyn & Bacon, 1982), pp. 308–312.
16. *See* William H. Davidson, *Global Strategic Management* (New York: Wiley, 1982).
17. For a theoretical perspective on the subject, *see* A. Louis Calvet, "A Synthesis of Foreign Direct Investment Theories and Theories of the Multinational Firm," *Journal of International Business Studies,* Spring/Summer 1981, pp. 43–60.
18. David J. Richardson, "On Going Abroad, The Firm's Initial Foreign Investment Decision," *Quarterly Review of Economics and Business,* Winter 1979, pp. 14–21.
19. Ian Allan, "Return and Risk in International Capital Markets," *Columbia Journal of World Business,* Summer 1982, pp. 3–21.
20. *Evaluating New Projects Abroad,* Management Monographs No. 45 (New York: Business International Corporation, undated), pp. 14–15.
21. *See* Sara L. Gordon and Francis A. Lees, "Multinational Capital Budgeting," *California Management Review,* Fall 1982, pp. 22–32.
22. F.D.S. Choi and G. G. Mueller, *An Introduction to Multinational Accounting* (Englewood Cliffs, NJ: Prentice-Hall, 1978), pp. 37–46.
23. David K. Eiteman and Arthur I. Stonehill,

Multinational Business Finance, 2nd ed. (Reading, MA: Addison-Wesley, 1979), pp. 540–541.

24. Frederick D. S. Choi and Vinod B. Bavishi, "A Crossnational Assessment of Management's Geographic Disclosures," *Working Paper* (Storrs, CT: Center for Transnational Accounting and Financial Research, University of Connecticut, 1983).
25. Hanns-Martin W. Schoenfeld, "International Accounting: Development, Issues and Future Directions," *Journal of International Business Studies,* Fall 1981, pp. 83–99.
26. Jeffrey S. Arpan and Lee H. Radebaugh, *International Accounting and Multinational Enterprises* (Boston: Warren, Gorham and Lamont, 1981), pp. 52–56. *Also see* H. P. Holzer and J. S. Chandler, "A Systems Approach to Accounting in Developing Countries," *Management International Review,* vol. 22, no. 2 (1982), pp. 23–32.
27. Michael J. Kane and David A. Ricks, "The Impact of Transborder Data Flow Regulation on Large United States Based Corporations," *Columbia Journal of World Business,* Summer 1989, pp. 23–30.

CHAPTER • 5

Regional Market Agreements

CHAPTER FOCUS

After studying this chapter, you should be able to:

- Describe the rationale behind regional market agreements
- Discuss how market agreements affect international marketing
- Examine the historical perspectives of market agreements
- Discuss the European Community and its various aspects, such as the Europe 1992 program and the Monetary Union
- Describe other market agreements, especially the North American Free Trade Agreement

A previous chapter discussed the worldwide postwar efforts to restore free trade.

These included elimination of tariff barriers through the General Agreement on Tariffs and Trade (GATT) and stabilization of currencies through the International Monetary Fund (IMF). At the same time these efforts went forward on the international level, an interest in economic cooperation at the regional level also developed, resulting in different forms of market agreements. Regional economic cooperation is based on the premise that, while responding to global agreements to promote trade, nations in a region connected by historical, geographic, cultural, economic, and political affinities may be able to strike more intensive cooperative agreements for mutually beneficial economic advantages.

An outstanding example of regional economic cooperation is today's ***European Community (EC),*** often called "the (European) Common Market."* At the time of development of the Marshall Plan, the United States strongly felt that European nations should seek an adequate economic integration to cope with the problems of reconstruction. Such economic integration, it was argued, would permit Western Europe to emerge both in a market the size of the United States and in the viable competitive position necessary for achieving economies of scale via mass production. Simultaneously, however, the self-interest of the United States was also a force in the initial stimulus for the European economic integration. The creation of a large, and at least somewhat homogeneous, market was certainly beneficial to U.S. corporations.

Economic cooperation has an effect on international marketing, and different forms of market agreements among nations have different effects. The international marketer should be aware of early attempts at regional cooperation and economic integration like the European Community and the cultivation of existing market agreements in different parts of the world.

Effects of Market Agreements

Market agreements affect international marketing in a variety of ways. *First, the scope of the market is broadened.* For example, after the formation of the Common Market, the French market ceased to be just a French market; it became a part of the larger Common Market. Such an expanded market provides a *flexibility* that would not be feasible dealing with individual countries. For example, under one type of market agreement called a *free trade area agreement,* internal trade barriers among member countries are abolished and a company may move products from one country to another freely. This permits a company to achieve economies of scale not only in production but also in product promotion, in distribution, and in other aspects of business. For example, the establishment of the Common Market made it feasible for the Ford Motor Company to integrate its operations in Germany and Britain.

*Originally called the European Economic Community (EEC) in 1958, the name was changed in 1980 to European Community (EC).

> A new management organization was created to make all the critical decisions for both the British and German companies. There were obvious operating economies in the arrangement—the duplicate dealer organizations in third markets could be eliminated and responsibility went where the skill was: body development work was concentrated in Germany, power train development concentrated in Britain. The pooling cut the engineering bill in half for each company, provided economies of scale with double the volume in terms of purchase—commonization of purchase, common components—and provided the financial resources for a good product program at a really good price.[1]

Since the formation of the EC, U.S. business activity in the region has grown significantly. U.S. investment in the EC increased fourfold during the 1970s. In 1970, for example, 30 percent of U.S. investment abroad was in the EC and 30 percent was in Canada. By 1990, U.S. investment in Canada had increased almost four times, while investment in the EC had gone up almost seven times to $164 billion. In 1987 EC investments in the United States amounted to nearly two-thirds of all foreign investments in the United States, about $183 billion.

Second, market agreements change the nature of competition. For example, before the formation of the Common Market, many American multinational corporations found little local competition in Western Europe, but afterward local companies were encouraged to expand quickly. They became factors in the market, through mergers and such, with the encouragement of member governments. In the computer area, Siemens A.G. (German), Compagnie Internationale pour L'Informatique (French), and Philips N.V. (Dutch) entered into a joint venture to compete effectively against IBM.

Despite IBM's best efforts, in 1985 the EC denied IBM the opportunity to join European firms for basic research to close Europe's technology gap with the United States and Japan. This research was sponsored to use Esprit, a $1 billion program focusing on basic information technology, and encourage Britain's ICL, France's Bull, Italy's Olivetti, former West Germany's Nixdorf, and the Netherland's Philips to cooperate with each other to compete against giants such as IBM.[2] Such cooperation among businesses need not necessarily be between companies of different nations. In Italy, for example, Montecatini and Edison companies merged to form Montedison.

Third, market-agreement firms expand through mergers and acquisitions and thereby become highly competitive outside their market area as well. For example, after the formulation of the Common Market, French and German companies were able to compete aggressively against U.S. and Japanese multinationals worldwide.

Finally, market-agreement countries are able to make decisions favorable to all member-country companies. It would not be feasible for an individual country to enforce such measures. For example, Common Market antitrust policies could adversely affect an American company and its subsidiaries or licensees that previously had been given exclusive rights in, say, Italy and the Netherlands.[3] The following list summarizes other implications of economic integration for marketing.[4]

1. Successful integration can lead to an increased growth for the region, providing opportunities to penetrate a larger market. The previous national markets may have been too small to permit efficient operation, or even to provide enough potential sales to interest a company. The regional market provides opportunity both for mass production and also for mass marketing.
2. Growth in income within the region can lead to increased exports for both member and nonmember countries. Often the increased income leads to increased imports by the region in order to meet its industrial requirements and to satisfy the demand for a variety of consumer goods.
3. The amount of trade diversion differs among the various product lines, but it is potentially large for agricultural products when the regional markets seek to protect local producers. Manufacturers that produce differentiated products in high demand are not likely to be as subject to diversion as those producing simple and undifferentiated goods.
4. Trade creation and diversion possibilities may lead international businesses to invest in production and marketing facilities within the region in order to get behind the tariff wall and to minimize nontariff barriers. Such facilities may also serve as supply points for marketing products to other regions as well as to other countries within the region.
5. Increased competition within the region makes marketing more difficult, but international firms often are able to capitalize on their effective marketing organizations. Thus, they should have an advantage in the more competitive world.
6. The desire to increase competition among its members in order to achieve efficiency sometimes leads to changed antitrust policy, and new standards of fair competition may be imposed. In this matter traditional business customs and organizations may be upset, and more aggressive marketing may result.
7. In some instances local industries may be favored to improve the regional community's position relative to outsiders. Thus, in the EC, governments sought to develop or maintain high-technology industries such as computers and aircraft. Governments may foster mergers among the region's firms in critical industries and governmental aid may subsidize these industries.

It is important to mention also that economic integration, while leading to a variety of benefits, can create some problems. Consider, for example, the potential for trouble with the freedom of labor movement within the European Community. With relatively poor countries like Spain and Portugal having joined the group, controversy over guest workers from these countries, in Germany in particular, is likely. In the long run, the freedom of labor movement may become illusory. Further, free entry for Spanish and Portuguese agricultural products has worsened the EC's agricultural problems, boosting output of such products as olive and citrus fruit and thus depressing prices. This is likely to put further pressure on the EC's budget, two-thirds of which is already spent on supporting farm subsidies.[5]

Another problem is the jeopardy into which existing agreements of a nation are thrown when it joins a market group.[6] Entry into the EC caused Great Britain's commitments to the Commonwealth to diminish. Agricultural overproduction and inefficiencies are always potentially controversial among member countries since no nation wants its output outpriced by cheap imports. As a matter of fact, agricultural exports have been a chief issue of conflict between the United States and the EC, and to a large extent responsible for the Uruguay Round deadlock, as was discussed in Chapter 2.

A market agreement does not create a homogeneous market; it simply broadens the market base. Within the enlarged, heterogeneous market, segments ought to be identified for the development of effective marketing strategy—each segment served by a unique marketing mix. Such an approach might not be possible for each individual country, however. Many marketers erroneously thought that with the establishment of the Common Market, Western Europe would present a single homogeneous market. Even the individual consumer was supposed to lose his or her individuality.

> The European consumer would come alive, and he was to have had the politeness of a Frenchman, the calmness of an Italian, the sense of humor of a German, the puritanism of the Danes, the sense of organization of the Belgian, the liveliness of a Dutchman, an Englishman's flair for cuisine, the soberness of an Irishman, and the frivolity of the Luxembourg people.[7]

While there apparently is not a homogeneous market of consumers, there are homogeneous segments within the Common Market that must be recognized and served through unique marketing programs.

Early Attempts at Regional Economic Integration

Current efforts toward regional economic integration among nations of the world began with the creation of the European Economic Community (EEC) in 1958, born through a long history of trial and deliberation. In 1948, the Organization for European Economic Cooperation (OEEC) was established to administer the Marshall Aid program. Very soon, it became obvious to all concerned that European nations would have to seek some form of economic cooperation in order to emerge as a large autonomous market.

The drive toward European economic unity continued to gain momentum in the early 1950s, although many leaders doubted that perpetual cooperation, other than on an ad hoc basis, would ever be feasible. The proponents of the movement met with their first success with the establishment of the European Coal and Steel Community (ECSC) in 1952. The ECSC was created to develop a common market in coal, steel, and iron ore. The six countries participating in this effort were France, Germany, Italy, Belgium, the Netherlands, and Luxembourg. The success of the ECSC led these six nations to venture further into the 1958 establishment of the EEC and its long-term plans. Initially, it was established as a customs union that was gradually to include both industrial and agricultural goods and to lead to the abolition of restrictions on trade among member nations and the creation of common external tariffs. The EEC's organizers looked to eventual economic union among the member countries to enable free movement of people, services, and capital, and gradual development of common social, fiscal, and monetary policies.

Simultaneously with the formation of the EEC, another seven-nation regional group was established. Unable to come to agreement within the OEEC, the United Kingdom, Denmark, Sweden, Norway, Switzerland, Austria, and Poland formed the European Free Trade Association (EFTA) in 1960.

With Europe as an example, regional agreements have come into existence all over the world—in Africa, in the Arab world, in Latin America, and in Asia. Communist countries also made their own regional cooperative arrangements.

The Bases of Cooperation

Economic cooperation among nations is mainly dictated by economic, political, geographic, and social factors. Nations may be willing to cooperate with each other simply as a matter of economic necessity.[8] For example, seventy-seven poor countries located distantly around the world have joined together to form a group called the New International Economic Order (NIEO), which negotiates concessions from richer countries for the purpose of enhancing NIEO member trade.[9]

Nations also may cooperate for political reasons. The Commonwealth is an interesting example of a political union of nations. Commonwealth countries are economically far apart from each other. For example, Australia is among the developed nations while Pakistan is a Third World country. Geographically, the Commonwealth countries are spread over different continents. Canada is in North America, Great Britain in Europe, Nigeria in Africa, and India in Asia. Even some political similarities of the past are different today as nations pursue different political modes—Burma is a military dictatorship; New Zealand, a democracy. The commonality of these nations is their historical partnership in the British Empire.

Geographic proximity is another factor that facilitates economic cooperation and integration among nations. Presumably countries in the same geographic region have a better appreciation of each other's strengths and weaknesses, and together they may come to realize synergies that would make them economically stronger. For example, a mass market is necessary for mass production. Nations located near each other would be better able to develop a mass market and could recognize this potential and join together. A notable example of such cooperation among nations in geographic proximity to one another was the formation of the European Community, or Common Market.

Finally, countries also may associate with each other on the basis of social customs, traditions, taboos, and culture. Arab countries, for example, share a long Islamic heritage. Such bonds favor economic union.

The Success of Cooperation

A question may be raised as to what factors account for the success of economic integration. Briefly, economic cooperation is likely to flourish when member countries have diverse products and raw materials. The most successful case of economic integration has been the European Community. Nations belonging to the EC have more or less complementary economies, diverse industries, different natural resources, and varying agricultural bases. Further, it is desirable that member nations be of compatible economic status in terms of balance-of-payments position and level of development.

Types of Market Agreements

There are five principal forms of market agreements among nations: free trade area, custom union, common market, economic union, and political union. Such agreements are differentiated on several bases.

Free Trade Area (FTA)

The free trade area (FTA) type of agreement requires nations to remove all tariffs among the members. Let us assume there are three nations—A, B, and C—that agree to an FTA agreement and abolish all tariffs among themselves to permit free trade. Beyond the FTA, A, B, and C may impose tariffs as they choose. For example, if nation X trades extensively with B, B may have very low tariffs for goods imported from X while A and C impose high tariffs on goods from X. Under an FTA agreement, B is free to continue its *preferred* relationship with X while A and C are at liberty to decide their own external tariff policies. The European Free Trade Area (EFTA) and the Latin American Free Trade Area (LAFTA) illustrate the free trade area type of agreement.

Customs Union

A customs union, in addition to requiring abolition of internal tariffs among members, further obligates the members to establish common external tariffs.[10] To continue with example countries A, B, and C, under a customs union agreement (instead of an FTA), B would not be permitted to have a special relationship with country X. A, B, and C would have to have a common tariff policy toward X. A customs union agreement exists among Caribbean countries. Their cooperative effort started as a free trade area and later developed into a customs union. As mentioned earlier, the EC began as a customs union.

Common Market

In a common market type of agreement members not only abolish internal tariffs among themselves and levy common external tariffs, but they also permit the free flow of all factors of production (capital, labor, technology) among themselves.[11] Our illustration countries A, B, and C, under a common market agreement, not only would remove all tariffs and quotas among themselves and impose common tariffs against other countries such as country X, but also would allow capital and labor to move freely within their boundaries as if they were one country. This means, for example, a resident of A is free to accept a position in C without a work permit. Likewise, an investor in B is at liberty to invest money in A, B, or C without restriction from either home or host government when transferring funds for investment.

Economic Union

Under the economic union arrangement, common market characteristics are combined with harmonization of economic policy. Member countries are expected to pursue common monetary and fiscal policies. Ordinarily this means synchronizing taxes, money supply, interest rates, and regulation of capital market, among other things. In effect the economic union calls for a supranational authority to design an economic policy for an entire group of nations. The EC, to a great extent, can be called an economic union. This designation is justified by the fact that the community has a common agricultural policy and shares the European monetary system.

Political Union

A political union is the ultimate market agreement among nations. It includes the characteristics of economic union and requires, in addition, political harmony among the members. Essentially, it means nations merging with each other to form a new nation.

In its pure form, an example of the political union does not exist. In the 1950s, however, Egypt, Syria, and Yemen formed a short-lived political union. To an extent, the Commonwealth of Nations and perhaps the newly formed Commonwealth of Independent States can be characterized as politically based agreements. In the future, in a very limited sense, the EC with the European Parliament in place could be considered a political union.

Market Agreements in Force

Most current market agreements are organized by geography. Some agreements are not formed according to region, however, but extend over different geographic areas of the world.

Europe

European nations have been by far the most aggressive in seeking economic integration. They have formed the European Community, the now-defunct European Free Trade Association, and the Council for Mutual Economic Assistance.

European Community (EC) Often called the European Common Market, the EC agreement came into existence in January 1958. Its purpose was to abolish over a twelve-year period all customs tariffs and other economic barriers among the six member countries: Germany, France, Italy, the Netherlands, Belgium, and Luxembourg. In 1973, the United Kingdom, Denmark, and Ireland joined the EC. Greece became a full member in 1982. Spain and Portugal joined the EC as full members on January 1, 1986. As it stands today, the EC is the word's largest exporter, producing over one-fourth of world exports.

The European Community today represents a true customs union, having abolished all customs duties and restrictions on trade in industrial goods within the community while imposing common external tariffs and supporting free internal movement of labor and capital. In the area of agriculture, the EC has developed a protective common agricultural policy that consists of a support system designed to promote domestic agricultural production and guaranteed farm incomes.

The European Community's 1957 Rome Treaty called for the eventual formation of an economic union. While some progress has been made toward this end in the form of a common antitrust policy, complete economic and monetary union, not to mention political union, has a long way to go. However, the name change from European Economic Community to European Community in 1980 indicates the broadened political role this group is likely to play in coming years.

A number of other countries are linked with the Common Market as associate members. Turkey is one. The EC also has preferential trade agreements with a number of Mediterranean countries and with the countries in the European Free Trade Association.

Following the Lomé (capital of Togo) Convention in 1975 and its latest extension in 1990 (the fourth Lomé Convention), the EC agreed to a trading program with sixty-six African, Caribbean, and Pacific (ACP) countries that is valid for five years (i.e., 1990–1995). The fourth Lomé agreement consolidates and builds on the earlier Lomé agreements, and provides, in particular, trade opportunities and development aid to selected Third World countries from EC members.[12] It establishes a vast, privileged domain of cooperation among multiform (economic, commercial, and even cultural) northern (the members of the EC) and southern (the associated states of Africa, the Caribbean, and the Pacific) countries.

Today, the EC is a viable world economic force with as large a market as the United States. If the present trend continues, the EC will grow in coming years as other countries join the group. Turkey and Sweden, for example, may soon become full members. Similarly, some Eastern European countries may seek entry into the EC.

Due to the EC program, Western European nations are doing more together than ever. The Common Market is expanding, both in members and in terms of trade, after settling a protracted dispute over budgetary shares. New cooperation agreements on matters important in future European development—space, broadcasting, and computer research—were negotiated in 1985 among countries and companies.

In 1990, exports by Common Market countries to other Common Market countries grew by 22 percent in local currency terms to the equivalent of 430.5 billion. In the U.S. view, Western Europe's appreciation of the economic importance of trade has been traditionally poor. But to Western Europe, expanding trade has been, and continues to be, the greatest achievement of the Common Market.

The rate of expansion in European trade during 1990 was seven times the rate of economic growth. This means several things. First, trade is acting as a propellant to Europe's overall economy—exactly what the continent's leaders had in mind when they launched the Common Market over thirty years ago. The key provision of the treaty, the elimination of tariffs among member states, touched off a trade boom that continues to this day.

Despite the tremendous achievements of the EC, in the mid-1980s, the organization faced a variety of problems (see International Marketing Highlight 5.1).

International Marketing Highlight 5.1

Crazy Quilt of Regulations

If a commercial truck driver who left New York and drove the 5,000 or so kilometers to Los Angeles respected all the applicable work and rest rules, he could drive that entire distance at an average speed of 60 kilometers per hour. If that same rule-obeying driver in the same heavy lorry were to leave the Midlands in the United Kingdom, pass by London, and drive down to Athens, also a distance of some 5,000 kilometers, he would be able to average only 12 kilometers per hour. It is worth noting that 12 kilometers per hour happens to be the speed of a horse and cart.

A critical examination of the EC showed that it never really became a common market. After the first heady years, various kinds of nontariff barriers once again began to choke off trade between member nations. A common currency, even a single free capital market, remained little more than a goal for the distant future. Less soaring aims, like harmonizing economic policies and standardizing member countries' value-added taxes, also appeared remote. Freedom of trade in services hardly existed at all, and there was little consensus on how to bring it about. The EC's common agricultural policy (CAP), which guarantees farmers high prices without limiting production, had produced huge surpluses that disrupted international markets and strained the EC budget. Yet farmers were not happy; their gripes about prices and market share erupted in violence.

The most disappointing failure, however, is lack of progress in creating a true common market in manufactured goods, the EC's original reason for existence. Before the EC's birth, Europe was a maze of protectionism. Tariffs and quotas were the most visible and significant barriers, but they were backed by a host of regulations and other protectionist devices, some more than one-hundred years old. After the tariffs and quotas were eliminated, much of their protectionist function was gradually taken over by the nontariff barriers, many of which have proliferated over the years (see International Marketing Highlight 5.2).

The EC members realized that as markets and industries globalize, those constraints—physical, technical, and fiscal—are no longer endurable. Further, as the forces of globalization have increased, the influence of European countries, both political and economic, has weakened. During the first half of the 1980s, Europe lost jobs at 0.5 percent per year, while its economy, roughly the same size as that of the United States, grew at 1.5 percent per year. At the same time, the unemployment rate in Europe climbed from 4 percent to around 6 percent. These numbers pointed to a troubling decline in the international competitiveness of European companies.

International Marketing Highlight 5.2

How Nontariff Barriers Hindered European Growth

A recent study by the EC Commission listed no fewer than fifty-six different categories of nontariff barriers, ranging from discrimination in government procurement contracts through national health and technical regulations to sheer customs chicanery at national borders. Many customs restrictions, such as taking currency in or out of France and Italy, are more stringent now than they were in the past. The time wasted getting goods through borders adds significantly to European industry's costs—as much as $1 billion a year. The total cost to industry of complying with all of the customs formalities is estimated at more than $10 billion, or between 5 percent and 10 percent of the value of the goods traded. This amounts to a substantial hidden tariff. In 1983, several truckloads of West German freezers were turned back at the French border for failing to have new certification documents in French, a requirement that had been introduced almost overnight. At the Italian border, customs officials often are simply unavailable, which halts truck traffic. Moreover, Italy still requires, as it did before 1958, that any pasta sold there must be made of durum wheat, not the soft wheat normally used for pasta-type products elsewhere. In Germany, a law whose origins go back several centuries specifies that beer sold there may be made only of barley malt, hops, and water. Since brewers in France, Belgium, and the Netherlands, like those in the United States, now use other grains or additives, this means that not a single bottle of Kronenbourg, Stella Artois, or Heineken can be sent across the Rhine.

Governments take action under many guises that discriminate against foreign products. France and Italy, for instance, impose disproportionately heavy taxes on big, powerful cars, which suits their automobile manufacturers whose output is concentrated in the small-car end of the line. As buyers of goods and services—telecommunications equipment, for example, or pharmaceuticals for national health services—governments can be decidedly protectionist.

Source: European Community Press and Information Service, New York, March 1985.

Thus, to create jobs, restore international competitiveness, and boost the value to European customers of the goods and services available to them, the EC members were led to adopt a new course, that is, the Europe 1992 program.

The twelve member countries of the EC have committed to integrating into a single internal market by the end of 1992. The result will be a $4 trillion market of 320 million people. This Internal Market Program will make sweeping changes in virtually every aspect of business life, and will greatly alter the way U.S. firms do business in Europe.

Initially described in a 1985 EC Commission White Paper, the Internal Market Program consists of 285 legislative directives intended to eliminate present barriers to the free movement of goods, people, and capital among the twelve EC member states. Internal Market Directives will reach into every aspect of

International Marketing Highlight 5.3

Europe 1992: Industries Most Affected

1. Industries that are losing protection and becoming more susceptible to competition:
   - financial services (banking and insurance)
   - pharmaceuticals
   - telecommunications services
2. Industries shifting from fragmented local to integrated communitywide markets:
   - distribution
   - food processing
   - transport (trucking)
3. Industries gaining technical economies of scale through sale of homogeneous goods and services:
   - electronics
   - packaging
   - white goods and other consumer products
4. Industries dependent on public procurement:
   - computer equipment and services
   - defense contractors
   - telecommunications equipment
5. Industries where the single market leads to import substitution, i.e., EC goods instead of imports:
   - chemicals
   - electrical components and products
   - office equipment
6. Industries where price disparity exists between countries with different indirect taxation (VAT) levels:
   - consumer good and services

Source: Business International, November 27, 1989, p. 365.

commercial activity, from eliminating border controls and duplicative customs documents, to setting uniform product standards, to establishing guidelines for company mergers. By 1992, 80 percent of all regulations affecting business in the EC will be EC regulations and directives instead of national laws. Major parts of the Europe 1992 program are summarized in Exhibit 5.1.

European officials believe that the integration of the EC market will increase economic growth and employment, and lead to greater consumption and imports. A study by the EC Commission predicts that the removal of existing barriers may result in a 5 percent increase in EC gross domestic product, more than $260 billion, through more economies of scale and greater economic efficiency.[13]

European industry should receive the most direct benefits from the program.

EXHIBIT 5.1 Highlights of the Europe 1992 Program

By the end of 1992, the European Community intends to have implemented 285 regulations to create a single internal market. The following specific changes represent the major part of the 1992 program.

In standards testing, certification

Harmonization of standards for:

- Simple pressure vessels
- Toys
- Automobiles, trucks, and motorcycles and their emissions
- Telecommunications
- Construction products
- Personal protection equipment
- Machine safety
- Measuring instruments
- Medical devices
- Gas appliances
- Agricultural & forestry tractors
- Cosmetics
- Quick frozen foods
- Flavorings
- Food emulsifiers
- Extraction solvents
- Food preservatives
- Infant formula
- Jams
- Modified starches
- Fruit juices
- Food inspection
- Definition of spirited beverages & aromatized wines
- Coffee extracts & chicory extracts
- Food additives
- Materials & articles in contact with food
- Tower cranes (noise)
- Household appliances (noise)
- Tire pressure gauges
- Hydraulic diggers (noise)
- Detergents
- Liquid fertilizers & secondary fertilizers
- Lawn mowers (noise)
- Medicinal products & medical specialities
- Radio interferences
- Earthmoving equipment
- Lifting and loading equipment

New rules for harmonizing packing, labeling, and processing requirements

- Ingredients for food & beverages
- Irradiation
- Extraction solvents
- Nutritional labeling
- Classification, packaging, and labeling of dangerous preparations
- Food labeling

Harmonization of regulations for the health industry (including marketing)

- Medical specialties
- Pharmaceuticals
- Veterinary medicinal products
- High-technology medicines
- Implantable electromedical devices
- Single-use devices (disposable)
- In-vitro diagnostics

Changes in government procurement regulations

- Coordination of procedures on the award of public works & supply contracts

- Extension of EC law to telecommunications, utilities, and transport
- Services

Harmonization of regulation of services
- Banking
- Mutual funds
- Broadcasting
- Tourism
- Road passenger transport
- Railways
- Information services
- Life & nonlife insurance
- Securities
- Maritime transport
- Air transport
- Electronic payment cards

Liberalization of capital movements
- Long-term capital, stocks
- Short-term capital

Consumer protection regulations
- Misleading definitions of products
- Indication of prices

Harmonization of laws regulating company behavior
- Mergers & acquisitions
- Trademarks
- Copyrights
- Cross-border mergers
- Accounting operations across borders
- Bankruptcy
- Protection of computer programs
- Transaction taxes
- Company law

Harmonization of taxation
- Value added taxes
- Excise taxes on alcohol, tobacco, and other

Harmonization of veterinary & phytosanitary controls
- An extensive list of rules covering items such as:
  - Antibiotic residues
  - Bovine animals and meat
  - Porcine animals and meat
  - Plant health
  - Fish & fish products
  - Live poultry, poultry meat, and hatching eggs
  - Pesticide residues in fruit & vegetables

Elimination and simplification of national transit documents and procedures for intra-EC trade
- Introduction of the Single Administrative Document (SAD)
- Abolition of customs presentation charges
- Elimination of customs formalities & the introduction of common border posts

Harmonization of rules pertaining to the free movement of labor and the professions within the EC
- Mutual recognition of higher education diplomas
- Comparability of vocational training qualifications
- Specific training in general medical practice
- Training of engineers
- Activities in the field of pharmacy
- Activities related to commercial agents
- Income taxation provisions
- Elimination of burdensome requirements related to residence permits

---

Source: Business America, August 1, 1988, p. 7.

The ability to compete in a continental scale market and to avoid duplication of administrative procedures, production, marketing, and distribution systems will offer great advantages.

A unified EC market can offer tremendous opportunities to U.S. companies, both those located in Europe and those exporting. At the same time, however, U.S. companies may face tougher competition from their European counterparts (see International Marketing Highlight 5.3).

U.S. company sales in the twelve-nation European Community are over $600 billion, almost four times greater than sales to Japan. Achieving a single EC internal market should mean greater economic growth for Europe, which, in turn, will bring increased demand for American products. In addition, the uniformity of trade and financial regulations will allow U.S. companies easier access to all the EC countries by eliminating the need to meet national registration requirements in each country. This will mean that a product or service that meets the EC requirements in one member state can then be freely marketed throughout the European Community. U.S. industries will thus be able to reach a greater number of European consumers at a lower cost.[14]

The 1992 program deals with three general objectives: the removal of physical barriers, the removal of technical barriers, and the removal of fiscal barriers through standardization of value added tax (VAT) rates and excise taxes.

The removal of physical barriers would eliminate the present regulations and procedures that give rise to such border controls as vehicle safety checks or animal and plant inspections. One important aspect of the program, and one with an immediate impact, was the adoption as of January 1, 1988, of a Single Administrative Document, which eliminates the need for duplicative customs documents for goods shipped to and within the European Community.

Perhaps the most significant aspect of the program from the point of view of U.S. industry will be the directives related to the removal of technical barriers. EC directives mandate the creation of uniform EC industrial standards, the opening of public procurement procedures, the removal of restrictions on trade in services and capital movements, and stricter guidelines against barriers to competition (see International Marketing Highlight 5.4).

The Europe 1992 program has been progressing on time, although there have been a variety of hindrances relative to the national interests of member nations. As a matter of fact, the 1991 historic accord on monetary and political union is a milestone that will transform the way Europe does business. The European Community's twelve government leaders launched a monetary union that will give Europe its own currency and central bank by the end of the century.[15] Like its precursor, the 1986 Single Europe Act, which paved the way for free trade within the EC after 1992, the accord promises to become a powerful force for even closer economic and political integration. The new European Currency Unit, or ECU, has the potential to become a strong rival to the dollar in international finance and trade.

The peaceful revolution that swept Eastern Europe in 1989 is one of the most significant global events of the past forty-five years. The EC and its member

International Marketing Highlight 5.4

Factors Determining Europe 1992's Effect on Marketing

There are four key imperatives that affect marketing strategy in a regional economy. These are: customer factors, business factors, corporate factors, and political factors. The first two, customer factors and business factors, combine to determine the potential of EC-wide marketing. The remaining two factors capture the readiness of the firm to adapt to 1992. The potential and readiness together ascertain the strategic thrust of the business. The marketing implications result from the strategic thrust of the business.

1. Customer Factors
   a. Usage patterns (culturally vs. functionally defined; diverse interest between users vs. concentration and/or networking of users; reflect traditional vs. new habits)
   b. Product images (local vs. national vs. global)
   c. Market development (local vs. concentrated vs. mass market)
   d. Product specifications (local vs. uniform)
   e. National identification (high vs. low)
   f. Communication process (high vs. low language content)
   g. Customer loyalty (high vs. low)
   h. Customer concentration (high vs. low)
   i. Segmentation criterion (geographic vs. pan-European lifestyle)
   j. Parallel importing (low vs. high)
2. Business Factors
   a. Scale economies (personal contact with customer necessary vs. mass communication possible; strong distribution outlets with resistance to change vs. integrated distribution network; complex channels with multiple layers vs. simple channels; labor-intensive manufacturing with high variable cost vs. asset-intensive with high fixed cost; low value added vs. high value added product; local sourcing vs. global sourcing; difficult to transport vs. easily transportable; stable technology vs. short life cycle; easily acquired technology vs. protected/proprietary technology; low vs. high R&D content)
   b. Nature of product (tailor-made vs. commodity like; old vs. new product)
   c. Access to distribution (local vs. universal)
   d. Profit economics (cost-benefit relationship of EC-wide marketing)
   e. Competitive advantage (low vs. high)
   f. Product benefits (local vs. universal
   g. Industry concentration (low vs. high)
   h. Emergence of new channels (low vs. high)
   i. Availability of media (low vs. high)
   j. Development of new media (low vs. high)

3. Corporate Factors
   a. Managerial talent (country-oriented management vs. multinational experience)
   b. Management orientation (risk-averse bureaucrats vs. professionals)
   c. Financial resources (weak vs. strong)
   d. Access to outside funding (narrow/illiquid financial market vs. easy access to capital)
   e. Existing commitments (low vs. high commitments to labor, stockholders, third parties)
4. Political Factors
   a. Product standards (national vs. EC)
   b. Media standards (national vs. EC)
   c. National interest (low vs. high stakes in business because of national security or trade balances, etc.)
   d. Political importance (low vs. high)
   e. "Fortress Europe" mentality (high vs. low)

Source: Subhash C. Jain and John K. Ryan Jr., "A Normative Framework for Assessing Marketing Strategy Implications of Europe 1992," *Journal of Euro-Marketing,* Vol. 1. Nos. 1/2, 1991, pp. 194–195.

states are uniquely placed to help their Eastern neighbors on their way to democracy. The EC, with more than thirty years of experience in bringing small and medium-size nations together in an economic unit, also serves as a model for bringing market-driven economic policies to the eastern part of the continent.

From the modest business that EC countries conducted with Eastern European nations, the contacts grew rapidly between 1988 and 1990 with the conclusion by the EC of trade and cooperation agreements with Hungary, Czechoslovakia, Poland, Bulgaria, and Romania.

But the rapid pace of events in Eastern Europe has also forced the EC to develop additional new responses. These so-called first-generation agreements are modest instruments with which to meet the challenge of helping the emergence of democracy and market economies in Poland and Hungary and the rest of Eastern Europe.[16] The Eastern European nations, of course, aspire to eventual membership in the EC. But this may not work out until their economies are strong enough to compete with more-developed nations.

European Free Trade Association (EFTA) The European Free Trade Association was formed in Stockholm in 1959 after a series of negotiations among those Western European countries that for one reason or another did not join the European Economic Community. (Great Britain, for example, had certain arrangements with Commonwealth countries that hindered joining the EEC.) Austria, Denmark, Norway, Portugal, Sweden, Switzerland, and the United Kingdom were the original seven members of the EFTA. Finland (as an associate) and Iceland joined later. Denmark and the United Kingdom ceased to be members in 1973 after joining the Economic Community.

The EFTA has been less ambitious than the EC in its endeavors toward economic integration. The EFTA agreement, achieved in 1966, called for progressive abolition of internal tariffs on nonagricultural products. The EFTA also removed quantitative import quotas. Organized as a free trade area, the EFTA agreement did not require members to enforce common external tariffs.

The EFTA agreement has led to an impressive increase in trade between the member countries. Its effect on external trade, however, was limited. Great Britain's withdrawal upon joining the Common Market caused EFTA's role to decline substantially. This was inevitable because the United Kingdom accounted for about half of EFTA's trade.

The twelve-nation European Community, the world's largest trading bloc, and the seven-member European Free Trade Association agreed in October 1991 to form a new common market, to be known as the European Economic Area. The agreement (after it is approved by each of the nineteen national parliaments) would allow for the free flow of most goods, services, capital, and people among its nineteen member nations and should go into effect just as a single regional market is formed by the EC on January 1, 1993.[17]

The agreement also paved the way for several new countries to seek full membership in the EC, which is rapidly moving toward social and political, as well as economic, integration. Of the seven members of EFTA, Sweden and Austria have already applied to join the EC, and Finland may do so soon, while Switzerland, Norway, Iceland, and Liechtenstein are still undecided.

Council for Mutual Economic Assistance (CMEA) In 1949 communist countries, led by the Soviet Union, formed the Council for Mutual Economic Assistance (sometimes called the Council of Mutual Economic Cooperation or COMECON) to coordinate trade and promote economic cooperation. Before it was disbanded as of January 1, 1991, CMEA's membership included Bulgaria, Czechoslovakia, East Germany, Hungary, Mongolia, Poland, Romania, the Soviet Union, Cuba, and Vietnam.

The CMEA was formed more as a political group than as an economic association. It was organized and tightly controlled by the Soviet Union.

Although some trade gains were recorded among its member nations, CMEA did not promote economic integration through product specialization in any significant way. This may be partly attributed to the fact that foreign trade among the centrally planned economies had been looked upon as a means of balancing shortages and surpluses generated by the domestic sector.

In general, market agreements require free trading unhindered by government controls to be effective. But in centrally planned economies, foreign trade is handled by state trading organizations; therefore, it has been difficult to figure out if an economic agreement has any effect. There is no way to find out if exports are subsidized or imports are accepted for strictly economic considerations.

This problem aside, COMECON boasted that it provided one-fourth of the world's industrial output. In 1984, COMECON members produced 35 percent of the natural gas in the world, 32 percent of the crude steel, and 32 percent of the bituminous coal. In other industrial products like chemicals, paper, and many consumer goods, COMECON's share in world output was a little over 20 percent.[18]

Africa

Influenced by the EC, a number of African countries have attempted to draw up market agreements in order to benefit from economic integration and cooperation. There are several major African market groups. The Afro-Malagasy Economic Union was formed in 1974 with Cameroon, Central African Republic, Chad, Congo-Brazzaville, Dahomey, Ivory Coast, Mali, Mauritania, Niger, Senegal, Togo, and Burkina as members. The East Africa Customs Union was formed in 1967 with Ethiopia, Kenya, Sudan, Tanzania, Uganda, and Zambia as members. The West African Economic Community (WAEC) was established in 1972 with Ivory Coast, Mali, Mauritania, Niger, Senegal, and Burkina as its member countries. The Maghreb Economic Community consisting of Algeria, Libya, Tunisia, and Morocco was formed. The Economic Community of West African States (ECOWAS) also was created with Benin, Cape Verde, Gambia, Ghana, Guinea, Guinea-Bissau, Ivory Coast, Liberia, Mali, Mauritania, Niger, Nigeria, Senegal, Sierra Leone, Togo, and Burkina as members.

Despite the fact that there are many market agreements in force in Africa, they have had no significant effect in promoting trade or economic progress because most African nations are small and have no economic infrastructure to produce goods to be traded among themselves. These nations depend to a very large extent on imports from developed countries. In return they export minerals and other natural resources. Even where natural resources, such as petroleum in the case of Nigeria, have brought monetary wealth, lack of mass education and economic experience has inhibited capitalizing on market agreements.

The Economic Community of West African States (ECOWAS) is a recent attempt by sixteen African countries to seek economic cooperation for their mutual advantage. The agreement called for complete economic integration by 1992. However, Nigeria accounts for almost two-thirds of the community's exports, and its latest economic woes, created by a decline in oil prices, have hindered smooth achievement of the goal of full integration.

Latin America

Of all the developing areas of the world, Latin America has struggled the longest for the benefits of economic integration and cooperation. Market agreement attempts have been made to have certain countries specialize in certain industries, such as textiles, metal working, or shoe manufacturing, in order to derive benefits of scale and experience. The United States has played a major role in helping Latin American countries with market agreements. Yet overall the low level of economic activity and the political instability in the region have repeatedly been stumbling blocks.

There are four major market agreements in operation in Latin America: (1) the Latin American Integration Association (formerly called the Latin American Free Trade Association or LAFTA), (2) the Central American Common Market, (3) the Andean Common Market, and (4) the Caribbean Community and Common Market.

The Latin American Free Trade Association (LAFTA), originally formed in

1960, was renamed the Latin American Integration Association (LAIA)[19] via the Treaty of Montevideo in August 1980. Its members are Argentina, Brazil, Chile, Mexico, Paraguay, Peru, Uruguay, Colombia, Ecuador, Venezuela, and Bolivia. LAFTA was the first attempt at economic cooperation among Latin American countries, but its large membership has hampered its effectiveness. The fact that some member countries (Argentina, Brazil, Chile, Mexico, and Venezuela) are economically more advanced than others, like Uruguay and Bolivia, has made it difficult to make agreements for free trade among themselves.

The Central American Common Market, comprised of Costa Rica, El Salvador, Guatemala, Honduras, and Nicaragua, was established in 1960. Its scope was more limited, and the countries, which are essentially on the same level of economic development, have found it mutually beneficial to implement the agreement.

The Andean Common Market was created in 1969 by Bolivia, Chile, Colombia, Ecuador, Peru, and Venezuela as a subgroup of LAFTA.[20] Chile is no longer a member, while Panama holds associate status in the group.

The Caribbean Community and Common Market (CARICOM) was formed in 1968. Its original members were Barbados, Guyana, Jamaica, Trinidad and Tobago, Antigua, Dominica, Grenada, Montserrat, St. Kitts-Nevis-Anguilla, St. Lucia, St. Vincent, and Belize.

Asia

Asia is a vast continent with a large population. In the past, meager industrial development combined with the diversity and size of the region gave little reason for market arrangements. But Japan and the Pacific countries, Australia and New Zealand, along with the United States and Canada, may enter into some sort of market arrangement. In fact, these countries created the Pacific Basin Economic Council to encourage intraregional trade, but it failed to develop into a market agreement.

In Southeast Asia, however, the emerging countries of Indonesia, Malaysia, the Philippines, Singapore, and Thailand have made a first attempt at establishing a market agreement. With these countries as members, the Association of South East Asian Nations (ASEAN) became operational in 1978. Brunei became a member later. The association seeks closer economic integration and cooperation through the establishment of complementary industries and investment incentives to nonmember countries. Although the group initially had setbacks in meeting its goals, it now shows slow progress.[21]

The ASEAN countries cover a total land area of more than three million square kilometers and have a combined population of nearly 300 million. They produce 85 percent of the world's natural rubber, 83 percent of its palm oil, 67 percent of its tin and copra, and 60 percent of its copper, along with substantial quantities of sugar, coffee, timber, various tropical fruits, and minerals. The area has substantial sources of food and energy, a large sea territory, and vast forest areas. Aside from its abundant natural resources, the region is a developing market with strong potential demand for consumer goods, capital goods, and technical skills. ASEAN's members include some of the world's fastest-growing economies, with projected GNP expansion of up to 6 percent annually.[22] In the 1990s, the region could emerge as a new center of world economic power because it is expanding not only more rapidly than other developing areas but also twice as fast as the industrialized countries. With such potential, the ASEAN region offers many attractive opportunities to U.S. exporters, investors, and service businesses.

The Indian subcontinent region, with a population of over one billion people, provides another possibility for a regional market group. In December 1985, seven nations of the region (India, Pakistan, Bangladesh, Sri Lanka, Nepal, Bhutan, and Maldives) put aside their differences and launched the South Asian Association for Regional Cooperation (SAARC). SAARC's initial purpose has been limited to cooperation in noncontroversial areas such as agriculture, rural development, telecommunications, postal services, transport, science and technology, meteorology, tourism, and sports. Important elements like the formation of a common market or a free trade zone have been omitted. However, even a small beginning in this region augurs well for the future, since there is a vast potential for mutually beneficial economic cooperation and growth.

Countries in the Arab region have already made some progress in making market agreements. Several market groups are operating there. One of these is the Arab Common Market (ACM) formed in 1964 with Egypt, Iraq, Kuwait, Jordan, and Syria as members. This group planned to achieve free internal trade within ten years, but it has not yet achieved this goal. External tariffs are likely to be regulated sometime in the 1990s.

The Regional Cooperation for Development (RCD) represented a new kind of regional agreement. It was created in 1964 among Iran, Pakistan, and Turkey for the purpose of undertaking such projects as the building of a hydroelectric dam to serve the entire region. Unlike other market agreements, this agreement did not provide for free trade between member nations or for the setting of common external tariffs, yet it did have a regional economic base and its aims were to benefit regional market potential. With the fall of the Shah of Iran, however, RCD virtually ceased to exist.

U.S.–Canada Free Trade Agreement

On January 2, 1988, President Reagan and Prime Minister Mulroney of Canada signed the U.S.–Canada Free Trade Agreement (FTA). This historic agreement represents the culmination of efforts stretching back more than one hundred years. FTA was designed to strengthen an already extensive trading relationship and enhance economic opportunity on both sides of the common border.

Each year the United States and Canada exchange more goods and services than any other two countries in the world. Bilateral trade in goods and services exceeded $200 billion in 1991. The elimination of tariffs and most other barriers to trade between the two countries under the FTA will increase economic growth, lower prices, expand employment, and enhance the competitiveness of both countries in the world marketplace.

While the FTA does not eliminate all trade problems between the United States and Canada, it does provide a consultative framework within which these problems can be managed before they create serious economic and political friction. Predictably, industries in both the United States and Canada can expect to undergo some structural readjustment in the years ahead to adapt to changing market conditions. However, the less-restricted trade permitted by the FTA will spur both the American and Canadian economies to higher growth rates, increased efficiency, and improved competitiveness with other trading partners.[23]

The FTA is fully consistent with U.S. and Canadian obligations under the General Agreement on Tariffs and Trade (GATT). It does not lessen commitments to achieve multilateral trade liberalization. Rather, it establishes useful precedents for such negotiations and encourages worldwide trade liberalization.

The agreement came into force on January 1, 1989. The two governments have established a joint Canada–U.S. Trade Commission to oversee its implementation. A secretariat in each capital (Washington, D.C., and Ottawa) is the principal government office responsible for that country's implementation of the agreement. In the United States, government agencies plan to continue seeking the views of business and industry as the FTA is implemented, including the possible expansion of the scope of the agreement.

The agreement contains provisions covering virtually every trading sector. The following is a summary of these provisions.

A. Management of Trade

Tariffs: Eliminates all tariffs on U.S. and Canadian goods by 1998. Some tariffs were removed immediately while the others will be phased out over five to ten years.

Rules of Origin: Rules of origin define goods eligible for FTA treatment and prevent "free riding." Goods wholly produced in the United States or Canada qualify for FTA treatment. Goods containing imported components qualify if sufficiently transformed to change tariff classification. In some cases there is an additional requirement that 50 percent of the cost of manufacturing be in the United States or Canada.

Customs: Ends customs user fees for goods and most duty drawback programs (in which importers have duty rebated) by 1994 for bilateral trade; ends duty waivers linked to performance requirements by 1998 (except for the Auto Pact; see following page).

Quotas: Eliminates import and export quotas unless consistent with GATT or explicitly grandfathered (allowed to remain in place) by the FTA.

National Treatment: Reaffirms GATT principle preventing discrimination against imported goods.

Standards: Prohibits use of product standards as a trade barrier and provides for national treatment of testing laboratories and certification boards.

Emergency Action: Allows temporary import restrictions in limited circumstances to protect domestic industries harmed by increased imports from the other country.

B. Agriculture and Industry

Agriculture: Eliminates all bilateral tariffs and export subsidies and limits or eliminates quantitative restrictions on some agricultural products, including meat. Eliminates Canadian import licenses for wheat, oats, and barley when U.S. crop price supports are equal to or less than those in Canada. Increases Canadian poultry and egg import quotas. For twenty years, allows tariffs on fruits and vegetables to be reimposed to protect the domestic market if prices fall below the five-year average.

Energy: Prohibits most import and export restrictions on energy goods, including minimum export prices. Requires any export quotas designed to enforce either short-supply or conservation measures to ensure continuation of the historical proportionate share of resources. Provides for Alaskan oil exports of up to 50,000 barrels per day to Canada under certain conditions.

Autos: Replaces eligibility rule for duty-free Auto Pact imports into the United States with tougher FTA rules of origin. (Most auto trade is already duty free under the 1965 U.S.–Canada Auto Pact.) FTA continues Auto Pact and programs allowing pact-qualified companies to import duty-free into Canada but does not allow new firms to qualify for pact membership. Permits U.S. auto and parts exports that meet the FTA rule to enter Canada at FTA tariff rates, which will be reduced to zero by 1998. Ends by 1996 Canadian non-Auto Pact production-based duty remission programs (under which producers pay less duty for automotive imports into Canada for meeting Canadian production requirements) and export-based programs for 1998 (those based on exports to the United States ended on January 1, 1989).

Wine and Distilled Spirits: Removes most discriminatory pricing and listing practices against wine or spirits imported from the other country. Prohibits new restrictions on beer.

Softwood Lumber: Preserves the 1986 memorandum of understanding with Canada on lumber pricing practices of Canadian provinces.

Cultural Industries: Exempts industries such as publishing, broadcasting, and films. However, if this exemption results in practices that restrain trade (otherwise inconsistent with the FTA), the injured party may take measures of equivalent commercial effect without resort to dispute settlement.

C. Services

Government Procurement: Expands the size of federal government procurement markets open to competitive bidding by suppliers from the other country.

Services: Precludes discrimination by either government against covered service providers of the other country when making future laws or regulations (transportation services are excluded).

Business Travel: Facilitates cross-border travel for business visitors—investors, traders, professionals, or executives transferred within the company.

D. Investment and Financial Services

Investment: Provides national treatment for establishment, acquisition, sale, conduct, and operation of businesses (exempts transportation). Commits Canada to end review of indirect acquisitions by U.S. companies and raises the threshold for review of direct acquisitions in most sectors to C$150 million (constant 1992 Canadian dollars). Bans imposition of most performance requirements (i.e., local content, export, import substitution, and local sourcing requirements) imposed on foreign investments.

Financial Services: Exempts U.S. bank subsidiaries from Canada's 16 percent ceiling on Canadian domestic banking assets held by foreign banks. Ends Canada's foreign ownership restriction on U.S. purchases of shares in federally regulated financial institutions. Assumes that reviews of applications by U.S. firms for entry into Canadian financial markets will be on the same basis as applications for Canadian firms. Permits banks in the United States to underwrite and deal in debt securities.

E. Resolving Disputes

General Dispute Settlement (except for cultural industries—publishing, broadcasting, film, etc.—financial services, countervailing duty, and antidumping cases): establishes a binational commission to resolve disagreements; allows for arbitration if the parties desire.

Dispute Settlement for Countervailing Duty and Antidumping Cases: Countries will continue to apply existing national laws, but court review of administrative agency determinations in either country will be replaced by a binational panel. The panel will apply the same standards and scope of review as would the relevant court.

Economists recognize that a quantitative assessment of the impact of the U.S.–Canada Free Trade Agreement on the U.S. economy as a whole is premature given the agreement's ten-year phase-in period and the fact that Canada's economy is only one-tenth the size of the U.S. economy.[24] Yet despite the economic downturn, the agreement is contributing to the increased flow of trade and investment between the U.S. and Canada (see International Marketing Highlight 5.5). In the future, our exports to Canada should accelerate as Canada's economy resumes stronger growth.

Much of the activity between the two countries so far occurs close to the border. In Washington state, Minnesota, New England, and upstate New York, there is increased investment from the Canadian side. As the agreement matures, other areas also are likely to feel the positive impact of the agreement. On the Canadian side, high labor costs, taxes, and interest rates, combined with the strong Canadian dollar, are creating distortions. Although some people blame the free trade agreement for their economic conundrum, overall there is optimism that in the long run it should be good for the country.[25] Some sources, in and out of the government, credit the agreement for softening the recession's effects on the Canadian economy.[26]

A North American Common Market—A Possibility

While Europe is marching toward economic integration, there are signs of increasing economic cooperation in North America as well. The U.S.–Canadian trade agreement is a step in that direction.

The idea of greater trade liberalization in North America has long appealed to liberals and conservatives alike. Some even dream of the eventual creation of a North American common market. The improved economic efficiency resulting

International Marketing Highlight 5.5

Success in Open Markets

The U.S.–Canada Free Trade Agreement has already achieved a number of notable successes in facilitating trade in investment:

Accelerated Tariff Removal. U.S. and Canadian companies are anxious to move to free trade, as has been demonstrated by the number of industry petitions to remove bilateral tariffs faster than specified in the agreement. Based on industry requests, the tariffs on some 400 products, accounting for almost $6 billion in bilateral trade, were removed in April 1990. Additional petitions are being considered for the second round of accelerated tariff elimination.

Standards Simplification. Under the agreement umbrella and through the efforts of the private sector, progress has been achieved in harmonizing standards. For example, twelve Canadian and U.S. standards have been combined to form one single binational heating and air conditioning standard. Now the manufacturers can produce only one standard; in addition, consumers have wider product selection at lower cost.

New Government Procurement Opportunities. Since implementation of the agreement, more than 200 additional Canadian government contracts, totaling nearly $13 million, have been awarded to U.S. companies of all sizes. Without the agreement, these contracts would not have been open to U.S. exporters.

Because of the agreement, Americans and Canadians are discovering new ways to work together in business, tourism, education, and the environment. For example, a New Brunswick manufacturer of file folders recently began buying paper stock from a U.S. company in Raleigh, North Carolina. Canadian tariffs on paper, previously as high as 25 percent, have been reduced by 60 percent, making American products more price competitive.

Source: Business America, April 8, 1991, p. 4.

from a North American economic agreement would surround the United States with a ring of prosperous countries better able to purchase U.S. goods and provide the United States with valuable products. Moreover, it would strengthen U.S. security by bolstering Mexico's economy and lessening the risk of wrenching political instability.

But the advantages to our neighbors are also great—freer access to the world's largest market and more capital investment and technology from the United States. In many respects, the countries complement each other well.

Canada, a sophisticated industrial economy, is resource-rich and population-poor. With only seven people per square mile, it has one of the world's lowest population densities—hardly a limitless market of new products. Mexico, a debt-ridden, developing country, desperately needs investment, technology, exports, and other economic spurs to growth. But it has an abundance of oil and people. Its population is growing rapidly, and the number of potential new workers is rising much faster than the number of jobs the economy is generating.

The United States needs resources, and, increasingly, it needs workers. Because of a sharp decline in the birth rate that started in late 1960s, the U.S. work force will grow by about 1 percent a year in the 1990s, down sharply from the 2.5 percent annual rate in the late 1970s. And, of course, the United States needs more markets for its exports.

A dialogue for creating a free trade area encompassing all of North America was begun on February 5, 1991, when the presidents of the United States and Mexico and the prime minister of Canada announced their intention to begin negotiations on a North American Free Trade Agreement (NAFTA). Successful negotiation of such an agreement would create the world's largest free trade area, comprising more than 360 million people with a combined annual output of $6 trillion.

After months of intensive study, all three governments concluded that a North American Trade Agreement will promote economic growth through expanded trade and investment. The benefits of continental free trade will enable all three countries to meet the economic challenges of the decades to come.

The staged elimination of barriers to the flow of goods, services, and investment, coupled with strong intellectual property rights protection (patents, trademarks, and copyrights), would benefit businesses, workers, farmers, and consumers. NAFTA would be a catalyst for economic growth and development in all three countries by increasing trade and investment, and the jobs that support them.[27]

Over the past several years, Mexico's trade and investment climate has changed dramatically, creating a congenial environment for NAFTA. The government has taken a variety of steps to deregulate the economy, thus raising business confidence (see International Marketing Highlight 5.6). A NAFTA would mean even greater access to the dynamic and growing Mexican market through the further reduction and eventual removal of tariffs and import permits, a more open services and investment regime, and the protection of intellectual property rights. U.S. business would enjoy a competitive advantage, free from tariffs and other barriers that would still apply to other competitors.

The nature of the two economies means that U.S.–Mexico trade, capital, and technology flows tend to be complementary and play to each country's comparative advantages. Industrial components, semimanufactured goods, and tropical products that U.S. and Canadian producers and consumers need are made in Mexico. U.S. producers sell machinery, capital goods, high-technology equipment, and temperate climate vegetables to Mexico.

By and large, the United States, Canada, and Mexico are not direct competitors in the same products. As a recent U.S. International Trade Commission study concludes, it is unlikely under a NAFTA that there would be wide-scale increases in imports in direct competition with U.S. production.

Indeed, our industries are becoming more integrated. Mexico has diversified its exports away from reliance on petroleum, and U.S. trade patterns have also

International Marketing Highlight 5.6

Mexico's Economic Reforms

Mexican President Salinas has implemented stunning economic reforms, raising business confidence and making the Mexican economy more open and competitive. The government budget deficit declined from 16 percent of gross domestic product (GDP) in 1987 to 4.3 percent in 1990. Inflation has fallen from 160 percent in 1987 to around 30 percent in 1990. Mexico's real GDP grew 3.9 percent in 1990, outpacing population growth for the third year in a row.

Far-reaching changes have improved many areas important to business. More than twenty-five areas of the Mexican economy have been deregulated, including trucking and many financial services. Mexico has sold or closed over 600 state-owned companies. In 1989, Mexico made substantial reforms in its rules for foreign investment, providing greater transparency, increased foreign participation, and greater efficiency in the application process. Now many sectors are expressly open to 100 percent foreign ownership.

Mexico joined the General Agreement on Tariffs and Trade (GATT) in 1986. Prior to this, Mexico's tariffs had been as high as 100 percent and licenses were required for virtually every import. As part of its accession to the GATT, Mexico bound its tariffs to a ceiling of 50 percent. Since then Mexico has unilaterally reduced its tariffs to a maximum of 20 percent and eliminated import licenses for most products. The current average applied tariff on U.S. goods is about 10 percent—comparable to Canadian tariffs before the U.S.–Canada FTA.

The result of these market openings is that U.S. exports to Mexico have doubled, growing from $12.4 billion in 1986 to $28.4 billion last year. Our agricultural exports totaled $2.5 billion in 1990, making Mexico our third-largest market. Consumer goods exports from the United States to Mexico have tripled, rising from $1 billion to $3 billion. Capital goods exports went from $5 billion in 1986 to $9.5 billion in 1990.

Source: Business America, April 8, 1991, p. 4.

been changing. The U.S.–Mexico relationship was once characterized by U.S. purchases of raw materials and sales of finished manufactures. In 1980, only 35 percent of Mexico's exports were manufactures; by 1990, this had increased to 75 percent. Clearly, the trading relationship is maturing.[28]

The way the three economies complement each other allows for greater room for growth and efficiency gains from free trade. Increasing economic ties through a NAFTA would result in net growth for the three partners.

Free trade agreements have promoted growth for the European Community, Australia, and New Zealand, among others. Even when trade agreements occur between economies with different levels of development, the net result has been positive. The accession of Greece, Spain, and Portugal to the European Community did not depress real wages within the EC. In fact, during the 1980s, real manufacturing wages rose in the Federal Republic of Germany, France, and the

United Kingdom by at least 20 percent. EC programs have resulted in the continued lowering of barriers to trade and investment and prompted a renewal of economic and job growth.

A North American Free Trade Agreement, which is expected to be concluded by 1996, will power the region's economic growth, productivity, and global competitiveness into the twenty-first century.

Other Forms of Agreements

We have discussed the important types of market agreements extant among nations in different regions of the world. In addition to these, various nations have made a variety of other arrangements for their economic benefit. For instance, four different forms of agreement are the Commonwealth of Nations, the Commonwealth of Independent States, commodity agreements, and producer cartels. Although the Commonwealth of Nations was mentioned in relation to political unions, it is not strictly speaking a political union. The only political bond among the Commonwealth nations existed in the past when they constituted part of the British Empire. In addition, commonality is hindered by the fact that the nations are geographically dispersed and represent different economic, political, and cultural perspectives. Yet the group survives. On the economic front, the member nations accord one another preferential treatment by agreeing to import from each other on a selective basis. Still, this situation has changed greatly since its beginnings in the post–World War II period, partially on political grounds and partially in response to individual economic interest. In particular, Great Britain's entry into the Common Market caused a decline in the economic role of the Commonwealth. Currently, the Commonwealth of Nations mainly provides member countries the opportunity to gather around a table on an annual basis in order to review matters of mutual concern. This format enables members to become acquainted with particular issues and later arrange mutually beneficial agreements if they desire.

The Commonwealth of Independent States (CIS) is a confederation of eleven countries that were previously part of the Soviet Union.[29] The shape that this agreement will ultimately take is difficult to say since its scope is not clear, but there is little doubt that it would be dominated by Russia, which has half of the former superpower's people and most of its resources and industrial base.

Some people are skeptical that the CIS will survive long. Most of the member republics, especially Ukraine, are deeply suspicious of Russian intentions. If the CIS does succeed, it could be a useful vehicle for smoothing economic reforms. The keys to its chances are whether Russia's President Yeltsin can overcome other republics' suspicions of Russia and whether he can improve living standards quickly. For reforms to forge ahead, he must persuade fellow CIS leaders to go along with a set of coordinated measures, such as synchronized price increases, mobility of labor, a free-trade system, and a unified monetary policy.

Another significant type of market agreement is the ***commodity agreement.*** Some have been entered into under the auspices of GATT to stabilize the price of commodities such as textiles, coffee, olive oil, sugar, tin, cocoa, and wheat. The underlying purpose of commodity agreements, which are made between producing and consuming countries, has been to prevent excessive price fluctuations that would be detrimental to the developing countries. Many of these countries are economically dependent on one commodity or another for economic health. This dependence does not fluctuate, as prices can, because of supply and demand conditions. For example, poor weather conditions in a producing country might spoil its crop and thus limit supply. Demand goes up and down in response to economic conditions in the consuming countries. Commodity agreements help producing countries receive stable earnings from the export of their commodities, while consuming countries are assured of adequate supplies of particular commodities.[30]

The term *producer cartel* refers to a unilateral agreement among producers of a commodity, or suppliers of a natural resource, to deal collectively as a group with the buyers for purposes of trading the commodity. The producer cartel became a popular mode of economic cooperation among producers of strategic commodities after the success of the OPEC petroleum cartel. Since 1975, a number of producer cartels have been organized by countries exporting bauxite, phosphate, chromium, rubber, and copper. However, it is unrealistic to expect other producer cartels to duplicate OPEC's record.

Interestingly, OPEC was established in 1960 and existed for over twelve years before exerting significant influence. As a matter of fact, between 1961 and 1972, the per-barrel price of Middle East crude oil went up slowly from $0.75 to $1.40. But by 1975, it soared to more than $10 per barrel and continued to climb to a high of $40 per barrel in 1980. But oil is a special commodity in two ways. First, its supply deeply affects patterns of life in developed countries, and second, a small number of countries in a hostile region of the world control a large part of world oil resources. Despite these facts, in early 1983 OPEC appeared to be losing its grip on world oil prices. The big 1,200 percent surge in oil prices since 1973 fundamentally changed the world energy picture. But the world adjusted—OPEC's higher oil prices encouraged conservation, fuel-switching, and more petroleum production outside OPEC's control. And to an extent, OPEC set off a worldwide recession. All in all, OPEC helped cripple oil demand so that crude oil prices dropped from about $40 per barrel to less than $12 in early 1988. Although the price rose again, to $17 a barrel in 1990, it may decline in the 1990s depending on political developments in the Middle East.

Summary

In the post–World War II period nations came to realize that the task of economic reconstruction and expansion could be achieved more smoothly through cooperation among governments. The cooperation took two forms: global and regional. Global cooperation was reflected in steps such as the establishment of the World Bank, the International Monetary Fund (IMF), and the General Agreement on Tariffs and Trade (GATT). Chapters 2 and 3 examined these efforts.

Regional cooperation took the form of economic integration through market agreements among nations in geographical proximity to each other. Five types of market agreements are free trade area, customs union, common market, economic union, and political union. Market agreements are based on commonality of interest among nations. For example, Third World countries share the common objective of economic development. Likewise, political systems and culture may influence nations to enter into economic cooperation. However, geographic proximity turns out to be the basis for market agreements more often than any other reason for cooperation. It is natural because, other things being equal, nations located in the same region are usually influenced by common social and economic environments.

Historically, the economic cooperation among nations that influences governments today first emerged in Europe. Six European countries—former West Germany, France, Italy, the Netherlands, Belgium, and Luxembourg—agreed to form what is popularly called the European Common Market or the European Community. Its example was followed by the establishment of market agreements in other parts of Europe and elsewhere throughout the world.

From the marketing viewpoint, the importance of market agreements lies in the potential generation of markets. Inasmuch as mass production can be justified only by mass markets, market agreements boost industrial development and economic activity. For example, the Common Market is about equal in size to the U.S. market. Thus, certain economies of scale, which previously could not be achieved in Western Europe, are now feasible as a result of the formation of the Common Market.

Review Questions

1. What factors lead nations to work toward economic integration?
2. What role did the United States play in the establishment of the European Economic Community?
3. Why did Great Britain not join the EEC at the time of its creation, but do so later?
4. List the differences between the arrangements of a free trade area and a customs union.
5. Is economic integration workable among Third World nations?
6. Examine why Japan might be hindered in establishing a market agreement in the Pacific region on the basis of your general knowledge of the factors that promote such arrangements?
7. In what way is the unification of the European market in 1992 likely to benefit U.S. businesses?

Endnotes

1. "Common Marketing for the Common Market," *Forbes*. July 1, 1972, p. 23. *Also see* John Drew, "European Markets: A Business Overview," *Europe,* July–August 1984, pp. 18–19.
2. "IBM Finds a Club that Doesn't Want it as

a Member," *Business Week,* February 11, 1985, p. 42.

3. Stefan H. Robock and Kenneth Simmonds, *International Business and Multinational Enterprises,* 2nd ed. (Homewood, IL: Irwin, 1983), p. 149. *Also see* "EC Backs French Ban on Japanese TV Sets," *The Asian Wall Street Journal Weekly,* March 9, 1981, p. 2.
4. Ruel Kahler, *International Marketing* (Cincinnati, OH: Southwestern Publishing Co., 1983), pp. 348–349.
5. Lawrence Ingrassia, "As Spain Joins the EC, Its Shielded Industries Get Ready for a Shock," *The Wall Street Journal,* October 14, 1985, p. 1: "The Haggling that May Stall Spain and Portugal's Entry into the EC," *Business Week,* May 28, 1984, p. 54.
6. *See* "What Bilateral Deals Mean for Trade," *The Economist,* February 6, 1988, p. 63.
7. Etienne Cracco and Guy Robert, "The Uncommon Common Market," in Ronald C. Curham, *1974 Combined Proceedings* (Chicago: American Marketing Association, 1975), p. 601.
8. *See* Bela Balassa, *The Theory of Economic Integration* (Homewood, IL: Irwin, 1961), pp. 1–21.
9. *See* Jack N. Behrman, "Transnational Corporations in the New International Economic Order," *Journal of International Business Studies,* Spring–Summer 1981, pp. 29–42.
10. R. Lipsey, "The Theory of Customs Unions: A General Survey," *Economic Journal,* vol. 70 (1960), pp. 496–513.
11. D. Swann, *The Economics of the Common Market* (Harmondsworth, England: Penguin Books, 1970).
12. "Lomé IV Convention," *Development Forum,* May–June 1989, p. 20.
13. Francine Lamoriello, "Completing the Internal Market by 1992: The EC's Legislative Program for Business," *Business America,* August 1, 1988, pp. 4–7.
14. Patrick W. Cooke and Donald R. Mackay, "The New EC Approach to Harmonization of Standards and Certification," *Business America,* August 1, 1988, pp. 8–9. *Also see* W. Free Brant, "The EC Single Internal Market: Implications for U.S. Service Industries," *Business America,* August 1, 1988, pp. 10–11; and Kevin Cote, "1992: Europe Becomes One," *Advertising Age,* July 11, 1988, p. 46.
15. "One Big Currency—And One Big Job Ahead," *Business Week,* December 23, 1991, p. 40.
16. "A New Economic Miracle," *Business Week,* November 27, 1989, p. 59.
17. Alan Riding, "Europeans in Accord to Create Vastly Expanded Trading Bloc," *The New York Times,* October 23, 1991, p. A1. *Also see* "Tearing Down Even More Fences in Europe," *Business Week,* November 4, 1991, p. 50.
18. *See* "COMECON's Crumbling Credit-Worthiness," *The Wall Street Journal,* September 18, 1985, p. 31.
19. *See* "New Latin American Association Carries on Traditions of LAFTA," *Business America,* April 6, 1981, p. 15.
20. "A Common Market of Sorts," *The Economist,* February 19, 1983, p. 25.
21. "ASEAN: Whatever For," *The Economist,* October 7, 1989, p. 40.
22. George Paine, Linda Droker, and John Sitnik, "ASEAN Economic Dialogue Returns to Washington," *Business America,* February 1, 1988, p. 2.
23. Alan Freeman, "Free-Trade Pact Creates Winners, Losers," *The Wall Street Journal,* February 7, 1989, p. A20.
24. "North American Free Trade Agreement: Generating Jobs for Americans," *Business America,* April 8, 1991, pp. 3–5.
25. Bernard Wysocki, Jr., "Canada Suffers Exodus of Jobs, Investment, and Shoppers to U.S.," *The Wall Street Journal,* June 20, 1991, p. 1.
26. Ann Reilly Dowd, "Viva Free Trade with Mexico," *Fortune,* June 17, 1991, p. 97.
27. *Business America,* April 8, 1991, pp. 3–5.
28. "Is Free Trade with Mexico Good or Bad for the U.S.," *Business Week,* November 12, 1990, p. 112.
29. "How Long Can Yeltsin Hold It All Together?" *Business Week,* January 13, 1992, p. 49.
30. Steve Mufson, "Third World Pleas on Commodity Prices Get No Sympathy in Developed Nations," *The Wall Street Journal,* October 2, 1985, p. 34.

Cases

Case 5: EQ Bank

On October 20, 1988, Michael Banks, political risk manager of EQ Bank in New York, was approached by Daniel Whitman, president of Enviro-systems, to arrange financing for the construction of a refuse recycling facility to be built in Senegal, Africa. This project called for shipping human refuse from the eastern seaboard of the United States to the West African country where the labor-intensive job of sorting would take advantage of the lower wage rate. The bulk of the refuse was to be sorted into recyclable components such as metals, glass, and plastics; the remainder was to be shredded, sterilized, and then seeded with a bacteria to ferment into a clean compost that would be superior to the local African soil. The human waste and some of the refuse was to be combined to produce methane. Both end products would be sold locally.

Banks was now preparing for a meeting, on November 15, 1988, with Joseph Gergacz, vice president of EQ's venture capital fund management division to discuss procedures for the project.

EQ Bank

EQ Bank, established in 1975, deals primarily in Africa. EQ Bank is a private non-deposit bank whose personnel see themselves as deal makers. They buy and sell a wide variety of African products, for both import and export. They also find buyers and suppliers for African manufactures and provide financial services and capital. Their variety of clients include private businesses, state-owned firms, governments, and international agencies that deal with Africa.

The company is divided into EQ Trade, EQ Aviation, EQ Capital Markets, and EQ Bank. These four units can operate separately or in concert depending on the needs of the client.

The import-export trade division is based on the belief that Africa's future depends on advanced technology and improving methods of production. To this end EQ Trade helps by providing a conduit for knowledge as well as products. It also encourages worldwide purchases of African products. They are manufacturers' agents for mining equipment (drills, bores, dump trucks, heavy earth moving machinery), surface transportation (fishing vessels, oil-field service vessels, railway locomotives and rolling stock, buses, commercial lorries, tractor-trailers), and commercial and general aviation (new and used aircraft, aircraft parts, ground service). They offer financial support in the form of supplier credit lines, short-term bridge financing, and currency hedging. They also act as consultants giving advice on markets, product information, and economic development assistance agency packages. The latter involves products that qualify for special treatment under bilateral or multilateral institutions providing grant or concession financing for development projects.

EQ Aviation is a worldwide network of airplanes, parts, and aviation services. Its personnel can provide the equipment to operate an airport and the expertise to form an airline.

EQ Capital Markets provides general managerial, financial, and technical skills in support of a wide variety of economic and business activities in Africa. Personnel in this division advise on mergers, acquisitions, divestitures, and joint ventures. They often counsel senior executives of African government ministries, financial institutions, state-owned enterprises, and private firms. They help corporations expand capital, structure debt and equity, and, in general, work to present the enterprise to the financial markets effectively and efficiently.

Through its affiliation with the Hong Kong Bank Group and other contacts in financial centers, EQ Capital Markets works to match capital with worthwhile projects in need of funds. It is also working to establish financial institutions in Africa.

Through its close relationship with African finance ministers and commercial banks, EQ Capital Markets is in an ideal situation to participate in debt-for-equity and debt-for-debt swaps—a practice personnel like to call debt arbitrage.

EQ Bank is the original EQ company. This merchant banking division concentrates most of its activities in trade and capital equipment financing. It is a registered Bahamian bank, and its personnel pride themselves on being able to create a variety of specialized financing structures tailored to specific client needs. They offer a variety of offshore banking services, including foreign currency exchange, hedging, interest rate futures, and interest rate swaps, all performed under the Bank Secrecy Act of the Bahamas.

The projects at EQ Bank were given to teams that had specific knowledge on the business aspects as well as a strong background in the region of Africa involved. With respect to the refuse conversion project, Banks worked with a Senegal and an Ivory Coast national. They were required to report their progress to their superior; however, when questioned on reporting procedures, Banks stated that he "reports occasionally, and sometimes not at all."

Banks had spent two years in the Peace Corps after graduating from Stanton College with a degree in philosophy. He then earned a master's degree in international affairs from Columbia University. After working for Chase Manhattan Bank for sixteen months, he returned to his undergraduate university and taught for one year. He then came to EQ Bank, and has been there for almost two years. He is a humanitarian and always stresses how he and his company are in business to help Africa, not just to make money.

The Rubbish

Currently the United States is producing 200 million tons of rubbish per year and it is disposed of by either landfill, incineration, or recycling. Burying is the cheapest and accounts for 90 percent of American disposal; however, this is likely to decrease in the future. Americans are voting to keep the smelly dump sites away from their homes and environmentalists are constantly campaigning to eliminate them altogether. Environmentalists are armed with many cases of poisoned land—completed dump sites where the rubbish is producing methane, thus making the land unusable.

Landfill sites are also being exhausted. One-third have closed since 1980, and more than half the cities on the East Coast will exhaust their sites by 2000. In New York fourteen sites have closed in the past ten years and now most of the city's 24,000 tons of trash per day is put into the Fresh Kills landfill on Staten Island. This site produces 5 million cubic feet of methane per year, enough to heat 50,000 homes. As landfill sites fill up, municipalities have looked to other locations. The notorious garbage barge, the Mobro, publicized this crisis when it spent two months in the summer of 1987 meandering around the Caribbean looking for a dump site for its 3,100 tons of New York's trash before returning home with it.

Incineration has the advantage of reducing the rubbish to ash, greatly decreasing the volume, and generating energy that by law, the local utility must buy. At this time there are several domestic American companies operating profitable incineration plants.

The major drawback to incineration is pollution. The smoke plume can contain hydrogen chloride and dioxin if the smokestack is not equipped with expensive scrubbing equipment. This added cost increases the incinerator's burning charge by almost 50 percent. However, not all states require such equipment and many believe that in the long run this will give incinerators a black eye. Also, the ash, which still must be disposed of, often contains dioxin and heavy metals. The introduction of these contaminants can be reduced with an extensive sorting of the input but this, too, is very expensive.

In other parts of the world recycling is a major solution to the problem of rubbish disposal. In Japan, for example, more than half of the waste paper is recycled and in Germany nearly 40 percent of the glass is recycled. Yet Americans only recycle 28 percent of their aluminum, 27 percent of their paper, and 10 percent of their glass. This seems to be a product of capitalism, as the sale of recycled material will not pay for the cost of collecting and reprocessing it in a free market.

The cost of landfills is estimated to be from \$40 to \$60 dollars per ton and incineration is between \$70 and \$120 per ton. This implies that a net gain to society would occur if a subsidy of up to \$40 per ton were made—potentially a politically dangerous move. But even if such a subsidy were granted, recycling only affects specific components and is only as effective as the consumers make it.

The newest approach to disposal problems comes from companies like Enviro-systems. Their system of converting rubbish into fertilizer by shredding, sterilizing, and seeding the waste with bacteria is already in use in France, producing 800,000 tons a year, and another plant in Pompano Beach, Florida, will open soon.

The Project

The people at Enviro-systems estimate that with the cheaper labor in Africa they will be able to collect, transport, and process rubbish for \$70 per ton. This low cost is due mainly to the wage rate in Senegal, which is approximately \$10 per day.

Senegal was selected not only for its low wage rate but also because it had a relatively stable dictatorship government that had been in power for the past twenty years. Furthermore, the country was in an economic decline, so the prospect of employing 700 to 800 people should outweigh the undesirable aspects of foreign rubbish processing.

The beauty of recycling is that the accepting country is paid to receive rubbish from municipalities and private collection agencies as well as being paid for the recycled product.

Enviro-systems estimates that it will require \$25 million to build the collection site in the United States and the facility in Africa, which will have a 4000 ton per day capacity. They would also like to purchase a 10,000 ton vessel for transporting the rubbish. They believe the project will be very profitable; in fact, they predict making \$378 million over the first six years.

The demand for fertilizer and methane in Africa is quite strong, and even though other disposal techniques are being explored, their impact on the demand for disposal is expected to be minimal. If the system is operational soon and the company lands some long-term contracts, the profit predictions may be fulfilled.

EQ Bank's Problem

To obtain financing EQ Bank must first convince the host country, Senegal, that the project will be beneficial to its society and not harmful to its environment. To help in this, Banks was trying to get endorsements from environmental organizations such as Greenpeace and the EPA. As a backup and bartering chip, he was also looking at nearby countries that would be acceptable.

EQ Bank then had to convince lenders of the viability of the project. Banks was planning to solicit funds from the World Bank, a very conservative donor group. In order to get funds from the World Bank, Banks knew that he would need to prove the soundness of the project both financially and environmentally, especially the latter. This aspect worried Banks, who did not have a technical background and was not quite sure what to look for or how to prove the system's safety. This is where the competition comes into play.

The Competition

Many of the large investment banking houses on Wall Street saw refuse recycling projects as a means to accomplish two goals. First, as the statistics presented above illustrate, there is a growing demand for this kind of facility, and investment bankers saw this project as a new niche in the market. They were working to develop a small staff of experts who understood the problems associated with installing such a facility and with environmental legislation, lobbying, and environmental engineering.

Secondly, this was an ideal opportunity to improve their public image. With all the negative publicity coming out of the insider trading scandals, firms like the former Drexel Burnham were eager to be involved in projects that were considered to be in the best interest of the country.

The Meeting

It is now the beginning of November, and Banks and his cohorts have approximately two weeks to formulate a strategy and gather the appropriate data to support it.

Case 6: Chiangmai Parasol Ltd.

*I*n September 1988, Maew Premprung received an order from a German restaurant chain to deliver 5,000 sun umbrellas before the end of the year. When she agreed on price and delivery conditions in June 1988, she had no idea that she might not even break even on this order. The price quoted in June, baht 1000 ($40 U.S.) per sun umbrella, CIF Hamburg, would at that time have realized a healthy profit. After checking the additional shipping, insurance, and packing costs of 200 baht per sun umbrella, she realized she might have made a mistake.

This case is printed here from *Selected Asian Cases of Small and Medium-Sized Enterprises in Export Marketing* (Geneva: International Trade Center UNCTAD/GATT, 1989).

Company Background

Chiangmai Parasol Ltd. was one of four sun-umbrella companies in the Chiangmai region of Thailand. The company was founded by Maew Premprung's father in 1939, and, being the only child, she had carried on the management of the company after her father's death in 1979. The company had originally been an enterprise operation out of her house; all of her sun umbrellas were distributed by a local retailer. When retail trade started to boom in 1980 due to the increasing popularity of Chiangmai as a tourist location, she decided to relocate her factory along one of the principal thoroughfares of Chiangmai. Soon her factory became a popular attraction for tour buses. Tour guides cooperated with her because she gave them a 10 percent commission on business generated by tour groups. The tourists would roam around the factory watching how the wooden handles were machine-turned and the bamboo was split in spokes by an electric slicer, and how the mixer stirred and blended the paint. This gave her factory a museum-like quality and added learning value to the umbrella's price. A special attraction was watching the hand painting of the umbrella's top, which allowed for creative input by the tourist thereby creating the image of a "custom-made" product. The closer contact of the tourist trade with her factory had led to a large amount of impulse-buying business. Allowing the customer to select and purchase a picture-like drawing and seeing his or her choice transferred to the umbrella's top by an artist had led to spiraling demand.

Problem Areas

Besides the present boom in business, Maew Premprung had learned from the economic downturn of 1982–1983 that her business was very dependent on the tourist trade. "No tourism, no business," was the saying of the president of the Chamber of Commerce. He had suggested extending her product line and moving more toward the production of larger sun umbrellas for restaurants and brandname carrying companies. He had further suggested that she should contact potential foreign customers directly and thus switch from indirect exporting through a middleman to direct exporting to the user.

Another idea, which she had picked up from a local workshop on export marketing, was to produce sun umbrellas that displayed foreign scenes such as the Eiffel Tower in Paris, the Statue of Liberty in New York, or even big sporting events like the Boston Marathon or the Wimbledon tennis tournament. The assumption was that people who visit these places or watch these events would be motivated to buy a sun umbrella as a souvenir.

Besides her sun umbrella line, many customers had suggested that she diversify into hand-painted umbrellas. One inherent disadvantage of producing only sun umbrellas was that European and American tourists bought her sun umbrellas simply as souvenirs as they did not have any functional purpose in the Northern hemisphere. One German customer had told her that of the five sun umbrellas she bought, all of them would be given away to friends in Bangkok because of the sun umbrellas' incompatibility with the cold German climate. The lack of functional value of her sun umbrellas to most foreign tourists had made her worry for a long time. Too much dependency on her customer's discretionary buying power had made the sun umbrella business very cyclical.

Maew Premprung had also introduced hand-painted lampshades and wall paper, but without much success. Umbrellas would represent a good alternative to sun umbrellas. However, these would contribute a reduced profit margin as the synthetic fabric for the umbrella had to be imported from Taiwan. Her sun umbrella tops were made of pressed paper covered with resin or wax. This material would not be durable in a rainy climate such as that in Germany.

Maew Premprung also worried about the rain-proofness of her biologically based dyes. She had not engaged in product testing to assess the color strength under different types of rainwater, ranging from acid-rich in the German Ruhr area to the salty type in many coastal areas of Europe.

When C. Kaufman, the German chain store manager, visited her factory, she was thrilled by his interest to place an order for large sun umbrellas for his restaurant chain. The order represented a breakthrough into sun-protection sun umbrellas with an opportunity to maintain her standard mark-up. More important, the order reflected a functional, rather than a discretionary, purchase. She figured that if she did a good job, more business could come her way from the restaurant sector as she had the unique ability to

EXHIBIT 1 Profit and Loss Account for the Year ending December 31, 1987 (in baht)

Sales	1,874,226
Cost of goods sold (variable including labor)	821,939
Gross margin	1,052,287
Fixed expenses	
Salaried retail saleswomen	26,154
Administrative expenses (owner's salary, electricity, vehicles, communication, machinery, repairs and maintenance, accountancy and legal assistance, bank charges, insurance, depreciation, sundries)	143,539
Lease-back charges (factory and store)	10,312
Financial charges	3,172
Local welfare obligations	10,000
Workers' profit participation fund	50,295
Total fixed expenses	243,472
Gross profit for the year	808,815

customize each umbrella's painting according to each customer's wishes. Specific promotional trademarks, brandnames, slogans, or scenes could be hand painted. It had become clear to her that foreigners regarded this as "art" and were most appreciative of her company's skills.

Maew Premprung looked again at her previous year's profit and loss statement ending 31 December (see Exhibit 1) and studied her fixed and variable costs. Could she afford to accept the order?

Case 7: International Machine Corporation

International Machine Corporation (IMC) manufactures food-processing and packaging equipment. IMC's revenues in 1983 amounted to $12 billion, of which 45 percent was generated outside the United States. IMC has subsidiaries in twenty-three countries and licensing arrangements in eight others.

IMC management was contemplating the establishment of a subsidiary in Mexico where it was thought that demand was sufficient for their product and that the local market and economy were expanding and would be receptive to such an investment. IMC had exported products to Mexico for several years. Before proceeding to invest money in the Mexican project, IMC wanted to determine the financial reliability of the project. IMC's president, Charles Furtell, asked Lewis Harvey, vice president of the International Division of the company, to work out a detailed financial analysis of the project. At his request, IMC's controller's office had supplied Harvey with considerable information.

Annual inflation was projected at 20 percent in Mexico and 10 percent in the United States. The current exchange rate, $1 for 22 pesos, was

This case is printed here with the permission of the authors, Vinod Bavishi of the University of Connecticut, and Hany A. Shawky of the State University of New York at Albany.

expected to remain fixed over the life of the investment.

Initial Investment

It was estimated that it would take one year to purchase and install plant and equipment.

Imported machinery and equipment would cost $9 million. No import duties would be levied by the Mexican government. With a small allowance for banking fees, the bill would come to 200 million Mexican pesos.

The plant would be set up on government-owned land, which would be sold to IMC for 20 million pesos.

IMC planned to maintain effective control of the subsidiary with ownership of 60 percent of equity. The remaining 40 percent was to be distributed widely among Mexico's financial institutions and private investors. Accordingly, IMC needed to invest $6 million U.S. in the project.

Working Capital

The company planned to maintain 5 percent of each year's sales as a minimum cash balance.

Accounts receivable were estimated to be seventy-three days of annual sales.

Inventory was estimated to be 20 percent of the following year's sales.

Accounts payable were estimated to be 5 percent of the year-end inventory.

Other payables were estimated to be 5 percent of sales for the current year.

Licensing and overhead allocation fees were to be paid annually at the end of the year.

Sales Volume

Sales volume for the first year was estimated to be 200 units.

Selling price in the first year was estimated to be 1,400,000 pesos per unit.

Sales growth of 10 percent was expected during the project life.

An annual price increase of 20 percent was contemplated.

Cost of Goods Sold

The U.S. parent company was expected to provide parts and components adding up to 180,000 pesos per unit in the first year of operation. These costs (in U.S. dollars) were expected to rise on an average of 10 percent annually, in line with the projected U.S. inflation rate.

Local material and labor costs were expected to be 420,000 pesos per unit, with an annual rate of increase of 20 percent.

Manufacturing overhead (without depreciation) was expected to be 28 million pesos the first year of operation. An average annual rate increase of 15 percent was expected.

Depreciation of manufacturing equipment was to be computed on a straight-line basis, with a project life of ten years and zero salvage value to be assumed.

Selling and Administrative Costs

Variable selling and administrative costs were expected to equal 10 percent of annual sales. These costs were likely to be incurred within Mexico and were expected to rise at 20 percent annually.

Semi-fixed selling costs were expected to equal 5 percent of annual sales. These costs were estimated to rise at 15 percent annually.

Licensing and Overhead Allocation Fees

The parent company would levy 70,000 pesos per unit as licensing and overhead allocation fees, payable at year-end in U.S. dollars.

This fee would increase 20 percent per year to compensate for Mexican inflation.

Interest Expense

Local borrowing could be obtained for working capital purposes at 15 percent. Borrowing would occur at the end of the year with the full year's interest budgeted in the following year.

Any excess funds could be invested in Mexican marketable securities with an annual rate of return of 15 percent. Investment was likely to be made at the end of the year, with the full year's interest to be received the following year.

Income Taxes

Corporate income taxes in Mexico were 42 percent of taxable income.

Withholding taxes on licensing and overhead allocation fees were 20 percent.

The parent company's effective U.S. tax rate was 44 percent, which was the rate used in analyzing investment projects. It could be assumed that the parent company could take appropriate credits for taxes paid to, or withheld by, the Mexican government.

Dividend and Terminal Payments

No dividend was planned to be paid for the first three years.

Dividends equal to 70 percent of earnings would be paid to the shareholders, beginning in the fourth year.

It was assumed that, at the end of the tenth year of operation, IMC's share of net worth in the Mexican subsidiary would be remitted in the form of a terminal payment.

Loss of Export Sales

At present, IMC was exporting about twenty-five units per year to Mexico. If IMC decided to establish the Mexican subsidiary, it was expected that the after-tax effects on income due to the lost exports sales would be $648,000, $742,000, and $930,000 in the first three years of operation, respectively.

IMC assumed it could not count on export sales for more than three future years, as the Mexican government was determined to see that such machinery was manufactured locally in the near future.

PART • 3

Environmental Factors Affecting International Marketing

CHAPTER • 6

Economic Environment

CHAPTER FOCUS

After studying this chapter, you should be able to:

- Describe the macroeconomic and microeconomic environment
- Examine the effect of the economic environment on marketing strategy
- Analyze the economic environment of a country
- Appreciate the emerging opportunities in developing countries

This chapter deals with the phenomenon of economic environment. In most cases, economic environment can be viewed from two different angles: the macro view or the micro view. From a macro view, people's wants and needs and the economic policy of a country establish market scope and economic outlook. A microenvironmental view focuses on a firm's ability to compete within a market.

Different countries provide varying market potential with respect to population. But potential per se does not mean that there is a realizable opportunity for any given firm. For example, a low level of economic activity in a country may force most people there to live modestly. In such a country, many goods and services taken for granted in the United States are truly luxuries. In addition, even if there is a market, the competition from both existing and other potential businesses may make it difficult for a new firm to establish itself. In brief, the economic environment of a country, both from the macro and micro viewpoints, largely defines the marketing opportunity for international business. The economic environment of the home country, to an extent, also influences marketing overseas. For example, the economic perspectives of the United States will have an effect on the international activity of U.S. firms.

This chapter begins with an examination of the factors that compose macro- and microeconomic environments. This explanation is followed by an illustration of the economic environment's impact on international marketing strategy. Finally, a framework for measuring economic potential and conducting opportunity analyses is furnished.

Macroeconomic Environment

A country's economy includes sources of domestic livelihood and the allocation of resources. Because not all of the world's economies operate at the same level of efficiency, it is necessary to form a clear idea of the economic situation of a particular host country in order to make adequate marketing decisions.

Population and Income

The most basic information to be considered is about the nature of the population, because the people, of course, constitute the market. Table 6.1 shows the population of different countries of the world, but population figures alone provide little information, since people must have the means in terms of income to become viable customers. Thus, Table 6.1 also shows population combined with per capita GNP, providing an estimate of consuming capacity. An index of consuming capacity depicts the absolute or aggregate consumption, both in the entire world and in individual economies. The consumption rate can be satisfied either domestically or through imports.

The information in Table 6.1 should be interpreted cautiously because it makes no allowances for the differences in the purchasing power of different countries. The point may be illustrated with reference to Thailand. Although its per capita GNP is lower than that of the U.S., the Thai bhat goes much further than the dollar. For example, one dozen eggs cost only \$.79 in Bangkok, while in New York they cost \$1.15; an apartment rents for \$950 in Bangkok, while

TABLE 6.1 Consuming Capacities of Selected Countries

COUNTRY	POPULATION*	PER CAPITA GNP†	INDEX OF CONSUMING CAPACITY‡
United States	248.8	20,910	5,202.4
Japan	123.1	23,810	2,931.0
Germany	62.2	20,440	1,271.3
France	56.2	17,820	1,001.4
United Kingdom	57.2	14,610	835.6
Italy	57.5	15,120	869.4
Canada	26.2	19,030	498.5
India	832.5	340	283.0
Australia	16.8	14,360	241.2
Brazil	147.3	2,540	374.1
Mexico	84.6	2,010	170.0
Sudan	24.5	330	8.0
The Netherlands	14.8	15,920	235.6
Belgium	10.0	16,220	162.2
Argentina	31.9	2,160	68.9
Switzerland	6.6	29,880	197.2
South Africa	35.0	2,470	86.4
Denmark	5.1	20,450	104.2
Philippines	60.0	710	42.6
Turkey	55.0	1,370	75.3
New Zealand	3.3	12,070	39.8
Peru	21.2	1,010	21.4
Israel	4.5	9,790	44.0
Ecuador	10.3	1,020	10.5
Uganda	16.8	250	4.2
Honduras	5.0	900	4.5
Paraguay	4.2	1,030	4.3

* *World Bank Report,* 1991. Figures in millions.

† *Statistical Abstract of the United States: 1991* (Washington, D.C.: U.S. Department of Commerce). Figures in U.S. dollars.

‡ Per capita GNP (gross national product) multiplied by total population in billions.

the rent for an equivalent apartment in New York is $1,680; the taxi fare for a five-mile ride in New York and Bangkok comes to $8.12 and $1.83, respectively.[1]

Two conclusions are obvious, however: (1) aggregate consuming capacity depends on total population as well as per capita income, and (2) advanced countries dominate as potential customers. In Chapter 1 it was noted that the U.S. multinational corporations are mainly active in Western Europe, Japan, and Canada. The reason for this is not difficult to find. In contrast, despite a large population, Bangladesh does not offer a realizable market potential. This is true also of other poor countries. It must be noted, however, that many countries belonging to the Third World as slowly emerging from their traditional poverty. Thus, it would be shortsighted to write them off.[2] As a matter of fact there is an interesting development taking place in the economic arena as far as the United States is concerned: Western Europe and Japan are becoming more competitive with the United States, while developing countries are becoming potential markets. Indeed U.S. exports to developing countries as a group already substantially exceed exports to its traditional trading partners.

Concept of Economic Advancement

Developing countries are becoming important markets. According to the concept of international product life cycle examined in Chapter 2, more and more developing countries may become significant markets (see International Marketing Highlight 6.1). It would be desirable for a marketer, therefore, to keep abreast

International Marketing Highlight 6.1

Grooming Markets in Developing Countries

Currently, Japan's Ministry of International Trade and Industry (MITI), which helped guide the postwar Japanese economic miracle, is focusing on Japan's less-developed neighbors to the south, especially Thailand, Malaysia, Indonesia, and the Philippines. MITI's economic plans for Malaysia, for example, include blueprints for new industries ranging from rubber sneakers to color-television picture tubes. The most elaborate document, written in concert with Malaysian planners, is seventy pages long and outlines, in astonishing detail, MITI's plans to make Malaysia one of the world's foremost producers of word processors, answering machines, and facsimile devices.

Always eager to study and coordinate, Japan's bureaucrats are working overtime these days on the economic transformation of the Asia-Pacific region—with the well-being of Japanese business and industry firmly in mind. Some of these grand plans exist only on paper. Yet, Japanese government aid is flooding into the region. So is Japanese private investment, in the form of factories and joint ventures.

More important than the amount of money is the methodical and sophisticated manner in which it is being spent. Far from using a case-by-case approach to foreign aid and investment, Japanese government and corporate strategists speak about shaping and even "coordinating" the economic development of the region. Implicit in this view is a division of labor. For example, as MITI sees it, Indonesia will pay special attention to textiles, forest products, and plastics. Thailand will focus on furniture, toys, and die-cast molds. And Malaysia will concentrate on sneakers, copiers, and television picture tubes.

The development strategy works like this: First, Japanese loans, mostly of government money, build up roads, bridges, and such. Second, the Japanese government sends technical experts. Third, Japanese loans filter down to industry within the Asian country, to finance joint ventures and other business alliances. Fourth, Japan opens its doors to imports from these offshore factories.

Source: Adapted from Bernard Wysocki, Jr., "In Asia, the Japanese Hope to 'Coordinate' What Nations Produce," *The Wall Street Journal,* August 20, 1990, p. 1.

of countries slowly reaching that point where market potential becomes worthwhile. Table 6.2 shows the economic status of different countries, based on GNP per capita. GNP per capita should not be relied on as the sole measure of the economic viability of a market, although it does provide a reasonable estimate of the market in cases where detailed analysis is not feasible.

Economic advancement is characterized by such factors as comparatively small allocation of labor force to agriculture; energy available in large amounts at low cost per unit; high level of gross national product and income; high levels of per capita consumption; relatively low rates of population growth; complex modern facilities for transportation, communication, and exchange; a substantial amount of capital for investment; urbanization based on production as well as exchange; diversified manufacturing that accounts for an important share of the labor force; numerous tertiary occupations; specialization of both physical and mental labor; surpluses of both goods and services; and a highly developed technology that includes ample media and methods for experiment. These factors can be utilized to examine economic standing. Needless to say, a large variety of information is needed to categorize countries on an economic development scale. For many characteristics, hard data may not be available and judgment becomes the determining factor.

As a generalization, the conditions in underdeveloped economies would be the mirror image, or reverse, of those that characterize economic advancement. This raises an interesting question. Can poor countries be converted into advanced countries through reversing the conditions that hamper economic progress? The answer to such a question is far from simple because economic development is not a simple, discrete process. Many historical, geographic, political, and cultural factors are intimately related to the economic well-being of a nation. For example, no wars have been fought on U.S. soil in the last hundred years, which to an extent helped the United States achieve its present economic greatness. The impact of this factor has been thoroughly covered elsewhere.[3]

Structure of Consumption

Nations' overall patterns of consumption can be viewed not only on the basis of potential but also on the basis of structure. While it is important to measure the volume of consumption among various cultures, nations, and societies, the characteristics of that consumption reveal its structure. Particularly conspicuous in this respect are differences in emphasis. Depending on economic factors, a country may have to emphasize producer goods over consumer goods. Also, what are considered necessities in one economy may be luxuries in another. In addition, consumption in most advanced countries is characterized by a higher proportion of expenditures devoted to capital goods than consumption in poor countries, where substantially more is spent on consumer goods.

However, proportionate expenditures for producer goods within a given economy are only moderately high if that economy enjoys the benefits of past (preferably long-term) capital accumulation. When a less-developed economy decides to become technically and economically more advanced, an extraordinary percentage of national income must be diverted to producer goods, especially if that economy is unable to attract substantial amounts of foreign currency in the

TABLE 6.2 Groups of Economies*

LOW-INCOME ECONOMIES	LOWER MIDDLE-INCOME	UPPER MIDDLE-INCOME	HIGH-INCOME ECONOMIES
Afghanistan	Argentina	Brazil	Australia
Bangladesh	Bolivia	Czechoslovakia	Austria
Benin	Chile	Gabon	Belgium
Bhutan	Colombia	Greece	Canada
Burkina	Costa Rica	Hungary	Denmark
Burma	Cuba	Iran	Finland
Burundi	Cyprus	Iraq	France
Central African Rep.	Dominican Rep.	Libya	Germany
Chad	Egypt	Oman	Hong Kong
China	El Salvador	Portugal	Ireland
Ethiopia	Guatemala	Republic of Korea	Israel
Ghana	Honduras	Romania	Italy
Guinea	Israel	South Africa	Japan
Haiti	Ivory Coast	Trinidad and Tobago	Kuwait
India	Jamaica	Uruguay	Luxembourg
Kampuchea, Dem.	Jordan	Venezuela	Netherlands
Kenya	Lebanon	Yugoslavia	New Zealand
Lao, PDR	Lesotho		Norway
Madagascar	Liberia		Saudi Arabia
Malawi	Mauritania		Singapore
Mali	Mongolia		Spain
Mozambique	Morocco		Sweden
Nepal	Nicaragua		Switzerland
Niger	Papua New Guinea		United Arab Emirates
Pakistan	Paraguay		United Kingdom
Rwanda	Philippines		United States
Sierra Leone	Poland		
Somalia	Senegal		
Sri Lanka	Syria		
Sudan	Thailand		
Tanzania	Turkey		
Togo	Yemen Republic		
Uganda	Zambia		
Vietnam	Zimbabwe		
Zaire			

*Countries not included in this table were not listed in the World Bank's Indicators.

Source: The World Bank, *World Development Report 1991,* (New York: Oxford University Press, 1991), pp. 204–205.

form of direct investment, loans, or other aid. This is one important reason why less-developed economies find the transition period to technical advancement so difficult.

The structural differences with regard to expenditures among nations can be explained by a theory propounded by the German statistician Engel. The ***law of consumption*** (Engel's law) states that poorer families and societies tend to spend a greater proportion of their incomes on food than well-to-do people. Table 6.3 substantiates Engel's law on a global scale. Shown is the percentage of per capita income spent for food, housing, clothing, and other purposes in selected countries. Third World countries like the Philippines and Kenya are shown to spend a larger percentage on food than countries like the United States. Further, in any country, rural people spend a larger percentage on food than urban dwellers (not shown in the table). Housing, in particular, receives a much smaller share of income in underdeveloped countries than in the advanced nations (see International Marketing Highlight 6.2).

The structure of consumption varies among developed countries too. While the average American home covers 1583 square feet and the typical European dwelling is more than 1050 square feet, Japanese families manage with 925

TABLE 6.3 **Consumption Expenditures of Selected Countries**

COUNTRY (BASE YEAR)	FOOD & BEVERAGE	CLOTHING & FOOTWEAR	HOUSING & OPERATIONS	HOUSEHOLD FURNISHINGS	MEDICAL CARE & HEALTH	TRANSPORTATION	RECREATION	OTHER*
Industrial Market Economies								
Belgium (1985)	19.7	6.8	17.7	10.7	10.6	13.1	6.6	14.8
Canada (1986)	16.2	5.7	22.4	9.7	4.2	15.8	11.3	14.7
France (1980)	19.4	6.2	17.8	8.2	10.5	6.8	8.1	13.0
Japan (1985)	20.8	6.1	18.6	6.3	10.4	10.7	10.6	16.5
Sweden (1980)	22.3	8.4	23.5	6.8	2.7	17.9	10.5	8.0
United Kingdom (1985)	21.1	6.7	18.4	7.2	1.3	18.3	10.1	17.0
United States (1980)	13.3	7.7	17.4	6.3	12.4	16.4	11.7	14.8
West Germany (1980)	23.6	8.6	19.8	9.7	3.1	16.4	10.7	8.2
Middle-Income Countries								
Mexico (1980)	37.4	8.2	12.6	12.4	4.0	9.1	5.6	10.8
Philippines (1972)	60.0	5.3	3.1	13.5	n.a.	2.3	n.a.	15.8
Republic of Korea (1985)	36.8	4.7	9.9	6.1	7.2	11.2	11.9	12.3
Low-Income Countries								
India (1980)	53.5	13.1	11.1	4.9	2.4	7.5	3.2	4.3
Kenya (1980)	n.a.							
Sri Lanka (1975)	52.7	10.1	4.2	5.5	1.3	18.3	4.1	3.9

**Other* includes expenditures for personal care, restaurants, and hotels.

n.a.: data not available.

Note: The expenditures are expressed as percentages of total consumption in constant prices.

Source: National Accounts Statistics: Main Aggregates and Detailed Tables 1988 (New York: United Nations, 1991). Table 2.6.

International Marketing Highlight 6.2

Acquiring a Vacation Spot

One CEO visited North Africa and fell in love with Morocco. Imagining frequent trips to this desert kingdom, he established a Marrakesh subsidiary for his firm, which manufactures kitchen cabinets. Unfortunately, he neglected to notice that most Moroccans don't have indoor kitchens, much less kitchen cabinets. The branch operation was a total failure. The lure of exotic climes had distorted this executive's previously sound business judgment.

Source: Charles F. Valentine, *The Arthur Young International Business Guide* (New York: John Wiley & Sons, 1988), p. 22.

square feet. The U.S. nuclear family boasts 2.2 cars on average; comparable households in the European community average 1.3 cars. In Japan, the average is 0.88. And while food costs absorb 26 percent of the typical Japanese household's income, the amount is less than 15 percent for the average American family, and about 20 percent for the Europeans.[4] As shown in Table 6.4, while the average

TABLE 6.4 Food Consumption Differences Among Nations

	FOOD MARKET AND HABITS		
COUNTRY	Per Capita Cereal Consumption (in pounds)	Per Capita Frozen-Food Consumption (in pounds)	Percent of Homes with Microwave Ovens
United States	9.8	92.4	80
Britain	12.8	48.2	43
[former] West Germany	2.0	33.4	21
Denmark	4.6	53.9	—
Sweden	—	51.7	—
France	1.1	40.5	16
Norway	—	38.3	—
Netherlands	—	34.8	8
Switzerland	—	33.2	—
Spain	0.4	—	13
Ireland	15.4	—	—
Australia	12.3	—	—
Canada	8.7	—	—
Belgium	—	—	10
Italy	—	—	3
Japan	0.2	18.6	—

Source: Kellogg Co. for cereal consumption; Birds Eye Wall Ltd. for frozen-food consumption; and GE Mintel Ltd. for homes with microwave ovens.

person in England eats thirteen pounds of cereal a year, per capita consumption in France is just one pound, and in Japan less than one-fourth of a pound. Americans eat about ten pounds of cereal each per year.

Other Economic Indicators

Population, income, and expenditure data provide basic insights into the economies of different nations. For a certain point in time, however, a variety of other aspects of economic environment may be pertinent in a given case. This economic information may be found in categories such as:

- Production indicators (such as the production of raw steel, automobiles, trucks, and electric power; crude-oil refinery runs, coal production, paperboard production, lumber production, and rail freight traffic)
- Prices (such as the price of gold, finished steel, aluminum, wheat, cotton, industrial raw materials, and foodstuffs)
- Finance (such as corporate bond yield, prime commercial paper, Eurodollar rate, money supply)
- Other indicators (such as index of industrial production, retail sales, installment credit debt, and wholesale and retail inventories)

It is not necessary for a marketer to gather information about and review all these indicators. As a matter of fact, complete information would be difficult to obtain from each and every country.[5] Thus, at any given time the choice of economic indicators to be examined is determined by the purpose of the project at hand. For example, a company contemplating manufacturing tires abroad needs to look into the foreign country's automobile and truck production data for a number of previous years as well as the data for those countries that are likely to import tires from the foreign country. A processed food manufacturer, on the other hand, would be interested in such information as inflation rate, foodstuff prices, and retail sales data. In brief, marketers should examine only those economic indicators that are relevant to their marketing decisions. Relevancy can be determined in part by the marketers' domestic operations but should also reflect the new situation in the foreign country.

Economic Systems

The economic system of a country is another important economic factor that a marketer must understand. Traditionally, there are two types of economic systems: capitalist systems and state-owned systems. The United States comes close to being a pure capitalist system. The state-owned, or Marxist, system is pursued in communist countries where all activities related to production and distribution are controlled by the state. Between the two extremes are many countries that follow mixed economic systems where certain industries are allowed to run freely while others are strictly or partially controlled.

The nature of economic systems affects the political/regulatory control of the economy. Today, the pure capitalistic system propounded by Adam Smith is a thing of the past. Even in the United States, there are some laws and conditions imposed on various businesses. The nature of these laws and other government regulations and controls will be examined in Chapter 9.

An interesting development of the recent past appears to have given rise to an economic system that is new to the modern world and links economic life with religion. Some Muslim countries have adopted a national economic perspective based on Islam. While the trend, led by Iran, is still emerging, it is difficult to say how far it will go or what impact it will have on marketers interested in doing business with Muslim countries, although insights into the Islamic type of economic system are provided by Pakistan's efforts:

> [Pakistan's] Islamization effort is understandable. Pakistan always has been fiercely Moslem [sic]. And the Koran, like the Bible, is laden with economic prohibitions, so that linking religion with economics would seem only natural.
>
> Analysts say the phenomenon may become a more frequent factor for non-Moslems to contend with in coming years. Pakistan isn't the only Moslem country to revamp its economic policies in line with Islamic teaching. Saudi Arabia also has moved in this direction, and other states are following suit. Pakistani effort contains three broad programs: The first is Zakat, a 2.5% tax on savings deposits, with the money going primarily for locally administered social programs. The levy, which went into effect last July [1981], is based on an Islamic dictum that the rich should look after their poorer brethren. The second is Ushr, a 10% tax on farm product income, scheduled to take effect soon. Officials describe the levy as the Moslem counterpart of Christian tithing, the setting aside of a tenth of one's income to the church. In a Moslem economy, the state and church are inseparable. The third is gradual elimination of interest. Although the Koran inveighs only against usury, Pakistan interprets the ban to include all forms of interest. Accordingly, interest gradually is being replaced by equity participation plans that reward investors with a share of profits.
>
> Although the effort has been slow starting, several federal financing agencies already have switched to equity-participation, and the government has begun requiring banks to offer special new savings accounts that shun interest payments in favor of shares.
>
> Details of the various provisions can be even more bewildering than the broad concepts of the plan.
>
> With the Ushr, for example, the full 10% tax applies only to irrigated land; unirrigated land, which ought to be less valuable, is taxed at only 5%. The theological rationale: yields from rain-fed land are more fully a gift from God, so the farmer ought to be grateful and return more of the profits to the state.
>
> So far, the Islamization effort is proceeding cautiously. Last year the Zakat yielded $50.8 million in new revenue, but the Ushr has been delayed, bogged down in administrative difficulties.
>
> Nevertheless, there's a good bit of skepticism about the program from both Moslem and non-Moslem analysts. Business leaders here say the Islamization measures have increased uncertainty about planning and new investment, and have added to the difficulty of doing business. And there could be more tax-cheating as some businesses seek to wriggle out of the new tax.[6]

Mutual Economic Dependence

The U.S. economy is profoundly related to the economies of other nations, particularly those of the advanced countries. The U.S. market is so large that despite its ability to supply most of its needs from domestic output, it is also a dominant factor in international trade. For example, what happens in Western Europe cannot be ignored by the United States. While there may be a time lag, happenings there are bound ultimately to affect the U.S. economy. It has been estimated that a recession in Western Europe affects the United States after a lag of about six months. Thus, when performing an economic analysis, an international marketer needs to consider the economic perspectives of the overall world economy, particularly those of its major trading partners and the host country.[7]

The depth of economic analysis varies from case to case. For example, if the enterprise concerns Saudi Arabia, economic development in the Pacific region can be discounted. On the other hand, if a project is related to Japanese industries, the economic environment in emerging countries of Southeast Asia must be reviewed.

Microeconomic Environment

Microeconomic environment refers to the environment surrounding a product and/or market of interest to a company. An examination of microenvironment indicates whether the company can successfully enter the market. Essentially the microeconomic environment concerns competition.

Sources of Competition

A U.S. company may face competition in an international market from three different sources: local business, other U.S. corporations, and other foreign companies. For example, if Chrysler Corporation were to consider entering the German market, it would compete against General Motors, Volkswagen, and Honda Motors of Japan (see International Marketing Highlight 6.3). Different competitors, however, may satisfy different types of demand: existing demand, latent demand, or incipient demand.[8] ***Existing demand*** refers to a product bought to satisfy a recognized need. ***Latent demand*** applies in a situation where a particular need has been recognized, but no products have been offered. ***Incipient demand*** describes a projected need that will emerge when customers become aware of it sometime in the future. To illustrate the point, consider demand in the computer industry. Overall, IBM may be strong in, let us say, Spain. But a firm like Next Inc. (former Apple Computer Inc. chairman Steven Job's new company) may choose to enter the Spanish market to serve *latent demand* there. This way Next Inc. avoids direct confrontation with IBM and Apple, at least in the short run.

Competition can also be analyzed by the characteristics of products. Three product categories are considered here: breakthrough products, competitive products, and improved products.[9] A ***breakthrough product*** is a unique innovation that is mainly technical in nature, such as a digital watch, a color television, or a jet plane. A ***competitive product*** is one of many brands currently available in the market and has no special advantage over the competing products. An ***improved product*** is not unique but is generally superior to many existing brands.

The nature of the competition that a company faces in entering an overseas market can be determined by relating the three types of products to the three types of demand. Upon examining the competition, a company should be able to ascertain which product/market it is most capable of pursuing. For example, let us assume Procter & Gamble is interested in manufacturing hair shampoo in Egypt and seeks entry into the emerging Arab market. The company finds that

International Marketing Highlight 6.3

Battle of Honey Nuts

After a year of planning, General Mills Inc. and overseas partner Nestlé S.A. are ready to launch their breakfast-cereal invasion of Europe. The first assault will be on France, Spain, and Portugal, with two of General Mills' biggest guns, Golden Grahams and Honey Nut Cheerios.

But Kellogg Co., which has been selling cereal to Europeans since the end of World War I, isn't waiting. In recent weeks, the company rolled out in Europe a new product called Honey Nut Loops, something it doesn't sell in the U.S.

General Mills says it isn't surprised at its archrival's preemptive effort. It will be interesting to find out what happens when Honey Nut Cheerios and the Kellogg product go head to head.

It could be a long and brutal fight. Switzerland-based Nestlé is the world's largest food company, General Mills is second only to Kellogg in cereals, and all three have enormous resources—and egos. Kellogg, which has lost market share to General Mills in the United States in recent years, isn't about to relinquish its dominance overseas. But the Nestlé–General Mills venture foresees $1 billion in sales in Europe alone by the year 2000 as it begins to live up to its name, Cereal Partners Worldwide.

Shipments of Honey Nut Cheerios and Golden Grahams soon will begin to France, Spain, and Portugal. Although Nestlé has several cereal plants in Europe, initially the two cereals will be made in General Mills's U.S. plants, then shipped in bulk to Europe for packaging at a Nestlé factory in Rumilly, France.

Source: Richard Gibson, "Cereal Venture Is Planning Honey of a Battle in Europe," *The Wall Street Journal,* November 14, 1990, p. B8.

in addition to a number of local brands, Johnson & Johnson's baby shampoo and Helene Curtis Industries' Suave shampoo are the *competitive* products in the market. Gillette has recently entered the market with its Silkience brand, which is considered an *improved* product. Most of the competition appears to be addressing the *existing* demand. No attempts have been made to satisfy *latent* demand or *incipient* demand. After reviewing various considerations, Procter & Gamble may decide to fulfill latent demand with an improved offering through its Head & Shoulders brand. Based on market information, the company reasons that a hair problem most consumers face in that part of the world is dandruff. No brand has addressed itself to that problem. Even Gillette's new entry mainly emphasizes silkiness of hair. Thus, analysis of the competition with reference to product offerings and demand enables Procter & Gamble to determine its entry point into the Arab market.

Competitive Advantage

The above analysis indicates an open space in the market for entry. But this in itself is not enough. Competitors may follow right on the heels of Procter & Gamble's entry steps. Thus, further analysis is needed to figure out the competitive advantage the company has over rivals, existing and potential. The following questions could be raised to analyze the competition:

- Who are the competition now, and who will they be in the future?
- What are the key competitors' strategies, objectives, and goals?
- How important is a specific market to the competitors, and are they committed enough to continue to invest?
- What unique strengths do the competitors have?
- Do they have any weaknesses that make them vulnerable?
- What changes are likely in the competitors' future strategies?
- What are the implications of competitors' strategies on the market, the industry, and one's own company?

While it may be relatively easy to pinpoint current competition in an international market, analysis of competition in the future is difficult because there is no way to figure out which companies from different parts of the world may become interested in the market in the future. In any event, the best way to examine competition is to draw up a demographic profile of the industry. Markets dominated by small single-industry businesses or small national competitors differ significantly from those dominated by multi-industry companies, and those in turn are different from those controlled by multinational or foreign companies.[10]

Obviously a U.S. MNC with multi-industry interests would have certain inherent strengths that a single-industry foreign national company could not match. For example, MNCs can often provide consumers with better and cheaper products or services, react faster to changing economic conditions, and more adroitly overcome or capitalize on market distortions created by governments than can national firms. These large companies have the resources to sacrifice profits in one country in order to penetrate or gain position there while using profits from another country to support this aggressiveness. They have the ability to work with governments, select the least costly source of supply, and even negotiate favorable trade concessions.

However, it is a mistake to believe that MNCs always have superior leverage. Local foreign competitors may be small, but they can be helped by their governments. For example, governments can require that foreign competitors reduce profitability in order to increase local employment levels or maintain the balance of trade. Governments can also ban a multinational firm from obtaining supplies in low-cost areas. Further discussion on the role of the government will be taken up in Chapter 8.

A simple listing of major competitors is not enough. It is also important to learn about their goals and aspirations. In fact, an attempt should be made to know competitors' total financial situations, including their serious problems as well as their advantages and opportunities.

Further, the competitors' relative strengths and weaknesses should be examined. Exhibit 6.1 lists areas to be considered in order to assess competitive strengths and weaknesses. Note that most areas of strength either are related to

EXHIBIT 6.1 Assessing Competitor's Areas of Strength

1. Excellence in product design and/or performance (engineering ingenuity)
2. Low-cost, high-efficiency operating skill in manufacturing and/or in distribution
3. Leadership in product innovation
4. Efficiency in customer service
5. Personal relationships with customers
6. Efficiency in transportation and logistics
7. Effectiveness in sales promotion
8. Merchandising efficiency—high turnover of inventories and/or of capital
9. Skillful trading in volatile price movement commodities
10. Ability to influence legislation
11. Highly efficient, low-cost facilities
12. Ownership or control of low-cost or scarce raw materials
13. Control of intermediate distribution or processing units
14. Massive availability of capital
15. Widespread customer acceptance of company brand name (reputation)
16. Product availability, convenience
17. Customer loyalty
18. Dominant market share position
19. Effectiveness of advertising
20. Quality salesforce

the excellence of personnel or are resource-based. Not all factors have the same significance for every product/market. Therefore, it is desirable first to recognize the critical factors that could directly or indirectly bear on a product's performance in a given market. For example, adequate distribution may be critical in a developing country with inadequate means of transportation and communication, while research and development might be strategic to gain the competitive edge in Western Europe.

An example of strength is provided by BMW car company. It is commonly known that selling foreign cars in Japan is not easy. Yet, in 1987, BMW sold almost 50,000 cars to the Japanese, and the number was expected to be four times as high in the early 1990s. With Japanese consumers' increasing interest in luxury cars, a new market segment has been emerging that was not being tapped by the Japanese companies. BMW took advantage of the situation. Avoiding the pitfalls that make doing business in Japan difficult, it established a comfortable niche for itself. After buying its own dealer network and expanding it, the company advertised heavily, set up a service-and-parts system, and lowered interest rates to single digits (5 percent), when consumer interest rates were 15 percent. In brief, despite the fact that Japan is a difficult market to enter, analysis of the microeconomic environment showed that BMW could successfully seek entry into the Japanese market.[11]

Japanese auto companies, in turn, have captured a major share (in 1991, approximately 30 percent) of the U.S. auto market. Let us assume Ford Motor Company decides to retaliate by exploring the possibility of entering the Japanese market. Despite all its strengths and experience in international business, however, Ford may find itself greatly constrained in its endeavors by one weakness—cost structure. Studies show that because of U.S. wage-price and managerial efficiency differentials, the Japanese companies can build a car and ship it to the United States for $2,000 to $2,300 less than it costs Detroit to produce an equivalent vehicle.[12] Thus, even if Ford were to assemble cars in Japan, other things being equal, it would still be severely handicapped because of the cost advantage of the local companies. Granted, Ford will pay lower wages in Japan, but this advantage would be wiped out by the experience that the Japanese have in Japan. In this instance, analysis of the microeconomic environment paints a discouraging picture for Ford's entry into the Japanese market.

Economic Environment and Marketing Strategy

The overall macroeconomic climate of the host country as well as the microeconomic environment surrounding the product/market has a significant effect on marketing strategy. The macroeconomic environment sets the limit of activity in different sectors of the economy. Thus, when the economy is booming, there will be plenty of jobs, consumers will be optimistic, and cash registers will ring often. In a booming economy situation, the international marketer will have more opportunity in the marketplace, although marketplace opportunities may attract new competition. But when an economy is down, unemployment may rise, interest rates may go up, sales could be more difficult to generate, and the international marketer's decisions will take a different shape.

Impact of Macroeconomic Environment

Brazil, as one of a few countries that are fast emerging into developed economies, provides a case where there would seem to be ample opportunities for U.S. international marketers. Yet during 1990 and 1991, the Brazilian economy was beset by a variety of problems that restricted the realization of opportunities there. By the end of 1988, the country had accumulated a huge external debt, over $100 billion attributed to oil imports, so that despite severe import restrictions, a record soybean crop, and excellent performance by manufactured exports, inflation ran about 250 percent during 1991. Although the economy maintained its approximate 4.8 percent annual growth rate, Brazil has severe problems. In addition, strict import restrictions limited the opportunity for exports to Brazil, and soaring inflation and falling consumer demand, attributed to Brazil's recession and delayed implementation of liberalization measures, required caution in establishing manufacturing there, since new plant construction would be costly. Further, Brazilian exports to the United States and other markets were less competitive in price. Thus, the short-run economic outlook for Brazil in 1992 appeared less than promising.[13]

Additionally, the health of an economy affects consumer confidence, which is then reflected in consumer buying plans. A favorable economic climate generates a spirit of optimism that makes consumers more willing to go out and spend money. The reverse occurs when economic conditions are unfavorable. In Brazil's case, 1990 and 1991 were not exciting years from the viewpoint of consumers. With high inflation and emphasis on exports to balance the trade deficit, Brazil's consumers had to tighten their belts.

While economic climate affects all businesses, some businesses are affected more deeply than others. International marketers should figure out the extent to which their business is susceptible to economic conditions. For example, in a depressed economy consumers tend to postpone buying durable goods. Thus, the economic environment in Brazil during 1991 seemed gloomy to consumer goods manufacturers interested in entering the market. It should be cautioned, however, that current economic environment is just one variable. Despite the fact that the short-run economic environment is less than conducive to profits, a company may enter an overseas market based on good long-term economic prospects in that economy and such other favorable factors as growing political stability or existence of low wage scales. The long-run perspective is the most important one if a firm has sufficient resources to endure waiting for the future favorable environment.

Impact of Microeconomic Environment

The following quote shows how the microeconomic environment of a product/market would affect marketing strategy:

> A very successful U.S. company, for many years a leader in its field, launched a cheaper version of its traditional product almost simultaneously in the United States and in Europe. The product design, pricing, and advertising copy—in fact, the whole marketing approach—were quite similar in both areas. The strategy was very successful at home, but in Europe sales fell far below expectations.
>
> What was the cause of the trouble? The company had neglected several significant differences between the two market areas:
>
> 1. In the United States it had a major share of the market, while in Europe it was an insignificant factor.
> 2. At home the company's product concept was in the mature phase of its life cycle, while in Europe it was at its beginning.
> 3. In the United States roughly 85% of all households knew the company and its products, whereas in Europe the awareness level was barely 5% and few consumers understood the nature of this innovative product.
> 4. As a result, the advertising copy that featured a low price without explaining the product concept was meaningful to most U.S. consumers but unsuitable for most of the European market.[14]

It is evident from this illustration that the U.S. company got into problems in Europe because its competitive strength there was meager (small market share), the product, relatively speaking, was new to the market (starting life cycle position), and the product presented an unfamiliar concept. In other words, the company did not orient its marketing program with the product/market environment existing in Europe.

Impact of the Domestic Economic Environment

While international marketers should be concerned with economic environment overseas, they should also be sensitive to economic perspectives in the United States, just as the reverse is true for domestic marketers. Thus, in appraising domestic economic development, short-run, foreign trade and international economic movements can no longer be ignored even when we are looking at the world's largest and most self-sufficient economy. Indeed, firms react to changing domestic and international economic environments and can be expected to shift their relative emphasis in promoting domestic versus foreign trade. During 1990, as the recession deepened in the United States, U.S. companies appeared to put greater stress on foreign markets than on U.S. markets. Similarly, in 1991, as the dollar fell, companies became more anxious to tap export markets. An empirical study on the subject indicated that during slack conditions in the United States, overseas markets provide a realistic alternative for maintaining business tempo. Based on his survey of 104 firms in Arkansas, Rao concluded:

> While there are wide variations as to the nature and extent of impact of the recent economic recession, more than one third of the reporting firms were adversely affected. During the recessionary period, about 40 percent of the respondents have intensified their overall export-marketing efforts. Some of the export facilitating developments such as the U.S. dollar devaluations and tax incentives have helped a number of manufacturer-exporters to expand their exports. During the recessionary period more than one third of the reporting firms have intensified their export-marketing efforts by arranging deliveries according to the needs of their customers, appointing more overseas agents and visiting overseas markets more frequently. Less than one third of the respondents have intensified various other types of export-marketing activities.[15]

Evidently, orientation toward overseas markets is somewhat related to the economic environment in the United States. This assertion is supported by the fact that in 1990 about a 12 percent share of the U.S. GNP was attributed to foreign business activity, while ten years previously it had been 5 percent.[16] Predictions regarding the U.S. economic environment in the 1990s and beyond appear to favor continuation of international business activity. Firms, therefore, should take advantage of this projection by gearing their objectives and goals toward developing appropriate foreign markets. To develop perpetual foreign markets, firms cannot simply shift gears in favor of overseas markets when something goes wrong in the domestic market, and then abandon foreign markets once the domestic economy picks up again. Such tactics are harmful to long-term market development abroad, and they damage the reputation of U.S. business.

Analysis of Economic Environments

Given the perspectives of macro- and microeconomic environment, an opportunity analysis may be performed to determine if it is worthwhile to seek entry into a foreign country's market. A conceptual scheme is helpful for analyzing economic environment in practice in order to assess marketing opportunities. The

EXHIBIT 6.2 Considerations in the Evaluation of Economic Environment

Financial Considerations

1. Capital acquisition plan
2. Length of payback period
3. Projected cash inflows (years one, two, and so forth)
4. Projected cash outflows (years one, two, and so forth)
5. Return on investment
6. Monetary exchange considerations

Technical and Engineering Feasibility Considerations

7. Raw materials availability (construction/support/supplies)
8. Raw materials availability (products)
9. Geography/climate
10. Site locations and access
11. Availability of local labor
12. Availability of local management
13. Economic infrastructure (roads, water, electricity, and so forth)
14. Facilities planning (preliminary or detailed)

Marketing Considerations

15. Market size
16. Market potential
17. Distribution costs
18. Competition
19. Time necessary to establish distribution/sales channels
20. Promotion costs
21. Social/cultural factors affecting products

Economic and Legal Considerations

22. Legal systems
23. Host government attitudes toward foreign investment
24. Host attitude toward this particular investment
25. Restrictions on ownership
26. Tax laws
27. Import/export restrictions
28. Capital flow restrictions
29. Land-title acquisitions
30. Inflation

Political and Social Considerations

31. Internal political stability
32. Relations with neighboring countries
33. Political/social traditions
34. Communist influence
35. Religious/racial/language homogeneity
36. Labor organizations and attitudes
37. Skill/technical level of the labor force
38. Socioeconomic infrastructure to support American families

conceptual scheme requires consideration of such variables as those shown in Exhibit 6.2. With the use of these variables, analysis of marketing opportunity centers on two sets of criteria: cost–benefit criteria and risk/reward criteria.*

Cost–Benefit Criteria Analysis

Cost–benefit criteria answer a series of questions that stress markets, competition, and the financial implications of doing business in a foreign country.

Markets Will people want our products? More importantly, will they want them enough to pay a price that will yield us a profit? Is the market large enough for the firm to venture in?

*Inasmuch as this chapter deals with economic environment only, the risk/reward criteria will be examined here solely with reference to economic situation. The risk/reward analysis should be extended by relating it to cultural environment (Chapter 7) and political environment (Chapter 8).

Competition What kind of competition will we have to face, and will the rules apply equally to all? Concern about equal treatment within a market comes from situations of altered marketplace. In many countries, ***altered marketplace competition*** comes from host governments, through direct ownership of competitors, subsidization, or participation. In such cases, the foreign business usually is at a disadvantage, even though it is pitted against inefficient local business, and therefore cannot compete on an equal footing.

Financial Examination How many resources (and how much of each) must be committed, and what will they cost? What return may be expected, and how long might it take to recover the investment?

Of course, there are other cost–benefit criteria. The level of training and skills of a national workforce is an important consideration, as well as the availability of educated, experienced local managers. Most MNCs have learned the value of having local or regional executives in host countries. For example, Sperry Rand Corporation in Japan shares a joint venture that is manned entirely by Japanese workers and executives.[17] In addition, transportation, the communications system, and the availability of local resources (especially energy) should be considered. This list could go on, but enough has been said to illustrate some of the assessable conceptual factors influencing market entry decisions.

Risk/Reward Criteria Analysis

The ***risk/reward criteria*** emphasize the overall constantly changing mix of situations in the social, political, and economic climates of a host country. In terms of economics, the macroeconomic characteristics of a nation will almost always affect the specific economics of business. The national economic objectives of the country, therefore, also figure in a firm's decision to explore entry there. For example, the firm needs to know how fiscal policy (the control of the nation's economy through taxes) translates into business taxation, or how income policy (wage/price guideposts) may affect wage and price controls. The firm also needs to know about a country's monetary policy (the control of the nation's economy through increasing or decreasing interest rates by the central bank; the Federal Reserve does it in the United States by establishing the rate at which commercial banks borrow from it). Does the country's policy place restrictions on international cash transactions, such as the repatriation of profits? What is the outlook, for example, for the cost and availability of credits? Is the currency strong, and, more important, what is the inflation situation?

Social/Cultural and Political Factors

Although it is convenient to categorize a country's environment into social/cultural, political, and economic aspects, they each overlap, and they all influence the intelligent analysis of any one aspect. In economic analysis, the social/cultural and political environments should be considered.

In the social area, the demographic characteristics of the population should be taken into account. The general level of education is an important indicator of the society's development, the likelihood of its accepting new ideas, and possibly, its attitude toward a foreign investor. The standard of living and the general expectations of the country tell a great deal. Is it a progressive society or a static one? Does it aspire to development, or is it frozen into old social patterns and mores? Are its expectations pragmatic or unrealistic? Class structure, where it exists, also yields information. In the past U.S. corporations too often overlooked the reality of class structure elsewhere because the idea of class structure is not well introduced in the United States. Projecting U.S. attitudes and domestic experience on other societies can create analytical problems.

The political area reflects both the social and economic situations and vice versa. However, some political aspects are particularly relevant to economic analysis:

- What kind of political system does the country have? Is it a democratic/parliamentary society? Or is it authoritarian and possibly repressive?
- Is the national leadership popular or unpopular? The answer might indicate the probability of radical change.
- By our standards, are the national policies successful or unsuccessful?
- What is the level of insurgency, if any? This might range all the way from random terror or occasional violence to guerrilla warfare or foreign supported insurgency. One of the most graphic signs of change in international business is that business must be prepared to defend itself not only economically, but also physically and ideologically in foreign countries.

If there is a common denominator of both the cost–benefit and risk/reward equations, it is stability. That is not to suggest that business should want some imposed stability at the price of reduced performance. Rather, what is desired is a reasonable level of stability in all of the areas just discussed. The aim should be to ensure that capital investment is recovered over a reasonable period, generates a satisfactory profit, and provides a base for the further expansion of international trade.

An Illustration

Decisions related to foreign market entry, expansion, and conversion, as well as phasing out from foreign markets, call for systematic frameworks for analysis, as discussed previously. Illustrated here is one method of putting a framework into practical use; other approaches are available to assess international marketing opportunities.[18] The suggested framework consists of three phases:[19]

1. Appropriate national markets are selected by quickly screening the full range of options without regard to any preconceived notions.
2. Specific strategic approaches are devised for each country or group of countries, based on the company's specific product technologies.
3. Marketing plans for each country or group of countries are developed, reviewed, revised, and incorporated into the overall corporate concept without regard to conventional wisdom or stereotypes.

Phase One: Selecting National Markets There are over 150 countries in the world; of these the majority may appear to offer entry markets. Many countries go out of their way to attract foreign investment by offering lures ranging from tax exemptions to low-paid, amply skilled labor. These inducements, valid as they may be in certain individual cases, have repeatedly led to hasty foreign market entry.

A good basis for decision is arrived at through a comparative analysis of different countries, with long-term economic environment having the greatest weight. First, certain countries, on account of their political situations (for example, Libya under Qadhafi) would be considered unsuitable for market entry. It might help to consult the index (discussed in the appendix to Chapter 8) that rates different countries for business attractiveness. The final choice should be based on the company's own assessment and risk preference. Further, markets that are either too small in terms of population and per capita income or economically too weak should be eliminated.

For example, a number of countries with populations of less than 20 million and annual per capita incomes below $2,000 are of little interest to many companies because of the limited demand potential.

The markets surviving this screening are then assessed for strategic attractiveness. A battery of criteria should be developed to fit the specific requirements of the corporation. Basically, the criteria should focus on the following five factors (industry/product characteristics may require slight modifications):

1. Future demand and economic potential of the country in question
2. Distribution of purchasing power by population groups or market segments
3. Country-specific technical product standards
4. "Spillover" from the national market (via standards, regulations, norms, or economic ties) to other markets (for example, the Andes Pact provides for low-duty exports from Colombia to Peru)
5. Access to vital resources (qualified labor force, raw materials sources, suppliers)

There is no reason to expand the list since additional criteria are rarely significant enough to result in useful new insights. Rather, management should concentrate on developing truly meaningful and practical parameters for each of the five criteria listed above, so that the selection process does not become unnecessarily costly and the results are fully relevant to the company concerned. For example, a German flooring manufacturer, selling principally to the building industry, selected the following yardsticks:

1. *Economic potential:* new housing needs, GNP growth
2. *Wealth:* per capita income, per capita market size for institutional building or private dwellings (the higher the per capita income, market volume, and share of institutional buildings, the more attractive the market)
3. *Technical product standards:* price level of similar products, for example, price per square meter for floor coverings (the higher the price

level, the more attractive the market tends to be for a technically advanced producer)

4. *"Spillover":* area in which the same building standards (especially fire safety standards) apply (for example, the U.S. National Electrical Manufacturers' Association standards are widely applicable in Latin America, and British standards apply in most of the Commonwealth countries)
5. *Resource availability:* annual production volume of PVC (an important raw material for the company)

Through these criteria, the analysis of economic potential was based on two factors: housing needs and economic base (see Figure 6.1). In specifying these criteria the company deliberately confined itself to measures that (1) could readily be developed from existing sources of macroeconomic data, (2) would show trends as well as current positions, and (3) match the company's particular characteristics as closely as possible.

Since German producers of floor covering employ a highly sophisticated technology, it would have been senseless to give a high ranking to a country with only rudimentary production technology in this particular facet. Companies in other industries, of course, would have to consider other factors—auto registrations per thousand population, percentage of households with telephones, density of household appliance installations, and the like.

The resulting values are rated, for each criterion, on a scale of one to five, so that by weighing the criteria on a percentage basis, each country can be assigned an index number indicating its overall attractiveness. In this particular case, the result was that, out of the forty-nine countries surviving the initial screening, sixteen were ultimately judged attractive enough—on the basis of market potential, per capita market size, level of technical sophistication, prevailing regulations, and resource availability—to warrant serious attention.

Interestingly, the traditionally German-favored markets of Austria and Belgium emerged with low rankings from this strategically based assessment because the level of potential demand was judged to be insufficient. Some new markets such as Egypt and Pakistan were also downgraded as offering an inadequate economic base. Likewise, even such high-potential markets as Italy and Indonesia were eliminated for objective reasons (in the latter case, the low technical standard of most products).

Phase Two: Determining Marketing Strategy After a short list of attractive foreign markets has been arrived at, the next step is to group these countries according to their respective stages of economic development. Here, the criterion of classification is not per capita income but the degree of market penetration by the generic product in question. For example, the floor covering manufacturer already mentioned grouped the countries into three categories, developing, take-off, and mature, as defined by these factors (see Figure 6.2):

1. *Accessibility of markets:* crucial for the choice between export and import production

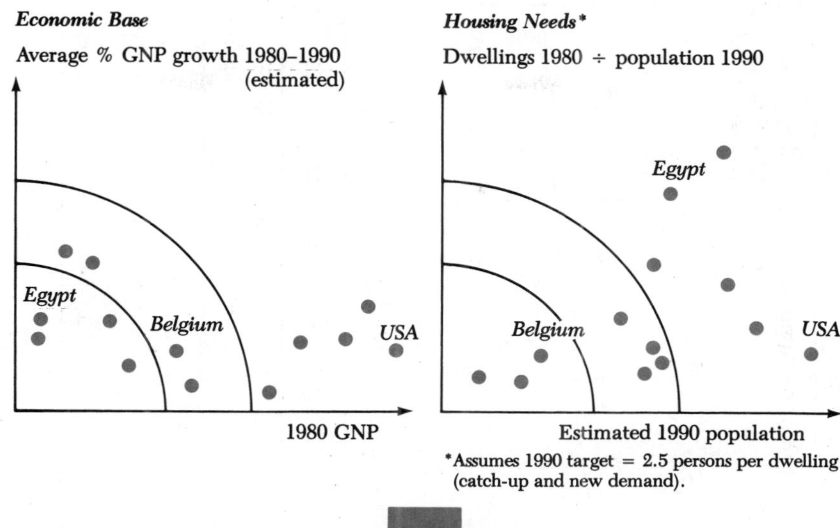

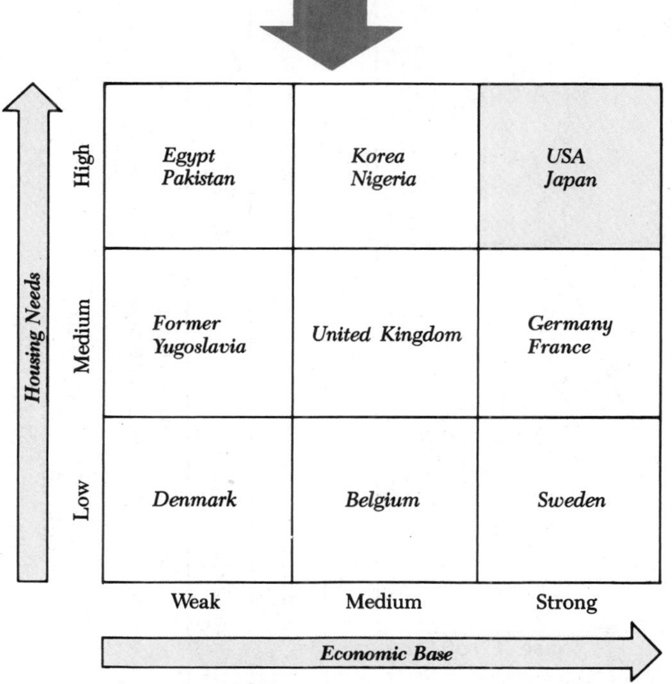

Examples: Sweden—needs only in replacement sector, Pakistan—economically too weak to meet needs.

FIGURE 6.1 Assessing Country Economic Potential: The Case of a Building-Industry Flooring Supplier

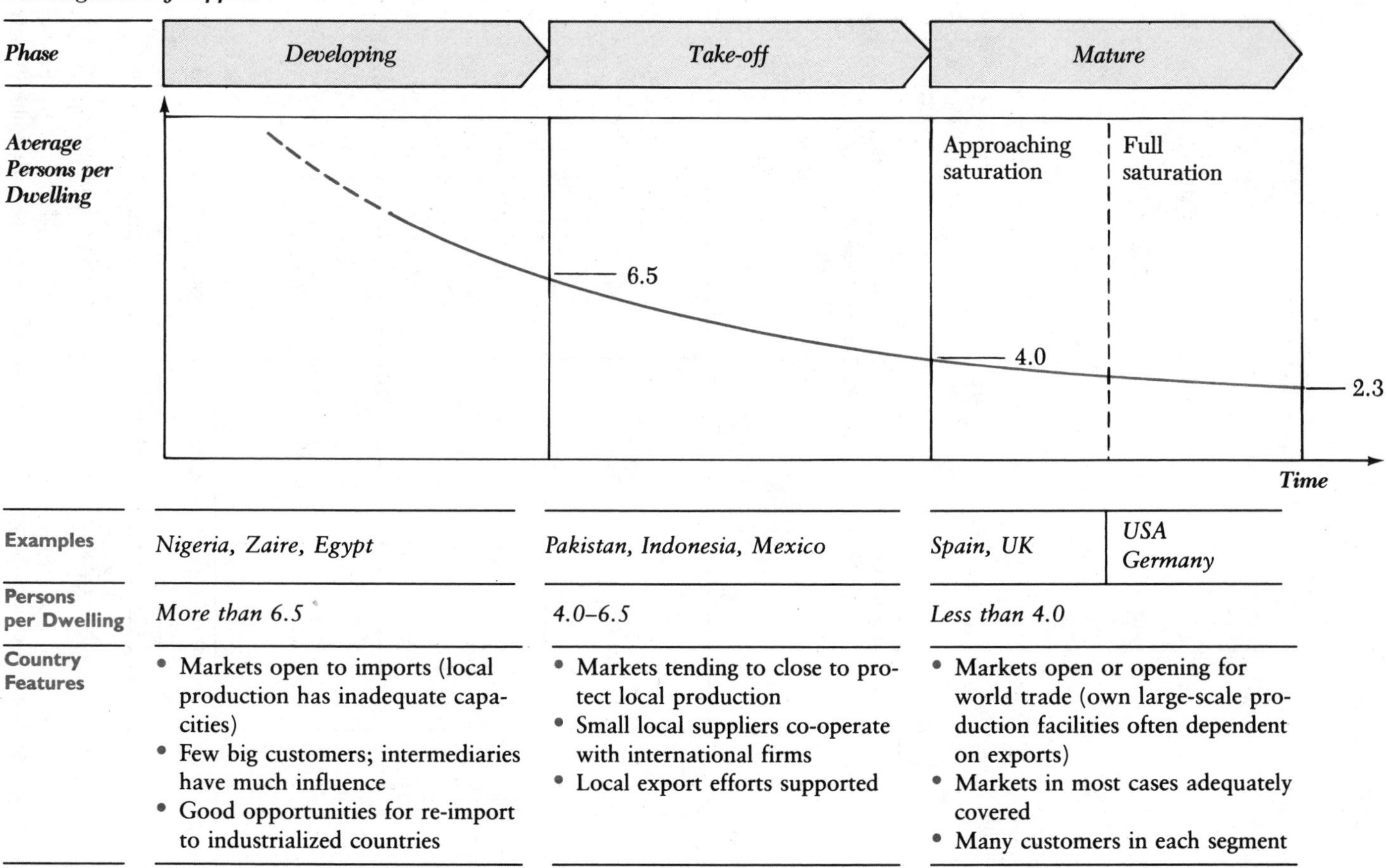

Examples	*Nigeria, Zaire, Egypt*	*Pakistan, Indonesia, Mexico*	*Spain, UK*	*USA Germany*
Persons per Dwelling	*More than 6.5*	*4.0–6.5*	*Less than 4.0*	
Country Features	• Markets open to imports (local production has inadequate capacities) • Few big customers; intermediaries have much influence • Good opportunities for re-import to industrialized countries	• Markets tending to close to protect local production • Small local suppliers co-operate with international firms • Local export efforts supported	• Markets open or opening for world trade (own large-scale production facilities often dependent on exports) • Markets in most cases adequately covered • Many customers in each segment	

FIGURE 6.2 Grouping Countries by Phase of Development

2. *Local competitive situation:* crucial for the choice between independent construction, joint venture, and acquisition
3. *Customer structure:* crucial for sales and distribution strategy
4. *Re-import potential:* crucial for international product/market strategy

The established development phases and their defining criteria must be very closely geared to the company situation, since it is these factors—not the apparent attractiveness of markets—that will make or break the company's strategic thrust into a given country.

This being the case, for each country or group of countries on the short list, management should formulate a generic marketing strategy with respect to investment, risk, product, and pricing policies, that is, a unified strategic framework applicable to all the countries in each stage of development. This step should yield a clear understanding of what the respective stages of economic development of each country entail for the company's marketing strategies (see Table 6.5).

Companies are too often inclined to regard "overseas" as a single market, or at least to differentiate very little among individual overseas markets. Another common error is the assumption that product or service concepts suited to a highly developed consumer economy will work as well in any foreign market. This is rarely true—different markets demand different approaches.

Across-the-board strategic approaches typically result in ill-advised and inappropriate allocation of resources. In less-developed markets that could be perfectly well served by a few distributors, companies have in some cases established production facilities that are doomed to permanent unprofitabiity. In markets already at the take-off point, companies have failed to build the necessary local plants, and instead have complained about declining exports only to finally abandon the field to competitors. And in markets already approaching saturation, companies have often sought to impose domestic technical standards where adequate standards and knowledge already exist or tried to operate like minireplicas of parent corporations, marketing too many product lines with too few salespeople. Again and again, product line offerings are weighted toward either cheaper or higher-quality products than the local market will accept. Clearly, the best insurance against such errors is to select strategies appropriate to the country.

Phase Three: Developing Marketing Plans In developing detailed marketing plans it is first necessary to determine which product lines fit which local markets, as well as the appropriate allocation of resources. A rough analysis of potential international business, global sales, and profit targets based on the estimates worked out in Phase One will help in assigning product lines. A framework for resource allocation can then be mapped out according to rough comparative figures for investment quotas, management needs, and skilled-labor requirements. This framework should be supplemented by company-specific examples of standard marketing strategies for each group of countries.

Table 6.6 illustrates the resource allocation process. Different product lines are assigned to different country groups, and for each country category different

TABLE 6.5 Developing Standard Strategies

PHASE	DEVELOPING	TAKE-OFF	MATURE
Basic Strategy	Test Market Pursue profitable individual projects and/or export activities	Build Base Allocate substantial resources to establish leading position in market	Expand/Round Off Operations Allocate resources selectively to develop market niches
Elements of Strategy			
Investment	Minimize (distribution and services)	Invest to expand capacity (relatively long payback)	Expand selectively in R&D, production, and distribution (relatively short payback)
Risk	Avoid	Accept	Limit
Know-how transfer (R&D)	Document know-how on reference projects	Use local know-how in • Product technology • Production engineering	Transfer know-how in special product lines; acquire local know-how to round off own base
Market share objective	Concentrate on key projects; possibly build position in profitable businesses with local support	Extend base with • New products • New outlets • New applications	Expand/defend
Cost leadership objective	Minimum acceptable (especially reduction of guarantee risks)	Economies of scale, reduction of fixed costs	Rationalize; optimize resources
Product	Standard technology, simple products	Aim for wide range, "innovator" role	Full product line in selected areas, products of high technical quality
Price	Price high	Aim for price leadership (at both ends)	Back stable market price level
Distribution	Use select local distributors (exclusive distribution)	Use a large number of small distributors (intensive distribution)	Use company sales force (selective distribution)
Promotion	Selective advertising • With typical high-prestige products • Aim at decision makers	Active utilization of selective marketing resources	Selected product advertising

strategic approaches are specified, for example, support on large-scale products, establishment of local production facilities, cooperation with local manufacturers.

The level of detail in this resource allocation decision framework will depend on a number of factors: company history and philosophy, business policy objectives, scope and variety of product lines, and the number of countries to be served. Working within this decision framework, each product division should analyze its own market in terms of size, growth, and competitive situations; as-

TABLE 6.6 A Specimen Framework for Resource Allocation

PHASE	SPECIMEN COUNTRIES	RESOURCE ALLOCATION BY PRODUCT DIVISION*					
		PVC Floor Coverings	Carpeting	Suspended Ceilings	Wall Paneling	PVC Tubes	Plastic-Coated Roof Insulation
Developing "Test market"	Nigeria	Intensive	No operations	Moderate	No operations	Intensive	Intensive
(Share of total resources: 20%)		Specific Plans • Develop own plastics-processing facilities • Acquire plastics processors					
Take-off "Build base"	Indonesia	Moderate	No operations	No operations	No operations	Moderate	Moderate
(Share of total resources: 50%)		Specific Plans • Give support in key projects • Cooperate with state-owned construction organization					
Mature "Expand/round off operations"	Spain	Moderate	Moderate	Intensive	Intensive	No operations	No operations
(Share of total resources: 30%)		Specific Plans • Develop local facilities for tufting and paneling • Acquire/cooperate with suppliers using unique product and production technology • Develop own distribution channel • Extend range to provide complete interior equipment program (system concept)					

*No operations (solid)
*Moderate (hatched)
*Intensive (dotted)

sess its profitability prospects, opportunities, and risks; and identify its own current strategic position on the basis of market share, profit situation, and vulnerability to local risks. Each product division will then be in a position to develop country-specific marketing alternatives for servicing each national market. Top management's role throughout is to coordinate the marketing strategy development efforts of the various divisions and constantly monitor the strategic decision framework.

The three-phase approach illustrated above exhibits a number of advantages.

- It allows management to set up, with a minimum of planning effort, a strategic framework that gives clear priority to market selection decisions, thus making it much easier for the divisions to work out effective product line strategies, unhampered by the usual "chicken or egg" problem.

- Division managers can foresee, at a fairly early stage, what reallocations of management, labor, and capital resources are needed and what adjustments may have to be imposed from the top due to inadequate resources.
- The company's future risk profile can be worked out in terms of resource commitment by country group and type of investment.
- The usual plethora of "exceptional" (and mostly opportunistic) product/market situations is sharply reduced. Only the really unique opportunities pass through the filter; exceptions are no longer the rule.
- The dazzling-in-theory but unrealistic-in-practice concept of establishing production bases in low-wage countries, buying from the world's lowest-cost sources, and selling products wherever the best prices can be had is replaced by a realistic country-by-country market evaluation.
- Issues of organization, personnel assignment, and integration of overseas operations into corporate planning and control systems reach management's attention only after the fundamental strategic aspects of the company's overseas involvement have been thoroughly prepared.

In brief, the three-phase approach enables management to profitably concentrate resources and attention on a handful of really attractive countries instead of dissipating its efforts in vain attempts to serve the entire world.

Opportunities in the Developing World

The framework just discussed is applicable for analyzing the economic environment in both developed and developing countries. However, further examination of opportunities in developing countries is appropriate for two reasons. First, more and more developing countries are pursuing the growth path. South Korea, Taiwan, Singapore, and Hong Kong were first, while Brazil and India followed. Now Eastern European countries have been opening up. Perhaps China will follow suit. The developing world is beginning to rely on the market mechanism to attract investment and technology and become industrialized. Second, government plays a significant role in business decisions. The bureaucrats approach foreign investment with much less sophistication and confidence than do private sector executives. Vachani summarizes the environmental differences in developing countries and how they affect multinational corporations (see Table 6.7).[20]

These characteristics suggest that in analyzing opportunities in the developing countries, a company should be willing to lay more emphasis on long-term potential than on short-term gains (see International Marketing Highlight 6.4). In addition, adequate treatment should be given to political and social variables.[21] Further, business conditions vary so much from one country to the other that a comparative (i.e., multicountry) analysis may be difficult. Availability of reliable and timely information makes the opportunity analysis more difficult in developing countries. Thus, there is no way to systematically evaluate such factors as sociopolitical conditions. Instead, a general feel for the situation is necessary, for which a trusted native could be of immense help.[22]

TABLE 6.7 Developing Country Attributes and Their Implications for MNCs

DEVELOPING COUNTRY ATTRIBUTES	IMPLICATIONS FOR MULTINATIONALS' OPERATIONS
Poor industrial infrastructure	Government preference for "high-technology" projects Few acquisition candidates Need to import components
Low consumer purchasing power	Difficult to sell high-price branded products Government may discourage aggressive advertising
Unsophisticated business environment	Poor media opportunities to sell branded products
Small markets	Need to export to achieve minimum efficient scale
Balance-of-payments problems	Government encourages exports, discourages imports Government restricts repatriation of funds
Suspicion of multinationals	Host discourages entry by acquisition Host discourages subsidiaries with high foreign equity
Colonial ties	Preference for multinationals from country with which ties existed
Outward orientation	Encourage exports Allow imports to aid exports Encourage foreign direct investment inflow for off-shore manufacturing
Inward orientation	Discourage foreign direct investment inflow High trade barriers

Source: Sushil Vachani, "Implications of Environmental Differences on Strategies of Multinationals' Manufacturing Subsidiaries," *Vikalpa,* July–September 1989, p. 4.

As a New York executive once pointed out, U.S. government or State Department assistance in social/political analysis is not necessarily reliable and may even be counterproductive. He cited as an example India and the Soviet Union, whose close relationship in matters of military technical assistance made the investment environment in India highly risky in official eyes. In reality, the investment climate in India was, and is, probably among the most stable and advantageous in the developing world. In other words, official analysis may be vulnerable to ideological bias.

In general, many U.S. firms' overall approach to developing-country foreign investment decision making is much less sophisticated than their developed-country approach. The former is often characterized by a lack of breadth in consideration of important variables, a biased perspective, and a lack of adequate preparation. The key to future improvement of opportunity analysis in developing countries may lie in the motivation generated by the inevitable increase in competition. In the past, the sheer power, dynamism, and momentum of U.S. business virtually ensured its success in almost any developing nation. As competition,

International Marketing Highlight 6.4

Procter & Gamble's Foreign Formula

The day after a 34-year-old Peruvian became manager of Procter & Gamble Co.'s Peru subsidiary in September 1988, the economy hit the skids. By the end of the year, inflation had soared to 2,000 percent. Key managers fled. Leftist terrorists kidnapped or murdered business leaders. The P&G subsidiary's sales plunged more than 30 percent, and the unit posted a loss. Money became tight.

But while many multinational companies pulled out of Peru, P&G remained. And now, the consumer-products company is expanding there.

Throughout Latin America, P&G is shaking the stranglehold of government price controls and its own strict U.S. culture. The Latin American division began as a fledgling detergent company but now is a $1 billion business that contributes 15 percent of P&G's international sales. The company expects the division, which has subsidiaries in nine countries and sells in ten others through distributors, to double its revenue again in five years. The division's profit margins exceed its international average.

P&G's success is attributed to an important lesson: U.S. management and marketing plans often don't work outside the United States. For example, Ace detergent, launched in Mexico in the early 1950s, was clobbered by local competitors. Developed for U.S. washing machines, the product had a low-suds formula. But at that time, many Mexicans washed their clothes in the river or in a basin of water, and they judged a detergent by its suds.

Eventually, the formula was changed. Similarly, P&G switched from cardboard boxes to plastic bags, which kept the detergent drier and were cheaper. Besides, many consumers shop every day and can afford only small amounts of detergent each time. Now, one top seller throughout Latin America is the 100-gram bag, enough to wash just one basket of clothes.

Source: The Wall Street Journal, June 5, 1990, p. 1.

particularly from Japan, becomes more significant, the recognition of shades of difference and finer distinctions with regard to opportunities becomes more important as well.

Capitalizing on Opportunities in Developing Countries

H. J. Heinz Company's expansion into developing countries illustrates the point.[23] On the theory that everyone needs to eat, Heinz looked for business opportunities around the globe. The company has been active abroad since 1905. In fiscal 1985, more than one-third of Heinz's sales came from foreign affiliates in the United Kingdom, Australia, New Zealand, and a few other nations, mostly in Europe. In the early 1980s, the company realized that it served only 15 percent of the world's population. It had not tapped the remaining 85 percent, which represents a huge potential. The company felt that improved living standards in the Third World would increase demand for Western-style foods such as ketchup.

Therefore, the company developed a plan to expand its operations in developing countries from less than $100 million in 1982 to $2.5 billion in 2000. In 1983 Heinz became the first foreign investor in Zimbabwe, acquiring 51 percent of Olivine Industries Inc., a maker of cooking oils and margarines. Since then the company has formed joint ventures in the Ivory Coast, Cameroon, and Thailand. The company has a long list of countries it wants to enter—South Korea, China, Malaysia, Nigeria, and Egypt—by carefully adapting its U.S. products to local tastes. In its entry decision, the company duly considers if the overseas investment and aid to Third World farmers could provide its processing operations with raw materials in the future. As a company spokesperson said: "Our strategy isn't just for today or next year, but [for] years from now. If we can grow enough in Zimbabwe, and make it cost-competitive, we might export raw materials to Heinz operations in Europe."

The company has different strategies for different regions of the world. It acquired local companies in Africa, while in Asia it would prefer joint ventures with successful local companies that understand local tastes and have access to distribution networks. As a company executive said, "We must be flexible and patient in seeking access to Third World markets. We have to convince them that we can offer something unique—new production techniques or the chance to manufacture a wide variety of foods. We have to negotiate with patience and many tea ceremonies. We introduced our brands to a vast awaiting audience and we now stand at the threshold of these new markets."[24]

Summary

The economic environment of a foreign country is an important factor that should be examined before an international marketer decides to enter its market. A country burdened with economic problems may lack stability and become vulnerable to political radicalism. On the other hand, a growing and burgeoning economy usually stimulates business activity and offers new opportunities. Thus, a careful review of economic conditions, both short- and long-term, is a prerequisite for a decision about entering an overseas market.

Economic environment can be divided into macro- and microeconomic environments. Macroenvironment describes the overall economic situation in a country and is analyzed using economic indicators such as GNP per capita, index of industrial production, rate of economic growth, inflation rate, balance-of-trade surplus (deficit), interest rates, unemployment data, and the like. The economic system of a country is also part of the macroenvironment. Two extreme types of economic systems are the capitalist system and state control. The latter is mainly found in socialist countries; most Western countries pursue a mixed form of capitalism.

Microenvironment refers to economic conditions relevant to a particular product/market. Analysis of microeconomic environment is largely performed with reference to competition. A firm should properly identify different sources of competition and examine its own strengths and weaknesses relative to major competitors. Equipped with a competitive advantage over its rivals, a firm will be able to develop a workable marketing mix.

Economic environment does affect international marketing decisions, whether changes occur in the macro- or microeconomic environments. The impact of the U.S. economic environment on international business activity should not be ignored. For example, U.S. firms enter the international market during a recession to sustain their business, only to withdraw as the domestic scene improves.

Conceptual schemes or frameworks are helpful for analyzing economic environment. Analysis can be performed with reference to cost–benefit criteria and risk/reward criteria. Cost–benefit criteria include markets, competition, and financial implications of doing business in a country. The risk/reward criteria include the broad social, economic, and political climates of a nation. The successful application of a conceptual scheme yields a marketing strategy that will foster the development of market plans appropriate to a particular foreign market at a particular time. The conceptual scheme can be used to analyze opportunities in developed and developing economies. In many cases, however, lack of adequate information on developing countries may mean depending more on the feel of the situation than on actual data.

Review Questions

1. Should different types of economic indicators be used to examine the macroeconomic environments of different countries? Discuss.
2. Discuss the following statement: "While advanced countries offer an immediate market opportunity, the competitive activity is excessively keen there. It may, therefore, be more advantageous for a firm to gain a permanent foothold in one or more developing countries, since often there is no competition to reckon with."
3. What are the distinguishing characteristics of Muslim economic ideas?
4. Present a scheme for analyzing the economic environment of Mexico from the viewpoint of an appliance manufacturer.
5. What relevance does Engel's law have in the analysis of economic environment for overseas business?
6. How can a firm examine its competitive advantage overseas?
7. What impact, if any, may the U.S. economic environment have on international marketing?
8. Illustrate how the economic perspectives of different countries are related.

Endnotes

1. "A Snapshot of Living Standards," *Fortune,* July 31, 1989, p. 92.
2. James E. Austin, *Managing in Developing Countries* (New York: The Free Press, 1990), Chapter 1.
3. Gunnar Myrdal, *The Asian Drama: An Inquiry into the Poverty of Nations* (New York: Pantheon, 1968).
4. "The Myth of the Japanese Middle Class," *Business America,* September 12, 1988, p. 49.
5. The most up-to-date statistics on a worldwide basis are available from the World Bank. *See World Development Report—1988* (New York: Oxford University Press, 1988).
6. Art Pine, "Pakistan Bends Economy to the Koran," *The Wall Street Journal,* September 9, 1981, p. 33.
7. Raymond Vernon, "Gone Are the Cash Cows of Yesteryear," *Harvard Business Review,* November–December 1980, pp. 150–55.
8. Subhash C. Jain, *Marketing Planning and Strategy,* 3rd ed. (Cincinnati, OH: Southwestern Publishing Co., 1990), p. 84.
9. Ibid.
10. *See* Michael E. Porter, *The Competitive Advantage of Nations* (New York: The Free Press, 1990), Chapter 11.
11. "How German Auto Makers Penetrated Japan's Market," *The Wall Street Journal,* May 17, 1988, p. 34. *Also see* Allan T. Demaree, "What Now for the U.S. and Japan," *Fortune,* February 10, 1992, p. 81.
12. *Business America,* April 25, 1988, pp. 4–5.
13. "Brazil: U.S. Outlook Not Promising Due to Uncertainties," *Business America,* April 20, 1992, p. 11.
14. Ulrich Wiechmann and Lewis G. Pringle, "Problems that Plague Multinational Marketers," *Harvard Business Review,* July–August 1979, p. 123. *Also see* "Heavy Electrical Machinery Firms Widen Quest for Business Overseas," *The Asian Wall Street Journal Weekly,* January 3, 1983, p. 15.
15. C. P. Rao, "Impact of the Domestic Economic Environment on International Business Involvement and Practices of Exporters," paper presented at the Academy of International Business Annual Meeting, Orlando, Florida, August 17–19, 1977, p. 12. *Also see* C. P. Rao, M. Krishna Erramilli, and Gopala K. Ganesh, "Impact of Domestic Recession on Export Marketing Behavior," *International Marketing Review,* Vol. 7, no. 2 (1990), pp. 54–65.
16. John Jelacic, "The U.S. Trade Outlook in 1991," *Business America,* April 22, 1991, p. 2.
17. See Jeremy Main, "How to Go Global and Why," *Fortune,* August 28, 1989, p. 70.
18. *See* Robert T. Green and Arthur W. Allaway, "Identification of Export Opportunities: A Shift-Share Approach," *Journal of Marketing,* Winter 1985, pp. 83–88; Susan P. Douglas, C. Samuel Craig, and Warren J. Keegan, "Approaches to Assessing International Marketing Opportunities for Small and Medium-Sized Companies," *Columbia Journal of World Business,* Fall 1982, pp. 26–31.
19. *See* Marie E. Wicks Kelly and George C. Philippatos, "Comparative Analysis of the Foreign Investment Evaluation Practices by U.S. Based Manufacturing Multinational Companies," *Business Studies,* Winter 1982, pp. 19–42; Robert Weigand, "International Investments: Weighing the Incentives," *Harvard Business Review,* July–August 1983, pp. 146–153; and Philip Kotler and Liam Fahey, "The World's Champion Marketers: The Japanese," *Journal of Business Strategy,* Summer 1982, pp. 3–13.
20. Sushil Vachani, "Implications of Environmental Differences on Strategies of Multinationals' Manufacturing Subsidiaries," *Vikalpa,* July–September 1989, pp. 3–12.
21. S. Tamer Cavusgil, "Guidelines for Export Market Research," *Business Horizons* November–December 1985, pp. 27–33.
22. *See* Susan Walsh Sanderson and Robert H. Hayes, "Mexico—Opening Ahead of Eastern Europe," *Harvard Business Review,* September–October 1990, pp. 32–43.
23. "Heinz Sets Out to Expand in Africa and Asia, Seeking New Markets, Sources of Materials," *The Wall Street Journal,* September 27, 1983, p. 77. *Also see* H. J. Heinz Company's annual report for 1985.
24. Anthony J. F. O'Reilly, "Establishing Successful Joint Ventures in Developing Nations: A CEO's Perspective," *Columbia Journal of World Business,* Spring 1955, pp. 3–9. *Also see* Gregory Stricharchuk, "Heinz Splits Up Star-Kist in Move to Raise World Canned-Fish Sales," *The Wall Street Journal,* November 2, 1988, p. B6.

CHAPTER • 7

Cultural Environment

CHAPTER FOCUS

After studying this chapter, you should be able to:

- Explain the meaning of culture and its various aspects
- Describe the impact of culture on product, price, promotion, and distribution decisions
- Analyze cultural implications for a product/market
- Discuss cultural adaptation
- Examine the process of cultural change

Doing business across national boundaries requires interaction with people and their institutions and organizations nurtured in different cultural environments. Values that are important to one group of people may mean little to another. Typical U.S. attitudes and perceptions of various things may be at variance with other people's ideas and views of the same things. In brief, there exist among nations striking and significant differences of attitude, belief, ritual, motivation, perception, morality, truth, superstition, and an almost endless list of other cultural characteristics.

Cultural differences deeply affect market behavior. International marketers, therefore, need to be as familiar as possible with the cultural traits of any country they want to do business with. International business literature is full of instances where stereotyped notions of countries' cultures have led to insurmountable problems. More than any other function of a business, marketing perhaps is most susceptible to cultural error, since marketing by definition requires contact with the people of the country concerned. Practically all marketing decisions are culture-bound.

The effect of culture on international marketing ventures is multifaceted. The factoring of cultural differences into marketing mix decisions to enhance the likelihood of success has long been a critical issue in overseas operations. With the increasing criticism leveled at multinational enterprises, cultural forces have taken on additional importance. Naiveté and blundering about culture can also be expensive.

This chapter begins by examining the meaning of culture and goes on to explore the profound effect of culture on marketing outside the United States. Various elements of culture are discussed. A framework for analyzing culture is introduced. The impact of the sociocultural fabric of the host nation on different marketing decisions is analyzed. Following this, a procedure for cultural adaptation overseas is recommended. Finally, the impact of foreign business on local culture as an agent of cultural change in the host country is examined.

The Concept of Culture

It was the middle of October and a marketing executive from the United States was flying to Saudi Arabia to finalize a contract with a local company to supply hospital furnishings. The next day, he met the Saudi contacts and wondered if they would sign the deal within two or three days, since he had to report the matter to his board the following Monday. The Saudi executive made a simple response: "Insha Allah," which means "if God is willing." The American felt completely lost. He found the carefree response of the Saudi insulting and unbusinesslike. He felt he had made an effort by going all the way to Saudi Arabia in order for them to question any matter requiring clarification before signing the contract. He thought that the Saudi executive was treating a deal worth over $100 million as if it meant nothing.

During the next meeting the American was determined to put the matter in stronger terms, emphasizing the importance of his board's meeting. But the Arabs again ignored the issue of signing the contract. "They were friendly, appeared

> happy and calm, but wouldn't sign on the dotted lines," the American later explained. Finally on orders from the president of his company, he returned home without the contract.

Why did the Saudi executives not sign the sales contract? After all, they had agreed to all the terms and conditions during their meeting in New York. But in Riyadh they did not even care to review it, let alone sign it.

Unfortunately, the U.S. executive had arrived at the wrong time. It was the time of Ramadan, holy month, and most Muslims fast. During this time, everything slows down, particularly business.[1] In Western societies, while religion is important, it is for most people only one aspect of life and business goes on as usual most of the time. In the Islamic countries, religion is a total way of life for the majority of people. It affects every facet of living. Thus, no matter how important a business deal may be, it would be undesirable to conduct a deal during the holy month. Such is the Arab value system. The executive from the United States, however, was not aware of Muslim culture.

Culture has been defined in different ways. Essentially, it includes all learned behavior and values that are transmitted to an individual living within the society through shared experience. A classic definition of culture is provided by Sir Edward Tylor:

> Culture is that complex whole which includes knowledge, belief, art, morals, law, custom, and any other capabilities and habits acquired by [individuals as members] of society.[2]

Culture develops through recurrent social relationships that form patterns that are eventually internalized by members of the entire group.

It is commonly agreed that a culture must have these three characteristics:

1. It is *learned,* that is, acquired by people over time through their membership in a group that transmits culture from generation to generation.
2. It is *interrelated,* that is, one part of the culture is deeply connected with another part such as religion and marriage, business and social status.
3. It is *shared,* that is, tenets of a culture extend to other members of the group.[3]

The concept of culture is broad and extremely complex. It encompasses virtually every part of a person's life. This suggests that culture serves virtually all human needs, both physical and psychological. Further, culture continues to evolve through constant embellishment and adaptation, partly in response to environmental needs and partly through the influence of outside forces. In other words, a culture does not stand still, but slowly, over time it may change. Finally, cultural differences are not necessarily visible but can be quite subtle and can surface in situations where one would never notice them.

A nation may embody more than one culture. Canada has a dual culture: English-speaking people and French Canadians. The two cultures may exhibit fundamental cultural differences. In Israel two distinctive cultures also exist, a so-called Western group consisting of European and U.S. immigrants whose culture

corresponds to their backgrounds, and a so-called Oriental group consisting of immigrants from Asian and African countries, most Arab-speaking Muslim societies. The contrasts between the two groups have been described this way:

> The oriental set of values corresponds to the values generally attributed to traditional societies described as: compulsory in their force, sacred in their tone and stable in their timelessness. They call for fatalistic acceptance of the world as is, respect for those in authority, and submergence of the individual in collectivity.
>
> In contrast to this, the norms and values of Israelis of western ancestry can be described as stressing acquisitive activities, an aggressive attitude toward economic and social change, and a clear trend toward a higher degree of industrialization. The oriental Israeli immigrants, having arrived later than the western immigrants, were expected to be absorbed in a western society, having a strong emphasis on specificity, universalism and achievement.[4]

Cultural Field

Knowledge of a culture can be gained by probing its various aspects—but which aspects? Since culture is such a vast concept, it is desirable to develop a field for cultural understanding. Exhibit 7.1 lists more than seventy universals that presumably are common to all cultures. While this list addresses all aspects of culture and thus provides insights into the entire field of culture, it may be unmanageably long to an international marketer.

Another way of gaining cultural understanding is to examine the following cultural elements within a country: material life, social interactions, language, aesthetics, religion and faith, pride and prejudice, and ethics and mores.

Material Life

Material life refers to economics, that is, what people do to derive their livelihood. The tools, knowledge, techniques, methods, and processes that a culture utilizes to produce goods and services, as well as their distribution and consumption, are all part of material life. Thus, two essential parts of material life are knowledge and economics.

Material life reflects standard of living and degree of technological advancement. In a hypothetical country, for example, a large proportion of the population is engaged in agriculture. Agricultural operations are mainly performed by manual labor; mechanization of agriculture is unknown. Modern techniques of farming such as use of fertilizers, pesticides, and quality seeds are unfamiliar. The medium of exchange is a barter system, markets are local, and living is entirely rural. Such a composite description suggests that the society is primitive. Opportunities for multinational business in a primitive environment will be limited.

By contrast, consider a different society where manufacturing industry serves as the major source of employment, and agriculture supports about one-tenth of the population. People live in urban centers and have such modern amenities as televisions, cars, VCRs, newspapers, and so on. Money is the medium of exchange. In such a culture, business across national boundaries would make sense.

EXHIBIT 7.1 Cultural Universals

age grading	food taboos	music
athletic sports	funeral rites	mythology
bodily adornment	games	numerals
calendar	gestures	obstetrics
cleanliness training	gift giving	penal sanctions
community organization	government	personal names
cooking	greetings	population policy
cooperative labor	hairstyles	postnatal care
cosmology	hospitality	pregnancy usages
courtship	housing hygiene	property rights
dancing	incest taboos	propitiation of supernatural beings
decorative art	inheritance rules	puberty customs
divination	joking	religous rituals
division of labor	king groups	residence rules
dream interpretation	kinship nomenclature	sexual restrictions
education	language	soul concepts
eschatology	law	status differentiation
ethics	luck superstitions	surgery
ethnobotany	magic	tool making
etiquette	marriage	trade
faith healing	mealtimes	visiting
family	medicine	weaning
feasting	modesty concerning natural functions	weather control
fire making	mourning	
folklore		

Source: George P. Murdock, "The Common Denominator of Cultures," in *The Science of Man in the World Crises,* Ralph Linton, ed. (New York: Columbia University Press, 1945), pp. 123–142.

The material life of a society cannot be described simply but falls on a continuum of material life whose two poles are traditional and industrialized. A position on the material-life continuum indicates a society's way of life. Each position would then become the basis of analyzing opportunities for an international marketer. For example, Brazil and Pakistan are both developing countries, but the study of material life in the two countries would show that Brazil is ahead of Pakistan, offering market opportunities for such projects as electrical appliances, stereos, and televisions. Pakistan, however, is still emerging from total dependence on farming, suggesting the importance of agricultural tools and inputs in that culture.

Social Interactions

Social interactions establish the roles that people play in a society and their authority/responsibility patterns. These roles and patterns are supported by society's institutional framework, which includes, for example, education and marriage.

Consider the traditional marriage of a Saudi woman. The woman's father chooses the husband-to-be. After agreeing on a small payment for the bride, the two men hold hands in front of a judge to finalize the marriage. The woman sees her husband for the first time when he comes to consummate the marriage. The social role assigned to women in the strict Islamic world is one of complete dependency on men; their authority and their command cannot be questioned. Women's place is always in the home. Outside the home, if women are seen at all, they are veiled. As has been said:

> Moslems [sic] believe in the segregation of men and women, with the exception of husbands and wives and close family members. Men who are strangers to the family are not even supposed to see a man's female relatives. Moslems are not receptive to the western concept of liberation of women. Males are more privileged. It is not uncommon, as an example, to witness some Moslem males traveling by air in the first-class section of an airliner and their wives in the back, flying economy.[5]

Social roles are also established by culture. For example, a woman can be a wife, a mother, a community leader, and/or an employee. What role is preferred in different situations is culture-bound. Most Swiss women consider household work (e.g., washing dishes, cleaning floors) as their primary role. For this reason, they resent modern gadgets and machines. Behavior also emerges from culture in the form of conventions, rituals, and practices on different occasions such as during festivals, marriages, get-togethers, and times of grief or religious celebration.[6]

Likewise, the authority of the aged, the teacher, and the religious in many societies is held high. The educational system, the social settings (celebrations and festivities), and customs and traditions reassert the prescribed roles and patterns of individuals and groups. A good example is the caste system in India. A person's social and occupational status is determined by birth in a certain family/community. Such is the strength of social heritage that, despite discrimination on the basis of caste being unconstitutional and legally punishable, the system still prevails today, especially in the rural areas.

With reference to marketing, the social interactions influence family decision making and buying behavior and define the scope of personal influence and opinion. In Latin America, as is true of Asian societies as well, the extended family is considered the most basic and stable unit of social organization. The extended family is the center for all economic, political, social, and religious life. It provides companionship, protection, and a common set of values with specifically prescribed means for fulfilling them. By contrast, in the United States the nuclear family (husband, wife, and children) is the focus of social organization.

An empirical study by Tan and McCullough showed how cultural differences affect the husband-wife influence in buying decisions. A Singapore husband played a more dominant role than his U.S. counterpart in family decision making.[7] Similar results were obtained in a study of Dutch and U.S. housewives. The U.S. wife played a more autonomous role than the Dutch wife in family decision making. Thus, social roles vary from culture to culture and are likely to affect marketing behavior.[8]

Language

Language as part of culture is considered not only in the literal sense as the spoken word, but also as symbolic communication of time, space, things, friendship, and agreements.[9] Communication occurs through speech, gestures, expressions, and other body movements.

The many different languages of the world do not literally translate from one to another, and the understanding of the symbolic and physical aspects of different cultures' communication is even more difficult to achieve. For example, a phrase such as "body by Fisher" translated literally into Flemish means "corpse by Fisher." Similarly, "Let Hertz put you in the driver's seat" translated literally into Spanish means "Let Hertz make you a chauffeur."[10] Nova translates into Spanish as "it doesn't go." A shipment of Chinese shoes destined for Egypt created a problem because the design on the soles of the shoes spelled "God" in Arabic. Olympia's Roto photocopier did not sell well because "roto" refers to the lowest class in Chile, and "roto" in Spanish means "broken."[11]

In addition, meanings differ within the same language used in different places. For example, English language meaning differs from one English-speaking country to another. A store sign in Hong Kong read, "Teeth extracted by the latest methodists," while the sign in a tailor's window in Jordan advised, "Order your summer suits. Because in big rush we will execute customers in strict rotation."[12] In England the words for "truck," "gasoline," and "cookies" are "lorry," "petrol," and "biscuits."[13]

As has been said:

> So you think you speak English? Most Americans assume a conversant ability in what they think to be their native tongue. But ever since the Colonials spun off from the kingdom 200-plus years ago, linguistic evolution has widened a considerable chasm of dialect between upstart and motherland. In truth, there is every justification for calling one language American and the other English.
>
> Since food (like money) is a universal language, Americans should encounter little difficulty in culinary communication. But . . .
>
> One is often advised to book a table rather than reserve one. . . . Asking for zucchini or eggplant is likely to draw a blank; try *courgettes* and *aubergines*. . . . French fries are *chips*. . . . Chips are *crisps*. . . . *Sandwiches* are sandwiches, but only a distant approximation of the more prodigious American concoctions. . . . *Puddings* may or may not include pudding; it's a traditional English term for desserts, which are also called *sweets*. . . . A *trifle* is no small matter; it's delicious pudding typically comprised of sherry-soaked cake topped with fruit, custard and whipped cream. . . . *Tea* is tea, of course, but tea is also *tea,* a late afternoon meal of sandwiches, cakes, or biscuits, and, of course, tea. . . . Those *biscuits,* incidentally, are cookies. . . . Tea by the cup may be called a *cuppa*. . . . *Bangers and mash? Bubbles and squeak? Pies, pasties, simple Simon?* Be bold, eat! Then after your meal, ask for the *bill,* not the check.
>
> If you're seeking sweaters, look for *jumpers*. . . . The gentleman looking for a vest and pants to match his jacket will be presumed to be either insolent or *crazy. Vest* implies undershirt, and *pants* implies underpants. Try a *waistcoat* and *trousers* instead. . . . You'll need *braces,* not suspenders, to hold up those trousers. . . . Ladies seeking knickers will be steered to the underwear department; try asking for *plus-fours* instead. . . . Shopping for a purse? Ask for a

> *handbag.* . . . Men carry *wallets* rather than billfolds, quite likely because they carry *notes* rather than bills. . . . Speaking of currency, a *quid* is to a pound as a buck is to a dollar. . . . Sneakers are commonly called *plimsolls.* . . . For that City look, buy a *bowler hat,* not a derby.
>
> *Streets* are streets, even though the English drive on the "wrong" side. . . . but a sidewalk is the *pavement,* and a crosswalk is a *zebra* (rhymes with Debra) crossing.
>
> The English politely wait in a *queue* (sounds like a cue), rather than line, for theater tickets. . . . *Theater* means live theater. . . . The movie theater is the *cinema,* where one is more likely to watch a *film* than a movie. . . . Buy your snacks at the *interval,* there'll be no intermission. . . . The best seats are the *stalls;* ask for orchestra seats and you'll be asked what instrument you play. . . . The balcony is the *gallery.* . . .
>
> Don't call someone from a phone booth; *ring* them from the *phone box.* And best of luck on your initial encounter with the *British Telcom* (Ma Bell). . . .
>
> A *bus* is a bus, but so is a *coach.* . . . The subway is the *Underground* or more commonly, the *tube,* whereas a *subway* is an underground walkway. . . . A truck is a *lorry,* and runs on *petrol.* . . .
>
> A desperate American seeking a bathroom may not find what he needs therein; better to ask for the *lavoratory, loo, gents, ladies, WC,* or simply *toilet.*[14]

Sometimes the same word may mean an entirely different thing in different cultures. "Table the report" in the United States means postponement; in England it means "bring the matter to the forefront." Therefore, an international marketer must be careful in handling the matter of language in business dealings, contracts, negotiations, advertising, and so on. Coca-Cola Co., for example, did not use the diet name in France since the word "diet" suggests poor health. Instead the company called it Coca-Cola Light.

Symbolic communication is equally important. To be on time for an appointment is an accepted norm of behavior in the United States. A person is looked down upon if he or she fails to be on time. But in many other cultures, people are not particular about time and an appointment at 11 A.M. may not mean 11 A.M. sharp, but only mean at *about* that time (see International Marketing Highlight 7.1). Something as simple as a greeting can be misunderstood. The form of greeting differs from culture to culture. Traditional greetings may be a handshake, hug, nose rub, kiss, placing the hands in praying position, or various other gestures. Lack of awareness concerning the country's accepted form of greeting can lead to awkward encounters.[15]

Aesthetics

Aesthetics include the art, the drama, the music, the folkways, and the architecture endemic to a society. These aspects of a society convey the concept of beauty and expression revered in a culture. For example, different colors have different meanings worldwide. In Western societies, wedding gowns are usually white, but in Asia white symbolizes sorrow.

The aesthetic values of a society show in the design, styles, colors, expressions, symbols, movements, emotions, and postures valued and preferred in a particular culture. These attributes have an impact on the design and promotion of different products.

International Marketing Highlight 7.1

Being on Time

Attitudes toward punctuality vary greatly from one culture to another and unless understood can cause confusion and misunderstanding. Romanians, Japanese, and Germans are very punctual, while many of the Latin countries have a more relaxed attitude toward time. The Japanese consider it rude to be late for a business meeting, but it is acceptable, even fashionable, to be late for a social occasion. In Guatemala, on the other hand, a luncheon at a specified time means that some guests might be ten minutes early while others may be forty-five minutes late.

Likewise, space and the way that a person occupies it communicates something about position in the terms of each culture. For example, a large office on the top floor of a building in the United States may mean that the person is important in an organizational hierarchy. Such a conclusion elsewhere would not always be right. Japanese executives usually share an office. Likewise, in the United States worldly possessions and material things are often used as symbols of success. A Lincoln Continental or a Mercedes automobile would signify achievement. But in many countries, such automobiles would not signal respect. Particularly in the Islamic countries, such emphasis on material possessions is frowned upon.

In many situations the symbolic language of communication is more important than the actual words, and people respond accordingly. Therefore, an international businessperson must understand cultural differences and behave accordingly to avoid inadvertently communicating the wrong message.

Religion and Faith

Religion influences a culture's outlook on life, its meaning and concept. Islam considers emphasis on material wealth ignoble. In Christianity, particularly in Western cultures, the ideal of people taking dominion of the earthly environment has combined with the Calvinist ethic of hard work and success to promote the idea of the acquisition of wealth as a measure of achievement. Hinduism, while it places no sanction on the acquisition of wealth, is fatalistic about the acquisition of riches. In general, the religion practiced in a society influences the emphasis placed on material life, which in turn affects the attitudes toward owning and using goods and services. Religious traditions may prohibit the use of certain goods/services altogether. For example, Hinduism prescribes vegetarianism, with special stress on abstinence from beef. Islam, on the other hand, forbids the eating of pork.

A fatalistic belief leads Asians to choose an auspicious time to buy a car or to plan a wedding. Car salespeople in Japan, for example, deliver a car to a consumer on a lucky day, while contractors check for an auspicious day before breaking ground, and insurance salespeople are careful to pick a good day before going for a customer's signature on a life insurance policy.[16]

Religion also influences male-female roles, as well as societal institutions and customs, such as marriage and funeral rites. Islam restricts the role of the female to the household. She is also confined to an inferior role. In addition, a Muslim man may have more than one wife, but a woman must practice monogamy.

Religion affects patterns of living in various other ways. It establishes authority relationships, an individual's duties and responsibilities both in childhood and as an adult, and the sanctity of different acts such as hygiene.[17] In the name of religion, Iranians in 1979 disrupted their whole country.[18] The Catholic church officially continues to prohibit the use of birth control devices. Animism, religion emphasizing magic practiced in many parts of Africa, demands human sacrifices. In general, organized religion and faith inevitably motivate people and their customs in numerous ways.[19] The impact of religion is continuous and profound (see International Marketing Highlight 7.2).

International Marketing Highlight 7.2

Cultural Diversity

When a manager from the dominant U.S. culture saw two Arab-American employees arguing, he figured he had better stay out of it. But the employees *expected* a third-party intermediary, or *wasta* in Arabic, and without one the incident blew up.

The expectation goes back to the Koran and Bedouin tradition. While the dominant American culture is likely to take an individualistic, win-lose approach and emphasize privacy, Arab-Americans tend to value a win-win result that preserves group harmony but often requires mediation.

A Latino manager starts a budget-planning meeting by chatting casually and checking with his new staff on whether everyone can get together after work. His non-Latino boss frets over the delay and wonders why he doesn't get straight to the numbers. Latino culture teaches that building relationships is often critical to working together, while the dominant American culture encourages "getting down to business."

Source: The Wall Street Journal, September 12, 1990, p. B1.

Exhibit 7.2 illustrates the role of religion in marketing with reference to Islam. Because religious traits and tenets may profoundly affect marketing, international marketers must be sensitive to the religious principles of the host country.

Pride and Prejudice

Every culture fosters a certain pride and prejudice in its inhabitants. Thus, even the culture most backward in the eyes of a Westerner will have a certain inherent pride in its traits and ways.[20] The Chinese are jealous of their cultural heritage, and they speak of it with great emotion. So do the Egyptians of their heritage. As a matter of fact, despite economic achievements, Americans feel deprived of cultural history in a country so young and diverse by nature (see International Marketing Highlight 7.3).

Cultural pride and prejudice make many nations reject foreign ideas and

EXHIBIT 7.2 Marketing in an Islamic Framework

ELEMENTS	IMPLICATIONS FOR MARKETING
I. Fundamental Islamic Concepts	
A. Unity. (Concept of centrality, oneness of God, harmony in life.)	Product standardization, mass media techniques, central balance, unity in advertising copy and layout, strong brand loyalties, a smaller evoked size set, loyalty to company, opportunities for brand-extension strategies.
B. Legitimacy. (Fair dealings, reasonable level of profits.)	Fewer formal product warranties, less need for institutional advertising and/or advocacy advertising, especially by foreign firms, and a switch from profit maximizing to a profit satisfying strategy.
C. Zakat. (2.5 percent per annum compulsory tax binding on all classified as "not poor.")	Use of "excessive" profits, if any, for charitable acts, corporate donations for charity, institutional advertising.
D. Usury. (Cannot charge interest on loans. A general interpretation of this law defines "excessive interest" charged on loans as not permissible.)	Avoid direct use of credit as a marketing tool; establish a consumer policy of paying cash for low-value products; for high-value products, offer discounts for cash payments and raise prices of products on an installment basis; sometimes possible to conduct interest transactions between local/foreign firm in other non-Islamic countries; banks in some Islamic countries take equity in financing ventures, sharing resultant profits (and losses).
E. Supremacy of human life. (Compared to other forms of life, objects, human life is of supreme importance.)	Pet food and/or products less important; avoid use of statues, busts—interpreted as forms of idolatry; symbols in advertising and/or promotion should reflect high human values; use floral designs and artwork in advertising as representation of aesthetic values.
F. Community. (All Muslims should strive to achieve universal brotherhood—with allegiance to the "one God." One way of expressing community is the required pilgrimage to Mecca for all Muslims at least once in their lifetime, if able to do so.)	Formation of an Islamic Economic Community—development of an "Islamic consumer" served with Islamic-oriented products and services, for example, "kosher" meat packages, gifts exchanged at Muslim festivals, and so forth; development of community services—need for marketing or nonprofit organizations and skills.
G. Equality of peoples.	Participative communication systems; roles and authority structures may be rigidly defined but accessibility at any level relatively easy.
	Products that are nutritious, cool, and digested easily can be formulated for Sehr and Iftar (beginning and end of the fast).

EXHIBIT 7.2 *(Continued)*

ELEMENTS	IMPLICATIONS FOR MARKETING
H. Abstinence. (During the month of Ramadan, Muslims are required to fast without food or drink from the first streak of dawn to sunset—a reminder to those who are more fortunate to be kind to the less fortunate and as an exercise in self-control.) Consumption of alcohol and pork is forbidden; so is gambling.	Opportunities for developing nonalcoholic items and beverages (for example, soft drinks, ice cream, milk shakes, fruit juices) and nonchance social games, such as Scrabble; food products should use vegetable or beef shortening.
I. Environmentalism. (The universe created by God was pure. Consequently, the land, air, and water should be held as sacred elements.)	Anticipate environmental, antipollution acts; opportunities for companies involved in maintaining a clean environment; easier acceptance of pollution-control devices in the community (for example, recent efforts in Turkey have been well received by the local communities).
J. Worship. (Five times a day; timing of prayers varies.)	Need to take into account the variability and shift in prayer timings in planning sales calls, work schedules, business hours, customer traffic, and so forth.
II. Islamic Culture	
A. Obligation to family and tribal traditions.	Importance of respected members in the family or tribe as opinion leaders; word-of-mouth communication, customer referrals may be critical; social or clan allegiances, affiliations, and associations may be possible surrogates for reference groups; advertising home-oriented products stressing family roles may be highly effective, for example, electronic games.
B. Obligations toward parents are sacred.	The image of functional products could be enhanced with advertisements that stress parental advice or approval; even with children's products, there should be less emphasis on children as decision makers.
C. Obligation to extend hospitality to both insiders and outsiders.	Product designs that are symbols of hospitality, outwardly open in expression; rate of new product acceptance may be accelerated and eased by appeals based on community.

(continued)

EXHIBIT 7.2 *(Continued)*

ELEMENTS	IMPLICATIONS FOR MARKETING
D. Obligation to conform to codes of sexual conduct and social interaction. These may include the following:	
1. Modest dress for women in public.	More colorful clothing and accessories are worn by women at home, so promotion of products for use in private homes could be more intimate—such audiences could be reached effectively through women's magazines; avoid use of immodest exposure and sexual implications in public settings.
2. Separation of male and female audiences (in some cases).	Access to female consumers can often be gained only through women as selling agents, salespersons, catalogs, home demonstrations, and women's specialty shops.
E. Obligations to religious occasions. (For example, there are two major religious observances that are celebrated—Eid-ul-Fitr, Eid-ul-Adha.)	Tied to purchase of new shoes, clothing, sweets, and preparation of food items for family reunions, Muslim gatherings. There has been a practice of giving money in place of gifts. Increasingly, however, a shift is taking place to more gift giving; because of lunar calendar, dates are not fixed.

Source: Mushtaq Luqmani, Zahir A. Quareshi, and Linda Delene, "Marketing in Islamic Countries: A Viewpoint," *MUS Business Topics,* Summer 1980, pp. 20–21.

International Marketing Highlight 7.3

Cultural Islands

Japan: The strongest work ethic, the greatest concern about the work ethic of the rest of the workforce, and strongly in favor of free trade.

South Korea: Strongly favors protectionism, puts country ahead of company, a strong sense of corporate responsibility toward employees, and more optimistic about the future.

India: More optimistic about the future and strongly favors protectionism.

Hungary: Organizationally different from companies in other countries and very focused on economic regeneration.

Source: Rosabeth Moss Kanter, "Transcending Business Boundaries: 12,000 World Managers View Change," *Harvard Business Review,* May–June 1991, p. 153.

imported products. But the reverse may also be true, and a perception of greatness attributed to another culture may lead to the eager acceptance of things reflecting that culture. For example, the Japanese are proud of their culture and economic achievement and prefer to buy Japanese manufactures. On the other hand, the words *Made in U.S.A.* marked on a product communicate quality and sophistication to people in many developing countries.[21] The Japanese respond to names. They like dealing with people of standing. It is for this reason that Mead Corporation, which has successfully operated in Japan for thirty-five years, had Nelson Mead, the son of the founder, handle that business.[22]

Ethics and Mores

The concept of what is right and wrong is based on culture. To be straightforward and openly honest are considered morally right in the United States, even if feelings are hurt. In Latin cultures, however, people avoid direct statements that would embarrass or make another uncomfortable. Thus, even if a Latin businessman does not mean to do business, he would appear to participate, only later to excuse himself from the transaction process.

In an empirical study of United States, French, and German managers, for example, substantial differences were noted on ethical issues. On an issue that may benefit the firm at the expense of the environment, the French and German managers were more likely to side with their employers and participate in what they perceived as a relatively minor infraction of environmental law. The American managers were less likely to approve a production run that would result in illegal air pollution.[23]

The differences in mannerisms between the Japanese and the Koreans also illustrate the point. The Japanese are correct and reserved; the Koreans informal and outgoing. A Korean saleswoman puts her hand on a customer's shoulder as she walks him to the door; a Korean executive invites a business acquaintance home to meet the family. Such acts of familiarity would be very unusual in Japan.[24] Graham noted that culture has significant influence on the process of business negotiations conducted by the executives in the United States, Japan, and Brazil. For example, substantial differences in bargaining style existed across the three cultures. Brazilians made fewer commitments and more demands. Their first offers were more greedy. Americans were more apt to offer a fair price, one that was closer to the eventual solution. Japanese consistently asked for higher profit solutions when making the initial offer in a negotiation[25] (see International Marketing Highlight 7.4).

Culture and Marketing

Culture influences every aspect of marketing. Figure 7.1 describes the linkage between culture and marketing action. A marketing-oriented firm should make decisions based on customer perspectives. Customers' actions are shaped by their lifestyles and behavior patterns as they stem from their society's culture. Thus, the products that people buy, the attributes that they value, and the principals whose opinions they accept, are all culture-based choices. As a matter of fact, it

International Marketing Highlight 7.4

Why Can't People Do Things the American Way?

Bill Hastings, the assistant director of marketing for a small American manufacturing company, visited Bangkok to investigate the possibility of distributing the company's products in Southeast Asia. Bill traveled with Cheryl Acosta, field director for the company's international operations. Neither of them had had any prior experience in Asia. Bill, in fact, had never traveled outside the United States. Both executives felt mildly apprehensive about being neophytes in the field, but they felt great excitement, too, as if they were the first explorers in an uncharted area. (Neither acknowledged that their counterparts in other companies probably had had years of international experience and had developed a mastery of Southeast Asian business practices.)

Bill and Cheryl attempted to complete a twelve-country marketing study in six weeks. Bill figured that once he obtained the facts and made a quick decision on how to proceed, sales would start rolling in. But they found the environment baffling and made little headway. Frustrated, they impulsively recommended a plan to headquarters that ended in a fiasco one year later.

"I can't understand what happened," Bill reflected in the aftermath. "The same method worked just fine when we started operations in Los Angeles."

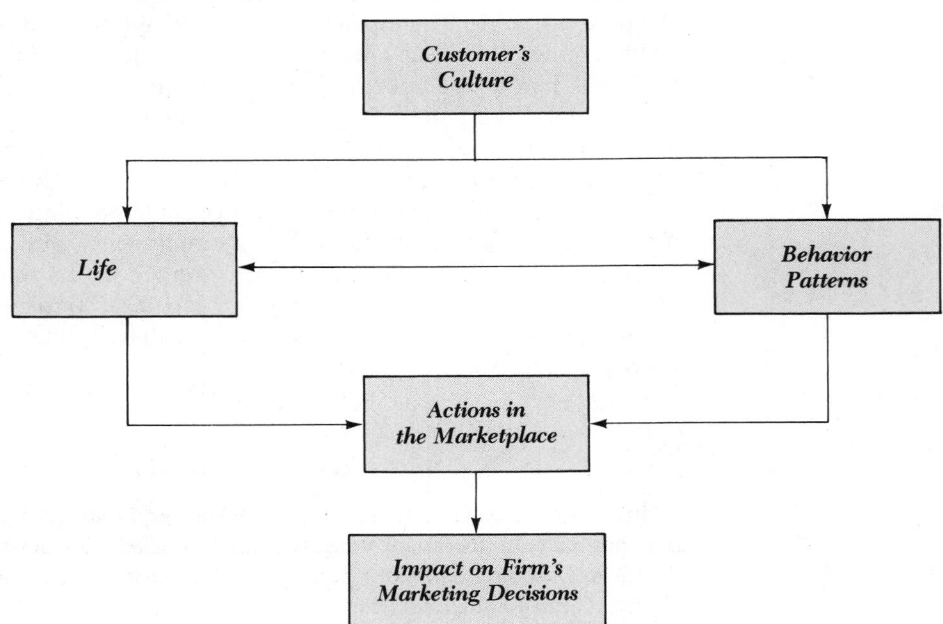

FIGURE 7.1 Impact of Culture on Marketing Decisions

is not an overstatement to say that a person's perspectives or resources, problems and opportunities to a considerable extent are generated and conditioned by culture. The influence of culture on marketing perspectives is cited in Exhibit 7.3 showing how Brazilians have reached negatively to products that were successful in the United States (see International Marketing Highlight 7.5).

A practical example of cultural impact is illustrated by the foods that people prefer. Of all the universals that constitute "culture," few, if any, are so ingrained

EXHIBIT 7.3 How Cultural Background Vary: An Example

Imaginative Brazilians do not always use products in the same way as Americans. "Marketers assume they can segment markets and position products, but Brazilian housewives find multiple uses for things," says Ian Gardner, a former Reckitt & Colman product manager. "If you try to sell a product specifically for cleaning floor surfaces, Brazilians will use it for disinfecting the toilet bowl, cleaning the cat, and washing the kids' hair."

Recently, sales of a certain brand of floor wax dropped mysteriously, says an American adman.

The perplexed manufacturer soon discovered many Brazilians had been using the floor wax as lighter fluid to ignite their Sunday barbecues.

When the company added more water to the solvent base, the floor wax became less flammable and Brazilians stopped buying it.

Products must be tailored to local tastes and customs. In Rio de Janeiro, consumers are used to butter that is usually slightly rancid from the tropical heat.

Unilever and Anderson-Clayton learned that to sell margarine successfully in Rio, it should taste slightly rancid.

Advertising as well as the product itself should be directed at the way Brazilians do things, like washing dishes. Brazilians squirt liquid detergent on a sponge rather than filling the kitchen sink with soapy water and submerging plates and silverware.

A recent commercial for a successful liquid dishwashing detergent featured a row of nuns, plates in hand, correctly doing the dishes by passing a soapy sponge down the line.

Why should [Brazilian] Portuguese speakers try to pronounce Kentucky Fried Chicken? "Some names are ridiculous, like [Pepsi's] Mountain Dew and [R.J. Reynolds'] Chesterfield," says Mr. Gardner. "Brazilians can't pronounce them."

Since its introduction in southern Brazil at the end of 1981, Mountain Dew has been working on the pronunciation problem with a mnemonic device. Ads read: "*Peca* [ask for] Mao-Tem-Du," a close approximation of Mountain Dew in a Brazilian accent.

"If you have to spend lots of money just to teach people to pronounce your product's name, there are much better ways to spend money," Mr. Gardner said.

Few Brazilians seem to be asking for Mountain Dew. A Pepsi marketing exec said the soft drink started very strong but sales have flattened. "But Brazilians can pronounce the name," he said. "They just need a little help."

Brazilians may have a similar problem when local beverage manufacturer Antarctica launches the national fruit flavored soft drink—called Guarana and pronounced "Gawra-nuh"—in the U.S. later this year.

Source: Laurel Wenz, *Advertising Age,* July 5, 1982, p. m–25.

International Marketing Highlight 7.5

Embarrassment in the Air

United Airlines' experiences in the Pacific market show how cultural mistakes could be embarrassing. As one of their officials reported:

> The map we inserted into our sales promotion brochure left out one of Japan's main islands.
>
> Our magazine ad campaign, "We Know the Orient," listed the names of Far Eastern countries below pictures of local coins. Unfortunately, the coins didn't match up with the countries.
>
> I leave to your imagination how Chinese businessmen felt taking off from Hong Kong during the inauguration of our concierge services for first-class passengers. To mark the occasion, each concierge was proudly wearing a white carnation . . . a well-known Oriental symbol of death.
>
> Perhaps the most embarrassing mistake was our inflight magazine cover that showed Australian actor Paul Hogan wandering through the Outback. The caption read, "Paul Hogan Camps It Up." Hogan's lawyer was kind enough to phone us long distance from Sydney to let us know that "camps it up" is Australian slang for "flaunts his homosexuality." The Paul Hogan story is particularly instructive. Americans often assume that the folks Down Under are just like Americans because we all speak English. This does not make for happy customers. Australians expect real cream in their coffee—not artificial whitener. And the American hand gesture for "thumbs up" has quite a different meaning Down Under. It does *not* mean "OK."

Source: John R. Zeeman, "Service—The Cutting Edge of Global Competition: What United Is Learning in the Pacific," a presentation before the Academy of International Business, Chicago, Illinois, November 14, 1987.

and consistently reinforced as are food habits. The daily physiological requirement of nutrition in some form exists for every human inhabitant in any society or culture—there is no escape from eating for an extended period. Food consumption, acquisition, and preparation also are interrelated with many of the other universals of the culture, including religious observances and ceremonies, feasting, folklore, and the division of labor.

The human perception of edibility has little to do with logical nutritional fulfillments. Culture creates the system of communication among humans about edibility, toxicity, and repleteness. Cultural pressures easily overrule physiological necessities; therefore, it becomes even more difficult for an individual alien to a culture to predict that culture's preference for or rejection of certain food habits.

Brazil. A full complement of climates, topography, and population provides a wide variety of foods in Brazil. West African slaves ritualized food preparation on one end of the continuum, while American-style hamburgers, hot dogs, and pizza wedges for snacks balance the wide spectrum acceptable in Brazil. One of the major staples, beans, are considered good only when they are cooked in clay or earthenware pots. Ritual offerings to the gods of certain vegetable dishes are made even today, mostly because of the West African influence. Keep in mind, however, that such acts are limited to certain classes or religious groups. The major portion of Brazil is highly urbanized and upscale. Corn is considered to have special powers. Coffee is a symbol of hospitality, customarily taken sweet, as the coffee beans are coated with sugar.

Canada. Food customs are difficult to define as so many ethnocultural groups reside in Canada. "Edibles" parallel those of the United States, and particular food traditions in certain areas are identical to adjacent U.S. areas (i.e., traditional Saturday night baked beans and steamed bread, boiled dinner, and fiddleheads in the Maritime provinces, just as in New England).

England. Food preparation tends to be simple. Tea is a mainstay, if not an institution. Breads, cakes, pies, and puddings make up a large part of the British menu. Rabbit, eel, and goose are far more common in England than in the United States. The English tradition of composure pervades their eating habits. Displaying an interest in food is considered ill-mannered, as is chewing anything more than a small bite of food at a time, or setting one's knife down while eating with a fork. Breakfast is tea, perhaps with bread, lunch is often a thin sandwich at a pub, and a light supper is simple in both ingredients and preparation.

France. Contrasting with the English concept of disinterest, France's appreciation of quality food and meticulous preparation is well known and well documented throughout historical publications. The French consider wine more basic and more appropriate than water at any time and for people of any age. Very little is wasted in food preparation. Vegetable water is not poured away but kept for food stock. Trimming and waste all go to the compost pile. "Anything that lives is edible" in France; snails, sea urchins, frog legs, horsemeat, rabbits, and eels are all common foods. Bakeries emphasize white bread (anything else is "health" bread and considered second class). Wine is never taken with a green salad, as the vinegar would disturb the palate's appreciation of the wine. Bread is the symbol of hospitality and used to cleanse the palate between courses. Smoking in many dining rooms is considered contemptuous of the food and drink offered. As the bread is hidden in the napkins in France, it is wise not to shake it out after sitting down.

Greece. Greeks never drink without food, and food is always shared with friends. Contrary to the French opinion, water is a symbol of hospitality and the most popular beverage in Greece. Water is an element of socialization: women gather at wells to procure water; men socialize at taverns where water is served. Refusal of any hospitable effort, including the sharing of much food, is an insult to both the host and hostess in Greece. The adage that "Greeks are either feasting or fasting" emphasizes the importance of food in the Greek Orthodox culture. Between Christmas and Epiphany all foods are hidden or disguised to prevent crippled ghosts (*Kallikandari*) from poisoning them. Modern Greeks will go to a pastry shop to eat and drink after a funeral as a form of ritual purification.

Japan. Traditional Japanese staples include fish, rice, vegetables, seafood, and tea. Although meat is permitted by religious custom, very little is consumed. Rice traditionally is believed to have medicinal qualities and is used in religious ceremonies as well. Sushi, although composed of vinegared rice and various other ingredients, is eaten with the fingers rather than with utensils. Buckwheat noodles are considered good luck and traditionally are shared on New Year's Eve. Dining etiquette is important to the Japanese. The rice bowl is always received or removed with both hands. Rice is never eaten all at once, but between other foods. Tea is often served in the same rice dish, so it is important to finish your rice if you want tea. Chopsticks are to be picked up with your right hand and laid one inch apart parallel to the place setting when not in use. It is polite to wait until older persons begin their meals before eating, and the sake cup is turned upside down to indicate politely that you've had enough.

India. Complex food habits and traditions are characteristic of a country having diverse religious faiths and the attendant subgroups. Thus, a comprehensive summary of India's various food habits is impossible. The following represents a small sampling. Kitchen and dining facilities of most homes are held in some degree of reverence, and shoes are not worn there. Because electrical appliances are not available in the majority of homes, food storage is not extensive and food preparation usually is limited to small stove cooking. Tea is favored in the north, coffee in the south. Religious taboos usually discourage the use of meat, even the intake of eggs. Pulse (a type of legume) is usually eaten in some form in one meal of the day and is referred to as *dal.* A wide variety of available freshly ground seasonings further personalizes food preparation. Food is prepared and eaten only with the right hand, and knives are never used outside of the kitchen where food is prepared. An after-dinner custom of chewing paan is practiced nationwide. The paan consists of a heart-shaped leaf enclosing special spices.

Iran. Very little seafood is used in Iran, and pork is forbidden by Muslin religion. Tea, coffee, and carbonated drinks are the leading beverages, while lamb, wheatbread, eggplant, and yogurt are staple foods. This is another country in which dining is accomplished with the right hand and knives are never seen in the dining room. Diners remove their shoes before entering the dining room and sit on soft cushions on the floor. Refusing coffee is taken as an insult, and coffee in very small cups traditionally is offered and served three times to a guest during which noisy sipping is quite acceptable.

Israel. Religious influences govern the diet of the Israelis as well as the design of each kitchen. Varying degrees of religious observances determine the extent of kitchen utensil duplication (one for meat, one for dairy), and only meats from animals who chew their cud and have a cloven hoof as well as fish with scales and fins may be eaten. The menu for Israelis is also as diverse as the number of religious sects there.

Italy. Plain bread and chicory are staples for Italian common people. Oil and pasta are cooking universals, and wine is treated as a food rather than an alcoholic medium. Green tomatoes are preferred over red tomatoes. It is against the rules of etiquette to leave a dining plate in front of a guest when it is obvious that the meal is finished.

Mexico. Tortillas (flatbread) and frijoles (beans) are on the daily menu of Mexicans, and the really hot spices are prepared mostly for the tourists. Fresh milk is not popular, but is used to serve cafe con leche. Dinnertime can last from 2:00 to 5:00 P.M. in the afternoon in Mexico, which includes the traditional siesta.

Spain. Gazpacho is a good example of Spain's staple foods—each region has it, and each region has its own way of preparing it the "correct" way. Spices tend to be more subtle than commonly thought. Social dining tends to center in restaurants rather than in the home.

Sweden. Sweden has a very Americanized diet and ranks close to the United States in frozen-food consumption. Processing foods by salting and smoking is quite common and popular. Reindeer meat is as common as pork and seafood. Strong, hot, black coffee is a part of every Swedish meal. The tradition of "skoal" is observed by a toast, a gulp, and a flash of your empty glass. Different courses during a meal are always served on fresh plates. The final ritual of a meal is to show appreciation for the hostess's efforts; the individual to her left starts by thanking her first, and then all other participants follow in sequence.

Venezuela. Yucca, plantains, corn, and beans are staple foods. Varieties of ants are considered a delicacy. Coffee, of course, is consumed daily.[26]

These descriptions are merely summaries; they do not encompass all trends, etiquettes, and traditions observed in the respective cultures, and each country deserves an in-depth report to provide meaningful data for planning a thorough marketing strategy. This is simply the appetizer before the main course—discovering the ramifications of cultural foods in the international marketplace (see International Marketing Highlight 7.6).

Empirical evidence on lifestyle and behavior differences is provided by Plummer.[27] Basing his findings on a number of cross-cultural consumer studies, he demonstrates significant differences among people belonging to different countries on a variety of dimensions. Some of these differences are illustrated in Exhibit 7.4. On the topic of housecleaning, for example, the normal attitude toward this chore appears much more casual in Australia, Germany, and the United States than in Italy and the United Kingdom. Likewise, people in the United Kingdom, Italy, France, and the United States hold a more traditional and conservative perspective of moral principle statements than those in Germany and Australia.

On the topic of personal hygiene Plummer found that "Americans would be

International Marketing Highlight 7.6

Gifts That People Prefer

Customs concerning gift giving are extremely important to understand. In some cultures, gifts are expected, and failure to present them is considered an insult, whereas in other countries, offering a gift is considered offensive. Business executives also need to know when to present gifts—on the initial visit or afterward; where to present gifts—in public or in private; what type of gift to present; what color it should be; and how many to present.

Gift giving is an important part of doing business in Japan. Exchanging gifts symbolizes the depth and strength of a business relationship to the Japanese. Gifts are usually exchanged at the first meeting. When presented with a gift, companies are expected to respond by giving a gift.

In sharp contrast, gifts are rarely exchanged in Germany and are usually not appropriate. Small gifts are fine, but expensive items are not a general practice.

Gift giving is not a normal custom in Belgium or the United Kingdom either, although in both countries flowers are a suitable gift if invited to someone's home. Even that is not as easy as it sounds. International executives must use caution to choose appropriate flowers. For example, avoid sending chrysanthemums (especially white) in Belgium and elsewhere in Europe since they are mainly used for funerals. In Europe, it is also considered bad luck to present an even number of flowers. Beware of white flowers in Japan where they are associated with death, and purple flowers in Mexico and Brazil.

Source: Business America, vol. 112, no. 2 (Special Edition 1991), pp. 26–27.

lost without their deodorant." The French and Australians, on the other hand, "appear less concerned about the use of a deodorant."[28] These differences vividly point out the importance of assessing cultural differences among nations before developing marketing strategy.

Similar differences in cross-national comparisons were discovered by Douglas. In her study of wives working at home and outside the home in the United States and France, she found that even after accounting for structural differences between the two countries, the U.S. wives tended to shop more in large supermarkets and less in neighborhood supermarkets and corner stores than French housewives. Further, the U.S. husbands seemed more likely to assist in grocery shopping, though infrequently, than French husbands.[29]

Muller and Bolger discovered major differences in the pattern of prepurchase information search for a new automobile between the two major cultural groups in Canada. First, French Canadians considered fewer cars during the search process than did English Canadians. Second, the French Canadian car buyers devoted less time to search than their English Canadian counterparts. Third, French Canadians conducted a generally less thorough and less extensive search for a new car than did English Canadians. Fourth, on the average, before choosing a new car, English Canadians made three times as many test drives as French Cana-

EXHIBIT 7.4 Cross-Cultural Differences

HOUSECLEANING		PERSONAL HYGIENE		MORALITY		CHILDREN		CHURCH	
"A house should be dusted and polished three times a week."		*"Everyone should use a deodorant."*		*"There is too much emphasis on sex nowadays."*		*"My children are the most important thing in my life."*		*"I attend church regularly."*	
100%	Agreement	100%	Agreement	100%	Agreement	100%	Agreement	100%	Agreement
86%	Italy	89%	United States	82%	United Kingdom	86%	Germany	77%	Spain
59	United Kingdom	81	French Canada	79	Italy	84	Italy/ French Canada	75	Italy
55	France	77	English Canada	69	English Canada	74	Denmark	73	French Canada
53	Spain	71	United Kingdom	66	United States	73	France	70	Germany
45	Germany	69	Italy	52	South Africa/ France/ French Canada	71	United States	65	United States
33	Australia	59	France	31	Australia	67	Spain	44	English Canada
25	United States	53	Australia	24	Germany	57	United Kingdom	36	United Kingdom
						56	English Canada	23	France
						53	South Africa	16	Australia
						48	Australia		

Source: Joseph T. Plummer, "Cross-Cultural Differences Among Consumers from Different Countries," *Journal of Advertising*, Summer 1977, pp. 10–11.

dians. To sum up, the French Canadian buyers of new autos search less than English Canadians, not only because of their traditional reliance on the family and on word-of-mouth communications, but for other reasons which were not made clear from this study.[30] Similarly, Schaninger, Bourgeois, and Buss found significant consumption, shopping, and media usage differences between the French-speaking, bilingual, and English-speaking Canadian families.[31]

But no matter who shops, or where, cultural differences always affect decision making when it comes to the product and its price, as well as to the way it is distributed and promoted.[32] Briefly, understanding and heeding cultural variables is critical to success in international marketing. Lack of familiarity with the business practices, social customs, and etiquette of a country can weaken a company's position in the market, prevent it from accomplishing its objectives, and ultimately lead to failure.

The Product

Two similar products are introduced into a country. One does extremely well; the other flops. Why? Although the performance of a product/market depends on a variety of factors, in many cases *failure is directly traceable to cultural blunders*. For example, Kentucky Fried Chicken was received well in France (as in

Germany and the United Kingdom), but McDonald's stumbled.[33] Similarly, the British prefer a wood handle on their umbrella while we in the United States find the plastic handle satisfactory. Apparently, what is a "right" product for one culture may be unsuitable for another culture.

A product that has been highly profitable in the United States may not achieve the same success elsewhere because the product attributes desired in the United States may not necessarily be desired in another part of the world. The Campbell Soup Company found out the hard way that the condensed soups so popular and acceptable in the United States were not liked in England. Accustomed to ready-to-eat soups, the English consumer found it hard to believe that water or milk could be added to soup without spoiling the taste.[34] Similarly, Phillip Morris ran into difficulties because of taste differences among nations. One of its popular brands was a dismal flop in Canada despite adequate promotion. Canadians have a preference for Virginia-type tobacco blends, which are different from what the popular brand had to offer.[35]

Sometimes a product that is unacceptable in its U.S. form may succeed if it is adapted to the culture of the new market. Mister Donut's success in Japan is the result of a series of minute but sensible modifications. Their coffee cup is smaller and lighter to fit the finger size of the average Japanese consumer. Even their donuts are a little smaller there than those in the United States. Similarly, Japanese mothers found the Beachnut babyfood jar too big. After the jar was made smaller, the sales increased. After years of painstaking market research, P&G finally realized that Japanese parents are very concerned with keeping their babies clean, and they change their children's diapers far more often than Americans do. In response, P&G devised Ultra Pampers, a more-absorbent diaper that keeps the child drier and makes frequent changing a less-messy task. P&G also discovered that in land-starved Japan, shelf and closet space is almost as precious to housewives as their children, so it made the diapers thinner so the same number fit in a much smaller box. The popularity of the new diapers spread rapidly, and today Ultra Pampers is the market leader in Japan.[36]

Another good example is the Barbie doll. This all-American best-seller did not do very well in Japan for a long time. Finally, Mattel Toys, its creator, gave the manufacturing license to Takara, a Japanese company. Takara's own survey revealed that most Japanese girls—and their parents—thought the doll's breasts were too big and the legs unrealistically long. After correcting these minor defects, and converting the Barbie doll's blue eyes to dark brown, Takara started selling the same doll under the same brand name and concept, and found that its production could not keep up with the demand. Takara sold some two million Barbie dolls in just two years. According to a Takara executive, dolls in Japan are a reflection of what girls want to be. With the target customer group in Japan being eighth-graders, this doll had to look more Japanese than the original version.[37]

In India, the Barbie doll had a slightly different problem. In a conservative country like India, the concept of boyfriend was unacceptable, so Ken did not accompany her. However, since brothers and sisters in India are much closer than in Western societies, Mattel created Mark as Barbie's brother for the Indian market.

The positioning of the product in different countries should be in line with the cultural traits of each society. Renault's strategy in different countries illustrates the point. In France, the Renault car was introduced as a little "supercar," which was fun to drive both on highways and within the city. In Germany, where auto buying is viewed as a serious matter, the emphasis was put on safety, modern engineering, and interior comfort. In Italy, road performance—road handling capacity and acceleration—was stressed. In Finland, the focus was on solid construction and reliability. For Holland, the Renault car had to be redesigned because the Dutch consider a small car cheap and mechanically inferior.[38] The same principle applies to the personal computer. American computer companies learned early on that they could not simply target Europe as one market, but must court each country market separately, acknowledging cultural differences. The French, for example, are very nationalistic, looking for more French-made parts in the product. The German market, on the other hand, has a very high perception of quality.[39]

In general, product positioning in a foreign market should match the country's unique cultural environment (see International Marketing Highlight 7.7).

The importance of perceived risk is subject to cultural influences as well. Thus, risk is a more important determinant of purchase behavior in the United States than in Mexico, where consumers are influenced by fatalism, the belief that humans have no control or recourse on the shape of things in the future. Therefore, for cultural reasons, the use of product warranties to reduce the risk of negative outcomes associated with purchases may not be as effective in Mexico as in the United States.[40]

Distribution

The cultural dimensions of a nation make certain distribution arrangements more viable. For example, in the United States Sears, Roebuck merchandises a big percentage of products under its own brand name. In Mexico, however, Sears has done two things differently in order to respond to pride aspects in the local culture. First, it buys over 90 percent of its items from national manufacturers. Second, it carries U.S. national brands made in Mexico to cater to well-to-do customers who like to distinguish themselves by using U.S. brands.

Channels of distribution may need to be modified to suit local conditions. Avon uses door-to-door and other direct selling in the United States. This provides men and women with the opportunity to make buying decisions in the privacy of their homes or workplaces. Such arrangements, however, did not work out abroad. European women considered calls by Avon representatives as intrusions on their privacy, and the representatives felt uncomfortable selling to friends in their homes for a profit.[41]

Cultural boundaries affect the mapping of sales territories. For example, a French company decided to divide sales territories in Africa based on market potential (respecting local administrative boundaries), something it had done successfully in the Western European market. This type of territory structure, how-

International Marketing Highlight 7.7

The Marlboro Man

What do college students in different countries think when considering Marlboro cigarettes? A researcher at Northwestern University posed this question and put it to the test by researching college students in five countries: Brazil, Japan, Norway, Thailand, and the United States. Small samples of students in each country participated in a word-association test by responding to the statement: "Smoking a Marlboro cigarette . . ."

Responses were sharply mixed. Thai students considered smoking a Marlboro cigarette to be relaxing. Norwegian students most closely linked smoking Marlboros to disease, and Brazilians associated the brand with pollution. U.S. students responded to "Smoking a Marlboro cigarette . . ." with words like "cowboy," "horse," and "macho"—all relating directly to Marlboro's longstanding advertising campaign. The Japanese associated smoking Marlboros with social occasions.

These different images point out that products and brands mean different things around the world because the cultural contexts in which they are interpreted vary greatly. This means that creative advertising needs to be adjusted to accommodate the specific cultural context in which it is placed. For example, because Japanese consumers associate Marlboro cigarettes with being sociable, Marlboro advertisements in Japan could show the cowboy with other cowboys rather than by himself. In Thailand, where consumers perceive cigarettes to be suggestive of relaxation, it may be most effective to show the cowboy in a subdued context rather than chasing wild horses.

Source: Lenore Skenazy, "How Does Slogan Translate," *Advertising Age,* October 12, 1987, p. 84.

ever, did not allow for the fact that the countries contained a number of tribes, each with a particular person authorized to buy in the community. The territory arrangements overlapped with these tribal areas and created a great deal of confusion in the assignment of sales responsibilities[42] (see International Marketing Highlight 7.8).

Promotion

Promotion practices, particularly advertising, are perhaps most susceptible to cultural error. Examples abound where advertising copy and design were culturally repugnant, and, therefore, totally ineffective. For example, in Thailand the Warner-Lambert Company used its U.S. ad for Listerine showing a boy and a girl being affectionate to each other. This type of appeal was ineffective since the boy-girl relationship shown was ultra-modern and hence against the cultural norms of Thailand's conservative society. A slight modification—two girls talking about Listerine—had a positive effect on sales.[43] Similarly, Colgate Palmolive Company introduced its Cue toothpaste in France only to find out later that *cue* in French is a pornographic word.[44] Pepsi ran into difficulties in Germany for using its U.S. ad, "Come alive, you're in the Pepsi generation," which in German

International Marketing Highlight 7.8

Cultural Response to Paris's Haute Couture

The cultural response of Paris's haute couture to serve Arab clientele highlights the influence of culture on distribution:

> The saleswoman at Nina Ricci's *haute couture* salon left her customer, a Saudi Princess, alone in the dressing room for a moment. When she returned, she found the princess prostrate on the floor, lying on a $5,000 white wool coat. She was using it as a prayer rug.
>
> Purveyors of luxury here, who have always catered to the most lucrative markets, are very sensitive these days to Arab cultures. Arabs are only about 15% of the 3,000-odd regular customers for high fashions and outnumbered four to one by Americans. But Arabs outspend everybody else. They buy big quantities. Arabs account for 50% to 60% of the $24 million spent annually at this city's [Paris] 23 couture houses.
>
> Ever since the Organization of Petroleum Exporting Countries precipitously increased oil prices in 1973, and wealthy Arabs in some numbers started spending petrodollars in Paris, vendors of goods have found it opportune to familiarize themselves with the customs of Middle Eastern society. And they have fashioned certain stereotypes—some of them cruel—about their *arriviste* clientele.
>
> Arab women won't undress in front of strangers and often want to take clothes home to try on. They tend to shop in groups—bringing along all the women in a household, from nanny to granny. They like their clothes to sparkle, and they don't like to wear black.
>
> Because they live in desert climates where it often is too hot to work by day, Arabs tend to be night owls, asking for private showings that might begin at 10 P.M. and end in the wee hours.

Source: Joan Kron, "An Arab Princess Is a Beautiful Bride in a $150,000 Gown," *The Wall Street Journal,* November 5, 1984, p. 1.

meant, "Come alive out of the grave."[45] Pepsodent's promise of white teeth backfired in Southeast Asia where betel nut chewing was an acceptable norm, and therefore, yellow teeth were taken for granted.[46] A P&G Camay soap commercial showed a Japanese husband in the room as his wife was bathing. The Japanese considered it an invasion of privacy and distasteful.[47]

Ajax's white tornado was not perceived as a symbol of power in many countries. Ultra Brite's sexy girl throwing kisses was ineffective in Belgium and the company was forced to drop the theme "Give your mouth sex appeal."[48] Carlsberg had to add a third elephant to its label of Elephant beer for an ad in Africa since two elephants are a symbol of bad luck there.[49] Usage of color in ads must be attuned to cultural norms as well. In Japan, as in many Asian countries, the color white is for mourning; purple is associated with death in many Latin American countries; and brown and gray are disliked in Nicaragua[50] (see International Marketing Highlight 7.9).

International Marketing Highlight 7.9

Taboos Around the World

Never touch the head of a Thai or pass an object over it, as the head is considered sacred in Thailand. Likewise, never point the bottoms of the feet in the direction of another person in Thailand or cross your legs while sitting, especially in the presence of an older person.

Avoid using triangular shapes in Hong Kong, Korea, or Taiwan, as the triangle is considered a negative shape in those countries.

Remember that the number 7 is considered bad luck in Kenya, good luck in Czechoslovakia, and has magical connotations in Benin.

Red is a positive color in Denmark, but represents witchcraft and death in many African countries.

A nod means "no" in Bulgaria, and shaking the head side-to-side means "yes."

Source: Business America, vol. 112, no. 2 (Special Edition 1991), pp. 26–27.

Pricing

The price that a customer may be willing to pay for a product depends on both its perceived and actual values. The value of goods imported from a Western country, for example, is perceived as much higher in developing countries. As an example, Indians perceive imported products as superior to those manufactured locally. For this reason, U.S./English brands sell at an inflated price. A story is told of an Indian who on a trip to England bought an expensive sweater for his wife from a London department store. He was disenchanted on returning home to find that the sweater had been manufactured in India.

An empirical investigation by Cattin and his colleagues showed that U.S. and French purchasing managers attached varying degrees of importance to products manufactured in different countries. For example, *Made in England* appeared to be more favorably perceived by the French, as promising more luxurious and more inventive products than *Made in U.S.A.* On the other hand, *Made in Germany* products were more highly regarded by American than French consumers. It would appear in countries where one's image is high, a premium price may be charged. On the other hand, where a national image is weak, an international business could do well to deemphasize "made in" information and perhaps seek entry in the market through a joint venture or some other form of close association with a domestic firm.[51]

Cultural Analysis—The Primacy of Host Country Viewpoint

The analysis of cultural differences is necessary for the formulation of international marketing strategy. Conceptually, cultural analysis may be based on any of the following three approaches: ethnocentrism, assimilation, and primacy of host country viewpoint.[52]

The *ethnocentrism approach* assumes "We are the best." Many U.S. companies are guilty of assuming that what is good at home should work in foreign markets as well.[53] The examples discussed in the previous section illustrate how ethnocentrism can lead to costly mistakes. The *assimilation approach* assumes that since the United States is a cultural melting pot, the cultural traits demonstrated in United States society are relevant anywhere. The third viewpoint, the ***primacy of host country approach,*** concerns market composition and emphasizes basing decisions on host country cultural traits. This approach considers domestic information as inappropriate to successful operation in markets outside the United States. The discussion that follows assumes the primacy of host country viewpoint.

Assessment of Culture

As assessment of a country's culture for marketing's sake involves analyzing the people's attitudes, motivations, perceptions, and learning processes. Exhibit 7.5 on the following page summarizes more specifically the cultural determinants. The information contained in this exhibit attempts to relate cultural traits to marketing decisions. For example, simply knowing about the religion or morality of a culture is not enough. What must be analyzed is whether or not the product slated to be introduced into the country has any direct or indirect connotations that conflict with the cultural patterns of the society. Similarly, an examination of advertising themes, phrases, words, or expressions should confirm viability of promotional decisions.

The cultural values of a nation may be studied through either observation or fieldwork. *Observation* requires living in a culture over a long period in order to become deeply involved in its pattern of living. *Fieldwork,* on the other hand, involves gathering information on a set of variables relative to the culture. While the observation method may be more desirable for a fuller understanding of the culture, from the standpoint of business it is impractical. Thus, the study of culture in the realm of international marketing must be based on fieldwork. One fieldwork approach for assessing culture has been worked out by Rokeach. He has developed a list of eighteen terminal and eighteen instrumental values (see Exhibit 7.6 on page 263). Rokeach's framework can be employed productively to discriminate people of culturally diverse backgrounds.[54]

Thus, one way to approach the cultural analysis of a country for the purpose of making marketing decisions might consist of two steps. First, a general notion of the culture is gained by using Rokeach's thirty-six values. This general information may be further interpreted by answering the specific marketing-related questions raised by Engel and his colleagues in Exhibit 7.5.

Hall's Map of Culture

A different way of understanding foreign cultures is recommended by Edward T. Hall. His framework, which he calls a map of culture, consists of a two-dimensional matrix containing different human activities, which he calls primary message systems. These activities are interaction, association, subsistence, bisexuality,

EXHIBIT 7.5 Outline of Cross-Cultural Analysis of Consumer Behavior

1. Determine Relevant Motivations in the Culture
   What needs are fulfilled with this product in the minds of members of the culture? How are these needs presently fulfilled? Do members of this culture readily recognize these needs?
2. Determine Characteristic Behavior Patterns
   What patterns are characteristic of purchasing behavior? What forms of division of labor exist within the family structure? How frequently are products of this type purchased? What size packages are normally purchased? Do any of these characteristic behaviors conflict with behavior expected for this product? How strongly ingrained are the behavior patterns that conflict with those needed for distribution of this product?
3. Determine What Broad Cultural Values are Relevant to This Product
   Are there strong values about work, morality, religion, family relations, and so on, that relate to this product? Does this product connote attributes that are in conflict with these cultural values? Can conflicts with values be avoided by changing the product? Are there positive values in this culture with which the product might be identified?
4. Determine Characteristic Forms of Decision Making
   Do members of the culture display a studied approach to decisions concerning innovations or an impulsive approach? What is the form of the decision process? Upon what information sources do members of the culture rely? Do members of the culture tend to be rigid or flexible in the acceptance of new ideas? What criteria do they use in evaluating alternatives?
5. Evaluate Promotion Methods Appropriate to the Culture
   What role does advertising occupy in the culture? What themes, words, or illustrations are taboo? What language problems exist in present markets that cannot be translated into this culture? What types of salespeople are accepted by members of the culture? Are such salespeople available?
6. Determine Appropriate Institutions for This Product in the Minds of Consumers
   What types of retailers and intermediary institutions are available? What services do these institutions offer that are expected by the consumer? What alternatives are available for obtaining services needed for the product but not offered by existing institutions? How are various types of retailers regarded by consumers? Will changes in the distribution structure be readily accepted?

Source: James F. Engel, Roger D. Blackwell, and David T. Kollat, *Consumer Behavior,* 3rd ed. (Hinsdale, IL: Dryden Press, 1978), p. 90.

territoriality, temporality, learning, play, defense, and exploitation.[55] Exhibit 7.7 explains briefly the ten primary message systems.

A person interested in learning about a culture need not study all ten aspects but can examine any one of them fully and gain an adequate understanding of the culture. Hall remarked: "Since each [aspect] is enmeshed in the other, one can start they study of culture with any of the ten and eventually come out with a complete picture."[56] For example, to understand buyer behavior, a marketer could analyze the culture by examining the association aspect; association

EXHIBIT 7.6 Terminal and Instrumental Values

TERMINAL VALUE	INSTRUMENTAL VALUE
A comfortable life (a prosperous life)	Ambitious (hardworking, aspiring)
An exciting life (a stimulating, active life)	Broadminded (open-minded)
A sense of accomplishment (lasting contribution)	Capable (competent, effective)
A world at peace (free of war and conflict)	Cheerful (lighhearted, joyful)
A world of beauty (beauty of nature and the arts)	Clean (neat, tidy)
Equality (brotherhood, equal opportunity for all)	Courageous (standing up for your beliefs)
Family security (taking care of loved ones)	Forgiving (willing to pardon others)
Freedom (independence, free choice)	Helpful (working for the welfare of others)
Happiness (contentedness)	Honest (sincere, truthful)
Inner harmony (freedom from inner conflict)	Imaginative (daring, creative)
Mature love (sexual and spiritual intimacy)	Independent (self-reliant, self-sufficient)
National security (protection from attack)	Intellectual (intelligent, reflective)
Pleasure (an enjoyable, leisurely life)	Logical (consistent, rational)
Salvation (saved, eternal life)	Loving (affectionate, tender)
Self-respect (self-esteem)	Obedient (dutiful, respectful)
Social recognition (respect, admiration)	Polite (courteous, well-mannered)
True friendship (close companionship)	Responsible (dependent, reliable)
Wisdom (a mature understanding of life)	Self-controlled (restrained, self-disciplined)

Source: M. Rokeach, *The Nature of Human Values* (New York: Free Press, 1973), p. 28.

EXHIBIT 7.7 The Primary Message System of Edward Hall's Map of Culture

1. *Interaction.* The interaction with the environment through different modes, such as speech and writing.
2. *Association.* The structure and organization of society and its various components.
3. *Subsistence.* The perspective of activities of individuals and groups that deal with livelihood and living.
4. *Bisexuality.* The differentiation of roles and functions along sex lines.
5. *Territoriality.* The possession, use, and defense of land and territory.
6. *Temporality.* The division and allocation of time and its use for various activities.
7. *Learning.* The patterns of transmitting knowledge.
8. *Play.* The process of enjoyment through relaxation and recreation.
9. *Defense.* The protection against natural and human forces in the environment.
10. *Exploitation.* The application of skills and technology to turn natural resources to people's needs.

Source: Excerpt from *The Silent Language* by Edward T. Hall, © 1959 by Edward T. Hall. Used by permission of Doubleday, a division of Bantam, Doubleday, Dell Publishing Group, Inc.

intersects with all other nine aspects just as they intersect with association. With each intersection, a variety of questions can be raised to gain cultural understanding. To illustrate the point, the intersection of association with learning may be examined by seeking answers to such questions as: How do different groups of the society learn about new things? Whose opinions are respected in each group? Similarly, the intersection of learning with association would be revealed in connection with such problems as how learning takes place through different sources in different groups.

The use of Hall's framework for international marketers is exemplified by Robock and Simmonds in an analysis of the play activity for a toy and games company.[57] Presumably, perspectives of play vary from one culture to another. To suit the marketing program to the cultural traits of the local market, Hall's framework would create eighteen categories of questions (see Exhibit 7.8). For example, categories 13 and 14 deal with learning as it emerges in play and play as it leads to learning.

Hall's approach provides an overall perspective on the culture through analysis of one or two primary message systems. In relation to the needs of business, this system works well because the time and expense for a comprehensive cultural perspective are not required. Only the particular element of the culture directly related to a particular international marketing decision needs to be analyzed.

Cultural Adaptation

Cultural adaptation refers to the making of business decisions appropriate to the cultural traits of the society. In other words, adaptation requires that the decisions should be sensitive to the local culture to ensure that the native customs, traditions, and taboos offer no constraint to their implementation.

The previous sections underscored the importance of culture as a factor in conducting business outside the United States. The impact of culture is ubiquitous in all marketing decisions. Obviously, international marketers must seek cultural adaptation overseas. All their decisions and actions should be fully congruent with local culture.

While the necessity for cultural adaptation is widely recognized, its realization can be difficult in practice. The major reason for this difficulty is what one author calls ***SRC,*** that is, the tendency to use a ***self-reference criterion,*** which can be explained this way: Whenever people are faced with unique situations, their own values are the measure for their understanding and response to the circumstances. Dependence on SRC comes naturally. For example, if someone in the United States is late for an appointment, that person will most likely feel guilty about it and apologize for being late—the value of punctuality and the importance of time have been instilled. The same person visiting an Arab country and scheduled for a business meeting would respond to the time of appointment with

EXHIBIT 7.8 A Business Application of Edward Hall's Map of Culture

INTERSECTIONS OF PLAY AND OTHER PRIMARY MESSAGE SYSTEMS	SAMPLE QUESTIONS CONCERNING CULTURAL PATTERNS SIGNIFICANT FOR MARKETING TOYS AND GAMES
1. Interaction/play	How do people interact during play as regards competitiveness, instigation, or leadership?
2. Play/interaction	What games are played involving acting, role-playing, or other aspects of real-world interaction?
3. Association/play	Who organizes play, and how do the organization patterns differ?
4. Play/association	What games are played about oganization; for example, team competitions and games involving kings, judges, or leader-developed rules and penalties?
5. Subsistence/play	What are the significant factors regarding people such as distributors, teachers, coaches, or publishers who make their livelihood from games?
6. Play/subsistence	What games are played about work roles in society such as doctors, nurses, firemen?
7. Bisexuality/play	What are the significant differences between the sexes in the sports, games and toys enjoyed?
8. Play/bisexuality	What games and toys involve bisexuality; for example, dolls, dressing up, dancing?
9. Territoriality/play	Where are games played and what are the limits observed in houses, parks, streets, schools, and so forth?
10. Play/territoriality	What games are played about space and ownership, for example, Monopoly?
11. Temporality/play	At what ages and what times of the day and year are different games played?
12. Play/temporality	What games are played about and involving time, for example, clocks, speed tests?
13. Learning/play	What patterns of coaching, tuition, and training exist for learning games?
14. Play/learning	What games are played about and involving learning and knowledge, for example, quizzes?
15. Defense/play	What are the safety rules for games, equipment, and toys?
16. Play/defense	What war and defense games and toys are utilized?
17. Exploitation/play	What resources and technology are permitted or utilized for games and sport, for example, hunting and fishing rules, use of parks, cameras, vehicles, and so forth?
18. Play/exploitation	What games and toys about technology or exploitation are used, for example, scouting, chemical sets, microscopes?

Source: Stefan H. Robock and Kenneth Simmonds, *International Business and Multinational Enterprises,* 4th ed. (Homewood, IL: Irwin, 1989), p. 426.

SRC and arrive on time for the meeting. If the other party fails to be on time, the visiting representative may be unhappy and angry and expect the latecomer to have the courtesy to apologize. Unfortunately, punctuality is not given the same priority the world over. To the Arab, the time of meeting would not mean that it has to be at the exact hour, but only means at about that time. For example, a 9 A.M. meeting does not communicate an exact time to the Arab but would be understood as some time in the morning. The tendency toward SRC is a stumbling block in cultural adaptation.

Framework for Adaptation

Lee proposes a four-step procedure for checking the influence of SRC in business adaptation:

- *Step 1.* Define the business problem or goal in terms of the cultural traits, habits, or norms of the United States.
- *Step 2.* Define the business problem or goal in terms of the foreign cultural traits, habits, or norms. Make no value judgments.
- *Step 3.* Isolate the SRC influence in the problem and examine it carefully to see how it complicates the problem.
- *Step 4.* Redefine the problem without the SRC influence and solve for the optimum business goal situation.[58]

To illustrate the implementation of this four-step procedure, consider the question: What automobile would be appropriate for the Pakistani market?

Step 1. In the United States, the automobile is a necessity for most of the people. Two cars per family is an accepted concept. Highway systems are designed for speeds of up to 70 miles per hour, but the legal limit for most highways is 55 miles per hour. Gasoline of high octane, both with and without lead, is available. Consumers look for comforts in the automobile such as air conditioning, AM/FM radio, cruise control, and leg room. Manufacturing techniques are sophisticated, and foreign exchange problems are unknown. Purchasers have a choice of buying either domestic or foreign-made automobiles. Introduction of yearly models of different cars is an accepted practice. Low-cost imports have achieved a significant share of the U.S. market and continue to challenge the viability of the domestic industry.

Step 2. Pakistan is a poor country. Over 60 percent of the people are illiterate and live in villages with muddy roads. Even in urban areas, lack of modern roads restricts speed to 35–40 miles per hour. Gasoline is very expensive—the equivalent of almost $3 for a U.S. gallon—and it is only 60 octane. The country is committed to a thoroughly Islamic way of life. Islamic thinking is finding its way into economic, political, educational, and family life. The Western attitude toward acquisition of goods and toward materialistic life is frowned upon. The rich have to live inconspicuously. The bicycle is the major mode of individual transportation and may be compared to having a good used car in the United States. Some people, a little more well-to-do, drive scooters, smaller versions of the motorcycle. Automobile ownership is a symbol of status and achievement. Ownership of an imported car is the equivalent of owning a Mercedes in the United States. With per capita GNP of $380 (1990 estimate), discretionary income is minimal.

Step 3. Review of steps 1 and 2 brings out the significant differences between the two countries. Even the cheapest American car, say a Chevette, would not match Pakistan's needs. In brief, an automobile manufacturer interested in entering Pakistan may not be able to successfully penetrate the market simply by modifying a U.S. model. Pakistan's needs call for a new product concept.

Step 4. The company seeking to enter the Pakistan market will be obliged to design an entirely new car. Such a car should be simple in all aspects: lightweight, few, if any, castings, and no compound body design; capable of giving very high mileage, say 80–100 miles per gallon, with cruising speeds up to 40 miles per hour. The car could simply be made of scrap iron with a low-powered engine and no frills. Such a car should be manufactured using local materials with minimum dependence on imported technology and/or parts. In other words, foreign exchange requirements of the project should be minimal. Overall, the feasible price for the car would have to be around $2,000.

Pakistan is not the only country that needs such a car. A large majority of Third World countries offer potential opportunities for a product of this type. Unfortunately SRC criteria, so deeply ingrained among Western auto manufacturers, have interfered with the development of an automobile for poorer nations. However, the experience of a nonprofit British-Dutch consortium, the Foundation for Transportation Development (FTD) in Lancaster, England, with their Africar is interesting. As has been said:

> Developed at a cost of $6.7 million, the vehicle has a body made of plywood—impregnated with epoxy to withstand the elements. Its angular contours are designed for easy production, but the shape also has low air drag to boost fuel economy. To smooth the ride, all four wheels have independent suspensions with hydraulic springs slung high off the ground for better clearance. With an air-cooled Citroën engine that needs minimum maintenance, the novel car has already proved its mettle in a rally from the Arctic Circle to the equator.
>
> Africar can turn a profit for licensed Third World producers on volumes of as few as 5,000 units per year.[59]

Areas of Adaptation

Essentially, there are three areas of foreign business adaptation: product, institutional, and individual.[60] The *product* may be marketed abroad as is, or it may be modified to fit the foreign country's climate, electrical specifications, color preferences, and the like, or it may be completely redesigned to match local requirements—a $2,000 automobile for the Third World. *Institutional* behavior includes adaptation of the organization and business interactions to match the host's perspective. For example, the U.S. firm in Spain may allow the workers time for a siesta during the day.

But most important, the adaptation of *individuals'* responses to foreign situations should strive to be free of SRC. Such adaptation may be required in all regards—the meaning of time, social behavior, play behavior, family interactions, and more. For example, adaptation may require that the female spouse of a U.S. executive not accompany him to a dinner party is an Islamic country. Unfortunately, in international situations, each culture is so deeply imbued with its own values that only what is normally seen and done appears appropriate and right.

Appropriate adaptive behavior is necessary to the successful conduct of foreign business. Adaptation should not be misinterpreted to mean that one should adapt the foreign country's attitudes and traits. Rather, one should, while inhibiting SRC, gain understanding and develop a spirit of tolerance and appreciation of different cultures.

Neglect of cultural factors limits marketing success, and can even lead to failure. Thus, marketing strategy should be duly attuned to local cultural traits. Exhibit 7.9 provides guidelines for cultural sensitization of marketing strategy. Although these guidelines are discussed with reference to Japan, they can, with modifications, be adapted to other countries.

Cultural Change

While international marketers must be aware that culture influences all aspects of a country's environment and that they therefore must be familiar with culture and then orient the marketing mix accordingly, they must also know that over time *cultures do change*.

This characteristic of culture brings up interesting possibilities. Products and services, which at one time may not be introduced into a particular culture, may become acceptable at a later time because of cultural change. In other words, cultural change affects acceptance of innovations. For example, back in the 1950s the filter cigarette was rejected in many Southeast Asian countries, because its basic for-health's-sake promotion over regular cigarettes made no sense in countries where the average life span was thirty years. After ten years, the filter cigarette slowly began to gain more acceptance. To an extent, the shift in attitude toward this product may be attributed to cultural change.

Basis of Cultural Change

The matter of cultural change is a controversial one and different anthropologists would specify different reasons for it. Although it may be disputed, one way of looking at cultural change is through economic development and Maslow's hierarchy-of-needs theory. Maslow ranked five human needs in lowest to highest order with lowest needs coming first: *physiological needs* (food, water, shelter, sex); *safety needs* (protection, security, stability); *social needs* (affection, friendship, acceptance); *ego needs* (prestige, success, self-esteem); and *the need for self-actualization* (self-fulfillment).[61] As a country begins to move from a subsistence economy, where fulfillment of physiological needs has been the major goal, to a situation where basic needs are easily achievable, new needs take precedence. This change forces cultural adjustments. In other words, as the economic well-

EXHIBIT 7.9 Guidelines for Making Marketing Strategy Sensitive to Japanese Culture

Relationships are everything: The primary frame of reference for success in Japan is to consider the context of relationships—to government, suppliers, distributors, customers, employees, etc.

Webs of tight relationships are what make Japan work. If they are effectively cultivated over the long term, desirable outcomes will result. The Westerner must virtually think "paranoid"—considering the other person's feelings and reactions all the time. This contrasts with the Western focus on good deals and contract terms, assuming that the relationships will take care of themselves. Think people (employees or consumers) first, companies second, and products third.

Generosity pays off: There are many practices that develop trust between Western marketers and the Japanese.

These include giving excellent service, attending to the details that make up quality, performing the favours and presenting the gifts that build mutual obligation, and taking the time to cater to the human side of Japanese businesspeople. Money or time saved according to the Western notion of efficiency in the short run may well result in social distance and system breakdowns in the longer run.

Teaming up the right people: Top management of the Western firm should regularly visit Japan to get to know the people there.

The Western head of the Japanese operation should be an executive with international, Asian, or preferably Japanese experience, to be assigned for a long while. Japanese personnel should include senior people with an impressive record and valuable contacts, and junior people who graduated from the upper ranks of the top-ranked Japanese universities. A network of consultants, Western and Japanese, should be retained as interpreters, market researchers, lawyers, advertising agencies, and the like. In cases where resources, reputation, and connections are needed to have a presence in Japan, a joint-venture partner should be found.

Avoiding confrontations: Problems always develop in relationships, especially when sharp differences between Western and Japenese ways exist.

To maintain harmonious relationships, no harsh words must be expressed. All people involved must save face and have their dignity in the group.

Actions speak louder: When one give his or her word in Japan, there is an obligation for it to be followed.

Therefore, carefully choose words that might lead to expectations of future actions or responsibility. This should lead to caution in making promises where there is no intention or small chance of acting on them. Actions, often small and symbolic, may count for more than a lot of nice English words in Japan.

Knowing the market: Japaneses consumers are different enough from their Western counterparts to necessitate at least a few key changes in product and marketing.

Market research in Japan must verify every assumption gained from Western success. Alterations may involve product quality, features, size, ingredients, service standards, packaging, promotional images and claims, and price level.

A substantial product advantage: Foreign products must possess some unique attributes that Japanese customers value and that aggressive Japanese competitors cannot easily imitate or improve upon.

This generally amounts to either of two types of advantages: a substantial technological edge, such as computer software, or a special image/style/brand name such as

(continued)

EXHIBIT 7.9 *(Continued)*

McDonald's fast foods and Levi jeans. Without these basic strengths, all other efforts will yield little if any staying power in Japan. If a solid advantage is possessed, it must be reinforced by at least meeting the competition on other performance dimensions of the marketing program—such as quality, price range, delivery, repair, and promotional spending.

Commitment to endurance: While the prize of Japanese business is one of the most lucrative in the world today, winning is a long and laborious task.

Remembering Murphy's Law ("if anything can go wrong, it will"), riding up the learning curve of marketing performance in Japan must be perceived by the Western company's top management as worth it. Large investments must be made for a long while—sometimes five to ten years—before the payoff appears. A modest marketing investment announces to all concerned that this firm is not taking Japan seriously so in turn the Japanese will not devote much effort to support it.

Source: Larry J. Rosenberg and Gregory J. Thompson, "Deciphering the Japanese Cultural Code," *International Marketing Review,* Autumn, 1986, pp. 55–56.

being of a society satisfies one level of needs, it gives rise to new needs whose satisfaction requires cultural change.

Consider the role of an Asian homemaker. In a village economy, she would be fully confined to her home. But a job for her husband in a factory in a nearby city enables the family to move to town. This move assures the family of basic needs fulfillment. There will be no more dependence on the farm for survival, but instead a weekly check. At this time safety needs become important. Safety requires buying groceries at the factory store as soon as they are available. In many developing countries items such as cooking oil, sugar, and bar soap are often in short supply. Thus, while the husband is at work, the wife must shop. This imposes a new role on the wife, a cultural change that results from economic prosperity. No longer are her activities confined within the home; now she can go out alone to shop, something that would have been culturally prohibited in the village.

Whether all aspects of a culture change when a single aspect changes is a question that may be answered by referring to Hall's classification of cultural aspects into formal, informal, and technical. *Formal* aspects constitute the core of a culture. They are most deeply rooted and are extremely difficult to change. Formal aspects are taught as absolute rights and wrongs. Nonobservance of formal aspects cannot be forgiven. *Informal* aspects are traits that one learns by being a member of the society. Everyone is supposed to be aware of these aspects. If an informal aspect is not adhered to, an expression of disapproval or concern would be shown. In other words, accommodation is feasible in relation to informal aspects. *Technical* aspects are transmitted in the form of instruction and have reasons behind them. Change can be most easily accomplished in technical cultural aspects. So long as change can be reasoned in a logical fashion, no emotions stand in the way.[62]

The definition of formal, informal, and technical cultural aspects will vary from country to country. For example, take the case of cigarette smoking among middle-class teenage girls. In India, this matter would be concerned with a formal aspect of the culture and completely rejected. In Latin America, it would be in conflict with an informal aspect of the culture. While parents might not like their daughters smoking, they might accept it after registering their disapproval. In Germany and Sweden, a young girl's smoking could be categorized as a technical aspect. Parents might not mind if the cigarettes are low-tar and, therefore, on technical grounds will resist smoking for health reasons. Once it is agreed that the cigarettes will be low-tar, there would be no objection to the girl's smoking.

MNCs as Agents of Change

A family's move from village to town, from farm work to factory work, describes how industrialization forces cultural change. A country may industrialize by exploiting its indigenous resources. But in the modern era, an important source of industrialization is the multinational corporation. An MNC rapidly and effectively transfers features of one cultural society to certain sectors of another perhaps very different society. In this process, it is uniquely capable of forcing cultural change.

> In fact, given the magnitude of international business, the prevailing pattern of close headquarters control over foreign affiliates, and the various linkages between foreign affiliates and host countries, the introduction of novel business value and behavioral patterns can be expected to have a profound impact on the cultural and social fabric of the societies in which international business is entrenched.[63]

MNCs transmit home country values in two ways: (1) through the vast network of affiliates, which introduce, demonstrate, and disseminate new behaviors while increasing and shaping the manufacturing sector of host countries, and (2) through the business service structure including advertising and business education.

Millions of people in host countries work for foreign affiliates of multinational corporations. While the latest data are not available, in the mid-1980s the United Nations estimated that about twenty-eight million people were directly employed by MNC affiliates in other countries. These people, while living in their own culture, spend their working lives in a foreign environment. Foreign affiliates are in most cases highly integrated with the parent corporation. They are subject to close headquarters control through a variety of mechanisms, notably majority equity ownership, managerial control in key decision areas, and the presence of expatriate managers among the senior employees of the affiliate. Thus, the working life of the affiliate to a large extent reflects the values common in the corridors of the parent corporation.[64] The affiliate employees may initiate, learn, and internalize new values and become channels to further diffuse these values in the host country culture at large.

The advertising media of MNCs is another avenue that transmits cultural values in host countries. The move of manufacturing companies to foreign countries has frequently been accompanied by a simultaneous move by advertising agencies. Of the top six advertising agencies of the world, five stem from the United States. Therefore, MNC affiliates in their marketing efforts abroad have easy access to the agencies handling parent company business. These foreign agencies transmit and reinforce attitudes that fit nicely with the requirements of the multinational corporation. Change in the acceptance of advertising was influenced by American practices. Today most European countries permit commercials on their broadcasting networks.

The role of advertising in the context of international marketing is summarized well in the following words:

> It should be noted that advertising does more than merely sell products and form consumption patterns; it informs, educates, changes attitudes, and builds images. For purposes of illustration, we may quote the statement of a marketing manager who answered the basic marketing question, "What do we sell?" in the following way: "Never a product, always an idea." In other words, the function of advertising agencies is to seek "to influence human behavior in ways favorable to the interests of their clients," to "indoctrinate" them.[65]

Another interesting development is the spread worldwide of U.S. business education. Business schools, especially the Harvard Graduate School of Business Administration, have trained thousands of foreign students through professional education in business. Additionally, many U.S. business schools have aided in the establishment of similar institutions in host countries. The Harvard Business School alone has helped Switzerland, Japan, France, Turkey, India, the United Kingdom, and a number of other countries in creating institutions for offering advanced education in business. In all these schools, staff and alumni from Harvard are an influential, if not dominant, group within the faculty, and in most cases, teaching and reading reflect a decidedly U.S. business philosophy. The coming generation of top managers in Europe, all more or less similarly trained to put the commercial interests of their enterprises above other considerations, are increasingly divorced from their particular national framework and reflect to various degrees the business philosophy of the top U.S. schools.[66]

The U.S. educated students, whether actually instructed in the United States of their homeland, generate and support ideas, values, and viewpoints that refer to the cultural traits revered in U.S. business circles. At the product/market level, they demand products and services in market categories where international marketers have traditionally had more experience. Included is a range of products from nutritious and more hygienically packaged goods to various kinds of household furnishings, appliances, and entertainment-oriented products. Also, new products are more easily accepted.

Summary

The cultural traits of a country have a profound effect on people's lifestyle and behavior patterns, and these are reflected in the marketplace. *Culture* is a complex term, and its precise definition is difficult. Broadly defined, however, it refers to all learned behavior of all facets of life and living transmitted from generation to generation. Cultural differences among countries can be subtle and zealously followed.

The study of culture includes material life (the means and artifacts people use for livelihood); social interactions between individuals and groups in formal and informal situations; language (spoken/written words, symbols and physical expressions that people use to communicate); aesthetics (art, drama, music); religion and faith; pride and prejudices; and ethics and mores. Cultural traits account for such differences among nations as color preferences, concept of time, and authority patterns. For example, in Western countries a bride's gown is usually white. In the far East, however, women wear white during mourning.

Cultural differences have impact on marketing decisions affecting product, price, distribution, and promotion. Two frameworks for analyzing culture are Rokeach's thirty-six values used to seek information on the cultural differences of national societies, and Hall's cultural map, with its two-dimensional matrix using ten human activities to generate a cultural analysis by focusing on the intersections of one with the nine others.

To conduct business successfully across national boundaries, marketers must adapt themselves to local cultures. A four-step framework for cultural adaptation, which encourages the avoidance of dependence on self-reference criteria (SRC), is important for developing an understanding perspective in new foreign situations. The tendency toward SRC reinforces the idea that what is good in America is good—and relevant—anywhere else as well.

A discussion of culture must also deal with cultural change. Cultures do change, but change is usually slow in coming. Industrialization is an important factor behind cultural change. Multinational corporations, through involvement in the industrialization process, serve as change agents in foreign cultures. Their worldwide networks of affiliates transmit the values of the parent corporation's culture. Cultural change also takes place through advertising media and through the internationalization of business education.

Review Questions

1. What elements of culture may be most relevant to marketing? Why?
2. How might a marketer of cosmetics assess significant cultural traits for his or her business in the Muslim world?
3. Americans share a variety of common traits with the English. Based on this assumption, will it be safe to conclude that the two societies have a more or less common culture?
4. Illustrate how an international marketer can use Hall's map of culture.
5. How has the spread of professional education in business affected local culture?
6. Describe how multinational corporations influence host country culture through their network of affiliates.
7. How could aesthetics, as an element of culture, affect marketing decisions in the international context?
8. Should an international marketer deliberately attempt to seek cultural change in a society?

9. "It is economic not cultural differences that count. Given the economic environment and income levels of the United States, people in any country, Muslim or Christian, would follow the U.S. lifestyle and materialistic living." Discuss this statement.

Endnotes

1. "Making Do During Ramadan," *Business Week,* April 8, 1991, p. 18A.
2. Edward B. Tylor, *Primitive Culture* (London: John Murray, 1871), p. 1.
3. Edward T. Hall, *Beyond Culture* (Garden City, NY: Anchor Books, 1977), p. 16. *Also see* Edward T. Hall, Learning the Arabs' Silent Language." *Psychology Today,* August 1979, p. 54.
4. Abraham Pizam and Arie Reichel. "Cultural Determinants of Managerial Behavior," *Management International Review,* no. 2 (1977), p. 66. *Also see* Barry Newman, "Singapore Fast Food: Try Pig Intestines—or Maybe a Big Mac," *The Wall Street Journal,* January 22, 1981, p. 1.
5. Karen Elliott House, "Saudi Marriage Mores Are Shaken as Women Seek a Stronger Voice," *The Wall Street Journal,* June 8, 1981, p. 1. *Also see* "Marriage-Minded Japanese Turn to Mama," *The Asian Wall Street Journal Weekly,* August 24, 1981, p. 13.
6. Changiz Pezeshkpur, "Challenges to Management in the Arab World," *Business Horizons,* August 1978, pp. 47–55.
7. Chin Tiong Tan and James McCullough, "Ethnicity and Family Buying Behavior." Paper presented at the Annual Meeting of the Academy of International Business, Cleveland, Ohio, October 1984.
8. Robert T. Green, Bronislaw J. Verhage, and Isabella C. M. Cunningham, "Household Purchasing Decisions," *Working Paper* (Austin, TX: University of Texas, 1983). *Also see* John I. Reynolds. "Developing Policy Responses to Cultural Differences," *Business Horizons,* August 1978, pp. 30–31.
9. Edward T. Hall, "The Silent Language in Overseas Business," *Harvard Business Review,* May–June 1960, pp. 88–96. *Also see* Sir Horace Phillips. "Language, the Passport to Global Business," *The Asian Wall Street Journal Weekly,* March 23, 1981, p. 11.
10. David A. Ricks, "How to Avoid Business Blunders Abroad," *Business,* April–June 1984, pp. 3–11.
11. David A. Ricks, "International Business Blunders: An Update," *B&E Review,* January–March 1988, p. 11.
12. Ibid., p. 12.
13. Vern Terpstra, *International Marketing* (Hinsdale, IL: Dryden Press, 1983).
14. Robert Howells, "Culture Clash: An American's Guide to English," *The Wall Street Journal,* October 30, 1984, p. 34.
15. *See* Jeffrey A. Rosenweig and Wayne D. Gantt, "Doing Business in Japan," *Emory Business Magazine,* Spring 1990, pp. 34–36.
16. "Before Buying Insurance, Consult This Calendar," *The Asian Wall Street Journal Weekly,* October 10, 1988, p. 8.
17. Geraldine Brooks, "Riddle of Riyadh: Islamic Law Thrives Amid Modernity," *The Wall Street Journal,* November 9, 1989, p. 1.
18. *See* Youssef M. Ibrahim, "Revolutionary Islam of Iran Is Neutralized by Policies of Bahrain." *The Wall Street Journal,* August 11, 1987, p. 1; and Karen Elliott House, "Rising Islamic Fervor Challenges the West, Every Moslem Ruler," *The Wall Street Journal,* August 7, 1987, p. 1.
19. P. Wright, "Organizational Behavior in Islamic Firms," *Management International Review,* no. 2 (1981), p. 87. *Also see* Ernest Dichter, "The World Customer," *Harvard Business Review,* July–August 1962, p. 116; S. G. Redding, "Cultural Effects on the Marketing Process in Southeast Asia," *Journal of Market Research Society,* April 1982, pp. 86–98.
20. Tim Carrington, "Chief of European Reconstruction Bank Faces Challenges on Financial and Cultural Fronts," *The Wall Street Journal*, November 26, 1990, p. A5.
21. *See* Robert A. Jackson, "Are American Buyers the Prisoners of Politicians?" *San Francisco State University School of Business Journal,* Summer 1984, pp. 33–40.
22. George Mellon, "Trade Curbs Would Threaten Many Companies," *The Wall Street Journal,* April 28, 1987, p. 35.

23. Helmut Becker and David J. Fritzsche, "A Comparison of the Ethical Behavior of American, French and German Managers," *Columbia Journal of World Business.* Winter 1987, pp. 87–96.
24. Lee Smith, "Korea's Challenge to Japan," *Fortune,* February 6, 1984, p. 94.
25. John L. Graham, "The Influence of Culture on Business Negotiations," *Journal of International Business Studies,* Spring 1985, pp. 81–96.
26. *See* Thelma Barer-Stein, *You Eat What You Are* (London: McClelland and Stewart, 1981); Mary Douglas, "Culture and Food," in *The Pleasures of Anthropology* (New York: New American Library, 1983); Peter Farb and George Armaelagos, *Consuming Passions* (Boston: Houghton Mifflin Co., 1980); Mac Marshall, *Beliefs, Behaviors and Alcoholic Beverages* (Ann Arbor: The University of Michigan Press, 1979). *Also see* "Beware When Bearing Gifts in Foreign Lands," *Business Week,* December 1976, pp. 91–92; Kathleen Reardon, "International Business Gift Giving Customs," *Working Paper* (Storrs: University of Connecticut, 1981).
27. Joseph T. Plummer, "Consumer Focus in Cross-National Research," *Journal of Advertising,* Summer 1977, pp. 5–15. *Also see* Vern Terpstra and Kenneth David, *The Cultural Environment of International Business,* 2nd ed. (Cincinnati, OH: Southwestern Publishing Co., 1985).
28. Ibid., p. 11. *Also see* I. G. M. Cunningham and Robert T. Green, "Working Wives in the United States and Venezuela: A Cross-National Study of Family Decision Making," *Journal of Comparative Family Studies,* Spring 1979, pp. 67–80.
29. Susan P. Douglas, "Cross-National Comparisons and Consumer Stereotypes: A Case Study of Working and Nonworking Wives in the U.S. and France," *The Journal of Consumer Research,* June 1976, pp. 12–20.
30. Thomas E. Muller and Christopher Bolger, "Search Behavior of French and English Canadians in Automobile Purchase," *International Marketing Review,* Winter 1985, pp. 21–30.
31. Charles M. Schaninger, Jacques C. Bourgeois, and W. Christian Buss, "French-English Canadian Subcultural Consumption Differences," *Journal of Marketing,* Spring 1985, pp. 82–92.
32. *See* Philip R. Harris and Robert T. Moran, *Managing Cultural Differences,* 2nd ed. (Houston, TX: Gulf Publishing Co., 1987).
33. Susan Douglas and Bernard Dubois, "Looking at the Cultural Environment for International Marketing Opportunities," *Columbia Journal of World Business,* Winter 1977, p. 102. *Also see* Ian R. Wilson, "American Success Story—Coca-Cola in Japan." in Mark B. Winchester, ed., *The International Essays for Business Decision Makers* (Dallas: The Center for International Business, 1980), pp. 119–127.
34. "The $30 Million Lesson," *Sales Management,* March 1967, pp. 31–38. *Also see* Henry Lane, "Systems, Values, and Action: An Analytic Framework for Intercultural Management Research," *Management International Review,* no. 3 (1980), pp. 61–70.
35. Robert D. Buzzell, "Can You Standardize Multinational Marketing?" *Harvard Business Review,* November–December 1968, pp. 102–113.
36. *Fortune,* November 6, 1989, p. 86.
37. Kenichi Ohmae, *Triad Power* (New York: The Free Press, 1985), pp. 102–104.
38. Susan Douglas and Bernard Dubois, "Looking at the Cultural Environment for International Marketing Opportunities," *Columbia Journal of World Business,* Winter 1977, pp. 106–107.
39. L. Erik Calonius, "As a Market for PCs, Europe Seems as Hot as the U.S. Is Not," *The Wall Street Journal,* August 19, 1985, p. 1.
40. Robert J. Hoover, Robert T. Green, and Joel Saegart, "A Cross-National Study of Perceived Risk," *Journal of Marketing,* July 1978, pp. 102–108. *Also see* Chin Tiong Tan and Christina Chua. "Effects of Attitudes and Social Influence in Bank Selection: A Study in an Oriental Culture," a paper presented at the Annual Meeting of the Academy of International Business, Washington, D.C., October 1982.
41. Susan Douglas and Bernard Dubois, "Looking at the Cultural Environment for International Marketing Opportunities," *Columbia Journal of World Business,* Winter 1977, p. 107. *Also see* Erdener Kaynak and Lionel A. Mitchell, "Cultural Barriers to the Full-Scale Acceptance of Supermarkets in Less-Developed Countries," a paper presented at the Annual Meeting of the Academy of International Business, New Orleans, October 1980.
42. Ibid.

43. R. S. Diamond, "Managers Away From Home," *Fortune,* August 15, 1969, p. 50.
44. Howe Martyn, *International Business—Principles and Problems* (New York: Collier-Macmillan, 1964), p. 78.
45. *Advertising Age,* May 9, 1960, p. 75.
46. *Also see* Matt Miller and Sundeep Chakravarti, "For Indians, a 2,000 Year-Old Habit of Chewing Red Goo Is Hard to Break," *The Wall Street Journal,* May 12, 1987, p. 28.
47. *Fortune,* November 6, 1989, p. 86.
48. S. Watson Dunn, "Effect of National Identity on Multinational Promotional Strategy in Europe," *Journal of Marketing,* October 1976, pp. 54–55.
49. J. Douglas McConnell, "The Economics of Behavioral Factors on the Multinational Corporation," in Fred C. Allvine, ed., *Combined Proceedings* (Chicago: American Marketing Association, 1971), p. 264. *Also see* Arndt Sorge and Malcolm Warner, "Culture, Management and Manufacturing Organization: A Study of British and German Firms," *Management International Review,* no. 1 (1981), pp. 35–48.
50. Charles Winick, "Anthropology's Contribution to Marketing," *Journal of Marketing,* July 1961, p. 59. *Also see* D. E. Allen, "Anthropological Insights into Customer Behavior," *European Journal of Marketing,* no. 5 (1971), pp. 45–47.
51. Philippe Cattin, Alain Jolibert, and Colleen Lohnes, "A Cross-Cultural Study of 'Made-in' Concepts," *The Journal of International Business Studies,* Winter 1982, pp. 131–142.
52. Nancy J. Adler, "Cultural Synergy: The Management of Cross-Cultural Organizations," in W. Warner Burke and Leonard D. Goodstein, eds. *Trends and Issues in OD: Current Theory and Practice* (San Diego, CA: University Associates, 1980), pp. 163–184.
53. "Hidden Agenda," *Marketing Insights,* Summer Issue 1990, pp. 40–45.
54. J. Michael Munson and Shelby H. McIntyre, "Personal Values: A Cross-Cultural Assessment of Self Values and Values Attributed to a Distant Cultural Stereotype," in H. Keith Hunt, ed., *Advances in Consumer Research,* vol. 5 (Ann Arbor, MI: Association for Consumer Research, 1978), pp. 103–104.
55. Edward T. Hall, *The Silent Language* (Garden City, NY: Doubleday, 1959), pp. 61–81.
56. Ibid., p. 61.
57. Stefan H. Robock and Kenneth Simmons, *International Business and Multinational Enterprises,* 4th ed. (Homewood, IL: Irwin, 1989), pp. 424–428.
58. James A. Lee, "Cultural Analysis in Overseas Operations," *Harvard Business Review,* March–April 1966, p. 110. *Also see* James R. Schiffman, "Korea Promises to Build a People's Car Affordable to Burgeoning Middle Class," *The Asian Wall Street Journal Weekly,* February 7, 1983, p. 11.
59. "A 'Jeep' that May Tame the Third World's Road," *Business Week,* February 13, 1989, p. 100.
60. James A. Lee, "Cultural Analysis in Overseas Operations," *Harvard Business Review,* March–April 1966, pp. 107–110. *Also see* D. George Harris, "How National Cultures Shape Management Styles," *Management Review,* July 1982, pp. 58–61; "Western Companies Vie to Dress East Europeans in Blue Jeans," *World Business Weekly,* February 23, 1981, p. 10.
61. *See* Abraham H. Maslow, *Motivation and Personality* (New York: Harper & Row, 1954).
62. Edward T. Hall, *The Silent Language* (Garden City, NY: Doubleday, 1959), pp. 110–113.
63. Karl P. Sauvant, "Multinational Enterprises and the Transmission of Culture: The International Supply of Advertising Services and Business Education." *Journal of Peace Research,* no. 1 (1976), p. 49.
64. Karl P. Sauvant, "The Potential of Multinational Enterprises as Vehicles for the Transmission of Business Culture," in Karl P. Sauvant and Farid G. Lavipour, eds., *Controlling Multinational Enterprises* (Boulder, CO: Westview Press, 1976).
65. Paul C. Harper, Jr., "The Agency Business in 1980," *Advertising Age,* November 29, 1978, p. 35.
66. *See* Shawn Tully, "Europe's Best Business Schools," *Fortune,* May 23, 1988, p. 106.

CHAPTER • 8

Political Environment

CHAPTER FOCUS

After studying this chapter you should be able to:

- Describe how political situations affect marketing decisions
- Discuss sources of political problems
- Examine different ways that governments may intervene in the affairs of foreign firms
- Explain how the political perspectives of a country can be examined
- Compare alternative strategies a company may pursue in the event of political intervention

The political environment of each country is unique. An apparently rich foreign market may not warrant entry if the political environment is characterized by instability and uncertainty. In brief, a thorough review of the political environment must precede commitment to a new market in a foreign country.

Furthermore, the political environments of countries do not remain static. Political changes and upheavals may occur after an international marketer has made a commitment and has an established business. The revolution in Iran exposed U.S. companies to potential losses of $1 billion and drove home the lesson that the political situation in a country must be reviewed on a continuing basis. Political environment connotes diverse happenings, such as civil difficulties (for example, the conflict between the communist government in Poland and Solidarity); acts of terrorism against businesses (for example, kidnappings, arson); and conflicts between countries in a particular region, which may be one-time occurrences like the war between India and China or perennial problems like the enmity between Israel and its Arab neighbors.

Political stability has been found to be one of the crucial variables that companies weigh when considering going overseas.[1] Unstable political environment subjects foreign business to risks such as violence, expropriation, restriction of operations, and restrictions on repatriation of capital and remittances of profits. If the risk is high in a particular politically unstable country, it is necessary to know how to monitor that country's ongoing political situation. This chapter examines the occurrence of political conflicts and difficulties in foreign countries and their effects on overseas business, and discusses ways to analyze politics and measure risk. Strategic responses to political change available to multinational marketers also are covered.

Politics and Marketing

A few years ago, the French president François Mitterrand invited Apple Computer executives to lunch at his residence, Élysée Palace. The Apple executives jumped at the invitation since for months they had been trying to sell their personal computers to the French government. The French government had authorized a $156 million purchase of teaching computers for the French school system, but Apple's foreign citizenship had hindered its efforts to get a piece of the order.

During the private, two-hour lunch, with a translator present, the Apple executives praised the government's computer program and offered to help in any way they could. But President Mitterrand rebuffed them. Later one aide said that the president had invited the Apple executives to discuss technological cooperation with French companies, not the educational computer purchase program.[2]

How Apple tried, and failed, to get a significant share of the computer order is a revealing tale of international marketing and politics. The total order, for 120,000 microcomputers, was the biggest single purchase of educational computers in Europe and part of an ambitious campaign to teach almost everybody in France how to use computers. Although Apple is the largest vendor of professional microcomputers in France, when the list of suppliers for the new program was announced, Apple received no order.

The head of Apple's subsidiary near Paris, a Frenchman, blamed the company's exclusion on lobbying by competitors and Apple's U.S. nationality: "The color of our passport is wrong."

On hearing about Apple's difficulties, the U.S. government complained to France about what it considered the unfair handling of the microcomputer order, raising the possibility of retaliatory moves in U.S. government contracting procedures. But other than registering its annoyance on the matter, the U.S. government did not pursue it, perhaps for political reasons.

Whether such nationalistic buying will get French students the best equipment is a matter of debate. Yet this clearly brings out the political underpinnings involved in conducting international marketing.

Marketing decisions in the international context are deeply affected by the political perspectives of both home and host countries.[3] For example, government decisions have significantly affected the U.S. automotive industry. Stringent requirements such as the fuel efficiency standards have burdened the industry in several ways.

Governments around the world help their domestic industries to strengthen their competitiveness through various fiscal and monetary measures. Such political support can play a key role in an industry's search for markets abroad. Without such assistance, an industry may face a difficult situation. The U.S. auto industry would benefit from United States government concessions favoring U.S. automotive exports. European countries, for example, rely on value-added taxes to help their industries. These are applied to all levels of manufacturing transactions up to and including the final sale to the user. However, if the final sale is for export, the value-added tax is rebated, thus effectively reducing the price in international commerce. Japan imposes a commodity tax on selected lines of products, including automobiles. In the event of export, the commodity tax is waived. The United States has no corresponding arrangement. Thus, when a new automobile is shipped from the United States to Japan, it receives no rebate or relief of its U.S. taxes upon export and also must bear the cost of the Japanese commodity tax (15 or 20 percent depending on the size of the vehicle) when it is sold in Japan[4] (see International Marketing Highlight 8.1).

The competition facing U. S. manufacturers, therefore, both at home and in international markets, is potent and resourceful. Moreover a number of these overseas competitors are wholly or partly state-owned and respond to the direction of their governments, which depend heavily on their export business for the maintenance of employment and the earning of foreign exchange. This makes politics important, deeply influencing the perspectives of international marketing (see International Marketing Highlight 8.2).

Politics may affect international marketing in various ways. In January 1985, Ford Motor Company divested itself of its auto operations in South Africa to take a 40 percent minority position.[5] About the same time, Japan liberalized tobacco imports by lifting restrictions on price, distribution, and the number of retail outlets that can handle their products, thus encouraging foreign suppliers to in-

International Marketing Highlight 8.1

Politics of Smoking

The federal government officially discourages cigarette smoking in the United States. But if people in other countries are going to smoke anyway, why shouldn't they puff away on American tobacco?

Armed with this logic, the Reagan administration strong-armed Japan, South Korea, and Taiwan to dismantle their government-sanctioned tobacco monopolies. This opened lucrative markets and created such growth for U.S. cigarette makers that skyrocketing Asian sales did much to offset the decline at home.

But Thailand, with a government tobacco monopoly of its own, is fighting U.S. pressure to open up, and U.S. tobacco companies are asking the Bush administration to take up trade sanctions against the Thais. That raises many questions about U.S. trade policy, including: Should Washington use its muscle to promote a product overseas that it acknowledges is deadly? Are trade disputes to be decided by lawyers and bureaucrats on the basis of commercial regulations, or should health and safety experts get into the act? Should the United States use trade policy to make the world healthier, just as it does to save whales, punish South Africa, or promote human rights?

Source: Business Week, October 9, 1989, p. 61.

tensify their marketing efforts.[6] In July 1985, Mexico approved the long-delayed, once-rejected 100 percent IBM-owned microcomputer plant to encourage more foreign investment.[7] After waiting for several years, toward the end of 1988, PepsiCo got the Indian government's approval for a joint venture there.[8] In 1991, after much politicking, the French government permitted IBM to link up with France's state-owned computer maker, Groupe Bull, to develop high-speed RISC computer technology.[9]

Conceptually, multinational enterprises are effected by politics in three areas: (1) the pattern of ownership in the parent company or the affiliate, (2) the direction and nature of growth of the affiliate, and (3) the flow of product, technology, and managerial skills within the companies of the group. Take, for example, the case of South Africa. The impact of politics on the strategies adopted by MNCs there leads to one important conclusion: The strategic choices made by MNC affiliates are a response more to political environment than to the interaction of market forces or to technological innovation. In other words, the government can substantially influence the strategy of MNC affiliates in ways that were thought impossible even a few years ago. In India, many MNC affiliates had to diversify into areas where neither the parent company nor the affiliate had the core capabilities. Competence ceased to be an important factor in strategy formulation compared to the need to comply with political directives and regulations. In general, the transfer of product and technology from the parent company in order to exploit new markets in the host country

International Marketing Highlight 8.2

Hidden Japan

Nowhere does the business-politics alliance work as well as in Japan. As a matter of fact, the Japanese have developed business-politics dealings into an art. The point is illustrated by Japan's *zoku,* informal "tribes" of Diet members from the ruling Liberal Democratic Party (LDP) who keep track of different interest groups and intercede if circumstances demand. For example, the LDP signs off on virtually all of the $3 trillion that Tokyo spends on public works. The related industries in turn make lavish contributions for party programs. According to experts, 2.8 percent of all construction revenues are funneled to the LDP through its construction *zoku.*

Collusion is a common practice in Japan. For example, in construction projects, before the formal bids are submitted for a job, the interested companies meet to decide whose turn it is and what the price should be. One way of quietly sharing information on bids to others is to write them down on the back of business cards that are exchanged during greetings. Everyone except the preagreed winner bids higher [than the winner]. Non-Japanese contractors do not even know about these meetings.

Thus, despite the U.S. government's efforts, American companies find it hard to compete in Japan for big projects. As has been said, "The *zoku* can make or break a foreigner's success in Japan."

Source: Business Week, August 26, 1991, p. 34.

meets with obstruction from the government unless the technology is in the areas specified by regulation.

The political impact does not end here. It has further ramifications on the MNC's worldwide operations. With regulations forcing MNC affiliates operating in controlled economies to move into areas where the parent company may or may not have prior experience, the parent company will find increasing difficulties in developing worldwide strategies to maximize their corporate interests. The large MNCs will have problems in achieving worldwide integration of resources, physical, human, and financial. Dilution of ownership will lead to erosion of the power of the parent company to control the management process in the affiliates. In short, the dissimilarity of business between the affiliates and the parent, along with reduced ownership by the parent, makes the latter primarily an investor. If this pattern continues, parent companies may soon find that they are no longer in a position to integrate their resources worldwide.

Sources of Political Problems

Figure 8.1 illustrates sources of political problems for firms doing business in foreign countries. Political impact on business comes mainly from political sovereignty and political conflict.

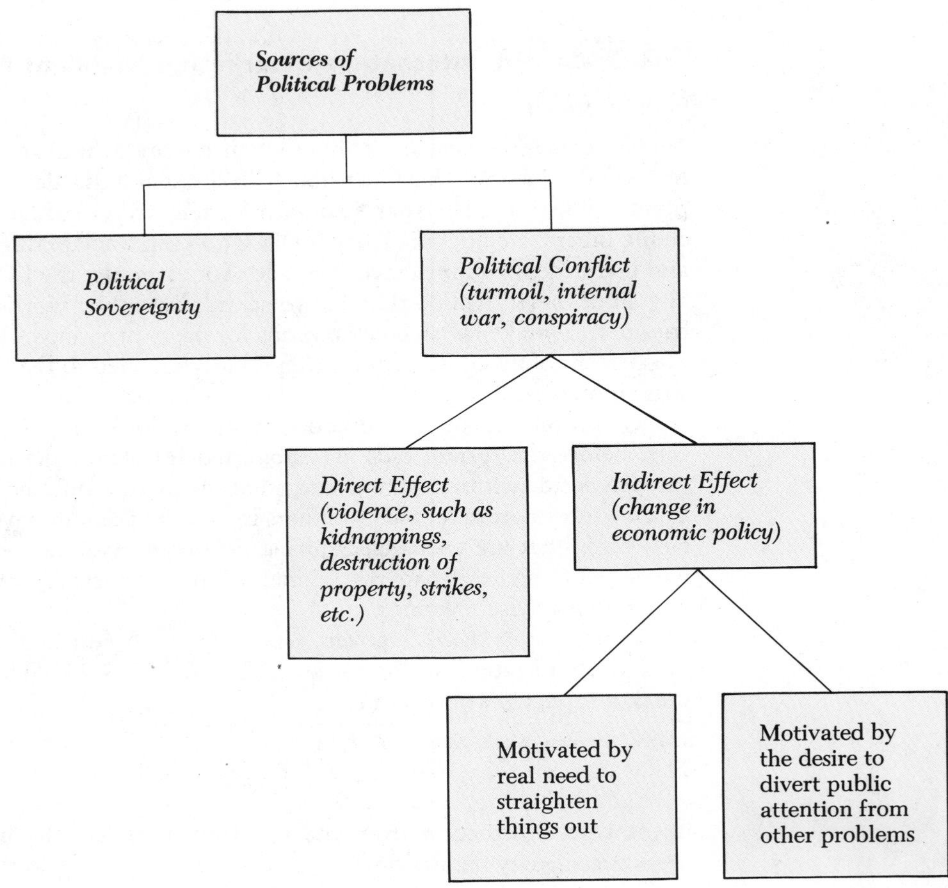

FIGURE 8.1 Politics and Foreign Business

Political Sovereignty

Political sovereignty refers to a country's desire to assert its authority over foreign business through various sanctions. Such sanctions are regular and evolutionary, and, therefore, are predictable. An example is increases in taxes over foreign operations. Many of the less-developed countries impose restrictions on foreign business to protect their independence (economic domination is often perceived as leading to political subservience). These countries are jealous of their political freedom and want to protect it at all costs, even if it means going at a slow economic pace and without the help of multinational corporations.

The political sovereignty problem mainly concerns developing countries. As Vernon states:

> Unlike the leaders of the industrialized countries, however, those in the developing countries have barely begun to enjoy the fruits, such as they are, of a separate national identity. Only a decade or so has gone by since they first began effec-

> tively to play off the great powers against one another, to create coalitions with other nations, and to share the subtle personal advantages that were once reserved to leaders of the industrialized states. In many developing countries, local business leaders also are enjoying a new experience. Like business [persons] in the industrialized nations, they have been learning how to protect the local market by persuading governments to impose import restrictions, and how to use the resources of public enterprises in effective partnerships. In a number of cases—a surprisingly large number of cases, in fact—they are even learning how to make multinational enterprises of their own.
>
> Finally, intellectuals and journalistic leaders in the developing countries are also exercising their sense of increased status, subject of course to some heavy restraints that their governments impose. To the extent that they are allowed, some are pressing for reforms in the liberal mold, such as programs for more effective taxation and better environmental controls, and some are committed to more revolutionary objectives, including the liquidation of capitalism.
>
> For these various leadership groups, multinational enterprises stand for several different things at once. Such enterprises are not merely multinational; they are also foreign, large, and privately owned. Accordingly, they can be used as stand-ins for so much that is deeply troubling in the developing world: for the threat of continued hegemony from the big industrialized countries; for industrial bribery and conspicuous wealth; and for all the seamy aspects of industrialization in general, including the abandonment of ancient values, the appearance of industrial pollution, and the appalling waste of misapplied resources.[10]

The industrialized nations, whose political sovereignty has been secure for a long time, require a more open policy for the economic realities of today's world. Today, governments are expected simultaneously to curb unemployment, limit inflation, redistribute income, build up backward regions, deliver health services, and not abuse the environment. These wide-ranging objectives make developed countries seek foreign technology, use foreign capital and foreign raw materials, and sell their specialties in foreign markets. The net result is that these countries have found themselves exchanging guarantees for mutual access to one another's economies. In brief, among the developed countries multinationalism of business is politically acceptable and economically desirable.

In many minds around the world, however, there are many different impressions and/or misconceptions about multinational corporations. MNCs can be blamed for everything from corrupting public officials and increasing social tensions to pursuing corporate policies that have negative impact on host and source countries alike. MNCs are held to be irresponsible to host governments and/or employees as they maximize their global profits while minimizing their global tax liabilities, exploiting host country factors of production while helping to create polarized societies, squeezing out local entrepreneurs and generating monopoly power while undermining national sovereignty and exacerbating international disparities in income distribution. MNCs are also accused of siphoning off needed capital from host countries while diverting local savings from productive national ventures; restricting host country access to modern technology; contributing to inflation; dominating key industrial sectors; and controlling host country technology, financial capital, and communication.[11] These negative impressions have been reinforced by MNCs' actions during difficulties in Latin America and Africa, and especially in the Congo (now Zaire), Panama, Chile, Libya, and Biafra.

Political Conflict

Many countries in different parts of the world undergo political conflict of various sorts. ***Political conflict*** can be irregular, revolutionary, and/or discontinuous, and basically may be categorized as turmoil, internal war, and conspiracy.[12] *Turmoil* refers to instant upheaval on a massive scale against an established regime (for example, the Islamic fundamentalists' mass protest against the Shah of Iran). *Internal war* means large-scale, organized violence against a government such as guerrilla warfare (for example, Vietnam's actions in Cambodia). *Conspiracy* represents an instant, planned act of violence against those in power (for example, the assassination of Egyptian President Anwar Sadat). Political conflict may or may not have an impact on business.[13] For example, while the ouster of the Shah of Iran incurred heavy losses for U.S. business there, the murder of Anwar Sadat made no difference to international business in Egypt at that time.

As a matter of fact, political change sometimes may lead to a more favorable business climate. For example, after the Peronist regime was overthrown in Argentina, the new government's policy was so favorable toward multinationals that the previously nationalized firms were returned to their owners. Similarly, Sukarno's departure from the Indonesian scene improved the business climate there, as did Nkrumah's absence from Ghana. After the assassination of Prime Minister Indira Gandhi in 1984, India's policy became highly favorable for international business. Gillette Company, for example, obtained the Indian government's permission to set up a razor blade plant after some eight years of asking. Similarly, Honda and Nissan successfully negotiated deals to produce cars in India. Suddenly, U.S. multinationals found India an attractive place to do business.[14]

It is important to make a distinction between political risk and political conflict. Political conflict in a country may lead to unstable conditions, but those conditions may or may not affect business. Therefore, political risk may or may not result from political unrest.[15] Businesses must analyze each occurrence of political conflict and assess the likelihood of its impact on business. Consider the case of the Philippines. During 1988, communist threats posed insurmountable problems for foreign companies although the economy had been doing well. For example, Dole Philippines' banana plantation was attacked and two warehouses were destroyed. Yet in the interest of long-term opportunity, Dole officials refused to take any drastic steps.[16]

The effect of political conflict on business may be direct or indirect. *Direct effects* would be violence against the firms in such forms as the kidnapping of an executive, damage to company property, a labor strike, and the like. Overall, direct effects are usually temporary and do not result in huge losses[17] (see International Marketing Highlight 8.3). *Indirect effects* occur because of changes in government policy. In other words, political conflict leads to some change in a government's economic perspective. Such change may come from a new attitude on

International Marketing Highlight 8.3

Executives in Peru Don't Leave Home Without It

Herbert Dunn, a former police officer and SWAT-team member in the United States, came to Peru in 1984 as a security consultant. He now teaches local executives how to defend themselves in a terrorist attack—a common occurrence in Peru.

With two major terrorist groups and a variety of smaller ones carrying out bombings, killings, and kidnappings, security is an obsession here. In 1990 alone, political violence claimed 3,384 lives—more than were lost in Lebanon's civil war in 1990—and caused material damage estimated by one research firm at $3 billion. That's about 15 percent of Peru's gross domestic product.

Many top businesspeople, some journalists, and even usually sedate political scientists don't leave home without a revolver. Visitors to corporate headquarters routinely check their guns, along with IDs, upon entering. Factories are fortified bunkers, surrounded by high walls and barbed wire, with armed guards looking out from watchtowers.

Even some of Lima's Kentucky Fried Chicken outlets have three armed guards at the entrance—not, as one resident jokes, to guard the quality of the product, but to keep the stores standing after two bomb attacks this year. Terrorists "seem to have an obsession about fried chicken," says Bustavo Gorriti, a journalist. "They must think it's the food of choice of the American plutocracy."

Source: The Wall Street Journal, April 10, 1991, p. 1.

the part on an existing government or through a new government. Further, the changes may be motivated by a sincere desire to straighten things out or simply to divert public attention from other domestic problems plaguing the country.

In many developing countries, for example, a variety of expectations may be raised that cannot be fulfilled, either economically or politically. Such a situation can lead to discontent and conflict. In Western societies discontent also occurs, but has an outlet through the ballot box. In transitional societies, such an outlet is usually not available and the main alternative is political conflict and unrest. Governments may dramatize their viability by sometimes rash nationalization of foreign business. Such actions divert attention from pressing problems by giving an appearance of taking effective measures, and may take advantage of antiforeign bias.[18]

From the viewpoint of foreign businesses, it is important to understand the nature of political conflict and the motivation behind government action. If a change in government policy is merely for symbolic purposes, it represents less risk to foreign businesses. Also, when new policy is expressed through the imposition of certain constraints, requirements, and/or controls on foreign businesses, it is important to assess the host government's administrative ability. The government must have the capacity to promulgate and enforce the new policy. If such capabilities are lacking, the new policy will remain a well-intentioned effort without any actual effects on foreign businesses.

Political Intervention

Carefully chosen overseas markets provide substantial opportunity. The opportunity, however, is coupled with risks of intervention by host governments seeking to further their own interests. Nations are not monolithic, or even bipartisan. Rather they are composed of different groups, each of which is intent on maximizing its individual interests. In countries where foreign investment plays a significant role in the economy, the goals of special interests frequently necessitate interference in the operations of foreign firms.[19] For example, if a foreign company is prominent is the economy of such countries as Zambia, Guinea, Chile, and Tanzania, the possibilities of government intervention are relatively great. While certainly not limited to developing countries, intervention in the affairs of foreign enterprise is more frequent in these countries. Developed countries respond to foreign enterprise by establishing their own multinationals to challenge foreign firms both on the homefront and abroad. Developing countries may have to intervene directly in the operations of multinational corporations operating in their lands in order to pursue their own special interests.

In general, intervention appears harsher to U.S.-based multinationals than the same action appears to French, English, or Japanese foreign companies. This can be attributed to the fact that the recently independent nations of Asia and Africa remain remarkably sympathetic to their former colonial rulers, partly because of familiarity, education, and language and partly because it is safer to deal with the people they know.

Political intervention can be defined as a decision on the part of the host country government that may force a change in the operations, policies, and strategies of a foreign firm.[20] The intervention may range from some sort of control to complete takeover or annexation of the foreign enterprise. The magnitude of intervention would vary according to the company's business in the country and the nature of the intervention.[21] There are different forms of intervention: expropriation, domestication, exchange control, import restrictions, market control, tax control, price control, and labor problems. Figure 8.2 shows different ways that governments may intervene in the affairs of foreign firms. Also specified are the likely effects of political intervention on marketing mix variables.

Expropriation

Of all the forms of political intervention, ***expropriation*** is most pervasive. As defined by Eiteman and Stonehill, it is:

> Official seizure of foreign property by a host country whose intention is to use the seized property in the public interest. Expropriation is recognized by international law as the right of sovereign states, provided the expropriated firms are given prompt compensation, at fair market value, in convertible currencies.[22]

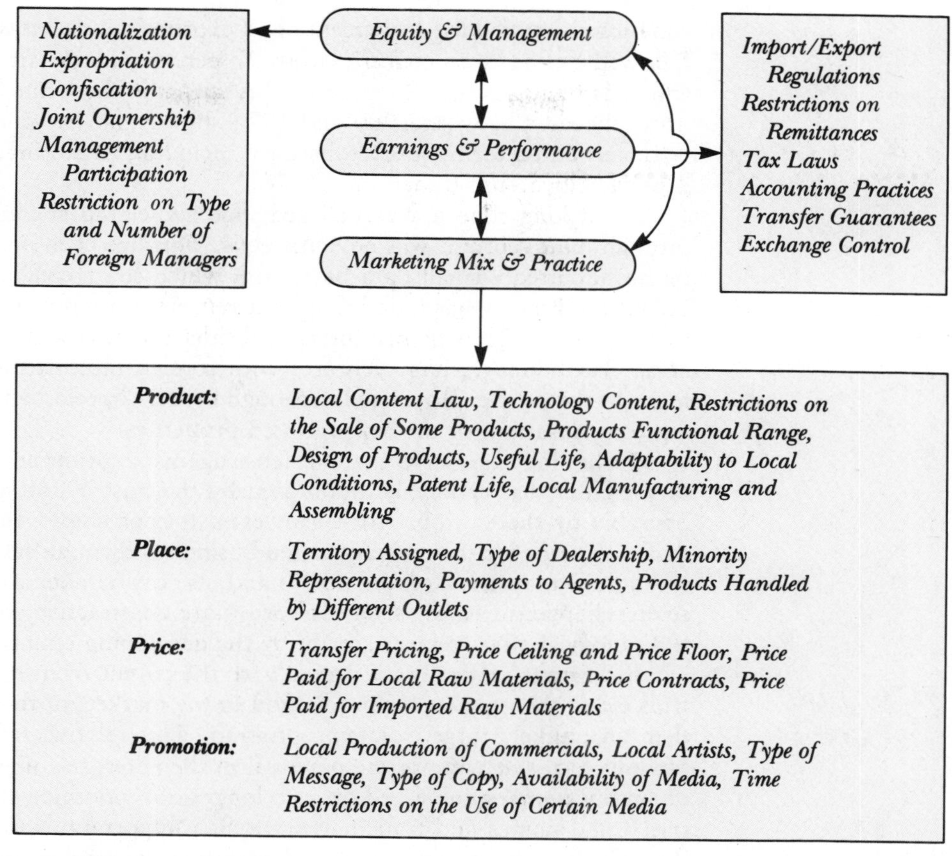

FIGURE 8.2 A Classification of Governmental Intervention in the Operations of Foreign Firms

Source: Humayun Akhter and Robert F. Lusch, "Political Risk and the Evolution of the Control of Foreign Business: Equity, Earnings and the Marketing Mix," *Journal of Global Marketing*, Spring 1988, p. 117.

The second part of this definition points out the source of much of the controversy associated with expropriation. Other terms used interchangeably with expropriation are nationalization and socialization. *Nationalization* refers to a transfer of the entire industry within that country from private to public ownership with no discrimination as to foreign ownership or local ownership. *Socialization,* also referred to as communization, differs from nationalization in that it is a transfer of all the industries within the country. *Confiscation* means expropriation without compensation.

Patterns of expropriation have been differentiated according to industry, geographic region, type of ownership, technology, degree of vertical integration, asset size, and politicoeconomic situation.[23] Based on geographic region, Latin

America accounted for 49 percent of all expropriations between 1960 and 1976, followed by the Arab countries with 27 percent, black Africa with 13 percent, and Asian nations with 11 percent.[24] A study by the United Nations of foreign firm takeovers between 1960 and 1974 shows that two-thirds of all takeovers were accounted for by just ten nations, including Argentina, Chile, Cuba, Peru, Algeria, Libya, and Iraq.[25]

For a long time it was believed that ownership shared with host nations through joint ventures was advantageous. This has been proved false. Although on an admittedly small data base from which strict conclusions would not be permitted, Bradley has found that joint ventures with host country governments, as opposed to wholly owned foreign subsidiaries, have a greater rate of expropriation. Furthermore, joint ventures with foreign multinationals are eight times more likely to be expropriated, although owners have a better chance of obtaining compensation for the expropriated properties.[26]

Technology can serve as the defense against expropriation, if the technology of the enterprise cannot be duplicated by the host country or cannot be made operable by the expropriators. However, former employees are sometimes induced to work for these expropriated businesses through salary incentives. Low-technology industries, on the other hand, are easily taken over, even though this seldom happens because such enterprises are unattractive, lacking the glamor of technological advancement sought by the developing countries.

If a firm is vertically integrated with the parent firm so that the parent controls either the supplies for production or the market for the product, the firm is then an unlikely target for expropriation. This relative safety comes from the obvious fact that without the parent firm the enterprise would be inoperable or its output unmarketable and thus no longer of economic value to the host country. Brand names and trademarks are also important; without the U.S. brand identification, for instance, it would be difficult to market some products successfully.

Another area to be analyzed and compared is that of asset size.[27] According to Bradley, a firm with total assets in excess of $100 million has a fifty times greater chance of being expropriated than a firm with assets of less than $1 million, the reason being that the political and economic gains from expropriation of a small firm would not justify the costs to the host country in negative reactions of the business community, world lending institutions, and foreign governments.

The politicoeconomic backdrops against which expropriations have taken place have been associated with sweeping and violent upheavals, which transformed the basic governmental structure and politicoeconomic ideologies of the nations involved.[28] Recent trends have shifted from those of ideologies and politics, to a more functional need for the economic development desired by the less-developed countries. In light of this trend, expropriations have become more selective, directed toward those foreign-owned enterprises whose policies or aspirations have collided with the economic plans and priorities of the developing nation. To lessen vulnerability in this area, a firm should assess the proper behavior necessary to fit in with the economic interests and objectives of the host nation.

This historical study of trends and patterns in expropriation provides insight into the factors that could help forecast possible expropriation.

Domestication

Domestication, which can be thought of as *creeping expropriation,* is a process by which controls and restrictions placed on the foreign firm gradually reduce the control of the owners. Although domestication may lead ultimately to expropriation, in a way it offers a compromise to both parties. The multinational corporation continues to operate in the country while the host government is able to maintain leverage on the foreign firm through imposing different controls. Domestication involves several measures, including:

- Gradual transfer of ownership to nationals
- Promotion of a large number of nationals to higher levels of management
- Greater decision-making powers accorded to nationals
- More products produced locally rather than imported for assembly
- Specific export regulations designed to dictate participation in world markets[29]

From the viewpoint of the host country, domestication is preferable to expropriation for a variety of reasons:

1. The embarrassment that expropriation often causes on the international scene can be avoided.
2. There is no effect on the country's credit rating among international financial institutions, unlike that following expropriation.
3. The host country does not need to run the expropriated business on its own. In businesses where new technical and managerial know-how processes are needed for successful operation, linkage with the multinational corporation is often more than convenient.
4. The host country is not singled out as bad risk by academicians, consultants, and present and potential investors. In other words, domestication, in contrast with expropriation, helps to maintain an aura of favorable political climate in the country.
5. Domestication partially satisfies the leftist sentiment in the host country.
6. It provides to the host country enough control to carefully scrutinize and regulate activities of the foreign firm. In this way, any truly negative effects of the MNC's operations in the host country are discovered and prompt corrective action taken, either through negotiations or through legislation and decree for further control.

Other Forms of Intervention

In addition to expropriation and domestication, there are various means of government intervention in foreign enterprise. The intervention usually takes the form of legislative action and/or a decree enacted in the best national interest. Further, intervention appears to apply to both domestic and foreign businesses. But a deeper probe often reveals that certain aspects of the law/decree are irrelevant for domestic business and are meant specifically to control foreign business. For example, a clause in a decree restricting repatriation of profits to stockholders outside the country would be meaningless for native companies.

The following means of intervention are discussed below: exchange control, import restrictions, market control, tax control, price control, and labor restrictions.

Exchange Control Countries having difficulties with the balance of trade often impose restrictions on the free use of foreign exchange. For example, import of luxuries from outside the country is restricted. Similarly, restrictions are placed on the remittances from the country involving hard currency. The exchange control may also be an effort to encourage domestic industry.

Exchange control measures affect foreign business in two ways. First, profits and capital cannot be returned to the parent company at will. Second, raw material, machinery, spare parts, and the like cannot be liberally imported for operating purposes.

Most developing countries utilize exchange control to regulate their hard currency balances. The need for such regulations is one important reason for restrictions on imports of consumer goods (for example, cars, appliances, clothing, perfumes) in most emerging countries. Sometimes even developed countries may resort to exchange control. One example is France in 1981 after the socialist government took over.[30]

Import Restrictions Import restrictions are primarily for the support of native industries. Consider a foreign pharmaceutical company traditionally importing certain compounds and chemicals from the parent company. If the host country places restrictions on imports, the company may be forced to depend on local sources of supply for these new materials. This can create two types of problems for the foreign firm. First, the local product may be of inferior quality, which would affect the quality of the finished product. Second, locally the product may be in such short supply that the pharmaceutical manufacturer cannot acquire it in adequate quantity.

Presumably governments legislate import restrictions with the total industry, and not a particular company, in mind. Thus, the difficulties likely to be faced by a foreign company do not figure in the discussion. Further, when a country wants to encourage domestic industry as a matter of industrial policy, import restrictions are adopted with the realization that the local product will be inferior, at least initially. Strictly from the point of view of the government, import restrictions seem reasonable, but they ordinarily jeopardize the functions of foreign business.

Market Control The government of a country sometimes imposes control to prevent foreign companies from competing in certain markets. For example, until recently Japan had prohibited foreign companies from selling sophisticated communications equipment to the Japanese government. Thus, AT&T, GTE-Sylvania, and ITT could do little business with Japan.

The Arab boycott of companies doing business with Israel is an interesting example of market control. Since the Arab states have not recognized Israel's right to exist, the Arabs hope that the boycott eventually will bring about the collapse of the state of Israel.[31] Although many countries have given in to Arab demands, the U.S. government has adopted strict laws to prevent companies from becoming susceptible to the Arab blackmail.

Tax Control Governments may also impose excessive and unconventional taxes on foreign business. For example, a new form of excise tax for which there is no precedent may be placed on the output of a foreign firm. Such taxes are imposed for three reasons. First, an out-of-the-way burden on foreign companies is an indirect way of warning them that they are not wanted in a country any longer. Second, when a country is in dire need of new revenues, an additional tax burden on foreign companies appears not only politically prudent but economically convenient. And third, taxes can be retaliatory if a government, for example, learns that foreign corporations have abused differences in international taxation and have deprived the country of due revenue.

Taxes per se do not hinder foreign enterprise. But problems do arise over excessively discriminatory taxes or taxes imposed at variance with the company's agreement with the government. For example, the host government may have agreed to give a tax holiday to a company, say for five years, to establish its operations in the country. Three years later, the government chooses to reverse its position for some reason, such as a new government's refusing to live with the agreement entered into by its predecessor.

Price Control For the sake of the public interest in difficult economic times, countries often resort to price controls. Even in the United States, the price control weapon has been used many times. For example, President Nixon imposed price controls in the early 1970s to fight inflation. Likewise, many states control the price that a vendor may charge for milk. Up until recently, the price of gasoline was regulated.

Similarly, countries use price control devices in various ways to improve their economies. For example, a country may set an official price on essential products such as drugs, heating oil, sugar, and cereals. Price control becomes a special problem if it is imposed randomly; for example, a price limit is placed on a company's finished product, but the prices of the raw materials used in the production of that product are left to market forces. Further, if the product of a particular foreign country has been singled out for price control without any economic rationale, such a measure amounts to undesirable intervention in the working of a foreign firm.

Labor Restrictions In many nations labor unions are very strong and have great political clout. Using its strength, labor may be able to talk the government into passing very restrictive laws that support labor at heavy cost to business. Traditionally, labor unions in Latin America have been able to prevent layoffs, plant shutdowns, and the like, even when business could not afford to meet such demands. Labor unions are gradually becoming strong in Western Europe as well. For example, Germany and a number of other European nations require labor representation on boards of directors.

Foreign firms may find it difficult to accommodate labor demands transformed into laws. Even where there are no labor laws to comply with, there may be labor problems. Problems can reach such a level that the foreign enterprise is left with no other choice but to leave.

An interesting example of labor problems is provided by Hitachi's experience in England. The company, a Japanese electronics manufacturer, was authorized by the British government to set up a TV assembly plant in northern England. The project was expected eventually to provide 500 jobs in a region badly hit by unemployment. As the company began its project, British labor unions bitterly campaigned against the plant, contending that the Japanese entry would destroy the domestic industry and in the long run cost the country 2,000 jobs. The matter became so serious that it had to be decided by the prime minister. The government backed out of the agreement, and the company had to withdraw.[32]

Political Perspectives

Given today's climate of global economic and political change and the experience of widespread nationalizations and expropriations in the 1960s and 1970s, there is a growing recognition in the business world of the need for a company to "look before it leaps" when considering entry into a foreign country. Any multinational marketer would be well-advised to compile a thorough analysis of the political risks peculiar to a foreign country's political system as well as risks peculiar to the company's industry in foreign settings.

History shows that far and away the riskiest ventures are those in countries of the Third World where appeals to nationalism are most damaging to multinationals. But the so-called revolution of rising entitlements that haunts Western business may be reflected in fundamental shifts in national policies toward foreign investment if popular frustration over stagnant economies increases. Consequently, traditionally "safe" investment havens would have to be viewed in a different light.[33]

On the other hand, the Third World countries cannot simply be ignored. For the United States, the developing countries are increasingly important both economically and politically. They are major suppliers of raw materials including, of course, oil; moreover, they constitute the most rapidly growing U.S. export markets. For example, from 1985 to 1990 U.S. exports of capital goods to developing countries doubled from under $48 billion to over $97 billion. In fact, taken as a group, developing countries (excluding OPEC countries) now account for more U.S. exports than the Western European countries. During the recessionary period of the early 1990s, while U.S. exports to industrial countries stagnated or declined, exports to developing (including oil-exporting) countries continued to expand. Without that demand for U.S. goods, unemployment and production would have been far worse. In 1990 about 25 percent of $410.35 billion in direct overseas U.S. investments was in developing countries. The Third World also accounts for around 40 percent of the $380.5 billion in U.S. bank claims on foreigners. Profits and interest from these investments and loans play an important role in offsetting U.S. trade deficits.

The political perspectives of a nation can be studied using factors such as those in the following list:

- Type of government
- Stability of government
- Quality of host government's economic management
- Change in government policy
- Host country's attitude toward foreign investment
- Host country's relationship with the rest of the world
- Host country's relationship with parent company's home government
- Attitude toward assignment of foreign personnel
- Extent of anti-private-sector influence or influence of state-controlled industries
- Fairness and honesty of administrative procedures
- Closeness between government and people

The importance of these factors varies from country to country. Nevertheless, it is desirable to consider them all to ensure a complete knowledge of the political outlook for doing business in a particular country.

Type of Government

World governments can be realistically grouped in four categories: democratic republics, communist dictatorships, dictatorships, and monarchies. In each category there is a spectrum of variation. Democratic governments are formed through regular elections and have different party systems. In the United States and England, two major political parties are active. Italy and France have several political parties. In India and Mexico, one dominant party controls. Although economic policies are an important issue in democracies, different parties hold different views on how the country's economy can be strengthened. In England the two major parties, Labour and Conservative (or Tory), have different economic approaches. A Labour government usually seeks greater government control, while a Tory government stands for programs similar to those of the Republican party of the United States.

Communist governments are rigidly regulated by complete government control of all business activity. Such governments exist in Cuba, the People's Republic of China, Vietnam, North Korea and Burma. Communist countries maintain various types of ties with foreign business. Because China desires to achieve economic progress through using Western technology and skills, the business climate there has been favorable. On the other hand, Burma has totally isolated itself from the rest of the world. The attitude of the Chinese government swings with changing events. It is convinced that the best way for the country to survive is to keep the screws on political dissent but also energize the economy with free-market reforms.

Dictatorships are authoritarian regimes. These governments are run either by military dictators, such as in Thailand, or by civilian dictators, such as in South Korea. Military dictators often eventually adopt a civilian posture, usually by holding an election that gives the appearance of a government elected by popular vote.

Authoritarian governments can be further categorized according to economic philosophy. They may be left wing or Marxist oriented, or right wing and directed toward free enterprise. Angola and Nicaragua reflect, for instance, left-wing characteristics, while both Indonesia and Nigeria follow right-wing policies.

Finally, monarchy refers to a government whose ruler derives power through inheritance. A country may have a monarchy and yet be democratic, such as Great Britain, whose Queen Elizabeth II is titular head of the country but not head of the British government. But in many countries, the government is actually run with the monarch as the head. Saudi Arabia and Jordan have monarchies. The Shah of Iran was a reigning monarch. A monarch may have inclinations to either the left or the right.

Any review of a country's political system and its impact on foreign business must remain free of stereotyped notions. Political philosophies change over time. Thus, what a government or a party stood for in the 1960s may not hold true in the 1990s. Obviously, current and emerging perspectives should be analyzed and understood.

Government Stability

In many countries, there are frequent changes of government. In such a climate, a foreign business finds that the government has changed by the time it is ready to implement an agreement. In other words, the government with whom the initial agreement was arranged was different from the one currently in office. Such changes may create difficulties in implementing the agreement because the new government may or may not subscribe to the commitments made by its predecessor.

Thus, it is important for international marketers to examine before making agreements whether the current government will continue to be in office to implement agreements made with it (see International Marketing Highlight 8.4). In a democratic situation, the incumbent party's strength and/or the alternative outcomes of the next election can be weighed to assess the likelihood of a change in government. In other situations, a variety of symptoms could point toward the instability of a government:

- Public unrest (demonstrations, riots, or other demonstrations of social tension)

International Marketing Highlight 8.4

Change in Command

Sam Parry was the assistant director of a corporate team investigating the prospects of a manufacturing venture in a small Caribbean country. After six weeks in the field, the team received a request from the government to address the head of state and his cabinet about their proposal. The team spent several days preparing a presentation. At the last minute, however, the project director was called away; she assigned Sam to address the assembled leaders in her place.

Sam had spent enough time helping to prepare the presentation that he felt comfortable with it. He even practiced his introduction to the prime minister—the honorable Mr. Tollis—and to the prime minister's cabinet. Finally, the day arrived for the address. Sam and the team were received at the governmental palace.

Once settled into the prime minister's meeting room, Sam opened the presentation. "Honorable Mr. Tollis," he began, "and esteemed members of the cabinet. . . ."

Abruptly, the prime minister interrupted Sam. "Won't you please start over?" he asked with a peeved smile.

Sam was taken aback. He hadn't expected his hosts to be so formal. They always seemed so casual in their open-necked short-sleeved shirts while Sam and his team sweated away in their suits. But Sam soon regained his composure. "Most honorable Mr. Tollis and highly esteemed members of the cabinet. . . ."

"Be so kind as to begin again," said the prime minister, now visibly annoyed.

"Most esteemed and honorable Mr. Tollis—"

"Perhaps you should start yet again."

Shaken, Sam glanced desperately at his team, then at the government officials surrounding him. The ceiling fans rattled lightly overhead.

One of the cabinet ministers sitting nearby took pity on Sam. Leaning over, the elderly gentleman whispered, "Excuse me, but Mr. Tollis was deposed six months ago. You are now addressing the honorable Mr. Herbert."

Source: Charles F. Valentine, *The Arthur Young International Business Guide* (New York: John Wiley & Sons, 1988), p. 400.

- Government crises (opposition forces trying to topple the government)
- Armed attacks by one group of people on another, or by groups from a neighboring country
- Guerrilla warfare
- Politically motivated assassinations
- Coup d'état
- Irregular change in top government leaders

A report covering these points would provide good evidence of a government's stability or instability.

Government Economic Management

Another factor to be examined is the quality of the host government's economic management. A country that manages its economic affairs according to sound economic principles, whether through free economics or socialist policies, will, all things being equal, provide a more favorable environment than a country governed by political emotions and abrupt practices. The economic environment of a country should be studied in the political context with reference to:

- The ability of the government to sustain its internal and external debt
- The country's pursuit of stable and diversified economic growth
- The country's ability to generate an adequate amount of foreign exchange
- The nature of the various fiscal and monetary means used to steer the economy
- The quality of the long-term planning of economic policy and its implementation

As an example, a country that continues to live on borrowed funds, either from private sources or international agencies like the IMF, and frequently defaults on payments demonstrates poor economic management.

Change in Government Policy

More than anything else, MNCs dislike frequent policy changes by host countries. Policy changes may occur even without a change in government. When this type of environment exists, it makes things so uncertain that foreign business cannot know what it is getting into. It is important, therefore, for the foreign business to analyze the mechanism of governmental policy changes. Information on the autonomy of legislatures and study of the procedures followed for seeking constitutional changes can be crucial.

Attitude Toward Foreign Investment

Many nations look upon foreign investment with suspicion. This is true of both developed and developing countries. Take, for example, Japan, where it would be extremely difficult for a foreign business to establish itself without first generating a trusting relationship in order to gain entry through a joint venture opportunity. Developing countries, on the other hand, are usually afraid of domination and exploitation by foreign business. In response to national attitudes, nations legislate a variety of laws and regulations to prescribe the role of foreign investment in their economies. It is appropriate, therefore, to review the host country's regulations and identify underlying attitudes and motivations. Indirectly, the success of other multinational businesses in a country indicates a favorable attitude.[34]

The International Stance of Government

Countries that maintain amicable political relationships with the rest of the world and have respect for international law and order show political maturity. These countries can be expected to behave in a responsible fashion. Iran, for example, in the post–Shah period behaved erratically without regard for international treaties and obligations. Uganda during Dada's regime fell in the same category. Usually, extreme cases can be easily identified. For less spectacular situations, membership in regional and international organizations as well as adherence to bilateral and multilateral principles and agreements provides evidence of a country's relationship with other nations.

Relationship with Parent Company's Home Government

In theory, multinational corporations have no political alignment. Yet a company originating in the United States will continue to be known as a U.S. company even though it may derive a major portion of its revenues and profits from operations outside the United States. Nestlé, for example, generates close to 50 percent of its revenues in the United States and only 4 percent in its home country, Switzerland. Nevertheless, it is identified as a Swiss company. Thus, the relationship between the host country government and the parent company government also will affect, either directly or indirectly, the MNC. Thus the international U.S. marketer should trace the history of the relationship between the host country's government and the United States government. Do the two governments agree on issues debated in international agencies? Are there any points of discord between the two countries? Are there reasons to believe that relations between them will improve or deteriorate in the future? (see International Marketing Highlight 8.5)

Attitude Toward Foreign Managers

A company making an investment in a foreign country needs to make sure that its business there is managed effectively. Among other factors, a crucial determinant of success in overseas operations is the assignment of experienced persons in key positions. But in a country where appointment of local nationals to key positions is a requirement and where qualified nationals are in short supply, there are bound to be difficulties.

Anti-Private-Sector Influence

An interesting development of the post–World War II period has been the increased presence of government in a wide spectrum of social and economic affairs that were previously ignored. As an example in the United States, concern for the poor, the aged, minorities, consumers' rights, and the environment has spurred government response and the adoption of a variety of legislative measures. In a great many foreign countries, such concerns have led governments to take over businesses to be run as public enterprises. Sympathies for public-sector enterprises, successful or not as businesses, have rendered private corporations suspect and undesirable in many countries. Also, it should not be mistakenly thought that public-sector enterprises are limited to developing countries. Great Britain and France have many government corporations, from airlines to broadcasting companies to banks and steel mills.

Obviously, in nations where there is an ongoing bias against home-grown private businesses, a multinational company cannot expect a cordial welcome. In such a situation, the MNC would have to contend with being a private business and being foreign. Sound business intelligence and familiarity with the industrial policy of the government and related legislative acts and decrees should provide clarification of the role of the private sector in any given economy.

International Marketing Highlight 8.5

Copyright Struggle in New York

A copyright squabble in 1988 between two small companies in New York's Chinatown over videotapes of Taiwanese soap operas illustrates how a relationship between governments could erupt into a political problem. U.E. Enterprises Inc., accused of pirating the Taiwanese television programs, claims that Taiwanese nationals no longer are entitled to copyright protection, as a result of the decision by the United States to recognize the People's Republic of China as the "sole legal government" of China in 1979. That decision, the defendants claim, negated the United States–Taiwan Friendship, Commerce and Navigation Treaty of 1948, which is the legal framework for trade as well as copyright agreements between the United States and Taiwan. The defendant's case relies on a complex argument that a law passed by Congress in 1979, purporting to maintain normal trade relations with Taiwan after recognition of the People's Republic, is constitutionally invalid because it effectively amended the treaty by changing the parties from the Republic of China to the "governing authorities of Taiwan." Only the president, with the consent of the Senate, has the power to make or amend treaties, U.E. Enterprises' attorneys say. On the other hand, legal experts feel that the very existence of the act refutes U.E.'s defense. The Justice Department, which filed a brief in the case, agreed.

On the surface, the case concerns only the unauthorized use of Taiwanese products in the United States. But the disputed treaty also protects U.S. companies, such as International Business Machines Corp., E-II Holdings Inc.'s Samsonite Unit, Walt Disney Co., and many others, from the pirating of their products in Taiwan. Because of this the case received wide publicity.

While the judgment was against U.E. Enterprises, the case highlights the significance of political relations between countries.

Source: The Wall Street Journal, October 25, 1988, p. B8.

Administrative Procedures

Every country has its own unique administrative scheme. The scheme emerges from such factors as experience, culture, the system of reward and punishment, availability of qualified administrators, and style of leadership. Additionally, the availability of modern means of transportation and communication helps to streamline governmental administration. Businesses often complain about the U.S. federal bureaucracy and its states' agencies, but if they were to compare U.S. administration with other nation's, they would be pleasantly surprised to learn that government in the United States is far more efficient than elsewhere. It is not extraordinary in many African countries for administrators to be altogether unavailable, the telephones not to work, or files to be lost. Similar difficulties would not be unusual in either Asia or Latin America. Such hindrances, in addition to the usual red tape, make business dealings uncomfortable and unpleasant. While a company may not bypass an overseas opportunity solely because of this factor, knowledge about the inefficiency of administrative machinery might lengthen schedules and force patience through understanding. The wisdom of engaging the services of a local broker or an agent could also be considered.

Closeness of Government to People

Iran's 1979 crisis suggests that economic development cannot be imposed on a nation; rather, it must evolve over time. The breakneck speed with which the Shah of Iran invested billions of dollars in development in the late 1960s and early 1970s created a fragile society. The Shah imposed a modern infrastructure, an industry dependent on foreign technology, and a Western lifestyle on a Muslim society that was opposed to change. This swift modernization, with GNP per capita increasing from $200 to over $2,000 in a decade's time, triggered a reaction that led to the Shah's fall. The people, in other words, could not absorb modernization quickly enough to adapt their lives accordingly, and they revolted. Religious priests became the leaders of a people disillusioned by Western living and material progress.

The Islamic revolution in Iran provides a classic case of how the distance between government and people can lead to the total disruption of a country. Many political scientists have noted the similarities between Saudi Arabia's modernization and Iran's. There also, a tribal nomadic society is being transformed seemingly overnight into an industrial society with modern amenities and facilities.[35] To an extent, South Vietnam presented a similar problem. The government kept developing programs, with U.S. aid, that widened the distance between the government and the people.

It is sometimes difficult to ascertain whether the people and the government of a country are in accord. The United States government, despite all its resources, failed to foresee that the Shah would fall. However, contact with journalists, religious leaders, and the intelligentsia of a country can provide some insights into the feelings of ordinary citizens toward their government and its programs. In traditional societies, where a windfall such as oil revenues suddenly offers an opportunity for multinational business, it would be prudent to investigate the sentiments of the people before making major commitments.[36]

Political Models

On the basis of the factors discussed so far, a country can be categorized as having one of the following political slants: state-centric international politics, pluralistic national politics, bureaucratic organizational politics, or transnational politics. Each of these political model systems presents different kinds of risk for doing business.

The state-centric model of international politics assumes that national governments seek power and status in relation to one another, that they do so in the context of a competitive, decentralized international political system, and that they utilize whatever internal political resources are available in pursuit of their international objectives. National governments' actions are thus assumed to be functions of the officials' desire for international power and status and of their reactions to political pressures exerted by other national governments.

The pluralistic model of national politics assumes that national governments are responsive to the diverse and conflicting interests and pressures of multiple interest groups within a political system. Group interests and pressures are expressed through electoral processes but are especially important in legislative and administrative processes, where they take the form of lobbying activities. National governments' actions are thus assumed to be functions of the officials' desire to remain in office and/or of their reaction to internal political pressures.

The bureaucratic organizational politics behavior model assumes that national governments' actions are the result of organizational processes within government bureaucracies. Intragovernmental conflicts are generated, for instance, by the differing policy preferences of individual officials and agencies. These variances arise from conflicting organizational interests, differences in career experiences, differences in ties to domestic clientele groups, and other factors. This model also suggests that government policies are slow to change because of bureaucratic inertia.

The transnational politics model emphasizes the increasingly important role played in world politics by organizations other than those of national governments. Thus, not only MNCs but also international organizations and nongovernmental associations, such as transnational interest groups, are all assuming greater influence, often at the expense of national governments.

Each model contains numerous variables and propositions about relationships among the variables. Each one is also evident in an abundance of impressionistic case studies, systematic quantitative studies, and historical narratives. However, even this abbreviated discussion suggests the utility of these models in political risk assessment, for they can be used to develop a lengthy and systematic list of potential sources of political risk.[37]

Political Risk Assessment

Political risk assessment (PRA) is useful for three reasons:

1. To identify countries that may turn out to be the Irans of tomorrow. (PRA should sound a warning signal of mounting political risks so that a firm can protect itself by minimizing its exposure.)
2. To identify countries unnecessarily discounted as politically unsound, for example, Angola and Rhodesia (Zimbabwe), and to identify countries where political conditions have changed for the better, for example, Egypt.
3. To provide a framework to identify countries that are politically risky, but not so risky as to be automatically ruled out. (Most developing countries fall into this category.)

Methods of Political Risk Assessment

Corporations utilize any number of methods to analyze political risk. The currently favored approaches are the so-called qualitative grand tour and old hand approaches, the delphi technique, and the use of quantitative methods.

Grand Tour This approach involves an executive or a team of executives visiting the country in which investment is being considered. Usually, prior to the visit, there has been some preliminary market research. Upon arrival, there are usually meetings with government officials and local businesspersons. The results of this type of visit can be very superficial, representing only selected pieces of information and thereby possibly camouflaging undesirable aspects of the market.

Old Hand This approach relies on the advice of an outside consultant or a person deemed to be an expert. Usually such persons are seasoned educators, diplomats, local politicians, or businesspersons. The capability and experience of the advisor is the factor determining the quality of this report.

Delphi Technique This technique involves asking a group of experts to share their opinions independently on a given problem, in a form that can be scored in order to produce a statistical distribution of opinion. The experts are shown the resulting distribution and given the chance to alter their original views. The process is repeated several times. And for some kinds of problems, it has been found that the average opinion of the group at the last round is usually more nearly correct than any of the individual views in the beginning.

To use this method, a group of experts would be asked to rate different political factors, for example, the stability of government, the role of its armed forces, and its political conflicts. Based on the final expert opinion, a go or no-go decision can be made.

Quantitative Methods In addition to qualitative methods, many businesses have tried quantitative methods to judge political risk.[38] Among the quantitative methods, discriminant analysis is the most rigorous. This technique involves developing a mathematical relationship among a series of quantifiable factors in order to predict (within specified probability ranges) the likelihood of certain events. Banks have utilized this technique before granting loans to foreign countries. This technique requires collection of different forms of quantitative data, complex analysis of data using an appropriate computer program, and expert interpretation of the results.

Political Risk Assessment Models

Political risk assessment is rapidly becoming a fact of U.S. corporate life. The surge of interest in PRA began with the unexpected fall of the Shah's regime in Iran and was reinforced by the overthrow of apparently secure governments in Nicaragua and South Korea. Several independent political risk consultants are available to help corporate clients develop general political risk summaries or provide studies of specific countries. The best known risk-raters are the Economist Intelligence Unit (EIU), a New York based subsidiary of The Economist Group, London; the *International Country Risk Guide* (*ICRG*); and BERI S.A.[39] According to the Economist Intelligence Unit, a rating of A, or 0–20 points, is the least risky; followed by B, 25–40 points; C, 45–55 points; D, 60–75 points; and E, 80–100 points. The ratings break down into three categories: medium-term lending risk, covering such factors as external debt and trends in the current account, with a maximum score of 45 points; political and policy risk, including factors such as the consistency of government policy and the quality of economic management, with a maximum score of 40 points; and short-term trade risk, including foreigh-exchange reserves, with a cap of 15 points.

The *International Country Risk Guide* is put out by a U.S. division of International Business Communications Ltd., London. *ICRG* offers a composite risk rating, as well as individual ratings for political, financial, and economic risk. The political variable, which makes up 50 percent of the composite figure, includes factors such as government corruption and how economic expectations diverge from reality. The financial rating looks at such things as the likelihood of losses from exchange controls and loan defaults. Economic ratings take into account such factors as inflation and debt service costs. The maximum, or least-risky, score is 100 for the political category and 50 each for financial and economic risk. For the composite score, 85–100 is considered very low risk; 70–84.5, low risk; 60–69.5, moderate risk; 50–59.5, moderately high risk; and 0–49.5, very high risk.

BERI S.A.'s political risk index (PRI) reviews fifty-four countries three times a year.

Consider Brazil. EIU puts Brazil in category C, giving it a total score of 55. The reason behind this poor showing is easy to see. The economy is struggling to cope with a debt load of over $100 billion, inflation hit 250 percent in 1991, and the economy also remains fairly closed. *ICRG* gives Brazil an overall score of 62, ranking it 54th out of 129 countries. Brazil gets 67 out of 100 for political risk, 34 out of 50 for financial risk, and 23 out of 50 for economic risk.

On the other hand, Mexico's prospects are bullish, and the investment climate has rarely been better. President Carlos Salinas de Gortari is pushing ahead with an ambitious plan to open up the country to foreign competition, and is aggressively pursuing a free-trade pact with the United States. Inflation is slowing. Though oil income has fallen because of the oil-price drop, the decline was expected and has done little to hurt confidence.

In its 1990 report, EIU gave Mexico a risk rating of 50, adding five points to the previous rating because of a high current-account deficit. Mexico still stays in EIU's *C* category.

In *ICRG*'s ratings, Mexico gets a score of 70.5 and a rank of 32. For political risk, it gets 71; for financial risk, 41; and for economic risk, 28.5.

Among Southeast Asian countries, Thailand is perceived as one of Asia's most attractive investments. Economic growth is strong, wages are relatively low, and the government is hospitable to foreign investment. The country is once again under military rule after a brief period of democracy. EIU gives Thailand a score of 25, putting it in the B category. Political risk drags down the score. *ICRG* gives Thailand a score of 68, ranking it 40th. Political risk is scored at 57, financial risk at 42, and economic risk at 37.

Indonesia is rated a medium-risk country. Though the government of President Suharto is authoritarian, it follows conservative fiscal and monetary policies and has steadily slashed restrictions on domestic and foreign investment in recent years. EIU gives Indonesia an overall rating of B. It has raised Indonesia's medium-term lending-risk rating to B from C, reflecting an expected improvement in the debt service as a percentage of gross domestic product. *ICRG* gives

Indonesia a score of 68.5, putting it in the moderate-risk category. But the country gets a relatively weak 57 for political risk, reflecting rising discontent with authoritarian rule and corruption. Indonesia chalks up a strong 44 for financial risk and 35.5 for economic risk.

In Eastern Europe, EIU rates Hungary 55, which puts it in the C category. *ICRG* ranks it 54th, with a composite score of 62, made up of 68 for political risk, 32 for financial risk, and 24 for economic risk. EIU gives Poland a score of 45, putting it in the D category. Poland gets a composite score of 61 from *ICRG,* putting it in 56th place (62 for political risk, 29 for financial risk, and 31 for economic risk). Finally, EIU gives Czechoslovakia a rating of 45, putting it in the C band. *ICRG* gives the country a composite risk rating of 69.5, ranking it 36th. Political risk comes in at 73, financial risk at 36, and economic risk at 30.

The general perspective provided by these studies does not help in monitoring political developments in a practical fashion. Too often, consultants' reports are of dubious usefulness to subsidiary managers, since they are mainly oriented to corporate headquarters. The objectives of a good political risk analysis system should not be to collect and evaluate information but rather to include the best political intelligence in decision making.[40] Toward this end, a specific study tailored to a particular purpose is more useful. Although there is some debate about the usefulness of the indexing services, the client lists of the three organizations include a number of Fortune 500 companies. For those interested in pursuing this subject in more depth, the appendix at the end of this chapter summarizes the procedures used by BERI S.A. in judging the political risk associated with different countries.[41]

Types of Political Risk

Two types of political risks, macro and micro, can be distinguished. Macro risks refer to actions and policies of a country directed at all foreign enterprises. Micro risks are actions and policies affecting selected fields of foreign business in a country. Both micro and macro risks can be further split between societally related and government-related actions and policies and internally and externally based events (see Table 8.1).[42]

Briefly, MNCs face a broad spectrum of political risk. It can be viewed as governmental and societal actions and policies, originating either within or outside the host country and negatively affecting either a select group or the majority of foreign business operations and investments. Understanding the origins and nature of the different types of political risk is important before establishing a system for monitoring political changes.

Strategic Response

When a company has become susceptible to political risk or has been politically victimized, it must make an effort to salvage its position. While there is little a company can do to ward off internal violence or political instability in the host country, it can employ a number of responses to discourage expropriation or generally to strengthen its position. As one author has stated:

TABLE 8.1 A General Framework for Political Risk Assessment

MACRO		MICRO	
Societal-Related	Governmental-Related	Societal-Related	Governmental-Related
Internal Revolution Coups d'etat Civil war Factional conflict Ethnic/religious turmoil Widespread riots/terrorism Nationwide strikes/protests/boycotts Shifts in public opinion Union activism	*Internal* Nationalization/expropriation Creeping nationalization Repatriation restrictions Leadership struggle Radical regime change High inflation High interest rates Bureaucratic politics	*Internal* Selective terrorism Selective strikes Selective protests National boycott of firm	*Internal* Selective nationalization/expropriation Selective indigenization Joint venture pressure Discriminatory taxes Local content/hiring laws Industry-specific regulations Breach of contract Subsidization of local competition Price controls
External Cross-national guerilla warfare International terrorism World public opinion Disinvestment pressure	*External* Nuclear war Conventional war Border conflicts Alliance shifts Embargoes/international boycotts High external debt service ratio International economic instability	*External* International activist groups Foreign MNC competition Selective international terrorism International boycott of firm	*External* Diplomatic stress between host and home country Bilateral trade agreements Multilateral trade agreements Import/export restrictions Foreign government interference

Source: Jeffrey D. Simon, "Political Risk Assessment: Past Trends and Future Prospects," *Columbia Journal of World Business,* Fall 1982, p. 67.

In sum, host governments should not be seen by MNC top managers exclusively as an impediment to global strategic freedom, to be avoided at all cost. Occasionally they may provide enough of a helping hand—through privileged market access, export credits, and subsidies—for smaller MNCs to face global competition, to make it worthwhile for those smaller, often weaker, MNCs to relinquish wholeheartedly some strategic freedom to gain competitive strength through government support. Host governments can thus either hamper or help global strategies, depending on their policies and on the strategic options of the affected firms. It is important, therefore, to make an analysis of host government goals, policies, and actions an integral part of the strategy formulation process in a global business.[43]

Strategic Choices

Essentially, a company has three strategic options to choose from in response to political difficulties in a host country. These responses are to adapt, to withdraw, and to take counteractive measures.[44] For example, IBM completely withdrew from India because the company could not live with the restrictions imposed by the government on freedom of strategy in product development, pricing, and other areas. Nestlé, on the other hand, accepted India's infringements in return for continued presence in the market. CPC International, du Pont, and Brown Boveri (a European company) likewise seek market presence rather than complete withdrawal. The third choice, counteractive response, amounts to making a new move to gain a competitive advantage based on company strengths and the needs of the host government. For example, Honeywell merged its French subsidiary, Honeywell Bull, with the French government company, Compagnie International pour l'Informatique, which was losing money. This arrangement gave Honeywell access to the French market and qualified it to receive French government grants for R & D (see International Marketing Highlight 8.6).

Keep in mind, however, that no single strategy works best in a single country

International Marketing Highlight 8.6

Managing Government Intervention

Bristol-Myers pursued the counteractive strategy in Indonesia. It had successfully marketed one of its nutritional products in Indonesia, which was centrally obtained from its Nijmegen facility in Holland. This worked well for Bristol-Meyers since the Indonesian market wasn't developed enough to justify the cost of building a plant there to service this market. The problem started when the Indonesian government decided to close its borders to the "finished product" that Bristol-Myers had introduced so successfully into the market. Bristol-Myers had to decide whether to find an alternative that could circumvent the new regulation or withdraw from the Indonesian market. Bristol-Myers decided to follow the former route. The concerned product was composed of a highly sophisticated powder that was blended with a heat-sensitive key raw material and canned. Bristol-Myers solved the problem by ascertaining what the Indonesian government really meant by "finished product." It worked closely with the ministry of health and the ministry of economics in Indonesia to come up with a mutually acceptable solution: Bristol-Myers was permitted to import a "base" powder that it would blend with an indigenous raw material. Bristol-Myers successfully subcontracted with an Indonesian company to produce and blend the raw material with the base. The "finished product" was subsequently canned, carried the Bristol-Myers label, and continued to be sold in Indonesia.

or even in a single industry. If the MNCs' managers are flexible and imaginative in responding to government demands, the consequences could be surprisingly favorable. Encarnation and Vachani found that new product lines and markets, risk diversifications, and higher earnings are among the benefits MNCs operating in India enjoyed in the wake of that country's "hostile" equity laws. Some, for example, negotiated for manufacturing licenses and other concessions in exchange for "Indianization." Others successfully sought entry to new markets, hitherto forbidden.[45] The choice, of course, among the three options depends on the bargaining power of the company in respect to the bargaining power of the host government.

MNCs' Bargaining Power

The bargaining power of MNCs stems from such factors as technology, economies of scale, and product differentiation. Companies with technology badly needed by the host country and unobtainable on comparative terms elsewhere bargain from a leverage position. For example, in the late 1970s Indonesia desperately sought to boost its oil exploration activity. This goal required sophisticated technology, and Indonesia was willing to go to any length to get it. In other words, oil companies negotiated with the Indonesian government on very favorable terms since they had the necessary technology.[46] Mexico willingly permitted IBM to establish a wholly owned microcomputer plant. The Mexican government was concerned that without a major microcomputer plant the local market would consist of outmoded and overpriced products. But if a company like IBM entered the market, it could pull other companies in the production chain along with it.[47]

Economies of scale, which a foreign firm might realize through its worldwide production and distribution arrangements, also yield a unique bargaining strength. If the low cost of the local multinational firm's output is directly related to the MNC's worldwide network or vertical integration (via the establishment of specialized plants in various countries and the transfer of components or end products among them), the host country will hesitate to intervene out of fear that any intervention would cancel out the benefits that the firm derives from being a part of the network. In the case of Marcona Mining's iron milling operation in Peru, for example, the firm signed long-term supply agreements with its customers that stipulated that, in the event of nationalization, the contracts with its Peruvian subsidiary would be considered void and that Marcona Mining would supply its customers from its other milling operations. When the firm was expropriated, the Peruvian government found it had no outlet for iron ore concentrate. Since the trade in this commodity is based almost entirely on long-term controls, there was no well-developed spot market to which the Peruvian government could turn.[48]

Product differentiation (that is, differentiation based on the nature of the product and product quality/performance attributes, and not on consumer perceptions) can serve as another area of strength in foreign firms' bargaining with the host governments. For example, a firm producing quality agricultural machinery will have greater leverage in dealing with a host government than will a cosmetics manufacturer.

To sum up, firms with technical, operational, and managerial requirements that are within the reach of the abilities of the host nation will have little bargaining power. Such firms are more likely to experience intervention that those in complex fields. For example, there is considerable local pressure on governments in Kenya, Indonesia, Brazil, and India to restrict such areas as consumer goods manufacturing, retailing, importing and exporting, and distribution to nationals only.

Bargaining Power of the Host Country

The bargaining power of the host country mainly depends on two factors: control of market access and inducements. The host country controls access to the market in many ways. It may restrict entry for other competitors, or it may open up rights to restricted markets. For example, Spain attracted Ford Motor Company by making it feasible for the company to sell enough cars there. Similarly, Japan has permitted foreign companies to sell communications-related products to its government, which may serve as an incentive for such firms as Western Electric to become more active in that market.

In addition, host countries may offer such inducements as R&D funds, tax holidays, market information, land subsidies, and financial concessions (repatriation arrangements) to attract the businesses sought. For example, ITT's European units have received large government grants to develop communication equipment tailored to local conditions.

Making a Response

The strategic response a company makes to intervention by the host country should depend on the bargaining power on each side. Bradley recommends the following strategies for improving the odds in international investing:

- Seek joint ventures with local private parties.
- Concentrate proprietary research, product development, and process technology in the United States.
- Ensure that each new investment is economically dependent on the parent corporation in the United States. (For example, establish the parent as the sole supplier of essential materials.)
- Avoid local branding or establish a single global trademark.
- Adopt a low-profile, multiplant strategy, with a number of investments in different countries.[49]

To conclude, the major benefits to a host country from a foreign investment usually appear at the beginning. Over time, the incremental benefits become smaller and the costs more apparent. Unless the firm continually renews these benefits, by introducing more products, say, or by expanding output and developing export markets, it is likely to be subject to increasing political risks.[50] The common government attitude is to ignore the past and instead to ask what will be done for them in the future. In a situation where the firm's future contributions are unlikely to evoke a favorable government reaction, the firm had best concentrate on protecting its foreign investments by striking a balance between the company's goals and those of its host. For example, a company may introduce higher technology products and thereby foster the government's economic plans.

Briefly, even antibusiness revolutionary regimes leave some room for innovative companies. In Nicaragua, MNCs thrived after the revolution with new strategies and innovative counterproposals. For example:

- They helped the government develop joint ventures between MNCs and state cooperatives that have resulted in new opportunities in Latin America and Eastern Europe.
- They changed production processes to keep prices low, reduce variable costs, and stimulate demand.
- They analyzed political reactions more carefully on any proposed deal in order to negotiate more skillfully.
- They loosened ties with the local private sector to make more direct links with the government.
- They increased monetary incentives to workers and helped union leaders in their dealings with the government.
- They found numerous ways to generate foreign exchange.[51]

Experience shows that foreign business can operate successfully in unstable political climates provided multinational marketers take the initiative in making strategic adjustments in operations and in relations with government, labor, and headquarters.

Summary

An international marketer needs to examine carefully the political environment of a country before making major commitments in that country. The political situation of a country may or may not be conducive to profitable business there.

Political problems related to foreign business occur mainly because of political sovereignty, a country's desire to assert its authority, and political conflict—either internal ones such as civil war or external troubles with another country. Such troubles may lead a country to intervene politically in the affairs of private business, particularly those of foreign firms. Intervention may range from some form of control to complete takeover, or expropriation, which is the official seizure of foreign property by a host country. Other forms of intervention include exchange control, import restrictions, market control, tax control, price control, and labor restrictions. At one time political intervention mainly occurred in developing countries. Now even industrially developed countries seek to control foreign enterprises in various ways.

The possibility of political intervention makes it necessary for a foreign marketer to carefully analyze the political situation of a country before investment there. This analysis can be made through study of the country's type of government (such as republic, dictatorship, and so forth); the stability of the government; the government's economic management; the frequency of changes in government policy; the attitudes that the country maintains toward foreign investment, other governments, the parent company's home government, foreign managers, and private business; the viability of the government's administrative procedures; and the closeness between the government and its people. On the basis of the preceding factors, the foreign firm can determine the political risk of doing business with a given country. Various methods or models can be employed for political risk assessment.

In theory, a company should not enter a politically unsafe country. However, things sometimes change within a country after entry has been made. For example, traditionally Iran provided a workable environment. But, beginning in 1978, it became an extremely high-risk country. What can a company do if problems arise afterward? There are three strategic responses for a company to make in response to political intervention: adapt and accept infringements and mold the business operations to suit the foreign government's requirements; withdraw and call it quits even if it means taking a loss of property; and attempt counteractive measures by making counterproposals that would provide the government with what it wants and at the same time allow the company a few concessions. In the final analysis, the host government's willingness to grant concessions to the foreign enterprise would depend on the MNC's own bargaining leverage. For example, a host government would be willing to concede to the terms of a multinational enterprise involved in business that is of strategic national importance and that cannot be replaced. On the other hand, a company manufacturing consumer goods, such as bar soaps and shampoo, may not have much bargaining power with the host government.

Review Questions

1. Why is it necessary for international marketers to study political environment? How can foreign politics affect marketing decisions?
2. What are the underlying causes of political unrest? Discuss.
3. Discuss different ways in which a host government may intervene in the affairs of a multinational firm.
4. Define the term *expropriation.* What can a company do to counteract expropriation?
5. What factors should a company study to gain insight into a country's politics?
6. Why is it desirable to undertake political risk assessment?
7. Examine the alternative responses a company can use to strengthen its position with the host government.

Endnotes

1. *See* H. Schollhammer and D. Nigh, "The Effect of Political Events on Foreign Direct Investments by German Multinational Corporations," *Management International Review,* no. 2 (1984), pp. 5–27. *Also see* Stephen J. Korbin, *Managing Political Risk Assessment* (Berkeley: University of California Press, 1982).
2. Richard L. Hudson, "Apple Computer vs. French Chauvinism: Politics, Not Free Trade, Wins in the End," *The Wall Street Journal,* February 22, 1985, p. 34.
3. *See* Roberto Friedmann, "Political Risk and International Marketing," *Columbia Journal of World Business,* Winter 1988.
4. "Toyota's Fast Lane," *Business Week,* November 4, 1985, p. 42. *Also see* "Asian Auto Makers Find a Back Door to the U.S. Market," *Business Week,* December 9, 1985, p. 52; "Import or Die," *The Economist,* February 19, 1983, pp. 11–12.
5. "The Screws Are Tightening on U.S. Companies," *Business Week,* February 11, 1985, p. 38.
6. "Foreign Cigarette Makers Aim for Bigger Share of Japan Market," *The Asian Wall Street Journal Weekly,* October 28, 1985, p. 23.
7. Steve Frazier, "Mexico Hopes Its Approval of IBM Plant Encourages More Foreign Investment," *The Wall Street Journal,* July 25, 1985, p. 25.
8. Anthony Spaeth and Amal Kumar Naj, "PepsiCo Accepts Tough Conditions for the Right to Sell Cola in India," *The Wall Street Journal,* September 20, 1988, p. 44.
9. *Business Week,* February 10, 1992, p. 43.
10. Raymond Vernon, "Multinational Enterprises and National Governments: Exploration of an Uneasy Relationship," *Columbia Journal of World Business,* Summer 1976, p. 11.
11. Jack N. Behrman, "Transnational Corporations in the New International Economic Order," *Journal of International Business Studies,* Spring-Summer, 1981, pp. 29–41. *Also see* Urban C. Lehner, "Neither Side Wins in Breakup of DOW Venture in Korea," *The Asian Wall Street Journal Weekly,* January 10, 1983, p. 1.
12. Stephen J. Korbin, "Why Does Political Instability Result in Increased Investment Risk?" *Columbia Journal of World Business,* Fall 1978, pp. 113–122.
13. Joel Davidow, "Multinationals, Host Governments and Regulation of Restrictive Business Practices," *Columbia Journal of World Business,* Summer 1980, pp. 14–19. *Also see* B. Lloyd, *Political Risk Management* (London: Keith Shipton Developments, Ltd., 1976).
14. Louis Kraar, "India Bids for Business," *Fortune,* January 6, 1986, p. 86. *Also see* Rosalind Rachid, "Indian Interests Hail Gandhi's Reform Steps," *The Journal of Commerce,* December 30, 1985, p. 34.
15. Stephen J. Korbin, "Assessing Political Risk Overseas." *The Wharton Magazine,* Winter 1981/1982, pp. 25–31. *Also see* Suleiman K. Kassicieh and Jamal R. Nassar, "Revolution and War in the Persian Gulf: The Effect on MNCs," *California Management Review,* Fall 1983, pp. 88–99.
16. Lynne Reaves, "U.S. Marketers Fend Off Turmoil in Philippines," *Advertising Age,* May 16, 1988, p. 10.
17. *See* William H. Carley, "A Secret Exxon Report Shows How Company Handled a Kidnapping," *The Wall Street Journal,* December 2, 1983, p. 1.
18. *See* "South Korea: A Paradise Lost for Investors," *Business Week,* September 6, 1982, p. 44. *Also see* William A. Stoever, "A Business Analysis of the Partial Nationalization of Zambia's Copper Industry, 1969–1981," *Journal of International Business Studies,* Spring 1985, pp. 137–163.
19. *See* Xiao-Hong Sun and Peter D. Bennett, "The Effect of Political Events on Foreign Direct Investment in Marketing," *Journal of Global Marketing,* Spring 1988, pp. 7–28.
20. Thomas A. Poynter, "Government Intervention in Less Developed Countries: The Experience of Multinational Companies," *Journal of International Business Studies,* Spring–Summer 1982, p. 13.
21. Ranjan Das, "Impact of Host Government Regulations on MNC Operation: Learning from Third World Countries," *Columbia Journal of World Business,* Spring 1981, pp. 85–90.
22. David K. Eiteman and Arthur I. Stonehill, *Multinational Business Finance* (Reading, MA: Addison-Wesley, 1979), p. 186.

23. David G. Bradley, "Managing Against Expropriation," *Harvard Business Review,* July–August 1977, pp. 75–83. *Also see* J. Frederick Truilt, "Expropriation of the Foreign Investment: Summary of the Post World War II Experience of American and British Investors in Less Developed Countries," *Journal of International Business Studies,* Fall 1970, pp. 31–38; Roger B. Hawkins, Steven Mintz, and D. Provissiero, "Government Takeovers of U.S. Foreign Affiliates," *Journal of International Business Studies,* Spring 1976.
24. David G. Bradley, "Managing Against Expropriation," *Harvard Business Review,* July–August 1977, pp. 75–83.
25. *Transnational Corporations in World Development: Third Survey* (New York: United Nations, 1983). *Also see* Thomas M. Gladwin and Ingo Walter, *Multinationals Under Fire: Lessons in the Management of Conflict* (New York: Wiley, 1980).
26. David G. Bradley, "Managing Against Expropriation," *Harvard Business Review,* July–August 1977, pp. 75–83.
27. Ibid.
28. Adeoye A. Akinsanya, *The Expropriation of Multinational Property in the Third World* (New York: Praeger, 1980).
29. Philip R. Cateora, "The Multinational Enterprise and Nationalism," *MSU Business Topics,* Spring 1971, p. 52.
30. "Europe's Economic Malaise," *Business Week,* December 7, 1981, p. 74.
31. *See* Jack G. Kaikati, "How Multinational Corporations Handle the Arab Boycott," *Columbia Journal of World Business,* Spring 1978, pp. 98–109. *Also see* "Mexican Government Will Require Permits for 90% Imports," *The Wall Street Journal,* July 9, 1982, p. 27.
32. Richard F. Janssen, "Hitachi Bid to Build Television Plant in Britain, Creating Jobs, Provokes a Storm of Opposition," *The Wall Street Journal,* November 1, 1977, p. 46.
33. Humayun Akhter and Robert F. Lusch, "Political Risk: A Structural Analysis," in S. Tamer Cavusgil, ed., *Advances in International Marketing* (Greenwich, CT: Jai Press, 1987), pp. 81–102.
34. *See* Gerald Pollio and Charles H. Riemenschneider, "The Coming Third World Investment Revival," *Harvard Business Review,* March–April 1988, pp. 114–127. *Also see Business America,* March 13, 1989, pp. 16–17; and *Statistical Abstract of the United States—1989* (Washington, D.C.: U.S. Government Printing Office, 1989), p. 835.
35. *See* "Saudi Arabia's Dilemma: Too Much, Too Fast," *Business Week,* December 8, 1980, p. 53. *Also see* J. Whitcomb Kennedy, "Risk Assessment for Affiliates Based in Less Developed Countries," *Columbia Journal of World Trade,* Summer 1984, pp. 76–79.
36. *See* David T. Beaty and Oren Harari, "South Africa: White Managers, Black Voices," *Harvard Business Review,* July–August 1987, pp. 94–105.
37. Thomas L. Brewer, *American Foreign Policy: Contemporary Introduction* (Englewood Cliffs, NJ: Prentice-Hall, 1980), Chapter 2. *Also see* Thomas L. Brewer, "Political Risk Assessment for Foreign Direct Investment Decisions: Better Methods for Better Results," *Columbia Journal of World Trade,* Spring 1981, pp. 5–12; Briance Mascarenhas and Ole Christian Sand, "Country-Risk Assessment Systems in Banks: Patterns and Performance," a paper presented at the 1984 Annual Conference of the Academy of International Business, Cleveland, Ohio.
38. *See* P. Nagy, "Quantifying Country Risk: A System Developed by Economists at the Bank of Montreal," *Columbia Journal of World Business,* Fall 1978, pp. 135–147; Elizabeth Goldstein and Jan Vanous, "Country Risk Analysis: Pitfalls of Comparing Eastern Bloc Countries with the Rest of the World," *Columbia Journal of World Business,* Winter 1983, pp. 10–16.
39. Discussion in this section draws heavily on Monua Janah, "Rating Risk in the Hot Countries," *The Wall Street Journal,* September 20, 1991, p. R4. *Also see* William D. Coplin and Michael K. O'Leary, "World Political/Business Risk Analysis for 1987," *Planning Review,* January/February 1987, pp. 34–40; Also see: Jean-Claude Cosset and Jean Roy, "The Determinants of Country Risk Ratings," *Journal of International Business Studies,* vol. 22, no. 1 (First Quarter 1991), pp. 135–142.
40. *See* Thomas W. Shreeve, "Be Prepared for Political Changes Abroad," *Harvard Business Review,* July–August 1984, pp. 111–118. *Also see* James Merrill, "Country Risk Analysis," *Columbia Journal of World Busi-*

ness, Spring 1982, pp. 88–91; Briance Mascarenhas and Ole Christian Sand, "Country-Risk Assessment Systems in Banks: Patterns and Performance," *Journal of International Business Studies,* Spring 1985, pp. 19–36.

41. William D. Coplin and Michael K. O'Leary, "1991 World Political Risk Forecast," *Planning Review,* January/February 1991, pp. 16–23.
42. Jeffrey D. Simon, "Political Risk Assessment: Past Trends and Future Prospects," *Columbia Journal of World Business,* Fall 1982, pp. 62–71 *Also see* Attila Yaprak and Keith T. Sheldon, "Political Risk Management in Multinational Firms: An Integrative Approach," *Management Decisions,* vol. 22, no. 6 (December 1984), pp. 22–29.
43. C. K. Prahalad and Yves L. Doz, *The Multinational Mission* (New York: The Free Press, 1987), p. 68.
44. Yves L. Doz and C. K. Prahalad, "How MNCs Cope with Host Government Intervention." *Harvard Business Review,* March–April 1980, pp. 149–157.
45. D. J. Encarnation and Sushil Vachani, "Foreign Ownership: When Hosts Change the Rules," *Harvard Business Review,* September–October 1985, pp. 152–160.
46. "Foreign Countries Offer Wide Range of Incentives to Invest," *The Asian Wall Street Journal Weekly,* August 24, 1981, pp. 12–14.
47. Steve Frazier, "Mexico Hopes Its Approval of IBM Plant Encourages More Foreign Investment," *The Wall Street Journal,* July 25, 1985, p. 25.
48. Brad Bueermann, "Marcona Mining: A Study in Risk Avoidance," unpublished paper, Stanford University, Graduate School of Business, June 1979.
49. David G. Bradley, "Managing Against Expropriation," *Harvard Business Review,* July–August 1977, pp. 75–83. *Also see* Stephen Weiss-Wik, "Enhancing Negotiators' Successfulness," *Journal of Conflict Resolution,* December 1983, pp. 706–739.
50. Alan C. Shapiro, "Managing Political Risk: A Policy Approach," *Columbia Journal of World Business,* Fall 1981, pp. 63–69.
51. James E. Austin and John C. Ickis, "Managing After the Revolutionaries Have Won," *Harvard Business Review,* May–June 1988, pp. 103–109.

APPENDIX

BERI S.A. Procedures for Assessing Political Risk*

The BERI S.A.'s Political Risk Index (PRI) is a service to companies and banks with multinational operations. The objective of PRI is to gauge the business climate in different countries. The concept focuses wholly on sociopolitical conditions in a country by:

- Creating a multicomponent system with flexibility to weigh key factors
- Utilizing a permanent panel of experts with a political science rather than a business orientation.
- Providing data that can move independently of other BERI S.A. risk measures
- Using three periods: present conditions, +5 years conditions, and +10 years conditions

First Step in the System

The expert rates the present conditions for each of the eight causes shown in the first two lists below from 7 (no problems) to 0 (prohibitive problems). Then, the two symptoms in the third list are rated on the same scale in the present. The perspective is from the viewpoint of an international corporation rather than private enterprise owned by nationals. This subtotal involves a maximum of 70 for the perfect country.

Six Internal Causes of Political Risk

- Factionalization of the political spectrum and the power of these factions
- Factionalization by language, ethnic, and/or religious groups, and the power of these factions
- Restrictive (coercive) measures required to retain power
- Mentality, including xenophobia, nationalism, corruption, nepotism, willingness to compromise

**Political Risk Information* (Long Beach, CA: BERI S.A., 1983).

- Social conditions, including population density and wealth distribution
- Organization and strength of forces for a radical left government

Two External Causes of Political Risk

- Dependence on and/or importance to a hostile major power
- Negative influences of regional political forces

Two Symptoms of Political Risk

- Social conflict involving demonstrations, strikes, and street violence
- Instability as perceived by nonconstitutional changes, assassinations, and guerrilla wars

Second Step in the System

One or more of the causes may have a very positive impact on the overall political risk. The second subtotal of the system permits discretionary use of 30 points. Experts typically allocate ±20 to a low-risk country, ±10 for moderate risk, etc., and usually opt to allocate no additional points to a prohibitively risky country. The perfect country would receive a rating of 100 as a result of steps one and two.

Forecast of PRI

Steps one and two are repeated for each of the +5 years and +10 years periods. The points awarded to a country under present conditions serve as a basis for changes in the future.

Interpretation of the Ratings

Four categories of political risk have become apparent from usage:

1. 7–100 Low risk. Political changes will not lead to conditions seriously adverse to business. No major sociopolitical disturbances are expected.
2. 55–69 Moderate risk. Political changes seriously adverse to business have occurred, but governments in power during the forecast period have a low probability of introducing such changes. Some disturbances will take place.
3. 40–54 High risk. Political developments seriously adverse to business exist or could happen in the near future. Major sociopolitical disturbances are occurring periodically.
4. 0–39 Prohibitive risk. Political conditions severely restrict business operations. Loss of assets is possible. Disturbances are part of daily life.

CHAPTER • 9

Legal Environment

CHAPTER FOCUS

After studying this chapter, you should be able to:

- Describe two types of legal systems
- Discuss jurisdiction of laws
- Examine relevant host country laws, U.S. laws, and international laws and conventions
- Explain arbitration and how companies may resort to it to resolve conflict in a foreign environment

Multinational enterprise in its global exercise must cope with widely differing laws. A U.S. corporation not only has to consider U.S. laws wherever it does business, but also must be responsive to the host country's laws as well. For example, without requiring any proof that certain market practices have adversely affected competition, U.S. law makes them violations. These include horizontal price fixing between competitors, market division by agreement between competitors, and price discrimination. These laws must be respected by a U.S. corporation regardless of its place of business. Simultaneously, local laws must be adhered to. For example, in Europe a clear-cut distinction is made between agencies and distributorships. Agents are deemed auxiliaries of their principal; distributorships are independent enterprises. Exclusive distributorships are considered restrictive in Common Market countries. The foreign marketer must be careful in making distribution arrangements in, say, France, so as not to violate the regulation concerning distributorship contracts.

Worldwide, different countries pursue legal systems of varied complexity and dimension. In some countries, laws only provide a broad guide, and the interpretation is left to the courts. In other countries, laws spell out virtually every detail. A foreign enterprise, therefore, has to be scrupulously careful to ensure that it fully abides by local laws and regulations. From the marketing standpoint, a U.S. company doing business in other countries should be primarily concerned with laws pertaining to competition, price setting (for example, price discrimination, resale price maintenance), distribution arrangements (for example, exclusive dealership), product (for example, wholesomeness, packaging, warranty and service, patents and trademarks), personal selling (for example, white-collar employment/labor laws), and advertising (for example, media usage, information provision).

In addition, there are both host country and U.S. laws relative to taxes, tariffs, licensing, and other areas related to business that should be understood and complied with, along with certain international laws and conventions that affect marketing decision making in the global context. The international marketer should also understand the use of arbitration as an alternative to legal recourse.

The impact of legal aspects on marketing is illustrated by an Italian law allowing wine coolers to be sold there. Although Italy had been producing wine coolers for export for years, existing law had prohibited wine from being mixed with other ingredients, basically to protect consumers from tampered wine. The new law prevents the beverage from being called a wine cooler. Instead, it's to be described as a wine-based "fantasy" beverage with a minimum of 75 percent wine and grape juice. The Italian word *fantasia* also means multicolored. No artificial flavors, sugar, or water are allowed.

Both Riunite and Cantina Sociale di Foggia launched their wine beverages in Italy within days of official publication of the law.[1]

International Legal Perspectives

Two important aspects of international legal systems are pertinent to marketing: the philosophical bases of the laws and the jurisdiction of these laws.

Common Law Versus Code Law

Philosophically, two types of legal systems may be distinguished: common law and code law. ***Common law*** is based on precedents and practices established in the past and interpreted over time. Common law was first developed in England, and most of the countries that at one time or another formed a part of the British Empire follow this system. ***Code law*** is based on detailed rules for all eventualities. Code law was developed by the Romans and is popularly practiced by a large majority of free world countries. Most countries of the free world may be divided into those that follow common law, as do Great Britain, the United States, Australia, India, and Kenya, and those that have code law, as do Italy, France, Germany, Mexico, and Switzerland.

It is important for an international marketer to be familiar with the genesis of a country's law, for it frequently has far-reaching effects on all kinds of decisions. For example, right to a property (which would cover such things as trademark) in a common law country would depend on the history of use of the property, that is, in a dispute which party actually used the trademark on its package and in its advertising campaign. According to code law, however, the right of property would be established based on which party actually registered the trademark. Assume two companies, say Alpha and Beta, are claiming rights to a trademark. Alpha registered the trademark but never used it. On the other hand, Beta has been using it all along in various commercial ways without ever bothering to register it. Legally, in a common law country, the trademark would belong to Beta Company. In the code law country, however, it would be the property of the Alpha Company.

Similarly, so-called acts of God in contractual obligations are interpreted differently in the two legal systems. Consider a Japanese company that entered into contracts with firms in England and Italy to deliver certain electronic equipment on a specified date. When a hurricane on the high seas destroyed the Japanese shipment, the company could not fulfill the contract. In both England and Italy, this is considered an act of God, and the Japanese company would not be held liable for not meeting the contractual terms. However, assume the shipment was destroyed not by a hurricane but by a breakdown in the air conditioning system of the building where the goods were stored. In this case, the common law might not release the Japanese exporters from noncompliance because air conditioning failure during summer heat can be expected and therefore is not an act of God. Under code law, both circumstances would most likely be considered acts of God.

The division between code law and common law countries, broad in nature, narrows in actual practice. Some common law countries also have specific codes, particularly in the area of commerce, that must be followed. Furthermore, although two countries follow the same system, the interpretation in a particular case may differ, based on the experiences and precedents in the two environments. For example, air conditioning failure might be considered an act of God in Egypt, even though it is a common law country, because air conditioning is limited there and the climate is sultry most of the year.

An emerging development is the difference between the legal system of free countries and communist rules. This difference becomes significant as former communist countries liberalize their economies and come in contact with people/companies from the capitalist world (see International Marketing Highlight 9.1).

Jurisdiction of Laws

Remarkably enough, while business across national boundaries is an accomplished fact, there is no international body to make rules and oversee their fulfillment by different parties. Thus, a business incorporated in a particular country carries the burden of complying with the laws of both the incorporating nation and the host country. For example, a large U.S. manufacturer may have subsidiaries incorporated/registered in different parts of the world. Such expansion makes the parent company liable to the laws of all the nations where it does business.

Major problems occur when laws of more than one country must be respected and these laws have different values. In other words, if a conflict occurs between two contracting parties, the question arises as to which nation's laws should be used to resolve the problem. If the contract contains a jurisdiction clause stipulating which country's legal system should be used to settle disputes, the matter can be settled accordingly. However, if the parties have failed to include a jurisdiction clause in the contract, two alternatives exist: (1) settle the dispute by following the laws of the country where the agreement was made or (2) resolve the dispute by applying the laws of the country where the contract has to be fulfilled. If the two alternatives are likely to lead to different conclusions, each party naturally would like to settle the issue according to the legal system that favors its position. Obviously this may lead to legal and counterlegal actions, presumably in different courts, perhaps in different countries. An alternative to legal action is arbitration, which will be discussed in a later section.

Consider the Bhopal tragedy in which over 2,000 people died from a gas leakage accident in a Union Carbide plant in India in 1984. The Indian government would have liked the question of compensation to survivors settled in the U.S. courts, because the U.S. courts have been more liberal than the Indian courts in granting compensation to victims in such cases. Despite India's viewpoint, Union Carbide would have preferred that the case be settled in the Indian courts, in the hope that their liability would be reduced substantially. In the end, the case was settled in India (for readers' interest, it was an out-of-court settlement).

Host Country Laws

Countries enact laws to control foreign businesses in their economies. Some of the laws are discriminatory against foreign goods and businesses. Laws are sometimes designed to allow reciprocity with nations on good trading terms with the country. In some instances, extremely favorable laws may be passed to attract foreign investment. In general, the legal environment of a country for foreign commerce depends on that country's economic objectives and its obligations and position in relation to worldwide commerce. In some situations, however, the laws may have political aims as well. For example, a government may decide to

International Marketing Highlight 9.1

Trial of a Salesman

Kwok Siu-wah, a Hong Kong salesman, was alleged to have defrauded three Shenzhen (China) companies of $12,800 by altering shipping invoices between May 1984 and July 1985. He was detained in July of 1985. In December, the Shenzhen Public Security Bureau turned the case over to the prosecutor's office, which demanded that Mr. Kwok repay the money. Because he was not able to do so, court proceedings were instituted against him. Simultaneously, the court temporarily confiscated the travel documents of Mr. Kwok's son, Kwok Wai-hung, who was not charged. The January 1986 verdict sentenced the elder Kwok to seven years in prison.

Since Hong Kong will come under Chinese rule in 1997, a comparison of the proceedings of the Shenzhen court with the proceedings of a Hong Kong court today is interesting.

In a Hong Kong court, the identity and authority of all the participants are made clear at the outset. In Shenzhen, however, the accused was isolated and opposed by all other participants in the case, who were themselves united under party leadership. None of the identities of the court personnel—police, lawyers, court staff, the plaintiff, or the accused themselves—were made public.

Moreover, the Public Security Bureau, the prosecutor's office, the court, and the plaintiff were united in a pursuit of the defendant and his family in an attempt to persuade them to turn over $12,800.

In Hong Kong, even though a defendant has confessed, a court must still render its verdict according to the evidence and to statements made in court. In the Shenzhen case, it was pointed out that the documents allegedly altered by the defendant also bore the signatures of every responsible official of the company he allegedly defrauded. Yet none of these officials was called to present evidence before the court. Instead, the court delivered its verdict based solely on the confession of the defendant—a man who had been isolated for six months prior to the trial.

Under these circumstances, the defendant's confession could have been influenced by threats, coercion, and possibly even mistreatment. The fact that Mr. Kwok's accusers never appeared in court to give evidence and that Mr. Kwok was not allowed to cross-examine them also leads one to raise the possibility that the charges in the case resulted not from Mr. Kwok's actions alone, but from actions involving him with Chinese officials in the alleged fraud. Was the money taken by Mr. Kwok alone, or was it split with others? The joint pursuit of this money by Shenzhen's police, prosecutor, and plaintiff makes one wonder about motives that have not been revealed. The fact that Mr. Kwok's accusers were not brought before the court for cross-examination raises the question of whether there was an attempt at some sort of cover-up.

In the courtroom—a temporary location rather than a formal, permanent site—the defendant was seated on a low stool, giving onlookers an impression of guilt before he had even been sentenced. The plaintiffs did not appear in court.

The defense attorney told the defendant's wife, "You should not entertain any suspicions, nor should you make complaints to any one."

At the beginning of the trial, the travel documents of the defendant's son, Kwok Wai-hung, were confiscated. He was not allowed to return to Hong Kong until his mother disclosed his plight at a news conference in Hong Kong. His release was apparently the result of the publicity that attended the incident in Hong Kong and China's fear of Hong Kong public opinion.

When the case concluded, the court stated that "During the period when the case was under investigation, this court had, according to the law, educated the defendant's wife Tin Yun-kiu, daughter Kwok Siu-ling, and son Kwok Wai-Hung, that they should pay back the sum embezzled by the defendant. This was totally legitimate."

Source: The Wall Street Journal, March 10, 1986, p. 7.

restrict all imports in order to promote a natural feeling among the people and their political supporters. On the other hand, political considerations may require a country to liberalize its laws pertaining to foreign business. For example, in 1988 in the wake of a high U.S. trade deficit and under pressure from Washington, Taiwan reduced tariffs on some 3,500 items by an average of 50 percent, including telecommunications, medical equipment, pharmaceuticals, sophisticated electronic equipment, forest products, agricultural goods, and cigarettes.[2] South Korea and Japan, other trading partners of the United States with whom it had a substantial negative trade balance, have been similarly tilting their trade policy toward the United States.

Laws that bear on entry into foreign markets take several forms, including tariffs, antidumping laws, export/import licensing, investment regulations, legal incentives, and restrictive trading laws.

Tariffs

A ***tariff*** is a tax that a government levies on exports and imports. If the tax is charged on exports it is called *export duty.* The tax associated with imports is referred to as *import duty* or *customs duty.* The purpose of export duty is to discourage selling overseas to maintain adequate supply at home.

The import duty is levied for different reasons: to protect home industry from being outpriced by cheap imports, to gain a source of revenue for the government, and to prevent the dilution of foreign exchange balances through consumer goods purchased by a few privileged people. In developing countries, where new industries cannot compete with imports from the Western world and their resources are limited, the import duty serves as an important measure to promote economic development. And, while most of the reasons for levying import duties make little sense in the United States and other industrialized countries, the influx of Japanese imports, particularly automobiles, has led many concerned groups in the United States to recommend heavy import duty on the Nissans and the Toyotas.

An import duty may be assessed either according to the value of the product (called ad valorem) or on a unit basis (called specific duty), or both. Computation of specific duty is easier, because the price factor does not come into the picture as it does in ad valorem duty.

A related term, called subsidy, is relevant here also. A *subsidy* is a reverse tariff. Many countries provide a subsidy for local manufactures for export abroad. For example, South Korea provides a subsidy to its steel manufacturers to compete effectively in the world market. A subsidy may also be provided to local products to make them competitive against imports. For example, the United States government subsidized certain types of steel to protect the U.S. industry against Japan's.

Antidumping Laws

Dumping is a type of pricing strategy for selling products in foreign markets below cost, or below the price charged to domestic customers. Dumping is practiced to capture a foreign market and to damage rival foreign national enterprises. For example, foreign car manufacturers have been charged with dumping cars in the United States. Japanese television manufacturers and steel companies also have been similarly charged.

Host governments often pass laws against dumping with a view to protecting local industries. Dumping can be a problem for developed and developing countries alike. Thus, the U.S. Treasury Department in 1976 found that twenty-three of twenty-eight foreign automakers had been dumping cars in the United States. It demanded that the foreign manufacturers increase their car prices. Subsequently, Volkswagen, for instance, raised its 1977 car price an average of 2.5 percent. In the same way, on the recommendation of the International Trade Commission, under the provisions of the 1974 Trade Act, the Treasury Department set minimum steel import price levels to enable U.S. manufacturers to compete against Japanese steelmakers.[3] Among the developing countries, Brazil has passed antidumping legislation against imports from the United States and Japan. Similar laws exist in South Korea, Taiwan, India, and Nigeria.

In theory, the practice of dumping cannot be criticized. A business should be free to set any price it finds would be beneficial in the long run. Thus, different prices may be set in different markets, based on the demand and the competition. The counterargument, however, is that price differentials are intended strictly to weaken competition and over the long run will hurt everyone. Particularly in international business, dumping does inhibit the orderly development of national industry. From this viewpoint, attacks on rival markets by dumping amount to destructive as well as unscrupulous means of securing market position. It is for this reason that countries pass antidumping laws.

Export/Import Licensing

Many countries have laws on the books that require exporters and importers to obtain licenses before engaging in trade across national boundaries. The purpose of an export license may be simply to allow for the statistical tracking of export activities. Licensing may also help to ensure that certain goods are not exported at all, or at least not to certain countries. Chapter 17 discusses United States government prohibition of exportation of certain defense-related goods to certain countries and government requirements for permission to sell bombers and fighter planes to any country. Readers may recall the debate in the Congress in 1981 about the sale of F-16 fighter planes to Saudi Arabia, which finally was approved.

Import licensing is enforced to control the unnecessary purchase of goods from other countries. Such restraints save foreign exchange balances for other important purposes like the import of pharmaceuticals, chemicals, and machinery. India, for example, has strict licensing requirements for the import of cars and other durable consumer goods.

Foreign Investment Regulations

One of the primary aims of laws and regulations on foreign investment is to limit the influence of multinational corporations and to achieve a pattern of foreign investment that contributes most effectively to the realization of the host country's economic objectives. There are several broad areas of legislation concerned with foreign investment. Such laws curtail:

- Foreign investment decision making through procedures affecting the selection of foreign investment, control of takeovers, prohibition or restriction of foreign investment in certain sectors, and elaboration of incentive schemes
- Regulation of ownership, managerial control, and employment through local participation requirements in ownership and management; limitation of expatriate employment and local employment quotas
- Taxation and regulation of financial transactions through determination of locally taxable income to inhibit avoidance of double taxation; control of capital and profit repatriation; incentives for profit reinvestment; regulation of local and foreign borrowing[4]

General Motors Corporation's problems in Germany show how investment laws could pose difficulty. The affair stems from GM's sale of its unprofitable Terex subsidiary, which made earthmoving equipment, to IBH Holding AG of Mainz in 1980. Over the next two years, before IBH declared bankruptcy in 1983, GM made four equity investments in the increasingly troubled German holding company. But in return, the automaker received immediate repayments of millions owed to it by IBH.

Such a maneuver, called "round-tripping," is generally considered illegal, unless properly disclosed, in Germany—though not in the United States. The Germans contend that it could hide a company's true financial condition and thus mislead investors and creditors.

Criminal investigation was launched against GM and its chairman Roger Smith. It took two years for the problem to be settled and GM to be exonerated of any wrongdoing. Meanwhile, however, before making a routine visit to Germany in 1986, Mr. Smith directed GM attorneys to seek assurances from a German prosecutor's office that he would not be arrested. He further requested the audit committee of the GM board to conduct its own review to satisfy itself that he had acted properly.[5]

To illustrate some foreign investment laws and how they work, Table 9.1 shows patterns of foreign direct investment regulation in selected developing countries.

Legal Incentives

Investment incentives enacted to attract foreign investment are an important part of government policy in most developing countries. In a few cases, the regulation of investment through incentive schemes is still the only significant regulation of foreign investment. Although incentive benefits are rarely exclusively reserved for foreign enterprises, in certain countries foreign private investment is in fact the main or sole beneficiary of incentives, because local capital and entrepreneurship cannot undertake the kind of investment encouraged by the incentives. On the other hand, there are some instances where incentives are restricted to local enterprises, joint ventures, or enterprises with a minority foreign participation.

Depending on the basic approach to investment regulation, incentives may be awarded automatically to all enterprises meeting the conditions specified in the relevant legislation, or incentives may be granted for a specific performance or contribution to the host country's economy, such as export promotion and diversification, the development of a backward area, the transfer of modern technology, the encouragement of applied research in the host country, and so forth. Incentives also are often awarded on the basis of case-by-case negotiation in accordance with ad hoc criteria.

The main incentive to the establishment of an enterprise is ordinarily an income-tax holiday of several years' duration. Some governments are inclined to reduce the length of such tax holidays when they involve important tax revenue losses. Tax measures such as accelerated depreciation (which are often used in developed countries as stimulants to investment) have proved less effective for various reasons as incentives in the economic environment of developing countries where the main interest is in new investment rather than the encouragement of expenditure on plant replacement. Other fiscal incentives obtainable in developing countries include the waiver of import duties on equipment and materials essential for production, exemptions from property taxes, and numerous minor tax concessions granted by the provinces or localities where the enterprise is located.

Restrictive Trading Laws

In addition to the tax incentive laws, many governments adopt measures that restrict imports or artificially stimulate exports. Usually such laws are referred to as nontariff barriers to international trade. There are several major types of nontariff barriers.[6]

- *Government participation in trade:* subsidies, countervailing duties, government procurement, and state trading
- *Customs and entry procedures:* valuation, classification, documentation, and health and safety regulations
- *Standards:* product standards, packaging, and labeling and marking

TABLE 9.1 Patterns of Foreign Direct Investment Regulation in Selected Developing Countries

PARAMETER	PATTERN I*	PATTERN II†	PATTERN III‡
I. Administration	Case-by-case screening largely restricted to award of *incentives* (nondiscriminatory)	Case-by-case screening at establishment (degree of discrimination varies)	Separate administration for foreign investment Screening at establishment
II. Investment screening criteria	Emphasis on functional contributions of investment Little indication of extensive cost/benefit analysis Screening largely for award of incentives	Emphasis on functional contributions and conditions of investment Little indication of extensive cost–benefit analysis	Criteria formulated for cost–benefit analysis, often extensive Includes social cost criteria in some cases
III. Ownership	Few requirements Few sectors closed to foreign investment	Joint ventures prevalent	Strict regulations on ownership and investment (except Brazil) A large number of closed sectors
IV. Finance	Few repatriation limitations	Few repatriation limitations	Repatriation ceilings in most areas (except Mexico and Chile) Screening of foreign loans Special control of payments to parent company
V. Employment and training	Announced localization policies but little headway in practice	Local quotas for work force Few local quotas for management	Specific across-the-board localization requirements
VI. Technology transfer	No controls	No controls	Screening and registration of all technology imported
VII. Investment incentives	Long-term tax incentives for establishment	Establishment incentives limited to five years—in most cases nonrenewable	Incentives tied to specific contributions, but incentives may be curtailed for foreign-owned firms
VIII. International dispute settlement	Adherence to international dispute regulation Regional investment regulation: East African Community, West African Economic Community	Same as Pattern I Regional investment regulaton: Arab Economic Union	Local adjudication and regional harmonization of investment regulation: Andean Common Market, Central American Common Market (CACM)

*Mostly Asia (excluding India), Africa, and CACM.
†Mostly Middle East and North Africa.
‡Mostly South America.
Source: National Legislation and Regulations Relating to Transnational Corporations (New York: United Nations, 1978), pp. 13–14.

- *Specific limitations:* quotas, exchange controls, import restraints, and licensing
- *Import charges:* prior import deposits, credit restrictions for imports, special duties, and variable levies

  For example, suppose Germany imposes an 11 percent value-added tax on a domestic product and a 13 percent tax adjustment at the border on a product of identical price and quality imported from the United States. This would induce German buyers to choose the German product over the U.S. import because the tax is 2 percent lower. On the contrary, if a German exporter were given a rebate of 13 percent, he would be able to sell at 2 percent below U.S. price levels and would benefit from an equivalent export subsidy.[7]

- *Other measures:* voluntary export restraints whereby agreement is made between two trading countries to limit the exports of a specific product to a particular level, such as the agreement between Japan and the United States to limit Japanese car exports to the United States; and orderly marketing agreements, which are specific agreements between trading partners whereby they agree to negotiate trade restrictions (see International Marketing Highlight 9.2).

International Marketing Highlight 9.2

Tough Move on Gum Control

Like spitting, public chewing may wind up on the wrong side of the law in the sternly ruled island republic of Singapore. The government has banned the manufacture, sale, and importation of chewing gum. Mere possession of the stuff is not illegal yet, but offending sellers face fines of up to $1,200 and importers could get a year in jail. Gum, explains a government spokesman, "causes filthiness to our public facilities."

Singapore's subway trains have been halted several times recently when wads of chewing gum jammed their doors. The gum lobby argues that gum does not clog doors, people do. The government is unmoved.

Gum fanciers arriving from abroad must declare any gum they have with them on their customs forms. They will be allowed to bring in small amounts for their personal use, but the government reserves the right to define how much that may be.

Source: Time, January 13, 1992, p. 31.

U.S. Laws

Both U.S. corporations and their U.S. officers working abroad remain liable to the laws of the United States. For instance, individuals must comply with U.S. Internal Revenue Service (IRS) laws, and corporations are bound by U.S. antitrust laws. One application of the U.S. antitrust laws to an American company overseas is the Gillette Company case. In a February 1968 suit, the Justice Department sought an injunction against Gillette for its acquisition of shares in Braun AG of Germany. The Justice Department held that Gillette's acquisition of Braun would restrict competition in shaving devices in the United States, given the fact that Braun makes electric razors and that Braun had previously relinquished to a third company its right to sell in the U.S. market until 1976.[8]

There are some laws, however, that have been specially enacted to direct multinational marketing activities, such as the Foreign Corrupt Practices Act of 1977. Basically, the intention of these laws is to protect American economic interests, ensure national security, maintain recognized standards of ethics, and promote fair competition. There are particular U.S. laws that a marketer should pay heed to when engaged in international activities.

Laws Affecting Foreign Trade

The United States, relative to other nations, has a liberal attitude toward exports and imports. However, there are many regulations that an exporter must be aware of in the conduct of business. The government prohibits trading with some nations, for example, North Korea, Vietnam, and, until 1972, the People's Republic of China. Likewise, exportation of several products, among them defense-related equipment, must be cleared with the U.S. Department of Commerce by obtaining a license permitting shipment (licensing requirements will be discussed in Chapter 17). The Omnibus Trade and Competitiveness Act of 1988 affects U.S. exporters in many ways (principal features of this act are discussed in Chapter 2).

The government of the United States also imposes restrictions, via the Internal Revenue Service, on pricing for intracompany foreign transactions. The IRS ensures that prices are not underestimated to save U.S. taxes. For example, a U.S. corporation may export certain goods to its subsidiary, say, in Germany, at a very low price. This would reduce the corporation's U.S. taxes. It is for this reason that the IRS is authorized to review pricing and demand change, if necessary, in such company-to-company overseas transfers.

In regard to imports, the United States markets traditionally were open to all nations with few restrictions. However, for health and safety reasons, food products from many developing countries are prohibited. For example, in 1985 the Food and Drug Administration detained Sri Lankan tea imports for special testing following terrorist threats to contaminate that nation's black tea with cyanide. Sir Lanka provides about 11 percent of U.S. tea imports, or about 21 million pounds of black tea annually. Another example occurred in 1989. For several weeks Chilean grapes and other fruits were prohibited from entering the U.S. since some of these products had been poisoned.

But things changed in the 1970s, when more and more U.S. companies showed signs of crumbling, often from an inability to compete in the world market. The textile, tire, and auto industries cut production or closed down entire factories, largely because U.S. consumers purchased imports. Consequently, workers and industries applied continuing pressure for tougher tariffs and trade quotas.

While the federal government basically subscribes to free trade and has supported GATT and the worldwide effort toward this goal, various legislative and nonlegislative measures have been adopted to protect domestic U.S. industry. For some products, like automobiles, import duties were increased. For other products, like textiles, quotas were imposed on imports from various countries. For steel, the government set minimum prices on imports to make domestic steel competitive.

It is encouraging, however, that both U.S. business and union leaders recognize that in the long run they may have more to lose than to gain by strengthening U.S. trade barriers. Many international economic experts believe that an open trade policy with a comprehensive trade adjustment assistance program is the most beneficial course for both U.S. workers and business, as well as for Third World economies. International trade not only allows countries to acquire material they need, but also encourages greater efficiency through competition, specialization, and economies of scale (the greater the production, the lower the unit cost). In the end, everyone benefits.

Since the mid-1970s, Third World nations have dramatically increased their exports of manufactured goods. The income from those exports has helped to pay for the imports they need. Between 1980 and 1990, goods produced in developing countries and shipped to industrialized nations, including the United States, increased from $200 billion to $395 billion. Exports account for nearly 80 percent of the total foreign exchange earnings in developing countries, and for about 8 percent of all manufactured goods actually bought by U.S. consumers.

As developing countries' per capita income increases, their demand for manufactured imports also increases. Countries that have become middle-income economies, such as Taiwan, South Korea, and Mexico, also have become important trade partners of the United States. In 1990 the United States exported $130 billion worth of goods to the developing nations—one-third of all U.S. exports. This amount almost equals the combined U.S. exports to Western and Eastern Europe.[9]

However, manufactured imports present a real threat to domestic U.S. industries. If imports greatly undersell domestic products, domestic industries may fail and jobs are lost. Endangered industries and workers encourage the government to (1) increase tariff and trade barriers, thereby preserving the status quo by making the domestic products competitive with the imports, or (2) pursue a comprehensive trade and adjustment policy that promises balanced growth of the national and world economy.

Increased protection presents the more politically expedient course, but not necessarily the wisest. If tariffs are raised and import quotas established, one unhappy result might be retaliation by other countries in the form of similar trade restrictions, thus shrinking U.S. export markets. In 1990, the sale of U.S. goods and services abroad accounted for 10 percent of the U.S. gross national product. The loss of markets forces domestic production levels down, creating more job losses. In 1990, one out of six U.S. manufacturing jobs depended on exports.

Moreover, the U.S. consumer, especially in the low- to middle-income brackets, benefits from imports from developing countries. According to a recent Overseas Development Council (ODC) report, imports from the Third World consist mainly of lower-price-range consumer goods—shoes, clothing, and small appliances. Such purchases generally help lessen the impact of inflation. The ODC report cites a survey of actual U.S. retail sales showing that imports from developing countries cost 16 percent less than U.S. products of the same quality. How much more do U.S. goods cost? According to the ODC, domestic sugar costs $660 million more than the imported product; television sets, $55 million more; and footwear, $1,200 million more.[10]

Lower prices, greater markets, and wider job opportunities all make an open trade policy attractive, but there are drawbacks. According to the ODC reports, the electronics, textile, and leather industries, among others, would be hurt. Also, workers hurt by foreign imports generally are poorer, less educated, less skilled, and older. Taking the adverse effects into account, the U.S. open trade policy incorporates benefits for people and businesses adversely affected by imports. Workers are provided with other jobs, basic education, job training, and income maintenance during transition periods under the government-funded 1978 Trade Adjustment Assistance (TAA) program.

Antitrust Laws

As noted earlier, the U.S. antitrust laws apply to U.S. corporations in their international dealings as well as in their domestic transactions. More specifically, U.S. businesses must carefully ascertain if antitrust laws would be violated in any way in the following situations:

- When a U.S. firm *acquires* a foreign firm
- When a U.S. firm *engages in a joint venture* abroad with another American company or a foreign firm
- When a U.S. firm *enters into a marketing agreement* with a foreign-based firm[11]

The Justice Department has become very strict in the application of U.S. antitrust laws on foreign operations of U.S. corporations. Justice Department enforcement takes several forms.

- In 1980 the Justice Department initiated criminal grand jury probes into allegations that U.S. and foreign competitors illegally set the prices of uranium, phosphate, and ocean shipping rates.
- In 1981 it reviewed the overseas licensing agreements of some two dozen multinationals to see whether their prices or territorial arrangements unreasonably prevented overseas producers from selling in the United States.
- In 1982 it investigated oil company reactions to the new two-tier pricing system for foreign crude along with other aspects of their relations with oil-producing countries.

The Justice Department's interest in applying antitrust laws to MNCs is evident in the fact that during the five-year period of 1974–1979, ten cases were filed against companies, compared with only three cases in the eight years before that. Among the products affected by suits were lithium, watches, books, industrial diamonds, bank security equipment, and mink. A case filed in February 1982 charged that Pan American World Airways, Trans World Airlines, Inc., and Lufthansa German Airlines criminally conspired to fix prices of excursion flights for military personnel and their families between Germany and the United States. Among all the reasons that provoke enforcement of antitrust laws, the struggles that involve the problem of market allocation stand out.

In January 1977, a new sovereign immunity law went into effect, giving the government another weapon to use for foreign antitrust actions. MNCs cannot insulate themselves from the antitrust law restraints on trade by going outside the United States: the law empowers the Justice Department to sue foreign governments. The law says that the federal government no longer need show any deference to the commercial activities of foreign governments; they may be charged for lawbreaking just as any other commercial venture. The Justice Department has always taken that position, but the new statute makes it clear to federal judges that government lawyers have the backing of Congress.

The 1977 law creates one difficulty: Where does political activity (which is immune from U.S. prosecution) begin and commercial activity end? The United States and Germany would probably find no difficulty in agreeing that Lufthansa, although state-owned, is a commercial activity. But business operations of great national importance to a particular country, such as oil production in the Persian Gulf states, may be considered commercial activities by Washington, and therefore subject to antitrust law, while the same is considered a political activity by the foreign government.

Aggravating tensions with other governments is often a concern in foreign antitrust situations. And these difficulties are sure to continue. In 1961, Britain, France, and other European countries passed laws allowing their governments to bar removal of certain shipping documents from their territories. These laws were later used to stymie grand jury investigations of ocean shipping rates. Australia passed a law to block the release of information that the uranium grand jury wanted. Canada also was upset because of prosecution of potash producers in which Freeport Minerals, International Minerals & Chemical, AMAX, and three other U.S. companies were accused of assuring the Saskatchewan government that if it ordered cutbacks in potash production there, they would not compensatorily increase U.S. production of the fertilizer.[12]

Foreign Corrupt Practices Act (FCPA)

The Foreign Corrupt Practices Act, passed by Congress in 1977, makes stringent antibribery provisions prohibiting all U.S. companies on file with the Securities and Exchange Commission from making any unauthorized payments. These payments include those made to foreign officials, political parties, and/or candidates. The law prescribes a one million dollar penalty to a corporation for violation of the law. Corporate officers connected with illegal payments may be fined $10,000 or be subjected to a five-year imprisonment, or both.

How FCPA may create hindrances is illustrated with reference to the Coca-Cola Company's deal with the former Soviet Union. In 1986, Coca-Cola signed a $30 million, six-year agreement to expand its business in the U.S.S.R. Until then, Coke was sold only in Moscow shops for tourists, and the company's Fanta orange soda was available in a few other cities. Published reports indicated that the Coca-Cola Company paid bribes to people in the Soviet Union to crack the Soviet market. Subsequently, a federal grand jury initiated an investigation to determine if the allegations of wrongdoing were correct. Although the company was finally proven innocent, it had to endure subpoenas of its documents and other inconveniences to prove its innocence[13] (see International Marketing Highlight 9.3).

International Marketing Highlight 9.3

Making Payments to Seek Business

In October 1989, a federal grand jury indicted Young & Rubicam on charges it paid kickbacks to Jamaican businessman Arnold Foote, Jr., to help the agency win the tourist account in 1981. According to the indictment, Mr. Foote in turn bribed Eric Anthony Abrahams, at the time Jamaica's minister of tourism, to award the account to Y&R. The agency subsequently created the award-winning "Come Back to Jamaica" campaign for the tourist board.

As part of the settlement, the Justice Department agreed to drop charges that Y&R violated federal racketeering prohibitions. But the ad agency pleaded guilty to conspiring to violate the Foreign Corrupt Practices Act, and to making $132,000 in payments.

In making the plea, Young & Rubicam acknowledged that it had "reason to know" that when it paid Mr. Foote, he would in turn make payments to the tourism minister, Mr. Abrahams. The ad agency paid a $500,000 fine to end the case.

Source: The Wall Street Journal, February 12, 1990, p. B4.

In part, the FCPA is an effort to extend American moral standards to other countries. The act also seeks to enlist U.S. MNCs as instruments of United States foreign policy. The FCPA, therefore, marks a major attempt by the U.S. government to enforce a series of noneconomic foreign policy objectives through private enterprise, whose principal purpose and rationale has traditionally been considered to be economic. The act places American corporations doing business abroad in an awkward position. On the one hand, they must comply with U.S. law, and on the other, they have to compete with other foreign countries whose governments do not prohibit such payments. In some nations where American business is conducted, bribery is commonplace; the FCPA could weaken the competitive position of U.S. corporations in such countries.[14] It has been remarked that:

> In France, the export-conscious defense ministry is nicknamed "Ministry of Bribes." Over the years, allegations of payoffs by Dassault, the French aircraft maker, have been aired in the Dutch Parliament, a Swiss military tribunal, and the British press.
>
> In [the former] West Germany, Bonn's tax collectors permit resident corporations to deduct foreign bribes, known as "sonderspesen" or "special expenses"; interviews of German executives by Business International Corporation turned

up a finding that "companies dislike the practice, disapprove of it, but adjust to local requirements."

In Britain, corrupt payments even to British Government officials qualify for tax deduction.[15]

Although macroeconomic research on the subject shows that the FCPA did not adversely affect U.S. trade,[16] the United States cannot force its moral principles and concepts of right and wrong on the whole world. Questionable payments will continue whether U.S. corporations participate or not. International bribery might be controlled through an international agreement effected through GATT or the IMF.

The Omnibus Trade and Competitiveness Act of 1988 amended the FCPA in many respects to lessen concern among U.S. companies about the scope of the statute. The primary change concerns payments to third parties by a U.S. firm "knowing or having reason to know" that the third party would use the payment for prohibited purposes. Under the new law, the U.S. firm must have actual knowledge of or willful blindness to the prohibited use of the payment. The act also clarifies the types of payments that are permissible and do not run afoul of the prohibition against bribery.[17] For example, under the FCPA as originally enacted, payments to low-level officials who exercise only "ministerial" or "clerical" functions were exempt. Unfortunately, this provision provided little guidance to companies in determining whether a given foreign official exercised discretionary authority: special problems arose in countries in the Middle East and Africa where foreign officials can be employed part-time. The trade act provides a U.S. business with better guidance by specifying the types of payments that are permissible rather than which individuals can receive them. The act specifies that a payment for a routine governmental action, such as processing papers, stamping visas, and scheduling inspections, may be made without subjecting the businessperson to the worry of whether this type of payment may lead to criminal liability. The changes in the law make it easier for U.S. exporters to do business in foreign countries by removing concerns about inadvertent violations.[18]

Antiboycott Laws

From time to time nations attempt to bring pressure on each other through programs of economic boycott. The early 1980s Arab boycott of companies doing business with Israel is an example of such a tactic. Most Arab states do not recognize Israel and hope that an economic boycott will contribute to Israel's collapse.

The oil fortunes of the Arab countries have given them significant economic clout to implement the boycott. The Arab boycott blacklists companies that deal with Israel with the intention of squeezing Israel from all directions and forcing the country into economic isolation.

The United States government has adopted various measures to prevent U.S. companies from complying with the Arab boycott. For example, the Tax Reform Act of 1976 included a measure that denied foreign income tax benefits to companies that subscribed to the boycott. The law preempts any state or local regulations dealing with boycotts fostered or imposed by foreign countries. The following are the major provisions of the antiboycott laws:

- To prohibit U.S. persons or firms and their foreign-controlled subsidiaries from refusing to do business with (1) firms blacklisted by a boycotting country and (2) boycotted friendly countries pursuant to foreign boycott demands
- To prohibit U.S. person or firms and their foreign-controlled subsidiaries from refusing (or requiring any other person to refuse) to employ, or otherwise discriminate against, any U.S. persons or firms on grounds of race, religion, sex, or national origin in order to comply with a foreign boycott
- To prohibit U.S. persons or firms and their foreign-controlled subsidiaries from furnishing information about another person's race, religion, sex, or national origin, where such information is sought for boycott-enforcement purposes
- To prohibit U.S. persons or firms and their foreign-controlled subsidiaries from furnishing information about past, present, or prospective relationships with boycotted countries or persons or firms blacklisted by a boycotting country
- To prohibit U.S. persons or firms and their foreign-controlled subsidiaries from furnishing information about whether any person is a member of, has made contributions to, or is otherwise associated with or involved in the activities of any charitable or fraternal organization that supports a boycotted country
- To prohibit U.S. banks from paying, honoring, confirming, or otherwise implementing letters of credit that contain an illegal boycott condition or requirement[19]

Laws to Protect Domestic Industry

The United States government has legislated many laws to protect domestic industry. From time to time, the government sets quotas on imports. For a number of years the sugar import quotas were set so as to preserve about half the market for U.S. producers. Often, quotas are split among several countries interested in exporting to the United States. Such allocation is partly influenced by political considerations. For example, a certain proportion of a quota may be assigned to a developing country even though its price is higher than that of other exporters. For a few years early in the 1980s, the U.S. government had imposed quotas on Japanese car imports. Recently, a debate has been going on in the federal government about limiting Japanese textile exports to the United States by establishing quotas for different categories of textiles.

Quotas, while providing relief to domestic industry, turn out to be only temporarily effective. In the long run, a domestic industry must stand on its own. If a domestic industry is inherently inefficient, quotas amount to a support of inefficiency, which is counterproductive. But if quotas are used to buy time so an infant industry can mature and compete effectively, that may be appropriate and productive. To illustrate the point, consider the arguments in favor of and against quotas on car imports.

For Import Auto Quota

- For each 100,000 units of auto production shifted from Japan to the United States, an additional 20,000 to 25,000 jobs would be restored to the automobile industry.
- Increased cash flow from added market share would provide capital for modernization and retooling.
- Import restraints would signal the financial community that government has a commitment to basic industry, making borrowing easier.
- Without restraints on imports, the competitive disadvantage of Detroit companies vis-à-vis the Japanese makers would permit the Japanese makers to increase their market share in the United States when the economic recovery got going.
- Import restrictions would be only slightly inflationary because with excess capacity, automakers would increase production rather than raise prices.

Against Import Auto Quota

- A quota would do little to help the industry itself, adding a maximum of 50,000 jobs and doing that only as long as a quota remained in force. The benefits would be minor compared with the benefits from prompt enactment of an economic recovery program.
- While a quota would add something to the industry's cash flow, more cash could be put in the hands of the companies if the United Auto Workers could be persuaded to forgo their cost-of-living wage increases for six months to a year.
- A quota would add to the price of automobiles, costing American consumers up to $3 billion each year and adding marginally to the rate of inflation.
- A quota on autos would set off demands by other industries for protection from foreign competition. At the same time it would reduce pressure on both labor and management for reform in the auto industry itself.[20]

After evaluating all the pros and cons for continuing quotas to restrict Japanese cars, they were abolished in 1985.

Another governmental way of supporting U.S. industry is to limit government purchases to domestic manufacturers. A number of state governments, for example, give preference to U.S.-made products. The United States government sometimes attaches conditions to foreign aid to developing countries, stipulating that the aid money must primarily be spent on goods manufactured by U.S. companies or their subsidiaries.

Laws to Eliminate Tax Loopholes

There are many federal laws meant to eliminate tax loopholes. A prominent example is legislation against tax havens. *Tax havens* are countries that provide out-of-the-ordinary privileges to multinationals in order to attract them to their lands. Tax havens make it more profitable for companies to locate there than in the United States. Doucet and Good categorize four types of tax havens:

1. Countries with no taxes at all, such as the Bahamas, Bermuda, and the Cayman Islands.
2. Countries with taxes at low rates, such as the British Virgin Islands.
3. Havens that tax income from domestic sources but exempt income from foreign sources, such as Hong Kong, Liberia, and Panama.
4. Countries that allow special privileges, which generally are suitable as tax havens only for limited purposes.[21]

Corporations find tax havens a legal way to save on taxes. Their response, however, to a country's offer is not motivated simply by tax benefits alone. Political stability in the country, availability of adequate means of communication and transportation, economic freedom for currency conversion, and availability of professional service serve as important criteria when a company locates itself in a tax haven. Before 1961, U.S. law permitted companies to establish foreign-based corporations in places where it was feasible to accumulate income earned abroad; U.S. taxes were not paid on this income until it was remitted to America. This essentially amounted to an arrangement whereby the United States government provided an interest-free loan to corporations. The Revenue Act of 1962 eliminated the deferral of taxes for companies set up strictly to save taxes. Since then, the tax havens have been faced with a steady barrage of anti-tax avoidance laws to reduce further the havens' attractions.[22]

Tax Treaties

Tax treaties are arrangements between nations that prevent corporate and individual income from being double-taxed. The United States has tax treaties with over thirty-five nations. Thus, foreigners who own securities in U.S. corporations and who are from countries with which there is a tax treaty pay a withholding tax of about 15 percent, while those from non-tax treaty countries pay a 30 percent tax.

The tax treaties are meant to provide a fair deal to individuals and corporations from friendly countries, which encourages mutual beneficial economic activity. Usually, under a tax treaty, the country where the primary business activity takes place is provided the right to be the principal receiver of tax revenue. A small proportion of the tax, however, may accrue to the other nation. Take, for example, the case of a Pakistani exporter with a business in the United States. Since there is a tax treaty between the United States and Pakistan, the income of the Pakistani businessman, as far as his U.S. operations are concerned, would be taxable under the U.S. Internal Revenue Service rules. But he would pay only a negligible tax in Pakistan.

Businesses, particularly the MNCs, use tax treaties in various ways to seek maximum benefits. Consider the following situations:[23]

- A tax treaty between the United States and England requires a 15 percent withholding tax on dividends.

- A tax treaty between the United States and the Netherlands specifies a 5 percent withholding tax.
- A tax treaty between the Netherlands and Great Britain calls for a 5 percent withholding tax. Additionally, dividends from foreign sources are not taxed in the Netherlands.

According to these arrangements, a U.S. company may establish a holding company in the Netherlands, which might receive dividend income from a British subsidiary. Finally, the dividends may be remitted to the parent company in the United States. The combined tax in the whole process will amount to 10 percent rather than 15 percent.

Tax treaties between the United States and different countries are reviewed from time to time. This permits periodic changes in treaty agreements to accommodate changes in the country's domestic monetary and fiscal policies. Usually, a treaty spells out the procedure for consultation and negotiation between officials of the two countries, should disagreements occur.

U.S. Government Support

Nations provide many kinds of support to their companies to enable them to compete successfully for foreign business. For example, companies belonging to OECD countries are often eligible for such government support as low-cost or no-cost bank guarantees, low-cost or no-cost working capital loans, and protection from price escalation. According to a U.S. Department of State report:

> The French government has provided partial compensation for inflationary cost rises incurred in export production since 1948. The Compagnie Française d'Assurance pour le Commerce Exterieur (COFACE) has administered the program since 1960. The insurance assists primarily export of capital goods and services clearly of French origin to non-European Community markets. For military equipment, it is available only for sales to developing countries. The minimum contract value is 2 million francs ($500,000) with a maximum contract period of one year. COFACE charges a premium of 1 percent on the value of the contract.
>
> Compensation is calculated by subtracting a deductible element for "normal international price increases" for the period of the contract from an index of cost increases (based on internal French price indices) and applying the resultant percentage to the initial contract value. The standard deductible is presently 6.5 percent per year and is based essentially on the estimated annual inflation rate of the French government for the next four years. For large contracts or those with long lead times compensation is computed on a case-by-case basis.[24]

Traditionally, this type of support has not been available from the U.S. government. In the fall of 1985, however, the U.S. government established a program of bank guarantees, similar to those of other OECD countries. Congress approved the creation of a "war chest" of $300 million to allow the Export-Import Bank (see Chapter 17) to match or beat competitors' subsidies for the benefit of U.S. exporters.[25] In 1992, under pressure from the United States during President Bush's trip to Japan, the Japanese automakers promised to increase their purchases of U.S. parts from $9 billion annually to $19 billion in four years and import an estimated 20,000 more U.S. cars a year.[26]

International Laws

A variety of international laws regulate business across national borders. International law is an area of study in and of itself. It would be impossible to discuss here, even perfunctorily, all the different types of international laws related to business. The General Agreement on Tariffs and Trade (GATT), the International Monetary Fund (IMF), and the World Bank were discussed in Chapter 3. Suffice it to say here that the agreements under these institutions compose international laws of sorts that influence business in different ways. The GATT regulations are particularly relevant for marketers since they deal with trade restrictions and barriers that affect market potential.

To give the reader an idea of other areas covered by international law and the agencies that administer these laws, a brief discussion of particular international laws follows.

Protection of Property

Property here refers to patents, trademarks, and the like. In the United States, businesses seek protection of their property under the U.S. laws. For example, a trademark can be registered. In an overseas situation, a multinational enterprise runs the risk of piracy. Stories are told that jeans manufactured in Hong Kong are given the Calvin Klein brand name and sold in Europe at half the usual price. Computer pirates in Taiwan incur the wrath of International Business Machines Corporation. IBM-compatible computers are sold widely in Taiwan by scores of small companies, who manufacture counterfeit machines in violation of IBM's copyrights.[27] The U.S. Patent Trademark Office estimates that intellectual property losses for U.S. industry, measured in terms of lost licensing opportunities and cost of enforcement, totalled at least $30 billion in 1988 alone[28] (see International Marketing Highlight 9.4).

Companies spend millions of dollars to build up and establish trademarks and brand names. Consider, for example, Coca-Cola, Tide, and Corningware's cornflower pattern. If a foreign firm steals a company's established brand name and uses it on a locally conceived and manufactured product, the interests of the established company could be hurt. It would mean not only losing potential markets, but also perhaps gaining a bad name for poor performance if a disappointed customer did not know that a product was an imitation.

The intellectual property protection problem is not limited to U.S. companies. Multinationals from other parts of the world face similar problems. For example, Hitachi Ltd. has accused Korea's Samsung Electronics Co. of using its technology to make dynamic random access memory chips. Hitachi also has a problem with the U.S.'s Motorola, Inc. It has sued the latter, charging that its MC88200 chip infringes on a Hitachi patent.[29]

The traditional way of protecting property outside the home country is by obtaining parallel protection in each host country. This process, however, is cumbersome and expensive. For example, it costs one large company almost $2 million to obtain foreign patents. This process is diverse, expensive, and is replete with risks that the patent will not be granted because the standards for patentabil-

International Marketing Highlight 9.4

Rounding Up Counterfeiters

Levi Strauss & Co. touts its trousers as "America's original jeans." But these days, so do a lot of others. The famous apparel maker is fighting an unprecedented explosion of counterfeit pants. In 1991, Levi seized 1.3 million pairs of knockoffs, more than five times as many as it usually confiscates in a year. But the new knockoffs, most of which are made in China, differ from the crude copies the company has seen in the past.

Counterfeiters have crossed the threshold. The typical consumer would not be able to detect that they are buying counterfeits. The fakes bear labels saying that they're made in the U.S. and proclaiming that their colored tab and stitched pocket design are registered trademarks to help you identify garments made only by Levi Strauss & Co.

Only someone well-versed in the "construction and engineering" of Levis could tell the difference. There are a few identifying marks on the real McCoys, but Levi doesn't want to tell consumers what they are for fear of tipping its hand to counterfeiters. (One difference is that real Levi labels note that they are "made from recycled paper.")

Though the fake Levis look nearly identical, the company contends they may fall apart at the seams. After a few washes, belt loops fall off, rivets rust, and shrinkage control is not what it should be. Levi contends that poor-quality jeans will hurt its reputation.

Counterfeiters are trying to cash in on the huge demand for Levi jeans overseas. Though fakes have been seized in thirty-one countries, most are destined for the booming European market, where Levis are a status symbol, commanding up to $100 a pair. In 1990 alone, the company's sales in Europe, where Levi sells mostly jeans, rose 55 percent. But Levi can't meet worldwide demand for its best-selling button-fly "501" jeans, most of which are manufactured in the United States.

Counterfeiters are eager to take up the slack. To combat them, Levi has spent about $2 million on more than 600 investigations, relying on a network of informants in Asia and Europe and trying to build paper trails on the middlemen who drive the market.

Source: The Wall Street Journal, February 19, 1992, p. B1.

ity in some countries are not compatible with accepted practices in other countries. Fortunately, there are international conventions and agreements that can make it easier to secure property rights. (Before describing these conventions, however, it should be noted that overall international arrangements for property protection are insufficient and inadequate, and brand name/trademark piracy is not actually alleviated.)

The real problem arises when the question of copyright infringement is not clear cut. Consider the fight between Lego System (a Danish company), the world's leading maker of children's building blocks, and a U.S. company, Tyco, popularly know for its model trains. Tyco spotted Lego's lack of competition and launched its own high-quality Lego copies called Super Blocks at retail prices 25 percent below Lego's. Thanks in part to its hard-hitting advertising campaign ("If you can't tell the difference, why pay the difference?"), in 1986 Tyco captured more than one-fifth of the $100 million U.S. market for blocks. Lego sued Tyco for copyright infringement in Hong Kong, where Tyco's blocks were made before production was shifted to Taiwan. Following a trial in 1986 that cost each company $2 million, the Hong Kong lower court decided in favor of Lego. But the appeals court reversed parts of the decision, and both toy makers have appealed to the London Court of Arbitration. In early 1987, the London court upheld the decision of the appeals court.[30]

Interestingly, owing to philosophical differences between code and common law, sometimes injured parties lose in legal dispute. For example, under common law, the right to property is established by actual use, while under code law the right emerges from legal registration. Thus, if a pirate registered a well-known brand (say, Colgate) in a code law country (say, Italy), in a legal dispute the actual owner (the Colgate Palmolive Company) may lose to the pirate, at least in Italy. Of course, if the country in question happens to be a friendly country, the United States government may be willing to help.

There are several important international conventions for property protection:

International Bureau for the Protection of Industrial Property. This bureau was established by the Paris Convention, to which over fifty nations including the United States subscribed. Currently the membership includes some ninety-four countries. Under this convention, once a company has filed for a patent in one country, it has priority for twelve months in seeking the patent in all other member countries. Further, the convention requires each member country to extend to the nationals of other member countries the same rights it provides to its own nationals.

The Inter-American Convention. Most Latin American countries and the United States are parties to this convention. This convention provides its members protection similar to that of the Paris Convention for inventions, patents, designs, and models.

Madrid Arrangement for International Registration of Trademarks. This forum has twenty-six members in Europe. The United States is not a member of the Madrid Convention. Under the Madrid arrangement, the member countries grant automatic registration in all countries through registration in one of the countries upon payment of the required fee. For example, if a company registers a trademark in Spain, a member country, registration is simultaneously ensured in the other twenty-five member countries after the appropriate payments are made.

The Trademark Registration Treaty. In the early 1970s sixteen European nations signed a convention to establish a European patent office. Under this convention, the patent office makes one grant for all the member countries under a single European patent law. The European patent office became operational in 1978 in Munich, Germany.

Intellectual property protection has improved in several problem countries in recent years (particularly Taiwan, Indonesia, and China). This has largely been the result of political pressure from the United States (see International Marketing Highlight 9.5). The following is a checklist for guarding intellectual property protection:

International Marketing Highlight 9.5

Saudi Copyright Law

Saudi Arabia passed a copyright law to curb widespread piracy of such material a videotapes and computer software. The law, approved by King Fahd in December 1989, was in response to pressure from the United States, where the Motion Picture Association of America has claimed industry losses of about $200 million a year due to piracy of videotapes in Saudi Arabia alone. The new law strictly forbids piracy, but diplomatic sources said much will depend on how the Saudis enforce the law.

Source: The Wall Street Journal, January 17, 1990, p. A16.

- Find out how the country protects intellectual property, if at all. The key is how intellectual property laws are enforced; many countries have tough laws, but their enforcement of these laws is often lax or inconsistent (e.g., South Korea).
- Register your copyrights and trademarks in countries in which you do business. This affords better protection by giving you access to the country's legal system (and usually to police and customs officials as well). Foreign courts seem to accept the concept of trademark more readily than the concept of copyright; hence, trademarks are generally easier to enforce abroad than copyrights.
- Clearly spell out dispute resolution procedures in contracts. Arbitration often avoids time-consuming foreign court procedures. In contrast to many legal systems, U.S. court procedures appear lightning-fast and simple. For example, a U.S. corporation has an intellectual property dispute with a distributor/licensee in Portugal. Because arbitration was not specified in the contract, the case must go to court in Portugal. It will take approximately two years before the case is even heard, much less resolved. However, companies should be aware that, although arbitration is usually quicker than litigation, it is not necessarily less expensive than going through the courts. The primary advantage of arbitration, of course, is the potential savings in time.

- Explore entering into licensing contracts with likely problem competitors, especially in countries without strong intellectual property laws. This is a preemptive strategy based on the premise "if you can't beat 'em, join 'em." Such a strategy at least ensures some financial returns in a high-risk environment.
- Consider distributing only older material overseas, especially in countries where the state of technology is somewhat less advanced (e.g., two- or three-year-old software). This will not only provide a market for older products, but better cushion the bottom line against piracy.
- Establish relations and cooperate with local customs officials and police. In Japan, Singapore, and Hong Kong, tough police actions are possible against pirates. Provided they are given reasonable evidence of piracy, officials will conduct raids on the pirates and destroy the infringing merchandise.
- Hiring a private investigator to gather evidence of piracy and work with local officials can also be beneficial. This proved successful for a prominent U.S. computer manufacturer in Taiwan. When conducting such a proactive intellectual property protection policy, companies may also wish to hire local lawyers familiar with the intellectual property laws and their enforcement.[31]

UN Treaties and Conventions

The United Nations has established a number of autonomous bodies and agencies to encourage worldwide economic cooperation and prosperity.

World Health Organization. WHO's work concerns the improvement of health conditions. It deals with such matters as drug standardization, epidemic control, health delivery systems, and related programs.

International Civil Aviation Organization. (ICAO promotes safe and efficient air travel through regulating flow of air traffic, air-worthiness standards, airport operations, and related communications (see International Marketing Highlight 9.6).

International Telecommunications Union. ITU regulates international communications via radio, telephone, and telegraph. For example, ITU controls and allocates radio frequencies and facilitates intercountry telegraph and telephone communications.

Universal Postal Union. UPU facilitates postal communication. For example, it conducts settlements among nations related to revenue sharing.

International Labor Organizations. ILO protects workers' rights, promotes worker welfare, and enhances the effectiveness of their organizations.

International Telecommunications Satellite Consortium. INTELSAT is another organization that deals with matters of telecommunications. Its work mainly concerns new satellite communications technology.

International Standards Organization. ISO is another specialized UN agency. It is particularly important because its administration bears directly on marketing. ISO promotes standardization of different products and pro-

International Marketing Highlight 9.6

Multinational Airlines

No American company owns a British airline, no French company a German one, no Japanese an American airline. Why, in this multinational age? The short answer is that commercial flight is governed by the Chicago Convention, an international treaty that has made the foreign ownership of airlines a game not worth playing. That convention forced postwar international airlines into cartelized business systems like the railways (which go under), instead of freer trading systems like road haulage (which prosper).

When the Chicago Convention was signed in 1944, other countries feared that the United States would dominate a free market in the airline business. This was a prospect they would not accept. Air transport embodied the newest technology of the time. National airlines carried national prestige. So a series of bilateral deals between countries carved up markets into protected pairs, blocking the emergence of multinational airlines.

There are signs that this system's days are numbered. British Airways (BA) has been privatized. The Dutch government now owns less than 40 percent of KLM. Governments from Turkey to New Zealand plan to sell all or part of their flag carriers. America has deregulated its domestic market, and wants more liberal international regime.

Other changes are on the way. Though foreign airlines still cannot pick up a passenger from, say, Pittsburgh and drop him in Washington, D.C. (a route BA flies every day), some American airlines believe that foreigners will eventually be allowed to compete in the American domestic market. The European Community is committed to liberalize air services within its jurisdiction.

Several airlines have already started to think globally. Ansett, an Australian airline, went into a joint venture to operate scheduled services in New Zealand last year. In August, Ansett bought 20 percent of America West airlines, a regional carrier based in Arizona (American law limits foreign ownership to 25 percent of an American carrier).

SAS, which is half-owned by three Scandinavian governments (Norway, Sweden, and Denmark) and half-owned by private investors, has long thought globally. Its chief executive, Mr. Jan Carlzon, tried to merge SAS with Sabena and then, when the Belgian carrier rejected him, with British Caledonian, where he was defeated by BA and British jingoism. Mr. Carlzon is now considering linking with Aerolineas Argentinas.

Source: The Economist, April 23, 1988, p. 71.

cesses. The ultimate purpose is to encourage world trade and business without hindrance from design/style/feature variations among nations. As an example, the ISO has over one hundred committees that are actively engaged in developing uniform international standards in various fields.

The impact of these agencies on international business varies. (For example, an airframe industry is affected by the ICAO regulations; a WHO agreement might apply to a pharmaceutical company.) But the importance of the need for standardization does not vary. For example, a grinding machine still usable in the United States would be unsuitable in England for such reasons as differences in electric current and weight measures (in England, current is 220 and the metric system has always been used). Thus, in order to sell a U.S.-made grinding machine the tolerance measurement would have to be varied to conform to measurements commonly used in Great Britain. Similarly, the electrical wiring would require change for the machine to operate on the higher voltage.

Consider the European telecommunications industry:

> In Spain, the busy signal is three pips a second; in Denmark it's two. Telephone numbers within French cities are seven digits long; in Italy they're almost any length. German phones run on 60 volts of electricity; elsewhere, it's 48. Only about 30 percent of the technical specifications involved in phone systems are common from one country to the next.[32]

Metric Transition

The differences in standards are among the major hindrances to world trade and business development. These differences have led to market opportunity losses for U.S. companies in many nations. This is one area where international cooperation is overdue.[33] Traditionally, U.S. industry and government have played almost no role in seeking common standards worldwide. This may be attributed to the fact that the overseas business of U.S. firms is proportionately small. In the future, however, U.S. businesses are more likely to participate actively in the standardization effort. The U.S. Department of Commerce's National Institute of Standards and Technology (NIST), which previously was known as the National Bureau of Standards (NBS), has been given several new assignments to boost U.S. industry in the world marketplace by seeking standardization. The assignments result from the 1988 Omnibus Trade and Competitiveness Act, which addresses the problem by moving the United States closer to the metric system, now used by most of the world's population. The "inch-pound" system of measurement used in the United States, known as the Customary or "English" system, was abandoned even by the English when the United Kingdom switched to the metric system in the early 1970s.

The 1988 act states that the metric system is "the preferred system of weights and measures for United States trade and commerce." It directs the federal government to provide leadership in metric conversion and calls for a preference in government purchasing for metric products. The act requires federal agencies to use the metric system wherever it is practical to do so in procurements, grants, and other business-related activities, by October 1, 1992. The agencies have notified grantees, contractors, and suppliers of the new requirements and of time schedules for meeting the government's deadline.

The act specifies that the federal government has a responsibility to develop procedures and techniques to assist industry, especially small business, as it voluntarily converts to the metric system. Individual groups and industries are still free to decide whether to convert and to determine conversion timetables according to their own needs.

The trade act requires government and industry to use metric units in documentation of exports and imports as prescribed by the International Convention on the Harmonized Commodity Description and Coding System. The Harmonized System is an international goods classification system designed to standardize commodity classification for all major trading nations. The international metric system (SI) is the official measurement system of the Harmonized System.

Congress spelled out in the act the reasons it believes the United States would benefit from converting to the metric system:

> World trade is increasingly geared towards the metric system of measurement.
>
> Industry in the United States is often at a competitive disadvantage when dealing in international markets because of its nonstandard measurement system, and is sometimes excluded when it is unable to deliver goods which are measured in metric terms.
>
> The inherent simplicity of the metric system of measurement and standardization of weights and measures has led to major cost savings in certain industries which have converted to that system.
>
> The metric system of measurement can provide substantial advantages to the Federal Government in its own operations.

The European Community is proceeding aggressively with plans to standardize differing national specifications and testing and certification procedures into a single EC-wide body of uniform standards and regulations. This can offer real advantages to U.S. businesspeople interested in a large market for their goods. A U.S. product that meets the EC requirements in one member state can then be freely marketed throughout the European Community.[34]

UN Guidelines on Consumer Protection

After more than six years of work, in April 1985 the United Nations General Assembly adopted by consensus a set of guidelines on consumer protection. The guidelines cover the following basic consumer principles:[35]

- Insurance of the physical safety of consumers and their protection from potential dangers caused by consumer products
- Protection of consumers' economic interests
- Consumers' access to the necessary information to make informed choices according to their individual wishes and needs
- Availability of effective consumer redress
- Freedom to form consumer groups or organizations and the opportunity of such organizations to be consulted and to have their views represented

These guidelines are important because without acceptance of such principles and strong information links on products that have been banned or severely restricted in various countries, sales could continue unabated. In other words, profit motive may override consideration for the harm many products may induce.

Implementation of these guidelines by countries currently lacking adequate consumer protection will enable them to cope with these and similar consumer problems.

Regional Laws

Regional laws pertain to specific areas involving a group of countries tied together through some kind of regional economic cooperation. (Chapter 5 examined different forms of regional groupings.)

Market groups may legislate laws applicable to multinational companies conducting business within the member countries. The most progressive market agreement is represented by the European Community, or Common Market. The EC has debated a variety of legislative measures that would deeply affect multinational enterprises. For example, there was consideration of a proposal that would not only force the head offices of MNCs with European-based subsidiaries to make disclosures of their global operations to local labor unions twice a year, but also would oblige them to inform and consult with the labor unions on any major decision affecting workers. Another proposal would require MNCs to consolidate the accounts of European subsidiaries. A third proposal, related to product-liability standards, would effectively eliminate the need for plaintiffs to show negligence to justify injury claims. Under a fourth proposal, workers would sit on the boards of all public companies. The most radical of all is a proposal to make corporate directors *personally* liable for damages should minority stockholders or creditors or even employees of a subsidiary suffer as a result of a corporate headquarters' decision favoring the interests of the parent company and its stockholders.[36]

These kinds of proposals are not accepted quickly; the EC lawmaking process is unparalleled for ponderousness. Proposals to harmonize the national laws of the twelve members of the EC must first be endorsed by a majority of the sixteen European commissioners (two each from Britain, France, Germany, and Italy, one each from the rest, and all appointed for four-year terms by their governments). Draft-stage directives then go to the 460-member European Parliament in Strasbourg, whose main role is to propose amendments for the commissioners' consideration. After receiving the parliament's views, the commission prepares a final draft of the directive and submits it to the Council of Ministers, composed of the appropriate cabinet-level officers from each national government. With the council's consent, a proposal becomes a legally binding EC directive, but even then it does not become law automatically. Enacting legislation to fulfill the intent of EC directives remains a prerogative of national parliaments. For example, in 1985 a European Community product liability directive was adopted by the Council of Ministers after more than eight years of talks. The directive allows consumers to collect damages for injuries from defective products without showing that the manufacturer was at fault. Member nations should pass laws that comply with the directive within three years.

Arbitration

Despite their best efforts, U.S. businesspeople working at the international level may run into difficulties from time to time with people, companies, and/or organizations in foreign countries. The conflict may be with the host country government; a native firm, either in the public or private sector; or an international firm belonging to a third country. The difficulty may arise because of differing interpretations of the contractual terms or because of opposing positions on an ad hoc issue that was not anticipated at the time the contract was made. There are three ways for an international firm to resolve conflicts. First, the two parties mutually agree to settle the differences. Second, the firm decides to sue the other party. Third, the conflicting parties agree to arbitration. Of the three alternatives, the first one is the best, if at all possible. Usually, however, the conflicting parties cannot realistically be expected to resolve their differences between themselves. As far as legal action is concerned, for a variety of reasons, it may not be in the best long-term interest of the international marketer. Legal action against a native firm would surely affect the reputation of the foreign enterprise, no matter how strong the case of the latter might be. Further, there is no guarantee that the court would make a fair, unbiased decision on behalf of the domestic party. Finally, the legal route can be messy, time consuming, and expensive.

For example, taking legal action in a trade case can range from an average $54,700 for a Section 301 violation (an unfair foreign trade practice) to $715,000 or more for a Section 337 case (an infringement or theft of intellectual property rights, such as patents, trademarks, and copyrights.) Similarly, legal costs in a dumping case may range from $151,000 to $553,300, while an import threat to national security may cost $181,300 to $537,500.[37]

Therefore, arbitration is usually the best recourse of a multinational firm to resolve conflict in a foreign environment. *Arbitration* can be defined as a process of settling disputes by referring the matter to a disinterested party for a review of the merits of the case and for a judgment, which may or may not be binding on the conflicting parties. Traditionally, the disputing parties resorted to ad hoc arrangements for arbitration because prior to 1966 there was no international authority to serve as arbitrator between an international marketer and a host country party. Currently, there are a number of arrangements available for arbitration.

1. *The International Center for Settlement of Investment Disputes (ICSID)* was established in 1966 by the World Bank convention to enable private investors to obtain redress against a foreign state for grievances arising out of an investment dispute. The convention established strict rules for arbitration that may explain in part why it is seldom used:

   > The Convention provides that, where both parties have consented to arbitration under the auspices of the Center, neither may withdraw its consent unilaterally; and should either party refuse to submit to the jurisdiction of the Center thereafter, an award can nevertheless be entered which will be final, binding, and enforceable without relitigation, in all nations that are members of the Convention. To facilitate the enforcement of awards, each member nation is obliged to designate a domestic court or other authority responsible for enforcement of awards made.[38]

   ICSID has not been able to play the role expected by the signatories who created the convention. The problem is that large developing countries, important prospects for direct foreign investment, are not ICSID members. Most of the Latin American countries are among the nonsignatories; they subscribe to the Calvo doctrine for representation of their position. *The Calvo doctrine,* named after an Argentine jurist, provides that a foreign investor by virtue of making an investment implicitly agrees to be treated by the host government as a national and gives up the right to involve any outside agency or home government in the resolution of a dispute.

In brief, ICSID has received lukewarm support from host countries as an arbitrator of disputes.

2. *The Inter-American Commercial Arbitration Commission* serves to arbitrate disputes between businesses of twenty-one Western hemisphere countries including the United States.
3. *The International Chamber of Commerce (ICC)* is an association of chambers of commerce worldwide. It has established a court of arbitration that has set rules used in conducting arbitration proceedings.

   Perhaps, of all the arrangements for arbitration, ICC is the most successful. Of two hundred decisions that the ICC Court of Arbitration made in recent years, only about twenty-two were questioned by the disputants. Of these twenty-two, twenty-one decisions were upheld in the courts when further legal action was pursued.

   The ICC arbitration procedure is rather simple. In the first instance, it tries to settle the dispute through mutual conciliation. If that fails, each party is allowed to choose one member of the Court of Arbitration from its current list of distinguished lawyers/jurists/judges. The third member is appointed by ICC. The Court of Arbitration schedules hearings and, after reviewing the facts presented by the plaintiff and the defendant, makes a decision.
4. *The American Arbitration Association (AAA)* is basically a U.S. tribunal originally established to conduct arbitration among businesses in the United States. More recently, the AAA extended the scope of its activities outside the U.S.
5. *The Canadian-American Commercial Arbitration Commission (CACAC)* serves as arbitrator between U.S. and Canadian businesses.
6. *The London Court of Arbitration* has jurisdiction that is restricted to cases that should legally be arbitrated in the United Kingdom. The decisions of this court are legally binding on the parties in dispute under English law.

A number of other agencies and organizations arbitrate in disputes about foreign direct investment. One of these is the *International Court of Justice (ICJ).* ICJ, also sometimes referred to as the World Court, is a special judicial UN agency. ICJ can be approached for the arbitration of disputes between sovereign nations. Thus, if the United States government decides to take up a matter on behalf of a U.S. company that is in a conflict with a government overseas, the dispute can be referred to ICJ for decision. Needless to say, the federal government would pursue the matter only if it involved a national issue. Since ICJ only deals with disputes between nations, and not those between individuals or their companies, and since the government would involve itself only if the matter is of national importance, ICJ has not been extensively used for the settlement of investment disputes.

Another agency is the *Permanent Court of Arbitration.* The PCA was established by the Hague Conventions of 1899 and 1907. It consists of a small bureau at the Hague and a panel of arbitrators, four from each member country. The arbitrators are chosen from the panel members whenever a case must be examined. PCA has played an insignificant role in connection with international investment disputes. Like the ICJ, use of PCA for arbitration in international investment disputes comes only through the U.S. federal government.

Finally, arbitration may also be conducted by the various *International Claims Commissions.* The ICC is an ad hoc arbitration arrangement. When a substantial number of claims between two countries accumulate, an ICC arbitration tribunal may be established by agreement between the interested nations. ICC's use requires that the United States government espouse and raise the MNC's claim against another nation. To invoke the jurisdiction of any of the last three bodies, the foreign nation in question must consent to arbitration.

Summary

A U.S. corporation involved in international marketing should comply not only with United States laws but also with host country laws. Worldwide, different countries follow different sets of laws. An international marketer should be particularly familiar with host country laws pertaining to competition, price setting, distribution arrangements, product liability, patents and trademarks, and advertising.

To fully grasp a country's laws, it is essential to understand the legal philosophy of the country. Countries may follow common law or code law. Common law is based on precedents and practices; England, for example, is a common law country. Code law is based on detailed rules; Mexico, for example, is a code law country. The legal basis of a country can affect marketing decisions in multifaceted ways.

Another important legal environment aspect is the jurisdiction of laws. The question of which laws will apply in which particular matters must be known. In some instances, those of the country where the agreement was made apply; in others, those of the country where the business was conducted apply. It is desirable to have a jurisdictional clause in agreements. If there is none, when a conflict of interest occurs, it may either be settled through litigation or be referred for arbitration.

In addition to heeding both United States law and host country laws, international marketers must be aware of treaties and international conventions. By and large, the relevant laws of the host country would be those concerning tariffs, dumping, export/import licensing, foreign investment, foreign investment incentives (provided by the government to attract foreign business), and restrictions on trading activities. The relevant U.S. laws would be laws affecting foreign trade, antitrust laws, antiboycott laws, laws to protect domestic industry, laws to prevent loopholes in the existing tax laws (tax haven laws), tax treaties, and laws that pertain to U.S. government support of U.S. business abroad.

Some international treaties and conventions are concerned with the protection of property, such as patents, trademarks, models, and the like, in foreign countries. Some international laws have provisions for the encouragement of both worldwide economic cooperation and prosperity and the realization of international products and processes standardization.

If a legal conflict occurs between parties from different countries, one way of resolving it is through arbitration. There are a number of organizations available for arbitration of disputes: the International Center for Settlement of Investment Disputes, the Inter-American Commercial Arbitration Commission, the International Chamber of Commerce, the American Arbitration Association, the Canadian-American Commercial Arbitration Commission, and the London Court of Arbitration.

Review Questions

1. Distinguish between code law and common law. Illustrate how the differences between the two may affect marketing decisions.
2. Explain how one might determine which country's laws would be applicable in the event of a dispute.
3. Define the term *dumping*. Why do countries pass antidumping laws?
4. Do U.S. antitrust laws apply to U.S. corporations in their international dealings? If so, how does this affect the competitive position of U.S. corporations?
5. What sort of support could the U.S. government provide to help U.S. corporations compete effectively against non-U.S. multinationals?
6. What is arbitration? Discuss the role of the International Chamber of Commerce as an arbitration agency.

Endnotes

1. *Advertising Age,* April 2, 1988, p. 34.
2. Ford S. Worthy, "Tightwad Taiwan Starts to Spend," *Fortune,* December 5, 1988, p. 177.
3. Warren J. Keegan, *Multinational Marketing Management,* 3rd ed. (Englewood Cliffs, NJ: Prentice-Hall, 1984), p. 346. *Also see* "Antidumping Levies Assessed on Imports from Three Nations," *The Wall Street Journal,* March 7, 1980, p. 14.
4. *National Legislation and Regulations Relating to Transnational Corporations* (New York: United Nations, 1978), p. 1.
5. Doron P. Levin and Thomas F. O'Boyle, "GM's Chairman Runs into Bizarre Problem Under German Law," *The Wall Street Journal,* June 10, 1987, p. 1.
6. Stephan H. Robock and Kenneth Simmonds, *International Business and Multinational Enterprises,* 3rd ed. (Homewood, IL: Richard Irwin, Inc., 1983), p. 139. *Also see* Urban C. Lehner, "U.S. Battle to Sell Baseball Bats in Japan Illustrates Difficulty of Cracking Market," *The Asian Wall Street Journal Weekly,* January 24, 1983, p. 4.
7. A. O. Cao, "Nontariff Barriers to U.S. Manufactured Exports," *Columbia Journal of World Business,* Summer 1980, p. 95.
8. Raymond Vernon, "Antitrust and International Business," *Harvard Business Review,*

September–October 1968, p. 86. *Also see* Robert H. Brumley, "How Antitrust Law Affects International Joint Ventures," *Business America,* November 21, 1988, pp. 2–4.

9. John Jelacic, "The U.S. Trade Outlook in 1991," *Business America,* April 22, 1991, pp. 2–7.
10. James Bednar, "Trade Adjustment: Aid to U.S. Workers," *Agenda,* September 1980, p. 21.
11. Vern Terpstra, *International Market* (Hinsdale, IL: Dryden Press, 1983). *Also see* "Antitrust Guide in International Operations," United States Department of Justice, Antitrust Division, January 26, 1977, p. 63.
12. "Antitrust Grows Unpopular," *Business Week,* January 12, 1981, p. 90.
13. "Coke Said to Face Inquiry Over Sales in Soviet Union," *The Wall Street Journal,* June 13, 1988, p. 22.
14. Jack G. Kaikati and Wayne A. Label, "American Bribery Legislation: An Obstacle to International Marketing," *Journal of Marketing,* Fall 1980, pp. 38–43. *Also see* Brooks Jackson, "Overseas Bribery Gets a Lot Less Attention After Cutbacks by the Justice Department," *The Wall Street Journal,* February 22, 1983, p. 33.
15. Jerry Landauer, "Proposed Treaty Against Business Bribes Gets Poor Reception Overseas, U.S. Finds," *The Wall Street Journal,* February 28, 1977, p. 28.
16. *See* John L. Graham, "Foreign Corrupt Practices: A Manager's Guide" *Columbia Journal of World Business,* Fall 1983, pp. 89–94. *Also see* John L. Graham, "The Foreign Corrupt Practices Act: A New Perspective," *Journal of International Business Studies,* Winter 1984, pp. 107–122.
17. "Doing Business Abroad with Fewer Restraints," *The Wall Street Journal,* June 5, 1990, p. B1.
18. *Business America,* October 24, 1988, p. 3.
19. Sandra MacRae Huszagh, "Exporter Perceptions of the U.S. Regulatory Environment," *Columbia Journal of World Business,* Fall 1981, pp. 22–31; Samuel Rabino, "An Examination of Barriers to Exporting Encountered by Small Manufacturing Companies," *Management International Review,* no. 1 (1980), pp. 67–74.
20. John F. Stacks, "The Administration's Split on Auto Imports," *Fortune,* May 4, 1981, p. 158.
21. Jean Doucet and Kenneth J. Good, "What Makes a Good Tax Haven?" *Banker,* May 1973, p. 493. *Also see* "The U.S. Targets a Tax Haven," *Business Week,* April 19, 1982, p. 106.
22. Caroline Doggart, *Tax Havens and Their Uses 1987* (London: Economist Intelligence Unit, 1987).
23. John D. Daniels, Ernest W. Ogram, Jr., and Lee H. Radebaugh, *International Business: Environments and Operations,* 2nd ed. (Reading, MA: Addison-Wesley, 1979), p. 480. *Also see* George C. Walt, Richard M. Hammer, and Marianne Burge, *Accounting for the Multinational Corporation* (New York: Financial Executives Research Foundation, 1977), p. 610.
24. Daniel M. Searby, "Doing Business in the Mideast: The Game Is Rigged," *Harvard Business Review,* January–February 1976, pp. 56–64. For further discussion on Eximbank and OPEC, see Chapter 17.
25. "The New Trade Strategy," *Business Week,* October 7, 1985, p. 90.
26. Allan T. Demaree, "What Now for the U.S. and Japan," *Fortune,* February 10, 1992, p. 80.
27. "IBM Hints for Taiwanese Pirates," *The Wall Street Journal,* October 16, 1984, p. 32. *Also see* Günter Hauptman, "Intellectual Property Rights," *International Marketing Review,* Spring 1987, pp. 61–64.
28. *Business International,* May 29, 1989, p. 166.
29. "Japanese Reverse Tack on Patent Protection," *The Wall Street Journal,* October 24, 1989, p. B1. *Also see* Thomas J. Maronick, "European Patent Laws and Decisions: Implications for Multinational Marketing Strategy," *International Marketing Review,* Summer 1988, pp. 31–40.
30. Erik Bjerager, "Denmark's Lego Challenges Imitators of its Famous Toy Blocks Across Globe," *The Wall Street Journal,* August 5, 1987, p. 18.
31. *Business International,* May 29, 1989, p. 166.
32. Richard L. Hudson, "European Officials Push Idea of Standardizing Telecommunications—But Some Makers Resist," *The Wall Street Journal,* April 10, 1985, p. 32.
33. *See* "Memo to U.S. Computer Makers: Standardize or Else," *Business Week,* October 3, 1988, p. 34.
34. *Business America,* August 1, 1988, p. 9.

35. "U.N. Rallies to Consumers," *Development Forum,* July–August 1985, p. 14.
36. *See Opening Up the Internal Market* (Brussels: EC, 1991).
37. Virginia M. Citrano, "So, Sue Me," *Northeast International Business,* May 1989, p. 38.
38. William R. Hopkins, "How to Counter Expropriation," *Harvard Business Review,* September–October 1970, p. 109.

PART • 3

Cases

Case 8: The Clondike Works

In March 1989, Robert Lenore, an executive in the International Division of the Clondike Works, was faced with deciding what tactics the company could employ against a Taiwanese manufacturing company that was exporting counterfeit products labeled with the "Clondike" name. Among many products, the company was most concerned about power-lock tape rules, of which it had lost 50 percent of its sales to the Taiwanese competitor.

The Taiwanese firm had duplicated the tape lock and sold it with either the "Clondike" name or a close fascimile for $2.00 to $2.50 below the Clondike price. Clondike's biggest customers for the power tape lock were in the Middle East, and during the previous two years the sales there had dropped over 50 percent. Mr. Lenore expressed deep concern over what could be done to rectify this situation.

The Clondike Works

In 1840, James and Patrick Clondike earned a reputation for manufacturing quality hardware products with Yankee craftsmanship. This reputation for quality continued to grow over the years, and Clondike always stood behind the quality of its work. For example, Clondike "Life Span" hinges were guaranteed for the life of the building in which they were installed. Over 10,000 of these hinges were used in the twin towers of the World Trade Center in New York City.

As the company's product lines grew, so did its quality control capability. New techniques and procedures, and new instruments and controls had been added to ensure that Clondike's reputation for quality could keep pace with the nation's growing technological sophistication. Because of its high standards, "Clondike" was the preferred name in tools, as well as builder's hardware. During the 1970s, the company registered tremendous growth. Its sales increased from $1 billion in 1981 to $1.8 billion in 1988. Earnings in 1988 amounted to about 6 percent of sales. The company was headquartered in Newton, Massachusetts.

Product Lines

Clondike manufactured and sold over 20,000 products. These products were divided into three product lines: consumer products ("do-it-yourselfers"), industrial products, and construction and maintenance products. The "do-it-yourselfer" (DIY) industry was seen as a major strategic thrust for Clondike works. Products in this category were introduced to enable the consumers to do everyday repair work, simple construction, and other types of improvements. The products in the DIY line were grouped into five categories: hand tools, hardware, drapery hardware, garden tools, and automatic garage door openers. DIY products accounted for about 42 percent of Clondike's sales. Industrial products were categorized into five groups: air tools, electrical tools, hand tools, hydraulic tools, and systems. Clondike's industrial products, sold worldwide, contributed about 35 percent toward the company's sales. Construction and maintenance products were divided into five categories: hand tools, electrical tools, hardware, doors, and hydraulic tools, and provided 23 percent of Clondike's sales.

Clondike International

International sales accounted for more than 42 percent of Clondike's total business. Besides the United States, Clondike had manufacturing operations in nine countries—England, France, Germany, Italy, Australia, Colombia, Brazil, Guatemala, and Mexico. The company had sales offices in thirty-three countries around the globe. International sales of the company's products began through overseas representation fifty years ago. The steady sales growth of Clondike's products in overseas markets was based largely upon the customer's approval of Clondike quality.

Internationally, the company was extremely diversified, which added to its strengths and protected it against currency fluctuations. For example, during the 1970s when the U.S. dollar was very strong, U.S. products were more expensive compared with products of countries whose currencies were weak against the dollar. Thus, the distributors in Europe found it to their advantage to source out of England, France, or Germany. During the 1980s, the U.S. dollar was weak and U.S. products were in great demand on the export market because they were cheaper. Many Middle Eastern orders, which formerly had gone to England or Europe, began coming to the United States because of the difference in currency values, and Clondike was able to make the best of the situation.

Competition from Taiwan

Clondike's 3-meter, 1½-inch-wide 10-foot power lock was sold all over the world. "Power lock" is a Clondike trademark registered in the United States. Its reproduction and sale throughout the Middle East, Africa, and Asia by the Taiwanese manufacturers were illegal. Originally the quality of the Taiwanese product had been inferior to the Clondike product, but in recent years the reproduction had been improved to a level comparable to the Clondike product.

The Taiwanese manufacturers capitalized on Clondike packaging and its logo and name to sell their product by outright use of the word *Clondike* on a label and package that duplicated Clondike's. In some instances, the Clondike logo was utilized by simply rearranging the design, colors, and background. In other cases, the imitation product was stamped with a look-alike "Clondike" name—minus the "e." In most ways, it was difficult to distinguish between the reproduction and Clondike's product. The only discernible difference was the stamped USA logo on the original products. Most dealers overseas exhibited the forged product side-by-side with the original product, and customers could not distinguish between the two, except by the prices.

Customer Loyalty

Clondike experienced customer losses based solely on price criteria. Sales had dropped over 50 percent in the previous two years in the firm's primary market—the Middle East, Far East, and Nigeria. In addition, costly labor and high overhead costs placed constraints on Clondike's ability to compete with the Taiwanese producer. Clondike's experience was comparable to the U.S. automotive industry's competition from the Japanese, whose labor costs were $10 to $12 per hour compared with U.S. costs of $14 to $16 per hour. Because of a similar discrepancy, the Taiwanese were able to offer quality goods, manufactured with cheap labor at prices well below their U.S. competition.

In an effort to compete with the Taiwanese on a price basis, Clondike attempted to supply the Middle East with tape locks produced in England, France, and Mexico. However, customer loyalty to the U.S.-made product discouraged the purchase of products manufactured elsewhere. Foreign customers were intrigued with the prestige of buying a product manufactured in the United States. Clondike's attempt to sell a less-expensive product proved unsuccessful, and it returned to supplying foreign dealers from the United States.

The Effects of International Politics, Economics, and Legislation

In early 1988, Clondike tried to take legal action against the Taiwanese firm. It proved to be a difficult task. There are no international courts and no enforceable laws. Legal action, therefore, had to be pursued through either the U.S. or the Taiwanese courts. Of basic importance to international legal action are (1) the cooperation given by the foreign government and (2) the strength of the company's representation in the foreign country.

Cooperation from the Taiwanese government was negligible for economic reasons. At the time, Taiwan was experiencing a difficult period of economic growth and development. The increase in its exports had a positive influence on its balance of payments. Therefore, the manufacturing and exporting of Taiwanese tape locks were good for the economy, even if they were illegally manufactured. Also, export was the only market for counterfeit products since selling them within Taiwan would result in court action for patent infringement.

Politically, Taiwan and the United States were no longer staunch allies. The United States had withdrawn its ambassador to Taiwan, and the UN had expelled the Taiwanese representatives. Such political actions precluded any cooperation from the Taiwanese government. As Mr. Lenore pondered the facts, he realized a decision had to be made regarding what action Clondike would take against Taiwanese counterfeiting. Part of the answer, he realized, was to stay in the market rather than pull out altogether. Also, there was reassurance in the idea that 50 percent of something was better than 50 percent of nothing.

Case 9: All Shave in Saudi Arabia

On a hot summer day in 1990, Mike Lacey lay on his bed and watched as the fan went around. He felt whipped and didn't really know what to do next. All week he had been trying to influence Mustafa Almin, and he had had no more effect than the fan was having on the heat of Riyadh.

This case is printed here with the permission of the authors Ellen Cook, Philip Hunsaker, and Mohammed Ali Alireza of the University of San Diego.

Three years ago the All Shave Company, of which Mike was Middle Eastern manager, had been very successful exporting razors and blades to Saudi Arabia. Then, in the face of possible import restrictions, the company had turned over its business to a new company financed by the Almin family. The family members were leading Saudi industrialists who had built a fortune on the production of steel products, like picks and shovels, and were then interested in expanding to new fields. All Shave received a minority interest in the new business in return for its trade name and technical aid.

The contract with the Almin family had also specified that they would "actively promote All Shave products." Mike thought that it was clearly understood that this meant continuing the aggressive promotion that had been used in Saudi Arabia to build the company's sales in the 1970s from nothing to a high level. Under Almin management, however, All Shave sales had dropped steadily. It was soon evident that the Almins were not pushing sales, and in visits and correspondence, the company applied increasing pressure for more activity.

When nothing happened, Mike finally decided he would go to Saudi Arabia and stay until he could find a way to get the Almins moving. That was over six weeks ago. After spending the first month in the field, Mike had worked up a detailed program designed to reestablish All Shave's market position. He had found All Shave products were being sold from Almin warehouses with virtually no sales effort and that promotion was limited to a few newspaper advertisements and a scattering of posters distributed by the Almin family's industrial sales reps. No additional salespeople had been added for All Shave accounts. The selling activity fell far short of All Shave's former program and that of its leading competitor.

For the past week, Mike had been trying to convince Mustafa Almin, the sixty-year-old head of the family, to adopt a better program. But he had argued in vain. Mike had pointed to the low sales volume and to the Almins' limited program, which he pointed out did not meet their agreement. He had supported his proposals in the greatest detail, arguing particularly that All Shave's previous success and the present results achieved by their competition proved that strong promotion was worthwhile.

Mustafa Almin expressed appreciation for Mike's interest and efforts but had agreed to nothing. He explained that a sales drop was inevitable with the change to the Saudi manufacturer. Although sales were lower, the company was making a reasonable profit. He said that to fulfill the contract terms he had undertaken newspaper advertising even though he did not believe in it. He felt its blatant character reflected on the prestige of the Almin family name.

Mustafa Almin believed that a good product was its own best advertisement and on that basis the Almin family had built a great business. He also observed that the closest competitor sold a higher-quality blade than All Shave and it was quite probable that this, rather than promotion, accounted for their success. In any case, several British concerns in related fields did very little advertising, and since they had been in India for many years, Mr. Almin felt their approach to the market was probably sounder.

Mike found it hard to counter these arguments. He was sure he was right, and equally sure that Mr. Almin was a very competent businessman who should be able to see the logic of Mike's proposals. He had great respect and liking for Mr. Almin, and he believed that once Almin grasped the value of promotion, he would do great things for All Shave in Saudi Arabia.

But how could he convince him?

Mustafa Almin settled himself to relax before the evening meal and reflected for a moment on the events of the past week. He had spent a great deal of time with the boy from the United States. He was a good boy, full of energy and ideas. He wished he could do something to help him. He drove so hard, and for what? This whole arrangement with the All Shave Company had turned out rather differently from what the Almins had expected. The product was good, and left to themselves, his family could develop it into a good business, as they had with the rest of their operations.

But they were not left to themselves. Instead, there had been constant pushing and arguing. These people from the United States never seemed to be satisfied with anything. Now they sent this young man who scarcely knew Saudi Arabia to tell the Almins how to run their business. It was not pleasant at all. He hoped the young man would give up soon.

Case 10: Aries Helicopter

In November of 1985, William Lance, an executive in the international marketing department of Aries Helicopter, was trying to resolve a problem that had arisen with a licensing agreement between Aries Helicopter and Smythe Aircraft Ltd. of Great Britain. The British company was consistently competing with and winning contracts from Aries Helicopter for the AH-61, a rescue/utility helicopter used in many countries around the world. Aries Helicopter had licensed Smythe Aircraft Ltd. to build the AH-61 for exclusive selling rights in Great Britain and limited rights for other countries in Western Europe. As it turned out, the British-made AH-61 was almost identical to the American-made AH-61, except for price. Lance now wondered what to do; their company's licensee was now a formidable opponent that was consuming as much as 40 percent of Aires Helicopter's expected AH-61 sales in Western Europe.

Aries Helicopter

Aries Helicopter was a division of AllTech Industries. AllTech began in the early 1940s as the United Aerospace Corporation and originally consisted of three other companies besides Aries Helicopter. One company was a jet engine manufacturer, the other two were high-tech systems manufacturers for the aeronautical industry. In the early 1970s, United Aerospace Corp. diversified its interests by acquiring several firms, including an air conditioning manufacturer and an industrial/residential elevator firm. All these companies joined to form AllTech Industries.

Product Line

The Aries product line included medium- to heavy-duty helicopters for industrial/utility as well as military uses. The product line was constantly changing because of rapid expansion in helicopter technology and because of increased awareness of the capabilities of the helicopter in rescue, military, and industrial uses. Aries built a sleek executive helicopter, the AH-76, aimed at big business and offshore oil drilling markets. Another entry was the AH-53, which was a heavy-lift helicopter that could be adapted to many uses in all areas of the military. Another model, the AH-60, was a medium-weight, extremely versatile helicopter: it was an excellent weapons platform for the military and its excellent performance characteristics far exceeded those of other current utility helicopters. Then there was the AH-61. This helicopter was specially designed for rescue missions. The AH-61 could land on water and lift medium to heavy loads for quite a distance. The AH-61's superior rescue mission capabilities increased the worldwide demand for such a helicopter. No other company had yet built such a high-quality product with such high-tech instrumentation.

Realizing that a good profit could be made in the international market, Aries began investigating how to enter this market.

Competition

Aries Helicopter had several domestic competitors in the helicopter market, including Boeing Vertal, Hughes Helicopter, and their closest competitor, Bell Helicopter. Although the Aries helicopters clearly were more expensive than those of their competitors, Aries was still the market leader by a fairly comfortable margin. Most of the competitors' helicopters were light-duty, relatively cheaply built products that really couldn't compete with Aries' high-quality products. The competitors were doing well, however, because they had found their own market niches in light-duty helicopters.

Aries Helicopter also had several European competitors that would have to be dealt with if

Aries expected to have a profitable international business: Aerospatiale of France, MBB of Germany, Augusta of Italy, and Smythe Aircraft Ltd. of Great Britain. Aries had roughly a ten-year advantage in technology over all of these companies, which led the Aries executives to conclude that a profitable market probably existed in European countries as well as in South American countries and Australia. The main problem was how to break into these foreign markets. In many cases, the governments of these countries refused to allow Aries' products to be sold. They cited many reasons, such as taking jobs away from their own helicopter manufacturers and taking money from their economies. Some countries simply refused to buy American-made products. They did not want to be identified with American products and would rather buy their own domestically produced product even if it was inferior. These were only a few of the market-entry difficulties that Aries Helicopter encountered.

Entry into Foreign Markets

Aries Helicopter had several market-entry technique options. They could use straight exporting, which required the least amount of risk but was not amenable to most foreign governments. They could license another company in a foreign country to build their helicopters and receive royalties on products made, as well as a fee for the technology to make them. Aries could enter into a joint venture with one or more other companies in foreign countries, which would open up many foreign markets to them, but at a much higher risk. Finally, they could establish manufacturing facilities in foreign countries, which was the highest risk alternative and usually was not easily accessible. Aries Helicopter opted to license foreign companies to build their products.

The circumstances surrounding the licensing contract between Aries Helicopter and the foreign company that Aries chose to deal with (i.e., Smythe Aircraft Ltd.) will be reviewed before the actual terms of the agreement. As mentioned, a ten-year differential in technology existed between Aries Helicopter and its European competitors. The production base of the AH-61, or the current number of contracts for each AH-61, was beginning to wane in the domestic market. Production was slowly declining because of the decreased demand, which meant that the actual cost of each AH-61 was more expensive for Aries Helicopter. From all indications, AH-61 was nearing the end of its product life cycle in the domestic market because of the industry's great strides in technology. The market for the AH-61 in Europe and in other foreign countries, however, was just beginning to catch on. The demand was increasing just as Smythe Aircraft's production base was expanding, which meant that each aircraft cost Smythe less than it cost Aries Helicopter to produce.

The Licensing Contract

The licensing agreement between Aries Helicopter and Smythe Aircraft Ltd. was signed in July 1979. It would enable Smythe to manufacture the AH-61 until July 1989, a period of ten years. At that time, if everything was running smoothly, Smythe had the option of continuing the agreement for another five years. At the end of those five years, the contract would be reevaluated. The licensing fee was approximately $20 million and included all the technology involved in the research and design of the AH-61 and any technology that would or could improve on the AH-61. Smythe, in turn, promised to reciprocate and allow Aries Helicopter to have any future technical improvements that they could make as they built the aircraft. In addition to the fee, Aries Helicopter would collect royalties of $80,000 per aircraft manufactured. The agreement also included specific areas in which the British firm would be allowed to sell their aircraft. Smythe Aircraft Ltd. would, of course, have exclusive selling rights in Great Britain, where there was an established need for such aircraft and a need for jobs to manufacture such aircraft. They would also have exclusive selling rights in all outlying territories that were under British control. As for the rest of Europe and the globe, Smythe would have to compete with other foreign companies that Aries had license agreements with and Aries Helicopter itself. There were a few exceptions, however, where Aries Helicopter had exclusive rights and Smythe Aircraft Ltd. was restricted from selling. One of these areas was Australia.

The Problem

In the late 1970s and early 1980s everything went well between Smythe and Aires. Smythe's production base was just starting up, so that Aries could compete with Smythe's costs through exporting. The aircraft's reputation grew, and soon there was quite a demand in the international marketplace. The Smythe version of the AH-61 was selling well outside of Great Britain as well as domestically. The Smythe Aircraft people soon coined the term *Ocean King* for their version of the AH-61 because it was selling so well. The name caught on quickly and stuck so tenaciously in international circles that even Aries' AH-61 was now labeled the Ocean King. This was all fine and well except that Aries was slowly losing its market identity as the real manufacturer of the AH-61—a loss that was not clearly understood until Aries' waning production base and Smythe's rising production base caused a discrepancy in the price of the two versions of the AH-61. At that time Aries' sales began to decline because Smythe's product was cheaper. This new twist in sales occurred late in 1983. Aries' executives began to look into the problem, never really thinking it would amount to much. The British version of the AH-61 was running around $750,000 as compared with Aries' $950,000. With such a difference in price, one could easily see the start of a major problem. Aside from the price discrepancy, other factors were interfering with the smooth running of Aries' and Smythe's license agreement. Smythe Aircraft began to develop some of their own technical improvements for the helicopter's onboard electrical systems. New sensors and computer components made the Ocean King superior to the Aries AH-61. According to the licensing contract, Smythe was supposed to provide Aries with these improvements to allow Aries to keep its aircraft up to date. Smythe did not make these improvements known to Aries. Concomitantly, Aries was much more concerned with the technology of their new helicopter line rather than with that of an aircraft whose product life cycle was near its end. Smythe Aircraft was now getting 60 percent of its sales in markets other than its own. In addition, Smythe Aircraft executives were sure they could make handsome profits in Australia, a territory that was off limits under the licensing agreement. Smythe Aircraft knew that but at the same time realized that Aries Helicopter took no action when Smythe improved the Ocean King without either consulting or providing Aries with the new technical improvements. Smythe Aircraft decided to take the chance and begin selling the Ocean King in Australia. The British government, incidentally, was also forcing Smythe into this maneuver by threatening to nationalize the firm if it did not sell the helicopters to Australia. Smythe wanted to keep its independence and needed the sales to do so. In 1985, Smythe Aircraft Ltd. began selling their Ocean King helicopters to the Australian government.

Aries Helicopter's Response

Aries executive Lance was now faced with two counts of breach of contract by Smythe Aircraft Ltd. with regards to the AH-61 helicopter. He wondered what to do. He did not want to do anything drastic to jeopardize the relationship built up over the years between Aries and Smythe, since this relationship was a long-term and profitable one. At the same time, Aries Helicopter could not take such abuse in the international marketplace. Something must be done. Lance had several options: compete with Smythe Aircraft, which was sure to be costly for Aries; wait four more years until the license agreement expired, which would cost Aries a considerable amount of sales but would be not as costly as competing directly; or withdraw the license in worldwide territory, which would end any Aries–Smythe business dealings. Lance and a special board of executives assembled to assess this situation finally decided to threaten Smythe Aircraft Ltd. with withdrawal of the license in the hope that this action would force Smythe into renegotiating the contract. If Smythe could be brought to negotiations, Aries could establish guidelines that would maximize revenue and profit. One guideline would be to limit worldwide sales territory to specific countries with an option to negotiate additional countries on a case-by-case basis. A second guideline would be an increase in the royalties per aircraft from $80,000 to $125,000 and an increase in spare parts cost. The last guideline would be to limit the description of the aircraft to what is now being built. In other words, no more technical improvements could be made on the Ocean King now being sold. Although Lance could only wait for Smythe Aircraft's response to the threat of withdrawal of its worldwide license, Lance had a good idea that Smythe would come around.

Two weeks later, Aries helicopter received Smythe Aircraft's response, and it was negative. Backed by the British government in their endeavors, Smythe simply refused to negotiate. This was no small blow for Lance, who, together with his special committee, had failed to deal effectively with a formidable opponent. Lance now had to devise a new course of action.

Case 11: McDonald's (Taiwan), Inc.

It was a sunny Friday afternoon in September. Noticing the recent developments in the fast-food industry, Mr. David T. Sun, president of McDonald's (Taiwan), Inc., was pondering how to react to the competition.

Background—McDonald's Enters Taiwan

McDonald's (Taiwan), Inc., was founded in 1983. Both Mr. Sun and McDonald's Corporation shared 50 percent equally in the interests. Mr. Sun, a native Taiwanese, had been working with a computer company in the United States for more than ten years. Before he resigned from the computer company, Mr. Sun had contemplated establishing an entrepreneurship of his own. During the early 1980s, many Taiwanese firms approached fast-food chains in the United States to discuss franchising, but no one was successful because the U.S. fast-food chains questioned whether a potential market existed in Taiwan for U.S. fast-food operations. Mr. Sun, however, convinced McDonald's through an in-depth investigation of the general environment and the fast-food market in Taiwan (see Exhibits 1 and 2).

Before McDonald's entered the market in 1983, there were 6,800 fast-food stores and restaurants in Taiwan. Most of them were family-owned and offered typical Chinese foods. The average revenue of stores varied from $200 to $2,000 per day. All of them emphasized cooking and packing.

This case is printed here with the permission of the authors, Barry Masor, Morris Mayer, and Hazel Ezell of the University of Alabama.

EXHIBIT 1 General Information on Taiwan, 1983

Area: 14,000 square miles.
Population: 18 million.
Population growth rate (1970–1982): 2.3 percent.
Per capita income: U.S. $2,027.
Per capita income growth rate (1970–1982): 8.2 percent.
Industrial work force: 3.1 million
Inflation: 6.8 percent.

In July 1983, McDonald's (Taiwan), Inc., revealed its plans for entering the Taiwanese market in January 1984. The announcement shocked the fast-food industry. The native chains were lobbying the congress in Taiwan to boycott the "invasion of the American giant." Before its entry, McDonald's gained a lot of publicity. The discussion about McDonald's could be heard all over the country. The Taiwanese government was concerned with the matter. In general, the government held a positive attitude toward the company. A government official said, "There is no reason to reject the application of McDonald's. And, the government hopes that McDonald's will be able to bring new techniques, management, and foods to our people to accelerate the innovation of native chains. In addition, the company intends to buy potatoes, onions, and milk from our farmers. So, McDonald's is welcome!"

The company decided to adopt the management, production, layout, and marketing strategies on the U.S. principle. The only change was that the taste was slightly adapted to meet the preferences of consumers. In the meantime, the company announced that it intended to open fifty stores and to generate $120 million of sales within five years.

In January 1984, the first McDonald's store opened in the newly developed business area of Taipei, which is the largest city in Taiwan and has a population of 2.2 million. The revenue of the first month was amazing. The average daily revenue was about $25,000. The store set a new record for McDonald's.

The company's advertising emphasizes the theme of McDonald's—quality, service, cleanliness, and value. Newspaper, TV, and bulk distribution of fliers were employed. The advertising of the chain is designed to implicate fun and excitement when eating in the chain. "Uncle McDonald's" was introduced to attract children. Children were invited to eat at McDonald's and get a gift from Uncle McDonald. And McDonald's became the best place for parents to reward their children.

McDonald's Fast Food Promotion Center, a nonprofit organization, was founded by the chain to gain more publicity.

EXHIBIT 2 Data Related to Market for Fast Food in Taiwan

	1981	1982	1983	1984*	1985*	1987*
DINING-OUT POPULATION (MILLION/DAY)	1.89	2.04	2.25	2.50	2.85	3.10
AVERAGE EXPENSE ($ PER LUNCH)	1.00	1.25	1.38	1.50	1.75	2.00
VOLUME ($ BILLION/YEAR)	0.50	0.68	0.85	1.04	1.39	1.74

*Estimated.
Source: Food Development Center, Republic of China, 1984.

Raw material is a headache for the chain because some local materials do not meet the requirements of the chain. To assure standardized quality and products, machines, potatoes, juices, and dishes were imported from the United States. Thus, the company paid more import taxes and it risked delivery delay.

Personnel presented a difficult problem for the company. Most native chains have no training program for their personnel. To offer high-quality products and friendly service, the company employed an intensive training program, which was described by a local newspaper as "tough and thorough training." Everyone in the company was asked to smile and say "Thanks!" when working. The company also adopted the fringe benefit policy of the U.S. company, which pays life insurance premiums for its employees. In addition to a basic salary, employees also received a bonus from the company. Other employee benefits included free meals.

In April 1984, the second McDonald's store of the company opened in the recreation area of Taipei, which contains twenty theaters and more than 1,000 apparel, shoe, and gift shops. This area used to be the business center of Taipei and still has dense traffic after office hours. The revenue of the second store was about $10,000 per day.

The third store opened in Kaohsiung in July 1984. Kaohsiung, a harbour city, is located in southern Taiwan. The city is the second-largest city in Taiwan and had a population of 1.1 million in 1983. Because people in southern Taiwan are more conservative, the business of the third store was around $6,000 per day, which is less than the first two stores. The quarterly revenue of each store in 1984 is shown in Exhibit 3.

Competitive Arena

Seeing the success of McDonald's, many domestic enterprises approached the fast-food chains in the United States, in Japan, and even in France. It seemed that every entrepreneur in Taiwan hoped to catch the fast-food train. During the last half of 1984, many companies announced the franchising or opening of foreign fast-food stores.

Before mid-1984, the only competitors of McDonald's were the typical Chinese fast-food chains and family-owned restaurants, which were no threat to McDonald's. The market situation had changed dramatically after mid-1984.

Murasaki

Murasaki, a Japanese chain, opened in July 1984. The chain became the second foreign chain to enter the market. The Japanese chain planned to open thirty stores in Taipei, with a total of one hundred stores in Taiwan. The chain provided consumers with sixty kinds of light food and Japanese-style decoration and service. The philosophy of the chain is to simplify the production process in order to serve consumers within one minute after an order is placed. The average price per lunch at the chain is about 20 percent higher than that of local chains. The major consumers of the chain were people of ages over 40. The average daily revenue of a store in the chain is around $5,000.

Kentucky Fried Chicken

Kentucky Fried Chicken was franchised to President Enterprise Corporation, the largest bakery in Taiwan, in September 1984. The chain opened its first store in March 1985. The investment in the first store amounted to U.S. $500,000. The chain planned to open ten stores in five years and one hundred stores if subfranchised. The chain adopted the design, decoration, and production from its franchisor. The average revenue of the chain was $5,000 per day. In August 1985, the chain opened the second store. As the chain learned its lesson from the first store, the floor of the second store was changed to plastic tile instead of carpet, and ratten tables and chairs were used to replace wood tables and chairs. The major consumers of the chain were working people. Because people had

EXHIBIT 3 Quarterly Revenue of Each Store, 1984

	FIRST STORE	SECOND STORE	THIRD STORE
FIRST QUARTER ($ MILLION)	1.945	—	—
SECOND QUARTER ($ MILLION)	1.867	0.862	—
THIRD QUARTER ($ MILLION)	1.753	1.073	0.487
FOURTH QUARTER ($ MILLION)	1.834	1.104	0.548

Source: Company records (data disguised).

become used to fried chicken long before the chain entered the market, the menu of the chain was totally accepted by consumers. The average price per lunch at the chain is about 25 percent higher than that of local chains. The advertising theme of the chain was: "It's finger-lickin' good."

Free Time

Free Time, a French chain, opened its first store in September 1985. The chain had planned for eighteen months before its opening. Free Time was equipped with 300 seats and French-style design and decoration. The menu of the chain is similar to that of McDonald's. The only differences were:

1. The chain put a paper ring around hamburgers to keep fingers from touching the hamburgers and to heighten the image of the chain.
2. The chain has food insurance for its consumers. The chain's consumers are eligible to a claim in any damage resulting from having eaten a meal at the chain.

The chain emphasizes a relaxing and romantic atmosphere in its advertising. The major consumers of the chain are working people and young lovers. The average revenue of the chain is around $7,000 per day. In a press conference, the president of the franchised chain announced that he intended to open twenty stores within five years.

Wendy's

Wendy's was introduced to Taiwan in June 1985. The first store of the chain was located on the ground floor of a new department store in Taipei. The chain adopted the management philosophy, production, design and decoration, and marketing strategies of its U.S. principle. The advertising themes of the chain were "Quality is our recipe," "Hot off the grill," and "Choice of topping." The chain planned to open ten stores within two years. The average revenue of the chain was around $8,000 per day. The chain opened another three stores three months after the first's inauguration. The major consumers of the chain come from the middle- and high-income levels.

McDonald's Operating Results

During the first half of 1985, McDonald's opened another four stores. One was in Taichung, the third-largest city in Taiwan, which has a population of 600,000. The other three stores were in Taipei. The average daily revenue of the new stores was around $6,000. The revenue of the stores opened in 1984 declined. However, experts in the fast-food industry estimated that the net profit of the chain was at least 25 percent of sales. Exhibit 4 shows the quarterly sales revenue for the first three stores.

As the chain was expanding. Mr. Sun noticed the following situation:

1. It is very difficult to get competent personnel.
2. Good locations were being occupied by competitors.

To assist in developing strategies for the very competitive market, Mr. Sun asked his marketing manager to bring him the results of a market survey conducted recently by the marketing department. Exhibits 5–11 present the findings.

EXHIBIT 4 **Quarterly Sales Revenue of First Three Stores, 1985**

	FIRST STORE	SECOND STORE	THIRD STORE
FIRST QUARTER ($ MILLION)	1.538	0.983	0.685
SECOND QUARTER ($ MILLION)	1.416	0.857	0.653
THIRD QUARTER ($ MILLION)	1.374	0.803	0.679

Source: Company record (data disguised).

EXHIBIT 5 **The Number of Stores in Each Foreign Chain, as of September 1985**

McDonald's	7
Wendy's	4
Kentucky Fried Chicken	2
Free Time	2
Murasaki	3

Source: Company records.

EXHIBIT 6 **Menu and Price at Each Chain**

	MCDONALD'S	WENDY'S	FREE TIME	KENTUCKY FRIED CHICKEN
MAXI HAMBURGER	0.75	0.80	0.75	—
MAXI CHEESEBURGER	1.00	1.13	1.00	—
SUPERCHEESE	1.50	1.63	1.50	—
CHICKENBURGER	1.38	2.00	1.88	1.63
FISHBURGER	1.45	1.60	1.75	—
FRENCH FRIES				
LARGE	0.70	—	0.75	0.75
SMALL	0.45	—	0.50	0.50
SHAKE	1.00	1.25	1.00	0.90
COCA-COLA				
LARGE	0.60	0.60	0.50	0.50
SMALL	0.40	0.40	0.40	0.40
COFFEE	0.60	0.60	0.60	0.60
SUNDAE	0.90	0.90	0.90	—
APPLE PIE	—	—	1.00	0.90
LUNCH	—	—	—	2.25
DINNER	—	—	—	3.10

Source: Company records.

EXHIBIT 7 Major Purchasing Factors of Importance to Consumers

	PERCENT
LOCATION	35%
PRICE	11
TASTE	16
SERVICE	12
REPUTATION	7
CLEANLINESS	9
OTHERS	10

Source: Company records (data disguised).

EXHIBIT 8 Demographic Profile of McDonald's Consumers

	PERCENT
AGE	
UNDER 5	5%
6–12	9
13–18	20
19–24	25
25–30	18
31–40	14
41–50	6
OVER 50	4
PROFESSION	
WHITE COLLAR	32
BLUE COLLAR	9
STUDENT	44
HOUSEWIFE	10
OTHERS	5

Source: Company records (data disguised).

EXHIBIT 9 Patronage Frequency per Month

	PERCENT
LESS THAN ONCE	70%
2–3	13
4–5	8
OVER 5 TIMES	5
DON'T KNOW	4

Source: Company records (data disguised).

EXHIBIT 10 The Comparative Performance of Each Chain

	MCDONALD'S	DOMESTIC	WENDY'S	KENTUCKY FRIED CHICKEN	FREE TIME	MURASAKI
LOCATION	+	–	+	+	+	+
PRICE	+	+	–	–	–	–
TASTE	*	*	*	*	*	*
SERVICE	+	–	+	+	+	+
REPUTATION	+	–	–	*	–	–
CLEANLINESS	+	–	+	+	+	+

Note: + = Better than average
* = Average
– = Worse than average

Source: Company records.

EXHIBIT 11 Population Trend of Taiwan, 1980–1990

	PERCENT		
	1980	1985	1990
AGE:			
UNDER 5	12%	10%	7%
6–15	19	18	16
16–25	18	19	17
26–35	13	14	16
46–60	14	13	14
OVER 60	9	10	12

Source: Statistics Bureau, Republic of China.

PART • 4

Perspectives of International Markets

CHAPTER • 10

International Marketing Research

CHAPTER FOCUS

After studying this chapter, you should be able to:

- Explain the importance of marketing research in the context of international business
- Discuss the procedure for undertaking marketing research across national boundaries
- Identify sources of secondary data both in the United States and abroad
- Describe the problems of conducting primary research overseas
- Examine the perspectives of an international marketing information system

The prime function of marketing is to make and sell what buyers *want,* rather than simply selling whatever can be most easily made. Therefore, what consumers require must be assessed through marketing research so that a firm can direct its activities toward optimal marketing through the satisfaction of those requirements.

The role of marketing research is equally important in domestic and international marketing. The worldwide marketing research industry had a value of about $3.8 billion in 1985. Of this, the largest single market was the United States, accounting for some $1.8 billion or about 47 percent of the total. Europe accounted for $1.4 billion, 35 percent of the total global marketing research expenditures. Japan, Australia, and New Zealand added another 9 percent. Canada accounted for 4 percent. The remaining $156 million, about 4 percent of the world total, came from the Third World. Half of the amount was spent in Latin and South America, mainly Mexico, Brazil, Argentina, and Venezuela. The Far East, excluding Japan, accounted for $38 million. The African total would have been very small if not for the $15 million of the $17 million total spent by South Africa. The Middle East, with Saudi Arabia the main market, contributed about $10 million and is a growth area, but one that has shown some slowing in recent years. India, Pakistan, and Sri Lanka added a further $9 million.[1]

The differences in international environments make conducting marketing research more difficult.[2] Consider the research information needed by these potential international marketers in order for them to make decisions on how to proceed:

> A manufacturer of a specialized industrial product, iron fitting, believes that there is potentially a good market for export and wants to begin to develop it. Neither the company's management nor any of its sales force, however, has knowledge of possible markets or of the nature of the competition.
>
> A large U.S. corporation is contemplating building a factory in Western Europe. Management wonders if its product should be changed to suit the new market.
>
> A pharmaceutical company has to decide how to price a prescription drug item manufactured in its factory in Brazil for the Latin American market. Should the same pricing schedule used in the United States be followed? If not, what criteria should be used to set the price?
>
> A soft drink company must determine how effective its U.S. advertising strategy will be in promoting its product in Southeast Asia.

Such situations are examples of international marketing problems that require marketing research. In each case, the firm's past experience cannot provide an adequate basis for decision. In fact the information necessary to support management action is more likely to be found outside the organization. Specialized trade journals or government studies or discussions with professional-level personnel who have special industry expertise are likely to be helpful. Or if all these fail, it may finally become necessary to undertake a customer survey.

This chapter examines the meaning of marketing research and provides a framework for conducting such research. The two types of research, primary and secondary, are differentiated and their procedures discussed. Alternative ways of organizing international marketing research and the need for the establishment of an international marketing information system are included.

Meaning of Marketing Research

The term ***marketing research*** refers to gathering, analyzing, and presenting information related to a well-defined problem. The focus of marketing research is a specific problem or project with a beginning and an end. Marketing research differs from *marketing intelligence,* which is information gathered and analyzed on a continual basis. Further, intelligence is evaluated information, whose credibility, meaning, and importance have been established.

Often in practice, marketing research is used interchangeably with the term *market research,* which is conceptually narrower in scope because it deals with information concerned with current and potential customers—who they are; why they buy a product or service; and where they buy it, when they buy it, what they buy, and how they buy it. Marketing research, in addition to market research information, also deals with information relative to *marketing mix variables:* product, price, distribution, and promotion; marketing organizational matters; and the marketing environment. A *marketing information system* is the organization of market research, marketing research, and marketing intelligence into a workable system.

The procedures and methods of conducting marketing research are conceptually the same for both domestic marketing and international marketing. For example, before collecting data the researcher must have a clear idea of the research problem. Likewise, only an appropriate sample will yield valuable results. Procedural similarities aside, international marketing research differs from domestic marketing in three major ways:

1. The effects of the international environment on the whole company as a profit-oriented unit are considered. For example, the marketing research project concerned with the ramifications of a substantial price hike in a particular foreign country must consider questions that do not apply to the domestic market; for example, will the company's subsidiary be nationalized if prices are increased beyond a certain level? (See International Marketing Highlight 10.1.)
2. Many concepts and frameworks (i.e., market segmentation), which constitute the core of marketing decision making in the domestic arena, may be unusable in international marketing, not because the concept cannot be transferred, but because the information necessary to make such a transfer is not available. For example, if there is a lack of current income distribution data on a country, any analysis of the demand for a product

International Marketing Highlight 10.1

Local Culture and Market Potential

The chairman of a large American soft drink company decided that the firm should target Indonesia for sales of its most popular beverage. With a population of nearly 180 million people, Indonesia is the fifth most populous country in the world. Management considered this huge potential market irresistible and worked out a bottling and distribution arrangement to serve the country. The company sold the soft drink syrup to a bottler, who then bottled the drink and distributed it.

Unfortunately, sales were terrible. The drink simply didn't sell. The marketing campaign flopped despite predominantly good initial research, including research into the local competition and government attitudes, because the chairman and his project directors forgot to consider two major factors. First, Indonesia does have 180 million inhabitants, but most of them live in rural areas still functioning within a preindustrial economy. Most Indonesians simply don't have much money. Second, many of them prefer sweet, coconut-based drinks; they are unaccustomed to American-style carbonated beverages. A market for American drinks does exist, but almost exclusively in the major cities. That market—consumers with Western tastes and sufficient disposable income to purchase foreign-style beverages—totals only about 8 million people.

---

will assume incorrect income categories and, therefore, cannot mean much for practical purposes.

3. Finally, the ethnocentric nature of marketing makes cultural differences among nations a significant factor. Thus, culture in a domestic market can be considered to be naturally understood, but in international marketing the culture must be fully investigated.

To illustrate the point, consider a recent study that explored the effect of a monetary incentive on the questionnaire response rate. Receipt of one U.S. dollar increased the response rate from Japanese businesspeople but decreased the response from Hong Kong businesspeople. The author noted:

> In this study, Japanese business executives were more compliant than Hong Kongese in general, and the monetary incentive was successful in more than doubling the response from Japan but decreased the response from Hong Kong. These findings may be biased because of the small sample, the sampling frame, or the questionnaire content. However, the results may imply a cultural difference either toward responding to questionnaires, or toward monetary incentives. The cross-cultural researcher should be aware of such problems, and explore the effect of monetary incentives prior to the mass mailing or surveys. Theoretically, monetary incentives may increase response rates in any culture or country; however, the type (local or foreign currency) and amount may be important factors.[3]

Such factors raise a variety of conceptual, methodological, and organizational issues in international marketing research relating to:

1. The complexity of research design, caused by operation in a multicountry, multicultural, and multilinguistic environment
2. The lack of secondary data available for many countries and product markets
3. The high costs of collecting primary data, particularly in developing countries
4. The problems associated with coordinating research and data collection in different countries
5. The difficulties of establishing the comparability and equivalence of data and research conducted in different contexts
6. The intrafunctional character of many international marketing decisions
7. The economics of many international investment and marketing decisions.[4]

Framework for International Marketing Research

Most marketing research studies proceed through a common series of major tasks:

- Define the problem and the information needed for support of management's decision-making process.
- Identify alternative sources of information.
- Plan and execute data collection.
- Analyze the data and prepare a report.

Defining the Problem

This first task, which sounds deceptively simple, may be the pivotal task in the entire study. In defining the problem, two important considerations are market structure and product concept. ***Market structure*** refers to the size of the market, its stage of development, the number of competitors and their market shares, and the channels through which the market is approached. The importance of market structure in problem definition is shown by a 1963 *Reader's Digest* study, which reported that French and German consumers ate significantly more spaghetti than Italians.[5] This finding was wrong. The study had concerned itself with only packaged, branded spaghetti, and not *total* spaghetti consumption. Because much of the spaghetti sold in Italy has been unpackaged and unbranded, the results of the study were totally invalid. The *Reader's Digest* researchers should have clearly defined the kind of spaghetti consumption to be studied in each of the different countries (see International Marketing Highlight 10.2).

In addition, a product may be viewed differently in different cultures. Thus, even before attempting to define the marketing research problem for study, exploratory research may be necessary to understand the ***product concept,*** that is,

International Marketing Highlight 10.2

Health Clubs in Singapore

A widely franchised health club opened a facility in Singapore. With its young, urban population and a widespread appreciation of Western culture, Singapore seemed a site destined for success. Moreover, the club's physical appearance and stock of equipment equaled or surpassed that of comparable facilities in the United States.

Yet the club couldn't sign up enough members. Despite the Singaporeans' interest in sports, the club attracted few of them and ended up catering to the relatively small expatriate community instead. Citizens of Singapore felt little enthusiasm for the American-style health club; they were more attracted either to Western competitive sports or to Chinese calisthenics and other traditional Asian forms of exercise.

Source: Charles F. Valentine, *The Arthur Young International Business Guide* (New York: John Wiley & Sons, 1988), p. 74.

the meaning of the product in a particular environment. In this way, problem definition will be appropriate to the concept of the product held in the particular country of interest.

Berent points out that milk-based products are viewed very differently in the United Kingdom and Thailand.[6] In England, they are usually consumed at meals and bedtime for their sleep-inducing, soothing, relaxing properties. In Thailand, the same products are consumed on the way to work and often away from home, for they are considered invigorating, energizing, and stimulating.

Let us assume a multinational marketer is interested in finding out the potential market for a brand of yogurt in England and Thailand. The problem definition in the two countries will have to be stated differently. In the United Kingdom, the yogurt might be primarily perceived by the consumers as a healthful and relaxing product to be used prior to retiring. In Thailand, the research problem would determine if yogurt would be considered mainly an energy food used to start the day.

Identifying Alternative Information Sources

After the problem has been defined, where the necessary information may be found and how to obtain it must be determined. In some cases, the study may be confined to ***secondary data,*** that is, published information that has been collected elsewhere. It may be available free (for example, government statistics), for a price (for example, syndicated research supplies), or through restricted distribution sources (for example, trade association statistics).

Let us assume that Ford Motor Company is interested in assembling its new world car in India in collaboration with an Indian company. Before committing itself to the joint venture, Ford would like to study the car's market potential in India over a ten-year period. Fortunately, the Indian government collects a variety of socioeconomic-demographic information on a regular basis. This information is conveniently available. Ford, therefore, can use with confidence such secondary information as population projections, income data, consumer expenditure patterns, and rural-urban population shifts to assess the market potential. The appendix at the end of this chapter lists important sources of secondary data for international marketers.

Sometimes internal data are also useful. Existing files, in fact, can often provide important insights into the question at hand. In the above example, Ford might have found that it already had sufficient information on population trends in India gathered when the company had earlier negotiated for the assembly of tractors there. Thus, there would be no need for another source of information.

In cases where no amount of investigation of secondary sources or of internal data provides the required information, ***primary data*** will have to be compiled from scratch through interviews and other direct collection of information. Primary data may be gathered in various ways (to be discussed later) from trade association representatives, governmental experts, managerial personnel, and/or the buying public.

For example, a company may be interested in introducing its prefabricated houses in Latin America. The company would have to study house-buying behavior in the target countries. Since this type of information may not be conveniently available from secondary sources, primary data gathering may be necessary. The importance of such information for decision making is revealed in a study on the subject done in the United Kingdom.

> Home ownership in different countries could also have completely different implications. The proverb that "a man's home is his castle" is far more applicable in the United Kingdom (where castles can in fact be found) than in the United States, where the geographic and social mobility of the population means that the regular exchange of homes is a commonplace experience during the life cycle of most families. Therefore, the decisionmaking patterns of husband and wife, and the amount of effort spent in making a home-buying decision, should be quite different between these two countries.[7]

Thus, before entering the market with prefabricated houses in Latin America, the company has to learn through primary research in which ways houses might mean home in various locales.

Data Collection

The actual collection of data must be planned and executed carefully. While data collection will be discussed at length in later sections of this chapter, it should be noted here that tracking down reliable, usable data sources can be time consuming. This is particularly so when a variety of sources is pursued concurrently. In fact, the search can go on with decreasing returns unless personnel with knowledge of the country appraise what progress is being made.

Interview questions must be tested for their appropriateness so that they produce the desired results. A sound approach is to conduct professional-level interviews in two phases: (1) collect basic data and (2) explore interview questions not anticipated at the start of the project.

Once basic data have been collected, the process of cross-checking can begin.

This step requires that all information be examined critically for its relevance. Cross-checking establishes the reliability of data by comparison of one source with another. It is important to document the criteria used by the project team to determine the reliability of collected data.

Analysis, Interpretation, and Report Preparation

For the final step, the preparation of the report, the data must be analyzed and interpreted.[8] Here also, attention should be paid to a country's cultural traits. For example, in an examination of the beer market, it was found that beer was perceived as an alcoholic drink in Northern European countries, but it was considered a soft drink in Mediterranean countries. Thus, other products listed with beer as alternative drinks would influence the research findings. Similarly, in Japan noncarbonated fruit juices are often substituted for bottled soft drinks. This seldom occurs in the United States.[9] In brief, *the significance of different concepts of the product in various countries must be taken into account.*

Reports must be complete, factual, and objective. It is particularly important to communicate the reliability as well as the limitations of the facts presented. Particular attention should be given to the following aspects of a report:

1. Data sources must be identified. Different sources of data warrant varying degrees of confidence. For example, information on a Third World country obtained from the United States Agency for International Development is probably more reliable than the information available from the government of that country.
2. Data projection must be explained. As a matter of fact, the statistical computations should be simplified as much as possible. Detailed description of the statistical/mathematical procedures followed can be included in an appendix at the end of the report.
3. The identity of all those interviewed should be included as well as their titles or qualifications. (This rule does not apply to consumer research.) This requirement may have to be relaxed when anonymity has been guaranteed.
4. The alternative courses of action developed from analysis and interpretation of the data must be labeled as such, clearly reserving to management the responsibility for selecting the appropriate course of action.

Information Requirements of International Marketers

The nature of marketing decisions does not vary from country to country, but the environment differs from country to country. For this reason, the sort of information required to complete a marketing study may vary from one country to another. For example, in a situation where a marketer is free to set prices based on competition, a detailed analysis of competition should be made. But in a country where the price is set by government, information on governmental cost analysis would be of greater importance. The fact that environment determines what kind of information is needed makes international marketing research efforts quite different from domestic marketing research work.[10]

Figure 10.1 shows the types of marketing studies a company may want to conduct in different areas, such as promotion, distribution, price, products, or markets. Each of these area studies takes a different form of information, as the following discussion makes clear.

Market Information

Market research is required for testing, entering, or leaving a market and deals with market performance, market shares, and sales analysis and forecasting. *Marketing performance research* involves market measurements, either to compare a company's performance against specified standards or to project a possible

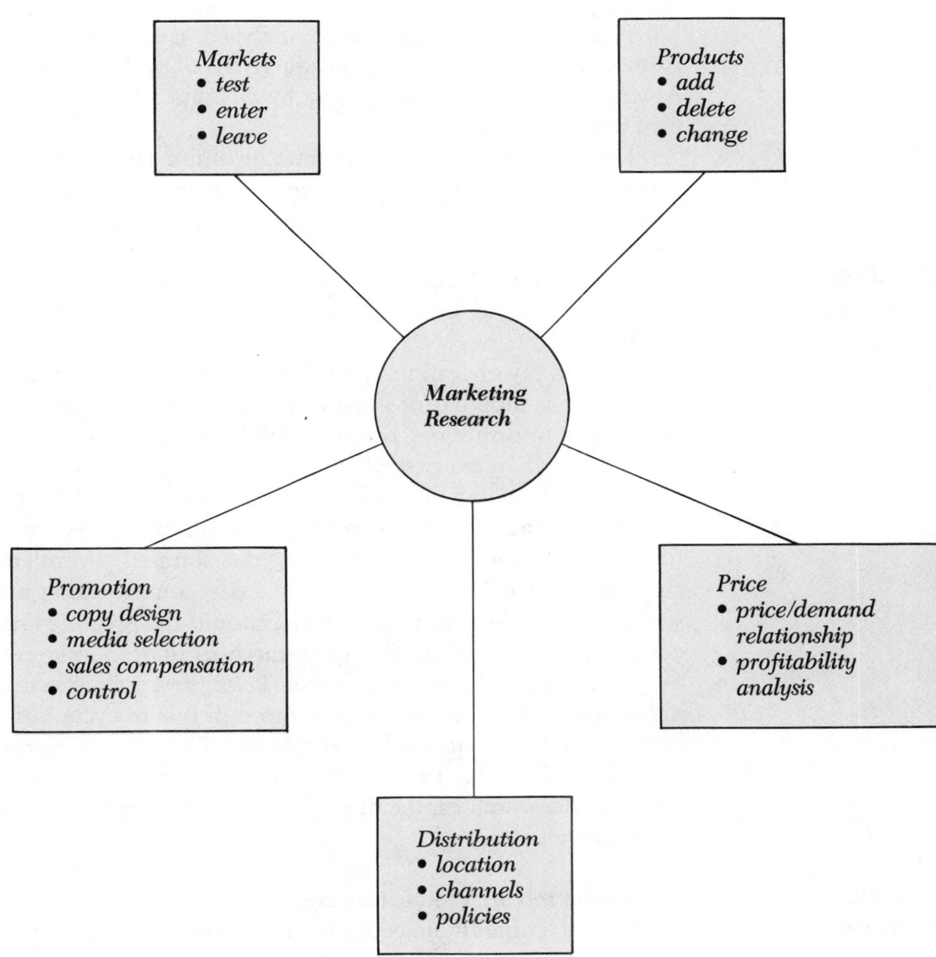

FIGURE 10.1 Types of Marketing Studies Required for Doing Business Abroad

future outcome. *Market potential* refers to the total market demand under optimal conditions; *market forecast* shows the expected level of market demand under the given conditions. To illustrate, when Pepsico decided to expand its Pizza Hut business into certain Middle Eastern countries, like Saudi Arabia, it conducted beforehand market potential research for five years in each country.

Market share refers to a company's proportion of total sales in an industry during a set time, usually a year. The market shares held by competitors shape marketing strategy for a company. The competitor with a respectable market share will have a cost advantage over its rivals. This cost advantage can be passed on to the customers through lower prices, which in turn strengthens the company's hold on the market. Because of the strategic importance of market share, business corporations keep constant watch on its fluctuations. Data supplied by industry associations, if properly analyzed, usually show respective market shares.

Past *sales information* can be analyzed in different ways: by amount of profit from different products, by productivity of sales territory (for example, Latin America or Western Europe), or by customer type. Sales analysis can pinpoint problems.

Sales forecasts refer to estimates of future sales of a product during a specific period. The sales forecast is the single most important basis for preparing budgets.

Product Information

Product research means both product line research and individual product research. This kind of research bears on when to add, delete, or change the product.

A company operating overseas must often decide which product line it should add, which it should drop, and which needs rejuvenation. These decisions require a variety of information. Consider this example. A large paper products company manufactured an expensive line of writing paper, as well as other kinds of paper products. The company had about a 30 percent market share in Latin America, but the demand had been constant for a number of years. As part of a program for simplification of product lines, the company wondered if there had been changes in the office environment in Latin countries that made the use of expensive paper obsolete. In other words, should the product line be abandoned? The company undertook marketing research to find an answer to this question.

A manager may also require marketing research information on each individual product. As a product passes through its life cycle, different marketing programs must be developed for every stage. Thus, it is important to place a product on its life cycle curve in order to choose the appropriate marketing program, and marketing research can be of real value in plotting a product's life cycle in different countries.

Promotion Information

Promotion research indicates research for advertising and personal selling. Companies consult the findings of objective research before spending money on advertising campaigns in order to select appropriate copy and appeals and make the best media selection. A trading stamp company operating in Europe, for example, redeemed stamps saved by consumers in two ways, either in merchandise or in travel. Over the years it was found that more and more customers preferred overseas travel to merchandise. For the company, however, merchandise was more profitable; so the company considered starting an ad campaign to entice consumers into redeeming their stamps in merchandise. The company wondered if a merchandise catalog, which emphasized the virtue of material acquisitions as status symbols, would be persuasive in Europe. The production of the catalog would cost about two million dollars, and the catalog's market effectiveness had to be tested beforehand.

Personal selling, just as advertising, must produce profits. Consider the complaint of the sales manager of a U.S. pharmaceutical company: "My salespeople in Italy are not productive enough even though we pay them a lot more than the industry average there." Marketing research can provide insights into problems related to *personal selling,* which involves questions about how many salespeople to hire and how much to pay them, how to form sales territories, and how much time to spend on retaining old customers and how much on developing new accounts.

Distribution Information

Distribution research consists of channel research and location research. *Channel research* can help a company decide which channels to use for distribution of its products. Marketing research can provide information on the availability of channels and their relative desirability.

A water systems manufacturer, for instance, traditionally used manufacturer's representatives for the distribution of its water pumps in the Canadian market. The company, however, was becoming dissatisfied with manufacturer's representatives and wanted to use its own sales force. A marketing research firm was asked for a study of the effect on sales of making such a change.

Location research concerns decisions about warehousing, inventory, and transportation. For example, the decision to own a warehouse in Germany or to use a public warehouse there requires marketing research.

Price Information

A company sets the prices of its products to meet both short-term and long-term objectives. To set prices, information about the ability of consumers to pay, about dealer reaction, and about the effect of price on demand is necessary. Studies that measure the public perception of a product's quality in relation to price also help in making pricing decisions.

Environment Information

No matter which sort of international marketing study is planned, the researchers must take into account the foreign country's environment in all its aspects: legal, political, social, cultural, and attitudinal, as shown by both the buying habits of its consumers and the business practices of its enterprises. Naturally, familiarity with the environment is equally important in domestic marketing, but knowledge of domestic environment can come more easily from personal experience. For example, if a U.S. company is interested in doing business in China, it must learn about a political system that is different from what is taken for granted in the U.S. political structure.

General Research Information

All marketing research requires three general groups of overall information in addition to the more specific categories already discussed:

1. General information about:
   a. Community-type conditions (for example, political happenings—campaigns, elections; cultural events—county fairs, special annual ethnic or religious celebrations; national events—sports, championships, holidays)
   b. Business conditions (for example, business ethics and traditional associations)
   c. Lifestyles and living conditions, that is, social and cultural customs and taboos (for example, marriageable age for men and women and the role of women in society). (See International Marketing Highlight 10.3.)

International Marketing Highlight 10.3

Hands-On Market Research

When Sony researched the market for a lightweight portable cassette player, results showed that consumers wouldn't buy a tape player that didn't record. Company chairman Akio Morita decided to introduce the Walkman anyway, and the rest is history. Today it is one of Sony's most successful products.

Morita's disdain for large-scale consumer surveys and other scientific research tools isn't unique in Japan. Matsushita, Toyota, and other well-known Japanese consumer goods companies are just as skeptical about the Western style of market research. Occasionally, the Japanese do conduct consumer attitude surveys, but most executives don't base their marketing decisions on them or on other popular techniques.

Of course, Japanese corporations want accurate and useful information about their markets as much as U.S. and European companies do. They just go about it differently. Japanese executives put much more faith in information they get directly from wholesalers and retailers in the distribution channels. Moreover, they track what's happening among channel members on a monthly, weekly, and sometimes even daily basis.

Japanese-style market research relies heavily on two kinds of information: "soft data" obtained from visits to dealers and other channel members, and "hard data" about shipments, inventory levels, and retail sales. Japanese managers believe that these data better reflect the behavior and intentions of flesh-and-blood consumers.

Source: Reprinted by permission of *Harvard Business Review.* An excerpt from "Market Research the Japanese Way" by Johny K. Johansson and Ikujiro Nonaka, May–June 1987, p. 16.

   d. General economic conditions (for example, the standards of living of various groups of people and the economic infrastructure—transportation, power supply, and communication)

2. Industry information about governmental decisions affecting the industry; resource availability (for example, labor and land); current or potential competitors (that is, general information about their markets and their problems); competition from U.S. companies, local companies, and/or third country companies; industry policy, concerted actions in the industry, and so forth.
3. Study-related information: collateral data generated to complete a specific market research study. For example, a study concerned with market potential needs information on supply and demand in market areas of current and potential interest (for example, capacity, consumption, imports, exports). On the other hand, a study concerned with the introduction of a new product requires information about existing products, the technical know-how available in the country, sources of raw material, and leads for joint ventures.

The amount of information to be gathered in a given case depends on the cost–benefit relationship of such information. For example, let us assume a company has an opportunity to export machinery to Kenya. Although normally the company checks on the credit rating of an importer before making a shipment, such a delay might ruin a particular transaction. The company figures out that, if the importer does not make the payment as stipulated, it stands to lose $2,000 after accounting for the advance from the importer. On the other hand, the company could have a market research firm do a study on the credit worthiness of the importer for $3,000 in a very short time. In other words, the cost exceeds the benefit and the study is not worth it. This example, while oversimplified, illustrates the importance of relating the cost to benefit in terms of time and money before deciding to undertake marketing research.

Finally, the nature of information required will vary based on the objective of research.[11] To illustrate the point, Exhibit 10.1 lists the type of information a firm needs to determine the export potential. The firm must examine different types of environments as well as undertake market and product research.[12]

Gathering Secondary Data at Home

There are two kinds of data—primary and secondary. Primary data are gathered by the researcher. Secondary data, on the other hand, refer to information collected by someone else, either an individual or an organization. Exhibit 10.2 characterizes the two kinds of data. Research based on secondary data may be conducted either at home or abroad. This section discusses secondary research in the United States.

U.S. Sources of Data

There are five sources of information in the United States: international agencies, the United States government, consulting firms, foreign government offices, and banks.

EXHIBIT 10.1 Information Needs for Determining Export Potential

STAGE ONE: PRELIMINARY SCREENING

Preliminary screening involves defining the physical, political, economic, and cultural environment.

Demographic/Physical Environment
- Population size, growth, density
- Urban and rural distribution
- Climate and weather variations
- Shipping distance
- Product-significant demographics
- Physical distribution and communication network
- Natural resources

Political Environment
- System of government
- Political stability and continuity
- Ideological orientation
- Government involvement in business
- Government involvement in communications
- Attitudes toward foreign business (trade restrictions, tariffs, nontariff barriers, bilateral trade agreements)
- National economic and developmental priorities

Economic Environment
- Overall level of development
- Economic growth: GNP, industrial sector
- Role of foreign trade in the economy
- Currency, inflation rate, availability, controls, stability of exchange rate
- Balance of payments
- Per capita income and distribution
- Disposable income and expenditure patterns

Social/Cultural Environment
- Literacy rate, educational level
- Existence of middle class
- Similarities and differences in relation to home market
- Language and other cultural considerations

The export marketer will eliminate some foreign markets from further consideration on the basis of this preliminary screening. An example would be the absence of comparable or linking products and services, a deficiency that would hinder the potential for marketing products.

STAGE TWO: ANALYSIS OF INDUSTRY MARKET POTENTIAL

Market Access
- Limitations on trade: tariff levels, quotas
- Documentation and import regulations
- Local standards, practices, and other nontariff barriers
- Patents and trademarks
- Preferential treaties
- Legal considerations: investment, taxation, repatriation, employment, code of laws

Product Potential
- Customer needs and desires
- Local production, imports, consumption
- Exposure to and acceptance of product
- Availability of linking products
- Industry-specific key indicators of demand
- Attitudes toward products of foreign origin
- Competitive offerings
- Availability of intermediaries
- Regional and local transportation facilities
- Availability of manpower
- Conditions for local manufacture

STAGE THREE: ANALYSIS OF COMPANY SALES POTENTIAL

The third stage of screening process involves assessing company sales potential in those countries that prove promising based upon the earlier analyses.

Sales Volume Forecasting
- Size and concentration of customer segments
- Projected consumption statistics
- Competitive pressures
- Expectations of local distributors/agents

Landed Cost
- Costing method for exports
- Domestic distribution costs
- International freight and insurance
- Cost of product modification

Cost of Internal Distribution
- Tariffs and duties
- Value-added tax
- Local packaging and assembly
- Margins/commission allowed for the trade
- Local distribution and inventory costs
- Promotional expenditures

Other Determinants of Profitability
- Going price levels
- Competitive strengths and weaknesses
- Credit practices
- Current and projected exchange rates

Source: S. Tamer Cavusgil, "Guidelines for Export Market Research," *Business Horizons,* November–December 1985, pp. 30–31.

International Agencies The United Nations, the World Bank, and the International Monetary Fund gather a variety of economic and social information on different countries of the world. This information is available to the public. For example, the United Nations yearbook provides information on worldwide demographics.[13] Also the World Bank's *The World Development Report* summarizes information on living patterns via such indicators as daily calorie supply, life expectancy at birth, and school enrollment.[14] The International Monetary Fund (IMF) provides historical information on national economic indicators (GNP, industrial production, inflation rate, money supply) of its member countries. This information is available on computer tapes.[15]

The information available from these international organizations, however,

EXHIBIT 10.2 Characteristics of Primary and Secondary Data

PRIMARY DATA	SECONDARY DATA
• From knowledgeable individuals at the professional level	• From published sources or collected by others
• May be costly in time and travel	• Usually free or low cost
• May tend to be subjective	• Can be collected quickly
• Must be pilot-tested	• May be biased or incomplete
• Can be very specific to problems at hand	• May be out of date
• Cannot require disclosure of proprietary information	• Requires careful analysis of limitations

has two drawbacks. First, the information is based on data supplied by each member country. It is difficult to determine what criteria and means have been used. In some cases, the reliability of the data should be questioned because the information compiled has been passed along by various bureaucrats who may have slanted the data for their own purposes. Second, the information is dated. It takes time for an international organization to gather information from all over the world, analyze it, and make it available to the public in summary form.

Most university libraries and public libraries in major cities carry the UN and the World Bank publications. The IMF information may be available only in more specialized libraries.

U.S. Government The U.S. Department of Commerce is the single most important source of secondary information. Forty-eight international trade administration district offices and nineteen branches offices of the U.S. Department of Commerce in cities throughout the United States and in Puerto Rico provide information and professional export counseling to businesspeople. Each office is headed by a director, supported by trade specialists and other staff. These professionals can help a company's decision makers gain a basic understanding of profitable opportunities in exporting and assist them in evaluating the company's market potential overseas.

Each district office can give information about:

- Trade and investment opportunities abroad
- Foreign markets for U.S. products and services
- Services to locate and evaluate overseas buyers and representatives
- Financing aid for exporters
- International trade exhibitions
- Export documentation requirements
- Foreign economic statistics
- U.S. export licensing and foreign national import requirements
- Export seminars and conferences

Most district offices maintain an extensive business library containing the department's latest reports.

The U.S. Department of Commerce information is obtained in two ways: on a regular basis, from periodicals such as *Business America,*[16] and on an ad hoc basis, from special reports prepared on opportunities for American companies, for example, in Saudi Arabia.

The U.S. Department of Commerce informs businesses not only about international business conditions abroad but also about events and happenings in Washington and their impact on international business. Information is available on all phases of marketing. Table 10.1 shows what kinds of information different U.S. government sources supply. Useful information may also be available from other departments/agencies of the federal government such as the U.S. State department's Agency for International Development (USAID) or the U.S. Depart-

TABLE 10.1 Match Your International Business Requirements with the Appropriate Government Programs or Services

If you are seeking information or assistance regarding → Use ↓	*Potential Markets*	*Market Research*	*Direct Sales Leads*	*Agents/Distributors*	*Licenses*	*Credit Analysis*	*Financial Assistance*	*Risk Insurance*	*Tax Incentives*	*Export Counseling*	*Export Regulations*	*Overseas Contracts*	*Marketing Strategies*	*Trade Complaints*	*Customs Advantages*
U.S. & Foreign Commercial Service	•	•	•		•					•	•		•	•	
District Export Councils										•					
Trade Opportunities Program			•	•	•							•			
Agent/Distributor Service				•											
Overseas Business Reports	•	•													
Foreign Economic Trends	•	•													
Small Business Administration		•					•			•					
International Chambers of Commerce											•				
Export Statistics Profiles	•	•													
Export Information System Data Reports	•	•													
Annual Worldwide Industry Reviews	•	•													
International Market Research	•	•													
Country Market Surveys	•	•													
Custom Statistical Service	•	•													
Product Market Profile	•	•													
Market Share Reports	•	•													
Country Market Profiles	•	•													
Country Trade Statistics	•	•													
Background Notes		•													•
International Economic Indicators	•	•													
World Traders Data Reports						•									
Commercial News USA	•		•	•											
Export-Import Bank							•								
Export Mailing List Service	•	•	•	•											
Commerce Trade Shows	•	•	•	•	•	•							•		
Commerce Trade Missions	•	•	•	•	•	•							•		
Export Development Offices		•													
Catalog Exhibitions			•												
Major Projects Program												•			
Overseas Private Investment Corporation						•		•							
Private Export Funding Corporation							•								
Foreign Sales Corporation							•		•						
Commerce Business Daily	•		•												
Free Ports & Free Trade Zones															•

Source: A Basic Guide to Exporting (Washington, D.C.: U.S. Department of Commerce, 1986), p. 87.

ment of Agriculture. Most of these organizations issue newsletters and other publications. An international marketer could subscribe to those pertinent to particular products or markets.

U.S. Consulting Firms Many management consulting firms (including accounting firms) specialize in services for U.S. business abroad. Some of these firms conduct original research. Their findings are available to the international marketer. One such firm is Business International Corporation, headquartered in New York City. It puts out a number of publications (newsletters issued periodically, studies issued on a regular basis, and ad hoc studies). Another firm that specializes in providing secondary data is Predicasts of Cleveland, Ohio. Similarly, the major accounting firms issue a variety of finance and accounting related information on different countries of the world. For example, Price Waterhouse regularly publishes booklets on select countries, providing perspectives on doing business there.

U.S. Foreign Government Offices Almost all countries maintain embassies in Washington, D.C. In addition, these countries have consulates and UN mission offices in New York City. A country may have more than one consulate office in the United States. For example, the government of Brazil maintains consulate offices in New York, Chicago, Dallas, and Los Angeles, in addition to their embassy in Washington, D.C. Usually, an embassy has a commercial attaché who may be a good source of secondary information on the country. The consulate and the UN mission usually have basic information on their country to offer the researcher. For example, let us assume research is being done to prepare a market-potential study in order to decide whether a company should assemble televisions in Nigeria. Inport data on television sets in Nigeria for the past five years are needed. The Nigerian consulate in New York might have a government publication that quickly and easily provides such information.

Other units of a foreign government in the United States can serve as important sources of data. For example, a hotel chain interested in constructing a hotel in the Caribbean island of St. Lucia may find the St. Lucian government tourist office in New York City an important source of information on tourist trade there.

Many governments maintain special offices in the United States for the purpose of promoting trade and business with U.S. companies. For example, the Indian government's Indian Investment Center in New York City offers all sorts of business-related information. If the center does not have the information, it can guide the research to the proper source.

U.S. Multinational Banks Both U.S. banks active worldwide (such as Citicorp, BankAmerica Corp., Chase Manhattan Bank National Corp.) and branches of foreign banks in the United States are additional sources of secondary information. Many of these banks maintain libraries. They usually offer free access to customers, present and prospective. In some instances, however, a bank may have information a researcher seeks in one of its reports, but the data may not be made available. It is worthwhile, nevertheless, to contact a multinational bank for secondary data.

Advantages of Secondary Research at Home

Secondary research conducted in the United States is less expensive and less time consuming than research abroad.[17] The research at home keeps commitment to future projects at a low level: no contacts have to be made overseas, and no high-level decisions have to be made on exploring markets outside the United States. Research in the home environment affords easy communication with sources of information. In addition, requests for certain kinds of information are often more favorably received by foreign sources located in the United States where political pressure and business customers do not inhibit response. Research undertaken in the United States about a foreign environment also gains objectivity. The researcher is not constrained by overseas customs or mores and can apply the same standards of quality and analysis as would be used for a project related to domestic business.

Disadvantages of Secondary Research at Home

Secondary research undertaken in the United States has various limitations. First, current information may be scarce in the United States. After all, there is a time lag between data gathering in a foreign country and its transmission to the United States. Further, certain things may be uncovered in the foreign environment that ultimately will bear on the project. For example, a company may be exploring the feasibility of establishing a plant in Saudi Arabia to manufacture air conditioners. Research done in the United States is likely to reveal good potential there for air conditioners based on secondary data such as high per capita income, hot climate, low rate of air conditioners per hundred households, and encouragement by the Saudi government. However, these data omit an important fact about Saudi living: a large proportion of the people live in mud houses. Additionally, there are regions without electricity. Such facts would become immediately obvious to a researcher on the spot.

Secondary Research Abroad

An alternative to doing secondary research in the United States is undertaking secondary research abroad. It should be recognized that the abundance of information available in the United States from both government and private sources is not found in most countries of the world, including the developed ones. Since World War II, however, interest in collecting socioeconomic information has greatly increased. As countries progressed economically, it became important to collect and publish statistical information on commercial matters on a regular basis. As a matter of fact, it may be claimed that availability of reliable secondary data is directly related to the level of economic development of a country. Even among Third World countries, data-gathering activity has greatly improved since the 1970s. This may be attributed partly to the United Nations' efforts to impress upon countries the desirability of keeping national statistical information accurate and current.

Foreign Sources of Information

The following are the major sources of secondary information for an international marketer:

Government Sources The single most important source of secondary information in a country is the national government. The quality and quantity of information will vary from country to country, but in most cases information on population statistics, consumption standards, industrial production, imports and exports, price levels, employment, and more is conveniently available. On the other hand, data on retail and wholesale trade may be found only in certain countries. The government data are usually available through a government agency or major publishers in the country. In many countries, marketing-related information gathered by the government is not separated from other sorts of information. Thus, the researcher must go through a plethora of information to choose what is relevant.

Private Sources In many countries there are private consulting firms (like Business International Corporation, New York City; and Predicasts, Cleveland, Ohio), which gather and sell commercial information (see International Marketing Highlight 10.4). Information from private sources may in fact have been collected by the government originally. But consulting firms analyze and organize it in such a manner that business executives can more easily make sense of it. The

International Marketing Highlight 10.4

Direct Mail Responders Love to Shop

The 1990 Target Group Index (TGI) survey by the British Market Research Bureau found that people who respond to direct-response advertising are less brand-loyal and more likely to experiment in their purchasing behavior.

The TGI is a national product and media survey. It measures the use of over 3,000 brands in more than 200 product areas and the use of 450 other services. The survey can be used to link responsiveness data with geographic and demographic information to more accurately target cold mailings.

Although the traditional image of the direct mail respondent is someone who doesn't like to shop, the response to the TGI survey contradicts this notion.

People who respond to direct mail enjoy their shopping more than anyone else, even though they are also the busiest people. They also hunt for bargains more enthusiastically, and are more likely to try new brands.

The TGI also found that in the past twelve months at least 62 percent of the adult population (over age 15) in the United Kingdom purchased goods through a mail order catalog or responded to a direct-response advertisement, or did both.

Seventeen million adults (39 percent) responded to direct-response ads, and 19.5 million (43 percent) made purchases through mail order companies.

Source: Direct Mail Information Service, 14 Floral Street, Covent Garden, London WC2E 9RR, United Kingdom.

commercial attaché at the U.S. Embassy should be able to provide the names and addresses of the local consulting firms. For example, International Information Services Ltd. (IIS), a global product pick-up service located in Sussex, United Kingdom, provides answers to such specific issues as the most popular pizza flavors in France and retail pricing structure for shampoos in Venezuela compared with that of its neighbors in Colombia and Brazil. Each day over 400 IIS shoppers visit supermarkets in 120 countries searching for information requested by clients such as Coca-Cola, General Foods, Procter & Gamble, Nestlé, and Unilever. The information gathered by IIS shoppers is stored, along with data from the company's comprehensive library of foreign trade publications, in a computerized data base, enabling IIS to offer clients continuous updates on new food, household, and pharmaceutical products introduced worldwide. IIS uses these data to compile bimonthly indexes of the new products.[18]

Research Institutes, Trade Associations, Universities, and Similar Sources Although not every country in the world has trade associations or research institutes, in both developed and developing countries (like India, Brazil, South Korea, Egypt), such sources could be important sources of secondary data. In some countries, they are set up with the help of international agencies and/or the government. Information on these sources should be sought from the appropriate U.S. embassy.

Local Businesses A U.S. company may be in contact with one or more businesses in a foreign country. These contacts can serve as important sources of secondary data. Even if these businesses have collected no data on their own, they could gather and communicate data available through other local sources such as those mentioned earlier.

U.S. Embassies The U.S. embassy (including the resources of other U.S. government agencies abroad, such as the Agency for International Development) may also provide secondary data on the country. Embassy personnel may have gathered information on a particular industry in a country in order to understand its impact on U.S. business at home (for example, the impact of the Japanese auto industry on U.S. automobile companies might be better understood with information from the U.S. embassy in Japan). Embassy appointees may be requested to be mindful of U.S. trade prospects for particular raw materials (for example, the U.S. embassy in Colombia would be aware of Colombian coffee bean trade). In addition, the embassy could lead the marketing researcher to other sources of secondary data in the country, such as trade associations or research institutes.

Problems with Foreign Secondary Data

Secondary data available in a foreign country suffer in comparison with similar information available from U.S. sources at home. The researcher must be aware of problems and deficiencies when interpreting information. The following brief summaries deal with some of the difficulties with the reliability of foreign secondary data.

The Underlying Purpose of Data Collection As mentioned earlier, the single most important source of marketing-related secondary data in a country is the government. The government as a political institution may not approach data collection with the same objectivity as a business researcher. This problem is particularly severe in developing countries where governments may enhance the information content in order to paint a rosy picture of economic life in the country. In this way, political considerations overshadow the reliability of the data.

It is worth noting that the United States as a society is more open than other countries. No matter how embarrassing data may apppear to be for the government or the nation, the free flow of information is considered desirable. This, however, is not true elsewhere. It is not surprising, therefore, that the plight of the poor in the United States seems exaggerated when measured by standards of poverty in developing countries. The researcher must ascertain that the data available are accurate within the limits of its source and that there are no hidden assumptions that might distort the information from the researcher's point of view.

Currency of Information Information gathering is an expensive activity. When the government has limited resources, data gathering becomes a lower priority. Thus, information may not be gathered as frequently as desirable. The researcher needs to be very careful that the information available overseas has not become outdated. For an example close to home, in the U.S. a sensible decision about a housing project could not be made on the basis of 1960s' house prices.

Reliability of Data It was mentioned above that political considerations may affect the reliability of data. In addition, the reliability of data may be affected by data collection procedures. For example, the sample may not be random, so that the results cannot be assumed to reflect the behavior of the total population. Even when a good sampling plan has been laid out, it may not be properly adhered to (i.e., the interviewers might substitute subjects when those required by the sampling plan cannot be reached). In brief, numerous factors may affect the reliability of data.[19]

It may be difficult for the researchers to judge the reliability of secondary data available in a country, and it would be dysfunctional to try to test that reliability. If the researchers are indeed very concerned with reliability, they would be better off undertaking primary data gathering. Researchers should judge for themselves how far to accept the data on the basis of inputs from different contacts in the country about their own experiences with secondary data there.

Data Classification Another problem has to do with the classification scheme of the available data. In many countries data reported are too broadly classified for use at the micro level. For example, in Malaysia the category "construction equipment, machinery, and tools" includes large bulldozers as well as hand-operated drills. Thus, a company interested in manufacturing heavy construction machinery in Malaysia cannot get a clear idea about the current availability of such equipment in the country from the information given under such a category.

However, the problem of data classification is being solved. The international trading community has for years had to confront the lack of a standardized goods classification system for products being traded in the international marketplace. The use of diverse systems has complicated the preparation of documents, hampered the analysis of trade data, created uncertainty in the negotiation and interpretation of trade agreements, and slowed the movement of traded goods. But, as countries adopt the Harmonized Commodity Description and Coding System, information across countries will be similarly classified, eliminating many of the problems that arise from the use of a nonstandardized system. In the U.S. the Harmonized System (HS) was adopted on January 1, 1988, requiring all U.S. exporters and importers to conform to the revised classification.

The Harmonized Commodity Description and Coding System is an international goods classification system designed to standardize commodity classification for all major trading nations. The system assigns all products a six-digit code, which would be used by all countries for both imported and exported goods. The HS was developed under the auspices of the Customs Cooperation Council (CCC) in Brussels, Belgium, and is based on the Customs Cooperation Council Nomenclature (CCCN), formerly known as the Brussels Tariff Nomenclature (BTN). It is more detailed and contains many new subdivisions to reflect changes in technology, trade patterns, and user requirements.

The Harmonized System replaces the Tariff Schedules of the United States Annotated (TSUSA) and Schedule B. The U.S. import and export schedules under the HS will be nearly identical and completely compatible. The only differences will occur with regard to level of detail; in some areas, such as textiles, the import schedule will need to be subdivided in much finer detail than is necessary for exports. In addition, both the U.S. import and export schedules will be identical through the first six digits with those of trading partners adopting the Harmonized System. Under the current system, a product may be given one code when it is imported, a separate code when it is exported, and various other codes in foreign countries. If the Harmonized System were applied on a worldwide basis, any single product would share a common six-digit base code. National subdivisions beyond the six-digit level are possible for tariff and statistical purposes.

The system will also provide U.S. exporters with information concerning the tariff classification of their goods in other countries as well as a procedure for bringing goods classification disputes before an international customs council.

Use of a common system would accelerate the movement of goods and their associated paperwork. International traders would no longer have to redescribe and recode goods as they move through the international marketplace. All this elimination of the above-mentioned obstacles would save time and money.

The Harmonized System consists of 5,019 four-digit headings and subheadings. Developing countries will be able, under certain circumstances, to adopt the system at the four-digit level; developed countries, however, must use all six digits. The first two digits represent the chapter in which the goods are found, the next two digits represent the place within the chapter where the goods are described, and the next two digits represent the international subdivisions within the heading. The United States will further subdivide the 5,019 six-digit international headings and subheadings into approximately 8,800 eight-digit rate lines, or classification lines, and into approximately 12,000 ten-digit statistical reporting numbers. This represents an increase in rate lines of about 1,500 and a decrease of about 2,000 in the statistical reporting numbers from the present system.

Comparability of Data Multinational corporate executives often like to compare information on their host countries about such matters as review of market performance, strategy effectiveness in different environments, and so on. Unfortunately, the secondary data obtainable from different countries are not readily comparable. Keegan reports, for example, that in Germany purchases of televisions are considered expenditures for recreation and entertainment, while in the U.S. television purchases are in the category of furniture, furnishing, and household equipment.[20] These discrepancies make brand share comparison nearly impossible.

Availability of Data Finally, in many developing nations, secondary data are very scarce. Information on retail and wholesale trade is especially difficult to obtain. In such cases primary data collection becomes vital.

Primary Data Collection

An alternative to secondary data is primary data collection. Primary data presumably provide more relevant information because they are collected specifically for the purpose in mind. However, the collection of primary data is an expensive proposition in terms of both money and time. Thus, the underlying purpose must justify the effort. For example, when a company has to make a decision about appointing a dealer for the occasional sale of its product in a developing country, it is not necessary to have primary data on the long-term market potential. On the other hand, if the company is considering the establishment of a manufacturing plant in the country, it may be important to undertake a market potential study.

Problems of Primary Data Collection

Primary data collection in a foreign environment poses a variety of problems not encountered in the United States.[21] These problems are related to social and cultural factors and the level of economic development, and can be grouped under three headings: (1) sampling problems, (2) questionnaire problems, and (3) the problem of nonresponse.

Sampling Problems A good piece of research should reflect the perspectives of the entire population. This is feasible, however, only when the sample is randomly drawn (see International Marketing Highlight 10.5). Unfortunately in many countries it is difficult to get completely representative information on the socioeconomic characteristics of the population because such information is lacking or, at best, is inadequate. Most samples in the end are biased. Cateora adds:

International Marketing Highlight 10.5

Who Drinks More Wine?

According to a recent study, the Italians drink the most wine of any country—about 116 liters per capita a year, compared with seventy-seven for the French and just over nine for the British. But another study disagrees. It gives the French first place in the wine-drinking competition, finding that annual per capita intake in France is seventy liters and that the Italians drink only sixty-two liters a year. (The difference may well be in the way the population is defined or the way the questions were asked.)

No matter what the reason, the study by the French Inter-Professional Office of Wine (ONIVINS) says that the French have cut their wine consumption. More than half of the 12,400 people interviewed in this study said they abstain from drinking wine.

In 1980, according to ONIVINS, nearly one-third of the French drank wine daily, compared with only 18 percent this year. Families spend less time together and eat together less often, forcing wine to take a back seat to other options such as mineral water and soft drinks. The ONIVINS study also found that the French are choosing to drink higher-quality wine, when they choose to drink wine.

Source: The European, August 10–12, 1990.

> In many countries, telephone directories, cross-index street directories, census tract and block data, and detailed social and economic characteristics of the universe are not available on a current basis, if at all. The researcher then has to estimate characteristics and population parameters, sometimes with little basic data on which to build an accurate estimate. To add to the confusion, in some cities in South America, Mexico, and Asia, street maps are unavailable; and in some large metropolitan areas of the Near East and Asia, streets are not identified nor houses numbered.[22]

Limitations aside, directories are available to help the international marketing researcher draw an adequate sample, especially in the industrial marketing area. *Boltin International,* for example, provides names and addresses of more than 300,000 firms in 100 countries, under 1,000 product classifications, by trade and by country.[23] Another source is *Kelly's Manufacturers and Merchants Directory,* which lists firms in the United States and other major trading countries in the world.[24]

Even if a workable random sample is drawn, inadequate means of transportation may prevent interviewing people as planned. For example, in developing countries, many areas, especially rural ones, are quite inaccessible. Thus, data gathering may have to be confined to urban areas. Further, only a small percentage of the population may have telephones. The World Bank statistics indicate, for example, that there are only four telephones per thousand population in Egypt, six in Turkey, and thirty-two in Argentina. In many countries the postal system is so inefficient that letters may not be delivered at all or may reach the addressee only after a long delay. In Brazil, for example, an estimated 30 percent of the domestic mail is never delivered.[25] In brief, it may be extremely difficult to obtain a proper random sample, especially in developing countries.

Questionnaire Problems In many countries different languages are spoken in different areas. Thus, the questionnaire has to be in different languages for use within the same country. In India, for example, fourteen official languages are spoken in different parts of the country, while most government and business affairs are conducted in English. Similarly, in Switzerland, German is used in some areas and French in others. In the Republic of Congo, the official language is French, but only a small part of the population is fluent in French. Unfortunately, translating a questionnaire from one language to another is far from easy. In the translating process many points are entirely eclipsed, because many idioms, phrases, and statements mean different things in different cultures. A Danish executive observed:

> Check this out by having a different translator put back into English what you've translated from the English. You'll get the shock of your life. I remember "out of sight, out of mind" had become "invisible things are insane."[26]

This translation problem may be partially averted with the help of computers; however, experience with computers shows that they cannot fathom the subtleties of language.[27]

Problem of Nonresponse Even if the interviewee is successfully reached, there is no guarantee that he or she will cooperate and furnish the desired information. There are many reasons for nonresponse. First, cultural habits in many countries virtually prohibit communication with a stranger, particularly for women. For example, a researcher simply may not be able to speak on the phone with a housewife in an Islamic country to find out what she thinks of a particular brand. Second, in many societies such matters as preferences for hygenic products and food products are too personal to be shared with an outsider. In many Latin American countries, a woman may feel ashamed to talk with a researcher about her choice of a brand of sanitary pad, hair shampoo, or perfume. Third, respondents in many cases may be unwilling to share their true feelings with interviewers because they suspect the interviewers may be agents of the government, for example, seeking information for imposition of additional taxes. Fourth, middle-class people, in developing countries in particular, are reluctant to accept their status and may take false claims in order to reflect the lifestyle of wealthier people. For example, in a study on the consumption of tea in India, over 70 percent of the respondents from middle-income families claimed they used one of the several national brands of tea. This finding could not be substantiated since over 60 percent of the tea sold nationally in India is unbranded, generic tea sold unpackaged. Fifth, many respondents, willing to cooperate, may be illiterate, so that even oral communication may be difficult. In other words, their exposure to the modern world may be so limited and their outlook so narrow that the researchers would find it extremely difficult to elicit adequate responses from them. Sixth, in many countries, privacy is becoming a big issue. In Japan, for example, the middle class is showing increasing concern about the protection of personal information. Information that people are most anxious to protect includes income, assets, tax payments, family life, and political and religious affiliation.[28] Finally, the lack of established marketing research firms in many countries may force the researcher to count on ad hoc help for gathering data. How far such temporary help may be counted on to complete a job systematically can only be guessed.

Resolving the Problems

There are no foolproof methods to take care of all the problems discussed above. The following suggestions, however, may help to eliminate some of the problems.[29]

The international marketing research effort should be undertaken in conjunction with a reputable local firm. Such a firm may be a foreign office of a U.S. advertising firm like J. Walter Thompson, a U.S. accounting firm like Price Waterhouse, or a locally owned firm belonging to a third country like a Japanese advertising agency in Italy. The resources of the cooperating firm will be invaluable; for example, its knowledge of local customs, including things like the feasibility of interviewing housewives while husbands are at work; its familiarity with the local environment, including modes of transportation available for personal interviews in smaller towns; and its contact in different parts of the country as sources for drawing a sample.

From the beginning, a person fully conversant with both sound marketing research procedures and the local culture should be involved in all phases of the research design. Such a person can recommend the number of languages the questionnaire should be printed in and what sort of cultural traits, habits, customs, and rituals to keep in mind in different phases of the research. Such a person may be a U.S.-educated marketer or a person with good business education or experience, preferably in marketing.

The questionnaire may first be written in English, and then a native fluent in English can translate it into the local language(s). A third person should retranslate it into English. This retranslated version can then be compared with the original English version. The three people involved should work together to eliminate differences in the three versions of the questionnaire by changing phrases, idioms, and words. Ultimately, the questionnaire in the local language should accurately reflect the questions in the original English questionnaire.

If feasible, the persons hired to conduct the interviews should have prior experience. The local cooperating firm discussed earlier may be helpful here. In any event, complete instructions and training should be given before work starts. As a matter of fact, the conducting of interviews should be practiced. Ways to ensure that the interviewers follow the instructions must be found for proper sampling control. For example, the researcher might accompany the interviewer sporadically.

Finally, the researcher should draw the best possible sample. If the sample is not random, the researcher should employ appropriate statistical techniques in analyzing the collected information so that the results reflect the reality of the situation.

Organization for International Marketing Research

International marketing research can be carried out both at the headquarters in the United States and in the host country. Marketing research at the headquarters is useful in two areas: short-term planning and budgeting, and strategy formulation. For example, yearly forecasts of sales for different products in different countries will be a part of the annual budget. But a study undertaken to determine if a new product successfully sold in the United States should be introduced in international markets would have a strategy focus.

Marketing research studies in host countries are concerned mainly with day-to-day operations, tactics to achieve designated goals, and short-term marketing planning. For example, a study may examine the factors responsible for poor sales performance in the previous quarter. Similarly, marketing research may be undertaken to decide if a concentrated six- or ten-week advertising campaign is preferable to spreading advertising over the whole year. Naturally, sales forecasting will be done to develop budgets. As mentioned above, the headquarters may also make sales forecasts. Thus, for discussion of annual plans and budgets, the host country manager would use his or her forecasts as the basis for resource allocation, while the headquarters' people use their forecasts to negotiate and approve the country budgets.

Marketing research is unquestionably an important function that must be conducted both at the headquarters and in the host countries. The persons to take charge at the two different locations would vary from company to company. For example, at NCR a staff assistant reporting to the vice president of international marketing is responsible for marketing research at the corporate headquarters. The marketing research function for NCR in host countries is performed at different levels according to the importance of each country to the parent company. In Japan, in the United Kingdom, and in Germany, NCR has large marketing research departments simply because the company is extremely active in these markets. On the other hand, in a country like Pakistan where NCR commitment is meager, marketing research study might be assigned to an outside consultant.

In addition to undertaking marketing research at the corporate level and in the host countries, in many companies marketing research may also be conducted at the regional level. A company may divide its international operations into regions; for example, Western Europe, Far East, Latin America, Middle East, Africa, and Southeast Asia. Each country manager in a region would report to the regional executive. Under such arrangements the regional executive may seek marketing research information to formulate regional marketing strategy or to develop the marketing perspective of a country within the region. There may be a specific person responsible for marketing research in the region, or one of the staff persons may carry this responsibility.

What is important to recognize is that marketing information is important at all levels. However, the process of gathering, analyzing, and reporting market-related information may not necessarily be called marketing research. Further, marketing research responsibility may not necessarily be assigned to a marketing person. Of course, the extent of marketing research that a company undertakes would vary according to the style of management and the importance of a particular foreign country for a given product.

International Marketing Information System

Earlier in this chapter, three terms were introduced: *market research, marketing research,* and *marketing intelligence.* An international marketing information system is a formal way of structuring the information flow through these three modes. Large, complex organizations may do business in a great number of countries with any number of products and services. This complexity combined with today's difficult and demanding business environment makes it particularly important for international marketers to have adequate and timely information available in order to make the right moves.

The following mishap illustrates the critical need for information:

> "I never dreamed this would happen to us," exclaimed the chairman of the American drug firm G.D. Searle & Co. (sales over $600 million) in an interview published in *Business Week.* The company was apparently unaware that it would be investigated by a Senate subcommittee on health involving charges that the company mishandled research data on two of its best selling products. It is obvious that this company—like many others—did not have an adequate "early warning" capability or intelligence system which could have enabled management to anticipate the crisis. One result of the threat: a corporate committee of social scientists was established to study economic and political trends and their potential effect on the company.
>
> Another recent example of an intelligence mishap involved Westinghouse Corporation's agreement to sell utility companies 80 million pounds of uranium at an average contracted price of $10 a pound over a period of twenty years. At the time the agreement was signed, Westinghouse owned only about twenty percent of the contracted amount of uranium. Since then, its price rose to $40 and if the company would have fulfilled the terms of the agreement it could have lost about $2 billion. Obviously top management were unaware that such an agreement was being negotiated, an intelligence failure concerning internal operations.[30]

Steps for Establishing an Information System

Figure 10.2 shows the essential steps for developing and maintaining an international marketing information system. As indicated in Figure 10.2, five essential components must be considered: determining information needs, identifying information sources, gathering information, analyzing information, and disseminating information. Information will be needed at corporate headquarters, regional offices, and country locations. Another way of looking at information needs is to differentiate between strategic and operational information. Still another way of categorizing information is suggested by Keegan (see Table 10.2).

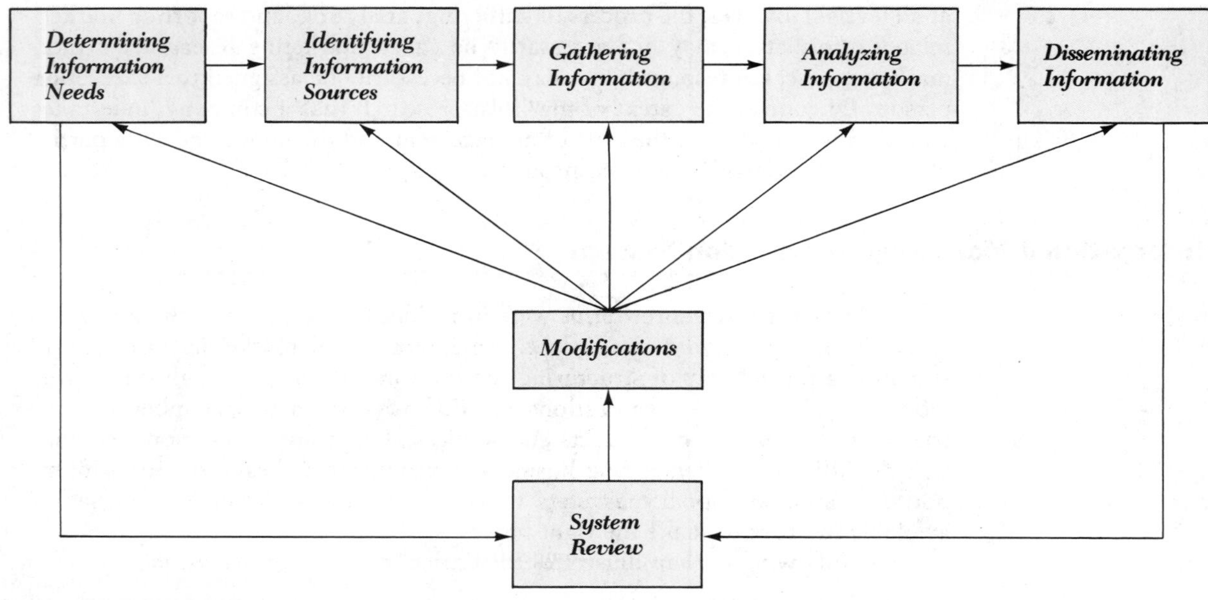

FIGURE 10.2 Components of an International Marketing Information System

Following his framework, the information may be grouped into six broad areas with thirty-one categories.

It is difficult to suggest a general framework for classifying the information needs of all or any particular companies. Every company should work out its own information categories, which may be based on one scheme or another. Which kind a company will establish is influenced by the marketing information needs of the company and the attitude of top management toward systematic information management. Whatever the ultimate system is—highly structured and/or computerized or primitive, unstructured, and manual—it must meet in sophistication and range the anticipated information needs it will be called on to supply.

Aspects of System Use

The information sources may be internal and external. Both internal and external sources may be further divided between international and domestic sources. Another way of classifying sources of information is to distinguish between secondary and primary sources. And the information may be gathered in various ways—by mail, by telephone, or via computer terminal through remote entry. Some information may be gathered regularly, and some may be collected on an ad hoc basis. Also, information may be gathered in a structured fashion or simply in an open-ended fashion. In gathering information, duplication should be avoided, as it is wasteful in most cases to gather the same information from different sources. In certain cases, though, duplication can be used as a control device. Next, the gathered information must be analyzed for use in the most

TABLE 10.2 Thirty-One Categories for a Global Business Intelligence System

CATEGORY	COVERAGE
	I. Market Information
1. Market potential	Information indicating potential demand for products, including the status and prospects of existing company products in existing markets
2. Consumer/customer attitudes and behavior	Information and attitudes, behavior, and needs of consumers and customers of existing and potential company products. Also included in this category are attitudes of investors toward a company's investment merit
3. Channels of distribution	Availability, effectiveness, attitudes, and preferences of channel agents
4. Communications media	Media availability, effectiveness, and cost
5. Market sources	Availability, quality, and cost
6. New products	Nontechnical information concerning new products for a company (this includes products that are already marketed by other companies)
	II. Competitive Information
7. Competitive business strategy and plans	Goals, objectives. Definition of business; the "design" and rationale of the company
8. Competitive functional strategies, plans, and programs	Marketing: Target markets, product, price, place, promotion. Strategy and plan: finance, manufacturing, R&D, and human resources
9. Competitive operations	Detailed intelligence on competitor operations. Production, shipments, employee transfers, morale, etc.
	III. Foreign Exchange
10. Balance of payments	Government reports
11. Nominal and real interest rates	Expert estimation
12. Inflation rate compared to weighted trading partner average	PPP theory
13. Estimate of international competitiveness	Expert judgment
14. Attractiveness of country currency and assets to global investors	Currency demand
15. Government policy re: country competitiveness	Expert assessment
16. Country monetary and fiscal policy	Expert assessment
17. Spot and forward market activity	Market reports
18. Expectations and opinions of analysts, traders, bankers, economists, business people	General assessment

(continued)

TABLE 10.2 (*Continued*)

CATEGORY	COVERAGE
	IV. Prescriptive Information
19. Foreign taxes	Information concerning decisions, intentions, and attitudes of foreign authorities regarding taxes upon earnings, dividends, and interest
20. Other foreign prescriptions and laws	All information concerning local, regional, or international authority guidelines, rulings, laws, decrees other than foreign exchange and tax matters affecting the operations, assets, or investments of a company
21. Home country prescriptions	Home country incentives, controls, regulations, restraints, etc., affecting a company
	V. Resource Information
22. Human resources	Availability of individuals and groups, employment candidates, sources, strikes, etc.
23. Money	Availability and cost of money for company uses
24. Raw material	Availability and cost
25. Acquisitions and mergers	Leads or other information concerning potential acquisitions, mergers, or joint ventures
	VI. General Conditions
26. Economic factors	Macroeconomic information dealing with broad factors, such as capital movements, rates of growth, economic structure, and economic geography
27. Social factors	Social structure of society, customs, attitudes, and preferences
28. Political factors	"Investment climate," meaning of elections, political change
29. Scientific/technological factors	Major developments and trends
30. Management and administrative practices	Management and administrative practices and procedures concerning such matters as employee compensation, report procedure
31. Other information	Information not assignable to another category

Source: Warren J. Keegan, *Global Marketing Management,* 4th ed. (Englewood Cliffs, NJ: Prentice-Hall, Inc., 1989), pp. 226–227.

convenient form. Finally, the information needs to be disseminated to all designated users. Some information may be made widely available to all managers and those above them. Other information may be restricted for senior people in the organization. Information may be disseminated on a regular basis or irregularly. Still other information may be available only on request.

The system design should be reviewed from time to time to ensure it still meets the demands placed on it. The review should also evaluate the cost–benefit relationship of the entire system. The review may recommend modifications in any one or more of the system components.[31]

Most large multimarket, multiproduct companies have some sort of multinational marketing information system in operation. It is difficult to say, however, how many of these systems can be labeled "sophisticated" or "advanced." But the increasing popularity of the international data networks made available by such companies as Control Data Corporation, Data Research Inc., and General Electric Company indicates that companies are moving toward the establishment of computerized information systems.[32] These systems may serve information needs of marketing and of other functional areas of the business as well in the following manner:[33]

1. To aid in decisions relating to international market expansion, for example, whether new countries are potential candidates for market entry or existing products might be carried into new markets
2. To monitor performance in different countries and product markets based on criteria such as return on investment and market share, so as to diagnose where existing or potential future problems appear to be emerging and, hence, where there is a need to adapt current marketing tactics or strategies
3. To scan the international environment in order to assess future world and country scenarios and to monitor emerging and changing environmental trends
4. To assess strategies with regard to the allocation of corporate resources and effort across different countries, product markets, target segments, and modes of entry to determine whether changes in this allocation would maximize long-run profitability.

Summary

The techniques and tools of international marketing research do not vary according to whether research is done in the United States or abroad. An international marketing research project essentially follows domestic procedures: problem definition, research design, data collection, analysis, and report preparation. However, several factors make international marketing research more challenging and more difficult.

The two sources of data are secondary data and primary data. Secondary data may be gathered either in the United States or abroad. There are a variety of sources of information from which secondary information may be gathered at home; foremost among them is the U.S. Department of Commerce. Secondary information available in host countries may be plagued by problems of timeliness, reliability, and comparability. But the collection of primary data abroad also poses difficulties, such as inability to draw a random sample, unwillingness of the sample population to cooperate, and inability to develop an adequate questionnaire.

Despite the inherent problems, a researcher can adopt measures to solve some, if not all, of the difficulties involved. Two helpful measures are the involvement of U.S. talent in data collection and cooperation with respectable foreign marketing information sources.

The international research activity may be formally organized at home or in the host country, or at both locations. Further, the marketing research organization may be just a one-person department or a large entity in accordance with the scope of marketing activity in a country. A company deeply involved in business around the globe should establish an international marketing information system with formal structuring to determine information needs, to identify information sources, and to gather, analyze, and disseminate information.

Review Questions

1. What factors make the conducting of international marketing research more difficult than domestic marketing research?
2. What are the principal sources of secondary data in the United States?
3. What difficulties are associated with secondary data on marketing in host countries?
4. Discuss the problems a researcher may face in primary data collection overseas.
5. What factors account for the unreliability of secondary data in foreign countries?
6. What steps may be taken to resolve the problems of primary data collection in the developing countries?
7. What kind of companies should consider developing an international marketing information system?
8. What help can be expected from international agencies in the search for secondary data?

Endnotes

1. "Third World Research Is Difficult, But It Is Possible," *Marketing News,* August 29, 1987, p. 50.
2. *See* Kjell Gronhaug and John Graham, "International Marketing Research Revisited," in S. Tamer Cavusgil, ed., *Advances in International Marketing* (Greenwich, CT: Jai Press, Inc., 1987), pp. 121–138.
3. Charles F. Keown, "Foreign Mail Surveys: Response Rates Using Monetary Incentives," *Journal of International Business Studies,* Fall 1985, p. 153. *Also see* Robert J. Hoover, Robert T. Green, and Joel Saergert, "A Cross-National Study of Perceived Risk," *Journal of Marketing,* July 1978, pp. 107–108.
4. Susan P. Douglas and C. Samuel Craig, *International Marketing Research* (Englewood Cliffs, NJ: Prentice-Hall, Inc., 1983), p. 16.
5. *European Market Survey* (Pleasantville, NY: Reader's Digest Association, 1963).
6. Paul H. Berent, "International Research Is Different: The Case for Centralized Control," in *International Marketing Research: Does It Provide What the User Needs?* (Amsterdam: European Society for Opinion and Marketing Research, 1976), pp. 110–111.
7. Charles S. Mayer, "The Lessons of Multinational Marketing Research," *Business Horizons,* December 1978, p. 9.
8. Essam Mahmoud and Gillian Rice, "Use of Analytical Techniques in International Marketing," *International Marketing Review,* Autumn 1988, pp. 7–14. *Also see* David R. Wheeler, "Content Analysis: An Analytical

Technique for International Marketing Research," *International Marketing Review,* Winter 1988, pp. 34–40.

9. Charles S. Mayer, "The Lessons of Multinational Marketing Research," *Business Horizons,* December 1978, p. 10.
10. *See* S. Tamer Cavusgil, "Qualitative Insights into Company Experiences in International Marketing Research," in V. H. Kirpalani, ed., *Changing Currents in International Marketing* (Chicago: American Marketing Association, 1984).
11. *See* Van R. Wood and Jerry R. Goolsby, "Foreign Market Information Preferences of Established U.S. Exporters," *International Marketing Review,* Winter 1987, pp. 43–52.
12. *See* Johny K. Johansson and Ikujiro Nonaka, "Market Research the Japanese Way," *Harvard Business Review,* May–June 1987, p. 16.
13. *See Statistical Yearbook of the United Nations* (New York: United Nations, an annual publication).
14. *See World Development Report* (Washington, D.C.: World Bank, an annual publication).
15. *See International Financial Statistics* (Washington, D.C.: International Monetary Fund, an annual publication).
16. *See Business America* (Washington: D.C.: U.S. Government Printing Office, a biweekly publication).
17. *See* Leonard M. Field, "How to Gather Foreign Intelligence Without Leaving Home," *Marketing News,* January 4, 1988, p. 24.
18. "Product Pick-Up Firm Samples International Supermarkets," *Marketing News,* March 1, 1985, p. 10.
19. *See* Ravi Parameswaran and Attila Yaprak, "A Cross-National Comparison of Consumer Research Measures," *Journal of International Business Studies,* Spring 1987, pp. 35–50.
20. Warren J. Keegan, *Multinational Marketing Management,* 3rd ed. (Englewood Cliffs, NJ: Prentice-Hall, 1984), p. 224.
21. *See* Erdener Kaynak, "Difficulties of Undertaking Marketing Research in the Developing Countries," *European Research,* November 1978, pp. 251–259. *Also see* Mary Goodyear, "Qualitative Research in Developing Countries," *Journal of the Marketing Research Society,* vol. 24, no. 2 (1982), pp. 80–96.
22. Philip R. Cateora, *International Marketing,* 5th ed. (Homewood, IL: Irwin, 1983), pp. 267–268.
23. *Boltin International* (Los Angeles, CA: Boltin International, an annual publication).
24. *Kelly's Manufacturers and Merchants Directory* (New York: Kelly's Directories Ltd., an annual publication).
25. Susan P. Douglas and C. Samuel Craig, *International Marketing Research* (Englewood Cliffs, NJ: Prentice-Hall, Inc., 1983), p. 224. *Also see* David Jobber and John Saunders, "An Experimental Investigation into Cross-National Mail Survey Response Rates," *Journal of International Business Studies,* Fall 1988, pp. 483–490.
26. Ferdinand F. Mauser, "Losing Something in Translation," *Harvard Business Review,* July–August 1977, p. 14.
27. J. Terence Gallagher, "A Problem of Translation," *The Asian Wall Street Journal Weekly,* September 30, 1985, p. 11c.
28. "Japanese Grow Anxious to Protect Their Privacy," *The Asian Wall Street Journal Weekly,* November 11, 1985, p. 23. *Also see* Naresh K. Malhotra, "Administration of Questionnaires for Collecting Quantitative Data in International Marketing Research," *Journal of Global Marketing,* vol. 4, no. 2 (1991), pp. 63–92.
29. *See* John Monaco, "Overcoming the Obstacles to International Research," *Marketing News,* October 24, 1986, p. 22.
30. E.D. Jaffee, "Multinational Marketing Intelligence: An Information Requirements Model," *Management International Review,* vol. 19, no. 2 (1979), pp. 53–60.
31. Benjamin Gilad, "The Role of Organized Competitive Intelligence in Corporate Strategy," *Columbia Journal of World Business,* Winter 1989, pp. 29–36.
32. William R. King, "Information, Technology, and Corporate Growth," *Columbia Journal of World Business,* Summer 1985, pp. 29–34. *Also see* Uma Sekaran, "Methodological and Theoretical Issues and Advancements in Cross-Cultural Research," *Journal of International Business Studies,* Fall 1983, pp. 61–74.
33. Susan P. Douglas and C. Samuel Craig, *International Marketing Research* (Englewood Cliffs, NJ: Prentice-Hall, Inc., 1983), pp. 278–279.

APPENDIX

Sources of Secondary Data

The following represents selected sources of information for international marketing purposes.

A. Information Available from International Agencies

1. *The United Nations.* United Nations publications can be obtained from:

   United Nations Publications
   Sales Office
   New York, NY 10017

   a. *Statistical Yearbook of the United Nations* (annual)

      The *Statistical Yearbook* is a major source of world economic data. It includes information on population, manpower, agriculture, manufacturing, mining, construction, trade, transport, communications, balance of payments, consumption, wages and prices, national accounts, finance, international capital flows, housing, health, education, and mass communications.

   b. *Economic Survey of Europe* (annual)

      Review of current developments in the European economy. *Economic Bulletin for Europe,* issued twice annually, supplements the *Survey.*

   c. *Economic Survey of Asia and the Far East* (annual)

      Review of current situation concerning agriculture, industry, transport, trade, and balance of payments. *Economic Bulletin for Asia and the Far East,* issued three times annually, supplements the *Survey.*

   d. *Economic Survey of Latin America* (annual)

      Review of regional economic developments. *Economic Bulletin for Latin America,* issued twice annually, supplements the *Survey.*

   e. *Economic Developments in the Middle East* (annual)

      Review of developments concerning agriculture, industry, petroleum, foreign trade, and balance of payments.

   f. *World Economic Survey* (annual)

      World economic report. A comprehensive review of world economic trends and issues.

g. *World Trade Annual*

Information from the twenty-four principal trading countries of the world, providing statistics of trade by commodity and country.

h. GATT publications (available from UN Publications Sales Office)

i. Analytical Bibliography—Market surveys by products and by countries

ii. *Guide to Sources of Information on Foreign Trade Regulations*

iii. Compilation of Basic Information on Export Markets

iv. *Compendium of Sources: International Trade Statistics*

v. *Manual on Export Marketing Research for Developing Countries*

vi. *World Directory of Industry and Trade Associations*

vii. *Directory of Product and Industry Journals*

2. *Organization for Economic Cooperation and Development.* OECD publications can be obtained from:

OECD Publications Office, Suite 1305
1750 Pennsylvania Avenue, N.W.
Washington, D.C. 20006

a. OECD Economic Surveys

Each title in this series of economic studies is a booklet published annually by the Organization for Economic Cooperation and Development pertaining to one of the twenty-one OECD member countries. Each booklet has information concerning recent trends of demand and output, prices and wages, foreign trade and payments, economic policy, and prospects and conclusions.

b. *OECD Economic Outlook* (semiannual)

A survey of economic trends and prospects in OECD countries. The survey examines the current situation and prospects regarding demand and output, employment, costs and prices, and foreign trade for OECD as a whole and in some of the major countries. Trends of current balances, monetary developments, and capital movements as factors affecting international monetary developments are also considered.

c. *Monthly Statistics of Foreign Trade*

This bulletin is intended to serve as a timely source of statistical data on the foreign trade by OECD member countries. The data cover not only overall trade by countries, but also a number of seasonally adjusted series, volume and average value indices, and trade by SITC sections.

3. *International Monetary Fund (IMF).* IMF publications can be obtained from:

International Monetary Fund
Washington, D.C. 20431

a. *International Financial Statistics* (monthly)

Statistical information on such financial matters as international liquidity, interest rates, prices, and money supply.

4. *The World Bank.* World Bank publications can be obtained from:

The World Bank
1818 H Street, N.W.
Washington, D.C. 20433

a. *World Bank: Annual Report* (annual)
b. *World Development Report* (annual)
   Reviews economy, assesses the impact of external factors on development, and considers future scenarios.
c. *World Tables* (annual)
   Presents annual data for most of the Bank's members in a four-page table for each economy.
d. *Publications Update* (monthly)
   Lists various research publications of the Bank. For example, *see* William W. Ambrose, Paul R. Hennemeyer, and Jean-Paul Chapon, *Privatizing Telecommunications Systems: Business Opportunities in Developing Countries,* 1990.

5. *International Chamber of Commerce.* ICC publications can be purchased at the following address:

The ICC Publishing Corporation, Inc.
801 Second Avenue, Suite 1204
New York, NY 10017

a. *ICC/E.S.O.M.A.R. International Code of Marketing and Social Research practice*
   This code provides individuals and organizations with a basic set of rules so that marketing and opinion research can be conducted in accordance with accepted principles of integrity and fair competition.
b. *International Code of Direct Mail and Mail Order Sales Practice*
c. *International Uniform Definitions for the Distributive Trade*
   A list of current definitions that permit international comparison of types of establishments, outlets, and selling methods.
d. *Marketing: Discipline for Freedom*
e. *Media Information for Advertising Planning*
f. *Advertising Agencies: Their Services and Relationship with Advertisers and Media*

B. Information Available from U.S. Government Sources

1. *U.S. Department of Commerce.* The following publications (a–n) can be purchased by writing to:

The Superintendent of Documents		Publications Sales Branch
U.S. Government Printing Office	or:	Room 1617
Washington, D.C. 20402		U.S. Dept. of Commerce
		Washington, D.C. 10130

a. *A Basic Guide to Exporting*
   Provides step-by-step approach to exporting. It is especially useful for firms with little or no export experience.
b. *Foreign Trade Report FT410* (monthly)

Provides a statistical record of shipments of all merchandise from the United States to some 100 countries.

c. *International Economic Indicators* (quarterly)

Lists trade trends for the United States and seven principal industrial countries.

d. *International Demographic Data* (updated periodically)

Details demographic profiles of developing countries and Eastern European economies.

e. *Market Share Reports* (annual)

Show U.S. participation in foreign markets during the last five years. Cover eighty-eight countries for 1,000 manufactured products.

f. Overseas Business Reports (yearly)

Some sixty percent of the reports are issued showing background data on both developed and developing countries.

g. *Foreign Economic Trends and Their Implications for the United States* (yearly)

Some 150 reports are issued giving country-by-country trade and economic statistics and trends.

h. Global Market Surveys

Market research studies conducted in selected countries for specific U.S. products.

i. Country Market Sectoral Surveys

Reports showing the most promising export opportunities for U.S. firms in selected countries.

j. Trade Lists

Provide names and addresses of potential buyers, distributors, and agents for different industries in selected countries.

k. *Business America* (biweekly)

Covers domestic and international news.

l. Country Studies

Each study classifies and analyzes the country's economic, military, political, and social systems and institutions, as well as the impact that cultural factors have on the country's lifestyle.

m. *European Trade Fairs: A Guide for Exporters*

Provides expert advice on participating in trade fairs.

n. *Custom Statistical Service for Exporters*

The service includes current data and market trends on thousands of products in more than 200 nations. Data are arranged by time frames from one month to five years, and by dollar and unit value, quantity, growth rate, and market-share percentages.

2. Other Government Sources

a. *Aids to Business* (Overseas Investment)

Explains how the Agency for International Development can assist U.S. firms interested in developing nations.

b. *Export Marketing for Smaller Firms*

Small Business Administration publication tells how smaller business firms can either expand their export trade or enter the export market.

c. *Export-Import Bank of the United States*

Describes U.S. export financing programs.

d. *Agricultural Economy and Trade*

Published by the U.S. Department of Agriculture. Describes overseas business opportunities in the agricultural sector.

C. Information Available from Commercial Publishers

1. Books

a. Bartels, Robert. *Global Development and Marketing.* Columbus, OH: Grid Inc., 1981.

b. Buzzell, Robert D., John A. Quelch, and Christopher Bartlett. *Global Marketing Management: Cases and Readings,* 2nd ed. Reading, MA: Addison-Wesley Publishing Co., 1992.

c. Cateora, Philip C. *International Marketing,* 7th ed. Homewood, IL: Richard D. Irwin, Inc., 1990.

d. Cundiff, Edward W., and Marye Tharp Hilger. *Marketing in the International Environment.* Englewood Cliffs, NJ: Prentice-Hall, Inc., 1984.

e. Czinkota, Michael R., and Ilkka A. Ronkainen. *International Marketing,* 2nd ed. Chicago: Dryden Press, 1990.

f. Douglas, Susan P., and C. Samuel Craig. *International Marketing Research.* Englewood Cliffs, NJ: Prentice-Hall, Inc., 1983.

g. Jain, Subhash C., and Lewis R. Tucker, Jr., eds. *International Marketing: Managerial Perspectives,* 2nd ed. Boston: Kent Publishing Co., 1986.

h. Jeannet, Jean-Pierre, and Hubert D. Hennessey. *International Marketing Management: Strategies and Cases.* Boston: Houghton Mifflin Co., 1988.

i. Kahler, Ruel. *International Marketing,* 5th ed. Cincinnati, OH: Southwestern Publishing Company, 1983.

j. Kaynak, Erdner. *Transnational Retailing.* Hawthorne, NY: Walder de Gruyter, Inc., 1988.

k. Keegan, Warren J. *Global Marketing Management,* 4th ed. Englewood Cliffs, NJ: Prentice-Hall, Inc., 1989.

l. Kirpalani, V. H. *International Marketing.* New York: Random House, Inc., 1984.

m. Peebles, Dean M., and John K. Ryans, Jr. *Management of International Advertising.* Newton, MA: Allyn & Bacon, Inc., 1984.

n. Robock, Stefan H., and Kenneth Simmonds. *International Business and Multinational Enterprises,* 4th ed. Homewood, IL: Richard D. Irwin, Inc., 1990.

o. Terpstra, Vern. *International Marketing,* 4th ed. Hinsdale, IL: Dryden Press, 1987.

p. Thorelli, Hans B., and Helmut Becker, eds. *International Marketing Strategy,* rev. ed. New York: Pergamon Press, 1982.
q. Vernon, Raymond, and Louis T. Wells, Jr. *Manager in the International Economy,* 5th ed. Englewood Cliffs, NJ: Prentice-Hall, Inc., 1986.

2. Reference Material
   a. *Business International Weekly Report.* New York: Business International Corporation, weekly issue. Reports important events of interest to managers of worldwide operations.
   b. Doing Business in . . . series. New York: Business International Corporation.
   c. *Encyclopedia of Geographic Information Sources.* Detroit: Gale Research, 1990.
   d. *European Markets: A Guide to Company and Industry Information Sources.* Washington, D.C.: Washington Researchers, 1989.
   e. *European Statistics: 1987–88* and *International Marketing Statistics: 1989–90.* Detroit: Gale Research. Designed for market planners and researchers, provides information on social, economic, and consumer trends in 140 countries.
   f. *International Marketing Data and Statistics* (annual). London: Euromonitor Publications, Ltd. Presents statistical information on all basic marketing parameters for over 100 countries.
   g. *Exporter's Encyclopedia* (annual). Import regulations and procedures required for shipping to every country in the world, as well as information on preparing export shipments. Lists world ports, steamship lines, airlines, government agencies, trade organizations. Special sections on packing, marine insurance, export terms, and many other areas of foreign trade. Price includes twice-monthly supplementary bulletins and newsletters. Available from Dun and Bradstreet International, P.O. Box 3224, Church Street Station, New York, NY 10008.
   h. *Multinational Business, Retail Business, Special Industry Reports.* New York: The Economist Intelligence Unit.
   i. *Predibrief.* Cleveland, OH: Predicasts. Industry news reports for thirty-five countries.
   j. *Reference Book for World Traders.* Loose-leaf handbook covering information necessary for planning exports to and imports from all foreign countries, as well as market research throughout the world. Kept up to date by monthly supplements. Available from Croner Publications, Inc., 211–213 Jamaica Avenue, Queens Village, NY 11428.
   k. *Sources of European Economic Information,* 4th ed. Cambridge, England: Gower Publishing Co., Ltd., 1989.
   l. *The World in Figures,* 5th ed. London: The Economist Newspaper Limited, 1990.
   m. *World Advertising Expenditures,* 1990 edition. New York: Starch INRA Hooper Group of Companies, 1991.

n. *Worldcasts.* Cleveland, OH: Predicasts. These are short-term and long-term economic forecasts in select industries for different countries.
o. *The Europa Year Book,* vol. 1 and vol. 2 (annual). London: Europa Publications, Ltd. An authoritative reference work providing a wealth of detailed information on the political, economic, and commercial institutions of the world.
p. *The Statesman's Year-Book* (annual). London: the Macmillan Press, Ltd. A statistical and historical annual of the states of the world.

3. Magazines and Newspapers

   The Wall Street Journal
   The New York Times
   Nihom Keizai Shimbun, Japan
   Financial Times, England
   Frankfurter Algemine, Germany
   Business Week
   Fortune
   Forbes
   The Asian Wall Street Journal Weekly

4. Service Organizations

   An important source of foreign market information are service organizations such as banks and consultants. Most large international banks have periodicals and special reports on international market developments.

CHAPTER • 11

Global Marketplace

CHAPTER FOCUS

After studying this chapter, you should be able to:

- Compare market opportunities in different parts of the world
- Discuss the dimensions of global markets
- Describe the forces behind market globalization
- Explain the rationale for segmenting the international market
- Evaluate different criteria for grouping countries

The World Bank lists 124 countries. It is difficult to imagine that a marketer would be interested in serving the entire global market. Granted, some companies such as Kodak and Coca-Cola are active in over 100 countries. But such a vast coverage of market develops gradually. Initially a company may enter just one country or a few countries. From there on the scope may broaden as the company brings other countries within its fold.

Obviously, the company must choose among the countries of the world in order to identify its target markets. Worldwide there is great contrast economically, culturally, and politically among nations. These contrasts mean that an overseas marketer cannot select target countries randomly, but must employ workable criteria to analyze the world market and choose those countries where the company's product/service has the best opportunity for success. While individual countries have peculiarities, they also have similarities that they share with other countries, and such bases render some grouping device feasible.

But what are the characteristics of that global marketplace, the international market? What is the rationale for grouping countries into segments? What procedure would a company employ to segment the international market? How can in-country segmentation be achieved?

Global Market

The most basic information needed to appraise global markets concerns population, because the people, of course, constitute the market. The population of the world reached an estimated 5.3 billion in 1990. According to the latest estimates from the Population Division of the United Nations, this total is expected to increase to 6.2 billion by 2000 and to almost 8.5 billion by 2025. Current world population is growing at about 1.7 percent per year. This is a slight decline from the peak rate of 1.9 percent, but the absolute number of people being added to the world's population each year is still increasing. This figure is expected to peak in the mid-1990s at about 90 million additional people per year (see International Marketing Highlight 11.1).

Population growth rates vary significantly by region. Europe has the lowest rate of population growth at only about 0.3 percent per year. Several European countries are experiencing declining populations, including Austria, Denmark, Germany, Luxembourg, and Sweden. Growth rates are also below 1 percent per year in North America.

The regions with the highest population growth rates are Africa (3 percent per year), Latin America (2 percent per year), and South Asia (1.9 percent per year). China, the world's most populous country, is growing at only about 1.2 percent per year. Even so, that rate means that China's population increases by over 12 million people each year. The world's second-largest country, India, is growing at over 1.7 percent per year. It is expected to grow from 850 million today to the 1 billion mark by about 2003.

One striking aspect of population growth in the developing countries is the rapid rate of urbanization. The urban population is growing at less than 1 per-

International Marketing Highlight 11.1

Babies Are Our Only Customers Worldwide

Gerber Products Co. is going global with a host of child-care products in an effort to break out of its mild-mannered, domestic baby-food niche.

The company has been fine-tuning its "superbranding" campaign for years. It feels it has developed a real following among mothers, and it is going to utilize its brand name to market products in three different categories: food and formula, baby-care products, and clothing.

Market research shows that moms around the globe recognize and trust the Gerber logo. The company's baby food already is sold in Mexico, Puerto Rico, Europe, and the Far East. Sales have expanded into Poland, Egypt, Russia, and Eastern Europe.

However, internationally the company is an infant. About 95 percent of the babies born in the world are born outside the United States. Yet right now, international sales account for only about 5 percent of the company's total sales.

Gerber will introduce the baby-food lines in new international markets first, then follow with baby-care products and apparel.

Source: Marketing News, September 16, 1991, p. 22.

cent in Europe and North America, but it is growing at almost 3.5 percent in the developing world. Today thirteen of the twenty largest urban agglomerations are in the developing world. By 2000, seventeen of the twenty largest cities will be in the developing world. The only developed-country cities in the top twenty will be Tokyo, New York, and Los Angeles. The world's largest cities will be Mexico City (26 million), Sao Paulo (24 million), and Calcutta and Bombay (both over 16 million).[1]

The above information shows that the total markets in Europe and North America will not be increasing; population will not add much to total market size. Of course, these populations are growing older, so that certain segments will have increasing numbers. For example, the total population of Europe will increase only 2.8 percent from 1990 to 2000, but the over-65 population will increase by 14 percent during the same period.

While the population variable provides a snapshot of market opportunity in a country, a variety of other factors must be considered to identify viable markets. For example, in the developing world, the increase in numbers does not necessarily mean increased markets for U.S. business. The fastest growing region, Africa, is also experiencing low or negative rates of economic growth per capita. Much of Latin America is hampered by huge external debts that force those countries to try to limit imports while using their resources to generate foreign exchange for debt service. In most of these cases, the problem of foreign debt will have to be solved before the growing populations in the developing world will translate into large markets for U.S. business.

Taking into account factors such as urbanization, consumption patterns, infrastructure, and overall industrialization, different parts of the global market are examined below.

Triad Market

The *triad market* refers to the United States and Canada, Japan, and Western European countries. They account for approximately 14 percent of the world's population, but they represent over 70 percent of world gross product. As such, these countries absorb the major proportion of capital and consumer products, and, thus, are the most advanced consuming societies in the world. Not only do most of the product innovations take place in these countries, but they also serve as the opinion leaders and mold the purchasing and consumption behavior of the remaining 84 percent of the world's population.

For example, over 90 percent of the computers worldwide are used by triad countries. In the case of numerically controlled machine tools, almost 100 percent are distributed in the triad market. The same pattern follows in consumer products. Triad accounts for 92 percent of the demand for electronic consumer goods. What these statistics point to is that a company that ignores the market potential of the triad does so at its own peril.[2]

An interesting characteristic of the triad market is the universalization of needs. For example, not too long ago manufacturers of capital equipment produced machinery that reflected strong cultural distinctions. West German machines reflected that nation's penchant for craftsmanship while American equipment was often extravagant in its use of raw materials. But these distinctions have disappeared. The best-selling factory machines have lost the "art" element that distinguished them and have become much more similar, both in appearance and in the level of skills they require. The current revolution in production engineering has brought ever increasing global standards of performance. In an era when productivity improvements can quickly determine their life or death on a global scale, companies cannot afford to indulge themselves in a metallic piece of art that will last 30 years (see International Marketing Highlight 11.2).

At the same time, consumer markets have become fairly homogeneous. Ohmae notes:

> The Triad consumption pattern, which is both a cause and an effect of cultural patterns, has its roots to a large extent in the educational system. As educational systems enable more people to use technology, they tend to become more similar to each other. It follows, therefore, that education leading to higher levels of technological achievement also tends to eradicate differences in lifestyles. Penetration of television, which enables everyone possessing a television set to share sophisticated behavioral information instantaneously throughout the world, has also accelerated this trend. There are, for example, 750 million consumers in all three parts of the Triad (Japan, the United States and Canada, the nations of Western Europe) with strikingly similar needs and preferences. . . . A new generation worships the universal "now" gods—ABBA, Levi's, and Arpege. . . . Youngsters in Denmark, West Germany, Japan, and California are all growing up with ketchup, jeans, guitars. Their lifestyles, aspirations, and desires are so similar that you might call them "OECDites" or Triadians, rather than by names denoting their national identity.[3]

International Marketing Highlight 11.2

Who Sells What, Where?

There may be "global markets" out there, but "global brands" have not captured them yet. This was the finding of a survey of U.S.-based manufacturers of consumer nondurable goods. Of the eighty-five brands included in the survey, twenty-nine, or 34 percent, were not marketed outside the U.S. at all. Others were only marketed marginally abroad.

Companies surveyed showed a clear preference for selling their goods in markets culturally similar to the United States: Canada and the United Kingdom. While one might argue that Canada was targeted so frequently because of its geographical proximity to the United States, the choice of the United Kingdom cannot be so easily explained. It is as far away as many other foreign countries, and its population and economy are smaller than several other foreign markets.

Among the survey's other key findings:

- *Canada is the star.* Canada was the largest foreign market by far for U.S. brands (thirty-three of the fifty-six sold abroad). In fact, for thirteen brands, Canada is the only foreign market. The U.K. was a distant second, being the largest foreign market for five brands. Mexico was next, with four brands, followed by [the former] West Germany with three.
- *Few mega-brands.* There were only fourteen "mega-brands," ones that could be termed truly global in that they were marketed in more than fifty countries. Those most internationalized were mainly soft drinks, cleaning products, and over-the-counter drugs. Food products rely less on standard branding worldwide.
- *Older products are more international.* An interesting finding was that a majority (57 percent) of the brands sold abroad were launched before 1960. This challenges the notion that new brands are more likely than older brands to be designed for global markets.
- *No name changes.* One might expect the limited distribution of U.S. brands overseas to be offset somewhat by foreign production of exports under different brand names, but this is not the case. Few survey respondents indicated that they sell similar items abroad under different brand names.

Source: International Marketing Review, vol. 6 (1989), pp. 7–19; and *Journal of Advertising,* no. 17 (1988), pp. 14–22.

There are many reasons for the similarities and commonalities in the triad's consumer demand and lifestyle patterns. First, the purchasing power of triad residents, as expressed in discretionary income per individual, is more than ten times greater than that of residents of developing countries. For example, television penetration in triad countries is greater than 94 percent, whereas in newly industrialized countries it is 25 percent, and for the developing countries less than 10 percent. Second, their technological infrastructure is more advanced. For example, over 70 percent of triadian households have a telephone. This makes it feasible to use such products as facsimile, telex, and digital data transmission/processing equipment. Third, the educational level is much higher in triad nations than in other parts of the world. Fourth, the number of physicians per 10,000 in triad countries exceeds thirty, which creates demand for pharmaceuticals and medical electronics. Fifth, better infrastructure in the triad leads to opportunities not feasible in less-developed markets. For example, paved roads make rapid adoption of radial tires and sports cars possible.

Pacific Rim

The Pacific Rim's growing power is the corporate challenge of the 1990s. The long-anticipated emergence of the countries in the region (South Korea, Singapore, Taiwan, Hong Kong, Malaysia, Thailand, Indonesia, and the Philippines) as economic powerhouses is shaping up. Steel consumption in the region (including Japan) is higher than in the U.S. and in Europe. Similarly, demand in the Pacific Rim (again, including Japan) for semiconductors exceeds that of the EC.

Some view Pacific Rim nations as a better business bet than Eastern Europe. According to them, Eastern Europe's embrace of free enterprise is just the first step. The hard part will be catching up with the work habits and entrepreneurship of a capitalistic system. These countries will find it difficult to shed the effects of forty years of Marxism-Leninism to become "gung-ho" like the Japanese and citizens of the newly industrializing economies.

The Pacific Rim offers a variety of opportunities for American companies, from cars to telecommunications equipment, airline seats and banking services, and a host of other products. However, it is a very competitive market. Not only are potent Japanese companies active in this market, but so are aggressive, growing conglomerates from other countries in the region. Asian producers outside Japan have already gained 25 percent of the global market for personal computers.

Without the fanfare of a common market, the Pacific Rim is becoming an economically cohesive region. A new division of labor in manufacturing is taking place. Japan and the "four dragons"—Singapore, Hong Kong, Taiwan, and South Korea—provide most of the capital and expertise for the region's other nations, which have an abundance of natural resources and labor.

Unlike Japan, other countries in the region are more amenable to buying Western products and forming manufacturing alliances with Western companies. Singapore in particular is promoting what it calls a "growth triangle, " in which multinational companies can offset the high wages of Singapore's skilled workers by also using lower-paid, less-skilled workers in nearby Indonesia and Malaysia.

American investments in the region generally pay off handsomely. A U.S. Department of Commerce study showed average annual returns of 31.2 percent in Singapore, 28.8 percent in Malaysia, 17.9 percent in South Korea, 23.6 percent in Hong Kong, 22.2 percent in Taiwan, and 14.1 percent in Japan versus 15.2 percent for U.S. investments in all foreign countries.[4] For all its burgeoning strength, however, the Pacific Rim faces risks. The region's political stability in the long run could be shaken here and there as strong leaders hand over power.

Yet the risks of not tapping its potential are global. If U.S. companies do not establish a firm position in the region, competitors from Japan, Taiwan, and Korea will gain more strength at home for even bigger assaults on markets in America and Europe.

Postcommunist Countries

The pace of the political transformations that have swept through Eastern Europe and the former Soviet Union is unprecedented. With irresistible force, the peoples of these communist countries have toppled their governments. With this, a new market is taking shape in the region. The tattered nations are lurching toward a Western economic orbit, and when they reach it, Western Europe's focus will shift eastward. Europe's accent will become more Germanic and Slavic, and its potential economic might will grow to a staggering size—nearly as large as the United States and Japan combined. The West stands to gain new markets as well as a labor supply that is well-trained and socially stable. It is a tantalizing prospect that Europe may produce the world's next economic miracle, harnessing the rich dynamism of the West to the untapped talent and energy of the East.

Yet the immediate task of rescuing the backward economies of Eastern Europe is an enormous challenge. Unwinding the command economies without heaping too much pain on the populace is a Herculean job. Privatizing industrial units, keeping inflation down, coping with massive layoffs are difficult tasks. So far, the biggest economies—Czechoslovakia, Hungary, and Poland—are making the most progress. Yugoslavia, racked by ethnic conflict, split into different nations, which are at war with each other. Less-developed Romania and Bulgaria are barely out from under their former rulers.

The difficulties ahead are large, but if the East can forge new links with the West without inflaming the continent's old nationalist passions, the world may well be headed for a "Pax Europa," with prosperity helping to ensure the peace.

At this time, Eastern Europe is more of a market for foreign investment and aid than manufactured goods. Since communism crumbled in 1989, foreign investors have been looking hard at Eastern European countries. By the end of 1990, almost 10,000 foreign joint ventures had been established in Poland, Hungary, and Czechoslovakia. Once the changeover to the market economy is complete, these countries should become attractive markets to serve. How long this may take is difficult to predict.

Experts claim that Eastern Europe's progress depends on two factors: its ability to attract adequate capital and the ability of the people to tolerate hardships during the changeover. According to one estimate, the cost of modernizing industry and infrastructure in Eastern Europe would be $500 billion over the next ten to fifteen years.[5] Considering the enormity of the task, it may be safe to say that Eastern Europe markets may not evolve into mass markets on Western lines for another twenty years. In the interim, this will be an ad hoc opportunity for capital equipment, telecommunications, and, from time to time, limited amounts of consumer goods.[6]

The Commonwealth of Independent States poses similar problems. Russia is taking drastic steps to liberalize its economy quickly. The country is adopting a high-risk austerity program to stabilize its collapsed economy and integrate it with the rest of the world's. Select features of Russia's radical economic program include:

- *Prices:* Freed most wholesale and retail prices on January 2, 1992. The annual inflation rate soared to 300 percent
- *Spending:* Cut most industrial subsidies, slashed weapons orders by 85 percent, and pledged to shrink the budget deficit from 15 percent to 1 percent of GNP
- *Taxes:* Imposed a tax of 15 percent on food and 28 percent on other goods and an even heavier levy on corporate profits and many commercial transactions
- *Money:* Floated the ruble against the dollar on January 2, 1992, allowing its market value to plunge below one cent; asked the West for a $6 billion stabilization fund to make the ruble convertible by July 1992
- *Industry:* Predicts a 20 percent plunge in industrial production in 1992; plans to sell off 25 percent of state-owned enterprises and property by the end of 1992.[7]

Russian leaders are convinced that only a radical reform program can save the country from a return to dangerous central control. But many wonder if too much is being done too soon. Although prices have begun to increase at a slower pace, and more food is available in stores, enterprises around the country are hurting badly, and unemployment is increasing sharply.

Time is clearly of the essence. With economic pain stirring, Russia could become explosive. On the other hand, Russia could emerge as a healthy economy in the late 1990s.[8]

To Westerners, Russia offers both a challenge and an opportunity. By and large, companies are optimistic about the country, and they are carefully watching its progress. If the economic measures succeed, Russia will offer all sorts of attractive opportunities.

Among other members of the commonwealth, the Baltics (Estonia, Latvia, and Lithuania) are expected to switch to market economies sooner than others. With a total population of less than eight million, these countries are mere blips on the map of Europe, but they have a highly motivated, well-trained, and low-paid work force.[9] Baltic workers are more productive than Russian workers and the Baltic countries could emerge as a viable market if their goods could be sold for hard currency in Western Europe. That is highly uncertain, however. Isolated from the West for more than fifty years, much of what they make is not competitive in today's European market—even at lower prices. Even so, there are plenty of companies willing to wait for several years. The Baltics provide a viable place to establish a manufacturing or service operation for serving the emerging Russian market.

Opportunities in other former Soviet republics are hard to pinpoint at this time. Five of them (Azerbaijan, Uzbekistan, Turkmenistan, Kyrgyzstan, and Tajikistan) have joined Iran, Turkey, and Pakistan to become a part of an Islamic common market.[10] Presumably, their economic perspectives would be determined by the policies pursued by their Muslim brethren. Largely Christian Georgia and Armenia will stay closer to Russia in their endeavor to revamp their economies. The direction that Moldavia, Ukraine, and Belorussia may adopt is uncertain. For example, Moldavia might link up with Romania, while Ukraine and Belorussia may follow an independent course.[11] In any event, considering their smaller populations, they are unlikely to offer any substantial market opportunity.

Latin American

As governments cut tariffs, welcome foreign companies, and unshackle their economies, market opportunities in Latin America abound. The severe miseries of the 1980s shocked the Latin countries into abandoning the statism, populism, and protectionism that have crippled their economies since colonial times. One after another in the late 1980s, governments in Latin America have thrust their businesspeople into the free market, cutting tariffs, welcoming foreign investment, and unloading hopelessly unprofitable state enterprises. Debt is becoming manageable and incomes are growing.

The United States has a better opportunity in the region since it has the inside track. Western European nations are largely occupied with Eastern Europe, and the Japanese remain focused mainly on developed countries.

Latin America offers a better opportunity, especially for U.S. firms, than Eastern Europe. It can feed itself and has a business infrastructure, albeit rickety. U.S. trade with the region is already fifteen times greater than with Eastern Europe. According to Peter Drucker, Latin America holds the key to the U.S. trade deficit.[12]

Although opportunities beckon, Latin America still suffers from acute economic problems. For example, inflation continues to be high and the debt problem still looms large. Slow or disappointing progress could turn the poor against free markets and back to a populist, anti-Yankee leader. Nonetheless, the rewards often outweigh the risks. Latin American consumers prefer U.S. products. Capital goods companies (e.g., telecommunications, transportation systems, mining and manufacturing equipment) have a special opportunity as these countries make investments to globalize their businesses.

China and India

China and India are by far the two most populous developing countries on earth. Notwithstanding the large differences in history, politics, and culture that separate them, the size of their populations and the vastness of their lands have stimulated similar responses to the changing global business environment. Both countries seek self-sufficiency, and at the same time are liberalizing their economies to link themselves to the global network.

Since the Tiananmen Square killings in 1989, China has become suspect in Western capitals. Yet business opportunities in the country continue to grow. For example, Procter & Gamble launched its China efforts in the Guangzhou region in 1988, focusing on two products, Head & Shoulders shampoo and Oil of Olay skin cream. Both were quick hits. Avon started in 1990 and sold six months' worth of inventory in the first thirty days. Capital goods companies—for instance, Lockheed and Westinghouse—had similar experiences.[13]

Despite communism, capitalistic values are slowly permeating select parts of the country, particularly the delta area closer to Hong Kong. As Hong Kong accedes to China, the level of business activity in the country, and hence the market opportunity, should accelerate. If a firm has the patience to endure endless negotiations and maddening bureaucratic tangles, China is a potentially growing market.

India's economic growth has occurred in a political culture that places a high value on national self-reliance and social equity. Thus, despite the fact that India is the world's largest democracy, in the realm of business it has pursued socialist policies. In recent years, however, dismayed by discouraging economic performance, India has started liberalizing the economy. The current government has taken drastic measures to encourage foreign investment and promote capital markets and exports. The government wants to establish a worldwide economy through large-scale liberalization by freeing foreign investment conditions, cutting down protection for Indian industry, and streamlining bureaucratic procedures.

At the same time, India is in the throes of a middle class revolution that could transform its attitude to ward business. The middle class accounts for some 200 million people and is growing rapidly. The rise of the middle class has sparked a boom in a variety of consumer products, durable and nondurables, a market once confined to a wealthy few.

More and more foreign companies are taking advantage of the changing business conditions in India. Recently, such well-known corporations as Timex, Kellogg, and PepsiCo have entered the Indian market, something that would have been impossible in the mid-1980s.

As the liberalization measures become established, India perhaps offers a better market opportunity than China. As *Business Week* notes:

> Indeed, India looks surprisingly good in comparison with China. Ten years of trading with China have taught U.S. Asian-based executives some hard lessons. Unlike China, India allows relatively free repatriation of profits. India also has great private wealth, with 5% of its population, or some 40 million upper-crust citizens richer than most Americans will ever be. China has only its egalitarian masses.[14]

Markets in Developing Countries

A basic management reality in today's economic world is that businesses operate in a highly interdependent global economy, and the 100-plus developing countries are very significant actors in the international business arena. They are buyers, suppliers, competitors, and capital users. In order to determine market opportunity in developing countries, it is important to recognize the magnitude and significance of these roles.

Traditionally, Third World countries (including India and China, some Pacific Rim nations, and most Latin American countries) have provided a market for about one-third of all U.S. exports. The largest U.S. exports to developing countries are machinery and transport equipment, agricultural products, and chemicals, but all major product categories share in these markets.

U.S. business with the Third World follows closely the economic growth trends recorded in those countries. For example, U.S. exports declined sharply in the early and middle 1980s as purchasing power in those countries was reduced by debt-service problems, declining commodity prices, and the global recession. By 1987, however, the Third World market recovered more rapidly. U.S. exports to those countries showed a 16 percent gain over the preceding year, compared with increases of only 9 percent in sales to developed countries.[15]

As we move toward and into the twenty-first century, developing countries will become even more important in the global economy. Market opportunity in these countries rests on their ability to develop economically. That development will depend on two factors: (1) on their governments' willingness to encourage growth through liberal monetary and fiscal policies, and (2) on the capacity of their managers to operate the productive apparatus in an efficient, effective, and equitable manner.

Dimensions of the Global Market

A statistical perspective of the world market is helpful to international marketers to equip them with basic information on socioeconomic life in the world via macro data. Presumably, such information should assist in segmenting the international market and in formulating marketing strategy. The macro information presented in the form of an appendix at the end of this chapter is taken from a 1988 *Business International* report. The report is primarily based on information available from such international organizations as the United Nations, the World Bank, and the International Monetary Fund.

Table A–11.1 furnishes information on population, income, and trade. This table also gives information about the average hourly wage for different nations. In most developed countries, the average hourly wage is over $5, while in most developing countries it is less than $1. In some countries (Sri Lanka, for example), it is as low as $0.19 an hour.

Table A–11.2 shows private consumption expenditures, and total stock of durable goods (e.g., passenger cars, trucks, and buses), service facilities (e.g., telephone access lines), and consumption of basic materials (e.g., cement, steel). As can be expected, total private consumption expenditures are much higher in industrialized countries than those in the middle- and low-income brackets. By the same token, ownership of passenger cars and other durable goods, as well as consumption of energy and basic materials, is skewed in favor of advanced countries. As a matter of fact, it is the low level of energy consumption and meager use of such materials as steel and cement that characterize less-developed countries.

Based on the kind of information included in the appendix, Business International has identified the twelve largest markets in the world (see Table 11.1). Interestingly, of these twelve markets, one-fourth are the developing countries of China, Brazil, and India. Based on this information, it will be foolhardy for a company to treat all developing countries alike. Apparently, there are countries that offer a better market opportunity than the industrialized countries.

An interesting characteristic of global markets is their emerging universality. In other words, a one-world market exists for products ranging from cars to

TABLE 11.1 **Size, Growth, and Intensity of World's Twelve Largest Markets**

	MARKET-SIZE (% OF WORLD MARKET)			MARKET INTENSITY (WORLD = 1.00)			FIVE-YEAR MARKET GROWTH (%)
Major Market	1978	1983	1988	1978	1983	1988	1988
United States	23.30	20.96	18.08	4.82	4.40	3.99	17.50
U.S.S.R.	14.32	13.16	12.17	2.14	2.03	1.97	9.15
China	3.84	6.64	11.56	0.16	0.26	0.61	333.25
Japan	9.14	9.07	8.10	3.31	3.42	3.29	12.15
Germany	4.92	4.93	3.95	3.55	3.91	3.47	5.63
Italy	3.04	4.06	3.69	3.09	3.35	3.38	10.96
France	3.67	3.77	3.39	3.10	3.38	3.22	9.96
United Kingdom	3.47	3.38	2.85	2.75	2.87	2.70	19.79
Brazil	2.24	2.21	2.58	0.82	0.78	0.88	25.79
India	1.33	1.53	2.44	0.08	0.09	0.17	155.95
Spain	2.30	2.41	2.12	2.64	2.87	2.76	18.33
Canada	2.23	2.02	1.94	4.25	3.81	3.92	22.09

Notes: **Market Size** shows the relative dimensions of each national or regional market as a percentage of the total world market. The percentages for each market are derived by averaging the corresponding data on total population (double-weighted), urban population, private consumption expenditure, steel consumption, cement and electricity production, and ownership of telephones, passenger cars, and televisions. **Market Intensity** measures the richness of the market, or the degree of concentrated purchasing power it represents. Taking the world's market intensity as 1.00, BI has calculated the intensity of each country or region as it relates to this base. The intensity figure is derived from an average of per capita ownership, production, and consumption indicators. Specifically, it is calculated by averaging per capita figures for cars in use (double-weighted), telephones in use, televisions in use, steel consumption, cement and electricity production, private consumption expenditure (double-weighted), and the percentage of population that is urban (double-weighted). **Market Growth** is a five-year average of the growth rates for several indicators: population, steel consumption, cement and electricity production, and ownership of passenger cars, trucks and buses, and televisions.
Source: Business International, July 30, 1990, p. 256.

consumer electronics to carbonated drinks. Firms today are engaged in world competition to serve consumers globally (see International Marketing Highlight 11.3). It must be cautioned, however, that each nation still has its own cultural peculiarities. Thus, a firm cannot assume that in each and every case what is good for the home country is good for the world.

A number of broad forces have led to growing globalization of markets.[16] These include:

- *Growing similarity of countries.* Because of growing commonality of infrastructure, distribution channels, and marketing approaches, more and more products and brands are available everywhere. This manifests similar buyer needs in different countries. Large retail chains, television advertising, and credit cards are just a few examples of once isolated phenomena that are rapidly becoming universal.
- *Falling tariff barriers.* Successive rounds of bilateral and multilateral agree-

International Marketing Highlight 11.3

Global Disorientation

She arrives on her British Airways flight, rents a Toyota at the Hertz desk in the terminal, and drives to the downtown Hilton hotel. She drops into a chair, flips on the Sony TV, and gazes glassily at this week's scandal on "Dallas." Room service delivers dinner along with the bottle of Perrier and the pack of Marlboro cigarettes she ordered. While eating dinner she catches herself nodding off, but is brought back to consciousness by a sudden feeling of disorientation. Is she in Sydney, Singapore, Stockholm, or Seattle? Her surroundings and points of reference over the past few hours have provided few clues.

With the expansion of the international economy and the growth of international business in the post–World War II era, the marketplace has taken on a recognizably similar face in countries around the globe. No longer is the overseas traveler surprised to see a familiar logo flashing from a neon sign or to find a favorite brand from home on sale in a foreign location. But the most interesting phenomenon is not just that multinational companies have entered foreign markets. Increasingly, it has become evident that the same few companies compete against each other for leadership positions in numerous national markets worldwide. In automobiles, construction equipment, consumer electronics, cameras, office copiers, airframes, computers, and a variety of other industries, not more than half a dozen MNCs dominate the major markets worldwide.

Source: From a note entitled "Global Competition and MNC Managers, " by Christopher A. Bartlett, Harvard Business School, 1985.

ments have lowered tariffs markedly since World War II. At the same time, regional economic agreements such as the European Community have facilitated trade relations among member countries.

- *Strategic role of technology.* Technology is not only reshaping industries but contributing to market homogenization. For example, electronic innovations permit the development of more compact, lighter products that are less costly to ship. Transportation costs themselves have fallen with the use of containerization and larger-capacity ships. Increasing ease of communication and data transfer make it feasible to link operations in different countries. At the same time, technology leads to an easy flow of information among buyers, making them aware of new and quality products and thus creating demand.

Global markets offer unlimited opportunities. But competition in these markets is intense. To be globally successful, companies must learn to operate and compete as if the world were one large market, ignoring superficial regional and national differences. Corporations geared to this new reality can benefit from enormous economies of scale in production, distribution, marketing, and management. By translating these benefits into reduced world prices, they can dislodge competitors who still operate with the perspectives of the 1970s and 1980s. Companies willing to change their perspectives and become global can attain sustainable competitive advantage (see International Marketing Highlight 11.4).

International Marketing Highlight 11.4

Why Go Global?

The rules for survival have changed since the beginning of the 1980s. Domestic markets have become too small. Even the biggest companies in the biggest countries cannot survive on their domestic markets if they are in global industries. They have to be in all major markets. That means North America, Western Europe, and the Pacific Rim countries.

Take, for example, the pharmaceuticals business. In the 1970s, developing a new drug cost about $16 million and took four to five years. The drug could be produced in Britain or the U.S. and eventually exported. Now, developing a drug costs about $250 million and takes as long as twelve years. Only a global product for a global market can support that much risk. No major pharmaceuticals company is in the game for anything other than global products. That helps explain a series of mergers of major drug companies, most recently the marriage of Bristol-Myers and Squibb.

Source: Fortune, August 1989, p. 70.

Segmenting the Global Market

A ***market segment*** refers to a group of countries that are alike in respect to their responsiveness to some aspect of marketing strategy. ***Market segmentation*** may be defined as a technique of dividing different countries into homogeneous groups. The concept of segmentation is based on the fact that a business cannot serve the entire world with a single set of policies because there are disparities among countries—both economic and cultural. An international marketer, therefore, should pick out one or more countries as target markets. A company may not find it feasible to do business immediately with the entire spectrum of countries forming a segment. In that case, the firm may design its marketing programs and strategies for those countries it does enter and draw upon its experience with these countries in dealing with new markets.

The importance of segmentation can be illustrated by a reference to Massey-Ferguson Ltd., a Toronto-based farm equipment producer. As far back as 1959, this company decided to concentrate on sales outside of North America and thus avoid competing head-on with Ford Motor Company, Deere & Company, and International Harvester Company. It took the company years to implement successfully its segmentation strategy before reaching a point where it derives almost 70 percent of its sales outside of North America. As a matter of fact, as the market matured in North America, Massey continued to grow and earn substantial income, since demand overseas accelerated in the 1980s. While Ford, Deere, and International Harvester struggled hard to maintain profitability, Massey-Ferguson, because of its decision to avoid the North American segment, showed a fine performance.

To survive and prosper in the increasingly competitive global marketplace, many companies are learning to find and dominate "niche markets." For companies of all kinds and sizes, nichemanship is rapidly becoming the new business imperative.

Simply defined, a niche is a relatively small segment of a market that the major competitors or producers may overlook, ignore, or have difficulty serving. The niche may be a narrowly defined geographical area. It may relate to the unique needs of a small and specific group of customers, or it may be some narrow, highly specialized aspect of a very broad group of customers. In some cases, the niche market may actually be very large—particularly if the company operates globally.

The possibilities are virtually endless. So too are the opportunities, as effective niche strategies can be extremely profitable.

By focusing on a niche market, companies often develop an excellent understanding of their customers' operations—and how those customers make money. This understanding in turn provides an edge when it comes to identifying opportunities for new products and marketing programs. And this emphasis on a niche provides a very clear focus for the development of business strategies and action plans.

The importance of niche strategy may be illustrated by the experience of Linear Technology, a Canadian firm.[17] It successfully carved out a niche in the world integrated circuit ("chip") business. Although this market as a whole is dominated by major Japanese and American firms, Linear Technology dominates the global market for one narrow segment—audio amplifier chips for hearing aids. Even in Japan, it has achieved more than a 50 percent market share in competition with companies like NEC. By having a broad product line within its specialized area and by focusing on the needs of one set of customers, it has managed to beat all competitors.

A basic problem in market segmentation is how it should be accomplished. Virtually all international marketers segment the world market, but typically their criteria do not provide categories that are truly significant. Traditionally, geography has been employed to divide the world. However, segmentation based on geography overlooks the possibility of economic and cultural differences among countries.

For example, the countries of the Middle East in no way constitute a homogeneous market. Iran, Iraq, Kuwait, the United Arab Emirates (UAE), Saudi Arabia, Egypt, and Lebanon are all very different. Lebanon has had special problems, while all the others have different legal and political systems. The Emirates have no formal business laws at all, Saudi Arabia has a fairly new and sophisticated statute, while Egyptian law has a long history and is based on French law. Lately, the Middle Eastern countries have made attempts to present a common economic posture through regulating tariffs, duties, and the like. Despite that, a

U.S. business cannot take full advantage of the fragmentation of bureaucracies and laws because the natural fragmentation of Middle Eastern markets is reinforced by nationalist tendencies. Therefore, it is not possible for a company simply to go into the cheapest or most liberal country and expect to maximize its profit by trading into the whole area from that base.

The Middle East description illustrates the point that world markets need to be grouped judiciously. It requires carefully finding and verifying the dimension(s) to be employed in classifying the countries.

Segmentation Process

Five procedural steps should be followed to gain information and insights into the segmentation criteria suitable for classifying world markets:

1. Develop a market taxonomy for classifying the world markets.
2. Segment all countries into homogeneous groups having common characteristics with reference to the dimensions of the market taxonomy.
3. Determine theoretically the most efficient method of serving each group.
4. Choose the group in which the marketer's own perspective (its product/service, strengths) is in line with the requirements of the group.
5. Adjust this ideal classification to the constraints of the real world (existing commitments, legal and political restrictions, practicality, and so forth).

A company interested in expanding business overseas can utilize this procedure by first deciding on a criterion for classifying the countries for its product. Not all countries should be analyzed, but only those that appear to offer a viable potential. For example, a computer manufacturer may segment countries based on need: those requiring simple machines (first-generation computers); those requiring medium-size computers (say, second-generation computers); and those requiring large, sophisticated computers. The company may find it is well placed to serve the second segment, those countries that require medium-size computers. Let us assume the following countries fall into this segment: South Korea, Brazil, Taiwan, Singapore, Mexico, Hong Kong, and Nigeria. To serve this targeted segment of countries, the company may establish three assembly plants, one in Nigeria, one in Brazil, and one in South Korea (assuming other countries in the geographic area would be served through exports from these three countries). But because the computer industry often encounters a lack of scientific personnel in such foreign countries, the company may consider establishing an assembly plant in India (instead of South Korea), which has a large pool of scientific talent, to serve the Asian part of its segment. It may do so even though the Indian market is highly competitive and the Indian government usually does not permit the establishment of a wholly foreign owned subsidiary. This is what is meant by adjustment of the ideal system to the real world.

Criteria for Grouping Countries

As is true in domestic market segmentation, countries of the world can be grouped using a variety of criteria. For example, a company may group world markets (countries) based on a single variable such as per capita GNP or geography. Similarly, religion or political system may serve as a criterion for grouping countries. Alternatively, the classification of countries may be based on the combination of a few selected variables. One may use just a few variables, such as political system, geography, and economic status (GNP per capita), or use a large number of variables, similar to what is done in establishing lifestyle or psychographic segments in domestic marketing.

Our discussion is developed based on economic status grouping, geographic grouping, political system grouping, grouping by religion, cultural grouping, multiple-variable grouping, intermarket grouping, and quality of life grouping. The discussion ends with a recommended scheme for country classification.

Of the different ways for grouping countries together, the choice of an appropriate method will depend on the reasons for segmenting the world market. The main purpose of grouping is usually related to the nature of the product. For example, a defense equipment manufacturer may classify countries based on their political systems. But for an appliance company, economic status may be a more appropriate choice.

> The manner in which countries are to be grouped will depend, to a large extent, on the nature of a company's product or product lines. Companies marketing capital goods may find that Rostow's classification of countries into five economic states is the most effective way to view operations. On the other hand, companies in the consumer durable-goods field may find that grouping countries by personal consumption expenditures is a more meaningful way to study worldwide activities. A series of composite indicators developed for each group may prove to be of substantial help in evaluating overseas division and area performance, and in applying the lessons learned in one market to the formulation of plans and strategies for the other areas.[18]

Economic Status Grouping

The simplest way to form economic groups is to classify countries on the basis of GNP per person. For example, countries may be grouped as industrialized countries with GNP per capita over $4,000; middle-income countries (GNP per capita between $800 and $4,000); and low-income countries with GNP below $800. If we follow this scheme, about fifty countries will fall in the low-income category, thirty-five in the middle-income category, and thirty will be considered industrialized (ignoring the centrally planned economies.)[19] (Economic status groupings should be differentiated from regional market agreements, discussed in Chapter 5, which are formed using more than strictly economic considerations.)

There is no empirical study showing that the economic status classification of countries by GNP per capita is a viable system. Based on domestic marketing experience, however, it is questionable if a single variable should be used to group countries into homogeneous categories. For example, GNP per capita of Kuwait, Libya, and Saudi Arabia would put them in the category of industrialized countries, but these countries by no means constitute the same market as industrial countries such as the United States, Germany, Italy, and so on. Additionally, emphasis on economic status alone in classifying countries misses the crucial impact of cultural differences among nations.

The grouping of countries based on GNP per capita assumes, like other economic criteria for segmentation, that market behavior is directly related to income. In domestic marketing a number of studies have questioned the relevance of income as a discerning variable. In the international arena as well, sole reliance on GNP per capita for international comparisons is considered inadequate. For example, in 1989 Ghana had a per capita GNP of $390 compared with India's $340. But if the purchasing power of a dollar in the two countries is considered, the per capita GNP for Ghana comes out to be $510, while that for India is $580.

> However serious poverty in the developing world may be, there is something suspicious about estimates showing that the 957 million citizens of countries with 1970–75 per capita incomes of less than $200 have an average income of $132, while the citizens of the United States live with fifty-three times that much. If this $132 figure indicates that people are living on the quantity of goods and services that could be bought in the United States for 36 cents per day, it poses a substantial puzzle. At that level of real income, a large proportion of these people would quickly die; yet the populations of these countries are growing very rapidly and, in general, life expectancy is increasing at the same time.[20]

Based on the current international situation, a slightly different way of forming segments is to group countries in the following five categories: First World, Second World, Third World, Fourth World, and Fifth World. These categories may be defined in the following terms.[21]

First World This includes the advanced industrial nations of Europe, North America, and Asia that accept a more-or-less capitalistic, market-oriented economy. The core of the First World consists of members of the OECD (Organization for Economic Cooperation and Development); that is, the industrialized West and Japan. New Zealand and Australia also qualify, and Greece and Spain are borderline cases.

Second World This group includes high-income oil exporters and newly industrialized countries. These countries have in the past fifteen years achieved significant economic progress, either through investing their oil revenues (for example, Saudi Arabia) or by competing aggressively in the international markets, such as South Korea.

Third World This group is made up of countries that need time and technology, rather than massive foreign aid, to build modern, developed economies. These include nations whose development may be guaranteed by other key resources and nations that are developed enough to attract foreign investment and borrow on commercial terms. Examples of the former group are Zambia (copper) and Morocco (phosphate). Mexico, Brazil, and India fall into the latter group.

Fourth World This group includes the 1.5 billion people of the world's hitherto centrally planned communist-run nations, with the exception of former Yugoslavia, which has a mixed economy, and the People's Republic of China.

Fifth World The 200 million inhabitants of the Fifth World live in hard-core poverty. Many Fifth World countries have few presently known resources. Usually a large part of the population is engaged in subsistence farming or nomadic herding, and some are isolated from the outside world. Life expectancy is below fifty years, and nutritional intake is significantly less than the minimum considered necessary for health. Notable examples are Mali, Chad, Ethiopia, Somalia, Rwanda, and Bangladesh.

Table 11.2 identifies countries in each group. The above groupings, while interesting and seemingly relevant, do not appear to lend themselves to practical use. Assignment of different countries to these categories is arbitrary. Besides, no evidence exists to support the viability of these categories from the standpoint of marketing.

Geographic Grouping

One popular way of grouping nations is to classify them along regional lines. Many multinational corporations organize their worldwide operations into such regions as Western Europe, Latin America, Far East (including Australia and New Zealand), Middle East, and Africa. A variety of reasons makes geographic grouping of countries an acceptable criterion for overseas marketers. First, geographic proximity makes it easier to manage countries blocked together. For example, all countries in Latin America can be managed, say, from a regional headquarters in Brazil. Both transportation and communication are easier to handle on a regional basis. Consider, if Argentina is grouped with Italy, Spain, and New Zealand, while Brazil is grouped with South Korea, Taiwan, and India (assuming some viable basis), how difficult it would be for an executive to manage these far-flung countries theoretically grouped together.

As a matter of fact, one might even argue that nations in the same geographic regions should share common cultural traits with each other. This added facet gives credence to geographic grouping. One more factor that supports regional classification of countries is the post–World War II organization of countries into trading groups, such as the European Economic Community (EEC), now the EC or so-called Common Market, Latin American Free Trade Association, and the European Free Trade Area. These organizations are regional in character; that is, countries in the same geographic region decided to join with each other to become large economic entities. Typically, members of a group agree to trade freely with each other without any barriers, as do the Common Market countries. In fact the EC countries go even further and levy common external tariffs. From the point of view of an international marketer, the existence of common economic arrangements among nations by means of groups will mean that entry into one country will automatically smooth entry into another country belonging to the same group; the same marketing strategy perspective can be applied to one or all. Thus, geographic division of countries appears sound.

Despite these reasons, geographic lumping of countries to form market seg-

Economic Grouping of Countries

FIRST WORLD (INDUSTRIAL MARKET ECONOMIES)	SECOND WORLD (HIGH INCOME OIL EXPORTERS AND NEWLY INDUSTRIALIZED COUNTRIES)	THIRD WORLD (EMERGING COUNTRIES)		FOURTH WORLD (EAST EUROPEAN ECONOMIES)	FIFTH WORLD (LEAST-DEVELOPED COUNTRIES)
Australia	Hong Kong	Algeria	Jordan	Albania	Afghanistan
Austria	Kuwait	Angola	Kenya	Bulgaria	Bangladesh
Belgium	Libya	Argentina	Korea, Rep.	Czechoslovakia	Benin
Canada	Malaysia	Bolivia	Lebanon	Hungary	Bhutan
Denmark	Oman	Brazil	Liberia	Poland	Botswana
Finland	Saudi Arabia	Burma	Mexico	Romania	Burkina Faso
France	Singapore	Cameroon	Mongolia	Russia	Burundi
Germany	South Korea	Chile	Morocco	Others	Cape Verde
Ireland	Taiwan	China	Nicaragua		Central African Republic
Italy	United Arab Emirates	Colombia	Nigeria		Chad
Japan		Congo, People's Rep.	Pakistan		Comoros
Luxembourg		Costa Rica	Papua New Guinea		Democratic Yemen
Netherlands		Cuba	Paraguay		Djibouti
New Zealand		Cyprus	Peru		Equatorial Guinea
Norway		Dominican Republic	Philippines		Ethiopia
Spain		Ecuador	Portugal		Gambia
Sweden		Egypt, Arab Rep.	Senegal		Guinea
United Kingdom		El Salvador	South Africa		Guinea-Bissau
United States		Ghana	Sri Lanka		Haiti
		Greece	Syrian Arab Rep.		Kiribati
		Guatemala	Thailand		Lao People's Dem. Rep.
		Honduras	Tunisia		Lesotho
		India	Turkey		Malawi
		Indonesia	Uruguay		Maldives
		Iran, Islamic Rep.	Venezuela		Mali
		Iraq	Vietnam		Mauritius
		Israel	Yemen Arab Rep.		Mozambique
		Ivory Coast	Yemen, PDR		Madagascar
		Jamaica	Yugoslavia		Myanmar
			Zambia		Nepal
			Zimbabwe		Niger
					Rwanda
					Samoa
					Sao Tome and Principe
					Sierra Leone
					Somalia
					Sudan
					Togo
					Tuvalu
					Uganda
					United Rep. of Tanzania
					Vanuatu
					Yemen
					Zaire

ments is not always sound. Geographic proximity of countries does not automatically guarantee they will present the same market opportunity for international business. For example, the Philippines and Thailand do not provide as viable markets as Singapore, Malaysia, South Korea, Taiwan, and Hong Kong, even though all these countries are in the same geographic region. Similarly, Mexico is geographically part of the same continent as the United States and Canada, but Mexico obviously differs culturally and economically from the other two.

What Rossman says about Latin America applies to other parts of the world as well:

> Many U.S. marketers think everything between the Rio Grande River and Tierra del Fuego at the southern tip of South America is the same, including the 400 million inhabitants. In fact, the Dominican Republic is no more like Argentina than Sicily is like Sweden.
>
> Many Latin Americans don't speak Spanish, including 140 million Portuguese-speaking Brazilians and the millions in other countries who speak a variety of Indian dialects.[22]

In general, geographic classification of countries for the purposes of international marketing may not be the most desirable alternative to use.

Political Grouping

Another way of grouping countries is to classify them by their political perspective. For example, countries may be categorized politically in the following types: democratic republics, dictatorships, communist dictatorships, and monarchies. These categories are used simply to facilitate discussion. As appropriate to a marketer's purposes, these categories may be refined further. Political segments may be established with reference to party systems. For example, the two-party system of the United States, the multiparty system of Italy, Israel, and Germany, or the single-party system of Mexico and India could be used. Dictatorships may be military or civilian.

Once a suitable set of political categories has been worked out, countries in each category or group may then be considered as homogeneous for purposes of developing marketing strategy. In other words, a different marketing strategy may be developed for each political group that would be relevant for the firm's international business with all the countries in that group.

If politics is used as the segmentation criterion for grouping countries, Nigeria, Bangladesh, and Argentina would have belonged in the same category in 1988. For example, all then had military dictators, with inclinations toward holding free elections to establish democratic governments. But from the vantage point of the multinational marketer, their political closeness did not render them potentially similar customers. Argentina was economically much closer to the Western European countries. Nigeria's economic potential is linked with oil prices. Bangladesh, on the other hand, highly populated like Japan, ranked among the low-income countries of the world. The differing economic perspectives of the three countries seem to negate their grouping according to political environment in order to develop a common marketing strategy. One strategy would not be adequate to serve these markets.

The concept of political grouping appears most relevant to categorizing communist countries. Because of common marketing approaches like centralized buying, barter, and countertrade that were practiced in Eastern Europe, these countries, in the past, could be served with a common marketing strategy.

Grouping in Religion

Religion constitutes an important element of society in most cultures. It thus greatly influences lifestyle, which in turn affects marketing. Following this logic, religion could work out to be a viable criterion for grouping countries. What has been said of Latin America applies to many other parts of the world with different religions.

> The life of the family and of the individual is greatly and continuously involved with the Church. One must not exaggerate the implications of this relationship of the individual, the family, and the community to the Church. But one should also be careful not to underestimate it. It gives the life a certain quality and adds something to the meaning of daily activities which is lacking in the United States.[23]

Religion can be defined as the quest for the values of the ideal life and as involving three phases: the ideal, the practices for attaining the value of the ideal, and the theology or world-view relating the quest to the surrounding universe. This definition covers virtually all aspects of a country's life—its aesthetics, its material culture, its social organization, its language, even its politics and economics.

Animism, Hinduism, Buddhism, Judaism, Islam, and Christianity are the major religions of the world. Religion as an aspect of cultural environment is discussed in Chapter 7. Briefly, however, animism is a prehistoric form of religion—ancient religion without religious texts and specific words but with some magic. Animism today is found all over the world but is practiced most obviously in African countries. Some Latin American countries have animistic tendencies as well.[24]

Hinduism, defined more as a way of life than a religion, is practiced mostly in India. Considered to be 4,000 years old, it reflects a complex set of tenets and beliefs but lacks a common creed or dogma.

> Hinduism has no dogma; it is not even a religion when you come to think of it; it is a way of life. This in itself makes the task of change harder. You are not up against dogma, you are just up against a total way of life, which is much more difficult to change than dogma.[25]

Buddhism sprang from Hinduism in India in the sixth century B.C. Buddhists are found mainly in Southeast Asia and Japan. In Burma, Sri Lanka, Thailand, Laos, and Kampuchea it is the dominant religion. There are some Buddhists in Western countries and, presumably, in the People's Republic of China as well.

Islam is practiced by over 500 million people living in about thirty countries. The Islamic countries are located mainly in the Middle East, Northern Africa, and South Asia. Islam tends to define a total way of life that its adherents should follow. It includes legislation that organizes all human relationships.

Christianity, sometimes referred to as the religion of the Western world, is found all over the globe. With the Protestant Reformation, Christianity began to emphasize individuality more than other religions. Although marked differences exist between the two major divisions of Christianity, Roman Catholicism and Protestantism, basically it stresses similar values such as achievement and thrift. Interestingly, the Protestant countries in particular rank economically among the highest in the world in terms of GNP per capita.

The effect of religion on lifestyle makes it a relevant criterion for grouping countries. Table 7.2 shows, for example, how Islam affects business. Yet the formulation of a common marketing strategy for a group of countries following Islam, or any one religion, may not suffice. Both Pakistan and Saudi Arabia are strong adherents of Islam. But the economic differences between the two countries would invalidate lumping them together for marketing decision making. Saudi Arabia, with a per capita GNP of $6,020 (1989 estimate) is a customer for a variety of consumer and industrial products. On the other hand, Pakistan, with its per capita GNP of $370 (1989 estimate), offers a very low potential for international marketers. Similarly, France and the Philippines, both primarily Catholic countries, cannot be served by following the same marketing perspective. In brief, while religion via culture plays an important role in determining lifestyle, by itself it may not serve as a viable criterion for grouping countries.

Cultural Classification

It is conceivable that countries can be classified in stereotyped cultural groupings. Presumably countries in a cultural group should be amenable to the same marketing strategy. To an extent, cultural groupings make sense since lifestyle is affected intimately by culture, and hence this form of classification for marketing decision making should be adequate. The problem here, however, is what constitutes a cultural category. Unless we use a variable like religion to serve as a surrogate for culture, it will not be easy to establish cultural categories.

The Human Relations Area Files, Inc., associated with Yale University, has identified about 700 major cultural groups in the world, further collapsing of which resulted in over sixty blue-ribbon culture types.[26] Even if only sixty categories are used, it will be an enormous task for an international marketer to relate all the different countries of the world to each of these categories and formulate an individualized strategy for each of the sixty cultural groups.

Multiple-Variable Grouping

A number of studies have been reported in marketing literature that used a large number of variables to form country clusters.[27] The argument behind the use of multiple variables has been that countries relate to each other in accordance with their cultural, religious, socioeconomic, and political characteristics. Therefore, it is desirable to form international segments using variables in all these areas rather than simply grouping countries on the basis of geographic proximity or economic status.

An important grouping study using cluster analysis was done by Sethi. He used twenty-nine variables to cluster ninety-one countries.[28] The method adopted by Sethi requires two procedural steps. First, a large number of variables should be collapsed into smaller, more meaningful groups of clusters. These groups are called ***variable clusters*** or ***V-clusters,*** and are discriminatory variables pertaining to countries such as GNP per capita, cars per capita, and single-family homes per capita. Second, objects (for example, countries) should be scored on the basis of each V-cluster. With the use of O-analysis (one method for accomplishing the second step), a large number of countries are classified into subgroups called O-clusters (or O-types). Each country is scored for each of the V-cluster dimensions mentioned in the first step. These scores are used to identify O-types or countries with similar characteristics.

Sethi's analysis vis-à-vis the first step gave the following four V-clusters:

1. Aggregate production and transportation, or C_1
2. Personal consumption, or C_2
3. Trade, or C_3
4. Health and education, or C_4

Table 11.3 shows the variables included in each V-cluster. With the use of the second step seven O-types or groups of countries are identified.

For identifying the seven O-type groups each country received a score for each of the V-cluster variables shown in Table 11.3. These scores resulted in seven O-types or country clusters. These country groups may then be used for developing marketing strategy—a different strategy for each O-type.*

Intermarket Segmentation

The multiple-variable approach assumes that countries with similar social-economic-political perspectives should be combined into segments. The approach falsely assumes that countries are indivisible, heterogeneous units. In recent years, a refined approach has been advanced: the formation of intercountry segments.[29] Groups of customers who are alike in different countries form segments. In other words, each country's market consists of different segments. A particular segment in a country may be very much like a similar segment in one or more other countries. These similar segments belonging to different countries may be combined to form a viable intermarket segment (see International Marketing Highlight 11.5).

Assume a U.S. chemical manufacturing company is interested in foreign expansion. The company manufactures different types of chemicals such as pharmaceuticals, fine chemicals, and fertilizers. In its attempts to segment the world market, the company may find small farmers in developing countries a segment worth serving. These customers, whether from Pakistan or Indonesia or Kenya or Mexico, appear to represent common needs and behavior patterns. Most of them till the land using bullock carts and have very little cash to buy agricultural inputs. They lack the education and exposure to appreciate fully the value of using fertilizer and depend on government help for such things as seeds, pesti-

*Advanced readers may find it interesting to know that the higher a country scores on C_1, C_2, and C_4 (C_3 was found to be indeterminate), the more developed it tends to be. However, it is difficult to rank country clusters on a continuum of development since intercomparisons of V-clusters and O-clusters must be made on all four dimensions.

TABLE 11.3 V-Clusters of Country Characteristics

V-CLUSTERS	VARIABLES
C_1: Aggregate production and transportation	Number of air passengers/km Air cargo (ton/km) Electricity production Number of newspapers Number of cities with a population of over 100,000 Population
C_2: Personal consumption	Income per capita GNP per capita Cars per capita TV sets per capita Energy consumption per capita Hospital beds Newspaper circulation Electricity production per capita Telephones per capita Radios per capita School enrollment per capita in population 15–19 years old College, university, and professional school education per capita in population 15–64 years old
C_3: Trade	Imports/GNP Exports/GNP Consumer price index
C_4: Health and education	Illiteracy among adults 15 years and older Percent of population in agriculture Life expectancy Physicians per capita Number of cities with a population under 100,000 School enrollment per capita in population 5–14 years old Political stability

Source: Eugene D. Jaffe, *Grouping: A Strategy for International Marketing* (New York: AMACOM, 1974), p. 17, adapted from S. Prakash Sethi, "Comparative Cluster Analysis for World Markets," *Journal of Marketing Research,* August 1971, pp. 350–351.

cides, and fertilizer. They acquire their farming needs from local suppliers and count on word-of-mouth to learn and accept new things and ideas. Thus, even though these farmers are in different countries continents apart, and even though they speak different languages and have different cultural backgrounds, they may represent a homogeneous market segment.

Take the case of the Mercedes-Benz. Considered a luxury car, it has a worldwide market niche among the well-to-do. Even in Japan Mercedes is considered

International Marketing Highlight 11.5

Segmenting the Global Market

A critical element in fending off the competition is being aware of who one's consumer is and what that consumer wants. Global Scan, an annual survey developed by the advertising agency, Network Backer Spielvogel Bates Worldwide Inc., that measures style of life and consumer attitudes and purchasing patterns of over 15,000 customers in fourteen countries (Australia, Canada, Colombia, Finland, France, Germany, Hong Kong, Indonesia, Japan, Mexico, Spain, the United Kingdom, the United States, and Venezuela), has classified global consumers into five distinct categories: strivers, achievers, pressured, traditionals, and adapters. Although all five consumer classes were found to exist in almost all of the Global Scan countries, segment sizes vary widely—sometimes dramatically—from one country to the next. The same five consumer groups can be found in the United States and in Japan—countries with totally different histories and cultures. The Japanese strivers and achievers, for instance, have more in common with their U.S. counterparts than they do with their own parents.

Global Scan has determined that, throughout the world, more strivers (26 percent) set highest priority on good service than all other groups, followed closely by achievers (22 percent). In fact, service will become increasingly important as these two segments age—or grow wealthier.

- *Strivers*. These are defined as young people on the run. Their median age is 31, and their average day is nonstop. They push hard to achieve success, but they are also hard pressed to meet all their goals. They are materialistic, look for pleasure, and insist on instant gratification. Short of time, energy, and money, they seek out convenience in every corner of their lives. Strivers think that others are getting more out of life—and most are envious.
- *Achievers*. Those who fall into this category are slightly older and several giant steps ahead of the strivers. They are affluent, assertive, and on the way up. Opinion leaders and style-setters, they shape the world's mainstream values. Achievers are hooked on status and high on quality; together with the strivers, they create the youth-oriented values that drive society today.

Source: Business International, July 23, 1990, p. 237.

the most popular foreign luxury car.[30] Similarly, a designer of men's clothing may find that elites of different countries compose a market segment themselves. Likewise, the teenagers of different countries may work out to be a viable segment. Table 11.4 illustrates the perspectives of these intermarket segments.

While the concept of intermarket segmenting is relevant on a worldwide basis, it is especially workable within a region. For example, women all over the world could be considered mistakenly to have similar cosmetic-usage behavior patterns. It is widely recognized that lifestyle behavior is deeply affected by culture. Muslim women are supposed to veil in public; some Latin women consider

TABLE 11.4 Behavioral Aspects Related to the Identification of Global Consumer Segments

	GLOBAL ELITES	GLOBAL TEENAGERS
SHARED VALUES	Wealth, success, status	Growth, change, future, learning, play
KEY PRODUCT BENEFITS SOUGHT	Universally recognizable products with prestige image High-quality products	Novelty, trendy image, fashion statement Name brands/novelty
DEMOGRAPHICS	Very high income, social status and class/well-traveled/well-educated	Age 12–19, well-traveled, high media exposure
MEDIA/COMMUNICATION	Upscale magazines, social-selective channels (i.e., cliques), direct marketing, global telemarketing	Teen magazines, MTV, radio, video, peers, role models
DISTRIBUTION CHANNELS	Selective (i.e., upscale retailers)	General retailers with name brands
PRICE RANGE	Premium	Affordable
TARGETED BY GLOBAL FIRMS SUCH AS	Mercedes Benz, Perrier, American Express, Ralph Lauren's Polo	Coca-Cola Co., Benetton, Swatch International, Sony, PepsiCo, Inc.
RELATED MICROSEGMENTS/ CLUSTERS	Affluent women, top executives, highly educated professionals, professional athletes	Preadolescents, female teens, male teens,
FACTORS INFLUENCING THE EMERGENCE OF THE SEGMENT	Increased wealth, widespread travel	Television media, international education

Source: Salah S. Hassan and Lea Prevel Katsanis, "Identification of Global Consumer Segments," *Journal of International Consumer Marketing,* vol. 3 (2), p. 24. Copyright 1991 by the Haworth Press, Inc (Binghamton, NY).

excessive cosmetic usage as self-indulgence. Thus, from the viewpoint of a cosmetic company, stereotyping people globally may prove to be unproductive. Instead, grouping people in a region where culture and economic conditions do not vary substantially from country to country may represent a viable segment. The intermarket concept is increasingly talked about with reference to Western Europe. Consider the following 1981 comment:

> The 6,400,000 upmarket, educationally elite readers of those magazines (i.e., *Scientific American, Time, Newsweek, The Financial Times,* and *The Economist*) have more in common with each other than with their fellow countrymen who are less well off—over 70 percent of them speak English in their business

> lives and therefore have a common means of communication. . . . The growing awareness of shared "lifestyle" traits, transcending national boundaries, may well usher in a new era of Europe-wide marketing and advertising strategies.[31]

Applying the concept of intermarket segmentation in Europe, many companies are pursuing the idea of a *Eurobrand,* that is, a product/brand destined for a market consisting of niches in different Western European countries. The development of satellite communication makes it feasible to simultaneously reach customers in different countries, which would not have been possible through the traditional television channel.[32]

Estee Lauder Inc. recently made its first foray into intermarket marketing with a strategy to sell products designed specifically for the West Coast of the U.S. and Japan. The cosmetics company's Aramis division launched a line of men's fragrances, called NewWest, in the fall of 1988 in California and Japan. At least initially, the company did not plan to sell the products elsewhere in the U.S. Such intermarket strategies have also been pursued by Campbell Soup Company and Chrysler Corp.[33]

Portfolio Approach

A new approach based on strategic planning frameworks for classifying countries has been recommended by Rizkallah.[34] This ***portfolio approach,*** as shown in Figure 11.1, proposes dividing countries on a three-dimensional basis: country potential, competitive strength, and risk. Following this method, eighteen country segments are obtained.

Country potential in the portfolio approach refers to the market potential for a firm's product/service in a given country and is based on such factors as population size, rate of economic growth, real gross national product, per capita

Competitive Strength

Risk	Strong	Average	Weak	*Country Potential*
High				High
				Medium
				Low
Low				High
				Medium
				Low

Source: Elias G. Rizkallah, "Multiple Product: Multiple Market Allocations—A Portfolio Approach," a paper presented at the Academy of International Business Annual Meeting in New Orleans, October 24, 1980, p. 10.

FIGURE 11.1 An International Market Taxonomy Matrix for Classifying Countries

national income, distribution of population, industrial production/consumption patterns, and the like. Both internal and external factors determine *competitive strength*. In a given country, the *internal factors* include the firm's market share; its resources; and facilities, including knowledge of the unique features of that country and the skills and facilities it owns to match these features. *External factors* include strength of competitors in the same industry, competition from industries of substitute products, and the structure of the industry locally and internationally. *Risk*—that is, political risk, financial risk, and business risk (like change in consumer preferences)—is any factor that causes variation in profit, cash flow, or other outcomes generated by involvement in a country.

The author of this approach claims the following advantages for the portfolio approach:[35]

- It is three-dimensional, which implies greater representativeness of the multinational environment.
- Its dimensions are relevant to marketing.
- It treats risk as a separate dimension, which makes it closer to the real world situation, since many countries of the world could have high potential and be attractive but have different degrees of risk.
- Each of the preceding dimensions is a composite measure of a variety of subfactors. For example, neither GNP nor income level, each by itself, is adequate as a descriptor of overall country potential.
- It uses an eighteen-cell matrix with three levels each of the country potential and competitive strength dimensions, and two levels of risk. This is important because the world contains not only highs and lows, but middle positions as well.

This approach presents an interesting method for achieving country segments. It requires, however, an abundance of information, both internal and external to the firm, which may not be easy to collect and analyze. Additionally, this approach is more relevant for use at a product/market level than at a headquarters level. Thus, a company involved in marketing a number of products/services abroad will have to work out a number of segmentation schemes. The scheme, however, makes strategic sense and provides an important framework for analyzing opportunities for chosen products in select markets that appear to be potentially viable.

In-Country Segmentation

So far the discussion has dealt with grouping the countries of the world from the point of view of the multinational corporation. However, the concept of segmentation also is relevant within a particular country. Just as marketers segment their markets in the United States, in each country there may be a variety of submarkets or segments that vary substantially from one another. The marketing strategist should identify these segments and choose those that are to be served.

One may use simple demographic and socioeconomic variables, personality and lifestyle variables, or situation-specific events (such as use intensity, brand loyalty, attitudes) as the bases for segmentation. For example, a U.S. food company segmented the French market into modern and traditional segments, defining the modern French consumer as liking processed foods while the traditional type looks upon them as a threat. A leading industrial manufacturer discovered that the critical variable for segmenting the Japanese market was the amount of annual usage per item, not per order or per any other variable. A toiletries manufacturer used geographic criteria—urban versus rural markets in West Africa. Exhibit 11.1 provides an inventory of different bases for market segmentation. Most of these bases are usually covered in a principles of marketing text. For a detailed account, however, reference may be made to an advanced book on the subject such as the one by Frank, Massy, and Wind.[36]

Besides products and customers, a market can also be segmented by level of customer service, stage of production, price-performance characteristics, credit arrangements with customers, location of plants, characteristics of manufacturing equipment, channels of distribution, and financial policies.

The key is to choose a variable or variables that so divide the market that customers in a segment have similar responsiveness to some aspect of the marketer's strategy. The variable should be measurable; it should represent an objective value such as income, rate of consumption, or frequency of buying, not simply a qualitative viewpoint such as the degree of customer happiness.[37] Also, the variable should create segments that may be responsive to promotion. Even if it were feasible to measure happiness, segments based on the happiness variable cannot be reached by a specific medium. Thus, happiness cannot serve as an appropriate criterion because it is not easily manipulated.

Once segments have been formed, the next strategic issue is deciding which segment should be selected. The segment chosen should fulfill the following conditions:

1. It should be one in which the maximum differential in competitive strategy can be developed.
2. It must be capable of being isolated so that the competitive advantage can be preserved.
3. It must be valid, even though imitated.

EXHIBIT 11.1 Bases for Segmentation

1. Demographic factors (age, income, sex, etc.)
2. Socioeconomic factors (social class, stages in the family life cycle)
3. Geographic factors
4. Psychological factors (lifestyle, personality traits)
5. Consumption patterns (heavy, moderate, and light users)
6. Perceptual factors (benefit segmentation, perceptual mapping)
7. Brand and loyalty patterns
8. Product attributes

The success of Volkswagen in the United States can be attributed to its fit into a market segment that has two unique characteristics. First, the segment served by VW could not be adequately served by conventional U.S. cars or modifications of them. Second, the manufacturing economies of scale could not be brought to bear by U.S. manufacturers as a whole to the disadvantage of VW. However, American Motors, like Volkswagen, was successful in identifying a special segment to serve with its compact car, the Rambler. In the long run, the critical difference between Volkswagen and American Motors was that American Motors could not protect its segment from the superior scale of manufacturing volume of the other three U.S. automobile manufacturers.

Summary

Worldwide there are about 5.3 billion consumers belonging to over 124 countries. Not all people, however, are viable consumers. The global market may be split into different regions such as the triad market, Pacific Rim market, postcommunist countries, Latin America, China and India, and developing countries. Different regions offer different market opportunities. The richest and most advanced among these is the triad market.

An interesting aspect of today's international business is the globalization of markets. World markets are slowly becoming homogeneous, requiring companies to develop marketing programs to serve consumers across national boundaries. A company interested in marketing abroad needs to decide which countries to enter and how those countries may be grouped together in homogeneous categories. The use of categories limits the need for developing marketing programs for each country separately and permits countries in each group to be served through a common marketing perspective.

Countries may be classified by such criteria as their economic status, geographic location, cultural traits, religious perspective, political system, socioeconomic-political characteristics, or common intermarket characteristics. In addition, a new approach for grouping countries, the portfolio method, recommends grouping countries based on three factors: competitive strength, risk, and country potential.

The concept of segmentation in the context of international marketing ought to be examined at another level, that is, segmenting the in-country market. Just as the U.S. market is segmented by marketers in different ways, it may be desirable to segment the market within each country and choose one or more segments to be served. The process of accomplishing in-country segmentation is essentially the same in international marketing as in domestic marketing.

Review Questions

1. What factors make the triad market most attractive?
2. What forces account for the growing globalization of markets?

3. Between the Pacific Rim market (excluding Japan) and the Eastern European market, which one appears to offer better market opportunities?
4. What is the rationale behind grouping countries together?
5. Even countries that appear to be the same in so many ways, Great Britain and Canada, for example, are nevertheless very different. Thus, does grouping of countries really help in making sound marketing decisions?
6. Discuss the following: "Philosophical imposition of political boundaries as the starting point in the matter of segmenting the world market is superfluous and dysfunctional. Why should we segment countries? We should rather segment the customers of the world. After all, it may be hypothesized that high-income people, whether living in the United States, France, Brazil, India, Nigeria, Egypt, Sweden, or Mexico, provide a similar potential for a product. If this is true, then it is the customer segmentation on a worldwide basis that should be sought and not country classification. Like income, education, geography, political views, age, and a host of other demographic and socioeconomic criteria may be used to segment the world market."
7. What are the variables used in the portfolio approach to classify countries? What problems do you anticipate in adapting the portfolio approach in practice?

Endnotes

1. *The Futures Group Reports,* March 1989.
2. Kenichi Ohmae, *Triad Power* (New York: The Free Press, 1985).
3. Ibid., p. 23.
4. Louis Kraar, "The Rising Power of the Pacific," *Fortune,* Pacific Rim Issue, 1990, p. 80.
5. Shawn Tully, "What Eastern Europe Offers," *Fortune,* March 2, 1990, p. 51. *Also see* W. W. Rostow, *The States of Economic Growth* (New York: Cambridge University Press, 1960); and Bertill Liander, Vern Terpstra, M. Y. Yoshimo, and Aziz A. Sherbini, *Comparative Analysis for International Marketing* (Boston: Allyn & Bacon, 1967), p. 27.
6. "Reawakening: A Market Economy Takes Root in Eastern Europe," *Business Week,* April 15, 1991, p. 46. *Also see* Janusz Bugajski, "Eastern Europe in the Post-Communist Era," *Columbia Journal of World Business,* Spring 1991, pp. 5–9.
7. "Yeltsin's Economic Shock Trooper," *Business Week,* February 24, 1992, p. 67.
8. "After Yeltsin's Strong Medicine, A Few Twitches of Life," *Business Week,* March 2, 1992, p. 50.
9. Paul Hofheinz, "Opportunity in the Baltics," *Fortune,* October 21, 1991, p. 68.
10. *The Wall Street Journal,* February 18,1992, p. 1.
11. "As the Empire Shrinks, Russian Nationalists Vie for Power," *Business Week,* February 5, 1990, p. 40.
12. Jeremy Main, "How Latin America is Opening Up," *Fortune,* April 8, 1991, p. 84.
13. Ford S. Worthy, "Where Capitalism Thrives in China," *Fortune,* March 9, 1992, p. 71.
14. "India is Becoming the New Asian Magnet for U.S. Business," *Business Week,* May 1, 1989, p. 132D.
15. *The Global Century: A Source Book on U.S. Business and the Third World* (Washington, D.C.: National Cooperative Business Association, 1989).
16. George S. Yip, "Global Strategy in a World of Nations," *Sloan Management Review,* Fall 1991, pp. 29–39.
17. Federal Industries (a Canadian firm) Annual Report, 1986.
18. Millard H. Pryor, Jr., "Planning in a Worldwide Business," *Harvard Business Review,* February 1965, p. 132. *Also see* Gary L. Bergstrom and Mark England-Markun, "In-

ternational Country Selection Strategies," *Columbia Journal of World Business,* Summer 1982, pp. 42–45;; and "Value Segments Help Define International Market," *Marketing News,* November 21, 1988, p. 17.

19. *World Development Report, 1988* (New York: Oxford University Press, 1988), pp. 222–223.
20. Morris David Morris, *Measuring the Condition of the World's Poor* (New York: Pergamon Press, 1979), p. 12.
21. *See* Richard D. Steade, "Multinational Corporations and the Changing World Economic Order," *California Management Review,* Winter 1978, p. 87. *Also see* "Poor vs. Rich: A New Global Conflict," *Time,* December 22, 1975, pp. 34–35; James W. Howe, *The U.S. and World Development: Agenda for Action, 1975* (New York: Praeger Publishers, 1974), p. 38.
22. Marlene L. Rossman, "Understanding Five Nations of Latin America," *Marketing News,* October 11, 1985, p. 10.
23. Frank Tannenbaum, *Ten Keys to Latin America* (New York: Knopf, 1962), p. 65. *Also see* Lane Kelley and Reginald Worthley, "The Role of Culture in Comparative Management: A Cross-Cultural Perspective," *Academy of Management Journal,* no. 1 (1981), pp. 164–173.
24. *See* Vern Terpstra and Kenneth David, *The Cultural Environment of International Business,* 2nd ed. (Cincinnati, OH: South-Western Publishing Co., 1985), pp. 77–116.
25. Prakash Tandon, "Maturing of Business in India," *California Management Review,* Spring 1972, p. 80.
26. *See Nature and Use of the HRAF Files* (New Haven: Human Relations Area Files, Inc., 1974).
27. *See* Ellen Day, Richard J. Fox, and Sandra M. Huszagh, "Segmenting the Global Market for Industrial Goods: Issues and Implications," *International Marketing Review,* Autumn 1988, pp. 14–27.
28. S. Prakash Sethi, "Comparative Cluster Analysis for World Markets," *Journal of Marketing Research,* August 1971, pp. 348–354. *Also see* Kenneth Matsuura, *A Classification of Countries for International Marketing,* Master's thesis, University of California, Berkeley, 1968.
29. *See* Sudhir H. Kale and D. Sudharshan, "A Strategic Approach to International Segmentation," *International Marketing Review,* Summer 1987, pp. 60–70.
30. "How Germany Sells Cars Where Detroit Can't," *Business Week,* September 9, 1985, p. 45.
31. Eugene Bacto, "Eurobrand: A New Approach to Marketing," *Advertising Age/Europe,* October 1981, pp. 3 and 9; Joel Stratte-McClure, "Not Divided but United by Lifestyle," *Advertising Age's Focus,* January 1982, p. 12.
32. John K. Ryans, Jr., "Have Communications Technological Developments Made Current European Marketing Practices/Strategies Obsolete? a presentation made at the Netherlands School of Business, July 5, 1982. *Also see* Gerald D. Sentell, "Modern, Traditional, and Transnational Consumer Groups in a Developing Dual Economy: An Empirical Investigation of Thai Consumers," a paper presented at the Academy of International Business Meeting, Washington, D.C., 1982.
33. "Estee Lauder Hoping to Sell Men's Perfume to Affluent Japanese," *The Asian Wall Street Journal Weekly,* September 26, 1988, p. 8.
34. Elias G. Rizkallah, "Multiple Product: Multiple Market Allocations—A Portfolio Approach," a paper presented at the Academy of International Business Annual Meeting in New Orleans, October 24, 1980.
35. Ibid.
36. *See* Ronald E. Frank, William F. Massy, and Yoram Wind, *Market Segmentation* (Englewood Cliffs, NJ: Prentice-Hall, 1972). *Also see* Thomas V. Bonoma and Benson P. Shapiro, *Segmenting the Industrial Market* (Lexington, MA: D.C. Heath and Company, 1983).
37. Robert A. Garda, "A Strategic Approach to Market Segmentation," *The McKinsey Quarterly,* Autumn 1981, pp. 16–29. *Also see* Ivor Mitchell and Tom O. Amioku, "Brand Preference Factors in Patronage and Consumption of Nigerian Beer," *Columbia Journal of World Business,* Spring 1985, pp. 55–68; Vern Terpstra, "Critical Mass and International Marketing Strategy," *Journal of the Academy of Marketing Science,* Summer 1983, pp. 269–282.

APPENDIX

Macro Information on Global Markets

The statistical information on the following pages has been reproduced from "Indicators of Market Size for 117 Countries," *Business International,* July 8, 1991.

Because the coverage of countries is not uniform for all indicators and because the variation around central tendencies can be large, readers should exercise caution in comparing the summary measures for different indicators, country groups, and years or periods.

Readers should also exercise caution in comparing indicators across countries. Although the statistics presented are drawn from sources generally considered the most authoritative and reliable, some of them, particularly those describing social features and income distribution, are subject to considerable margins of error. In addition, variations in national practices mean that the data in certain instances are not strictly comparable. The data should thus be construed only as indicating trends and characterizing major differences between countries.

Sources used by *Business International* editors include: *Monthly Bulletin of Statistics* (UN); *OECD Economic Surveys: Direction of Trade Statistics* (IMF); *International Financial Statistics* (IMF; U.S. Department of Commerce; Agency for International Development; *World Automotive Market* (Johnston International Publishing Corp.); *The World's Telephones* (American Telephone and Telegraph); *World Radio-TV Handbook* (AT&T Communications); *Statistical Yearbook* (UN); *Yearbook of Labor Statistics* (ILO); *Yearbook of National Accounts Statistics* (UN); *Yearbook of Energy Statistics* (UN); International Iron and Steel Institute; *Key Indicators of Developing Member Countries of ADB* (Asian Development Bank); *Selected World Demographic Indicators by Countries, 1950–2000* (UN); central banks' and government publications.

TABLE A–11.1 Basic Indicators

	POPULATION				GROSS DOMESTIC PRODUCT			NATIONAL INCOME
	Total 1989 (millions)	Avg. Annual % Increase 1984–89	Working Age 1989 (millions)	Avg. Annual % Increase 1984–89	Total 1989 ($ billions)	Avg. Annual Real % Increase 1985–89	Per Capita 1989 ($)	Total 1989 ($ billions)
WESTERN EUROPE								
EC								
BELGIUM	9.93	0.1	6.7	0.1	156.8	3.1	15,794.0	141.3
DENMARK	5.13	0.1	3.5	2.0	106.2	2.9	20,694.0	92.1
FRANCE	56.16	0.4	37.1	5.7	955.9	3.1	17,020.0	836.2
GERMANY	61.99	0.3	42.4	−1.2	1,189.1	3.3	19,183.0	1,055.6
GREECE	10.03	0.3	6.7	3.3	54.2	2.7	5,401.0	48.8
IRELAND	3.51	−0.1	2.2	2.7	33.9	4.1	9,669.0	26.3
ITALY	57.52	0.2	39.5	7.3	865.8	3.7	15,053.0	753.0
LUXEMBOURG	0.38	0.8	0.3	3.5	8.0	6.0	21,111.0	8.7
NETHERLANDS	14.83	0.6	10.3	3.9	223.7	3.1	15,084.0	198.9
PORTUGAL	10.47	0.7	6.9	5.4	45.4	4.1	4,338.0	42.6
SPAIN	38.81	0.2	25.8	4.4	380.0	4.6	9,791.0	334.8
UNITED KINGDOM	57.20	0.3	37.5	3.8	831.7	4.0	14,540.0	745.3
TOTAL EC	325.96	0.3	218.8	3.7	4,850.8	—	14,881.0	53,004.6
EFTA								
AUSTRIA	7.62	0.2	5.1	1.1	126.5	3.0	16,598.0	108.1
FINLAND	4.96	0.3	3.3	0.2	115.5	4.6	23,278.0	95.8
ICELAND	0.25	1.1	0.2	7.1	5.2	3.7	20,611.0	4.3
NORWAY	4.23	0.4	2.7	3.0	90.9	4.2	21,488.0	73.8
SWEDEN	8.50	0.4	5.5	2.5	189.9	3.2	22,342.0	163.3
SWITZERLAND	6.65	0.6	4.5	3.3	177.2	3.4	26,639.0	167.6
TOTAL EFTA	32.21	0.4	21.5	2.0	705.0	0.0	21,889.0	612.8
TURKEY	56.74	3.0	34.8	19.7	78.5	6.3	1,384.0	76.1
TOTAL WESTERN EUROPE	414.91	0.6	275.1	5.3	5,634.3	—	13,580.0	53,693.5
EASTERN EUROPE								
BULGARIA	8.99	0.1	6.0	1.4	36.2	4.6	4,030.0	—
CZECHOSLOVAKIA	15.65	0.2	10.2	0.9	50.5	3.2	3,225.0	—
E. GERMANY	16.67	0.0	11.2	−0.2	148.6	—	8,796.0	—
HUNGARY	10.38	−0.5	6.9	−1.5	28.9	1.3	2,783.0	—
POLAND	37.85	0.5	24.5	1.6	82.2	4.1	2,172.0	—
ROMANIA	23.15	0.5	15.3	3.8	42.1	3.8	1,819.0	—
USSR	288.75	1.2	187.4	4.5	1,020.2	3.8	3,533.0	—
YUGOSLAVIA	23.69	0.6	16.1	3.1	73.0	0.8	3,083.0	—
TOTAL EASTERN EUROPE	425.30	0.9	277.7	3.6	1,481.7	—	3,127.0	—
MIDDLE EAST								
BAHRAIN	0.49	3.6	0.3	3.9	3.5	1.8	7,110.0	2.0
EGYPT	53.08	2.4	29.3	1.9	58.8	2.8	1,108.0	—
IRAN	54.20	3.4	28.7	3.0	361.0	−1.0	6,661.0	155.7
IRAQ	18.28	3.9	9.3	4.1	66.2	−1.7	3,621.0	—
ISRAEL	4.51	1.6	2.7	1.9	43.9	2.6	9,730.0	23.6
JORDAN	4.10	4.0	2.0	4.2	4.5	0.8	1,093.0	4.0
KUWAIT	2.05	4.6	1.2	5.0	23.1	2.3	11,259.0	29.3
LIBYA	4.38	6.2	2.3	6.4	22.2	−1.6	5,080.0	—
OMAN	1.42	3.6	0.7	3.0	8.4	4.3	5,909.0	—
QATAR	0.42	8.4	0.3	8.2	6.6	—	15,829.0	—
SAUDI ARABIA	14.43	5.3	7.5	5.0	83.0	−2.4	5,751.0	98.0
SYRIA	11.72	3.4	5.8	3.5	18.2	2.1	1,551.0	—
UNITED ARAB EMIRATES	1.55	3.7	0.9	0.2	27.3	−0.9	17,592.0	17.4
YEMEN ARAB REPUBLIC	7.77	3.0	3.8	1.7	6.8	8.7	871.0	4.8
TOTAL MIDDLE EAST	178.40	3.3	94.8	3.0	733.5	—	4,111.0	—
AFRICA								
ALGERIA	24.60	3.2	12.8	3.7	47.2	1.9	1,918.0	—
ANGOLA	9.80	2.9	5.1	2.8	7.4	8.8	757.0	—
BURKINA FASO	8.77	2.7	4.7	2.7	1.9	6.9	221.0	—
CAMEROON	11.54	3.2	6.1	3.1	10.7	0.6	929.0	6.8
CONGO	1.94	2.8	1.0	2.6	2.3	0.1	1,170.0	1.3
ETHIOPIA	49.51	3.6	25.5	3.2	6.0	1.8	121.0	—
GABON	1.13	3.5	0.7	4.5	3.7	0.4	3,240.0	—

TABLE A–11.1 (*Continued*)

AVERAGE HOURLY WAGE		TOTAL EXPORTS		TOTAL IMPORTS		IMPORTS FROM U.S.		IMPORTS FROM JAPAN		IMPORTS FROM EC	
1989 ($)	Avg. Annual % Increase 1984–89	1989 F.O.B. ($ millions)	Avg. Annual % Increase 1984–89	1989 C.I.F. ($ millions)	Avg. Annual % Increase 1984–89	1989 C.I.F. ($ millions)	Avg. Annual % Increase 1984–89	1989 C.I.F. ($ millions)	Avg. Annual % Increase 1984–89	1989 C.I.F. ($ millions)	Avg. Annual % Increase 1984–89
11.19	10.9	99,707	14.3	98.179	12.4	4,454	6.3	2,231	16.0	70,209	13.6
14.27	13.6	28,020	12.3	26,616	10.2	1,831	16.3	1,026	13.5	13,303	11.4
8.72	11.2	178,967	13.1	193,015	13.3	14,641	13.1	7,849	24.5	114,137	15.5
13.74	13.3	341,389	15.2	269,646	12.2	20,362	13.4	17,143	22.8	137,898	12.7
4.49	7.9	7,050	9.4	15,522	11.0	597	16.9	918	8.7	9,890	17.1
8.03	6.0	20,781	16.8	17,469	12.7	2,810	12.3	998	25.5	11,383	12.3
9.03	12.0	141,034	14.1	153,181	12.9	8,339	10.3	3,526	22.1	86,834	18.2
9.52	10.7	—	—	—	—	—	—	—	—	—	—
11.91	12.3	107,299	10.4	104,049	11.0	8,711	9.7	3,137	18.4	65,816	14.2
2.16	14.3	12.672	19.7	18,983	20.3	841	−3.4	582	26.1	12,816	32.2
6.50	14.7	44,394	13.8	71,419	20.5	6,490	15.4	3,419	32.7	40,810	34.1
8.87	12.1	152,339	10.3	197,683	13.8	21,294	11.7	11,631	19.0	104,062	16.1
—	—	1,133,652	13.3	1,165,762	13.1	90,370	11.6	52,460	21.1	667,158	15.7
9.81	13.6	32,469	15.9	38,896	14.9	1,412	15.9	1,925	26.7	26,408	17.4
12.89	16.0	23,305	11.9	24,432	14.8	1,545	20.8	1,793	22.0	10,913	19.3
—	—	1,411	14.6	1,419	12.5	156	23.1	68	22.5	697	11.6
14.63	12.6	26,952	7.8	23,254	11.3	1,684	6.2	880	10.4	10,074	9.9
12.20	13.5	51,082	12.0	48,204	13.0	3,952	13.1	2,945	19.6	26,531	13.2
14.04	11.6	51,547	15.4	58,206	15.1	3,717	14.9	2,645	20.4	41,261	15.8
—	—	186,766	12.6	194,411	13.9	12,466	13.3	10,256	19.5	115,884	15.1
1.53	34.8	11,572	11.1	15,880	8.8	1,727	10.7	580	11.2	6,621	15.7
—	—	1,331,990	12.9	1,376,053	12.8	104,563	11.6	63,296	20.6	789,663	15.4
—	—	2,212	3.2	4,241	7.2	199	41.6	180	17.9	1,770	11.1
1.28	5.5	6,934	5.7	7,720	9.8	59	2.2	61	−1.4	2,870	15.3
4.63	14.1	6,096	4.6	7,288	9.2	103	9.1	104	−3.4	1,979	20.1
1.04	8.4	10.217	3.6	10,053	4.7	160	−0.6	121	11.0	3,138	15.0
0.84	0.8	13,098	2.4	10,053	−0.9	179	7.0	142	19.0	2,799	8.8
1.03	—	14,270	6.1	9,752	4.1	156	−9.6	97	8.6	758	−2.3
1.69	2.7	40,042	1.6	57,163	6.3	4,698	17.0	3,376	5.1	15,145	7.2
0.96	8.7	13,599	5.9	14,833	4.5	762	10.3	219	25.4	5,886	13.6
—	—	92,869	3.0	106,270	5.2	5,554	10.5	4,081	4.8	28,459	8.9
—	—	2,715	−1.5	2,944	−2.6	219	−2.6	292	7.0	622	2.3
—	—	2,634	3.7	7,378	−6.1	1,137	0.7	403	−8.6	2,791	−8.0
—	—	13,439	1.5	9,590	−6.5	66	−6.8	1,010	−10.6	2,829	−5.4
—	—	12,079	8.3	10,297	2.9	1,291	17.5	538	2.5	3,667	21.5
6.35	10.6	10,649	13.0	13,741	7.8	2,360	6.0	355	16.9	6,666	4.9
1.66	—	1,195	11.8	2,324	−2.8	320	3.6	79	−15.9	657	−0.5
—	—	11,257	1.2	6,452	−1.0	940	5.6	734	−14.2	2,003	2.9
—	—	7,560	−5.2	5,716	−2.8	51		245	5.9	3,391	3.0
—	—	3,721	3.4	2,447	−0.2	187	2.0	366	−4.8	896	12.8
—	—	2,570	−9.4	1,502	5.6	111	3.7	231	1.5	536	2.1
—	—	31,894	−0.7	25,591	−3.2	3,934	−5.3	3,025	−12.5	10,457	10.0
—	—	3,005	18.8	2,098	−11.1	166	193.4	88	6.6	876	3.1
—	—	17,030	4.5	9,559	6.8	928	3.8	1,438	3.1	2,972	0.1
—	—	990	221.1	1,698	−1.2	78	10.2	68	−15.8	407	2.6
—	—	120,738	1.2	101,337	−2.1	11,788	−0.9	8,872	−10.1	38,770	2.0
—	—	9,569	−3.4	8,977	−2.0	834	11.4	291	−16.9	5,573	8.3
—	—	3,036	10.4	1,443	8.6	107	2.3	28	30.0	995	10.3
—	—	125	12.9	489	14.5	12	−5.4	21	24.0	225	5.9
—	—	1,789	18.1	1,381	6.7	46	−16.1	74	1.0	873	−1.9
—	—	1,135	1.2	600	0.4	13	4.6	16	−5.9	411	1.2
—	—	499	5.8	1,245	6.3	82	−4.7	57	0.4	519	5.0
—	—	1,570	−0.6	941	4.4	51	20.0	39	−2.6	573	2.5

(*continued*)

TABLE A–11.1 (*Continued*)

	POPULATION				GROSS DOMESTIC PRODUCT			NATIONAL INCOME
	Total 1989 (millions)	Avg. Annual % Increase 1984–89	Working Age 1989 (millions)	Avg. Annual % Increase 1984–89	Total 1989 ($ billions)	Avg. Annual Real % Increase 1985–89	Per Capita 1989 ($)	Total 1989 ($ billions)
AFRICA (*continued*)								
GHANA	14.57	3.3	7.5	3.8	5.1	6.0	353.0	5.7
IVORY COAST	12.10	4.2	5.9	2.9	9.4	0.3	774.0	—
KENYA	24.87	4.9	11.2	4.7	8.3	4.4	333.0	5.6
MADAGASCAR	11.60	3.2	6.0	3.0	2.3	1.6	202.0	—
MALAWI	8.02	3.2	4.1	3.1	1.6	3.3	198.0	—
MAURITIUS	1.03	1.0	0.7	1.8	2.1	6.5	2,015.0	1.4
MOROCCO	24.52	2.6	13.7	2.8	22.4	4.5	913.0	22.6
MOZAMBIQUE	15.30	2.5	8.1	2.2	1.3	−0.8	85.0	3.3
NIGERIA	109.17	3.2	53.7	3.1	21.5	0.6	197.0	—
SENEGAL	7.17	2.4	3.8	2.3	4.7	1.8	652.0	4.1
SIERRA LEONE	4.05	2.5	2.1	1.3	0.7	0.8	170.0	1.2
SOUTH AFRICA	34.49	2.2	20.3	3.6	88.9	1.7	2,577.0	70.6
TANZANIA	24.80	3.3	11.7	2.6	3.1	2.6	131.0	2.9
TUNISIA	7.99	2.6	4.7	3.2	10.1	3.5	1,261.0	10.5
UGANDA	17.80	3.5	8.7	3.4	4.5	3.1	251.0	—
ZAIRE	34.49	2.8	17.7	2.6	3.3	2.4	98.0	2.0
ZAMBIA	7.80	3.9	3.8	3.3	3.4	1.9	433.0	1.9
ZIMBABWE	9.12	2.7	4.8	3.9	5.3	3.7	577.0	4.9
TOTAL AFRICA	476.20	3.2	244.3	3.2	277.0	—	582.0	—
NORTH AMERICA								
CANADA	26.22	1.0	17.8	0.9	550.4	4.3	20,990	367.3
UNITED STATES	248.76	1.0	163.9	0.8	5,163.2	3.9	20,756	4,646.4
TOTAL NORTH AMERICA	274.98	1.0	181.7	0.8	5,713.6	—	20,778	5,013.7
LATIN AMERICA								
LAIA								
ARGENTINA	31.93	1.3	19.5	1.5	60.3	−0.3	1,887	—
BOLIVIA	7.19	2.8	3.8	2.8	4.6	0.7	640	—
BRAZIL	147.40	2.1	88.6	2.4	482.0	4.7	3,270	214.9
CHILE	12.96	1.7	8.2	1.5	25.4	6.3	1,958	—
COLOMBIA	31.19	2.1	18.7	2.4	39.8	4.0	1,275	2.3
ECUADOR	10.49	2.9	5.8	3.3	10.4	3.2	990	8.1
MEXICO	84.49	2.1	49.8	3.8	200.7	1.4	2,376	104.8
PARAGUAY	4.16	3.0	2.3	3.5	4.4	4.0	1,052	3.9
PERU	21.79	2.6	12.4	3.0	51.8	1.2	2,378	13.2
URUGUAY	3.08	0.6	1.9	0.7	8.4	2.4	2,733	7.8
VENEZUELA	19.25	2.7	11.2	3.0	43.1	1.3	2,240	57.3
ANCOM SUBTOTAL	89.91	2.5	51.9	2.8	149.7	—	1,665	80.9
TOTAL LAIA	373.92	2.1	222.3	2.7	930.8	—	2,489	426.6
CACM								
COSTA RICA	2.96	4.1	1.8	4.1	5.3	4.7	1,774	4.7
EL SALVADOR	5.21	1.7	2.7	1.7	6.4	1.5	1,237	6.1
GUATEMALA	8.94	2.9	4.6	3.0	8.4	1.9	939	1.0
HONDURAS	4.95	3.2	2.6	4.0	4.9	3.5	987	4.1
NICARAGUA	3.74	3.4	1.9	3.8	1.2	−3.1	328	3.1
TOTAL CACM	25.80	2.9	13.6	3.1	26.2	—	1,016	—
CARIBBEAN								
BARBADOS	0.26	0.8	0.2	1.5	1.5	3.2	5,929	—
CUBA	10.50	1.0	7.3	2.2	34.1	0.5	3,245	—
DOMINICAN REPUBLIC	7.02	2.3	4.1	3.1	6.7	2.3	953	6.1
GUYANA	1.02	1.6	0.6	2.4	0.3	−3.3	249	0.3
HAITI	5.61	1.5	3.2	2.9	2.1	−0.1	373	2.0
JAMAICA	2.37	0.8	1.4	1.6	3.9	1.5	1,639	1.9
NETHERLAND ANTILLES	0.19	1.1	—	—	1.5	1.3	7,642	—
PANAMA	2.37	2.2	1.4	3.0	4.5	−1.5	1,919	4.2
PUERTO RICO	3.26	−0.3	2.0	−0.1	28.2	3.9	8,638	18.2
TRINIDAD & TOBAGO	1.26	1.5	0.8	1.8	4.3	−4.6	3,444	3.5
TOTAL CARIBBEAN	33.86	1.3	21.1	2.3	87.0	—	2,570	36.1
TOTAL LATIN AMERICA	433.59	2.1	257.0	2.7	1,044.1	—	2,408	481.7

TABLE A–11.1 (*Continued*)

AVERAGE HOURLY WAGE		TOTAL EXPORTS		TOTAL IMPORTS		IMPORTS FROM U.S.		IMPORTS FROM JAPAN		IMPORTS FROM EC	
1989 ($)	Avg. Annual % Increase 1984–89	1989 F.O.B. ($ millions)	Avg. Annual % Increase 1984–89	1989 C.I.F. ($ millions)	Avg. Annual % Increase 1984–89	1989 C.I.F. ($ millions)	Avg. Annual % Increase 1984–89	1989 C.I.F. ($ millions)	Avg. Annual % Increase 1984–89	1989 C.I.F. ($ millions)	Avg. Annual % Increase 1984–89
0.55	—	1,071	24.3	1,308	18.9	135	23.1	66	18.6	549	4.3
—	—	3,153	3.6	2,469	10.5	87	−0.1	70	6.8	1,287	2.2
0.78	3.8	1,157	2.6	2,569	11.9	156	20.8	230	8.3	1,028	11.2
—	—	336	1.5	614	11.1	8	−16.0	25	30.9	235	1.3
0.33	—	267	−1.4	503	14.5	18	30.2	48	23.3	210	13.9
0.45	8.3	986	22.9	1,324	23.9	21	151.5	121	36.9	453	13.1
—	—	3,405	9.8	5,527	7.4	480	10.1	66	−8.9	2,983	8.0
—	—	359	29.4	780	12.4	45	36.5	43	29.8	291	5.8
—	—	11,050	2.0	5,280	4.9	541	4.0	292	−2.8	2,587	5.4
—	—	869	10.5	1,228	5.3	76	13.9	28	14.9	736	4.7
0.07	—	137	−0.3	183	2.7	8	3.3	11	2.9	74	6.9
2.71	−0.6	22,220	5.8	16,949	4.7	2,343	3.3	1,686	1.5	7,174	5.7
—	—	312	−1.3	717	−2.4	18	−8.4	69	−3.1	307	−4.0
—	—	2,978	11.2	4,326	7.0	242	5.5	60	−2.4	2,879	7.7
—	—	270	−5.8	490	12.6	25	71.1	31	18.7	206	5.6
—	—	1,726	13.5	1,447	20.9	134	10.5	75	109.5	950	18.8
—	—	1,322	19.7	889	10.6	50	9.1	89	45.4	368	18.1
1.70	—	1,451	7.8	1,040	2.5	121	20.3	46	0.7	393	4.7
—	—	70,792	3.1	62,719	3.7	5,653	1.2	3,582	−2.8	31,879	3.9
11.50	3.4	120,673	6.2	117,146	8.7	74,556	7.4	8,066	13.2	13,272	14.9
13.02	5.3	363,807	11.3	493,652	7.7	—	—	97,110	10.2	88,821	7.1
—	—	484,480	9.9	610,798	7.8	74,556	7.4	105,176	10.4	102,093	7.9
0.79	—	9,842	5.9	4,287	0.4	768	−0.7	268	−3.1	1,250	3.7
0.23	—	819	2.4	784	17.8	159	16.3	41	28.2	106	18.9
1.26	10.1	34,409	6.0	20,029	6.2	4,187	11.3	1,322	18.8	3,893	17.3
1.09	−1.6	8,191	18.0	6,496	14.6	1,283	12.7	502	15.4	1,267	16.6
—	—	5,734	11.7	5,066	3.1	1,844	4.1	552	6.7	1,009	4.4
0.49	—	2,348	−0.8	1,854	2.2	614	3.2	258	1.8	385	5.1
1.62	2.1	24,752	2.4	25,082	21.9	16,801	23.8	1,323	26.8	3,269	20.5
0.98	0.5	1,281	45.3	677	8.2	119	32.9	88	28.4	104	8.6
0.75	6.7	3,491	3.5	2,016	11.7	664	11.7	83	−2.9	410	10.5
—	—	1,638	12.5	1,271	11.3	109	12.2	38	25.1	262	16.3
2.94	—	12,433	−2.1	6,881	2.9	3,071	0.5	283	2.6	1,983	8.4
—	—	24,825	0.1	16,601	2.7	6,352	2.0	1,176	1.0	3,893	6.0
—	—	104,938	4.0	74,443	8.4	29,619	12.6	4,758	9.8	13,938	11.0
1.20	5.2	1,437	8.2	1,743	10.3	705	12.9	116	8.7	212	6.7
—	—	573	−3.6	1,319	6.5	573	13.1	46	10.3	169	11.7
—	—	1,277	9.6	1,739	4.7	687	11.7	88	6.8	310	12.7
—	—	973	5.2	1,083	3.2	566	12.2	98	28.2	110	−1.2
—	—	286	−5.3	522	−1.7	2	798.7	19	11.6	107	−3.0
—	—	4,546	3.1	6,406	4.7	2,533	9.9	367	9.4	908	5.6
—	—	195	−10.2	678	1.3	238	−3.7	39	10.5	127	9.5
1.26	—	1,313	10.1	2,709	6.5	3	35.0	59	−19.0	713	2.7
1.20	—	928	2.0	1,974	9.7	815	13.9	285	45.0	226	14.5
—	—	251	4.6	215	1.1	86	18.1	11	40.4	40	6.1
—	—	220	5.0	426	−1.8	235	−1.9	23	−2.2	56	7.1
—	—	967	7.0	1,801	10.1	890	11.2	74	34.5	223	13.7
6.25	—	938	−16.8	2,491	4.1	454	51.8	73	83.7	420	110.5
—	—	297	4.1	1,338	4.2	374	−1.8	142	42.6	195	20.9
5.73	2.7	—	—	—	—	—	—	—	—	—	—
—	—	1,553	−4.2	1,227	−7.9	633	−0.2	28	−30.2	192	−11.8
—	—	6,662	3.2	12,859	0.5	3,728	14.7	734	−0.5	2,192	5.8
—	—	116,146	1.2	93,708	4.2	35,880	6.9	5,859	7.8	17,038	9.6

(*continued*)

TABLE A–11.1 *(Continued)*

	POPULATION				GROSS DOMESTIC PRODUCT			NATIONAL INCOME
	Total 1989 (millions)	Avg. Annual % Increase 1984–89	Working Age 1989 (millions)	Avg. Annual % Increase 1984–89	Total 1989 ($ billions)	Avg. Annual Real % Increase 1985–89	Per Capita 1989 ($)	Total 1989 ($ billions)
ASIA								
AFGHANISTAN	15.81	−2.2	8.7	−2.3	—	—	—	—
BANGLADESH	106.51	1.8	56.7	2.6	20.3	3.6	191	—
CHINA	1,119.70	1.4	761.4	2.3	422.5	10.2	377	351.3
HONG KONG	5.76	1.3	4.0	1.4	62.9	7.6	10,918	—
INDIA	811.82	2.0	479.0	2.0	236.5	5.7	291	250.8
INDONESIA	179.14	2.1	109.5	3.3	94.0	5.6	525	88.9
JAPAN	123.12	0.5	85.9	1.0	2,833.7	4.6	23,016	2,675.4
DEM. KAMPUCHEA	7.80	2.2	4.9	1.4	—	—	—	—
KOREA, NORTH	21.90	2.7	13.0	3.2	—	—	—	—
KOREA, SOUTH	42.38	1.0	27.8	1.2	211.9	9.7	4,999	172.8
LAOS	4.00	2.6	2.2	2.6	0.5	4.9	126	—
MALAYSIA	16.96	2.4	10.2	2.9	37.5	5.2	2,210	—
MYANMAR	40.81	1.6	24.0	1.8	18.1	−0.1	442	8.5
NEPAL	18.44	2.6	10.1	2.9	2.8	5.7	154	2.3
PAKISTAN	108.68	3.1	56.1	2.3	42.0	6.2	386	47.0
PHILLIPPINES	60.10	2.4	34.0	2.6	44.4	1.3	738	41.5
SINGAPORE	2.68	1.2	1.9	1.5	28.4	6.3	10,582	21.1
SRI LANKA	16.81	1.5	10.5	2.0	7.0	3.5	417	—
TAIWAN	20.10	1.1	13.2	1.1	151.5	9.3	7,538	127.3
THAILAND	55.45	1.8	35.2	2.9	69.7	8.4	1,257	63.7
VIETNAM	64.40	1.9	36.3	1.8	—	4.7	—	—
TOTAL ASIA	2,842.40	1.7	1,784.2	2.2	4,283.6	—	1,507	3,850.5
OCEANIA								
AUSTRALIA	16.81	1.6	11.2	1.7	282.9	4.5	16,827	252.2
NEW ZEALAND	3.31	0.5	2.2	0.8	41.8	1.7	12,618	36.2
TOTAL OCEANIA	20.12	1.4	13.4	1.6	324.6	—	16,134	288.4

TABLE A–11.2 Structure of Consumption

	PRIVATE CONSUMPTION EXPENDITURE					PASSENGER CARS		TRUCKS AND BUSES	
	1989 Total ($ billions)	Avg. Annual Real % Increase 1987–91	1988 % for Food	1988 % for Clothing	1988 % for Household	1989 (thousands)	Cumulative % Increase 1984–89	1989 (thousands)	Cumulative % Increase 1984–89
WESTERN EUROPE									
EC									
BELGIUM	98.3	3.1	20.2	6.6	10.3	3,736	13.2	378	8.6
DENMARK	56.0	0.8	23.5	5.9	6.8	1,596	10.8	302	19.4
FRANCE	571.4	3.1	19.8	6.4	8.2	22,520	8.3	4,570	38.1
GERMANY	644.3	3.1	22.6	8.4	9.2	29,190	15.0	1,859	9.8
GREECE	37.5	2.0	37.6	7.2	7.7	1,438	31.6	675	21.8
IRELAND	19.2	3.3	38.8	6.6	7.7	749	5.3	127	38.0
ITALY	537.1	3.7	25.3	9.4	8.9	23,500	11.9	1,990	8.6
LUXEMBOURG	4.5	—	21.6	6.4	10.3	—	—	—	—
NETHERLANDS	132.7	2.7	19.1	7.2	8.1	5,251	10.0	538	41.2
PORTUGAL	28.9	5.7	38.6	10.7	9.0	1,427	25.6	422	22.0
SPAIN	238.4	4.8	27.1	7.6	7.8	10,787	21.6	2,073	30.7
UNITED KINGDOM	532.0	3.1	17.4	7.2	6.7	21,348	23.3	3,151	97.6
TOTAL EC	2,900.4	—	—	—	—	121,542	14.7	16,085	34.0
EFTA									
AUSTRIA	70.1	3.1	22.6	10.0	7.9	2,785	12.8	272	16.7
FINLAND	59.7	3.9	23.2	5.5	7.0	1,796	22.7	238	24.0

TABLE A-11.1 (*Continued*)

AVERAGE HOURLY WAGE		TOTAL EXPORTS		TOTAL IMPORTS		IMPORTS FROM U.S.		IMPORTS FROM JAPAN		IMPORTS FROM EC	
1989 ($)	Avg. Annual % Increase 1984–89	1989 F.O.B. ($ millions)	Avg. Annual % Increase 1984–89	1989 C.I.F. ($ millions)	Avg. Annual % Increase 1984–89	1989 C.I.F. ($ millions)	Avg. Annual % Increase 1984–89	1989 C.I.F. ($ millions)	Avg. Annual % Increase 1984–89	1989 C.I.F. ($ millions)	Avg. Annual % Increase 1984–89
—	—	721	3.0	1,306	9.1	5	2.4	102	−2.0	50	−6.9
0.15	—	1,305	7.7	3,609	6.4	282	3.5	437	11.6	411	2.7
0.19	—	51,751	16.0	58,316	19.8	6,918	14.0	10,105	10.5	8,777	24.9
2.70	12.0	73,114	21.4	72,149	21.0	5,933	15.0	11,950	12.9	7,179	17.9
0.38	—	16,003	10.6	21,165	8.3	1,894	7.2	1,325	9.0	5,107	10.5
—	—	21,936	1.3	16,467	5.1	2,216	−0.2	3,832	4.1	2,594	4.9
10.98	14.6	274,597	10.3	209,635	9.6	48,253	13.0	—	—	28,137	24.9
—	—	13	70.0	34	8.0	—	—	—	—	4	16.7
—	—	772	3.5	1,231	9.4	—	—	216	−3.7	139	33.1
2.99	22.1	62,371	17.1	61,556	15.6	15,824	19.7	17,612	19.1	6,678	19.7
—	—	98	94.2	122	28.7	1	—	27	39.6	8	24.1
—	—	25,049	9.7	22,588	11.9	3,803	12.0	5,438	12.0	3,137	12.1
—	—	250	1.8	311	6.5	9	−6.0	76	−3.0	69	6.1
—	—	231	24.5	593	17.0	10	138.6	79	15.9	69	14.2
—	—	4,660	13.1	7,107	4.3	1,095	15.4	928	2.0	1,522	5.6
0.35	0.9	7,754	8.6	11,165	13.9	2,133	5.8	2,174	22.3	1,251	16.5
2.71	7.4	44,769	14.4	49,694	12.9	8,522	16.8	10,612	16.9	6,218	16.8
0.26	5.4	1,540	1.9	2,187	3.7	147	−0.8	293	−0.7	367	7.4
3.27	19.7	66,201	17.5	52,249	20.7	12,148	21.7	16,237	22.6	6,612	24.5
0.51	—	20,028	22.9	25,296	22.0	2,796	18.9	7,771	26.0	3,603	24.7
—	—	740	27.1	741	8.1	12	−8.7	185	8.3	153	18.7
—	—	673,903	12.7	617,521	12.9	112,001	13.9	89,399	13.5	82,085	18.3
10.25	4.1	37,037	9.7	44,609	12.0	9,261	13.1	8,320	10.8	9,843	12.2
7.34	10.9	8,849	10.3	8,810	7.9	1,430	8.5	1,620	5.6	1,712	7.4
—	—	45,886	9.8	53,419	11.2	10,691	12.4	9,940	9.7	11,555	11.3

TABLE A-11.2 (*Continued*)

TELEPHONES	TELEVISIONS		PERSONAL COMPUTERS	STEEL		CEMENT		ELECTRICITY		ENERGY CONSUMPTION	
1989 (thousands)	1990 (thousands)	Cumulative % Increase 1985–90	1989 (thousands)	1989 (K MT)	Cumulative % Increase 1984–89	1989 (K MT)	Cumulative % Increase 1984–89	1989 (billion kwh)	Cumulative % Increase 1984–89	1988 kg Oil Equiv. per capita	Cumulative % Increase 1983–88
5,138.0	3,965	32.2	841	3,998.0	−8.2	6,720.0	17.7	66.43	23.7	3,911	12.6
4,398.0	3,505	31.0	506	1,798.0	15.8	2,004.0	20.1	28.45	26.0	3,505	10.2
34,345.0	28,600	33.0	4,301	17,565.0	13.4	25,992.0	14.4	406.90	32.5	2,566	−6.3
41,734.0	37,757	3.2	6,110	35,712.0	15.0	28,500.0	−1.4	440.59	12.1	3,916	1.1
4,523.0	2,281	32.6	—	1,938.0	19.5	12,528.0	−7.3	31.01	24.9	1,978	30.8
942.0	1,005	10.4	—	522.0	25.5	1,332.0	−10.4	13.70	22.0	2,493	8.4
30,716.0	25,867	9.6	2,789	27,994.0	28.8	39,708.0	3.7	210.84	17.4	2,537	16.9
—	92	0.0	—	—	—	550.0	55.8	1.38	52.7	8,231	13.0
9,750.0	7,025	4.9	1,563	4,710.0	14.6	3,540.0	11.5	73.14	16.5	4,766	4.8
1,109.0	1,679	4.6	—	1,903.0	58.7	6,468.0	6.7	25.72	28.5	1,083	17.6
15,477.0	19,072	83.4	2,058	12,343.0	75.7	27,372.0	7.6	141.23	19.6	1,614	2.5
29,518.0	26,395	7.7	6,024	17,400.0	21.4	16,512.0	23.3	311.20	11.0	3,464	3.4
177,650.0	157,243	18.0	—	125,883.0	22.3	171,226.0	6.9	1750.58	18.7	2,947	3.7
4,309.0	3,650	12.0	442	2,975.0	24.0	4,752.0	−3.0	50.17	20.0	2,811	12.2
3,028.0	2,470	6.2	507	2,274.0	10.9	1,608.0	−2.9	50.76	17.4	4,054	23.6

(*continued*)

TABLE A–11.2 (*Continued*)

	PRIVATE CONSUMPTION EXPENDITURE					PASSENGER CARS		TRUCKS AND BUSES	
	1989 Total ($ billions)	Avg. Annual Real % Increase 1987–91	1988 % for Food	1988 % for Clothing	1988 % for Household	1989 (thousands)	Cumulative % Increase 1984–89	1989 (thousands)	Cumulative % Increase 1984–89
WESTERN EUROPE (*continued*)									
ICELAND	3.1	—	20.9	8.7	12.3	134	34.0	17	30.8
NORWAY	45.8	0.7	25.4	10.8	7.3	1,622	13.4	314	46.7
SWEDEN	99.0	2.7	21.2	7.6	6.1	3,483	13.0	281	26.0
SWITZERLAND	101.5	2.3	26.2	4.4	5.3	2,745	7.6	251	23.0
TOTAL EFTA	379.2	—	—	—	—	12,565	13.2	1,373	27.2
TURKEY	50.8	7.1	52.9	6.3	10.2	1,310	58.6	643	23.7
TOTAL WESTERN EUROPE	3,330.4	—	—	—	—	135,417	12.1	18,101	33.1
EASTERN EUROPE									
BULGARIA	—	—	33.4	10.2	16.5	1,138	89.7	146	−2.7
CZECHOSLOVAKIA	22.8	2.1	39.0	6.9	12.9	3,000	16.5	461	13.8
E. GERMANY	—	4.3	47.5	12.5	12.1	3,462	9.7	279	31.8
HUNGARY	14.1	−0.3	47.5	7.6	9.2	1,790	33.2	223	4.7
POLAND	42.5	−5.6	39.2	9.3	6.2	4,519	31.9	1,001	23.3
ROMANIA	33.8	0.0	33.1	10.0	5.5	307	22.8	192	28.0
USSR	—	4.3	42.8	18.9	8.0	12,688	8.1	9,387	−2.4
YUGOSLAVIA	36.0	0.5	51.5	7.6	8.0	3,089	7.5	846	213.3
TOTAL EASTERN EUROPE	149.2	—	—	—	—	29,993	15.5	12,535	4.3
MIDDLE EAST									
BAHRAIN	1.4	—	—	—	—	109	65.2	30	20.0
EGYPT	47.3	1.9	—	—	—	425	−0.9	248	2.9
IRAN	188.4	0.5	46.9	9.3	5.5	1,557	−2.1	551	7.4
IRAQ	—	—	—	—	—	251	0.4	269	1.5
ISRAEL	27.0	5.9	27.6	7.1	9.8	739	21.9	145	16.0
JORDAN	3.5	4.3	40.7	5.6	4.9	136	0.7	68	13.3
KUWAIT	10.8	−4.7	28.3	7.8	11.7	583	7.6	206	3.0
LIBYA	8.8	—	—	—	—	448	5.2	322	−0.6
OMAN	3.3	—	—	—	—	112	16.7	63	−56.8
QATAR	1.7	—	—	—	—	88	15.8	39	−35.0
SAUDI ARABIA	38.7	—	—	—	—	1,378	7.9	1,477	−10.7
SYRIA	12.3	0.1	—	—	—	118	22.9	138	−28.5
UNITED ARAB EMIRATES	11.4	−4.1	—	—	—	281	28.9	153	20.5
YEMEN ARAB REPUBLIC	4.7	—	—	—	—	20	0.0	59	−1.7
TOTAL MIDDLE EAST	388.0	—	—	—	—	6,245	7.2	3,768	−5.6
AFRICA									
ALGERIA	25.2	—	—	—	—	725	25.6	480	31.5
ANGOLA	4.3	—	—	—	—	122	−5.4	41	−4.7
BURKINA FASO	1.5	—	—	—	—	11	0.0	13	0.0
CAMEROON	8.7	1.7	—	—	—	90	8.4	79	14.5
CONGO	1.2	−8.4	—	—	—	26	4.0	20	5.3
ETHIOPIA	4.3		—	—	—	43	7.5	21	5.0
GABON	1.7	−4.8	—	—	—	—	—	—	—
GHANA	3.9	4.0	—	—	—	58	−3.3	46	2.2
IVORY COAST	6.5	−3.0	—	—	—	168	5.0	91	4.6
KENYA	5.1	2.7	—	—	—	133	6.4	149	16.4
MADAGASCAR	2.0		—	—	—	48	−4.0	43	−2.3
MALAWI	1.2	3.1	—	—	—	15	0.0	16	6.7
MARITIUS	1.4		—	—	—	34	3.0	14	27.3
MOROCCO	15.3	4.3	—	—	—	565	25.6	227	13.5
MOZAMBIQUE	1.0		—	—	—	84	−5.6	24	0.0
NIGERIA	20.5	2.0	32.9	3.6	2.5	773	1.6	606	−2.4
SENEGAL	3.4	3.8	—	—	—	90	45.2	28	−24.3
SIERRA LEONE	0.7	—	—	—	—	23	21.1	7	−30.0
SOUTH AFRICA	50.9	2.6	33.4	7.0	10.3	3,115	8.3	1,126	−6.8
TANZANIA	2.9	—	—	—	—	44	4.8	52	4.0
TUNISIA	6.5	1.8	—	—	—	171	21.3	177	12.0
UGANDA	4.0	—	—	—	—	13	−59.4	13	0.0
ZAIRE	2.5	0.8	—	—	—	94	0.0	86	1.2

TABLE A–11.2 (*Continued*)

TELE-PHONES	TELEVISIONS		PERSONAL COMPUTERS	STEEL		CEMENT		ELECTRICITY		ENERGY CONSUMPTION	
1989 (thousands)	1990 (thousands)	Cumulative % Increase 1985–90	1989 (thousands)	1989 (K MT)	Cumulative % Increase 1984–89	1989 (K MT)	Cumulative % Increase 1984–89	1989 (billion kwh)	Cumulative % Increase 1984–89	1988 kg Oil Equiv. per capita	Cumulative % Increase 1983–88
125.0	76	4.1	—	—	—	134.0	11.7	4.48	8.5	4,104	17.6
2,579.0	1,466	7.1	452	1,138.0	−18.8	1,380.0	−10.8	119.88	12.8	4,658	5.3
7,410.0	3,750	15.1	796	3,865.0	4.0	2,200.0	−1.8	139.34	13.0	3,439	3.7
6,051.0	2,760	8.2	724	2,526.0	11.4	5,436.0	30.0	51.66	7.3	2,645	3.8
23,502.0	14,172	10.4	—	12,778.0	8.0	15,510.0	4.9	416.29	13.5	3,361	8.3
7,467.0	10,530	31.6	—	7,390.0	40.2	23,808.0	51.3	47.62	74.1	658	19.2
208,619.0	181,945	15.0	—	146,051.0	21.7	210,544.0	5.3	2214.49	18.3	2,676	3.3
1,790.0	2,100	0.2	—	2,667.0	−10.7	4,968.0	−13.1	44.33	−0.8	4,009	1.8
3,978.0	8,012	31.8	62	11,016.0	0.6	10,884.0	3.4	86.08	9.8	4,320	−0.8
3,977.0	12,600	2.4	54	8,557.0	−1.4	12,264.0	6.1	118.39	13.5	5,435	7.9
1,770.0	4,265	0.4	55	2,809.0	−21.3	3,852.0	−7.1	29.57	12.4	2,667	3.5
4,830.0	9,950	5.1	104	13,555.0	−11.1	17,112.0	2.8	145.49	7.9	3,314	7.3
—	4,010	1.3	—	12,207.0	3.0	13,260.0	2.1	75.85	5.8	3,293	3.6
37,532.0	95,000	15.3	—	166,319.0	7.7	140,436.0	8.1	1,722.00	15.3	4,821	17.9
4,550.0	6,530	60.0	75	4,562.0	−9.0	8,556.0	−8.1	83.03	13.7	1,751	10.9
58,427.0	142,467	14.3	—	221,692.0	4.2	211,332.0	10.4	2,304.73	13.4	4,364	14.4
141.0	186	9 .4	—	46.0	−62.6	—	—	3.32	49.8	10,668	18.0
1,455.0	4,300	11.4	—	4,652.0	98.0	10,056.0	118.6	35.41	51.1	465	12.6
2,104.0	2,678	7.1	—	5,179.0	11.2	12,519.0	17.5	38.77	17.5	916	10.1
886.0	1,200	33.3	—	891.0	1.5	9,162.0	63.6	23.45	44.8	517	19.7
2,285.0	1,175	30.6	—	823.0	41.4	2,292.0	21.3	19.56	34.2	1.982	14.1
—	286	19.2	—	393.0	11.3	1,932.0	−4.6	3.26	70.2	685	5.4
362.0	800	37.9	—	51.0	−95.4	984.0	−12.5	20.00	55.9	5,649	21.5
500.0	500	192.4	—	553.0	176.5	2,722.0	−12.0	16.00	123.7	2,497	8.5
80.0	1,015	12.8	—	285.0	−37.1	—	—	3.90	105.3	2,360	−70.7
135.0	160	33.3	—	164.0	446.7	306.0	88.9	4.50	35.7	20,053	32.1
1,238.0	3,750	21.0	—	2,691.0	−43.0	9,525.0	15.2	42.20	37.8	4,361	62.4
685.0	700	16.7	—	125.0	−85.5	3,972.0	−7.2	8.11	14.0	769	0.3
544.0	170	30.8	—	—	—	3,266.0	57.9	13.15	29.7	13,208	142.9
—	300	971.4	—	—	—	—	—	0.82	121.0	130	−1.5
10,415.0	17,220	21.3	—	15,853.0	−16.0	56,736.0	5.3	232.45	41.1	1,252	24.4
1,052.0	1,600	6.7	—	2,522.0	−2.3	6,505.0	36.2	14.97	46.5	860	31.1
82.0	52	40.5	—	—	—	354.0	—	1.81	4.0	63	−27.6
17.0	42	110.0	—	—	—	—	—	0.13	2.4	19	−13.6
61.0	5	233.3	—	—	—	586.0	−2.0	2.40	12.8	186	−35.9
26.0	6	20.0	—	—	—	15.0	−46.4	0.29	25.3	277	307.4
153.0	75	66.7	—	—	—	250.0	—	0.82	1.2	18	28.6
14.0	40	90.5	—	—	—	137.0	−29.4	0.88	20.3	806	0.5
77.0	175	182.3	—	—	—	477.0	71.6	4.75	80.8	70	7.7
88.0	810	138.2	—	—	—	700.0	—	2.21	6.8	153	10.9
357.0	195	156.6	—	204.0	2.0	1,200.0	1.7	2.84	27.6	65	−9.7
44.0	65	30.0	—	—	—	24.0	−35.1	0.52	10.0	40	90.5
50.0			—	—	—	84.0	20.0	0.62	28.4	30	−6.3
74.0	128	45.5	—	—	—	—	—	0.64	36.5	279	41.6
362.0	1,210	17.1	—	686.0	−14.1	4,644.0	30.0	8.83	33.0	243	3.0
65.0	21	200.0	—	—	—	73.0	−100.0	0.48	−91.4	23	−65.7
260.0	650	41.3	—	600.0	−40.0	3,336.0	20.9	9.93	13.9	113	−33.5
36.0	234	17.0	—	—	—	393.0	—	0.76	17.0	87	−23.0
15.0	34	13.3	—	—	—	24.0	—	0.17	−31.6	53	−1.9
4,744.0	3,445	14.8	—	7,644.0	27.1	6,936.0	−14.2	156.74	27.6	1,932	−4.9
131.0	16	60.0	—	63.0	−7.4	300.0	—	0.88	1.3	26	−13.3
333.0	650	62.5	—	589.0	2.3	3,960.0	42.6	4.49	10.7	492	−0.8
61.0	110	44.7	—	—	—	20.0	0.0	0.66	5.1	19	5.6
32.0	22	69.2	—	53.0	−37.6	400.0	—	5.39	16.8	46	−11.5

(*continued*)

TABLE A–11.2 (*Continued*)

	PRIVATE CONSUMPTION EXPENDITURE					PASSENGER CARS		TRUCKS AND BUSES	
	1989 Total ($ billions)	Avg. Annual Real % Increase 1987–91	1988 % for Food	1988 % for Clothing	1988 % for Household	1989 (thousands)	Cumulative % Increase 1984–89	1989 (thousands)	Cumulative % Increase 1984–89
ZAMBIA	2.6	−0.2	—	—	—	96	−4.0	67	−1.5
ZIMBABWE	2.6	1.2	30.1	10.3	12.9	173	−2.8	80	0.0
TOTAL AFRICA	180.0	—	—	—	—	6,714	9.1	3,506	2.7
NORTH AMERICA									
CANADA	321.7	3.7	15.7	6.3	13.6	11,800	10.0	3,600	7.0
UNITED STATES	3,450.1	2.6	13.6	7.3	6.2	140,655	12.2	42,813	17.1
TOTAL NORTH AMERICA	3,771.8	—	—	—	—	152,455	12.0	46,413	16.3
LATIN AMERICA									
LAIA									
ARGENTINA	43.7	−1.1	38.8	4.5	5.1	4,186	18.2	1,494	9.9
BOLIVIA	3.6	1.8	—	—	—	75	127.3	136	189.4
BRAZIL	257.4	2.5	32.0	13.2	13.2	9,527	2.7	2,434	21.6
CHILE	17.1	5.8	—	—	—	669	35.7	297	29.1
COLOMBIA	25.9	2.9	38.6	6.0	5.5	645	−21.3	617	208.5
ECUADOR	7.4	1.8	33.6	10.1	5.4	69	−9.2	163	−5.2
MEXICO	130.5	1.2	38.8	8.4	13.0	5,410	15.8	2,385	24.5
PARAGUAY	3.4	3.7	—	—	—	60	71.4	30	7.1
PERU	39.8	0.4	41.0	9.8	11.6	391	3.7	221	11.1
URUGUAY	6.1	3.6	—	—	—	167	−0.6	81	−5.8
VENEZUELA	28.1	−0.2	45.5	4.3	5.2	1,601	7.1	573	−33.1
ANCOM SUBTOTAL	104.8	—	—	—	—	2,781	−0.7	1,710	15.9
TOTAL LAIA	562.9	—	—	—	—	22,800	8.7	8,431	18.8
CACM									
COSTA RICA	3.2	4.3	—	—	—	82	3.8	72	18.0
EL SALVADOR	5.3	5.4	—	—	—	52	0.0	65	1.6
GUATEMALA	7.1	2.8	—	—	—	95	0.0	93	0.0
HONDURAS	3.6	3.6	—	—	—	27	0.0	52	6.1
NICARAGUA	1.0	−2.5	—	—	—	31	−8.8	28	−3.4
TOTAL CACM	19.2	—	—	—	—	287	0.0	310	4.7
CARIBBEAN									
BARBADOS	1.1	—	—	—	—	35	20.7	8	33.3
CUBA	33.9	—	—	—	—	19	—	33	—
DOMINICAN REPUBLIC	5.1	2.1	—	—	—	114	14.0	72	12.5
GUYANA	0.1	—	—	—	—	22	−26.7	9	−25.0
HAITI	2.0	—	—	—	—	32	10.3	21	61.5
JAMAICA	2.3	1.9	42.1	5.3	6.3	93	−13.1	16	−44.8
NETHERLANDS ANTILLES	—	—	—	—	—	68	7.9	15	15.4
PANAMA	3.0	−3.5	—	—	—	177	43.9	49	−2.0
PUERTO RICO	—	—	20.1	12.0	10.8	1,295	27.0	227	21.4
TRINIDAD & TOBAGO	2.4	−6.0	—	—	—	244	37.1	79	43.6
TOTAL CARIBBEAN	50.0	—	—	—	—	2,099	25.0	529	23.3
TOTAL LATIN AMERICA	632.2	—	—	—		25,186	9.7	9,270	18.5
ASIA									
AFGHANISTAN	—	—	—	—	—	31	−6.1	25	−3.8
BANGLADESH	18.5	3.5	—	—	—	32	−31.9	34	3.0
CHINA	254.1	5.3	51.4	13.9	13.5	900	800.0	3,425	101.5
HONG KONG	36.4	7.0	16.7	21.5	14.8	178	−2.7	154	40.0
INDIA	178.3	6.6	53.5	13.1	4.9	1,628	59.6	1,480	38.6
INDONESIA	50.1	3.7	53.4	4.3	8.0	966	29.5	1,333	34.5
JAPAN	1,595.8	4.3	19.9	5.8	6.0	30,776	13.4	21,674	24.7
DEM. KAMPUCHEA	—	—	—	—	—	—	—	—	—
KOREA, NORTH	—	—	—	—	—	—	—	—	—
KOREA, SOUTH	112.6	9.1	37.8	5.1	6.1	1,211	160.4	987	104.3
LAOS	—	—	—	—	—	—	—	—	—
MALAYSIA	19.5	6.6	45.1	7.0	10.6	1,172	15.6	351	39.3
MYANMAR	9.9	—	—	—	—	27	−6.9	42	−2.3
NEPAL	2.3	—	—	—	—	—	—	—	—
PAKISTAN	30.1	4.3	—	—	—	457	22.5	308	23.7
PHILLIPPINES	32.4	4.9	60.8	5.3	13.4	377	4.4	506	−5.4

TABLE A–11.2 (*Continued*)

TELEPHONES	TELEVISIONS		PERSONAL COMPUTERS	STEEL		CEMENT		ELECTRICITY		ENERGY CONSUMPTION	
1989 (thousands)	1990 (thousands)	Cumulative % Increase 1985–90	1989 (thousands)	1989 (K MT)	Cumulative % Increase 1984–89	1989 (K MT)	Cumulative % Increase 1984–89	1989 (billion kwh)	Cumulative % Increase 1984–89	1988 kg Oil Equiv. per capita	Cumulative % Increase 1983–88
95.0	120	33.3	—	6.0	−53.8	408.0	112.5	6.74	−32.2	168	−32.3
287.0	200	12.4	—	211.0	58.6	780.0	27.5	8.03	81.4	504	50.0
8,516.0	9.905	27.9	—	12,578.0	−4.0	31,606.0	−43.6	235.97	22.7	298	−6.7
20,126	15,700	12.5	4,000	13,904	6.2	11,844.0	37.6	512.59	17.0	7,378	11.1
125,836.0	215,000	51.9	50,744.0	102,351	−7.9	71,388.0	1.3	2,778.65	−2.6	7,011	7.6
145,962.0	230,700	48.4	54,744.0	116,255	−6.4	83,208.0	5.2	3,291.24	0.0	7,026	7.7
3,922.0	6,800	4.6	94.0	2,431	−20.9	6,024.0	2.4	46.50	3.5	1,381	13.2
194.0	535	15.6	—	46	−23.3	420.0	35.5	1.88	24.6	228	−18.3
14,059.0	28,000	12.0	222.0	12,462	16.8	26,508.0	36.0	214.17	20.0	545	17.5
866.0	3,200	82.9	—	1,077	64.2	1,885.0	50.2	16.91	25.3	737	15.2
2,498.0	3,350	21.8	—	1,337	18.5	6,648.0	25.9	38.34	28.3	595	0.2
691.0	825	33.1	—	277	−8.9	2,126.0	42.3	5.60	33.2	497	6.2
9,359.0	12,350	45.3	334.0	7,256	0.0	23,760.0	27.0	101.88	17.1	1,156	−3.3
112.0	350	52.2	—	—	—	275.0	79.7	2.90	215.2	162	5.9
736.0	2,080	137.7	—	530	12.1	3,300.0	69.5	14.14	20.6	365	−14.9
529.0	650	47.7	—	—	—	435.0	8.5	7.00	−3.4	560	14.5
1,749.0	3,500	55.6	122.0	2,661	27.4	5,256.0	9.9	57.77	30.3	2,149	−5.0
5,868.0	10,290	47.9	—	4,851	19.7	15,204.0	8.7	117.73	28.5	834	−4.0
34,715.0	61,640	24.8	773.0	28,077	9.2	76,637.0	29.8	507.09	19.7	833	4.6
410.0	611	35.8	—	120	−17.2	557.0	44.3	3.19	4.0	344	7.2
136.0	425	41.7	—	55	−14.1	455.0	4.6	1.87	11.0	160	23.1
128.0	475	131.7	—	102	3.0	880.0	79.2	1.79	5.6	116	−12.8
69.0	330	17.9	—	45	−22.4	41.0	−91.5	1.09	2.8	131	−16.0
50.0	220	15.8	—	—	—	256.0	−14.1	1.07	9.8	205	−11.3
793.0	1,913	34.2	—	322	−12.0	2,189.0	11.1	9.01	6.3	167	−2.3
111.0	68	23.6	—	—	—	228.0	256.3	0.48	25.3	1,027	13.6
553.0	2,100	40.0	—	1,091	6.6	3,756.0	12.2	15.24	24.0	1,064	9.0
549.0	728	86.7	—	131	7.4	1,235.0	16.8	5.30	32.2	285	−30.3
33.0	.40	—	—	—	—	—	—	0.39	−3.8	330	−25.0
50.0	27	35.0	—	—	—	240.0	9.6	0.45	15.6	37	0.0
168.0	353	64.2	—	—	—	360.0	39.0	2.59	13.0	658	−26.0
65.0	61	5.2	—	—	—	—	—	—	—	148	—
252.0	458	30.9	—	—	—	349.0	6.7	2.57	13.0	420	−17.0
—	900	10.4	—	—	—	1,236.0	44.6	14.40	14.7	1,722	−13.8
212.0	370	15.6	—	153	159.3	384.0	−5.9	3.47	15.7	3,994	3.8
1,993.0	5,105	37.1	—	1,375	14.2	4,728.0	−28.7	44.87	19.4	852	−5.8
37,501.0	68,658	25.9	892.0	29,774	9.1	83,554.0	23.5	560.97	19.4	795	3.4
—	129	29.0	—	—	—	70.0	−46.2	1.11	8.2	174	262.5
—	492	48.6	—	425	21.1	348.0	27.5	7.72	79.8	47	46.9
10,893.0	126,000	27.3	490.0	69,504	15.6	204,144.0	88.6	594.59	57.7	530	23.5
2,891.0	1,400	9.5	155.0	2,313	27.8	2,136.0	15.6	24.16	34.8	1,397	16.8
4,420.0	20,000	52.7	144.0	20,036	64.2	44,568.0	50.9	245.14	44.9	201	23.3
1,015.0	7,112	10.5	—	2,334	−12.5	15,660.0	76.1	36.51	67.4	205	5.1
66,636.0	68,600	6.1	7,029.0	93,278	25.4	80,316.0	1.8	799.70	23.3	2,745	12.5
—	60	15.4	—	—	—	—	—	0.70	−30.0	19	850.0
—	250	25.0	—	—	—	9,979.0	24.7	53.00	29.3	1,881	−0.2
14,195.0	8,700	13.7	705.0	18,300	72.3	30,120.0	47.6	94.48	61.9	1,412	37.8
8.0	32	6.7	—	—	—	—	—	1.10	2.3	25	13.6
1,646.0	2,350	125.5	98.0	2,022	−17.4	4,800.0	38.4	21.48	57.4	956	14.5
80.0	68	112.5	—	—	—	444.0	43.2	2.46	30.2	45	0.0
67.0	35	75.0	—	—	—	215.0	451.0	0.59	86.4	18	63.6
740.0	2,080	107.0	—	1,883	57.0	6,936.0	54.0	35.38	39.1	184	12.9
986.0	6,150	86.4	—	2,182	170.0	3,624.0	−1.0	25.93	23.0	196	−8.4

(*continued*)

TABLE A–11.2 (*Continued*)

	PRIVATE CONSUMPTION EXPENDITURE					PASSENGER CARS		TRUCKS AND BUSES	
	1989 Total ($ billions)	Avg. Annual Real % Increase 1987–91	1988 % for Food	1988 % for Clothing	1988 % for Household	1989 (thousands)	Cumulative % Increase 1984–89	1989 (thousands)	Cumulative % Increase 1984–89
SINGAPORE	13.2	8.4	25.5	9.2	10.6	251	8.2	237	91.1
SRI LANKA	5.5	2.1	43.1	10.6	4.4	155	9.2	139	15.8
TAIWAN	78.8	10.3	32.7	4.9	5.1	1,979	145.2	524	28.1
THAILAND	41.0	9.6	39.6	12.1	8.1	817	70.2	1,423	115.3
VIETNAM	—	—	—	—	—	—	—	—	—
TOTAL ASIA	2,478.8	—	—	—	—	40,957	23.5	32,642	35.0
OCEANIA									
AUSTRALIA	163.5	3.0	21.2	6.4	7.8	7,244	9.2	1,978	10.0
NEW ZEALAND	25.6	—	13.7	4.1	9.0	1,550	5.7	315	7.1
TOTAL OCEANIA	189.1	—	—	—	—	8,794	8.5	2,293	9.6

Notes

Population figures are midyear UN estimates. Working age is defined as ages 16 to 64 inclusive.

Gross domestic product (GDP) is the total value at current market prices of all goods and services produced by residents of a country before deduction of depreciation charges on fixed capital.

National income is the sum of the incomes of nationals of a country, whether resident or not, before deduction of direct taxes.

Average wages in manufacturing are subject to inconsistencies in reporting and definitions of manufacturing, as well as differences in the workweek and treatment of overtime, benefits, payments in kind, etc.

Total exports are presented f.o.b. (approximately the seller's price before transportation).

Private consumption expenditure is the value of final expenditure by households and private nonprofit institutions on current goods and services, less sales of similar goods.

Passenger cars in use denotes motor vehicles seating fewer than eight persons, including taxis, jeeps, and station wagons.

Trucks and buses in use includes vans, lorries, buses, and tractor and semitrailer combinations (except trailers and farm tractors).

Telephone sets in use comprises both public and private telephones in use, including those connected to a PBX.

Television sets in use is a total number of receiving sets in each country.

Personal computers refers to the total installed base of personal computers.

Steel consumption is apparent consumption of crude steel (that is, production plus imports minus exports) disregarding inventory changes.

Cement production includes all types of cement products.

Electricity production combines generation of electricity by utility firms for public use and production by companies for their own use.

TABLE A–11.2 (*Continued*)

TELE-PHONES	TELEVISIONS		PERSONAL COMPUTERS	STEEL		CEMENT		ELECTRICITY		ENERGY CONSUMPTION	
1989 (thousands)	1990 (thousands)	Cumulative % Increase 1985–90	1989 (thousands)	1989 (K MT)	Cumulative % Increase 1984–89	1989 (K MT)	Cumulative % Increase 1984–89	1989 (billion kwh)	Cumulative % Increase 1984–89	1988 kg Oil Equiv. per capita	Cumulative % Increase 1983–88
1,220.0	985	23.1	121.0	3,021	33.0	1,704.0	−32.1	14.04	49.3	5,165	14.0
166.0	750	66.7	—	—	—	624.0	52.9	2.86	26.3	85	−11.5
—	6,660	27.2	722.0	14,100	131.7	18,044.0	26.8	76.91	59.3	2,346	—
1,000	6,000	60.9	130.0	3,548	52.4	15,024.0	82.2	37.34	69.5	391	45.9
115.0	2,200	10.0	—	—	—	1,954.0	115.4	5.70	35.7	80	−11.1
106,078.0	260,053	23.6	9,593.0	232,946	31.4	440,710.0	42.3	2,080.88	39.1	474	26.1
8,727.0	8,300	7.8	1,994.0	6,390	5.6	6,888.0	48.0	140.35	24.3	4,860	16.0
2,403.0	1,390	16.8	—	595	−26.3	720.0	−12.5	28.82	8.7	3,401	36.3
11,130.0	9,690	9.0	1,994.0	6,985	1.8	7,608.0	38.9	169.18	15.2	4,580	23.0

Energy consumption is denominated in per capita oil equivalent. Coal equivalent can be calculated by dividing the oil equivalent figure by 0.687623.

Currency conversion. For the presentation of GDP and private consumption expenditure on a comparative basis, *BI* has converted data in local currencies to U.S. dollars, using average exchange rates for the year from the *Monthly Bulletin of Statistics* (U.S.). In cases in which multiple exchange rates are used, a choice was made based on *BI*'s best judgment.

Although conversion to a common currency is often essential for comparisons between countries, it should be recognized that a degree of distortion is inevitably involved. An important contribution to this distortion is the fact that exchange rates apply only to goods in world trade. Countries vary in their degree of involvement in international trade, which results in differences in the volumes and prices of nontraded goods among economies.

Variation in national accounting. East European countries and the former Soviet Union use net material product instead of gross domestic product as a measure of economic activity for the nation as a whole. This concept deliberately excludes certain services, including government services, and is thus 20 percent to 30 percent lower than GDP would be if these services were counted.

PART • 4

Cases

Case 12: Idéale Imprimerie

Well established as the leading printer in Morocco, Idéale Imprimerie is located in Casablanca, the country's commercial capital. In the spring of 1991, the management of Idéale identified an attractive opportunity for market expansion, namely, local production of wallpaper. Production of wallpaper would be within their field of expertise, and some evidence existed to suggest that this would be an important growth market in the future. The only problem appeared to be the lack of published data on consumer demand and purchasing patterns. This information would be necessary for decisions concerning production plant capacity, production scheduling, product lines, and distribution. Curious to know more about the feasibility of such a venture, the managing director of Idéale Imprimerie contacted the national business school, the Institut Supérieur de Commerce et d'Administration des Entreprises (ISCAE), for help in evaluating this new market.

The Company

Idéale Imprimerie is recognized as the leader in its sector for printing on both paper and cartons. With its group of 175 employees, it dominates the sector not only by its size, but also by its reputation. Any reference in the business community to "Idéale" is immediately understood. Idéale's premises cover three times the surface area of its closet competitor, Belles Impressions. About fifteen other small printers compete in specific segments of the market, specializing in certain production processes, types of materials (e.g., billboards, handouts, letterhead stationery), or regions of the country.

Idéale was set up in 1975. The managing director, Maurice Pichot, is actively assisted by two working directors, Luigi Ghislanzoni and Mohamed Boukhari. This small team has the advantage of familiarity with the French market (Maurice), the Italian market (Luigi), and the local market (Mohamed). They are constantly on the lookout for new ideas that will give their company a competitive edge, in order to maintain their leadership position.

The Market Environment

Morocco is a Muslim Arab kingdom situated at the western end of the Mediterranean. Because Morocco was formerly a French protectorate (until 1956), the French influence still persists through use of the French language in business. Elsewhere, Moroccan Arabic is the everyday language. Topographically and politically Morocco is part of North Africa and a member of the "Maghreb" trading group composed of Morocco, Algeria, and Tunisia. Recent involvement in the war with Algeria over possession of the western Sahara has had serious repercussions on the Moroccan

This case is printed here with the permission of the author, Lyn S. Amine of St. Louis University.

economy. Current national problems focus on management of the heavy burden of foreign debt. Long-term development objectives include maintenance of a free market economy directed by five-year plans; rapid modernization of the way of life (compatible with Islamic traditions); and the general emancipation of the people through education, health services, and equal employment opportunities. However, unemployment, underemployment, and illiteracy are major problems among a population of approximately 20 million, 50 percent of whom are under age 20.

The concept of marketing is steadily growing in significance in the business community. Instrumental factors include the presence of numerous multinational marketing companies (Nestlé, Unilever, Procter & Gamble, Ford, International Harvester—some of which are "Moroccanized" in name, ownership, and management); the existence of a university-level business school in Casablanca (ISCAE); and the activities of five major advertising agencies (Shem's, Univas, TOP, KLEM, Cinémapresse) and one international marketing research agency (Middle East Marketing Research Bureau).

Notable characteristics of Moroccan business customs are:

- A relentless drive to preserve business and administrative secrecy at all levels
- A general fascination with novelty and innovation in all its forms
- Widespread and rapid imitation of successful new ideas

Marketing research activities of any type meet with much resistance, being considered an invasion of privacy by businesspeople and consumers alike. However, once successful inroads are made, then "me-too" activities will soon follow.

The Product Market

Traditionally homes in Morocco were built to the classic Arab model: single-family homes with two floors built around an open courtyard. Floors and walls are decorated by ceramic tiles, and ceilings are covered with wood carvings or stucco reliefs. Modern homes consist of villas with two floors or two- to three-bedroom condominium apartments for sale or rent. These modern homes represent the target market for wallpaper. From 1973 until the present time, nine importers were the sole source of wallpaper supply for the local market. Therefore, an opportunity for import substitution existed that would benefit from government support grants accorded to "infant" industries.

Idéale's initial research requirements specified items such as historical import data by value and volume, domestic sales records, discretionary income by type of household (traditional or modern), home construction data, and general lifestyle data.

Marketing Research Efforts

Intensive searching by Ghislanzoni revealed four potentially useful sources of secondary data. However, all suffered from various deficiencies.

Import Statistics

Although recorded for ten years prior to the date of Idéale research, imports of wallpaper were recorded by weight (kgs) and value (thousands of dirhams). Wallpaper is sold by the roll, and different qualities and designs have different weights. Since the number of rolls was not specified, Idéale management could not even speculate on the number of "modern" households buying wallpaper over the past ten years.

Domestic Water-Heater Industry Study

This study was completed by the national economic development bank (BNDE) and offered two types of indirectly useful data, population growth statistics and annual home construction figures. The BNDE's objective was to determine the market for large, electric, domestic water heaters. Pichot and his colleagues considered it

TABLE 1 Summary of Calculation of Consumption of Wallpaper (by number of rolls; Years 1–11)

	YEAR 1	2	3	4	5	6	7	8	9	10	11
A	14,174	14,529	14,893	15,267	15,692	16,124	16,570	17,025	17,450	17,887	18,334
B = 20%A	2,834.8	2,905.8	2,978.6	3,053.4	3,138.4	3,224.8	3,314	3,405	3,490	3,577.4	3,666.8
$C = \frac{B}{5}$	566.96	581.16	595.72	610.68	627.68	644.96	662.80	681.0	698.0	715.48	733.3
D = 10%C	56.69	58.11	59.57	61.06	62.76	64.49	66.28	68.1	69.8	71.54	73.3
E = 25%D	14.17	14.52	14.89	15.26	15.69	16.12	16.57	17.02	17.45	17.88	18.3
F = E×30	425.1	435.6	446.7	457.8	470.7	483.6	497.1	510.6	523.5	536.4	549.9
G	425,100	435,600	446,700	457,800	470,700	483,600	497,100	510,600	523,500	536,400	569,900

A = Population of Morocco in thousands.
B = Estimated one-fifth of the population with substantial purchasing power: *Libération*.
C = Estimate of five persons per household.
D = One-tenth of the population estimated responsible for the largest part of consumer expenditures: *Libération*.
E = Estimate of potential proportion of wallpaper purchasers (10 percent).
F = Estimated consumption of 30 rolls per household (in thousands): survey data.
G = Total estimated consumption by number of rolls.

reasonable to assume that if a home featured this important "modern" convenience, then in all probability family lifestyle (along with home decorations) would also be more modern than for families in traditional homes. Consequently they thought these modern homes could be considered legitimate members, actual or potential, of the target market for wallpaper sales.

Boukhari had heard importers claim that the expected life of the product was five years. The "ballpark" figure for number of modern households (equal to the proxy market for water heaters) was therefore divided by five to establish a base number of assumed customer households per year. Population growth statistics of 5 percent per annum gave some indication of expected expansion rates of the total consumer market, but not specifically of the identified "modern" segment.

Study of the Potential Market for Locally Produced Wallpaper

Although of great apparent relevance, this research by the Office for the Development of Industry (ODI) proved virtually useless. As imports

TABLE 2 Calculation of Consumption of Wallpaper Using Proxy Data (by number of rolls; Years 6–11)

	YEAR 6	7	8	9	10	11
A	6,444	7,546	9,986	11,612	12,462	14,297
B	35,051	35,051	35,051	35,051	35,051	41,495*
C = (A+B)	41,495	42,597	45,037	46,663	47,513	55,792
D = (C×30)	1,244,850	1,277,910	1,351,110	1,399,890	1,425,390	1,673.760

A = Number of new homes equipped with a water heater: BNDE.
B = Number of existing homes equipped with a water heater, less an estimated 15 percent of traditional homes, spread equally over the five-year period to reflect assumed demand among established households.
C = Total number of estimated customer households.
D = Total estimated consumption by number of rolls, assuming thirty per household: survey data.
*Year 11 would be the first year of expected replacement purchases, assuming a product life of five years.

TABLE 3 Calculation of Imports of Wallpaper (by number of rolls; Years 1–11)

YEAR	KILOGRAMS*	DIRHAMS (IN THOUSANDS)*	ROLLS†
1	14,465	182	20,090
2	19,348	283	26,872
3	43,449	463	60,346
4	78,439	707	108,943
5	81,624	670	113,367
6	81,510	680	113,208
7	109,468	1,351	152,039
8	207,579	1,804	288,304
9	265,625	2,176	368,924
10	472,917	3,356	656,829
11	511,255	3,211	710,076

**Annuaires Statistiques des Importations*, Dept. of Commerce, Morocco
†Weight per roll varies from 500 gm to 1300 gm, standard quality weight being 500 to 600 gm and deluxe quality 1200 to 1300 gm. A guesstimated average weight per roll of 720 gm was used to convert weight of imports into number of rolls.

were recorded by weight, ODI researchers had calculated future demand per inhabitant also by weight. The study assumed that all consumers, traditional or modern, urban or rural, were potential customers with the result that the final weight per inhabitant was infinitesimal.

Income Distribution Study

Again, although of great apparent use, the propagandist nature of this study, entitled "Inequality for How Long?" and published by the local periodical *Libération,* made Pichot cautious in using these statistics. The study asserted that 65.4 percent of national income was owned by 20 percent of the population making up the "class A." Moreover, a mere 10 percent of class A was responsible for 37 percent of total consumer expenditure. Many members of class A would clearly be customers for wallpaper along with other luxury and status items. Pichot, Ghislanzoni, and Boukhari therefore assumed that the maximum size of the target market (in terms of individuals) would include this 20 percent of the national population. Making the further assumption of five persons per household, they were then able to estimate the number of households in the target market.

Some informal visits to the showrooms of

TABLE 4 Comparison of Estimated Values Calculated Using Proxy Data and Improvisation (Years 6–11)

	YEAR 6	7	8	9	10	11
Table 1	483,600	497,100	510,600	523,500	536,400	549,900
Table 2	1,244,850	1,277,910	1,351,110	1,399,890	1,425,390	1,673,760
Table 3	113,208	152,039	288,304	368,924	656,829	710,076
Average value	613,886	642,350	716,671	764,105	872,873	977,912
Percentage change	—	+4.6%	+11.6%	+6.6%	+14.2%	+12.0%

the nine importers by specially briefed staff members yielded the following lifestyle information:

- Consumers shop for wallpaper as a complementary decoration to fitted carpets (in place of traditional rugs) and modern living room and bedroom sets.
- Generally, the wife makes all decisions regarding quality and style.
- Customers are members of the upper class consisting of professional, technical, and commercial leaders and high-ranking administrators.
- Homes are modern and situated in the new and/or prestigious residential areas in Casablanca (whose estimated population is about 3 million).
- Average annual household consumption of wallpaper is about thirty rolls.

The Decision

Idéale's management turned over all these data to the marketing department at ISCAE. Recognizing that use of "guesstimates" and proxy data would not produce statistically reliable results, Pichot requested only a go/no go decision regarding the advisability of entering the wallpaper market as a local producer. What would you recommend as members of the marketing department at ISCAE?

Case 13: California Foods Corporation

In early 1990, the international marketing manager at California Foods Corporation (CFC), Lois Verbrugge, was considering how to react to the continuing decline of CFC grape juice sales in the Puerto Rican market. In 1989, the marketing staff in the international division estimated that sales of CFC grape juice had fallen off by approximately 30 percent from the previous year. To determine why this loss of volume had taken place, extensive consumer research was utilized. But, as of February, Ms. Verbrugge and her staff had not come up with any clear-cut remedies for CFC's problems in the Puerto Rican market.

Company Background

CFC was a wholly owned subsidiary of the Federation of Grape Growers' Associations. The federation purchased the California Foods Corporation in 1956 as part of a strategy to integrate its business forward into the processing and distribution of grape products. CFC continued in 1990 to operate as an agribusiness largely as it had in 1956. The federation supplied the grapes, and CFC handled all processing and marketing of the products. CFC's sales had increased every year since the takeover by the federation. CFC was generally considered the foremost leader in the juice industry. It set the standards for progressive marketing techniques and new product development for the industry. With sales reaching a quarter billion dollars in 1989, the growers and CFC were the largest grape growing, processing, and marketing enterprise in the world.

Originally, CFC had produced only grape-related products: grape jams, grape jelly, frozen grape concentrate, grape drink, and grape preserves. In recent years, however, CFC had expanded to include nongrape products, too. Between 1970 and 1982, CFC introduced thirty-six new products. In 1990, CFC incorporated a complete line of fruit juices with a selection of fruit drinks and a line of fruit-flavored preserves.

CFC's International Division

CFC distributed an assortment of products to foreign markets with the majority of sales derived from juices and fruit drinks. It marketed its products to over forty countries. Major markets included Puerto Rico, Mexico, and Japan. CFC products were distributed by food brokers and distributors to retail stores and food service institutions. In 1988, the International Division experienced record sales and greater than expected profitability. Sales slipped slightly during 1989, largely the result of sales erosion in the Puerto Rican market.

The Juice and Drinks Market in Puerto Rico

Most of the juice consumption in Puerto Rico was composed of imported products. Some of the more popular brands competing for market share were CFC, Seneca, Pueblo, and Grand Union. There was only one domestic grape juice producer, selling under the name Richy. Richy had been in business for a few years, but its impact on the market had been minimal. Table 1 outlines the imported volumes of juices and drinks into Puerto Rico over the last three years.

As the table reveals, grape juice imports (California Foods' and others) were declining rather sharply. Still, the grape juice market was by far the largest juice market in Puerto Rico.

The "fruit drink" category was quite large too and was growing, especially the miscellaneous/all-others subgroup, which included Tang's imported powdered grape and orange drinks. Because many Puerto Ricans equated powdered grape with grape juice, it was possible that at least some of CFC grape juice's volume loss could be traceable to these imports, although no hard evidence existed.

Frozen concentrates represented another competing group that was large and had shown strong growth in the preceding three years. Again, the miscellaneous/all-others subgroup had shown steady growth. Perhaps some of CFC grape juice's loss could be attributable to a shift of sales across generic categories.

CFC's Entry into Puerto Rico

CFC's first experience in Puerto Rico came in the 1950s when it introduced CFC grape juice. At that point, grape juice was practically unheard of by the majority of Puerto Ricans. Despite this, the introduction was a resounding success and CFC grape juice became the best-selling juice in Puerto Rico.

Rumor had it that CFC grape juice's success was traceable to the Puerto Rican beliefs that grape juice was good for men's virility and for women's hemoglobin during their menstrual cycles. Pseudomedicinal drinks were concocted by mixing egg with grape juice. The resulting mixture was referred to as an "egg punch." To take advantage of this seemingly unique consumer behavior, CFC launched an "egg punch" campaign in 1985. One television spot showed a young Puerto Rican man at a disco drinking an egg punch and subsequently departing with an attractive young woman. Print advertising featured a mother nursing her newborn and copy expounding the nutritional value of grape juice.

Grape juice was indeed CFC's biggest seller in Puerto Rico. Sales for 1989 were 412,000 cases. Frozen concentrated grape juice accounted for sales of 32,000 cases during 1989. Other CFC products were Calfood fruit drink, California instant powdered grape drink, CFC grape soda, and CFC strawberry soda.

Consumer Research

In order to ascertain the causes for CFC's rapid decline in grape juice sales, an "Awareness, Usage, and Attitude Study" was compiled in February 1990 to update the marketing department's understanding of Puerto Rican grape juice consumers. Two hundred personal interviews were done with people who had used grape juice during the previous two years. The study was administered by a Puerto Rican consulting group. Results are listed in Table 2.

The results of the study showed that the demand for orange juice had increased tremen-

TABLE 1 Juices and Drinks Imported into Puerto Rico

	THOUSANDS OF CASES (NOT EQUIVALENTS)			PERCENT OF CHANGE
	1987	1988	1989	1988–1989
Fruit juices				
Vegetable juice	20.6	23.4	23.9	+2.1
Tomato juice	45.5	21.2	26.3	+24.6
Apple juice	84.5	109.0	105.6	−3.1
Citrus juice	203.5	198.7	183.4	−7.7
Nectars	—	5.0	1.8	−64.0
Pineapple juice	22.5	22.9	29.1	+27.1
Prune juice	25.8	23.3	29.5	+26.6
Grape juice CFC	569.1	586.5	412.1	−29.7
Other	40.6	37.1	26.6	−28.3
Fruit drinks				
RJR	114.1	161.0	116.3	−27.8
Borden*	92.9	124.4	132.6	+6.6
Miscellaneous/all others†	260.5	296.4	356.0	+20.4
Fruit juice—frozen and concentrated				
Citrus Central	184.8	236.6	219.5	−7.2
CFÇ	34.4	24.4	32.5	+33.2
Miscellaneous/all others	378.1	431.5	499.8	+15.8

*Includes Orange Burst instant breadfast drink, Wyler's ades.
†Includes Tang powdered grape and orange drinks.
Source: Maritime Reports (Washington, D.C.: U.S. Government Printing Office, 1990).

dously since 1988. Both current and previous study users of CFC grape juice were drinking much more orange juice by 1990. In addition, the percentage of respondents who did not use orange juice was practically nil.

Current users of CFC juice continued to drink large quantities of grape juice, as the figures reveal. In fact, 86 percent of all CFC users said that they drank as much, or more, grape juice in 1989 as they had previously. However, among the previous CFC users, there were many more who had decreased their consumption of grape juice than had increased it. Therefore, it was implied that they were not switching from

TABLE 2 Consumption Results of Sample of Puerto Rican Grape Juice Users During 1988 and 1989

	PREVIOUS USERS (n = 45)				CURRENT CFC USERS (n = 155)			
Juices	More	The Same	Less	Don't Use	More	The Same	Less	Don't Use
Orange	57.7%	28.9%	11.1%	2.3%	43.5%	42.2%	11.7%	2.6%
Grape	13.3	37.8	24.5	24.4	38.9	47.4	13.0	0.7
Pineapple	22.2	26.7	33.3	17.8	23.3	29.9	31.1	15.7
Grapefruit	15.6	11.1	51.2	22.1	5.2	16.9	45.4	32.5
Fruit drinks	17.7	20.0	35.5	26.8	13.6	29.2	23.3	33.9
Fruit nectar	20.0	35.6	26.7	17.7	13.6	30.5	30.5	25.4
Powdered drinks	31.1	17.8	24.4	26.7	9.1	32.5	34.4	24.0

one grape juice brand to another, but drinking more orange juice instead. Over 57 percent of previous CFC users drank more orange juice by 1990 than they had in early 1988.

The main motive for the purchase of grape juice by mothers in the sample was because their children had asked for and/or liked it. The study also revealed that Puerto Ricans perceived grape juice to be both tasty and nutritious. On the negative side, respondents who were buying less grape juice had a variety of reasons for not buying it; most notably, very high price and preference for other juices were mentioned.

It was discovered that previous CFC users replaced grape juice with three other types of beverages: other canned juices (pineapple, orange, grapefruit), natural juices (orange, grapefruit, tamarind, lemon), and carbonated drinks (Pepsi, Coca-Cola, and the like).

Researchers had asked the question "Why aren't you using more CFC grape juice?" The most frequent response indicated that CFC's price was too high and that the respondents tried to buy products that were more economical. Secondary reasons suggested that they did not like the taste and preferred other flavors to grape. Table 3 summarizes consumers' reasons for buying either less or no grape juice in general and of CFC's in particular.

CFC had performed a similar consumer study in 1985 to determine grape juice drinkers' attitudes toward CFC grape juice. One section of the 1985 questionnaire involved consumers' opinions of the characteristics of CFC grape juice. Likewise, part of the 1990 survey was devoted to similar questioning. In both studies, respondents rated CFC grape juice on the basis of eight criteria, on a scale from 1 to 6. The figures in Table 4 represent average ratings for each of the product characteristics.

Both studies seemed to suggest that CFC grape juice had been, and still was, well regarded in the Puerto Rican market. There had not been too much change in the general opinion that CFC grape juice was a good-tasting, nutritious, high-quality product. In consumers' minds even the price had become more reasonable in relation to the generally stormy economic conditions. So, what seems to be the problem with CFC grape juice in the Puerto Rican market?

The study data appear to support the notion that CFC grape juice is held in high esteem in Puerto Rico, yet a solution to CFC's sales problem is needed. With this in mind, Ms. Verbrugge arranged a meeting with Jeff Hartman, Market Research Manager, to discuss and review the situation. Ms. Verbrugge wanted to examine the problem in more detail and was prepared to commit additional funds for marketing research. Before making any decision, however, she wanted Mr. Hartman's assessment of the situation.

TABLE 3 Respondents' Reasons for Not Buying Grape Juice

	REASONS FOR NO LONGER SERVING GRAPE JUICE	REASONS FOR NO LONGER SERVING CPC GRAPE JUICE
High price	22.6%	23.2%
Only use it occasionally	9.7	4.4
Prefer other flavors	29.0	22.2
Harmful to stomach/diet	12.9	10.3
Prefer natural juices	16.1	6.7
Not accustomed to using it	n.a.	8.9
Prefer powdered drinks	n.a.	8.7
Other	9.7	15.6
Total	100.0%	100.0%

TABLE 4 Averaged Ratings of CFC Grape Juice (Scale of 1 to 6)

	1990 STUDY (n = 200)	1985 STUDY (n = 200)
Sweetness	4.95	3.96
Taste	4.96	4.73
Economy	3.86	3.47
Nutrition	5.06	5.24
Naturalness	4.91	5.05
Best for children	4.97	4.92
Best for adults	4.88	4.74
Quality	5.13	5.17

Case 14: Currency Concepts International

Dr. Karen Anderson, Manager of Planning for Century Bank of Los Angeles, settled down for an unexpected evening of work in her small beach apartment. It seemed that every research project Century had commissioned in the last year had been completed during her ten-day trip to Taiwan. She had brought three research reports home that evening to try to catch up before meeting with the bank's Executive Planning Committee the next day.

Possibly because the currency-exchange facilities had been closed at the Taiwan Airport when she first arrived, Dr. Anderson's attention turned first to a report on a project currently under consideration by one of Century Bank's wholly owned subsidiaries, Currency Concepts International (CCI). The project concerned the manufacture and installation of currency-exchange automatic teller machines (ATMs) in major foreign airports.

CCI had been responsible for the development of Century Bank's very popular ATM ("money machine"), now installed in numerous branches of the bank, as well as in its main location in downtown Los Angeles. The current project was a small part of CCI and Century Bank's plan to expand electronic banking services worldwide.

As she started to review the marketing research effort of Information Resources, Inc., she wondered what she would be able to recommend to the Executive Planning Committee the next day regarding the currency-exchange project. She liked her recommendations to be backed by solid evidence, and she looked forward to reviewing results of the research performed to date.

This case is printed with the permission of the author, Grady D. Bruce of the California State University, Fullerton.

Activities of Information Resources, Inc.

Personnel of Information Resources, Inc., had decided to follow three different approaches in investigating the problem presented to them: (1) review secondary statistical data; (2) interview companies that currently engage in currency exchange; and (3) conduct an exploratory consumer survey of a convenience sample.

Secondary Data

The review of secondary data had three objectives:

1. To determine whether the number of persons flying abroad constitutes a market potentially large enough to merit automated currency exchange
2. To isolate any trends in the numbers of people flying abroad
3. To determine whether the amount of money that these travelers spend abroad is sizeable enough to provide a potential market for automated currency exchange

The United States Department of Transportation monitors the number of people traveling from United States airports to foreign airports. These statistics are maintained and categorized as follows: citizen and noncitizen passengers, and civilian and military passengers. Since this study was concerned only with Americans who travel abroad, only citizen categories were considered. Furthermore, since American military flights do not utilize the same foreign airport facilities as civilian passenger flights, the military category was also excluded. The prospect that non-Americans might also use these facilities causes the statistics to be somewhat conservative. The figures, for 1978, were summed for each foreign airport; the results by geographical area are shown in Exhibit 1. The top ten gateway cities from all American ports are shown in Exhibit 2.

The second objective, to determine any growth trends in air travel, was addressed by studying the number of Americans flying abroad in the last five years. Exhibit 3 shows the number of American travelers flying to various geographic areas and the associated growth rates in each of those areas. Europe, clearly, has the greatest number of travelers; and, although it did not show the greatest percentage growth in 1978, it does have the largest growth in absolute numbers. Generally, growth rates in overseas air travel have been good for the last four years; at this time, these trends appear to be positive from the standpoint of a potential market. However, there are also some potential problems on the horizon. As the world's energy situation increasingly worsens, there is the possibility of significant decreases in international travel.

In order to address the third objective, whether the amount of money spent by American travelers abroad constitutes a potential market, per capita spending was examined. Exhibit 4 shows per capita spending, by geographic area, for the last five years as well as yearly percentages of growth. The category that includes the Far East, "other areas," shows the highest per capita spending. This may be the result of the relatively low prices found in the Far East.

Europe shows the second-highest figures for per capita spending; this area also exhibited strong growth in the last year. These figures indicate that Americans are spending increasing

EXHIBIT 1 American Citizens Flying Abroad in 1978 to Foreign Ports of Entry with Over 25,000 Arrivals

Europe	3,725,952
Caribbean	1,930,756
Central America	1,356,496
South America	301,347
Far East	516,861
Oceania	133,584

Note: Included in these area totals are all ports of entry that receive more than 25,000 passengers annually (68 per day). Ports of entry with a lower through-put rate were excluded.

Source: United States Department of Transportation. *United States International Air Travel Statistics,* 1978, Washington, D.C.

EXHIBIT 2 Most Frequented Foreign Ports of Entry from All American Ports

PORT	PASSENGERS
1. London, England	1,420,285
2. Mexico City, Mexico	641,054
3. Frankfurt, Germany	446,166
4. Hamilton, Bermuda	378,897
5. Nassau, Bahamas	361,791
6. Tokyo, Japan	320,827
7. Freeport, Bahamas	309,288
8. Paris, France	295,823
9. Rome, Italy	272,186
10. Acapulco, Mexico	226,120

Source: Based on data provided in United States Department of Transportation, *United States International Air Travel Statistics,* 1978, Washington, D.C.

EXHIBIT 3 Growth in Number of Americans Flying Abroad 1974–1978 (Thousands)

	1974	% CHANGE	1975	% CHANGE	1976	% CHANGE	1977	% CHANGE	1978
European and Mediterranean	3,325	(4.2)	3,185	10.6	3,523	11.3	3,920	5.2	4,105
Western Europe	3,118	(4.1)	2,990	10.0	3,245	11.2	3,663	6.9	3,914
Caribbean and Central America	2,147	(3.8)	2,065	6.6	2,201	—	2,203	7.4	2,365
South America	423	5.7	447	(2.5)	436	10.8	483	6.6	515
Other Areas	572	14.9	657	12.2	737	6.4	784	2.7	805
Total	9,585	8.5	9,344	36.9	10,142	39.7	11,053	28.8	11,704

Source: United States Department of Commerce, *Survey of Current Business,* June 1979, Washington, D.C.

EXHIBIT 4 Per Capita Spending by Americans Traveling Abroad 1974–1978

	1974	% CHANGE	1975	% CHANGE	1976	% CHANGE	1977	% CHANGE	1978
Europe	542	11.1	602	1.3	610	—	612	17.2	717
Caribbean and Central America	319	19.4	381	(6.6)	356	—	359	4.5	375
South America	494	9.5	541	(1.7)	532	(1.1)	526	12.9	594
Other Areas	786	1.9	802	0.9	809	3.7	839	20.0	1,007
All Areas	486	12.6	547	—	545	1.8	555	14.6	635

Source: United States Department of Commerce, *Survey of Current Business,* June 1979, Washington, D.C.

amounts of money abroad; even when inflation is taken into consideration, these figures are positive.

Information Resources, Inc., concluded, therefore, that Europe holds the greatest market potential for introduction of the new system. As Dick Knowlton, coordinator of the research team, said, "Not only are all of the statistics for Europe high, but the short geographic distances between countries can be expected to provide a good deal of intra-area travel."

Company Interviews

In an attempt to better understand the current operations of currency exchange in airports, four major firms engaged in these activities were contacted. While some firms were naturally reluctant to provide information on some areas of their operations, several were quite cooperative. These firms, and a number of knowledgeable individuals whose names surfaced in initial interviews, provided the information that follows.

In both New York and Los Angeles, there is only one bank engaged in airport currency exchange: Deak-Perera. American Express, Bank of America, and Citibank, as well as Deak-Perera, are engaged in airport currency exchange in a variety of foreign locations. Approval of permits to engage in airport currency exchange activity rests with the municipal body that governs the airport and is highly controlled. It appears that foreign currency exchange is a highly profitable venture. Banks make most of their profits on the spread in exchange rates, which are posted daily.

Both Citibank and Bank of America indicated that they attempt to ensure their facilities' availability to all flights. The more profitable flights were found to be those that were regularly scheduled, rather than chartered. The person more likely to use the facilities was the vacationer rather than the businessperson. Neither bank could give an exact figure for the average transaction size; estimates ranged from $85 to $100.

It was the opinion of bank/Deak employees, who dealt with travelers on a daily basis, that the average traveler was somewhat uncomfortable changing money in a foreign country. They also believed it to be particularly helpful if clerks at the exchange counter converse with travelers in their own language. A number of years ago Deak attempted to use a type of vending machine to dispense money at Kennedy Airport. This venture failed; industry observers felt that the absence of human conversation and assurance contributed to its lack of success.

Most of the exchanges perform the same types of services, including the sale of foreign currency and the sale of travelers checks. The actual brand of travelers checks sold varies with the vendors.

American Express has recently placed automated unmanned travelers check dispensers in various American airports. This service is available to American Express card holders and the only charge is 1 percent of the face value of the purchased checks; the purchase is charged directly to the customer's checking account. As yet, the machines have not enjoyed a great deal of use, although American Express has been successful in enrolling its customers as potential users.

Methods of payment for currency purchases are similar at all exchanges. Accepted forms of payment include: actual cash, travelers checks, cashier checks drawn on local banks, and Master Charge or Visa cards. When using a credit card to pay for currency purchase, there is a service charge added to the customer's bill, as with any cash advance.

Traveler Interviews

To supplement and complement the statistical foundation gained by reviewing secondary data sources, the consumer interview portion of the study was purposefully designed to elicit qualitative information about travelers' feelings toward current and future forms of exchanging currency. Approximately sixty American travelers were interviewed at both the San Francisco and Los Angeles International Airports, due to the accessibility of these locations to Information Resources' sole location. An unstructured, undisguised questionnaire was developed to assist in channeling the interview toward specific topics (see Appendix A). Questions were not fixed and the question order was dependent on the respondent's answers. Basically, the guide served to force the interview conversation around the central foreign currency exchange theme. The interviews were conducted primarily in the arrival/departure lobbies of international carriers and spanned over four weeks, beginning in mid-December 1979. A deliberate attempt was made to include as many arriving as departing passengers to neutralize the effect of increasing holiday traffic. Additionally, to reduce interviewer bias, three different interviewers were used. Interviews were intentionally kept informal. And Dick Knowlton cautioned the interviewers to remain objective and "not let your excitement over the product concept spill over into the interview and bias the responses."

The interviews were divided almost evenly between those who favored the concept and those who did not. Those who did perceive value in the concept tended also to support other innovations such as the automated teller machine and charging foreign currency on credit cards. Those who would not use the currency exchange terminals wanted more human interaction and generally did not favor automation in any form; a fair proportion also had had previous problems exchanging foreign currency. However, even those who did not favor the currency exchange idea did seem to prefer the system of having twenty-four-hour availability of the machines, and of using credit cards to get cash under emergency situations.

The respondents represent a diverse group of individuals ranging in age from eighteen to eighty years, holding such different positions as oil executive, photographer, housewife, and customs officer. Primarily bound for Europe, Canada, and Mexico, the interviewees were mainly split between pleasure-seekers and those on business. Only three individuals interviewed were part of tour groups, and of these three, only one had previously traveled abroad. The majority of the others had been out of the United States before and had exchanged currency in at least one other country. Many had exchanged currency in remote parts of the world, including Morocco, Brazil, Australia, Japan, Tanzania, and Russia. Only five individuals had not exchanged money in airports at one time or another. The majority had obtained foreign currency in airports and exchanged money in airports primarily in small denominations for use in taxi cab fares, bus fares, phones, and airport gift shops, as well as for food, tips, and drinks. Most respondents agreed a prime motive for exchanging money in airports was the security of having local currency.

Exchanging currency can become a trying ordeal for some individuals. They fear being cheated on the exchange rate; they cannot convert the foreign currency into tangible concepts (for example, "how many yen should a loaf of bread cost?"); they dislike lines and associated red tape; and many cannot understand the rates as posted in percentages. Most individuals exchange money in airports, hotels, or banks, but sometimes there are no convenient facilities at all for exchanging currency.

People like to deal with well-known bank branches, especially in airports, because they feel more confident about the rate they are receiving. However, major fears of individuals are that money exchange personnel will not understand English and that they will be cheated in the transaction. Furthermore, a few people mentioned poor documentation when they exchange currency in foreign airports.

The travelers were divided as to whether they exchange currency before or after they arrive in the foreign country, but a few said that the decision depended on what country they were entering. If a currency, such as English pounds, could easily be obtained from a local bank before leaving the United States, they were more likely to exchange before leaving. However, in no case would the traveler arrange for currency beyond a week in advance. Most preferred to obtain the foreign currency on relatively short notice—less than three days before the trip. Of the individuals on tours, none planned to obtain currency in the foreign airport. Apparently, the tour guide had previously arranged for the necessary transportation from the airport to the hotels, and there would be only enough time to gather one's luggage and find the bus before it would depart, leaving no time to enjoy the facilities of the airport which required foreign currency. All three tour individuals did mention that they planned to obtain foreign currency once they arrived at the hotel. All individuals mentioned that they had secured their own foreign currency, but a few of the wives who were traveling with their husbands conceded that their spouses usually converted the currency in the foreign airport.

Very few of the interviewees had actually used an automated teller machine, but the majority had heard of or seen the teller machines on television. Those who had used the automated machines preferred their convenience and were generally satisfied with the terminal's performance. Many of those who had not used the automated teller machines mistrusted the machine and possible loss of control over their finances. Concerns about security and problems with the machines breaking down were also expressed. One woman described the teller machines as being "convenient, but cold." Apparently, many people prefer having human interaction when their money is concerned.

As noted earlier, approximately thirty of the respondents would favor the exchange terminals over their normal airport currency exchange routine, while the same number would have nothing to do with the machines. However, the majority of potential users qualified their use by such features as competitive rates, knowing the precise charges, or knowing they could get help if something went wrong. Individuals who indicated no preference were included in the favorable category, simply because they would not refuse to try the machine. Most of the indifferent people seemed to indicate they would try such a machine if some type of introductory promotional offer was included, such as travel information, currency tips, or a better rate.

With virtual unanimity, the respondents felt that twenty-four-hour availability made the currency exchange machines more attractive, yet that alone would not persuade the dissenters to use the terminals. Some individuals felt that a machine simply could not give the travel advice that could be obtained at the currency exchange booths.

The opportunity to charge foreign currency against a major credit card, such as Master Charge or Visa, was a definite plus in the minds of most respondents. One individual clearly resented the idea, however, feeling that he would "overspend" if given such a convenient way to obtain cash. Respondents offered a number of suggestions concerning implementations of the product concept and a number of specific product features:

1. Add information about the country.
2. Provide small denominations, and include coins.
3. Have it communicate in English.
4. Put in travelers checks to get cash.
5. Put in cash to get foreign currency.
6. Post rates daily.
7. Keep rates competitive and post charges.
8. Have television screen with person to describe procedure.
9. Place the machines in hotels and banks.
10. Have a change machine nearby that can convert paper money.
11. Place machine near existing currency exchange facilities for convenience when normal lines become long.
12. Demonstrate how to use the machine.
13. Use all bank credit cards.

Appendix A: Interview Guide for International Travelers (U.S. Citizens)

These interviews should remain as informal as possible. The object is not to obtain statistically reliable results, but to get ideas that will help to stimulate research. These questions are not fixed; the order, however, is sometimes dependent on answers the respondents give.

Introduce Yourself

1. Are you going to be traveling to a foreign country? Arriving from a foreign country? A United States resident?
2. Where is/was your final destination?
3. Why are you traveling (business, pleasure, a tour)?
4. How often do you travel outside of the United States?
5. Have you ever exchanged currency in a foreign country. (If no, go to #6.) Where? Does anything in particular stand out in your mind when you exchanged currency?
6. Have you ever changed money in an airport? (If no, go to #7.)
7. Where do you plan to exchange currency on this trip?
8. Where do you change money normally?
9. Have you ever had any problems changing currencies? Explain circumstances.
10. Normally, would you change money before entering a country or after you arrive? If before, how long in advance? Where? (Probe.)
11. Are you familiar with automated teller machines that banks are using? (If not, explain.) Have you used one of these machines?
12. What are your feelings toward these machines?
13. If a currency exchange terminal, similar to an automated teller machine, was placed in your destination airport, would you use the machine or follow your normal routine?
14. Would 24-hour availability make the currency exchange machines more attractive? Would you use the terminals at night?
15. None of the currency exchange machines currently exists. What features or services could be provided so that you might choose to use a terminal rather than other currency exchange facilities?
16. If you could charge the foreign currency received to a major credit card, such as Master Charge or Visa, would you be more likely to use the machine?
17. Demographics—Age range (visual)
    Occupation?
    Sex?
    Traveling alone?

Case 15: A. G. Nashbandi Manufacturing

It was two weeks after having finished a workshop on market entry strategies into the Middle East, sponsored by the Philippine Trade Training Centre, that Mr. Nashbandi made the decision to diversify his export markets and participate in a trade fair in Dubai, in November.

This case is printed here from *Selected Asian Cases of Small and Medium-Sized Enterprises in Export Marketing* (Geneva: International Trade Center UNCTAD/GATT, 1989).

History of the Company

A. G. Nashbandi Manufacturing was founded in 1979 as a single proprietorship to produce ladies' and children's undergarments for the Philippines market. The company positioned its products for the lower-income brackets, using 100 percent Nylon Tricot and Polyrayon as the raw material instead of the more expensive cotton. The company experienced a major crisis when in 1983, due to mismanagement of the company, bank loans could not be paid back and the company had to be refinanced. This unfortunate experience had left a credibility gap with the banking network in the area. A constant shortage of working capital and the unwillingness of the local banks to provide long-term financial support had led to various financial emergency measures, like factoring the company's invoices, requesting excessive suppliers' credit, and financing through a Hong Kong bank based on a family member's collateral. The company had been forced to maintain a conservative operation, producing a standard product line of undergarments, in order to avoid risk at all costs. Due to their location in the rural area outside Manila, the low labor costs had led the company to compete on price.

The Results of the Workshop

The workshop had made Mr. Nashbandi aware of the substantial growth of Filipino exports of women's and girls' undergarments to Kuwait during the period 1986–87 (from zero to $55,533 U.S.). He saw also opportunities in the export of girls' and women's synthetic nightwear (a total value of $137,212 in 1987), product lines that would be compatible with his present manufacturing capability. The announced trade fair in Dubai in November 1989 would be attended by Kuwaiti buyers and his participation would be subsidized by the Filipino Textile and Garment Board.

The Marketing Strategy

With a Filipino population of 75,000 in Kuwait, Mr. Nashbandi wondered if he should make it his target market, rather than the native Arab one. He wondered if more loyalty and natural interest would exist among Filipinos for a product made in the Philippines.

Identifying the manufacturing source through a Filipino brandname would enable him to enhance communication with his target market. By the same token, he wondered if underwear and nightwear are bought because of brand names or for other reasons.

No unemployment existed among the Filipinos because all adult single Filipinos or the heads of Filipino households have to be employed in Kuwait in order to maintain their working visas. He wondered also if his markup could benefit from the higher disposable income. Should he trade up and introduce some higher quality standards into his undergarments and nightwear?

The Filipino community represents a rather closely knit society abroad, which made him think of using "party selling" in private homes as a promotional tool. In addition, he could engage in direct mailing of brochures based on mailing lists obtainable from the Philippines consulate in Kuwait. This would also allow him to mail-order and bypass the middleman. Another promotional alternative was to merchandise his undergarments and nightwear from a hotel room for one or two weeks after advertising to the Filipino community the time and place. It would give him direct contact with the ultimate consumer and, besides, with only little out-of-pocket expense, provide him two additional mark-ups: the importer-distributor's and the retailer's.

Bypassing the middlemen would free him from making the difficult choice of using agents or merchants. The agent meant much more risk for him, as he remained responsible for the merchandise. The only variable costs would be the agent's commission, which would occur only after the agent's sale. He would increase his own profit contribution by using agents; however, his risk would be higher as well. The merchant, represented by the importer, wholesaler, or distributor, would reduce his risk considerably but also lower his profit margin. The merchant would buy outright, pay him through a letter of credit upon delivery of the merchandise, and assume merchandising responsibility thereafter. In the Philippines market, he had experimented with agents and merchants and he was never totally satisfied with either one. Perhaps he could cater to the Filipino target market in Kuwait directly and use middlemen for other Arab markets.

The product mix he considered most difficult to decide on. He realized that synthetic fibers used for undergarments or nightwear are much less comfortable than natural fibers, especially cotton. The very hot climate in Kuwait during the summer months and the superior purchasing power might well give cotton fibers a comparative advantage. The presence of almost universal central air conditioning in Kuwaiti homes complicated the choice between synthetic and cotton fibers even more. Would a blend of 65 percent cotton and 35 percent synthetic fibers be the solution? He realized that he would have to import this fabric because of its unavailability in the Philippines, which would drive up his costs. All-cotton yarn made in the Philippines was available, but the domestic market demand exceeded its supply by about 50 percent. This might mean that he would have to import cotton yarn as well and do the knitting in a bonded warehouse to avoid paying import duties. This would require two manufacturing centers.

On the other hand, his Filipino target market in Kuwait might continue to buy garments made out of synthetic fibers, maintaining their previous habits from the Philippines. Further, most of the Filipino workers might try to maximize their net earnings by saving money wherever they can. Synthetic underwear tends to be lower in price than cotton or cotton blends. Besides, the present exports of undergarments and nightwear from the Philippines are made of all-synthetic fabrics. When he checked again the total Filipino export value of these product lines to Kuwait, he remembered from a workshop that China and Thailand have made major gains in their world market undergarment shares because of their switching to 100 percent cotton products. The prices they were able to charge were also superior to those of garments made from synthetic fibers.

Case 16: Curtis Automotive Hoist

In September 1990, Mark Curtis, president of Curtis Automotive Hoist (CAH), had just finished reading a feasibility report on entering the European market in 1991. CAH manufactured surface automotive hoists, a product used by garages, service stations, and other repair shops to lift cars for servicing. The report, prepared by CAH's marketing manager, Pierre Gagnon, outlines the opportunities in the European Economic Community and the entry options available.

Mr. Curtis was not sure if CAH was ready for this move. While the company had been successful in expanding sales into the United States market, Mr. Curtis wondered if this success could be repeated in Europe. He thought that with more effort, sales could be increased in the United States. On the other hand, there were some positive aspects to the European idea. He

This case is printed here with the permission of the author, Gordon H. G. McDougall of Wilfrid Laurier University, Québec.

began reviewing the information in preparation for the meeting the following day with Mr. Gagnon.

Curtis Automotive Hoist

Mr. Curtis, a design engineer, had worked for eight years for the Canadian subsidiary of a U.S. automotive hoist manufacturer. During those years, he had spent considerable time designing an above-ground (or surface) automotive hoist. Although Mr. Curtis was very enthusiastic about the unique aspects of the hoist, including a scissor lift and wheel alignment pads, senior management expressed no interest in the idea. In 1980, Mr. Curtis left the company to start his own business with the express purpose of designing and manufacturing the hoist. He left with the good wishes of his previous employer who had no objections to his plans to start a new business.

Over the next three years, Mr. Curtis obtained financing from a venture capital firm, opened a plant in Lachine, Québec, and began manufacturing and marketing the hoist, called the Curtis Lift.

From the beginning, Mr. Curtis had taken considerable pride in the development and marketing of the Curtis Lift. The original design included a scissor lift and a safety locking mechanism that allowed the hoist to be raised to any level and locked in place. As well, the scissor lift offered easy access for the mechanic to work on the raised vehicle. Because the hoist was fully hydraulic and had no chains or pulleys, it required little maintenance. Another key feature was the alignment turn plates that were an integral part of the lift. The turn plates meant that mechanics could accurately and easily perform wheel alignment jobs. Because it was a surface lift, it could be installed in a garage in less than a day.

Mr. Curtis continually made improvements to the product, including adding more safety features. In fact, the Curtis Lift was considered a leader in automotive lift safety. Safety was an important factor in the automotive hoist market. Although hoists seldom malfunctioned, when they did, it often resulted in a serious accident.

The Curtis Lift developed a reputation in the industry as the "Cadillac" of hoists; the unit was judged by many as superior to competitive offerings because of its design, the quality of the workmanship, the safety features, the east of installation, and the five-year warranty. Mr. Curtis held four patents on the Curtis Lift, including the lifting mechanism on the scissor design and a safety locking mechanism. A number of versions of the product were designed that made the Curtis Lift suitable (depending on the model) for a variety of tasks, including rustproofing, muffler repairs, and general mechanical repairs.

In 1981, CAH sold twenty-three hoists and had sales of $172,500. During the early years, the majority of sales were to independent service stations and garages specializing in wheel alignment in the Québec and Ontario market. Most of the units were sold by Mr. Gagnon, who was hired in 1982 to handle the marketing side of the operation. In 1984, Mr. Gagnon began using distributors to sell the hoist to a wider geographic market in Canada. In 1986, he signed an agreement with a large automotive wholesaler to represent CAH in the U.S. market. By 1989, the company sold 1,054 hoists and had sales of $9,708,000 (Exhibit 1). In 1989, about 60 percent of sales were to the United States with the remaining 40 percent to the Canadian market.

Industry

Approximately 49,000 hoists were sold each year in North America. Typically hoists were purchased by an automotive outlet that serviced or repaired cars, including new car dealers, used car dealers, specialty shops (for example, muffler shops, transmission, wheel alignment), chains (for example, Firestone, Goodyear, Canadian Tire), and independent garages. It was estimated that new car dealers purchased 30 percent of all units sold in a given year. In general, the specialty shops focus on one type of repair, such as mufflers or rustproofing, while "nonspecialty"

EXHIBIT 1 Curtis Automotive Hoist—Selected Financial Statistics (1987 to 1989)

	1989	1988	1987
Sales	$9,708,000	$7,454,000	$6,218,000
Cost of Sales	6,990,000	5,541,000	4,540,000
Contribution	2,718,000	1,913,000	1,678,000
Marketing expenses*	530,000	510,000	507,000
Administrative expenses	840,000	820,000	810,000
Earnings before tax	1,348,000	583,000	361,000
Units sold	1,054	847	723

*Marketing expenses in 1989 included advertising ($70,000), four salespeople ($240,000), marketing manager and three sales support staff ($220,000).
Source: Company records.

outlets handle a variety of repairs. While there was some crossover, in general, CAH competed in the specialty shop segment and, in particular, those shops that dealt with wheel alignment. This included chains, such as Firestone and Canadian Tire as well as new car dealers (for example, Ford) who devote a certain percentage of their lifts to the wheel alignment business, and independent garages who specialized in wheel alignment.

The purpose of a hoist was to lift an automobile into a position where a mechanic or service person could easily work on the car. Because different repairs required different positions, a wide variety of hoists had been developed to meet specific needs. For example, a muffler repair shop required a hoist that allowed the mechanic to gain easy access to the underside of the car. Similarly, a wheel alignment job required a hoist that offered a level platform where the wheels could be adjusted as well as providing easy access for the mechanic. Mr. Gagnon estimated that 85 percent of CAH's sales were to the wheel alignment market to service centers such as Firestone, Goodyear, and Canadian Tire and to independent garages that specialized in wheel alignment. About 15 percent of sales were made to customers who used the hoist for general mechanical repairs.

Firms purchasing hoists were part of an industry called the automobile aftermarket. This industry was involved in supplying parts and service for new and used cars and was worth over $54 billion at retail in 1989, while servicing the approximately 11 million cars on the road in Canada. The industry was large and diverse; there were over 4,000 new car dealers in Canada, over 400 Canadian Tire stores, over 100 stores in each of the Firestone and Goodyear chains, and over 200 stores in the Rust Check chain.

The purchase of an automotive hoist was often an important decision for the service station owner or dealer. Because the price of hoists ranged from $3,000 to $15,000, it was a capital expense for most businesses.

For the owner/operator of a new service center or car dealership the decision involved determining what type of hoist was required, then what brand would best suit the company. Most new service centers or car dealerships had multiple bays for servicing cars. In these cases, the decision would involve what types of hoists were required (for example, in-ground, surface). Often, more than one type of hoist was purchased, depending on the service center/dealership needs.

Experienced garage owners seeking a replacement hoist (the typical hoist had a useful life of ten to thirteen years) would usually determine what products were available and then make a decision. If the garage owners were also mechanics, they would probably be aware of two or three types of hoists but would not be very knowledgeable about the brands or products currently available. Garage owners or dealers who were not mechanics probably knew very little about hoists. The owners of car or service dealerships often bought the product that was recommended and/or approved by the parent company.

Competition

Sixteen companies competed in the automotive lift market in North America: four Canadian and twelve United States firms. Hoists were subject to import duties. Duties on hoists entering the U.S. market from Canada were 2.4 percent of the selling price; from the U.S. entering Canada the import duty was 7.9 percent. With the advent of the Free Trade Agreement in 1989, the duties between the two countries would be phased out over a ten-year period. For Mr. Curtis, the import duties had never played a part in any decisions: the fluctuating exchange rates between the two countries had a far greater impact on selling prices.

A wide variety of hoists were manufactured in the industry. The two basic types of hoists were in-ground and surface. As the names imply, in-ground hoists required that a pit be dug "in-ground" where the piston that raised the hoist was installed. In-ground hoists were either single-post or multiple-post, were permanent, and obviously could not be moved. In-ground lifts constituted approximately 21 percent of total lift sales in 1989 (Exhibit 2). Surface lifts were installed on a flat surface, usually concrete. Surface lifts came in two basic types, post-lift hoists and scissor hoists. Surface lifts, compared to in-ground lifts, were easier to install and could be moved, if necessary. Surface lifts constituted 79 percent of total lift sales in 1989. Within each type of hoist (for example, post-lift surface hoists), there were numerous variations in terms of size, shape, and lifting capacity.

The industry was dominated by two large U.S. firms, AHV Lifts and Berne Manufacturing, who together held approximately 60 percent of the market. AHV Lifts, the largest firm with approximately 40 percent of the market and annual sales of about $60 million, offered a complete line of hoists (that is, in-ground and surface) but focused primarily on the in-ground market and the two-post surface market. AHV Lifts was the only company that had its own direct sales force; all other companies used (1) only wholesalers or (2) a combination of wholesalers and company sales force. AHV Lifts offered standard hoists with few extra features and competed primarily on price. Berne Manufacturing, with a market share of approximately 20 percent, also competed in the in-ground and two-post surface markets. It used a combination of wholesalers and company salespeople and, like AHV Lifts, competed primarily on price.

Most of the remaining firms in the industry were companies that operated in a regional market (for example, California or British Columbia) and/or offered a limited product line (for example, four-post surface hoist).

Curtis had two competitors that manufactured scissor lifts. AHV Lift marketed a scissor hoist that had a different lifting mechanism and did not include the safety locking features of the Curtis Lift. On average, the AHV scissor lift sold for about 20 percent less than the Curtis Lift. The second competitor, Mete Lift, was a small regional company with sales in California and Oregon. It had a design that was very similar to the Curtis Lift but lacked some of its safety features. The Mete Lift, regarded as a well-manufactured product, sold for about 5 percent less than the Curtis Lift.

Marketing Strategy

As of early 1990, CAH had developed a reputation for a quality product backed by good service in the hoist lift market, primarily in the wheel alignment segment.

EXHIBIT 2 North American Automotive Lift Unit Sales, by Type (1987 to 1989)

	1987	1988	1989
In-ground			
Single-post	5,885	5,772	5,518
Multiple-post	4,812	6,625	5,075
Surface			
Two-post	27,019	28,757	28,923
Four-post	3,862	3,162	3,745
Scissor	2,170	2,258	2,316
Other	4,486	3,613	3,695
Total	48,234	50,187	49,272

Source: Company records.

The distribution system employed by CAH reflected the need to engage in extensive personal selling. Three types of distributors were used: a company sales force, Canadian distributors, and a U.S. automotive wholesaler. The company sales force consisted of four salespeople and Mr. Gagnon. Their main task was to service large "direct" accounts. The initial step was to get the Curtis Lift approved by large chains and manufacturers and then, having received the approval, to sell to individual dealers or operators. For example, if General Motors approved the hoist, then CAH could sell it to individual General Motors dealers. CAH sold directly to the individual dealers of a number of large accounts including General Motors, Ford, Chrysler, Petro-Canada, Firestone, and Goodyear. CAH had been successful in obtaining manufacturer approval from the big three automobile manufacturers in both Canada and the United States. CAH had also received approval from service companies such as Canadian Tire and Goodyear. To date, CAH had not been rejected by any major account but, in some cases, the approval process had taken over four years.

In total, the company sales force generated about 25 percent of the unit sales each year. Sales to the large "direct" accounts in the United States went through CAH's U.S. wholesaler.

The Canadian distributors sold, installed, and serviced units across Canada. These distributors handled the Curtis Lift and carried a line of noncompetitive automotive equipment products (for example, engine diagnostic equipment, wheel balancing equipment) and noncompetitive lifts. These distributors focused on the smaller chains and the independent service stations and garages.

The U.S. wholesaler sold a complete product line to service stations as well as manufacturing some equipment. The Curtis Lift was one of five different types of lifts that the wholesaler sold. Although the wholesaler provided CAH with extensive distribution in the United States, the Curtis Lift was a minor product within the wholesaler's total line. While Mr. Gagnon did not have any actual figures, he thought that the Curtis Lift probably accounted for less than 20 percent of the total lift sales of the U.S. wholesaler.

Both Mr. Curtis and Mr. Gagnon felt that the U.S. market had unrealized potential. With a population of 248 million people and over 140 million registered vehicles, the U.S. market was over ten times the size of the Canadian market (population of 26 million, approximately 11 million vehicles). Mr. Gagnon noted that the six New England states (population over 13 million), the three largest mid-Atlantic states (population over 38 million), and the three largest mid-Eastern states (population over 32 million) were all within a day's drive of the factory in Lachine. Mr. Curtis and Mr. Gagnon had considered setting up a sales office in New York to service these states, but they were concerned that the U.S. wholesaler would not be willing to relinquish any of its territory. They had also considered working more closely with the wholesaler to encourage it to "push" the Curtis Lift. It appeared that the wholesaler's major objective was to sell a hoist, not necessarily the Curtis Lift.

CAH distributed a catalog-type package with products, uses, prices, and other required information for both distributors and users. In addition, CAH advertised in trade publications (for example, *Service Station & Garage Management*), and Mr. Gagnon traveled to trade shows in Canada and the U.S. to promote the Curtis Lift.

In 1989, Curtis Lifts sold for an average retail price of $10,990 and CAH received, on average, $9,210 for each unit sold. This average reflected the mix of sales through the three distribution channels: (1) direct (where CAH received 100 percent of the selling price), (2) Canadian distributors (where CAH received 80 percent of the selling price), and (3) the U.S. wholesaler (where CAH received 78 percent of the selling price).

Both Mr. Curtis and Mr. Gagnon felt that the company's success to date was based on a strategy of offering a superior product that was primarily targeted to the needs of specific customers. The strategy stressed continual product improvements, quality workmanship, and service. Personal selling was a key aspect of the strategy; salespeople could show customers the benefits of the Curtis Lift over competing products.

The European Market

Against this background, Mr. Curtis had been thinking of ways to continue the rapid growth of the company. One possibility that kept coming up was the promise and potential of the European market. The fact that Europe would become a single market in 1992 suggested that it was an opportunity that should at least be explored. With this in mind, Mr. Curtis asked Mr. Gagnon to prepare a report on the possibility of CAH entering the European market. The highlights of Mr. Gagnon's report follow.

History of the European Community

The European Community (EC) stemmed from the 1953 Treaty of Rome in which five countries decided it would be in their best interest to form an internal market. These countries were France, Spain, Italy, West Germany, and Luxembourg. By 1990, the EC consisted of twelve countries (the additional seven were Belgium, Denmark, Greece, Ireland, the Netherlands, Portugal, and the United Kingdom) with a population of over 325 million people.* In 1992, virtually all barriers (physical, technical, and fiscal) in the EC were scheduled to be removed for companies located within the EC. This would allow the free movement of goods, persons, services, and capital.

In the last five years many North American and Japanese firms had established themselves in the EC. The reasoning for this was twofold. First, these companies regarded the community as an opportunity to increase global market share and profits. The market was attractive because of its sheer size and lack of internal barriers. Second, in 1992, companies that were established within the community were subject to protection from external competition via EC protectionism tariffs, local contender, and reciprocity requirements. EC protectionism tariffs were only temporary and would be removed at a later date. It would be possible for companies to export to or establish in the community after 1992, but there was some risk attached.

*As of September 1990, West Germany and East Germany were in the process of unification. East Germany had a population of approximately 17 million people.

Market Potential

The key indicator of the potential market for the Curtis Lift hoist was the number of passenger cars and commercial vehicles in use in a particular country. Four countries in Europe had more than 20 million vehicles in use, with West Germany having the largest domestic fleet of 30 million vehicles, followed in order by France, Italy, and the United Kingdom (Exhibit 3). The number of vehicles was an important indicator because the more vehicles in use meant a greater number of service and repair facilities that needed vehicle hoists and potentially the Curtis Lift.

An indicator of the future vehicle repair and service market was the number of new vehicle registrations. The registration of new vehicles was important as this maintained the number of vehicles in use by replacing cars that had been retired. Again, West Germany had the most new cars registered in 1988 and was followed in order by France, the United Kingdom, and Italy.

Based primarily on the fact that a large domestic market was important for initial growth, the selection of a European country should be limited to the "Big Four" industralized nations: West Germany, France, the United Kingdom, or Italy. In an international survey companies from North America and Europe ranked European countries on a scale of 1 to 100 on market potential and investment site potential. The results showed that West Germany was favored for both market potential and investment site opportunities while France, the United Kingdom, and Spain placed second, third, and fourth, respectively. Italy did not place in the top four in either market or investment site potential. However, Italy had a large number of vehicles in use, had the second-largest population in Europe, and was an acknowledged leader in car technology and production.

Little information was available on the competition within Europe. There was, as yet, no dominant manufacturer, as was the case in North America. At this time, there was one firm in Germany that manufactured a scissor-type lift. The firm sold most of its units within the German market. The only other available information was that twenty-two firms in Italy manufactured vehicle lifts.

Investment Options

Mr. Gagnon felt that CAH had three options for expansion into the European market: licensing, joint venture, or direct investment. The licensing option was a real possibility as a French firm had expressed an interest in manufacturing the Curtis Lift.

In June 1990, Mr. Gagnon had attended a trade show in Detroit to promote the Curtis Lift. At the show, he met Phillipe Beaupre, the marketing manager for Bar Maisse, a French manufacturer of wheel alignment equipment. The firm, located in Chelles, France, sold a range of

EXHIBIT 3 Number of Vehicles (1988) and Population (1989)

COUNTRY	VEHICLES IN USE (THOUSANDS)		NEW VEHICLE REGISTRATIONS (THOUSANDS)	POPULATION (THOUSANDS)
	Passenger	Commercial		
West Germany	28,304	1,814	2,960	60,900
France	29,970	4,223	2,635	56,000
Italy	22,500	1,897	2,308	57,400
United Kingdom	20,605	2,915	2,531	57,500
Spain	9,750	1,750	1,172	39,400

wheel alignment equipment throughout Europe. The best-selling product was an electronic modular aligner that enabled a mechanic to utilize a sophisticated computer system to align the wheels of a car. Mr. Beaupre was seeking a North American distributor for the modular aligner and other products manufactured by Bar Maisse.

At the show, Mr. Gagnon and Mr. Beaupre had a casual conversation in which each explained what their respective companies manufactured; they exchanged company brochures and business cards, and both went on to other exhibits. The next day, Mr. Beaupre sought out Mr. Gagnon and asked if he might be interested in having Bar Maisse manufacture and market the Curtis Lift in Europe. Mr. Beaupre felt the lift would complement Bar Maisse's product line and the licensing would be of mutual benefit to both parties. They agreed to pursue the idea. Upon his return to Lachine, Mr. Gagnon told Mr. Curtis about these discussions, and they agreed to explore this possibility.

Mr. Gagnon called a number of colleagues in the industry and asked them what they knew about Bar Maisse. About half had not heard of the company, but those who had commented favorably on the quality of its products. One colleague, with European experience, knew the company well and said that Bar Maisse's management had integrity and would make a good partner. In July, Mr. Gagnon sent a letter to Mr. Beaupre stating that CAH was interested in further discussions and enclosed various company brochures including price lists and technical information on the Curtis Lift. In late August, Mr. Beaupre responded stating that Bar Maisse would like to enter a three-year licensing agreement with CAH to manufacture the Curtis Lift in Europe. In exchange for the manufacturing rights, Bar Maisse was prepared to pay a royalty rate of 5 percent of gross sales. Mr. Gagnon had not yet responded to this proposal.

A second possibility was a joint venture. Mr. Gagnon had wondered if it might not be better for CAH to offer a counter proposal to Bar Maisse for a joint venture. He had not worked out any details, but Mr. Gagnon felt that CAH would learn more about the European market and probably make more money if they were an active partner in Europe. Mr. Gagnon's idea was a 50–50 proposal where the two parties shared the investment and the profits. He envisaged a situation where Bar Maisse would manufacture the Curtis Lift in their plant with technical assistance from CAH. Mr. Gagnon also thought that CAH could get involved in the marketing of the lift through the Bar Maisse distribution system. Further, he thought that the Curtis Lift, with proper marketing, could gain a reasonable share of the European market. If that happened, Mr. Gagnon felt that CAH was likely to make greater returns with a joint venture.

The third option was direct investment where CAH would establish a manufacturing facility and set up a management group to market the lift. Mr. Gagnon had contacted a business acquaintance who had recently been involved in manufacturing fabricated steel sheds in Germany. On the basis of discussions with his acquaintance, Mr. Gagnon estimated the costs involved in setting up a plant in Europe at: (1) \$250,000 for capital equipment (welding machines, cranes, other equipment), (2) \$200,000 in incremental costs to set the plant up, and (3) carrying costs to cover \$1,000,000 in inventory and accounts receivable. While the actual costs of renting a building for the factory would depend on the site location, he estimated that annual building rent including heat, light, and insurance would be about \$80,000. Mr. Gagnon recognized these estimates were guidelines but he felt that the estimates were probably within 20 percent of actual costs.

The Decision

As Mr. Curtis considered the contents of the report, a number of thoughts crossed his mind. He began making notes concerning the European possibility and the future of the company.

- If CAH decided to enter Europe, Mr. Gagnon would be the obvious choice to head up the direct investment option or the joint venture option. Mr. Curtis felt that Mr. Gagnon had been instrumental in the success of the company to date.
- While CAH had the financial resources to go ahead with the direct investment option, the joint venture would spread the risk (and the returns) over the two companies.
- CAH had built its reputation on designing and manufacturing a quality product. Regardless of the option chosen, Mr. Curtis wanted the firm's reputation to be maintained.
- Either the licensing agreement or the joint venture appeared to build on the two companies' strengths; Bar Maisse had knowledge of the market and CAH had the product. What troubled Mr. Curtis was whether this apparent synergy would work or whether Bar Maisse would seek to control the operation.
- It was difficult to estimate sales under any of the options. With the first two (licensing and joint venture), it would depend on the effort and expertise of Bar Maisse; with the third option, it would depend on Mr. Gagnon.
- CAH's sales in the U.S. market could be increased if the U.S. wholesaler would "push" the Curtis Lift. Alternatively, the establishment of a sales office in New York to cover the eastern states could also increase sales.

As Mr. Curtis reflected on the situation he knew he should probably get additional information—but it wasn't obvious exactly what information would help him make a "yes" or "no" decision. He knew one thing for sure—he was going to keep his company on a "fast growth" track—and at tomorrow's meeting he and Mr. Gagnon would decide how to do it.

PART • 5

International Marketing Decisions

CHAPTER • 12

Product Policy and Planning

CHAPTER FOCUS

After studying this chapter, you should be able to:

- Discuss the perspectives of international product planning
- Debate the pros and cons of following standardization versus customization of product in overseas markets
- Describe various aspects of new product introduction in international markets
- Explain the factors that affect global adoption and diffusion of new products
- Compare various branding alternatives for international markets
- Examine the role of international product warranties and services

The product decision is among the first decisions that a marketing manager makes in order to develop a marketing mix. Traditionally, product decision in international marketing simply has meant exporting products already produced and marketed in the United States. In the future, and even now, such a simple perspective on product policy will not work. Today U.S. companies face strong competition from European and Japanese companies, as well as from newly industrialized countries and third world nations. At the same time, foreign markets have become more sophisticated and an American product may not be acceptable any longer simply because it is an American product.

Thus, the product decision must be made on the basis of careful analysis and review. The nature, depth, and breadth of the product line; the possibilities of new product development and product innovation; the importance attached to product design (the adaptation and customization of products to suit local conditions vis-à-vis standardization); the decision on foreign R&D; and a planned screening and elimination of unsuccessful products bear heavily on success in foreign markets.

This chapter examines these product-related issues and suggests conceptual approaches for handling them. Also discussed are international packaging and labeling matters, international brand strategy, and warranty and service policies.

Meaning of Product

Products are all around us, and yet it is not easy to define precisely what a product is. The difficulty is that the same product may have a different significance for people in different countries. A refrigerator is a necessity in the United States because people tend to depend on a variety of frozen foods and weekly shopping. In Mexico, however, as in other developing countries, food shopping most commonly occurs on a daily basis. A refrigerator there is a luxury for the rich to store either leftovers or perishable foods for a short time.

A definition of *product,* thus, must be comprehensive in order to serve an operational purpose. A product can be defined as a bundle of attributes that satisfies a customer demand. It may be offered in the form of a tangible item, a service, or an idea. For example, the attributes of a wine are flavor, taste, consistency, and its quality as a thirst quencher or cool refreshment. Different wines have different attributes, and each brand is intended to meet the demands of a particular set of target customers. Likewise, the attributes of a corporate jet plane are width of cabin, fuel economy, flight range, speed, and noise level. Businesspersons around the world would prefer different sets of attributes in choosing a plane for their use.

Putting it differently, customers do not simply buy products in the physical sense, they buy *satisfaction,* which is derived from the product's attributes, various features, and characteristics. This fact has important ramifications in the defining of product objectives.

A company can offer different versions of the same product and thus broaden its product line by catering to the needs of heterogeneous segments of the market.

In the United States, the Coca-Cola Company is a *full-line* soft drink manufacturer producing Classic Coke, New Coke, Diet Coke, Sprite, Minute Maid, and other soft drinks to cater to the needs of different target groups. Outside the United States, the company offers just Coca-Cola in most countries. Thus, the Coca-Cola Company is considered a full-line manufacturer at home, but a limited-line manufacturer internationally.

International Product Planning

International product planning involves determining which products to introduce into which countries; what modifications to make in the products; what new products to add; what brand names to use; what package designs to use; what guarantees and warranties to give; what after-sales services to offer; and finally, when to enter the market. All these are crucial decisions requiring a variety of informational inputs. Chapter 10 on marketing research specifies different ways and sources for gathering appropriate information. Basic to these decisions are three other considerations: (1) product objectives, (2) coordination of product planning activities between headquarters and subsidiary, and (3) foreign collaboration.

The process of product planning in the international context is diagrammed in Figure 12.1. A company interested in an international market should first define its business intent based on the objectives of both the corporation and the host country. The product objectives of a company would flow from the definition of its business. Ultimately, the offering should provide satisfaction to the customer, which would be reflected in the realization of the goals of both the corporation and the host country.[1]

Product Objectives

Product objectives emerge from host country and corporate objectives combined via the business definition. The company's goals usually are *stability, growth, profits,* and *return on investment.* Stated differently, the corporate objectives may be defined in terms of *activities* (the manufacture of a specific product, or export to a particular market), *financial indicators* (to achieve a targeted return on investment), *desired position* (its market share and relative market leadership), and all these in combination with each other. The parent company usually also has a series of objectives on behalf of the various *stakeholders' interests* for which it is accountable. Host country objectives vary depending on the country's economic, political, and cultural environment. For example, the typical goals of a less-developed country would be to seek faster economic growth, to build a balanced industrial sector, to create employment opportunities, and to earn foreign exchange. On the other hand, the objectives of an oil-rich country might be to provide a modern living standard to its masses in a short time without disrupting the cultural structure of its society and/or to diversify its economy to reduce its dependence on oil over the long term.

Obviously the objectives of the host country and the company are poles apart. In any emerging market worldwide, however, no company can hope to

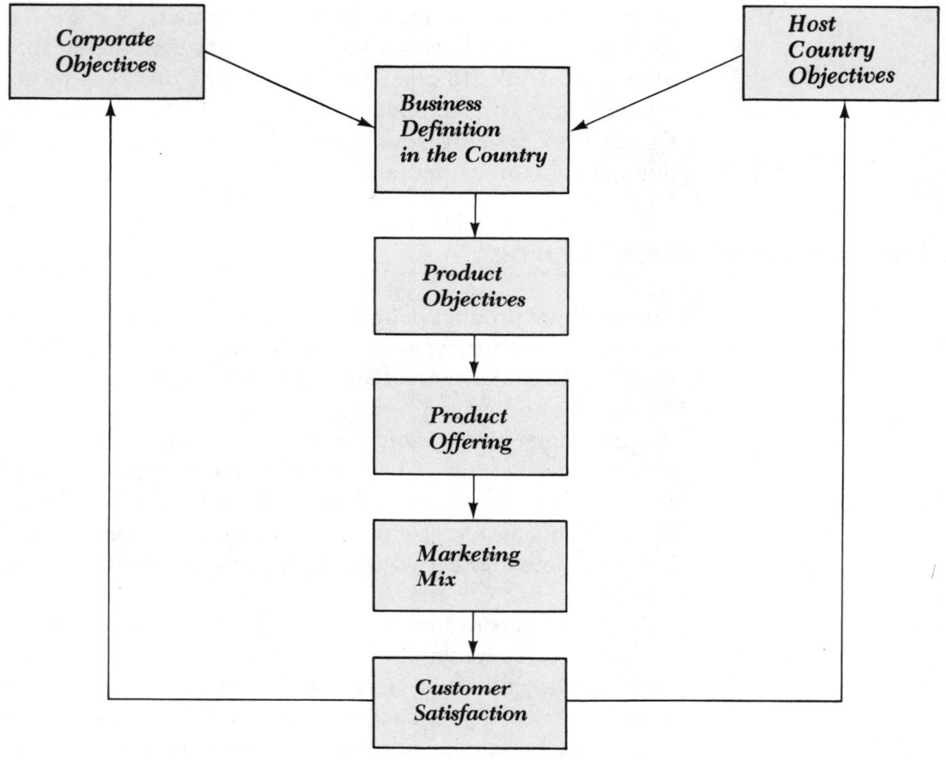

FIGURE 12.1 Perspectives of International Product Planning

succeed without aligning itself with the national concerns of the host country. There are no models to use in seeking a description of such an alignment. Conceptually, however, a macroanalysis of a country's socioeconomic perspectives should provide insights into its different concerns and problems. The company can then figure out if its business would help the country in any way, directly or indirectly. The business definition should then be developed accordingly. For example, the shortage of foreign exchange might be a big problem for a country. A multinational marketer's willingness to pursue a major effort of export promotion in the country would amount to an objective in line with the country's need. On the other hand, a company simply interested in manufacturing and selling such consumer goods as toiletries and canned foods, in a nation that is interested in establishing a basic infrastructure for industrial development in the country, may not be serving the national interest.

The definition of product objectives should emerge from the business definition. Product objectives can be defined in physical or marketing terms. "We sell instant coffee" is an example of defining objectives in physical terms. In marketing terms, the objective statement would emphasize the satisfaction of a customer need. The latter method is preferred because it reinforces the marketing concept.

To illustrate the point, assume that RCA is interested in establishing a plant for manufacturing consumer electronics in Egypt. The product objectives may be defined in the following manner:

- *RCA corporate objective.* Earn a minimum of 25 percent return on investment in any developing country.
- *Egypt's national concerns.* Create employment opportunities and build up faltering foreign exchange balances.
- *Business definition.* Establish a large consumer electronics plant in Egypt to compete effectively in the Middle East.
- *Product definition.* Meet the electronic home-entertainment needs of the masses.

Product Planning

The perspectives of international product planning can be categorized between issues of day-to-day concern on the one hand and strategic issues on the other. The day-to-day issues arise in implementing decisions already made. For example, following up on the RCA example, an issue may arise concerning the need for extra precautions to be taken to protect working televisions from dust. This issue applies only to the Middle East market where the climate requires that windows be open all the time, and where the winds carry a lot of dust into the houses. The issue would be handled appropriately by local managers. If any specific technological help is needed, it would be sought from the parent corporation on an ad hoc basis.

Strategic issues require major commitments, which must be taken up with the parent corporation. For example, using the RCA illustration, the question might be raised whether color picture tubes for TV sets should be imported from RCA in the United States or from a relatively new Japanese subsidiary located in Egypt. Another strategic question could arise with reference to trading with a country that is not on friendly terms with the United States. Let us assume Egypt does a lot of trade with Uganda. Assume further that the United States has a trade embargo against Uganda. Will it be all right for the RCA subsidiary in Egypt to export electronic goods to Uganda in view of the U.S. government's trade embargo? Strategic questions cannot be handled by subsidiary management alone and must be referred to the parent organization.

It is difficult to accumulate an inventory of decisions to label as day-to-day or strategic. It all depends on the individual situation. The subsidiary management must decide if the matter involved is strategic enough to require input from or a decision by the parent. At the risk of overgeneralization, an issue/matter/decision can be considered strategic:

- If the United States government comes into the picture
- If substantial investment needs to be made
- If previously agreed upon arrangements would be overturned by a decision
- If long-term financial interests of the parent are affected

- If the host government appears to be imposing regulations that might affect the long-term survival of the company
- If technical problems have arisen that cannot be handled locally
- If certain accusations have been made against the subsidiary that could flare up in labor trouble or have other ramifications

In addition to ad hoc problems, which may be day-to-day or strategic, the parent should require inputs in the form of the subsidiary's plans. Product planning for established product lines and plans for the development and marketing of new product lines would then be prepared by each host country/geographic area and separately submitted to corporate management for approval.

Foreign Collaboration/Investment

Often international businesses seek foreign collaboration in order to enter world markets. Such collaboration may take shape in a licensing agreement or in a joint venture with a business in the host country. Traditionally, the concept of foreign collaboration has been explained with reference to the international product life cycle. As discussed in Chapter 2, essentially this has meant that U.S. exports dominate the world market, and then the producers from other developed countries become increasingly competitive, first in their markets and then in third-country markets, and finally in the U.S. market. The cycle may be repeated with successive challenges from producers in less-developed countries.

In theory, a U.S. corporation should seek foreign collaboration in the third and fourth stages of the international product life cycle; that is, when it is competitively more desirable to produce abroad and compete effectively in foreign markets, as well as in the United States, through importing from the foreign source. The theory would work if worldwide markets were perfect. This, of course, is not so. Host governments insist on establishing plants even when the plants are not economic propositions in the international context. For example, a country may opt for a steel mill although it can import steel from a neighboring country much more economically. In brief, market imperfections brought about by tariff and nontariff barriers intrude upon the practical application of theory. As a matter of fact, in some industries, such as the automobile industry, the theory may fail because investment requirements at the third and fourth stages are tremendous. Thus, we should not expect auto industries to move from Japan and Europe to emerging developing countries.

An international marketer can still seek foreign collaboration by producing a specialized product in another country in order to take advantage of the peculiar strengths of that country. For example, labor in some nations is cheap, particularly in most developing countries. Some other countries have a big pool of scientific talent—India, for example. By collaborating with a foreign company to produce and/or distribute a product, a multinational marketer can gain competitive leverage.[2]

Coca-Cola Company's recent collaboration with Nestlé S.A. of Switzerland illustrates the point. The two companies have undertaken a multimillion dollar effort to market canned coffee, either warm or cold, to Koreans. If the effort succeeds, the Coca-Cola Nestlé Refreshments Co. would roll out Nescafé canned coffee through Asia, Europe, and the United States.[3]

Product Design Strategy

An important question that multinational marketers need to answer is whether the same product approach will be adequate in foreign markets. In other words, a decision must be made about which is the more appropriate of two product design strategies—standardization or customization. ***Standardization*** means offering a common product on a national, regional, or worldwide basis. ***Customization*** means adaptation, that is, making appropriate changes in a product to match local perspectives. On the one hand, the environmental differences between nations abroad are great. The degree of difference recommends product customization or adaptation over standardization in order to cater to the unique situation in each country. On the other hand, there are potential gains to consider in product standardization.[4] International marketers must examine all the criteria in order to decide the extent to which products should vary from country to country.

Decision Criteria

Whether to standardize or to customize is a vexing question with which international marketers have long wrestled. It is simple enough to figure out the rationale for standardization. Nothing new needs to be done to make the offering ready for any market. The literature, however, is full of illustrations showing how standardization has led to complete market failure. General Electric Company's debacle in the small appliance field in Germany and Polaroid's difficulties with the Swinger camera in France are classic examples. At the same time, Volkswagen's success worldwide with the Beetle supports standardization. Excessive concern with local customization can be troublesome, too. Holland's Philips Company learned the hard lesson that it cannot afford to customize televisions for each European market separately. Standardization became necessary to obtain R&D and manufacturing efficiencies.[5] Because neither strategy alternative is superior on its merits, certain criteria can be used instead to determine if adaptation would be desirable and, if so, to what extent.[6]

Nature of Product Research on the subject shows that foreign product design strategy varies with the nature of the product. More standardization is feasible in the case of industrial goods than for consumer goods. Among consumer goods, nondurables require greater customization than durables, because nondurable consumer goods appeal to tastes, habits, and customs. These traits are unique to each country; therefore, adaptation becomes significant.[7] An alternative to customization, however, is to limit the target market to a small identifiable segment.

Market Development Different national markets for a given product are in different stages of development. A convenient way of explaining this phenomenon is through the product life cycle concept. Products go through several life cycle stages over a period of time, and in each stage different marketing strategies are appropriate. The four stages usually identified in the life cycle of a product are introduction, growth, maturity, and decline.

If a product's foreign market is in a different stage of market development than its U.S. market, appropriate changes in the product design become desirable in order to make an adequate product/market match. The claim is that Polaroid's Swinger camera failed in France because the company pursued the same strategy there as in the United States, when the two markets were in different stages of development. The U.S. market was in the mature stage, while the French market was in the introductory stage.[8]

Even within a country one segment may be ready for a standardized product, while the product must be appropriately adapted for other segments. For example, Hill and Still found that products targeted to urban markets in lesser-developed countries need only minimal changes from those marketed in developed countries. On the other hand, the rural markets in LDCs require greater adaptation.[9]

Cost–Benefit Relationship Product adaptation to match local conditions involves costs. These costs may relate to R&D, physical alteration of the product's design, style, features, changes in packaging, brand name, performance guarantee, and the like. As far as standardization is concerned, no R&D is required since manufacturing technology and quality control procedures have been established. Performance has been tested and improved. In brief, standardization brings certain cost savings. One important cost, however, that standardization may involve and that is difficult to quantify is opportunity cost. If the product is customized, presumably it would have a greater appeal to the mass market in the host country. Thus, to determine whether adaptation would be in order, a cost–benefit analysis in terms of what it would cost to customize and what benefits may be expected in the form of market growth must be undertaken. The cost–benefit analysis should then be compared with the growth and profitability that would result from standardization. The net difference should indicate the relative desirability of seeking product adaptation.

Legal Requirements Different countries have different laws about product standards, patent laws, and tariffs and taxes. These laws may require product adaptation. For example, in Europe the 220-volt electrical system is used. This has led European governments to set stringent safety standards for such products as irons—cord connections must be stronger, radio interference must be shielded, and so on.[10] Likewise, foreign auto manufacturers must adapt their cars for export to the United States because of the U.S. government safety standards and emission control requirements (see International Marketing Highlight 12.1.).

Competition In the absence of current and potential competition, a company may continue to do well in a market overseas with a standard product. But the presence of competition may require customization to gain an advantage over the rivals by providing a product that ultimately matches local conditions. For example, the firms from the newly industrializing countries of Asia successfully

International Marketing Highlight 12.1

Oh, How Life Would Be Easier if We Only Had a Europlug

Those of you who have traveled Europe know of the frustration of electrical plugs, different electrical voltages, and other annoyances of international travel. But consider the cost to consumers and the inefficiency of production for a company that wishes to sell electrical appliances in the European "common" market.

Philips, the electrical appliance manufacturer, has to produce twelve kinds of irons to serve just its European market. The problem is that Europe does not have a universal standard. The ends of irons bristle with different plugs for different countries. Some have three prongs, others two; prongs protrude straight or angled, round or rectangular, fat, thin, and sometimes sheathed. There are circular plug faces, squares, pentagons, and hexagons. Some are perforated and some are notched. One French plug has a niche like a keyhole; British plugs carry fuses.

Europe's plugs and sockets are balkanized partly because different countries have different voltages and cycles. But the variety of standards also has other causes, such as protecting local manufacturers. The estimated cost of the lack of universal standards is between $60 billion and $80 billion a year, or nearly 3 percent of the EC's total output of goods and services.

Source: The Wall Street Journal, August 7, 1985, p. 1.

compete by rapidly adapting their products to changing markets and adopting more innovative product strategies. In this way the MNCs from these countries are able to gain leverage against the MNCs from the industrialized countries. Thus, the latter must anticipate and understand market requirements better than ever and appropriately adapt their products to be competitive.[11]

Traditionally Kodak could get away by selling a standard film globally because it was so rich, efficient, and powerful. But with changing competitive conditions, Kodak cannot succeed with parochial attitudes. It is not the only company in the market anymore. Now, for instance, Kodak sells film in Japan with the ruddier flesh tones preferred by the Japanese.[12]

Support System The support system refers to institutions and functions that are necessary to create, develop, and service demand. These include retailers, wholesalers, sales agents, warehousing, transportation, creditors, and media. The availability, performance, and cost of the support system profoundly affect the product design strategy. For example, frozen foods cannot be marketed in countries where retailers do not have facilities with freezers. The point can be illustrated by a reference to Lever Brothers' attempts to introduce packaged foods in developing countries. In the absence of refrigeration facilities at the retail level (as well as in homes), the frozen vegetables could not be introduced. The company, therefore, developed and sold a line of dehydrated vegetables, such as peas, carrots, and beans, in countries like India, Pakistan, Thailand, and the Philippines.

Physical Environment The physical conditions of a country (i.e., climate, topography, and resources) may also require product adaptation. For example, such products as air conditioners in a hot climate, as in the Middle East, require additional features for satisfactory performance. Differences in the size and configuration of homes affect product design for appliances and home furnishings. European kitchens are usually smaller than U.S. kitchens. Further, European homes generally do not have basements. Thus, compactness of design in such appliances as washers and dryers is a necessity since they must be accommodated within a crowded area.

Market Conditions Cultural differences, economic prosperity, and customer perceptions in the foreign country would also influence the decision to adapt a product. Britishers prefer a slightly more bitter taste in soup than Americans do. This required the Campbell Soup Company to modify soup ingredients in Britain to cater to the local taste. The masses in many countries cannot afford the variety of products that U.S. consumers consider essential. To bring such products as automobiles and appliances within the reach of the middle class in developing countries, for example, the products must be appropriately modified to cut costs without reducing functional quality. Finally, foreign products in many cultures are perceived as high-quality products. In such cases, standardization would be desirable. On the other hand, if the image of a country's products is weak, it would be strategically desirable to adapt a product so that it could be promoted as a different, rather than typical, product of the country. For example, U.S. automobiles are considered substandard. Thus, entry by American auto manufacturers into Japan would require changes in the product design to gain acceptance in Japan.[13]

Standardization: A Common Practice

Other things being equal, companies usually opt for standardization. A recent study on the subject lends support to the high propensity to standardize all or parts of marketing strategy in foreign markets. For example, an extremely high degree of standardization appears to exist in brand names, physical characteristics of products, and packaging.[14]

> More than half the products that MNCs sell in less developed countries originate in the parent companies' home markets. Of the 2,200 products sold by the 61 subsidiaries in the sample, 1,200 had originated in the United States or the United Kingdom.[15]

The arguments in favor of standardization are realization of cost savings, development of worldwide products, and achievement of better marketing performance. Standardization of products across national borders eliminates duplication of such costs as research and development, product design, and packaging. Further, standardization permits realization of economies of scale. Also, standardization makes it feasible to achieve consistency in dealing with customers and in product design. The consistency in product style—features, design, brand name, packaging—should establish a common image of the product worldwide to help increase overall sales.[16] For example, a person accustomed to a particular brand is likely to buy the same brand overseas if it is available. The global exposure that brands receive these days as a result of extensive world travel and mass media requires the consistency feasible through standardization. Finally, standardization may be urged on the grounds that a product that has proved to be successful in one country should do equally well in other countries that present more or less similar markets and similar competitive conditions (see International Marketing Highlight 12.2).

International Marketing Highlight 12.2

Gillette Tries to Nick Schick in Japan

For Gillette Co., the leading razor maker in most parts of the world, Japan has always been a sore spot. The company, which averages a 65 percent market share in 70 percent of its markets, hobbles along with a 10 percent share of the razor and blade market in Japan.

What has barred the giant Gillette from growing in Japan isn't a closed market, unfair Japanese customs, or anything else Japan is often accused of. It is rival American Warner-Lambert Co., owner of the Schick brand name. Although Schick trails Gillette in the U.S., it has gained 62 percent of Japan's "wet-shaving" razor and blade market by using the Japanese style of marketing.

Now, the battle is heating up as both sides promote new products worldwide. Armed with its popular Sensor brand, Gillette is launching a new strategy. While Schick stresses its Japanese way of marketing, Gillette is emphasizing its "Americanness." It is airing the same ads it runs in the U.S. and selling Sensor in the same packages, with the brand name in bold English letters and a Japanese version of it only in tiny letters in a corner. The company vows to double market share in Japan in the next three to five years. Previously, Gillette had TV ads made just for the Japanese market, although it did use foreign models and sports personalities.

Source: The Wall Street Journal, February 4, 1991, p. B1.

Rewards of Adaptation

Although standardization offers benefits, too much attachment to standardization can be counterproductive. Marketing environment varies from country to country, and thus a standard product originally conceived and developed in the United States may not really match the conditions in each and every market (see International Marketing Highlight 12.3). In other words, standardization can lead to substantial opportunity loss.

> Pond's cold cream, Coca-Cola, and Colgate toothpaste have been cited as evidence that a universal product and marketing strategy for consumer goods can win worldwide success. However, the applicability of a universal approach for consumer goods appears to be limited to products that have certain characteristics, such as universal brand-name recognition (generally earned by huge financial outlays), minimal product knowledge requirements for consumer use, and product advertisements that demand low information content. Clearly, Coca-Cola, Colgate toothpaste, McDonald's, Levi jeans, and Pond's cold cream display these traits. Thus, whereas a universal strategy can be effective for some

International Marketing Highlight 12.3

Taking on Japanese Flavor

Fast-food outlets in Japan are trying to become more Japanese, offering burgers dipped in teriyaki sauce and making buns out of rice.

McDonald's Japanese subsidiary, the country's biggest fast-food chain, has added a sandwich of fried chicken soaked in soy sauce to its menu. The company tested the 320-yen ($2.25) item, called Chicken Tatsuta, and found that it sold nearly as well as the Big Mac.

Japanese-style burgers appeal to consumers because they seem more healthful. Moreover, tastes are changing. When U.S. chains first entered Japan two decades ago, what Japanese consumers were looking for in a hamburger was America. But now, consumers say they've gotten the American taste down, and they're asking if we have something else. Wendy's restaurants in Japan offer sandwiches with deep-fried pork cutlets—usually served with a bowl of rice—as well as a version of the teriyaki burger.

Source: The Wall Street Journal, June 19, 1991, p. B1.

> consumer products, it is clearly an exception rather than the general rule. Those who argue that consumer products no longer require market tailoring due to the globalization of markets brought about by today's advanced technology are not always correct.
>
> An MNC that intends to launch a new product into a foreign market should consider the nature of its product, its organizational capabilities, and the level of adaptation required to accommodate cultural differences between the home and host country. An MNC should also analyze factors such as market structures, competitors' strategic orientations, and host government demands.[17]

The international marketplace is far more competitive today than in the 1960s, and most likely will remain so. Thus, some sort of adaptation might provide a better match of the product with local conditions for competitive advantage.[18] Vachani and Wells, for example, argue that based on a study of the product decisions of Indian subsidiaries of five multinationals, there remain important consumer segments that have special needs that are not met by global products.[19] Ohmae's charges against American companies for not adapting their products to Japanese needs are also revealing.

> Yet, American merchandisers push such products as oversize cars with left-wheel drive, devices measuring in inches, appliances not adapted to lower voltage and frequencies, office equipment without *kanji* capabilities and clothes not cut to smaller dimensions. Most Japanese like sweet oranges and sour cherries, not visa versa. That is because they compare imported oranges with domestic *mikans* (very sweet tangerines) and cherries with plums (somewhat tangy and sour).[20]

There are several patterns and various degrees of differentiation that firms can adopt to do business on an international scale. The most common of these are obligatory and discretionary product adaptation. An *obligatory,* or minimal, product adaptation implies minor changes or modifications in the product design that a manufacturer is forced to introduce for either of two reasons. First, it is mandatory in order to seek entry into particular foreign markets. Second, it is imposed on a firm by external environmental factors, including the special needs of the foreign market. In brief, obligatory adaptation is related to safety regulations, trademark registration, quality standards, and media standards. An obligatory adaptation requires mostly physical changes in the product. *Discretionary* or voluntary product adaptation reflects a sort of self-imposed discipline and a deliberate move on the part of an exporter to build stable foreign markets through a better alignment of product with market needs and/or a cultural alignment of the product.

Swiss-based pharmaceutical maker Ciba-Geigy's efforts in adapting its products to local conditions are noteworthy. Basic to the company's adaptation program are the quality circles. These circles include local executives with line responsibilities in packaging, labeling, advertising, and manufacturing. They are responsible for determining if (1) Ciba-Geigy's products are appropriate for the cultures in which they are sold and meet the users' needs, (2) products are promoted in such a way that they can be used correctly for the purposes intended, and (3) when used properly, products present no unreasonable hazards to human health and safety.[21]

Adaptation: An Example[22]

A French product, Yoplait yogurt, was planned for introduction into the U.S. market in 1969 as a standard product. Yet certain adaptations in container size and package labeling became necessary to cater to the requirements of the U.S. market.

In 1977, when General Mills agreed to produce and market Yoplait yogurt in the United States, eight flavors of yogurt, in addition to plain yogurt, were sold under the Yoplait trademark. By 1980, Yoplait had extended its product line to eleven different flavors: plain, peach, raspberry, lemon, apple, cherry, pineapple, strawberry, orange, blueberry, and mix-berry, a mixture of blueberry and raspberry. Additional flavors were produced to enlarge the line and maintain the customer interest.

The original Yoplait yogurt marketed in the United States was exactly the same as the Yoplait yogurt marketed in France in terms of its flavors, color, texture, and taste. Nothing had been done to change and adapt it to American consumer tastes. This, as a matter of fact, was General Mills' strategy to position Yoplait as "the yogurt of France, made in America." In the 1980s, however, the company added two lines of yogurt—breakfast yogurt (a blend of yogurt and grains) and custard yogurt—both in different flavors, which were unique to the U.S. market. This strategy was intended to expand the market by focusing on subsegments. A few years later, the product line was extended to include "light" yogurts to serve additional subsegments in five different flavors (strawberry, raspberry, cherry, blueberry, and strawberry-banana).

The container, although it had exactly the same shape in both countries (it is a trademark of Sodima-Yoplait of France), was slightly bigger in the United

States (170 grams instead of 120 grams). This difference was in response to differences in French and American eating habits: yogurt was perceived differently in the two countries. In France, yogurt was primarily considered a dessert to be eaten at the end of lunch or dinner, both big meals there. In America, yogurt was regarded as a lunch meal or as a healthful, nonfilling snack. Given the different eating habits, and consequently the different positioning of yogurt in each country, the Yoplait container was made bigger in the United States, where consumers expected to eat more yogurt at a time than in France.

The different positioning of yogurt in the United States had another marketing consequence. Since it is not perceived as a family meal food, but more as an individually eaten food, it is sold in individually priced containers. In France, where it is regarded more as a family dessert, Yoplait is sold in packs of four, six, or eight individual containers.

The packaging of Yoplait also had to comply with federal labeling regulations by printing on its containers consumer information, such as the percentage of U.S. recommended daily allowance (RDA) information.

Developing an International Product Line

Continued success in overseas markets requires the individual designing of a viable product line for each country. To achieve this viability, the composition of the product line may need to be periodically reviewed and changed. Such environmental changes as customer preferences, competitors' tactics, host country legal requirements, and a firm's own perspectives (including its objectives, cost structure, and spillover of demand from one product to another) can all render the current product line inadequate. Thus, it may become necessary to add new products and/or eliminate existing products. Additions to the product line may take different forms. A firm may simply extend additional domestic products abroad. Alternatively, certain specific products may be sought for a particular foreign country, either locally abroad or in the home country. Finally, new products may be developed for international markets. Also, product(s) may be either eliminated or selectively cut from a line in some countries. There are various ways of obtaining an optimum product line for different international markets.

Extension of Domestic Line

The extension of domestic products to foreign markets follows the logic of the concept of international product life cycle. Companies develop products for the home market that prove successful and lead to some export orders. As the exports grow, the firm considers setting up a warehouse, a sales branch, or a service center in the foreign locale. Later the firm finds it more economical to assemble or manufacture the product in the host country.

Relating this process to product line extension, a firm may initially market a few products overseas. As those markets grow or change, an opportunity may emerge to extend the line by selecting additional products from the domestic line for overseas distribution. A TRW subsidiary in the 1960s, for example, exported fractional horsepower motors to Egypt, Nigeria, India, and a number of other developing countries. In the 1970s many of these countries started manufacturing sophisticated equipment that required large horsepower motors. This change at the customer level made the company's international division choose additional motors for export to these countries. The Coca-Cola Company began marketing Coca-Cola in Japan in 1958. As the market developed, it appeared viable to introduce additional beverages. Thus, Fanta was added in 1968, and Sprite in 1970. By 1973 these other flavors were outselling Coke.[23]

Introducing Additional Products to the International Line

Products may be added to the line for two reasons: (1) to serve an unfulfilled customer need in a particular market overseas or (2) to optimize the existing marketing capacity. For example, a chemical company selling fertilizer and pesticides overseas in developing countries may discover a dire need for quality seeds and thus may add seeds to its line. Alternatively, the same company may feel it has established a good distribution network to serve rural customers and that it is not being fully utilized. The company may, therefore, consider products that could be successfully distributed to their rural customers. Such products may or may not be related to the company's business. For example, in Japan Coca-Cola markets two fruit drink products, a canned coffee-flavored noncarbonated drink, and a carbonated orange fruit drink (both under the "Hi-C" name) that it does not sell in the United States. Similarly, Coca-Cola markets potato chips in Japan, a business unknown to the company at home.[24] Campbell Soup Company sells gourmet cookies in Europe and Japan and not in the United States.[25]

The implementation of this strategy alternative can be illustrated with reference to Colgate-Palmolive Company's experience. Colgate distributes internationally a variety of products that belong to other companies. For example, Colgate sold Wilkinson razor blades for their British manufacturer. Colgate did the same for Henkel's (a German company) Pritt Glue Stick.[26]

MNCs often add products differently to their parent country market than to the international market, where product line strategy alternatives are pursued in response to the needs and opportunities of world markets. The products for addition to the line are determined according to inputs or product specifications received from different markets abroad. Insofar as possible, attempts are made to develop one standardized product to serve customers worldwide.

The decision to add a product to the line is influenced by such considerations as marketing compatibility, finances, organization, and environment. Marketing compatibility involves the match between the new addition and the current and potential marketing compatibilities of the parent company and its foreign subsidiary in matters such as product, price, promotion, and distribution. The closer the proposed product is to current marketing perspectives, the easier it would be to market the product successfully. A low compatibility, however, may affect profitable marketing. Thus, in the earlier example, the chemical company may find adding seeds to its line more compatible than offering leased agricultural machinery.

Sound business judgment requires a full examination of the financial risks and opportunities relative to the product addition under consideration. The common criteria for use in determining the financial compatibility of the proposed addition are profitability and cash flow implications.

The environmental compatibility includes concern for the customer, competitive action, and legal/political problems. The inclusion of a product in the line should not pose any problem for either existing or potential customers. At the same time, the competitive reactions to the company's product addition should be projected and evaluated. If the political/legal problems are likely to become a big stumbling block, it might be best to cancel plans to add the product.

Introducing a New Product to a Host Country

For the purposes of this discussion, a new product is defined as one that is new to the host country, but not new to the international market. For example, when Kodak started distributing its pocket camera in Southeast Asia in 1982, it was a new product to Sri Lanka, Pakistan, Thailand, and other countries in the region. But in the other markets, like the United States, Western Europe, and Japan, it was not a new product. Many decisions are required for the introduction of new products in foreign markets. These include decisions about which products to introduce in different foreign markets; decisions about timing and the sequence of introduction; and whether to introduce the product as it is marketed in the United States, that is, in the standardized form, or to adapt it to the peculiar requirements of the host country.

An empirical study on new product introductions overseas showed that U.S. corporations frequently introduced new products first to countries culturally similar to the United States.[27] Thus, Great Britain, Canada, and Australia were the leading recipients of new U.S. international offerings, accounting for almost half the new product introductions, and other developed countries accounted for more than one-third. Only one-sixth of new product introductions were made in developing countries. New product introductions to foreign markets also varied by industry. New products in the category of office machines, computers, and instruments were introduced across national boundaries in less than half the cases. On the other hand, textiles, paper, and fabricated metal innovations were entered in foreign markets in 85 percent of the cases. As far as timing is concerned, the U.S. corporations have been introducing new products to overseas markets faster than before. For example, the percentage of foreign introductions within one year of domestic introduction went up from 5.6 percent of all innovations in the period from 1945 to 1950 to 38.7 percent between 1971 and 1975. This testifies to the growing importance of new products for successful competition in international markets. Although no empirical evidence is available, presumably, in the wake of increasing competition, this percentage should prove to have been still higher in the 1980s, and should go up further in the 1990s (see International Marketing Highlight 12.4).

Alternative Ways of Seeking New Products for Foreign Markets A company can develop a new product for a foreign market either internally or by acquisition of another company. Internally, new products are developed through R&D. R&D may be conducted in either the home or the host country. For example,

International Marketing Highlight 12.4

Where Japan Will Strike Next

Primed with an arsenal of high-tech products from filmless cameras to mid-engine sports cars, the Japanese are also preparing to branch out across the globe in services from credit cards to construction. They are confident—even arrogant—about their ability to innovate in technology, not just to capitalize on technology borrowed from somebody else. With the billions that Japanese companies have amassed at home and abroad, they are poised for a quantum jump in their already impressive share of world markets.

Some samples of what are soon to be launched from Japan:

- Tape recorders the size of a matchbox, without cassettes or moving parts.
- High-definition televisions with twenty-one-foot screens that have movie-theater clarity.
- TV sets that double as home computers.
- Flat TV screens you can hang on your living room wall.
- Translation telephones, with simple vocabularies at first, that handle multilingual conversations almost instantaneously.
- Semiconductor chips the size of silver dollars that act as electrical transformers.
- Air conditioners that use a third less power than today's.
- Microminiaturized personal computers a fraction the size of the IBM PS/2 and Apple Macintosh.
- Robots that sew, smooth concrete floors, hoist slabs into place, or wash windows better and faster than people do.
- Sports cars that are just as good as the Ferraris and Lamborghinis that cost more than twice as much.

Source: Fortune, September 25, 1989, p. 42.

Colgate-Palmolive developed in the United States a manual washing device—an all-plastic, hand-powered washer for developing countries. But IBM developed IBM 2750 and 3750 electronic private business telephone exchanges within the United Kingdom.[28] For most companies, however, R&D is centralized at home. (A later section will examine the role of foreign R&D in international product policy in detail.)

Many companies add new products through acquisitions. For example, Gillette acquired Braun AG of Germany in order to add electric shavers to its line. Similarly, Gulf Oil acquired Shawinigan Chemical of Canada to enter the field of carbon block. International Telephone and Telegraph (ITT) acquired Rimmel Ltd. of England to enter the cosmetics field.[29]

Rationale Behind New Products A firm may introduce new products in foreign markets as either a defensive or an offensive measure. Defensively, the new product is expected to help the company compete effectively. For example, a well-established company may be challenged by competition. In response to this, the introduction of a new product may appear to be the most desirable course against the competition. For example, with coffee drinking gaining in popularity over tea, the Brooke Bond Tea Company, a British company, decided to introduce its own brand of coffee in a number of Southeast Asian countries. Alternatively, a new product may be introduced to satisfy host government requirements for business related to national development. For example, Union Carbide, a chemical company, seriously considered adding men's shirts to its portfolio of businesses in India.

New products may also be added because the corporation had earlier licensed its company/brand name to someone else. For example, Union Carbide had to develop a new product/brand for Europe because a German firm had the license for Eveready.

New products may also be introduced as an offensive weapon for growth. For example, Polaroid Corporation sought growth by developing a conventional film since the instant photography market had matured and showed no signs of survival. Branded as Polaroid Super Color, the film was introduced in Spain and Portugal in 1986. In 1988, the company entered it in several other markets.[30]

The rationale for new product introduction can take three shapes: (1) to serve a segment hitherto ignored, (2) to satisfy an unfulfilled need, and (3) to adapt a domestic product for better product/market match. Often there is no single reason, but rather a number of considerations figuring into a new product decision.[31]

Overall, new products are appearing more frequently because so-called product life cycles (from drawing board until the last is sold) are getting shorter as companies cut their development times and reorganize their factories to build new things more quickly. Products survive for a shorter time in the market because they are rapidly outdated by products from rivals who are speeding up their operations, too. The incentive for successful innovation is great. Premium prices can be charged for novel things, particularly if they create new markets. IBM did this with its personal computers. America's Compaq then stole some of IBM's market by developing the next generation of IBM-compatible computers before IBM.[32]

The following example of the lives of devout Muslims illustrates the way in which new product opportunities can develop in overseas markets. Muslims must face Mecca and pray five times each day. Because the proper time for each prayer is measured from either sunrise or sunset, it changes from day to day and greatly from place to place. In addition, the Koran specifies that the body face Mecca within 2½ degrees. The Muslim faithful can obtain charts of every part of the globe that show the direction to Mecca, but attaining the proper accuracy can be tough, even with a compass. Therefore, Sensortron Technology Ltd. brought high technology to bear on the problem. The company, which was founded in Monaco by an American, Romm Doulton, developed two pocket-sized aids. One points to Mecca, the other emits an electronic *Hadan,* or call to prayer. Both have microprocessors that calculate the direction of Mecca based on a person's proximity to one of 11,000 programmed locations. Sensortron figured its potential market is 10 percent of the world's half a billion Muslims.[33]

New Product Development Process Usually, six steps are involved in new product development: *idea, screening, evaluation, prototype product, market testing,* and *entry.* Organizations spend varying amounts of time on each step. At each step, management must make a go or no-go decision. As a product progresses from one step to the next, it requires a greater commitment of resources.

Idea derives from different sources, the principal ones being host government, customers, subsidiary employees, and international agencies, such as the World Health Organization. The ideas received go through the *screening* process to choose the promising ideas for detailed consideration. Screening begins by matching the product idea with the overall objectives of the subsidiary in the host country. Next comes a determination of product feasibility vis-à-vis the resources of both the subsidiary and the parent company, including finances, raw materials, energy, past experience, management skills, patents (for example, the ownership of a technical design/process), and the like.

Product ideas that seem feasible are carried on through the *evaluation* step. Evaluation mainly concerns total market potential and demand analysis. At this time, accounting information such as fixed costs, unit variable cost, and likely price is used to conduct the break-even analysis to figure out the point at which the company would be at a no-profit/loss situation in terms of either volume or dollar sales.

Once the evaluation step has been completed, the management must make the go or no-go decision. If it is *go,* the idea is next given physical shape in the form of a *prototype product.* Engineering and production groups work jointly in this task. Marketing astuteness demands *market testing* before final commitment to full-scale commercialization. Testing the market helps in two ways: (1) it furnishes information on the chances of product acceptance and (2) it indicates an appropriate strategy. If the market tests are encouraging, the company should go ahead with *entry* of the product into the market.

Conceptually, the whole process appears to be logical and sequentially possible. However, a variety of difficulties can arise that might require accepting shortcuts or even omissions of certain things. For example, the test marketing may be rendered difficult for lack of a marketing research firm specializing in market testing in the host country. Similarly, if the product development effort is located outside the host country, the coordination between engineering/production and the host country marketing group would prove difficult. Further, the host government requirements can pose problems in systematically following the product development procedure. For example, the target date for full-scale introduction may have to be altered. Finally, internal organization and management style may hinder smooth and timely development of new products. As one writer points out:

> Despite many inspiring advances, however, corporate America still suffers from handicaps that will impair its ability to keep up with the rapid evolution of prod-

> ucts. An oft cited complaint is the lengthy lead times between the moment an idea is conceived and the time it finally rolls off an assembly line. In U.S. auto plants, that process takes as long as five years, twice as long as in Japan.[34]

Difficulties aside, new products provide a viable route for growth as much in foreign markets as at home (see International Marketing Highlight 12.5).

International Marketing Highlight 12.5

Better than the Best

Getting the Lexus out of Toyota, whose forte is rolling out wheels for the world's millionaires, is like producing beef Wellington at McDonald's. Toyota had to target its customer precisely, create all-new management organizations, rethink components down to the tiniest screw, and invest more time and money—six years and over $500 million—than anyone had originally imagined.

Toyota set out to do what nobody else had done: design a sedan that would travel 150 mph while carrying four passengers in relative quiet, comfort, and safety—and without incurring the American gas-guzzler tax. Even though 65 mph is the legal limit in the U.S., Toyota figured Lexus owners would want to brag about outrunning radar.

Those specifications dictated breakthroughs in aerodynamics, noise dampening, suspension, and, most of all, the engine. The company devised a nine-stage process to reach each design target. It included: discussing how goals would be met, making continual follow-ups, and trying wherever possible to have it both ways. For example, the company wanted the optimum solution—the biggest engine with the least noise—even though the two objectives are difficult to reconcile. Compromise was unacceptable. "We had to push the engineers to achieve the vision we wanted to create," said the chief engineer. Despite obstacles aplenty, the product looks like a stunning success.

Source: Fortune, August 14, 1989, p. 63.

Management of Product Line

Based on the experiences of successful companies, a few generalizations can be made about profitably managing an international product line. These suggestions relate to market segmentation, product design, product quality, product innovation, and economies of scale.[35] First, any product added to the line, whether entirely new or extended overseas from the home country, must be directed toward a well-defined target group.[36] For example, Riunite became the largest-selling imported wine in the United States through advertising itself as a beverage drink for young consumers: "More than a wine, it's a beverage. It can be drunk by anybody who is legal, anywhere, at any time of day. Its real competitors are soft drinks, beer, vodka and tonic, and iced tea."[37]

Further, it is helpful to distinguish products according to aesthetic appeal and functional design. This holds true for both consumer and industrial goods. Additionally, well-made, long-lasting products obtain a permanent place in the market that competitors find difficult to challenge. Inasmuch as foreign markets vary, a novel product created to match the characteristics of a particular market can be an extremely useful step to gain an advantage over competition selling "me-too" products extended from the parent company. Product innovation is especially helpful for mature industries with static demand. Finally, a cost advantage over the competition provides a strong, enviable position. Thus, realization of economies of scale in managing the product line is a desirable objective. For example, Japanese automakers traditionally have occupied an unbeatable position in the U.S. market, based largely on a cost advantage of almost $2,000 over an equivalent U.S.-built car. While the U.S. automobile companies might be able to match other advantages, such as gas mileage, the Japanese cost position is formidable. (Lately this advantage has partially vanished due to the decline in the value of the dollar against the yen.)

Overseas R&D

Research and development is essential to originating new products. United States corporations spend billions of dollars annually on R&D. For example, in 1987 American industry spent over $123 billion on R&D over and above the R&D supported by the federal government. Although U.S. companies make significant investments in R&D, their performance is lagging behind the Japanese. For example, of the top ten patent winners in the U.S. in 1980, seven were U.S. companies (G.E., RCA, U.S. Navy, AT&T, IBM, Westinghouse, and General Motors), two were European, and one was Japanese. In 1990, however, five were Japanese companies, three were U.S. (G.E., Kodak, and IBM), and two were European.[38]

Most of the R&D activity of MNCs is centralized in the United States. A Conference Board study on the subject, conducted in the early 1970s, indicated that U.S. R&D expenditures overseas came to about 10 percent of the total.[39] The overseas R&D is concentrated mainly among the large multinationals, just as domestic R&D is highly concentrated among the large industrial corporations.

Terpstra lists several reasons that lead companies to centralize R&D in the home country:[40]

- Critical mass and economies of scale (By expanding R&D in the home country, a company can realize economies of scale rather than incur initial costs.)
- Easier communication (Social and cultural barriers such as language differences are avoided.)
- Better protection of know-how (A company finds it easier to protect its research output and patents at home than abroad.)
- More leverage with host government (Host country's interest in seeking R&D would make the overseas company more vulnerable to foreign government action.)
- Ease of control of coordination (R&D activity can be controlled better by centralization of the entire program in one country; centralization permits better coordination with marketing and production.)

Although U.S. multinationals and those of other nations centralize the major portion of R&D in their home countries, companies do undertake some R&D abroad as well. Foreign R&D is explained by factors such as adaptation of home products abroad; response to subsidiary pressures; response to host government incentives for local R&D; public relations tool; local professional talent; cost savings; broader base for seeking new product ideas; proximity to markets; and continuation of R&D activities of a firm acquired abroad.[41]

Obviously, there are many reasons that justify undertaking overseas R&D. In the future, it would be reasonable to expect more and more companies to initiate or enlarge their R&D activity abroad. This can be predicted from the known facts that the foreign marketplace is becoming highly competitive and that host countries are becoming very aggressive in seeking technology. Today, U.S. MNCs have to compete against non-U.S. MNCs, not only from Europe but also from the developing countries. The sharing/transferring of technology serves as an effective tool for entry into many countries. An obvious form of technology transfer takes place when the parent company engages in research and development activities abroad.[42]

Proctor & Gamble's experience illustrates how research and development is becoming an international process for more and more companies. P&G recently introduced Liquid Tide, which, by drawing on ideas and technology from around the world, has a distinctly international R&D connection. A new ingredient that helps suspend dirt in wash water came from the company's research center near P&G's Cincinnati headquarters; the formula for Liquid Tide's surfactants, or cleaning agents, was developed by P&G technicians in Japan; and the ingredients that fight the mineral salts present in hard water came from P&G's scientists in Brussels.[43] Thus, by pooling its research and development strength worldwide, P&G was able to develop a successful product that would not have been feasible if it had relied only on its R&D in the United States, since certain technologies are more advanced in particular countries because of endemic needs and conditions.[44]

Unilever, a company whose core products include soaps and detergents, as well as margarine and other inexpensive edible oils, provides another example of an MNC that has globalized its R&D. The company has four major laboratories that conduct basic research: one in the Netherlands, one in India, and two in the United Kingdom. It also has some forty applied research centers in foreign subsidiaries, twenty-four of which are in LDCs. Unilever makes a practical organizational distinction between basic research and applied research, granting subsidiaries responsibility for the latter.[45]

Product Elimination

In international marketing, primary attention is frequently given to the problem of developing, adding, and modifying new products. Less emphasis is placed on product deletion decisions. This section discusses the importance of international product deletion and its strategic implications.

In recent years worldwide material shortages have caused many MNCs to reappraise their product mixes. The worsening scarcities of raw materials, price controls in some countries, increasing entry difficulties, tariffs, and the fear of a global energy crunch have forced multinational companies of every size, shape, and kind to reexamine their overseas product mix and make appropriate changes in it. Very often a small proportion of a company's products, say 20 to 30 percent, accounts for a large percentage, say between 60 and 80 percent, of its profits. The majority of the products, accounting for most of the losses or a smaller proportion of profits, should be examined very carefully. In many cases, the breadth and depth of the worldwide product line is greater than that of the domestic line. Weak products, on the basis of estimated future contribution to the product line, must be phased out to prevent dispersion and fragmentation of effort.

Additionally, the rapid rate of change in international marketing conditions mandates continual monitoring of products to weigh their relevancy in the light of new customer needs, competitive offerings, and environmental conditions. Further, as in domestic business, elimination of weak products also reduces the level of inventories at the international level. These inventories are subject to risk because of uncertainties in the fluctuating exchange rates. Thus, elimination of "sick" products reduces exchange risks.

There are many reasons for failure of overseas products. Honeywell, Inc., decided to sell a substantial part of its 47 percent interest in its French subsidiary, Honeywell Bull, in 1981 because of continuing losses.[46] J.C. Penney decided to pull out of Belgium in 1981 since economic and political conditions made it impossible to operate profitably there. For example, Belgium's strict price controls made it difficult for the company to pass along cost increases to customers.[47] Volkswagen AG closed its U.S. manufacturing operations in 1987 under pressure from Japanese competitors and poor U.S. sales, which had been linked to an image problem that hurt the company's U.S.-produced cars.[48] ITT Corporation closed most of its telecommunications operations in Argentina primarily because of unstable economic conditions—delays in payments from the government-owned telephone company and a lack of new orders.[49]

Another important reason for product deletion overseas is customer rejection of the product. For example, after three years and an advertising campaign of $2 million, the Campbell Soup Company decided to close its Brazilian canned soup operation. Campbell failed to interest Brazilian cooks who felt they could serve only soup that they could call their own.[50] Campbell's offerings—mostly vegetable and beef combinations packed in extra large cans bearing a variant of the familiar red and white label—failed to catch on. Instead, Brazilian cooks seemed to prefer the dehydrated products of competitors, such as Knorr and Maggi, which they could use as soup starters and add ingredients of their own. Campbell's soup was considered an emergency solution when cooking time was short.

Like the Campbell Soup Company, Gerber Products Company also decided to leave the Brazilian market. The company failed to convince mothers to use baby food as an everyday feeding item despite an award-winning advertising campaign telling mothers they would have more time to show affection to their infants if they were not bent over a sink preparing food. The company underestimated a cultural factor. Brazilian mothers are not willing to accept that prepared baby food is a good substitute for food freshly made by themselves—or, more likely, by their live-in maids, since most women in Brazil who can afford to buy prepared baby food can afford to have a maid.[51] In general, Brazilian women like to use prepackaged baby food only for convenience, when visiting friends and relatives or going to the beach.

All in all, appropriate organizational procedures for systematic review of products must be established. Specific criteria to evaluate product performance, such as minimum level of sales, market share, profitability, and condition of the product line, should be set. The criteria can be established by local organizational units relative to specific market conditions, by headquarters' management, or by both, depending on the organizational structure. Some coordination of these criteria is ordinarily desirable. The review of products based on these criteria can be carried out on a market-by-market and/or on a regional or global basis depending on the uniformity of the product mix in different markets. Typically, however, some informational input from local organizational units is necessary.

Adoption and Diffusion of New Products

A paramount concern in the introduction of new products is acceptance by the public. One way of determining whether a new product would be accepted by a sufficient number of potential customers is through an analysis of expected product adoption and diffusion in the foreign market.

Customers do not instantly buy new products. They go through a step-by-step mental process of acceptance or rejection of a new product. Typically, this process occurs in sequential stages:[52]

- Awareness (Being exposed to a new product, consumers become aware of it.)
- Knowledge (Consumers develop enough interest in the product to seek additional information.)
- Evaluation (An attitude forms, negative or positive, about the product.)
- Trial (Consumers buy the product to see if it indeed meets their needs.)
- Adoption (The product is accepted for continuing use after satisfactory experience during trial.)

Not all customers pass through all these stages in their adoption of new products. For example, a customer may move straight from awareness to evaluation to adoption. Similarly, different customers take varying amounts of time to move from stage to stage. Further, the time lapse between stages also varies with the nature of the product. For an inexpensive product, the whole process may involve only a few minutes. But the adoption process for an expensive product may require months.

A classic study on the subject showed how a new product is accepted by people over time. Initially, only a small percentage of people accept it. A little larger percentage follows. Eventually the product is accepted by the masses. As shown in Figure 12.2, the adoption over time can be represented by a bell-shaped curve. Based on this conceptualization, five categories of customers can be identified: innovators, early adopters, early majority, late majority, and laggards. Innovators constitute a small proportion. The real market develops when early and late majority consumers enter the market.

The classification shown in Figure 12.2 is arbitrary. The actual shape of the curve and the percentage of people in each category depend on the nature of the product/market. The framework is based mainly on studies in the field of rural sociology, that is, farmers' acceptance of new practices. It has not been tested in the marketing of modern-day products.

While the actual adoption might not pattern itself so neatly, it is reasonable to expect a tendency toward such a distribution. Assuming this, the adoption framework can be utilized to forecast the initial demand for a new product in a foreign country and how the demand would mature with time. Thus, even where economies of scale are important for a product to achieve satisfactory performance, a company may not establish production facilities if customers cannot be expected to enter the market for several years.[53]

In international marketing, the concept of the diffusion of new products is essential. *Diffusion* refers to how a new product captures a target market. The adoption process is concerned with acceptance by individuals, while the diffusion process emphasizes the aggregate of individual decisions to adopt a new product.

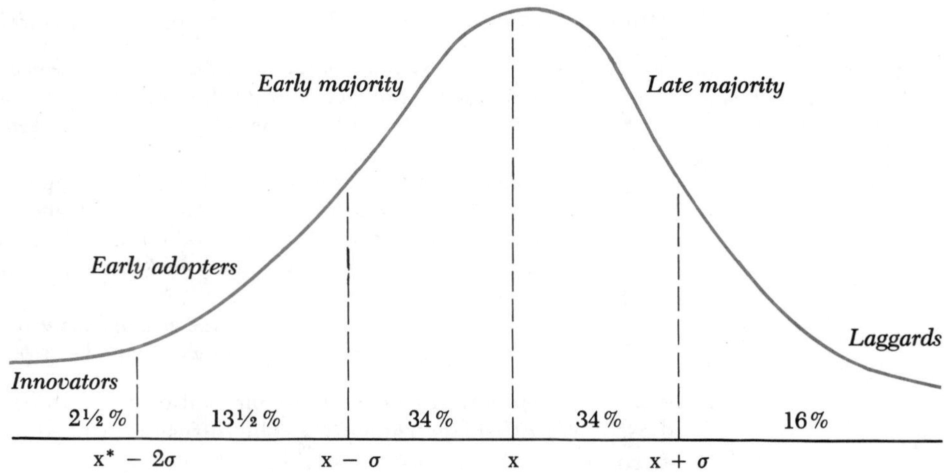

*(x = mean time for adoption)

Source: Everett M. Rogers, *Diffusion of Innovation* (New York: Macmillan, 1962), p. 306.

FIGURE 12.2 New Product Adoption Segments

Thus, an analysis of the diffusion process in a country/culture indicates if the new product would be acceptable.

Research on the subject shows that diffusion is influenced by a number of organizational factors such as effectiveness of communication between the parent and the subsidiary.[54] In addition, a variety of product-related and market-related characteristics facilitate diffusion. The product-related characteristics are relative advantage, compatibility, complexity, divisibility, and communicability. The market-related characteristics include innovativeness of target customers and their clearer perception of need and economic ability.

Product-Related Characteristics

Relative Advantage Relative advantage refers to the degree of superiority of the new product compared with current offerings. If the new product is perceived as more beneficial, that is, it appears to make a stronger promise of need fulfillment, it is likely to diffuse more quickly. One of the major causes of faster diffusion of superior products is word-of-mouth from the innovator, or initial adopter, to other customers.

Compatibility The higher the compatibility of the new product to the current ones, the more rapidly it will diffuse. Compatibility refers to social/cultural perspectives and the consistency of the product with existing tastes, values, and behaviors. Socially, a product requiring little change will be more readily accepted. Change is painful because it necessitates adjustments, both physical and mental, in established patterns. New products, or innovations, can be classified into three categories in order to judge compatibility. They may be labeled *continuous* innovations, *dynamically continuous* innovations, or *discontinuous* innovations.

> A continuous innovation has the least disrupting influence on established patterns. Alteration of a product is involved, rather than the establishment of a new product. Examples: fluoride toothpaste; new-model automobile changeovers; methol cigarettes.
>
> A dynamically continuous innovation has more disrupting effects than a continuous innovation, although it still does not generally alter established patterns. It may involve the creation of a new product or the alteration of an existing product. Examples: electric toothbrushes; the Mustang automobile; Touch-Tone telephones.
>
> A discontinuous innovation involves the establishment of a new product and the establishment of new behavior patterns. Examples: television; computers.[55]

A product representing continuous innovation would diffuse more rapidly than those in the other two categories. The diffusion of products in the last category, discontinuous innovation, would require the longest time.

Complexity A product that is easy to comprehend and use would be diffused relatively quickly. A complex product requires detailed instructions for customer use. A customer must not only be made aware of the new product but also be educated in its use; the more complex the product, the slower the learning process. Nestlé baby formula ran into difficulties in many African countries because mothers in rural sections of Africa did not understand the quantities of baby formula they needed to buy in order to feed their babies adequately and they watered the formula down.[56]

Divisibility If a product is available for trial on a limited basis, it diffuses far more rapidly. Customers can try it without making major commitments. In other words, divisibility reduces the risk to the customer, because a product can be sampled or can be had on a returnable basis—for example, ten days' free trial.

Communicability A product with attributes that can be conveniently communicated to the target customers and so distinguish it from other products can be more readily diffused. In other words, the degree to which the benefits/qualities of a product are obvious to potential customers dictates the pace of diffusion. By the same token, if a product is visible in a culture, it tends toward fast diffusion.

Market-Related Characteristics

Customer Innovativeness Wherever customers by virtue of their social/cultural traits are open and prone to accept new things, diffusion becomes easier. Thus, diffusion occurs more rapidly in Western societies than in Eastern cultures. Within the same country, different cultural groups show different tendencies toward acceptance of a new product. For example, in Israel most Arab Jews would be less inclined to accept new innovations than would most European Jews.

Need Perception In situations where customers have a clear perception of their needs, new products are more likely to be diffused rapidly, because it is easier to determine if the product matches the need. Where customers do not know whether they need the product or not, diffusion would be rather slow, even if the product is desirable. For example, in many developing countries birth-control-related products are not diffused since customers are not convinced of the need, or aware of the option, to limit family size. In such situations, even when birth-control devices are offered free, they are not accepted.

Economic Ability Despite the presence of all the characteristics favorable to rapid diffusion, a new product may fail if the customers are unable to afford it. Thus, the economic ability of the customers would be another determining factor in the rate of diffusion. Many poor countries failed in their family planning campaigns because couples could not afford birth-control pills.

Impact of Diffusion Process on New Products

The characteristics that affect the diffusion process can be added up for an estimate of the length of diffusion time. While the exact time of product spread cannot be predicted, the approximate length of time can be identified. If the diffusion time is longer than anticipated or desirable, it may become necessary to make some changes in the new product to achieve more rapid diffusion. For example, the product design may have to be simplified to make it convenient for the customers to understand and use the product. Likewise, new features added to the product could provide an additional advantage to the users vis-à-vis the competing products.

As a matter of fact, adjustments may have to be made in the entire marketing mix to increase the pace of diffusion. However, the variable most related to diffusion, other than the product variable, is promotion. For example, promotional perspectives could be reoriented to provide customers an opportunity to try the product before making a commitment.

Foreign Product Diversification

Diversification refers to seeking unfamiliar products or unfamiliar markets, or both, for the purpose of expansion. Every company is at its best offering certain familiar products; diversification requires substantially different and unfamiliar knowledge, thinking, skills, and processes. Thus, diversification is at best a risky strategy, and a company should choose this path only when current product/market orientation seems to provide no further opportunities for growth.

Most large multinationals are diversified and have no need to undertake product diversification solely for international business. In other words, their diversification is usually planned in the home market, say, the United States, and once the diversified product succeeds in the United States, it can be introduced in foreign markets as well.

For a variety of reasons, however, a company may decide to diversify in a particular market overseas. First, in a particular country government pressure may force a foreign company into unrelated areas. As mentioned earlier, Union Carbide considered entering the field of men's dress shirts in India to fulfill a government regulation.[57] Second, a special opportunity in a field may lead a company to diversify in that country. For example, a U.S. hotel chain might enter the car rental business in Latin America but not in the United States, where there is fierce competition in the car rental business. Third, a strictly one-product international company may diversify overseas if its main business has reached maturity. Take the case of the Hoover Company, for example. In the United States, it is basically a vacuum cleaner company. In Europe, the company has long been active in washing machines as well. The European business accounted for more than 50 percent of Hoover's sales. In the late 1970s and early 1980s, the European business slowed down because of recession and aggressive, low-priced continental competitors, causing chronically depressed earnings. The company, therefore, decided to adopt a new strategy that included diversifying into a new line of cleaners and washing machines just for the European market, particularly Britain.[58]

Similarly, Unilever has diversified into different fields to strengthen its position in the U.S. market. In 1987, the company paid $3.1 billion to acquire Chesebrough-Pond's, which sells personal-care items and cosmetics including Pepsodent, Vaseline, Pond's, Q-tips, and Faberge. In August 1989, for a total of $1.5 billion, Unilever acquired Elizabeth Arden, whose products include Visible Difference cosmetics, Elizabeth Taylor's Passion perfume, Erno Laszlo skin-care products, and Red Door salons. In July 1989, it acquired Calvin Klein Cosmetics, which sells Eternity and Obsession fragrances.[59]

Brand Strategy

Corporate identification is a valuable asset in marketing, in both domestic and international markets. Firms face the choice of linking the company closely with its products and brands or of establishing market strength for each individual product line or brand. In the context of international business, the factors that usually determine policy on identification are further complicated by problems of nationalism, language and cultural differences, and customer preferences that vary with the distinctive characteristics in each market. Despite these difficulties, a company must make decisions on multinational identification about the use of brand names, use of trademarks, and names of subsidiaries.

Brand Alternatives

An overseas marketer has several alternative ways to decide on the brand name:

- Use one name with no adaptation to local markets.
- Use one name but adapt and modify it for each local market.
- Use different names in different markets for the same products.
- Use the company name as a brand name under one house style or the corporate umbrella approach.

One Brand Name Worldwide This strategy is useful when the company primarily markets one product that is widely distributed, and the brand name does not seem to conflict with local cultures of different societies. Coca-Cola, for example, is marketed around the globe under the brand name Coke without any adaptation to local markets.

The worldwide use of one brand name provides a greater identification of the product with the company on an international basis. It helps to achieve greater consistency and coordination of advertising and promotion on a worldwide basis. It permits clear identification of a brand with a company noted for quality or technical superiority. It eliminates confusion with products of other companies. Finally, a great sense of consumer familiarity through customer identification of trademarks is realized[60] (see International Marketing Highlight 12.6).

International Marketing Highlight 12.6

Power Brands

What would happen if you tried to compare the world's best-known brand with those held in the highest esteem? To find out, Landor Associates, a San Francisco design consulting firm, assembled a list of what it calls "brands with global image power."

Landor surveyed 10,000 consumers in the United States, Western Europe, and Japan, asking them to judge 6,000 brands by both measures. The top ten: Coca-Cola (a U.S. brand); Sony (Japanese); Mercedes-Benz (German); Kodak (U.S.); Disney (U.S.); Nestlé (Swiss); Toyota (Japanese); and McDonald's, IBM, and Pepsi Cola (all U.S.).

Source: Landor Associates, San Francisco, 1991.

Modifying Brand Name in Each Market Some factors overseas may lead a company to adapt a brand name to suit local conditions. Nestlé, for example, introduced several new products in Europe in the 1960s by modifying the brand name for each country. Its soluble coffee was introduced in Germany under the name "Nescafé Gold" and in Britain under "Nescafé Gold Blend."

Very often when a company leaves its home market, it tries to shake its so-called foreignness. Back in 1950 when the Campbell Soup Company entered the British market on a national scale, it attempted to take advantage of its Scottish-origin name. Each of its brands of soups was introduced at a tasting party for the press with a number of Campbell families living in Britain. These ranged from the Duke of Argyll, head of the Campbell clan, right down to Donald Campbell, the racing motorist. To add further to the name, some 5,000 Campbells in the London telephone directory were sent a sample can of Campbell's soup. Today, Campbell Soup is thought to be a British company by a large portion of its consuming public in Britain.[61]

The adaptation of the parent brand name to local conditions would also be affected by media considerations. For example, Unilever sold one of its detergents in Germany under the brand name Radion, but for special reasons it was sold under another name in Austria. For a few years this worked out well. But then a great majority of Austrians began to watch German TV programs and read German magazines. Thus, German advertisements gained importance among Austrians. In the case of Radion detergent, however, this was a problem since it was sold under a different brand name in Austria. The company finally decided to substitute Radion for the Austrian brand name.

Different Brand Names in Different Markets

Local brands are often used when the brand name cannot be translated into the local language; when a product is manufactured, sold, and consumed locally; when it is a leading selling brand and part of a new local acquisition; and when the company wants to play down its foreignness and be thought of as a local company.[62]

A local brand name is necessary for products for which there has been no local manufacturer and the imported international brand is too expensive for the typical local consumer. The British American Tobacco Company has a number of markets where it caters to the full range of purchasing power. It provides cigarettes at the lowest possible prices for the mass consumer (through purely local brands, unheard of elsewhere), as well as international brands for the relatively wealthy minority who can afford them.

Individual brand names permit greater identification of the product by consumers with a name more suited to the local language or jargon. For example, in the United States Frigidaire was synonymous with the word "refrigerator," but this could not be the case in a non-English-speaking market. The local brand name, however, may have a strong market following; in the case of acquisition, it would be preferable to retain the local name, perhaps linking it with the corporate name of the acquiring company. For example, the local name on the package could be underscored with the caption "A Product of the XYZ Company." A local brand name or trademark can support a general campaign by the company to "go local" in its total approach to the market. A local trademark or brand name lessens the impact on other company products and the total corporate image if the new product proves to be a failure.

Company Name as Brand Name Many companies use standard trademarks for all their products, but are flexible in the case of brand names, taking into consideration local market conditions, local consumer motivation, language and translation problems, and other market factors. Some use both worldwide brands and local brands according to each market situation, and thus avoid the major disadvantage of a worldwide brand policy—inflexibility.

Trademarks in the form of symbols, logos, letters, and initials have all become forms of corporate identification. Just as the brand name is identified with the product, the trademark goes further and identifies both the product and the company. The double task carries a much stronger corporate message back to the consumer. Whereas the brand name may contend with the company name for first place, the trademark usually complements and reinforces it.

Some companies can benefit from the double impact of a trademark that is the same as or similar to the company name. Levi Strauss & Company has profited from Levi's jeans' identity. However, success in foreign markets has brought with it the problem of keeping others from using the same name, because as international sales have increased, so have the infringements upon Levi trademarks. (The problem of infringements will be discussed in a later section.)

The dilemma of brand name versus company name is a contested issue. Even the largest international companies, such as Unilever, Shell, and Imperial Chemicals Industries (ICI), differ on this point. Shell and ICI promote products under the company name and are heavy corporate advertisers. Unilever promotes brands and products and does not emphasize its corporate name, especially in areas outside its home territory.

The 3M Company (Minnesota Mining and Manufacturing) is an example of a firm that has successfully taken the umbrella approach and has created a family look around its products. Faced with an ever-growing number of a new products and a constant need for new brand names, 3M decided on a corporate packaging theme for all its products. Previously, names and packaging had not conveyed the impression of one versatile company offering products to industry, to commercial business, and to the home consumer. The new corporate design system consists of three rectangular elements. One rectangle always carries the 3M logo, another the product identification, and the third the divisional identification, such as the Scotch™ plaid of the retail tape and gift wrap division. 3M considers the one look worldwide more important internationally than in the United States, since identity and packaging problems had become quite difficult internationally with multiple sources of supply, different languages, and various modes of distribution.

Brand Piracy

One persistent problem that well-known brands face in foreign markets is counterfeiting. Consider, for example, the irritation it would cause Procter & Gamble to find out that its Crest brand name is being used falsely on a toothpaste sold for one-fifth the Proctor & Gamble price in various markets abroad. Unfortunately, the laws pertaining to brand piracy in many countries are loose, with little punishment for shady practices.

Of the many factors that encourage brand piracy, two stand out. First, a variety of U.S. goods are held in high esteem, particularly those of long standing, such as Singer sewing machines. In the developing countries, goods from advanced countries, especially the luxury goods, serve as status symbols and most of the time are in short supply. Thus, a ready-made market exists for imported brands that the counterfeiter likes to exploit. Second, the technological knowledge required to produce a counterfeit product is readily available. For example, a person in Taiwan interested in counterfeiting a Seiko watch will encounter little difficulty in acquiring the know-how and parts required.

As U.S. companies do more manufacturing offshore, developing countries acquire the technology to produce bogus goods. But not all offenders are foreign. According to a *Business Week* report 20 percent of the world's fakes are made in the United States, mostly by marginal producers who cannot make a profit legally. No one knows the exact number of shoddy goods being traded, but experts estimate that up to $60 billion in annual world trade is in fakes.[63]

Three forms of piracy can be labeled: imitation, faking, and preemption.[64] *Imitation* amounts simply to copying an established brand. For example, a manufacturer in Italy may produce cheap jeans and put on the Calvin Klein label for sale as a genuine Klein product. *Faking* refers to identifying the fraudulent product with a symbol, logo, or brand name that is very similar to the famous brand. For example, in Europe several companies have sold jeans under the brand names of "Lewis" (in France) and "Levy's" (in Germany), which are pronounced very similarly to Levi's. A Hong Kong firm advertises its blue jeans under its own brand name, but displays the figure of the Levi Strauss trademark, "The Levi's Saddleman," with the only difference being that the branding iron in the hand of the saddleman is replaced by a horsewhip.[65] Here is another example:

> Recently, McDonald's filed a request for a temporary injunction against McDavid's, a Tel Aviv hamburger outlet. The restaurant looks distinctly American—from the plastic counters and beeping digital cash registers to the Uncle Sam hat atop the McDavid's symbol. The owner of McDavid's was quoted as saying that he had had McDonald's 120-page manual for its franchise owners translated into Hebrew.[66]

Piracy through *preemption* of brand names is feasible in those countries where the law permits wholesale registration of brand names. In such countries, a person may register in his or her name a large number of well-known brand names, and then either sell these names to those interested in counterfeiting or better still to the multinational when it is ready to move into the country. In Monaco, for example, a person registered 300 famous brand names such as Chase Manhattan, Bankers Trust, du Pont, Sears, Texaco, NBC, and CBS.

Needless to say, brand piracy can cause unfair competition to multinational enterprises in many markets. Worse still is the export of the counterfeit product to the home market. For example, while the loss of a particular country as a market may not cause much worry to Proctor & Gamble, a fake product in the United States sold at a meager price would create a real problem.

Unfortunately, MNCs have little protection in the form of international laws to protect their brands overseas. There are some conventions, such as the Paris Convention and the Madrid Convention, discussed in Chapter 9, that make it convenient to obtain registration of the brand simultaneously in member countries. Other than that, the international marketer is left with few alternatives. Legal recourse overseas can be ill-advised since it would be difficult to ensure an unbiased decision. Besides, legal action is expensive and can result in adverse publicity in the foreign market. Thus, the only option of the international firm to protect its brand is either to withdraw from the market where it must compete against imitations and fakes or to promote its product in such a way as to make the customer aware of false brands. The best defense for business victimized by brand piracy is to strike back rather than to rely on government agencies. In this regard, the experience of Paris-based Cartier is illuminating. Despite Cartier's best efforts, Mexican officials were uncooperative about pursuing a Mexico City retail store owner who was selling fake Cartier products, even with forty-nine legal decisions against him. So Cartier opened its own store directly across the street and forced the retailer to strike a deal: in return for not selling forgeries, he would become Cartier's sole local distributor.[67]

A few years ago a coalition of twenty-five U.S. and European businesses helped to mitigate the problem of invasion of the U.S. home market. Through their efforts, an amendment in U.S. customs laws now requires officials to confiscate counterfeit goods at the port of entry.

Identifying Country of Origin

A related question here is the identification of country of origin on a product. For example, should a U.S. company use the "Made in the USA" label on its product? The answer to this question depends on the market for which the product is destined. There was a time when U.S. products were held in high esteem worldwide. Traditionally, therefore, as far as U.S. companies were concerned, identifying the country of origin was considered very desirable. However, more recent events suggest that the country of origin not be identified indiscriminately.

Nagashima's study on the subject indicated that in contrast to made-in-the-USA products, the image of made-in-Germany products has improved greatly. Similarly, the made-in-Japan image has been significantly upgraded over the years.[68] Cattin and colleagues arrived at similar conclusions in a study of U.S. and French purchasing agents. The French purchasing managers appeared to perceive made-in-England labels more favorably than made-in-USA labels. On the other hand, made-in-Germany labels did not appear as valuable among the French purchasing managers as among the American managers, because the former perceived such items as more expensive, more heavy-industry-oriented, less technically advanced, and subject to less pride of ownership.[69]

Han and Terpstra's recent study showed that consumer perceptions of product quality vary across product perspectives, i.e., U.S.-branded/U.S.-made, U.S.-branded/foreign-made, foreign-branded/U.S.-made, and foreign-branded/

foreign-made. However, the sourcing country stimuli came out stronger than brand name when the consumers evaluated bi-national products.[70]

Thus, the made-in-the-USA label is not the sole mark of prestige, technical advancement, and innovativeness.[71] Additionally, in many developing countries, nationalist sentiments favor locally produced products. In the light of these developments, an international marketer may choose not to use the "made in" attribute as a regular practice. Where laws require such identification, the company has no choice. For example, goods entering the United States must be identified by their origin. But in countries where there are no such legal requirements, the "made in" identification should be used if research findings and business acumen indicate that the identification would benefit the business (see International Marketing Highlight 12.7).

International Marketing Highlight 12.7

What America Makes Best

A deep concern for product quality is turning many U.S. manufacturers into the world's top competitors. Among the many products that restore the definition of quality to the words "Made in America" are:

- F-16 aircraft (General Dynamics)
- Computer workstations (Sun Microsystems)
- Biotechnological drugs (Genentech)
- Pacemakers (Medtronic)
- Satellites (Hughes Aircraft)
- Stereo speakers (Advent, Allison, Infinity)
- Towels and bed sheets (many companies)

Source: Fortune, March 28, 1988, p. 40.

Private Branding for Foreign Markets

Private branding refers to identifying a product with the brand name of another business. For example, a food processor may can soups and put the A&P label on them. Private branding is a common practice in the United States whereby large retailers sell a variety of products under their house brand. The question is to what extent this practice is relevant in international marketing.

An essential requirement for private branding is the existence of a developed distribution system in the market, particularly at the retail level. Thus, only developed societies such as Japan and a few countries in Western Europe qualify for successful private branding outside the United States. In other words, U.S. businesspersons may find it advantageous to enter a country, say, England, by producing private brands for a large retailer there. The danger with such a decision is that the U.S. exporter is entirely at the mercy of the English retailer: the manufacturer's name is not known. As the product becomes popular, the retailer might want to strike such a hard bargain that the U.S. producer is caught in an unfavorable cost/profit situation, and ends the association. This is likely to happen because the retailer can easily find alternative sources of supply for the product both in the United States and elsewhere. It is for such reasons that H.J. Heinz Co. is opposed to the retailers' big push into private labels in Britain. While Heinz's major competitors, Campbell Soup and Nestlé, have succumbed to pressure from the food chains, Heinz decided against private branding. To compete with private-label brands, which retail up to 15 percent less than its own products, Heinz has had to hold down its prices, step up new-product introductions, and boost advertising. Although these tactics have adversely affected short-term profits, Heinz feels confident that consumers will continue to consider its products superior and demand them despite higher prices. Thus, the retailers eventually will lose their leverage.[72]

Even in nonfood areas, private branding at the international level is slowly becoming popular. For example, Polaroid agreed to let Minolta Camera Co. of Japan sell the Spectra Pro, its most expensive consumer instant camera, in the United States as the Minolta Instant Pro. Polaroid considers the agreement to be a logical move to find new ways to grow through private branding.[73] Private branding for U.S. retailers by foreign companies, however, is quite prevalent. For example, J.C. Penney has an array of its electronic products and appliances (radios, toasters) manufactured in Southeast Asia under the J.C. Penney brand.

International Packaging

Good marketing practice requires that products be offered to customers in serviceable shape and pleasing form. Thus, the product must be moved in a proper fashion from the production point to the retail shop. Therefore, packaging plays an important role that can be described basically in two ways—physical and psychological. Physically, the packaging should be sturdy enough to undergo all the strain involved in shipment. The psychological aspect involves the package as a promotional tool. In general, international packaging decisions ought to take into account the requirements of four groups of people: customers, shippers, distributors, and host governments.

Customer Requirements Packaging requirements for the customer will vary from country to country, based on socioeconomic-cultural factors. Customer characteristics should be examined in order to make sound packaging decisions. The aesthetics of the package is the first important consideration. The shape of the package and the logo, symbols, and figures used on it; the words and phrases describing the product; and the color scheme must all be appropriately attuned to the cultural traits of the host country. While in developing countries the major emphasis in packaging is on visual aesthetics, in developing countries the overall physical quality of the package is important because the package will most likely be kept and used as a container. Thus, the package itself may become a selling point. The higher the quality of the package, however, the higher the cost. If package costs substantially increase the product price, demand will be adversely affected. Another aesthetic factor to reckon with is size. An eight-ounce jar of coffee may be all right in the United States, but thoroughly inappropriate in a tea-drinking nation where coffee is used infrequently.

Climate is another consideration in foreign packaging decisions. The package chosen should be sturdy enough to withstand extreme climatic conditions. For example, food product packaging may have to be redesigned for shipping to zones of high temperature, such as Saudi Arabia. Package failure would mean that customers would be buying a stale product and the brand name would earn a bad image.[74]

Finally, packaging should be safe in every way, both when it is used to house the product and during after-use. It is particularly important that after-use should not lead to any bad side effects, including ecological concerns. The disposal of the package should not be hazardous to humans or pets and should not lead to pollution of the environment.

Shipper Requirements Regardless of the mode of transportation, the main concern of shippers involved in international marketing is getting goods to their destination without damage, theft, or loss, and doing that with the least possible cost. The key to accomplishing this is in efficient packing and packaging methods. The major questions to answer in order to design proper packaging for international shipment are: Where is the shipment going? Will it be stacked? For how long and where (in a warehouse or in an open space)? What are the handling requirements (net weight and type of load)? Are there any unusual or additional requirements? Sometimes these questions are difficult to answer in advance. In such cases, a consulting firm with expertise in packaging for international shipments can be helpful.

Distributor Requirements The distribution channels for dispersion and conversion of products for worldwide markets require that theft, pilferage, and damage of shipped goods be avoided through proper packaging. For example, advertising the company or product on the shipping case is inadvisable. Not only does it involve unnecessary printing cost, but it is also an invitation to pilferage. Most of the requirements of channels of distribution in international marketing are similar to domestic marketing channels. For example, the package should not waste shelf space, should handle easily, and should permit easy and efficient price marking/labeling. Foremost, the package should protect the contents and be aesthetically attractive to promote the product at the point of purchase.

Government Requirements Government requirements in the area of packaging are mainly related to labeling and marking. Labeling applies to retail packages and is intended to provide consumers with essential information about the contents of the package in order to assure them that both the package and its contents conform to the regulations in force within the market. Marking regulations concern only the transport container and normally do not affect the labeling on the retail package inside.

To illustrate government labeling requirements, many countries with two common languages require bilingual labeling. Likewise, nations on the metric system require provision of information on weight and measure in metric designation. Canada's law pertaining to labeling illustrates the point. It requires:

1. That the identity of the product by its common or generic name or its function be shown on the principal display panel in English and French
2. That the net quantity of the product be declared in metric units and in the French and English languages
3. That the person by or for whom the product was manufactured be identified sufficiently for postal purposes

Special "other information" requirements are set forth for food products related to the use of artificial flavorings.[75]

International Warranties and Services

Customers buy not only the physical product but also the benefits that the product provides. To assure the customer that the product will do what it is meant to do, it is usual in U.S. domestic business to provide a warranty. The question arises whether such a warranty should be extended internationally. Similarly, certain products, particularly consumer durables and industrial products, require servicing throughout their useful life. International marketers have to decide on servicing arrangements for products sold overseas.

Warranties

A ***warranty*** is a guarantee from the manufacturer that the product will perform as stipulated. There are various reasons for companies to give warranties. First, a warranty serves as a competitive tool. A good warranty policy tends to differentiate the product in the marketplace. It enhances the customer's confidence in the product. Second, a warranty sometimes helps in gaining additional business. For example, the warranty may hold good only if the product is regularly serviced. Thus, to keep the warranty viable, the customer might contract with the company for servicing. (To illustrate the point, in March 1975, Boeing sold six jet airliners to Iraqi Airways for $200 million. Along with the sale went a service contract for $20 million for training personnel and servicing the airliners.[76]) Third, an explicit warranty limits the liability of the company should the product fail to come up to the expectations of the buyer.

The design of a warranty policy raises an important managerial question: Should a standard warranty be provided worldwide, or should the warranty be customized for each country or region? For example, on most electronic toys, manufacturers provide one-year guarantees in the United States. Whether this one-year warranty should be extended to toys sold outside the United States is a question that must be investigated.

The answer to this question would involve a variety of considerations. First among these considerations is the nature of the market. If the international market is represented as one market, such as the Common Market where goods move freely within the market, it is desirable to offer a standard warranty. *Competition* within international markets would be another consideration. For example, the company may not have an elaborate warranty policy at home, but in an international market it might be forced into matching the warranty offered by competitors. For example, in 1986 Ford did not offer extensive warranties on most of its cars in the United States. But outside the United States, Ford continued its two-year or 60,000-kilometer warranty. The warranty may have to be different if the conditions of the use of the product vary in different markets. A warranty may have to be made much more restrictive if wear and tear on the product because of, say, climatic conditions is likely to be excessive. For example, in the dusty conditions and hot climate of Saudi Arabia, equipment such as air conditioners would wear out in a shorter period than in Switzerland. A company, therefore, may offer a more liberal warranty in Switzerland than in Saudi Arabia. Another consideration is the nature of the product. Conventionally, a warranty on certain products is limited to basic performance. In such cases, a standard warranty could be offered worldwide. For example, Allis Chalmers, Bell & Howell, Brunswick (bowling equipment), Caterpillar, AB Dick, Parker Pen, Sunbeam, and Volkswagen offer a basic performance warranty common to all markets.[77] A final consideration in deciding between a standard and localized warranty is the ability of the company to service the product under warranty. Servicing requires servicing facilities. If it is not feasible to have facilities in all the markets and countries the company sells in, it may offer different warranties to fit the situation.

Service

Service constitutes an offer to maintain the original product through overhauling, replacement of parts, adjustments, and the like. Most industrial products and many consumer durables require servicing on a regular basis. Provision of service on an international basis is important on two accounts. First, service must be provided to comply with the warranty policy. For example, if a piece of equipment carries a year's warranty on certain parts and functions, the manufacturer should make arrangements to ensure that the terms of the warranty are adequately fulfilled by providing appropriate service facilities. Second, service ranks as a promotional tool. When a product by its very nature periodically requires after-sale service, the company that provides such a service has an edge over a competitor who does not offer service.[78]

International customer service has not received the same degree of attention from U.S. firms as has domestic customer service. Typically, U.S. exporters delegate the responsibility for service to third parties such as importers. Consequently, the service needs of foreign customers often are handled ineffectively.[79]

The formulation of a service policy requires an objective assessment of needs. The need may vary by country, depending on such factors as intensity of use, climatic conditions, and the technical skills of the people using the product. For example, in the United States higher labor costs mean that various industrial machine tools are used much more intensively than in Japan. In an extreme climate, a product is very likely to require greater care. Also, when the people using the product have marginal skills, the need for service escalates.

A prerequisite to an offer of service is an adequate supply of spare parts. Companies often fail in this regard and thereby earn a bad reputation among their customers. The problem in supplying parts is that many products come in different models and parts frequently vary from model to model. Furthermore, a product may have a large number of parts, some of which are exorbitantly expensive, and a service facility has to carry all of them. There is no easy solution to this problem. Usually companies consult their own past experience to work out a list of parts that often need replacing and then carry these parts in the inventory.

Providing service also necessitates trained personnel to perform the servicing. Most companies handle the training process in one of two ways: Either the native service personnel are trained in their own country by one or more technicians from the United States, or they are brought to the United States for training. Usually training involves on-the-job experience as well as classroom instruction. Training on high-technology products is rendered on an ongoing basis. Many companies have teams of trainers who visit country after country to update local personnel on new materials/processes/parts related to the product.

In conclusion, a good service program is helpful, directly and indirectly, in getting feedback from customers on various aspects of the marketing mix. The service organization, based on customer inputs, can serve as a catalyst to generate ideas on product improvement. Similarly, this information can shed light on other aspects of the marketing mix.

Summary

Decisions about products involve such issues as what products and product lines to introduce in various countries; to what extent a product should be adapted or modified to match local customs and characteristics; whether new products should be introduced; where the R&D effort should be concentrated; whether the firm should diversify into unrelated areas; which products should be eliminated; how products should be packaged; what brand policy to pursue; what after-sale services to offer; and what guarantees the company should provide on various products.

Product means a bundle of attributes put together to satisfy a customer need. The product objectives for each country or market should be defined separately and be based on overall corporate objectives on the one hand, and on the concerns of the individual national governments on the other. Product planning decisions, both immediate and strategic, are based on product objectives.

Product design is a major strategic issue. A company can either offer a standard product worldwide or adapt it to local requirements. Adaptation can be physical (for example, changes made in the electrical wiring system of a machine to match voltage requirements of a country) or cultural (for example, a color change in response to a cultural preference). The decision to standardize or adapt is dictated by the nature of the product, market development, cost–benefit considerations, legal requirements, competition, support system, physical environment, and market conditions. Generally companies try to market a standardized product internationally. Although this helps in cost savings, standardization can also lead to missed opportunities.

To operate overseas successfully, periodic review of the product line is necessary. Product line development essentially involves three alternatives: (1) extension of the domestic line, which refers to the introduction of domestic products to overseas markets; (2) adding additional products to the overseas line even if the company does not carry those products domestically; and (3) adding new products. New products for international markets can be either developed internally or acquired. The rationale behind the addition of new products and the procedure for undertaking new-product development are complex marketing issues. Product review may also result in product elimination. There are several reasons for product elimination and different ways of implementing elimination decisions.

Another issue examined is the R&D activity. Some companies undertake R&D across national boundaries, but companies largely centralize R&D activity at home for a variety of reasons. More recently, however, R&D effort in host countries has been initiated by some companies. There are relative pros and cons of centralization versus decentralization of R&D.

The diffusion of innovations in overseas markets involves adoption and diffusion processes that are affected by a series of factors. In fact, the diffusion process itself may have an impact on new products.

There are four alternatives for formulating an international brand strategy: using one name worldwide, using one name with adaptations for each market, using different names in different markets, and using the company name as a family name for all brands. An important problem that companies face in brand management is that of brand piracy, the illegal use of famous brand names in various ways. In the absence of any international law to protect the brands, each company must independently guard its brand from invaders. The identification of country of origin on the product as well as private branding for international markets are decisions that must be made in relation to specific situations.

International packaging is influenced by such considerations as customers, distribution channels, shippers, and host governments. The service/warranty component provides a company with an important opportunity to differentiate its product from the competition.

Review Questions

1. What are the advantages of product standardization worldwide?
2. Under what circumstances should the product be adapted to local conditions?
3. Distinguish between obligatory and discretionary adaptation. Give examples.
4. Illustrate the logic behind the extension of the domestic product line to overseas markets.
5. What factors influence a decision to add products to the overseas product line?
6. Discuss the rationale behind the introduction of new products across national boundaries.
7. What factors help in the successful management of the international product line?
8. Why do MNCs mainly centralize R&D at home?

9. What alternative strategies can a company adopt to brand its international products?
10. What factors enhance the diffusion of innovations overseas?

Endnotes

1. *See* Masaaki Kotabe, "Corporate Product Policy and Innovative Behavior of European and Japanese Multinationals: An Empirical Investigation," *Journal of Marketing,* April 1990, pp. 19–33.
2. Igal Ayal, "International Product Life Cycle: A Reassessment and Product Policy Implications," *Journal of Marketing,* Fall 1981, p. 96. *Also see* "Brazil Raises Exports of High Technology, to Pace Third World," *The Wall Street Journal,* October 6, 1981, p. 1.
3. Samon Darlin, "Coke, Nestlé Launch First Coffee Drink," *The Wall Street Journal,* October 25, 1991, p. B1.
4. Subhash C. Jain, "Standardization of International Marketing Strategy: Some Research Hypotheses," *Journal of Marketing,* January 1989, pp. 70–79. *Also see* Robert D. Buzzell, "Can You Standardize Multinational Marketing?" *Harvard Business Review,* November–December 1968, pp. 1, 2, and 113; Robert Bartels, "Are Domestic and International Marketing Dissimilar?" *Journal of Marketing,* July 1968, pp. 56–61; Stewart H. Britt, "Standardizing Marketing for the International Market," *Columbia Journal of World Business,* Winter 1974, pp. 39–45; Warren J. Keegan, "Multinational Product Planning: Strategic Alternatives," *Journal of Marketing,* January 1969, pp. 58–62.
5. Donald S. Henley, "Evaluating International Product Line Performance: A Conceptual Approach," in *Multinational Product Management* (Cambridge, MA: Marketing Science Institute, 1976), pp. II-1–II-19.
6. *See* Subhash C. Jain, "Standardization of International Marketing Strategy: Some Research Hypotheses," *Journal of Marketing,* January 1989, pp. 70–79.
7. Susan P. Douglas and Christine D. Urban, "Lifestyle Analysis to Profile Women in International Markets," *Journal of Marketing,* July 1977, pp. 53–54. *Also see* Emmanuel J. Cheron, Thomas C. Padgett, and Walter A. Woods, "A Method for Cross-Cultural Comparisons for Global Strategies," *Journal of Global Marketing,* Fall/Winter 1987, pp. 31–52.
8. Jose De La Torre, "Product Life Cycle as a Determinant of Global Marketing Strategies," *Atlantic Economic Review,* September–October 1975, pp. 9–14.
9. John S. Hill and Richard R. Still, "Effects of Urbanization on Multinational Product Planning: Markets in Lesser-Developed Countries," *Columbia Journal of World Business,* Summer 1984, pp. 62–67.
10. Robert D. Buzzell, "Can You Standardize Multinational Marketing?" *Harvard Business Review,* November–December 1968, pp. 1, 2, and 113.
11. Wenlee Ting, "The Product Development Process in NIC Multinationals," *Columbia Journal of World Business,* Spring 1982, pp. 76–81.
12. Seth Luboro, "Aim, Focus, and Shoot," *Forbes,* November 26, 1990, p. 67.
13. Allan T. Demaree, "What Now for the U.S. and Japan," *Fortune,* February 10, 1992, p. 90.
14. Ralph Z. Sorenson and Ulrich E. Wiechmann, "How Multinationals View Marketing Standardization," *Harvard Business Review,* May–June 1975, pp. 38–56.
15. John S. Hill and Richard R. Still, "Adapting Products to LDC Tastes," *Harvard Business Review,* March–April, 1984, pp. 93–94. *Also see* John S. Hill and William L. James, "Product and Promotion Transfers in Consumer Goods Multinationals," *International Marketing Review,* vol. 8, no. 2 (1991), pp. 6–17.
16. *See* "Brazil: U.S. Jeans Makers Find a Market that Fits," *Business Week,* August 30, 1982, p. 39.
17. W. Chan Kim and R. A. Manborgue, "Cross-Cultural Strategies," *Journal of Business Strategies,* Spring 1987, p. 31. *Also see* M. P. Kacker, "Export-Oriented Product Adaptation—Its Patterns and Problems," *Management International Review,* no. 6 (1976), pp. 61–70.

18. Warren J. Keegan, Richard R. Still, and John S. Hill, "Transferability and Adaptability of Products and Promotion Themes in Multinational Marketing—MNCs in LDCs," *Journal of Global Marketing,* Fall/Winter 1987, pp. 85–101. *Also see* Kamran Kashani, "Beware the Pitfalls of Global Marketing," *Harvard Business Review,* September–October 1989, pp. 91–98.
19. Sushil Vachani and Louis T. Wells, Jr., "How Far Should Global Products Go?" *Vikalpa,* April–June 1989, pp. 3–10.
20. Kenichi Ohmae, *Triad Power* (New York: The Free Press, 1985), pp. 101–102.
21. W. Chan Kim and R. A. Manborgue, "Cross-Cultural Strategies," *Journal of Business Strategies,* Spring 1987, p. 30.
22. Based on a case study titled "Sodima-Yoplait" completed by a French student, Marie Colongo, under the supervision of Subhash C. Jain, University of Connecticut, 1986. Subsequently updated in 1988.
23. Ian R. Wilson, "American Success Story—Coca-Cola in Japan," in Mark B. Winchester, ed., *The International Essays for Business Decision Makers,* vol. 5 (Dallas: The Center for Business, 1980), p. 121.
24. Ibid.
25. "Campbell Soup Unit's Cookies Will Be Sold in Japan by Meiji Seika," *The Asian Wall Street Journal Weekly,* September 30, 1985, p. 22.
26. Vern Terpstra, "International Product Policy: The Role of Foreign R&D," *Columbia Journal of World Business,* Winter 1977, p. 25.
27. William H. Davidson and Richard Harrigan, "Key Decisions in International Marketing: Introducing New Products Abroad," *Columbia Journal of World Business,* Winter 1977, pp. 15–23.
28. *See* Georges Leroy, *Multinational Product Strategy* (New York: Praeger, 1976).
29. Ibid. *Also see* Richard Klavans, Mark Shauley, and William E. Evan, "The Management of International Corporate Venture: Entrepreneurship and Innovation," *Columbia Journal of World Business,* Summer 1985, pp. 21–28.
30. "A New Focus for Polaroid: Conventional Film," *Business Week,* July 25, 1988, p. 36.
31. Attila Yaprak, "Formulating a Multinational Marketing Strategy: A Deductive, Cross-National Consumer Behavior Model," an unpublished doctoral dissertation, Georgia State University, 1978.
32. "Another Day, Another Bright Idea," *The Economist,* April 16, 1988, p. 82.
33. "Computers That Point Moslems Toward Mecca," *Business Week,* March 25, 1985, p. 846.
34. "Taking on the World," *Time,* October 19, 1987, p. 47.
35. *See* Ralph Z. Sorenson II, "U.S. Marketers Can Learn from European Innovators," *Harvard Business Review,* September–October 1972, pp. 89–99.
36. *See* Johny K. Johansson and Hans B. Thorelli, "International Product Positioning," *Journal of International Business Studies,* Fall 1985, pp. 57–76; Ivor S. Mitchell and Tom O. Amioku, "Brand Preference Factors in Nigerian Beer," *Columbia Journal of World Business,* Spring 1985, pp. 55–67.
37. Charles G. Burck, "The Toyota of the Wine Trade," *Fortune,* November 30, 1981, p. 155.
38. Thomas A. Stewart, "The New American Century," *Fortune,* The New American Century Issue, 1991, p. 12.
39. *See* Daniel Creamer, *Overseas Research and Development by United States Multinationals, 1960–1975* (New York: The Conference Board, 1976).
40. Vern Terpstra, "International Product Policy: The Role of Foreign R&D," *Columbia Journal of World Business,* Winter 1977, pp. 24–32. *Also see* Tamara J. Erickson, "Worldwide R&D Management: Concepts and Applications," *Columbia Journal of World Business,* Winter 1990, pp. 8–13.
41. *See* Paul Shrivastava, "Technological Innovation in Developing Countries," *Columbia Journal of World Business,* Winter 1984, pp. 23–30.
42. *See* Susan Moffat, "Picking Japan's Research Brains," *Fortune,* March 25, 1991, p. 84.
43. Paul Ingrassia, "Industry Is Shopping Abroad for Good Ideas to Apply to Products." *The Wall Street Journal,* April 29, 1985, p. 1.
44. *See* Alecia Swasy, "P&G Gambles That Smaller Is Better with New Super-Concentrated Detergent," *The Wall Street Journal,* October 16, 1989, p. B7.
45. W. Chan Kim and R. A. Manborgue, "Cross-Cultural Strategies," *Journal of Business Strategy,* Spring 1987, pp. 28–35.

46. "Honeywell Keeps a Foot in France—for Now," *Business Week,* December 7, 1981, p. 45.
47. "The Frustrations Behind Penney's Cutback," *Business Week,* November 16, 1981, p. 60.
48. Joseph B. White and Thomas F. O'Boyle, "Volkswagen AG to Close or Sell Its U.S. Plant," *The Wall Street Journal,* November 23, 1987, p. 2.
49. "ITT Corp. May Close Unit in Argentina," *The Wall Street Journal,* February 22, 1985, p. 34.
50. "Campbell Soup Fails to Make It to the Table," *Business Week,* October 12, 1981, p. 66.
51. "Gerber Abandons a Baby-Food Market," *Business Week,* February 8, 1982, p. 45.
52. *See* Everett M. Rogers and F. Floyd Shoemaker, *Communications of Innovations* (New York: Free Press, 1971). *Also see* Hirokazu Takada and Dipak Jain, "Cross-National Analysis of Diffusion of Consumer Durable Goods in Pacific Rim Countries," *Journal of Marketing,* April 1991, pp. 48–54.
53. Zoher E. Shipchandler, "Change in Demand for Consumer Goods in International Markets," in Subhash C. Jain and Lewis R. Tucker, Jr., eds., *International Marketing Managerial Perspectives,* 2nd ed. (Boston: Kent Publishing Co., 1986).
54. Sumantra Ghoshal and Christopher A. Barlett, "Creation, Adoption, and Diffusion of Innovations by Subsidiaries of MNCs," *Journal of International Business Studies,* Fall 1988, pp. 365–388.
55. Thomas S. Robertson, "The Process of Innovation and the Diffusion of Innovation," *Journal of Marketing,* January 1964, pp. 15–16.
56. H. Anton Keller, "Behind WHO's Ban on Baby Formula Ads," *The Wall Street Journal,* June 29, 1981, p. 1.
57. Yves L. Doz and C. K. Prahalad, "How MNCs Cope with Host Government Intervention," *Harvard Business Review,* March–April 1980, p. 149.
58. "Hoover: Revamping in Europe to Stem an Earnings Drain at Home," *Business Week,* February 15, 1982, p. 144. *Also see* Sushil Vachani, "Distinguishing Between Related and Unrelated International Geographic Diversification: A Comprehensive Measure of Global Diversification," *Journal of International Business Studies,* vol. 22, no. 2 (Second Quarter 1991), pp. 307–322.
59. The New, Improved Unilever Aims to Clean Up in the U.S.," *Business Week,* November 27, 1989, p. 102.
60. *See* Sak Onkvisit and John J. Shaw, "The International Dimension of Branding: Strategic Considerations and Decisions," *International Marketing Review,* vol. 6, no. 3 (1989), pp. 22–34. *Also see* Robert Johnson, "Naming a New Product Is Tough When the Best Names Are Taken," *The Wall Street Journal,* January 19, 1988, p. 31.
61. This and other examples in this section are taken from *Choosing Corporate, Product, and Brand Names for Worldwide Marketing* (New York: Business International Corporation, 1966), pp. 24–32.
62. *See* "Brand Awareness Slips When It Crosses International Borders," *Marketing News,* November 21, 1988, p. 16.
63. "The Counterfeit Trade," *Business Week,* December 16, 1985, p. 64.
64. *See* Jack G. Kaikati and Raymond LaGrace, "Beware of International Brand Piracy," *Harvard Business Review,* March–April 1980, p. 46. *Also see* "The Pirates of Taiwan," *Dun's Business Month,* February 1983, p. 13.
65. *Choosing Corporate, Product, and Brand Names for Worldwide Marketing* (New York: Business International Corporation, 1966), pp. 24–32.
66. Jack A. Kaikati and Raymond LaGrace, "Beware of International Brand Piracy," *Harvard Business Review,* March–April 1980, p. 54.
67. "The Counterfeit Trade," *Business Week,* December 16, 1985, p. 64.
68. Akira Nagashima, "A Comparative 'Made In' Product Image Survey Among Japanese Businessmen," *Journal of Marketing,* July 1977, pp. 95–100. *Also see* Donald G. Howard, "Understanding How American Consumers Formulate Their Attitudes About Foreign Products," *Journal of International Consumer Marketing,* vol. 2 (1989), pp. 7–24; Paul L. Sauer, Murray A. Young, and H. Rao Unnava, "An Experimental Investigation of the Processes Behind the Country of Origin Effect," *Journal of International Consumer Marketing,* vol. 3 (1991), pp. 29–60; John R. Darling and

Van R. Wood, "A Longitudinal Study Comparing Perceptions of U.S. and Japanese Consumer Products in a Third/Neutral Country: Finland 1975 to 1985," *Journal of International Business Studies,* vol. 21 (Third Quarter 1990), pp. 427–450.

69. Philippe J. Cattin, Alain Jolibert, and Colleen Lohnes, "A Cross-Cultural Study of 'Made In' Concepts," *Journal of International Business Studies,* Winter 1982, pp. 131–141. *Also see* Warren J. Bilkey and Eric Nes, "Country-of-Origin Effects on Product Evaluations," *Journal of International Business Studies,* Spring–Summer 1982, pp. 89–100; Erdener Kaynak and S. Tamer Cavusgil, "Consumer Attitudes Towards Products of Foreign Origin: Do They Vary Across Product Class?" *International Journal of Advertising,* no. 2 (1983), pp. 147–157; Chem L. Narayana, "Aggregate Images of American and Japanese Products: Implications of International Marketing," *Columbia Journal of World Business,* Summer 1981, pp. 31–35.

70. C. Min Han and Vern Terpstra, "Country-of-Origin Effects for Uni-National and Bi-National Products," *Journal of International Business Studies,* Summer 1988, pp. 235–256. *Also see* Graham J. Hooley and David Shipley, "A Method for Modelling Consumer Perceptions of Country of Origin," *International Marketing Review,* Autumn 1988, pp. 67–76.

71. *See* Brenda Sternquist and Tomoyoshi Ogawa, "Japanese Consider U.S. Products Inferior," *Marketing News,* September 26, 1988, p. 4.

72. "Heinz Struggles to Stay at the Top of the Stack," *Business Week,* March 11, 1985, p. 49.

73. "Polaroid and Minolta: More Developments Ahead," *Business Week,* July 16, 1990, p. 32. *Also see* Ron Suskind, "Minolta Puts Name on Polaroid," *The Wall Street Journal,* August 29, 1990, p. B1.

74. *See* "Export Packages—What Is Required for Fresh Fruits and Vegetables," *International Trade Forum,* July–September 1988, p. 14.

75. "Law and Rulings," *Modern Packaging,* July 1975, p. 55. *Also see* Hans B. Thorelli, "Consumer Information Policy in Sweden—What Can Be Learned?" *Journal of Marketing,* January 1971, pp. 50–55.

76. "Boeing Gets Baghdad's Aircraft Business," *Business Week,* August 4, 1975, p. 35.

77. *Business International,* June 16, 1967, p. 187.

78. *See* Norman E. Marr, "Understanding Customer Service for Increased Competitiveness," *International Marketing Review,* Autumn 1987, pp. 45–53. *Also see* "A Big Selling Feature for Exporters: The Assurance of After-Sales Service," *Business America,* February 15, 1988, pp. 19–20.

79. Martin Christopher, Richard Lancioni, and John Gattorna, "Managing International Customer Service," *International Marketing Review,* Spring 1985, pp. 65–70. *Also see* Brent Bowers and Damon Darlin, "Hotels in the U.S. and Japan Are Squaring Off in Services Game as Field Becomes Globalized," *The Asian Wall Street Journal Weekly,* September 26, 1988, p. 6.

CHAPTER • 13

International Pricing Strategy

CHAPTER FOCUS

After studying this chapter, you should be able to:

- Describe the importance of the pricing decision in the international context
- Explain the parent company's role in pricing
- Discuss factors that must be considered in setting prices
- Compare the cost approach versus the market approach for price setting
- Examine factors that affect transfer pricing
- Discuss issues of dumping and leasing

Pricing is a particularly critical and complex variable in overseas marketing strategies. The pricing decision ultimately affects an organization's ability to stay in the market. At the same time, the uncertainties of entirely unpredictable forces, such as costs, competition, and demand, threaten with numerous pitfalls for international pricing. This chapter develops a framework for understanding the international pricing process with a description of the problems and tactics of international marketers.

International pricing has several processes and ramifications. Corporate headquarters has a role in making pricing decisions. Different price-setting approaches are available, and a variety of concerns influence pricing decisions including intrafirm pricing, dumping, and leasing. An international marketer must work with facility through all these complex variables.

Importance of Pricing

Pricing, an important decision in any business, be it domestic or international, directly affects revenue and thus profitability. Further, appropriate pricing aids proper growth, as development of a mass market depends to a large extent on price. For businesses dependent on acquiring business contracts through competitive bidding, such as the construction and mining industries and drilling companies, a poor pricing decision threatens survival. Too high a price may mean no business, while a lower price may lead to an unprofitable operation. In many cases, the price indicates a product's quality.[1] If the Mercedes car, for example, were priced in the same range as the Oldsmobile, the Mercedes would lose some of its quality image. Finally, price affects the extent of promotional support to be allocated to a product.

Parent Company's Role in Pricing

One basic question in overseas pricing pertains to the role of the parent corporation. The parent company must decide how much say it wants to reserve for itself in international pricing, including whether the pricing decision will be made centrally or delegated to foreign subsidiaries. To an extent the pricing role of the parent company is determined by the emphasis put on price competition in the total marketing mix.

Strategic Significance of Pricing

The role assigned to the pricing variable in developing the marketing mix depends on its strategic significance. Traditionally, U.S. companies have relied more on nonprice competition than on pricing. For example, Terpstra found that U.S. companies generally avoid price competition in the Common Market and more often go after competitive leverage through advertising, selling, and product differentiation.[2] This sort of behavior can be attributed to the fact that U.S. manufacturing costs are usually high, which makes it difficult to compete pricewise. Further, the quality of U.S. goods has been considered high, which permitted targeting the product for a segment in which price did not matter.

In the last few years, however, price competition has been stressed more than before. Sales promotion, presale and postsale service, advertising and product differentiation, and product quality are no longer depended upon exclusively.[3] This change has been necessitated partly by the importance of focusing on mass markets overseas, particularly in Western Europe. A small decrease in price can be an effective way of increasing penetration in many foreign markets, especially wherever there is considerable price consciousness and where products are not highly differentiated. For example, the Italian appliance industry in the 1960s made significant inroads in the Western European markets through price competition. By 1965 Italian-made refrigerators accounted for 32 percent of the total French market, and for 40 percent to 50 percent of the Benelux market (Belgium, the Netherlands, and Luxembourg).[4] Furthermore, costs in many countries, Germany for example, have been rising faster than in the United States. Thus, price competition is feasible in some cases.

Leff makes an interesting case for penetrating Third World markets through judicious use of pricing. The high elasticity of demand for consumer products and the highly skewed income distribution in developing countries lead him to recommend making changes in the pricing/output strategy. In this way, mass markets can be developed, enabling the multinational corporation to achieve higher profits and larger growth, and enabling the host country to enhance the rate of economic development.

> Marketing executives in the less-developed countries frequently complain of the small and narrow markets for many consumer products. The relatively small size of markets for nonagricultural consumer products is not surprising in light of the economic and demographic conditions in the less-developed countries. Faced with this situation, marketing executives have tried to enlarge the markets for their products with advertising, promotion, and other techniques of modern marketing. The scope for using such techniques effectively is not always great, however. Suggested here is an alternative approach to the marketing of many consumer products in the less-developed countries. This is an approach which would expand markets and optimize returns by implementing a pricing policy to reduce the (real) relative price of a company's products, in order to bring them within the reach of the broader population. Such a pricing policy generally receives relatively little attention as compared with other elements in the marketing mix. There are special reasons why a strategic pricing policy along these lines might be expected to have particularly fruitful effects in the conditions of the less-developed countries. Furthermore, apart from its relevance for marketing per se, pricing policy also has important implications for top-level corporate strategy in developing country markets.[5]

Uniform Versus Differentiated Pricing

To what extent the setting of uniform prices is desirable in worldwide markets is a question that multinational companies perpetually face. Some international marketers argue for uniform prices. Others, however, observe that the obvious differences in the markets of various countries favor the use of an internationally differentiated pricing policy. In brief, pricing in overseas markets is a controversial issue involving legal, economic, governmental, and marketing aspects, both in the practice of differentiated pricing and in price uniformity.

In theory, it is desirable on economic grounds to set different prices in different markets, because demand and supply differ from country to country. This occurs under any form of imperfect competition, such as pure monopoly, oligopoly, and monopolistic competition.

> In evaluating each foreign market, the firm may find that there exist different demand elasticities than those encountered in the home market. Hence it behooves the firm to take advantage of these different demand elasticities by charging the appropriate price in each market.[6]

Thus, it makes economic sense for the multinational firm to vary prices from market to market. Such a strategy, however, may cause the firm to be charged with dumping in the host country. So from a legal standpoint it may be desirable to set a uniform price globally. The host country may frown upon differentiated pricing since it may expose the domestic firm to foreign competition. Such an argument would even be economically justified in the case of an infant industry.

Empirical research on the subject corroborates the conceptual framework. Boddewyn found that over two-thirds of consumer-nondurable marketers and almost 50 percent of industrial-good manufacturers among U.S. MNCs adapted pricing to local conditions. This adaptation is justified on the grounds that manufacturing costs, competitor's prices, and taxes all vary from country to country, making local market considerations a critical factor in pricing.[7]

Despite the importance of differentiated pricing, some firms try to standardize at least the relative price level. As a matter of fact, some sort of uniformity in international pricing ensures adequate product positioning and control.

All in all, the decision between uniform and differentiated pricing would be dictated by such factors as competitive conditions, life cycle position of the product, product diffusion process, regulatory considerations, channel structure, company objectives, and consumer price perceptions. If the competitive position of the firm does not vary from market to market, it may be worthwhile to pursue a uniform pricing strategy. A firm essentially in a monopoly or differentiated oligopolistic situation may price its product uniformly on a global scale. For example, Boeing sells a highly differentiated jetliner. To all intents and purposes, therefore, it charges the same price for its planes everywhere, whether they are sold in the United States or Europe. Even the Third World countries pay the same price. In the introductory product stage when the product is not highly diffused, markets are limited to a few daring or innovative customers. These customers constitute homogeneous segments even though they may be geographically apart. Thus, a new product may initially be priced uniformly throughout the world. Further, if the diffusion process of an innovation has a similar pattern worldwide, standardized pricing will make sense. The perspectives of pricing—uniform versus differentiated—are also affected by local laws. Even when other conditions favor a standard price worldwide, local taxes, for example, may oblige a company to price the product higher in a particular country than elsewhere.

The wholesale and retail distribution structure of a country also influences the price decision. A *Business International* study found, for example, that radio and television sets were priced lowest in Germany; prepared foods were more expensive in Italy and least expensive in the Netherlands. Such differences were attributed to retail structure.[8] Thus, where the channel structure is inefficient, additional distribution costs will be incurred, which must be absorbed through accelerating prices, resulting in nonuniformity of price worldwide.

The corporate objectives in a country may vary. Such differences in objectives would make standardized pricing ineffective. For example, a company may enter one market to develop a mass market through penetration and plan to be there for a long time. On the other hand, its entry in another country may be considered an ad hoc opportunity, expected to last a few years until the domestic industry, currently in its infancy, matures. Such a difference in objectives would suggest the development of different pricing strategies in the two countries. In the latter case, skimming the cream off the top of the demand curve will make sense. In the first case, however, a penetration pricing strategy would be in order.

Finally, the price perceptions of customers may vary from country to country, requiring differentiated pricing. For example, in the competitive environment of Western Europe, an American product may be perceived as the equivalent of local products and hence must be competitively priced. But the same product in a developing country might be perceived as superior in quality, and a low standard price would disturb the customer. Hollander says:

> Entirely aside from the problem of competitive or political reprisals, consumers' suspicions and doubts about the quality of the merchandise in foreign-seeming or innovative stores can easily be identified if the prices seem unbelievably or unreasonably cheap. Moreover, foreign markets will often reject "low end," i.e. low-priced, low-quality products. Some highly publicized ventures organized around price appeals, such as GEM (American discount stores in England) and INNO-France (Belgian department stores in France), have been marked failures.[9]

Responsibility for Price Setting

The corporate headquarters should spell out who is responsible for price setting. Three ways to allocate price-setting responsibility are (1) headquarters only decides, (2) each overseas subsidiary decides independently, and (3) decisions are jointly made between the parent and the subsidiary. Because of differences in local manufacturing and market situations, it would appear impractical for the parent organization to set the price for foreign markets. Many companies assign pricing responsibility exclusively to country managers.

Most frequently, however, companies follow some sort of joint decision-making procedure. The parent company specifies a basic framework for pricing, leaving considerable leverage for overseas affiliates to set actual prices. The framework may consist of a formula to be adopted for figuring out base price or simply a few guidelines. The following is an example of a price guideline issued by one headquarters to each of its foreign affiliates.

> Our products should command a premium price, although not necessarily the top price in the market, and therefore should appeal to the consumer to whom superiority . . . is important.[10]

Pricing Factors

The factors to consider in international pricing exceed those in strictly domestic marketing not only in number, but also in ambiguity and risk. Domestic price is affected by such considerations as pricing objectives, cost, competition, customer, and regulations. Internationally, these considerations apply at home and in the host country. Each of these considerations composes a number of components that vary in importance and interaction in different nations.[11] This section reviews pricing factors and looks at their influence on pricing in international business operations.

Pricing Objectives

Pricing objectives should be closely aligned to marketing objectives, which should in turn be derived from overall corporate objectives. Essentially, objectives can be defined in terms of profit or volume. The profit objective may take the shape of either a percentage markup on cost or price or a target return on investment. The volume objective is usually specified as a desired percentage of growth in sales or as a percentage of the market share to be achieved. Sometimes businesses define their pricing objectives in such general terms as *image building* (that is, pricing should project a certain image of the product/company), *stability* (that is, pricing should realize a stable level of sales and profits), and *ethics* (that is, the setting of a price should meet the ethical standards of good and fair business).

Two questions must be answered in setting price objectives: (1) Who should set the pricing objectives in different countries (the parent organization or the host country subsidiary)? (2) Should there be common objectives worldwide, or should objectives vary by country? (These questions will be examined in later sections.) Suffice it to say here that, inasmuch as market conditions differ in each country, it would be dysfunctional to set common pricing objectives globally. Further, no matter who sets the final price, both parent/regional and subsidiary inputs should be properly reviewed before making the decision. For example, what price the market will bear should be properly related to the parent corporation's profit goal.

Cost Analysis

Cost is one important factor in price determination. Of all the many cost concepts, fixed and variable costs are the most relevant to our discussion. ***Fixed costs*** are those that do not vary with the scale of operations, such as number of units manufactured. Salaries of the managerial staff, office rent, and other office and factory overhead expenses are examples of fixed costs. On the other hand, ***variable costs,*** such as costs of material and labor used in the manufacture of a product, bear a direct relationship to the level of operations.

It is important to measure costs accurately in order to develop a cost-volume relationship and to allocate various costs as fixed or variable. Measurement of costs is far from easy. Some fixed, short-run costs are not necessarily fixed in the long run; therefore, the distinction between variable and fixed costs matters only in the short run. For example, in the short run the salaries of the marketing staff in the home office would be considered fixed. However, in the long run, the sales staff could be either increased or cut, no longer making sales salaries a fixed expense.

Further, some costs that initially appear fixed can be considered variable costs when properly traced. A company manufacturing different products can keep a complete record of the sales manager's time spent on each product and thus may treat this salary as variable. However, the cost of that record keeping will far exceed the benefits to be derived from making the salary a variable cost. Also, no matter how well a company maintains its records, some variable costs cannot be allocated to a particular product or line of business. In the final analysis, allocation of costs must be examined on the merit of each particular case.

The impact of costs on pricing strategy can be studied by considering the following three relationships: (1) the ratio of fixed costs to variable costs; (2) the economies of scale available to a firm; and (3) the cost structure of a firm vis-à-vis competitors. If the fixed costs of a company in comparison with variable costs form the higher proportion of its total costs, adding sales volume will be a great help in increasing earnings. Consider, for example, the case of an airline whose fixed costs are as high as 60 percent to 70 percent of total costs. Once fixed costs are recovered, the additional tickets sold add greatly to earnings. Such an industry would be termed *volume sensitive.* There are some industries, such as the paper industry, where variable costs constitute the higher proportion of total costs. Such industries are *price sensitive* because even a small increase in price adds much to earnings (see International Marketing Highlight 13.1).

If substantial economies of scale are obtainable through a company's operations, market share should be expanded. In considering prices, the expected decline in costs should be duly taken into account—that is, prices may be lowered to gain higher market share in the long run. The concept of obtaining lower costs through economies of scale has often been referred to in the literature as *experience effect,* which means that all costs go down as accumulated experience in-

International Marketing Highlight 13.1

Pricing at Replacement Cost

Why did gas prices go up so fast? It's hard to blame consumers for wondering why gas should increase by 10 to 20 cents a gallon just five days after Iraqi tanks rolled into Kuwait City—the oil companies were selling gasoline from old, cheap crude, weren't they?

The real answer is a combination of accounting and price-setting practices for crude oil. The last-in first-out method of accounting for inventory that most U.S. oil companies use causes them to price products according to the cost of replacing them, not according to historical cost. Reason: When it's time to figure profits for a given quarter, the cost of the most recently purchased oil is what gets subtracted from revenues. Since that cost went up quickly, oil companies must increase revenues quickly as well to maintain profit margins.

Source: Joel Drefuss, "Gas Pump Economics 101," *Fortune,* September 10, 1990, p. 42.

creases. Thus, if a company acquired a higher market share, its costs would decline, enabling it to reduce prices. If a manufacturer is a low-cost producer, maintaining prices at competitive levels will earn additional profits. The additional profits can be used to promote the product aggressively and increase the overall scope of the business. If, however, the costs of a manufacturer are high compared with other competitors, prices cannot be lowered in order to increase market share. In a price-war situation, the high-cost producer is bound to lose.

Competition

The nature of competition in each country is another factor to consider in setting prices. The competition in an industry can be analyzed with reference to such factors as the number of firms in the industry, the relative sizes of different members of the industry, product differentiation, and ease of entry. In addition, competitive environment can be categorized as privileged position, leadership, chaotic, or stabilized competition, as shown in Table 13.1. The privileged position amounts to a monopoly situation. The supply of spare parts is one example in this category, particularly in industrial markets. The leadership position refers to oligopolistic competition in which the leader reaps high margins while the followers receive only adequate margins. The chaotic situation also operates in oligopoly. Only long-run programs can rescue a company from chaos. Finally, the stabilized competition applies to a monopolistic situation where a high degree of product differentiation prevails.

The impact of market structure on pricing is illustrated in the following quotation with reference to the Japanese market:

> The oligopolistic structure of Japanese industry is the main reason for widespread price coordination. In most branches of industry, many company or industrial groups exist, each of which has strong connections in the financial sector, in the Diet and in the bureaucracy. Any attempt by one of these companies to engage in heavy price competition could provoke such a powerful negative reaction from the others that it would probably produce more harm than benefit. Furthermore, price coordination and resale price maintenance (RPM) have various advantages for manufacturers. In the Japanese market, with its overwhelming number of small retail outlets, RPM also serves to protect the small retailers. When prices are uniform, consumers do not have much incentive to prefer large outlets (which can cut prices as a result of economies of scale) over small, more expensive shops. Thus, price coordination and RPM are strongly supported by small retailers, who in sheer numbers are a politically visible segment of the population.
>
> Examples of price coordination and industrial cooperation are clearly evident. In the summer, electric fans that are identical in color, shape, quality and price are on the market—but are produced by several different companies. Even discount prices tend to be coordinated. In Akihabara, Tokyo's largest consumer electrical goods shopping area, numerous outlets will offer identical models of vacuum cleaners at discount prices. Although each shop sells the products of different manufacturers, the discount prices are all at the same level.[12]

Customer Perspective

Customer demand for a product is another key factor in price determination. Demand is based on a variety of considerations among which price is just one. These considerations include the ability of customers to buy, their willingness to

TABLE 13.1 Competitive Environment

POINTS OF DIFFERENTIATION	COMPETITIVE ENVIRONMENT			
	Privileged Position	Leadership	Chaotic	Stabilized Competition
Definition	Lack of significant direct competition	Leader has ability to set price level Leader affects degree of variation from basic level	Price level and variation are unpredictable and frequently changing	Firms have pricing latitude Price levels and variations adjust smoothly to each firms's strategy
Characteristics	High degree of technical/service differentiation High cost of entry Good customer, competitor intelligence Considerable latitude in pricing	Few competitors, high cost of entry Leader has high market share Leader has recognized technical and marketing leadership, and generally is low-cost producer Leader has reputation for good pricing decisions Leader is able to communicate its policies Leader's actions are predictable	Price is the major competitive tool "Commodity" products—everybody viewed the same Customers are price sensitive, or made to be price sensitive Tendency to excess capacity No recognized leader and no restraint	No recognized industry price leader No firm has dominant market share Firms employ product differentiation and market segmentation Competition based on technology, service, delivery; not based on price Infrequent price changes
Implications	High margins and profits Responsibility for market development	Good margins and profits for leader Acceptable margins and profits for followers Customers are satisfied	Nobody making even acceptable profits Customer probably dissatisfied	Good or acceptable margins for all Customers are satisfied

Source: Donald S. Henley, "Evaluating International Product Line Performance: A Conceptual Approach," in *Multinational Product Management* (Cambridge, MA: Marketing Science Institute, 1976), pp. II-13–II-16.

buy, the place of the product in the customer's lifestyle (whether a status symbol or a daily-use product); prices of substitute products; the potential market for the product (whether there is an unfulfilled demand in the market or if the market is saturated); the nature of nonprice competition; consumer behavior in general; and segments in the market. All these factors are interdependent, and it may not be easy to estimate their relationships accurately.

Demand analysis involves predicting the relationship between price level and demand, simultaneously considering the effects of other variables on demand. The relationship between price and demand is called ***elasticity of demand,*** or sensitivity of price, and it refers to the number of units of a product that would be demanded at different prices. Price sensitivity should be considered at two different levels: total industry price sensitivity and price sensitivity of a firm.

Industry demand for a product is elastic if demand can be substantially increased by lowering prices. If lowering price has little effect on demand, it would be considered inelastic. Environmental factors, which vary from country to country, have a direct influence on demand elasticity. For example, when gasoline prices are high, the average U.S. consumer seeks to conserve gasoline. If gasoline prices should go down, people would be willing to use gas more freely. Thus, in the United States, the demand for gasoline can be considered somewhat elastic. On the other hand, in a Third World country like Egypt, where only a few rich people own cars, no matter how much gasoline prices change, the total demand would not be greatly affected, making it inelastic.

When the total demand of an industry is highly elastic, the industry leader may take the initiative to lower prices. The loss in revenues due to increased prices will presumably be more than compensated for by the additional demand generated, thus enlarging the total dollar market. Such a strategy will be highly attractive in an industry where economies of scale are possible. Where demand is inelastic and there are no conceivable substitutes, prices may be increased, at least in the short run. In the long run, however, the government may impose controls, or substitutes may be developed.

An individual firm's demand is derived from the total industry demand. An individual firm seeks to find out how much market share it can command in the market by changing its own prices. In the case of undifferentiated, standardized products, lower prices should help a firm in increasing its market share, as long as competitors do not retaliate by matching the firm's prices. Similarly, when business is sought through bidding, lower prices should help. In the case of differentiated products, however, market share can even be improved by maintaining higher prices (within a certain range). The products may be differentiated in various real and imagined ways.

For example, a manufacturer in a foreign market who provides adequate warranties and after-sale service might maintain higher prices and still increase market share. Brand name, an image of sophistication, and the impression of high quality are other factors that can help in differentiating a product and hence afford an opportunity to increase prices and not lose market share. Of course, other elements of the marketing mix should reinforce the image suggested by the price. In brief, a firm's best opportunity lies in differentiating the product. A differentiated product offers more opportunity for increasing earnings through higher prices.

Government and Pricing

Government rules and regulations pertaining to pricing should be taken into account in setting prices. Legal requirements of both the host government and the United States government must be satisfied.

Chapter 9 discusses different legal aspects that affect marketing decisions. In brief, the provisions of U.S. antitrust laws (for example, the Robinson-Patman Act related to price discrimination) would apply to any foreign pricing decision that would adversely affect competition in the United States. For example, suppose an electronics company exports integrated circuits (ICs) to South Korea at a price lower than the one it charges U.S. customers. Suppose further that the Korean importer uses these ICs to assemble computer terminals that are exported to the United States to compete against U.S.-made terminals. If the Korean company gets an advantage over the U.S. terminal manufacturers because of the lower price it pays for the ICs bought from the United States, the IC manufacturer could be charged with price discrimination.

A host country may have different laws concerning price setting. These may range from guidelines for the setting of prices to complete procedures for arriving at prices, amounting to virtual control over prices.[13]

The exact nature of government regulations in the area of pricing would depend on the legal and philosophical principles of the nation.

> Perhaps the most obvious difference can be found in the realm of legal and philosophical approaches toward competition. Europe, Japan, and the U.S., for example, have far different approaches toward competition policy. In the U.S., antitrust has a long history. Structure and conduct are the principal bases upon which public policy toward competitive activity is formulated. In Europe, antitrust has a history of less than 15 years. Performance is far more important than structure and conduct which would be unheard of in the U.S., *provided* that performance in terms of public benefits (price, products, service, stable employment, etc.) is acceptable. The Japanese, if the literature is to be believed, coordinate industry, financial institutions, unions, and governments in a manner impossible to duplicate in the other advanced countries. In the developing countries, antitrust is virtually unknown and competition may even be seen as wasteful of fixed plant and equipment.[14]

Government regulations evolve over time. For example, relatively new antitrust laws have been enacted in the European Community (EC). These laws may be even more stringent than those of the United States. The first company cited for violations in the EC was United Brands for selling bananas at lower prices in the Netherlands than in other countries.

Briefly, the international pricing decision depends on such factors as pricing objective, cost, competition, customer, and government requirements. An empirical study on the subject, however, has shown total costs to be the most important factor in setting international price. The competitors' pricing policies rank as the next important factor, followed by the company's out-of-pocket costs, return on investment policy, and the customer's ability to pay.[15]

International Price Setting

International pricing is affected by such factors as differences in costs, demand conditions, competition, and government laws. The impact of these factors on pricing is figured in by following a particular pricing orientation. This section examines different pricing orientations and discusses export price setting. Perspectives of price setting in foreign markets are also considered.

Pricing Orientation

Companies mainly follow two different types of pricing orientation: the cost approach and the market approach. The ***cost approach*** involves first computing all relevant costs and then adding a desired profit markup to arrive at the price. The cost approach is popular because it is simple to comprehend and use and leads to fairly stable prices. This approach, however, has two drawbacks. First, definition and computation of costs can become troublesome. Second, this approach brings an element of inflexibility into the pricing decision.

This approach arrives at a tentative price based strictly on costs. The final price emerges after making adjustments, dictated by considerations of government, demand, competition, company objectives, and others. The principal emphasis, however, continues to be on costs, which forces inflexibility. More than that, a problem arises in defining the meaning of cost. Should all (both fixed and variable) costs be included or only variable costs? What proportion of fixed costs should be included, if any? Particularly, should costs related to R&D and parent corporation administrative overhead costs be included? The answers to these questions are far from easy.

A conservative attitude would favor using full costs as the basis of pricing. On the other hand, an incremental cost pricing could allow for seeking business otherwise lost. Exhibit 13.1 illustrates this point. The Natural Company would not be able to conduct its foreign business if it insisted on recovering the full unit cost of $11.67. If the full costing method were the decision criterion, the company would actually pass up the opportunity to add $3,000 to profit.

The profit markup applied to the cost to compute final price may simply be a markup percentage arbitrarily decided upon. Alternatively, the profit markup may represent a desired percentage return on investment.

For example, if the total investment in a business is $16,000,000 and the total cost of annual output (averaged over the years) is $25,000,000, the capital turnover ratio would be $16,000,000/$25,000,000, or 0.8. Multiplying the capital turnover ratio, 0.8, by the desired return on investment, say, 20 percent, would give a markup of 16 percent (0.8 × 0.20) on standard cost. It can be shown as:

$$\textit{Percentage markup on cost} = \frac{\textit{Total invested capital}}{\textit{Standard cost of annual normal production}} \times \textit{Percentage desired return on investment}$$

This method is an improvement over the pure cost-plus method since markup is derived more scientifically. But the determination of rate of return poses a problem. Academically, the rate of return should be based on the minimum fair return on investment. In other words, rate of return has to be equal to, or more than, the current cost of capital. In actual practice, a certain amount usually comes to be accepted as a fair return. Thus, 15 percent is considered a normal return in manufacturing industries, while 8 percent to 10 percent suffices in services indus-

EXHIBIT 13.1 Full Costing Versus Incremental Costing

The following is an illustration of the full costing and incremental costing methods. The Natural Company has a production capacity of 20,000 units per year. Presently the company is producing and selling 15,000 units per year. The regular market price is $15.00 per unit. The variable costs are listed below.

Material	$5/unit
Labor	$4/unit
Total Variable Cost	$9/unit

The fixed cost is $40,000 per year.
The income statement reflecting the situation above would appear as follows:

Income Statement		
Sales (15,000 @ $15.00)		$225,000
Cost: Variable Cost (15,000 @ $9.00)	$135,000	
Fixed Cost	40,000	175,000
Profit		$ 50,000

Now suppose the company has the opportunity to sell an additional 3,000 units at $10.00 per unit to a foreign firm. This is a special situaiton and would not have an adverse effect on the price of the product in the regular market.

If Natural Company uses the full costing method to make its decision, the offer would be rejected. The reasoning behind this is that the price of $10.00/unit does not cover the full cost of $11.67/unit ($175,000 ÷ 15,000 = $11.67). By using the full costing method as a decision criterion, the company would actually be giving up $3,000 in additional profits.

If the incremental costing method is used, the offer would be accepted, and thus, a gain of $3,000 in profits would be realized. The incremental costing method compares additional costs to be incurred with the additional revenues that will be received if the offer is accepted.

Additional Revenue (3,000 @ $10.00)	$30,000
Additional Costs (3,000 @ $ 9.00)	27,000
Additional Income	$ 3,000

The difference between the two decision methods results from the treatment of fixed cost. The full costing method includes the fixed cost in the cost per unit calculation. The incremental cost method recognizes that no additional fixed costs will be incurred if additional units are produced. Therefore, fixed costs are not considered in the decision process.

The following is an income statement comparing the results of the company with and without the acceptance of the foreign offer:

(continued)

EXHIBIT 13.1 (*Continued*)

Income Statement

	Rejecting the offer	Accepting the offer
Sales (15,000 units @ $15.00)	$225,000	$225,000
(3,000 units @ $10.00)	—	30,000
Total Sales	$225,000	$225,000
Costs: Variable (@ $9.00/unit)	$135,000	$162,000
Fixed	40,000	40,000
Total Cost	$175,000	$202,000
Net Income	$ 50,000	$ 53,000

NOTE: An important factor in such a decision is considering what the effects of accepting the offer will be on regular market price. If the additional sales were made in the regular market at the $10.00 price, it could depress the regular market price below $15.00. This would severely hamper operations in the future.

tries. In this method, markup is linked to the total investment and, therefore, does not consider changes in price of cost components.

Under the ***market approach*** pricing starts in a reverse fashion. First, an estimate is made of the acceptable price in the target segment. An analysis is performed to determine if this price would meet the company's profit objective. If not, then the alternatives are either to give up the business or to increase the price. Additional adjustments in price may be required to cope with competitors, host country government, expected cost increase, and other eventualities.

Both the cost and market approaches essentially consider common factors in determining the final price. The difference between the two approaches involves the core concern in setting prices. The market approach focuses on pricing from the viewpoint of the customer. Unfortunately, in many countries it may not be easy to develop an adequate price-demand relationship, and therefore implementation of the market approach may occur in a vacuum. It is this kind of uncertainty that forces marketers to opt for the cost approach (see International Marketing Highlight 13.2).

Export Pricing

In theory, export pricing is based on either of the two pricing approaches. In most cases, however, the cost approach turns out to be a more viable approach. The difficulty of gaining adequate knowledge of the foreign market and the desire to ensure satisfactory profit on export transactions leads companies to choose the cost approach.

Whichever approach is preferred, export pricing is affected by three factors:

1. The price destination (that is, who it is that will pay the price—the final consumer, independent distributors, a wholly owned subsidiary, a joint venture organization, or someone else)
2. The nature of the product (that is, whether it is raw or semiprocessed

International Marketing Highlight 13.2

Approach to Price Setting

Seiko Epson, the Japanese computer peripherals manufacturer, sets floor prices at headquarters after considering costs, recommendations from executives in the company's various manufacturing divisions and country markets, and a corporate profit markup target for the particular product. Starting from this figure, product division presidents at headquarters establish flexibility parameters. The low-end products, such as Epson's LQ-500 series printer, are usually restricted to a variability range of less than 5 percent, while the prices charged for high-end products like computers and laser-jet printers can range from 10 percent to 25 percent above or below the base price. Salespeople in headquarters are allowed to negotiate prices within these parameters with country-level sales affiliates. In view of the rapid technological change and rapid entry of new products in that industry, this sort of price flexibility is considered essential by marketing staff.

Source: Marketing Strategies for Global Growth and Competitiveness (New York: Business International, no date), p. 64.

material, components, finished or largely finished products; or services or intangible property—patents, trademarks, formulas, and the like)

3. The currency used for billing (that is, the currency of the purchaser's country, the seller's home country currency, or a leading international currency)

The *price destination* is an important consideration since different destinations present different opportunities and problems. For example, pricing to sell to a government may require special procedures and concessions not necessary in pricing to other customers. A little extra margin might be called for. On the other hand, independent distributors with whom the company has a contractual marketing arrangement deserve a price break. Wholesalers and jobbers that shop around have an entirely different relationship with the supplier than the independent distributors.

As products, raw materials and commodities give a company very little leeway for maneuvering; there is usually a prevalent world price that must be charged, particularly when the supply is plentiful. But if the supply is short, the seller may be able to demand a higher price. Similarly, when it is a sellers' market, the seller can make the buyer pay for adverse exchange fluctuations, and vice versa.[16]

A pricing choice in export pricing that a company must consider is whether to set a common price or different prices for domestic and international markets. Although some companies have common prices, more often, for reasons discussed in the previous section, a firm develops two price lists, one for the domestic and one for the foreign market. The salesperson or distributor for a particular foreign market receives the foreign price list, which would be used in discussing price with customers. Usually, a company would charge the same price to a given customer even if a product is supplied from various plants. For example, a Brazilian order might be filled from either a U.S. plant or a plant in Italy. Normally, the Brazilian market would be served from the United States and the U.S. price list would be used. In an emergency, if the order must be filled from Italy, the parent company would absorb the extra cost of shipping the product from Italy in order to maintain stable prices.

Often, a margin is built into the price list so that, if necessary, it is feasible to adjust prices in response to local market conditions. Such conditions would include overall competitiveness based on production and related costs, the export incentives other governments give their manufacturers, and the actual margin another producer has in a given country.

Price lists are periodically reviewed for adjustments. In the economic environment of the 1980s, such review became more frequent. For example, a chemical MNC reviewed prices every three months instead of semiannually, mostly because of world supply/demand conditions. Usually, exporting firms give anywhere between thirty to ninety days' notice of an impending price increase, depending on the nature of the product.

As far as currency conditions are concerned, the appropriate strategy would depend on the currency used and its relative strength. For example, if domestic currency is used, Cavusgil recommends alternative strategies depending on whether it is weak or strong (see Table 13.2).

A company may make sales on a spot basis or for future delivery. For sales on a spot basis, prices are determined according to the daily exchange rate at the time of the order. On orders for future delivery, a company may either quote at the current rate or use a forward rate. The final decision on the use of the exchange rate will depend on the company's overall export exposure and its past experience with exchange losses.[17]

Figure 13.1 illustrates list price determination. The flow-diagram charts the experience of two companies, one French and one Belgian, both active in the French market. The diagram outlines the process for setting list prices and the decision criteria used at crucial points in the process. One periodical notes:

> Planning prices and volumes is the key to effective marketing management for capital-intensive producers of industrial goods. For firms selling more or less homogeneous products (chemicals, basic metals, etc.), volume/margin trade-offs are particularly crucial. Unused production capacity begs to be filled with orders that at least provide contribution above variable cost, although this can often result in a profitless search for volume. Since no producer can expect to maintain prices higher than competitors for similar products delivered under given conditions for any period of time, prices must be competitive and any differential advantage is usually quickly matched. Hence, prices and volumes of each product are under continuous review as conditions constantly shift in many end-use markets over which the industrial producer has little or no control and about which information may be relatively scant.[18]

Price Escalation

The retail price of exports is usually much higher than the domestic retail price for the same product. This escalation in foreign price can be explained by such costs as transportation, customs duty, and distributor margins, all associated

TABLE 13.2 International Pricing Strategies Under Varying Currency Conditions

WHEN THE DOMESTIC CURRENCY IS WEAK	WHEN THE DOMESTIC CURRENCY IS STRONG
Stress price benefits.	Engage in nonprice competition by improving quality, delivery, and after-sale service.
Expand product line and add more costly features.	Improve productivity and engage in vigorous cost reduction.
Shift sourcing manufacturing to domestic market.	Shift sourcing and manufacturing overseas.
Exploit export opportunities in all markets.	Give priority to exports to countries with relatively strong currencies.
Use a full-costing approach, but employ marginal-cost pricing to penetrate new or competitive markets.	Trim profit margins and use marginal-cost pricing.
Speed repatriation of foreign-earned income and collections.	Keep the foreign-earned income in host country; slow down collections.
Minimize expenditures in local or host country currency.	Maximize expenditures in local or host country currency.
Buy needed services (advertising, insurance, transportation, etc.) in domestic market.	Buy needed services abroad and pay for them in local currencies.
Bill foreign customers in their own currency.	Bill foreign customers in the domestic currency.

Source: S. Tamer Cavusgil, "Pricing for Global Markets," in *Marketing Strategies for Global Growth and Competitiveness* (New York: Business International, no date), p. 61.

with exports. The geographic distance that goods must travel results in additional transportation cost. The imported goods must also bear the import taxes in the form of customs duty imposed by the host government. Further, the completion of the export transaction may require the passage of the goods through many more channels than in a domestic sale. Each channel member must be paid a margin for services it provides, which naturally increases cost. Also, a variety of government requirements, domestic and foreign, must be fulfilled, incurring further costs.

The process of price escalation is illustrated in Exhibit 13.2. It is evident that the retail price for exported goods is about 60 percent more than the domestic retail price. For example, about $80 more is spent on transportation alone. An additional $90 is accounted for by the import tariff. Finally, the agent costs for the exported goods amount to about $371, compared with $194 for domestic distribution.

The price escalation could raise the final price to the foreign customer so much that demand drops. An exporter has various means to counteract such a problem:

1. Ship modified or unassembled products, which might lower transportation costs and duties

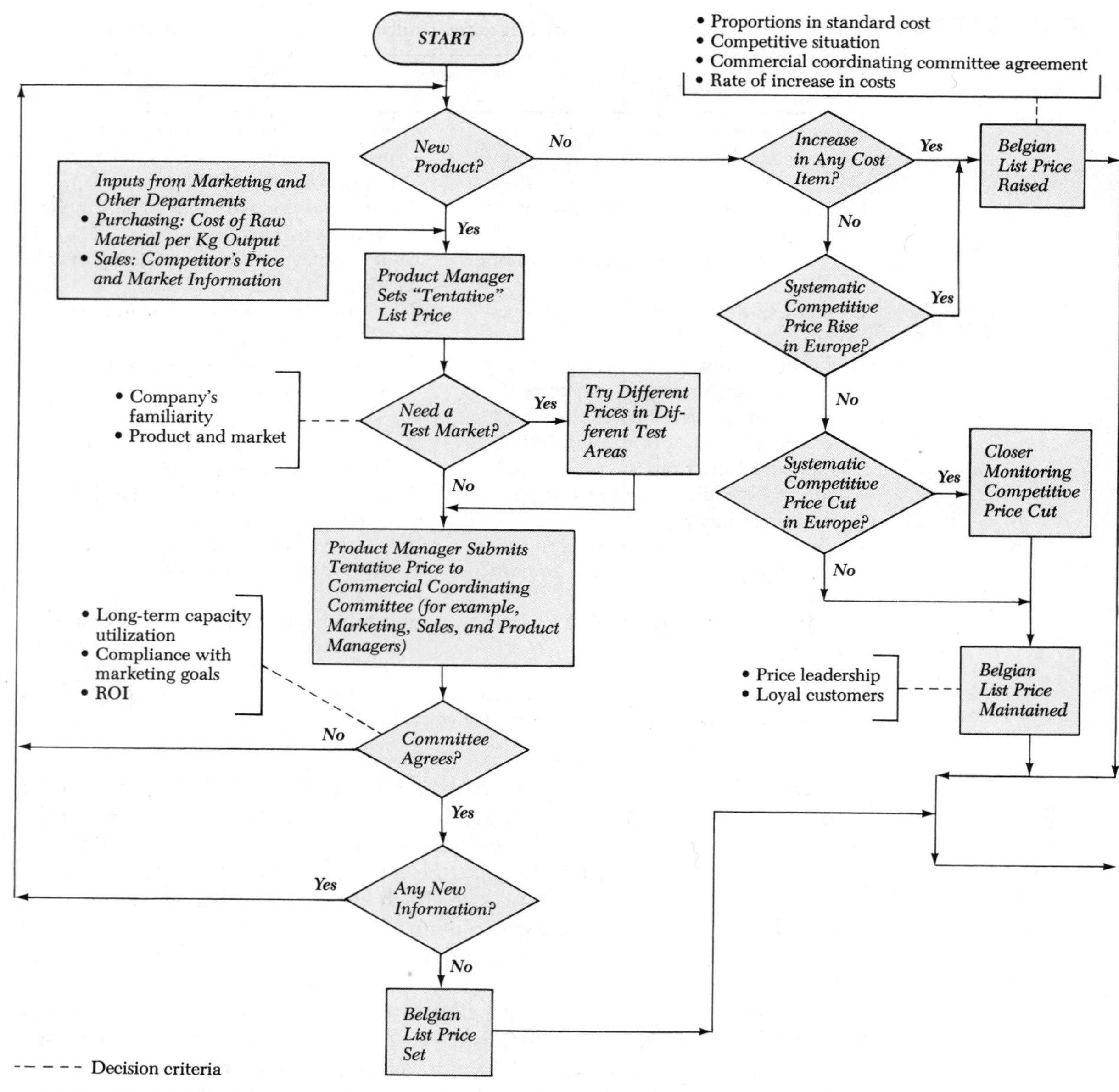

FIGURE 13.1 List Price Determination

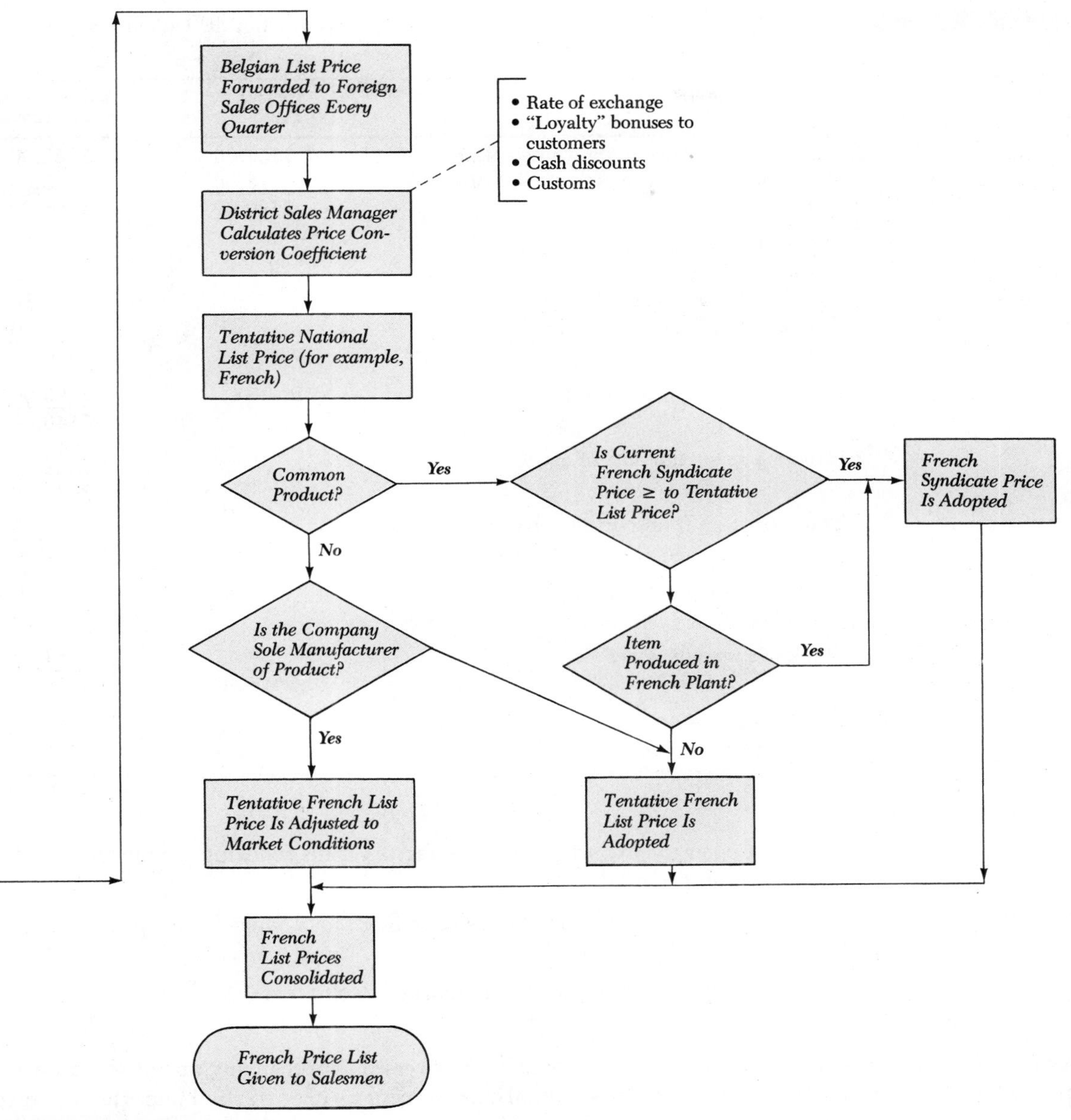

FIGURE 13.1 (*Continued*)

Source: John U. Farley, James M. Hulbert, and David Weinstein, "Price Setting and Volume Planning by Two European Industrial Companies: A Study and Comparison of Decision Processes," *Journal of Marketing*, Winter 1980, p. 48.

EXHIBIT 13.2 An Example of Price Escalation (Export from the United States to the Middle East)

	DOMESTIC TRANSACTIONS	MIDDLE EAST TRANSACTION
Manufacturing price in the United States	$362.00	$362.00
Transportation to wholesaler/point of shipment	18.00	23.00
	$380.00	$385.00
Export documentation (i.e., bill of lading, counselor's invoice)		4.00
Handling for overseas shipping		2.50
Overseas frieght and insurance		58.50
		$450.00
Import tariff: 20 percent of landed cost		90.00
		$540.00
Handling at foreign port of entry		3.00
		$543.00
Transportation from port of entry to importer		17.00
		$560.00
Importer margin (on sale to wholesaler): 10 percent		56.00
		$616.00
Wholesale margin: 8 percent	30.40	49.28
	$410.40	$665.28
Retail margin: 40 percent	164.16	266.12
Final retail price	$574.56	$931.40

2. Lower the export price at the factory, thus reducing the multiplier effect of all the markups
3. Get its freight and/or duty classifications changed for a possible lowering of these costs
4. Produce within the export market to eliminate the extra steps.[19]

Export Price Quotation

An export price may be quoted to the overseas buyer in any one of several ways. Every alternative implies mutual commitment by exporter and importer and specifies the terms of trade. The price alters according to the degree of responsibility that the exporter undertakes, which varies with each alternative.

There are five principal ways of quoting export prices: ex-factory; free-alongside-ship (F.A.S.); free-on-board (F.O.B.); cost, insurance, and freight (CIF); and delivered duty-paid. The ex-factory price represents the simplest arrangement. The importer is presumed to have bought the goods right at the exporter's factory. All costs and risks from thereon become the buyer's problem. The ex-factory arrangement limits the exporter's risk. However, an importer may find an ex-factory deal highly demanding. From another country, it could prove difficult to arrange for transportation and to take care of the various formalities associated with foreign trade. Only large companies, such as Japanese trading companies, can handle ex-factory purchases in another country smoothly.

The F.A.S. contract requires the exporter to be responsible for the goods until they are placed alongside the ship. All charges incurred up to that point must be borne by the seller. The exporter's side of the contract is completed on receiving a clean wharfage receipt indicating safe delivery of goods for foreign embarkation. The F.A.S. price is slightly higher than the ex-factory price since the exporter undertakes to transport the goods to the point of shipment and becomes liable for the risk associated with the goods for a longer period.

The F.O.B. price includes actual placement of goods aboard the ship. The F.O.B. price may be F.O.B. inland carrier or F.O.B. foreign carrier. If it is the former, then the F.O.B. price will be slightly less than the F.A.S. price. But if it is F.O.B. foreign carrier, then the price will include the F.A.S. price plus cost of transportation to the importer's country. Usually an F.O.B. contract requires the following seller and buyer obligations.

The Seller Must:

1. Deliver the goods on board the vessel named by the buyer at the port of shipment on the date specified in the contract
2. Bear all cost payable on or for the goods until they have effectively been placed aboard the ship or other mode of transportation
3. Suitably pack the goods for the mode of transportation specified
4. Provide documentation indicating proof of delivery of goods aboard the mode of transportation

The Buyer Must:

1. Arrange for transportation specifying the mode of transportation to the port of departure
2. Bear all cost and risk from the time the goods have been placed on board the mode of transportation.[20]

Generally, U.S. companies prefer quoting export prices as F.O.B. This limits their responsibility to activities in the United States. In fact, companies usually favor F.O.B. inland carrier over F.O.B. foreign carrier.

Under the CIF price quotation, the ownership of the goods passes to the importer as soon as they are loaded aboard the ship, but the exporter is liable for payment of freight and insurance charges up to the port of destination. Finally, the delivered duty-paid alternative imposes on the exporter the complete responsibility for delivering the goods at a particular place in the importer's country. Thus, the exporter makes arrangements for the receipt of the goods at the foreign port, pays necessary taxes/duties and handling, and provides for further inland transportation in the importer's country. Needless to say, the price of delivered duty-paid goods is much higher than the goods exported under the CIF contract.

Price Setting in Foreign Markets

The pricing decision of an MNC for a foreign market is essentially based on the same considerations as those affecting pricing in the domestic market. As discussed earlier in this chapter, these considerations include overall parent company objectives, the competition, the customer, costs, and government regulations. In the international field, however, there is a range of additional factors to be examined before finalizing the price. First, the price in various regions of the world should be kept fairly uniform. Such parity prevents unrelated dealers in home markets from competing with the overseas company units. For example, if a firm in Europe makes and sells products identical to those it makes and sells in the United States, a customer in Europe would not have any reason to prefer one source over another except for a significant price differential. If the price for a given product sold in Europe goes up substantially above the selling price in the United States, the European customer will very likely import the U.S.-made product and undercut the U.S. firm's European manufacturing subsidiaries.

Second, ethical considerations in the foreign market differ from those in the domestic market. For example, a pharmaceutical company may find it ethically desirable to sell drugs in developing countries at a lower margin despite the feasibility of realizing a higher profit. Third, price segmentation becomes more significant in the foreign market. The nomads of the Sahara, although they are extremely poor, need expensive clothes because of harsh conditions and extreme temperatures. As a matter of fact, a small market for expensive products always exists anywhere in the world. For example, the Lamborghini car sells for over $60,000. The largest single market for this car is Portugal, the country with the lowest per capita income in Europe.[21]

Fourth, U.S. businesspersons characteristically like to maximize short-term performance. In foreign markets, however, it may be preferable to seek long-term gains, even if less-than-optimum profits are earned in the initial years. Thus, pricing to realize a designated rate of return may have to be staggered over several years. In this way, the return in the first few years would be lower, but much higher in the later years, averaging out overall to a figure considered satisfactory by the parent corporation (see International Marketing Highlight 13.3).

Finally, government plays a much more prominent role in pricing in almost all countries outside the United States. In many countries, prices are strictly controlled and all price changes have to be cleared with the government before taking effect.[22] Price control is not limited to developing countries. In the 1970s, for example, a number of European countries (Belgium, France, Ireland, the Netherlands, Spain, Sweden, and the United Kingdom) instituted price controls.

Ordinarily, price control means that an application to increase price must be filed with the government, together with supporting data of cost increases. Government approval may take several months, and often the price increase only takes effect after an additional several months.[23] In other words, a future price increase is publicly announced several months ahead of time. This leads to obses-

International Marketing Highlight 13.3

Giveaway Pricing

Japanese companies definitely conduct business differently. Consider Japan's number one computer maker, Fujitsu Ltd., which won a contract to design a computer system for the city of Hiroshima by bidding 1 yen, or 0.7 cents. Fujitsu's strategy is simple: give away the design job, which hopefully should lead to the city's equipment orders. Japanese companies hope that once they get the inside track, they will enjoy a lifetime of orders. Such lowball pricing is a common practice in Japan. In the past, Fujitsu and NEC Corp. had both submitted a 1 yen bid to design a library computer system. They drew straws and Fujitsu won. Earlier, Fujitsu had won a contract to design a telecommunications system in Wakayama Prefecture by bidding 1 yen.

The lowball pricing highlights Japanese companies' managerial philosophy: Shoot for the long-term. They don't mind giving away business in the short run and dividing up the bidding with their Japanese competitors to ultimately hype the market share, the end-game of Japanese business strategy.

Giveaway pricing shows how difficult it is to break into the Japanese market. Even if other structural barriers to trade, i.e., distribution system, exclusionary business practices, and land-use policies, are eliminated, the rigged bids would be an insurmountable hurdle for U.S. companies to cross.

Another kind of price distortion practiced in Japan is the government's price floor enforcement, applicable in such industries as airlines, insurance, agriculture, and fertilizer, whereby the business is divided up in cartels. This way competitors are prevented from entering the market.

Source: Business Week, November 20, 1989, p. 50.

sive buying to beat the price increase. The price control problem can eventually force a company to leave a country. The following case is an illustration:

> Gerber Products Co. had been operating in Venezuela since 1960. Unprofitable operations forced the firm to sell out in 1979. The company blamed price controls as a major factor in losses. Some of Gerber's products were still being sold at prices set in 1968. The government had refused repeated requests for price increases. The price squeeze forced Gerber to cut output from eighty-eight varieties to as low as twelve. The company reportedly lost $500,000 in the first six months of 1979.[24]

Transfer Pricing

Transfer pricing refers to the pricing of goods/services among units within the corporation. It serves as a measure of the economic performance of profit centers within the enterprise. It differs from market price, which measures exchanges between a company and the outside world, for the net effect of transfer pricing is borne by the same organization. The determination of transfer prices in multinational corporations is an important issue because a substantial proportion of international exchanges consists of transactions between a parent corporation and its affiliates. For example, in the case of the United States, 55 percent of 1988 exports and 41 percent of 1988 imports were within related firms. Similarly, in the case of OECD countries, about one-third of merchandise imports and exports represented transfers among affiliated enterprises.[25]

Factors Affecting Transfer Pricing

Economic theory holds that price reflects demand and supply. For intracompany transactions, however, the parent corporation can control transfer pricing because the exchange is little more than an accounting entry between units of the same corporation. The principal objective of the parent corporation in setting intrafirm prices is to maximize the long-term economic interests of the total corporation. In this endeavor one or more affiliates of the company may often end up losing which leads to conflicts that must be resolved. Essentially, transfer pricing decisions are affected by the following factors:

1. Income tax liability within the host country
2. Income tax liability within the United States
3. Tariffs and/or customs duties within the host country
4. Exchange controls within the host country
5. Profit repatriation restrictions within the host country
6. Quota restrictions within the United States
7. Credit status of the U.S. parent firm
8. Credit status of the foreign subsidiary or affiliate
9. Joint-venture constraints within the host country.[26]

The importance of these factors varies from company to company and according to the location of affiliates. Empirical studies, however, indicate that income tax liability is the most important variable influencing transfer pricing.[27] This conclusion is based mainly on research conducted to investigate MNCs' experiences vis-à-vis industrialized countries. In the case of developing countries, however, Kim and Miller ranked profit repatriation restrictions, exchange control constraints, and joint-venture constraints within the host country as the three most important factors affecting the pricing decision.[28] Despite the importance of different factors in different parts of the world, the motivation behind transfer pricing is the same—maximize overall corporate performance.

To illustrate the point, consider the ramifications of no international rules on the allocation of costs and income for tax or other purposes. In the absence of uniform enforced standards of tax base division, the multinational corporations can set their transfer prices to minimize tax liability. This may require discretionary transfer pricing and profit shifting to affiliates in low-tax jurisdictions. Tax rate differentials, import duties, and foreign exchange restrictions may all influence the pattern of profit sharing. The profits may be shifted from a parent to an affiliate or between affiliates in various ways, such as by creating interdivision costs (for example, sales commissions), fees for contracted services, salaries, interest, rent, purchase premiums, discounts, and royalties.[29]

Transfer Pricing Methods

For setting transfer prices, companies usually set guidelines like the following:

- All domestic and foreign units are profit centers, and transfers must be set at levels that yield a reasonable profit to both the selling and buying units.
- Profit is divided according to functions performed in producing and marketing goods to unrelated buyers.
- Gross margins (the spread between production and distribution costs and the sale to an unrelated buyer) are divided more or less evenly between domestic producing and foreign marketing units.
- Overall impact on consolidated profit is the paramount consideration, and profit is taken where it is best for the total corporation.

Such guidelines are meant to provide a broad perspective for arriving at prices. The actual price is left to the discretion of the manager concerned, since differences in corporate objectives and environmental conditions may not permit a uniform method. For instance, in order to cover certain costs, transfer prices may be raised in countries that limit or refuse to allow royalties as a deductible business expense for a local subsidiary or in countries with exchange controls on dividends that delay remittances. Prices to high-tariff countries may be kept as low as legal requirements permit. A company that is attempting to enter a foreign market, or to expand its share of a market, frequently suppresses initial administrative, research, or other expenses when establishing costs in its transfer price.[30]

Many companies, however, prescribe more specific procedures for setting intrafirm prices. Such procedures are built around three major approaches: cost-based, market price, and negotiated pricing. The cost-based approach requires the inclusion of designated overheads and expense items in computing costs. Additionally, a profit markup may be added to the cost. The price resulting from the cost formula may be modified to accommodate special circumstances surrounding a particular case. The market price requires setting the transfer price in such a way as to allow the marketing unit to meet competitive prices. Unfortunately in many situations, however, competition is lacking. For example, tailor-made components produced, say, by an IBM subsidiary for its foreign affiliates may not have a going market price. If such a price does exist, it may be a price created by the multinational enterprise itself, as in the case of replacement parts produced by General Motors for General Motors cars.[31]

Incidentally, since the transfer price has a variety of repercussions both at home and in host countries, many governments have developed rules for setting transfer prices following the "arm's length" principle, which is more or less arriving at the price based on competitive conditions.[32] In practice, the arm's length approach yields decisions by national tax authorities. Companies that strictly follow the arm's length principle set their own formula subject to the concurrence of the tax authorities. One executive reported:

> The basis of the arm's length price is the alternate disposition price in the open market, except in a few cases where no established market price exists for a product. In these instances, the price of a similar product is selected as a base and the price is adjusted for quality difference from the reference product.[33]

Government involvement in the setting of transfer prices is understandable. In addition to profit shifting and tax avoidance in safe havens, transfer pricing can also affect the international price structure in critical arenas, thereby possibly fueling the current inflationary process or creating a balance-of-payments problem.

In many industries, the products planned for transfer from the parent or another affiliate are commonly available from sources outside the corporate family. In such cases, many companies let their contracting units negotiate the transfer price. The negotiated price may be based on market price or landed cost plus an agreed-upon profit markup.

Handling Interdivisional Conflicts

Decentralized units of a corporation usually are profit centers. Each profit center's rewards and benefits are dependent on its bottom-line performance. Thus, if the transfer pricing system affects the profits of a unit, it is likely to lead to a conflict between the units involved. Interdivisional conflict because of transfer pricing is unhealthy and should be avoided or minimized by setting the transfer price in such a way that a balance exists between each division's perception of the other's advantage in the transfer situation. If one of the divisions enjoys an advantage, the performance of the other division is adversely affected.

An empirical study on the subject showed that where either the supplier or the customer division is seen as making excessive profits from transfer pricing transactions, interdivisional conflict is increased; that is, conflict results not only from the real impact of a transfer price on a unit's performance but also from the perception about the impact on the divisions involved. It is necessary, therefore, to provide adequate information to both the affiliates to prevent misconceptions about impact. Further, arrangements should be made through some sort of organizational set-up at headquarters to handle any conflict. The thrust of the conflict-handling effort should be to remove the imbalance that may favor one unit over the other.

Dumping

Dumping refers to the practice of pricing exports at levels lower than the domestic price. Strictly as a business strategy, dumping is a way of setting differential prices to achieve certain objectives. Thus, if a product is sold in the United States in two different markets at different prices (assuming this is feasible within the Robinson-Patman Act), there is nothing wrong with that practice. However, in the context of the international market, if this strategy is used intentionally to destroy a domestic industry, it becomes a matter of concern for the host country government on behalf of the greater interest of its nation. It is for this reason that many nations have antidumping laws on the books.

An international marketer must make sure that pricing decisions are free from liability for dumping in the host country. Countries usually levy a heavy penalty against dumping, which may cause the imported goods to be much higher than the market price.

Actually the problem of dumping is more prevalent in developed markets. It is in these markets that exporters find the best opportunity for growth. Dumping is one way to render the domestic industry noncompetitive. If carried to its extreme, dumping can force the domestic manufacturers out of business. Once that happens, the price of imported goods can be increased. In brief, an exporter may practice dumping with lower profits in the short run, but with extremely high profits in the long run. As an example, the United States is a large market. Overall, U.S. tariff barriers are very low. Exporters from Japan, South Korea, Brazil, and even from Europe find it a lucrative market to expand in. Dumping provides an opportunity to exporters to undercut the price of U.S.-manufactured goods. Thus, in the past, many exporters have been charged with dumping, particularly the Japanese (for example, TV manufacturers and steelmakers). Responding to the steel industry's pleas, the Treasury Department set up the trigger price program in 1978. Minimum prices were established for different types of imported steel. Prices below the minimum prices would automatically initiate an investigation of possible dumping.

It is desirable, of course, to avoid making a pricing decision that might lead to a dumping charge. Consideration of dumping, however, raises an important question: Is it really bad? After all, cheap imports are generally a very good thing, and it is in the national interest to encourage competition. Few economic principles are better tested than the notion that every nation should specialize in what it can produce best, and then import other goods sold at costs lower than those it would take to produce them at home—just as within the United States, Michigan imports oranges and Florida imports coal.

Presumably, no one would oppose a decision by OPEC to dump oil in the United States at a price below U.S. cost of production, even though cheap OPEC oil would harm some domestic producers. International trade is always harmful in some way to those competing against the imports. But while some gain and others lose from the importation of cheap goods, the gains generally outweigh the losses.

Understandably, businesspersons focus on what they think they have lost, as the U.S. steel and U.S. automobile industries have. More than any other sector, steelmakers argue that foreign steel dumping threatens thousands of U.S. jobs as well as the industry's very existence. Although the industry has bounced back from its low point in the early 1980s, it still regards itself as endangered (see International Marketing Highlight 13.4).

There is a rule of thumb in economics that people who demand protection against *unfair* competition are generally seeking protection against *competition*. Industries that have sought protection against dumping have justified their claims with xenophobic accusations of predatory conspiracies designed to destroy U.S. industry and exploit the United States. The argument goes that dumping leads to increased dependence and vulnerability, and therefore, antidumping restric-

International Marketing Highlight 13.4

Anti-Dumping Duty: A Protectionist's Weapon

Protectionists in rich nations often use anti-dumping duties against firms that charge less for their products in export markets than they do at home, or that sell at prices below their costs. Such a pricing strategy is designed to gain market share at the expense of local competitors. Unfortunately, it is not easy to establish the dumping charge given the plethora of prices and products, the volatility of exchange rates, and the difficulty in assessing costs.

The point may be illustrated with reference to the East Asian exporters of acrylic sweaters to the United States during 1990. America's Knitwear and Sportswear Association complained that South Korea, Hong Kong, and Taiwan were dumping the sweaters in the U.S. market.

The U.S. government carefully examined the matter and South Korea was found not guilty. Hong Kong, however, had to pay an anti-dumping duty of 6 percent. However, Taiwan's producers were the worst hit, with 21 percent duty. Interestingly, all involved agree that Taiwanese firms are no more guilty or innocent of dumping than their counterparts in South Korea or Hong Kong. Being small and disorganized, however, they were severely hit.

South Korean firms got away because they are large and vertically integrated. Their cost and pricing systems were too complex to permit American textile companies to muster adequate evidence to establish their allegations.

Hong Kong firms, although smaller than Korea's, successfully defended themselves by hiring a well known New York law firm. For example, in one case they avoided a quota on two piece suits by sewing the tops and bottoms together and importing them as jumpsuits. In another case, they got around a quota on ski jackets by cutting off the sleeves and exporting them as vests (jerkins), whose quota had not been filled. Later on, the sleeves were reattached in America with zippers.

Source: The Economist, November 23, 1991, p. 72.

tions are demanded in the interest of national security and to eliminate the possibility of economic blackmail.

There very well may be cases where dumping is harmful. But since we cannot distinguish these cases from the multitude of cases of beneficial dumping, or from alleged dumping that is really only ordinary international trade, a dumping policy decision really amounts to the choice of the direction in which society is to err. Should it have a policy that restricts all dumping or take the risk of permitting some harmful dumping in order to get the benefits of freer trade?

Free Trade Versus Protectionism

To err in the direction of free trade has its costs, and these costs will be inequitably distributed by being concentrated in a few industries and their groups of workers. But to err in the opposite direction is even more costly. An expansion of antidumping laws risks an international trade war as countries retaliate by erecting new trade barriers of their own. Through such actions, U.S. inflation could accelerate and U.S. exporters could be wiped out. A trade war in the early 1930s was one reason why the depression was so severe. Ironically, one of the industries most vulnerable to such a trade war is steel, which, despite its woes, exports billions of dollars of steel products.

All international trade—fair or otherwise—inflicts costs on some Americans, costs that should be shared with, and offset by, other Americans. However, this sharing should be through adjustment assistance by which businesses and workers get help in moving out of less-efficient, declining industries that compete with imports and into more-efficient, expanding export industries. No matter how well disguised, protectionism is self-defeating.

Meeting the Import Challenge

Many businesses face competition from imports. Foreign goods are often sold at prices that seem so ridiculously low that they can only be explained as dumping. A company can consider several strategic options to protect its markets from imports and possibly develop new opportunities for its products. A company facing competition from imported goods should:

- Evaluate its underlying competitive position and that of foreign competitors.
- Assess whether it is feasible to drive the domestic value-added component down to the same level as that of the import.
- Look at import competition in the context of changes in world production and trade factors. Adopting this approach will help differentiate between the short- and long-run impact of imports.
- Clearly understand the impact of changes in either its own or the foreign competitor's value-added and raw-material components.
- Be aware that the basis for import competition will vary with the country of origin. European imports require a different response than Japanese imports, and these, in turn, will require still a different response than that for, say, Korean or Taiwanese imports.
- When there are fundamental differences in cost that cannot be eliminated, attempt to change the product. The domestic producer should ensure, however, that value-added additions to its products result in differences in real value in the marketplace and that the foreign producer cannot emulate them. If the foreign competitor can follow with relative ease, the foreign competitor's leverage is actually increased.
- Segment the market so that efforts are concentrated where competitive leverage is greatest. Attempting to match imports across a wide spectrum of products can often be disastrous. The domestic producer should be both thoughtful and explicit in the method of segmentation.
- Fully assess the impact of volume on value-added. If this is significant, and if reasonable changes in volume can be made, then this, combined with the ability to purchase raw material at internationally competitive prices, can

bring about significant changes in total cost. As a result, the domestic producer could possibly become competitive with imports. The remaining domestic producers may then face an abrupt change in their respective strategies for competing with domestic competitors as well as a need to change the strategy for competing with imports.[34]

Leasing

In domestic marketing, leasing serves as an important alternative to outright buying, especially in the area of industrial marketing. In recent years, however, leasing has emerged in international marketing as well. For example, several years ago TAW Company founded TAW International Leasing, Inc., to rent different types of heavy equipment, especially in Africa.[35] Similarly, Clark Equipment Company leases equipment overseas through its Clark Rental Corporation subsidiary.[36] As a matter of fact, leasing strategy is employed by essentially all capital goods and equipment manufacturers active in foreign markets.

A variety of conditions operating in foreign markets make leasing a viable pricing strategy to pursue. These conditions are capital shortage, availability of maintenance and servicing personnel, intermittent need, customer's unwillingness to make a long-term commitment, and the tax advantages of leasing. Capital shortage may make it difficult for customers to buy certain equipment. This is particularly true in the case of developing countries. Leasing, however, provides a way to procure use of the equipment. By the same token, leasing permits the international marketer an entry into the market, which otherwise might be closed because of capital shortage.

Further, many kinds of equipment require regular maintenance and servicing. Customers may shy away from buying equipment because they fear a lack of adequate servicing. Leasing, however, transfers the burden of servicing and maintenance onto the lessor and relieves the customer of the worry about servicing. In many situations, a customer may be unwilling to buy a product outright either out of concern about possible technological obsolescence or because its relevance for the business is unclear. In such cases, leasing provides a viable compromise. The customer can use the equipment without being stuck with it. As a matter of fact, in many leasing arrangements, the customer is given an option to buy the product at a specified price after having the opportunity to use it for some time. Finally, many countries offer investment incentives that are available for both outright purchase and leased equipment/plant. Where capital shortage becomes a hindrance to an outright purchase, the incentive still can be sought through leasing. To the U.S. marketer, leasing offers an additional advantage: the entire lease price or rental may be written off as an expense for income tax purposes. The marketer may even be willing to pass on a portion of this tax benefit to the overseas customer.

Advantages aside, leasing poses two problems. First, how should the leasing price be set? Second, what may a lessor do if the customer overseas abruptly calls the deal off? For example, in the United States, an attempt is usually made to recover the total cost of the leased equipment in about half its useful life. Thus, the leasing charge/rental during the second half of life would be strictly profit. However, the life of the equipment may be longer or shorter in a foreign setting depending on the intensity of use and the conditions under which the use takes place. Thus, the establishment of the useful life of the product might not be easy. Further, it would be difficult to compute the monetary value of risks involved in a long-term foreign transaction. Finally, the inclusion of foreign inflation factors in setting the lease price would pose problems too because computation of inflation rates and related forecasts are not reliable.

A still greater problem occurs when a foreign party backs out of a deal. For example, in 1974 the Zambian government canceled its contract with TAW to rent 330 tractors and 400 trailers. TAW had gone out of its way to manufacture the equipment custom-designed for heavy-duty usage on inferior roads at a time when U.S. business was good and parts were short. The Zambian government's decision created a big problem for TAW. How was it to dispose of the equipment?[37]

Despite the problems that leasing may pose, in the years to come leasing is likely to become more popular. In recent years, many governments have facilitated marketing overseas through leasing plans. For example, the French government tried to establish a market for its Concorde, the supersonic jetliner, through backing a leasing program.[38] Similarly, the U.S. Export-Import Bank provides guarantees on foreign leasing by U.S. companies. Such support helps companies venturing into new foreign markets through leasing.

Summary

Prices determine the total revenue and to a large extent the profitability of any business. Because of the crucial importance of pricing, top management often plays a significant role in making pricing decisions. Top management must decide the strategic significance of pricing in the marketing mix. For example, U.S. companies traditionally have competed overseas based on nonprice factors. Lately, however, more and more companies emphasize price competition. Further, top management's goals must determine the extent to which uniform versus differentiated prices are set worldwide. It is argued usually that dissimilar conditions in overseas markets favor differentiated prices. However, it is felt that standardized pricing increases overall corporate effectiveness. Finally, top management assigns the pricing responsibility either to headquarters or to subsidiaries, or jointly between them.

In making any pricing decision, the following factors deserve consideration: pricing objectives, cost, competition, the customer, and government regulations. In international marketing, these factors must be examined both at home and in the host country. Each factor, composed of a number of components, varies in each nation both in importance and in interaction.

Prices in overseas business are set by following either a cost approach or a market approach. The cost approach involves computing all relevant costs and adding a profit markup to determine the price. The market approach examines price setting from the customer's viewpoint. If the price that appears satisfactory to the potential customer does not meet the company's profit goal, either the business is given up or the price is increased. Thus, either approach brings a viable decision on price.

Export pricing is affected by three additional considerations: the price destination, the nature of the product, and the currency used in completing the transaction. Usually companies prepare separate price lists for different overseas markets. The price list contains a profit margin that makes it feasible to adjust the price following local market conditions, including competitive price, the government's export incentives in some countries, and the flexibility for competitive reduction of the price.

Price escalation is an important consideration in export retail pricing. The retail price of exports usually is much higher than the domestic retail price for the same good. This difference can be explained by the added costs associated with exports, such as transportation, customs duty, and distributor margin. To counteract the excessive escalation of export prices, a variety of strategic alternatives is available to management.

Price setting by multinational marketers in foreign markets essentially follows the procedure practiced in domestic markets. Internationally, however, a few additional factors become important. The price in various regions of the world should be kept relatively uniform to avoid competition for company units from unrelated dealers in the home market. Especially in developing countries, the ethics of pricing requires careful examination. Also price segmentation acquires more significance in foreign markets. Further, it may not always be desirable to pursue short-term pricing goals in foreign markets. Finally, governments outside the United States play a significant role in pricing.

An important topic in international marketing concerns pricing intracompany transfer of goods and services, that is, prices for goods and services exchanged within the corporate family. When transactions between units of the same enterprise take place across national frontiers and the units are subject to different environmental factors, such as customs duties, tax rates, and currency risks, adjustments in transfer prices can be used to advance various corporate goals and increase overall corporate profits. Since the transfer price has repercussions for both the home and host countries, many governments have designed rules to monitor such prices. In the United States, for example, the IRS requires setting transfer prices according to the arm's length principle, which more or less means arriving at the price based on competitive conditions.

The chapter ends with a discussion on dumping and leasing. Dumping refers to the practice of pricing exports at lower levels than the domestic price for the same goods. As dumping may adversely affect domestic industry, many nations have legislated antidumping laws. As an alternative to outright purchase, leasing is slowly emerging in importance in international marketing. While setting leasing prices presents difficulties for various reasons, it nevertheless provides a good entry into markets otherwise inaccessible because of capital shortage.

Review Questions

1. What role does corporate management play in price setting for international markets?
2. What arguments favor a strategy of differentiated pricing in international markets?
3. Under what circumstances may uniform prices make sense?
4. Briefly discuss various factors that affect the pricing decision internationally.
5. Differentiate between the cost and market approaches to pricing.
6. What is meant by price escalation? What strategic options are available to international marketers to counteract escalation in export prices?
7. Under what circumstances might dumping be useful to the people of the importing country? Explain.
8. What advantages does leasing offer in international markets?

Endnotes

1. Bill Saporito, "Why the Price Wars Never End," *Fortune,* March 23, 1992, p. 68. *Also see* Johny K. Johansson and Gary Erickson, "The Price-Quality Relationship and Trade Barriers," *International Marketing Review,* Autumn 1985, pp. 52–63.
2. Vern Terpstra, *American Marketing in the Common Market* (New York: Praeger, 1967), pp. 109–110.
3. J. J. Boddewyn, "American Marketing in the European Common Market, 1963–1973," in *Multinational Product Management* (Cambridge, MA: Marketing Science Institute, 1976), pp. VII-1–VII-25.
4. Robert D. Buzzell, "Can You Standardize Multinational Marketing?" *Harvard Business Review,* November–December 1968, p. 104.
5. Nathaniel H. Leff, "Multinational Corporate Pricing Strategy in the Developing Countries," *Journal of International Business Studies,* Fall 1975, p. 55.
6. Peter R. Kressler, "Is Uniform Pricing Desirable in Multinational Markets?" in Subhash C. Jain and Lewis R. Tucker, Jr., eds., *International Marketing: Managerial Perspectives* (Boston: CBI Publishing Company, Inc. 1979), p. 389.
7. J. J. Boddewyn, "American Marketing in the European Common Market, 1963–1973," in *Multinational Product Management* (Cambridge, MA: Marketing Science Institute, 1976), pp. VII-1–VII-25.
8. "Why Common Market Does Not Mean Common Prices," *Business International,* February 2, 1973, p. 47.
9. Stanley C. Hollander, *Multinational Retailing* (East Lansing, MI: Division of Research, School of Business Administration, Michigan State University, 1970), p. 169.
10. Ralph Z. Sorenson and Ulrich E. Wiechmann, "How Multinationals View Marketing Standardization," *Harvard Business Review,* May–June 1975, p. 42.
11. *See* Alan Roberts, "Setting Export Prices to Sell Competitively," *International Trade Forum,* July–September 1988, pp. 10–13, 30–31.
12. Raphael Elimelech, "Pricing for the Japanese Market," in Subhash C. Jain and Lewis R. Tucker, Jr., eds., *International Marketing: Managerial Perspectives,* 2nd ed. (Boston: Kent Publishing Co., 1986), pp. 285-297.
13. *See* Victor H. Frank, J., "Living with Price Control Abroad," *Harvard Business Review,* March–April 1984, pp. 137–142.
14. Donald S. Henley, "Evaluating International Product Line Performance: A Conceptual Approach," in *Multinational Product Man-*

agement (Cambridge, MA: Marketing Science Institute, 1976), pp. II-10–II-11.

15. James C. Baker and John K. Ryans, Jr., "Some Aspects of International Pricing: A Neglected Area of Management Policy," *Management Decisions,* Summer 1973, pp. 177–182. *Also see* "Factors that Influence Pricing Decisions, *International Management,* June 1981, p. 3.
16. Sharon V. Thach and Catherine N. Axinn, "Pricing and Financing Practices of Industrial Exporting Firms," *International Marketing Review,* vol. 8, no. 1 (1991), pp. 32–46.
17. *See* Damon Darlin, "Most U.S. Firms Seek Extra Profits in Japan, at the Expense of Sales," *The Wall Street Journal,* May 15, 1987, p. 1.
18. John U. Farley, James M. Hulbert, and David Weinstein, "Price Setting and Volume Planning by Two European Industrial Companies: A Case Study and Comparison of Decision Processes," *Journal of Marketing,* Winter 1980, p. 46. *Also see* Peter G. P. Walters, "A Framework for Export Pricing Decisions," *Journal of Global Marketing,* vol. 2, no. 3 (1989), pp. 95–111.
19. Vern Terpstra, *International Dimensions of Marketing* (Boston: Kent Publishing Company, 1982), p. 141. *Also see* Pamela Sherrid, "Learning the Tricks of the Japanese Trade," *Fortune,* November 20, 1978, p. 63.
20. Warren J. Keegan, *Multinational Marketing Management* 3rd ed. (Englewood Cliffs, NJ: Prentice-Hall, 1984), p. 511.
21. Carl McDaniel, Jr., *Marketing* (New York: Harper & Row, 1982), p. 739.
22. *See* Amanda Bennett, "Peking Is Finding It Difficult to Let Prices Float," *The Wall Street Journal,* February 22, 1985, p. 34.
23. Venkatakrishna V. Bellur, Radharao Chagauti, Rajeswarnrao Chagauti, and Saraswati P. Singh, "Strategic Adaptations to Price Controls: The Case of the Indian Drug Industry," *Journal of the Academy of Marketing Science,* Winter–Spring 1985, pp. 143–159.
24. Vern Terpstra, *International Dimensions of Marketing* (Boston: Kent Publishing Company, 1982), p. 151.
25. U.S. Department of Commerce. (Based on an ad hoc inquiry.)
26. Seung H. Kim and Stephen W. Miller, "Constituents of the International Transfer Pricing Decision," *Columbia Journal of World Business,* Spring 1979, p. 71. *Also see* Jane O'Burns, "Transfer Pricing Decisions in U.S. Multinational Corporations," *Journal of International Business Studies,* Fall 1980, pp. 23–39.
27. Jeffrey S. Arpan, "Multinational Firm Pricing in International Markets," *Sloan Management Review,* Winter 1973, pp. 1–9. *Also see Interdivisional Transfer Pricing,* Business Policy Study No. 122 (New York: National Industrial Conference Board, 1967).
28. Seung H. Kim and Stephen W. Miller, "Constituents of the International Transfer Pricing Decisions," *Columbia Journal of World Business,* Spring 1979, pp. 69–77.
29. Mohammad F. Al-Eryani, Pervaiz Alam, and Syed H. Akhter, "Transfer Pricing Determinants of U.S. Multinationals," *Journal of International Business Studies,* vol. 21, no. 3 (Third Quarter 1990), pp. 409–426.
30. A. Smallman, "Transfer Pricing and Its Misuse," *European Journal of Marketing,* vol. 13, no. 4 (1979), pp. 167–168.
31. Raymond Vernon, *Storm over the Multinationals: The Real Issues* (Cambridge, MA: Harvard University Press, 1977), p. 129.
32. Richard A. Musgrave and Peggy B. Musgrave, *Public Finance in Theory and Practice* (New York: McGraw-Hill, 1976), pp. 716–736.
33. James Greene, "Intercorporate Pricing Across National Frontiers," *The Conference Board Record,* October 1969, p. 44. *Also see* C. S. Jones, "Transfer Pricing and Its Misuse: Some Further Considerations," *European Journal of Marketing,* vol. 15, no. 7 (1981), pp. 51–53.
34. Ireland J. Stewart, "Meeting the Challenge of Import Competition," *Business,* May–June 1981, pp. 45–46.
35. "Zambia: The TAW Truck Deal Runs Out of Gas," *Business Week,* April 27, 1974, p. 56.
36. *Business Abroad,* May 13, 1980, p. 15.
37. "Zambia: The TAW Truck Deal Runs Out of Gas," *Business Week,* April 27, 1974, p. 56.
38. "Concord Leasing Plan to Facilitate Marketing Is Approved by France," *The Wall Street Journal,* August 17, 1973, p. 18.

CHAPTER • 14

International Channels of Distribution

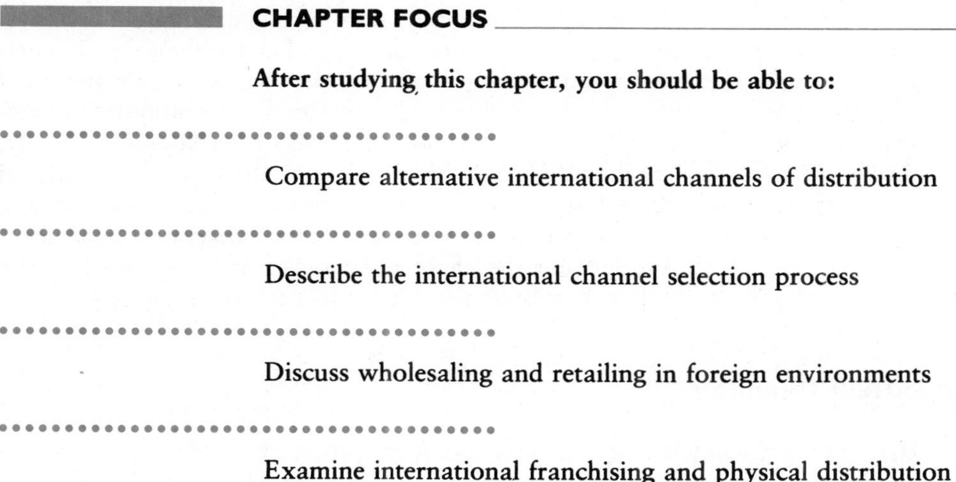

CHAPTER FOCUS

After studying this chapter, you should be able to:

- Compare alternative international channels of distribution
- Describe the international channel selection process
- Discuss wholesaling and retailing in foreign environments
- Examine international franchising and physical distribution

As for domestic marketing, the distribution process for international programs involves all those activities related to time, place, and ownership utilities for industrial and ultimate consumers. The selection, operation, and motivation of effective channels of distribution are often crucial factors in a firm's differential advantage in international markets. The diverse activities and culturally differentiated roles of channel intermediaries make the formulation of distribution strategies a challenge for any firm entering foreign markets.[1]

The channels of distribution available in a country are the result of culture and tradition. For example, in Japan there are usually too many channels involved in the distribution of a product. In the developing countries, channels of distribution are scattered, small in scope, inefficient, and insufficient. An international distribution system must be adapted to the country's established practices. Channel innovations ought to emerge from customer need rather than through an arbitrary attempt to streamline the distribution system.[2]

This chapter describes the alternative channels of distribution for an international marketer to consider. There are examples of different types of intermediaries, both domestic and foreign, for distribution across national boundaries. Guidelines are provided for selecting, motivating, and controlling the channels most appropriate for a firm's distribution mix. In addition, wholesale and retail patterns in overseas markets are examined. Also explored is the rationale of overseas franchising relationships along with their patterns of development. Finally, the perspectives of international physical distribution are discussed. International distribution, which requires special knowledge of complex rate structures and tariffs, presents many unique problems. These call for an adequate management information system. Throughout the chapter, examples are given to illustrate how to achieve an effective distribution system in international markets.

Alternative Distribution Channels

Distribution channels are the link between producers and customers. As Figure 14.1 shows, there are various ways of creating this link. Basically, an international marketer distributes either directly or indirectly. Direct distribution amounts to dealing with a foreign firm. The indirect method means dealing through another U.S. firm that serves as an intermediary. The choice of a particular channel link will be founded on considerations to be discussed in a later section of this chapter.

Channel Theory

It has long been held that the channels of distribution available in a country depend on its stage of economic development, which is reflected in the per capita real income and the sociopsychological, cultural, or anthropological environment. From this premise, it can be concluded that:

- The more-developed countries have more levels of distribution, more specialty stores and supermarkets, more department stores, and more stores in the rural areas.

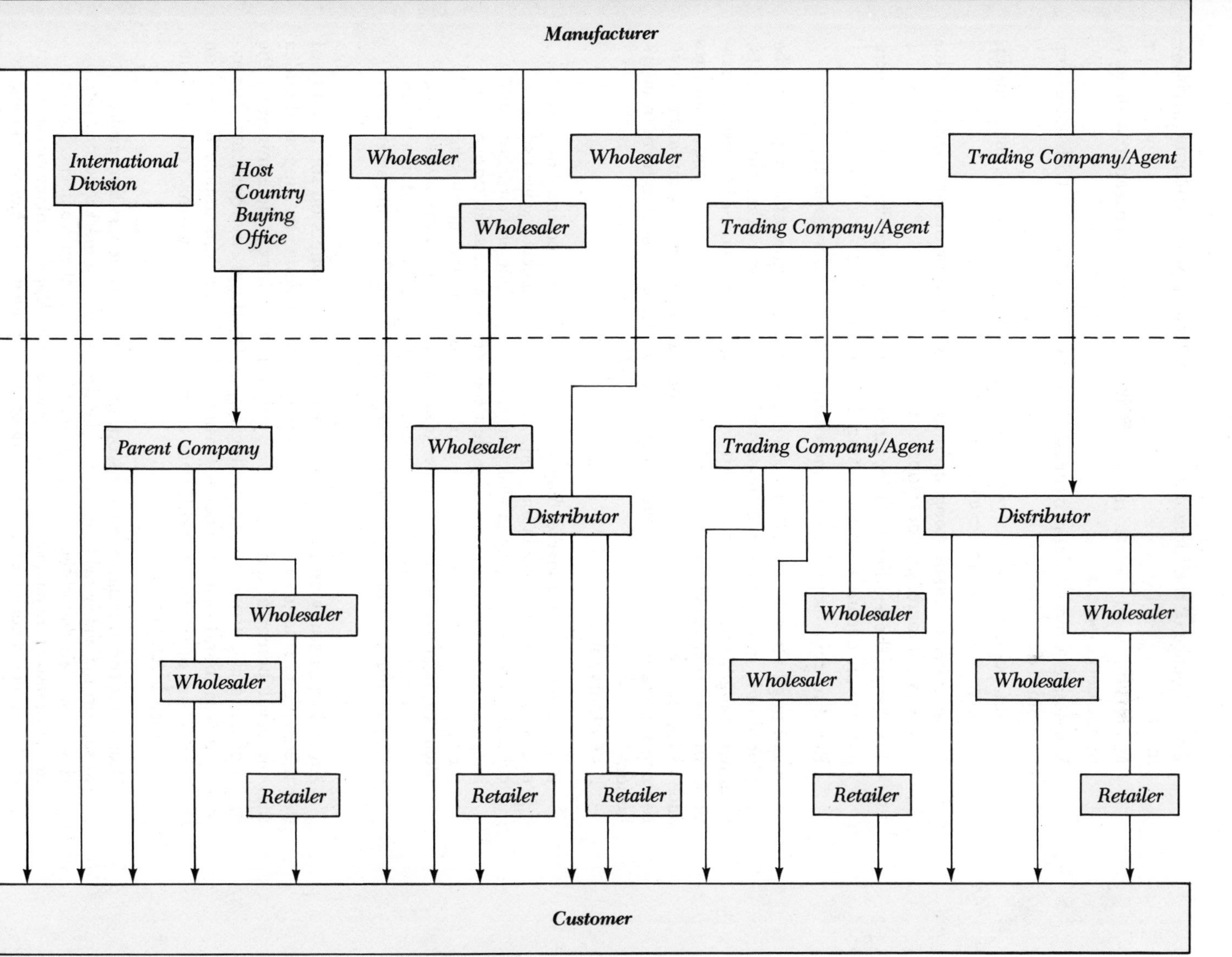

Note: Middle agents above the dotted line are U.S. based. Those below the dotted line are foreign channels.

FIGURE 14.1 Selected Channels of Distribution in International Marketing

- The influence of the foreign import agent declines with economic development.
- Manufacturer-wholesaler-retailer functions become separated with economic development.
- Wholesaler functions approximate those in North America with increasing economic development.
- The financing function of wholesalers declines and wholesale markups increase with increasing development.
- The number of small stores declines and the size of the average store increases with increasing development.
- The role of the peddler and itinerant trader and the importance of the open-garden-fair decline with increasing development.
- Retail margins improve with increasing economic development.[3]

According to this theory, changes in the channel structure of a country can be introduced only in response to changes in its economic and other environments. Channel changes cannot be enforced from without. At the cost of oversimplification, for example, supermarket distribution would not work in poor countries such as Egypt, Kenya, Sudan, and Pakistan because the economy and other environments operating in those countries are not conducive to such a form of distribution.[4]

As Goldman notes:

> It is difficult for a supermarket fully to utilize its cost saving potential in a situation where the supply system for produce and meats is highly fragmented, agricultural products are badly graded, supermarkets are not part of a vertically integrated system and in many cases must compete with the small store owners for supplies in the central wholesale market. In addition, the supermarket must often bear high overhead costs, suffer from antiquated municipal laws limiting hours and modes of operations, face major employee training and motivation problems and must pay disproportionately higher taxes than the small food stores.[5]

An empirical study on the subject, however, casts doubts on the viability of this theory. The results of the study showed little evidence to support the idea that the development of a distribution system in a country is determined by the limits of its social, economic, technological, and cultural environments. For example, it was found that channel structure and relationships mainly depend on the relative size of the firms at different channel stages, rather than on the country's level of development.

> Despite the comprehensiveness and scope of the survey there was little evidence to support the widely held theory that the development of marketing structure closely parallels that of the social, economic, and cultural environment. Except in certain respects in Japan and Ceylon, the level of development of the marketing environment did not appear to be an important determinant of the organizational or attitudinal characteristics of firms, or of channel structure and relationships.

> Nor were marketing structures of countries similar at comparable levels of development. In general, there was often a high degree of variation among firms within a country with regard to both firm characteristics and channel relationships.
>
> These results suggest that the influence of environmental factors on marketing structure may be considerably less important than is frequently postulated. In particular, the variation among firms within a country suggests that individual firms may respond in different ways and in varying degrees to environmental conditions. No consistent pattern of response emerged at the national level.
>
> Alternatively, the relationship between environmental factors and the marketing system may be more complex and indirect than that tested. The timing of technological conditions may be a crucial factor. For example, the introduction of advanced marketing technology from a highly industrialized nation to a developing country may distort the relationship between the level of development and marketing structure. The appropriate methodology would be a study of the evolution of marketing structures over time in various countries rather than a comparative survey of countries at different levels of development.[6]

Apparently, the relationship between a country's channel structure and its environment remains undefined. How else to explain the channels of distribution in a country is a matter of speculation. All that can be said, given the current state-of-the-art, is that distribution channels, like any other socioeconomic phenomenon, evolve slowly from a multitude of factors, some direct and some indirect. We do not quite know what these factors are, let alone their relationships.

Distribution Channels in Japan: An Example

Each country, rich or poor, has its own unique distribution system, evolved over time. International marketers must carefully examine the various aspects of a country's established distribution system to determine how to obtain distribution for their goods.

Despite the fact that Japan is the second economic power in the world today, its distribution system has been labeled outmoded, complex, cumbersome, and inefficient. The purpose of focusing this discussion on Japan is to emphasize that distribution structure is country-specific, and it would be naive for international marketers to enforce their own new distribution system on a country. Thus, distribution channels must be used as they are, and efforts should be made to fit into the country through the established patterns.

In general, the Japanese system encompasses a wide range of wholesalers and other agents, brokers, and retailers, differing more in number than in function from their American counterparts. There are myriad tiny retail shops. An even greater number of wholesalers supplies goods to them, layered tier upon tier, many more than most U.S. executives would think necessary.[7] For example, soap may move through three wholesalers plus a sales company after it leaves the manufacturer before it even reaches the retail outlet. A steak goes from rancher to consumer in a process that often involves a dozen middle agents. Furthermore, as Figure 14.2 shows, Japan's distribution channels have traditionally been segregated by product type, with the consequent development of many specialized marketing routes.

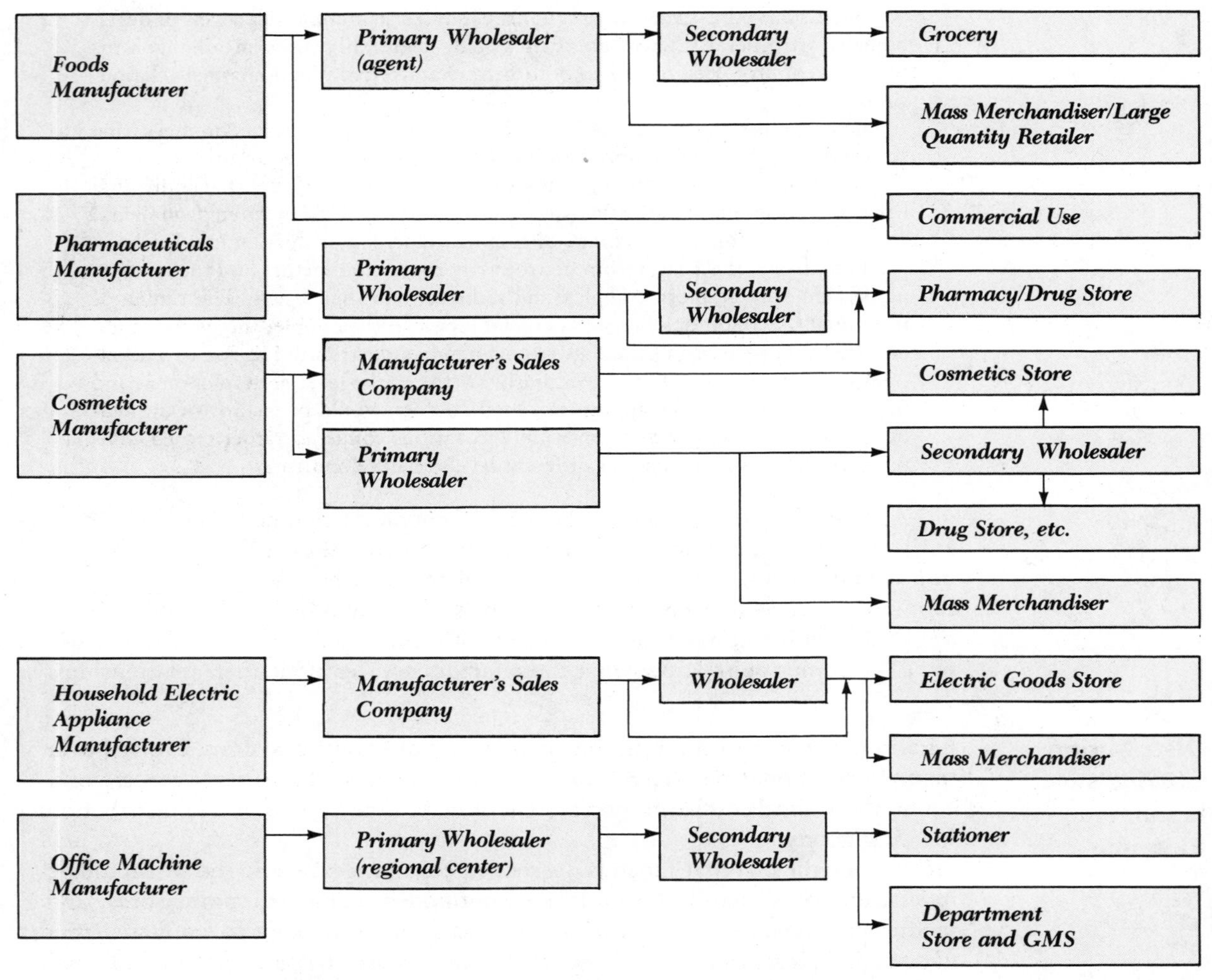

Source: Kaoru Kobayashi, "Marketing in Japan: Distribution Channels," *Tradepia International,* Winter 1980, p. 23.

FIGURE 14.2 Flowcharts of Selected Distribution Channels in Japan

The Japanese distribution system stems from the early seventeenth century when cottage industries and a burgeoning urban population spawned a merchant class. And despite Japan's economic achievements, the distribution system has remained remarkably faithful to its antique pattern. The system endures in part because most Japanese companies typically operate with little equity capital and much debt. Manufacturers supply goods to wholesalers in return for promissory notes ranging up to about six months; thus, while wholesalers can manage on a relatively small amount of capital, manufacturers can spread their risks by dealing with many wholesalers. In this way, the financial structure complements the distribution system.[8]

The distribution network also reflects other traditionally close ties among many Japanese companies. These ties go far beyond personal relationships. For example, Japanese wholesalers are usually willing to take back unsold goods from retailers; the large number of wholesalers enables them to spread this risk too. In addition, wholesalers often provide special rebates to retailers according to the stores' sales volume, and many small steelmakers get special financing from their own wholesalers when they expand production capacity.

The Japanese place much greater emphasis on the development of strong personal relationships with users in order to ensure a stable supply over a long period at a stable price. Their system fosters such relationships.[9] Businesses in the United States tend to rely on price competitiveness and product satisfaction to establish supply.

The Japanese distribution system is built into the fabric of its society. It is a sort of welfare system that provides a living for so many people that the government does not have to pay welfare. In this way, the seemingly inefficient distribution system serves an important social function: It has been a flexible make-work device, acting as a buffer to absorb excess workers, particularly those on the verge of retirement. Many observers expect this social role to increase as the current slowdown in Japan's economic growth shrinks employment in manufacturing.[10]

Another reason for the longevity of Japan's distribution system is that it serves most companies well. Some suppliers, for instance, keep their inventories at or near their customers' headquarters to ensure rapid deliveries. Foreign companies, of course, can't compete with such service unless they maintain substantial stockpiles and facilities in Japan.

Consumers also are served well. Lacking much storage space in their small homes, most Japanese homemakers shop several times a week and prefer convenient neighborhood shops. The little shops often strengthen their position by doing more for customers than just selling goods. In brief, Japanese distribution channels are more complex than comparable channels in the United States. But the dominant view in Japan is that the system suits the needs of Japanese consumers.[11] For example, while furniture stores in the United States may take up to ten weeks for delivery, Japanese consumers usually receive delivery within a week.

Moreover, statistics indicate that the distribution system is not likely to change soon.[12] According to government figures, the number of mom-and-pop retailers employing four or fewer workers increased almost 60 percent between 1975 and 1990 to 2 million outlets. During the same period, the number of similar-size wholesalers rose to more than 413,000 from about 250,000.[13] In 1986, the latest years for which complete figures are available, 5.9 million workers were employed in various wholesale operations and 8.8 million worked in retail outlets.[14] The papa-mama stores control 56 percent of Japan's retail sales (versus 3 percent for U.S. mom-and-pops and 5 percent in Europe).[15]

Japan has one retailer for every seventy-four people, compared with one for every 144 Americans. Similarly, Japan has one million bars and restaurants, more than three times as many per person as in the United States. More than half of these establishments are independent operators, so they need frequent deliveries in small quantities. Wholesalers of perishable foods make as many as three drop-offs a day. Campbell Japan Inc.'s typical delivery of soup to a retailer is minuscule by U.S. standards: six cans. Campbell's average shipment to wholesalers is three to five twenty-four-can cases. That and a 19 percent duty increase the price of a can of tomato soup in Tokyo to $1.45, compared with $.39 in New York.[16]

In conclusion, the way the Japanese distribution channels are structured and managed presents one of the major reasons for the failure of foreign firms to establish major market position in Japan.[17] Further, despite the fact that the Japanese channels have been held inefficient and cumbersome, they seem to serve the customer well (see International Marketing Highlight 14.1).

Although no crucial differences in the functions of distribution exist among the European nations, the United States, and Japan, nevertheless distribution is directly connected with the final consumer and is naturally affected by social, cultural, and historical conditions peculiar to each country.[18] The customs and practices in the distribution of products can differ substantially from one country to another, yet basically fulfill the same functions of channeling products from manufacturers to consumers.

International Channel Members

The previous section mentioned two forms of distribution: direct and indirect. Either way, a company may go through one or more agents or merchant intermediaries. The essential difference between them concerns the legal ownership of goods. In one method, an agent, without taking title to the goods, distributes them on behalf of the principal, the manufacturer. In the other method, merchant intermediaries do business in their own names and hold title to the goods they deal in. Figure 14.3 identifies important types of intermediaries. The type of intermediaries and their names vary from country to country and from industry to industry in the same country. For this reason, the discussion here is limited to certain intermediaries popularly used worldwide for distribution across industries.

Indirect Distribution Through Agents

Important among these types of agents are export management companies, manufacturers' export agents, cooperative exporters, Webb-Pomerene associations, foreign freight forwarders, commission agents, and country-controlled buying agents and trading companies. While these agents do not take title, they do take possession of goods. However, they have different duties in respect to continuation of relationship with the principal (long-term versus ad hoc); degree of control maintained by the principal (complete versus slight versus none); pricing authority accorded to the agent (full versus partial versus advisory); affiliation with buyer or seller; number of principals served at a time (few versus many); involvement or noninvolvement with shipping or handling of competitive lines; provision of promotional support (continuous versus one-time versus none); extension

International Marketing Highlight 14.1

Customer Service—The Japanese Way

My husband and I bought one souvenir the last time we were in Tokyo—a Sony compact disk player. The transaction took seven minutes at the Odakyu Department Store, including time to find the right department and to wait while the salesman filled out a second charge slip after misspelling my husband's name on the first.

My in-laws, who were our hosts in the outlying city of Sagamihara, were eager to see their son's purchase, so he opened the box for them the next morning. But when he tried to demonstrate the player, it wouldn't work. We peered inside. It had no innards! My husband used the time until the Odakyu would open at 10:00 to practice for the rare opportunity in that country to wax indignant. But at a minute to 10:00 he was prempted by the store ringing us.

My mother-in-law took the call and had to hold the receiver away from her ear against the barrage of Japanese honorifics. Odakyu's vice president was on his way over with a new disk player.

A taxi pulled up fifty minutes later and spilled out the vice president and a junior employee who was laden with packages and a clipboard. In the entrance hall the two men bowed vigorously.

The younger man was still bobbing as he read from a log that recorded the progress of their efforts to rectify their mistake, beginning at 4:32 P.M. the day before, when the salesclerk alerted the store's security guards to stop my husband at the door. When that didn't work, the clerk turned to his supervisor, who turned to his supervisor, until a SWAT team leading all the way to the vice president was in place to work on the only clues, a name and an American Express card number. Remembering that the customer had asked him about using the disk player in the U.S., the clerk called thirty-two hotels in and around Tokyo to ask if a Mr. Kitasei was registered. When that turned up nothing, the Odakyu commandeered a staff member to stay until 9 P.M. to call American Express headquarters in New York. American Express gave him our New York telephone number. It was after 11 P.M. when he reached my parents, who were staying at our apartment. My mother gave him my in-law's telephone number.

The younger man looked up from his clipboard and gave us, in addition to the new $280 disk player, a set of towels, a box of cakes, and a Chopin disk. Three minutes after this exhausted pair had arrived they were climbing back into the waiting cab. The vice president suddenly dashed back. He had forgotten to apologize for my husband having to wait while the salesman had rewritten the charge slip, but he hoped we understood that it had been the young man's first day.

My Tokyo experience contrasts sharply with treatment I've received at home. In late July, without explanation or apology from Bloomingdale's, a credit of $546.66 appeared on my American Express statement for china ordered January 12, paid for April 17, and never received.

Source: Hilary Hinds Kitasei, "Japan's Got Us Beat in the Service Department Too," *The Wall Street Journal,* July 30, 1985, p. 30.

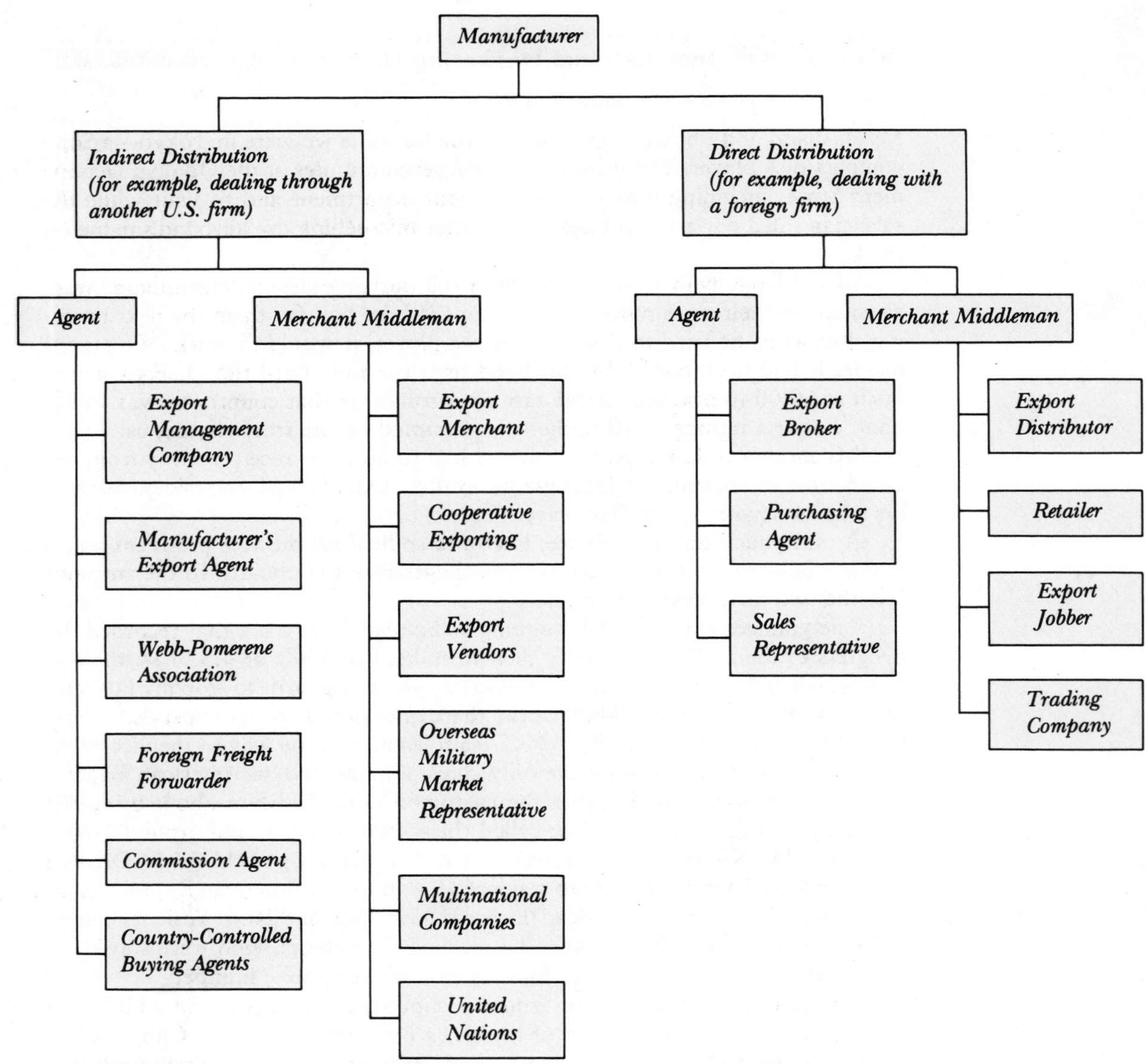

FIGURE 14.3 **Intermediaries in International Distribution**

of credit to principal (regularly versus occasionally versus rarely versus never); and provision of market information (good versus fair versus poor).[19]

Export Management Company (EMC) An export management company is an independent export organization that serves different companies in their export endeavors. The EMC regards the exporter as a client, not as an employer. The

EMC deals in a number of allied but noncompetitive lines. Usually, the EMC handles the entire export function for a manufacturer. In all contacts and communications overseas, the EMC operates under the client's name, using client stationery and promotional materials, such as catalogs.[20] EMCs differ in the scale of their operations. Some handle export sales for as few as four or five manufacturers; others serve as many as fifty companies. A typical firm represents ten manufacturers. EMCs are especially helpful to small companies that are unable to afford experienced and skilled export managers. EMCs understand foreign cultures. They are up-to-date on international politics, logistics, taxation, and legal problems. They provide a viable alternative for small firms to launch themselves in the export business.[21]

EMCs come in all sizes. The EMC provides a full range of services to manufacturers, relieving them of all the tasks involved in the process. The EMC obtains orders for its principals/clients by making contacts overseas and fills the orders, observing necessary formalities in packaging, documentation, and shipping.

An EMC may be just a one-person operation, or it may employ as many as a hundred people. Some firms are relatively new, while others have decades of experience. Large export management firms often maintain overseas offices in strategic locations. Senior executives of these firms frequently travel overseas to seek orders and develop relationships with the customers. Exhibit 14.1 outlines the major benefits of export management firms.

There are about 1,200 EMCs in the United States. Most are located in the larger seaport cities. The important sources for locating an EMC are the U.S. Department of Commerce, port authorities, and banks handling foreign trade. The National Federation of Export Management Companies, based in Washington, D.C., and local chambers of commerce are also good sources. An exporter should attempt to find an EMC that specializes in its product type, has in place a well-organized and controlled worldwide distribution system, is well-financed and managed, and is willing and eager to devote significant amounts of managerial effort and money to launching its product.

EMCs generate their income either from commissions or from discounts on goods they buy for resale overseas. The commission/discount varies from 10 percent or less to 30 percent or more, based on the services provided and the difficulty of the marketing task.

EMCs are used by both large and small companies, simply because they can undertake exporting more effectively and generally at a lower cost than other channels. Further, it is quite common for exporters to use multiple EMCs. A single EMC may not be able to reach all world markets. In addition, EMCs usually come to specialize by product. Thus, a company that deals in diverse products may use several EMCs.

Interestingly, EMCs usually do not take title, although some EMCs do accept title and credit risk and, in some cases, even physical possession.[22]

Manufacturer's Export Agent (MEA) Manufacturer's export agents provide services similar to those provided by the export management company with the exception that they cover limited markets. Further, the contractual relationship

EXHIBIT 14.1 Benefits of Export Management Companies

- *Credit assistance.* The EMC often does its own financing. It pays the manufacturer in dollars before the export order leaves the United States, relieving the client of any credit risk. Depending on the specific product category, the foreign buyer may need as much as 180 days' credit, or more. By providing the credit, the EMC helps bring buyer and seller together.
- *Licensing.* Import barriers, transportation charges, or local competition may make the effective promotion and sale of the manufacturer's goods impractical or impossible. The EMC will, when warranted by the sales potential of the market, frequently arrange for the local production of the manufacturer's products under either a joint venture or a royalty-yielding license arrangement with the U.S. manufacturer. Armed with knowledge of the market through continuing activities in it, the EMC normally supervises the implementation of such contracts and monitors performance on behalf of the U.S. manufacturer.
- *Demonstrations.* Some EMCs also arrange for overseas demonstrations and proper technical indoctrination of foreign users or representatives, by either the EMC's or the manufacturer's technical staff, depending on the nature of the products.
- *Shipping expenses.* The EMC saves its clients money by consolidating shipments. It can ship thousands of dollars worth of products from several principals to one overseas customer, consolidating the orders at the port and shipping them on one ocean bill of lading.
- *Specialization.* Because the EMC specializes in allied but noncompetitive products, it helps the sales of each individual line. Suppose, for example, that the EMC handles construction equipment. An overseas contractor asks for a price quotation on power shovels but also needs other earthmoving equipment. The EMC is in a position to offer trucks, trailers, pneumatic hammers, rotary drills, and related equipment from its various principals, benefiting all concerned, including the overseas customer who deals with a single source of supply.
- *Overseas travel.* Most EMCs consider overseas travel a normal function of their operations. However, some bill their clients for their routine overseas travel on a cost-share basis, depending on the number of manufacturers represented on the trip.

Source: The Export Management Company (Washington, D.C.: U.S. Dept. of Commerce, 1976), p. 28.

is short-term only, from a few months to a year or two. Sometimes the contract applies only to a particular transaction. The MEA acts under his or her own name and receives a commission for services. Thus, while an international marketer might deal with one export management company, he or she would be represented by several MEAs. Because the MEA does not serve the export department of the principal as an EMC does, he or she cannot be relied upon to perpetuate business for an export-minded company.

Webb-Pomerene Association A Webb-Pomerene association is formed among competing U.S. manufacturers, especially and exclusively for the purpose of exports according to the Webb-Pomerene Act of 1918. An agreement in the form of a Webb-Pomerene association is exempt from antitrust laws.

The members of a Webb-Pomerene association can engage in different international marketing activities to their mutual advantage. For example, they can set prices, combine shipments, jointly undertake marketing research or share information with each other, and allocate orders among different members of the association. It is estimated that there are currently over thirty active Webb-Pomerene associations.

Foreign Freight Forwarder Foreign freight forwarders specialize in handling overseas shipping arrangements. Their services can be utilized for handling goods from a U.S. port to the foreign port of entry. Occasionally, they may handle inland shipments also. A foreign freight forwarder receives a discount or fees from the shipping company. For extra services such as packing, they would be paid by the export manufacturer.

Commission Agent Commission agents represent foreign customers interested in buying U.S. products. They serve as so-called finders for their principals and locate the appropriate goods at the lowest price. The commission agents receive a commission for their services from their foreign clients.

Country-Controlled Buying Agent This type of agent is an official buyer of a foreign government, seeking to buy designated goods for his or her country. Many developing countries, for example, maintain supply missions in the United States with a number of officers who are entrusted with the task of procuring different goods for their countries.

American Trading Company (ATC) The ATC is a relatively new form of indirect channel that can be formed under the Export Trading Company Act of 1982 (also see Chapter 17). The goal of this act is to increase U.S. exports by encouraging more efficient provision of export trade services to producers and suppliers alike, by improving the availability of trade finance, and by removing the antitrust disincentive to export activities.[23] Before the Export Trading Company Act, U.S. firms were handicapped in forming trading companies because of the fear of antitrust prosecution and inadequate capitalization. Since the passage of this legislation, however, there has been an increasing interest among businesses of all sizes to form trading companies.

Although the act provides a legal basis for the development of ATCs, the shape of their operating characteristics (i.e., type of product exported, the export role adopted—agent or merchant—services provided, etc.) is left in the hands of private business. Because the whole concept of trading companies is new to the United States, it is too early to say what products they normally will handle, how they will be managed, and what services they will concentrate on. Thus far, agribusiness firms are taking more interest in trading companies than are any other types of business.[24]

Empirical research on the subject indicates that ATCs are likely to be more diversified both in handling products and in geographic coverage. In addition, unlike the EMCs, the ATCs have the potential to be much larger in size and operations. By the same token, decision making in ATCs should be diversified, since the membership would be shared by firms (e.g., banks, manufacturers, EMCs) with different backgrounds and cultures.[25]

Indirect Distribution Through Merchant Intermediaries

Merchant intermediaries located in the United States serve as middle agents for manufacturers in their export endeavors. Export merchants, other manufacturers, export vendors, overseas military market representatives, multinational companies, and the United Nations principally fill this role.

The merchant intermediaries invariably take title to the goods and deal in their own names. They may or may not undertake delivery of the goods, and the services they provide vary. Likewise, the authority exercised by these intermediaries differs. For example, the export merchant usually has pricing authority, but a cooperative exporter does not.

Export Merchant Export merchants buy directly from manufacturers according to their specifications, taking title to the goods. They have overseas contacts through which the goods are sold either to wholesalers or retailers. They assume all the risks and sell in their own names. Their compensation consists of a markup percentage that is based on market conditions. In general, an export merchant resembles a domestic wholesaler.

Cooperative Exporter Cooperative exporter is the name given to any company that has an established system of handling exports for its own goods and distributes products overseas for other manufacturers on a contractual basis. For example, Colgate-Palmolive Company has been distributing Wilkinson blades in many international markets.[26] Colgate also acts as a distributor for Pritt Glue Stick (a product of Henkel of Germany) and Alpen cereal produced by Wheetabix Company of England. Lately, Colgate and Kao Corporation of Japan have formed a joint venture to manufacture toiletry products in the United States. The products of this venture would be distributed worldwide through the former's distribution network.[27] Similarly, Sony Corporation serves as a distributor in Japan for different U.S. and European companies. Through its Sony International Housewares, Sony distributes for such companies as Whirlpool, Regalware, and Heath Company.[28] Kao Corporation of Japan, a diversified chemical and detergent company, markets Dow Chemical Co.'s corrosion-resistant vinyl ester resin, a type of fiberglass-reinforced plastic used in industry.[29] Whirlpool used Sony in Japan, Perrier marketed the Swiss chocolate Lindt in the United States, Breck Shampoo used Schick in Germany, and Champion Spark Plug used a Nanjing spark plug manufacturer to distribute its products in China.[30]

These cooperative arrangements are also called *piggybacking*. The cooperative exporter may assume the role of an EMC or may just serve as a commission agent for a short period in select markets. The principal asset of cooperative exporters is their experience in dealing overseas as manufacturers themselves. Therefore, they are more aware of and sympathetic toward the problems of the manufacturer interested in developing export markets.

Export Vendor Export vendors are companies that specialize in buying poor-quality and overproduced goods for distribution overseas. The companies buy goods outright, taking title to them. They ship the goods to one or more countries and sell them through their established contacts. Such intermediaries are useful in times of depressed business conditions in the United States and/or when a company for some reason gets stuck with certain unwanted products. For example, many small U.S. manufacturers used such intermediaries to get rid of goods they produced for the 1980 Olympic Games in Moscow. Since the U.S. did not participate in the games, these goods could not be sold in a normal way.

Overseas Military Market Representatives These are representatives who specialize in selling to U.S. military post exchanges (PXs) and commissaries. More than $3 billion annually in consumer goods, not all of them made in the United States, is sold by U.S. military PXs and commissaries overseas. The bulk of this market is made up of the joint Army-Air Force PX system. PX managers abroad decide what to buy. Commissary managers are restricted by a "brand name contracts" list but still have considerable discretion. All PX and commissary orders are placed through central headquarters in the United States.

The PX and commissary system primarily serves young consumers, among whom ethnic products are popular. Usually, these products are purchased in bulk at top discounts. These representatives generally work for a commission but on occasion will buy on their own for resale. Some representatives handle all types of consumer products; others are specialized.

Multinational Companies Some 5,000 U.S. companies, through overseas subsidiaries, have overseas operations including factories, branch and regional offices, and in some countries elaborate residential compounds for American personnel. (American compounds with more than 1,000 residents are not unusual in the Middle East.)

Not all of these companies are committed to buy products from the U.S. Usually they do, however, for three important reasons: (1) their staff is familiar with products from the U.S.; (2) purchasing of major items can be done in the home office; (3) it is cheaper to consolidate purchasing and buy the same brand for all subsidiaries.

The multinational company market generates massive demand for plant machinery, supplies, testing equipment, vehicles, spare parts, process control systems, training equipment, computer systems, appliances, office machines, furniture, and other goods. Residents of the compounds require all types of household appliances, fixtures, foods and other consumables, educational equipment and materials, and entertainment and leisure products.

United Nations The UN's purchasing is spread out among a number of agencies. Some have headquarters in the United States, others in Europe. Any member nation can compete for this business. Each agency is specialized.

The UN agencies themselves do not purchase goods in the same quantities as do projects financed by organizations such as the World Bank. The UN agencies often act as advisors rather than actual buyers.

A good example is UNESCO (the United Nations Educational, Scientific, and Cultural Organization). A $50 million educational development project in Zaire, for instance, may be jointly financed by the government of Zaire, the African Development Bank, and the World Bank, but designed (including product specifications) by UNESCO advisors. Purchasing and contracting will be done by the Ministry of Education of Zaire, probably with advice from the same UNESCO team who helped write the specifications.

Other UN agencies operate in much the same manner. A notable exception is UNICEF (the United Nations Children's Fund). UNICEF maintains in Copenhagen a large warehouse with substantial stocks of basic equipment and teaching aids for primary schools in developing countries. UNICEF ships from Copenhagen and issues replacement orders as stocks are depleted.

In the United States all UNICEF buying is done through the UN's New York headquarters. To qualify as a vendor one must submit catalogs and specifications, and sometimes samples for evaluation. UNICEF has very strict requirements governing the types of products included on its basic list and carried in its regular inventory.

Direct Distribution Through Agents

A company may deal with different types of agent intermediaries overseas. These agents do not take title to the goods and usually work for a commission. The product involved, and the way it is marketed in the United States, will provide a clue as to who might be employed to undertake overseas distribution—sales representatives, purchasing agents, or export brokers.

Sales Representative These agents resemble a manufacturer's representative in the United States. A manufacturer supplies the sales representatives with literature and samples to conduct sales in a predesignated territory. These representatives usually work on a commission basis, assume no risk or responsibility, and are under contract for a definite period. They may operate on either an exclusive or nonexclusive basis, and they do not handle competing lines. They serve as a good source of market information.

Purchasing Agent These agents are also referred to as buyers for export, export commission houses, or export confirming houses. They are active in U.S. markets, seeking goods of interest to their foreign principals. Their product quality and price demands stem from the requirements of the principals.

Usually, foreign purchasing agents represent governments or big contractors, either for a specified time or for a particular task. In any event, they do not provide continual service and stable volume to vendors. For example, a foreign government might authorize a purchasing agent to buy designated goods in the United States for the completion of a large mill or plant. Once the mill or plant is constructed, the purchasing agent ceases to be active.

Purchasing agents receive commissions from their principals. A transaction with a purchasing agent is completed, as in domestic marketing, with the agent handling all packing and shipping details. A purchasing agent may represent several principals requiring the same goods and may deal with different competing vendors.

Export Broker An export broker brings the foreign buyer and U.S. seller together. Usually, export brokers receive a commission or fee from the seller for their services. They take neither title nor possession of goods and assume no financial responsibility relative to the export transaction. Export brokers generally are used in the export of commodities such as grain and cotton. Only rarely is the export broker involved in the export of manufactured goods.

Direct Distribution Through Merchant Intermediaries

The foreign merchant intermediaries take title to the goods and sell them under their own names. They may or may not take possession of the goods. They render services similar to a domestic wholesaler. Major types of foreign merchant intermediaries are export distributors, foreign retailers, export jobbers, and trading companies.

Export Distributor The export distributors purchase goods from a U.S. manufacturer at the greatest possible discount and resell them for a profit. They are especially active in distributing products that require periodic servicing. They commit themselves to provide adequate service to the customers through carrying a sufficient quantity of spares and parts, maintaining facilities, and providing technicians to perform all normal servicing operations.

Export distributors buy in their own names and usually maintain an ongoing relationship with the exporter. Export distributors have exclusive sales rights in a country or region and receive easy payment terms from exporters.

Foreign Retailer In some cases U.S. manufacturers deal directly with foreign retailers, particularly in the case of consumer goods. For example, Campbell Soup Co. sells its Pepperidge Farm Cookies in Japan by directly dealing with a 3,300-store 7-Eleven chain throughout Japan.[31] The contact may be made either through a traveling salesperson or by mail using catalogs or brochures. In many countries, large retailers perform a dual role. While they sell directly to consumers through their own outlets, they also distribute imported goods to smaller retailers. Thus, exports handled by the retailer may receive wide coverage.

Export Jobber Export jobbers determine customer needs overseas and fill them by making purchases in the United States. Some jobbers reverse the process, filling needs of U.S. customers by supplying imported products. The jobbers mainly deal in staples, openly traded products for which brand names have little importance.

Trading Company In modern times the so-called trading companies usually are associated with Japan. Actually, the concept of the trading company is much older.[32] During colonial times many European countries, particularly Britain and France, used trading companies to develop trade with other nations. For example, the East India Company was England's major means to enter India. Similarly, the French trading companies Cie Française de l'Afrique Occidentale and Ste Commerciale de l'Ouest Africain were active in Africa.[33]

In Japan, the trading company originated as a commodity dealer that outgrew its wholesale functions. When the country was opened to the West, the trading company primarily served as a buffer between Japanese merchants and foreign businesses. Then Japan began to industrialize. Having neither raw materials at home nor an empire to exploit, the new industry needed imports. Rather than depend on foreigners, they adapted their trading companies to the task of acquiring the raw materials in addition to moving Japanese goods overseas.

Japanese trading companies have been very successful in promoting Japan's exports. They offer a broad range of services, from marketing research to financing, and present a relatively inexpensive way for the small or medium-size firm to do international marketing.

Some major functions of trading companies include trading and distributing, risk-hedging in exchange rates and commodity price fluctuation, domestic and overseas marketing of exported and imported technology, management consulting, participation in manufacturing, joint ventures abroad in resource developments and urban and rural development, and organizing new industries. The only functions that trading companies do not perform are production and retailing, but they may become involved even in these activities through joint ventures.[34]

There are approximately 7,000 trading companies in Japan today, but only about 300 of them are engaged in foreign trade. The six largest trading companies in Japan, referred to as the Big Six, are Mitsubishi Corporation, C. Itoh & Company, Nissho-Iwai Company, Sumitomo Shoji, Marubeni Corporation, and Mitsui & Company. They had combined sales of over $375 billion in 1986.[35] They are responsible for bringing in about 68 percent of Japan's imports and shipping out about 44 percent of its exports. These six companies have over 500 offices outside Japan, employing over 15,000 people.[36]

The big trading companies control 56 percent of Japan's foreign trade. Together, they are the main exporters of almost every product (except cars and electrical appliances) that is exported directly by manufacturers. Japanese trading companies have expert knowledge about the lures most attractive to distributors of Japanese exports in all major foreign countries. By contrast, foreign exporters cannot compete so easily in Japan, because they will usually have to sell through a trading company that is part of a Japanese group probably making a competing product.[37]

In addition to privately controlled trading companies such as those in Japan, many countries have state-controlled trading companies. Such companies are active in countries like those in Eastern Europe where business is conducted by a few government-sanctioned and -controlled trading outfits. (Currently, attempts are in progress, especially in Poland and Czechoslovakia, to privatize their trading companies.) In many countries the state-controlled trading companies may be the only means of doing business. In many other nations, however, trading companies bridge the gap between Western business style and local cultural practices for conducting business.

Dealing with Intermediaries

After an exporter successfully locates prospective intermediaries, terms of agreement must be defined between them. A written agreement often avoids later disputes and misunderstandings. However, some companies have a simple agreement, leaving details to be settled when and as question arise. As long as the intent of both parties is good, it is feasible to work without spelling out every detail in a written document. Yet it is still considered a better alternative to prepare a written contract after the manufacturer has investigated the channel member's overall integrity, financial soundness, community standing, share of the market, and other product lines carried. Exhibit 14.2 shows the items included in a typical agreement.

In addition to the items shown in the sample agreement, it is desirable to specify that the intermediary will not deal in competing lines, disclose confidential information, or make agreements that bind the exporting firm in any way. Further, the place and time for the title to the merchandise to pass from the seller to the buyer should be clearly stated because of tax implications in the countries of both the exporter and the intermediary. Finally, the contract should avoid articles that directly or indirectly conflict with U.S. antitrust laws.

Company-Owned Distribution

An alternative way for a company to arrange for distribution in other countries is to establish its own distribution instead of going through intermediaries. An exporter may choose this alternative for three reasons: to enhance coverage with the objective of increasing sales, to maintain complete control over foreign distribution, and to seek distribution when channels are unavailable.

Foreign company-owned channels not only take a long time to establish, but also may not always provide the desired sales results. Difficulties are likely to occur, especially when a change is made in channel arrangements. For example, if an exporter drops existing channels in favor of company-owned distribution, it will face tough competition from them. Further, in many countries it may not be easy to find qualified individuals to serve as salespersons. As a matter of fact in many nations, Japan for example, a company may face insurmountable problems in seeking distribution of its own. Occasionally, a joint venture with a host

EXHIBIT 14.2 Items to Include in an Agreement with Foreign Intermediaries

- Names and addresses of both parties
- Date when the agreement goes into effect
- Duration of the agreement
- Provisions for extending or terminating the agreement
- Description of product lines included
- Definition of sales territory
- Establishment of discount and/or commission schedules and determination of when and how paid
- Provisions for revising the commission or discount schedules
- Establishment of a policy governing resale prices
- Maintenance of appropriate service facilities
- Restrictions to prohibit the manufacture and sale of similar and competitive products
- Designation of responsibility for patent and trademark negotiations and/or pricing
- The assignability or nonassignability of the agreement and any limiting factors
- Designation of the country (not necessarily the United States) and state (if applicable) of contract jurisdiction in the case of dispute

Source: A Basic Guide to Exporting, a publication of the United States Department of Commerce (Washington, D.C.: U.S. Government Printing Office, 1981), p. 66.

country business is preferable to a strictly company-owned distribution. The host country business may already have a distribution set-up. The joint venture route provides the exporter an opportunity to enhance control and market coverage without the problems of building channels from scratch.

Channel Management

Channel management covers selecting appropriate channels of distribution and making them work. The selection process requires decisions on distribution structure and choice of specific channel members. Once the selection is made, the goal is to make the channel arrangements work adequately. This requires maintaining cordial relationships and minimizing conflicts.

Channel Selection

The channel selection process in international marketing is similar to the one for a domestic situation. Usually, the selection process involves establishing channel objectives and feasible channel alternatives, evaluation of alternatives, and the choice of appropriate channels.

Establishing Objectives The objectives of an international channel of distribution derive from total marketing objectives in the foreign market. Channel objectives are concerned with a clear-cut definition of the target customers. Implicit in the definition of target customers is the decision about whether the company wants intensive, selective, or exclusive distribution. Intensive distribution is an attempt to reach the mass market, and it requires a broad-based channel structure. Selective distribution is letting a designated channel undertake distribution on a monopoly basis.

Objectives should not only designate the target customers, but also specify the type of service to be rendered to each group of customers. For example, the acceptable time lag between the receipt of an order and delivery of goods should be clearly defined. Similarly, an original equipment manufacturer should state not only the types of services the company intends to make available but also with what frequency.

Establishing Feasible Channel Alternatives The characteristics of customers, product, intermediaries, competitors, marketing environment, and company's strengths and weaknesses determine the various possible alternatives for the distribution of a line of products.[38] If the number of customers is large and/or geographically widespread rather than concentrated, and if they make their purchases in smaller quantities at frequent intervals, the company will have to opt for intensive distribution, that is, a large number of channel outlets. Another factor to be considered here is the desire of the customer to deal with a particular type of channel. For example, the customer in a country may dislike the idea of buying groceries from large supermarkets. In other words, a customer's susceptibility to different selling methods is an important factor to be considered.

A variety of product characteristics have an effect on the selection of channels of distribution. Perishable goods require direct channels. Bulky but inexpensive products can use long channels. Shorter channels are employed when the unit value of a product is high, as in the case of computers, and/or when the product has to be custom-made, like air-conditioning equipment for a large building. Proximity to the customer helps in cutting down costs as well as in rendering good service. Also, products requiring installation and regular maintenance would call for shorter channels of distribution. Most capital equipment falls into this category.

The kinds of channels available constrain channel selection. The company should consider the terms demanded by different channel constituents and evaluate them in comparison with services and benefits provided including factors such as channel location, credit granted, quality of the sales force, warehousing facilities, reputation in the market, outlay on advertising, and overall experience. Consideration must also be given to the demands of the intermediaries from the company (i.e., what the channels expect from suppliers in such matters as decision-making authority, services, and financial assistance). Depending on other factors such as customer and product characteristics, the company will choose those channels that make the maximum impact in the market at minimum cost.

Host country trade practices concerning the distribution of a particular product is another influential variable. For example, innovations may not be easily accepted in all countries. Even today many Swiss homemakers prefer buying groceries from mom-and-pop-type outlets.

The environment of the host country constitutes another variable to weigh in making a channel selection decision. For example, the economic structure affects the suitability of a particular channel. In free economies, it is common practice to use private agents/distributors who buy and resell at a markup. Most agents/distributors function as parts of local companies that deal in a large number of product lines ranging from candy to sophisticated machine tools. In state-controlled markets, like those of Iraq, Burma, South Yemen, and Syria, international marketers must do business with state-owned trading companies operating on very low margins that cover physical distribution costs but usually no other necessary marketing activities. In such countries, international marketers often retain the services of private agencies to promote their products to the final consumers.[39] Poor economic conditions may not justify committing the company to excessive fixed costs, and thus distribution through wholesalers may be deemed the best alternative. A depressed economy may also demand cutting down on nonessential services.

Further, cultural conditions might militate against the utilization of a particular type of channel. Consider the factors implicit in the following comment:

> Furthermore, the British housewife is not yet freely attuned to the informal aspects of typical supermarket shopping. She likes the modern convenience of the supermarkets but still expects the social relationships, which are traditional among shopkeepers and their customers. As a means to that end, some have scheduled staple buying: fats and oils on Monday: flour and sugar on Tuesday; and so on. That tends to formalize the daily shopping social. Thus, executives of U.S. food manufacturers doing business in the United Kingdom must realize that British culture assigns a role to the supermarkets that differs from the role

in the United States. Successful channel management must take that role into account through the strategies used.[40]

The final factor in evaluating channel alternatives is the company's own strengths and weaknesses in the overseas market. A well-known company of long standing in the market will tap channels more easily than the new entrant. A financially strong company need not necessarily opt for channels that absorb a part of the distribution costs of inventory, transportation, advertising, and/or training. Similarly, a company with a large number of products for the same market could deal directly with the customers.

All these factors serve as a basis for determining the feasible alternative channels of distribution. Generally, the company would have three channel alternatives: selling direct to the customers, selling through intermediaries based in the United States, and selling through foreign distributors. In practice, however, channels in international marketing can be a labyrinth of complicated relationships. For example, the company might sell directly in some countries while employing U.S.-based distributors in another country and utilizing overseas distributors in still other cases.

Evaluation of Alternative Channels Each channel alternative should be evaluated on the basis of three factors: coverage, control, and cost. Coverage refers to both qualitative and quantitative coverage of customers and is determined by an analysis of customers, including such factors as their geographic locations, sales potential, and service requirements. Usually, customers are grouped into homogeneous categories. Each channel alternative can then be evaluated for different customer segments according to geographic coverage, coverage of big accounts, meeting the needs of different segments, and the like. If deemed necessary, different weights can be assigned to these factors. Often, it will be found that no one channel provides optimum coverage for each segment. Thus, to cater to different segments, the company may be obliged to choose more than one channel.[41]

Control refers to the discretion that the company has, or wants to have, in seeing the goods through to the customers. Dealing with some intermediate agents leaves the company in better control of various activities such as establishing prices, recommending cooperative advertising, and suggesting inventory level. On the other hand, some intermediaries will demand flexibility in pricing, the right to refuse to enter into cooperative advertising, freedom in deciding how much inventory they would like to carry, and so forth. In brief, going through the agent/distributor necessitates sharing control. If a company wants complete control, it must develop company-owned distribution. Direct distribution, however, requires patience and ingenuity (see International Marketing Highlight 14.2).

A third factor in evaluating channel alternatives is cost. Direct distribution by the company is usually more costly if the sales base is small, but it gives the company full control over distribution. In the final analysis, a balance has to be struck between cost, coverage, and control. No one factor can be considered in isolation. Probably a composite index should be utilized to measure each channel.

International Marketing Highlight 14.2

"Boutique" Marketing System

Fieldcrest Mills' bed and bath division decided in 1976 to export its "boutique" marketing system to Western Europe and Japan. "It seemed an obvious thing to do," the president explains. "Department stores in those countries were decades behind the United States. They still looked on towels and sheets as mundane products with no fashion pizzazz whatever. And just like our stores decades ago, they were selling unattractive products at virtually no profit, sort of like a public service to customers."

The firm embarked on a campaign to convince department stores in Europe and Japan that they could, like their U.S. counterparts, make money by selling high-fashion (that is, high markup) towels and sheets. At first there was considerable resistance to Fieldcrest's selling efforts. The owner of a Stuttgart department store flatly rejected the offer of a written guarantee that installation of a Fieldcrest boutique would double the profits generated on that floor space within two years.

But Fieldcrest eventually succeeded in convincing a number of overseas department stores to take a fling. Stores in Hamburg, Munich, London, and Tokyo agreed to install boutiques in especially favorable locations—usually on the main floor near the cosmetics counters, where customer traffic is heavy. Fieldcrest provided the design and even the lighting systems at its own cost. Foreign consumers are now developing a taste for those fashionable U.S. bed and bath products. At London's famed Harrods, the Fieldcrest boutique has become one of the most successful profit centers. As a result of its boutique concept, Fieldcrest's exports jumped in 1980 by a most respectable 58 percent.

Source: Herbert E. Meyer, "How U.S. Textiles Got to Be Winners in the Export Game," *Fortune,* May 5, 1980, p. 261.

The channel with optimum coverage and control at minimum cost would be the obvious choice.

Choosing the Channels After alternative channels have been evaluated, the one most appropriate to the stated objective should be chosen. In practice, however, it may be difficult to state the objective in concrete terms for clear matching with each alternative. Thus, subjective judgment becomes important in the final decision. Management should not only consider the implications of the short run, but also allow sufficient flexibility to meet changing requirements. Sometimes a channel is chosen as a stopgap arrangement that will allow for a new alternative in the future.

Pros and Cons of the Use of Intermediaries

Independent intermediaries play a significant role in the total global marketing effort of many companies. Although even some large companies use intermediaries for seeking distribution in smaller foreign markets or for distribution of certain product lines in larger markets, the distribution through intermediaries is especially important for smaller companies, which generally do not have the scale of operations, financial resources, or experience to operate more directly in foreign markets.

The popularity of this mode of distribution has been attributed to the many advantages that intermediaries provide in foreign markets. A distributor brings immediate new assets to the multinational marketer by providing local market know-how, knowledge, and contacts with little expenditure on the part of the exporter.[42] In the case of selling computers in the Middle East, one writer notes:

> Although you know more about the product, inevitably the local guy will know more about the market. And make no mistake—market knowledge is more important than product knowledge in getting sales in the Middle East.[43]

Further, the overseas distributor adds to the effective capital available for a company's worldwide marketing efforts, because distributors have funds of their own, as well as local borrowing power that a firm located in another country may not have. Further, intermediaries afford an opportunity for the stocking and sale of a company's product in a new market at negligible cost. The cost of a company-owned local operation, involving support staff, office space and equipment, overhead, and the like is worthwhile only when a certain volume of business and a certain operating margin are achieved. A distributor may be able to do a good job with a smaller volume by spreading his costs among many lines of products.

The point can be illustrated with this example. A chemical company charges its distributors of textile fibers F.A.S. price less 3 percent. That 3 percent would never cover the costs of maintaining a sales force, local travel expenses, or overhead. But the distributor handles other noncompetitive products—such as textiles machinery—with larger margins. The irregularity of this machinery business is balanced by the steadiness of the fiber sales. Spreading the costs makes it possible for the distributor to carry economically and profitably both lines of goods where neither might be viable separately (see International Marketing Highlight 14.3).

On the other hand, there are some serious disadvantages to using independent distributors. First, the manufacturer has less direct control over an independent distributor than over his or her own employees. Second, there is a risk of violation of U.S. or Common Market antitrust laws when a distributor is being directed, particularly in the area of pricing. Third, the manufacturer may have little contact with, or knowledge of, the retail outlets used by the distributor. Fourth, the manufacturer has little or no control over the marketing, sales techniques, and credit policies of the distributor. Finally, in some cases, it may be very difficult and costly for the manufacturer to cancel an agreement.

Briefly, then, a company should use distributors in markets where sales volume would not justify its own distribution or when it does not have the staff and know-how to set up its own operations. A firm may or may not change a satisfactory distributor arrangement when local volume could pay the costs of a company's own operation. In some markets, such a volume may never be reached, but in others when it is reached, the distributor relationship is retained for any

International Marketing Highlight 14.3

Schick Versus Gillette in Japan

In Japan, a product's success often depends on how widespread the distribution network is. And that is a classic strength of Schick. After entering the market along with Gillette and other foreign makers in 1962, when Japan liberalized the razor market, Schick decided to leave distribution to Seiko Corp. Seiko imports Schick razors from the United States and now sells them to 150,000 wholesalers nationwide.

Gillette, meanwhile, flopped when it tried to crack the market on its own and never caught up with Schick. Instead of going through a sole Japanese agent like Seiko, Gillette mainly tried to sell razors through its own salespeople, a strategy that failed because Gillette didn't have the distribution network available to Japanese companies—which was crucial. Now Gillette is making another try on its own. It has doubled salespeople in Japan to forty, and for the first time held lavish parties last year for wholesalers.

Source: The Wall Street Journal, February 4, 1991, p. B1.

of a host of reasons. Alternatively, the company may acquire or just continue to use the distributor as an adjunct to its own operations in the market.[44]

Selection of Intermediaries

Finding reliable distributors is a major challenge for firms entering markets in other countries. There are a number of potential sources of overseas distributors ranging from local trade and banking houses to chambers of commerce, officials of foreign embassies in the United States, and various state and the U.S. departments of commerce. Of all of these, the U.S. Department of Commerce provides the most thorough information. It offers several aids to assist U.S. exporters, which are described in Chapter 17. There is, however, one important service, titled Agent/Distributor Service (A/DS), that is designed exclusively to help U.S. firms identify suitable representatives abroad for a fee. The exporters may seek the names of agents and/or distributors abroad who have indicated an interest in handling specific products from the United States.

The following four criteria could be employed to identify suitable intermediaries: financial strength, good connections, the number and kinds of other companies represented, and the quality of local personnel, facilities, and equipment.

Financial Strength Sales in foreign markets take time to mature. Yet the distributor must invest in personnel and equipment ahead of the actual business activity if the organization is to have an effective beginning. Thus, the prospective distributor must be financially sound and should have the strength and will to take the risks involved. Financial strength involves both credit standing and cash flow position.

Good Connections In a large number of countries, business is conducted on a personal basis. In many cases, the government is deeply involved in business. Thus, for agents and distributors to be effective, they should be well connected both in private and in government circles. They should be regarded as respectable businesspersons by all concerned and follow established traditions and practices.

Other Business Commitments Information should be gathered on other commitments that the potential intermediary is involved in. For example, someone currently dealing in noncompeting goods and enjoying a good reputation for providing service, handling complaints and problems, and carrying inventory might be a viable candidate. Information on performance can be sought from the companies he or she has been representing. In addition to an encouraging reputation, any experience gained through handling complementary goods would be advantageous in representing the firm's products. However, sound business practice prohibits distributors from handling competing lines.

Personnel, Facilities, and Equipment The number and quality of the representative's employees, equipment, and facilities should be examined. After all, the reputation of the foreign firm in the host country depends on the activities and behavior of the people representing it. The people should not only be skilled and qualified in their trade but also have good public relations. Further, the distributor's facilities and equipment should be adequate, as well as properly located. If certain equipment is lacking, the distributor should be willing to make additions. Often potential representatives are willing to hire more people and purchase additional facilities and equipment, if selected. To ensure that the distributor lives up to such promises, these provisions should be specified in the agreement.

The following are additional considerations in the selection of intermediaries:[45]

- Capability to provide adequate sales coverage
- Overall positive reputation and image as a company
- Product compatibility (synergy or conflict?)
- Pertinent technical know-how at staff level
- Adequate infrastructure in staff and facilities
- Proven performance record with client companies
- Positive attitude toward the company's products
- Mature outlook regarding the company's inevitable progression in market management

Channel Control and Performance

Distribution in foreign locales through intermediaries always entails compromise. The compromise involves the loss of control over the MNC's foreign marketing operations in exchange for relatively low-cost representation. Although some control must be relinquished to intermediaries even in domestic markets, in foreign markets it is more significant because the firm has no permanent presence abroad. A distributor, the only means of accomplishing all the related tasks—selling, servicing, providing market information—often falls short of the manufacturer's expectations. The independent distributor represents an entity separate from the exporter, and their goals may not match exactly. Despite the fact that the exporter/manufacturer lacks full control of foreign distribution, he or she still wants adequate information. This raises the dilemma of how to encourage high performance by channels that are not a part of the firm's own network.

No matter how one looks at it, companies using independent distributors will have great difficulty in controlling them. It is difficult for the exporter to make sales forecasts, set sales targets, and develop customer-contact plans when there is no access to the distributor's books, sales reports, or other records. Thus, the manufacturer should not depend on controls to optimize distributor performance but instead use motivational methods.

> A distributor wants to do the best possible job for each of his manufacturers, but he really cannot. So he concentrates on (1) where he makes the most money and (2) where he has the least aggravation or the greatest personal pull. The following are some thoughts on how we can build loyalty:
>
> 1. Build your distributor with your company: bring him into your picture; discuss future plans as they affect his area with him; seek his advice.
> 2. Give your distributor an attractive profit margin; try to keep in mind that you want to be in business with him for several years; make him want to continue the relationship.
> 3. Be sure he has credit terms which make him competitive, or more so, in amount and length of payment.
> 4. Maintain regular correspondence, and make sure he can clearly understand what you have to say.
> 5. Make a point of commenting on successful distributors in whatever communication you use in his area (advertising, publicity, house organs, sales bulletins, and so on).
> 6. Keep your obvious control to a minimum; as his performance improves, your supervision can be reduced.
> 7. If financing is needed locally and you have the ability to help, do so if his situation justifies this.
> 8. Bring the distributor to the United States on occasion and let him see what goes on.
> 9. Offer a scholarship to the children of a successful distributor.
> 10. Establish a recognition system: recognition certificates, cash prizes, trips, and so on.
> 11. Make available remembrance items: giveaways with your company name—perhaps, if warranted, with his name too.[46]

An empirical study on the subject notes that the performance of an overseas distributor is affected by such relational factors as formalization, standardization, reciprocity, intensity, and conflict.[47] *Formalization* refers to the extent to which the relationship is agreed upon and made explicit. *Standardization* indicates the extent to which the established roles and trading routines are followed. *Reciprocity* means the extent to which the manufacturer and distributor are *both* involved in decision making, despite the traditional domains of each party. *Intensity* is the level of contact and resource exchange between the parties. Finally, *conflict* refers to the level of tension and disagreement between the two parties. The findings of this study strongly recommend that high performance is associated with certain relational characteristics. High performance requires that the two parties:

- Adapt their roles and routines (or make them less standardized)
- Display a commitment to developing business in the market in question (or focus on contact and resource intensity)
- Exhibit lower levels of intercompany tension and disagreement (or conflict)

In addition, the manufacturer should demonstrate (1) a genuine interest in the foreign market and in the overseas distributor, (2) a willingness to adapt his or her ways of doing business to be an effective competitor abroad, and (3) an ability to minimize disagreements with the overseas distributor.[48]

Modification of Channel

Environmental forces, internal or external, may force a company to modify existing channel agreements. A shift in the trade policy/practice of a country, for instance, may render distribution through a state trading organization obsolete. The experience of companies in the Common Market is relevant here. Multinational companies in the EC area, in response to the 1992 single internal market program, have been changing their distribution channels from covering only one national market to covering two or more national markets and serving areas reflecting natural rather than national boundaries. Similarly, technological changes in product design may require service calls to customers more frequently than the current channels can manage, and thus require the company to opt for direct distribution.

Ordinarily, a company new to the international market starts distribution through intermediaries. The company has little, if any, knowledge of the conditions overseas and has neither the insight nor capabilities necessary to deal successfully with the vagaries of the market. For good reasons, therefore, intermediaries are patronized. With their knowledge of the market, they play an important role in establishing demand for a company's products. But once the company attains a foothold in the market, it may discover that it does not have enough control of distribution to make further headway. At this time, modification becomes essential. The perspectives of Japanese companies illustrate the point.

> In marketing, too, the Japanese have avoided "going global" all at once. When they have an exportable product, they test it out in South East Asia and a few U.S. cities (notably Los Angeles) to learn how to market it abroad. When the situation looks risky, they ask trading companies to do the overseas marketing on their behalf, again so as to prevent their lack of a critical resource—in this case marketing know-how—from becoming a bottleneck to their international growth.
>
> Such caution does not reflect a lack of interest in overseas trade. On the contrary, the company will typically dispatch a high-caliber liaison officer, usually on the CEO's orders, to such places as New York, Chicago and Los Angeles, with a specific mission to develop plans for eventual direct marketing. Many of

> today's top corporate executives have been on such a mission at some time in their career. The fact that the company may ask trading companies to handle its initial overseas marketing, or may accept OEM deals under well-known American or European brands, is likely to reflect a methodical, one-step-at-a-time approach to the long-term goal of becoming a global brand.
>
> It is clear in hindsight that such Japanese companies as Canon, Ricoh, Panasonic, and Pentax all had the ambition to become world leaders, but in each case they started with trading-company, dealer, and/or OEM arrangements. Once confident of their product quality and cost competitiveness, they began to address their marketing inefficiencies and gradually to by-pass, first, the trading companies and, eventually, their distributor and OEM partners. Some of them do still accept OEM relationships, but they will soon begin to insist on own-brand marketing also. Dual-brand strategies have in any case been hard to administer in the United States as a result of antitrust legislation, internal administrative complexities, and conflicts over engineering resource allocation. It was because of such difficulties that Pentax left Honeywell and Ricoh left Savin. Both aspire eventually to become global marketers in their own right.[49]

Managerial astuteness requires that the company do a thorough study before deciding to change existing channel arrangements. No matter how long a U.S. company has been engaged in business with other countries, there are customs and conditions that may constrain a nonnative firm in establishing its own distribution system. In other words, hurried measures could create insurmountable problems, resulting in loose control and poor communications. Further, the affected intermediary agents should be taken into the company's confidence about future plans and compensated for any breach in terms. Any modification of channels should tally with the total marketing system. This requires consideration of the effect of a modified plan on various ingredients in the marketing mix, such as pricing, promotion, and so on. The managers in different departments (as well as the customers) should be informed so that the change does not come as a surprise. In other words, care must be taken to ensure that a modification in channel arrangements causes no distortion in the overall distribution system.

Wholesaling in Foreign Environments

An international marketer interested in overseas distribution must acquire complete knowledge of the existing wholesale and retail patterns of the host country. Such knowledge reveals what sort of distribution is feasible; what economic, social, and cultural factors influence the distribution structure of the country; and what legal and political requirements must be followed. The following two sections examine different aspects of wholesaling and retailing in foreign markets.

Overall, wholesalers worldwide perform such functions as purchasing, selling, transportation, storage, financing, information gathering, production planning, risk management, and even management consulting. But in some countries, some of the functions are reserved for manufacturers or retailers or both. Briefly, functions performed by wholesalers vary from country to country. Table 14.1 provides statistical information on wholesaling in foreign markets.

TABLE 14.1 Wholesaling in Selected Countries

COUNTRY	NUMBER OF WHOLESALERS	NUMBER OF WHOLESALE EMPLOYEES	EMPLOYEES PER WHOLESALER	RETAILER PER WHOLESALER	POPULATION PER WHOLESALER
United States	416,000	5,355,000	13	5	564
Ireland	3,073	42,100	14	11	1,139
Austria	12,890	148,900	12	3	582
Sweden	27,913	193,200	7	3	145
Soviet Union	1,000	120,000	120	481	174,922
Belgium	57,079	177,400	3	2	174
United Kingdom	80,104	1,087,000	14	3	698
Israel	4,862	36,900	8	8	782
Japan	429,000	4,091,000	10	4	278
India	116,000	—	—	32	5,612
Turkey	24,592	87,200	4	20	1,923
Chile	561	15,900	28	42	20,856
Brazil	46,000	442,000	10	61	2,820
South Korea	45,568	173,200	4	21	878
Italy	120,366	547,000	5	8	473
Egypt	1,766	42,300	24	1	25,595
Yugoslavia	1,110	138,100	124	70	20,000

Sources: United Nations Statistical Yearbook, 1983–1984, pp. 866–889, and 1979–1980, pp. 404–419; and *Statistical Abstract of the United States,* 1986, p. 774.

Status and Role of Wholesalers

The status and role of wholesalers vary from country to country.[50] In developing countries, they play a crucial role by handling imports as well as products of small, domestic manufacturers and by financing the flow of goods between the producers and retailers.[51] Despite their importance in many developing countries, wholesalers are held in low esteem for two reasons. First, the major economic emphasis in developing countries is on production since goods are scarce in virtually all sectors. Second, wholesale trade, like retail, in many countries is dominated by foreigners. The local population, therefore, looks down upon wholesalers as they consider them to be getting rich by exploiting them. For example, in many African countries, like Kenya and Sierra Leone, people of the Indian subcontinent control the trading sector of the economy. About 75 percent of Kenya's retail and wholesale business even today is controlled by Asians. Similarly, the Chinese have been dominant in the Philippines and Indonesia. European companies control a large proportion of Malaysia's and Singapore's trade.[52]

Further, the size of wholesaling operations differs significantly from country to country. In Finland, four wholesaling houses handle the major portions of all trade. One of these four houses, Kesko, controls over 20 percent of the market.[53] On the other hand, Japan is known for its myriad wholesalers linked to each other in a multilevel arrangement.

Services Offered by Wholesalers

Services provided by wholesalers are related to competition. In a country like India, where there are virtually hundreds of wholesalers, the margins are low and the competition is fierce. In such an environment, wholesalers provide a variety of services from financing to inventory maintenance. On the other hand, the large trading companies usually provide a good service mix, but at a substantial cost to the manufacturer/retailer. In most industrialized countries, the emerging trend toward vertical integration has squeezed the wholesaler from both sides. The wholesalers, therefore, have tried to streamline by carefully limiting the areas of operation and strictly controlling them. For example, wholesalers continue to be a major factor in Western Europe in food products. Thus, even though Kraft Incorporated distributes in Germany through company-owned channels, it must provide the wholesalers their commission without receiving any services.[54]

Merchandising Policies

Smaller wholesalers usually limit their business to handling a particular family of goods. Whenever they expand, they venture only into related goods. Large wholesalers, however, deal in different products without any underlying relationship among them. For example, Hamashbir Hamerkazi, a large wholesale group in Israel, handles different kinds of products and has interests in twelve large manufacturing firms.[55]

Margins and Efficiency

The margins and efficiency of wholesalers depend on the services they provide and the competition they face. Where competition is lacking, wholesalers run an inefficient operation. The wholesaling function simply amounts to an intermediate function for the flow of goods. The inefficiency of operations has no relationship to margins. When the business develops into a monopoly and the goods are in short supply, margins are rather high, despite the low level of services (related to credit, storage, shipping, market research information). Keen competition, however, raises the level of services that wholesalers provide without simultaneous improvement in either the margins or efficiency. In brief, wholesaling worldwide is not marked by efficiency; with poor efficiency and keen competition, the margins are meager.

Retailing in Overseas Markets

Diverse retailing patterns can be observed from country to country, even more than in wholesaling.[56] Retailing in many respects is a localized activity, deeply influenced by prevailing social and cultural norms and government controls.[57] An international marketer should gain as much insight into the retailing practices of the host country as necessary for his or her marketing endeavors.

Worldwide Retailing Patterns

Retailing operations vary widely in size. Some countries have large stores comparable to those in the United States. In other nations, retailing is a small family business. Harrods of England, Mitsukoshi of Japan, and Au Printemps of France are well-known names in retailing. These stores have a large clientele and carry an extensive line of merchandise along the lines of a typical department store in the United States. For example, Mitsukoshi serves over 100,000 customers every day. Contrast this with retailing in Pakistan and Nigeria, where retailers in a large city number in the thousands and carry one or two lines of goods, serving a very few customers. The relative size of retail patterns is illustrated in Table 14.2. Relatively speaking, not only is the number of retail stores in the developing countries much greater than in the industrialized nations, but also by contrast the number of customers served is low. As a matter of fact, even among developed countries retailing patterns vary significantly. For example, in 1982 the average sales volume per store was $523,000 in the United States, $408,000 in Great Britain, and $182,500 in Japan.[58]

The level of services that retailers provide to manufacturers varies according to their size. Thus, large retail houses generally carry inventory, render financial help, display and promote merchandise, and furnish market information. On the other hand, smaller retailers would depend entirely on the manufacturer or wholesaler. On their own, they would carry a limited quantity of products (which might lead to out-of-stock items) and would expect the vendor to provide credit. Promotion and merchandise display material would have to be handled by the manufacturer or the wholesaler.

The smaller retailers carry limited lines of goods in limited variety. Usually, their operations are run inefficiently and their margins are low. On the other

TABLE 14.2 **Retailing in Selected Countries**

COUNTRY	1990 POPULATION (IN THOUSANDS)	1988 GNP PER CAPITA (U.S. DOLLARS)	NUMBER OF RETAILERS	NUMBER OF RETAIL EMPLOYEES
United States	250,410	19,840	1,923,000	15,072,000
Ireland	3,500	8,710	32,332	79,900
Austria	7,644	16,330	37,524	227,000
Sweden	8,526	20,880	75,709	315,300
Germany	78,475	19,900*	—	1,977,000
Belgium	9,909	15,110	131,798	205,000
United Kingdom	57,366	14,080	231,674	2,642,500
Israel	4,409	9,790	40,000	85,000
Japan	123,642	23,290	1,721,000	6,376,000
India	849,746	329	3,760,000	5,328,000
Turkey	56,704	1,263	491,600	692,000
Chile	13,083	1,609	23,800	33,400
Brazil	152,505	2,473	2,817,000	1,968,000
South Korea	43,045	3,950	945,800	945,800
Ghana	15,165	349	2,182	5,800
Italy	57,664	13,860	927,372	1,742,000
Egypt	54,706	1,455	2,136	48,200
U.S.S.R.	—	—	659,700	4,814,000
Yugoslavia	23,842	2,596	79,679	341,300

*West Germany only.

Sources: Population and GNP per capita information are for 1983 and are from *The World Development Report 1991*. Data on retailing establishments are from the *United Nations Statistical Yearbook*, 1979–1980, pp. 404–419; 1983–1984, pp. 866–890; and *Statistical Abstract of the United States*, 1984, p. 799.

hand, large-scale operations are able to achieve economies of scale and infuse professionalism into the operations. Their margins are relatively high, but at the same time so are their services.

An international marketer would have difficulty dealing directly with smaller retailers. Thus, in nations where retailing is a mom-and-pop business, the wholesaler becomes important. By the same token, new ideas and innovations overseas at the retail level can be successfully introduced only in countries that have large retail houses.

Theory of International Retailing

Any institutional framework in a country is a function of its environment. In the area of international retailing, this thesis is supported by empirical work on the subject.[59] For example, supermarkets were found to be more common and retail outlets much larger in countries with relatively higher GNPs per capita. As a matter of fact, time lags in the development of retailing innovations and improvements appeared similar in length to lags in environmental development. In brief, it can be theorized that the retailing structure (that is, the number of inhabitants per retail establishment and sales per retail establishment) emerges from the environmental characteristics of the country. The environmental determinants of retail structure are personal consumption expenditures per capita, passenger car ownership, and geographical concentration of population. The theory of retailing propounded here has a variety of implications for multinational marketers. Arndt says that reported results

> appear to have important strategic implications for multinational retailers who, more often than not, establish modern retail institutions such as supermarkets and discount stores. . . . Conceptual framework may be used by multinational retailers as a base for forecasting the optimal timing to establish retail operations within a new country. The framework may also facilitate decisions regarding the magnitude of investments such as the number of stores to be established in a particular country and their approximate size.[60]

For example, Western capital-intensive mass-market technology clearly is ill-suited to serve low- and middle-income consumers in the Third World. Instead, the traditional labor-intensive food retailer is more suitable for marketing staples to the bulk of the world's population—that is, neither so primitive as to offer no escape from low production and low income, nor so highly sophisticated as to be out of the reach of poor people.

Until recently, the transfer of capital-intensive marketing technology was recommended as a solution to Third World problems. The horizontally and vertically integrated systems surrounding institutions known as supermarkets were considered generators of substantial benefits as a result of economies of scale, self-service, and a shortened distribution channel. Supermarkets supposedly help to by-pass the public wholesale markets; replace the crowded, old-fashioned, noisy, disorderly, dirty but picturesque food stands in municipal retail bazaars; and do away with street vendors who cause health and safety hazards in busy downtown areas. In short, the small limited-line retailers of consumer staples—

plus the long, labor-intensive, and haphazardly coordinated distribution chain—were being arrogantly brushed aside as inadequate, inefficient, and irrelevant.

The experience of the past twenty-five years, however, shows that Western marketing technology is too big and too expensive. It does not create the jobs needed to absorb the rapidly expanding labor force in the Third World, and it is not appropriate for the small firms and businesses that make up the bulk of the economic activity in developing countries. Further, evidence has been presented that shows competition can emerge when the traditional institutions are well managed.[61]

Global Retailing Trends

Worldwide, various changes are emerging on the retail scene.[62] Although most changes are limited to advanced nations, different sorts of retailing trends are evident even among developing countries.

Adoption of U.S. Retailing Innovations Such U.S. retailing innovations as self-service supermarkets, discount houses, and suburban shopping centers gradually are finding their way into most European countries and Japan. The growth of discounting in Germany illustrates the point. Starting with the first discount store in 1953, the number of discounters exceeded 1,000 by the 1970s. The new discount houses, called *verbraucher markte* (consumer markets), are in some cases larger than a typical discount store in the United States. Similarly, discounting has taken off in France, where 1960s supermarkets have evolved into hypermarkets, selling not just food but furniture, clothing, and hardware. To illustrate the point, cat food costs 2.80 francs at a hypermarket compared with 5.30 francs at a neighborhood shop.

Incidentally, hypermarkets did not succeed in the United States. For example, Wal-Mart Stores Inc. established four hypermarkets in different cities to penetrate suburban markets. But, the company had trouble in running them profitably. Similarly, K-mart Corporation's hypermarket failed to meet expectations.[63]

Discounting is becoming popular in Japan as well. Daiei Inc. has 204 stores that conduct American-style discounting business. Its cut-rate stores are shaking up Japan's protective distribution system, where manufacturers tend to dictate prices to retailers.[64] For example, in a Tokyo department store a pair of designer jeans costs $63, while in a suburban discount store the same product costs $39. Similarly, a Gucci bag, a pair of Reebok shoes, a JVC video camcorder, and a pound of sirloin steak cost $176, $67, $1,454, and $23, respectively, in the department store, but at a discounter the price is $105, $47, $701, and $9, respectively.[65]

American retailing innovations are also finding their way to developing countries. For example, McDonald's, Kentucky Fried Chicken, Pizza Hut, Burger King, Ponderosa, and Wendy's are thriving in many Southeast Asian areas including China.[66]

Even mail-order business is catching up. For example, mail-order business traditionally had a shoddy image in Japan. Only such products as contraceptive devices and aphrodisiacs, which reputable stores refused to sell, were convenient to channel through mail. With more Japanese women working and with mail-order houses trying hard to improve their image, the mail-order business has begun to boom. Well-known companies have begun selling jewelry, kitchen utensils, fur coats, baby clothes, and even automobiles by mail. This trend is visible in other countries as well.[67]

Further, the share of business for the large retailers has been increasing as retailing becomes concentrated in fewer hands. This trend is noticeable throughout Western Europe with the exception of Italy.[68] In Japan, large department stores have captured about 10 percent of domestic retail sales. But their strong market position has been overtaken by so-called supers or general merchandise stores, which handle about 15 percent of retail sales. Self-service and convenience chain stores have also grown rapidly and together hold another 15 percent of the market.[69]

Internationalization of Retailing The growing interest among the large retailers of industrialized countries in expansion overseas is another noticeable change. Sears, Roebuck & Company has ventured into Mexico, South America, and Spain: J.C. Penney Company moved into Belgium and Italy; Safeway entered Great Britain, Germany, and Australia; Federated Department Stores found its way into Madrid. Likewise, Avon representatives and Tupperware parties have become common in a number of countries. Since 1984, Toys 'R' Us Company has opened megastores in Canada, Britain, Singapore, Germany, France, Italy, and Japan.[70]

The internationalization of retailing, however, is not limited to U.S. business. Harrods, Britain's best-known department store, has branched out into Japan.[71] France's Au Printemps department store opened stores in Japan, Singapore, Saudi Arabia, South Korea, and Turkey. In 1987, it opened its first U.S. store in Denver and plans to open many more in the 1990s.[72] The following is a list of selected European interests in U.S. retailers (see International Marketing Highlight 14.4):

INVESTOR	COUNTRY	U.S. RETAILER
Tengelmann	Germany	A & P
Haniel	Germany	Srivner
Rewe-Leibbrand	Germany	SDC/Furr's
Asko	Germany	SDC/Furr's
Albrecht	Germany	Benner-Tea, Albertson
Cavenham	United Kingdom	Grand Union
Promodes	France	Red Food, Houchens
Ahold	Netherlands	First National
Delhaize	Belgium	Food Lion, Food Giant
Otto-Versand	Germany	Spiegel
Marks and Spencer	United Kingdom	Brooks Brothers

Social Marketing An interesting trend in the developing countries has been the retailers' entry into social marketing. For example, retailers in Kenya, Jamaica, and India willingly display and sell contraceptives to support their governments' efforts to popularize family planning.[73] This shows the awareness of even small businesses/retailers in developing countries toward the need for social programs and their willingness to participate. It seems that the primitive distribution networks in developing countries can be counted on for delivery of medically and socially oriented products, ideas, and services. In other words, psychologically, physically, and economically, the retailers are accessible for distribution of such products as health-related foods, over-the-counter medicines, and nutrition and hygiene information, even though each of them may run a small, inefficient operation.

Cooperative Retailing The emergence of consumer retail cooperatives is another trend that deserves mention. Traditionally, consumer cooperatives have been popular in Europe. For example, consumer cooperatives control almost one-fourth of food sales in Switzerland. Presumably, the two largest Swiss coop-

International Marketing Highlight 14.4

Low Prices, Swedish Meatballs, and a Squad of Baby Sitters Are Helping this Retailer Buck the Recession

Ikea, the cheeky furniture company from Sweden, has nearly doubled sales to $3.2 billion over the past four years, and now has ninety stores in twenty-two countries, including recent openings in Hungary and Poland. Now Ikea plans to shake the dowels out of America's retail furniture business. The company is launching a bicoastal blitz in the United States, with store openings in metropolitan New York and Los Angeles. The privately held company expects to have eight of its enormous stores (each is about six times the size of an average supermarket) in the L.A. and New York markets by 1993.

Ikea's offer is value intelligently presented, and it is as persuasive a selling proposition as consumers are ever likely to hear. The response to the store opening in Elizabeth, New Jersey, about fifteen miles from Manhattan, bordered on riot. The New Jersey Turnpike was backed up for nine miles as 26,000 shoppers jammed into the place on its first day of business, racking up $1 million in sales and doubling Ikea's opening-day record. Months later, embarrassed Ikea workers were still telling shoppers that the $285 armchairs, $116 oak veneer bookcases, or couches they wanted were out of stock. One harried clerk was taking *reservations* to place orders on a particular bookcase, which like most items was selling at 20 percent to 40 percent below competitive offerings. Mangers had underestimated sales by 40 percent.

Like most successful businesses, Ikea idolizes the customer. Shoppers move through a cleverly designed layout that allows them to look, get information, and make purchase decisions without any sales help. A couch, for instance, is displayed both in a real-life setting and in a group of other couches for sale so people can compare.

Buying furniture is a consumer's nightmare. There are no standards for quality, no rationale for pricing. The selling methods often resemble those employed by used-car dealers, practices Ikea makes endless fun of in its advertising. What consumers really need are information and time to browse, and at Ikea they get plenty of both. The key selling tool is a catalogue that includes prices and specifications. On the floor, each piece of furniture is graded by a code called *Mobelfakta,* an adaptation of the Swedish testing-board standards that identify materials, construction, and durability characteristics on an A, B, C scale.

As for time, take all you want: Ikea staffers will mind the toddlers in a playroom. The company also provides an infant changing room and someone to warm the baby's bottle. There are a restaurant and a snack bar that sell Swedish specialties at low prices, which gives people some places to think their decisions through. If they can't make up their minds on big-ticket furniture purchases, and the company doesn't necessarily expect them to, the family can wander through the lower level, called the Marketplace, which is stacked with glassware, linens, rugs, and other household items at deep discounts.

To keep prices down, Ikea designs all its furniture for low-cost manufacture and distribution, and contracts out to suppliers in nearly fifty countries, many located in Eastern Europe and the [former] Soviet Union. Ikea's next move is to find more suppliers in the United States. Would-be applicants should prepare for high volume and high standards.

Source: Fortune, March 11, 1991, p. 72.

eratives have over one-third of Swiss households as members. In Japan consumers' cooperative union stores, which are nonprofit institutions, are fast emerging as a viable force in food retailing.[74]

The cooperative movement at the retail level, however, is spreading much faster in the developing countries of Asia and Africa. In many countries (for example, Mexico and India), government-sponsored cooperative societies have been formed to undertake distribution of essential products. The presence of the cooperatives reduces the volume of trade handled by private retailers and increases the government's control over trade. Interestingly, however, cooperatives do not succeed in many nations because in an economy of scarcity cooperatives are often out of stock of the most-needed goods and products. This forces consumers to depend on private sources for their crucial purchases, even though it means paying a higher price.

International Franchising

Expansion into international markets represents a major growth opportunity for domestic franchise operations. This section focuses on the entry motivations, ownership practices, marketing strategies, and problems associated with U.S. franchise operations abroad.

The term ***franchising*** has many connotations; therefore, its meaning must be delineated in the context of private enterprise, where it refers to "a form of marketing or distribution in which a parent company customarily grants an individual or relatively small company the right or privilege to do business (for a consideration from the franchisee) in a prescribed manner over a certain period of time in a specified place."[75] An important aspect of a franchise arrangement is the continuing relationship between the parties.

The current growth of the franchise industry is of recent origin and is strictly an American phenomenon. However, franchising as an alternative way of seeking distribution has been known for years. Many years ago, Germany beer brewers negotiated exclusive arrangements for sale of their brands outside their home market. In the United States, the Singer Sewing Machine Company is credited with the first attempts to establish worldwide franchising operations. Similarly, the Bata Show Company of Czechoslovakia (now operated from Canada) instituted franchising about the same time. Today of course, franchising has expanded to such diverse businesses as fast-food restaurants, business services, construction, hotels and motels, and recreation and entertainment. Overall, franchising accounts for over one-fourth of retail sales in the United States.

Perspectives of International Franchising

Companies are primarily motivated by three factors in the expansion of their franchising operations internationally: market-growth opportunities, profit potential, and the desire to be known as an international firm. Companies usually initiate franchising in other countries on a limited scale—one or two countries with a few outlets in key locations. Initial success, however, leads to further expansion. Like the international expansion of U.S. business in general, foreign franchising operations usually start with Canada, Western Europe, and Japan. For example, Canada has the largest number of U.S. franchise operations, followed by England and Japan.[76] Fast foods and business services account for over 50 percent of international franchising operations of U.S. firms. In 1987, 354 U.S. franchisors operated 32,000 outlets in foreign countries, and their gross sales amounted to almost $6 billion.[77]

Marketing Strategy

Firms entering overseas markets by establishing franchising operations must determine if they will follow a standardized or differentiated strategy with reference to product, price, and promotion. Most firms follow a standardized approach, particularly the soft drink and business services organizations. However, some fast-food companies have made adaptations in their overseas operations, particularly in the product area, in response to particular cultural habits and customs of different nations. For example in Japan, Denny's serves ginger pork, curried rice, and dishes flavored with soy sauce. McDonald's offers tomato and beet-root in Austria; in France it serves wine with meals. Dairy Queen is attempting to penetrate the Middle East market by adding *roti,* a type of bread, and a fried vegetable and meat dish to the fare.

Price is duly adjusted to local competition. Promotion also varies, depending on media availability. For example, the use of television in foreign markets is much less popular. The dominant means of promotion are radio and different forms of sales promotions.

Problems with U.S. Franchising in Other Countries

Companies face a variety of problems in their efforts to engage in international franchising. Some are similar to those faced in domestic markets, but differ in intensity and severity.

Other problems may be classified as:

- *Governmental and legal restrictions.* Tax structure, barriers against foreign ownership, and limitation of profit repatriation are some of the problems causing trouble for more than 60 percent of the international franchising firms.
- *Selection of method of operation.* The method of operation depends largely on the business practice of the host nation, the availability of qualified franchisees, and the availability of capital.
- *Choice of location.* The selection of proper site is a crucial factor in the success of the franchise.
- *Availability of supplies.* Two business inputs—qualified personnel and food materials—face scarcity problems in Japan and Europe.
- *Adjustment to local tastes and customs.* Recognizing local traditions and tastes is of utmost importance. Culture, habits, consumer behavior, and desires vary widely from nation to nation.
- *Operational problems.* Once opened, the outlet faces problems that threaten its continued existence. The two prevalent challenges facing international franchising have been competition and the ability to adapt to local conditions while maintaining one's uniqueness. Monitoring the customs and habits of the host country is always necessary in order to discover or anticipate changing trends.
- *Limited expansion opportunities.* The international franchising industry has been a relatively recent development. Progress has been rapid, however, and the large U.S. franchisers all have outlets in foreign nations, with plans for further expansion. Analyses indicate that, although there are difficulties that must be overcome, expansion opportunities do exist and the future of international franchising appears optimistic.[78]

International franchisers must ascertain the basic practicability of transporting their business system to a foreign country and engage in a thorough market research study before attempting to expand internationally. Many American firms stumble because of their mistaken assumption that what works at home will work overseas as well.[79] The success of international franchising will probably depend on the ability to adjust to a culture with different attitudes, values, and beliefs.

Future Trends

For numerous reasons, the international franchising operations of U.S. corporations should grow at a fast pace in the 1990s. First, as the people in Western Europe and Japan move away from downtown areas into suburbs and as more and more women start working, the fast-food industry should prosper. Second, there has been a gradual break in the tradition of going home for lunch, particularly in France, Germany, England, and Scandinavian countries. This is attributed to tightening of working hours, forced by the need to increase productivity. Third, the rise in discretionary income in Europe and Japan has enhanced the need for convenience foods. For example, companies like McDonald's and Kentucky Fried Chicken are showing annual sales increases of 50 percent a year. Fourth, franchising permits a substantial involvement of the local entrepreneur (for example, in the franchisee-owned ownership arrangement) right from the beginning. This makes entry into the country easier. Fifth, even among the emerging developing countries or otherwise large Third World countries, franchising has a great potential because it permits mass distribution, involves native businesspersons, and offers a standard product/service at a price trimmed by economies of scale. In conclusion, the future of franchising operations in the international markets appears promising, and more and more companies may seek foreign market entry through franchising.[80]

International Physical Distribution

International physical distribution (PD) encompasses the logistics or movements of goods across countries from the sources of supply to the centers of demand. In other words, it is concerned with getting the right product to the right place at the right time, in good condition and at reasonable cost. Warehousing, transportation, and inventory are the major components of physical distribution. The final purpose of physical distribution activity is to provide adequate service to the customer. For satisfactory performance of this function, the various components of PD should be properly integrated for worldwide distribution.

Importance of International Physical Distribution

The importance of international physical distribution is illustrated by Japan. Two large metropolitan areas in Japan—Tokyo and Osaka—consume approximately 85 percent of all gasoline sold in Japan. The physical distribution system for a particular oil company serving Japan is made up of four different levels of intermediary agents—a national wholesaler, a regional wholesaler, a local wholesaler, and a retailer. The gasoline is physically delivered to the national wholesaler, who then has it delivered to the regional one, then on to the local one, and finally the retailer. There is nothing odd about this distribution system until one stops to consider that all channel members are located within the same metropolitan area. It would be considerably more convenient and far cheaper to ship the gasoline directly from the oil company's tanks to the retailer. However, because of the cultural environment in Japan, it may not be entirely feasible to streamline this distribution system. Nevertheless, the example serves to indicate that, by evaluating and implementing an alternative system, the delivery cost of the gasoline could be lowered. For example, an American manufacturer trying to penetrate the Japanese consumer goods market satisfied the cultural requirements by routing the paperwork through various levels of appropriately compensated intermediaries while distributing the product itself directly.[81] Distribution is a marketing area that management might have a tendency to view as a so-called cost sink without realizing that considerable savings can be achieved by proper analysis and revision of distribution systems.

The physical distribution of goods is usually accepted as it is. It is rarely realized that this is one area that offers a great potential for increasing efficiency. In no other function is there as much waste, duplication, and indifference as there is in the moving of goods from one country to another.

Even in a strictly domestic business with many plants, warehouses, and markets, physical distribution is considered to be a difficult function. Added to this in the international context are the complexities of national borders, customs of trade, tariffs and duties, carrier performances, nationalism, monetary exchange, and the necessity of filing numerous documents.

Management of International Physical Distribution

The three important aspects of physical distribution are warehousing, transportation, and inventory management. The basic decisions to be made concerning warehousing are how many warehouses of what size a company needs (if any at all), and in which country they should be located. The decision on warehousing requires information such as where the firm's customers, both current and potential, are geographically located around the world; what is the pattern of their current demand, and what demand pattern is likely to emerge in the future; and what level of customer service should be followed. The last item refers to the number of days within which the the customer order would be filled. Often customers are categorized based on their importance for the company. The service level is varied in different categories. All this information is analyzed before making the warehousing decision.

The transportation decision mainly involves the choice of a mode of transportation for shipping the goods both internationally and locally within a foreign nation. This decision is affected by such factors as the availability of transportation, nature of product, size of shipment, distance to be traveled, type of demand (routine versus urgent demand), and cost of different shipping alternatives.[82]

Inventory management deals with stocking inventory to fill customer orders. It involves two decisions—how often to order in a given period and how much to order. The costs involved with these decisions are inversely related. For example, if too many orders are placed in a year, the ordering costs go up. On the other hand, if large quantities are bought at a time, the total number of orders is reduced and hence the total ordering cost, but the costs of carrying large purchases go up. Thus, an optimum point must be found for the number of orders and the size of each order. This can be figured by using different forms of informational inputs and an appropriate mathematical formula. (Such details, however, are beyond the scope of this book.)

So far the three aspects of physical distribution have been discussed separately. For an integrated decision on international physical distribution, however, these three aspects should be considered simultaneously. This amounts to considering physical distribution as a system with three components—warehousing, transportation, and inventory management.

The logic of applying a systems approach to physical distribution is simple. Because the costs involved in administering warehousing, transportation, and inventory functions are interrelated, they must be considered simultaneously for effective decision making. For example, if the number of warehouses is increased, transportation costs will decrease but inventory costs will increase—inventory will have to be duplicated at more places. Similarly, if an attempt is made to decrease inventory costs by cutting down inventory levels, transportation costs will go up. Obviously, an optimum decision mandates that all relevant costs be considered in an integrated fashion and in relation to the desired service level.[83]

International Physical Distribution: An Example

Illustrated here are the highlights of Eastman Kodak Company's international physical distribution arrangements as an example of how a large MNC moves goods internationally.[84] For Kodak, proper distribution means getting the right product to the right place at the right time, in good condition, and at a reasonable cost. To achieve this, Kodak has developed a highly integrated worldwide distribution system.

International Organization Sophistication, coordination, and cooperation are required in order for Kodak to provide a wide range of products manufactured in both the United States and foreign factories to all of its corporate installations around the world. The center of Kodak's organization in this important area is the International Distribution Operations Committee. The committee provides a focal point for the Distribution Division's interface with the International Photographic Division and also develops and evaluates new ideas in the export area.

Inventory Management Kodak's inventory management system consists of two subsystems. The automatic replenishment subsystem determines the timing and amount of an order to be placed with one of the manufacturing companies. If stock is below a predetermined reorder point, the system prepares a replenishment order that is reviewed by the local planning department, thereby eliminating the time the stock planner usually spends in clerical review of the product line and leaving more time for true planning. In addition the system automatically establishes control points used in the reorder cycle, which is the second part of the inventory management process. This system provides each of Kodak's computerized foreign facilities with an effective and efficient means of maintaining properly balanced inventories.

The results of the dual process are replenishment orders sent to Kodak manufacturing plants from one location to another. Transmission of computerized information is relayed over telephone lines in Northern Europe among six nonmanufacturing companies. One large computer in Sweden services smaller computer systems in Denmark, Norway, Finland, Belgium, and Holland. Each night, replenishment orders from these six Kodak companies are transmitted from Sweden to New York and then to Rochester. By reducing lead time, inventories at the ordering locations can also be reduced. In attempting to maintain a proper worldwide balance of inventories, the main considerations are efficiency, accuracy, and timing.

Shipping Kodak's General Transportation group coordinates product movement from Rochester to foreign markets. Kodak's goods are shipped to New York City by truck and then by either ocean or air freight. In-transit time accounts for the majority of time between the issuance and receipt of an order by a foreign company. Therefore, the General Transportation group must try to make this time as short as practical, and the product as safe as possible, during the in-transit time interval. Also, they must schedule the timing and method of shipment so that Kodak gets the best possible rates for the service it uses.

Warehousing Kodak's international distribution system is based on the assumption that the supplying factory has sufficient inventory in its distribution center to fill the order. This is the most important link in the entire chain of events. Along with its marketing and manufacturing divisions, Kodak's Distribution Division is responsible for ensuring that the factory distribution centers will have the product when it is needed. This means that Rochester must maintain close contact with the international marketplace to see that sales requirements for the foreign market are properly incorporated into the marketing, distributing, and manufacturing chain of events.

This function is performed by International Estimating, and an international information system has been developed to aid them in the task. This information system consists of three parts. Weekly information is provided to International Estimating for a select number of key items. The second part generates monthly stock and product sales data in card format from each of the international companies to the supplying factory. The final portion of the system operates on a quarterly basis and is involved with medium-term forecasting. The last step helps International Estimating in establishing sales estimates to present to marketing as the first step in the production scheduling process.

Summary

Once opportunities in other countries have been determined, arrangements must be made to get the product to the market. Essentially a company has two options concerning foreign distribution: establish company-owned channels or deal with different types of intermediaries. Initially, most companies use an existing system of distribution rather than attempting to build their own channels.

An important consideration in channel selection for overseas distribution is the availability of appropriate channels. Theory has it that the channel structures of a country reflect the stage of its economic development. According to this concept, channels of distribution in developed countries would be similar to those in the United States, while in developing countries channels would be fragmented, smaller in operation, and inefficient. Unfortunately, limited research on the subject fails to support this theory. Presumably the contradiction occurs because the channel structure of a country is more complex than has previously been suggested. For example, Japan is an advanced country, yet the Japanese channels of distribution are labeled by some as outmoded, complex, cumbersome, and inefficient.

Different types of intermediaries are active in the field of international distribution. Essentially, they can be categorized either as domestic agents and merchant intermediaries who provide channels of indirect distribution, or as foreign agents and merchant intermediaries who make it feasible to distribute directly. An essential difference between agents and merchant intermediaries is that the agents do not take title to the goods and operate only on behalf of their principals. The merchant intermediaries take title to the goods and conduct business on their own.

An international marketer should select appropriate channels and make them work. The selection process includes the establishment of channel objectives, feasible alternatives, and the choice of appropriate channels.

Once the distribution channel is determined, reliable foreign distributors must be found. The U.S. Department of Commerce provides different forms of services in this area. The actual selection of an intermediary is based on criteria such as the candidates' financial strength, their connections, the number and kind of other companies they represent, and the quality of their local personnel, facilities, and equipment.

Overall, independent intermediaries play a crucial role in international marketing. Their knowledge of the market and of the relevant business customs and practices adds to the strength of the manufacturer/exporter. They are especially important for smaller companies. Even some large companies with particular products prefer distributors over company-owned channels.

Use of intermediaries necessitates that manufacturers relinquish part of the control of the channel. It is important, therefore, for the manufacturer to design and implement an appropriate program to motivate channel members for effective performance.

An international marketer should gain knowledge of the host country's wholesale and retail patterns. Such knowledge will provide insights into the social, economic, political, and cultural factors that will affect distribution. Wide variations exist in the wholesaling and retailing characteristics of developed and developing countries. As a matter of fact, even among the advanced countries, channels differ significantly.

A discussion on physical distribution concludes the chapter. Physical distribution concerns the flow of goods from the manufacturer to the customer. Essentially, there are three aspects of physical distribution—warehousing, transportation, and inventory management—and they are related to each other. For an optimum physical distribution decision, they should be considered as a system. Physical distribution is one area where cost savings through efficiency are feasible provided the decision is systematically made.

Review Questions

1. What accounts for the differences in available channels in developed and developing countries?
2. Examine the distinguishing characteristics of Japanese distribution channels.
3. Discuss the role played by an export management company in international distribution.
4. Why do multinational companies undertake distribution for other multinationals? What are the pros and cons of such piggybacking?
5. Discuss the importance of trading companies in foreign trade. Why are there no U.S. trading companies comparable in size and scope to the Japanese trading companies?
6. What criteria should an international marketer adopt in channel selection?
7. What factors weigh heavily with international firms in the selection of particular distributors/dealers?
8. What steps can a firm take to motivate the channel members to perform effectively?

Endnotes

1. Jack Nadel, "Distribution: The Key to Success Overseas," *Management Review,* September 1987, pp. 10–17.
2. *See* Adel I. El-Ansary, "How Better Systems Could Feed the World," *International Marketing Review,* Spring 1986, pp. 39–49. *Also see* Suk-Ching Ho and Ho-fuk Lau, "Development of Supermarket Technology: The Incomplete Transfer Phenomenon," *International Marketing Review,* Spring 1988, pp. 20–30.
3. George Wadinambiaratchi, "Channels of Distribution in Developing Economies," *The Business Quarterly,* Winter 1965. *Also see* Leon V. Hirsch, *Marketing in an Underdeveloped Economy: The North Indian Sugar Industry* (Englewood Cliffs, NJ: Prentice-Hall, 1962); and George Wadinambiaratchi, "Theories of Retail Development," *Social and Economic Studies* (a publication of the University of West Indies), December 1972, pp. 391–403.
4. *See* Erdener Kaynak, "The Introduction of a Modern Food Retailing Institution to Less-Developed Economies: Problems and Opportunities," in Michael G. Harvey and Robert F. Lusch, eds., *Marketing Channels: Domestic and International Perspectives* (Norman, OK: Center for Economic and Management Research, School of Business Administration, The University of Oklahoma, 1982), pp. 52–58.
5. Arieh Goldman, "Adoption of Supermarket Shopping in a Developing Country: The Selective Adoption Phenomenon," *European Journal of Marketing,* vol. 16, no. 1 (1982) pp. 25–26.
6. Susan P. Douglas, "Patterns and Parallels of Marketing Structures in Several Countries," *MSU Business Topics,* Spring 1971, p. 48.
7. Yoshihiro Tajima, *Outline of Japanese Distribution Structures* (Tokyo: The Distribution Economics Institute of Japan, 1973).
8. *See* Michael R. Czinkota, "Distribution of

Consumer Products in Japan," *Industrial Marketing Review,* vol. 2, no. 3 (1985), pp. 39–51. *Also see* L. Joseph Rosenberg, "Cultural Background: Implication and Effects on Japanese Distribution Channels," in Michael G. Harvey and Robert F. Lusch, eds., *Marketing Channels: Domestic and International Perspectives* (Norman, OK: Center for Economic and Management Research, School of Business Administration, The University of Oklahoma, 1982), pp. 52–58.

9. *See* Robert E. Weigand, "Japan's Changing Marketing Channels," *Working Paper,* The University of Illinois at Chicago, 1988. *Also see* Jean L. Johnson, Tomuaki Sakano, and Naoto Onzo, "Behavioral Relations in Cross-Culture Distribution Systems: Influence, Control and Conflict in U.S.-Japanese Marketing Channels," *Journal of International Business Studies,* vol. 21, no. 4 (1990), pp. 639–656.
10. *See* Yoshi Tsurumi, "Managing Consumer and Industrial Systems in Japan," *Sloan Management Review,* Fall, 1982, p. 42.
11. William Lazar, Shoji Murata, and Hiroshi Kosaka, "Japanese Marketing: Towards a Better Understanding," *Journal of Marketing,* Spring 1985, pp. 69–81.
12. Masayoshi Kanabayashi, "Japan's Complex Distribution System Hinders Foreign Companies' Efforts to Sell Goods There," *The Wall Street Journal,* May 3, 1978, pp. 44.
13. "Selling in Japan Gets Less Befuddling," *Business Week,* February 20, 1989, p. 122D.
14. *See Statistics of Commerce (1985)* (Tokyo: Japanese Ministry of International Trade and Industry).
15. Damon Darlin, "Papa-Mama Stores in Japan Wield Power to Hold Back Imports," *The Wall Street Journal,* November 14, 1988, p. 1.
16. "Selling in Japan Gets Less Befuddling," *Business Week,* February 20, 1989, p. 122D.
17. Randolph E. Ross, "Understanding the Japanese Distribution System: An Explanatory Framework," *European Journal of Marketing,* vol. 17, no. 1 (1983), pp. 5–13.
18. *See* Rowland C. Chidomere, "Environmental Factors and Distribution of Household Appliances in Nigeria," *International Marketing Review,* Winter 1986, pp. 44–51.
19. Philip R. Cateora, *International Marketing,* 7th ed. (Homewood, IL: Irwin, 1990), pp. 572 and 578.
20. "The Export Management Company" (Washington, D.C.: U.S. Department of Commerce, 1976).
21. *See* Daniel C. Bello and Nicholas C. Williamson, "Contractual Arrangement and Marketing Practices in the Indirect Export Channel," *Journal of International Business Studies,* Summer 1985, pp. 65–82.
22. John J. Brasch, "Using Export Specialists to Develop Overseas Sales," *Harvard Business Review,* May–June 1981, pp. 6–8. *Also see* John J. Brasch, "Export Management Companies," *Journal of International Business Studies,* Spring–Summer 1978, pp. 59–71.
23. Donald G. Howard and James M. Maskulka, "Will American Export Trading Companies Replace Traditional Export Management Companies?" *International Marketing Review,* Winter 1988, pp. 41–50.
24. Don Stow, "Export Trading Companies: An Update," *Business America,* January 20, 1986, p. 9.
25. Daniel C. Bello and Nicholas C. Williamson, "The American Export Trading Company: Designing a New International Marketing Institution," *Journal of Marketing,* Fall 1985, pp. 60–69.
26. "Why Colgate Sells Other People's Products," *Business Week,* April 20, 1974, p. 108.
27. Colgate-Palmolive, Kao Join to Create Hair Products Line," *The Asian Wall Street Journal Weekly,* January 24, 1983, p. 22.
28. "How Sony Piggybacks Foreign Products in Japan," *Business International,* February 1, 1974, p. 38.
29. "Kao Takes Over Sales of Dow Chemical Vinyl Ester in Japan," *The Asian Wall Street Journal Weekly,* October 7, 1985, p. 21.
30. Vern Terpstra and Chwo-Ming J. Yu, "Piggybacking a Quick Road to Internationalization," *International Marketing Review,* vol. 7, no. 4 (1990), pp. 52–63.
31. "Campbell's Taste of the Japanese Market Is MM-MM Good," *Business Week,* March 28, 1988, p. 42.
32. *See* Lyn S. Amine. "Toward A Conceptualization of Export Trading Companies in World Markets," in S. Tamer Cavusgil, ed., *Advances in International Marketing,*

(Greenwich, CT: Jai Press, Inc., 1987), pp. 199–238.

33. Paul J. McNulty, "Predecessors of the Multinational Corporation," *Columbia Journal of World Business,* May–June 1972, pp. 73–80.
34. Tom Roehl, "The General Trading Companies: A Transactions Cost Analysis of Their Function in the Japanese Economy," in Michael G. Harvey and Robert F. Lusch, eds., *Marketing Channels: Domestic and International Perspectives* (Norman, OK: Center for Economic Research, School of Business Administration, The University of Oklahoma, 1982), pp. 86–100.
35. "Corporate Scoreboard," *Business Week,* July 20, 1987, p. 162.
36. Bradley K. Martin, "Japan's Trading Giants Look to Year 2000," *The Wall Street Journal,* March 31, 1986, p. 23.
37. *See* Lyn S. Amine and S. Tamer Cavusgil, "Japanese Sogo Shosha and the U.S. Export Trading Companies," a paper presented at the Academy of International Business Annual Conference, Cleveland, Ohio, 1984.
38. *See* Bert Rosenbloom and Trina L. Larsen, "International Channels of Distribution and the Role of Comparative Marketing Analysis," *Journal of Global Marketing,* vol. 4, no. 4 (1991), pp. 39–54.
39. Dant T. Dunn, Jr., "Agents and Distributors in the Middle East," *Business Horizons,* October 1979, p. 71.
40. Jac L. Goldstucker, "The Influence of Culture on Channels of Distribution," in *Proceedings of the Fall Conference* (Chicago: American Marketing Association, 1968), p. 470.
41. *See* Saul Klein, "Selection of International Marketing Channels," *Journal of Global Marketing,* vol. 4, no. 4 (1991), pp. 21–37.
42. *See* Daniel C. Bello, David J. Urban, and Broinslaw J. Verhage, "Evaluating Export Middlemen in Alternative Channel Structures," *International Marketing Review,* vol. 8, no. 5 (1991), pp. 49–64.
43. A. Duguid and E. Jacques, *Cases and Studies in Export Organizations* (London: Her Majesty's Stationery Office, 1971); and D. A. Tookey, *Export Marketing Decisions* (Middlesex, England: Penguin, 1975), p. 72.
44. Erin Anderson and Anne T. Coughlan, "International Market Entry and Expansion via Independent or Integrated Channels of Distribution," *Journal of Marketing,* January 1987, pp. 71–82.
45. *See Finding and Managing Distributors in Asia* (New York: Business International Corporation, 1983), p. 92. *Also see A Basic Guide To Exporting,* (Washington, D.C.: U.S. Department of Commerce, January 1992), pp. 4.6–4.7.
46. Robert Douglas Stuart, *Penetrating the International Market* (New York: American Management Association, 1965), pp. 87–88.
47. Philip J. Rosson and I. David Ford, "Manufacturer-Overseas Distributor Relations and Export Performance," *Journal of International Business Studies,* Fall 1982, pp. 57–72. *Also see* Gary L. Frazier, James D. Gill, and Sudhir H. Kale, "Dealer Dependence Levels and Reciprocal Actions in a Channel of Distribution in a Developing Country," *Journal of Marketing,* January 1989, pp. 50–69.
48. Philip J. Rosson, "Success Factors in Manufacturer-Overseas Distributor Relationships in International Marketing," in Erdener Kaynak, ed., *International Marketing Management* (New York: Praeger Publishers, 1984), pp. 91–107. J. J. Boddewyn, "American Marketing in the European Common Market," in *Multinational Product Management* (Cambridge, Mass.: Marketing Science Institute, 1976), pp. VII-1–VII-25).
49. Kenichi Ohmae, "Myths and Realities of Japanese Corporations," *The McKinsey Quarterly,* Summer 1982, p. 17.
50. *See* Robert Bartels, ed., *Comparative Marketing: Wholesaling in Fifteen Countries* (Homewood, IL: Irwin, 1963).
51. *See* Raef T. A. Hussein and Robert A. Robicheaux, "Power and Conflict in Jordanian Food Distribution Channels," *Journal of International Food and Agribusiness Marketing,* vol. 1, no. 3/4 (1989), pp. 69–92.
52. John Borrell, "Anti-Asian Sentiments in East Africa Worry the Region's Indian Communities," *The Wall Street Journal,* September 2, 1982, p. 20.
53. Vern Terpstra, *International Marketing,* 4th ed. (Hinsdale, IL: Dryden Press, 1987), p. 388.
54. Ibid., p. 390.
55. Philip R. Cateora, *International Marketing,* 7th ed. (Homewood, IL: Irwin, 1990), p. 589.

56. *See* Stanley Hollander and J. J. Boddewyn, "Retailing and Public Policy: An International Overview," *Journal of Retailing,* Spring 1974, pp. 55–66.
57. Erdener Kaynak, *Transnational Retailing* (Hawthorne, NY: Walter de Gruyter, Inc., 1988).
58. *United Nations Statistical Yearbook, 1983–1984.*
59. Johan Arndt, "Temporal Lags in Comparative Retailing," *Journal of Marketing,* October 1972, pp. 40–45. *Also see* Susan P. Douglas, "Patterns and Parallels of Marketing Structures in Several Countries," *MSU Business Topics,* Spring 1971, p. 48.
60. Ibid., p. 45.
61. Frank Meissner, "Capital-Intensive Supermarket Technology Can't Serve Needs of Poor in Third World," *Marketing News,* November 27, 1981, p. 15.
62. *See* Madhav Kacker, "Coming to Terms with Global Retailing," *International Marketing Review,* Spring 1986, pp. 7–20.
63. "Wal-Mart Gets Lost in the Vegetable Aisle," *Business Week,* May 28, 1990, p. 48.
64. "A Retail Rebel Has the Establishment Quaking," *Business Week,* April 1, 1991, p. 39.
65. Carla Rapport, "Ready, Set, Sell—Japan Is Buying," *Fortune,* September 11, 1989, p. 159.
66. Maria Shao, "U.S. Fast Food Chains Sprout in Taiwan as Affluence Creates New Appetites," *The Asian Wall Street Journal Weekly,* September 9, 1985, p. 16. *Also see* "McWorld?" *Business Week,* October 13, 1986, p. 78; and "Kentucky Fried Chicken Finds Favor in Bejing," *Asian Wall Street Journal Weekly,* September 26, 1988, p. 25.
67. Masayoshi Kanabayashi, "Busy Japanese Turning to Mail Order, Which They Once Spurned as Shoddy," *The Wall Street Journal,* June 26, 1985, p. 301. *Also see* "The Japanese Go on a Mail-Order Shopping Spree," *Business Week,* September 7, 1987, p. 44; and "Next, a Mail-Model," *The Economist,* January 16, 1988, p. 65.
68. Vern Terpstra, *International Marketing,* 4th ed. (Homewood, IL): Irwin, 1987, p. 391.
69. Kaoru Kobayashi, "Marketing in Japan," *Tradepia International,* Winter 1980, pp. 22–23.
70. "Toys 'R' Us Goes Overseas and Finds That Toys 'R' Them Too," *Business Week,* January 26, 1987, p. 71. *Also see* "Guess Who's Selling Barbies in Japan Now," *Business Week,* December 9, 1991, p. 72; and "Toy Joy," *The Economist,* January 4, 1992, p. 62.
71. "Harrods Ventures Beyond Britannia," *Business Week,* April 19, 1982, p. 36.
72. "Printemps Finds Tough Climbing in the Rockies," *Business Week,* November 28, 1988, p. 101. *Also see* "Purveyors to All Nations," *The Economist,* December 5, 1987, p. 20; "Clothing Makers Go Straight to the Consumer," *Business Week,* April 29, 1985, p. 114; Madhav Kacker, "Coming to Terms with Global Retailing," *International Marketing Review,* Spring 1986, pp. 7–20; and *The Economist,* October 22, 1988, p. 68.
73. T. R. L. Black and John U. Farley, "Retailers in Social Program Strategy: The Case of Family Planning," *Columbia Journal of World Business,* Winter 1977, pp. 33–43.
74. Bradley K. Martin, "Japan's Mom-and-Pop Stores Cooped Up," *The Wall Street Journal,* September 18, 1985, p. 23.
75. *See* Lawrence S. Welch, "Diffusion of Franchise System Use in International Operations," *International Marketing Review,* vol. 6, no. 5 (1989), pp. 7–13.
76. *Business America,* May 9, 1988, p. 27.
77. *Business America,* May 9, 1988, p. 27. *Also see* "Franchising Is Still Proving Its Validity as a Marketing Method," *Business America,* March 16, 1987, p. 18.
78. Luu Trankiem, "International Franchising: A Way to Capture Foreign Markets," *Los Angeles Business and Economics,* Summer–Fall, 1979, p. 27.
79. Joann S. Lublin, "For U.S. Franchisers, a Common Tongue Is Not a Guarantee of Success in the U.K.," *The Wall Street Journal,* August 16, 1988, p. 25.
80. *See* Niazamettin Aydin and Madhav Kacker, "International Outlook of U.S.-Based Franchisers," *International Marketing Review,* vol. 7, no. 2 (1990), pp. 43–53.
81. L. Soorikian, "Planning and Control in International PD," *Transportation and Distribution Management,* January–February 1974, p. 36. *Also see* James L. Heskett and Peter F. Mathias, "The Management of Logistics in MNCs," *Columbia Journal of World Business,* Spring 1976, pp. 52–62.

82. Michael R. Czinkota, "Logistics: The Critical Ingredient in International Marketing," in Michael G. Harvey and Robert F. Lusch, eds., *Marketing Channels: Domestic and International Perspectives* (Norman, OK: Center for Economic and Management Research, School of Business Administration, The University of Oklahoma, 1982), pp. 24–29.

83. Jacques Picard, "The Management of Physical Distribution in Multinational Corporations," *Columbia Journal of World Business,* Winter 1982, pp. 67–73.

84. Robert E. Schellberg, "Kodak: A Case Study of International Distribution," *Columbia Journal of World Business,* Spring 1976, pp. 32–38.

CHAPTER • 15

International Advertising

CHAPTER FOCUS

After studying this chapter, you should be able to:

- Compare the pros and cons of using standardized versus localized advertising
- Examine the development and availability of international media
- Describe the steps in an international advertising program
- Discuss global advertising regulations
- Explain the role of advertising agencies internationally

Promotion is the fourth and and final decision about marketing mix. Promotion means communication with the customer. The creation of awareness, interest, desire, and action is the universal aim of the promotion mix. Coordinating and integrating promotion with other aspects of a marketing strategy are often quite difficult to achieve in overseas markets. The quality, availability, and scheduling of promotional tools all influence the degree of success realized by a product or service.

Promotion includes advertising, personal selling, sales promotion, and publicity. Advertising refers to the corporate-sponsored messages transmitted through the mass media. Personal selling involves person-to-person contact with the customer. Sales promotion consists of different techniques (for example, samples, trading stamps, point-of-purchase promotion, coupons, contests, gifts, allowances, and displays) that support and complement advertising and personal selling. Publicity includes seeking favorable comments on the product/service and/or the firm itself through a write-up or presentation in mass media for which the sponsor is not charged. The focus of this chapter is on advertising. (Personal selling and other forms of promotion will be examined in Chapter 16.)

There are several important considerations in the design of international advertising and what it communicates. One important strategic consideration is whether to standardize advertising worldwide or to adapt it to match the environment of each country. Another consideration is the availability of media, which varies around the world. The development of advertising programs for foreign markets should take these differences, as well as advertising regulations in international markets, into account. The expertise of international advertising agencies can be valuable.

Perspectives of International Advertising

Worldwide, advertising plays a crucial role. In the case of many products/markets, a successful advertising campaign is the critical factor in achieving sales goals. As a matter of fact, more and more companies consider successful advertising to be requisite to profitable international operations.[1]

Global advertising expenditures were estimated to be $223.4 billion in 1988, and projected to increase to $650 billion by the year 2000. Outside the United States, advertising expenditures could rise from $180 billion in 1990 to $300 billion by 2000.[2] These are impressive projections. Marketers abroad more and more are emulating U.S. advertising practices. The broad dimensions of the U.S. advertising industry changed significantly between 1960 and 1990. The total amount of money spent for advertising rose from a little less than $12 billion to more than $88 billion, more than a sevenfold increase. During the same period, the economy of the United States also increased approximately six times. Advertising as a percentage of GNP should rise in many countries as their media and marketing practices move increasingly in directions pursued in the United States. For example, with the advent of current development in China, the advertising

International Marketing Highlight 15.1

Television Advertising in Asia

Commercial television in Asia has emerged and expanded, stimulating fresh marketing efforts. Japan, the most mature television advertising market in Asia, has seen its market more than double since 1982 to $8.2 billion. And two of the largest potential consumer markets on the continent—China and India—have opened their doors to commercial television by expanding Western programming. General evening viewing in India is expected to climb to 400 million people by 1995.

Television ad expenditures in Asia do not come close to matching those of Western Europe, but the pace of growth has been more dramatic. In fact, between 1980 and 1986, Asian ad expenditures (excluding Japan) climbed 58.6 percent, versus 27.5 percent in Europe.

The signs of change can be discerned in television advertising data for selected Asian nations. For its survey, *World Advertising Expenditures* (1982–1987), Starch, INRA, Hooper Inc. recorded these gains:

- India, up from $16.2 million to $108 million;
- Japan, up from $3.6 billion to $8.2 billion;
- South Korea, up from $194 million to $430 million;
- Malaysia, up from $21 million to $66 million;
- Taiwan, up from $95 million to $266 million.

Source: Business International, February 20, 1989, p. 54.

industry has been growing at a rate of 50 percent a year[3] (see International Marketing Highlight 15.1).

Table 15.1 summarizes advertising expenditures during 1990 in selected countries. As might be expected, advanced countries account for a greater proportion of the expenditures than do Third World nations. As a matter of fact, it may be postulated that advertising expenditures are significantly related to economic development.

Advertising is a key tool in international marketing. While the rationale for advertising may vary from country to country and among industries within a country, its overall relevance remains beyond question.[4] Like any other tool, of course, advertising can be misused and misapplied. But as long as the ethics of advertising are maintained, it serves a useful purpose. Advertising is important for the following specific reasons.[5] First, advertising involves a significant commitment of funds—the cost of effective and ineffective advertising varies little. Further, an effective advertising campaign represents a tangible resource, transferable from one market to another. Obviously every effort must be made to achieve effective advertising performance and so create a durable asset. Second, for many companies advertising is their sole representative internationally. The

TABLE 15.1 **A Comparison of Population, Advertising Expenditures, and GNP**

COUNTRY	1990 POPULATION (IN MILLIONS)	TOTAL 1990 ADVERTISING EXPENDITURES (MILLIONS U.S. $)	1990 PER CAPITA ADVERTISING EXPENDITURES (U.S. $)	1990 ADVERTISING AS A % OF GNP
Argentina	32.29	$ 829.7	$ 25.7	1.1%
Australia	17.01	3,847.9	226.3	1.3
Austria	7.64	1,012.0	132.4	0.7
Bahrain	.50	11.0	21.8	—
Belgium	10.02	1,283.3	128.1	0.8
Bolivia	7.31	64.7	8.9	1.4
Brazil	150.20	3,186.5	21.2	0.8
China, People's Republic	1,133.70	523.0	.5	0.1
Colombia	32.84	476.4	14.5	1.2
Costa Rica	2.80	67.9	24.2	1.3
Cyprus	.70	4.8	6.8	0.1
Denmark	5.14	1,377.2	268.0	1.2
Dominican Republic	7.14	58.5	8.2	1.0
Ecuador	10.56	45.7	4.3	0.5
Finland	4.98	1,800.2	361.6	1.4
France	56.45	12,891.9	228.4	1.2
Germany, Federal Republic	62.00	13,944.4	224.9	1.0
Greece	10.05	526.1	52.4	0.9
Guatemala	9.20	16.4	1.8	—
Hong Kong	5.78	861.4	149.1	1.3
India	849.51	895.8	1.1	0.3
Indonesia	181.58	286.9	1.6	0.3
Ireland	3.50	321.1	91.6	1.0
Israel	4.64	587.9	126.8	1.2
Italy	57.59	5,709.7	99.1	0.6
Japan	123.50	38,433.6	311.2	1.2
Kenya	24.37	20.5	.8	0.2
Korea, South	42.79	2,826.1	66.0	1.2
Malaysia	17.75	321.7	18.1	0.8
Malta	.35	14.5	41.1	0.6
Mexico	86.16	2,199.3	25.5	1.0
Netherlands	14.93	4,334.7	290.3	1.7
New Zealand	3.41	624.5	183.4	1.4
Norway	4.24	1,233.3	290.7	1.3
Oman	1.55	11.9	7.7	—
Pakistan	113.69	89.6	.8	0.2
Panama	2.42	54.0	22.3	1.2
Portugal	10.37	415.6	40.1	0.8
Qatar	.44	10.8	24.6	0.2
Saudi Arabia	14.90	139.7	9.4	—
Singapore	2.72	314.8	115.7	0.9
Spain	39.33	10,350.2	263.2	2.4
Sri Lanka	17.00	21.1	1.2	0.3
Sweden	8.55	2,729.3	319.1	1.3

(continued)

TABLE 15.1 (*Continued*)

COUNTRY	1990 POPULATION (IN MILLIONS)	TOTAL 1990 ADVERTISING EXPENDITURES (MILLIONS U.S. $)	1990 PER CAPITA ADVERTISING EXPENDITURES (U.S. $)	1990 ADVERTISING AS A % OF GNP
Switzerland	6.69	4,098.0	612.6	1.9
Taiwan	16.00	1,569.3	98.1	—
Trinidad and Tobago	1.28	23.5	18.3	0.5
United Arab Emirates	1.59	69.5	43.7	—
United Kingdom	57.48	15,816.0	275.1	1.7
United States	250.94	128,640.0	512.6	2.4
Venezuela	19.74	439.2	22.3	0.9
Zambia	8.12	4.2	.5	0.1
Zimbabwe	9.81	26.3	2.7	0.4

Source: World Advertising Expenditures (New York: Starch, INRA, Hooper and International Advertising Association, 1992), pp. 16–17.

image and impression created by advertising reflect on the entire corporation. If advertising succeeds in establishing and maintaining desired market images, it can pave the way for expansion. Third, advertising should establish the desired position for a product in a market. Once this position has been achieved, any local disturbances and changes, such as price-related effects, are less significant. Fourth, global advertising requires a certain degree of centralization, which in itself becomes a measure of control over global activities. Finally, advertising provides the most cost-effective method for communicating with potential buyers and creating markets in other countries (see International Marketing Highlight 15.2).

It is worth noting that the purposes of advertising as well as the methods employed vary between developed and developing countries. For example, stimulation of consumer demand is often a goal in industrialized countries in order to promote the growth of output and employment. In developing countries, however, where supplies of consumer goods are in short supply, the same purpose would be dysfunctional. Rather, diversion of demand from supply-constrained products to those that are plentiful would be a sound alternative aim.[6]

Very often international advertisers fail to appreciate the differences that exist between the industrialized nations and Third World countries. This blindness leads to unprecedented problems. Exhibit 15.1 illustrates how global advertisers create the problems by their initial failures to appreciate the differences between developed and developing countries.

Determining Advertising Strategy: Standardization Versus Localization

An important strategic decision for international marketers to make is whether the basics of an advertising campaign developed at home can be transferred to other nations with changes like translation into local languages. Many marketers

International Marketing Highlight 15.2

International Coffee War

When you think of coffee, what country do you think of? When researchers asked that question in 1959, most U.S. consumers replied, "Brazil." The National Federation of Coffee Growers of Colombia found to their dismay that the country of Colombia received almost no mentions.

Obviously the Colombia coffee growers felt a major awareness campaign was needed. They also wanted U.S. consumers to identify brands with 100 percent Colombian coffee as quality or premium. This might sound like an impossible mission. Who, after all, cares which country grows the coffee beans?

The Colombian coffee growers federation accepted the challenge. It developed the slogan "The Richest Coffee in the World" and the character of Juan Valdez as a spokesperson who taught consumers how to identify brands that contain 100 percent Colombian coffee. The Valdez character also explained the unique properties of Colombia that enabled it to grow the best coffee in the world.

DDB Needham ads established the premium image by featuring upscale settings with discriminating consumers enjoying 100 percent Colombian coffee. For example, one ad featured a businessman sitting in a lush grand parlor in front of a fireplace reading *The Wall Street Journal* and drinking a cup of Colombian coffee. The copy featured only the headline: "50% Tax Bracket, 100% Colombian Coffee," the Juan Valdez logo, and the campaign slogan.

By the mid-1980s unaided awareness of Colombia as a coffee-producing country reached an all-time high of 96 percent. Additionally, 62 percent of consumers believed that Colombia grows the best coffee. In the great coffee war Colombia took the offensive away from Brazil. In 1983 only thirty-five coffee brands featured the Colombia logo. Today, 640 brands are in the program. People are willing to pay 15 percent more for the Colombian coffee compared with the blends.

Source: "The Richest Coffee in the World," DDB Needham Case Study, unpublished document.

strongly believe that a successful advertising concept will do well anywhere. Critics, however, are quick to reject standardization on the ground that cultural differences between nations require advertising to be tailored to each country. This section examines the arguments for and against global transferability of advertising and proposes an analytical approach to the formulation of advertising strategy.

Standardized Approach

Many practitioners and scholars believe that universal advertising can work advantageously. A Swedish executive, for example, found that savings bank promotions were successfully transferable all over Scandinavia.[7] Similarly, Fatt supports a standardized approach, believing that "the desire to be beautiful is universal.

EXHIBIT 15.1 Illustrations of Problems International Advertisers Face in Developing Countries

---

The Medium Is Not Always the Message

The level of the media technology in most developing countries amounts to one radio and one television station. Making matters worse is an increasing hostility toward foreign dominance of Third World media. In the early 1970s, 40 percent of Peruvian, 50 percent of Bolivian, and 85 percent of Costa Rican prime time programming were packaged, commercials and all, by U.S. networks. In reaction some Third World countries banned foreign investment in all areas of communications.

Esperanto, Anyone?

Not long ago the residents of a Middle Eastern country saw an auto ad about a new suspension system that, in translation, said the car was "suspended from the ceiling." Since there are at least thirty different dialects in the eighteen Arab countries, there is plenty of room for error. Not even print ads are free from the dangers of dialect; by making a wrong choice in calligraphy styles, for example, an advertiser could offend a conservative Moslem nation.

Not with My Wife, You Don't

Whether glamor queens such as Revlon's Lauren Hutton or symbols of Middle American wholesomeness like Betty Crocker, women play an important role in American advertising. In a number of developing nations, however, one must tread cautiously when escorting people into Rosie's diner. In Saudi Arabia, for example, advertisers were recently told they could no longer use women—veiled or unveiled.

Hold the Pickles, Hold the Lettuce, Hold the Hamburger

As the Armour meat-packaging company found when it tried to open a branch office in Goa, India, one cannot milk a sacred cow. Cultural taboos vary from nation to nation; it is imperative that advertisers learn about and avoid them.

You Can't Fight City Hall

In Bahrain, an independent state in the Persian Gulf, outdoor advertiser Poster Projects Company learned the hard way that feuds with the government are bad for business. During a dispute with Poster Projects over the imposition of the world's biggest outdoor advertising tax, Bahrain municipal officials sneaked out at the crack of dawn one Saturday and tore down every billboard Poster Projects had erected a week earlier. The company capitulated, ending the dispute. One might complain that "there oughtta be a law," but there usually isn't.

Blondes Have More Fun . . . or Do They?

American advertising is populated with fair-haired, freckle-faced children and lanky, Athletic adults with year-round tans. In the Third World most people have black hair, brown eyes, and skin tones that range from black to brown to yellow. Imagine for a moment switching on your television and discovering that all the men in the commercials are wearing turbans. This is precisely the jarring effect a typical American commercial has on a resident of the Third World.

Great Expectations

In a country where anyone from a peanut salesman to an ex-actor can be president, upward mobility is an inalienable right. Advertising frequently appeals to the Horatio Alger within us, encouraging a desire for bigger, better, and newer. Keeping up with the Joneses may be a fine way for Americans to pass time, but in many Third World

EXHIBIT 15.1 (*Continued*)

nations where 60 percent of the wealth is held by 10 percent of the people (compared to 27 percent in the U.S.), it's almost impossible. In the 1974 book *Global Reach,* the authors describe a phenomenon found in several Peruvian villages: a small stone is painted to resemble a transistor radio and "peasants too poor to buy a real one carry it for status."

Source: "Mistakes People Make," *Grey Matter,* no. 1 (1981), a publication of Grey Advertising Inc., p. 3.

Such appeals as 'mother and child,' 'freedom from pain,' 'glow of health,' know no boundaries."[8]

Empirical research on the subject and the experiences of many marketers confirm that such sentiments abound among advertisers. In a field study, Dunn found that successful U.S. ads were indeed transferable to Europe and even the Middle East.[9] In their study sample of Fortune 500 firms, Donnelly and Ryans discovered that 90 percent of the firms to at least some degree extended their U.S. advertising approach to nondomestic situations.[10] International Playtex's recent experiences with the Jhirmack line of hair-care products support the standardized approach.

> The more we deviate from our original marketing plans, the more problems we encounter . . . our packaging, advertising and promotion are virtually identical and only vary when local regulations prohibit certain activities.[11]

International Playtex, Inc.'s efforts in developing a standardized campaign for its Wow bra are all the more revealing. The company traditionally ran forty-three versions of its ads worldwide, employing different ad agencies in various countries. For Wow, the company assigned the entire global business to Grey Advertising, Inc. The ad theme was based on a single feature: Wow provides the extra support features of underwire bras without using uncomfortable wires. The company uses a plastic that took three years to develop. Beyond the basic theme, however, the commercial for each market had to be fine-tuned to meet local requirements. For example, the most noticeable change in the commercial had to be made for South Africa, where TV standards don't allow women to be shown modeling bras. In this market, fully clothed models hold up the bra on a hanger, while in other countries the models wear the bras. Further, some commercials had to be twenty-nine seconds long, while others had to be thirty seconds long, because some countries want one second of silence at the beginning of the ad, while others do not. Certain national preferences also had to be observed: the French like lacy bras, while Americans prefer plainer, opaque styles.

Creating a global commercial that met government regulations and industry standards in different countries required good logistics. Grey Advertising, for example, showed Playtex foreign managers videotapes of potential models for ads. Three models were selected by consensus from over fifty prospects. Overall, the standardized approach did pay off. The Wow campaign allowed Playtex to present one unified message and save money. Grey was able to produce the Wow ad for a dozen countries for $250,000; the average cost of producing a single U.S. ad is $100,000.[12]

There is an apparent trend toward standardization. A number of companies, including A.T. Cross Pencil Company, Deere & Co., and Levi Strauss & Co., have been reported as favoring standardization.[13] Proponents of the standardized approach advance various reasons to support their viewpoint.[14] First, there is the cost savings. Once an advertising concept is developed, it can be transferred to other nations with minor additional cost. Second is the realization of economies of scale made possible by the centralization of worldwide advertising authority to the home office. Third, standardization permits full utilization of home office advertising expertise hard won on the field. Fourth, it prevents the generation of disparate messages in different nations, which eventually may blur the established image of the product. Fifth, the common approach to advertising ensures proper concern for corporatewide objectives in promoting the product. Finally, similarities in the usage of media among specific segments across nations justify the standardized approach. For example, Urban's study on the subject showed that French and American women belonging to the same socioeconomic groups revealed similar media usage behavior (see Exhibit 15.2).[15] Culture aside, this means that a particular type of segment in one country exhibits behavior comparable to that of a similar segment in another country. Thus, businesspeople in France may not differ from those in the United States, Egypt, or Singapore. Presumably, then, a standard advertising strategy, can be employed to reach businesspeople in many countries (see International Marketing Highlight 15.3).

Localized Advertising

Customization of advertising for each nation is justified on the grounds of cultural differences among countries. A strong proponent of this school of thought is anthropologist Edward T. Hall.[16] The international marketing literature is full of examples illustrating how efforts at standardization have backfired. Consider the following example:

> A worldwide leader in the toilet goods field built up one of its toothpaste brands to a leadership position in its home market with a promise of decay prevention. Given this success, the same promise was used to introduce the product in Latin American markets. The company was well-established in that part of the world, and together with its advertising agency developed on-site a new advertising campaign to carry the decay-prevention message—an execution tailored to those markets in every detail. At the end of one year of broad-scale advertising and selling effort, the product was withdrawn. It had achieved only a 3 percent share of market instead of the 15 percent achieved in the United States.
>
> A leading producer of farm equipment was particularly pleased with the success of a North American advertising campaign which was built around the testimonials of small farmers. The manufacturer felt that this campaign combined the traditional virtues of an endorsement by actual users with the added element of those customers to whom economy of use was a vital factor in their purchase decision. For these reasons, the testimonial campaign was introduced into Europe. The advertising vice president was dismayed to receive an urgent Telex

EXHIBIT 15.2 Media Usage Patterns: U.S. and French Women

1. In both the United States and France, women who are employed full-time report watching less television than do women who stay at home. In the United States, full-time workers listen to more radio than do homemakers.
2. In both the United States and France, women with college-level educations watch less television and read more newspapers and magazines than do women with less formal education. In France, the better-educated women listen to less radio than women with less education.
3. In both the United States and France, women with higher incomes watch less television. In the United States, these women read more newspapers and magazines than do women with lower incomes. Also, they listen to more radio. In France, higher-income women listen to less radio than do their lower-income counterparts.
4. Socioeconomic influences on television usage are similar in both the United States and France.
5. Within each country, the influence of socioeconomic variables is the same for newspapers and magazines.
6. In the United States, income significantly differentiates consumption levels of all media categories; in France, education is of importance with respect to all media.
7. There are striking similarities in cross-national consumer media use patterns of all media except radio.
8. In both the United States and France, women employed full-time read more news magazines and fashion magazines then do full-time homemakers.
9. In both the United States and France, college-educated women read more news, household, fashion, women's service, and popular interest magazines than do grammar-school educated women. Also in both countries, college-educated women read fewer confessions magazines.
10. In both the United States and France, women with higher incomes read more news, household, and popular interest magazines, and fewer confessions magazines. In the United States, higher-income women also read more women's service magazines and sex magazines than do lower-income women. In France, the higher-income women read more business and fashion magazines than their lower-income counterparts.

Source: Christine D. Urban, "A Cross-National Comparison of Consumers' Media Use Patterns," *Columbia Journal of World Business,* Winter 1977, pp. 53–64.

from the largest distributor organization demanding that the campaign be withdrawn after only two weeks. The distributor had been flooded with telegrams from his dealers. They all found the campaign to be insulting and described it like this: "Most of our farms in Europe are small to begin with. When you stress 'smallness' so much, our customers think you are talking about peasants. And who likes advice from them?"[17]

Briefly, product-related attributes influence buyer behavior differently around the globe. Thus, a standard approach to advertising may not be practical. For example, General Motors' Nova car did not do well in Latin America since *no va* translated into Spanish means "doesn't go." Emphasis on "whiteness" from

International Marketing Highlight 15.3

Gillette's Panregional Approach

Gillette has organized its advertising plans according to regional and cultural clusters: pan-Latin America, pan-Middle East, pan-Africa, and pan-Atlantic. This is the result of what Gillette calls convergence, which is based on the belief that the company can identify the same purchase incentives and needs among consumers in regions or in countries that are linked by culture, consumers' habits, and development of the company's market for products.

For example, Gillette may use the same European-style advertising for Australia, New Zealand, and South Africa. In Asia, the company will link the less economically developed countries of Malaysia, Thailand, the Philippines, and Indonesia. It will market Singapore, Hong Kong, and Taiwan together, but handle Japan, China, and India separately.

The overall objective of Gillette's panregional strategy, which sells some 800 products in 200 countries, is to approximate a global marketing strategy while remaining sensitive to regional and national differences. Every two years Gillette conducts research on brand usage of its products and those of competitors in most major markets.

Source: Business International, February 20, 1989, p. 51.

a laundry detergent will not work in Brazil because Brazilians do not wear white clothes. Chileans buy their coffee strictly on the basis of price, but for Germans good coffee is a must for which they would pay any price.[18] Kentucky Fried Chicken is viewed as an ordinary meal in the United States, while the Japanese consider it to be a treat.[19] A television candy commercial for South Africa with a circus elephant had to be changed since the animal is sacred to the Venda people, the segment to which the ad was directed. Besides, the royal title of the wife of the king of neighboring Swaziland is "she-elephant," and it was feared the ad might offend that country.[20] Students of West African culture recommend against printing an advertisement on white paper there. In West Africa, white is associated with death and it might be perceived as a death notice. Grammatical errors in copy annoy the French. The macho image of a model wearing a hard hat does not excite Latin Americans. They prefer their macho men in suits suitable for executives. Testimonial advertising is considered "pushy" and "phony" among the Japanese.[21]

Perhaps the classic success story of standardized advertising has been Exxon's campaign built around the slogan: "Put a Tiger in Your Tank." This was translated into numerous languages worldwide. For example, in French it read: "Put a tiger in your motor." Ryans, nevertheless, has questioned whether this campaign was really as universal as acclaimed.[22]

Gillette, in its efforts to introduce its Trac II razor to Europe in 1972, found out that products in the toiletries category are geared to cultural traits and lifestyles and thus the U.S. advertising approach would fail abroad. In its attempt to develop localized advertising, the company changed the Trac II name to G II in some nations, since marketing research showed that *trac* in some of the Romance languages meant "fragile." Similarly, the copy design was adapted to match the local perspective. The U.S. copy showed builders constructing a new and unique razor. In Europe a sports analogy made sense, emphasizing synchronization of two moves to score a goal, or the closest shave through G II.[23]

Although product attributes and functions are generally similar in different countries, the perception of these attributes varies from nation to nation. Thus, the common needs of people belonging to different nations do not mean necessarily that the same products will be appreciated in the same ways. This suggests that standardized advertising will not work globally.

> Product [need] universality cannot imply global message appeal. . . . [Israeli and American women] might manifest the same need for cosmetics (i.e. preservation of beauty), but this certainly does not mean that an Israeli woman perceives the American cosmetic ad the same way it is perceived by the American. Therefore, understanding consumer wants, needs, motives, and behavior is a necessary condition to the development of an effective promotional program.[24]

A standardized advertising approach seems particularly unsuited in developing countries because an international advertiser is likely to encounter marked differences in lifestyle, level of wealth, market structure, and various other aspects of the environment in the countries. Amine and Cavusgil, for example, found localized advertising more appropriate in Morocco, since knowledge of local environment and campaign targeting are essential for effective advertising.[25]

Strategy Selection

The determination of international advertising strategy is not a simple matter of choosing between standardization and localization. Conditions differ from nation to nation. Further, while one campaign may have been successfully transferred, another campaign might flop in the same country.[26] Besides, even where localization appears satisfactory, companies naturally do not want to give up the benefits of standardization. To resolve the problem, strategy should be formulated after careful analysis and consideration. The recommended procedure consists of three steps: apply choice criteria, analyze advertising transferability, and make organizational arrangements.

Choice Criteria The extension of the home country advertising program to a host country is affected by the following factors: host country environment, advertising objectives relative to the host country, target market, product characteristics, media availability and cost–benefit relationship. Although it may not be feasible to combine all these influencing factors into a quantitative model, an international advertiser should find even a qualitative, sequential examination of these criteria helpful.

Environmental factors. Exhibit 15.3 lists thirty-one factors that have been identified through empirical research as helpful in making decisions on advertising transferability across national boundaries. Not all these factors would be relevant in every case. It would be desirable, therefore, to diagnose and identify the most salient environmental concerns for a product/market.

EXHIBIT 15.3 Thirty-One Environmental Variables Useful for Formulating Advertising Strategy*

Rate of economic growth of country
Per capita income and distribution of income
Average size of household
Level of literacy
Level of educaiton
Vocational training
Social class structure
Attitudes toward authority
Attitudes toward the United States
Degree of nationalism in country
Attitudes toward achievement and work
Attitudes toward risk taking
Attitudes toward wealth and monetary gain
Similarity of ethical and moral standards to U.S. standards
Availability of time on commercial broadcast media
Adequate coverage of market by broadcast media
Availability of satisfactory outdoor media
Availability of satisfactory print media
Independence of media from government control
Political organization and stability
Import/export rate of country
Legal restraints on advertising within the country
Availability of prototype campaigns
Relative importance of visual versus verbal in ad message
Experience and competence of personnel in foreign subsidiary and distributor
Experience and competence of personnel in foreign agency or branch of U.S. agency
Eating patterns and customs
Importance of self-service retailing
Import duties and quotas in country
Development and acceptance of international trademark or trade name
Applicability of product's theme or slogan to other markets

---

*Listed in order of decreasing importance.

Source: S. Watson Dunn, "Effect of National Identity on Multinational Promotional Strategy in Europe," *Journal of Marketing,* October 1976, p. 52.

For example, factors considered important from the viewpoint of consumer goods companies in developed countries are level of education; level of literacy; attitudes toward risk taking, achievement, work, wealth, and monetary gain; experience and competence of personnel in foreign agency or branch of U.S. agency, foreign subsidiary, or distributor; degree of nationalism in the country and attitudes toward the United States; rate of economic growth of country; per capita income and distribution of income; import duties and quotas in the country; development and acceptance of international trademark and trade name; eating patterns and customs; importance of self-service retailing; attitudes toward authority; social structure; applicability of product or slogan to other markets; independence of media from government control; and availability of satisfactory media.[27] Clearly, a different set of factors would be applicable to industrial goods. Likewise, the factors relative to developing countries are likely to be different. However, if the overall perspectives of the environmental factors vis-à-vis the host country are similar to those of the United States, standardization might be feasible. A significant difference in the environment, however, would suggest localized advertising.

Advertising objectives. Advertising objectives vary from market to market. Advertising does not lead directly to sales. A sale is a multiphased phenomenon, and advertising can be used for transferring the customer from one phase to the next. One writer states: "Advertising attempts to move consumers from unawareness of a product or service—to awareness—to comprehension—to conviction—to action."[28] Presumably, customers in the host country may not be at the same point in the product adoption cycle as those in the home country. If this is so, the advertising objectives of the two markets would differ and thus the home-country advertising concept might not work in the host country. For example, a television manufacturer's advertising objectives for Mexico would have to be different from those for the United States because in the United States television is in the maturity stage of the product life cycle, while in Mexico it is in the growth stage. In Mexico, the major focus of advertising may be to move the customer from awareness to comprehension, while in the United States from conviction to action. Thus, the U.S. advertising concept for marketing televisions would not be effective in Mexico.

Target market. If the proposed ad campaign for another country is aimed toward a segment that is more or less similar in characteristics to the segment served in the United States, standardized advertising would appear satisfactory. But, if the target segments differ, a localized campaign would be desirable. For advertising purposes, Ryans proposes dividing the market into three consumer categories:

1. International sophisticates: a select group of well-to-do and successful people who are mainly in the developed countries and who have international exposure because of travel, education, responsibility, and the like.
2. Semisophisticates: a large group of middle- and high-income individuals who are largely in developed countries and who have substantial discretionary income.
3. Provincials: people who have a narrow outlook and ethnocentric orientation.[29]

Of the three groups, the first one would be most receptive to standardized advertising. The provincial group can effectively be reached through localized advertising. The semisophisticates may or may not be convinced by the standardized approach, depending on the nature of the product.

Product characteristics. The nature of the product involved is another factor determining the usage of standardized international advertising.[30] According to Britt, product attributes include both purchase and usage consumption patterns, psychological characteristics associated with the product (e.g., attitude), and cultural criteria.[31] Table 15.2 includes questions that should be raised relative to consumption patterns, psychological characteristics, and cultural criteria. For example, under consumption patterns one of the questions is "Do the same family members motivate the purchase in all target countries?" If the answer to this question is positive, standardized advertising would be attractive.[32] Although it may not be feasible to specify a definite "yes" or "no" answer to all the questions raised in Table 15.2, a sense of direction can be gained by considering the questions. If the consideration of a product yields an affirmative sense of direction, then the use of standardized advertising would be recommended. Localized advertising would be preferable in cases where a negative sense dominates.

Media availability. Media availability is another consideration that determines the feasibility of using standardized advertising. For example, a U.S. television ad would not be suitable in India since commercial advertising on television is limited there. Because of legal restrictions in France, the International Playtex Company could not use coupons and door-to-door samples as it could in the United States for a promotion campaign for its Jhirmack line of hair-care products. The company was, therefore, obliged to launch in-store demonstrations.[33]

Cost–benefit relationship. In the final analysis, the choice between the standardized approach and localization should be based on a careful consideration of cost–benefit. If the cost of local adaptation exceeds the benefit that such an adaptation might provide, it is desirable to opt for standardized advertising. On the other hand, it would be reasonable to incur costs, as a form of investment, if the localized advertising could open up new opportunities that might be lost by sticking to the standardized advertising concept.[34]

Transferability Analysis There are two aspects to consider in advertising propositions for international transfer: the buying proposal and the creative presentation. The *buying proposal* refers to the content, not the form, of the advertisement.[35] Its focus is on the most persuasive and most relevant elements of the advertisement. The *creative presentation* assists in transferring the buying proposal into an advertising message, which consists of the headline idea and all the visual and verbal elements of the advertisement. Table 15.3 illustrates the difference between the two aspects. A buying proposal is far easier to transfer across national boundaries than are creative presentations because certain needs are basic worldwide and customer motivations for such products do not vary much. For example, expectations for a laundry detergent may not differ from nation to nation. Similarly, emphasis on punctuality by an airline would catch the fancy of businesspersons who fly frequently, regardless of their nationality.

Despite acceptable worldwide primary benefits, even the transferability of a buying proposal may be negatively affected by three factors:

TABLE 15.2 International Advertising Strategy: Impact of Product Characteristics

CONSUMPTION PATTERNS—PURCHASE AND USAGE	PSYCHOLOGICAL CHARACTERISTICS—ATTITUDES TOWARD PRODUCT AND BRAND	CULTURAL CRITERIA—SOCIETAL PROHIBITIONS
1. Is the product or service purchased by *relatively the same consumer income group* from one country to another? For example, if a preponderance of camera-purchasing Italians are in the upper quintile income bracket, while Japanese camera-owners are evenly dispersed along the entire income spectrum, standardized advertising appeals would not be effective. 2. Do *the same family members motivate the purchase* in all target countries? For instance, the housewife's demand for more leisure time typically motivates the purchase of dishwashers in both Canada and Britain. This makes standardized advertising more attractive. 3. Do *the same family members dictate brand choice* in all target countries? The family member who motivates the purchase is often not the same person to select the brand. For example, a child's desire for a sugarcoated cereal may not take away the mother's choice of corn flakes. If the same people dictate the brand choice in the different target countries, standardization is more feasible than otherwise. 4. Do *most consumers expect a product to have the same appearance?* In the United States, for example, the typical housewife engages in much more one-stop shopping than her European counterpart, and Americans usually have more shelf space at home. Conse-	1. Are *the basic psychological, social, and economic factors* motivating the purchase and use of the product or service the same for all target countries? For instance, persons in the travel industry must try to ascertain if going away on a vacation provides the same psychological uplift for Belgians or Brazilians as for Americans. Or when marketing food is the concern, advetising executives should be aware that in the Netherlands health attitudes may be quite different from those in nearby Belgium or France. 2. Are *the advantages and disadvantages of the product or service* in the minds of consumers basically the same from one country to another? 3. Does *the symbolic content of the product or service* differ from one country to another? Fro instance, there are certain U.S. products associated with status (Cadillacs, Theatre Guild membership) and others with glamor (imported perfumes, stylish clothes). This underlying symbolic content may not exist in the international market, making a standardized appeal virtually worthless. 4. Is *the psychic cost of purchasing or using the product or service* the same, whatever the country? For example, the purchase of female birth-control devices generally imposes a higher psychic cost in more fundamentalist, religious, and rural societies than in Stockholm.	1. Does *society restrict the purchase and/or use of the product or service* to a particular sex, age group, religious group, or education level? The restrictions can be either legally enforced or socially imposed as a result of the particular mores of the people. 2. Is there a *stigma attached to the product or service*—the brand name, advertising content, or type of artwork in one or more of the target countries? An unfortunate example concerns a U.S. aircraft manufacturer: "Intent on building a worldwide reputation as a manufacturer of superb defense weapons, it ran ads in France boasting about the 'military machine' it had produced. The reaction of the French was simple: 'Warmonger!' They had suffered from the impact of war in a way the United States has never experienced and cannot understand." 3. Does usage of the product or service as suggested by advertising interfere with *tradition in one country and not the others?* After all, tradition is a potent factor.

(*continued*)

TABLE 15.2 (*Continued*)

CONSUMPTION PATTERNS—PURCHASE AND USAGE	PSYCHOLOGICAL CHARACTERISTICS—ATTITUDES TOWARD PRODUCT AND BRAND	CULTURAL CRITERIA—SOCIETAL PROHIBITIONS
quently, the American may purchase big economy-sized boxes of laundry detergent, while the Swiss housewife may tend to purchase smaller, sixteen-ounce boxes. 5. Is *the purchase rate the same* regardless of the country? Many French housewives will make a *daily* stop at the local butcher for the evening's meat, whereas Americans usually go to the store for meat only once or twice a week. 6. Are *most purchases made at the same kind of retail outlet?* To pursue the above example, the French housewife will buy meat at the butcher (a specialized outlet), whereas the American usually shops in food centers (broad and expansive mixed-merchandise outlets). This makes advertising standardization difficult. 7. Do *most consumers spend the same amount of time* making the purchase? In other words, products classified as shopping goods or convenience goods in Germany are not necessarily so categorized in Brazil. 8. Do *most consumers use the product or service for the same purpose or purposes?* The French and Israelis normally bathe less frequently than Americans. Perfumes, therefore, may have more of a deodorant appeal in these countries than in the United States. A standardized advertising strategy would ignore this fact. As another exmple,	5. Does *the appeal of the product or service for a cosmopolitan market* differ, thus crossing national boundaries? In other words, does the fact that a product or service is widely known and distributed affect the way people in different countries perceive it? 6. Is *the brand name equally known and accepted* in all target countries? For example, Coca-Cola is a well-recognized brand name throughout most of the world, and this tends to make a standardized campaign quite effective. However, the brand name must also be accepted, not simply well known. Esso and Pfizer are two companies that undertook extensive computer research before naming a product for international use. The brand name must avoid unpleasant connotations, slang expressions, and difficult pronunciations. 7. Are *customer attitudes toward the package* basically the same? This question concerns both the shape and kind of package (for example, Pringles' cardboard canisters versus Lay's paper bag) as well as the words and pictures on display. 8. Are *customer attitudes toward pricing* basically the same? Americans who pay approximately $1.25 for a gallon of gasoline consider it an outrageous price, whereas Europeans accustomed to paying around $3.00 think that Americans have a bargain.	

(*continued*)

TABLE 15.2 (*Continued*)

CONSUMPTION PATTERNS—PURCHASE AND USAGE	PSYCHOLOGICAL CHARACTERISTICS—ATTITUDES TOWARD PRODUCT AND BRAND	CULTURAL CRITERIA—SOCIETAL PROHIBITIONS
bicycles primarily satisfy recreational needs in the United States, but they primarily provide a transportation function throughout much of the rest of the world. 9. Is *the product or service used in different amounts* from one target area or country to another? And a related question, does *the usage rate* (once a day, twice a week, etc.) *vary from country to country?* Wines are enjoyed much more often in France and Mexico than in Scandinavia or the United States. Yet orange juice is not a fixture at the breakfast table in Norway or Sweden, as it is in the United States. Variations in usage must be reflected in marketing strategies for these products. 10. Is *the method of preparation the same* in all target countries? A restaurant chain would not want to advertise its crisp broccoli in a country where its patrons usually like the broccoli stalks thoroughly cooked and tender. 11. Is *the product or service used along with other products or services?* If so, are these other products or services the same in all target countries? For example, an advertisement for cheese alongside a sudsy stein of beer would be consistent with German eating habits, but wine would be a more appropriate substitute if the cheese processor advertised in France.	9. Is *brand loyalty the same* throughout target countries for the product or service under consideration? For example, the French are much more likely to shop for clothes according to the manufacturer's name than are the Spanish. 10. Will *past advertising strategies conflict* with the projected standardized approach? A company that has traditionally promoted a bold, aggressive image may run into trouble designing a standardized campaign emphasizing subtle competence. 11. Are *the media of the target countries* suitable for a common advertising strategy? A standardized television campaign would hardly be advisable in a country such as Panama, where only the relatively rich can afford to own television sets.	

Source: Steuart Henderson Britt, "Standardizing Marketing for the International Market," *Columbia Journal of World Business,* Winter 1974, pp. 39–45.

TABLE 15.3 Differences Between Advertising Proposition and Presentation

PRODUCT CATEGORY	BUYING PROPOSAL	CREATIVE PRESENTATION
Leisure-time driving	Off-the-road technology	Jeep's "We wrote the book on 4-wheel drive"
Toothpaste	Cosmetic benefits	Colgate's "Ring of confidence"
Bank trust department	Conservative management	Chase Manhattan's "Nest egg"
Laundry detergents	Heavy-duty cleaning	Procter & Gamble's "Tide gets out the dirt kids get into"
Airline travel	In-flight service quality	British Caledonian's "The airline other airlines hate"

Source: Reprinted by permission of *Harvard Business Review.* An exhibit from "Improved Payoffs from Transnational Advertising" by James Killough, July–August 1978, p. 105.

1. Traditional beliefs (For example, some vacationers from some nations are more concerned about the wholesomeness of food than clean beaches and large hotel rooms.)
2. Contemporary behavior (For example, traits and preferences may have formed in variance from the traditional belief, such as an emphasis on natural foods among the younger generation.)
3. Product familiarity (For example, du Pont capitalized on the familiarity of its Teflon brand in its European advertising.)

A review of a buying proposal in the light of these three factors would indicate whether the primary benefits of the product will be relevant in the host country. If the answer is "yes," the buying proposal can be transferred with reasonable expectations for success.

The creative presentation, on the other hand, is difficult to transfer in its original form. The following barriers limit an intact transfer of creative presentation:

- Cultural barriers (In most Anglo-Saxon countries, women are accepted without question as family spokespersons, but much less so in Latin America and seldom in Muslim countries.)
- Communication barriers (Something accepted as funny in one country might be considered silly in another. Exxon's tiger ad, putting a cartoon character in the gas tank, did not make sense to the Swedes.)
- Legislative barriers (Laws and regulations imposed on the advertising industry differ among nations.)
- Competitive barriers (Competition for a product varies from one national

market to another and sometimes necessitates changes in advertising viewpoint for proper positioning.)

- Implementation barriers (such barriers might include poor printing and reproduction because of the level of facilities available, and the necessity of using local landscapes and models to avoid negative connotations.)

It would be naive to expect that a standardized creative presentation would succeed globally. Therefore, appropriate marketing research must be conducted to determine what elements of the creative presentation can be retained, what must be eliminated or replaced, and what should be added. As a matter of fact, once the creative presentation has been reworked, the advertisement should be tested in the prospective market before becoming final.

Organizational Support Whatever strategy is selected, its successful implementation requires appropriate organizational arrangements. If the standardized approach is adopted, the company should establish and adequately staff the international advertising office. For example, Deere & Company has organized its international advertising at a central office at its headquarters that develops yearly several hundred pieces of advertising in as many as twelve languages with the assistance of one advertising agency.[36]

Similarly, if a localized strategy is decided on, then communication links must be established to coordinate the advertising efforts of far-flung subsidiaries. Such a coordination not only would serve as a control device, but also should lead to cost savings. The advertising expertise developed at headquarters should be shared with subsidiary advertising people to avoid the necessity of reinventing the wheel, so to speak, for each operation.

In conclusion, it should be noted that no particular strategy is appropriate for all companies at all times. In fact, two companies in the same industry may well pursue different strategies (see International Marketing Highlight 15.4). Some companies adhere to a policy of standardization. This group includes such multinationals as International Playtex Company, British Airways, and Philip Morris Inc. For example, Phillip Morris has used the Marlboro-country concept and has kept the basic Marlboro look in all its ads worldwide. Traditionally, British Airways had decentralized advertising arrangements and its local managers enjoyed a great deal of autonomy. However, the decentralized arrangement led country managers to position British Airways in different markets differently. Therefore, in 1983 British Airways introduced a widely publicized global advertising campaign to present a common image worldwide. The campaign included the well-known ninety-second Manhattan Landing television commercial created by the Saatchi & Saatchi advertising agency, one of the leading proponents of global advertising.[37]

At the other end of the spectrum are those companies that have delegated almost the entire advertising responsibility to locals. Nestlé S.A., for example, utilizes 130 different ad agencies in over forty countries and has given near autonomy to country managers. There are companies in between the British Airways

International Marketing Highlight 15.4

Nike vs. Reebok: Marching to Different Drummers

Nike, the worldwide sports and fitness company, has created a global advertising program and tailored it regionally to local markets. The basic vehicle is the popular "Bo Knows" commercial that was used in the company's U.S. campaign. In that ad, Bo Jackson, an American professional football and baseball star, was seen taking part in a wide variety of other professional sports, such as tennis and basketball, while wearing Nike shoes and apparel. Well-known professional athletes from other sports exclaimed that "Bo knows" their sports as well.

For international use, Nike used Jackson in a similar ad while including athletes whose names where well known in the target countries, such as cricket star Ian Botham for ads that ran in the United Kingdom and soccer star Ian Rush for ads that ran in France, Sweden, Denmark, and Norway. The ads ran in the local European language without subtitles.

In contrast, another leading U.S. athletic shoe producer, Reebok, bases its international ad strategy on addressing the individual needs and national brand identities of each country while remaining under a global umbrella theme. Individual strategies may differ from country to country and are designed to capitalize on international talents and unique country differences, but the common thread of a global brand identity remains consistent.

For the most part, Reebok's foreign advertisements feature actors and athletes famous in each country, who promote the company's shoes in campaigns devised locally. However, U.S. commercials and print ads are often adapted for foreign use. For example, Reebok's new brand image campaign, "It's Time to Play," is in use in France, but with a revised edit that is more in tune with the demographics of that market.

Source: Marketing News, December 4, 1989, p. 10.

and Nestlé styles that pursue a patterned approach, establishing basic guidelines for global advertising centrally and leaving development of individual campaigns to locals. In the final analysis, whatever the advertising strategy, a company must consider local factors. Even products that had been considered sure winners have been hurt by a failure to reckon with local realities. General Foods' Maxwell House was dismayed to find that the great American coffee had little respect among the Germans. Similarly, Procter & Gamble's Crest fluoride appeal did not mean much to English customers.[38] The theory that people are alike and that they have the same generic needs and preferences does not always hold true in international advertising.

A recent study of U.S. and Japanese advertisements, featuring products and services in a home setting, showed significant differences between the two countries. The Japanese advertising emphasized status to a much greater degree than did U.S. ads. The reverse was true with personal efficacy, which was more prominent in U.S. ads[39] (see International Marketing Highlight 15.5).

Media

The global growth of the advertising industry is directly related to the development and availability of mass media. Mass media are most highly developed in the United States, followed by Britain, Germany, France, Japan, and Italy. In the less-developed countries, where a majority of the world population lives, the mass media are far behind. This is evident in the information contained in Table 15.4 and Table 15.5.

Table 15.4 shows the number of newspapers (local and regional/national) and magazines (consumer/trade and technical) for selected countries. Although the number of newspapers is one indicator of the media resources of a country, the extent of their circulation also matters. For example, in 1990 Pakistan had as many as 168 local and regional newspapers, but their total circulation was rather small, limited to about 5.3 million (figure not given in the table). On the other hand, that same year, Japan achieved a circulation of over 16.5 million (figure not given in the table) with seventy-nine local and regional newspapers. Thus, in many countries, the lag is not in overall numbers of newspapers published, but in the extent of the circulation. In some countries, however, poor media development is a factor, as typified by such a large country as South Korea with only 68 newspapers in 1990. On the other hand, Mexico has typified media inefficiency. In 1990, 317 magazines achieved a circulation of 6 million there. By comparison, Sweden with 239 magazines had a circulation of 7 million in 1990 (see International Marketing Highlight 15.6).

Table 15.5 examines the broadcasting media of radio and television. In the United States and many other industrialized countries, television constitutes the most important medium for advertising, accounting for anywhere from 15 percent to 27 percent of advertising expenditures.[40] In the developing countries, television is still in its primitive stages. As a matter of fact, in many poor countries, television cannot be considered a mass medium; even if television is available, television commercials are more or less prohibited. Thanks to the development of transistor technology, radio is becoming a popular mass medium worldwide.

Advertising and Mass Media

Advertising is the principal source of revenue for most commercial mass media throughout the world. Although the dependence of media on advertising revenues is generally considerable, cross-national comparisons show some variations.[41] In the case of most developed countries including the United States, television relies heavily on advertising revenues. In those countries where television is subsidized or owned by the government, as in Western European countries, the high costs of transmission require considerable support from commercial advertising. But in those countries where the TV owner pays an annual fee to the government for television viewing, as in Italy, Finland, and Sweden, advertising revenues are not so significant. Newspapers and magazines are not as dependent on advertising revenues. In some countries the reader pays most of the cost, while in others the advertiser does. The dependence of radio on advertising revenues also varies by country and is lowest in Western Europe.[42]

International Marketing Highlight 15.5

Is Global Branding More Myth Than Reality?

Despite the prominence of some well-known global brands, a recent study indicates that most U.S.-based MNCs do not seriously pursue the ideas of global branding. According to the survey, which examined U.S.-based manufacturers of consumer nondurable goods, "global markets" may be out there, but global brands have not yet captured them. Of eighty-five brands included in the survey, twenty-nine (or 34 percent) were not marketed outside the United States at all, and many of the remaining brands were only minimally marketed abroad (see table below).

Largest Foreign Markets for U.S. Brands

	NUMBER OF BRANDS FOR WHICH LISTED COUNTRY IS LARGEST FOREIGN MARKET	NUMBER OF BRANDS FOR WHICH LISTED COUNTRY IS SECOND-LARGEST FOREIGN MARKET
Canada	33	2
United Kingdom	5	9
Mexico	4	0
Germany	3	5
Japan	2	4
Australia	2	4
France	1	1
Italy	1	2
Nigeria	1	1
Norway	1	0
Missing	3	14
Total	56	42

Companies surveyed showed a clear preference for selling their goods in markets culturally similar to the U.S. market, i.e., Canada and the United Kingdom (see table). While one might argue that Canada was targeted so frequently because of its geographical proximity to the United States, the choice of the United Kingdom cannot be so easily explained. It is as far away as many other foreign countries, and its population and economy are smaller than those of several other foreign markets.

Source: Marketing Strategies for Global Growth and Competitiveness (New York: Business International Corp., October 1990), p. 36.

TABLE 15.4 1990 Media Information: Newspapers and Magazines for Selected Countries

COUNTRY	NEWSPAPERS			MAGAZINES		
	Total	Local & Regional	National	Total	Consumer	Trade & Technical
Argentina	255	—	255	850	450	400
Australia	—	—	—	—	—	—
Austria	197	164	33	129	59	70
Bahrain	—	—	—	—	—	—
Belgium	17	—	17	64	64	—
Bolivia				—	—	—
Brazil	1,939	1,939	—	745	195	550
China, People's Republic	773	—		5,751	—	—
Colombia	32	30	2	110	52	58
Costa Rica	4	—	4	31	6	25
Cyprus	13	—	13	21	7	14
Denmark	—	—	—	—	—	—
Dominican Republic	10	1	9	36	34	2
Ecuador	41	37	4	26	20	6
Finland	—	—	—	—	—	—
France	—	—	—	—	—	—
Germany, Federal Republic	—	—	—	—	—	—
Greece	225	195	30	540	30	510
Guatemala	6	2	4	25	15	10
Hong Kong	43	43	—	613	—	613
India	—	—	—	—	—	—
Indonesia	109	107	2	109	104	5
Ireland	73	60	13	90	30	60
Israel	147	135	12	—	—	—
Italy	—	—	—	—	—	—
Japan	84	79	5	3,889	—	—
Kenya	8	3	5	70	45	25
Korea, South	68	35	33	145	97	48
Malaysia	41	21	20	165	115	50
Malta	8	—	8	26	16	10
Mexico	332	332	10	317	120	197
Netherlands	78	70	8	1,200	—	1,200
New Zealand	133	127	6	500	—	—
Norway	—	—	—	—	—	—
Oman	—	—	—	—	—	—
Pakistan	180	168	12	1,640	1,630	10
Panama	7	2	5	4	3	1
Portugal	51	15	36	88	54	34
Qatar	—	—	—	—	—	—
Saudi Arabia	—	—	—	—	—	—
Singapore	14	—	14	3,700	3,700	—
Spain	120	110	10	3,200	200	3,000

(*continued*)

TABLE 15.4 (*Continued*)

COUNTRY	NEWSPAPERS Total	NEWSPAPERS Local & Regional	NEWSPAPERS National	MAGAZINES Total	MAGAZINES Consumer	MAGAZINES Trade & Technical
Sri Lanka	86	—	86	—	—	—
Sweden	157	152	5	239	30	209
Switzerland	220	220	—	2,050	50	2,000
Taiwan	226	—	226	193	193	—
Trinidad and Tobago	6	—	6	—	—	—
United Arab Emirates	—	—	—	—	—	—
United Kingdom	1,680	1,660	20	6,677	2,373	4,304
United States	1,622	1,620	2	15,350	11,050	4,300
Venezuela	—	—	—	—	—	—
Zambia	9	3	6	3	2	1
Zimbabwe	16	14	2	38	18	20

Source: World Advertising Expenditures (New York: Starch, INRA, Hooper and International Advertising Association, 1992), pp. 48–49.

Throughout the world, a trend toward commercialization of mass media is apparent. In the printed media this trend is reflected in the substantial increase in the commercial content of newspapers and magazines. In the case of television, the amount of time devoted to advertising is not very significant compared with the proportional amount of space in newspapers and magazines. This is partly because the amount of advertising time allowed on television is regulated in most countries. In Mexico, for example, a maximum of 12 percent of total broadcasting time may be used for advertising, and individual advertisements may not exceed two and one-half minutes in length. However, worldwide there has been a tendency toward the commercialization of television. In Colombia, where the control of television was originally in the hands of the state, the system was modified to allow for the sale of time to commercial interests. Israel commercialized its system in 1976. Even in Europe the traditionally strong state-owned systems have shifted one by one to allow some commercial support. Italy has become one of the world's most commercial and competitive television markets. The United Kingdom opened a commercial channel in 1955, which claims to have taken away more than half of the BBC's viewers. Switzerland, which long held out against television advertising, has yielded to commercial support. In France and the Netherlands, television became commercial in 1968. Although in many countries, including Belgium, Denmark, Sweden, and Norway, government broadcasts still carry no TV advertising, deregulation is sweeping the television industry in Europe. Guided by free market policies, governments are selling their own stations or letting entrepreneurs into the game.[43] Cable networks, as discussed below, covering as many as eighteen countries have started broadcasting programs from different countries.

The demand for time to broadcast commercials and increased programming costs have led to a dramatic rise in the cost of television advertising. To begin

TABLE 15.5 **1987 Media Information: Television Sets and Radio Receivers for Selected Countries**

COUNTRY	TELEVISION SETS Total (millions)	TELEVISION SETS Per 1,000 Population	CABLE Subscribers (thousands)	RADIO RECEIVERS Total (millions)	RADIO RECEIVERS Per 1,000 Population	CINEMAS
Argentina	9.8	310.7	600	10.4	329.5	511
Australia	7.0	429.8	—	26.2	1,619.3	514
Austria	1.9	252.7	447	—	—	470
Bahrain	—	—	—	—	—	—
Belgium	3.5	355.0	2,950	—	—	371
Bolivia	0.3	36.8	—	0.6	87.6	45
Brazil	27.8	196.8	—	59.5	421.3	1,423
Canada	9.1	351.9	—	—	—	—
Chile	3.2	253.6	80	5.6	446.7	180
China, People's Republic	90.0	84.2	—	300.0	280.7	—
Colombia	5.0	169.5	200	9.0	305.1	—
Costa Rica	0.3	92.3	90	0.4	147.6	35
Cyprus	0.2	243.0	—	0.2	316.6	20
Denmark	2.1	411.4	—	3.8	744.4	315
Dominican Republic	4.9	732.6	100	6.0	893.4	79
Ecuador	—	—	—	—	—	350
El Salvador	0.4	76.4	20	1.2	241.3	30
Finland	2.6	525.6	345	—	—	328
France	—	—	—	—	—	2
Germany, Federal Republic	23.4	384.7	3,800	—	—	3,281
Greece	3.5	349.9	—	—	—	220
Guatemala	0.9	110.8	80	2.5	291.5	50
Hong Kong	1.6	295.9	—	4.8	873.9	110
India	16.0	20.1	10	50.0	62.7	12,400
Indonesia	9.0	53.0	—	—	—	2,115
Ireland	1.0	276.9	320	1.8	498.5	101
Israel	1.0	228.6	—	1.1	251.5	250
Italy	19.0	331.3	—	14.3	248.6	5,500
Jamaica	0.4	170.1	—	1.4	582.7	33
Japan	83.0	679.6	4,935	153.0	1,252.8	2,109
Jordan	—	—	—	—	—	—
Kenya	1.0	45.3	—	4.2	190.1	67
Korea, South	9.3	221.2	—	9.8	233.5	676
Kuwait	—	—	—	—	—	—
Lebanon	0.5	181.2	—	0.6	235.5	50
Malaysia	2.0	120.8	—	2.2	132.9	205
Malta	1.2	3,333.3	—	0.2	611.1	14
Mexico	11.9	144.7	152	12.9	157.4	1,000
Morocco	3.0	130.6	—	—	—	250
Netherlands	—	—	—	—	—	—
New Zealand	0.9	282.3	—	3.5	1,046.1	154
Nigeria	5.3	49.2	—	84.0	787.0	147
Norway	—	—	—	—	—	—
Oman	—	—	—	—	—	—

(continued)

TABLE 15.5 *(Continued)*

COUNTRY	TELEVISION SETS Total (millions)	TELEVISION SETS Per 1,000 Population	CABLE Subscribers (thousands)	RADIO RECEIVERS Total (millions)	RADIO RECEIVERS Per 1,000 Population	CINEMAS
Pakistan	1.5	14.6	—	12.5	122.0	—
Panama	0.2	105.6	3	0.4	155.8	22
Peru	3.1	148.1	—	—	—	—
Philippines	4.1	70.4	25	8.0	137.3	940
Portugal	2.4	237.4	—	—	—	324
Puerto Rico	1.5	448.3	225	1.7	508.1	115
Qatar	—	—	—	—	—	—
Saudi Arabia	—	—	—	—	—	—
Singapore	0.5	206.5	—	0.6	247.1	42
South Africa	—	—	—	—	—	400
Spain	13.0	334.5	—	—	—	2,083
Sri Lanka	0.6	39.7	—	3.0	183.4	200
Sweden	3.3	388.9	—	—	—	1,236
Switzerland	2.3	353.8	1,100	—	—	431
Taiwan	4.3	219.1	—	2.8	145.8	600
Thailand	6.3	117.1	—	8.2	153.2	262
Trinidad and Tobago	0.3	265.8	—	0.4	344.2	20
Turkey	8.5	160.8	—	7.0	132.5	88
United Arab Emirates	—	—	—	—	—	—
United Kingdom	33.0	580.5	—	—	—	1,252
United States	87.4	359.1	39,700	482.3	1,981.7	8,600
Venezuela	3.1	169.7	500	3.2	176.6	436
Zambia	0.2	29.2	—	0.9	127.8	22
Zimbabwe	0.2	21.4	—	0.8	83.3	92

Source: World Advertising Expenditures (New York: Starch, INRA, Hooper and International Advertising Association, 1988), pp. 52–53.

with, compared to the United States, media costs are much higher in foreign markets and, as a recent study of nine major global markets shows, the costs are increasing at a rate of 10 percent to 15 percent annually. In part, the increase can be explained by shortages of advertising time. In the United Kingdom, for example, instead of paying fixed rates, companies bid for television advertising time, which escalates the prices. Moreover, stations follow a preempt system. Even though a company has booked a spot at $57,000, another company that is willing to pay more will get it.[44]

Relative Importance of Different Media for Advertising

A comparison of advertising expenditures by media category around the world reveals that print is still the most important: 40 percent of the reported expenditures by fifty-three countries in 1990 were made in newspapers and magazines. Television is second with 24 percent, and radio is third with 7 percent. The remaining expenditures go to media such as outdoor posters and transit advertising, cinema, direct mail, exhibits, sales promotion, and reference publications.[45]

International Marketing Highlight 15.6

24,629 Journals—in Ninety-Two Languages

Despite the low literacy rate of around 40 percent, perhaps no country matches India in the number of newspapers published in an incredible variety of languages, shapes, sizes, and opinions.

Newspapers and periodicals are published in ninety-two languages—the sixteen main languages recognized by the constitution, seventy-six others, and a few foreign languages.

At the end of 1987, the total of newspapers and magazines was 24,629 of which 2,151 were dailies, 7,501 weeklies, 3,366 biweeklies, 8,123 monthlies, and the rest quarterlies and annuals. In contrast, the United States has 1,642 dailies and about 8,000 weeklies.

Although English is the mother tongue of fewer than 250,000 people in India, the overall circulation of the English-language press is second only to that of Hindi. While the Hindi press had a total readership of 14 million, English was next with 10 million, followed by Malayalam with 6 million.

Hardly any major urban center is without at least two English papers. New Delhi alone has six English dailies, compared to two in Washington and five in London.

About 30 percent of newspapers published in the country are concentrated in the four metropolises of Delhi, Bombay, Calcutta, and Madras. Among multiple-edition dailies, *The Indian Express,* published in eleven centers in English, leads with a circulation of 632,199, followed by another English daily, *The Times of India,* with a circulation of 573,552 in six editions.

Source: India Abroad, August 25, 1989, p. 12.

Of course, patterns and levels of expenditures vary from country to country, and from region to region (see Table 15.6). Differences in media expenditures do not always reflect the preferences of advertisers, since in several countries, particularly in Europe, there are restrictions on television and radio advertising. Thus, print advertising is relatively high in Western Europe and Australia and relatively low in Latin America. On the other hand, television advertising is well above average in Latin America and Asia and below average in Western Europe and the Middle East/Africa. The use of television as an advertising medium continues to expand proportionately faster than the use of other media, with the most pronounced increases occurring among the less-developed countries. Radio advertising is very popular in Latin America but is less so in Western Europe, where commercial radio is even more limited than commercial television.[46] Despite variations among regions and countries, a trend has emerged: advertising expenditures on television are increasing, while expenditures on print and radio advertising are decreasing in relative terms. The growing importance of television advertising is due largely to the continuing increase in the number of TVs throughout the world. The growth rate of TV sales in different nations between

TABLE 15.6 Distribution of Advertising Expenditure in 1990 by Media and Select Countries (millions of U.S. dollars)

COUNTRY	TOTAL	PRINT	TELEVISION	RADIO	CINEMA	OUTDOOR TRANSIT	DIRECT ADVERTISING	MISCELLANEOUS
Argentina	829.1	262.3	250.9	72.4	27.7	79.6	58.4	78.8
Australia	3,548.0	1,869.7	1,057.9	335.2	63.3	221.9	—	—
Austria	1,012.0	566.0	264.7	119.3	—	62.0	—	—
Bahrain	11.0	6.1	4.9	—	—	—	—	—
Belgium	1,223.5	527.4	321.4	21.5	13.8	134.5	204.9	—
Bolivia	64.6	14.0	46.8	2.7	0.5	0.6	—	—
Brazil	3,186.5	1,121.8	1,825.9	153.0	—	63.6	—	22.2
China, People's Republic	523.1	159.7	117.4	19.1	0.5	—	126.0	100.4
Colombia	476.4	103.3	283.4	89.7	—	—	—	—
Costa Rica	67.9	26.1	32.7	—	9.1	—	—	—
Cyprus	4.8	1.6	2.2	0.9	—	—	—	0.1
Denmark	1,377.2	897.1	129.3	22.6	12.1	19.6	—	296.5
Dominican Republic	58.5	11.3	37.6	7.4	0.2	1.9	—	0.1
Ecuador	45.8	9.4	27.4	3.9	0.1	0.7	0.4	3.9
Finland	1,800.2	1,167.3	210.3	62.5	1.3	40.8	318.0	—
France	12,891.9	3,627.0	2,523.3	619.8	84.5	1,138.6	—	4,898.7
Germany, Federal Republic	13,944.4	8,429.8	1,708.2	550.8	136.2	420.9	2,698.5	—
Greece	526.2	232.8	221.1	35.6	1.3	35.4	—	—
Guatemala	16.3	4.8	10.5	1.0	—	—	—	
Hong Kong	861.3	363.0	421.9	37.9	11.2	27.3	—	—
India	895.8	599.9	177.1	22.9	4.6	91.4	—	—
Indonesia	286.9	172.2	26.1	53.5	4.1	31.0	—	—
Ireland	321.1	168.8	84.9	35.2	—	22.1	—	10.1
Israel	587.9	415.3	20.0	30.1	4.5	42.0	20.6	55.4
Italy	5,709.7	2,466.9	2,908.1	91.7	—	243.0	—	—

Japan	38,433.6	11,971.1	11,164.4	1,612.7	—	4,347.7	3,628.7	5,709.0
Kenya	20.5	9.6	3.0	4.0	0.6	1.2	0.2	1.9
Korea, South	2,826.2	1,370.0	845.2	134.7	—	476.3	—	—
Malaysia	321.6	153.5	130.7	5.5	1.1	26.2	—	4.6
Malta	14.6	9.5	4.0	0.2	—	0.6	0.3	—
Mexico	2,199.3	314.4	1,649.1	235.8	—	—	—	—
Netherlands	4,334.6	2,232.4	331.7	59.9	7.1	80.7	1,277.9	344.9
New Zealand	624.5	281.2	210.1	83.6	—	—	—	49.6
Norway	1,233.4	730.9	20.0	8.0	9.6	17.6	447.3	—
Oman	11.9	6.9	5.0	—	—	—	—	—
Pakistan	89.6	39.9	39.2	2.5	0.2	4.6	—	3.2
Panama	54.0	16.0	32.0	3.5	0.5	2.0	—	—
Portugal	415.6	154.9	181.7	32.6	—	46.4	—	—
Qatar	10.7	7.3	3.4	—	—	—	—	—
Saudi Arabia	139.7	89.4	50.3	—	—	—	—	—
Singapore	314.7	200.3	95.4	6.6	1.9	8.3	—	2.2
Spain	10,348.3	4,051.8	2,393.8	784.9	58.9	363.0	1,299.9	1,396.0
Sri Lanka	21.0	12.7	3.8	2.5	0.1	1.9	—	—
Sweden	2,729.3	1,706.8	39.9	—	11.8	78.9	891.9	—
Switzerland	4,098.0	1,895.3	162.7	41.0	22.3	299.5	1,677.2	—
Taiwan	1,569.2	710.4	458.1	84.7	5.5	35.3	44.5	230.7
Trinidad and Tobago	23.4	7.4	0.4	5.2	0.2	0.8	0.4	—
United Arab Emirates	69.4	47.9	21.5	—	—	—	—	—
United Kingdom	15,726.0	9,055.6	4,149.4	200.9	69.6	503.3	1,747.2	—
United States	128,640.0	42,174.0	28,405.0	8,726.0	—	1,084.0	23,370.0	24,881.0
Venezuela	439.2	136.5	285.7	8.5	—	8.5	—	—
Zambia	4.1	3.3	0.4	0.2	—	—	—	0.2
Zimbabwe	26.3	17.9	4.6	3.0	0.5	0.3	—	—

Source: World Advertising Expenditures (New York: Starch, INRA, Hooper and International Advertising Association, 1992), pp. 36–37.

1980 and 1990 has been anywhere from twice to 200 times higher than that of population growth.[47]

Mention must be made of two emerging media, cable TV and satellite TV, which are expected to have significant effects on advertising in the 1990s and beyond.[48] It is predicted, for example, that by the year 2000, 125 million European families will watch the same television programs, despite the cultural impediments.[49] The European communication satellite (ECS-1), used by major pan-European TV stations in the U.K., Germany, France, Italy, the Netherlands, and the U.S., has a range of coverage beyond the EC, including some parts of Eastern Europe and the former Soviet republics. Table 15.7 lists the percentage of homes connected to cable stations in different countries.

Table 15.8 shows the coverage available to advertisers through satellite channels. As an example, McDonald's used the Sky Channel's children's program to launch its program, "Fun Factory," which scored high viewing figures among children throughout the region.

The advertising game in Europe is changing, and the global companies will be the first to benefit. With the market for satellite TV growing, Europe's broadcasting regulators have accepted that national monopolies on TV transmissions are no longer defensible. For example, the arrival of pan-European satellite broadcasting has breached the long-standing barrier to television advertising in Sweden. It is expected that Swedish TV will go commercial within a few years.

TABLE 15.7 Penetration of Cable TV in Europe (percentage of homes)*

	CATV	MATV	TOTAL
Belgium	79%	5%	84%
Netherlands	60	15	75
Switzerland	26	10	36
Ireland	25	2	27
Denmark	10	50	60
Norway	13	14	27
Austria	8	3	11
United Kingdom	8	5	13
Finland	5	34	39
Germany	5	37	42
France	3	39	42
Sweden	3	48	51
Greece	0	0	0
Italy	0	0	0
Portugal	0	0	0
Spain	0	0	0
United States			45%
Japan			10%

*The cable companies predict that 40 million to 60 million European homes will be cabled by 1995.
Source: Business International, "Ideas in Action," April 14, 1986.

TABLE 15.8 European Satellite Channels Currently Carrying Advertising

CHANNEL	LANGUAGE	HOMES REACHED	COUNTRIES OF RECEPTION
Sky Channel	English	4,051,178	Netherlands, Switzerland, [former] West Germany, Finland, Norway, United Kingdom, Austria, Sweden, Luxembourg, France, Denmark, Belgium
Music Box	English	2,544,000	Netherlands, Switzerland, United Kingdom, Finland, [former] West Germany, Sweden, Austria, Denmark
TV-5	French	2,000,000	Belgium, Finland, France, [former] West Germany, Netherlands, Norway, Sweden, United Kingdom, Switzerland
SAT-1	German	460,000	[former] West Germany
Children's Channel	English	110,000	United Kingdom
Screen Sport	English	100,000	United Kingdom, Sweden, Finland
RAI	Italian	n.a.	Belgium
New World Channel	Multilingual	—	—

Source: From Rein Rijkens and Gordon E. Miracle, *European Regulation of Advertising* (Amsterdam: North Holland, 1986), p. 175, quoted from *Campaign,* August 30, 1985, vol. 35, as reported by David Wood. Copyright 1986 by Elsevier Science Publishers, Physical Sciences and Engineering Division.

Satellite TV is not limited to Europe alone. Developing countries are experimenting with satellite broadcasts to reach the masses. India, for example, has launched a satellite to reach people in remote villages, making broadcasts of the same program in different languages. Currently such broadcasts are limited to social programs such as family planning, but may eventually be opened for commercial advertising.

International Advertising Program

The development of an international advertising program depends on the advertising strategy that an MNC pursues. For the sake of discussion, let us assume that a company has decided to decentralize its advertising and let its overseas subsidiaries play a major role in determining their advertising program. The parent corporation maintains sufficient control through periodic review and approval authority over the final budget. The advertising program essentially includes nine steps:

1. Provision of guidelines by headquarters
2. Definition of advertising goals
3. Preparation of a campaign plan

4. Review and approval of plan
5. Copy development and testing
6. Media planning
7. Budget approval
8. Campaign implementation
9. Measurement of advertising effectiveness

Basically, an advertising program, in both domestic and international advertising, involves decisions concerning the media, the message, and the budget allocation. However, differences in number and types of media in conjunction with cultural and other environmental aspects necessitate tailoring themes, messages, presentations, and illustrations to the target market.

> It is the advertising environment embracing language, culture, socio-economic conditions which change from one country to another, not the approach taken to plan and to prepare effective advertising campaigns.[50]

Head Office Guidelines

The head office guidelines should include procedural, discretionary, and format guidelines.

Procedural Guidelines These should include what should be done and when. For example, the guidelines may specify that no commitments be made to the media except with budget approval. Likewise, subsidiaries may be required to prepare a minimum of four different ads and market test them to single out the final copy. Procedural guidelines are requirements that must be followed. Their purpose is to bring about global consistency in advertising. These guidelines essentially draw upon the parent corporation's past experience.

Discretionary Guidelines These are bits of advice that a subsidiary may or may not choose to accept. The following is an example of such a guideline: "Experience in the United States and elsewhere supports the usage of testimonial advertising. You may, therefore, consider using a local model to promote the product."

Format Guidelines These define any form, design, or procedure that should be followed in planning the campaign. These guidelines also include dates that must be adhered to. The major purpose of format guidelines is to make it easy for the corporation to impose and maintain control over the advertising activities of the subsidiaries.

Advertising Goals

Advertising goals should be appropriately related to product/market objectives. Thus, a subsidiary serving two markets (business customers and household consumers) may have different advertising goals in the two markets. Because advertising produces changes in attitudes, advertising goals should be defined in order to influence attitudinal structures. Accordingly, advertising may be undertaken to: (1) affect those forces that strongly influence the choice criteria used for evaluating brands belonging to the product class; (2) add characteristic(s) to those considered salient for the product class; (3) increase/decrease the rating for a salient product class characteristic; (4) change perception of the company's brand with regard to some particular salient product characteristic; and (5) change perception of competitive brands with regard to some particular salient product characteristic. Based on these additudinal perspectives, advertising objectives may be defined as:[51]

- Increasing consumer's or buyers' *awareness* of the product . . . either generally or comparatively
- Improving the product's *image* among consumers or buyers . . . either generally or comparatively
- Increasing a target group of opinion leaders' or consumers'/buyers' *awareness* of the company . . . either generally or comparatively
- Increasing the company's *image* among a target group of opinion leaders or consumers/buyers . . . either generally or comparatively
- Increasing the product's *sales* or market share among consumers or buyers . . . either generally or comparatively (These objectives are more appropriate for retail or direct-response advertising.)

A good definition of objectives aids in writing appropriate copy and in selecting the media. The firm's headquarters should make sure that the objectives have been defined by the proper managerial person.

Campaign Plan

The campaign plan outlines what sort of advertising campaign the subsidiary has in mind. It spells out the dimensions of strategy and media and indicates the preliminary budget estimates. For example, a subsidiary may plan along the following lines:

- Develop ad copy using a female model to promote the product, and run it simultaneously in six different magazines every other month for one year.
- Estimate the impact of the campaign by twice exposing 60 percent of the target customers to the new version of the product.
- Remember that the rationale behind this campaign is to reinforce the product's image among customers and counteract the competitor's recent entry into the market with a product similar to ours.
- Measure the effectiveness of the campaign by having an ad agency do a recognition test with a sample of women in the third, sixth, and ninth months of the campaign.
- Continue to position the product among women between 20 and 40 years of age from middle-income families.
- Estimate that the costs of this campaign during the first year will be $2 million.
- Decide that, for implementation of this plan, approval is needed by December 15.

Review and Approval of Plan

Headquarters should review each subsidiary's advertising schemes to ensure that they will contribute to the realization of the subsidiary's marketing goals and to assess that the planned campaign is realistic and entails a proper use of resources. In the review process it is important to judge matters from the viewpoint of the individual subsidiary's business and related environments. In other words, headquarters managers should avoid using self-reference criteria. Where insufficient information has been provided by the subsidiary, further information should be requested. Finally, reviewers at corporate headquarters should remember that events do not move at the same pace in every country. Thus, every effort should be made to meet the deadline set by the subsidiary.

Copy Development and Testing

Copy refers to the content of an advertisement. In advertising, the term *copy* is used in a broad sense to include words, pictures, symbols, colors, layout, and any other ingredients of an ad. Copywriting is a creative job, and its quality depends to a large extent on the creative genius of persons in the advertising agency or the company. However, creativity alone may not produce good ad copy. The marketing managers should provide their own conception of the copy and furnish adequate information on the product, objectives, target customers, competitive activity, and legal aspects. The copywriter uses these facts as well as talent and imagination to develop ad copy. Before finalizing copy, it should be screened and revised as necessary. Sometimes several versions of the copy are developed and tested simultaneously, and the final version is chosen on the basis of test results.

In point of fact, the copywriter should follow the managerial process to create good copy successfully. First, the work should center on an objective. Consideration should then be given to whether the ad will be in black and white or in color, and what format (vertical or horizontal) can best convey the message. The competition must be evaluated to find a mark of distinction for the brand in question. In brief, copywriting may be a flash of inspiration on the part of an advertising genius, but it is also a systematic, logical, step-by-step presentation of ideas. Among other things, copy should be believable and easily understood by the audience.

Often subsidiaries have available various ads used in the United States and elsewhere in the world. If the copy of one of the available ads appears basically appropriate, it may well be worthwhile to use it. But such "foreign" copy should be adapted for local conditions. This point is especially noteworthy when expatriate managers have to make ad copy decisions (see International Marketing Highlight 15.7).

To avoid snarls, it is best for subsidiary management to work closely with their advertising agency. The task of adaptation becomes easier if the agency that initially worked on the campaign has an office in the subsidiary's country. Multinational ad agencies have global experience and contacts that facilitate locating and using the best talent for adapting the ad to local conditions. Interestingly, often local native-born managers are as bad as expatriate managers in the

International Marketing Highlight 15.7

Problems with Using "Foreign" Ad Copy

Suppose that an American manufacturer had been selling his designer jeans coast-to-coast with the help of a catchy jingle set to a disco beat. He decides teenagers in France would like his product as much as those in California or New York, so he gets ready to export. To save money, he hires a French major from a local university to translate the words of his jingle. The music, he feels, needs no translation.

In fact, he transfers his advertising campaign in its entirety to France; after all, it works in the States.

Should he settle back and wait for the francs to roll in? Or should he prepare to fall flat on his face?

Unfortunately, he'd better brace for a crash. In his attempt to go overseas, our marketer has made three errors, any of which could be fatal:

1. He has hired a non-native speaker to translate his message.
2. He is assuming that a commercial that appeals to Americans will sell to the French.
3. He has made no studies of the French market itself.

It's wide-eyed and naive to believe that a straightforward translation of any ad will work. The disco beat marries itself well to English, because English is a concise tongue. It's not discursive like French or the other Romance languages; the accents and rhythm are different. For the ad to be effective, the manufacturer must rewrite his commercial entirely, and discard the English lyrics completely.

Or consider the case of the American maker of heavy-duty wrapping paper who hired a language "scholar" to translate an ad from English to Japanese. The scholar invented a brand new Japanese character (ideograph or word-picture) to represent the product. As a result, Japanese readers were treated to a product that called itself "He who envelops himself in ten tons of rice paper."

Source: Ann Helming, "Pitfalls Lie Waiting for Unwary Marketers," *Advertising Age,* May 17, 1982, p. M-8. Copyright 1982 by Crain Communications Inc.

localization of ad copy. Long-accustomed to the outside world (perhaps with a U.S. business education), they may be quite divorced from the realities of life in their home countries and may approach the task with imported ideas.

The final test of the appropriateness of copy is the marketplace. Three or four different versions should be sample-tested, using appropriate statistical procedures. Unless a subsidiary is very well equipped, the copy-testing task should be assigned to the agency. The final copy should be selected based on test results. In some cases it may become necessary to develop yet another entirely new copy if none of the original ones appears sufficiently effective.

Media Planning

The decision on media is made simultaneously with the copy decision. It is influenced by media availability, media coverage, and media cost.

Media availability elsewhere in the world is more restricted than in the United States. Even in developed countries like Switzerland, commercial advertising is permitted only during certain hours. In Germany, Europe's richest and largest national market, TV spots are kept to barely 40 minutes a day and none on Sunday.[52] Many countries ban the advertising of certain products. For example, Venezuela bans foreign cigarette and liquor advertising.[53] In England, the government once questioned the high expenditures budgeted by Unilever and Procter & Gamble for advertising detergents.[54] In brief, in media planning, careful analysis is necessary to figure out first what media are practical before making the actual selection.

Media coverage varies from country to country. The average is affected by the range of exposure and ownership of receivers. Ownership is a problem in the developing countries, where only a small percentage of the populations own radios and/or televisions. Printed media present similar problems. The masses may be illiterate, may not afford to subscribe to newspapers and magazines, or may live beyond circulation centers. In addition, the heterogeneity of a country with different languages or cultural and religious groups may make it difficult to reach enough people through a single campaign. A related problem here is the availability of coverage statistics. In many countries, the sole source of such information is the government, whose figures may be overstated for political reasons, besides being haphazardly gathered and/or outdated. In other countries, absolutely no information may be available on the coverage of different media, except the best guesses of bureaucrats. In other words, Starch's coverage data and Nielson's ratings are not widely known outside the United States. In any event, subsidiary management should gather as much information on media coverage as possible in order to select the media focus.

The final consideration is cost. In many countries media prices are subject to negotiation. Thus, the cost could be affected by the bargaining abilities of the subsidiary management. On the other hand, in some countries media rates are arbitrarily set and increased without any market justification. This often happens where media are government-controlled and do not depend solely on advertising revenues to operate. Further, in less-developed countries, media costs are relatively high compared with those in the advanced nations. In newspaper advertising, the most popular medium worldwide, the rates are much higher in the developing countries in proportion to circulation. Besides, the real cost of reaching potential buyers with advertising messages may also be high because the media are not readily available and a large proportion of the population is scattered in rural areas. After considering all the problems, subsidiary management must judiciously choose the best media available for its purposes.

Budget Approval

Budget approval is generally granted during the review process, but some companies keep budget approval pending until the copy has been developed and tested and the media planning completed. Although it may seem odd that subsidiaries proceed to develop and test copy as well as undertake media selection without budget approval, changing business environments, which are subject to political situations like threatened nationalization and/or business conditions that are declining because of competition, may make it essential to postpone commitments.

Campaign Implementation

Once budget approval has been received, the campaign should be undertaken as planned. Contingency plans are also necessary in case of unexpected difficulties. For example, one company in Pakistan had planned an ad using a female model to promote a brand of bar soap. Everything seemed fine during the planning stages. As release time approached, the Pakistani government banned all use of female models in ads. In such eventualities, contingency plans can save the day.

The thrust of the program may also require change if initial feedback on the campaign is discouraging. In any event, a certain amount of flexibility can accommodate changes for an effective campaign.

Measuring Effectiveness

There are various means to measure advertising effectiveness. Such research can be undertaken both before and after an ad is run. Pretesting measures include:

- Opinion and attitude ratings, gathered by questioning a sample of the prospective audience
- Projective techniques, which are indirectly elicited responses from the audience using motivation research techniques
- Laboratory testing, gathered by exposing a sample of customers to the ad and asking their reactions

Posttesting measures include:

- Recognition and recall
- Changes in attitude ascribable to the ad
- Inquiries and sales measures; for example, the return of a card included with the ad

The methods discussed thus far are the same as those utilized in domestic marketing. However, their utilization may not be feasible in every nation. The facilities, talent, and resources needed for advertising effectiveness studies may be lacking.

Problems

Many problems can arise overseas to hinder the smooth development of an advertising program. Some countries lack facilities for fine printing. In other nations, government restrictions on advertising cause difficulties. In still other cases, illiteracy and language differences within the same country have an adverse effect. Mostly these problems arise in developing countries.

There are no easy answers for these problems. In some cases, advance planning and patience may help. For example, if an ad must be approved by the country government beforehand, enough time should be allotted so that, if a delay occurs in the process, the prompt release of the ad is assured. Similarly, if some printing/recording must be done in the home country for lack of facilities in the host country, advance planning is vital. Beyond that, an advertiser must accept the problems as an environmental constraint in doing business internationally.

Global Advertising Regulations

Most countries impose some regulations on advertising. The purpose behind these regulations is twofold: (1) to protect the consumers against misleading advertising and their own gullibility and (2) to protect smaller businesses from the competitive threats of large corporations.[55] It is interesting to note that advertising regulation is more common in developed societies than in developing countries. This may be explained by the fact that the advertising industry is still in its infancy in most developing countries, and therefore ignored as yet.[56] Besides, not all developing countries have the administrative machinery to enforce regulations.

Exhibit 15.4 illustrates the types of issues that lead to regulation in different parts of the world. For example, while France and Mexico resist the use of foreign language, the Muslim countries regulate the use of foreign material themes and illustrations. Essentially, advertising regulation is focused on specific areas (see International Marketing Highlight 15.8):

EXHIBIT 15.4 Major Issues and Countries to Watch

Advertising to children	Canada, Scandinavia, United States
Class action by consumer associations	EC Commission, United States
Comparison advertising	EC Commission (encouragement), France (possible relaxation), Philippines (ban), United States (encouragement)
Corrective ads	United States, EC Commission
Feminine hygiene commercials (mandatory prescreening)	Canada (British)
Infant formula promotion	World Health Organization/UNICEF (severe restriction)
Privacy protection and transborder data flows	France, Norway, Sweden, United States
Reversal of the burden of proof on the advertiser	EC Commission, Scandinavia, United States
Sexism in advertising	Canada, Netherlands, Scandinavia, United Kingdom, United States
Use of foreign languages in advertisements	France, Mexico, Québec Province
Use of foreign materials, themes, and illustrations	Korea, Muslim countries, Peru, Philippines
Wording used in food and drug ads	Belgium, European Community, United States

Source: J. J. Boddewyn, "The Global Spread of Advertising Regulation," *MSU Business Topics,* Spring 1981, pp. 5–13.

International Marketing Highlight 15.8

War on Smoking

While cigarette smoking in the United States is declining, in many countries overseas it is a growth industry. But these are protective markets not open to outsiders. Consider Thailand's $744 million cigarette market, which was finally opened to imports under heavy pressure from U.S. trade negotiators only after Thailand imposed high import duties, a cumbersome customs-clearance procedure, and stiff restrictions on cigarette advertising.

What is interesting about Thailand's efforts to curb American tobacco imports is that it relied heavily for help on an alliance of local and international antismoking activists. As a spokesperson from the American Cancer Society, an alliance member, notes, "The Thais complained to us that your government is trying to force U.S. cigarettes down our throats." Now these antismoking groups are actively campaigning against smoking throughout Asia, and have seriously hurt the U.S. tobacco industry.

As U.S. companies stepped up their efforts to develop the Asian markets, the antismoking activists intensified their efforts to keep them away. For example, a fourteen-nation group called the Asian Consultancy on Tobacco Control met in Hong Kong to formulate a four-year strategy to prevent smoking in the area. The group's aim is to persuade Asian countries to adopt uniform tobacco-control regulations and thus prevent U.S. companies from making inroads in the region.

Source: "Asia: A New Front in the War on Smoking," *Business Week,* February 25, 1991, p. 66.

- Certain classes of product/services, such as alcoholic beverages, tobacco, nonprescription pharmaceuticals, and financial and real estate deals
- Mail-order distribution
- Ads targeted toward children
- Foreign ownership of advertising agencies
- Comparative advertising
- "Puffery" or superlative claims—for example, "this brand is *the* best"
- Use of foreign language/words, models, backgrounds, and illustrations
- Media—for example, time limits for advertising
- Sexism in advertising

Table 15.9 exemplifies regulations on advertising in Western Europe. Regulations affecting advertising in various regions of the world have grown both in number and stringency over the years.

Some examples of regulation of the financial aspects of advertising include:

- India announced an upper limit of $10,000 for advertising expenses for all companies doing business in India; expenditures over that limit were to be taxed at the rate of 50 percent. Widespread cancellation of advertising in

TABLE 15.9 Some Regulations on Advertising in Western Europe

	THE MOST SENSITIVE AREAS			
	Tobacco	Alcohol	Pharmaceuticals (general public)	The Use of Superlatives
Germany	Forbidden: to make any suggestion that smoking is not dangerous; to encourage young people to smoke; and to use the terms "pure" or "natural"	No restrictions so far, but this is now under review	Banned	Allowed where the superiority can be proved, though the rules are stricter in some areas
Belgium			Banned for products aimed at cancer, TB, polio, and diabetes; some other restrictions	
France	Any reference to health is banned	Forbidden entirely when it comes to drinks with a high alcohol content; less strict for others	Forbidden for any product the cost of which is refunded by Social Security	Forbidden on TV to all intents and purposes
Italy	Banned	The brand name can be promoted, but not the product	Must have special clearance; no ads for contraceptives	
Netherlands	Voluntary restraint	Voluntary restraint	Voluntary restraint	Accepted where it is backed by facts. Since no law exists, advertisers tend to be cautious
Great Britain	"Every packet carries a government health warning" will have to be mentioned in all advertising	No legal controls, but voluntary restraint	Forbidden in the case of cancer; restrictions on others; firms are not allowed to claim that they can cure a disease	
Sweden	Some form of warning is being studied, as is a total ban	Forbidden to mention the price or the catalogue number	Allowed, but with very strict controls	Forbidden when excessive; allowed if presented as a subjective opinion

TABLE 15.9 (*Continued*)

MENTION OF RIVAL FIRMS	TV ADVERTISING	FALSE ADVERTISING CLAIMS: Burden of Proof	Penalties	The Right of Consumer Associations to Bring a Lawsuit
Theoretically not allowed; but many exceptions	Voluntary restrictions to tobacco advertising	On the plaintiff in the case of unfair competition (with *prima facie* evidence from the defendant); it stays with the government for foods and medicines	Both penal and civil; in some cases consumer associations can ask for imprecise claims to be withdrawn	Only where the cases do not involve either foods or medicines
Banned if misleading, denigratory, or not relevant	Does not exist	On the plaintiff	Both penal and civil; injunctions possible	On condition that they are members of the Consumer Council
Banned if denigratory	No advertising for tobacco, alcohol, or anything else	Under study: on the plaintiff, but advertisers must produce any evidence on demand	Both penal and civil; under study: ads containing corrections	Under study
Forbidden to mention names	More careful investigation than in other media	On the plaintiff	Both penal and civil	None
Acceptable if no names are given and if it is not denigratory	Boards of control check pharmaceutical products and drinks	On the plaintiff	Both penal and civil	None
Banned if denigratory; must contain facts that can be proved	Cigarette advertising is banned and advertising of drinks restricted	On the plaintiff	Both penal and civil (fines of up to £400)	None
Forbidden if defamatory or injurious	Does not exist	In civil cases, on the defendant; in criminal cases, on the relevant government department	Penal and civil; sometimes the rapid withdrawal of the manufacturing license	In general through the ombudsman; otherwise, consumer associations can go to law

Source: "Transnational Corporations in Advertising," *Technical Paper* (New York: United Nations, 1979), p. 52.

reaction to this law, however, caused the withdrawal of this tax, as the government was concerned with the effects that the cancellation of advertising might have on the level employment.

- In Costa Rica, a law provides for the national majority ownership of the media and the agencies.
- In Venezuela, Colombia, Ecuador, and Peru, a maximum of 19 percent of foreign ownership of advertisement agencies is stipulated by law.
- In Germany, TV advertising on the commercial stations is restricted to twenty minutes per day in blocks of five to seven minutes between 5:00 P.M. and 8:00 P.M. with no advertising on Sundays and holidays. In the Netherlands since April 1, 1978, TV commercials must be confined to five-minute blocks in the evenings.
- In Turkey, the state-owned commercial TV carries twelve minutes of non-commissionable advertising each evening in three-minute blocks.

Some examples of regulation of the language and content of advertising include:

- "Puffery," or the use of superlatives claiming that the product advertised is the best of its kind, is usually tolerated on the grounds that consumers do not take such hyperbolic claims too seriously, and that such claims do not significantly affect competition, since specific or easily identifiable competitors are not named. However, in Germany, such claims cannot be used if worthy of belief, and in Austria if otherwise provable.
- There is emerging in both the developed and the developing countries a growing motivation for restrictions on foreign-made commercials to discourage misleading advertisements where foreign brand names, for example, are used to convey the impression that a local product is in fact a foreign one. Regulations in this area tend to spread on a regional basis. An effort is being made in the Philippines, Indonesia, and Malaysia to enhance a major native language at the expense of English and of minority languages.
- In Denmark, Germany, and Italy, medical product advertising must be supervised as to content.
- In Germany, France, Belgium, Austria, Italy, and the Netherlands, restrictions on comparative advertising are enforced.
- A French law forbids the use of foreign words and expression when French equivalents can be found in the official dictionary. This reaction against "Franglais" (anglicized French) applies particularly to TV commercials. A similar law was recently passed by Belgium.
- Peruvian regulations stress the protection and enhancement of the national culture and of the "Peruvian way," and therefore endeavor to ban foreign-inspired models and materials.
- The Philippine government encourages the use of Tagalog because of "a

desire for preserving the national heritage and independence from foreigners."

- The Actors and Announcers Equity Association of Australia imposes a limit of 20 percent on foreign materials with no "local talent" content. It will usually accept foreign talent if local actors or announcers are paid in parallel or if a fee is paid to the association.
- China is expected to introduce regulations banning foreign cigarette and liquor advertising.
- Not satisfied with ordering advertisers to stop showing women in Western-style clothes, to keep them a safe distance from male models, and to tone down garment ads, the Pakistani government announced that it would not permit mass media to use women at all for commercial purposes.[57]

Industry Self-Regulation

The growing trend toward governmental action has led the advertising industry to attempt self-regulation in order to prevent undesirable governmental regulations. Self-regulation also shields the industry from unfair internal competition. Standards are set, and objective arbitration settles complaints and disputes outside the framework of government. The degree of self-regulation throughout the world varies from country to country according to each country's cultural and social values and level of development. The appendix at the end of this chapter summarizes advertising self-regulation in selected countries.

Most self-regulation measures are spearheaded by advertising industry associations. In many countries, Belgium for one, specialized self-regulatory bodies have been formed to deal with problems related to advertising. Large advertising agencies and even the media in some countries have set their own standards or codes of conduct.

Advertising Agencies

Advertising agencies serve advertisers. As multinational corporations have circled the globe, their advertising agencies as well as involved banks and accounting firms have followed suit. The principal reason that advertising agencies go international has been to continue to serve their clients both at home and abroad. Chapter 1 examined the domination of the multinational scene by U.S. corporations. This domination is even more apparent in the case of advertising agencies. As seen in Table 15.10, of the ten largest advertising agencies in the world, all but two are U.S.-based.

Globally, the major thrust of the advertising agencies' business is in the developed countries. Their principal clients focus most of their activities in these countries. It has been estimated that over 85 percent of their income is derived from activities in developed countries. The major portion of their income from developing countries originates in Latin America.[58]

TABLE 15.10 The Top Ten Ad Agencies Worldwide

AGENCY, HEADQUARTERS	WORLDWIDE BILLINGS (MILLIONS)	U.S. BILLINGS AS % OF WORLDWIDE
Dentsu Inc., Tokyo	$10,063.2	n.a.
Saatchi & Saatchi Advertising Worldwide, New York	6,049.9	46
Young & Rubicam, New York	6,250.5	50
Backer Spielvogel Bates Worldwide, New York	5,143.2	42
McCann-Erickson Worldwide, New York	4,772.3	29
Ogilvy & Mather Worldwide, New York	4,828.0	44
BBDO Worldwide, New York	4,550.0	58
J. Walter Thompson Co, New York	4,407.5	42
Lintas: Worldwide, New York	3,957.6	38
Hakuhodo Inc., Tokyo	4,449.2	n.a.

Source: Crain Communications Inc., 1990.

Advertising agencies use various modes of foreign entry. One form of foreign entry is the opening of a local office. Such an arrangement permits complete control over the nature and size of the foreign office. However, it is a costly alternative, as it takes eight to ten years for a new office to generate enough clients to become financially self-sufficient. Another alternative is to acquire full or partial interest in existing agencies. This offers an ongoing business with a trained staff and a roster of clients. But in practice it is difficult to impose control over an acquired business that has established procedures of its own. A third alternative is to form a joint venture that may later develop into full ownership. Finally, a holding company can be formed. The choice of mode of entry would depend on the captive business, availability of a viable firm for acquisition, future prospects, financial resources of the agency, and national regulations.

A multinational firm uses a home-based advertising agency in order to achieve and maintain control. Even when strategy decisions are delegated to nationals, if a subsidiary works with the same agency that the MNC uses in the United States, then there is sufficient assurance that the overall advertising function should be performed satisfactorily.

Often multinational enterprises retain the same agency for U.S. and international advertising. One problem with the use of a foreign agency is a lack of cultural insight into the market. Frequently, however, the foreign agency will have local employees. In nations where the dearth of local talent may force an agency to depend entirely on expatriate managers, chances are there is no local agency, leaving the MNC no choice but to use the foreign agency. Overall, the trend among MNCs is toward employing one individual advertising agency worldwide rather than a separate agency in each country. This practice is reinforced by the desire to avoid diverse advertising approaches and the consequent loss of overall advertising effectiveness.

As in the United States, a foreign advertising agency (unless prohibited by the national law) receives a 15 percent discount from the media on the business it places. This constitutes the main source of revenue for ad agencies. In some countries, however, there is a movement away from the 15 percent compensation plan to a schedule of fees. Further, in many countries local agencies aggressively compete against the multinational agencies by passing along a portion of their discount to their clients. Fifteen percent is a standard charge for a routine advertising job. In cases where a client requires help beyond the simple work of creating copy and scheduling the media, the agency normally charges more.

Summary

The promotion of goods and services is an important part of the marketing mix. The purpose of promotion is to inform, persuade, and remind the customer that certain goods and services are available. The four ingredients of promotion are advertising, personal selling, sales promotion, and publicity.

Advertising is an American institution born of U.S. economic progress. However, the rest of the world is catching up fast. World advertising expenditures, other than those of the United States, are likely to rise from $130 billion in 1988 and $180 billion in 1990 to $300 billion in 2000.

An important decision for international advertisers to make is whether the advertising campaign should be standardized worldwide or localized. Standard advertising has advantages in that a successful campaign in one country is likely to be effective in another nation as well. Further, standard advertising is economical. On the other hand, localized advertising recognizes cultural differences among nations. An effective advertising campaign in the United States will not necessarily be well received in, say, Saudi Arabia because of differences in cultural traits, language, economic life, and the like. For example, a female ad model is not likely to be acceptable in a Muslim country. In the final analysis, the choice between standard and local advertising should be based on such environmental considerations as levels of education; experience and competence of personnel in the foreign agency; degree of nationalism and rate of economic growth in the country; eating patterns and customs of the country; attitudes toward authority; and independence of media from governmental control. If overall environmental differences are significant, then advertising should be localized. Besides the environment, other criteria to be weighed before using a standardized campaign overseas are advertising objectives relative to the host country, target market, product characteristics, media availability, and cost—benefit relationship.

The growth of global advertising is directly related to media development. Unfortunately, in many countries media have not yet developed adequately. Besides, many nations strictly regulate media availability. Statistical information reflects worldwide media differences. Unlike those in the United States, overseas media do not derive revenues solely from advertising.

The steps to follow to build an international advertising program are provision of headquarters guidelines, definition of advertising goals, preparation of a campaign plan, review and approval of plan, copy development and testing, media planning, budget approval, campaign implementation, and measurement of advertising effectiveness.

Overseas countries impose different regulations on advertising. While the thrust of the regulations varies from nation to nation, the essential focus is on certain classes of products/services; mail-order distribution; ads targeted toward children; foreign ownership of advertising agencies; comparative advertising; superlative claims in ads; use of foreign language/words; and media. Many U.S. advertising agencies have expanded outside the United States.

Review Questions

1. What factors argue for an internationally standardized approach to advertising?
2. Is the fact of cultural differences among nations strong enough to justify localized advertising?
3. Define the terms *buying proposal* and *creative presentation*. How do they affect standardized or localized advertising?
4. In the United States, advertising is the principal source of revenue for the media. Is this true in other countries? If not, how do media derive their incomes?
5. List the various steps for developing an international advertising program.
6. Illustrate with examples the types of regulations that countries overseas impose on media.
7. Why is it desirable for a U.S. company to use a U.S.-based advertising agency in other countries?

Endnotes

1. *See* Robert F. Roth, *International Marketing Communications* (Chicago: Crain Books, 1982), p. 7.
2. "U.S. Outspends the World in Ads," *Marketing News,* February 2, 1988, p. 15. *Also see* "Strong Spending: Foreign Ad Budgets Again Beat U.S.," *Advertising Age,* March 28, 1988, p. 6.
3. "China Is Planning to Hold Its First Advertising Parley," *The Asian Wall Street Journal Weekly,* December 2, 1985, p. 11.
4. Peter S. H. Leeflang and Jan C. Reuiji, "Advertising and Industry Sales: An Empirical Study of the West German Cigarette Market," *Journal of Marketing,* Fall 1985, pp. 92–98.
5. James Killough, "Improved Payoffs from Transnational Advertising," *Harvard Business Review,* July–August 1978, pp. 102–110.
6. Nathaniel H. Leff and John U. Farley, "Advertising Expenditures in the Developing World," *Journal of International Business Studies,* Fall 1980, pp. 64–79.
7. Erik Elinder, "How International Can Advertising Be?" in S. Watson Dunn, ed., *International Handbook of Advertising* (New York: McGraw-Hill, 1964), pp. 59–71.
8. Arthur C. Fatt, "The Danger of 'Local' International Advertising," *Journal of Marketing,* January 1976, p. 61. *Also see* Gordon E. Miracle, "Internationalizing Advertising Principles and Strategies," *MSU Business Topics,* Autumn 1968, pp. 29–36.
9. S. Watson Dunn, "The Case Study Approach in Cross-Cultural Research," *Journal of Marketing Research,* February 1966, pp. 26–31. *Also see* Michael Colvin, Roger Heeler, and Jim Thorpe, "Developing International Advertising Strategy," *Journal of Marketing,* Fall 1980, pp. 73–79.

10. James H. Donnelly, Jr., and John K. Ryans, Jr., "Standardized Global Advertising: A Call as Yet Unanswered," *Journal of Marketing,* April 1969, pp. 57–60. *Also see* George Fields, "How to Scale the Cultural Fence," *Advertising Age,* December 13, 1982, p. 4–11.
11. "Playtex Conditions Its Strategies," *Advertising Age,* May 17, 1982, p. M-16.
12. "Playtex Kicks Off a One-Ad-Fits-All Campaign," *Business Week,* December 16, 1985, p. 48.
13. Dean M. Peebes and John K. Ryans, Jr., *Management of International Advertising: A Marketing Approach* (Rockleigh, NJ: Allyn & Bacon, 1984), p. 73.
14. Dean M. Peebles, John K. Ryans, Jr., and Ivan R. Vernon, "Coordinating International Advertising," *Journal of Marketing,* January 1978, p. 28.
15. Christine D. Urban, "A Cross-National Comparison of Consumers' Media Use Patterns," *Columbia Journal of World Business,* Winter 1977, pp. 53–64.
16. Edward T. Hall, *The Silent Language* (New York: Doubleday, 1959). For discussion on cultural influences see Chapter 8.
17. James Killough, "Improved Payoffs from Transnational Advertising," *Harvard Business Review,* July–August 1978, p. 103.
18. B. G. Youovich, "Maintain a Balance of Planning," *Advertising Age,* May 17, 1982, p. M-7.
19. Based on an interview with a Kentucky Fried Chicken executive.
20. *Washington Post,* January 11, 1982, p. 38.
21. Ann Helming, "Pitfalls Lie Waiting for Unwary Marketers," *Advertising Age,* May 17, 1982, p. M-8.
22. John K. Ryans, Jr., "Is It Too Soon to Put a Tiger in Every Tank?" *Columbia Journal of World Business,* March 1969, pp. 69–75. *Also see* Dennis Chase and Eugene Bacot, "Levi Zipping Up World Image," *Advertising Age,* September 19, 1981, p. 34.
23. Jamie Talan, "Gillette Company on Track with Sharp Marketing for GII," *Advertising Age,* May 17, 1982, p. M-14.
24. Jacob Hornik, "Comparative Evaluation of International vs. National Advertising Strategies," *Columbia Journal of World Business,* Spring 1980, p. 43.
25. Lyn S. Amine and S. Tamer Cavusgil, "Mass Media Advertising in a Developing Country," *International Journal of Advertising,* vol. 2 (1983), pp. 317–330.
26. Roger Blackwell, Riad Ajami, and Kristina Stephan, "Winning the Global Advertising Race: Planning Globally, Acting Locally," *Journal of International Consumer Marketing,* vol. 3, no. 2 (1991), pp. 97–120.
27. S. Watson Dunn, "Effect of National Identity on Multinational Promotion Strategy in Europe," *Journal of Marketing,* October 1976, pp. 50–75.
28. E. Jerome McCarthy, *Basic Marketing—A Managerial Approach,* 7th ed. (Homewood, IL: Irwin, 1981), pp. 487–488.
29. John K. Ryans, Jr., "Is It Too Soon to Put a Tiger in Every Tank?' *Columbia Journal of World Business,* March 1969, pp. 69–75.
30. John S. Hill and William L. James, "Consumer Nondurable Products: Prospects for Global Advertising," *Journal of International Consumer Marketing,* vol. 3, no. 2 (1991), pp. 79–96.
31. Steuart Henderson Britt, "Standardizing Marketing for the International Market," *Columbia Journal of World Business,* Winter 1974, pp. 39–45. *Also see* Robert T. Green and Eric Langeard, "A Cross-National Comparison of Consumer Habits and Innovator Characteristics," *Journal of Marketing,* July 1975, pp. 34–41.
32. Barbara Mueller, "An Analysis of Information Content in Standardized vs. Specialized Multinational Advertisements," *Journal of International Business Studies,* vol. 22, no. 1 (First Quarter 1991), pp. 23–40.
33. "Playtex Conditions Its Strategies," *Advertising Age,* May 17, 1982, p. M-16.
34. *See* Robert D. Buzzell, "Can You Standardize Multinational Marketing?" *Harvard Business Review,* November–December 1968, pp. 102–113.
35. Discussion is based on James Killough, "Improved Payoffs from Transnational Advertising," *Harvard Business Review,* July–August 1978, pp. 102–110.
36. Ibid., p. 104.
37. John A. Quelch, "British Airways," a Harvard Business School case.
38. S. Watson Dunn, "Effect of National Identity on Multinational Promotion Strategy in Europe," *Journal of Marketing,* October 1976, pp. 50–57.
39. Russell W. Belk and Richard W. Pollay, "Materialism and Status Appeals in Japa-

nese and U.S. Print Advertising," *International Marketing Review,* Winter 1985, pp. 38–47.
40. *See World Advertising Expenditures* (Mamaroneck, NY: Starch INRA Hooper, Inc., 1989), pp. 32–33.
41. The discussion in this and the following section is adapted mainly from "Transnational Corporations in Advertising," a technical paper issued by the United Nations, 1979.
42. F. Callahan, "Does Advertising Subsidize Information?" *Journal of Advertising Research,* no. 18 (1978), pp. 19 and 22.
43. Andrew C. Brown, "Europe Braces for Free-Market TV," *Fortune,* February 20, 1984, p. 74. *Also see* "The Media Barons Battle to Dominate Europe," *Business Week,* May 25, 1987, p. 158; "En Garde: The Battle of French Television Has Begun," *Business Week,* February 24, 1986, p. 50; and Shawn Tully, "U.S.-Style TV Turns on Europe," *Fortune,* April 13, 1987, p. 5.
44. Tim Harper, "U.K. Eyes New Channel to Ease Demand Prices," *Advertising Age,* May 16, 1988, p. 68.
45. *World Advertising Expenditures* (New York: Starch, INRA, Hooper and International Advertising Association, 1992), pp. 36–37.
46. *See* Cynthia Webster, "The Effect of Nationality on Media Usage Patterns: A Study of Consumers From Countries of Various Levels of Development," in James E. Littlefield and Magdolna Csath, eds., *Marketing and Economic Development* (Budapest, Hungary: Karl Marx University of Economic Sciences, 1988), pp. 238–241.
47. *See Statistical Yearbook,* different issues (Paris: UNESCO). *Also see* W. D. Davidson, J. Boyland, and F. Yu, *Mass Media: Structure and Effects* (New York: Praeger, 1976).
48. *Business Week,* July 17, 1989, p. 104.
49. S. Tamer Cavusgil and Karl Hutchinson, "Pan-Europe TV Opens up New Multinational Markets," *Marketing News,* March 27, 1987, p. 8.
50. Erdener Kaynak and L. A. Mitchell, "A Comparative Study of Advertising in Canada, the United Kingdom, and Turkey," a paper presented at the Academy of International Business Annual Conference, October 1984, Cleveland, Ohio.
51. Dean M. Peebes and John K. Ryans, Jr., *Management of International Advertising* (Rockleigh, NJ: Allyn & Bacon, 1984), p. 25. *Also see* Norihiko Suzuki, "The Changing Pattern of Advertising Strategy by Japanese Business Firms in the U.S. Market: Content Analysis," *Journal of International Business Studies,* Winter 1980, pp. 63–72.
52. "The Media Barons Battle to Dominate Europe," *Business Week,* May 25, 1987, p. 158.
53. *Advertising Age,* July 5, 1982, p. M-14.
54. Vern Terpstra, *International Marketing,* 3rd ed. (Chicago: Dryden Press, 1983), p. 414.
55. *See* J. J. Boddewyn, "Advertising Regulation in the 1980s: The Underlying Global Forces," *Journal of Marketing,* Winter 1982, pp. 27–35. *Also see* J. J. Boddewyn, "The Global Spread of Advertising Regulation," *MSU Business Topics,* Spring 1981, pp. 5–13; James R. Wills, Jr., and John K. Ryans, Jr., "Attitudes Toward Advertising: A Multinational Study," *Journal of International Business Studies,* Winter 1982, pp. 121–130; and Jean Boddewyn, "The One and Many Worlds of Advertising: Regulatory Obstacles and Opportunities," *International Journal of Advertising,* vol. 7, no. 1 (1988).
56. *See* Rein Rijkens and Gordon E. Miracle, *European Regulation of Advertising* (New York: Elsevier Science Publishing Co. Inc., 1986).
57. *Advertising Age,* September 7, 1981, p. 26; *Advertising Age,* July 12, 1982, p. 24; *Advertising Age,* December 6, 1982, p. 3.
58. "Transnational Corporations in Advertising," a technical paper issued by the United Nations, 1979.

APPENDIX

Self-Regulation in Selected Countries

	CENTRAL SELF-REGULATORY BODIES	VOLUME OF ACTIVITY	OTHER SELF-REGULATORY ACTIVITY	TREND
Argentina	Comision Inter-Societaria de Autorregulation Publicitaria (CIAP)	33 denunciations in 1977	Cigarette industry and media advertising	Situation stable
Australia	Advertising Standards Council (ASC)	611 complaints in 1977	Media council, Australian Federation of Consumer Organizations (AFCO)	Increasing government involvement
Austria	Oesterreichischer Werberat (Austrian Advertising Council); Fachverband Werbung (advertising agency association); and another advertising association	Medium	Association for Consumer Information; Chamber of Workers	Action is "concerted," with advertising industry, government, consumerists cooperating together
Belgium	Jury d'Ethique Publicitaire	196 cases in 1977	Comité de la Publicité pour les Médicaments (pharmaceuticals self-regulation)	Toward more government regulation, because of consumer pressure
Brazil	Inter-Associative Commission of Brazilian Advertising		None	Level of consumer concern low; no trend to government intervention
Canada	Canadian Advertising Advisory Board (CAAB), top level with two review bodies: Advertising Standards Council, Conseil des Normes de la Publicité; regional councils in Winnipeg, Vancouver	357 complaints in 1977	None	All quarters report satisfactory situation

(*continued*)

	CENTRAL SELF-REGULATORY BODIES	VOLUME OF ACTIVITY	OTHER SELF-REGULATORY ACTIVITY	TREND
Denmark	Consumer ombudsman; dissemination through Danish Advertising Agencies Association and Danish Daily Publishers Association	Very active	None	Ombudsman system working well
France	Bureau de Vérification de la Publicité	2,987 investigations in 1977	None	Increasing government regulation, including "corrective advertising" law; also cooperation between advertising, government, and consumer organizations
Germany	Zentralausschuss der Werbewirtschaft e. V. (ZAW)	250 cases investigated in 1977	Various industries have own codes; agency legal staffs check conformity	Reluctance to increase volume of self-regulation; increasing legislation
Greece	None	None	None	Two attempts to form self-regulatory groups unsuccessful
Netherlands	Reklameraad (advertising board)—radio and TV; Reklame Code Commissie (advertising code commission)—most media other than broadcast	Very active	Each firm (advertiser, agency, media) has an "ethical officer" to handle self-regulation; KOAGG (regulatory board for pharmaceutical and medical products)	Consumerist agitation about broadcast advertisements; advertiser concern about Common Market moves
	None	None	No report	Self-regulation body being studied by Indian Society of Advertisers; considerable consumer complaint against both advertisers and government regulators

	CENTRAL SELF-REGULATORY BODIES	VOLUME OF ACTIVITY	OTHER SELF-REGULATORY ACTIVITY	TREND
Iran	None	None	Tehran agency association members subscribe to ICC Code, handle ad hoc self-regulation	Movement toward central body; increasing press concern over consumer protection
Ireland	Advertising Standards Committee (ASC)	Very low	All advertising industry associations have own self-regulatory operations	Increasing government regulation and restrictions
Israel	Israel Advertising Association and Advertisers Association of Israel, jointly with Israel Consumers Council	2 cases per month	ABC (Audit Bureau of Circulations) and MABAF (media body for non-newspaper publications) handle certain aspects	No serious government intervention because of satisfactory cooperation of three bodies
Italy	Instituto dell'Autodisciplina Publicitaria (IAP)	57 cases in 1973	None	Stable
Japan	Japan Advertising Review Board (JARO)	317 complaints in 1977	None	Much importance has been attached to self-regulation
Mexico	None		Seven major advertising industry associations have committees to handle self-regulation questions	Greater government regulation; efforts toward central voluntary group
Norway	Norwegian Marketing Association (prior review)	Extensive	Each agency appoints executive responsible for checking advertisements	Consumer ombudsman and market council handle advertising regulation; no change foreseen
Philippines	Philippine Board of Advertising (PBA)	No report	Moderately active consumer group	Increased government regulations

(*continued*)

	CENTRAL SELF-REGULATORY BODIES	VOLUME OF ACTIVITY	OTHER SELF-REGULATORY ACTIVITY	TREND
South Africa	Advertising Standards Authority of South Africa (ASA)	97 cases in 1977	Various advertising industry associations continue to be active in self-regulation; each agency has "code enforcer" to check advertisements	ASA working to be assigned central role, forestall increasing legislation
Spain	Autocontrol de la Publicidad, S.A.	No report	Consumer groups	Government control increasing and action by consumer groups
Sweden	Consumer ombudsman and industry's private consulting unit; some industries have formal or informal self-regulation	4,000 cases in 1973		Consumer ombudsman and market council handle all regulation
Switzerland	Schweizerische Kommission zur Uberwachung der Lauterkeit in der Werbung	±200 cases per year	None	Stable
United Kingdom	Advertising Standards Authority, with its Code of Advertising Practices Committee (print and sales promotion)	300+ cases per year	Industry associations have own committees; major agencies and advertisers have legal counsel; Tobacco Advisory Committee handles self-regulation of cigarette and tobacco advertising	0.1 percent subscription of display advertising billings will strengthen ASA/CAP; new government Office of Fair Trading given wide powers to regulate advertising and marketing practices
United States	National Advertising Review Board (NARB)	±250 cases per year	Major companies and agencies have legal counsel to check advertisements; all important industry associations have codes and committees; media have individual and group codes, review mechanisms	High level of controversy, strong consumerist pressure for increased legislation and government action; NARB/NAD still establishing itself

	CENTRAL SELF-REGULATORY BODIES	VOLUME OF ACTIVITY	OTHER SELF-REGULATORY ACTIVITY	TREND
Venezuela	None		Consumer group	Policy of new government not yet defined; no plans for self-regulation

Source: Adapted from James P. Neelankavil and Albert B. Stridsberg, *Effective Advertising Self-Regulation* (New York: International Advertising Association, 1980).

CHAPTER • 16

Multinational Sales Management and Foreign Sales Promotion

CHAPTER FOCUS

After studying this chapter, you should be able to:

- Discuss the role of personal selling in international business
- Examine the problems of expatriates and third country nationals
- Describe the formulation and implementation of policy guidelines regarding the transfer of people from nation to nation
- Define the steps in building foreign sales promotion and public relations programs

Personal selling, sales promotion, and public relations are all devices of a company's total promotional scheme, but each one has certain characteristics that assign it a unique role. When a company begins selling in export markets, or switches from export selling to international marketing, or launches a new product line or service in a new foreign market, or takes an established line of products into a new country or region, it invariably has more promotion tasks to undertake than funds available. In other words, marketers' aspirations with respect to foreign marketing almost always exceed their ability or willingness to allocate funds. This chapter highlights the significance of different types of promotion and examines their relevance in different foreign situations. Unfortunately, no ready-made formulas are available to give priority to different forms of promotion. However, the discussion here identifies considerations that may help in determining where and how to begin.

Sales Personnel and Personal Selling Abroad

Sales personnel in international business can be classified in two ways, either by the task they perform or by their nationality. Principally, there are three categories of selling tasks: sales generation, sales support, and missionary work. *Sales generation* is the creative task of helping the customer to make a purchase decision. *Sales support* is concerned with after-sale service. *Missionary work* is undertaken by a manufacturer's salespersons to stimulate demand to help the distributors. When classifying sales personnel by nationality, there are also three categories: expatriates, natives, and third country nationals. *Expatriates* are home country employees on deputation in the host country. For example, a G.E. sales manager from the United States assigned to launch the G.E. sales effort in Spain would be considered an expatriate. *Natives* are employees belonging to the host country. A Spanish national working for G.E. as a salesperson in Spain is a native. *Third country nationals* are employees transferred from one host country to another. For example, a French national transferred to Spain would be defined as a third country national.

For the most part, U.S. companies do not transfer selling personnel abroad. There are two reasons for this. First, selling requires deep familiarity with the local culture, which an expatriate cannot be expected to have, and second, it is extremely expensive to assign expatriates to selling positions. Such reasons lead companies—IBM as an example—to depend mainly on nationals for selling jobs. Similarly, Unilever only employs nationals of a country for marketing jobs in that country.[1] There are occasions, however, when companies may assign expatriates to work, usually for short periods, in the selling area.[2] Such a practice is more commonly followed in the marketing of big-ticket items. The expatriate who has a proven track record at home can be quite helpful in resolving difficult foreign situations, and/or in serving as a catalyst for the natives. For example, Otis Elevator had to assign a sales engineer from the home office to provide after-sale service for its elevators in a large office complex in Singapore for a year. This became necessary because the native salesforce had failed to ensure smooth functioning of its elevators. Likewise, NCR Corporation uses expatriates to provide on-the-job training to natives. As a matter of fact, the company has a cadre of seasoned salespeople who travel from country to country assisting native salesforces in selling the company's products. Many big-ticket items require selling directly from the home office, which usually involves expatriates. For example, Boeing bids for selling airliners to foreign airlines from its headquarters in Seattle. Its salespeople, mainly expatriates, travel extensively worldwide to call on its customers. In 1983, Greece decided to rejuvenate its air force by buying 100 new fighter bombers. This amounted to over $3 billion worth of business, Greece's biggest-ever defense contract. A number of U.S. aircraft companies and European companies sent sales personnel to Athens to make sales presentations and contacts.[3]

The management of a native salesforce is a local matter to be handled according to business practices in the host country. From the viewpoint of parent corporations, therefore, the major concern is with expatriates and third country nationals. Foreign sales positions are demanding assignments that require long hours of hard work, perseverance, and self-sacrifice. Developing the long-term relationships necessary for successful selling in a foreign environment takes tremendous effort.

Expatriates

The recruitment, transport, and risks connected with sending expatriate salespeople overseas are time consuming and expensive, ranging from two-and-a-half to three times the costs involved with an equivalent domestic salesperson. In addition, an MNC risks a loss of time and money if the salesperson fails to stay the length of the assignment. Productivity may suffer too if the person becomes a so-called brownout—someone who stays on the foreign assignment but becomes inefficient because either he or she or the family is unhappy.[4] Also, an expatriate's lack of knowledge or disregard for the host country's cultural practices may damage a company's reputation or cause the loss of a critical contract. Finally, the MNC should be concerned with the repatriation of expatriates in order to reassimilate them into the stream of domestic corporate activity without loss of efficiency (see International Marketing Highlight 16.1).

In addition to using expatriates for sales positions overseas for limited periods, many companies place expatriates in foreign subsidiaries for reasons that may be hard to accept. A study by Galbraith and Edstrom offers four reasons for using expatriates. While the study deals with foreign placement in general, it has equal application for the assignment of salespeople overseas. The reasons were (1) to fill a position, (2) to utilize managerial talent, (3) to give an executive international experience, and (4) to facilitate coordination and control with the parent company.[5]

The first reason usually results from a technical position becoming vacant in a subsidiary located in a developing country, where the lack of technically qualified personnel motivates the move. One example is the recruitment of engineers for high-paying positions in the Middle East. According to the study, this reason accounted for 60 percent to 70 percent of all transfers.

The second reason, to use managerial talent, is explained by the authors as

International Marketing Highlight 16.1

Indifference at Home

In a survey of personnel managers at fifty-six multinational companies based in the United States:

56 percent say a foreign assignment is either detrimental to or immaterial in one's career.

47 percent say their returning expatriates aren't guaranteed jobs with the company upon completion of their foreign assignments.

65 percent say their expatriates' foreign assignments are not integrated into their overall career planning.

45 percent view returning expatriates as a problem because they are so hard to fit back into the company.

20 percent consider their company's repatriation policies adequate to meet the needs of their returning expatriates.

Source: Moran, Stahl & Boyer, New York.

follows: "a job opportunity and a promotable individual do not always occur in the same subsidiary." This situation complements the first. An absence of opportunity at home and a need overseas would encourage the transfer of a talented individual to a subsidiary outside the United States.

The third reason, to provide international experience for executives, was cited by U.S. firms in the study as the second most important criterion for foreign assignment. This consideration, however, is not independent of the need to fill a position. If there are qualified local managers and the transfer occurs, then the probable reason is valuable international experience and exposure. Knowledge gained during the assignment would increase the firm's global perspective in relation to existing markets. Firsthand information is always preferable. This leads to the fourth reason, coordination and control, which is particularly crucial in situations where the firm is initiating large efforts to crack a local market, where the organization is implementing policy changes, or where the firm lacks confidence in developing countries.

It is quite logical to bring in expatriates for specific so-called fire-fighting assignments (for example, to supervise and/or train locals) or for a developmental assignment, that is, to expose a promising executive to multinational experience. The problems occur when people are sent overseas for historical, egocentric, or nationalistic reasons like: "But we've always had an expatriate do that job. No one can manage that operation except an American." Political maneuvering within a company can also cause problems, like sending an employee overseas to clear the way for another person to take up an emerging position. Retreading the path of least resistance—that is, the best solution is always to bring in an American whenever there is any problem—can be counterproductive.

Third Country Nationals

In recent years, a new trend has been to assign employees at all levels from one host country to another. This trend has arisen for two reasons. One, in many countries of the world there is a surplus of workers, while other countries lack adequate workforces. For example, Saudi Arabia's population is about 6 million people. If a company is developing fast there, it may need a large salesforce but find it difficult to find suitable Saudis to fill sales positions. Saudi Arabia is, therefore, forced into accepting salespeople from other developing countries, like Pakistan, India, or South Korea.[6] Too, a company often needs a salesperson with certain requisite experience for a subsidiary. Looking around, the company discovers the most appropriate person for the job is a third country national (see International Marketing Highlight 16.2).

Third country individuals face unique organizational problems (see Exhibit 16.1). For example, third country employees naturally want to know to which organization, the parent corporation or the host country company, they belong in regard to promotion and benefits and their feeling of identity. To manage third country employees effectively, both headquarters and host country management should study their special problems. An appreciation of their needs enhances performance for the benefits of the corporation. Although the episode in International Marketing Highlight 16.3 concerns an executive, it is equally relevant for salespersons. The story illustrates the type of management thinking and planning that ought to precede actual transfer of people across national boundaries. Cultural biases, financial interests, and individual preferences all play a role in a person's life. A person's success in one environment doesn't guarantee success

International Marketing Highlight 16.2

Wooing Third Country Nationals

Multinational firms are tapping more third country nationals for overseas posts. Nationality matters less as businesses race to enlarge their ranks of global managers. So-called TCNs—neither Americans nor local nationals—often win jobs because they speak several languages and know an industry or foreign country well. The average number of third country nationals per U.S. company rose to forty-six in 1989 from thirty-three in 1988.

Pioneer Hi-Bred International employs twenty-nine TCNs in key jobs abroad, triple the number five years ago, partly because they accept difficult living conditions in Africa and the Middle East. Raychem has a dozen such foreigners in top European posts, up from eight in 1986. The numbers are going to increase as Europe's falling trade barriers ease relocation. A French citizen runs the company's Italian subsidiary, a Belgian is a sales manager in France, while a Cuban heads the unit in Spain.

Scott Paper, whose TCN managers have increased to thirteen from two in 1987, will step up recruitment of young foreigners willing to move around Europe or around the Pacific.

Source: The Wall Street Journal, September 16, 1990, p. B1.

EXHIBIT 16.1 Problems Faced by Third Country Nationals

- *Blocked promotions.* The tendency of MNCs to reserve top positions at headquarters for parent country managers.
- *Transfer anxieties.* The third country managers' anxieties caused by uncertainty about the timing of their next transfers, the countries to which they will be transferred, the positions to which they will be assigned, and the extent of managerial autonomy involved in their next assignments.
- *Income gaps.* The tendency of third country managers to feel deprived in terms of income in comparison to parent country managers, and the tendency of host country managers to feel deprived in comparison to third country managers.
- *Unfamiliarity and adaptability difficulties.* The natural tendency of newly arrived third country managers to make mistakes and their compulsion to cover them up.
- *Avoidance of long-range projects.* The tendency of third country managers to concentrate on short-range, nonrisk, and demonstration-type projects.
- *Inappropriate leadership style.* The tendency of third country managers to imitate the managerial style prevalent at headquarters.
- *Nonparticipative decision making and screening of information.* The tendency of third country managers to adopt a detached leadership style because of their perception of headquarters as their positive reference group.
- *Insufficient authority in industrial relations.* The tendency of MNCs to delegate insufficient authority to third country managers in top positions for dealing with critical industrial relations issues in their subsidiaries.
- *Lack of commitment of top-ranking third country managers to the perpetuation of the host country organization.* The conviction of host country managers that third country managers are less committed to the perpetuation of the host country organization and to the welfare of their host country subordinates.

Source: Yoram Zeira and Ehud Harari, "Managing Third Country Nationals in Multinational Corporations," *Business Horizons,* October 1977, p. 84.

elsewhere. A company needs a sound policy for moving people from country to country.

Formulating Policy Guidelines

The high rate of expatriate failure among U.S. multinationals is a matter of great concern. It stems from several factors: the family situation, lack of cross-cultural relational abilities, the short duration of overseas assignments, problems of repatriation, overemphasis on the technical competence criterion to the disregard of other important attributes such as relational abilities, and inadequate training for cross-cultural encounters.

Companies can no longer afford to transfer people from nation to nation without having an appropriate policy for a guide. Too many people and too much money are involved. While the common practice is to hire natives for sales positions, the number of short-term specific assignments for solving ad hoc problems is on the increase, which requires bringing in expatriates or third country nationals.

International Marketing Highlight 16.3

Managing Third Country Nationals

The scene is the West Coast headquarters of a worldwide high-technology company. It is late in the afternoon and an all-day conference involving the personnel director and the vice president of international operations is in progress.

What is the problem? The problem is Pierre. Who is Pierre? He is not just another militant employee off the assembly line. Pierre is a key executive, two levels from the top of the organization, and, heretofore, regarded as a comer headed for a key top-management position in the United States upon conclusion of his current assignment.

How did Pierre get in this fix? He was hired in Paris and managed the French subsidiary until it achieved significant market penetration in France. One day Pierre woke up and found that the job had lost challenge. There was nowhere for him to go. He was a big fish in a small pond. About the same time, the company was beginning operations in Australia. What was better logic than to send Pierre from France to Australia to utilize his flair for building up the business? After he had opened up operations in Australia, there were vague plans to move him back to headquarters.

Pierre was a task-oriented man. For six months he left his family in Paris, took a flat in Sydney, and worked day and night, making only two brief return trips to France. Then he moved his family to Australia and the trouble began.

The problems started simply enough. How did he get paid? The French subsidiary wanted him off their books. "No problem," said the personnel director, "we will pay you like an American. After all, you work for an American company, so we will pay you in U.S. dollars."

Pierre received his first paycheck and could not believe it. When transferred to the U.S. scale, he made less money than in France. (Top management salaries in parts of Western Europe have reached parity and in many cases have surpassed their U.S. counterparts—this is not even considering benefits, which have historically been much better in Europe than in the United States.)

Pierre took the salary reduction in stride, primarily because he was too involved in building up the market and did not have time to worry about it then. After his family had been there one month, the U.S. dollar was devalued and the Australian dollar revalued. Since Pierre used U.S. dollars to buy Australian dollars, his purchasing power was cut.

The problems then increased in intensity. There was the matter of taxes. He was in Australia and legally responsible for Australian taxes. But Pierre's Australian taxes were more than he would have paid had he stayed in Paris. The first of many cables was sent to corporate headquarters.

"What about my salary and taxes?"

"Pay him like an American, tax him like an American," said the personnel director.

The next round of cables soon followed. "But I am not an American; I am a Frenchman. I want a French salary and French tax levels, and while I'm at it, what about my French profit sharing? Do I lose this while in Australia?" (In

France, many companies set aside, at least by U.S. standards, a rather liberal amount of money for profit sharing.) "What about my company car?" (Having a company car is another European custom for top management.) "How about vacation?" (Holidays in France are longer.) "How about home leave? When can I go back to France?"

As if this were not enough, further cables kept rolling in. "What about housing? I pay more housing in Sydney than I did in Paris."

Then there was education. Who would pay the fee for correspondence courses to keep Pierre's children involved in the French education system?

The crowning blow was when Pierre asked for a cost-of-living allowance. "It couldn't cost him more to live in Sydney than in Paris!" shouted the vice president of international operations. "What's happened to Pierre? He has turned into a greedy, me-first employee. Is this the kind of manager we want representing us overseas? Get him back here; let's talk this out now!"

Pierre gladly caught the next plane. How did all this happen? What caused Pierre's metamorphosis? It was another common fault of multinational companies engaging in the movement of people across borders. In the heat of battle, decisions are made to move people without being thoroughly thought out. Moreover, these decisions are made without an underlying philosophy and plan.

Source: David M. Neor, *Multinational People Management* (Washington, D.C.: Bureau of National Affairs, 1975), pp. 9–11.

The policy should cover determination of the most appropriate nationality, the selection of the nonnative salesperson, plans for repatriation and reassignment, work assignments, and the development of native salespersons by the nonnative selected. In actuality, companies may not have a thoroughly articulated policy for expatriates and third country nationals that covers all these points. But increasingly companies attach importance to the problems that occur when people work in different cultures. As an example, Westinghouse Corporation has defined the following corporate procedure for assignment, repatriation, and reassignment of international employees:

> **Background**
>
> The long-term interest of the Corporation is best served by limiting international assignments to those management and professional employees who have an established record of competence. International assignments can be a valuable supplement to the normal training and development programs for the high-potential employee.
>
> Management and professional people with international experience are an invaluable corporate asset, and every effort should be made to assure that experience gained by employees through such assignments is retained and properly utilized.
>
> Consequently, all organization units assigning personnel internationally should develop specific plans for the selection, assignment, and repatriation of management and professional employees. Consistent with the needs for international staffing, organization units should identify competent employees who have the desire and potential to successfully undertake an assignment abroad.

Guidelines
1. Pre-assignment—a pre-assignment orientation program should be planned and implemented on a timely basis to assure that candidates and their dependents are fully prepared to undertake international assignments. Organization units assigning personnel internationally will define in writing all known conditions of assignment, including but not limited to the employee's salary, allowances, duration of assignment, etc. The employee should be provided copies of all applicable policies and procedures. 2. Repatriation and reassignment—Organization units should periodically review the status of their international assignees and develop specific repatriation plans for each employee. Where performance continues to be satisfactory, it is the responsibility of these units to assure that personnel selected for international assignments will have upon return a position at least equivalent to the level held by the employee prior to accepting the international assignment. For coordination reasons, it is also the responsibility of these units to keep Key Personnel Services advised of their repatriation plans or problems. 3. Application—This procedure applies to all organization units assigning personnel internationally, as well as to all management and professional personnel who accept an international assignment, with the exception of those engaged in service and other activities which normally require international travel or who are assigned for a limited time to specific international customer contracts abroad.[7]

Abroad as at home, poor supervision and inappropriate policies produce negative results. Deficiencies in management away from home can be costly. More and more attention, therefore, is likely to be given to recruiting, selecting, developing, and motivating managers for overseas assignments, however brief the assignment.

Tung suggests that to enhance expatriate success and minimize failure, U.S. multinationals (1) adopt a longer-term orientation with regard to expatriate assignments and provide support mechanisms at corporate headquarters to allay concerns about repatriation, (2) develop a more international orientation, and (3) provide more rigorous training programs to prepare expatriates for cross-cultural encounters.[8]

Implementing Policy Guidelines

The first step after formulating a policy for the management of both expatriates and third country nationals is the pursuit of this policy to administer adequately the selection, orientation and training, compensation, and placement procedures inaugurated for salespeople for positions away from home.

Selection

Selection is crucial to the success for an overseas appointment. It is desirable to establish adequate selection criteria and to adapt the criteria carefully to ensure that the right person is chosen. Exhibit 16.2 lists considerations of selection. Potential candidates could be rated as either satisfactory or unsatisfactory on each of the criteria listed. Then the person showing the highest satisfactory ratings overall could be the final choice. In addition to the factors included in the

EXHIBIT 16.2 Interview Criteria for International Candidates

Motivation

- Investigate reasons and degree of interest in wanting to be considered.
- Determine desire to work abroad, verified by previous concerns such as personal travel, language training, reading, and association with foreign employees or students.
- Determine whether the candidate has a realistic understanding of what working and living abroad requires.
- Determine the basic attitudes of the spouse toward an overseas assignment.

Health

- Determine whether any medical problems of the candidate or family might interfere with the success of the assignment.
- Determine whether the candidate is in good physical and mental health, without any foreseeable change.

Language ability

- Determine potential for learning a new language.
- Determine any previous language(s) studied or oral ability (judge against language needed on the overseas assignment).
- Determine the ability of the spouse to meet the language requirements.

Family considerations

- How many moves has the family made in the past between different cities or parts of the United States?
- What problems were encountered?
- How recent was the last move?
- Are there any special adjustment problems that you would expect?
- How is each member of the family reacting to this possible move?
- Do special educational problems exist within the family?

Resourcefulness and initiative

- Is the candidate independent; can the candidate make and stand by decisions and judgments?
- Does the candidate have the intellectual capacity to deal with several dimensions simultaneously?
- Is the candidate able to reach objectives and produce results with available personnel and facilities, regardless of the limitations and barriers that might arise?
- Can the candidate operate without a clear definition of responsibility and authority on a foreign assignment?
- Will the candidate be able to explain the aims and company philosophy to the local managers and workers?

Resourcefulness and initiative

- Does the candidate posses sufficient self-reliance, self-discipline, and self-confidence to overcome difficulties or handle complex problems?
- Can the candidate work without supervision?
- Can the candidate operate effectively in a foreign environment without normal communications and supporting services?

(continued)

EXHIBIT 16.2 (*Continued*)

Adaptability

- Is the candidate sensitive to others, open to the opinions of others, cooperative, and able to compromise?
- What are the candidate's reactions to new situations, and efforts to understand and appreciate differences?
- Is the candidate culturally sensitive, aware, and able to relate across the culture?
- Does the candidate understand his own culturally derived values?
- How does the candidate react to criticism?
- What is the candidate's understanding of the U.S. government system?
- Will the candidate be able to make and develop contacts with his peers in the foreign country?
- Does the candidate have patience when dealing with problems?
- Is the candidate resilent; can he bounce back after setbacks?

Career planning

- Does the candidate consider the assignment anything other than a temporary overseas trip?
- Is the move consistent with the candidate's progression and that planned by the company?
- Is the candidate's career planning realistic?
- What is the candidate's basic attitude toward the company?
- Is there any history or indication of personnel problems with this employee?

Financial

- Are there any current financial and/or legal considerations that might affect the assignment, e.g., house purchase, children and college expenses, car purchases?
- Are financial considerations negative factors, i.e., will undue pressures be brought to bear on the employee or family as a result of the assignment?

Source: David M. Noer, *Multinational People Management* (Washington, D.C.: The Bureau of National Affairs, 1975), pp. 55–57.

sample list, the candidate's spouse should be involved in the selection process right from the start. Many failures stem from the spouse's reluctance to transfer in the first place and an inability to adapt to host country conditions. An expatriate rated as having a marginal chance of success might do very well because of a supportive spouse. It is, therefore, crucial to consider spouse evaluation in an expatriate selection system. Further, before accepting the assignment, the candidate and his or her spouse should be given an opportunity to see the country. An advance trip of a week or so cannot give anyone a thorough understanding of a country's culture, but, if properly done, it enables the prospective expatriate to make a more intelligent decision (see International Marketing Highlight 16.4).

Orientation and Training

Sales personnel slated for foreign assignment should be oriented to the new job and provided relevant training. Essentially, orientation and training should cover the terms and conditions of the assignment, language training, and cultural training[9] (see International Marketing Highlight 16.5).

International Marketing Highlight 16.4

Spouses Must Pass Test Before Global Transfers

Employees' families are playing a bigger role in international transfers. The inability of spouses or children to adapt to their new surroundings is the number one cause of failure in overseas transfers, including premature returns, job-performance slumps, and other problems. With overseas postings costing an average of $225,000 to $250,000 a year, companies are trying to smooth the way.

Many companies include spouses in the screening process for overseas assignments, including a formal assessment of such qualities as flexibility, patience, and adaptability. Fort Motor interviews spouses before the move. Exxon also meets with the spouses or children. Minnesota Mining & Manufacturing offers spouses educational benefits and uses electronic mail to introduce employees' children to peers in the target country. 3M recently found new housing for one Japanese executive in the U.S. so his sixty-five pound dog could rejoin the family.

The programs are largely a response to pressure from employees. As many as 75 percent of international transfers end in such family problems as marital discord or adjustment problems in children. Companies are finding that it's difficult to get someone to go unless they address those issues.

Source: The Wall Street Journal, September 6, 1991, p. B1.

Terms and Conditions of the Assignment The employee should be provided with a clear and concise overview of the company's expatriate policies, procedures, and compensation system; information on housing, transportation, and schools in the host country; and information on moving arrangements.

Language Training Language training is perhaps the most basic type of knowledge that a foreigner needs for a productive life in a host country. Language is the key to a country's culture. It permits understanding of the subtleties of the country and the reasons why certain things are done differently. A language can be learned in different ways: in a language school with a regular program lasting several months; through a short, intensive program offered either by a commercial school or a local university, or at home through a self-study program. Do-it-yourself kits are available for home study programs in the form of records, cassette recordings, books, telephone conversations with instructors, and different combinations of these alternatives. Regardless of the method, the one central ingredient in learning a language is proper motivation on the part of the employee and family. It is incumbent upon the multinational employer to emphasize the need for language training.

Cultural Training Both academic and interpersonal cultural training should be given. Academic training includes the provision of things like books, maps, brochures, films, and slides. The interpersonal training consists of making arrangements for candidate and family to make a trip to the host country, in addition to

International Marketing Highlight 16.5

The Colgate-Palmolive Global Marketing Training Program

Few companies pour as much money and management expertise into training marketing managers as New York-based Colgate-Palmolive. Although much smaller than Lever Brothers and Procter & Gamble, Colgate derives 60 percent of its revenue from abroad. The company prides itself on its ability to penetrate new markets (sometimes before its giant competitors arrive) and maintain good profitability. To retain its position as one of the world's preeminent consumer products companies, Colgate decided years ago to develop a program to ensure itself of a steady supply of superior marketers with the skills to operate almost anywhere.

The "Global Marketing Training Program" Colgate created, which gives its participants a two-year immersion in global marketing, has acquired considerable prestige since its establishment. Admission is highly competitive and is sought by some of the brightest B.A.'s and M.B.A.'s from the world's best colleges and business schools. Successful applicants must have not only excellent academic credentials but also leadership skills, fluency in at least one other language in addition to English, and some international-living experience, for example, a year of study in a country other than the applicant's own.

The program itself consists of assignments in various departments at Colgate, with a strong emphasis on marketing functions. A typical rotation includes some time in finance and manufacturing and larger blocks of time at Colgate's ad agency, in market research, and in product management. The trainees serve for seven months as field salespeople in the United States, and they actually perform the job rather than merely accompanying regular salespeople on their rounds.

The program gives trainees the basic skills global marketing managers need. The participants learn to use computers, devise budgets, formulate sales promotion strategies, manage work groups, and so on. They also begin to develop relationships that will help them when they start to operate in the international environment.

Most of Colgate's new marketing "graduates" are sent to markets in developing countries. Some are initially assigned to work in the United States, but they, too, are soon posted overseas. Because non-U.S. markets are so important to Colgate, it does not automatically bring its international marketers back to the United States after a foreign assignment, as do many other MNCs. Often, the marketers go directly from one overseas post to another, becoming, in essence, career internationalists.

Source: Business International, September 10, 1990, p. 306.

meeting with host country natives living in the United States and people who have lived previously in the host country.[10]

The following information was specifically designed for U.S. expatriates in Japan. With modification, however, this may apply equally well to other situations.

A Few "Don'ts"

Don't lose your temper in front of the Japanese. Their proverb, *Tanki wa sonki* ("A short temper means a lost spirit"), illustrates how they feel.

Don't regard human problems coldly, for this violates their emotional sensitivity.

Go out of your way to avoid being egotistical, unrelenting, harsh, or abrasive, for these four disagreeable characteristics have been attributed to us in popular fiction, and Japanese who are unfamiliar with Americans are looking for such behavior.

Do not engage in flattery or sugarcoat your compliments, for the Japanese consider people who talk this way as lacking in sincerity. There are plenty of nice things you can say and still be factual.

Do not try to high-pressure the Japanese into buying something or taking action. If pressed too hard, they may dig in their heels and take twice as long to make a decision. There are much more effective ways to influence them.

Don't use the table-pounding technique. The Japanese almost invariably respond negatively to such power tantrums—particularly in the case of Americans, for they react to their Occupation-era memories by firmly opposing American power plays, thus demonstrating their independence.

Don't tell them how to run their country. They think they are doing pretty well—and have evidence to back them up. Some Japanese feel that foreigners who give unsolicited advice are either ignorant of local circumstances or arrogant, even though the visitors may just be trying to be helpful.

A Few "Do's"

Be as courteous as you can, for the Japanese are on the whole an especially polite people and appreciate this behavior in others. (In public opinion polls in Japan, the British and French are regarded as the most polite. Americans are usually rated near the bottom.)

If you should become exasperated, remain cool and keep a smile on your face if you can. If you cannot do so, try to show no emotion. Do not allow your temper to goad you into saying something insulting or, worse, taking offensive action. The Japanese believe in their proverb, *Nama byoho wa okizu no moto* ("Crude tactics cause great injuries").

Go out of your way to be good-natured, practical, sociable, frank, responsible, and efficient, for these are desirable traits which Japanese expect to find in Americans. Don't disappoint them.

Speak a little Japanese if you can. They will appreciate the effort.

Avoid criticizing the United States, its institutions, and its leadership, for an American company cannot be considered separately from the whole. If foreigners are led to think that the country is falling apart, they will have doubts about its companies, too.

Learn as much as your time will permit about Japanese history, for without some understanding of the past it will be difficult to understand the present.

Recognize that the Japanese have reason to be proud of their culture and business accomplishments. They will appreciate Westerners who want to learn all they can about the country.[11]

Compensation

Salespeople away from their home base cost more because they must be paid extra compensation. The extra compensation covers three factors. First, it is a premium for climatic conditions in the host country, separation from friends and relatives, cultural shock, and subjection to situations of political instability and economic risk in conditions of unstable currencies. Second, it is an allowance for housing, children's schooling, return trips home on a periodic basis, income tax, and overall cost-of-living expenses. Third, there are certain perquisites common in host countries for particular positions, like car and driver, servants, and club memberships.

The elements of compensation and the amount paid under each heading differ from country to country depending on the living costs. According to Union Bank of Switzerland, for example, giving New York an index of 100, the cost-of-living index in Tokyo would be 199, Stockholm 131, Geneva 127, London 101, Frankfurt and Paris 95, Milan 94, Toronto 88, Sydney 84, Los Angeles 76, Hong Kong 72, Cairo 62, Mexico City 55, and Bombay 54 (based on a basket of 108 goods and services excluding rent for a typical European family of three).[12]

Table 16.1 shows what it takes to maintain a $110,000-a-year U.S. lifestyle for a family of four in different cities around the world. For example, in Hong Kong another $49,051 will be needed to support the same living, while in Mexico one will end up saving over $6,000.[13]

Exhibit 16.3 illustrates a typical expatriate compensation package. Note that the total additional compensation is over three times more in the United Kingdom than in the United States. Even in a developing country an expatriate may cost more depending on demand and supply conditions relative to different elements of compensation. In a city like Tokyo, housing would be very expensive since suitable apartments are very scarce. In many developing countries, housing is expensive because Western-style accommodations are difficult to locate, and a high premium must be paid for the few that are available. Similarly, if taxes are very high in a country and if the foreigner is taxed like a native, the company

TABLE 16.1 Living Expense Differences in Various Cities in the World

CITY	HOUSING	TRANSPORATION	TAXES	GOODS AND SERVICES	TOTAL
Hong Kong	$52,360	$15,878	$ 8,100	$12,713	$89,051
Tokyo	39,487	6,233	15,650	18,435	79,805
Geneva	22,667	5,674	19,983	17,397	65,721
Brussels	9,193	5,228	36,883	13,502	64,806
Frankfurt	12,345	5,518	25,989	14,628	58,480
Buenos Aires	19,103	4,854	21,016	10,596	55,569
Sydney	12,192	9,620	17,860	13,268	52,940
Paris	15,199	4,786	18,886	13,098	51,969
Amsterdam	11,014	5,081	19,723	13,508	49,326
London	15,269	6,254	10,681	13,846	46,050
Rio de Janeiro	13,703	4,216	14,748	11,125	43,792
Mexico City	8,175	2,893	12,480	10,139	33,687

Source: Reprinted from January 16, 1984 issue of *Business Week* by special permission, copyright © 1984 by McGraw-Hill, Inc.

EXHIBIT 16.3 The Price of an Expatriate

An employer's typical first-year expenses of sending a U.S. executive to Britain, assuming a $100,000 salary and a family of four.

Direct compensation costs	
Base salary	$100,000
Foreign-service premium	15,000
Goods and services differential	21,000
Housing costs in London	39,000*
Transfer costs	
Relocation allowance	$5,000
Air fare to London	2,000
Moving household goods	25,000
Other costs	
Company car	$15,000
Schooling (two children)	20,000
Annual home leave (four people)	4,000
U.K. personal income tax	56,000*
Total	$302,000

Note: Additional costs often incurred aren't listed above, including language and cross-cultural training for employee and family, and costs of selling home and cars in the U.S. before moving.
*Figures take into account payments by employee to company based on hypothetical U.S. income tax and housing costs.
Source: Organization Resource Counselors Inc., New York.

must bear the tax burden over and above what the employee would have paid in the United States or other home country.

Considering the expenses involved in transferring nonnatives to host countries, the company should make a careful study of the conditions of each country and undertake regular reviews of any changes. The overhead to keep watch on the changes in costs, taxation, facilities, and currency values is by no means negligible; experts in the field are high-priced, and their travel budgets are large. Nevertheless, the cost is a sound investment if as a result the company's team of valuable expatriates and/or third country nationals is fairly compensated and has confidence in the home office's policy toward them. These necessary perquisites secure their profitable contribution to the company's performance.

Placement

Once a salesperson accepts an overseas position, the company should provide adequate information to prepare for the departure to the host country. This information includes advice on such matters as how to apply for a passport; how to obtain necessary visas and immunizations; how expenses should be handled for reimbursement; how to obtain transportation and arrange accompanied baggage and unaccompanied baggage shipment; tax matters; and current status under the various company benefit, pension, stock, and insurance plans. Information is also needed on obtaining an international driver's license, making financial arrangements, deciding what clothing to take, and even reminding the salesperson to notify correspondents of a change of address. Some of these arrangements and details are quite complicated, and generous advice and counsel for each individual can smooth the passage of personnel and their families to transfer assignments.

Repatriation and Reassignment

Traditionally, salespeople have welcomed overseas assignments. It has meant taking extra compensation and seeing the world at company expense; besides, going abroad was considered to be a route to the executive suite. More recently, however, fewer jobs are opening up in Euro-capitals. The Middle East and the LDCs are the new foreign-assignment destinations, where hardship pay lives up to its name and the experience offers little beyond just that—experience. A returning salesperson faces a severe penalty for being out of the home office working environment and a severe shock when confronted with the domestic real estate market.

Fewer salespeople are willing to accept overseas positions, particularly those personnel who perceive the risk of an inferior position upon return. On a number of occasions, there has been no job for a returning expatriate, who has then spent months in a holding pattern. Many companies lose good marketing people for lack of job vacancies in the United States when their time comes to return.[14]

Returning home amounts to facing previously familiar surroundings. Yet, as the following quotes show, expatriates have found the reentry into the home environment more of a problem than going abroad.[15]

> Repatriating executives from overseas assignments is a top management challenge that goes far beyond the superficial problems and costs of physical relocation. . . . The crux of the matter is the assumption that since these individuals are returning home—that is, to a familiar way of life—they should have no trouble adapting to either the corporate or the home environment. However, experience has shown that repatriation is anything but simple.[16]

> Managers know that there is always a risk of being stuck, at least temporarily, in a mediocre job when they return.[17]

> Few, if any, executives ever come out ahead financially in a transfer back to the U.S. . . . An even more serious shock [than the financial shock], because it can have a long-range impact on the executive's career, is the re-adaptation to corporate life . . . a foreign assignment [tends to] . . . keep the executive out of the mainstream of advancement. . . . In some respects the more outstanding a performer the executive was overseas, the more uncomfortable his return will be.[18]

The returning executives themselves have made these comments:

> Going home is a harder move. The foreign move has the excitement of being new . . . more confusing, but exciting. Reentry is frightening. . . . I'll be happy to be home . . . I wonder if I can adjust back.
>
> There's some kind of traumatic reaction to it. It evidenced itself in my insomnia. There was something there . . . waking me up at 4 A.M.[19]
>
> Career . . . it didn't help. I got personal learning. I lost time. My career stopped when I left and started again when I returned.
>
> Colleagues view me as doing a job I did in the past. I had the experience before going . . . they don't view me as gaining while overseas.
>
> The organization has changed . . . work habits and norms and procedures have changed and I have lost touch with all that . . . I am a beginner again.
>
> Colleagues are indifferent to my international assignment.
>
> Before going overseas I thought that it might help my career. Within the home organization, international is more remote from domestic. You are visible only within international.
>
> I have no specific reentry job to return to. . . . I want to leave international and return to domestic. . . . Working abroad magnifies problems while isolating effects . . . i.e., you deal with more problems, but . . . [the home office] does not know the details of the good or bad effects . . . managerially, I'm out of touch with financial policies . . . I'll be less confident in managing. . . . If this job had been in North America, . . . my old management style would have worked.[20]

The repatriation problem is not limited to U.S. expatriates. Even Japanese returnees find it hard to assimilate their own culture after having spent a few years in the United States. Because most Japanese white-collar workers generally have a negative attitude toward overseas assignments, many returnees end up taking jobs with the U.S. subsidiaries in Japan.[21]

To alleviate the reluctance of personnel to be recruited for foreign assignments, companies are providing prospective expatriates with written guarantees on company foreign personnel policy. These repatriation agreements are really no more than general promises in writing that include a limit of a two- to five-year maximum on time spent abroad and assurances of return to a mutually acceptable job. Union Carbide assigns senior executives to act as sponsors for overseas managers, including salespeople. Sponsors scout six months prior to the expatriates' return to locate a suitable position. Union Carbide's Linde division has a seven-member committee to review overseas personnel and place returning employees. The Dow Chemical Company has ten full-time counselors who visit with each of the company's expatriate employees, including those in sales, once a year. The counselors let the expatriates know that they have not been forgotten and act as advocates for possible promotion considerations. Also, repatriation supervisors are assigned to expatriates to monitor compensation, performance, and potential career paths.

At Westinghouse, the originating suborganization (the business unit or group) assumes responsibility for placement of returning individuals in positions of appropriate responsibility at the conclusion of foreign assignments. Each expatriate receives a formal performance evaluation. If deemed unsatisfactory, the employee will simply be repatriated with no new position. If the review is acceptable, the employee will receive reasonable assurances of a position upon returning and will be counseled on the potential for promotion. The repatriation process begins with the identification of a new home position six months prior to the completion of the out-of-country assignment. Westinghouse also places its overseas personnel on a computerized corporate file that matches expatriate's qualifications with job openings.

The results of repatriation programs exhibit a pattern of success.[22] The success rate in getting overseas personnel to remain in their posts for the duration of the assignment is much higher when a satisfactory repatriation policy exists. It alleviates possible career anxieties.

Salespeople with international experience are an invaluable corporate asset. Repatriation agreements should ensure that the experience gained by personnel through such assignments is retained and properly utilized.

Adler's empirical work on the subject shows that a few ad hoc measures are not enough to resolve the problems of the returnees.

> **Predeparture Training**
> Since employees who adjust well overseas tend to be more effective at reentry, organizations should provide predeparture training for employees and their families.
>
> **Selection**
> Employees who are successful and satisfied prior to going overseas tend to be successful and satisfied at reentry. Sending failures will not bring home successes. It is therefore recommended that organizations select effective, rather than marginal, employees for overseas assignments.
>
> **Overseas Contact**
> Foreign-based employees who are aware of both the positive and negative changes in the organization tend to be more effective at reentry. It is recommended that management frequently inform foreign-based employees of current organization policies, projects, plans, etc.
>
> **Job Responsibility**
> The higher the job responsibility at reentry, the more effective is the returnee. It is recommended that reentry be planned from the employee's career perspective and not solely according to the demands of the overseas project.
>
> **Cross-Cultural Skills**
> Because awareness of cross-cultural skills is often tacit and because skills are often seen as not transferable to the home country, it is recommended that returnees be assisted in identifying their newly enhanced and acquired skills, and in finding ways to apply them within the home organization.
>
> **Xenophobic Home Country Managers**
> Since managers who have not worked in foreign countries frequently discount the value of the returnees' overseas experience, it is recommended that the home organization assist home country managers in recognizing and developing ways to use returnees' cross-cultural skills.

Similar Countries
Since reentry from all parts of the world can be equally difficult, it is recommended that reentry from more similar countries (e.g. same language and same level of economic development) be as well managed as reentry from more dissimilar countries.

External Validation
Since returnees whose experience is recognized and valued by the organization are more effective and use their cross-culturally acquired skills to a greater extent, and since a xenophobic response is common among home country managers, it is recommended that home country managers be taught how to value returnees and their foreign experiences.[23]

Actually, a systematic approach, which takes care of expatriates right from the beginning, is needed to resolve the repatriation problem. Harvey suggests a four-phase program for this purpose:[24]

1. Planning expatriation
   Development of foreign assignment with specific objectives in mind (i.e., corporate and career path)
   Development of assessment procedure of various environments
   Modification of objective performance measures
2. Preexpatriation phase
   Clear delineation/communication of executive's objectives in foreign assignments
   Development of a consensus on evaluation criteria for foreign assignments
   Information/awareness of repatriation problems
   Provision of necessary training for family and executive for foreign assignment
3. Expatriation phase
   Establishment/maintenance of formal communication channels with expatriate
   Supply of data on domestic activities and the importance of expatriate's assignments
   Systematic/periodic review of expatriate's foreign assignment
   Performance/evaluation of expatriate and adequate recognition/money
   Assessment of domestic job opportunities and their fit into career path of expatriate
4. Repatriation phase
   Intensive organization/environment update for executive
   Redefinition of motivation for domestic position
   Assistance with family reorientation

Movement of salespeople across national boundaries for temporary assignment in another country is most likely to continue. These people are of significant value. They serve as catalysts of new ideas and as risk takers—the MNC's people-on-the-spot, so to speak. Companies must undertake proper measures to equip them for ultimate gains and success in the foreign environments and bring them home for the ultimate gain of the corporation and their continued happiness and success in it.

International Sales Negotiations

Face-to-face negotiations with the customer is the heart of the sales job. Negotiations are necessary to reach an agreement on the total exchange transaction, comprising such aspects as the product to be delivered, the price to be paid, the service agreement, the payment schedule, and other issues. Briefly, negotiations are the means of deciding the terms of sales.

International sales negotiations have many characteristics that distinguish them from negotiations in the domestic setting. First and foremost, the cultural background of the negotiating parties is different, which may inhibit understanding of each other's viewpoint.[25] Second, political factors often complicate and delay international business negotiations. Third, in many cases, the host government must be involved in bringing the negotiations to a conclusion.

Sales negotiations may involve such issues as product features, service, price, delivery date, mode of payment, training of buyer personnel, and financing. While these issues are usually negotiated between buyer and seller in domestic situations as well, they assume greater importance in international marketing for a variety of reasons. Consider service. In the United States a company selling a product that requires periodic servicing will presumably have adequate service facilities and parts inventory. But if the product sale is negotiated in, say, Thailand, and the company's closest service facilities in the area are located in Japan, the customer would want certain assurances about timely servicing at a reasonable cost. The customer may demand that the company establish facilities in Thailand itself. On the other hand, the company may not find it financially feasible to do so. In such a situation, negotiations become essential. As a matter of fact, the Thai government may step in and refuse to grant foreign exchange until the company agrees to make local service arrangements.

Negotiating Process

The objective of a negotiating process is to reach an agreement of mutual benefit.[26] The process begins from a situation of *contention,* meaning each party has its own agenda to strike the deal. It ends with *conclusion,* whereby a mutually satisfying agreement has been reached. The distance from contention to conclusion is covered through the stages of clarification, comprehension, confidence, credibility, convergence, conciliation, and concession. The first stage, *clarification* and *comprehension,* involves seeking information to form a better idea of each other's position on significant issues. The second stage includes *confidence* and *credibility,* which refer to the formation of attitudes among the parties based on an appreciation of each other's requirements and the reasons behind them. At the conclusion of this stage, the two parties would reach a *convergence* of views on many aspects of the deal (see International Marketing Highlight 16.6). The third stage, *concession* and *conciliation,* requires the parties to reach a compro-

International Marketing Highlight 16.6

Preparations for Price Discussions

Importer's reaction to price offer	Exporter's possible response
1. The initial price quoted is too high; a substantial drop is required	Ask the buyer what is meant by too high; ask on what basis the drop is called for; stress product quality and benefits before discussing price.
2. Better offers have been received from other exporters.	Ask for more details on such offers; find out how serious such offers are; convince the buyer that the exporter's firm has a better offer.
3. A counteroffer is required; a price discount is expected.	Avoid making a better offer without asking for something in return, but without jeopardizing loss of interest; when asking for something in return make a specific suggestion, such as "If I give you a 5 percent price discount, would you arrange for surface transport including storage costs?"
4. The price of $..... is my last offer (the importer specifies a lower price).	Avoid accepting such an offer immediately; find out the quantities involved; determine if there will be repeat orders; ascertain who will pay for storage, publicity, after-sales service, and so on.
5. The product is acceptable but the price is too high.	Agree to discuss details of the costing; promote product benefits, reliability as a regular supplier, timely delivery, unique designs, and so on.
6. The initial price quoted is acceptable.	Find out why the importer is so interested in the offer; recalculate the costing; check competition; contact other potential buyers to get more details on market conditions; review the pricing strategy; accept a trial order only.

Source: Claude Cellich, "Negotiating Strategies: The Question of Price," *International Trade Forum,* April–June 1991, p. 12.

mise on the remaining unsettled issues through give and take. The final stage is the conclusion of negotiations. The shape of the negotiated agreement depends on the bargaining power of the two parties, which in turn is determined by the importance of the deal for each of them. For example, if the product involves substantial business for the seller now and potential additional sales later, the buyer would be in a relatively strong bargaining position. On the other hand, if the product is not readily available from another source, the seller will approach negotiations from a point of leverage.

In addition to the bargaining power of the two parties, negotiations are considerably affected by the negotiating skills of the people involved in the process. Issues such as how people perceive each other, how they interact, how the ambience of negotiations can be altered, how confidence and trust can be established, and how they threaten and intimidate each other will significantly influence the outcome.[27] These issues, along with the fact that the negotiating parties come from different economic, political, and cultural backgrounds and may speak different languages, make international negotiating a complex exercise. It is for this reason that many scholars consider international negotiating an art (see International Marketing Highlight 16.7).

Negotiating Strategies

Basic to negotiating well is the ability to put yourself in the other person's shoes, understand his or her way of thinking, recognize his or her perspective, and allocate sufficient time for the task. Even when you start from a point of weakness, there are strategies that a salesperson can pursue to negotiate to his or her advantage. For example:

1. Increase your variables and know your alternatives. Price is not the only flexible factor. Consider every aspect of the deal—R&D, specifications, delivery and payment arrangements. The more options you have, the greater your chances of success.
2. When attacked, listen. Keep the customer talking and you will learn valuable things about his or her business and needs.
3. To reduce frustration and assure the customer that you're hearing what he or she is saying, pause often to summarize your progress.
4. Assert your own company's needs. Too much empathy for the customer can reduce the emphasis on problem solving and lead to concessions.
5. Try to make your customer commit to the outcome of the whole negotiation. Make sure the full solution works for both parties.
6. Save the hardest issues for last.
7. Start high, concede slowly, keep your expectations high, and remember that every concession has a different value for buyer and seller.
8. Never give in to emotional blackmail. If the customer loses his temper, don't lose yours. Withdraw, postpone, dodge, sidestep, listen. As a last resort, declare the attack unacceptable but always refuse to fight.[28]

Negotiating style varies from culture to culture, and often involves language differences, cultural conditioning, approaches to problem solving, implicit assumptions, gestures and facial expressions, and the role of ceremony and formality. In preparing for and analyzing a negotiation, it is useful to review these dimensions fully. As has been said: "The negotiator must enter into the private world or cultural space of the other, while at the same time, sharing his or her own perceptual field."[29]

International Marketing Highlight 16.7

Negotiating in Korea

Korea is unique in Asia in that it has a bimodal industrial leadership elite. Its members are either in their fifties and sixties or in their thirties. The younger, postwar managers are a new breed; often they are descendants of founders. To assume that a youthful Korean negotiator has no clout is folly. On the contrary, the new generation is competent, dedicated, educated, trained, and often powerful. Korea's modern global orientation stems from these highly Westernized managers. Therefore, negotiations with younger Koreans will be quite occidental in their flavor, whereas discussions with the older power group will likely follow more traditional patterns.

Foreigners, whether customers or suppliers, ought to go to great lengths to observe the general protocol and tenor of Korean business discussions. Central to negotiating in Asia is the maintenance of proper interpersonal relationships. Koreans have regulated the tone of communications by structuring their society. Class, official status, sex, age, and education are identification tags that set the tone of discussions. A foreigner will be judged by—and often matched with—his or her peers in these status categories.

Behavior is the second regulator of relationships. Koreans are strong spirited and straightforward. Yet in business negotiations they can be low-key, diplomatic, and indirect. This subtlety is designed to protect the image of the participants. Their honor and privacy must be respected. This general approach precludes such tactics as abruptness or open criticism. Even strong disagreement should be clad in modest clothing. An atmosphere of conflict avoidance should prevail, to preserve the self-esteem of all participants.

Koreans make up with shrewdness for what they may lack in sophistication. They strike a hard bargain whether buying or selling. But, when selling, they certainly present a more hospitable, deferential, and pliable front.

The buying process invites two caveats. One has to do with price. Asians are preconditioned to haggle over price. Therefore, Koreans automatically raise their opening price in order to yield ritualistically later to make the deal. This practice makes the bottom price a matter of conjecture. The foreign buyer, as a result, should be prepared and should know what constitutes a good price. Second, Koreans have been known to take shortcuts. They quite reasonably ask, "If it works this way, why not that way?" But "that way" may involve a change in the product makeup and cost input. Therefore, clear-cut specifications are a must for the purchaser of Korean products.

Both younger Koreans and businesspeople in particular have a keen appreciation of time's importance and value. Though a buyer's time is more precious than that of a vendor, on the whole, business deadlines such as appointments receive prompt treatment. Korea's precarious position has forced a more practical view of time on the economic sector.

Because practically all decisions come from top levels of the Korean enterprise, visitors should make every effort to contact upper-echelon officers. Lower-level executives are afraid to manage. They have neither full information nor clear authority. This state of affairs leaves the owner-manager or the chief executive and his top-level team as an overworked decision-making group. They are occupied with both trivial and major deliberations. Frequently the top executive still rules by inspiration and through charisma.

Although Westerners attach great importance to a written contract, Koreans perceive a contract as a loosely structured statement of consensus—a "working contract" open to adjustment while it is in effect. Thus Koreans' propensity is to leave a number of clauses flexible. A common saying states that a signed contract is nothing but a place to begin tomorrow's negotiations. The foreigner is well advised to nail down all critical phases of agreement. Copious notes taken during negotiations will be very helpful.

Source: Doing Business in Korea (Menlo Park, CA: Business Intelligence Program, SRI International, no date), pp. 10–14.

Foreign Sales Promotion

Sales promotion devices tend to stimulate new attitudes toward the promoted product through the lure of getting something for nothing. The very feeling that something can be had for free creates a strong desire for the product among buyers no matter which country/region they belong to. Historically, sales promotion is a uniquely American phenomenon. But today sales promotion techniques are popularly used to supplement advertising and personal selling throughout the world (see International Marketing Highlight 16.8).

Besides increasing sales at the retail level, sales promotion helps in building the morale of the sales force. Some companies use sales promotion simultaneously with sales incentive schemes to make them complement each other. For example, in the 1970s, Hoover Company promoted its vacuum cleaners in England through providing a packet of one dozen throw-away vacuum bags as a lure. At the same time the company organized a sales contest for its dealers and salesforce for a vacation in the United States. Sales promotion also acts as a push-through device by making customers want the product. Once the image of a product is established among customers, dealers and retailers will be compelled to stock it. For example, Coca-Cola Company introduced its orange soda, Fanta, in many developing countries through free gifts of ballpoint pens and pencils and the like. Through consumer demand even the very small retailers were forced into carrying Fanta.

Devices of sales promotion can be classified on the basis of the function to be performed and the target to be reached. Three main types of sales promotion functions can be distinguished: sales promotion for introducing a new product, sales promotion for increasing the use of a product, and sales promotion for the direct enticement of customers at the retail level. Free samples, price-off coupons, and refund offers are the devices used for introducing new products. Price-off deals, premiums, contests, and sweepstakes, constitute the methods for securing greater use of a product. Trading stamps, retailer coupons, and point-of-

International Marketing Highlight 16.8

Globalization of Coupons

International coupon use is on the rise, a trend that will continue through the 1990s, according to a recent study.

"Coupon Distribution and Redemption Patterns Report," released by NCH Promotional Services, Chicago, examines the couponing and promotion trends in major world markets including the United States, Canada, the United Kingdom, Spain, Italy, and Belgium.

Although the United States remains the world's leading coupon market, with over 279.4 billion coupons issued in 1990, several other markets around the world are beginning to experience the same couponing growth that occurred in the U.S. during the early 1980s.

The European Community's recent gains in political and economic freedoms have given marketers the opportunity to use more creative promotional techniques. The European market has enormous, untapped promotional possibilities.

As distribution methods standardize and multinational firms introduce tried-and-true coupon promotion practices on a larger scale, the barriers to couponing will begin to dissolve.

The study said consumers in the United Kingdom and Belgium are the EC's most active coupon users. In 1990, an average of seventeen coupons per household were redeemed in the United Kingdom, and eighteen coupons per household were redeemed in Belgium. The United Kingdom, Europe's largest coupon market, has had redemption growth of 21 percent since 1989, the largest increase in the world.

The study also reported that the U.K.'s coupon industry outlook is bright, since seven out of ten consumers already use coupons regularly. Newspapers and magazines are the most popular means of distribution in the United Kingdom. Spain and Italy rely heavily on in- or on-pack promotions for their coupon distribution. In several European markets, door-to-door coupon distribution is common, although this technique is virtually unheard of in the U.S.

In other parts of Europe, couponing has had relatively stagnant growth. In Spain, distribution has declined over the past few years, and Italy's couponing has shown only modest increases. In both countries, an average of three coupons were redeemed per household, compared with seventy-seven in the United States and twenty-six in Canada.

Although couponing has just become legal in Denmark, other European countries have limited access to coupons. In Holland and Switzerland, major retailers refuse to accept coupons.

Source: "Global Coupon Use Up; U.K., Belgium Tops in Europe," *Marketing News,* August 5, 1991, p. 6. Copyright 1991 by the American Marketing Association.

purchase demonstrations are resorted to for action at the retail level. Sales promotion techniques can be consumer-oriented, and dealer- and distributor-oriented. Sampling, demonstrations, or instructions; premium offers or temporary price reductions; and contests and sweepstakes are consumer-oriented promotion devices. Intermediary- or agent-oriented techniques will include assistance in store layout, assistance in planning and developing strategy such as accounting and inventory instructions, cooperative advertising, dealers' sales training, provision of point-of-purchase materials, and money and merchandise allowances.

The above categorization is based on U.S. practices. The marketing environment in a foreign market, however, may require making appropriate adaptations in sales promotion offerings. As a matter of fact, in some nations a marketer may be forced into coming out with an entirely new sales promotion idea that is in line with the country's environment. Poor economic conditions in developing countries may suggest putting greater emphasis on the economic value of the offering, assuming the product is directed at the mass market. Legal restrictions in many countries call for adaptation. In Germany, giveaways (other than items of insignificant value such as calendars and diaries) are legally prohibited. Further, the sales promotion campaign should not create conflict in the marketplace so as to raise eyebrows in political circles. Inasmuch as some sales promotion campaigns must be implemented through wholesalers and retailers, their structure and practices would also be a consideration in planning a sales promotion campaign. For example, retailers in most developing countries are small, scattered, and disorganized. They may not be able to handle the equivalent of a cents-off type of sales promotion. Above all, the sales promotion offering should be culturally acceptable. The customization of sales promotion to match the perspectives of a country is well illustrated by Ford Motor Company's efforts in Brazil.[30] In the midst of high inflation, banks in Brazil were not willing to finance purchases of big-price items by low-income families. Ford Motor Company, therefore, established car-buying clubs of sixty members each. Each member made sixty monthly payments toward a car. A drawing was held each month and the member whose name appeared on the drawing received the car that month. This way the low-income Brazilian families continued to buy the cars without being burdened with high interest costs. The company, on the other hand, generated a guaranteed number of customers each month.

Management of sales promotion requires (1) a clear definition of *objectives* (for example, introducing a new product, increasing sales of an existing product, reducing seasonal declines in sales, countering competitor's gains, and registering new customers); (2) making *budget* allocations (which must be done in the context of a total promotional budget including advertising and personal selling); (3) drawing a *plan of action* covering such points as length of the campaign, details of sales promotion offerings, instructions required for the salesforce and middle agents, coordination needed with other departments of the company, media announcements, and cost estimates; and (4) an *evaluation* of the campaign to determine its viability for future use in the same country, and in other nations.

Public Relations Overseas

Public relations serves as a useful device for establishing a foothold and/or strengthening existing position in an overseas market. The public relations activity is directed toward an influential, though relatively small, target audience of editors and journalists who work for publications or in broadcasting aimed at a firm's customers and prospects. Since the target audience is small, it is relatively inexpensive to reach.

To do an effective public relations job overseas, an international marketer needs to hire an established public relations firm. It is desirable to look for a firm that has relevant experience and adequate resources. If the United States public relations firm of the company has an office in the host country, it may be retained there too. Alternatively, one may have to choose from among the local firms. After the public relations firm is recruited, the company should develop a dossier, that is, a package of information that editors may file for future reference. A typical dossier runs to ten pages and includes information on the company's capabilities, its technologies, its preeminence, and why it operates in the host country. The dossier may be supplemented with a corporate brochure, preferably in the host country language, identifying worldwide manufacturing, research and development, and sales/service locations. Usually, the dossier is accompanied by a letter inviting editors to contact a designated person for further information. The letter may also state that articles and releases will be regularly issued by the company in the future.

The company should decide, in consultation with the public relations firm, how an initial contact should be made with the target audience, editors and journalists. At this stage, the public relations firm is better known to the audience than is its client. As a matter of fact, some public relations firms are so well accepted in a country that a release on the company's behalf signals editors that the story is newsworthy, factual, and worth publishing. Thus, the public relations firm should play a lead role in establishing initial contact for the firm.

Future announcements and releases may either be custom-developed for the host country or extracted from among those prepared for the domestic market. In other words, a firm entering an overseas market may reuse some of its U.S. news releases, application case histories, technical and feature articles, trends articles, and the like. The appropriateness of domestic material in an overseas market may be judged by the host country marketing management and the public relations firm. Wherever necessary, however, original releases must be produced and issued as desired.

Once a story or article on the firm appears in print, it will be read by only a small fraction of customers. But it is important to get all the promotional value one can from a good placement. One way of doing this is to send story/article reprints in quantity to the firm's salespeople and distributor salespeople for use in their sales calls and mailings. The reprints support sales training programs, too. New salespeople can learn much about the company's products and applications from a file of articles.

International Marketing Highlight 16.9

Global Philanthropy

American Express—Developed an academic course to educate secondary school students on travel and tourism issues. Cost: $500,000.

DuPont—Sent 1.4 million water-jug filters to eight nations in Africa. Their synthetic fabric removes debilitating parasitic worms from drinking water. Cost: $400,000.

Alcoa—Teamed up with local authorities in southern Brazil to build a sewage plant serving 15,000 rural residents. Cost: $112,000.

H.J. Heinz—Funded infant nutrition studies in China and Thailand through Heinz's Institute of Nutritional Sciences in Chengdu, China. Cost: $94,000.

IBM—Donated computer equipment and expertise to Costa Rica's National Parks Foundation to develop strategies for preserving rain forests. Cost: $60,000.

Hewlett-Packard Co.—Donated computers to the University of Prague.

Source: Business Week, February 25, 1991, p. 91.

The activities outlined above help in establishing a good name for the company and its product during the start-up period. To continue to generate news and be visible in the long run, a variety of techniques can be used. These include interviews and the publicizing of talks by area executives, publicity for new product designs or services developed in or for the overseas area, case histories from customers' experiences in the area, special activities for key media, invitations to the press to cover company-sponsored seminars, meetings, and workshops, and photographs to meet an editor's express needs. These techniques assist in *localizing* the company. Beyond that, as the company becomes fully established, the public relations activities may include sponsored speeches and seminars, and management leadership in professional associations (see International Marketing Highlight 16.9).

The role of public relations abroad does not differ greatly from what it is in the United States, but somehow U.S. companies do not emphasize it overseas as thoroughly as at home.[31] The public relations activity internationally should not be directly limited to market a product/service. Public relations programs should serve as a company's antenna, gathering and analyzing information on events, trends, and legislation, and as a contact point with the firm's various audiences.

Summary

Personal selling is an important ingredient of any marketing program. Three sources of sales personnel are identified: expatriates (U.S. nationals working in a host country, say, England), natives (an English national working in England), and third country nationals (a French citizen transferred by a U.S. company to work in England). In the realm of international business, most personal selling jobs are handled by the local management. The head office, however, can provide useful support to local management on such aspects as selection, training, supervision, compensation, and evaluation.

The chapter concentrates on the problems involved in managing expatriates and third country nationals. Multinational corporations should have a well-defined policy for expatriates and third country nationals that deals with such matters as determining the most appropriate nonnative nationality selection in host country personnel situations, employment upon repatriation, and plans for natives' development. Also covered are various aspects of managing expatriates and third country salespeople: selection, orientation, training (including terms and conditions of the assignment, cultural training, and language training), compensation, and placement. Finally, the process of international sales negotiations and strategies for successful negotiations are discussed.

In ways similar to domestic marketing, sales promotion and public relations are also relevant to international marketing. The role of sales promotion in other countries does not vary from what it is in the United States. However, an appropriate sales promotion program for an overseas market should be geared to the local environment. For example, in a country where retailing organizations are small and scattered, it may be difficult to use the equivalent of cents-off coupons. Public relations provide a justification and an identity for the foreign enterprise in the economic sphere of the host country. It is desirable to hire the services of a public relations firm with relevant experience in order to get started on a solid program. Publicity programs, which give the firm and its products broad exposure to customers and prospects as well as third-party endorsement by the media, provide a cost-efficient use of a limited promotional budget.

Review Questions

1. Define the term *expatriate*. What problems are expatriates likely to face overseas?
2. Discuss the problems that pertain to the employment of third country nationals as salespeople.
3. What are the elements of policy guidelines for sales management overseas?
4. What precautions should be taken in selecting salespeople for overseas positions?
5. What type of training should be provided to expatriates?
6. Why do expatriate salespeople cost more? Illustrate with examples.
7. What steps may be adopted to adequately repatriate and reassign salespeople located abroad?
8. How does the retail structure of a host country affect the sales promotion program?
9. What role does a public relations firm play for an international marketer?

Endnotes

1. W. Chan Kim and R. A. Manborgue, "Cross-Cultural Strategies," *Journal of Business Strategy,* Spring 1987, p. 29.
2. "U.S. Concerns Are Hiring More Foreigners Abroad," *The Wall Street Journal,* May 29, 1981, p. 31.
3. "The Sale of the Decade?" *The Economist,* February 19, 1983, p. 43.
4. Michael G. Harvey, "The Multinational Corporation's Expatriate Problem: An Application of Murphy's Law," *Business Horizons,* January–February 1983, pp. 71–78.
5. O. Jay Galbraith and Anders Edstrom, "International Transfer of Managers: Some Important Policy Considerations," *Columbia Journal of World Business,* Summer 1976, pp. 100–112.
6. *See* "Singapore Affluence Is Making the Work Force Choosy," *Business Week,* December 7, 1981, p. 56.
7. *Corporate Procedure* (Pittsburgh: Westinghouse Electric Corporation, 1988), pp. 2–5.
8. Rosalie L. Tung, "Expatriate Assignments: Enhancing Success and Minimizing Failure," *Executive,* no. 2 (1987), pp. 117–126.
9. *See* Joann S. Lublin, "Younger Managers Learn Global Skills," *The Wall Street Journal,* March 31, 1991, p. B1.
10. *See* Mark Mendenhall and Gary Oddou, "Acculturation Profiles of Expatriate Managers: Implications for Cross-Cultural Training Programs," *Columbia Journal of World Business,* Spring 1986, pp. 73–80.
11. Reprinted by permission of *Harvard Business Review.* An excerpt from "How to Negotiate in Japan" by Howard F. Van Zandt, November–December 1970, p. 54. Copyright © 1970 by the President and Fellows of Harvard College; all rights reserved. *Also see* John Nirenberg, "Reducing Culture Shock for the Expatriate Managers," *San Francisco State University School of Business Journal,* Summer 1984, pp. 73–77.
12. *Business Week,* November 7, 1988. *Also see* Shawn Tully, "Where People Live Best," *Fortune,* March 11, 1991, p. 44.
13. "The Costs of Living Abroad vs. Standard City, USA," *Business Week,* March 7, 1983, p. 104. *Also see* "Residential Rents Are Rising Sharply in Asia's Expatriate Housing Market." *The Asian Wall Street Journal Weekly,* June 15, 1981, p. 17.
14. "How to Ease Re-Entry After Overseas Duty," *Business Week,* June 11, 1979, p. 48. *Also see The Wall Street Journal,* January 5, 1982, p. 1.
15. Michael G. Harvey, "The Executive Family: An Overlooked Variable in International Assignments," *Columbia Journal of World Business,* Spring 1985, pp. 84–92. *Also see* Joan M. Inzinga, "The Perceived Learning Needs and Intercultural Experiences of Corporate Expatriates: American and Asian Pacifics," Ph.D. dissertation, The University of Connecticut, 1988.
16. "Successful Repatriation Demands Attention, Care and Dash of Ingenuity," *Business International,* March 3, 1978, p. 65.
17. "How to Ease Re-Entry After Overseas Duty," *Business Week,* June 11, 1979, p. 48.
18. Lee Smith, "The Hazards of Coming Home," *Dun's Review,* October 1975, p. 72.
19. Nancy J. Adler, "Re-Entry: Managing Cross-Cultural Transitions," a paper presented at the Academy of International Business Meetings in New Orleans, October 1980.
20. Ibid.
21. Nan M. Sussman, "A Hard Homecoming for Japan's Expats," *The Asian Wall Street Journal Weekly,* January 13, 1986, p. 15.
22. Cecil G. Howard, "Integrating the Expatriate into the Domestic Organization," *Personnel Administrator,* January 1979, p. 63. *Also see* Cecil G. Howard, "How Best to Integrate Expatriate Managers in the Domestic Organization," *Personnel Administrator,* July 1982, pp. 27–33.
23. Nancy J. Adler, "Re-Entry: Managing Cross-Cultural Transitions," *Group and Organization Studies,* September 1981, pp. 355–356.
24. Michael C. Harvey, "The Other Side of Foreign Assignments: Dealing with the Repatriation Dilemma," *Columbia Journal of World Business,* Spring 1982, p. 55.
25. John L. Graham, Dong Ki Kim, Chi-Yuan Lin, and Michael Robinson, "Buyer-Seller Negotiations Around the Pacific Rim: Differences in Fundamental Exchange Processes," *Journal of Consumer Research,* June 1988, pp. 48–54.
26. Discussion in this section draws heavily on

Claude Cellich, "Skills for Business Negotiations," *International Trade Forum,* October/November 1990, p. 8.

27. Nigel C. G. Campbell, John L. Graham, Alain Jolibert, and Hans Gunther Meissner, "Marketing Negotiations in France, Germany, the United Kingdom and the United States," *Journal of Marketing,* April 1988, pp. 49–62.
28. Thomas C. Keise, "Negotiating With a Customer You Can't Afford to Lose," *Harvard Business Review,* November–December 1988, pp. 30–37.
29. Philip R. Harris and Robert T. Moran, *Managing Cultural Differences,* 2nd ed. (Houston: Gulf Publishing Co., 1987), p. 57.
30. "How Brazilians Beat the Credit Squeeze," *Business Week,* November 1, 1976, p. 50.
31. Oivind Mathisen, "Does the PR Role Differ in International Marketing Arenas?" *Advertising Age,* February 20, 1979, p. 56.

CHAPTER • 17

Export Marketing

CHAPTER FOCUS

After studying this chapter, you should be able to:

Describe perspectives of U.S. export trade

Discuss how the United States government encourages and hinders exports

Define the steps in conducting export business

Examine duty-free zones and barter trade

The United States is the world's largest exporter. Yet its exports are a meager percentage of the U.S. gross national product (GNP). The balance has shifted, however, to an extraordinary extent in the last decade. In 1970, the ratio of U.S. exports to GNP was 4.3 percent. Exports have more than doubled since then to 9.7 percent of GNP in 1991. But in comparison with the exports of European nations and Japan, U.S. exports (as a percentage of GNP) are still small. For Germany and the United Kingdom, exports amount to roughly 20 percent of GNP.

The international trade environment provides U.S. business with a variety of opportunities for export growth. The United States government is moving toward policies and procedures that encourage exports. The world economy began to recover in the early 1980s from a long recession. A decline in petroleum prices provided an additional boost to world economies, and narrowing inflation differentials among nations have always favored export growth.

But trends alone cannot prompt higher exports. U.S. businesses must make conscious efforts to boost exports. About 1 percent of U.S. companies accounted for about 80 percent of all 1991 U.S. exports. Big MNCs account for the vast bulk of export revenues. Nevertheless, most exporters are small companies. For example, the percentage of exporting manufacturers with fewer than 500 employees in 1987 was over 80 percent in rubber and plastics, machinery, furniture, instruments, fabricated metals, and chemicals.[1] There is continued potential opportunity for other U.S. companies to conduct export business successfully.

Some marketing managers do not fully explore potential sales abroad because of an uneasiness or lack of understanding about foreign credits and collections. Others shy away because of a fear that selling abroad involves too much red tape. Of course, selling abroad differs from selling in the domestic market, yet export sales can be handled without much difficulty if management has the vision and energy to make the attempt.

This chapter begins with an analysis of certain U.S. exports. Then, the procedural details for conducting an export business are outlined. Significant export management issues are discussed, and the emerging area of barter trading is examined.

U.S. Export Trade

The United States imports more merchandise than it exports, resulting in the problem of a negative balance of trade. To an extent, the negative trade balance is caused by excessive oil imports. During the 1950s, U.S. exports amounted to 18 percent of world trade. This declined to about 13.5 percent in 1970 during a period of indifference toward export trade. For example, either U.S. exports then were unique products that sold themselves—without significant competition from other countries—or export markets were used as last resorts to absorb periodic excess domestic inventories. Only a few companies were really committed to exporting. In the recent past, the United States government had no clear-cut policy for the encouragement of exports. Not until the mid-1960s did the United States government become particularly concerned about the U.S. balance of payments. During the decade of the 1970s, two compelling reasons to expand exports emerged. First, U.S. economic growth had slipped to less than 3 percent annually from about 4 percent over the preceding twenty years. U.S. companies began to consider export markets as a way of sustaining their own growth rates. Second, the dramatic increase in the price and consumption of imported oil made it essential to boost exports to help offset the huge outflow of U.S. dollars paid for oil. The U.S. share of world exports climbed as high as 20.6 percent in the early 1980s. It declined during 1984 through 1987 (19.2 percent) but rose to 20.5 percent in 1988, and stood at 13.0 percent in 1990.[2]

The U.S. potential for export growth is enormous. There is a $2 trillion market abroad, and with its capture come millions of jobs and income security for average Americans. So far only a fraction of U.S. export potential has been tapped. Eight out of ten new manufacturing jobs created between 1985 and 1990 were in export-related industries. Yet over 85 percent of U.S. manufacturers do not export at all. A $10 billion increase in exports generates about 193,000 American jobs both directly and indirectly. A similar increase in imports eliminates about 179,000 jobs. Thus, the export job-generation effect is about 7.8 percent larger than the import job-loss effect.[3]

Thousands of U.S. companies offer products and services that could be competitive abroad. Entry into export markets should help domestic business as well because, as the market expands via exports, economies of scale should be realized in lower costs of products both for overseas shipment and for those to be sold in the United States. Also, exports provide a cushion against slumps in the domestic market.

The Level and Direction of U.S. Export Activity

Exports are becoming ever more important to the U.S. economy, just at a time when expansion seems increasingly difficult. U.S. exporters find it difficult to keep pace with foreign competition. For example, during 1991 while U.S. industries exported $421.6 billion worth of goods to foreign customers, U.S. imports amounted to $488.1 billion. (See Table 17.1.) For seventeen years, the United States continued to incur trade deficits; from $9.3 billion in 1976 to $148.5 billion in 1985—the largest deficit on record, exceeding the 1984 record by over $40 billion. Since then, the picture has been a little more encouraging. Between 1985 and 1990, exports rose at a faster pace than imports. In 1991, while exports increased over 7 percent, imports registered a decline of 1.4 percent, although there was a substantial trade deficit of $66.5 billion.

This deficit refers to U.S. balance of trade and *not* to balance of payment. The ***balance of trade*** is the difference between merchandise exports and imports. The ***balance of payment,*** on the other hand, includes all international transactions, such as merchandise exports and imports; transfers under U.S. military agency sales contracts; travel and transportation by U.S. citizens abroad and by foreigners in the United States; and direct investments, foreign aid, and other payments. Such international transactions (excluding merchandise exports and imports) usually are called "invisibles" in international commerce. Their significant role for the United States is borne out by the fact that at times our deficits

TABLE 17.1 Merchandise Exports and Imports*

TYPE OF TRANSACTION	1960	1965	1970	1975	1985	1986	1987	1988	1989	1990	1991
Exports of goods and services	$19,650	$26,461	$42,469	$107,088	$213,100	$217,300	$254,100	$322,200	$363,800	$394,000	$421,600
Imports of goods and services	$14,758	$21,510	$39,866	$98,041	$361,600	$387,100	$406,200	$459,500	$473,200	$495,000	$488,100

*In millions of dollars.

Source: U.S. Department of Commerce, *Statistical Abstract of the United States: 1991* (Washington, D.C.: U.S. Government Printing Office, 1991), p. 763; *Business America,* April 6, 1992, pp. 2–5; and *Business America,* April 22, 1991, pp. 2–7.

in merchandise trade have been largely balanced or exceeded by growing positive "invisible" balances.

Table 17.2 shows different products exported and imported by the United States and the countries with which U.S. trade is conducted. American exports consist primarily of agricultural products and ready-for-sale manufactured goods, as well as component parts and intermediate products used in manufacturing—in other words, from soybeans to computers and aircraft, and from blue jeans to machine tools. The U.S. import list includes oil, autos, TVs, and other consumer and industrial goods. Among the ten key industries in U.S. foreign trade, aerospace, computer equipment, oil field machinery, medical equipment, and chemicals enjoy export surpluses, while cars and trucks, textiles and apparel, electronics, steel, and machine tools remain huge losers.

During the last ten years, U.S. trade has undergone interesting changes. First, trade with Pacific Basin countries has registered a significant increase, while trade with Western Europe has relatively declined. The Geneva-based General Agreement on Tariffs and Trade says transpacific trade overtook transatlantic trade in value for the first time in 1984. Second, trade with developing countries has been increasing faster than with developed countries. Third, the role of manufactured products has increased in importance over basic products. The above shifts reflect the changes in the world economy. More nations today participate in trade than ever before. U.S. trade is shifting away from its traditional markets of Canada and Western Europe to a broader base of nations, indicating that U.S. business is truly becoming international in character (see International Marketing Highlight 17.1).

The top fifty U.S. exporting companies are listed in Table 17.3. The total exports of each company, export rankings based on dollar volume, and rankings based on exports as percentages of sales are shown. Along with direct exporting to foreign customers, U.S. corporations have traditionally advanced in foreign markets through a worldwide network of subsidiary companies. These subsidiaries usually include both local manufacturers and companies that market products from the U.S. parent. Table 17.3 includes sales through foreign subsidiaries as well as those made directly. For example, General Motors, Ford, and IBM exported and sold over $1 billion of goods almost exclusively through foreign affiliates.

The direction of U.S. trade is indicated in Table 17.4. The Common Market countries account for almost one-fourth of U.S. exports. As a single country, Canada is the most important U.S. customer, followed by Japan. Moreover, almost one-third of U.S. exports are to Third World countries. As far as U.S. imports are concerned, Japan led with an 18.7 percent share in 1991, followed by Canada, which accounted for 18 percent. About 5 percent of U.S. imports in 1991 were from oil-producing countries—underlining the importance of crude oil and petroleum products as a crucial item. United States trade with Eastern European nations is meager.

U.S. Export Problems

The U.S. export situation is adversely affected by various factors. Chief among these are that (1) most corporate managers consider exports to be only marginal business and (2) while the U.S. government pays lip service to the promotion

TABLE 17.2 Value of Domestic Exports and General Imports of Selected Commodities by Area: 1989 (in millions of dollars)

		WESTERN HEMISPHERE		WESTERN EUROPE				ASIA		
SELECTED COMMODITIES	Total[1]	Canada	Mexico	United Kingdom	West Germany	France	Italy	Japan	China: Taiwan	South Korea
Domestic exports, total	350,017	74,977	24,117	19,643	16,069	10,919	6,929	42,764	10,975	13,208
Agricultural commodities	40,003	2,148	2,683	653	964	421	633	8,003	1,742	2,573
Nonagricultural commodities	310,014	72,829	21,434	18,990	15,105	10,498	6,296	34,761	9,233	10,635
Food and live animals	19,724	1,903	1,990	469	384	371	338	7,238	1,008	1,217
Meat and meat preparations	2,819	218	273	8	6	53	15	1,627	32	87
Grain and cereal preparation	15,458	209	976	35	66	15	112	2,452	682	950
Wheat and wheat flour	6,187	2	66	4	(Z)	(Z)	81	476	131	298
Corn	6,690	76	449	6	46	7	27	1,561	541	641
Beverages and tobacco	5,510	82	19	83	231	22	59	1,388	622	119
Crude materials, excluding fuels	26,627	2,288	1,493	798	1,255	445	906	7,233	1,361	2,872
Soybeans	3,997	37	309	73	180	46	59	866	447	220
Logs and lumber	4,965	439	143	90	108	26	158	2,732	132	310
Metal ores and scrap	5,313	819	225	238	236	61	66	1,159	264	617
Mineral fuels and related materials	9,823	1,678	712	259	102	334	632	1,510	516	344
Bituminous coal	4,242	683	1	203	32	269	490	595	170	172
Chemicals and related products	36,485	4,210	2,195	1,554	1,515	931	731	4,664	1,751	1,642
Manufactured goods	276,359	68,977	19,759	18,029	14,089	9,741	4,967	25,283	7,903	8,612
Textile yarn, fabric, articles	3,897	696	387	273	139	74	75	297	70	89
Iron and steel mill products	3,167	598	434	91	38	32	114	250	74	309
Machinery	139,994	15,634	8,327	8,579	5,690	5,093	1,969	8,467	3,459	3,658
Power generating	14,166	2,915	852	1,158	659	1,917	203	779	523	219
Agricultural[2]	2,305	735	108	121	65	209	28	103	11	22
General industrial	13,096	2,745	1,228	844	581	449	227	833	498	592
Office machinery and computers	23,184	2,572	691	3,017	2,339	1,274	683	3,001	435	624
Telecommunications[3]	7,669	803	1,161	745	277	147	142	848	367	225
Electrical[4]	23,921	3,752	3,477	1,437	1,134	725	436	1,925	1,216	1,088
Transport equipment	50,517	17,560	2,486	2,982	3,017	1,262	639	2,993	992	1,359
Automobile, motor vehicles[5]	25,480	15,891	2,080	360	724	379	91	852	745	156
Aircraft and parts	23,638	1,669	406	2,622	2,293	883	568	2,141	247	1,203
Professional, scientific, and controlling instruments	10,924	1,201	656	890	962	613	443	1,589	299	370
General imports, total	472,926	88,210	27,186	18,242	24,834	13,029	11,946	93,586	24,326	19,742
Agricultural commodities	22,099	2,923	2,290	227	542	775	612	210	152	53
Nonagricultural commodities	450,827	85,287	24,896	18,015	24,292	12,254	11,334	93,376	24,174	19,689

TABLE 17.2 (*Continued*)

SELECTED COMMODITIES	Total[1]	WESTERN HEMISPHERE		WESTERN EUROPE				ASIA		
		Canada	Mexico	United Kingdom	West Germany	France	Italy	Japan	China: Taiwan	South Korea
Food and live animals	20,685	3,521	2,391	164	273	150	218	290	341	188
Meat and meat preparations	2,565	557	(Z)	1	2	4	3	4	1	(Z)
Fish, including shellfish	5,397	1,213	393	29	3	23	2	172	216	147
Vegetables and fruit	4,937	252	1,068	18	79	20	38	34	80	18
Coffee	2,272	2	492	(Z)	40	(Z)	1	(Z)	—	(Z)
Beverages and tobacco	4,364	577	252	611	178	884	331	34	2	6
Crude materials, excluding fuels	15,370	7,983	627	162	160	116	103	178	89	52
Paper base stocks	3,078	2,686	8	(Z)	1	(Z)	—	(Z)	(Z)	—
Wood	3,521	3,157	102	1	4	1	15	(Z)	22	(Z)
Metal ores and scrap	3,883	1,213	176	39	53	22	3	22	8	4
Mineral fuels and related materials	52,649	7,770	4,299	1,663	105	154	333	140	(Z)	29
Crude petroleum	35,400	3,132	4,014	1,182	(Z)	—	23	(Z)		4
Petroleum products	14,234	2,093	256	473	45	144	300	53	(Z)	25
Natural gas	1,761	1,695	—	—	—	—	—	—	—	—
Chemicals and related products	20,752	3,934	582	2,030	2,828	1,502	722	2,373	349	185
Manufactured goods	379,597	68,269	19,596	15,638	24,105	11,721	10,847	92,924	23,892	19,466
Paper, paperboard	8,549	6,204	376	141	320	108	155	220	66	66
Iron and steel	10,578	1,657	307	400	844	648	241	2,476	133	479
Nonferrous metals	10,889	4,758	707	350	368	183	44	389	32	13
Machinery	126,758	11,490	9,739	5,478	8,770	3,626	2,380	43,959	8,387	6,961
Power generating	14,249	2,854	1,211	1,448	1,047	1,703	174	3,853	91	94
General industrial	14,470	1,731	725	950	1,948	372	694	4,118	922	447
Telecommunications[3]	23,182	950	2,669	195	165	119	34	10,057	1,938	2,220
Electrical[4]	32,338	2,443	4,202	844	1,882	573	266	9,217	2,309	2,675
Office machinery and data processing equipment	25,679	1,696	774	827	444	228	304	11,150	2,618	1,410
Transport equipment	79,003	27,640	2,437	2,375	6,200	2,401	975	29,439	884	1,900
Automobiles, buses, trucks	53,877	13,603	1,294	1,010	5,077	73	331	22,680	22	1,594
New passenger cars	44,703	12,871	1,175	950	5,051	73	281	19,921	22	1,594
Motor vehicle parts	15,269	5,850	1,073	354	924	551	256	5,162	266	94
Clothing	24,559	260	592	219	120	196	899	228	2,816	3,398
Footwear	8,393	55	170	34	31	56	816	7	2,005	2,183

— Represents zero. (Z) Less than $500,000. [1]Includes countries and regions not shown separately. [2]Agricultural machinery and parts and tractors, excluding tractor parts. [3]Includes sound recording and reproducing apparatus and equipment. [4]Electrical machinery, apparatus, appliances, and parts [5]Includes motor vehicle and tractor parts, except tires, engines, and electrical parts.

Source: U.S. Bureau of the Census, *Highlights of U.S. Export and Import Trade,* Report FT 990, December 1990.

International Marketing Highlight 17.1

America's Hottest Export: Pop Culture

There is good news for the United States these days on the export front: Around the globe, folks just can't get enough of America. They may not want our hardware anymore—our cars, steel, or television sets. But when they want a jolt of popular culture—and they want more all the time—they increasingly turn to American software: our movies, music, TV programming, and home video, which together now account for an annual trade surplus of some $8 billion. Only aerospace—aircraft and related equipment—outranks pop culture as an export.

Like it or not, Mickey Mouse, Michael Jackson, and Madonna—her overseas sales are two and a half times her domestic number—prop up what's left of our balance of trade.

Broaden the definition of pop culture to include licensed consumer products—say, Teenage Mutant Ninja Turtle bubble bath—throw in such culture-driven products as McDonald's burgers, Levi's jeans, and Coca-Cola's soft drinks, and you're looking at America's top seller abroad. Last year Walt Disney Co. sold $1.5 billion worth of consumer products—hats, watches, comic books—in Japan, where Coca-Cola earns more money than it does in the United States.

In the past five years the overseas revenues of Hollywood studios doubled, and in a couple of years they should surpass domestic. The $20-billion-a-year American music business—basically rock & roll—collects 70 percent of its revenue outside the U.S. Sales of U.S. television programming to Europe are estimated at about $600 million a year. Almost everybody in the world watches Cosby, and everybody in the world watched Dallas. The most popular film of all time in Israel and Sweden is "Pretty Woman, " which already has garnered more than $360 million worldwide at the box office and hasn't yet opened in the two biggest markets outside the U.S.—Japan and France.

Source: Fortune, December 31, 1990, p. 50.

of exports, it actually inhibits them through laws and regulations. Notably, the traditional business factors (the high costs of labor and capital, or low productivity) that at one time were considered responsible for limiting U.S. exports are no longer influential; U.S. companies are now competitive. Instead, exports are hurt by an overall negative attitude. Sometimes agricultural exports are discouraged because of domestic price pressures; other times military exports are blocked for political reasons, as are exports to communist countries and possibly the Arab countries in response to their boycott legislation against Israel.

There are historical reasons for the U.S. indifference toward international trade. In the 1950s and 1960s, the United States had little need of export markets because the home market was large enough to absorb mass production. But today, to balance the cost of oil imports, the United States needs to generate additional exports in the tens of billions of dollars. The continued U.S. disinterest in the export sector also costs jobs, corporate profits, and business growth.

TABLE 17.3 The Fifty Leading U.S. Exporters

RANK				EXPORT SALES		TOTAL SALES		EXPORTS AS PERCENT OF SALES	
1990	1989	COMPANY	PRODUCTS	$ Millions	Percent Change 1989–90	$ Millions	Fortune 500 Rank	Percent	Rank
1	1	Boeing, Seattle	Commercial and military aircraft	$16,093.0	46.0%	$ 27,595.0	13	58.3%	1
2	2	General Motors, Detroit	Motor vehicles and parts	10,315.9	1.3	126,017.0	1	8.2	40
3	4	General Electric, Fairfield CT	Jet engines, turbines, medical systems	7,128.0	(1.9)	58,414.0	6	12.2	27
4	3	Ford Motor, Dearborn, MI	Motor vehicles and parts	7,098.0	14.0	98,274.7	3	7.2	41
5	5	International Business Machines, Armonk, NY	Computers and related equipment	6,195.0	13.1	69,018.0	4	9.0	37
6	7	Chrysler, Highland Park, MI	Motor vehicles and parts	5,004.0	(7.1)	30,868.0	11	16.2	16
7	6	E.I. Du Pont de Nemours, Wilmington, DE	Specialty chemicals	4,352.0	(10.2)	39.839.0	9	10.9	29
8	8	United Technologies, Hartford	Jet engines, helicopters, cooling equipment	3,606.0	9.0	21,783.2	17	16.6	15
9	10	McDonnell Douglas, St. Louis	Aerospace products, missiles, electronic systems	3,538.0	22.2	16,351.0	24	21.6	10
10	9	Caterpillar, Peoria, IL	Heavy machinery, engines, turbines	3,435.0	4.4	11,540.0	39	29.8	4
11	11	Eastman Kodak, Rochester, NY	Imaging, information, and health products	2,957.0	2.9	19,075.0	20	15.5	18
12	15	Philip Morris, New York	Tobacco, beverages, food products	2,928.0	28.0	44,323.0	7	6.6	45
13	12	Hewlett-Packard, Palo Alto, CA	Computers, electronics	2,816.0	6.9	13,233.0	29	21.3	11
14	14	Motorola, Schaumburg, IL	Communications equipment, semiconductors	2,801.0	20.8	10,885.0	42	25.7	6
15	13	Unisys, Blue Bell, PA	Computers and related equipment	2,203.7	(8.2)	10,111.3	49	21.8	9
16	17	Occidental Petroleum, Los Angeles	Agricultural products, coal	2,077.0	4.1	21,947.0	16	9.5	34
17	16	Digital Equipment, Maynard, MA	Computers and related equipment	1,920.3	(8.7)	13,084.5	30	14.7	22
18	18	Allied-Signal, Morristown, NJ	Aircraft and automotive parts, chemicals	1,838.0	8.6	12,396.0	36	14.8	20
19	21	General Dynamics, St. Louis	Tanks, aircraft, missiles, gun systems	1,624.0	6.7	10,182.0	48	15.9	17
20	19	Weyerhaeuser, Tacoma	Pulp, paper, logs, lumber	1,560.0	(0.9)	9,024.3	54	17.3	13
21	22	Raytheon, Lexington, MA	Electronic systems, aircraft	1,435.0	7.1	9,362.3	52	15.3	19
22	25	Dow Chemical, Midland, MI	Chemicals, plastics, consumer products	1,344.0	16.2	20,005.0	18	6.7	43
23	20	Union Carbide, Danbury, CT	Chemicals, plastics	1,280.0	(18.0)	7,621.0	65	16.8	14
24	33	Intel, Santa Clara, CA	Microcomputer components and systems	1,202.3	20.5	4,124.6	119	29.1	5
25	31	Minnesota Mining & Mfg., St Paul	Industrial, electronic, and health products	1,199.0	17.7	13,021.0	31	9.2	36

26	26	Westinghouse Electric, Pittsburgh	Electrical products and electronic systems	1,195.0	5.7	12,915.0	33	9.3	35
27	24	Archer-Daniels-Midland, Decatur, IL	Protein meals, vegetable oils, flour	1,162.7	(3.79)	7,925.3	60	14.7	23
28	30	Merck, Rahway, NJ	Health products, specialty chemicals	1,156.3	11.3	7,824.1	63	14.8	21
29	35	Compaq Computer, Houston	Computers and related equipment	1,121.4	25.1	3,625.7	136	30.9	3
30	40	Sun Microsystems, Mountain View, CA	Computers and related equipment	1,117.3	48.7	2,480.7	181	45.0	2
31	23	Textron, Providence	Aerospace and consumer products	1,103.0	(8.8)	7,917.6	61	13.9	25
32	32	Exxon, Irving, TX	Petroleum, chemicals	1,101.0	8.0	105,885.0	2	1.0	50
33	27	International Paper, Purchase, NY	Pulp, paperboard, wood products	1,100.0	0.0	12,960.0	32	8.5	39
34	29	Hoechst Celanese, Bridgwater, NJ	Chemicals, plastics, fibers, pharmaceuticals	1,085.0	4.4	5,881.0	90	18.4	12
35	28	Monsanto, St. Louis	Herbicides, chemicals, pharmaceuticals	1,079.0	0.8	9,047.0	53	11.9	28
36	34	Aluminum Co. of America, Pittsburgh	Aluminum products	926.0	(1.0)	10,865.1	43	8.5	38
37	37	Xerox, Stamford, CT	Copiers, printers	900.0	16.9	18,382.0	22	4.9	47
38	38	Bayer USA, Pittsburgh	Chemicals, health and imaging products	865.0	13.9	5,903.7	89	14.7	24
39	48	FMC, Chicago	Armored military vehicles, chemicals	848.0	18.4	3,754.8	131	22.6	8
40	36	Rockwell International, El Segundo, CA	Electronics, automotive parts	835.0	4.4	12,442.5	35	6.7	44
41	44	Abbott Laboratories, Abbott Park, IL	Drugs, diagnostic equipment	814.5	18.9	6,210.3	82	13.1	26
42	41	Deere, Moline, IL	Farm and industrial equipment	758.0	2.2	7,881.0	62	9.6	33
43	42	Honeywell, Minneapolis	Building, industry, and aviation control systems	750.0	4.5	6,985.2	69	10.7	30
44	45	Amoco, Chicago	Chemicals	743.0	11.2	28,277.0	12	2.6	49
45	47	Bristol-Myers Squibb, New York	Drugs, medical devices, consumer products	741.0	16.1	10,509.0	46	7.1	42
46	46	Tenneco, Houston	Farm, construction, and auto equipment	711.0	10.4	14,893.0	26	4.8	48
47	50	Cooper Industries, Houston	Petroleum and industrial equipment; electronic products	662.7	16.0	6,222.2	81	10.7	31
48	*	Reynolds Metals, Richmond	Aluminum, plastic and paper products	639.0	13.5	6,075.7	88	10.5	32
49	49	Ethyl, Richmond	Specialty and petroleum chemicals	592.7	0.0	2,513.8	178	23.6	7
50	39	Lockheed, Calabasas, CA	Aerospace products, electronics, missile systems	588.0	(22.0)	9,977.0	50	5.9	46
		Totals		$118,544.8		$1,045,448.6			

*Not on last year's list

Source: James Beeler, "Exports: Ship 'em out," *Fortune, The New American Century* issue, 1991, p. 60.

TABLE 17.4 **U.S. Trade: 1991**

TOP 25 U.S. MARKETS U.S. Domestic and Foreign Merchandise Exports, 1991 (F.A.S. Value)			LEADING U.S. SUPPLIERS U.S. General Merchandise Imports, 1991 (Customs Value)		
		$ billions			**$ billions**
	Total Exports	**421.6**		**Total Imports**	**488.1**
1.	Canada	85.1	1.	Japan	91.6
2.	Japan	48.1	2.	Canada	91.1
3.	Mexico	33.3	3.	Mexico	31.2
4.	United Kingdom	22.1	4.	Germany	26.2
5.	Germany	21.3	5.	Taiwan	23.0
6.	South Korea	15.5	6.	China	19.0
7.	France	15.4	7.	United Kingdom	18.5
8.	Netherlands	13.5	8.	South Korea	17.0
9.	Taiwan	13.2	9.	France	13.4
10.	Belgium-Luxembourg	10.8	10.	Italy	11.8
11.	Singapore	8.8	11.	Saudi Arabia	11.0
12.	Italy	8.6	12.	Singapore	10.0
13.	Australia	8.4	13.	Hong Kong	9.3
14.	Hong Kong	8.1	14.	Venezuela	8.2
15.	Saudi Arabia	6.6	15.	Brazil	6.7
16.	China	6.3	16.	Thailand	6.1
17.	Brazil	6.2	17.	Malaysia	6.1
18.	Switzerland	5.6	18.	Switzerland	5.6
19.	Spain	5.5	19.	Nigeria	5.4
20.	Venezuela	4.7	20.	Netherlands	4.8
21.	Malaysia	3.9	21.	Sweden	4.5
22.	Israel	3.9	22.	Belgium-Luxembourg	4.1
23.	Thailand	3.8	23.	Australia	4.0
24.	Former U.S.S.R	3.6	24.	Israel	3.5
25.	Sweden	3.3	25.	Philippines	3.5

(*continued*)

Consequently, it is likely to lead to slower economic growth and, ultimately, to a slower rise in living standards.[4]

Following World War II, the participation of U.S. companies in the rebuilding of Europe was primarily through exporting. But, as country after country regained its strength, many U.S. companies built manufacturing plants and marketing operations abroad to serve local markets. Ironically, U.S. multinationals spread management skills, capital, and technology to a greater extent than they increased markets for U.S.-made products around the world. Japan was the exception because restrictions kept out most MNCs as well as many U.S. exports.

For nearly twenty years the economies of overseas production, compared with high costs at home, compelled U.S. companies to continue building plants abroad rather than exporting goods to serve foreign markets. But many of the factors that made that practice desirable no longer apply. For example, the per-

TABLE 17.4 (*Continued*)

U.S. TRADE BALANCES, 1991

Listing of U.S. Merchandise Trade Balances
General Imports, Customs Value; Domestic and Foreign Exports, F.A.S. Value

U.S. Surplus Positions	$ billions	U.S. Deficit Positions	$ billions
		Total	−66.3
1. Netherlands	+8.7	1. Japan	−43.4
2. Belgium-Luxembourg	+6.7	2. China	−12.7
3. Australia	+4.4	3. Taiwan	−9.8
4. United Kingdom	+3.5	4. Canada	−6.0
5. Former U.S.S.R.	+2.8	5. Germany	−4.9
6. Spain	+2.6	6. Nigeria	−4.5
7. Egypt	+2.5	7. Saudi Arabia	−4.4
8. Mexico	+2.1	8. Venezuela	−3.6
9. France	+2.0	9. Italy	−3.2
10. Turkey	+1.4	10. Thailand	−2.4
11. Kuwait	+1.2	11. Malaysia	−2.2
12. Argentina	+0.8	12. Angola	−1.6
13. United Arab Emirates	+0.7	13. South Korea	−1.5
14. Ireland	+0.7	14. Algeria	−1.4
15. Panama	+0.7	15. Indonesia	−1.3
16. Greece	+0.6	16. Sweden	−1.2
17. Chile	+0.5	17. Philippines	−1.2
18. Bahrain	+0.4	18. India	−1.2
19. Jamaica	+0.4	19. Singapore	−1.2
20. South Africa	+0.4	20. Hong Kong	−1.1
21. Israel	+0.4	21. Colombia	−0.8
22. Paraguay	+0.3	22. Gabon	−0.6
23. Leeward & Windward Is.	+0.3	23. Macao	−0.6
24. Iran	+0.3	24. Brazil	−0.6
25. Pakistan	+0.3	25. Sri Lanka	−0.5

Source: John Jelacic, "The U.S. Trade Outlook," *Business America,* April 6, 1992, p. 5.

centage increase in unit labor costs in the United States in the early 1980s was the lowest among the major industrial countries. The U.S. increase in hourly compensation over the same two years followed a similar pattern. What continues to be lacking is the determination to export.[5]

In other words, while there are still significant wage differences among countries, the gap is fast narrowing. For example, in 1984 the average hourly compensation for manufacturing workers in U.S. dollars was $5.85 in Britain, $6.35 in Japan, $7.42 in France, $7.46 in Italy, $9.55 in the Federal Republic of Germany, $11.00 in Canada, and $12.59 in the United States. The difference between the lowest wage in the industrialized countries and the United States was over $10 in the 1970s and now has been reduced to less than $7.[6]

It is estimated that, although 20,000 U.S. companies export, another

20,000 that could successfully sell in foreign markets are not doing so. The resulting asymmetry in U.S. trade relations with the rest of the world is typified by the auto industry. Very few of the big cars Detroit designs for the U.S. market are exported, while Europeans and the Japanese build smaller cars for world markets.[7] In 1991, combined they shipped 2.6 million cars to the United States. With the entry of the Japanese luxury cars into the U.S. auto market, the domestic industry is going to be further squeezed.[8]

There are also short-term causes for the U.S. lag in exports. The trade gap may reflect the interaction of two economic factors: (1) the slow economic recovery in Europe and Japan from the 1980s recession and (2) the fact that the United States is at the peak of its domestic business expansion. The result has been a strengthening of demand in the United States for foreign products and a weakening of demand in those countries for U.S. goods. Eventual reversal of the cycles should sharply improve the U.S. trade balance in the 1990s, as in 1975 when the United States ran up a record $11 billion surplus.

In addition, in the early 1980s the overvaluation of the dollar made U.S. exports artificially expensive to foreign buyers, and imports artificially cheap to American consumers. The decline in the value of the U.S. dollar, instigated by the central banks of major trading partners, has helped U.S. exports in the later half of the 1980s by giving American goods a price advantage in world markets while making foreign products more expensive in the United States. Price (although inclusive of quality, delivery service, and credit terms) is only one factor in world-market competition. Numerous nonprice barriers—ranging from foreign government "buy local" rules to excessive duties—mitigate the impact of currency changes on trade in many products (see International Marketing Highlight 17.2).

Further, as mentioned above, an increasing share of U.S. exports—anywhere from 25 percent to 50 percent—is now made up of intracompany shipments of materials, components, and finished products between parent companies of U.S. multinational concerns and hundreds of their own affiliates abroad. The MNCs' huge financial stake in overseas production combined with foreign government pressures against worker layoffs inhibits cutbacks of foreign output in order to step up exports from the United States—even if costs are lower.

At the same time, a number of countries impose barriers against U.S. exports. These barriers comprise government laws, regulations, policies, or practices that either protect domestic producers from foreign competition or artificially stimulate exports of particular domestic products. A recent U.S. government report classifies these barriers into eight different categories:

1. Import policies (for example, tariffs and other import charges, quantitative restrictions, import licensing, customs barriers);
2. Standards, testing, labeling, and certification (for example, unnecessarily restrictive application of sanitary standards, refusal to accept U.S. manufacturer's self-certification of conformance to foreign product standards);

International Marketing Highlight 17.2

Prince for Sale or Rent

The biggest rip-off in the music industry—the widespread transfer to cassettes of compact discs (CDs) that people rent in Japan—looks like it is being outlawed. The Japanese authorities, who have hitherto turned a blind eye to the practice, had until the end of December 1991 to put a stop to piracy that cost foreign record companies upwards of $1 billion a year in lost sales. Record producers in America and Europe wanted the Japanese to ban the rental of new CDs for one year following their release.

At present, the Japanese CD rental stores are supposed to hold back new record releases for one to three weeks. Few bother. But if Japan fails to come up with an answer soon, America will push ahead with the (rather fanciful) fifty-year renting moratorium it has proposed at the GATT trade talks.

Under Japan's present copyright laws, record companies can ban the renting of CDs and records for up to a year after release, and demand a royalty fee from rental stores for twenty-nine years thereafter. But the agreement applies only to Japanese CDs and records, not foreign ones. The stores pay a one-time fee of 400 yen ($3) for the right to rent each new Japanese release. With foreign CDs and records accounting for a third of the rental market in Japan, Western record companies understandably feel cheated.

Source: The Economist, December 21, 1991–January 3, 1992, p. 80.

3. Government procurement (for example, "buy national" policies and closed bidding);
4. Export subsidies (for example, export financing on preferential terms and agricultural export subsidies that displace U.S. exports in third country markets);
5. Lack of intellectual property protection (for example, inadequate patent, copyright, and trademark regimes);
6. Services barriers (for example, regulation of international data flows, restrictions on the use of foreign data processing);
7. Investment barriers (for example, limitations on foreign equity participation, local content and export performance requirements, and restrictions on transferring earnings and capital); and
8. Other barriers (for example, barriers that encompass more than one category listed above or that affect a single sector).[9]

Thus, the structure of international trade is moving further and further from the classical model of unimpeded commerce based strictly on comparative advantages. Eventually, the large reverse flow of foreign multinational investment now coming into the United States should help narrow the U.S. trade gap by substituting U.S.-made products for imports.

Currently, however, U.S. companies that already have well-established export networks are the only ones in a position to make aggressive use of the new price competitiveness of American products. Many U.S. companies turned away from exports in the 1960s when the U.S. dollar was overvalued. More recently, U.S. companies have been deterred from making costly investments in overseas sales and service organizations by laws, executive actions, and court rulings that impede exports. Unless a more favorable business environment is created for U.S. exporters, they will continue to lose world market shares to foreign rivals, regardless of business cycles or the variable U.S. dollar. A product's price does not make much difference if producers cannot reach or service foreign markets or get domestic products into foreign customers' hands (see International Marketing Highlight 17.3).

Table 17.5 shows how the United States is losing its markets to imports in industry after industry. This situation cannot be allowed to continue; U.S. businesspeople must learn to export aggressively.

Despite the gloomy picture that Table 17.5 depicts, there are products, such as pulp and wastepaper, electronic components and parts, and timber (see Table 17.6)

International Marketing Highlight 17.3

Obstacles Small Exporters Face

Small firms starting to export say the single largest source of information—the Department of Commerce—is also one of the biggest sources of frustration. They condemn trade-promotion programs throughout the federal government as unfocused, overlapping, and inefficient. Worse, U.S. commercial banks, citing too little profit and too much risk, routinely refuse to lend to small exporters. Talk of recession has amplified their concerns.

As more small companies search out business abroad, many say their two greatest needs, reliable trade information and trade financing, are in short supply.

When N&N Contact Lens International Inc. of Lywood, Washington, began looking for information on overseas markets two years ago, the local Department of Commerce office was stumped by simple, specific questions. Asked who sells contact lenses in Caracas, Venezuela, it gave the company lists, many of which were outdated, of distributors of such broad categories as "medical devices."

Among major industrialized nations, the United States spends the least per capita to promote exports. Number 1, Canada, shelled out eighteen times more in 1987, the latest year for which figures are available: $21.44 for each inhabitant versus $1.20 in the United States. The U.S. government itself brands the services of the U.S. and Foreign Commercial Service, a unit of the Commerce Department's International Trade Administration, as unfocused and inefficient.

Source: Mark Robichaux, "Exporters Face Big Roadblocks at Home, " *The Wall Street Journal,* November 7, 1990, p. B1.

TABLE 17.5 Share of U.S. Market Occupied by Imports

PRODUCT	1972	1989
Blowers and fans	3.6%	31.5%
Converted paper products	10.4	21.7
Costume jewelry	10.4	41.3
Dolls	21.8	58.9
Electronic computing equipment	0.0	13.5
Lighting fixtures	4.2	19.1
Precious metal jewelry	4.9	28.3
Primary zinc	28.4	55.1
Printing trade machinery	8.5	23.8
Radios and TVs	34.9	63.5
Semiconductors	12.3	38.8
Shoes	17.1	57.4
Luggage and personal goods	20.7	53.2
Men's and boys' outerwear	8.7	37.5
Men's and boys' shirts and nightwear	17.8	51.5
Musical instruments	14.9	27.8
Nitrogenous fertilizers	4.3	21.5
Power-driven hand tools	7.5	26.4
Sporting and athletic goods	13.0	28.8
Telephone and telegraph equipment	2.1	17.5
Tires and inner tubes	7.2	20.2
Women's blouses	14.9	41.4
Women's suits and coats	7.3	32.6
Wool yarn mills	6.1	19.9

Source: Different publications of the U.S. Department of Commerce.

TABLE 17.6 Fastest-Growing U.S. Exports

	GROWTH RATE 1985 THROUGH JUNE 1989 PERCENT CHANGE	AMOUNT JULY 1988 THROUGH JUNE 1989 IN BILLIONS
1 Music, video, and computer tapes; floppy disks	32.3%	$ 2.5
2 Cigarettes and other tobacco products	30.4	3.2
3 Meat	30.0	2.7
4 Pulp and wastepaper	27.1	4.1
5 Synthetic resins, rubber, and plastics	27.1	7.9
6 Electronic components and parts	25.0	11.5
7 Electromedical and radiological equipment	23.3	2.7
8 Electrical machinery and equipment	19.8	4.9
9 Timber	19.3	2.3
10 Animal feeds	19.0	3.4

Source: U.S. Department of Commerce.

in which American companies maintain leads. If adequate encouragement is provided, these products offer an opportunity to offset the U.S. trade balance.

U.S. Government Encouragement of Exports

Worldwide, governments play a vital role in encouraging exports. Traditionally, in the United States the issue of exports has not been given the status that issues such as tax reform, armaments, corporate corruption, the Arab boycott of Israel, and antitrust enforcement receive. But the importance of balancing the trade deficit has led the government in the past few years to adopt programs to boost exports.

The U.S. government aids exports through the Export-Import Bank, foreign sales corporations, Commerce Department programs, the Overseas Private Investment Corporation, and pressure on major trading partners to spur their economies. The Omnibus Trade and Competitiveness Act of 1988 has been hailed as landmark legislation intended to spur U.S. exports.

Export-Import Bank

The Export-Import Bank was created by the U.S. government in 1934 to provide low-cost financing to encourage exports of aircraft, nuclear plants, and other "big-ticket" items. The bank's lending capacity is based on appropriations approved by Congress. The bank's subsidy supposedly helps U.S. businesses to meet European and Japanese competition via-à-vis their export-subsidy programs. For example, the bank might lend money equal to 45 percent of the price of the American goods to prospective buyers at low rates of interest. In some cases, the bank has financed up to 85 percent of the price. As a matter of fact, in at least one case—a proposed $16 million sale of gas turbines to Malaysia by United Technologies corporation—the bank agreed to provide 100 percent financing. Despite the bank's program, it is not easy to match Japanese and European competition. For example, in the Malaysian deal, a Japanese company won the sale with a government-backed 4 percent twenty-year loan. General Electric Co. lost the contract for Thailand's new power plant generators to Japan's Fuji Electric Co., since Japan's export-finance agency offered a highly subsidized, last-minute loan.[10]

During the Reagan administration, the bank's lending authority was vastly enhanced. For example, export credit programs were strengthened by increasing the level of the Export-Import Bank ceiling on export guarantees. Further, in accordance with the provisions of the Export Trading Company Act of 1982, the bank's new ETC Loan Guarantee Program was developed in a way that should be especially helpful to small and medium-size minority and agricultural exporters and producers. For example, exporters can obtain short-term, preexport loans to be used to finance export-related activities when arrangements cannot be made in the private credit market.

In recent years, the Export-Import Bank redesigned and streamlined its loan, guarantee, and insurance programs to make them more accessible, especially to the small and medium-sized businesses with the greatest potential for increasing

U.S. exports and improving the balance of trade. The bank also works with cities and states on a program to educate local officials about trade assistance available from the U.S. government. Through its programs, the Export-Import Bank has supported nearly $200 billion in U.S. exports, including $50 billion in loans.[11]

Foreign Sales Corporations (FSCs)

Before the creation of FSCs, U.S. companies could establish domestic international sales corporations (DISCs) under the Revenue Act of 1971. The purpose behind the DISC legislation was to encourage businesses, especially small ones, to engage in export activity through the tax sheltering of income. A DISC could be established in any state with nominal capital of $2,500. To tax shelter the income, a minimum of 95 percent of the DISC sale had to be export-related and, whether the goods were grown, extracted, or manufactured in the United States, they must have come from an organization other than the DISC. In other words, the DISC acted as a parent company and served as an export channel. DISCs ran into conflict with some of the fair-trade rules of the General Agreement on Tariffs and Trade. After years of complaints from U.S. trading partners, GATT ruled in 1982 that DISCs are an "illegal" export subsidy. This ruling forced the U.S. government to abolish DISC legislation.

Thus, DISCs ceased after December 31, 1984. But to continue to encourage U.S. businesses to export, the Deficit Reduction Act of 1984 replaced DISCs with FSCs. An FSC is a foreign corporation not located in the U.S. Customs Zone that is allowed to earn some exempt and nontaxable income on its exports from the United States. In most cases this partial exemption can result in U.S. tax savings of up to 7.4 percent of the profit on the export transaction for a manufacturer/exporter and 14.7 percent for a trading company/exporter. The FSC is required to pay U.S. tax on the balance of its nonexempt income. The FSC's trade income dividends to its U.S. corporate shareholders are not taxable to them.[12]

The FSC legislation has an advantage over the DISC legislation: it allows a permanent tax exemption to the U.S. corporate shareholders on dividend distributions that may be as frequent as the FSC desires and that may be invested anywhere. However, the DISC legislation required investing the proceeds in qualified foreign assets. Thus, U.S. farmers and agricultural cooperatives can benefit from the FSC but not from the DISC. These benefits aside, overall FSCs provide for limited tax exemption and are more costly to operate.[13]

To become an FSC, a corporation must meet eight qualifications:

1. The corporation must be organized in a foreign country or U.S. possession.
2. There can be no more than twenty-five shareholders.
3. There can be no preferred stock.
4. The records of the corporation must be kept at a non-U.S. office.
5. The board of directors must have at least one nonresident.
6. It cannot be a member of a controlled group that also includes a DISC.
7. It must elect to be an FSC.
8. Foreign management and economic process requirements must be met.

The rules for FSCs are much stricter than were those of DISCs. Thus, despite the permanency of the advantage to corporate shareholders, FSCs are a poor substitute for DISCs. U.S. exports are expected to be hurt as a result of the change. In addition, foreign governments still may not be satisfied.

Commerce Department Programs

The U.S. Department of Commerce offers a variety of services through the International Trade Administration (ITA) to help businesses in their export activities. Forty-eight ITA district offices and nineteen branch offices in cities throughout the United States and in Puerto Rico provide information and professional export counseling to businesspeople. Each office is headed by a director, supported by trade specialists and other staff. These professionals can help a company's decision makers gain a basic understanding of profitable opportunities in exporting and assist them in evaluating the company's market potential overseas.

Each district office can give information about:

- Trade and investment opportunities abroad
- Foreign markets for U.S. products and services
- Services to locate and evaluate overseas buyers and representatives
- Export seminars and conferences

Most district offices maintain an extensive business library containing the department's latest reports.

The major elements of ITA programs are summarized below.[14]

U.S. and Foreign Commercial Services The U.S. and Foreign Commercial Services (US/FCS) were combined a few years ago to offer the American exporter coordinated trade assistance both at home and abroad. Overseas, the US/FCS maintains 126 offices in sixty-six countries that are considered to be the principal U.S. trading partners. More than 175 commercial officers direct export promotion activities at these sites and manage promotional programs developed by ITA.

Commercial officers gather data on specific export opportunities, country trends affecting trade and investment, prospects for specific industries, and other commercial intelligence. They also identify and evaluate importers, buyers, agents, distributors, and joint-venture partners linked with U.S. firms; and they monitor and analyze local laws and practices that affect business conditions.

The domestic side of the US/FCS operates, as mentioned above, forty-eight district offices in industrial and commercial centers throughout the nation. These offer a broad range of trade-related information, as well as one-on-one counseling by experienced trade specialists.

The district offices can tell exporters or prospective exporters about trade and investment opportunities abroad, foreign markets for U.S. products and services, financing aid, insurance from the Foreign Credit Insurance Association (FCIA), tax advantages of exporting, international trade exhibitions, export documentation requirements, economic facts on foreign countries, and export licensing and import requirements.

Besides the district offices, an export counseling unit in Washington, D.C., helps U.S. firms develop or expand markets abroad. Counselors advise exporters on the choice of support services and guide them in the use of export practices and procedures.

The report counseling unit also maintains an export information reference room in Washington, D.C., where interested persons may examine a wide range of information on major foreign projects under consideration by international financial institutions.

Publications That Assist Exporters A variety of publications are available to help exporters reach and expand foreign markets. The foremost of these publications are *Business America, Commercial News USA, A Basic Guide to Exporting, Market Share Reports, Global Market Surveys,* and *Overseas Business Reports.* For further details on these and other publications, see the appendix at the end of Chapter 10 (see International Marketing Highlight 17.4).

Commerce Export Assistance Programs ITA maintains a wide range of programs to help U.S. companies begin exporting and to locate or expand foreign markets. Major programs include:

> *Automated Information Transfer System (AITS).* AITS, a linked system of small computers, has been installed in most ITA district offices and nearly fifty overseas posts to make market-related information accessible worldwide on a timely, efficient, and inexpensive basis. The AITS system can match U.S. producers with overseas buyers interested in their products; retrieve trade leads, company contacts, and other information; and send messages from one ITA location to another.
>
> *Trade Opportunities Program (TOP).* Export opportunities, originating from either private or government sources overseas, are transmitted daily to TOP in Washington, D.C., by U.S. and Foreign Commercial Service posts around the world. As subscribers to TOP, U.S. business firms indicate the products or services they wish to export, the countries they are interested in,

International Marketing Highlight 17.4

The Export Yellow Pages

Reaching out to the global marketplace became much easier in 1992 with the inaugural publication of *The Export Yellow Pages.* Produced as part of a public/private initiative with the U.S. Department of Commerce—which spearheads distribution of 50,000 copies worldwide—*The Export Yellow Pages* is uniquely designed to help:

- Foreign firms buy U.S. products and services
- U.S. executives locate export service providers

Source: Business America, January 13, 1992, p. 34.

and the type of opportunities desired, whether direct sales, overseas representation, or foreign government tenders. The TOP system matches the product interests of foreign buyers with those indicated by U.S. subscribers, mailing the leads to subscribers on a daily basis.

New Product Information Service (NPIS). This program provides worldwide publicity for new U.S. products available for immediate export. Promotional descriptions are published in *Commercial News USA* magazine for dissemination to business and government leaders around the globe. Information on selected NPIS products is also broadcast overseas by the U.S. Information Agency's "Voice of America" radio shows.

Export Contact List Services. ITA collects and stores data on foreign firms in a master computer file called the *Foreign Trade Index (FTI).* Covering 143 countries, this file contains information on more than 140,000 importing firms, agents, distributors, service organizations, manufacturers, retailers, and potential end-users of U.S. products and services. The information is made available in various forms, such as mailing labels and computer printouts, to meet company requirements.

World Traders Data Reports (WTDRs). Prepared by U.S. commercial officers abroad, WTDRs are business reports providing background information on potential foreign trade contacts. Each report also contains a general narrative prepared by the U.S. commercial officer conducting the investigation as to the reliability of the foreign firm.

Agent/Distributor Service (A/DS). The A/DS provides U.S. firms with the names of agents and/or distributors abroad who have indicated an interest in handling specific products from the United States. ITA's commercial officers conduct "customized" on-site searches to identify representatives who are both interested and qualified to handle specific products.

Overseas Trade Fairs. ITA sponsors participation by U.S. firms in worldwide international trade fairs, assisting with many preshow promotional services such as marketing, provision of exhibit space, and design and construction of exhibits. The cost to the U.S. participant varies by country and event.

Commerce Assistance on Specific Markets. Commercial and economic information on most trading partners of the United States are available through ITA's international economic policy unit.

Assistance on Foreign Industry Sectors. Trade information on most industry sectors is available through the trade development unit in ITA.

Comparison Shopping. This is a custom-tailored service that provides firms with key marketing and foreign representation information about their specific products. Commerce Department staff conduct on-the-spot interviews to determine nine key marketing facts about the product, such as sales potential in market, comparable products, distribution channels, going price, competitive factors, and qualified purchasers.

Foreign Buyer Program. Exporters can meet qualified foreign purchasers for their products or services at trade shows in the United States. The Commerce Department promotes the shows worldwide to attract foreign buyer delegations, manages an international business center, counsels participating firms, and brings together buyer and seller.

Overseas Catalog and Video-Catalog Shows. Companies can gain market exposure for their product or service without the cost of traveling overseas by participating in a catalog or video-catalog show sponsored by the Commerce Department. Provided with the firm's product literature or promotional video, the Department's U.S. and Foreign Commercial Service will send an industry expert to display the material to select foreign audiences in several countries.

Overseas Trade Missions. Officials of U.S. firms can participate in a trade mission, which will give them an opportunity to confer with influential foreign business and government representatives. Commerce Department staff will identify and arrange a full schedule of appointments in each country.

Matchmaker Events. Matchmaker Trade Delegations offer introductions to new markets through short, inexpensive overseas visits with a limited objective: to match the U.S. firm with a representative or prospective joint venture/licensee partner who shares a common product or service interest. Firms learn key aspects of doing business in the new country and meet in one-to-one interviews the local people who can help them be successful.

Exporters Licensing Services This ITA activity assists U.S. firms in fulfilling their obligations under the Export Administration Act. The act helps to ensure U.S. national security and to further U.S. national foreign policies by controlling exports to certain destinations of certain kinds of sensitive, high-technology equipment and data.

Exporters Licensing group gives speedy advice to business executives who need to determine whether their exports require advance, validated licenses or who need help in filing the requisite applications.

Service Industries Development Program The Trade and Tariff Act of 1984 mandates that the Commerce Department establish a service industries development program. An essential element of this program is an updated survey of the services sector, which includes statistics on exports and imports of services, receipts, employment, and wages paid by service firms.

Improved data on service industries help analysis of this sector's contribution to the U.S. economy and advance the marketing of U.S. services abroad. With an eye to the future, an improved services data base reinforces Uruguay Round negotiations aimed at liberalizing services trade by providing a clear picture of the markets for U.S. service exports and how service imports affect the U.S. economy.

Foreign Requirements for U.S. Products and Services U.S. companies wishing to sell abroad must know how to deal with foreign national requirements, standards, testing, and certification requirements. The National Center for Standards and Certification Information (NCSCI), a branch of the Commerce Department's National Bureau of Standards, is the government's central repository for standards-related information about foreign countries.

Foreign Metric Regulations The Office of Metric Programs provides exporters with information about foreign metric import regulations. It also provides guidance and assistance on matters relating to U.S. transition to the metric system.

Overseas Private Investment Corporation (OPIC)

Established as a federal agency in 1969, OPIC provides insurance coverage for U.S. companies in countries where annual per capita income does not exceed $1,000. During the Reagan administration, this limit was raised to include countries with per capita income up to $2,200. Boosting this limit permitted OPIC to operate in such emerging developing countries as Brazil, where U.S. companies are offered the promise of quick growth.

OPIC offers twenty-year coverage to U.S. companies abroad, compared with the three-year policies typically available from private insurers.

OPIC has been designed to be self-sufficient. It operates on its own profit without congressional funds. In 1990, OPIC wrote $6.1 billion worth of insurance covering 100 countries. It is authorized to write up to $7.5 billion. Table 17.7 shows the political risk insurance payments made by the Overseas Private Investment Corporation in recent years.

In addition to the services described above, OPIC has special programs to meet specific needs of the investor involved in contracting and exporting, energy exploration, and development and leasing arrangements.

Many developing countries require foreign firms to post performance or advance payment guaranties in the form of standby letters of credit. OPIC political risk insurance for contractors and exporters protects against arbitrary or unfair drawing of these letters of credit. It also protects against confiscation of tangible

TABLE 17.7 OPIC Risk Payments

RISK	COUNTRY/YEAR	COMPANY	PAYMENT
Currency inconvertibility	Dominican Republic, 1983	American Can	$1,064,452
	Sudan, 1982	Equator Bank	3,219,455
	Ghana, 1981	Firestone Tire	7,116,636
	Zaire, 1980	Continental Milling	2,616,000
Expropriation	Iran, 1982	Carrier Corp.	2,395,000
	Benin, 1981	Morrison-Knudsen	3,978,692
	Iran, 1981	Cabot Corp.	2,584,986
	Chile, 1972	Chile Copper Co.	13,640,000
War damage	Nicaragua, 1983	American Standard	84,842
	Nicaragua, 1980	Sears, Roebuck	247,115
	Indonesia, 1978	Freeport Minerals	123,871
	Bangladesh, 1976	Belbagco Inc.	387,000

Source: OPIC (Overseas Private Investment Corporation).

assets or bank accounts and losses due to a government owner failing to live up to contract provisions.

Energy programs are special insurance and finance programs geared toward U.S. investors involved in oil, gas, oil shale, geothermal, mineral, solar, and other energy projects. OPIC can provide a loan guaranty of up to $50 million to finance as much as 50 percent of a new project deemed commercially feasible.

Leasing programs provide specialized insurance and finance services for U.S. investors involved in international leasing. Political risk insurance is available for cross-border operating and capital leases running for at least thirty-six months. Loan guaranties to leasing companies can range from $500,000 to $30 million, with the fees paralleling OPIC's general finance programs. Direct loans are available to foreign leasing projects in which small U.S. businesses have significant interests.

Pressure on Trading Partners

For many years, the United States government has tried to increase demand for U.S. products abroad by prodding the governments of Germany and Japan in particular to stimulate their economies and thus draw in more U.S. goods. This idea is based on the assumption that recovery abroad would stimulate U.S. exports.

In addition, the United States government has been pressuring the Japanese to reduce barriers that restrict the sales of U.S. goods in Japan. For example, traditionally the Japanese government required purchase of telecommunications equipment from native sources only. Recent pressure, however, has led Japan to partially eliminate this restriction and thus has opened the door for U.S. firms, such as Western Electric, a subsidiary of American Telephone and Telegraph, to explore export opportunities in Japan.[15] Similarly, pressure is being put on South Korea and Taiwan to open their markets to American goods.[16] Table 17.8 illustrates how barriers affect U.S. exports. For example, since Argentina and Brazil do not provide patent protection, U.S. pharmaceutical companies lose over $110 million in sales annually to copycat pharmaceuticals manufacturers.

Export Trading Company Act, 1982

This act was the first major export expansion legislation in more than a decade. It encourages businesses to join together and form export trading companies. It provides antitrust protection for joint exporting, and permits banking institutions to own interests in these exporting ventures. This act makes exporting practical for small- and medium-size firms by permitting them to join forces and hire specialists to handle all the complicated details of exporting without fear of antitrust prosecution and inadequate capitalization.[17] The following are the highlights of the provisions of the Export Trading Company Act.

Banking Provisions Bank holding companies and bankers' banks may invest up to 5 percent and loan up to 10 percent of their capital and surplus to an export trading company.

Bank holding companies and bankers' banks may own up to 100 percent of the stock of an export trading company.

The Federal Reserve Board (FRB) must approve any proposed investment.

TABLE 17.8 Barriers That Affect U.S. Exports

PRODUCT	COUNTRIES	BARRIER	SALES LOST BY U.S. (ANNUAL, ESTIMATED)
Grain	European Community	Price supports, variable duties	$2.0 billion
Soybeans	European Community	Price supports	$1.4 billion
Rice	Japan	Ban	$300 million
Beef	European Community	Ban on growth hormones in livestock	$100 million
Commerical aircraft	Britain, France, [former] West Germany, Spain	Subsidies to Airbus Industrie	Over $850 million
Telecommunications equipment	European Community, South Korea	Standards stacked against imports	No estimate
Telecommunications satellites	Japan	Ban on import by government agencies	No estimate
Pharmaceuticals	Argentina, Brazil	No patent protection	Over $110 million
Videocassettes, films	Brazil	Requirements to subsidize and market local films	Over $40 million
Computer software	Thailand	Poor patent protection	No estimate

Source: U.S. Department of Commerce.

Under this process, a bank need only notify the FRB of the intended investment. If no objection is made within sixty days thereafter, the bank may proceed with the intended investment.

A bank is exempted from the collateral requirements contained in the Federal Reserve Act for loans to its export trading company.

Antitrust Certification Provisions

The Commerce Department is the certifying agency, subject to the concurrence of the Justice Department.

Eligibility for certification is based on four specific antitrust standards.

Only the Secretary of Commerce, not the Justice Department, can revoke or modify a certificate.

A certificate holder has complete immunity from U.S. antitrust laws, except for private party lawsuits for actual damages. Such laws are subject to the following limitations: the trading entity must have violated the specific antitrust standards enumerated in the bill; a two-year-statute of limitations is applicable to any lawsuits; a certificate creates a presumption of lawfulness; the certificate holder can be awarded costs, including attorney's fees, if she or he prevails in any action brought against her or him.[18]

In the first three years after the ETC Act was passed, the Commerce Department issued seventy-six certificates providing antitrust protection to twenty-nine firms and individuals. Small and medium-sized firms constituted a majority of the holders of these certificates. Interestingly, the agribusiness community is taking more interest in the ETC program than other industries. Further, by the end of 1986, a total of forty-two bank ETCs had been formed with the approval of the Federal Reserve Board, and had invested $85 million in them.[19] Despite these achievements, the ETC program has received lukewarm support in the business community. Critics consider these achievements insignificant. Empirical research shows that such large companies as Sears, General Electric, Rockwell International, and General Motors would have formed export trading companies with or without the ETC legislation. Banks and small and medium-sized manufacturers, which were supposed to benefit most from the legislation, have not responded well.[20]

One reason for this lackluster support may be the ignorance of smaller companies about the act's relevance and usefulness to their business. The U.S. Department of Commerce's educational programs (e.g., conferences and publications) may encourage these firms to take advantage of the export opportunities furnished under the ETC Act.

Omnibus Trade and Competitiveness Act of 1988

On August 23, President Reagan signed the Omnibus Trade and Competitiveness Act of 1988. The major provisions of the act are discussed in Chapter 2. The act maintains U.S. commitment to free trade and provides better trade remedy tools to open foreign markets. It strengthens the ability of U.S. firms to protect their patented, copyrighted, and trademarked goods and ideas from international thievery.[21]

Further, the act supports the Uruguay Round trade talks to adapt or expand the GATT by improving existing rules with respect to agriculture and to dispute settlement, and by extending GATT discipline to new areas such as services, investment, and intellectual property.

The act also provides for the establishment of an interagency committee to assure the timely collection of accurate trade and economic data and to provide the private sector and government officials with efficient access to this data for policymaking and export promotion (see International Marketing Highlight 17.5).

U.S. Government Hindrance of Exports

Although the government encourages exports in various ways, several U.S. rules and regulations act as obstacles to increasing exports:

- The anti-Arab boycott rules, which require U.S. exporters to forgo Arab contracts that bar Israeli-made goods
- The Trade Act of 1974, which bars Export-Import Bank credit to most communist countries

International Marketing Highlight 17.5

Trade vs. Environment

In the past few years, a new problem has arisen concerning trade barriers and environmental laws. In these trade versus environment conflicts, developing nations with an abundance of natural resources are pitted against industrialized nations. For example, fishermen in Mexico were harvesting yellowfin tuna by using nets that trap scores of dolphins in the process. As a result, tens of thousands of dolphins drowned. In 1988 the United States banned all imports of tuna caught using this technique. However, in response to a Mexican complaint, a GATT panel ruled that such a ban was an unfair trade barrier. The GATT panel ruled against a member country restricting imports of a product merely because it came from a country with different environmental policies than its own.

At a time that a U.S.-Mexican free-trade treaty is in the works, this conflict between the two countries does not augur well. So far the Mexican government has not pushed the matter further despite the GATT ruling in its favor. But if other countries transhipping Mexican tuna are banned from exporting, they may protest under the GATT ruling.

Concern for the environment is laudable. But the problem is that countries pursue trade protectionism in the name of a "safe" environment. For example, Canadians protect their prized Pacific salmon against overfishing by virtually counting the catch. Atlantic lobsters are safeguarded by New England states by banning sales of adolescent crustaceans. Europeans demand that imported beef must be untainted by artificial growth hormones. As world trade grows, such conflicts are likely and there is no easy way to resolve them. Resource-rich developing nations see imperialism in the efforts of industrialized nations to force environmental reforms on them. Rich nations, on the other hand, fear deterioration of the environment as a genuine concern.

Source: "Save the Dolphins—or Free Trade, " *Business Week,* February 17, 1992, p. 130D.

- The Foreign Corrupt Practices Act of 1977, which imposes jail terms and fines for overseas payoffs by U.S. companies
- Limits on the sale and financing of nuclear plants (these restrictions have been designed to halt the spread of nuclear weapons)
- Human rights legislation, which denies credits to rights violators (loans have been withheld from South Africa and Chile, for example)[22]
- U.S. trade embargoes, which ban exports to Cuba, Vietnam, Zimbabwe, and many other countries
- Strategic controls restrictions, which stop exports with potential military uses to communist bloc countries[23]
- Antitrust laws, which prevent U.S. companies from bidding jointly on major foreign projects

- Restrictions on hi-tech exports to protect national security[24]

The United States policy in foreign trade matters continues to be based on *helping and reforming* other nations. Such a policy reinforces the view that major trading partners of the United States (Western European nations and Japan) are so weak that they require very substantial U.S. concessions in trade and other economic matters, and that the United States is so strong that it is immune from economic injury no matter what concessions are made by its government. The validity of such an appraisal is questionable, as is the expectation that other nations will accept U.S. values and ethics as a basis for their exports.

Among other remedial measures, it has been suggested that the United States government

- Provide a wide range of export credits, including Export-Import Bank loans or grants for engineering or economic studies of major infrastructure projects extending over a considerable period and involving high risk. With U.S. financing, U.S. engineers will get the jobs and they will specify U.S. equipment.
- Clarify the law on corrupt practices overseas and reduce the scope of liability. Present law is so loosely drafted that some companies fear they could get into trouble by paying commissions to local agents or fees to attorneys. To an extent this problem has been addressed by the Omnibus Trade and Competitiveness Act of 1988 (see Chapter 2).
- Review the antitrust laws and amend them to permit joint efforts and cooperation by competitive U.S. companies overseas. Antitrust should be limited to the borders of the United States.
- Stop using export restrictions in an effort to enforce human rights policies when suppliers from other nations are available to take over the business.[25]

Export Management

United States companies face a challenge to succeed in a time of growing protectionism and keen competition. While United States government programs are some help, the proper management of export activity at the company level is equally important. This section discusses select strategies to improve export performance.

Export markets offer a variety of opportunities. But to capitalize on these opportunities, companies should develop an export focus and do a thorough job in identifying products/markets. Consider Japan.[26] Often companies grumble about its closed markets, but they fail to realize that the new generation of Japanese crave U.S. goods and have plenty of purchasing power. In the year 2000, the generation born after 1955 will make up 42 percent of Japan's consumer market.[27]

Foreign products selling well in Japan are those not requiring much after-sale service, which foreign producers are relatively poor at providing, and those in which foreign producers maintain a competitive edge vis-à-vis their Japanese competitors in terms of either price or performance. These products are primarily nondurable consumer and specialty goods that satisfy individual tastes. Examples include black tea (market share of imports to the overall market equals 60 percent), canned soup (40 percent), neckties (25 percent), climbing ropes (90 percent), paper diapers (50 percent), skiing goods (30 percent), and fountain pens (35 percent).

Awareness of Emerging Markets

Third World countries are slowly evolving into important markets for U.S. products. While the U.S. continues to incur a trade deficit with Canada, Germany, and Japan ($7.5 billion, $9.4 billion, and $41.4 billion, respectively, in 1990), the trade surplus with the Third World during the same period went up. In future years, as Third World countries continue to develop their economies, they are likely to become more important markets for the United States.[28]

In 1970, OECD countries with 20 percent of the world's population accounted for 83 percent of the world's trade in manufactures. On the other hand, the developing countries (including China) with 70 percent of the world's population had just 14 percent of the world's trade in manufactures. The communist countries accounted for the balance. According to GATT estimates, in the year 2000, the OECD countries should conduct 63 percent of the world's trade in manufactured goods, a 20 percent reduction between 1980 and 2000. The share of the Third World countries should increase to 28 percent.[29]

In the matter of trade, the LDCs typically get less attention than OECD countries. Yet LDCs are significant markets. Companies need to expand their view and explore opportunities in the LDCs in a systematic matter.

A framework for selecting potential growth markets for exports is diagramatically depicted in Figure 17.1. Market attractiveness may be based on company competencies, industry practices, and competitive conditions. A sustainable competitive position in selected foreign markets can be built if a company is able to reach a minimum level of size and effectiveness; that is, critical mass. *Critical mass* is determined by the ability of the company to match the product, price, distribution, and promotion requirements of the market vis-à-vis competition. Once different markets are located on the grid, the approximate allocation of resources for foreign market development may be made as follows: In the lightly shaded areas, at the upper right-hand corner of the grid, are found attractive markets where the company already has a strong position. In these markets the appropriate strategy is usually to maintain that position or build it further. The heavily shaded areas indicate attractive markets where the company is within reach of critical mass. Here, the company can improve results by investing the necessary time and resources to gain the step-function benefits of crossing the threshold. The white areas of the grid are those markets with low attractiveness, or markets where it is unlikely that the company can reach critical mass. Here,

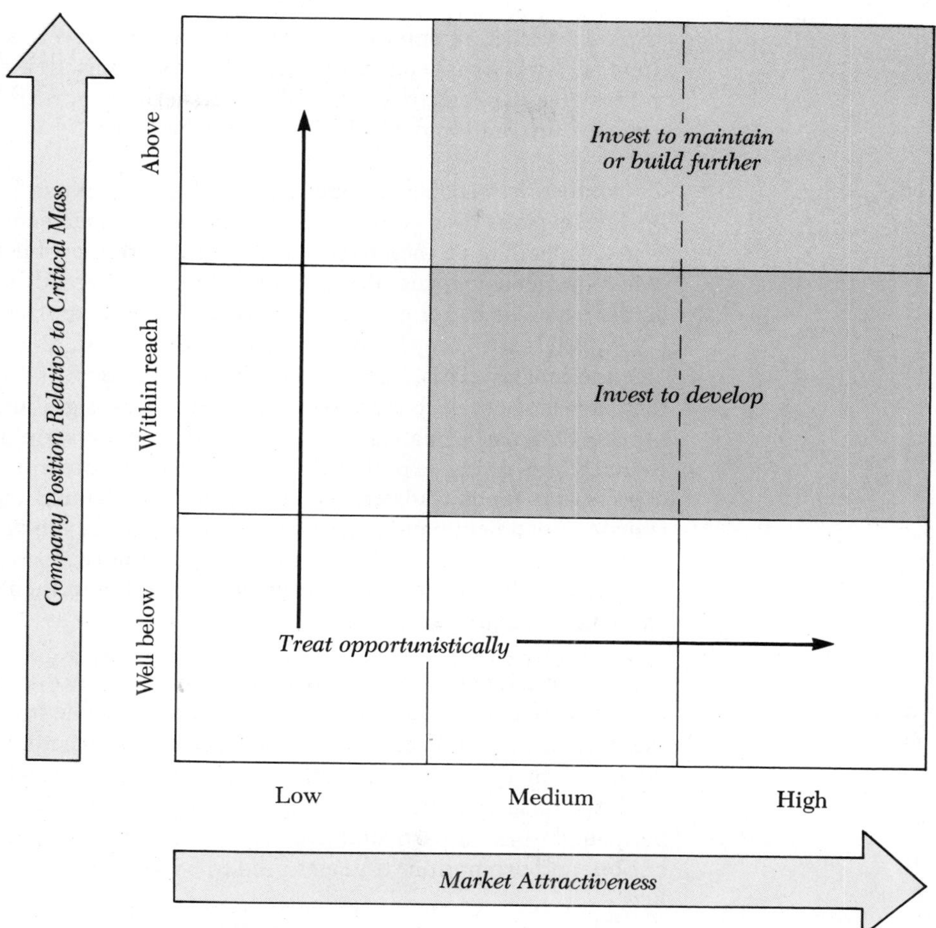

FIGURE 17.1 Setting Development Priorities in Overseas Markets

a strategy of careful opportunistic response and limited or reduced investment is probably called for.

Product Specialization

There was a time when U.S. products everywhere were considered superior across the board. In the past twenty years, however, other industrialized countries have achieved similar distinction in a variety of products. No longer are U.S. electronic goods considered the best. German machinery is often held superior to that of the United States. Moreover, many Third World countries are able to produce high-quality, low-technology products at significantly lower costs. In brief, U.S. corporations cannot expect to do well overseas with all products. A careful choice of both products and market is essential. For example, high-technology products have provided a unique opportunity for U.S. business to acquire leverage in entering export markets. However, other industrialized nations are slowly challenging the U.S. position in this area.[30] U.S. companies need to be active in protecting their advantage in the export of high-technology products (see International Marketing Highlight 17.6).

Appropriate Management Orientation

To compete effectively abroad and develop and expand foreign markets, U.S. businesspersons need to develop a particular management orientation. Different firms, depending on their experience, face different problems in the export arena. The management focus of each firm, therefore, should be directly related to its actual experience. For example, Czinkota divides exporters into three categories: (1) exporters with only a partial interest in exporting, (2) exporters who export on an experimental basis, and (3) experienced exporters.[31] As shown in Table 17.9, the perspective of each type of export operation is significantly different from the others. Obviously, management style and strategy should vary accordingly. To illustrate this point, experienced firms need to devote more attention to financial aspects and funds transfer, while new entrants should tackle packaging, funds transfer, document handling, and the mechanics of exporting. By the same token, as the dynamics of a firm's business change from the experimental to the experienced level, the nature of the problems changes, and then a different managerial emphasis is required.

Appropriate Export Strategy

Finally, for a longer-term effective export performance, a company must develop an appropriate marketing strategy. For the foreseeable future, the global environment dictates that U.S. export sales cannot be generated simply by repeating what a company does in the United States. Overseas markets should be properly analyzed to search out and identify product/market niches where a certain company might have a particular opportunity. Next, adequate product, price, distribution, and promotion strategies need to be formulated to serve those target markets.

The textile industry's export performance during the late 1980s illustrates how a well-planned strategy can pay off.[32] For example, U.S. textile exports (yarn, fabric, and carpeting) increased 50 percent, from $3.2 billion in 1980 to $4.8 billion in 1985. To accomplish this, the textile companies took three strategic measures.

First, they identified market segments that currently were not adequately served. For example, British carpetmakers mainly produced two types of carpets—woven wool carpet and synthetic carpet. The middle class could not afford the wool carpet because it was expensive; and the synthetic carpet looked cheap. To cater to the middle class, American mills introduced mid-priced carpeting in different shades, colors, and textures.

Second, riding on the tidal wave of enthusiasm for such U.S. fashions as blue jeans, U.S. textile producers started exporting denim and corduroy to European apparel makers. These foreign companies compete head-on with U.S. apparel makers, such as Levi Strauss. Thus, the move to supply denim to a customer's competitors was risky. But in the long run, the textile mills found it to be a sound strategy.

International Marketing Highlight 17.6

100 Products That America Makes Best

All-electric plastics injection-molding machine, Cincinnati Milacron
Aluminum foil, Reynolds Metals
Atomic clock, Frequency Electronics, Hewlett-Packard
Ball point pens, A.T. Cross
Balloon and laser angioplasty catheters, C.R. Bard, Eli Lilly, Trimedyne
Bamboo fly-fishing rods, Walt Carpenter
Bed sheets and towels, Burlington Industries, Dan River, Dundee Mills, Fieldcrest Cannon, J.P. Stevens, Springs Industries, West Point-Pepperell
Biotech drugs: t-PA, Genentech
Bobcat skid-steer loaders, Melroe
Boots and hunting shoes, Timberland, L.L. Bean
Brain electrical activity mapping system, Nicolet Instrument
Camera film (color), Eastman Kodak
Central office switching equipment, AT&T
Charcoal briquettes, Kingsford Products
Charge couple device image sensor, Eastman Kodak
Clothes dryers, Whirlpool
Combines, Case IH, Deere
Computer operating systems software: MS-DOS, Unix, VM, VMS, Microsoft, AT&T, IBM Digital Equipment
Copiers, Eastman Kodak, Xerox
Cotton denim, Cone Mills
Cruising sailboats, 37 feet and under, Pacific Seacraft
Crystal, Steuben Glass
Data parallel supercomputers, Thinking Machines
Digital plotters, Hewlett-Packard
Dishwashers, General Electric
Distributed database management technology, Tandem Computers
Ditch Witch trenchers, Charles Machine Works
Drugs: Capoten and Vasotec, Squibb, Merck
Dustbuster Plus hand-held cordless vacuum cleaners, Black & Decker
Electrodeposition primers, PPG Industries
Electrohydraulic servo valves, Moog
F-16 jet fighters, General Dynamics
Fast food: hamburgers, McDonald's
Financial, engineering, and scientific hand-held calculators, Hewlett-Packard
501 jeans, Levi Strauss
Flashlights, Mag Instrument
Flutes, Wm. S. Haynes
FM two-way radios, Motorola
Frequency and time interval analyzers, Hewlett-Packard
Fur coats, Peter Dion, Goldin-Feldman, Ben Kahn, Maximilian, Louis Milona
Glass fiber for communications, Corning Glass Works
Gore-Tex waterproof breathable fabric, W.L. Gore
Handbags, Coach Leatherware
Hay and forage equipment, Ford New Holland
Heating controls, Honeywell
Heavy earthmoving equipment, Caterpillar
Ice cream and sorbet, New York Fruit Ice
Industrial and commerical floor sweepers and scrubbers, Tennant
Instant camera films, Polaroid
Integrated voice and data communications systems (T-1 multiplexers), Network Equipment Technologies
Intelsat VI satellite, Hughes Aircraft
Ion chromatographs, Dionex
Jazz music
Jet aircraft: 747 family of planes, Boeing
Jet engines, General Electric
Kevlar fiber, Du Pont
Loader/backhoe, Case IH
Locomotives, General Electric
Longwall mining systems, Joy Technologies
Lycra spandex fiber, Du Pont
Magnetic resonance imaging scanners, General Electric
Marlboro cigarettes, Philip Morris
Mass spectrometers, Finnigan
Men's ready-to-wear suits, Oxford Clothes

Micro-precision machine and measuring tools, Moore Special Tool
Microprocessors: Motorola 68000 family, Intel 80X86 family, Motorola, Intel
Microwavable food in shelf-stable packaging: Impromptu, Top Shelf, General Foods, Geo. A. Hormel & Continental Can
Microwave ovens, Litton Industries
Minicomputers, Digital Equipment, Hewlett-Packard, IBM
Minisupercomputers, Alliant Computer Systems, Convex Computer
Multimeters, Hewlett-Packard, John Fluke Mfg.
Offshore drilling equipment, Cameron Iron Works
Oscilloscopes, Tektronix
Pacemakers, Medtronic
Paper towels, Procter & Gamble, Scott Paper
Personal computer applications software, Lotus Development, Microsoft, WordPerfect
Personal computers, Apple Computer
Pianos, Steinway & Sons
Post-it note pads, 3M
Powerboats, Cigarette Racing Team, Donzi Marine
Pressure transmitters for industrial process plants, Rosemount
Row-crop planters, Case IH
Scotch S-VHS videotape, 3M
Scotchcal drag reduction tape, 3M
Sheet and strip stainless steel, Allegheny Ludlum
Soft drinks, Coca-Cola
Stationery, Crane
Stereo loudspeakers, International Jensen, Allison Acoustics, Infinity Systems
Sunglass lenses, Corning Glass Works
Supercomputers, Cray Research
Symbion J-7 and Thoratec artificial hearts, Symbion, Thoratec Medical
Tampax, Tambrands
Technical workstations, Apollo, Silicon Graphics, Sun
Teflon, Du Pont
Telephone sets, AT&T
Thermos vacuum containers, Halsey Taylor/Thermos
Thin film hard disks, Komag, Seagate Technology
Tillage equipment, Krause Plow
Tractors, 100 hp and over, Deere
Washing machines, Maytag, Whirlpool

Source: Richard L. Kirkland, Jr., "Entering a New Age of Global Business," *Fortune,* March 14, 1988, p. 40.

Third, the textile producers introduced new product concepts overseas. For example, towels and sheets in Europe and Japan had been stable, commodity-type products in standard shapes and designs, without fashion appeal. U.S. companies decided to introduce a "boutique" marketing system to develop an export market for bed and bath textile products. One company that stands out in the successful pursuit of this strategy is Fieldcrest Mills.

An appendix at the end of this chapter provides a checklist of the principal kinds of marketing information that a company needs to develop export strategy.

Export Procedure

Many marketing managers fail to explore fully potential business abroad because of their uncertainty about, or simply lack of understanding of, export mechanics. While exporting is certainly more demanding than a strictly domestic business,

TABLE 17.9 Life Cycle Stages of U.S. Exporting Firms

TYPE OF EXPORT OPERATION	AVERAGE ANNUAL EXPORT SALES VOLUME	WHERE THEY EXPORT	ATTITUDE TOWARD EXPORTING	PROBLEMS	WHAT THEY HAVE TO IMPROVE	WHY THEY EXPORT
Partially interested	$200,000	Half export only to Canada, fewer than 10 customers.	Export occasionally. Don't actively solicit orders. Exporting not part of overall growth strategy.	Financing, communication, technical advice, gathering information on foreign business.	Packaging, funds transfer, document handling, mechanics of exporting.	Increased profits compared to domestic market.
Experimental	$1 million	1/3 export only to Canada	Considering export as a strategy for expansion. Some exploration of foreign markets.	Sales, gathering data on foreign business, adapting products to foreign needs, financial information.	Systematic investigation of foreign opportunities.	Profits, technological advantage over competitors, belief in product.
Experienced	$4 million (20% of total sales	1/6 export only to Canada. Each has at least 40 overseas customers.	Committed to exporting, part of overall corporate strategy. Actively seek export possiblities.	Communication, sales, gathering market information, customer service, foreign business practices.	Financing, funds transfer.	Unique product, higher profits, tax advantages, competitive pressure, market share.

Source: Michael R. Czinkota, "Assess Commitment and Motives; Identify Stage of Development When Managing Firm's Exports," *Marketing News,* June 26, 1981, p. 10.

by using the information provided by the U.S. Department of Commerce and employing agents and other professionals familiar with the formalities, export sales can be handled almost as easily as domestic sales. One need not travel abroad and meet with customers in person to be successful in exports. As with most any undertaking, there are basic procedural tasks involved in exporting.

Locating Customers

Overseas customers can be located in many ways. Large corporations have their established contacts. Firms new to exports can identify likely prospects overseas through the information available from the U.S. Department of Commerce. For example, as discussed earlier in this chapter, the *World Traders Data Reports* (WTDRs), a service of the Commerce Department, provide detailed commercial information on foreign firms—background information on the organization, year established, number of employees, sales area, type of operation, products handled, name of contact officer, general reputation in trade and finance circles, names of other foreign firms the company represents, and even a U.S. foreign service officer's comment on the firm's suitability as a trade contact.

Before proceeding with a prospect, it is advisable to examine the socioeconomic-political-regulatory environment of the importing country. Such an examination would indicate if an export can be successfully transacted. For example, many countries prohibit the importation of certain products. Some require that an import license be obtained from the government. Other countries impose restrictions on the quantity imported. Thus, if an import license is required, the exporting firm should insist that the importer obtain it first. Similarly, if a government levies a heavy import duty, the exporter should remind the interested overseas party of the impact of such a barrier on the final cost of the product.

Obtaining Export Licenses

Exporters should be aware of U.S. government regulations affecting the export of certain strategic commodities to certain destinations. Essentially, all items intended for export require an export license. This rule is mandated by the need for national security, and by the foreign policy and economic interests of the United States. The rule, however, applies neither to U.S. territories and possessions nor, in most cases, to Canada. There are two types of licenses: general and validated.

> A general license permits exportation within certain limits without requiring that an application be filed or that a license document be issued. A validated license authorizes exportation within specific limitations; it is issued only on formal application. Most goods can move from the United States to free-world countries under a general license. A validated license is required to export certain kinds of strategic goods regardless of the destination.[33]

An exporter needs to know whether a general or validated license is necessary and which office to contact to obtain the license. For most commodities, the license is granted by the Commerce Department's Office of Export Administration (OEA). For certain specific products and commodities, however, export licenses are provided by other U.S. government departments and agencies (see

Table 17.10).[34] For example, in the case of arms, ammunition, and other war-related items the license is given by the Department of State.

The type of license—general or validated—required for exporting is based on two considerations: country of destination and commodity to be exported. For export purposes, the U.S. government has classified countries (except Canada) into seven categories:[35] Q—Romania; S—Libya; T—all countries of the Western Hemisphere except Canada and Cuba; W—Poland and Hungary; Y—Albania, Bulgaria, Czechoslovakia, the Commonwealth of Independent States, and several communist countries; Z—North Korea, Vietnam, Haiti, Iraq, and Cuba; and V—all other countries except Canada. Exports to countries in the Z category are almost completely banned. There is a selective embargo, based on the type of commodity, on exports to countries in the Y group. In brief, different licensing requirements apply to countries in each category. Thus, exports to countries in the Y category would require a validated license, while those in the T category, a general license.

Items requiring a validated license include, but are not limited to, certain chemicals, special types of plastics, sophisticated electronic and communication equipment, scarce materials, and related technical data. By referring to the commodity control list of the Export Administration regulations available from the U.S. Department of Commerce, one can determine whether a validated export license is needed for a particular commodity to a particular country.

To obtain a validated export license, an application must be prepared following the procedures described in the Export Administration regulations. Where the value of the shipment is $5,000 or more and a validated license is needed, special forms generally must be completed by importers or their government to support the request for license.

A general license is a published authorization for the exporting of commodities that do not require a validated license. The majority of U.S. products exported require a general, not a validated, license. An exporter need not obtain formal authorization to ship products requiring a general license. Those products

TABLE 17.10 U.S. Export Licensing Authorities for Specific Commodities

COMMODITY	LICENSING AUTHORITY
Arms, ammunition, and other war-related products	Department of State
Atomic energy material (including fissionable materials and facilities for their manufacture)	Atomic Energy Commission
Gold and silver	Department of Treasury
Narcotic drugs	Department of Justice
Natural gas and electric energy	Federal Power Commission
Tobacco plants and seeds	Department of Agriculture
Vessels	Maritime Commission
Endangered wildlife	Department of the Interior

Source: U.S. Department of Commerce. *The Export Administration Regulations* (Washington, D.C.: U.S. Government Printing Office, 1981).

can be shipped by merely inserting the correct general license symbol or code on the export control document, that is, the shipper's export declaration. In other words, no formal application has to be made to export products for which a general license is needed.

Collecting Export Documents

A variety of documents is needed to complete an export transaction. The documents help to clear exported goods at shipping points and through customs, and to receive payment. Documentation requirements vary from country to country. The following documents are required most commonly.

Commercial Invoice A commercial invoice summarizes details of the sales contract and lists the names and addresses of the exporter, shipper, and consignee; date of order; shipping data; mode of shipment; delivery and payment terms; description of product; and prices, discounts, and quantities.

Some countries require additional information in the commercial invoice; for example, the invoice must be signed and notarized or countersigned by the exporter's chamber of commerce. Similarly, some countries require the invoice to be visaed by the resident consul of the importer's country. Details for the inclusion or attachment of additional information in the commercial invoice can be obtained from any of the forty-eight U.S. Department of Commerce district offices located in major cities across the nation.

Consular Invoice This term refers to a certificate pertaining to exports that should be obtained from the consulate office of the importer's country. A consular invoice is prepared on forms available from the consulate and often is in the language of the importing country. It is visaed by the resident consul, certifying the authenticity and correctness of the proposed shipment.

Certificate of Origin Many countries require a certificate, either on a prescribed form or on the exporter's letterhead, that specifies the origin of the merchandise. Usually such a statement is made on the commercial invoice, but some countries require an additional separate certificate. The certificate of origin makes it easier to establish possible preferential rates for import duties under a most-favored-nation arrangement.

Inspection Certificate An inspection certificate is an affidavit, either by the shipper or by an independent inspection firm, certifying the quality, quantity, and conformity of goods in relation to the order. Importers often request such a certificate to ensure the correctness of the shipment.

Shipper's Export Declaration This document summarizes shipping information and contains a description of the merchandise in a special nomenclature, both in words and by commodity identifying number per Export Administration regulations. The reference to a specific validated or general export license also appears on this document.

Export Packing List The export packing list summarizes information about the merchandise and facilitates shipping. The list is also used by customs officials to check the cargo at both the point of shipment and the port of entry. The list helps the importer to inventory the merchandise received. The list itemizes the material in each package; specifies the type of package (box, crate, drum); shows the package dimensions and weight; and provides the shipper's and buyer's references. The packing list is attached to the outside of one of the packages in a waterproof envelope marked "packing list enclosed."

Dock, or Warehouse, Receipt This document stipulates the receipt of goods at the pier or warehouse for further shipment abroad. This receipt is usually needed when the exporter has to deliver goods only to the U.S. port of export.

Insurance Certificate This certificate specifies the type and amount of insurance coverage. Virtually all shipments overseas are insured to protect the goods against political risks and damage by natural causes. An exporter can obtain an open cargo policy to cover all foreign shipments or insure individual shipments.

Bill of Lading This is the single most important export document. A ***bill of lading*** establishes the ownership of goods, testifies to the carrier's obligation to ship the goods, and serves as a receipt of goods from the carrier. A bill of lading may be negotiable or nonnegotiable. The nonnegotiable bill of lading is usually used for air shipments; the goods are addressed to the named consignee. However, most shipments are made via negotiable bills of lading. The goods may be consigned to the consignee or to a third party but are delivered to the bearer of the bill of lading, that is, the party presenting the properly endorsed bill of lading. Following commercial practice, a bill of lading, to be valid and acceptable, must be marked "Clean on Board." This amounts to a certificate by the carrier that the goods were received on board in good and satisfactory condition. Conversely, a bill of lading marked "Foul" by the carrier would mean that the goods were received on board either damaged or spoiled.

A bill of lading includes the name and address of the exporter, the forwarding agent, and the overseas consignee (both intermediate and ultimate); it identifies the carrier, the U.S. port of export, and the foreign port of unloading; and it includes the name of the party to be notified on arrival of the goods. It also contains details pertaining to the merchandise; nature of goods (e.g., "four boxes: textiles"), weight, value, and other pertinent information.

Packing and Marking

The importance of adequate packing for overseas shipment is discussed in Chapter 12 on product policy. Briefly, packing should be designed to prevent breakage and to protect against pilferage and exposure to moisture. Further, every effort should be made to keep package weight down to save on shipping costs, while ensuring that the package is sufficiently sturdy to withstand the violent handling, stacking, loading, and unloading so common to ocean shipping.

The package should be properly marked for easy identification. Legible and clear marking will ensure its shipment to the correct destination. Besides, it will help the consignee to identify the package without difficulty. Usually, overseas buyers specify special identification marks to be imprinted on the package. Frequently, exporters avoid showing trademarks or other clues that might reveal the contents of the shipment. Such precautions help to avoid pilferage.

Shipping Abroad

Shipping of merchandise to overseas destinations involves observing different formalities that not every exporter is able to handle independently. It is desirable, therefore, to enlist the services of a ***foreign freight forwarder,*** an agent who specializes in moving the cargo to overseas destinations. After the goods have been delivered to the port of export, the freight forwarder takes over to clear the goods through U.S. customs and deliver the cargo to the pier in time for loading aboard the selected vessel. In addition, a freight forwarder furnishes useful advice to the exporter relative to freight costs, port changes, consular fees, export documentation, and customs rules, both in the United States and the importer's country.

Shipment may be made from the United States by either air or ocean carrier; in the case of countries accessible by land, such as Mexico and Canada, trucks can also be used. Carrier companies provide various types of contracts for overseas shipments. For example, three types of ocean service are available: conference lines, independent lines, and tramp vessels. The conference and independent lines operate on a predetermined schedule, while tramp vessels sail on ad hoc arrangements and usually carry bulk cargo. Conference lines are carriers who have formed an association to establish common freight rates and shipping conditions. Exporters who contract to deal exclusively with conference lines ship at lower rates than noncontract shippers. Independent lines price their services individually and aggressively compete for noncontract exporters, vying with the conference lines.

The shipping arrangement is finalized after a ***booking contract*** is obtained, reserving space for the cargo on a specified vessel.

Receiving Payment

There are various methods of receiving payment for exports, such as cash in advance, open account, consignment sales, dollar draft, and letter of credit. The method of payment used and the terms and conditions agreed upon would depend on the credit standing of the importer, the exchange restrictions operating in the importer's country, and the competition the exporter faces. Usually the international services of a commercial bank are used to receive payment.

Cash in Advance As far as the seller is concerned, cash in advance is the safest method. Payment received before shipping the goods relieves the seller of worry about collection. Besides, the money is available for use right away. From the buyer's viewpoint, this is not a preferred method for two main reasons. First, certain foreign exchange restrictions prohibit paying cash in advance. Second, there is no guarantee of shipment of the merchandise as specified.

Overall, this method of payment is not used frequently; the trade conducted via cash in advance constitutes a small portion of the total trade.

Open Account In an open-account arrangement, goods are shipped without any prior financial deal. This is a risky method of receiving payments unless the seller is dealing with a known party whose financial integrity is held in high esteem. Even where there is no danger of not receiving payment under this mode of payment, the trade practice in the buyer's country may be to pay only when the goods have actually been received. In Third World countries exchange problems may create an additional difficulty if the buyer fails to receive foreign exchange.

This method is most often used between organizations under the same corporate umbrella, for example one subsidiary of a company ships goods to another subsidiary in another country. Open-account shipments are also feasible between large organizations in industrialized countries; for example, General Motors may ship parts to Volvo in Sweden.

Consignment Sales Consignment sales refer to an arrangement whereby goods are shipped to the overseas party while the seller retains title to the goods. The consignee makes payment to the seller after the goods have been sold. The consignment arrangement, like the open account, is feasible if the consignee's country provides a stable economic and political environment, and the consignee has a good reputation and offers a deal that is a sound business risk. Consignment sales are made mostly to exporters' overseas branches or affiliates.

Export Drafts An export draft is an unconditional order drawn by the exporter asking the importer to pay the designated amount either on presentation (sight draft) or at a future date mutually agreed upon (time draft). Usually the future date specified in the draft is 30, 60, 90, 120, or 180 days after presentation. The draft may name either the seller as the party to receive payment or a bank to handle collection.

If a bank is to handle payment, the exporter delivers the draft and shipping documents to the named bank. The bank then forwards them to its branch, affiliate, or correspondent bank in the importer's country. The branch contacts the buyer or the buyer's bank and demands immediate payment if it is a sight draft, or acceptance on the time draft. Once payment or acceptance is received, the shipping documents are delivered to the buyer.

An export draft can be drawn in U.S. dollars or in a foreign currency. A payment-on-draft agreement is usually used when the protection provided by a letter of credit (discussed next) is not necessary. This mode of receiving payment is less expensive and, therefore, enhances the exporter's competitive position in seeking export business.

Letter of Credit A frequently used method of receiving payment for exports is through the letter of credit. It is a document issued by a bank at the buyer's request in favor of the exporter. The document promises to pay the specified sum of money in the designated currency within a specified time upon receipt by the bank of shipping documents (bill of lading).

Essentially, there are two types of letters of credit: revocable and irrevocable. An irrevocable letter of credit, once given to and accepted by the seller, cannot be altered in any way without permission of the seller. On the other hand, a revocable letter of credit may be declared invalid by the buyer, either personally or through a bank, for any discretionary reason. Except for cash in advance, the irrevocable letter of credit offers the exporter the highest degree of protection. Inexperienced exporters, particularly when dealing with unknown parties, and especially in Third World countries, should find the letter of credit a safe way to secure themselves financially.

Exhibit 17.1 shows a sample irrevocable letter of credit. Typically a letter-of-credit transaction involves the following steps:

1. After the exporter and customer agree on the terms of a sale, the customer arranges for its bank to open a letter of credit. (Delays may be encountered if, for example, the buyer has insufficient funds.)
2. The buyer's bank prepares an irrevocable letter of credit, including all instructions to the seller concerning the shipment.
3. The buyer's bank sends the irrevocable letter of credit to a U.S. bank, requesting confirmation. The exporter may request that a particular U.S. bank be the confirming bank, or the foreign bank selects one of its U.S. correspondent banks.
4. The U.S. bank prepares a letter of confirmation to forward to the exporter along with the irrevocable letter of credit.
5. The exporter reviews carefully all conditions in the letter of credit. The exporter's freight forwarder should be contacted to make sure that the shipping date can be met. If the exporter cannot comply with one or more of the conditions, the customer should be alerted at once.
6. The exporter arranges with the freight forwarder to deliver the goods to the appropriate port or airport.
7. When the goods are loaded, the forwarder completes the necessary documents.
8. The exporter (or the forwarder) presents to the U.S. bank documents indicating full compliance.
9. The bank reviews the documents. If they are in order, the documents are air mailed to the buyer's bank for review and transmitted to the buyer.
10. The buyer (or agent) gets the documents that may be needed to claim the goods.
11. A draft, which may accompany the letter of credit, is paid by the exporter's bank at the time specified or may be discounted at an earlier date.[36]

Duty-Free Zones

In order to encourage international trade despite import barriers, many countries have resorted to the opening of foreign-trade enclaves. There are different types of such enclaves. Among these, however, duty-free zones (also called free-trade zones or foreign-trade zones) are the most popular. The ***duty-free zones*** are

EXHIBIT 17.1 Sample Letter of Confirmed Irrevocable Credit

CABLE: ANYBANK	ANYBANK OF WASHINGTON, D.C. 9600 Louisiana Avenue Washington, D.C.	TELEX: 000000 DATE: *May 1, 1986*

An Export Company
5353 Louisiana Avenue
Washington, D.C. 20200

ADVISED THROUGH: *First National Bank of Arlington, P.O. Box 40, Arlington, VA 22022*

Dear ______:

Our correspondents,

Banque Parisienne de Credit au Commerce et a l'Industrie, Paris, France

request us to inform you that they have opened with us their irrevocable credit in your favor for the amount of

Maximum Two Thousand Seven Hundred Fifty-Seven Dollars and 06/100 ($2,757.06)

by order of

An Importing Company, 45 Rue Jean Pierre, 75007 Paris

We are authorized to accept your 60-day sight draft, drawn on us when accompanied by the following documents, which must represent and cover full invoice value of the merchandise described below:

1) *Signed commercial invoice in six (6) copies.*
2) *Full set of clean ocean bills of lading, dated on board, plus one (1) nonnegotiable copy if available, issued to the order of Banque Parisienne de Credit au Commerce et a l'Industrie, notify: An Importing Company, 45 Rue Jean Pierre, 75007 Paris, indicating Credit No. 10173.*
3) *Insurance certificate in duplicate, in negotiable form, covering all risks, including war risks, strikes, and mines for the value of the merchandise plus 10%.*

Covering: *Perfume NO. 337*
As per pro forma invoice dated March 3, 1986
FOB Baltimore

Merchandise to be forwarded from Baltimore to Le Havre.
Partial shipments prohibited.
The cost of insurance is payable in excess of the credit amount and reimbursable to you against presentation of justification, when included in your drawings and added to your invoice.

The above-mentioned correspondent engages with you that all drafts drawn under and in compliance with the terms of this credit will be duly honored on delivery of documents as specified, if

presented at this office

on or before

June 30, 1986

We confirm the credit and thereby undertake that all drafts drawn and presented as above specified will be duly honored.

____
(Authorized Signature)

Source: Based on U.S. Department of Commerce, *A Basic Guide to Exporting* (Washington, D.C.: U.S. Printing Office, 1981), p. 36.

unique because they let businesses store, process, assemble, and display goods from abroad without paying a tariff first. Once these products leave a zone and are delivered within the United States, a tariff must be paid—but not on the cost of assembly, or on profits.[37] For example, a furnituremaker will have to pay a duty only on the imported raw wood used, not on the cost of assembling the item or on the profits. Consider Timex Co.'s example. It used the Little Rock, Arkansas, free-trade zone to store machinery it had bought overseas. By storing the equipment in the duty-free zone, the company deferred import duties until it had decided in which U.S. plant to use the foreign machinery. Finished goods can be stored in free-trade zones for reasons other than deferring customs duties. One firm ages wine in the New Orleans duty-free zone and thus defers import duties for years.[38]

If a product is re-exported, a company never has to pay a tariff. That means a U.S. cameramaker can assemble foreign parts in a Florida free-trade zone and ship the finished cameras to Latin America without paying U.S. duty.

Even if half the plants in these zones are foreign owned, it benefits the United States to have them because of the jobs created. Common for years in other countries, duty-free zones are becoming popular in the United States as the cost of doing business abroad rises.

Currently, there are 177 foreign-trade zones in the United States, in such large cities as New York, Boston, San Francisco, and Chicago; and in such remote places as Duluth, Minnesota; Little Rock, Arkansas; Bangor, Maine; and Burlington, Vermont. More than $53 billion worth of merchandise was processed in these zones in 1990, over one-third more than in 1980. About 1,780 business firms used foreign-trade zones during 1990. About 600 firms occupied zone facilities on a permanent basis.[39]

The cost advantages of foreign-trade zones are exemplified by Berg Steel Pipe Co., a German-French joint venture in Panama City's zone.[40] Berg produces large-diameter pipe for, among others, the oil industry, importing some of the needed steel plate from Germany and Italy for about $450 to $500 a ton. Imported as materials, the plate normally would be taxed at 6 percent. But with trade-zone status, Berg can convert the plate into pipe and move it into the U.S. market at the rate for finished products—1.9 percent—or export it free of tariff.

With such savings, companies of all kinds are setting up in foreign-trade zones. The variety of goods processed runs from Ambrosia Chocolate Co.'s bulk chocolate in Milwaukee to Xerox Corp.'s copiers near Rochester, New York. General Motors Corp. has eleven plants in foreign-trade zones, Ford Motor Co., twelve, and Chrysler Corp., nine. Other trade zones include Bethlehem Steel Corp.'s shipbuilding yard in Sparrows Point, Maryland, a Caterpillar Inc. engine plant near Peoria, Illinois, and three Eli Lilly & Co. plants in Indiana. Many foreign firms, such as Porsche, Nissan, and Mazda are active, too. And although both the tonnage and dollar value are dominated by giant corporations, more small than big companies are involved in foreign-trade zones.

Duty-free zones are especially useful for firms that:[41]

1. Import finished goods, component parts, or raw materials for eventual domestic consumption

2. Import finished goods, component parts, or raw materials for transshipment or re-export to a foreign port
3. Import merchandise that frequently is affected by customs quota delays
4. Receive considerable amounts of damaged or unsalable merchandise as a result of overseas shipment
5. Export domestically manufactured goods subject to high domestic excise taxes
6. Import and store merchandise subject to high domestic excise taxes
7. Import expensive or highly sensitive merchandise requiring extensive security and insurance coverage
8. Import merchandise high in foreign labor content
9. Face frequent delays in customs inspection classifications and other formalities
10. Import merchandise that must be processed, generating significant amounts of scrap or waste

Barter

An interesting development in recent years has been the emergence of barter, whereby goods/services are exchanged for goods/services without resorting to money-swapping. In other words, barter replaces money and credit as the medium of international exchange. Several types of barter deals are popular in the international market: counterpurchases, switch trading, clearing agreements, and buyback barter.

Counterpurchase (or Pure Barter)

Counterpurchase refers to a set of parallel cash agreements in which the supplier sells a service or product and orders unrelated products to offset the costs to the buyer.[42] For example, a few years ago Caterpillar Tractor sold tractors to a Latin American logger and sawmill operator and took coffins in exchange.[43] Here are some other examples:

> Canada is buying McDonnell Douglas F-18 aircraft worth $2.4 billion. In return, the company will help Canada find customers for goods and services worth $2.9 billion.
>
> Yugoslavia requires automakers to buy Yugoslav goods equal in value to components they ship to Yugoslav auto plants. Fiat buys autos from its Yugoslav licensee.
>
> Brazil asked bidders on a $130 million space satellite for pledges to export Brazil's goods. Canada's Spar Aerospace won jointly with Hughes Aircraft and will arrange imports of Brazilian products of equal value into Canada.
>
> Russia is buying construction machinery from Japan's Komatsu and Mitsubishi. The Japanese are taking Siberian timber.
>
> Colombia is asking equipment suppliers to buy its coffee. A Spanish government company did so in return for Colombia's purchase of buses from Spain's ENESA.[44]

In the past, countertrade was used primarily by the Soviet Union and by Eastern European and foreign-exchange-poor Third World economies. But recently these practices have spread as countries such as Canada, Switzerland, Sweden, and even the United States have joined this trend. One example of a countertrade deal is the New Zealand Meat Board's agreement to sell $200 million worth of frozen lamb to the Iranian government in exchange for crude oil. Another example is General Electric's agreement to sell Swedish products in overseas markets in exchange for a contract to build engines for Sweden's JAS fighters.[45]

Switch Trading

In a ***switch-trading*** arrangement additional parties are brought into the picture whereby part of the exchanged goods is shifted to the new party, often for cash. When one party has an unwanted balance of goods to be received from a second party, a third party in need of the goods offered by the first party is found to purchase the available goods, with the proceeds going to the second party. In one transaction Mitsui, a Japanese company, bought tanning material in the Soviet Union and delivered it to Argentina in return for plastic products. These Mitsui materials sold in the U.S. for cash.[46] Other examples:

> Hungary agrees to trade electrical equipment defined as worth 500,000 West German deutsche marks [DM] to Egypt in return for cotton that has an open market price of 500,000 DM. The electrical equipment goes to Cairo, and the cotton is prepared for shipment to Budapest. But the Hungarians do not want the cotton, so the foreign trade office sells the cotton to a French company for 450,000 DM. Hungary gets its hard currency, less a 5 percent to 10 percent commission that would be paid to the negotiation specialist.
>
> Greece has accumulated the equivalent of $1 million of credit in Romania through its sales of cotton and fresh oranges, but it has agreed to take Romanian goods—which it does not want—as payment. It asked a bank in Vienna to act as its switcher. The bank offers the equivalent of $700,000 in hard currency for the overvalued Romanian credit position. The Greeks accept the offer and purchase aircraft parts from Boeing in Seattle, something they wanted all along. The switcher finds a customer in Africa who is willing to accept the Romanian canned goods if the price is right. If the switcher has done his job properly, the prices will be acceptable to the Africans, and everyone else will benefit, too.[47]

Clearing Agreement

The objective of the ***clearing agreement*** is to balance the exchange of products over time between two governments without having to transfer funds by using an agreed-on value of trade, tabulated in nonconvertible "clearing account units." The contracting parties establish an exchange ratio of their respective currencies to determine the amount of goods to be traded. Usually, the exchange value is figured in U.S. dollars. An advantage of the clearing agreement is that flexibility is normally provided so that either side may accumulate a limited import/export surplus for the short term. The following example illustrates clearing agreements:

> Morocco and the [former] Soviet Union agree to exchange capital equipment and fresh oranges for a new phosphate plant. Morocco might prefer to buy the equipment elsewhere, but it has little foreign exchange, so it buys from the country that will take oranges in payment rather than hard currency. But Morocco

needs the equipment more than the Soviets need the oranges. At settlement date, Morocco corrects the deficit by either paying the difference in hard currency or hoping the Soviets will enter a new agreement and permit the deficit to be carried over to the next contract.[48]

Buyback Barter

Under ***buyback barter,*** one party's purchase of capital equipment (e.g., plant, process) is paid for through the output made feasible by the capital equipment. For example, a U.S. tire company may sell equipment to establish an auto-tire plant in Egypt and get paid for it through tires manufactured by the Egyptian plant. Similarly,

> Russia is buying phosphates from Occidental Petroleum. In a $20 billion deal, Oxy helped the Soviets build ammonia plants and is buying part of the output.
>
> China awarded a $500 million contract to Italy's Tecnotrade to expand mines and modernize a railroad. Tecnotrade agreed to buy coal for sale abroad.[49]

The barter agreements are really a form of protectionism because making any seller trade goods he or she would not otherwise buy eliminates part of free trade.[50] Countries in the former Soviet bloc have been the chief practitioners of barter. In recent years, they have been joined by OPEC and Third World countries. As a matter of fact, more and more industrialized countries are following the same route to sell such big-ticket items as aircraft.

While Japanese and European companies have adapted themselves to barter, U.S. companies find it hard to absorb such practices. Long accustomed to straight cash deals, they are being dragged very reluctantly into barter agreements. But because rival companies outside the United States are so accustomed to writing barter contracts, more and more U.S. companies are likely to be forced into barter. How barter-type deals can hurt business is illustrated by General Electric's efforts to sell computerized axial tomographic (CAT) scanners for Austria. G.E. lost the deal for CAT scanners for Austrian hospitals after the German competitor, Siemens, agreed to step up production of unrelated electronic goods from an Austrian plant it operates, preserving 4,000 jobs. It is estimated that barter currently accounts for 25 percent to 30 percent of world trade.[51]

Barter has been motivated by the following factors:

1. Manufacturing capacity in the developing countries has increased in the past decades, but their goods do not adequately compete in a free market against the products from industrialized nations. Barter makes it feasible for these countries to sell their goods internationally.
2. Recessionary conditions worldwide have forced companies in industrialized nations to generate business however possible. A company like McDonnell Douglas might agree to sell aircraft, even if it means receiving a less desired payment. For example, back in 1975 Douglas Aircraft sold seven DC-9 jets to Yugoslavia and agreed to help the Yugoslavs sell their products in the United States, products that included hams, transmission towers, iron castings, and rubber bumper guards.
3. The increase in oil prices put a heavy burden on Third World countries.

To alleviate the problem, oil-producing countries in many cases agreed to help these nations by accepting an exchange of manufactures for crude.

4. European nations have found barter to be the only way to expand East-West trade. The economic system of the communist nations rendered them unable to compete in the international markets with countries accustomed to market economies. The barter system provided the former Soviet bloc nations the opportunity to conduct foreign trade.
5. Third World countries prefer barter with foreign companies, particularly for the purchase of big-ticket items, to help reduce their expenditures of hard currency.

Barter trade is a wave of the future. While it tends to complicate overseas sales agreements, U.S. companies may have no choice. Stiff competition from European and Japanese companies, particularly in the case of high-value products, may force U.S. firms into barter deals.[52]

The point can be illustrated by General Electric Company's experience with Romania. G.E.'s recent $142 million agreement to sell electric turbine generators for a Romanian nuclear power plant would be the largest U.S. sale ever to that country. To get the sale, G.E. agreed to buy or market abroad Romanian products valued at up to the entire $142 million cost of the turbines. Moreover, G.E. agreed to provide technology that could eventually enable Romania to compete in G.E.'s own overseas markets. G.E. also helped convince the U.S. Export-Import Bank to grant its biggest-ever loan to Romania, $120 million, and the company pressed private banks to lend Romania as much as $200 million more.[53]

All of these extraordinary efforts (which fall loosely under the term *countertrade*) are necessary to sell products to countries that don't have the cash to pay for them. More and more, G.E. and other U.S. companies are finding out that having a good product isn't enough. Countries with low hard-cash reserves now look as closely at an exporter's countertrade and financing terms as they do at its product. If competitors from Europe and Japan are willing to offer countertrade, the American companies must be, too. After all, barter accounts for over one-third of the world trade and appears to be increasing at a fast pace.[54]

Summary

The United States is the largest exporter in the world. Compared with other nations, however, U.S. exports constitute a small percentage of the GNP. Because the United States alone provided a large and growing market for labor-expensive American manufactured goods, export markets had not held much attraction for U.S. businesses. The situation changed in the 1970s. In particular, the high cost of oil imports made it necessary for the United States to put greater emphasis on exports and to seek a positive trade balance. Moreover, the devaluation of the U.S. dollar and wage increases overseas made U.S. goods competitive worldwide.

The U.S. government has a variety of programs to encourage exports. Through the Export-Import Bank, the government provides low-cost financing for overseas customers to buy American goods. An exporter can establish a foreign sales corporation to save taxes on his or her export earnings. The U.S. Department of Commerce's forty-eight district offices provide export-related information and counseling. The Overseas Private Investment Corporation, a federal government agency, insures U.S. business activity abroad in less-developed countries. Exporters are permitted to join together, without fear of antitrust prosecution, to form export trading companies under the 1982 Export Trading Company Act. Stronger tools to open foreign markets and help U.S. exporters are provided by the Omnibus Trade and Competitiveness Act of 1988.

Although the government supports export growth in principle, many of its programs hinder export growth. For example, the anti-Arab boycott rules require U.S. businesses to forgo Arab contracts that bar Israeli-made goods.

Export markets provide a unique growth opportunity, but competition in these markets is fierce. Businesspersons, therefore, should adopt appropriate marketing strategies to conduct export trade profitably. They should be aware of emerging markets like those of the Third World countries; specialize in the export of technology products, where American business has a lead; adopt private measures (in addition to those available from the U.S. government) to strengthen their competitive position in relation to foreign competitors; and develop an appropriate orientation for managing export business.

Procedurally, exporting requires locating customers, obtaining an export license from the federal government (a validated or a general license); collecting export documents (such as bill of lading, commercial invoice, export packing list, insurance certificate); packing and marketing; shipping abroad; and receiving payment. Various methods of receiving payment include cash in advance, open account, consignment sale, dollar draft, and letter of credit. Of these, the last two are most popular.

The provision of customs-privileged facilities, via the establishment of free-trade zones, is a recent trend that many countries have adopted to encourage and facilitate international trade. The United States government has approved 177 foreign-trade zones in different communities.

The age-old practice of barter is recurring as a new force in international trade, whereby goods are exchanged for goods without money swapping. Initiated by the Soviet bloc, barter has spread to both the Third World and industrialized nations. Currently it accounts for 25–30 percent of world trade. Unaccustomed to noncash dealings, American companies have not been very enthusiastic about barter. Since it is likely to become more important, more and more U.S. corporations could be forced into barter agreements in the future.

Review Questions

1. Traditionally, what reasons explain America's meager interest in the export business?

2. Currently, why is it important for the United States to emphasize exports?
3. How does the Export-Import Bank help in enhancing U.S. exports?
4. Briefly, list the services of the U.S. Department of Commerce that assist exporters.
5. What is a foreign sales corporation? What role does it play in the context of U.S. exports?
6. How does the United States government hinder exports? Give illustrations.
7. What is a bill of lading? What functions does it serve?
8. Illustrate how a letter of credit helps in receiving payment for exports.
9. What is a free-trade zone? How does it help in increasing international trade?
10. Why is barter becoming important? What reasons account for U.S. companies' lack of interest in this activity?

Endnotes

1. Jeffrey A. Tannenbaum, "Weaker Dollar Enriches Some Exporters," *The Wall Street Journal,* October 5, 1988, p. 32.
2. *Business America,* April 22, 1991, p. 6.
3. Richard S. Belous and Andrew W. Wyckoff, "Trade Has Job Winners Too," *Across the Board,* September 1987, pp. 53–55.
4. *See* Subhash C. Jain, *Export Strategy* (Westport, CT: Greenwood Press, Inc., 1989).
5. *See* Michael R. Czinkota and Wesley J. Johnston, "Exporting: Does Sales Volume Make a Difference?" *Journal of International Business Studies,* Spring–Summer 1983, pp. 147–153. *Also see* E. Kaynak and Vinay Kothari, "Export Behavior of Small and Medium-Sized Manufacturers: Some Policy Guidelines for International Marketers," *Management International Review,* June 1984, pp. 61–69.
6. *Time,* October 7, 1985, p. 30.
7. *The Economist,* January 11, 1992, p. 60.
8. Allan T. Demaree, "What Now for the U.S. and Japan," *Fortune,* February 10, 1992, p. 80.
9. "Report Cites Significant Foreign Barriers to U.S. Exports," *Business America,* April 9, 1990, p. 9.
10. Michael R. Sesit, "Foreign Nations Offer Cheap Export Loans, Rile American Firms," *The Wall Street Journal,* September 19, 1985, p. 1.
11. Rob Garverick, "A Guide to Eximbank Programs," *Business America,* November 5, 1990, p. 10.
12. "Forming an FSC in the U.S. Virgin Islands," *Business America,* September 17, 1984, p. 3.
13. B. E. Lee and Donald R. Bloom, "Deficit Reduction Act of 1984: Change in Export Incentives," *Columbia Journal of World Business,* Summer 1985, pp. 63–67.
14. Discussion on U.S. Department of Commerce programs is adapted from "A Directory of Export Services," *Business America,* vol. 112, no. 2 (1991), pp. 8–12.
15. *See* "U.S. and Japan Make Progress on Trade Issues During Presidential Business Development Mission to Far East," *Business America,* January 13, 1992, pp. 13–14.
16. *See* "The Deficit Busters Go After Korea and Taiwan," *Business Week,* October 20, 1988, p. 42. *Also see* Yoon Je Cho, "Some Policy Lessons from the Opening of the Korean Insurance Market," *The World Bank Economic Review,* vol. 2 (1988), pp. 239–254.
17. *See* Joanne Hvala, Anne C. Perry, and Jean J. Boddewyn, "General Electric Trading Company: The Sogoshosha That Wasn't," *Journal of Global Marketing,* vol. 3, no. 4 (1990), pp. 7–32.
18. William Scouton, "Export Trading Companies—A New tool for American Business," *Business America,* October 18, 1982, p. 6.
19. James V. Lacy, "The Export Trading Company Act Is Alive, Healthy, and Promoting U.S. Exports," *Business America,* February 16, 1987, pp. 19–21.

20. Michael R. Czinkota, "The Business Response to the Export Trading Company Act of 1982," *Columbia Journal of World Business,* Fall 1984, pp. 105–111. *Also see* Steve Weiner and Robert Johnson, "Export Trading Firms in U.S. Are Failing to Fulfill Promise," *The Wall Street Journal,* May 24, 1984, p. 1.
21. "America's Frugal New Year," *The Economist,* December 19, 1987, pp. 13–14. *Also see* "The New Trade Act," *Business America,* October 24, 1988, pp. 2–6.
22. *See* Robert S. Greenberger and Jane Mayer, "Reagan, Bowing to Congress, Imposes Economic Sanctions on South Africa," *The Wall Street Journal,* September 10, 1985, p. 16.
23. "The Price of Technology Leaks," *The Wall Street Journal,* May 10, 1985, p. 24.
24. Tim Carrington, "Fight Over India's Bid for Computer Shows Disarray of U.S. Policy," *The Wall Street Journal,* February 24, 1987, p. 1.
25. John Autin, "President's Export Council Advises Administration on Major Trade Issues," *Business America,* January 21, 1985, pp. 24–25.
26. Erwin Dichtl, Hans-Georg Koeglmayr, and Stefan Mueller, "International Orientation as a Precondition for Export Success," *Journal of International Business Studies,* First Quarter 1990, pp. 23–40.
27. *See* Joel Dreyfuss, "How to Beat the Japanese at Home," *Fortune,* August 31, 1987, p. 80. *Also see Fortune,* May 11, 1987, p. 111; *KKC Brief,* October 1987.
28. James E. Austin, *Managing in Developing Countries* (New York: The Free Press, 1990), Chapter 1.
29. "Leap Forward or Sink Back," *Development Forum,* March 1982, p. 3.
30. Patricia Gray, "Asian Computer Firms Invade the U.S. Market," *The Wall Street Journal,* January 10, 1986, p. 1.
31. Michael R. Czinkota, "Assess Commitment and Motives: Identify Stage of Development When Managing Firm's Exports," *Marketing News,* June 26, 1981, p. 10.
32. *See* David A. Ricks, Jeffrey S. Arpan, Andy H. Barnett, and Brian Toyne, "Global Changes and Strategies for Increasing the International Competitiveness of the U.S. Man-Made Fibers Industry," *Columbia Journal of World Business,* Summer 1986, pp. 75–84.
33. *The Financing of Exports and Imports* (New York: Morgan Guaranty Trust Company of New York, 1980), p. 24.
34. U.S. Department of Commerce, *Export Control Regulations* (Washington, D.C.: U.S. Government Printing Office, 1981). *Also see* Robert M. Springs, Jr., "New Export Law on Aid to International Marketers," *Marketing News,* January 3, 1986, p. 10.
35. U.S. Department of Commerce, *Export Control Regulations* (Washington, D.C.: U.S. Government Printing Office, 1981).
36. U.S. Department of Commerce, *A Basic Guide to Exporting* (Washington, D.C.: U.S. Government Printing Office, November 1981), pp. 35–36.
37. T. Bettina Cornwell, "Foreign-Trade Zones in the United States: A Longitudinal Management Perspective," *International Marketing Review,* vol. 6, no. 6 (1989), pp. 42–52.
38. Peter Wright, "International Partnerships and Foreign Trade Zones: Strategies for Small Firms," *The Collegiate Forum,* Spring 1984, p. 4. *Also see* William R. McDaniel and Edgar W. Kossack, "The Financial Benefits to Users of Foreign-Trade Zones," *Columbia Journal of World Business,* Fall 1983, pp. 33–41.
39. Information for this section was obtained from Foreign Trade Zones Board, International Trade Administration, U.S. Department of Commerce, Washington, D.C. *Also see Business America,* January 27, 1992.
40. Ken Slocum, "Foreign-Trade Zones Aid Many Companies, But Stir Up Criticism," *The Wall Street Journal,* September 30, 1987, p. 1.
41. John Widdifield, "U.S. Businesses Still Are Neglecting to Take Advantage of Benefits of Foreign Trade Zones," *Marketing News,* December 23, 1983, p. 7.
42. *See* Jean-Francois Hennart, "Some Empirical Dimensions of Countertrade," *Journal of International Business Studies,* Second Quarter 1990, pp. 243–270.
43. "Better Barter?" *Fortune,* February 18, 1985, p. 105.
44. David B. Yoffie, "Profiting from Countertrade," *Harvard Business Review,* May–June 1984, p. 8. *Also see* "New Restrictions on World Trade," *Business Week,* July 19, 1982, p. 118.

45. Anant R. Negandi and Peter A. Donhowe, "It Is Time to Explore New Global Trade Options," *Journal of Business Strategy,* January–February, 1989, pp. 27–31.
46. Everett A. Martin and Thomas E. Ricks, "Countertrading Grows as Cash-Short Nations Seek Marketing Help," *The Wall Street Journal,* March 13, 1985, p. 29.
47. Robert E. Weigand, "International Trade Without Money," *Harvard Business Review,* November–December 1977, p. 28.
48. Ibid.
49. "New Restrictions on World Trade," *Business Week,* July 19, 1982, p. 118. *Also see* Falko Schuster, "Barter Arrangements with Money: The Modern Form of Compensation Trading," *Columbia Journal of World Business,* Fall 1980, pp. 61–66.
50. *See* Sarkis J. Khoury, "Countertrade: Forms, Motives, Pitfalls, and Negotiation Requisites," *Journal of Business Research,* vol. 12, no. 2 (1984), pp. 257–270; and Yusug A. Choudhry, Mary McGeady, and Ronald Stiff, "An Analysis of Attitudes of U.S. Firms Towards Countertrade," *Columbia Journal of World Business,* Summer 1989, pp. 31–38.
51. "New Restrictions on World Trade," *Business Week,* July 19, 1982, p. 118.
52. Cyndee Miller, "Worldwide Money Crunch Fuels More International Barter," *Marketing News,* March 2, 1992, p. 5.
53. Roger Lowenstein, "U.S. Firms Move to 'Countertrading,'" *The Wall Street Journal,* November 4, 1981, p. 16.
54. "Countertrade Increases Worldwide," *Development Forum,* March 1986, p. 16.

APPENDIX

A Checklist for Export Marketing

Market Potential

Segmentation

1. Are the ultimate consumers American tourists or foreign citizens?
2. Are we tapping the burgeoning middle class in industrialized nations?
3. Are our customers the wealthy elite in the underdeveloped countries?
4. Are our buyers affiliates of our company?

Size of Market

1. How large is the sales potential?
2. What volume could be sold at higher/lower prices?
3. What sales potential do we estimate for the next few years?

Special Opportunities

1. Would differential pricing be noticed—and be objectionable?
2. Do prices abroad fluctuate seasonally?
3. Could some particular price policy foster trust and long-term relations?
4. How does the delivered price relate to other elements of the marketing mix?

Marketing Mix

Individualizing and Adaptation

1. Should our product be modified (simplified or embellished) to increase its suitability for foreign markets?
2. How should we position our product to gain for it the appropriate level of price perception?
3. Could special packing or packaging enhance the value of our product?

4. Would freight, customs duty, and so on be substantially lower for separate components to be assembled abroad?
5. Is assembly abroad less expensive than in the United States?

Reducing the Buyer's Risk

1. Does our price include warranty service?
2. How quickly and assuredly are spare parts available?
3. Might feasibility studies cause our product to be specified?
4. In the country of destination, at what stage of the product life cycle is our offering?

Buyer-Seller Relationship

1. How closely can we estimate what the buyer is willing to pay?
2. What is our reputation for quality and commercial integrity?
3. Have we avoided misunderstandings about measurement units such as "ton" and commercial terms such as "CIF"?
4. Should our quotation include a cushion for later price concessions?

Channel

1. At what point in the distribution process is our price compared with those of competitors?
2. How many middle agents are in the distribution chain, and what functions do they perform?
3. Can we reduce the cost of distribution?

Foreign Market Environment

Degree of Market Control

1. Is the price of our commodity determined through market institutions?
2. How closely do we control the availabilities and prices of our line at the point of final sale?

Foreign Attitudes

1. How important is price in the purchasing decision?
2. Is the prevalent business philosophy "low turnover–big markup"?
3. Are high-priced goods subject to special tariff surcharges?
4. What is the business culture with respect to haggling, price-fixing, and boycotting of price-cutters?
5. Are price deals effective?
6. In what ways are we affected by any foreign laws in margins, prices, price changes, intercompany pricing, and "most favored customer clause"?

Competition

1. In our line, how active is worldwide competition?
2. Are the competitor's quotations valid?

3. Is our price level encouraging foreign imitators?

Some Alternatives

1. What do we learn from foreign competitors' prices about manufacturing opportunities abroad?
2. Have we considered licensing as an alternative to selling?
3. Could multilateral transactions in foreign exchange or foreign merchandise make our product's final price more attractive?

Cost Considerations

Commercial Risks

1. What are the costs and risks of submitting a foreign quotation?
2. Could our exported merchandise be shipped back to the United States and interfere with our domestic marketing?

Incremental Costs

1. Are foreign orders absorbing idle capacity?
2. Are we disposing of excess inventory?
3. Does potential foreign business warrant expansion that captures economies of scale?
4. Are we pricing a product line, a single product, or a one-time opportunity?
5. Have we separated our variable and fixed costs?
6. Do foreign orders require special production changes, extra shifts, or other costly adjustments?
7. What are the differential marketing and administrative costs of selling abroad?
8. What is the total impact of export sales on our costs?
9. How closely does the country of destination enforce its antidumping laws?

Special Risks and Opportunities

1. Have we costed out all possible modes of transportation?
2. Do our costs include insurance on our goods until we receive payment, even if the purchaser insists on insurance coverage?
3. Do our credit terms reflect various risks: (a) commercial, (b) inflation, (c) currency exchange rate, (d) blocking of remittances, (e) expropriation, (f) interest rate fluctuations?
4. Do export sales offer any tax advantages?
5. What is our profitability mix between original equipment and spare parts, or initial order and reorders?

Administrative Considerations

Internal Organization

1. What are our objectives in international business?
2. What are our specific goals with respect to the present quotation?
3. Who (title and location) is authorized to quote a binding price?
4. What intrafirm conflicting interests regarding international marketing must be resolved?
5. Do our affiliates in different countries compete against each other?

Price Policy

1. What is our basic price policy (such as, same FOB factory price to everybody)?
2. What is our stance toward competition—price higher, same, lower, ignored?
3. How flexible are we—to accommodate good customers, meet competition, offset new duties or changes in currency values?
4. How important is foreign business for us?
5. Could our foreign involvement harm our image domestically?

Procedures

1. Have we ensured compliance with applicable U.S. laws?
2. Do we use standard forms for preparing quotations?
3. Do our quotations have a time limit?
4. Do we formally review quotations accepted and rejected?

Intracompany Pricing

1. Is pricing a legal means of repatriating earnings?
2. Are we permitted to avoid foreign customs duties through high prices on raw materials and low prices on finished goods?
3. What is the influence of our intracountry pricing on income taxes in the United States and in the country of destination?
4. Are we quoting "arm's length" prices to our affiliates?

PART • 5 Cases

Case 17: The Kellogg Company

In 1990, Peter A. Horekens, marketing director for Kellogg Company, was faced with the problem of developing a market for ready-to-eat cereals in the Latin American region. Although Kellogg had no competition in the ready-to-eat cereal market in this region, they also had no market. Latin Americans did not eat breakfast as the Americans did. This problem was especially prominent in Brazil. To create a market and increase sales in this region, Horekens had to create a nutritious breakfast habit among the Brazilians.

Company Background

Kellogg Company, headquartered in Battlecreek, Michigan, was founded in 1906 by W. K. Kellogg to "help people help themselves." This focus had remained intact throughout the company's history. The company continued to operate successfully with sales in 1990 amounting to $3,215 million.

Scope of Business

The Kellogg Company manufactured and marketed a wide variety of convenience foods with ready-to-eat cereals topping the list. Other products included frozen and fresh baked pies, toaster pastries, soups, soup bases, seasonings, tea, frozen waffles, dessert mixes, and snack items. The company's products were manufactured in eighteen countries and distributed in 130 countries.

Kellogg subsidiaries included Mrs. Smith's Frozen Foods, Inc., Salada Company, and Fearn International Inc. Mrs. Smith's was a leader in the frozen food industry, and the product line included pies, desserts, entrees, and frozen waffles sold under the Eggo brand. Salada Company sold teas bags and other tea products. Fearn International produced quality food service items marketed under the brand name LeGout. The company also produced products for school service and health care markets. In addition, efforts had been concentrated on expansion into delicatessens and restaurant chains. Kellogg engaged in a variety of supporting activities, including grain milling and carton printing.

Distribution of products was handled through brokers and distributors, as well as through its own sales force. Jobbers—independent and chain store warehouses—made Kellogg products available in retail stores, restaurants, and feeding institutions worldwide. Ready-to-eat cereals were sold principally to the grocery trade for resale to consumers.

Kellogg faced intense competition in each of the consumer food areas in which it was engaged from manufacturers who offered products similar in nature or a variety of alternatives.

Kellogg research and development objectives were designed to generate new and improved products, processing methods, and packaging to keep ahead of the competition. Research and development budgeting allowed for this stress on innovation and new product development. Existing and new products were supported through increased budgets for advertising and promotion. Budgets were also increased to modernize and expand production facilities to meet the increased demand for Kellogg products and to keep costs down.

Kellogg had spent heavily and continued to increase its spending to stay at the top of its primary market—the ready-to-eat cereal market. But competition in the domestic market had led Kellogg to seek new markets. Among these, Latin America was at the top of the list. The primary market within Latin America was Brazil.

International Market

In 1990, Kellogg International operations accounted for 42 percent of Kellogg Company's sales of more than $3 billion. International operations were divided into four segments: Canada, the United Kingdom and Europe, Afro-Australasia, and Latin America. Among the products sold overseas were ready-to-eat cereals, frozen pizzas, drink products, entrees, snacks, desserts, and pharmaceuticals. The ready-to-eat cereal sales made up the majority of international sales.

In most of these foreign markets, Kellogg controlled more than half of the ready-to-eat cereal market. The United Kingdom was by far Kellogg's largest market. Internationally, sales in the ready-to-eat cereal market continued to increase, although in the past few years the competition also had increased. But in Latin America, consumption of ready-to-eat cereals was negligible.

The Latin American Market

The Latin American market, mainly Mexico and Brazil, showed great potential as a Kellogg's ready-to-eat cereal market. The demographics fit the ready-to-eat market; the only problem was Latin Americans did not eat the traditional American-style breakfast.

The Latin American market included a growing number of families with children. The population mix was becoming younger. The developing economy enabled consumers to spend more of their income on food. Kellogg wanted to increase sales in this Latin American region, especially Brazil, but consumers had turned their backs on the American-style breakfast. How was Kellogg to create a nutritious breakfast habit among the Brazilians?

The company asked J. Walter Thompson, Kellogg's advertising agency, to help instill the breakfast habit in Brazil. According to Horekens, "In general, Brazilians do what people in *novelas* do." *Novelas* are Brazilian soap operas. J. Walter Thompson tried to advertise Kellogg ready-to-eat cereal and instill the breakfast habit by advertising within a soap opera. The first experience of advertising within a soap opera failed; the advertisement portrayed a boy eating the cereal out of a package.

Kellogg wanted to teach the Brazilians how to eat a complete, nutritious breakfast, not just Kellogg's cereal. The commercial did not work because it made Kellogg ready-to-eat cereal seem more like a snack than a major part of a complete breakfast. Kellogg wanted to portray ready-to-eat cereal as a part of a complete, well-balanced, nutritious breakfast. Thus, they needed the cereal to be eaten in a bowl with milk along with other foods to make a complete breakfast.

The company believed that the growing population in this region would reinforce the importance of grains as a basic food source. The 1990 population in Brazil was 165 million, which made it the sixth most populated country in the world. The population was estimated to grow to 210 million by 2000. Within this population growth was an increase in the number of women of childbearing age, which further supported Kellogg's potential for a successful cereal market. The structure of the population in Brazil in 1990 was:

- Thirty-seven percent of population under age 15
- Forty-eight percent of population under age 20
- Twelve percent of population over age 50
- Six percent of population over age 60

These figures showed that the population of Brazil better fit the market for a ready-to-eat cereal, with the increasing number of children and elderly people as the two largest cereal-consuming segments.

The "cult of the family" continued to be the most important institution in the formation of the Brazilian society. This cultural ideal was reflected in the ways they conceptualized and evaluated the range of personal and social relations. This seemed to be the way Kellogg would have to demonstrate the importance of a nutritional breakfast—by playing up the family and its importance.

Through the use of the *novelas,* Kellogg made a second attempt to teach the Brazilians the importance of breakfast. Most Brazilian families watched these soap operas, composed mostly of family scenes. In their commercials, Kellogg opted for scenes that showed the family at the breakfast table. One member of the family, usually the father, took the cereal box, poured the cereal, and then added milk. This scene represented a complete "Kellogg" breakfast in a way that Brazilians could relate to. The advertisement focused first on nutrition, then on flavor, and finally on ease of preparation. As a result of this campaign, sales in Brazil increased. Kellogg controlled 99.5 percent of the ready-to-eat cereal market in Brazil; however, per capita cereal production was less than one ounce or several spoonfuls per Brazilian annually, even after advertising.

Although Kellogg controlled the market, there was not much of a market to control. Brazilians had begun to eat breakfast, but Horekens was not sure whether sales would continue to increase.

How can Kellogg further convince the Brazilians of the importance of eating a nutritious breakfast in order to establish a long-term market?

Case 18: Avon Products, S.A. de C.V.

In 1990, Philip Evans, marketing manager in the international division of Avon Products, Inc., met with his colleagues to consider long-range marketing strategy for Latin America, especially Mexico. A decidedly profitable market, Mexico and the rest of Latin America accounted for almost 15 percent of Avon's worldwide sales. The problem confronting Avon executives was how to sustain the growth rate it had generated in the past.

Company Background

Avon Products, Inc., a diversified company, included the Avon Division, Mallinckrodt, Inc., Tiffany & Co., and a direct-mail division.

The Avon division was the world's largest direct-selling business. Its two principal industry segments were the manufacture and sale of cosmetics, fragrances, and toiletries; and of fashion jewelry and accessories. Avon Products, Inc., sales in 1989 amounted to $4 billion, of which over 42 percent were from operations outside the United States. Operating profits from international business in 1989 amounted to about 53 percent. Net sales in 1989 from Latin American operations were $545.6 million. Of the total corporate-wide operating profits of $600 million in 1989, $81.6 million were generated in Latin America.

Avon's international division was formed in 1949 when the company expanded the distribution and salesforce to Canada. By late 1954, the company expanded its operations to include Puerto Rico and Venezuela. During the ensuing years, international operations grew at a rapid pace, first to Europe and Latin America and then to the Far East and Africa.

In Mexico, the company had a wholly owned subsidiary under the name of Avon Products, S.A. de C.V., headquartered in Mexico City. The Mexican subsidiary had three manufacturing laboratories and five distribution branches covering Mexico and the rest of Latin America.

Avon had captured its largest international market share in Latin America, where competition had been less fierce than in other foreign markets. In Mexico, the results had been truly phenomenal, largely because Latin hospitality blended well with the Avon approach. The Latins were much more apt to invite Avon representatives into their homes. Whereas U.S. representatives, on an average in each two-week campaign, won orders from fewer than thirty customers, Mexican representatives, in each three-week campaign, averaged fifty-four customers.

Products

The two principal businesses of Avon Products, S.A. de C.V., were the manufacture and sale of (1) cosmetics, fragrances, and toiletries, and (2) fashion jewelry and accessories. The products were sold directly to customers in their homes by Avon representatives, following the method used since Avon's founding in the United States in 1886. The company sold more than 650 products. Although the range of products sold in foreign countries was not as extensive as that sold in the United States, most of the products were substantially the same as those marketed domestically. The products marketed in Mexico were categorized as follows:

- *Fragrance and bath products for women.* These products consisted of perfumes, colognes, sachets, fragrance candles, pomanders, lotions, soaps, and powders. They were marketed in a number of fragrance lines, each based on a particular scent and packaging theme.
- *Makeup, skin-care, and other products for women.* These products included makeup items such as lipsticks, mascaras, and eye shadows; skin-care products; nail and hand-care items; and hair-care products such as shampoos, conditioners, and brushes.
- *Men's toiletry products.* Men's toiletries included colognes, after-shave lotions, shaving creams, talc, and soaps marketed in a number of fragrance lines, each based on a particular scent and packaging theme.
- *Daily need, children's, and teen products.* Daily need items included deodorants, antiperspirants, oral hygiene products, and household products such as room sprays. Children's and teen products included fragrance products and novelty products for young children.
- *Fashion jewelry and accessories.* The line included rings, earrings, bracelets, and necklaces for women, men, and children. Women's items accounted for most of the sales.

In Mexico, Avon cosmetics were affordable, medium-priced products that appealed to both women at home and the small number of women who worked outside the home.

Avon packaging consisted of glass and chrome bottles and ceramic jars tailored to meet the tastes of its primary market, the vast middle class.

Product Distribution

In Mexico and elsewhere in Latin America, Avon's cosmetics, fragrances, and toiletries were sold by a sizeable salesforce. The salesforce consisted of women known as representatives de Avon (Avon representatives). They served as independent dealers, and not as agents or employees of the company. They purchased products directly from the company and sold them directly to the residents of their communities.

With some exceptions in rural areas, each representative was responsible for one territory. Unlike U.S. sales territories, in Mexico there were 200 homes in an average territory. But like in the United States, Mexican representatives called on homes in their territories, selling primarily through the use of brochures highlighting new products and specially priced items for each three-week sales campaign. Product samples, demonstration products, makeup color charts, and complete sales catalogs were also used. The representatives forwarded orders every three weeks to a distribution center located just outside Mexico City. Each representative's orders were processed and assembled by Avon and delivered to her home using local delivery services.

Over the long term, Avon S.A. had planned for a 10 percent growth in its salesforce—a key determinant in keeping earnings growing at a healthy pace. The company's main method of building a salesforce was to shrink the size of sales territories once an area was covered. This tactic served to intensify sales efforts.

Avon's long-term prospect for recruiting representatives looked particularly bright in Mexico, since neighborhoods were receptive to door-to-door selling. Both personal contacts and local advertising were used to recruit representatives. As a local manager noted:

> Avon's coverage in Mexico was excellent. We were in every small town and village, as well as in the big cities. Sixty-five percent of Mexico's population is under the age of 25. We are a very young people and a very young country. As the younger generation's buying power increases, we will have many opportunities to create new products that are attractive to them.

Product Promotion

Avon directed its sales promotion and sales development activities toward giving direct-selling assistance to its representatives. This was done by making available such aids as product samples and demonstration products, as well as the Avon brochure. Avon sought to motivate its representatives through the use of special prize programs that reward superior sales performance. Periodic sales meetings were conducted by the district manager to which representatives were invited. The meetings were designed to keep representatives alert to the product line changes, to explain sales techniques, and to give recognition to representatives' superior performance. Mexican representatives took particular pride in receiving recognition for sales achievements, and because of that, management favored an increase in promotional activities in developing future strategy.

An additional promotional tool was introduced in Mexico in 1988—a program called "Opportunity Unlimited." Under this program, top-performing representatives, who qualified as group sales leaders, had the opportunity to earn commissions by stimulating sales increases in their groups of representatives. Representatives could continue to earn commissions as group sales leaders as long as they stimulated sales increases. This program anticipated that group sales leaders would increase group sales by such methods as searching for new representatives, training new representatives, and motivating and assisting established representatives. Mexico was a testing ground for "Opportunity Unlimited." If the program proved successful there, the company planned to introduce it in other foreign markets.

Product Manufacture

Avon S.A. manufactured and packaged almost all of its cosmetics, fragrances, and toiletries products. Although most of the Mexican products were based on U.S. products, Avon S.A. developed several of its own fragrances based on Mexican tastes. Packages, consisting of containers and packaging components, were designed by U.S.-based Avon and manufactured in Mexico.

The fashion jewelry line was generally developed by Avon's U.S. staff and manufactured in Puerto Rico and Ireland or by several independent manufacturers in the United States and shipped to the Mexican distribution center.

Mexican Cosmetics Market

The cosmetics market in Mexico was segmented by product and by final user. Men, women, and children used different products. Similarly, Mexicans of Indian heritage required different products than did those of Spanish descent. However, in both the groups, most products were purchased by women. So the focus of the industry was on women between the ages of 18 and 65. On an average, women spent $35 per capita annually on cosmetics for themselves and their families.

As Mexican society become more liberal, it was anticipated that teenagers (16 to 18) would become frequent users of a limited number of cosmetics. Avon had produced a line of cosmetics for U.S. teenagers called "Color Works," which was promoted as "not your mother's makeup." Test marketing was being done with this age group in Mexico to survey the acceptance of the line.

Mexican men, especially in the cities, tended to purchase more colognes and after-shave lotions than their U.S. counterparts. They preferred products with a musky, masculine scent. Avon believed that this segment would continue to grow 10 percent annually throughout the 1990s.

Competition

Avon faced competition from two sources: Max Factor, a U.S. firm with a subsidiary located in Mexico City, and Bella, a Mexican firm also based in Mexico City. Unlike Avon, these companies concentrated their retail distribution through supermarkets, department stores, and pharmacies. Of the two competitors, Bella concerned Avon the most.

Bella manufactured and marketed a full line of products in the medium-level price range. Its highly segmented and differentiated products were aimed at women with either light or dark complexions. Bella sales concentrated in the larger cities, such as Mexico City, Mazatlán, Veracruz, and Oaxaca. The large-city market was estimated to be about $424 million in 1989 and was expected to grow 12 percent annually in coming years.

Promotion was aimed at "La Bella Mujer Mexican"—the beautiful Mexican woman. Focused on ethnic pride, Bella maintained that their line of cosmetics was custom-made for the different complexions of Mexican women. As an attack on Avon's direct selling, Bella incorporated the use of catalog sales. A large number of households were mailed a seasonal catalog displaying the full line of products. Consumers placed their orders with a central distribution center, but the orders were delivered in person by a sales representative, who could then solicit additional orders. In the long run, Avon S.A. saw this as a threat to their door-to-door method.

Issues Confronting Management

Despite its healthy incursion into Mexico, the prospects for long-term growth for Avon, S.A. de C.V., appeared hazy, largely because the company faced a major turning point in the years ahead. Its expansion was derived primarily from its ability to move into, and then saturate, vacant territories in its sales network. As mentioned previously, once a territory was covered, Avon simply divided it into smaller areas and added new representatives to canvas customers on a more concentrated basis.

Such so-called downsizing had been occurring since the late 1950s when Mexican representatives were supposed to cover some 400 to 500 households. Naturally, very few managed to do this, so when the company started reducing the territories to 250 to 300, there was little impact on representatives' earning potential. The impact on the company's earnings, however, was tremendous. This strategy allowed Avon S.A. to more than triple its salesforce over a fifteen-year period.

By 1992, Avon S.A. expected to have completed a planned conversion to 100-home territories in Mexico, from a then current level of 150-home territories. Once this was accomplished, Avon S.A. was unsure about going lower. It became apparent that if Avon S.A. wanted to grow with the population and keep ahead of the rate of inflation, it must find other ways to build sales.

One alternative was to add new lines of products, particularly those that could be tailor-made to the Mexican market. But U.S.-based Avon executives were afraid that these new products would hurt existing products. Evans and his colleagues realized that planning was needed if Avon S.A. was to sustain growth and maintain profits in the future.

Case 19: Chivaly International

In early 1991, Martin Creich, product manager for Chivaly International's urethane foam product division, was considering a recommendation that the firm establish a regional sales office in Singapore. Since marketing its products in Indonesian markets in 1984, Chivaly had captured 10 percent of the urethane foam market. By establishing a sales office in Singapore, Creich could foresee increasing the Indonesian market share for Chivaly's urethane foam to 25 percent and expanding into Malaysian and Thai markets. In addition, a regional sales office would strengthen Chivaly's competitive posture, allowing the firm to conduct sales directly to distributors and commission agents.

Before presenting his recommendations to top management, Creich wanted to compile the necessary information to support his decision.

Chivaly Corporation

Chivaly was a major manufacturer of chemicals, metals, flax-based papers, cellophane, sports equipment, and home building products. Incorporated in South Dakota in 1892, the firm had since established its executive offices in Oklahoma City.

Urethane foam, a part of the chemical division, had been marketed since 1949 and was one of the world's most adaptable products. It was used primarily as cushioning material in chairs, beds, spring mattresses, auto upholstery, and other products that needed foam cushioning. As a result of the product's adaptability, its major chemical component, toluene duso cyanate (TDI), had become one of the world's largest chemical commodities. Chivaly was also a large producer of TDI, supplying the chemical division with adequate proportions of the commodity for urethane foam production.

Urethane foam was produced for the firm's worldwide markets in two plants located in Lake Charles, Louisiana, and in Mansville, West Virginia. Each plant separately produced more than 50,000 tons of urethane foam per year. Production inefficiencies resulted if either plant fell below the standard 50,000-ton level.

From a process standpoint, urethane foam was a difficult chemical to produce. The product's toxic and lethal components made production and process controls vital steps in manufacturing. Orders were shipped directly from each plant to Chivaly's distributors throughout the world.

International Markets

In 1990, approximately 16 percent of Chivaly's $2 billion in sales were derived from international markets. By 2000, the company planned to obtain a significant portion of its sales and profits from its overseas businesses. Management believed that investing substantial sums of capital to establish sales offices around the world would help the firm strengthen its international presence. Chivaly already had established offices in Mexico City, Caracas, Dublin, London, Paris, Frankfurt, Johannesburg, Madrid, Cape Town, and Sydney.

Chivaly's entry into specific foreign markets was a result of thorough market analyses. Specifically, the firm performed market profiles and market attractiveness analyses that considered pertinent factors such as target markets, resource requirements, cultural factors, and personnel requirements. After such basic information had been gathered, corporate representatives then traveled to the targeted countries to meet with regional sales representatives, who helped gather further information based on questionnaires distributed to local contacts. The corporate representatives then used this information to formulate a final area profile with analyses and recommendations, eventually determining which markets were most attractive. This process determined which consumers, commission agents, and distributors were to be used if the market proved profitable.

Indonesian Operations

Chivaly entered the Indonesian market in 1984, selling urethane foam on a freight alongside basis through a Japanese trading company. The trading company, in turn, sold the urethane to local companies in Indonesia. Chivaly's entry into the Indonesian market was haphazard. Initially, the firm knew nothing about the market or how their product was sold. As Chivaly's Indonesian operation grew, the firm established sales representatives in the region, providing a direct link to the market.

The Indonesian market was heavily influenced by corruption. Indonesians expected "royalty payments" in exchange for special treatment and favors. Chivaly representatives, however, had been instructed to refrain from participating in these payments. To avoid this situation, Chivaly sought clients whose executives were American-educated and familiar with Western business procedures.

Indonesia's cultural environment also restricted the way foreign firms could do business. For example, Indonesians preferred to do business with local people; therefore, Chivaly hired a large number of local people as sales representatives.

Chivaly also sold its urethane foam through local distributors. Sales were volume oriented, and long-term business relationships were valued more than short-term profits. Because American companies concentrated on profits, firms would often lose their distributors and commission agents. Asians also refused to wage price wars and, more often than not, refused to sell any product at a price higher than that of their competitors.

Indonesia had few political constraints; however, Chivaly was prohibited from opening regional offices in the country unless a majority of the subsidiary was owned by nationals. Chivaly also was prevented from purchasing and stockpiling urethane foam in local warehouses, which was a major factor in establishing an office in Singapore. As a free-trade zone, Singapore adopted a laissez-faire attitude toward free enterprise.

Chivaly's major Indonesian competitor was the German firm Bayer. Chivaly also competed on a smaller scale with Dow Chemical and BASF. There was little product differentiation among these suppliers. Factors that provided the competitive edge included service, local relationships, and the strength of letters of credit.

Bayer was the largest producer of urethane in the world, while Chivaly ranked second. As the first company to enter the Indonesian urethane foam market, Bayer had captured roughly 45 percent of the Indonesia market, with sales of over 7,500 tons of urethane.

Bayer's German production facilities provided the firm with huge production capacity and economies of scale. The firm used its extensive distribution network to distribute its full line of urethane foam chemical components to Indonesian markets. However, Bayer did not adapt to cultural factors. Sales representatives maintained a strict European attitude in business affairs, which proved a handicap in Indonesia.

There was little advertising in the urethane foam business. Sales were made strictly through sales contacts. Prices were based on open market demand. In 1990, the price for urethane foam components was $1,550 a ton.

Competitors often mislabeled chemicals for shipment to get cheaper freight rates. Because TDI was a Poison B chemical that caused several health hazards, the word *Tylene* was often painted over the TDI label in Indonesia. Tylene was a comparatively harmless chemical and could be shipped at lower freight rates. Chivaly made sure its products were always represented in the correct manner.

By 1990, Chivaly had captured 10 percent of the Indonesian market, but management believed they were underpricing their product. To combat its price problem, Chivaly wanted to achieve two objectives: (1) to sell 4,000 tons of TDI and (2) to increase its urethane foam market share to 25 percent. Management felt that the Singapore office would fulfill these objectives.

Case 20: Connecticut Corporation (Japan)

In late 1988, John Lindstrom, director of marketing for the International Beverage Division of Connecticut Corporation (CC), was faced with deciding what action should be taken to increase the market share for Bleinheau Vodka in Japan. Three strategies were open to him:

1. Increase promotional efforts on behalf of Bleinheau in Japan, and streamline distribution
2. License Suntory, Japan's largest liquor producer, to manufacture, label, and sell Bleinheau in Japan
3. Remove Bleinheau from the Japanese market

Connecticut Corporation entered the market in Japan in 1981 by licensing out Black Velvet Whiskey to the Suntory Company. In this arrangement CC gave Suntory the rights to produce, label, and sell Black Velvet in return for 10 percent of the profits. In 1985, however, CC opened up branch headquarters in Tokyo to export Bleinheau and other CC beverage products, such as Black and White Scotch, Wild Turkey, Club Cocktails, Grand Marnier cognac, and United Vintners wines from the United States and distribute them in Japan.

Because vodka was not yet popular in the Japanese spirit market, Bleinheau had not yet been able to gain the distribution and market share it wanted. Mr. Lindstrom believed that with the increasing popularity of Western-style drinks, vodka would soon gain the acceptance of the Japanese public.

Corporate Background

Connecticut Corporation is a multinational corporation, headquartered in Springfield, Massachusetts. In 1987, the firm's worldwide sales of $1,921,879,000 were divided among three categories. The following table shows the approximate percentage of sales attributed to each:

CATEGORY OF BUSINESS	PERCENTAGE OF SALES
Beverage operations	57%
Food operations	24
International operations	19
Total	100%

Connecticut International was responsible for the overseas manufacture and export, as well as the marketing, of all products sold by CC outside the United States. Those products included the ones that were part of the Food Group, both owned and franchised operations of Southern Fried Chicken, A-1 Steak Sauce, Ortega Taco Sauce and Taco Shells, and the ones that were part of the Beverage Operations, such as Bleinheau Vodka, Yukon Jack Whiskey, Black Velvet Whiskey, Irish Mist Liqueur, Arrow Brand Liquors, Lancer Wines, Inglenook Wines, and Club Cocktails.

Connecticut International's beverage operations were divided into two parts: Connecticut de Brazil, which included only the manufacturing, exporting/importing, and marketing in Brazil, and the Connecticut International Beverage Group, which housed, among others, Connecticut in Japan.

Marketing Environment

A study done by Steven Young, marketing research manager for Connecticut in Japan, showed the following facts about the environment the company faced in Japan:

- The overall spirits market environment in Japan is attractive. Although GNP will grow at a slower rate than it has in the past thirty years, it will outstrip the United States and other major industrialized nations. This should mean substantial discretionary income. This coupled with increased urbanization should contribute to the growth of quality spirits. Besides, the post–World War II population has been drinking more in the Western fashion, suggesting that vodka should gain in popularity.
- Because economic activity is contracting, unemployment is at the highest levels since 1946.
- Competition is strengthening. This is especially true of the domestic competition such as Suntory.
- The percentage of the population in the high and upper-middle income segments has increased.
- The consumer economy is relatively healthy as both disposable income and personal consumption expenditures are attractive relative to other countries. Also, recent trends in household expenditures favor increased consumption of services and nondurable goods at the expense of durable goods.
- Per capita alcoholic beverage consumption continues to increase rapidly along with disposable income, yet is still far from saturation

in comparison with other developed/underdeveloped countries.

- Media costs are the highest in the world and increasing.
- Domestic competitors such as Suntory tend to ignore profitability to achieve market share. This attitude fosters dumping. An example is the market for Scotch, which had a reputation as an expensive, high-quality item. Suntory began dumping, and now Scotch is no longer part of the high-quality market for gift giving and other such occasions for which Scotch traditionally had been used.

In summary, because of the size of its population, its stability, and its track record, Japan represented an attractive, although challenging, market with long-term economic prospects. In keeping with Japan's growth-oriented economy and tradition of following America, it would be reasonable to expect that the alcoholic beverage market, particularly the quality spirits market, would experience continued real growth in the foreseeable future, perhaps at a somewhat slower pace.

Advertising and Promotion

Whereas United States laws prohibited the advertising of hard liquor on television, it was not so in Japan. Therefore, a large part of Connecticut's advertising for Bleinheau in Japan was done through television and cinema media. Other forms of advertising media used by Connecticut Japan included posters and billboards, which showed different drinks that could be made with Connecticut products (including Bleinheau) and explained how to make them. In addition, the company provided various freestanding point-of-purchase displays for use in distribution centers where liquor was sold.

The copy used in all advertising centered around the idea of Bleinheau having "world popularity," especially of being "big in the United States," because anything considered popular in the United States has great appeal to the Japanese, especially the younger generation.

In addition to advertising, there were several types of promotion for Bleinheau.

1. Merchandise giveaways were directed at the dealers who supplied the bars and other types of wholesalers.
2. Bleinheau was directed to the general public through "Bleinheau Nights" in local night clubs and bars. On these nights, Bleinheau offered discounts on all drinks made with Bleinheau vodka. The company also had giveaways such as T-shirts and glasses with "Bleinheau" printed on them.
3. Tie-ins with other products were used. A tie-in was done with Canada Dry. In areas where Canada Dry had a strong market share, consumers could buy a six-pack of Canada Dry and get a bottle of Bleinheau at a very low price. In markets where Bleinheau held a strong position, the purchase of a bottle of Bleinheau entitled the consumer to a free bottle of Canada Dry.

Distribution

The distribution system in Japan was much different from that in the United States. To distribute their products in Japan, Connecticut had to work through a complicated multitiered distribution system. This system had been in a gradual state of change for years because overlapping and the sheer size of the distribution system had resulted in a profit squeeze, with some middle levels being forced to accept lower margins and even being bypassed in some cases. This trend was expected to continue in the 1990s.

Connecticut at that time had approximately 20 percent distribution in Japan. This had been achieved through five major wholesalers and seventeen secondary wholesalers. The problem lay in the fact that, while wholesalers were ultimately credited for every sale, they aggressively sold only their proprietary brands.

Competition

Connecticut's competition came not only from other rivals in the vodka market, but from all spirits marketers. For example, Scotch whiskey was very popular in Japan, holding over 75 percent of the spirits market through 1987. Vodka, on the other hand, had not yet become a popular drink in Japan.

In both the spirits market as a whole and the vodka market by itself, Connecticut's major competition came from the Suntory Company. In the vodka market, Nikka was Connecticut's second-biggest competitor.

Suntory Company

Suntory was the largest producer and seller of domestic spirits in Japan, as well as a major importer of whiskey into Japan. Suntory held the number one position in national whiskies and had entries in all the spirits categories. Further, Suntory held the number one position in vodka with a 57 percent market share (mostly through licensing from companies outside Japan). Suntory's strategy, however, was not aimed at this market, but instead at putting all its resources into maintaining its market share in whiskey.

Nikka

Nikka provided the only other strong competition in the vodka market in Japan, with an 18 percent market share. Assuming the anticipated activity in white spirits materialized, Nikka was expected to be second in market share in the domestic field, behind Suntory.

Other Brands

Of the remaining 25 percent of the market, Connecticut's Bleinheau held 8 percent and the other 17 percent belonged to several domestic and imported brands.

Japanese Consumer

Alcoholic beverage consumption was well accepted in Japan, but usage, penetration, and frequency (especially in regard to wine) were still low. For example, the Japanese rarely drank during the day. Central to this was the increased consumption of Western spirits occasioned by Westernization after World War II. Just as with products, traditions, and fashion, what was popular in the United States often was very attractive to the Japanese. Examples included blue jeans, golf, and tennis. The popularity of Westernized bars and nightclubs also was increasing. The incidence of alcoholic beverage consumption ("drank last week") was increasing among women but stable among men, as the following table shows:

DRINKING POPULATION

	1979	1981	1983	1985	1987
Male	26.8%	25.2%	26.5%	26.2%	25.8%
Female	8.0	9.0	10.5	11.5	11.8
Total	34.8%	34.2%	37.0%	37.7%	37.6%

Except for a few imported brands, the Japanese had little brand familiarity and/or loyalty with respect to alcoholic beverages. The Japanese consumer, however, was responsive to advertising and its creation of "in-ness," as shown with the growth of gin in 1981–1982 when it was heavily advertised and its subsequent deterioration when advertising support was pulled. The trendsetters in Japan were a small group of the post–World War II generation who were the most traveled, best educated, and affluent. The following table summarizes trends in liquor consumption in Japan:

TRENDS IN SERVED MARKET IN JAPAN (IN THOUSANDS OF CASES)

	1980	1987	1994†
Scotch whiskey	199	2,719	4,792
Vodka	25	43	320
Cognac	56	237	651
Others*	198	377	1,251
Total served market	478	3,376	7,014

*Including gin, rum, tequila, bourbon, and Canadian whiskey.
†Projected

Case 21: Ozark Glass Company

Ozark Glass, a division of Ozark-Mercantile, Inc., is a manufacturer of colored sheet glass located in a medium-size city in the Southwest. The company was founded in 1974 by Dr. Steven Connors and originally operated as an antique shop specializing in merry-go-round horses. The objective of the firm was simply to provide a hobby for Dr. Connors and his wife, Arlene.

By 1976, the company had expanded into a stained glass studio teaching interested consumers the hobby of stained glass. At this time, a stained glass artist joined the firm as a partner. The company then started to actively pursue the profitable do-it-yourself market. Classes were started to teach hobbyists how to work with stained glass. The classes increased the public's knowledge of uses for stained glass. One of the students became particularly interested in opening a store in Tulsa, Oklahoma, patterned after Ozark Glass. Thus, the concept of franchising stained glass products was developed. Six additional stores were soon opened.

The rapid expansion of the company led to an inability to purchase enough glass to satisfy the demands of the franchise stores. When the firm was unable to reach an agreement with its current supplier to open an additional facility under a joint agreement, Ozark Glass started its own 16,700 square foot manufacturing facility in April 1978.

The plant is one of only 15 stained glass manufacturing facilities in the United States. The plant employs 62 people and has a capacity to produce 250,000 pounds of glass a month. Since opening the plant, Ozark Glass has grown to the third-largest producer of stained glass in this country.

The plant is equipped with five furnaces that produce a product line consisting of 150 colors of glass. The product lines include three types of transparent glass: "Cathedral"—a single colored glass; "Streaky"—a glass containing two or more colors mixed together; and "Wispy"—glass that is streaked with white glass. In addition, the company produces two types of glass that transmit little or no image: "Semilescent"—glass that light transmits well through; and "Opalescent"—a dense glass that transmits light in reduced amounts.

The case is printed with the permission of the authors, C. P. Rao and James DeConinck of the University of Arkansas.

Growth Strategy

The company has experienced impressive growth since opening its manufacturing facility in 1978. In that year, total sales were $30,000, all domestically generated. By 1981, total sales had expanded to slightly more than $2 million and in 1985 total sales topped the $3 million level. Of particular importance has been the growth of the export market. Since 1979, export sales have shown a five-fold increase from $198,000 to slightly less than $1 million in 1985. The export market has accounted for approximately 35 percent of sales since 1981 (see Exhibit 1).

The Export Market

Ozark Glass company's exporting began when the company received inquiries from overseas readers of advertisements placed in U.S. trade publications. Although the company's advertising was not specifically directed at overseas readers, management aggressively pursued these inquiries by, first, sending a letter to each inquiry and, second, by phoning each prospect. The transoceanic phone call was especially impressive to the prospects.

These inquiries led to the company's first international sales to an Australian firm, Yencken Sandy Glass Industries, in December 1978. After a visit to Ozark Glass company's manufacturing facility, the Australian firm purchased $20,000 of merchandise.

EXHIBIT 1 Ozark Glass Company Gross Sales for the Period 1978–1985

YEAR	GROSS SALES	DOMESTIC SALES	EXPORT SALES
1978	$ 30,000	$ 30,000	None
1979	1,413,978	1,215,556	198,422
1980	1,859,668	1,364,431	495,237
1981	2,090,000	1,448,365	641,635
1982	2,324,080	1,508,328	815,752
1983	2,565,784	1,683,155	882,629
1984	2,824,928	1,844,678	980,250
1985	3,180,869	2,058,023	1,122,846

The Australian firm invited the president of Ozark Glass to Australia to conduct a series of seminars to six retail stores handling glass supplies on how to market and display stained glass. The seminars led to orders being placed from each of the six stores.

Ozark Glass was able to enter the New Zealand market after Yencken Sandy Glass Industries sold glass products to several New Zealand firms. Inquiries were soon received from these firms in New Zealand. Following a strategy similar to the one employed in Australia, a representative of Ozark Glass made a personal visit to explain how to display glass products and set up instructional classes to generate interest among hobbyists in working with stained glass. Despite intense competition from European manufacturers, Ozark Glass became the largest seller of stained glass in both Australia and New Zealand.

The success of Ozark Glass was attributable to a willingness to compete against European stained glass firms. Since the art of manufacturing stained glass had originated in Europe, many people in Australia and New England believed European glass was superior. This had caused American manufacturers to avoid competing in this market. Ozark Glass was able to successfully sell in this market because of its personal sales visits to potential clients and its willingness to assist customers in all aspects of the stained glass business. In addition, the use of a telex machine allowed the firm to communicate with international clients.

During 1980, the firm started to receive a small number of orders from Japan. These Japanese firms had also become familiar with Ozark Glass company's product line through advertisements in U.S. trade publications. The firm pursued these leads through the use of the telephone. Although some problems resulted because of the language barrier, the company concluded the Japanese firms did not understand what stained glass was but purchased the product because it was considered "Western."

The company contacted the Japanese firm from whom they had received orders, and requested permission to conduct a lecture on the uses of stained glass. Most of the stores agreed to allow Ozark Glass to visit their stores. An interpreter was provided by each store. Additional prospects were obtained from the U.S. Commerce Department.

The lectures enabled the company to convert many small clients into large customers and to also gain new prospects for future sales. The success in the Japanese market reinforced to the company the value of personal visits to increase sales.

Although both the Japanese and Korean markets appeared profitable, Ozark Glass lost both markets to a West Coast competitor whose cost was 79 cents per square foot compared to 90 cents per square foot for Ozark Glass. No effort was made to compete directly with the competitor. A once promising market was simply abandoned.

Perhaps Ozark Glass was willing to abandon the Far Eastern market because of increased activity in Europe. Even while the Far Eastern market had been expanding, the company had become interested in pursuing the difficult but lucrative European market. The company viewed the European market as attractive because of the lack of competition from other American firms. In addition, Ozark Glass was targeting the hobby market and anticipated no direct competition from European glass manufacturers. The difficulty in competing against European manufacturers was because of a perceived notion on the part of European customers about the inferiority of American glass.

In an effort to pursue the European market, Ozark Glass contacted the European office of the State Industrial Commission. The commission provided the company with a list of potential customers. The company aggressively pursued these leads through the use of telephone calls and letter writing. As anticipated, the pursuit of the European market was a difficult process because of the perceived superiority of European glass. As a way of convincing Europeans of the quality of American glass, the company adopted the following slogan, "European Quality From the Heart of America." Although penetrating the European market was difficult, Ozark Glass eventually obtained a German distributor for its glass products. The German client placed five orders for stained glass over the next eighteen months. Today, this company is Ozark Glass's largest customer in Europe. The success in Europe was considered a coup for the company since it was believed in industry circles that an American firm could not successfully compete in Europe.

The success in Europe was attributable to a difference in European glass, which is similar to window glass, compared to the glass sold by Ozark Glass, which is stained glass. This is important because Ozark Glass is targeting the stained glass hobby market and thus has no direct competitor in Europe.

The firm's success in exporting earned it a Presidential "E" award in 1981 (see Exhibit 2). This award is given to firms that have shown excellence in acquiring international sales. The award further enhanced the company's belief in its motto of "people sell people."

Export Marketing Strategy

Ozark Glass has relied on informality in developing its export marketing strategy. From an organizational structure perspective, both domestic and international sales are the responsibility of the national sales manager. This individual reports to the vice president of the company who in turn reports to the president. All three individuals have responsibility in developing plans for the overseas markets. The company has adopted a policy of flexibility instead of establishing a formal set of export objectives.

Export Objectives

In the early 1980s, Ozark Glass pursued the export market as the primary means of generating continued growth. The reason for this decision was that the company encountered few U.S. competitors in overseas markets. In fact, no other domestic manufacturer had international sales exceeding 5 percent of their gross sales. Because of the lack of European or American competition in the European market and the past success in international markets, Ozark Glass has high expectations for continued growth abroad.

Product Strategy

The company offers three sheet sizes of glass—10″ × 10″, 21″ × 25″, and 25″ × 42″—for both domestic and international clients. The

EXHIBIT 2 Firm Wins Exporting Award

Ozark Glass company's growth in export sales has earned the firm a Presidential "E" award from the U.S. Department of Commerce.

The award was presented to Dr. Steven Connors, president of Ozark Glass, and Ron Miller, vice president and general manager.

Ozark Glass rolls about 2.9 million pounds of stained glasses annually from its plant. One-third of its annual production is shipped to Germany, Switzerland, Italy, Scandinavia, Australia, New Zealand, Japan, Taiwan, Korea, South America, Mexico, and Canada.

The plant supplies twenty-seven Ozark glass retail franchises, a number of foreign and domestic retail customers, and four foreign manufacturers of ready-made Tiffany-style lamps and lighting fixtures.

United States hobbyists make up the fastest-growing market, according to Miller. These are about 500,000 do-it-yourself glass craft workers, and per capita spending on their hobby averages $200 a year.

Most stained glass stores offer classes in glass techniques. Ozark Glass stores also sell works by accomplished students on consignment. "We are especially proud of our shipment to Europe. We were told there was no market there since stained glass originated in Europe," said Miller.

Other advice that Europeans consider stainded glass a trade and would not be receptive to it as a craft was also mistaken, said Miller. The agent for Ozark Glass in Germany is succeeding in a market historically dominated by European glassmakers.

The Australian market, however, is primarily made up of professional stained glass workers, possibly because of the strong British influence of trade unions and apprenticeships.

Ozark Glass has opened a franchise in Osaka, Japan, and is considering a second store in Japan, where the stained glass hobby is catching on rapidly.

"The Japanese do very meticulous, exacting work. They tend to try difficult projects and they relish going to school. Typically, a Japanese student attends classes at least twice a year. Most U.S. students go six weeks to learn the two basic techniques, lead and copper foil," said Miller.

The factory produces 150 colors and combinations of glass. Cathedral glass is the transparent jewel tones. Opalescent is a milky, translucent glass. Streakies combine cathedral and opalescent glasses. Ozark Glass is one of the few makers of irridescent glass, which has a light-reflecting surface.

Last July, Connors brought in English glass engineer Michael Chambers as a technical consultant. Chambers is a graduate of Sheffield University, a leading school for glassmaking.

His expertise has meant "tremendous differences in the quality of our production and cost efficiency," said Miller.

Chambers's father and brother have applied for immigration permits, and their arrival will allow Ozark Glass to begin production of antique glass, now exclusively manufactured in Europe.

Molten stained glass is rolled into flat sheets, while antique glass is first blown into a cylinder. The process requires cutting away the top and bottom of the cylinder, slitting the sides, then reheating the piece and flattening it.

The result is a heavy, transparent glass containing irregular bubbles. Antique glass is used mainly in doors and such furniture pieces as china cabinets.

Ozark Glass began as an antique shop by Connors's wife, Arlene, in 1974. Mrs. Connors studied stained glass techniques in order to restore antique glass pieces she offered in the shop.

When she branched into stained glass classes, the Connors' found that materials were often scarce and shipments delayed.

They opened the office-warehouse factory complex in 1978 and launched their first four franchises by 1979. Mrs. Connors now designs windows and trains new franchises. She is assisted by Miller's wife, Penny, who also manages the local store.

Ozark Glass has now become the fourth-largest stained glass manufacturer in the U.S. It is one of the youngest and smallest firms to receive the presidental citation for exporting.

Selected by the U.S. Department of Commerce, award-winning firms must achieve export sales growth equal to or exceeding their domestic sales growth.

company does not offer special metric measurements for the international market.

Because of the perceived superiority of European glass, Ozark Glass places special emphasis on manufacturing a high-quality product. As mentioned earlier, Ozark Glass has adopted a slogan to emphasize the quality of its products when selling overseas—"European Quality From the Heart of America."

An important characteristic of high-quality stained glass is the ease with which it can be cut. According to industry experts. Ozark Glass products are among the industry's softest.

Promotion Strategy

Ozark Glass spends almost no money conducting market research and only about one percent of sales on advertising. Demographics or economic indicators are not used as part of management's strategy to obtain potential clientele. Instead the company relies on inquiries from advertisements in various trade publications followed by a personal visit from a management representative to generate sales abroad.

The company believes that the best way to generate long-term growth in international markets is to develop a strong franchise network. The company currently has three international franchises and anticipates opening two additional franchises in London and Mexico City.

The company has also been generating sales through exhibits at international trade shows in Germany, England, Mexico, Puerto Rico, and South America. In the past, trade shows have generated several small orders and new contacts. The company plans to increase participation at trade shows with special emphasis being placed on penetrating the South American market.

Pricing Policy

Ozark Glass follows a cost-plus pricing strategy. Two different price lists are used—one for franchise outlets and the other for wholesale accounts (see Exhibit 3). Both price lists contain seven levels of pricing ranging from the lowest-priced items (A) to the highest-priced items (G). The franchise price list contains prices that are 5 percent to 100 percent higher than the wholesale price list depending on the size of the order. Because of the higher profit margin on franchise sales, the company is actively attempting to expand its franchise network. Although franchise outlets generally are subjected to higher costs, no minimum order is required. In addition, on orders of $1,000 or more, franchise pricing is similar to the wholesale price list. For example, the following volume discounts are allowed:

GLASS WEIGHT	DISCOUNT
150 Pounds	15%
200 Pounds	20%
500 Pounds	33%
1,000 Pounds	33% and no freight charges

A minimum order of 1,000 pounds is required to qualify for the wholesale price list.

Ozark Glass prices its products by the pound. This has created a problem in both domestic and international markets. For example, several competitors price by the square foot and a conversion factor must be used when submitting quotes. By dividing the square foot price by 1.5, a comparison can be made to pound prices as quoted by Ozark Glass and prices by the square foot as quoted by many of the company's competitors. A similar problem exists when negotiating prices with an international account where pounds must be converted to square meters. The company has adopted a similar conversion equation to alleviate this problem.

Foreign Exchange Rates

Export sales have suffered during the past several years because of the strength of the dollar. Ozark Glass company's competitive pricing strategy advantage in Europe has been reduced. The company has had to cut its profit margin to maintain a slight pricing advantage over European competitors.

The fluctuating exchange rates have forced management to pay greater attention to day-to-day rates. For example, sales to Germany are evaluated on a daily basis. The company allows an additional 3 percent discount if the trading rate of the German mark is 2.7 times greater than the dollar.

The company employs no systematic strategy in evaluating the international market regarding currency fluctuations. The firm does not employ a finance specialist to aid in rate forecasting or engage in advance negotiations regarding fluctuating exchange rates when marketing to overseas accounts.

The company is anticipating greater international sales with the recent decline in the value of the dollar. Ozark Glass believes that with the decrease in the value of the dollar, international sales and profits should both increase. The firm is especially optimistic concerning sales to Europe.

Manufacturing Philosophy

All of the company's products are produced in one manufacturing facility. Sales are currently not exceeding the capacity of the facility although the plant does have room for increased expansion if it becomes necessary. Management does not anticipate the need for an additional manufacturing facility in the near future.

Although having only one manufacturing facility has some cost disadvantages when supplying certain markets, management believes that maintaining one facility allows it to maintain greater quality control over the product line. The company has achieved success in large part because of the quality of its glass in comparison with that of other manufacturers. Because of this, the company is reluctant to enter into any joint ventures or licensing agreements as a way of expansion.

The company's present location also allows for an abundant supply of sand, the most important raw material in the production of stained glass. The region also provides Ozark Glass with inexpensive natural gas to operate its glass furnaces, allowing the company to sell its products to European accounts at a price below those of European competitors.

Distribution Channels

A telex and long distance WATS lines are the primary means of conducting sales internationally. The company does employ sales agents in Germany and Canada to assist in direct sales to these two countries. The sales agents are used because many potential clients are unfamiliar with the use of stained glass and other related products. Management attributes the unfamiliarity with stained glass products to immaturity of the market. As the market matures, management anticipates the continued use of sales agents to generate business in remote areas.

A freight forwarder is employed to handle transportation of products to international accounts. The forwarder is responsible for coordinating both sea and land carriers and for handling all necessary paperwork, such as obtaining permits and authenticating bills of lading.

EXHIBIT 3 Ozark Glass Wholesale Price List

	PRICE PER POUND						
Price Code	A	B	C	D	E	F	G
Full Sheets	$1.80	1.89	2.15	2.33	2.60	2.55	3.30
Half Sheets	2.20	2.30	2.60	2.80	3.35	3.10	3.90
10 by 10's	2.79	2.92	3.33	3.60	4.20	3.95	5.10

Case 22: Hindustan Paper Corporation

In November 1972 an Indian company, Hindustan Paper Corporation (HPC), approached the Swedish company, Defibrator AB, and asked for an offer on a pulp mill. The offer was sent in March 1974. During this time a number of contacts were made between the parties to understand what the buyer really wanted, and the offer was revised a couple of times. After the offer several meetings were held between the project group from Defibrator and HPC. HPC received a number of offers but invited only Defibrator for face-to-face negotiations. These negotiations started in June 1976, lasted for two weeks, and ended in a deadlock. The parties could not agree on most of the issues that were under conflict right from the beginning.

The Seller

In 1931 Dr. Arne Asplund invented the defibrator process, a method for pulping wood and other lignocellulose materials. It can continuously defibrate the material mechanically. If the raw material is preimpregnated with a suitable cooking liquor before the mechanical defibration, the method can be adapted to several conventional chemical pulping processes.

Defibrator supplied its first plant in 1936. Within ten years Defibrator had emerged as a world leader in the pulp industry and by the time of this project had supplied to more than fifty countries.

Defibrator is considered an innovator and world leader in its field, and it has a certain goodwill in the market. The firm has, however, no monopolistic position and there are a number of competitors in the market; two of them submitted their offers for this project.

Whenever Defibrator submits an offer, it has a number of objectives:

- To obtain the order at the best possible price
- To obtain the order on such terms and conditions that it will not cause problems afterward (in case of guarantees and period)
- Not to damage their already established reputation by any act in a particular project
- To obtain the order to recover the expenses incurred on the offer.

India is a big market and this was Defibrator's first project in the country. The company therefore hoped that after this project it would capture the market in and around India. HPC gave the impression that it intended to buy a number of such projects in due course.

A number of subcontractors were involved in Sweden. Defibrator had permanent contracts with them, and these subcontractors were accustomed to work for Defibrator in all projects. However, it had to gather the prices and time requirements for the delivery from them before making an offer.

All negotiations, both technical and commercial, are carried out by the head office in Sweden. Defibrator organized a negotiating team led by a senior sales engineer and also including an attorney. A project group had already been organized within Defibrator that was responsible for the whole project. This group included the technical manager, the R&D manager, the laboratory manager, and the sales manager as chief of the group. The sales manager was the final authority and it was he who nominated the negotiating team.

When selecting the team members, it was customary to nominate individuals who had had some experience negotiating with the same or a similar buyer. In this case, no individual had experience negotiating with the same or another buyer from India but the negotiating team leader had some experience negotiating with buyers from other developing countries.

Defibrator had all the experience and re-

This case is printed with the permission of the author, Pervez N. Ghauri of the Oslo Business School.

sources for such projects, and also the skills and resources to organize an effective negotiating team. In the case of negotiation skills Defibrator had an advantage. They could organize a team of individuals who had experience negotiating such large deals. As regards resources available to the negotiating team, Defibrator's team had all the power and authority to negotiate and compromise on the issues of the contract. They did not have any deadline or target to meet.

Defibrator is an independent firm and works without any restrictions from the Swedish government. It has, however, some restrictions for such sales, particularly in cases where credit is given by a Swedish firm.

The Buyer

The buyer had a number of objectives. HPC was planning to expand rapidly in paper and pulp. It was thus keenly interested in acquiring the most suitable technology in the field.

HPC is a state-owned corporation, and the decisions about the project were made in the Parliament. HPC had to follow the rules of the government in its own interest as it was responsible to the government for all its decisions.

It was decided by the Parliament to purchase this project at any price, to overcome the acute shortage of paper in the country and to save foreign exchange, as at that time most paper was imported. The board of directors of Hindustan Paper Corporation was asked to negotiate for the project. All negotiations, compromises, and the agreement itself had to be approved by the government of India. The government has determined a policy (terms and conditions for purchase of such projects) that was followed in this case. Certain foreign exchange restrictions are in force and all purchases from abroad must be approved by the Department of Finance.

There was no nomination or selection of a team for negotiation or for the project, as it was the policy of the Indian government for the board of directors of HPC to assume responsibility for all negotiation and to deal with other matters regarding the project. The board of directors consisted of a chairman, project leader (general manager/technical services), two senior project officers (pulp), general manager (establishment), financial adviser, financial controller, deputy controller (purchases), purchase officer, and coordinator.

HPC had some experience negotiating with European firms, having recently concluded a contract with a German firm. Two members of the board of directors (which acted as the negotiating team) had studied in Europe (one of them in Scandinavia), so according to their own perception they had enough experience in dealing with foreign firms and some knowledge of the environment of the seller.

The HPC negotiating team had, however, limited powers and authority to negotiate and compromise on all the issues. The board of directors acted as the negotiating team but for major issues had to obtain the approval of the Department of Industries.

The parties had never done business with each other, nor with any other party in each other's country. There are many differences in the traditions of trade and in the social environment of the two countries. The parties were thus unfamiliar with each other's environment and ways of doing business.

The Indian government applied to West Germany for a government loan to finance the project. One of the conditions for this loan was that the project must be evaluated by a reputable foreign consultant. Sandwell & Co. from the United States was selected.

Defibrator had an agent in India who assisted in obtaining some information about the buyer and its environment and who served as a middleman between the parties in the early stages of the project.

The Project

HPC contacted Defibrator in November 1972 and asked for an offer for the pulp mill. The offer was sent in March 1974. One of the main reasons for this delay was that in the beginning Defibrator was not sure of the seriousness of the buyer. It did not have any knowledge of the buyer and its environment, which made it difficult for Defibrator to submit an offer.

Before making an offer Defibrator asked the buyer for a meeting, and HPC's technical staff visited Sweden a couple of times. The technical staff from Defibrator had discussions with the Indian visitors. A number of contacts were also made through correspondence and through Defibrator's agent in India.

In all these meetings and correspondence mainly technical issues were discussed. HPC had, however, hinted that it wanted to pay cash and that there would not be any problem with the foreign exchange restrictions of the government of India.

The offer was sent in March 1974. Two competitors of Defibrator also submitted offers for the same project. One of the engineers from Defibrator took the offer with him to India where he met the board of directors of HPC and discussed the details of the offer with the engineers. By this time some of the board members of HPC had traveled around the world and studied the technology properly. They examined the preliminary offers of all the vendors, including Defibrator. They prepared a report in which they rejected the offer from the local vendor and recommended Defibrator's machinery very strongly.

At Defibrator's end, several meetings were held among the project group. At these meetings the objectives of the buyer and the forthcoming tests were discussed, and the cost and price calculations, service responsibilities, and guarantees were worked out.

Another rough offer was prepared and submitted by Defibrator, but it was not accepted by HPC. Informal negotiations continued until April 1976, and took about two years. Several meetings were held. It was mostly the technical staff from both sides plus HPC's consultants and Defibrator's agent in India who attended these meetings. The technical issues were the prime subject of discussion at this stage.

HPC handed over a copy of the terms and conditions of the Indian government for purchase of such projects, which helped Defibrator to formulate its strategy for the negotiation. HPC also sent a copy of a contract draft it had concluded with a German firm for another package deal. This copy of the contract also conveyed a picture of the strategy of HPC and of the Indian government. Defibrator realized the strong financial position of HPC after some meetings and through the terms and conditions supplied. The terms of payment stated by HPC were much more favorable for Defibrator than those it demanded in its first offer.

It was during this period that Defibrator discovered that HPC's engineers and consultants preferred its technology.

After informal negotiations, HPC and its consultants prepared another report in which they strongly emphasized that Defibrator's machines were the only ones suitable for the project. A number of internal meetings were held at HPC and it was decided to enhance the capacity of the plant. All three vendors were asked to submit their final offers according to increased capacity.

After the informal meetings in April 1976, Defibrator started working on the final offer. The final offer was sent to HPC in May 1976. The parties knew that this was the final offer and would serve as a base for the contract; thus, almost all the issues were considered at this stage.

Defibrator learned of the report of the HPC's engineers and consultants in which they strongly recommended its machines. The results of laboratory tests were also very positive. All these things gave Defibrator a sense of power over HPC. The latter, on the other hand, knew that the machines of Defibrator were the most suitable ones and was inclined to cooperate with Defibrator. In other words, HPC realized that it was in some way dependent on Defibrator.

After receiving the offer from Defibrator, HPC started scrutinizing it with the help of its consultant. The board of directors of HPC was to act as its negotiating team, but they had to follow the already determined terms and conditions of the government. Their only function was to see how and on which issues Defibrator's offer and contract draft differed from the policy of the government. In other words, they did not try to perceive the strategy of the seller.

Defibrator, on the other hand, tried to formulate a strategy. With the help of HPC's conditions and a copy of the contract (supplied by HPC), Defibrator worked out a contract draft. This draft was sent to HPC with the demand that it should be accepted as an agenda for the forthcoming negotiations..

A negotiating team had been nominated at Defibrator with a senior sales engineer as the leader. The leader had some experience negotiating such deals with less-developed countries. The attorney of the company was included in the team to assist in the contract formulation and other legal matters.

HPC's team had to follow the policy of the government. In the words of their negotiating team leader, "We have clear and definite terms and conditions and policy for such purchases and we had to follow them, so there was no strategy formulation or changes thereto for this particular project." Furthermore, he continued, "we did not try to get knowledge about Defibrator's negotiating strategy as we knew enough of its technology and no other information was considered necessary."

Face-to-Face Negotiations

HPC, after having received and studied the final offer, invited Defibrator for formal negotiations in June 1976. The invitation was accepted by Defibrator and its negotiating team visited India. The parties to negotiation were: Defibrator, the board of directors of HPC, Sandwell & Co. (HPC's consultant), and Defibrator's agent in India. Defibrator's contract draft, already sent, was discussed but not accepted. The draft was discussed paragraph by paragraph and there was disagreement on most of the issues. There were many arguments on the wording of the contract.

Whenever a conflict arose, the session was interrupted and the parties retired to their chambers and worked separately. At the next meeting they submitted the proposals or wordings for the disputed paragraphs. The parties, however, failed to compromise on any of the disputed issues, and Defibrator was asked again and again to amend its contract draft if it was to serve as an agenda for the negotiations.

The session lasted for two weeks and a number of meetings were held. The following issues were under conflict right from the beginning, and could not be agreed upon:

Governing Law of the Contract. HPC demanded that Indian law regulate the contract as mentioned in the policy of the government. Defibrator's contract draft demanded that the contract be governed by the law of Switzerland. According to Defibrator, "We could not accept law that we do not understand. In case of any dispute later on, one must be able to save one's interest, and arrange for an attorney who understands the particular law."

Technical Documents. HPC in its terms and conditions demanded: "Technical details, drawings, etc., supplied by the vendor shall be the property of the purchaser and the vendor shall keep all such information, drawings, and design confidential. All such information supplied to vendor by purchaser will also be the property of the purchaser." Defibrator, in its contract draft, demanded: "All such drawings and specifications will be the property of the purchaser and the vendor shall keep them confidential. The purchaser will also keep them confidential and these documents and drawings will be used by the purchaser solely for the purpose of the equipment being sold."

Sales Conditions. HPC showed its inability to depart from the terms and conditions of the government while Defibrator demanded that the sales conditions prepared by the United Nations Economic Commission for Europe be followed.

Arbitration. HPC demanded that all disputes and differences should be referred for arbitration in accordance with provisions of the Arbitration

Act of 1940 in India. Defibrator demanded that arbitration should be settled in Zurich under the rules of the International Chamber of Commerce.

Bank Guarantee. One of the clauses in Defibrator's contract draft demanded that the purchaser would provide, simultaneously with advance payment, a bank guarantee from a first-class Indian bank or from the Indian Ministry of Finance, satisfactory to the Swedish Export Credit Guarantee Board, covering 90 percent of the contract price. During the negotiation HPC showed its inability to arrange the bank guarantee, and argued that with such terms of payment, they had never heard of such a bank guarantee. The negotiating team of Defibrator consulted the head office by telephone, but the clause could not be compromised. The head office told the team leader that they would look into the matter and could not give a decision at once.

Price of Training. In its preliminary offer Defibrator agreed to give training to HPC's engineers free of charge, but in the final offer a price was demanded for the training and HPC refused to accept this clause. It demanded that training should be given free of charge to three operation and three maintenance engineers.

Price. HPC demanded a 7 percent discount on the project price, but the issue was not thoroughly discussed.

In the opinion of Defibrator's team leader, "One of the most obvious reasons for the failure of this session was that the buyer seemed to have no or very little experience with contracts and negotiating such big deals." HPC held other views: "Many of the board members were not available and some of the records were not handy at the time. These things created too many difficulties to have any worthwhile discussions with the vendor."

Case 23: Sperry/MacLennan

In August of 1988 Mitch Brooks, a junior partner and director of Sperry/MacLennan (S/M), a Dartmouth, Nova Scotia, architectural practice specializing in recreational facilities, is in the process of developing a plan to export his company's services. He intends to present the plan to the other directors at their meeting the first week of October. The regional market for architectural services is showing some signs of slowing and S/M realizes that it must seek new markets. As Sheila Sperry, the office manager and one of the directors, said at their last meeting: "You have to go wider than your own backyard. After all, you can only build so many pools in your own backyard."

This case has been prepared by Mary R. Brooks of Dalhousie University as a basis for classroom discussion rather than to illustrate effective or ineffective handling of an administrative situation, and is printed here with her permission. The author gratefully acknowledges the support of the Secretary of State, Canadian Studies Program, in developing the case.

About the Company

Drew Sperry, one of the two senior partners in Sperry/MacLennan, founded the company in 1972 as a one-man architectural practice. After graduating from the Nova Scotia Technical College (now the Technical University of Nova Scotia) in 1966, Sperry worked for six years for Robert J. Flinn before deciding that it was time to start his own company. By then he had cultivated a loyal clientele and a reputation as a good design architect and planner. In the first year, the business was supported part-time by a contract with the Province of Prince Edward Island Department of Tourism to undertake parks planning and the design of parks facilities from park furniture to interpretive centers. At the end of its first year, the company was incorporated as H. Drew Sperry and Associates; by then Sperry had added three junior architects, a draftsman, and a secretary. One of those architects was John MacLennan, who would later become a senior partner in Sperry/MacLennan.

Throughout the 1970s, the practice grew rapidly as the local economy expanded, even though the market for architectural services was competitive. The architectural program at the Nova Scotia Technical College (TUNS) was graduating more architects wishing to stay in the Maritimes than could be readily absorbed. But that was not the only reason why competition was stiff; there was a perception among businesspeople and local government personnel that, if you wanted the best, you had to get it from Toronto or New York. The company's greatest challenge throughout this period was persuading the local authorities that they did not have to go to Central Canada for first-class architectural expertise.

With the baby boom generation entering the housing market, more than enough business came their way to enable Sperry's to develop a thriving architectural practice, and by 1979 the company had grown to fifteen employees and had established branch offices in Charlottetown and Fredericton. These branch offices had been established to provide a local market presence and meet licensing requirements during their aggressive growth period. The one in Charlottetown operated under the name of Allison & Sperry Associates, with Jim Allison as the partner, while in Fredericton, partner Peter Fellows was in charge.

But the growth could not last. The early 1980s was not an easy time for the industry and many architectural firms found themselves unable to stay in business through a very slow period in 1981–1982. For Sperry/MacLennan, it meant a severe reduction in staff and it also marked the end of the branch offices. Financially stretched and with work winding down on a multipurpose civic sports facility, the Dartmouth Sportsplex, the company was asked to enter a design competition for an aquatics center in Saint John, New Brunswick. It was a situation where they had to win or close their doors. The company laid off all but the three remaining partners, Drew, Sheila Sperry, and John MacLennan. However, one draftsman and the secretary refused to leave, working without pay for several months in the belief that the company would win; their faith in the firm is still appreciated today.

Their persistence and faith were rewarded. In 1983 Sperry won the competition for the aquatics facility for the Canada Games to be held in Saint John. The clients in Saint John wanted to build a new aquatic center that would house the Canada Games competition *and* provide a community facility that was self-supporting after the games were over. The facility needed to project a forward-thinking image to the world and act as a linchpin in the downtown revitalization plan. Therefore, it was paramount that the facility adhere to all technical competition requirements and that the design include renovation details for its conversion to a community facility sporting a new Sperry design element, the "indoor beach." The Saint John Canada Games Society decided to use Sperry for the contract and were very pleased with the building, the more so since the building won two design awards in 1985, the Facility of Merit Award for its "outstanding design" from *Athletics Business* and the Canadian Parks and Recreation facility of Excellence Award. Sperry had gained national recognition for its sports facility expertise and its reputation as a good design firm specializing in sports facilities was secured.

From the beginning, the company found recreational facilities work to be fun and exciting. To quote Sheila Sperry, this type of client "wants you to be innovative and new. It's a dream for an architect because it gives him an opportunity to use all the shapes and colors and natural light.

It's a very exciting medium to work in." So they decided to focus their promotional efforts to get more of this type of work and consolidate their "pool designer" image by associating with Creative Aquatics on an exclusive basis in 1984. Creative Aquatics provided aquatics programming and technical operations expertise (materials, systems, water treatment, safety, and so on) to complement the design and planning skills at Sperry.

The construction industry rebounded in 1984; declining interest rates ushered in a mini building boom that kept everyone busy for the 1984–1987 period. Jim Reardon joined the company in 1983 and quickly acquired the experience and knowledge that would ease the company through its inevitable expansion. John MacLennan, by then a senior shareholder in the firm, wanted to develop a base in the large Ontario market and establish an office in Toronto. Jim Reardon was able to take over John's activities with very little difficulty as he had been working very closely with John in the recreational facilities aspect of the business. Reardon became a junior partner in 1986.

With John MacLennan's move to Toronto in 1985, the company changed its name to Sperry/MacLennan in hopes that the name could be used for both offices. But the Ontario Association of Architects ruled that the name could not include "Sperry" because Drew Sperry was not an Ontario resident, and the Toronto office was required to operate under the name of MacLennan Architects. The Ontario office gradually became self-supporting and the company successfully entered a new growth phase.

Mitch Brooks joined the practice in 1987. He had graduated from TUNS in 1975 and had been one of the small number in his class to try and make a go of it in Halifax. The decision to add Brooks as a partner, albeit a junior one, stemmed from their compatibility. Brooks was a good production architect and work under his supervision came in on budget and on time, a factor compatible with the Sperry/MacLennan emphasis on customer service. The company's fee revenue amounted to approximately $1.2 million in the 1987 fiscal year; however, salaries are a major business expense and profits after taxes (but before employee bonuses) accounted for only 4.5 percent of revenue.

Now it is late August, and with the weather cooling Mitch Brooks reflects on his newest task, planning for the coming winter's activities. The company's reputation in the Canadian sports facility market is secure. The company has completed or has in construction five sports complexes in the Maritimes and five in Ontario, and three more facilities are in design. The awards have followed and, just this morning, Drew was notified of their latest achievement—the company has won the $10,000 *Canadian Architect* Grand Award for the Grand River Aquatics and Community Center near Kitchener, Ontario. This award is a particularly prestigious one as it is given by fellow architects in recognition of design excellence. Last week Sheila Sperry received word that the Amherst, Nova Scotia, YM-YWCA won the American National Swimming Pool and Spa Gold Medal for pool design against French and Mexican finalists, giving them international recognition. Mitch Brooks is looking forward to the task ahead. The partners anticipate a slight slowdown in late 1988 and economists are predicting a recession for 1989. With nineteen employees to keep busy and a competitor on the west coast, they decided this morning that it is time to consider exporting their hard-won expertise.

The Architecture Industry

In order to practice architecture in Canada, an architect must graduate from an accredited school and serve a period of apprenticeship with a licensed architect, during which time he or she must experience all facets of the practice. At the end of this period, the would-be architect must pass an examination similar to that required of U.S. architects.

Architects are licensed provincially and these

licenses are not readily transferable from province to province. Various levels of reciprocity are in existence. For this reason, joint ventures are not that uncommon in the business. In order to "cross" provincial boundaries, architecture firms in one province often enter into a joint venture arrangement with a local company. For example, the well-known design firm of Arthur Erickson of Vancouver/Toronto often engages in joint ventures with local production architects, as was the case for their design of the new Sir James Dunn Law Library on the campus of Dalhousie University in Halifax.

In the U.S., Canadian architects are well-respected. The primary difficulty in working in the U.S. has been founded in immigration policies, which limit the movement of staff and provide difficulties in securing contracts. These policies will be eliminated with the Free Trade Agreement and the reciprocity accord signed between the American Institute of Architects and the Royal Architectural Institute of Canada, a voluntary group representing the provincial associations.

As architects in Nova Scotia are ethically prohibited from advertising their services, an architect's best advertisement is a good project, well done and well received. The provincial association (Nova Scotia Association of Architects [NSAA]) will supply potential clients with basic information about licensed firms, their area of specialization, and so on. NSAA guidelines limit marketing to announcements of new partners, presentations to targeted potential clients, advertisements of a business card size with "business card" information, and participation in media events.

The provincial association also provides a minimum schedule of fees, although many clients view this as the maximum they should pay. Although architects would like to think that the client chooses to do business with them because they like their past work, the price of the service is often the decision point. Some developers prefer to buy services on a basis other than the published fee schedule, such as a lump-sum amount or a per square foot price. Although fee cutting is not encouraged by the professional organization, it is a factor in winning business, particularly when interest rates are high and construction slow.

As the "product" of an architecture firm is the service of designing a building, the marketing of the "product" centers on the architect's experience with a particular building type. Therefore, it is imperative that the architect convince the client that he has the necessary experience and capability to undertake the project and complete it satisfactorily. S/M has found with its large projects that the amount of time spent meeting with the client requires some local presence, although the design need not be done locally.

The process of marketing architectural services is one of marketing ideas. Therefore, it is imperative that the architect and the client have the same objectives and ultimately the same vision. Although that vision may be constrained by the client's budget, part of the marketing process is one of communicating with the client to ensure these common objectives exist.

Architects get business in a number of ways. "Walk-in" business is negligible and most of S/M's contracts are a result of one of the following five processes:

1. By referral from a satisfied client.
2. A juried design competition will be announced. (S/M has found that these prestigious jobs, even though they offer "runners-up" partial compensation, are not worth entering except to *win* as costs are too high and the compensation offered other entrants too low. Second place is the same as last place. The Dartmouth Sportsplex and the Saint John Aquatic Center were both design competition wins.)
3. A client will publish a "Call for Proposals" or a "Call for Expressions of Interest" as the start of a formal selection process. (S/M rates these opportunities; unless they have a 75 percent chance of winning the contract, they view the effort as not worth the risk.)

4. A potential client invites a limited number of architectural firms to submit their qualifications as the start of a formal selection process. (S/M has a prepared qualification package that it can customize for a particular client.)
5. S/M hears of a potential building and contacts the client, presenting its qualifications.

The fourth and fifth processes are most common in buildings done for institutions and large corporations. As the primary buyers of sports facilities tend to be municipalities or educational institutions, this is the way S/M acquires a substantial share of its work. While juried competitions are not that common, the publicity possible from success in landing this work is important to S/M. The company has found that its success in securing a contract is often dependent on the client's criteria and the current state of the local market, with no particular pattern evident for a specific building type.

After the architect signs the contract, there will be a number of meetings with the client as the concept evolves and the drawings and specifications develop. On a large sports facility project, the hours of contact can run into the hundreds. Depending on the type of project, client meetings may be held weekly or every two weeks; during the development of working drawings and specifications for a complex building, meetings may be as often as once a day. Therefore, continuing client contact is as much a part of the service sold as the drawings, specifications, and site supervision and, in fact, may be the key factor in repeat business.

Developers in Nova Scotia are often not loyal buyers, changing architects with every major project or two. Despite this, architects are inclined to think the buyer's loyalty is greater than it really is. Therefore, S/M scrutinizes buyers carefully, interested in those that can pay for a premium product. S/M's philosophy is to provide "quality products with quality service for quality clients," and thus produce facilities that will reflect well on the company.

The Opportunity

In 1987 the Department of External Affairs and the Royal Architectural Institute of Canada commissioned a study of exporting opportunities for architects on the assumption that free trade in architectural services would be possible under the Free Trade Agreement. The report, entitled *Precision, Planning, and Perseverance: Exporting Architectural Services to the United States,* identified eight market niches for Canadian architects in the U.S., one of which was educational facilities, in particular post-secondary institutions.

This niche, identified by Brooks as most likely to match S/M's capabilities, is controlled by state governments and private organizations. Universities are known not to be particularly loyal to local firms and so present a potential market to be developed. The study reported that "post-secondary institutions require design and management competence, whatever the source" (p. 39). Athletic facilities were identified as a possible niche for architects with mixed-use facility experience. Finally, the study concluded that "there is an enormous backlog of capital maintenance and new building requirements facing most higher education institutions" (p. 38).

In addition to the above factors, the study indicated others Brooks felt were of importance:

1. The U.S. has 30 percent fewer architectural firms per capita than Canada.
2. The market shares many Canadian values and work practices.
3. The population shift away from the Northeast to the Sunbelt is beginning to reverse.
4. Americans are demanding better buildings.

Although Brooks knows that Canadian firms have always had a good reputation internationally for the quality of their buildings, he is concerned that American firms are well ahead of Canadian ones in their use of CADD (computer-assisted design and drafting) for everything from conceptual design to facility management. S/M, despite best intentions, has been unable to get

CADD off the ground but is in the process of applying to the Atlantic Canada Opportunities Agency for financial assistance in switching over to CADD.

Finally, the study cautions that "joint ventures with a U.S. architectural firm may be required but the facility managers network of the APPA [Association of Physical Plant Administrators of Universities and Colleges] should also be actively pursued" (p. 41).

Under free trade, architects will be able to freely engage in trade in services. Architects will be able to travel to the U.S. and set up an architectural practice without having to become qualified under the American Institute of Architects; as long as they are members of their respective provincial associations and have passed provincial licensing exams and apprenticeship requirements, they will be able to travel and work in the U.S., and import staff as required.

Where to Start?

In a meeting in Halifax in January 1988, the Department of External Affairs had indicated that trade to the U.S. in architectural services was going to be one positive benefit of the Free Trade Agreement to come into force in January 1989. As a response, S/M has targeted New England for their expansion, because of its geographical proximity to S/M's home base in the Halifax/Dartmouth area, and also because of its population density and similar climatic conditions. However, with all the hype about free trade and the current focus on the U.S., Brooks is quite concerned that the company might be overlooking some other very lucrative markets for his company's expertise. As part of his October presentation to the board, he wants to identify and evaluate other possible markets for S/M's services. Other parts of the U.S., or the affluent countries of Europe where recreational facilities are regularly patronized and design is taken seriously, might provide a better export market, given their string of design successes at home and the international recognition afforded by the Amherst facility design award. Brooks feels that designing two sports facilities a year in a new market would be an acceptable goal.

As part of searching for leads, Brooks notes that the APPA charges $575 for a membership, which provides access to their membership list once a year. But this is only one source of leads. And of course there is the U.S. Department of Commerce Bureau of the Census as another source of information for him to tap. He wonders what other sources are possible.

S/M looks to have a very good opportunity in the New England market with all of its small universities and colleges. After a decade of cutbacks on spending, corporate donations and alumni support for U.S. universities has never been so strong, and many campuses have sports facilities that are outdated and have been poorly maintained. But Mitch Brooks is not sure that the New England market is the best. After all, a seminar on exporting that he attended last week indicated that the most geographically close market, or even the most psychically close one, may not be the best choice for long-run profit maximization and/or market share.

Case 24: El Norte Chemicals, Ltd.

*J*uan Cavasantes, assistant to the director of countertrade and Latin American specialist for El Norte Chemicals, collected his notes and headed for the boardroom. The El Norte board of directors was waiting to evaluate his proposal that El Norte Chemicals should swap various chemical products for wine from the country of

This case is printed here with the permission of the author, David K. Smith, Jr., of Michigan State University.

Bocotania. Cavasantes believed that the board should approve his proposal and hoped that the directors would agree to the proposed transaction quickly, so that he could import at least a few containers of Bocotanian wine in time for the upcoming Christmas and New Year's holidays.

The Company

El Norte Chemicals, Ltd. (hence, ENC), is a Delaware corporation formed in 1902. The company manufactures plastics, organic and inorganic chemicals, pharmaceuticals, and other specialty products including polymeric materials and fabricated products of various sorts. A substantial portion of ENC's business consists of high volume/low markup (and low value added) chemical products. Raw materials used by ENC to produce its products are as indicated in Table 1. In general, availability of these raw materials (feedstocks) has not been a problem.

Up until the Second World War, ENC was a atively small firm doing business primarily in the United States. After the war, however, the company expanded vigorously into petrochemicals. As indicated in Table 2, the average growth in ENC revenues associated with the move into petrochemicals was substantial.

In the 1970s, the growth rate realized over the previous two decades was no longer sustainable on petrochemicals alone. Consequently, ENC spent considerable time and effort working to identify new growth opportunities. Ultimately, a decision was made to shift from a primarily domestic focus to the solicitation of business on a global basis.

ENC's decision to adopt a global focus was accompanied by considerable soul-searching as to the corporate structure that would best support the new global focus. Ultimately, the centralized decision-making structure and culture that had evolved over the first seventy years of ENC's existence was scrapped. In its place, a decentralized structure based on relatively autonomous geographic regions was adopted. Figure 1 gives an overview of the struc-

TABLE 1 Major Feedstocks Utilized by ENC Chemicals, Inc.

Liquified petroleum gas
Naphtha
Natural gas
Benzene
Crude oil
Ammonia
Coal
Limestone
Salt
Styrene
Ethylene
Acrylonitrile
Octane
Propylene oxide
Cellulose
Butadiene
Aniline
Toluene diamine

TABLE 2 Growth in ENC Revenues over the Period 1950–81

YEAR	REVENUES (MILLION $U.S.)	YEAR	REVENUES (MILLION $U.S.)
1950	102	1966	425
1951	120	1967	450
1952	130	1968	455
1953	145	1969	460
1954	160	1970	465
1955	180	1971	475
1956	200	1972	495
1957	220	1973	554
1958	230	1974	620
1959	260	1975	690
1960	280	1976	770
1961	305	1977	860
1962	330	1978	970
1963	370	1979	1064
1964	395	1980	1225
1965	410	1981	1395

(a.) Pre-1970s Organizational Structure of ELN Chemicals, Inc.

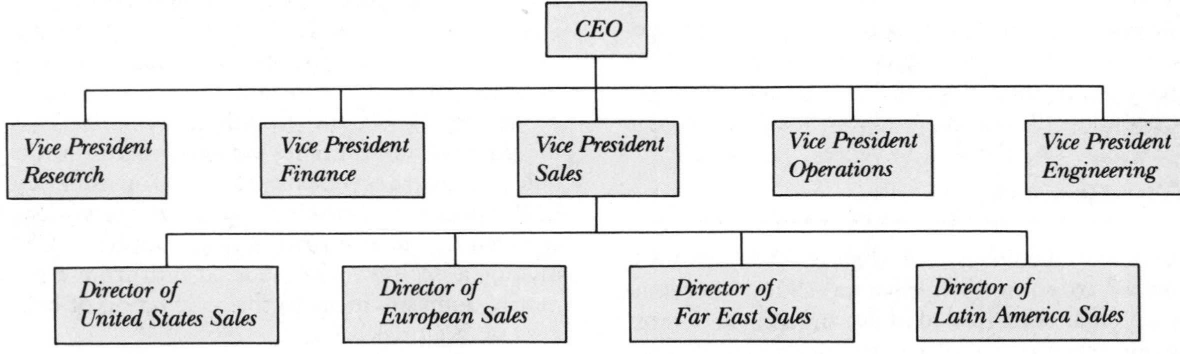

(b.) Post-1970s Organizational Structure of ELN Chemicals, Inc.

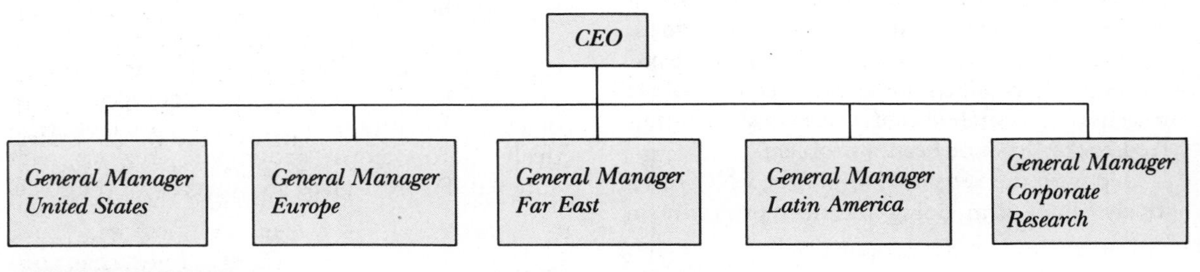

FIGURE 1 Evolution of ENC Chemicals, Inc., Organizational Structure

ture in existence at the time the decision to "go global" was made as well as the new decentralized structure.

Results associated with the decision to become a global supplier of chemical products were impressive. As Table 2 indicates, the growth in revenues during the 1970s not only matched but, in fact, exceeded the results produced during the years when growth had been petrochemical-induced.

While the growth in revenues during the decade of the 1970s was acceptable to management, ENC's profitability over this period was very erratic. Consequently, ENC's management began looking for ways to reduce the large oscillations in corporate profits and return on investment (ROI). Ultimately, management decided that ENC's heavy dependence on the sale of commodity and basic chemicals would be reduced by focusing corporate attention and resources on the development of specialty chemicals businesses.[1] Since the early 1980s, nearly all ENC's capital expenditures have been dedicated to the strengthening of ENC's specialty chemical businesses.

[1]The definitions ENC uses for commodity, basic, and specialty chemicals are as follows: commodity chemicals: chemicals that are not differentiable from those of competitors; basic chemicals: chemicals that can be differentiated from those of competitors because of the addition of services and/or technical capabilities; specialty chemicals: chemicals that offer characteristics that differentiate them from competing products.

Bocotania

Bocotania, located in South America, is approximately 1.2 million square kilometers—about one-sixth the size of the United States. Part of the country is very desolate, part is very mountainous, and part is covered by jungle vegetation. Total population is about 19 million people, many of whom are descendants of the Spaniards who conquered Bocotania in the 16th century. In addition, however, a large percentage of the population is composed of descendants of the Indians who controlled the area before the arrival of the Spaniards.

Bocotania has been richly endowed with a number of natural resources including silver, gold, and a variety of other nonferrous metals. Thus, a substantial portion of the Bocotanian economy is devoted to the mining, refining, and fabricating of nonferrous metal products of various sorts. Bocotania has a number of other natural resources as well, including timber and petroleum. In addition, the climate and soil conditions are conducive to the production of agricultural products such as sugar, cotton, coffee, fruits (including plums, apricots, peaches, grapes, and mangoes), vegetables (asparagus, broccoli, bell peppers), and spices (oregano).

Much of the political and economic life (as much as 90 percent of Bocotanian business ventures) has been and continues to be controlled by a small number of very powerful families of European heritage. Unfortunately, the Indians, with their very different languages and culture, have not been well integrated into the Bocotanian economy. Levels of literacy and education for Indians are substantially lower than for Bocotanians of European descent. Furthermore, it is very uncommon for Bocotanians of Indian descent to be promoted to positions of power and influence. As a consequence, the history of working conditions in factories and mines is very bad, and the dominant theme of union/management relationships for many years has been conflict rather than cooperation. More recently, the tensions and bitterness generated by the disenfranchisement of the large Indian population by the oligopolistic ruling families has manifested itself in the emergence of a violent guerrilla movement against the government and the status quo. Over the last five years, numerous mayors and other government officials living in rural areas have been murdered. To date, however, terrorism against business managers has not been a major problem.

ENC'S Involvement in Bocotania

ENC had entered the Bocotanian market in the late 1960s, during the waning days of the post-war petrochemical boom. At that time, ENC had discovered that relatively small and remote locations far from the intensely competitive triad markets of Europe, Japan, and the United States represented attractive pockets of business at above-average margins. Over the ensuing years, the company's involvement in Bocotania grew steadily, until at one point ENC's fully staffed office (that is, managers for most functions including traffic, credit, treasury, marketing and sales, etc.) was generating about $16 million of sales per year, all to local companies manufacturing for local consumption, and all at margins 10 percent higher than the 20 percent ENC was able to achieve at that time in the triad markets of Europe, Japan, and the United States. Products supplied by ENC to these local producers included low- and high-density polyethylene (for plastic bags), polystyrene (for disposable cups), ABS (for the plastic housing on electrical appliances), industrial chemicals such as caustic soda (used by paper and soap manufacturers), and agricultural chemicals (fungicides, insecticides).

While the decade of the 1970s had been good for Bocotania and for ENC's operations there, the decade of the 1980s was a disaster. With expectations buoyed by high prices for a number of their mineral products, Bocotanian managers borrowed heavily during the 1970s to expand and/or upgrade their mining and processing operations. Unfortunately, other producers worldwide reacted the same way, so when new facilities started operations early in the 1980s, world prices for nearly all of Bocotania's raw material-related products fell dramatically.

The initial effect of the decline in global resource prices was limited to the natural resource sector of the Bocotanian economy. Sales by ENC of floculants and other chemicals used in the mining industry decreased considerably during the early to mid-1980s. Over time, however, as resource-related companies declared bankruptcy and workers lost their jobs, the effect on the Bocotanian economy broadened. Manufacturers of a wide range of consumer and industrial goods began to suffer, too, as it became more and more difficult for Bocotanian buyers (individual and industrial) to acquire the funds necessary to purchase anything but the most basic necessities. Ultimately even companies manufacturing basic consumer goods began to suffer sales declines. Thus, ENC's sales of the plastics used for bags, cups, and a variety of other consumer products began to evaporate. For many people, purchases in 1988 were limited to bread, milk, and other essentials of existence. Demand for nonessential consumer goods had virtually disappeared, and the economy was shrinking. Of those ENC customers, both consumer and industrial goods companies, that were still in business, many were laying off staff or in the process of shutting down completely.

Enter ENC's Countertrade Unit

Early in 1989, with ENC revenues in Bocotania plunging, ENC's managing director in Bocotania asked Mike Jones, director of ENC Global Trading, to review this situation. Specifically, the managing director asked Jones to analyze the situation in Bocotania and to make recommendations as to how the Global Countertrade unit could help Bocotanian customers continue purchasing ENC chemicals, given the deteriorating economic environment in Bocotania.

In February of 1989, Jones and Cavasantes flew to Bocotania to review the situation. While their trip confirmed the dismal situation faced by most Bocotanian companies manufacturing for local consumption, it also uncovered a few bright spots in the economic picture. For example, some Bocotanian companies manufacturing primarily for export were actually doing quite well. This was especially true for producers and fabricators of copper. As indicated in Table 3, prices of copper have recovered from their mid-1980s low and are currently at historic highs. Jones and Cavasantes also found that export-oriented companies taking advantage of Bocotania's relatively low labor costs to export labor-intensive manufactured goods using locally available inputs could compete quite effectively in world markets. However, their review of ENC's customers confirmed the fact that few of these customers had any experience marketing in the international marketplace.

During their stay in Bocotania, Jones and Cavasantes spent a considerable amount of time talking with ENC customers. One evening, a manufacturer of plastic bags and disposable cups for local consumption who had until recently been one of ENC's largest customers commented that his family also ran a winery. This customer went on to say that he would be eager to buy considerable quantities of polyethylene and polystyrene for his plastics factory operations if ENC

TABLE 3 Nine-Year Trend in Copper Prices (price per pound)

Year	Price
1989	1.38
1988	1.01
1987	0.84
1986	0.63
1985	0.62
1984	0.65
1983	0.78
1982	0.67
1981	0.78

would accept wine as payment for these chemicals. When asked about the quality of the family wine, their customer smiled and asked if they had enjoyed the red and white wine that had been served earlier in the evening. As it happened, both Jones and Cavasantes had remarked earlier (and positively) on the quality of the wine they had been served, particularly the red.

The last night of their trip, Jones and Cavasantes reviewed the alternative business opportunities they had uncovered for ENC Global Countertrade during their trip. To qualify as an "opportunity," proposals had to involve products that met two criteria: (1) substantial quantities of consistent-quality products appeared to be available in Bocotania; and (2) informal discussions with bankers and/or government officials suggested that the Bocotanian government would be willing to allow an item to be countertraded. Products meeting these two criteria included nonferrous metallic compounds of various sorts, rare earths used by paint manufacturers to control the drying times for various sorts of paints, suits and/or other textile products sewn in Bocotania for export markets, and a couple of different vegetable products including asparagus and broccoli. Of these, Jones and Cavasantes knew that while ENC itself used moderate amounts of nonferrous metallic compounds, ENC had experienced problems with various nondomestic sources of these products and that, subsequently, ENC purchasing agents preferred to work with domestic sources. They also knew that paint dryers would require extensive testing and certification procedures to assure buyers that the properties of paints incorporating these rare earths would be those desired, that development of large, assured sources of supply of vegetables would be a multiyear challenge, and that development of substantial suppliers of high and consistent quality suits would take considerable time. Thus, their initial predisposition as they examined the proposals brought to them was to focus their attention and energies on wine. Jones urged Cavasantes to place the wine opportunity at the top of their priority list, and to follow up on it as soon as they returned to the States.

Because of the importance of the quality issue, Cavasantes' first step following their return to the U.S. was to deliver several bottles of their customer's wine to a testing agency. As indicated in Table 4 the tests confirmed the initial reactions of Jones and Cavasantes, which had been that both red and white were quite acceptable but that the red was more impressive.

Given an assurance of acceptable quality, Cavasantes turned next to consider the issue of distribution. His first move was to call a broker of brandy he knew in Houston, to learn a bit about the distribution of alcoholic beverages. Next, he went to his local liquor store to discover the names of the importers of the wines that were for sale there. He discovered that while many

TABLE 4 Evaluation of 1987 Vintage White and Red Wines from Bocotania

EVALUATIVE DIMENSION	SCORES Red	White
Empirical Evaluations		
color	+	=
sugar content	+	+
viscosity	+	−
Subjective Assessments		
aroma (nose)	+	+
body	+	=
mouth persistence	+	+
overall taste assessment	+	=
Other Issues		
bottle	+	=
label	+	+
residue	+	+
Summary Assessment Score	+	=

Note: Tests were conducted using as benchmarks a Yugoslavian red wine and a Czechoslovakian white wine that are well established and accepted in the United States. + indicates that the tested wine was evaluated more favorably than the benchmark wine, = indicates that the tested wine was evaluated as equal to the benchmark wine, and − indicates that the tested wine was evaluated as inferior to benchmark wine. Both benchmarks are priced at $2.99 retail.

of the wines available in his store were imported by nationwide distributors such as "Monsieur Henri," a few brands were imported by a small Chicago wholesaler named N. J. Phillips, Inc. Because Cavasantes suspected that "Monsieur Henri" had little need for one more brand, he called N. J. Phillips, Inc. He found that Nancy Phillips carried several smaller brands, that she had been importing wines for approximately five years, and that she was willing to consider adding Bocotanian wines to her product portfolio.

Based on the strength of her interest, Cavasantes flew to Chicago to provide Ms. Phillips with samples of both the Bocotanian red and white wines. While she preferred the red, she found both wines quite acceptable. By the end of Cavasantes' trip, Ms. Phillips had, on the basis of commitments from several Latin American specialty restaurants in the Chicago metropolitan area, agreed to accept half a container (400 cases of twelve bottles each) of Bocotanian wines as soon as they were available, assuming the retail price could be kept under $3.00 per bottle. In addition, using relationships with her suppliers, Ms. Phillips had initiated a search for importers like herself in the Detroit, New York, and West Coast markets who would be interested in sampling the Bocotanian wines and were big enough to be able to commit to the purchase of at least half a container per order.

On his flight back to ENC headquarters, Cavasantes reviewed the status of his efforts on the wine project. He was pleased with the results of the quality tests and with the progress he had made toward solving the distribution issue. His primary concern at the moment, he decided, related to the fact that the Bocotanian wine should carry a retail price not higher than $3.00 per bottle. As Cavasantes had discovered, both wholesalers and retailers of wine expected a 50 percent markup. While he felt certain that his source of Bocotanian wines would be open to negotiation on price, Cavasantes was not sure how far below the quoted price of slightly more than one U.S. dollar his source would be willing to go.

Presentation Day Minus One

This day, Cavasantes had expected to be able to devote himself to resolving the price issue. However, on his initial attempt to call Bocotania, he discovered that phone, fax, and telex connections to Bocotania were out of order. Later in the morning, before Cavasantes could try again to place his Bocotanian call, he received a call from Houston asking whether he could sell sixty metric tons of copper sulfate for a European seller. Because ENC people in Europe indicated that speedy attention to this opportunity could open important doors for them, Cavasantes felt obliged to respond immediately. As it happens, his secretary had just run a PIERS report on copper sulfate, showing the major importers of this material to the United States over the previous twelve months. Consequently, before lunch Cavasantes was able to place the copper sulfate for the European seller with a major user in Florida, at a price of $2.00 per pound. For acting as intermediary on this transaction, ENC Global Trading earned a commission of 10 percent.

After lunch Cavasantes again tried to place phone, fax, and telex messages to Bocotania. Again, he was unsuccessful. Cavasantes decided to draft his proposal regarding Bocotania wines to show the directors. With luck, he reasoned, he would get through to Bocotania early the next morning, and be able to fill in blanks in his proposal to the directors. As always, his guide for drafting this proposal was the set of framing guidelines that Jones had developed when ENC first began doing countertrade transactions (see Exhibit 1).

Presentation Day

Once again, phone and fax communications were out of order. However, Cavasantes was able to get a telex through to ENC's Bocotanian office. Thus, while Cavasantes knew he would not be able to get answers to his questions on price, he would at least be able to indicate to the directors that the question had been raised and that answers should be forthcoming shortly.

EXHIBIT 1 Items to Be Addressed in ENC Purchase-Side Countertrade Contracts

1) Identity of parties to the contract
2) Products to be purchased by ENC, and the quantities involved for some period of time (often a year)
3) Specifications (country and standard) that product specifications must match
4) Packaging and shipment methods to be used by seller
5) Assignment of responsibility for freight expenses (place to which products will be delivered F.O.B.)
6) Price ENC will pay for the product
7) Payment arrangements (how and when ENC will remit funds to the seller)
8) Documentation seller shall present to ENC to claim payments due them under this contract (often, one commerical invoice together with several copies, a clean-on-board bill of lading, an original certificate of origin together with a couple of copies, and an original packing list together with several copies)
9) Any ancillary materials to be included with each product (for example, a users manual, a warranty card, etc.)
10) Agreement by seller that ENC or any other buyer is entitled to resell these products using their own trademarks
11) A force majeure clause (means that in event of certain specified events such as floods, strikes, major mechanical problems, war, and acts of God the parties shall notify each other promptly of the condition and at that point the contract shall be suspended until the problem can be resolved)
12) Legal system that shall be used in event of litigation
13) Right of ENC and/or other involved parties including certification-to-standards inspectors to inspect the factory
14) Seller agreement to maintain an adequate inventory of spare parts and components for a period (say, five years) after the last shipment made under this agreement.
15) Agreement that seller will ship spare parts quickly (say, within fifteen days) after receipt of telex or fax requesting such shipment
16) Controlling definitions for commercial terms used in this agreement (often, International Rules for the Interpretation of Trade Terms [INCOTERMS], published by the International Chamber of Commerce, Paris, France
17) Starting date and period for which this contract shall be valid (often, one year)

PART • 6

Planning and Control

CHAPTER • 18

Organization and Control in International Marketing

CHAPTER FOCUS

After studying this chapter, you should be able to:

- Describe alternative organizational designs for international marketing
- Specify criteria for choosing an appropriate organization structure
- Examine delegation of authority to subsidiaries for marketing decisions
- Identify performance evaluation measures
- Examine conflicts and their resolution between parent and subsidiaries

Markets across national boundaries offer many opportunities for growth and expansion. In taking advantage of such opportunities, international marketers formulate diverse strategies to fit the various different markets and successfully compete in them. A basic requirement for the effective implementation of any strategy is appropriate organizational structure.

Theoretically, the structure of an organization should be commensurate to its task, technology, and external environment. In the context of international business, however, this concept is difficult to put into practice since a multinational firm is faced with diverse external environments with various environmental constraints. For example, efficient operation on a world scale requires a flexibility and point of view that are unnecessary in a strictly domestic enterprise. Managers, for example, may follow a decision process of global coordination and integration. But the political demands of a particular host country may require a more diverse and locally responsive decision process. These simultaneous pressures for greater integration and greater diversity create strain in structuring the organization. Thus, the matter of choosing an ideal structure that fits the international marketing strategy and responds to international market demands is an important and complex issue.

This chapter reviews alternative organizational designs that companies use to manage their complex, far-flung operations effectively. The criteria for choosing an appropriate organization structure are examined. Conditions that require organizational changes are analyzed. The question of delegating authority to foreign affiliates is discussed. Finally, different ways of controlling foreign operations and measuring their profitability are considered.

Alternative Organizational Designs

There are several ways to organize a multinational firm. This section discusses distinctive features of alternative organizational designs, relative advantages and disadvantages of each alternative, and the variables that influence the choice of a specific design.

Essentially, there are four organizational structure archetypes: (1) international division structure, (2) geographic structure, (3) product structure, and (4) matrix structure. A fifth type, the functional organization, is not considered because few multinationals adopt this structure. According to a study by Stopford and Wells of 170 multinationals, virtually none of them used this structure.[1] Its biggest disadvantage is too much centralization. This makes coordination of functional decisions difficult and equal interdependence between products and areas rare.

The company's selection of its organizational form has enormous implications for the marketing function. For example, if it is a matrix structure, the director of international advertising may have dotted-line responsibility for all the country advertising managers, who also must report to a local managing director. The director may not find this preferable, but will have to take this as a given. The point is that the multinational company is quite unlikely to say everything (finance, production, etc.) is organized on a geographic basis except for marketing, an area that can choose whatever structure it desires.

Factors Affecting Organizational Design

A multinational corporation must choose an organizational structure that maximizes decentralization while still providing for the coordination of independent activities. The structure is mainly determined by the following environmental factors.[2]

Quality of Management The decentralization of authority to the local level can become quite a problem because the quality of management varies from country to country. However, authoritative committees either at the corporate or regional level with majority control can be used to offset this potential problem.

Diversity of Product Lines Most firms with a high degree of product diversity decentralize on a product basis, rather than on an area basis. Firms producing a few similar products will not decentralize on a product basis, because of the high degree of interdependence among these products. But complete standardization is usually not practical or desirable for marketing decisions because of different market characteristics and consumers.

Size of Firm Firms that derive a substantial portion of business from foreign operations usually drop the international division structure in favor of a product or geographic structure, which facilitates growth. As long as its international business is small, a firm can operate effectively with an international structure.

Location of Subsidiaries and Their Characteristics A company that emphasizes local and regional variations will lean toward the geographic structure because specific geographic variations must be specifically catered to. On the other hand, a company whose subsidiaries are similar to those of the home country is unlikely to favor a geographic structure because a good degree of standardization can be used in promoting products. For example, the United States and Canadian markets are quite similar.

Economic Blocs Companies operating within a regional economic bloc usually integrate their subsidiaries within the bloc area to deal better with trade barriers and oversee these operations by establishing special regional organizational units. Such a design makes it feasible to provide adequate responses to the unique economic characteristics of the bloc arrangement.

The ultimate decision on a firm's international organizational structure is based on specific factors unique to that company's operating environment. Hence, no two firms, even in the same industry, will exhibit exactly similar structures. In the computer industry, for example, IBM, Sperry Rand Corporation, and Control Data all use different organizational structures. Sperry Rand operates with a product structure because of a diversified product line, while IBM, because of its large size, has an area organization. Control Data's product line and international business have not expanded to the point where more decentralized decision making is necessary and can thus operate effectively with a functional structure.[3]

International Division Organization

The international division form of organizational design is depicted in Figure 18.1. Under this structure, the firm's activities are separated into two units—one domestic and the other international. The main function of such an international division is to develop the firm's foreign business ventures. The executive at corporate headquarters who oversees the division is given line authority and is directly responsible for the profitability of the international division. The creation of such a division is a company's deliberate attempt to draw a distinction between its domestic and international business. Companies in a developmental stage favor this structure because they may not have enough trained executives to staff a worldwide organization effectively. Top management can thus be freed from foreign operations to work on domestic business (see International Marketing Highlight 18.1).

The drawback to this design is that a firm can easily grow too diverse for this particular structure. Further, corporate planning can become awkward because of the two autonomous units. The isolation of top management, which initially seems like a blessing, can become a curse. Conflicts may occur as operations aboard expand and business overseas grows. Thus, when the perspective of business enlarges, the international division structure becomes ineffective. Another inherent problem with this structure is that R&D cannot be easily decentralized, and, therefore, it tends to be domestically oriented. With the basic research domestically centered, R&D for overseas is usually diminished to only product modification.

Geographic Organization

A worldwide geographic structure can overcome the problems associated with the international division structure. Foreign and domestic operations are not isolated but integrated as if foreign boundaries did not exist (see Figure 18.2). Worldwide markets are segregated into geographic areas. Operational responsibility goes to area line managers, while corporate headquarters maintains responsibility for worldwide planning and control.

Companies that operate under a geographic structure usually share the following characteristics:[4]

1. Their product lines are less diverse.
2. Their products are sold to end-users.
3. Marketing is the critical variable.
4. All of their products are marketed through similar channels.
5. Products are changed for local consumer needs.

Geographic organization has many advantages. Delegation of line authority and responsibility is explicit. Coordination of product sales and manufacturing is enhanced, and overall there is a pooling of experience in problem areas. A significant disadvantage of this structure is that a large number of "super" executives are needed to run the organization effectively. Another drawback is that

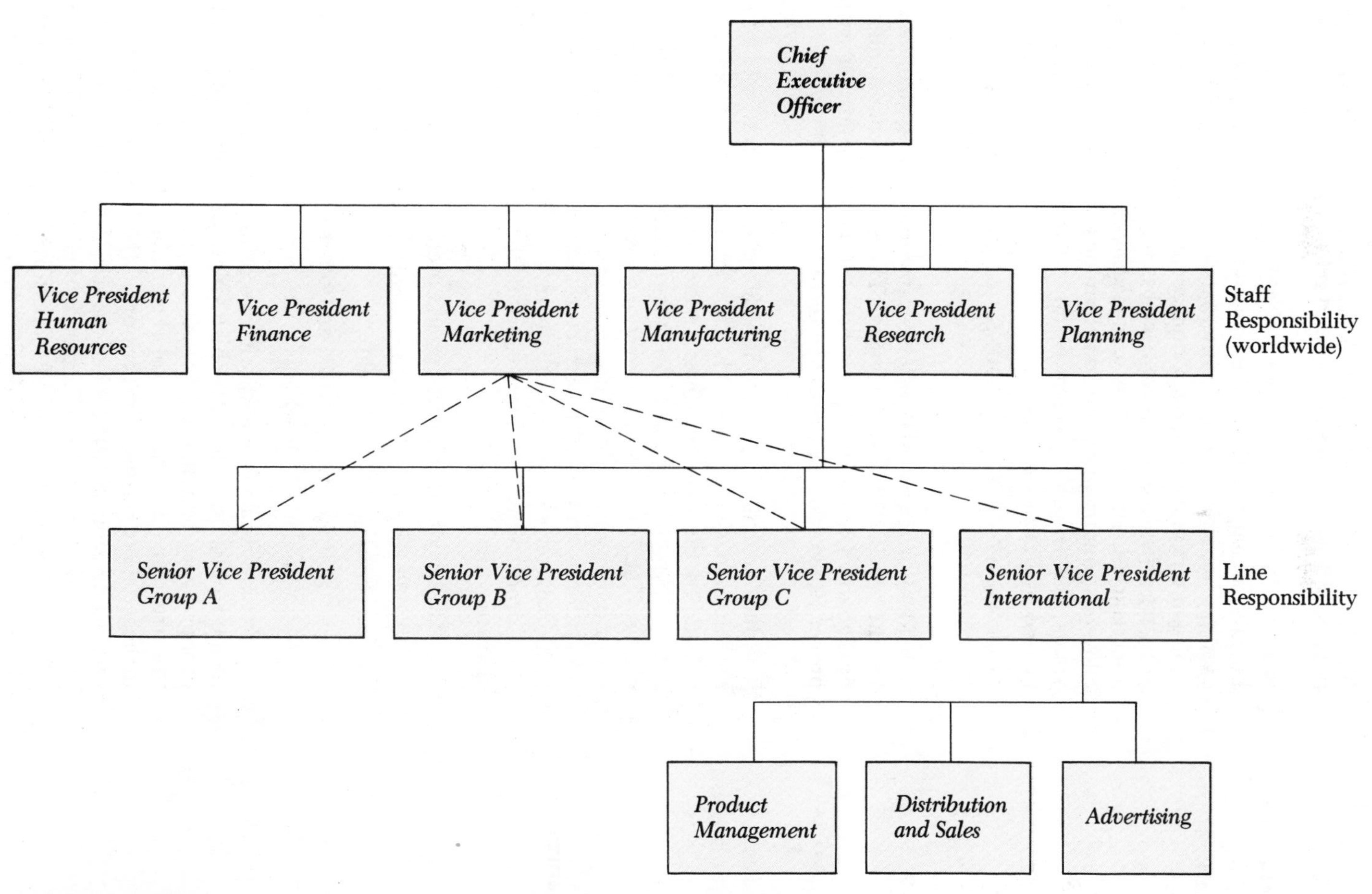

FIGURE 18.1 **International Division Organization Concept**

International Marketing Highlight 18.1

Organizing for International Success

Loctite, the engineering adhesives and sealants company, has consolidated all overseas activities under an International Group president based at corporate headquarters in Newington, Connecticut. Within the international group, operations are organized into three overseas regions, managed by a vice president and a secretary; Latin America is managed by the country manager of Brazil. Loctite allows its country managers to determine the product mix, design marketing programs, and set pricing policy within the context of an annual business plan approved by headquarters.

Source: Winning in the World Market (New York: American Business Conference, Inc., 1987), p. 32.

individual products may suffer because there is no single executive responsible for the specific product activities. The use of product managers at corporate headquarters can alleviate this problem by ensuring that each product line has proper penetration in world markets.

Product Organization

The third structure assigns worldwide responsibility to product group executives at the line management level. The coordination of activities in a geographical area is handled through specialists at the corporate staff level. As shown in Figure 18.3, emphasis is placed on the product line rather than on geographic differentials. The firm is segregated along product lines; each division is a separate profit center with the division head directly accountable for profitability. Decentralization is critical in this structure. More decisions are likely to be left to the local manager who is then usually more highly motivated.

Corporations that operate within the structure usually share the following characteristics:

1. They have a variety of end-users.
2. Their product lines are highly diversified and employ a high level of technological capability.
3. Shipping costs, tariffs, and other specific cost considerations dictate local manufacturing.

Decentralization of authority is a prime advantage of this structure. The motivation of division heads is high. New products can be added and old ones dropped with only marginal effect on overall operations. Another advantage of this structure is that the control of a product through the product life cycle can be managed more readily. Furthermore, MNCs do not have to abandon worldwide product division structure when the size of the foreign operations becomes large.[5]

A drawback of this structure is that coordination problems among various product divisions can arise. Product divisions must constantly be kept in check by top management. Also, division heads promoted to headquarters are likely to

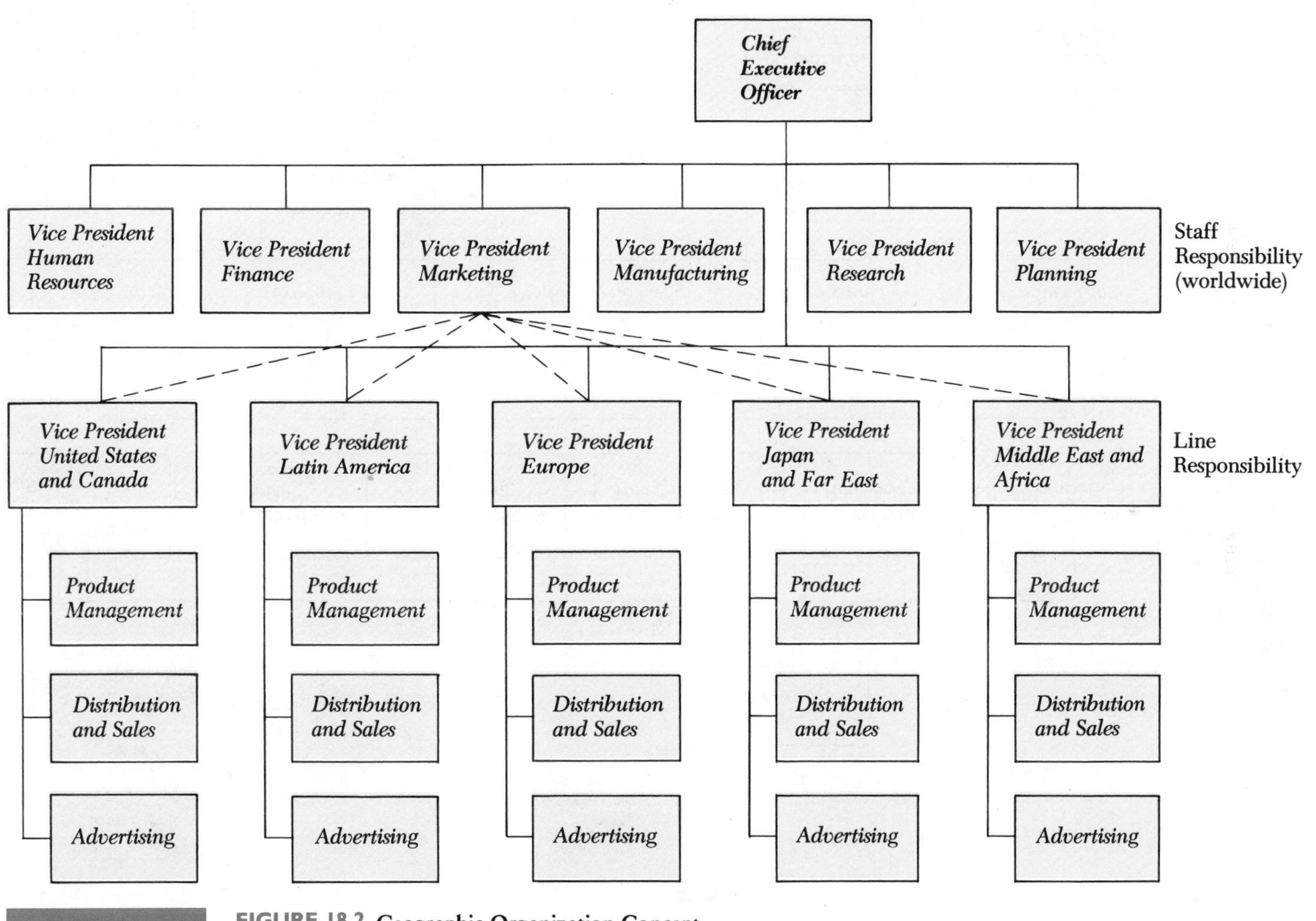
Chief Executive Officer
Vice President Human Resources
Vice President Finance
Vice President Marketing
Vice President Manufacturing
Vice President Research
Vice President Planning
Staff Responsibility (worldwide)
Vice President United States and Canada
Vice President Latin America
Vice President Europe
Vice President Japan and Far East
Vice President Middle East and Africa
Line Responsibility
Product Management
Distribution and Sales
Advertising
Product Management
Distribution and Sales
Advertising
Product Management
Distribution and Sales
Advertising
Product Management
Distribution and Sales
Advertising
Product Management
Distribution and Sales
Advertising

FIGURE 18.2 **Geographic Organization Concept**

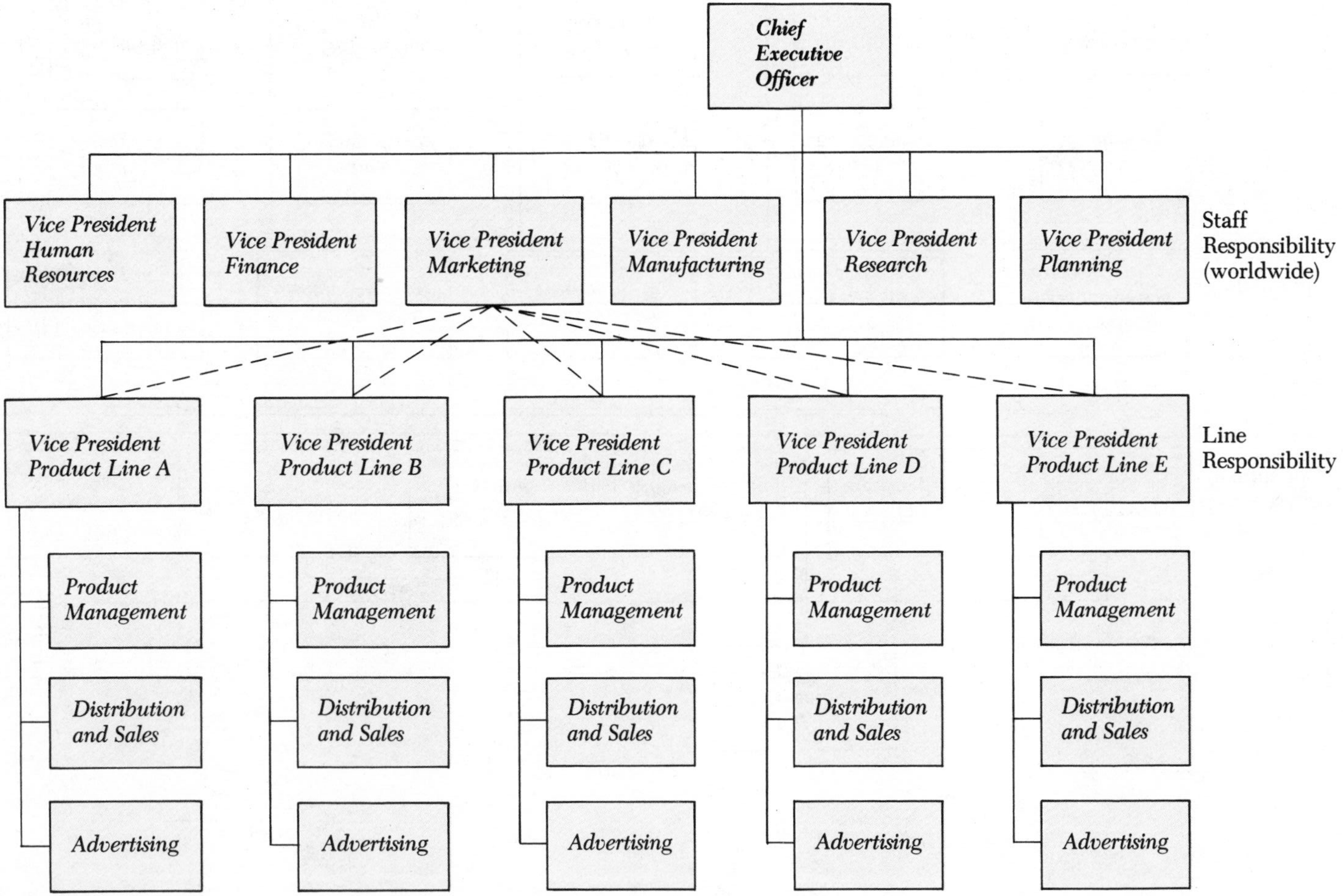

FIGURE 18.3 Product Organization Concept

be biased in favor of their former product area. The possibility of neglect of certain product areas exists. Many companies employ area specialists who are assigned the responsibility for overcoming that problem.[6]

Matrix Organization

One of the recent developments in organization design is the matrix structure. This structure, which first achieved prominence in the 1960s, has been adopted by many multinational corporations. The matrix structure offers greater flexibility than the single-line-of-command structures already discussed and reconciles this flexibility with coordination and economies of scale—the strength of large organizations. The main identifying feature of the matrix organization is that certain managers report to two bosses rather than to the traditional single boss; there is a dual rather than a single chain of command. Firms tend to adopt matrix forms when it is absolutely essential to be highly responsive to two sectors, such as product and geography; when uncertainties generate very high information processing requirements; and when there are strong constraints on financial and/or human resources.[7]

For the multinational firm the matrix organization is a solution to the problem of responding to economic and political environments. A matrix organization can have both geographic and product management components. The product management component would have worldwide responsibility for a given product line; the geographic management component would be responsible for all product lines in a national setting. Because the responsibilities overlap at the national product/market level, both are brought into play for major decisions. A national subsidiary product division must be able to relate to both in order to operate adequately.[8]

In the matrix organization it is expected that managers in the geographic area will defend positions favoring responsiveness to the local environment and that product managers will defend positions favoring efficiency and overall economic competitiveness. Because their past experiences and their interests do not coincide, geographic and product managers tend to behave differently in a given situation. This creates a duality of focus.[9]

Most matrix organizations adopt dual budgeting systems, whereby each arm of the matrix generates a complete budget. Parallel accounting systems provide independent controls. Dual personnel evaluation systems go hand in hand with dual budgeting to help sustain a power balance. If a person is to be directed by two superiors, both should take part in that person's evaluation. Employees with two bosses must know that both bosses have a part in each employee's evaluation. That way a commitment to both orientations is encouraged. Many matrix organizations insist that both superiors sit in when evaluation feedback is given to employees and that both advise employees of salary changes so that rewards will not be thought of as coming from one side of the matrix.[10]

In designing a matrix system, one has to be aware of its typical problems. Power struggles are a constant problem when the system is first applied. These struggles result from the dual command system, which has a tendency to create an imbalance of power as each side determines the limits of its influence. Besides tight control over the budgeting and evaluation systems, balance can be maintained by means of pay levels, job titles, and other means of increasing the status of the weaker side.

Another problem is the mistaken belief that matrix management is group decision making. It is not. Each matrix boss and his or her parallel in the other arm have separate functions that should seldom conflict. Their subordinates should work around any conflicting demands, coming to both bosses only as a last resort. The two bosses should rarely have to meet for decision making.[11]

Matrix structures have a tendency to collapse during economic crisis. In a crisis situation, matrix structures often become a convenient cause for poor management. A false need for decisive action may be felt, and as a result, the dual checking systems and double chain of command can seem to be excessive overhead. But these costs are offset by increased productivity because the matrix structure increases a firm's ability to react to changes in the environment. Collapse is mainly a problem only if the structure is used by a firm with no real need for it.

In conclusion, the matrix system is of great benefit to firms that have to react quickly to the environment. Corporations generally evolve into matrix forms rather than starting with them from scratch. Besides geographic and product matrices, there can be geographic and functional, or functional and product, matrix systems. Figure 18.4 shows an example of how the matrix structure of a multinational corporation may look.

Empirical Evidence

Empirical work on organizational structures of multinational enterprises by Halman shows that most firms have complex structures with some sort of matrix structure with product/market on one axis and geography on the other.[12] In most cases the international division, and/or regional office, serves as a buffer between top management and host country management. This tendency can be explained by the fact that top management cannot take the time and energy to deal with the great diversity of operations abroad and the wide variety of laws, cultures, customs, and other international factors. Nor can operating subsidiaries or branches abroad be exposed for long to the monolithic perceptions and policies of top corporate officers. Thus, international divisions are created to translate and buffer the communication between foreign operations and headquarters policy.

Organization Within Smaller Firms

Depending on the size of the firm, the responsibility for international marketing may be held by the president of the firm, be delegated to a line executive (for example, the vice president of sales), or be given to a staff person, like a marketing researcher or a strategic planner, as an additional duty. Occasionally, however, one person is appointed or hired to manage international operations in its entirety.

To illustrate the point, a chemical pump manufacturer in Ohio with annual sales of about $15 million handled its export business of about $3 million through the president's office. A high-technology firm in Boston (annual sales $16 million) with 50 percent of its business originating in Western Europe had a vice president of exports on par with the vice president of marketing (for do-

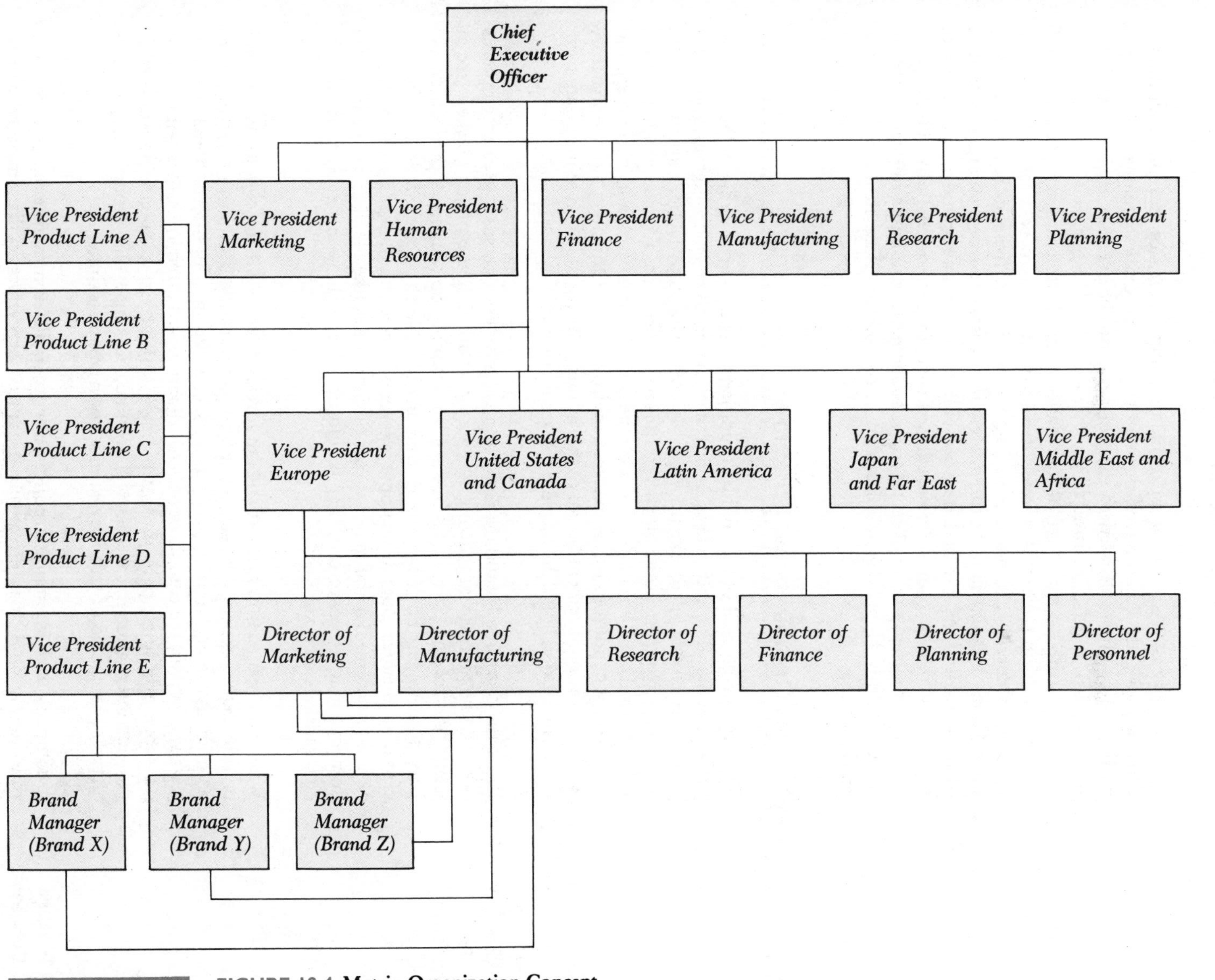
Chief Executive Officer
Vice President Marketing
Vice President Human Resources
Vice President Finance
Vice President Manufacturing
Vice President Research
Vice President Planning
Vice President Product Line A
Vice President Product Line B
Vice President Product Line C
Vice President Product Line D
Vice President Product Line E
Vice President Europe
Vice President United States and Canada
Vice President Latin America
Vice President Japan and Far East
Vice President Middle East and Africa
Director of Marketing
Director of Manufacturing
Director of Research
Director of Finance
Director of Planning
Director of Personnel
Brand Manager (Brand X)
Brand Manager (Brand Y)
Brand Manager (Brand Z)

FIGURE 18.4 **Matrix Organization Concept**

mestic business). A precision instruments company in Connecticut traditionally filled export orders as received through the domestic sales organization. After a while, the company decided to expand aggressively overseas. It hired an MBA for this purpose who reported to the president.

Clearly the organization of international marketing activity within a small firm depends on the extent of one's involvement in and commitment to overseas markets. Generally, initial international marketing activity is handled through the existing organization. As the interest in overseas business enlarges, a specific office is established for that purpose. That office may expand as the scope of business increases. It must be noted, however, that even one individual, if sufficiently committed and backed by top management, can make important strides in successfully launching or expanding a company's place in the international marketplace.

Choosing an Appropriate Organizational Structure

The organizing goal of international marketing is a structure that helps the company to respond to differences in international market environments and at the same time enables it to extend valuable corporate knowledge, experience, and know-how from the home market to the entire corporate system. In other words, the structure must be compatible with the organization's task and technology and the relevant conditions of the external environment.[13] Obviously no one structure will meet the requirements of all corporations. The choice of an appropriate form of organization should be based on several criteria.[14]

Foreign Markets Versus Domestic Markets

If a firm does a substantial proportion of business overseas, greater emphasis needs to be given in organizing foreign operations. If the major markets are at home, the foreign part of the business may simply be organized through an export department. For example, a company like Nestlé, which does over 90 percent of its business outside its home market of Switzerland, needs a global organization structure. But the major thrust of companies like Hershey Foods is on the domestic market; therefore, they would not attach the same importance to foreign markets as does Nestlé.

Evolution of Corporate Organization Structure

When an organization first expands to foreign markets, its foreign affiliates and/or subsidiaries report directly to the company president, or his or her delegate, without assistance from a headquarters/staff group. As international business grows, however, the complexity of coordination and direction will extend beyond the scope of a single person. Assembling a staff group to take responsibility for growing international activities will become necessary. This evolutionary process dictates the choice of structure at any given point in time.

The Nature of a Business and Its Related Strategy

A company with minimum product diversity in different markets (both domestic and international) may effectively organize itself functionally. In other words, when the same products are sold worldwide for similar end-users, through similar channels of distribution and advertising themes, the functional domestic setup may be extended overseas as well. Where product lines are diverse, and/or where local expertise is requisite to adequately serving the market, a geographic organizational structure may be more appropriate.

Management's Orientation

The cultural attitudes and orientation of a company's management toward different aspects of doing business overseas is another factor that affects the choice of an organization's structure.[15] These aspects include such considerations as management's attitudes toward foreigners and overseas environments, management's willingness to take risks and seek growth in unfamiliar circumstances, and management's ability to make compromises to accommodate foreign perspectives. Perlmutter has identified among international executives three primary orientations toward building multinational enterprises. These executives tend to be ethnocentric, or home country oriented; polycentric, or host country oriented; or geocentric, world oriented.[16]

An ethnocentric orientation considers home nationals more trustworthy and more reliable. Consequently, this orientation requires that home country methods and outlook be accepted overseas without question. The polycentric orientation acknowledges that host country cultures are different and believes that their people are difficult to understand. In line with this is the idea that local people know what is best for themselves and therefore local organizations should have local identities insofar as possible. The geocentric orientation views worldwide markets on an equal basis. Executives who subscribe to this global orientation seek the best personnel for key positions worldwide. The overseas affiliates, under this orientation, are considered an integral part of the corporation, rather than just satellites. The focus is on an amalgamation of worldwide objectives from local objectives with each part making its unique contribution from its particular competence. Table 18.1 describes how different aspects of organization design vary under the three orientations. For example, an organization operating with a world orientation is more complex and interdependent than it would be under either of the other two orientations.

Availability of Qualified Managers

The final criterion that determines the choice of organizational structure is the availability of internationally trained executives. If an adequate number of trained managers is not available, a company may be forced to accept a different structure for the short run than the one considered appropriate. In the long run, however, managers could be trained and the organization appropriately restructured. But the investment needed for developing internationally trained executives would have to be justified in terms of future potential and foreign business expansion plans.

To evaluate a company's justifiable long-run development of management talent, it is helpful to consider the different conditions under which each of the four organization designs (international division, product division, area division, and matrix organization) appear to be suitable. The scheme presented in Table 18.2 provides a generic framework for figuring out an appropriate organization for an international corporation. Particular schemes, however, may have to be modified to accommodate company-specific factors.

TABLE 18.1 Three Types of Headquarters Orientation Toward Subsidiaries in an International Enterprise

ORGANIZATION DESIGN	ETHNOCENTRIC	POLYCENTRIC	GEOCENTRIC
Complexity of organzaiton	Complex in home country, simple in subsidiaries	Varied and independent	Increasingly complex and interdependent
Authority; decision making	High in headquarters	Relatively low in headquarters	Aim for a collaborative approach between headquarters and subsidiaries
Evaluation and control	Home standards applied for persons and performance	Determined locally	Find standards that are universal and local
Rewards and punishments; incentives	High in headquarters, low in subsidiaries	Wide variation; can be high or low rewards for subsidiary performance	International and local executives rewarded for reaching local and worldwide objectives
Communication; information flow	High volume to subsidiaries orders, commands, advice	Little to and from headquarters. Little between subsidiaries	Both ways and between subsidiaries. Heads of subsidiaries part of management team
Identification	Nationality of owner	Nationality of host country	Truly international company but identifying with national interests
Perpetuation (recruiting, staffing, development)	Recruit and develop people of home country for key positions everywhere in the world	Develop people of local nationality for key positions in their own country	Develop best people everywhere in the world for key positions everywhere in the world

Source: Howard V. Perlmutter, "The Tortuous Evolution of the Multinational Corporation," *Columbia Journal of World Business,* January–February 1969, p. 12.

TABLE 18.2 Suitability of Basic MNC Organizational Structures to Corporate Concerns

	LEVEL OF SUITABILITY			
AREA OF CORPORATE CONCERN	International Division	Worldwide Product Division	Area Division	Matrix
Rapid growth	Medium	High	Medium	High
Diversity of products	Low	High	Low	High
High technology	Medium	High	Low	High
Few experienced managers	High	Medium	Low	Low
Close corporate control	Medium	High	Low	High
Close government relations	Medium	Low	High	Medium
Resource allocation				
Product considerations should dominate	Low	High	Low	Medium
Geographic considerations should dominate	Medium	Low	High	Medium
Functional considerations should dominate	Low	Medium	Low	High
Relative cost	Medium	Medium	Low	High

Source: Reprinted by permission of *Harvard Business Review.* An exhibit from "Reorganizing Your Worldwide Business" by J. William Widing, Jr., May–June 1973, p. 159.

Seeking Organizational Changes

Organizations operate in dynamic environments. Thus, no organizational structure can remain static. As the environment undergoes changes, appropriate changes must be made in the strategy, and structure follows strategy.

Need for Reorganization

Essentially, reorganization becomes warranted as a result of one or more of the following four factors: (1) sales growth, (2) adverse financial performance, (3) new products, and (4) changes in the external environment (for example, political upheaval in the country).[17] Consider a company that has recently entered international markets through filling infrequent export orders. The work involved has amounted to clerical functions handled by an experienced clerk in the sales department. Over the years, as sales grew, the nature of the foreign business changed, requiring a variety of managerial decisions. This triggered a structural reorganization. An international division was established that handled all matters related to business outside the United States.

Such causes for reorganization can be monitored by watching for specific indicators of organizational malaise, as shown in Table 18.3. For example, conflict among divisions or duplication of administrative services indicates that reorganization should be considered.

Management of Reorganization

Reorganization changes the status quo and established patterns of doing things. People within the organization may not have the capacity and/or willingness to adjust to structural changes. They may, therefore, resist changes. Such resistance can lead to disruption of intergroup and intragroup working relationships. For example, the domestic organization may neglect work strictly meant for international business. Resistance especially becomes a problem when reorganization calls for dilution of the responsibility and authority of an executive or group that hitherto wielded great influence and performed well.

To ensure organizational harmony, the change must be gradual and not brought about in a revolutionary fashion.[18] Nor can structural change be imposed unilaterally. More people than just those likely to be affected should be consulted before finalizing the reorganization; for example, it may be necessary to persuade senior management of the need for reorganization.

New Perspectives on Organization: Corporate Networking

As MNCs become ever larger through foreign acquisitions, joint ventures, or direct investments overseas, several have decided that the traditional ways of organizing just do not work for them, and no amount of tinkering can change that fact.[19] These companies tend to be technology oriented; they need to stay flexible, respond quickly to technological advances, and become or remain product innovators.

Such companies have decided that the only way they can accommodate their needs is to adopt a radical system of organizing people and work, called

TABLE 18.3 Indicators of Organizational Malaise Abroad

INDICATORS	CHARACTERISTICS
Conflicts among divisions or subsidiaries over territories or customers in the field	Most common when a company is expanding into new geographic areas. Also caused by the introduction of new products abroad and acquisitions or mergers.
Failure of foreign operators to grow in accordance with plans and expectations	May only apply to overall sales in a particular area, or to a particular product line. Obviously more acute if one's share of the market is falling even when sales are increasing.
Lack of financial control over operations abroad	Related to the company's philosophy of centralization versus decentralization and the degree to which authority is delegated to managers overseas. Further complicated by foreign tax laws and accounting conventions.
Duplication of administrative personnel and services	Most common when product lines go abroad as extensions of independent domestic divisions, or when major acquisitions are made.
Underutilization of manufacturing or distribution facilities abroad	Often occurs when various product lines extend operations abroad independent of each other, or when consolidation does not take place after a merger.
Duplication of sales offices and specialized field salesmen	Common with corporations selling technical products such as specialty chemicals or electronic equipment.
A proliferation of relatively small legal entities and/or operating units within a country or geographical area	Often results from establishing a new subsidiary each time a domestic division enters a new foreign country, until five, six or even more function side by side.
A proliferation of distributors	Overlapping coverage and conflicting interests.
An increase in complaints relating to customer service abroad	Often a symptom that field marketing personnel do not have a coordinated approach to handling a common customer.

Source: Reprinted by permission of *Harvard Business Review.* An exhibit from "Reorganizing Your Worldwide Business" by J. William Widing, Jr., May–June 1973, p. 155.

corporate networking. This can best be characterized as an "anti-organization" approach, in that its designers are consciously seeking to break through the constraints imposed by all the conventional organizational structures.

In a networked company, employees around the globe create, produce, and sell the firm's products through a carefully cultivated system of interrelationships. Middle-level managers from R&D, marketing, distribution, and other functions discuss common problems and try to accommodate one another. To foster flexibility rather than conformity, information does not necessarily travel along present organizational routes or chains of command as it does in other organizational systems.

Thus, marketing people in France would speak directly to manufacturing people in Singapore without going through the home office in, say, the United States. According to proponents of the network approach, lateral relationships spur innovation, new product development, and better quality control. They believe it is the only way a company can be truly innovative in today's bureaucratic world. Networking puts greater decision-making responsibility in the hands of middle managers, who are not required to clear every detail and event with higher-ups. The idea is to substitute cooperation and coordination, which are in everyone's interest, for strict control and supervision (see International Marketing Highlight 18.2).

Corporate networks require the various groups to stay in close contact with each other. Their success hinges on fast, reliable communication. It is no coincidence that networks have become popular at a time when electronic mail, facsimiles, teleconferencing, and other advanced telecommunications techniques have become accessible, inexpensive, and increasingly recognized as extremely valuable management tools.[20]

Pioneering work on network organization has been done by Bartlett and Ghoshal.[21] They classify companies involved in foreign business into four categories: multinational, global, international, and transnational. The first three categories represent traditional organization, while transnational refers to networking organization. Key characteristics of each type of traditional organization are:

- *Multinational:* Strong local presence through sensitivity and responsiveness to national differences
- *Global:* Cost advantages through centralized global-scale operations
- *International:* Use of parent company knowledge and capabilities through worldwide diffusion and adaptation

The multinational organization is decentralized. Control from headquarters is informal and personal, overlaid with simple financial controls. Top executives consider overseas operations independent profit centers that are part of the parent company's portfolio. This structure allows local organizations to tailor products to their home markets and helps firms avoid trade barriers. Multinational firms are sensitive and responsive to national differences. Local responsiveness gives the firm advantages over competitors but it has drawbacks. Because the multinational organization is so decentralized, knowledge developed within each

International Marketing Highlight 18.2

IBM's Network Experiment

In the past, IBM organized its overseas operations from an international division, IBM World Trade Corp., but has since departed from such a centralized approach. The company now organizes most of its overseas operations by regions, which are overseen by IBM World Trade Corp. as a nonadministrative umbrella, and uses a network to manufacture and market its products, such as the AS/400 mainframe computer.

The company's decision to try networking stemmed from management's desire to get the cutting-edge computer to market quickly with minimal roadblocks put in the way by the corporate hierarchy. Under the network system, research labs in California and Tokyo, manufacturing plants in Mexico and Italy, marketing teams in New York and Madrid, and distribution centers in Europe, as well as suppliers in various countries all contributed to launching the AS/400. In IBM's structure, outside suppliers are included as integral links in the network.

Electronic mail, teleconferencing, and other communication channels are used to link the groups. An ad hoc product-development team was formed, comprising managers, technicians, and marketing people around the world. These individuals went back to their regular jobs after the AS/400 became well established. In adopting a network, IBM abandoned its traditional decision-making process, "contention management," which required that conflicts between two managers working together on a project be resolved at a higher level of management. The network system encourages the two disputing managers to get together with a project leader via a teleconference and hammer out their differences as quickly as possible.

Source: Business International, July 9, 1990, p. 226.

unit rarely reaches the rest of the company. Efficiency also suffers since duplication is inherent in the structure and economies of scale are not fully exploited.

The multinational model was frequently adopted by companies prior to World War II, when communications technology was in its infancy and national markets varied dramatically. Overseas operations incapable of operating independently of the home office were not effective in that environment. In some cases, World War II actually forced companies to use a multinational structure when overseas subsidiaries were cut off from the parent company.

The global organization model is almost a mirror image of the multinational model. Highly centralized, the global organization considers overseas operations delivery pipelines to the global market. The corporate headquarters is a central hub maintaining tight controls over decision resources and information. Global companies consider the world one global market. They centralize production and operations. Centralization allows them to capture economies of scale and gain cost advantages. On the other hand, centralization makes firms less responsive to local needs and makes them more susceptible to tariffs and trade barriers.

The global organization model is typical of many Japanese companies. *Group behavior* and *interpersonal harmony* are strongly emphasized in Japanese culture. These cultural characteristics contributed to the adoption of the global organization model by many Japanese firms.

The international organization represents a "coordinated federation." Assets, resources, and responsibilities are decentralized but headquarters still coordinates many activities. Formal planning and control systems allow central management to coordinate overseas operations.

The control inherent in this system facilitates the transfer of knowledge and skills from the parent company to overseas divisions. Transferred knowledge can be adapted to meet local market needs. Decentralization with tight controls allows the international organization to capture some of the advantages of both the global and multinational models without the disadvantages. However, the international organization does not fully gain the advantages of global-scale economies or responsiveness that the other two models respectively have.

The international model often is adopted by companies with strong domestic positions. These companies move into overseas markets and produce miniature models of the home organization. Overseas operations are given flexibility to adapt to local markets but strong control and coordination is maintained by headquarters.

Bartlett and Ghoshal argue that until recently, most worldwide industries presented relatively one-dimensional strategic requirements. In each industry, either responsiveness, or efficiency, or knowledge transfer was crucial, and companies that possessed the matching structure were rewarded. Thus, if the strategic requirement of the industry was *responsiveness* (e.g., branded packaged products), a company following the multinational model found a good fit. Similarly, for companies in industries requiring strategic efficiency (e.g., consumer electronics), the global model was appropriate, while the international model was suitable for companies in industries where transfer of knowledge was a dominant strategic requirement (e.g., telecommunications switching).

In the 1980s, success in global industries depended not just on one dimension (responsiveness or efficiency or leveraging of parent company knowledge and competencies), but on all three at the same time. This need led to a new model of organization, the transnational structure. The transnational model, or network organization, draws on the strengths of the three traditional models as a means to achieve global competitiveness. Instead of making a blanket centralization or decentralization decision, the transnational organization makes selective decisions. Some operations and resources are centralized while others are decentralized. These decisions are made so that the entire company gains from the proper spread of resources and control. The structure relies on interdependencies to integrate all company units while allowing them to concentrate on their strengths and maintain the independence necessary for responsiveness. For example, if Division X has a strength in precision manufacturing technology, that will be its focus. Other divisions will depend on Division X for its expertise. However, precision manufacturing will not be monopolized by Division X.

The transnational configuration develops its strengths from three fundamental characteristics: dispersion, specialization, and interdependencies. New consumer trends, technological advances, and competitive strategies can develop anywhere in the world. The ability to sense and respond to these changes provides a competitive advantage, which is achieved through dispersed assets. Specialization of national operations allows the transnational company to capture minimum-scale efficiencies while retaining a dispersed structure. The current world competitive situation demands that company units engage in collaborative information sharing and problem solving, cooperative resource sharing, and collective implementation. That is, a transnational organization must employ relationships built on interdependencies.

The transnational organization requires highly flexible coordination processes to cope with both short-term shifts in specific role assignments and long-term realignments of basic responsibilities and reporting relationships. Furthermore, it must be capable of modifying roles and relationships on a decision-by-decision basis (see International Marketing Highlight 18.3).

Delegating Decision-Making Authority to Foreign Subsidiaries

Organizations are seldom totally centralized or decentralized. Complete centralization is not economical in most instances because of the administrative impossibility of making *all* of the tremendous number of decisions that would have to be made at the top management level. On the other hand, complete decentralization implies a collection of completely separate businesses, which is also undesirable. Subunits should be more than isolated investments. They should contribute not only to the success of the corporation but also to each other's success as well.

Determining the optimal degree of delegation amounts to an art. There are always trade-offs between control and delegation. Ideally, top management tries to choose a degree of decentralization that maximizes benefits over costs. But in practice, it may not be feasible to quantify either benefits or costs.

Factors That Affect Delegation

The extent and pattern of decentralization of authority in overseas affiliates varies from situation to situation. Empirical work on the subject, however, has indicated that ordinarily the degree of delegation rests on the following factors: the type of decision, the relative importance of international business and the size of the affiliates, the location of the MNC's home base, and the nature of the industry.

Type of Decision Marketing is a polycentric function that is deeply affected by local factors. Primary authority for international marketing decisions is, therefore, decentralized in favor of host country management. Aylmer's study of what kinds of decisions are made by whom provides some insights. This study involved the local management of the Western European operations of nine major U.S.-based consumer durable goods companies. Aylmer found that local management was responsible for 86 percent of the advertising decisions, 74 percent of the pricing decisions, and 61 percent of the channel decisions. Even where other

International Marketing Highlight 18.3

Imperial Chemical Industries: A Network Corporation

The archaic name is entirely appropriate: The sun never sets on ICI's far-flung nerve centers, and the company has probably moved as near as any to being truly global. The world's 38th-largest industrial corporation, ICI sells $21 billion a year of pharmaceuticals, film, polymers, agricultural chemicals, explosives, and other products.

In 1983, ICI began to abandon its traditional country-by-country organization and establish worldwide business units. The company concentrated its resources on its strongest ones. Within each, it focused activity where the most strength lay. Four of the nine new business units are headquartered outside Britain. Two are in Wilmington, Delaware—ICI is growing 20 percent a year in the United States but only 2 percent to 3 percent at home. A factory in Britain or Brazil producing advanced materials or specialty chemicals answers to a boss in Wilmington.

To avoid overlapping research around the world, labs were given lead roles near the most important markets. Advanced materials research went to Phoenix to be near clients in defense industries, while leather dye research went to the south of France, the heart of the market.

The strategic shift created wrenching changes. ICI reduced its manufacturing jobs in Britain by 10,000 to 55,000; other people were transferred or taken off pet projects. It's hard on people who have built national empires and now don't have such freedom. The company is asking people to be less nationalistic and more concerned with what happens outside their country. The upheaval has been especially worrisome to British employees, since ICI's stronger growth rate elsewhere attracts more resources.

The payoff is better decision making. Before, each territory would work up projects and have warring factions competing in London for the same money. Now with one person responsible for a global product line, it becomes immaterial where a project is located. The profits will be the same. When you start operating in this manner, it takes a lot of steam out of the defense of fiefdoms. In pharmaceuticals, for example, better—and quicker—decision making has helped ICI reduce the time lag in introducing new drugs to different markets from half a dozen years to one or two. ICI hopes eventually to make the introductions simultaneous.

A global company needs a world view at the top. Until 1982, ICI's sixteen-person board was all British. Now it includes two Americans, a Canadian, a Japanese, and a German. Among the 180 top people in the company, 35 percent are non-British.

British or non-British, they may go anywhere. The new chairman of ICI Americas Inc. is an Australian who also has worked for ICI in Britain and Canada. He quickly learned that a common language is no insurance against cultural shocks. When he went to England, he couldn't get any respect with his direct Australian manner, so he learned the oblique ways of the English. For example, he says, if an English boss reacts to a pet project by saying, "Perhaps you ought to think about this a little more," what he really means is "You must be mad. Forget it." In the U.S. he had to unlearn the lesson. He told a manager, "Perhaps you ought to think about this a little more." The manager took him literally. Asked why he had gone ahead, the man replied, "Well, I thought about it, like you said, and the idea got better."

Source: Jeremy Main, "How to Go Global—And Why," *Fortune,* August 28, 1989, p. 70.

organization levels were involved, local management often retained a strong voice in the final outcome of these decisions. As far as product design was concerned, decisions primarily rested with the parent organization.[22]

A similar study by Brandt and Hulbert generally substantiates Aylmer's findings. Their study was conducted among sixty-three U.S., European, Canadian, and Japanese subsidiaries located in Brazil. They concluded that, of the three major marketing areas— product, promotion, and pricing—product-related decisions sustained the most intervention from headquarters. Forty-five percent of the sixty-three subsidiaries involved replied that they received home office guidance regarding product design specifications. Forty-seven percent received help in making brand-name decisions. These two areas require extensive financial investment. For this reason the home office exercised greater control in any decisions made. Decisions concerning price guidelines received a minimal amount of assistance. Greater autonomy to the subsidiary was permitted because it was recognized that local management has a better knowledge of the competitive situation in the area and is more in tune with how customers and the local market will react to price changes[23] (see International Marketing Highlight 18.4).

Relative Importance of International Business and Size of Affiliates The relative importance of the firm's international operations and that of the local affiliates' position within the firm are two important organizational forces that affect the delegation of authority.[24] The frequency of higher management participation in local decision making is affected by the firm's international sales as a percentage of total sales—the higher the sales, the greater the frequency of high management participation in local decision making. For example, in Aylmer's research in one company with 50 percent international sales, top management was directly involved with the major marketing decisions. By contrast, the policy decisions of another company, where international sales accounted for less than 10 percent of total sales, were delegated to local management. The size of an affiliate also affects the delegation of authority. The larger the affiliate, the greater the authority shared with local management. In the case of smaller affiliates, parent company management more often imposes decisions on local management.[25]

Location of MNC's Home Base The delegation of decision-making authority to subsidiaries varies among multinational corporations of different nations.[26] According to Picard, U.S. subsidiaries of European corporations enjoy more

International Marketing Highlight 18.4

Managing a Global Business

Cray Research's organizational approach is designed to suit its product line. The supercomputer industry that it has pioneered epitomizes global business in its purest form, much like the large commercial airframe industry in which Boeing is the world leader. Worldwide installations and clients number in the low hundreds at most. The price tag on a supercomputer is high, averaging $12 million to $15 million. Each sale is a discrete event that moves through a complex and time-consuming cycle lasting anywhere from one and one-half to four years. And each purchase decision commits the buyer for a long period of time.

The focal point of the operation is Chippewa Falls, Wisconsin, the site of the company's research and development and manufacturing facilities, which Cray invites customers to visit. It sets prices centrally, and each sales contract is signed directly by Cray U.S. and the individual customer, regardless of location.

Cray's country organizations handle marketing, sales, and service functions and derive a commission on sales and revenues from service contracts. Sensitive, however, to the value that country managers can add, Cray allows them room for decisions in some areas. For example, the country manager has greater control over the marketing of used equipment in his territory, can determine trade-in credit for upgrades, and sets service fees.

In addition, Cray recognizes that country managers are key front- line players in dealing with customers. To enhance their status, it has the managers of six leading country subsidiaries report to internal boards of directors, which include their peers from various functions and U.S. regions and are chaired by executive vice presidents. This reporting relationship encourages collaborative behavior. Country managers also have direct access to Cray's CEO. Country managers are, however, expected to meet specific financial and technical criteria, both set centrally.

Source: Winning in the World Market (New York: American Business Conference, Inc., 1987), pp. 34–35.

autonomy than subsidiaries of U.S. corporations in Europe for several reasons (see International Marketing Highlight 18.5).

> Many European companies are understaffed at the top executive level relative to U.S. companies; therefore, not enough managerial attention and time can be given to the subsidiaries.
>
> Before modern telecommunications were developed, many European companies were already exporting a large portion of their production and were establishing sales subsidiaries overseas because their own local markets were too small. Lack of rapid telecommunications caused most decisions to be made at the local level.
>
> The American multinational corporations' tendency to control may stem from the fact that when they expanded after World War II, the overseas markets were very small compared to the domestic market.[27]

International Marketing Highlight 18.5

How Japanese Firms Delegate

According to a white paper on Japanese international trade, the widest range of autonomy allowed by Japanese parent companies to their local operations is in decisions on promotion and performance rating systems (in line with adjustment of personnel management to local cultures), supply sources for raw materials and parts, production and inventory volumes, and marketing strategy. The authority most zealously guarded by Japanese corporate headquarters was in the appointment of officers and in decisions on corporate finances (e.g., dividend payouts, long-term fund raising, capital expansions), research and development plans, and plant and equipment investments or expansions.

However, the imperative for centralized management among Japanese companies becomes truly apparent when compared with the management of foreign-affiliated enterprises operating in Japan. While overseas parents still control over half of decisions regarding the appointment of officers and long-term funding, their local subsidiaries in Japan seem to exercise far more control over determination of production and inventory volume, sourcing, sales price and marketing, personnel management, and even R&D. The comparison also reveals that relatively more control over marketing and pricing is held by Japanese corporate headquarters than by non-Japanese firms: About 60 percent of decisions on marketing strategy and selling prices could be made by local subsidiaries of Japanese firms, while over 80 percent of subsidiaries (even in joint ventures) of foreign firms could do so.

Source: H. Aoki, "The White Paper on International Trade 1989—Rapid Progress in Structural Adjustment," *Journal of Japanese Trade and Industry,* September 1, 1989.

Nature of the Industry The degree of delegation is affected also by the nature of the industry. For example, high centralization is more likely to occur among the firms in nonfood categories than among firms in the food category. In general, the nature of a company's products has an important influence on the delegation of authority to overseas affiliates. Consider the following:

> Food products . . . are generally perceived to be . . ."culture-bound"; this means they often become part of a national culture and their use pattern and meaning to consumers vary considerably from one country to the other. Coffee is an old product—350 years old in Europe, so local patterns and traditions surrounding coffee have been built up over many years. As a result, local taste preferences vary considerably from country to country, and even within a country; the café au lait of France and Switzerland, the thin slightly acid taste of Americans, the strong expresso in the small cup in Italy, coffee as a strong milk modifier in England and Australia, the smooth rich acidic taste of the Germans and the Scandinavians.[28]

Where highly culture-bound products require extensive custom-tailoring or marketing programs to meet local conditions, subsidiary management tends to play a dominant role in the process of marketing decision making.

Integration of Multinational Marketing Activities

A key problem of multinational corporations is how to tie the business activities of the subsidiaries together. There are different ways to integrate subsidiary operations, one of which is centralization. But centralization has limits. For example, there are products that are relatively culture-bound and require local adaptation. In such cases, the tailoring of marketing programs to local conditions requires that authority be transferred to subsidiaries. When sufficient centralization is not feasible, there are three other methods for integrating corporate activities: corporate acculturation, system transfer, and people transfer.[29]

The process of subsidiary acculturation involves assimilating corporate management's criteria for decision making into subsidiary management thinking. Through this process, subsidiary managers can manage the company's overseas operations with relatively little interference from headquarters.

Systems transfer refers to the use of a uniform framework for marketing planning and budgeting. This can serve to educate managers toward a disciplined analysis of business, provide headquarters with comparable data from all subsidiaries, standardize the process of decision making throughout the organization, and facilitate communication between headquarters and subsidiaries and among subsidiaries in different countries.

People transfer refers to the establishment of personal contact across borders among headquarters and subsidiary personnel. This includes long-term assignment of managers abroad, and short-term meetings between headquarters and subsidiary executives and among personnel from different foreign subsidiaries. People transfer can help to smooth out the differences of viewpoint that exist in a multinational organization.

Performance Evaluation and Control of Foreign Operations

Every company must have a performance evaluation and a control system to measure different operations. This need is particularly acute in the management of far-flung, hard-to-assess operations in different national markets. Broadly speaking, performance evaluation measures can be categorized as either financial or nonfinancial techniques. Nonfinancial techniques are measurements that range from personnel development to the building of long-term profitability. Financial techniques involve financial measurements against established standards, budget, previous performance, and other subsidiaries of present operations. The financial techniques can be further split into two groups: measurements against budgets and balance sheet ratios. All measures have their relative merits and demerits. Whatever performance measures are selected, the system should be kept as simple as possible; it should not burden managers with endless paperwork.

Further, measurements must preserve a proper balance between immediate results and long-term objectives. A higher rate of return in Brazil may be desirable in light of the economic and political instability threatening foreign investment in that country. But such a target may be unrealistic because of foreign-exchange losses, import restrictions, and other impediments. Many companies temper a poor performance in the present with expectations for future profitability dependent upon a continued presence in the market.

Controlling Multinational Operations

Controls are defined as checkpoints and are used to verify performance progress by comparison with some standard often defined by top management in the planning process. But as a corporation's size increases, the distance between top management and marketing operations grows, making the control and analysis process more difficult. At that point, effective controls have to be maintained. In a changing environment, information must come swiftly to ensure quick action in response to any success or failure. This timing factor has led to a trend toward tighter controls of foreign subsidiaries by U.S. corporations. It has been held, for example, that if Union Carbide Corp. had maintained tighter control over its Indian subsidiary, the Bhopal tragedy would not have happened.[30]

A second factor favoring stricter controls is the completion of the European Community's 1992 internal market program. Under this program EC countries will represent a single market without any barriers. As a consequence, U.S. firms have wisely relocated plants and reorganized distribution and marketing functions to include these Common Market countries. But control must go hand in hand with expansion. Tight control should ensure consistency in product and marketing performance.[31]

The third reason for adoption of strict controls is the correction of unsatisfactory performance by subsidiaries. Frequently, such failure is caused by a subsidiary manager's incompetence. But, for whatever reason, control over subsidiaries should improve, as well as provide, standards for achievement.

Further, since a multinational corporation typically has several foreign subsidiaries in different parts of the world, a good control system is important to ensure that these subsidiaries move together toward a common goal, spelled out by the corporate strategic plan. On the other hand, a poor control system can make the task of evaluation and adjustment a very cumbersome one. General Motors Corp., for example, operates in seventeen European countries. Its European operations have been hurt by the corporation's lack of a coherent strategy and strong management. Its Adam Opel subsidiary in West Germany often has been pitted against its Vauxhall Motors Ltd. unit in Britain. In the absence of proper controls, both companies lost money. Thus, in early 1986, GM decided to overhaul the organization and impose new control procedures in Europe.[32]

A good control system is also vital in evaluating the performance of top management in each subsidiary. Since the environmental conditions surrounding each subsidiary differ, it is impossible to use a completely standard system of evaluation. Some managers are forced to operate under far more severe conditions (cultural, economic, political) than others. A good control system allows for consideration of these variant factors in order to measure the true progress of an operation.

Finally, a good control system permits better strategic planning and implementation of the planning. According to Phatak, a management control system in a multinational company should meet ten basic requirements in order to ensure effective monitoring and evaluation of subsidiaries' performance.[33]

1. The control procedures and techniques to be used should be understandable and acceptable to the subsidiary heads involved.
2. The subsidiary heads should take an active part in formulating the control procedures and techniques to be used.
3. The subsidiary head being evaluated should actively participate in the appraisal process.
4. Each subsidiary should be given realistic objectives. These objectives should take into account each individual subsidiary's internal and external environments.
5. Financial as well as nonfinancial data should be utilized to evaluate subsidiary performance.
6. The control system should detect and report deviations from subsidiary plans as soon as, or before, they occur.
7. The subsidiary head should be evaluated on the basis of performance only in those areas under direct control. The evaluation should take into account those factors that influence subsidiary performance but over which the subsidiary has little or no control.
8. Control techniques should be tailored to the internal and external environments of the specific subsidiary.
9. The control system should not stagnate, but should be revised and improved as required by changes in the subsidiary's environment.
10. Top management must tie compensation to results achieved, and outstanding performance must be tangibly rewarded.

Financial Measures of Performance

A number of financial measures of performance are available and relied on by MNCs. Some of the more popular measures are income or profit contributions, cash flow, and performance relative to a budget. There is a consensus that no single measure of performance is adequate in and of itself. An ideal measure of the true economic benefit of a subsidiary would be arrived at by comparing the performance of the entire multinational corporation with and without that subsidiary. This is difficult, if not impossible, to accomplish operationally, particularly when there are many interrelated subsidiaries in the multinational network. As a practical alternative, corporations rely on a combination of different measures to assess the performance of their operations, both domestic and overseas.[34]

Budgets as Indicators of Performance Companies rely heavily on budgets to compare forecasts of the unit's results with actual results. The variance between the two is then analyzed to evaluate performance and to determine areas in need of improvement. A major problem in the use of budgets for performance evaluation is the setting of realistic, attainable numerical goals.

Income or Profit Contribution Accounting-based net income of a foreign operation is a logical and readily available index of performance. However, it can be an inaccurate measure of performance because profits can be manipulated, especially in the short run. For example, elimination of such staff functions as research may improve the profit picture for the purpose of performance evaluation. But in the long run, such cuts can also hurt profit performance. Further, net income is not a useful measure for evaluating managerial performance because it typically reflects allocation of corporate headquarters' costs, which are beyond the control of the foreign manager.

Profit contribution is a better measure of managerial success than net income. Profit contribution is unit operating revenues less all expenses directly traceable to the unit, and this figure is more likely to include items under the manager's control. The major limitation of profit contribution is that it omits the unit's share of headquarters' costs. Both net income and profit contribution neglect the investment base required to generate earnings.

Return on Investment (ROI) Evaluation by return on investment is frequently used since it is believed that the ultimate test of performance is the relationship of profit to invested capital. ***ROI*** is computed by dividing the net income by the net assets. There is a good deal of controversy about what items should be included in the profits (numerator) and the investment base (denominator), and how they should be measured.

As far as marketing is concerned, different factors affect ROI differently. Empirical work by Douglas and Craig provides interesting insights on this issue.[35] Overall they found that, at least in the short run, increased expenditure on marketing mix variables depressed levels of ROI. But in European markets, high price in conjunction with new product development and expenditure on advertising was positively related to ROI, while salesforce and other marketing type expenditures were negatively related to ROI. In other foreign markets, the authors found little effect of marketing mix variables on ROI, and that only superior-quality products could be related to ROI. They argue that the consequent ambiguity can be explained by the fact that the effectiveness of different types of promotional activity may vary from one market to another.

Douglas and Craig's work failed to reinforce the opinion popularly held in the United States that overseas market share leads to profitability, as little correlation was found between market share and ROI in European or other foreign markets. This result, however, may be due to manipulation of transfer pricing, where creative accounting is used to show losses in high-tax countries and profits in low-tax areas. In addition, the level of investment (joint venture, wholly owned subsidiary) may serve to obscure any relationship between ROI and marketing strategy.

Residual Income ***Residual income*** is equal to a foreign operation's net income less an investment carrying charge equal to the unit's investment base multiplied by the cost of capital. A benefit of this approach is that it relates income to the investment costs of producing that income. Also, suboptimal decisions are not made with regard to investments, as may happen with ROI. Residual income, however, is subject to the same measurement problems associated with ROI.

Cash Flow ***Cash flow*** is depreciation plus net income (after taxes). Benefits of the cash flow approach as a measure of profitability and performance are its familiarity to executives as a method and its compatibility with a capital budgeting framework. When figuring the items to be included in the cash flow computation for the foreign subsidiary, it is vital to include the returns to the rest of the corporate system rendered by the activities of the foreign operation. In addition, differential taxes levied on the foreign subsidiary, the cost of transferring funds back to the parent, and funds that can be repatriated to the parent should be included in the derivation.

Nonfinancial Measures

Concern for long-range profitability makes companies focus their concentration not only on the figures in the budget but also on what lies behind the figures. Measuring foreign subsidiary performance is intimately connected with evaluating a wide range of nonfinancial aspects, some quantifiable, some not. It is these underlying factors that ultimately affect profits, although they may not show up in short-term profit statements.

Nonfinancial measures can cover any aspect of running a business. To be effective, they should be defined as clear and precise objectives with definite times of completion. For example, if a subsidiary plans to introduce in January a new product that has been successful elsewhere, a nonfinancial objective for that product might state that by July a market study of specific dimensions must be completed.

There can be any number of nonfinancial measures of performance. Management should develop a checklist of meaningful measures that it intends to use to rate the relative performance of affiliates. The following factors may be included in such a checklist:

- Market penetration or market share trends, by product and class of trade
- Affiliate export sales results
- Number of days credit outstanding as compared with average in industry
- Spot surveys of service standards
- Salesperson workload appraisals of the time spent with customers and dealers and in promoting merchandising programs
- Periodic postcompletion audits of capital budget projects to confirm the credibility of the financial and operating forecasts that are made by local management
- General attitude of distributors, dealers, and large consumers toward company
- Comparison of unit manufacturing yields and production times in affiliates with corresponding standards in U.S. plants
- Productivity gains resulting from methods and systems improvements
- Training and management development—the availability of executives in the organization who are ready to assume greater responsibility
- Trends in worker reduction and employee turnover

- Extent of exchange exposure in countries where inflationary pressures are great and there is risk of devaluation
- Quality of affiliate management's relations with local government and community leaders
- Worthwhile new ideas or new proposals that have been advanced in the last year by local management
- Productivity trends that are a reflection of the efficiency with which capital and labor are employed—the suggested index being the ratio of sales volumes on key products to labor costs (inside and hired) plus depreciation

From marketing's standpoint, one of the most important nonfinancial measures is market penetration. For many products, particularly for consumer products, many companies use market penetration as a yardstick to measure how well business is doing in a given market. A given percentage of the market is required to support the necessary level of promotion for a product to sell effectively and generally obtain a high enough level of visibility to make an overall impression on the consumer. Measuring market penetration can best be done by comparing company sales with the market as a whole. After the size of the potential market has been estimated, the percentage of available business actually captured by the subsidiary should be calculated for total sales and for sales by product. When compared with forecast sales, these figures will give a good measure of how aggressive local management has been and where weak spots in the product line are holding back the overall effort. But market penetration should be appropriately qualified by the impact of other factors including degree of competition, local and foreign; impact of substitute products; treatment of export sales in view of local laws or incentives, production costs, or tariff position; weighting of captive sales to the total sales effort; and level of the sales effort (wholesale, retail, ultimate consumer).[36]

Evaluation of promotional effort must be basically qualitative, since it is difficult to establish a valid relationship between advertising and promotion expenses, and sales performance. Further, the suitability of promotional effort to the local market is most often the prime factor in evaluating effectiveness. Suitability of the product to the market may also have a significant effect on the marketing effort. Consumer preference evaluation, as well as social and cultural acceptance of the product, is especially important in areas where these factors may differ considerably from American norms. The subsidiary's staff is responsible for recommending and marketing the product that will best suit the local market.

Development of new products is closely linked to product suitability since the subsidiary must make recommendations from field experience as to product development and trends in the market. An evaluation measure used by some firms is the frequency and quality of new product suggestions from the field subsidiaries to the parent R&D department and of new promotion and sales techniques.

Distribution and service evaluation may be combined since the distributor is often responsible for after-sale servicing. The most frequently listed factors for evaluation in this area are most effective use of channels of distribution; attitudes of distributors, retailers, consumers; distributor performance; quality of after-sale servicing; and promptness in filling orders.

In all these areas, a long-term judgment question should always be present: Have actions been taken during the period under analysis that will help or hinder sales performance in subsequent periods?

Conflicts and Their Resolution

As is conceivable in any organizational setup, conflicts are bound to arise between different groups. In the context of international marketing such conflicts usually emerge from differing parent corporation and subsidiary points of view.

Certain problems severely block relationships between management in U.S. corporations and their foreign subsidiaries. For the following reasons, problems often arise in the control of foreign operations.

One of the biggest problems subsidiaries encounter in the control process is that corporate decisions are made too slowly. Delays in receiving important and urgent decisions from headquarters cause companies to miss out on many opportunities.

Subsidiary managers also find that too many reports have to be sent to headquarters. In most cases, they feel nobody reads these reports and that the importance of the information tends to be minimized. The result is that headquarters management often relies on information not from the subsidiary but from superficially formed impressions.

Another aspect of the control problem is attributed to low levels of credibility in both headquarters and the subsidiary management. Corporate executives tend to disregard the local manager's recommendations. As a result, in highly centralized and controlled companies, local managers must resort to persuasion to get their ideas accepted at headquarters. On the other hand, local managers tend to disregard headquarters' directives and doubt the soundness of its decisions because local managers often are uninformed about the reasons for the decisions or they cannot accept that a corporate executive is better informed or better qualified to make decisions. Thus, each distrusts the other's judgments and abilities.[37]

Finally, one of the biggest problems in the control relationship is headquarters' lack of knowledge about conditions abroad. Most U.S. companies with foreign subsidiaries underestimate the importance of social, cultural, economic, and political conditions with which foreign subsidiaries must deal. Many companies are just not well informed about such conditions.[38]

An empirical investigation by Wiechmann and Pringle provides interesting insights into the problems that concern marketing executives of large U.S. and European multinationals and their subsidiaries worldwide.[39] In a nutshell, it is not primarily competition, political and legal pressure, nonavailability of channels, and differing social and cultural outlooks that bother marketing executives in corporate headquarters and their foreign subsidiaries. The worst problems are internal, those emerging from friction between two groups. For example, marketing executives at the headquarters may charge marketing managers in foreign subsidiaries with failure to formulate long-term strategy, while subsidiary managers are bothered by the parent company's overemphasis on short-term financial performance.

Exhibit 18.1 summarizes the concerns of corporate marketing executives as well as those of subsidiary managers. Naturally, some conflict is inevitable, simply because the orientation of the two groups is different. The corporate people want detailed information on subsidiary operations to enable them to unify and integrate their far-flung operations. Subsidiary executives prefer less control and more authority and want to be treated as autonomous units. Some conflict and tension may be desirable to help avert obsolete approaches to management and to encourage continual dialogue between the parties. But some problems need to be eliminated, including such common areas of concern as deficiencies in the communication process, overemphasis on short-term issues, and failure to utilize fully the corporation's experience overseas.

To resolve shortcomings, the first step is to articulate the problems through the kind of information given in Exhibit 18.1. Then, the causes of conflict should be established. For example, a subsidiary's short-term perspective may be related to unique competitive conditions in its market area. Finally, an appropriate solution should be found. The remedy for each cause will be different. The solution may range from open discussion between the corporation and its subsidiary to organizational changes. In any event, as a lasting solution to conflict resolution, foreign subsidiaries must be adequately involved in both strategy formulation and implementation processes.

Bartlett and Ghoshal note:

> When Procter & Gamble launched Pampers in Europe, it directed the marketing strategy from European headquarters. The result: a big failure. The reason: P&G failed to take advantage of particular strengths of national units; country managers, bypassed in the planning, had no stake in the outcome.
>
> The failure led P&G to rethink the way it used local subsidiaries and to form the highly successful "Eurobrand teams," made up of line and staff officers of key national subsidiaries. Shouldering the load in marketing development with product configurations, advertising themes, and packaging, Eurobrand teams successfully introduced Vizir, a liquid detergent, in six countries within a year.
>
> In pushing new strategies like this, P&G and other successful MNCs diverge from traditional hierarchical structures in which the top formulates—and the national subunit simply implements— strategy and planning. By cooperating and co-opting capabilities, the parent's sales and market share get a big boost from the country unit's technical expertise, market knowledge, and competitive awareness—all without losing boundary-crossing benefits like scale economies.[40]

EXHIBIT 18.1 Key Problems Identified by Headquarters' Executives (1–6) and Subsidiaries' Executives (7–12)

1. Lack of qualified international personnel
- Getting qualified international personnel is difficult.
- It is difficult to find qualified local managers for the subsidiaries.
- The company can't find enough capable people who are willing to move to different countries
- There isn't enough manpower at headquarters to make the necessary visits to local operations.

2. Lack of strategic thinking and long-range planning at the subsidiary level
- Subsidiary managers are preoccupied with purely operational problems and don't think enough about long-range strategy.
- Subsidiary managers don't do a good job of analyzing and forecasting their business.
- There is too much emphasis in the subsidiary on short-term financial performance. This is an obstacle to the development of long-term marketing strategies.

3. Lack of marketing expertise at the subsidiary level
- The company lacks marketing competence at the subsidiary level.
- The subsidiaries don't give their advertising agencies proper direction.
- The company doesn't understand consumers in the countries where it operates.
- Many subsidiaries don't gather enough marketing intelligence.
- The subsidiary does a poor job of defining targets for its product marketing.

4. Too little relevant communication between headquarters and the subsidiaries
- The subsidiaries don't inform headquarters about their problems until the last minute.
- The subsidiaries do not get enough consulting service from headquarters.
- There is a communications gap between headquarters and the subsidiaries.
- The subsidiaries provide headquarters with too little feedback.

5. Insufficient utilization of multinational marketing experience
- The company is a national company with international business; there is too much focus on domestic operations.
- Subsidiary managers don't benefit from marketing experience available at headquarters, and vice versa.
- The company does not take advantage of its experience with product introductions in one country for use in other countries.
- The company lacks central coordination of its marketing efforts.

6. Restricted headquarters control of the subsidiaries
- The headquarters staff is too small to exercise the proper control over the subsidiaries.
- Subsidiary managers resist direction from headquarters.
- Subsidiaries have profit responsibility and therefore resist any restraints on their decision-making authority.

7. Excessive headquarters control procedures
- Reaching a decision takes too long because approval must come from headquarters.
- There is too much bureaucracy in the organization.

(*continued*)

EXHIBIT 18.1 *(Continued)*

- Too much paperwork has to be sent to headquarters.
- Headquarters staff and subsidiary management differ about which problems are important.
- Headquarters tries to control its subsidiaries too tightly.

8. Excessive financial and marketing constraints

- The emphasis on short-term financial performance is an obstacle to the development of long-term marketing strategies for local markets.
- The subsidiary must increase sales to meet corporate profit objectives even though it operates with many marketing constraints imposed by headquarters.
- Headquarters expects a profit return each year without investing more money in the local company.

9. Insufficient participation of subsidiaries in product decisions

- The subsidiary is too dependent on headquarters for new product development.
- Headquarters is unresponsive to the subsidiaries' requests for product modifications.
- New products are developed centrally and are not geared to the specific needs of the local market.
- Domestic operations have priority in product and resource allocation; subsidiaries rank second.

10. Insensitivity of headquarters to local market differences

- Headquarters management feels that what works in one market should also work in other markets.
- Headquarters makes decisions without thorough knowledge of marketing conditions in the subsidiary's country.
- Marketing strategies developed at headquarters don't reflect the fact that the subsidiary's position may be significantly different in its market.
- The attempt to standardize marketing programs across borders neglects the fact that our company has different market shares and market acceptance in each country.

11. Shortage of useful information from headquarters

- The company doesn't have a good training program for its international managers.
- New product information doesn't come from headquarters often enough.
- The company has an inadequate procedure for sharing information among its subsidiaries.
- There is very little cross-fertilization with respect to ideas and problem solving among functional groups within the company.

12. Lack of multinational orientation at headquarters

- Headquarters is too home-country oriented.
- Headquarters managers are not truly multinational personnel.

Source: Reprinted by permission of *Harvard Business Review.* An exhibit from "Problems That Plague Multinational Marketers" by Ulrich E. Wiechmann and Lewis G. Pringle, July–August 1979, pp. 120 and 122.

Summary

As the scope of a firm's international business changes, its organizational structure must be adequately modified in accordance with its tasks and technology and the external environment. There are four main ways of structuring an international organization: international division structure, geographic structure, product structure, and matrix structure. The organizational structure is affected by such factors as quality of management, diversity of product line, size of firm, subsidiaries' locations and their characteristics, and existence of regional economic blocks within the market. Each of the different structures has relative merits and demerits. An empirical study of international organizations shows that most firms, however, follow a complex structure along the lines of the matrix organization. Added to that, firms have the international division or regional office to serve as a buffer between the corporate and host country management.

The choice of an appropriate organizational form for international marketing activities is dictated by such considerations as the relative importance of foreign markets vis-à-vis domestic markets, the evolutionary pattern of the firm's organizational structure, the nature of business and its related strategy, management's orientation (home country versus host country versus world orientation), and availability of qualified managers.

Business is conducted in a dynamic environment. As the environment undergoes change, there should be appropriate responsive change in the structure. Change is triggered by such factors as sales growth, adverse performance, introduction of new products, and changes in the external environment. The need for reorganization becomes noticeable as these causes articulate themselves in the form of specific indicators of organizational malaise, for example, conflict among divisions or duplication of administrative services, among many other signs of trouble. The change should be managed in such a way that organizational harmony continues to be maintained. Thus, consultations with people likely to be affected by the change and gradual introduction of change would be in order.

An important decision for international marketing executives to make at the headquarters level is how much decision-making authority will be delegated to subsidiary management. To the extent that marketing is a *polycentric* function subject to influence by local factors, the primary responsibility for marketing decisions is delegated to local management. However, product- related decisions remain largely the prerogative of the parent corporation's management with subsidiary management dominating in decisions of price, promotion, and distribution. The extent of authority delegation differs also according to parent corporation national identity. For example, U.S. multinationals as a group prefer greater centralization than do European or Japanese multinationals. Similarly, the nature of a product also influences authority delegation decisions.

Performance evaluation and control of foreign operations are linked with organizational structure. There are two types of performance evaluation measures, financial and nonfinancial. Financial techniques include measurements against budgets and balance sheet ratios. Nonfinancial measures include market penetration, affiliate export sales results, salesforce workload appraisals, and the general attitudes of distributors, dealers, and large customers toward the company.

Organizational conflicts are inevitable between corporate executives and subsidiary management. One empirical study on the subject showed that the worst problems are internal, emerging from friction between the two groups. For example, both groups charge each other with pursuing short-term orientations. While some of the conflicts can be expected and tolerated because of the different perspectives of their work situations, efforts by and large must be made to eliminate the underlying causes of conflicts with improvements in the organizational structure to smooth the way.

Review Questions

1. What factors affect an organization structure in the context of international marketing?
2. What factors lead a company to opt for the matrix form of organization?
3. What criteria may a firm employ to determine an appropriate organization for structuring international business?
4. Differentiate between ethnocentric, polycentric, and geocentric orientations of international executives. How does each orientation affect organization structure?
5. What factors necessitate change in organizational design to accommodate international marketing?
6. To what extent are marketing decisions delegated to overseas subsidiaries' managers? What insights do empirical findings provide on this issue?
7. What different ways are there to integrate multinational marketing activities?
8. Discuss market penetration as a measure of performance evaluation in international marketing.

Endnotes

1. John M. Stopford and Louis T. Wells, *Managing the Multinational Enterprise* (New York: Basic Books, 1972). *Also see* Douglas N. Dickson, "Case of the Reluctant Multinational," *Harvard Business Review,* January–February 1983, p. 6.
2. Jacques Picard, "Determinants of Centralization of Marketing Decision Making in Multinational Corporations," in *Marketing in the 80's,* Proceedings of the Educators' Conference (Chicago: American Marketing Association, 1980), pp. 259–261.
3. *See* Rodman Drake and Lee M. Caudill, "Management of the Large Multinational: Trends and Future Changes," *Business Horizons,* May–June 1981, pp. 88–90.
4. Arvind V. Phatak, *International Dimensions of Management* (Boston: Kent Publishing Company, 1983), pp. 65–89.
5. *See* William G. Egelhoff, "Strategy and Structure in Multinational Corporations: A Revision of the Stopford and Wells Model," *Strategic Management Journal,* vol. 9 (1988), pp. 1–14.
6. William H. Davidson and Philippe Haspeslagh, "Shaping a Global Product Organization," *Harvard Business Review,* July–August 1982, pp. 125–132.

7. Paul R. Lawrence, Harvey F. Kolodny, and Stanley M. David, "The Human Side of the Matrix," *Organizational Dynamics,* Summer 1979, pp. 43–47. *Also see* William C. Goggin, "How the Multinational Structure Works at Dow Corning," *Harvard Business Review,* January–February 1974, pp. 64–65.
8. Y. L. Doz, *Power Systems and Telecommunications Equipment: Government Control and Multinational Strategic Management* (New York: Praeger, 1979), p. 209.
9. Ibid., p. 237.
10. Paul R. Lawrence et al., "The Human Side of the Matrix," *Organizational Dynamics,* Summer 1979, p. 47.
11. Stanley M. David and Paul R. Lawrence, "Problems of Matrix Organization," *Harvard Business Review,* May–June 1978, pp. 134–136.
12. Milton G. Halman, "Organization and Staffing of Foreign Operations of Multinational Corporations," a paper presented at the Academy of International Business Meeting, New Orleans, October 25, 1980.
13. *See* S. Samuel Craig, Susan P. Douglas, and Srinivas K. Reddy, "Market Structure, Performance and Strategy: A Comparison of U.S. and European Markets," in S. Tamer Cavusgil, ed., *Advances in International Marketing* (Greenwich, CT: Jai Press, Inc., 1987), pp. 1–22.
14. Stefan H. Robock, Kenneth Simmons, and Jack Zwick, *International Business and Multinational Enterprise,* 4th ed. (Homewood, IL: Irwin, 1989), pp. 270–272. *Also see* Gunnar Hedlund, "Organization In-between: The Evaluation of the Mother-Daughter Structure of Managing Foreign Subsidiaries in Swedish Multinational Corporations," *Journal of International Business Studies,* Fall 1984, pp. 109–124.
15. *See* David K. Tse, Kam-hon Lee, Lean Vertinsky, and Donald A. Wehrung, "Does Culture Matter? A Cross-Cultural Study of Executives' Choice, Decisiveness, and Risk Adjustment in International Marketing," *Journal of Marketing,* October 1988, pp. 81–95. *Also see* Lane Kelley, Arthur Whatley, and Reginald Worthley, "Assessing the Effects of Culture on Managerial Attitudes: A Three-Culture Test," *Journal of International Business Studies,* Summer 1987, pp. 17–32.
16. Howard V. Perlmutter, "The Tortuous Evolution of the Multinational Corporation," *Columbia Journal of World Business,* January–February 1969, pp. 9–18. *Also see* Yoram Zeira, "Ethnocentrism in Host-Country Organizations," *Business Horizons,* June 1979, pp. 66–74, and Nigel Piercy, "The Corporate Environment for Marketing Management and Marketing Budgeting," *International Marketing Review,* Spring–Summer 1984, pp. 14–32.
17. William G. Egelhoff, "Strategy and Structure in Multinational Corporations: An Information Processing Approach," *Administrative Science Quarterly,* September 1982, pp. 435–458. *Also see* "Tips to Consider Before Restructuring Your World Operations," *Business International,* July 4, 1980, pp. 210–211.
18. *See* Christopher A. Bartlett, "MNCs: Get Off the Organization Merry-Go-Round," *Harvard Business Review,* March–April 1983, pp. 138–146.
19. *See* Subhash C. Jain, *Marketing Planning and Strategy,* 3rd ed. (Cincinnati, OH: South-Western Publishing Co., 1990), Ch. 11. *Also see* "And Now the Post-Industrial Corporation," *Business Week,* March 3, 1986, p. 64.
20. *See* Jeremy Main, "How to Go Global—And Why," *Fortune,* August 28, 1989, p. 70.
21. Christopher A. Bartlett and Sumantra Ghoshal, *Managing Across Borders: The Transnational Solution* (Boston: Harvard Business School Press, 1989).
22. R. J. Aylmer, "Who Makes Marketing Decisions in the Multinational Firm?" *Journal of Marketing,* October 1970, pp. 25–30. *Also see* Donna G. Goehle, *Decision Making in Multinational Corporations* (Ann Arbor, MI: University Research Press, 1980); and J. Michael Geringer and Louis Hebert, "Control and Performance of International Joint Ventures," *Journal of International Business Studies,* Summer 1989, pp. 235–254.
23. Zada L. Martinez and David A. Ricks, "Multinational Parent Companies' Influence Over Human Resource Decisions of Affiliates: U.S. Firms in Mexico," *Journal of International Business Studies,* Fall 1989, pp. 465–488.
24. *See* Saeed Samiee, "Pricing in Marketing Strategies of U.S. and Foreign-Based Com-

panies," *Journal of Business Research,* vol. 15 (1987), pp. 17–30.

25. R. J. Aylmer, "Who Makes Marketing Decisions in the Multinational Firm?" *Journal of Marketing,* October 1970, pp. 25–30.
26. Stephen R. Gates and William G. Egelhoff, "Centralization in Headquarters—Subsidiary Relationships," *Journal of International Business Studies,* Summer 1986, pp. 71–92.
27. Jacques Picard, "How European Companies Control Marketing Decisions Abroad," *Columbia Journal of World Business,* Summer 1977, p. 120. *Also see* Hans Jansson, *Interfirm Linkages in a Developing Economy: The Case of Swedish Firms in India* (Uppsala, Sweden: Uppsala University, 1982); Charles Y. Young, "Demystifying Japanese Management Practices," *Harvard Business Review,* November–December 1984, p. 172.
28. Ulrich Wiechmann, "Integrating Multinational Marketing Activities," *Columbia Journal of World Business,* Winter 1974, p. 12.
29. Ibid., pp. 13–14.
30. Thomas M. Gladwin and Ingo Walter, "Bhopal and the Multinational," *The Wall Street Journal,* January 16, 1985, p. 28.
31. J. K. Johansson, "A Note on the Managerial Relevance of Interdependence," *Journal of International Business Studies,* Winter 1982, pp. 143–145.
32. "General Motors' Big European Overhaul," *Business Week,* February 10, 1986, p. 42.
33. Arvind V. Phatek, *Managing Multinational Corporations* (New York: Praeger, 1979), p. 222.
34. Lane Daly, James Jiambalvo, Gary Sundem, and Yasumasa Kondo, "Attitude Toward Financial Control Systems in the United States and Japan," *Journal of International Business Studies,* Fall 1985, pp. 91–110.
35. Susan P. Douglas and C. Samuel Craig, "Examining Performance of U.S. Multinationals in Foreign Markets," *Journal of International Business Studies,* Winter 1983, pp. 51–62.
36. David Norburn, Sue Birley, Mark Dunn, and Adrian Payne, "A Four-Nation Study of the Relationship Between Marketing Effectiveness, Corporate Culture, Corporate Values, and Market Orientation," *Journal of International Business Studies,* Third Quarter 1990, pp. 451–468.
37. Hari Bedi, "Tips for Dealing with Asian Managers," *The Asian Wall Street Journal Weekly,* November 18, 1985, p. 16. *Also see* Nancy J. Adler, "Cultural Synergy: The Management of Cross-Cultural Organizations," in W. Warner Burke and Leonard D. Goodstein, eds., *Trends and Issues in OD: Current Theory and Practice* (San Diego: University Associates, 1980), pp. 163–184.
38. *See* Julian Gresser and Andrew Osterman, "Competing with the Japanese on Their Own Turf," *The Wall Street Journal,* December 2, 1985, p. 20. *Also see* Robert Shuter, "When the Boss Is a Stranger in a Familiar Land," *The Wall Street Journal,* January 1, 1985, p. 20.
39. Ulrich E. Wiechmann and Lewis G. Pringle, "Problems that Plague Multinational Marketers," *Harvard Business Review,* July–August 1979, pp. 118–124.
40. Christopher A. Bartlett and Sumantra Ghoshal, "Tap Your Subsidiaries for Global Reach," *Harvard Business Review,* November–December 1986, p. ES26.

CHAPTER • 19

Marketing Planning and Strategy for International Business

CHAPTER FOCUS

After studying this chapter, you should be able to:

- Describe perspectives of marketing planning at the corporate and subsidiary levels
- Examine the steps in achieving planning effectiveness
- Discuss the current and future role of the United States in light of emerging changes
- List strategic changes that MNCs are likely to face in the 1990s

The essence of international marketing management is the development of appropriate objectives, strategies, and plans that culminate in the successful realization of foreign market opportunities. The world marketplace is marked by accelerating change requiring explicit statements of objectives and strategies.

Business across national boundaries became a dominant factor in world commerce after World War II. Today for a number of U.S. companies, as well as for many non-U.S. multinationals, sales and/or revenues from overseas exceed domestic business. The international marketplace is changing fast. In the 1960s, U.S. corporations had an edge in many ways, but no longer. In such markets as automobiles, steel, watches, textile goods, and electronic equipment, there is fierce competition. In addition to multinational enterprises from Europe and Japan, corporations belonging to Third World nations, such as South Korea, Taiwan, Brazil, and India, are increasingly participating in world markets, giving rise to new forms of competition.

Currently, multinational corporations are expanding at a rate of more than 10 percent a year, or twice the growth rate for gross world product. The prospect is that these business organizations will become even more important in the future. According to the projections of knowledgeable economists based on present trends, in the year 2000 the economy of the world will be more than half internationalized.

Although markets overseas are changing and the competition increasing, international markets offer attractive opportunities. As a matter of fact, markets across national boundaries frequently offer higher rates of return than domestic markets. But to make a mark in the international arena, a company needs to define its objectives clearly, choosing appropriate strategies, and develop adequate plans to implement the chosen strategies.

The purpose of this chapter is fourfold. First, perspectives of international marketing planning and strategy are examined. This analysis is followed by a discussion of a short-term operations marketing plan. Next, concepts and procedures for developing and formulating international marketing strategy are studied. Finally, the unfolding environment likely to have an impact on international marketing in the rest of this century is probed. This final section highlights the challenges that lie ahead for international marketing executives.

Dimensions of International Planning and Strategy

Planning practices for multinational markets are far behind those for domestic markets. This is particularly true of strategic planning.[1] Theoretically, international marketing planning and strategy should involve both subsidiary and headquarters management. Further planning should focus on operational matters as well as strategic issues. Currently, however, most marketing planning among multinational corporations is operational and short term. In a great many corporations, the effort amounts to a set of financial figures extrapolated for the next four to six quarters. In some cases the plan is put together by the headquarters staff with meager inputs from the subsidiary. In some corporations, however, the planning task is entirely delegated to subsidiary management. In the latter case, the headquarters' review is skimpy and only ritualistic.[2]

The challenge of successfully competing in the international field in the future will force corporations to become more systematic in their planning efforts.

> In a world of continuous and escalating change, the planning process has never been more difficult nor has delay in recognizing our errors and modifying our plans been more costly. Social and political forces join the customary economic variables to make planning more complex. We could, of course, respond to the difficulties of planning for an uncertain future by satisfying ourselves with the status quo and concentrating on attempts to do better the things we are doing today, thus addressing ourselves to historic markets, applications, processes, and programs. In fact, some of the popularity of this "small is beautiful" way of thinking may in reality be an expression of frustration with the problem of planning for growth. Most of us in industry reject this attitude, however, not only because we don't want to fly in ever-smaller circles but also, and more importantly, because we have a contract with our employees, shareholders, and customers, and the communities in which we operate to grow, and in so doing harvest the benefits of our growth-oriented service, social, and profit objectives.
>
> Every industry must look ahead—one year, five years, ten years—and plan for: (a) the future political, social and economic environment; (b) the evolution of that particular industry; and (c) how the industry must change to meet the problems and opportunities it judges it will face.[3]

Essentially, marketing planning at the subsidiary level is short-term planning related to the next twelve to fifteen months and not strategic planning, which usually has a long- run focus. A subsidiary's planning efforts should be duly coordinated with those at headquarters. Characteristically, it should be from the bottom up and should take into account the environmental realities surrounding its products/markets. In this effort, the parent corporation plays two roles. The first role involves facilitating linkage between corporate and subsidiary perspectives. This amounts to providing corporatewide perspectives relative to its overall mission and direction, both generally and with reference to the subsidiary/country market. The second role includes establishing a worldwide planning system. Such a system is achieved by developing planning procedures and communicating them to subsidiaries. An additional role that corporate headquarters must perform is to serve as a catalyst in creating a planning culture among the subsidiary executives.

At headquarters, marketing planning focuses on coordination and approval of plans submitted by subsidiaries, as well as formulation of corporatewide strategy. The strategy formulation in international business reflects not only the domestic experience of the company but also management's orientation toward multinational business. Three management orientations were discussed in the previous chapter: ethnocentrism, polycentrism, and geocentrism. A company with a geocentric perspective tends to look at world markets as a whole, with no demarcation between domestic and international business. Its strategic focus is global. But an executive with an ethnocentric orientation views international business as secondary, a place to dispose of "surplus" products left over after fulfilling domestic demand. The differences in these approaches have been illustrated by choices of branding policy.

- *Ethnocentric approach.* Branding policy in overseas companies stresses the parent company as a unifying feature but not necessarily the origin of the parent company.
- *Polycentric approach.* Each local company brands products on an independent basis, consistent with local country criteria.
- *Geocentric approach.* A worldwide branding policy exists only for those brands that are acceptable worldwide.[4]

Planning at the Subsidiary Level

Presumably, an overseas subsidiary would undertake both short-term marketing planning as well as strategic planning. The following section examines conceptual designs for formulating subsidiary plans. Also addressed are the problems that hinder the planning process. Finally, suggestions are made to resolve the problems.

Short-Term Planning

A short-term marketing plan constitutes the core of an overseas subsidiary's planning effort. It is operationally, not strategically, oriented. The plan covers marketing operations usually for about a year.

The complexity of planning varies among companies. In some cases it may amount to simple preparation of sales budgets. In more globally oriented firms, however, planning would involve multiple considerations to consolidate mutual interdependence between different overseas affiliates and the parent corporation.

The process of short-term marketing planning is depicted in Figure 19.1. The inputs for triggering the planning process are partly received from the parent corporation and partly generated within the subsidiary. The corporate headquarters shares with the subsidiary the perspectives of its mission and objectives. This input helps the subsidiary to define its overall goals and specific marketing objectives. Headquarters, in order to establish homogeneity among different subsidiaries' plans, may prescribe a standard procedure for conducting the planning process. For example, a standard format may be required for sales forecasts/budgets. Additionally, the parent organization would provide the subsidiary an analysis of the shape of things to come in the environment. The planning inputs gathered at the subsidiary level consist of external and internal factors. External factors are the emerging trends in the product/market environment (for example, competition, legislation to be enacted, demand shifts, and the like). Internal factors include past sales data and the scope of activities in other functional areas of the business.

Equipped with the above inputs, planning starts with a review of past sales and their extrapolation into the future. The extrapolated forecasts are duly revised in light of the planning inputs. For example, sales forecasts may need to be revised downward because of a newly established plant by a domestic competitor. Similarly, sales forecasts for a product/market may be increased if the subsidiary's production facilities expect to be able to manufacture an improved version of the product.

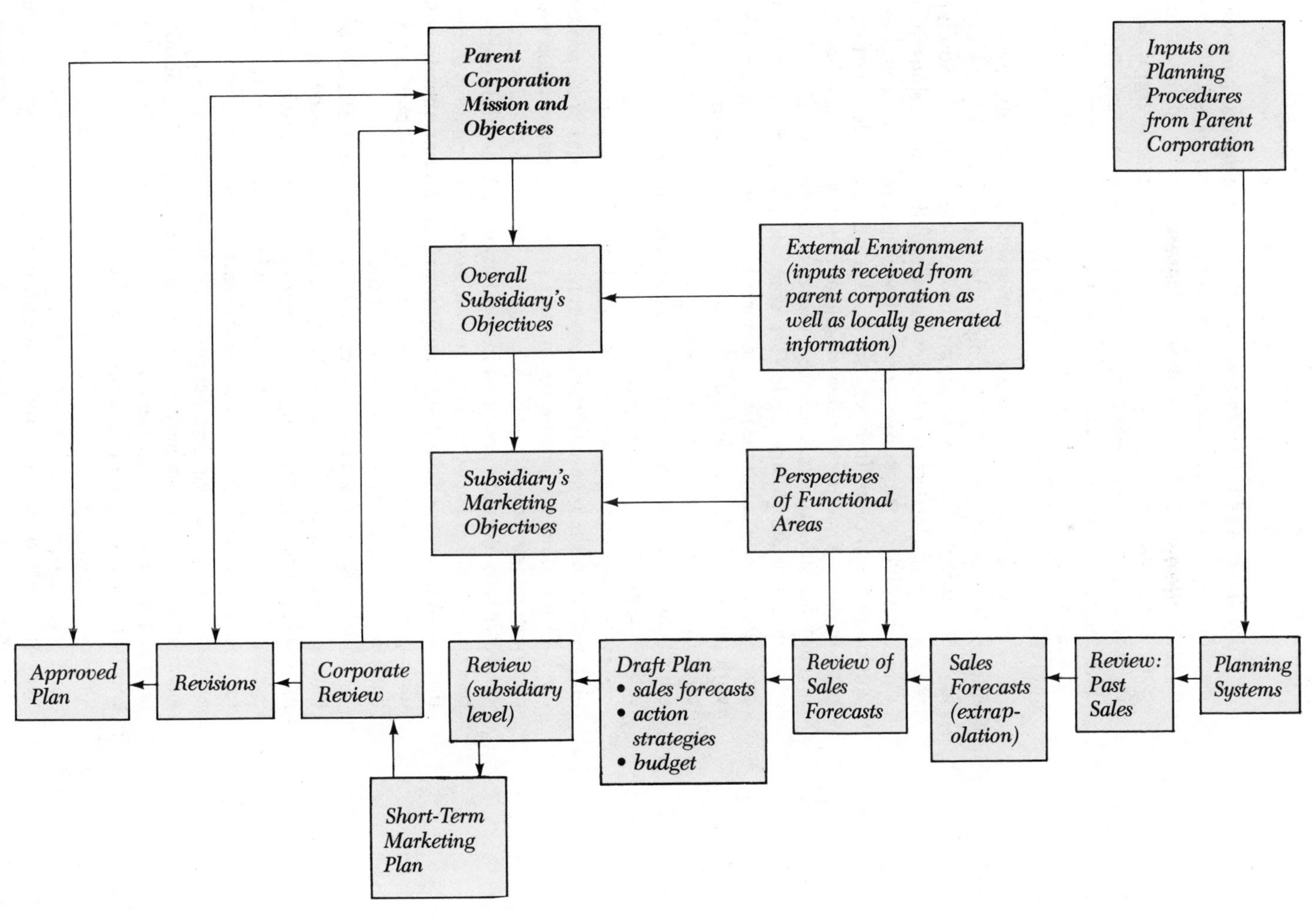

FIGURE 19.1 Framework for Short-Term Marketing Planning by Overseas Subsidiary

The final sales forecasts form the basis for generating action strategies and developing the budget. Action strategies refer to the perspective to be pursued in different areas of the marketing mix—product, price, promotion, and distribution. The budget would include sales revenues, gross margin, full details on selling and administrative expenses, promotional allocations, and other overheads. The budget may include data from the past one or two years to permit historical comparisons. The budget should be prepared in local currency as well as in U.S. dollars.

The marketing budget must be reviewed by the subsidiary management to add to and accommodate the companywide outlook. For example, the subsidiary's controller office would supply the cash-flow analysis. Similarly, the finance function would reflect the likely impact of the fluctuations in local currency value. Likewise, the budget would have appended a capital-expenditure and working-capital plan. In brief, the marketing budget does not constitute a complete budget. A variety of other financial information must be included before it is ready for submission to the corporate management.

Once the subsidiary review is complete, the short-term marketing plan emerges. This is submitted to the parent corporation for examination together with the subsidiary budget and other related information. Usually, the subsidiary plan and budget are presented to a corporate team in person. The meeting usually is held in the United States so the subsidiary executives have a chance to meet different corporate officers and visit various plants and facilities.

If the corporation is regionally organized, the subsidiary may present its plan and budget to the regional management. The regional management then assimilates all the plans within the region and makes a regionwide presentation to the corporate management.

Revisions may be demanded in the marketing plan and/or the accompanying budget. The subsidiary management can accept the revisions or defend their position through supplying appropriate information and arguments. Once a compromise is reached, the parent corporation approves the plan, and it becomes the basis for the subsidiary's operations in the next year.

Ideally, the short-term marketing plan should be initiated by the subsidiary management. Further, it should bear a close relation to the subsidiary's strategic plan, which presumably would be appropriately linked to overall corporate strategy. In practice, however, it would be naive to expect such a systematic effort, for two reasons. First, the state of the art may not permit drawing plans in a smooth, sequential manner. Second, lack of necessary data and of proper management orientation impede adherence to a conceptually sound system. For example, corporate management with an ethnocentric orientation would want the corporate way of planning adopted without consideration of the local environment.

Strategic Planning

Very few subsidiaries practice strategic market planning. As a matter of fact, anything beyond short-term planning mainly consists of longer-term extrapolations of the same plan. Such a perspective can be explained by two factors. First, the art of strategic planning is still emerging, and its articulation at the subsidiary level can be difficult. Second, many multinational corporations consider strategic planning to be the prerogative of the corporation and discourage subsidiary involvement. While centralization of strategic planning at headquarters may appear attractive, there is one crucial problem. Centrally developed strategic plans tend to consider the entire world to be similar, and thus, standardized strategies are formulated for all markets. Unfortunately, such an assumption cannot hold true. Markets outside the United States differ in many dimensions, and appropriate strategies to serve these markets cannot be formulated centrally.[5]

Process of Strategic Market Planning Two basic factors of strategic planning are markets and competition. Surrounding these factors are sociocultural, technological, political, and regulatory concerns, unique to each market. Strategic market planning should begin with customer analysis and end with differential marketing programs tailored to meet buyer needs, giving due consideration to environmental influences.[6]

After a thorough analysis of buyer needs and expectations, R & D should be approached for development of a customized product as necessary. Strategic directions for introducing new products and penetrating new markets should be developed. The customization may simply involve adaptation of package design/size or may require an entirely new version of the product. The remaining ingredients of the marketing mix should be custom designed similarly. Once the strategy is approved by the parent corporation, implementation of the program begins. The implementation of a strategy may take years, and in the process several go/no-go decisions would be made.

In the development of different market-related strategies, the impact of emerging environmental trends ought to be incorporated. For example, traditional wage rates in Germany rose proportionally to productivity increases. This discipline has been one of the strengths of the German economy. However, in 1983 and 1984, wage rates increased by an average of 14 percent each year.[7] Since productivity increases accounted for less than half this amount, how much could be realized in substantial price increases? Naturally, a complete study of competitive conditions would be required to make this decision.

Problems of Strategic Market Planning A variety of problems hinders a subsidiary's planning process. The first problem concerns the availability of adequate information. Both the subsidiary and the parent corporation can be blamed for this problem. Subsidiaries often lack the knowledge and resources to scan the environment systematically and gather adequate information from the external environment. Further, internal information may not be adequately organized. Not the least problem is that available information on national trends and so on is often outdated, particularly in such emerging countries as Brazil and South Korea, which are changing fast.

As far as headquarters is concerned, there may not even be a worldwide marketing information system in place. Thus, information at headquarters from different subsidiaries and different groups is not adequately collected, nor is the gathered information properly disseminated.

Furthermore, sometimes information is poorly coordinated. Thus, while there might be an abundance of information, the right information may be nowhere to be found. Conceivably, headquarters could request information from a subsidiary that headquarters itself had made available.

Lack of an established planning system is another problem. Emphasis on day-to-day matters by headquarters discourages strategic planning at the subsidiary level. In some cases, the planning system is too complex and unnecessarily cumbersome. Thus, a major portion of marketing managers' time in subsidiary companies is spent on responding to the needs of the parent corporation.

Another problem concerns the scarcity of trained managers. Subsidiaries often lack trained personnel to undertake planning. This problem can, however, be mitigated through training arranged by the parent corporation. Finally, if the plan is adhered to as a rigid instrument of control, it could lead to intracompany fighting and manipulations to ensure meeting cost and revenue projections. Such fighting leads to rivalries, which are obviously counterproductive. Manipulations result in a distorted picture of performance.

Seeking Planning Effectiveness

Effective planning at the subsidiary level should be encouraged through the setting of objectives, the training of planning professionals, the development of planning and communication systems, and a cordial, collaborative attitude between all the people involved. The core of these measures is cooperation between the subsidiary and the parent corporation (see International Marketing Highlight 19.1).

Objective Setting The subsidiary's objectives must not be directives from the home office, nor be defined solely by the subsidiary itself in isolation from corporate direction. Rather, the objectives should be jointly set so that both corporatewide perspectives and conditions peculiar to the subsidiary environment are weighed in arriving at the subsidiary objectives.

Cadre of Planning Professionals The corporation should develop a cadre of international strategic planning professionals. Such professionals should have awareness and insight into the country or region whose planning they coordinate. In other words, marketing planning at headquarters should not be entrusted to finance people who examine strictly in terms of set formulas and cut-off points. The planners at headquarters should be sensitive to the varying environment of each subsidiary before passing judgement on its financial performance.

Planning and Communication Systems Traditionally, multinational corporations have pursued standardized strategies worldwide. For example, if a corporate decision is made to increase market share for a particular product, that decision must be carried out globally. Standardization, however, ignores the realities of the marketplace in subsidiaries. The problem may be solved in two ways: (1) through overhauling the planning system to take into account the marketing environment of each subsidiary and (2) by developing appropriate data bases through effective communication between the subsidiary and the home office.

International Marketing Highlight 19.1

Planning Activities at the Subsidiary Level

Grand Metropolitan monitors the effectiveness of subsidiary marketing programs annually, but evaluation is conducted at the sector level more frequently and at the local level sales and marketing activity is often measured on a monthly basis.

At the start of each company year, long-term (i.e., four-year) objectives are updated and agreed upon and short-term objectives reviewed. (Long-term overall objectives are set by the individual sectors working in conjunction with representatives from the corporate planning department, but specific marketing tasks remain the exclusive province of the relevant sector managers.) Short-term marketing performance is judged by reference to these short- and long-term goals at regular intervals by local management and by sector management, both of which formally review progress at the end of each quarter.

In the autumn, each sector reviews its strategy and, if necessary, revises it. This review is finalized at the corporate center in December. Local marketing decisions are then amended in the light of any changes that have been agreed to. The review at this time is concerned with strategic concepts rather than specific quantified business objectives. These issues are settled at the subsequent set of meetings that take place in the spring, at which quantified objectives are agreed for actions consequent upon previously agreed strategies. The final step in the process is the submission and agreement of annual plans at local, sector, and corporate levels. This takes place in August/September.

Source: Marketing Strategies for Global Growth and Competitiveness (New York: Business International, no date), p. 74.

Collaborative Attitudes Both the subsidiary and the parent corporation should develop an attitude of cordiality toward each other. Neither can do an adequate job of marketing planning on its own. They should collaborate with each other, with the parent playing the staff role and the subsidiary assuming the line responsibility for marketing planning. This way headquarters would be able to bring its systems capability to the planning, while the subsidiary would contribute its deep knowledge of the marketplace.

Marketing Planning at the Corporate Level

Corporate management mainly plays two planning-related roles. First, it provides various informational inputs to the subsidiaries and reviews and approves their plans. Second, it develops a corporatewide strategic plan, which may be either one global strategic plan covering both domestic and international markets or two separate strategic plans, one each for domestic and international business. Presumably, companies with an ethnocentric or polycentric orientation would follow the latter course. Geocentrically oriented firms, however, would consider global markets as one market and would not make a distinction between domestic and international business.

Corporate headquarters' role in the planning efforts of subsidiaries has been examined in the previous section. Studied in this section are different aspects of a multinational corporation's strategic planning activity. Strategic planning among corporations is a new phenomenon that became popular in the 1970s. Initial efforts at strategic planning, as might be expected, were limited to domestic business. Strategic planning in international business is still in the developmental stage. Thus, overall experience in strategic planning for worldwide business is limited.

Strategic marketing planning constitutes only a part of the corporate strategic plan. *The true role of strategic marketing planning is to influence the behavior of competitors and the evolution of the market to the advantage of the corporation.* Stated differently, *marketing strategy is the concept of changing the competitive environment.* Thus, a marketing strategy statement includes a description of the new competitive equilibrium to be created, the cause-and-effect relationships that will bring it about, and the logical steps to support the course direction. A strategic marketing plan specifies that sequence and timing of the steps that will alter competitive status. Against today's background of mounting labor costs, sluggish growth in home markets, shifting exchange rates, and rising import barriers abroad, international strategy becomes increasingly significant (see International Marketing Highlight 19.2).

Shrinking profit margins from domestic operations impel MNCs more strongly than ever to make explicit strategy statements. Marketing figures prominently in these statements.[8]

Two related developments appear to signal the continued importance of strategic planning for international business. First, companies that derive a major portion of their sales and profit from overseas activities and look at markets abroad for future growth must depend on a well-prepared strategy to pursue appropriate paths. Second, given the changing patterns of competition since the 1970s, strategic planning is a critical factor for maintaining leverage in overseas markets.

Planning Process

The process for international strategic planning is depicted in Figure 19.2. The process consists of sequential steps to be followed. These steps are basic to strategic planning, irrespective of management's attitudinal orientation (see International Marketing Highlight 19.3).

The process begins with the firm's commitment to go international. A corporation enters overseas markets to pursue long-term profitable growth. As growth prospects in the domestic market diminish, international markets provide a strategic alternative. On the other hand, companies frequently opt for international business in response to an invitation by a foreign interest. The decision to go, or not to go, international must be based on such considerations as corporate mission and objectives, long-term opportunity potential, analysis of strengths and weaknesses, management philosophy, opportunities at home, and financial implications of foreign entry.[9] The decision to enter international markets may be an

International Marketing Highlight 19.2

Singapore Airlines—The Flying Beauty

It may be the world's 15th biggest carrier, but Singapore Airlines is consistently the most profitable. In the year ending on March 31, 1991, it made a net profit of S$913 million ($513 million) on sales of S$4.9 billion. Its balance sheet shows a mere S$438 million in long-term debt and a cool S$2.1 billion in cash. The carrier has the youngest fleet of any big airline—the average age of its forty-six aircraft is under five years. And it is the winner of countless awards for service.

The contrast with American and European airlines, many of which began to hemorrhage cash during the Gulf war and have yet to recover, could hardly be starker. This raises two intriguing questions: How has a tiny city-state with a population of under 3 million, and thus no automatic reservoir of passengers for its national carrier, managed to create a global airline? And can Singapore Airlines maintain its edge?

The recipe for success as described by Joseph Pillay, the airline's chairman since its formation in 1972, looks deceptively simple: "Our mission remains inviolable: offer the customer the best service that we are capable of providing; cut our costs to the bone; and generate a surplus to continue the unending process of renewal."

What has saved this from becoming just another empty mission statement is Singapore Airlines' relentless investment. It has forty new aircraft on firm order, and another twenty-five on option. The most important are 747-400s, which carry more people and fly farther than earlier versions of the jumbo. They also use 35 percent less fuel. Lower running costs and the ability to fly nonstop, a key factor in attracting high-yield business travelers, create bigger profits. These enable Singapore Airlines to pay cash for its aircraft. Another benefit of this virtuous circle is that aircraft can be sold before they are too old.

Source: The Economist, December 14, 1991, p. 74.

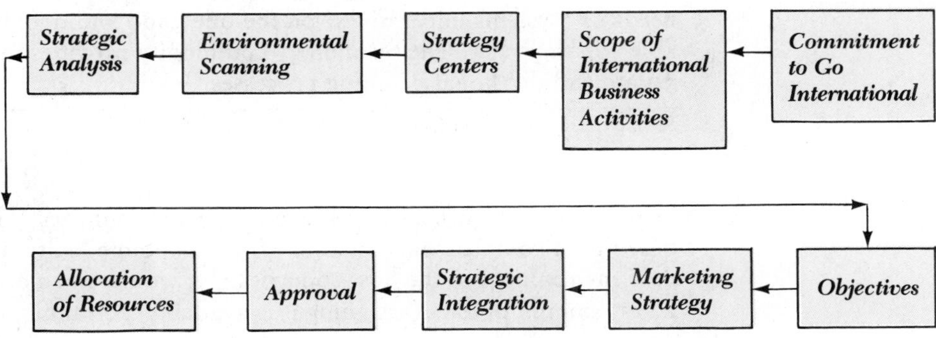

FIGURE 19.2 Process of Strategic Marketing Planning at the Corporate Level

International Marketing Highlight 19.3

How IBM Approaches Global Strategic Planning

IBM has developed an approach to global strategic planning that takes into account the divergence between headquarters and regions. The approach revolves around its unique needs and corporate culture. These include parallel planning process, the ability to direct and leverage the immense resources of the organization worldwide, the ability of corporate planners to promote cultural cross-fertilization and act as "broker" of creative ideas, and the use of global models to promote common goals.

The core of IBM's strategic planning process resides within the divisions. Each geographic and functional division generates its own strategic plan on an annual cycle, coordinated by the corporate planning office. The cycle culminates in "commitment plans," which comprise a five-year strategic plan and a two-year detailed business plan. The plans represent both a blueprint for the divisions' response to regional market needs and opportunities and a financial commitment to the corporation. There's a qualitative and a quantitative dimension and the latter becomes the measurement for the following year.

Concurrent with the commitment plan cycle, a "top-down" planning mechanism provides direction from senior management. A series of strategic planning conferences is attended by twenty top executives. The strategies emerging from these conferences are often far-reaching in their implications for the organization. An example is the company's commitment to the concept of "market-driven quality" in the late 1980s. Although the concept sounds general, it has had implications for every part of the vast organization. It has affected not only the marketing and production techniques, but the very way in which IBM measures its own progress. This sets the overall framework, defines the business, and establishes a long-range intent.

A third critical dimension to the planning process is product planning. Within IBM, there is a separate framework for technology-driven planning of new products and service concepts, where the time frame may be as long as a decade. A continual exchange takes place between the technological research function and the corporate and divisional strategies, providing input on customer needs or "systems imperatives" on the one hand and defining the "art of the doable" on the other. The technology community provides major input to the corporate and divisional planning processes.

Source: Business International, May 28, 1990, pp. 169–170.

open decision, or it may be relative to specific countries. The decision should be based on a complete examination of the economic, cultural, political, and business environment of the host countries.[10] It would be an arduous task to analyze a vast amount of data (assuming it is available) pertaining to different countries. As a shortcut, therefore, companies often choose countries with similar perspectives. Thus, Canada, Great Britain, France, and Germany are among the markets that appear more attractive culturally, politically, and economically to many U.S. companies. Chapter 6, on economic environment, presents a framework for selecting international markets for making investments. This same framework is relevant in the strategic decision process.

Strategic Business Units

After overseas product/market matches are established, the next step is to reorganize different parts of the business that would be involved internationally into strategy centers or strategic business units. ***Strategic business units (SBUs)*** are self-contained businesses that meet three criteria: (1) they have a set of clearly defined external competitors, (2) their managers are responsible for developing and implementing their own strategies, and (3) their profitability can be measured in real income, rather than in artificial dollars posted as transfer payments between divisions. Once SBUs are identified, appointments of SBU heads should be made.

The steps discussed so far are the purview of top management. Such work should be undertaken at the highest level with analytical support provided by corporate staff. It should be strongly emphasized that SBUs do not replace the traditional organizational lines. The operations continue to be planned and implemented as in the past. Over and above the traditional organization, however, SBU structure is created for determining strategy. Thus, an SBU may be established around products/markets in different divisions in different countries. For example, a company may manufacture color televisions in an electronic division in a country, while in another country radios and stereos are manufactured as a part of the home entertainment division. For strategy development purposes TVs, radios, and stereo equipment may be pulled together in an SBU.

Further strategic planning analysis henceforth is undertaken at the SBU level. In a large multiproduct, multimarket company, strategy cannot be developed at the top management level because it would be too complex a task for one office to examine the perspectives of all products/markets.

Each SBU conducts opportunity analysis of the different products/markets under its control. This analysis can be accomplished by the product portfolio approach popularized by the Boston Consulting Group (BCG).

Product Portfolio Approach—The BCG Framework

The BCG framework is based on the assumption that the firm with the highest market share relative to its competitors should be able to produce at the lowest cost. Conversely, firms with a low market share relative to competition will be high-cost producers. By comparing relative market share positions (high/low) with market growth rates (high/low), the firm can position its different businesses on a 2-by-2 matrix as shown in Figure 19.3.

Using the two dimensions discussed above, growth and market share, businesses can then be classified into four categories: stars, cash cows, question marks, and dogs. Businesses in each category exhibit different financial characteristics and offer different strategic choices.[11]

Stars High-growth market leaders are called ***stars.*** They generate large amounts of cash, but the cash they generate from earnings and depreciation is more than offset by the cash that must be put back into these businesses in the form of

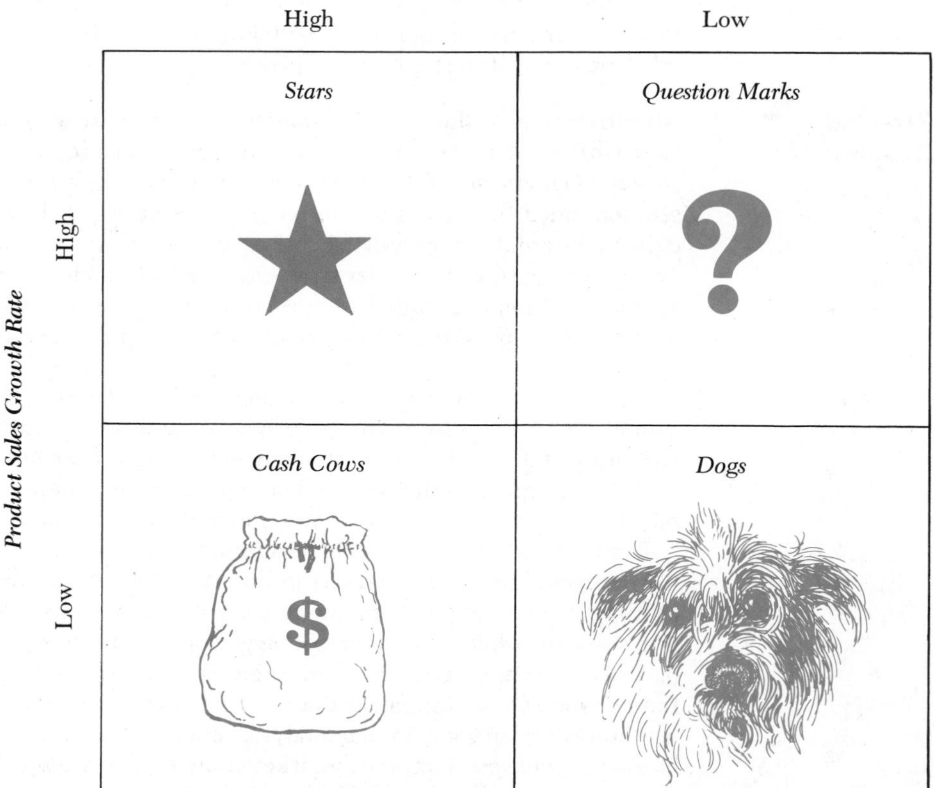

FIGURE 19.3 **Boston Consulting Group Framework**

capital expenditures and increased working capital. Such heavy reinvestment is necessary to fund the capacity increases and inventory and receivable investment that go along with market share gains. Thus, star products represent probably the best profit opportunity available to a company, and their competitive position must be maintained. If a star's share is allowed to slip, because it has been used to provide large amounts of cash in the short run or because of cutbacks in investment or the raising of prices (creating an umbrella for competitors), the star will ultimately become a dog.

The ultimate value of any product or service is reflected in the stream of cash it generates, net of its own reinvestment. For a star, this stream of cash is in the future, sometimes the distant future, and, to obtain real value, the stream of cash must be discounted back to the present at a rate equal to the return on alternative opportunities. It is the future payoff of the star that counts, not the present reported profit.

Cash Cows ***Cash cows*** are characterized by low growth and high market share. They are net providers of cash. Their high earnings coupled with their depreciation represent high cash inflows, while they need very little in the way of reinvestment. Thus, these products generate large cash surpluses, which help to pay dividends and interest, provide debt capacity, supply funds for R&D, meet overheads, and also make cash available for investment in other products. Thus, cash cows are the foundation on which everything else depends. These products must be protected. Technically speaking, a cash cow has a return on assets that exceeds its growth rate. Only if that is true will the cash cow generate more cash than it uses.

Question Marks Products that are in growth markets but have a low share are categorized as ***question marks.*** Because of growth, these products require more cash than they are able to generate on their own, since they have a low share of the market. If nothing is done to change its market share, the question mark will simply absorb large amounts of cash in the short run and later, as growth slows down, become a dog. Thus, unless something is done to change its future outlook, a question mark remains a cash loser throughout its existence and ultimately becomes a "cash trap."

What can be done to make a question mark more viable? One alternative is to gain market share increases for it. Since the business is growing, it can be funded to dominance so that it may become a star, and later a cash cow when growth slows down. This strategy is a costly one in the short run. An abundance of cash must be infused into the question mark in order for it to win a major share of the business, but in the long run this is the only way of developing a sound business from the question mark stage. The other strategy is to divest the business. Outright sale is more desirable. But, if this does not work out, a firm decision must be made not to invest further in the business, and the business must be allowed simply to generate whatever cash it can while none is reinvested.

Dogs Products with low market share and in a low growth position are called ***dogs.*** Their poor competitive position condemns them to poor profits. Because growth is low, there is little potential for gaining sufficient share to achieve a viable cost position. Usually they are net users of cash. Their earnings are low, and the reinvestment required just to keep the business together eats its cash inflow. The business, therefore, becomes a "cash trap" and is likely to regularly absorb cash unless further investment in the business is rigorously avoided. An alternative is to convert dogs into cash, if there is an opportunity to do so.

The usage of BCG framework for performing opportunity analysis in the context of international business is illustrated in Figure 19.4.[12] The top half of the figure shows product/market portfolios of competitors A and B. Competitor A is a market leader. In the United States and Canada its business has reached maturity, while in Europe it has a solid position. The cash cow position in the United States and Canada should generate extra cash for investment in the star markets of Europe. Competitor A has an insignificant position in Brazil and no

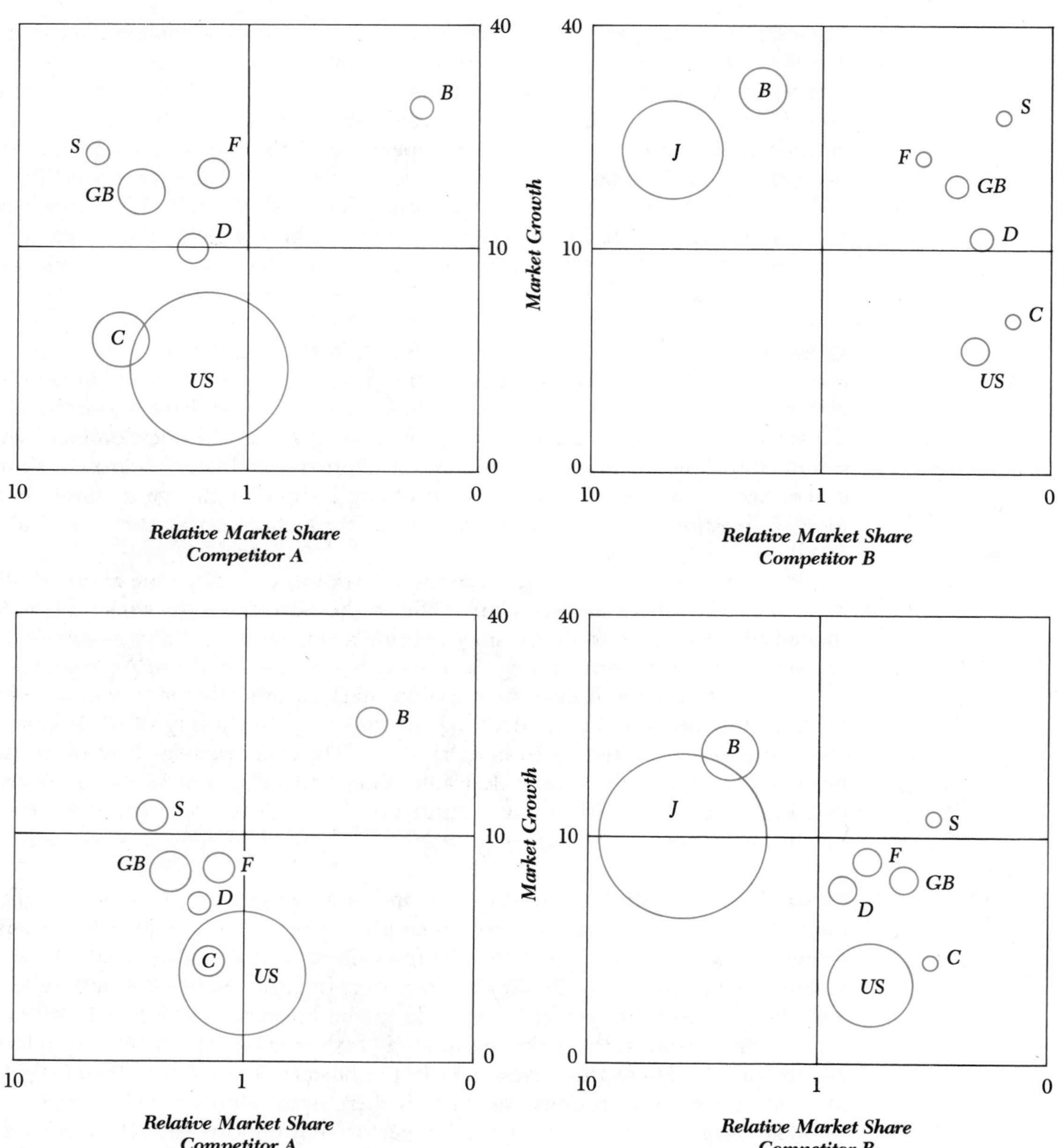

(B = Brazil, C = Canada, D = Germany, F = France, GB = Great Britain, J = Japan, S = Spain, US = United States)

Source: Jean-Claude Larréché, "The International Product-Market Portfolio," in Subhash C. Jain, ed., *Research Frontiers in Marketing: Dialogues and Direction,* Educators' Conference Proceedings (Chicago: American Marketing Association, 1978), p. 278.

FIGURE 19.4 Strategic Analysis Using the Product Portfolio Approach

entry in the Japanese market. On the other hand, B is a smaller competitor, but it occupies a dominant position in the two fast-growing and potentially large markets of Japan and Brazil. It is quite conceivable that in the future B may generate more total unit sales than A, and thus seek lower costs through greater scale effects. The cost leadership may make B more competitive also even in mature markets (the United States and Canada), which currently are A's stronghold. In brief, if competitor A does not take adequate strategic measures in its illustrated position, in five years its position is quite likely to be as depicted in the bottom half of Figure 19.4.

Following the BCG approach, a company may conduct an opportunity analysis by (1) analyzing its current international product/market portfolio, (2) analyzing the competitors' current international product/market portfolio, and (3) projecting its own and the competitors' future international product/market portfolios. The analysis may then be used to define objectives of each product/market. For example, competitor A in Figure 19.4 may set an objective to enter the Japanese market within a year's time. Likewise, objective(s) may be set to make a major commitment to the Brazilian market. Essentially, a product/market objective should be stated either in terms of growth rate, market share, or profitability.

Once objectives have been specified, alternative strategy options are generated. The preferred strategy will usually have a focus on one of the areas of the marketing mix, product, price, promotion, or distribution. For example, the preferred strategy may be to reduce prices to maintain market share. Here the emphasis of the strategy is on pricing. Thus, pricing would be labeled as the core strategy, the area of primary concern. However, in order to make an integrated marketing decision, appropriate changes may have to be made in the product, promotion, and distribution areas. The strategic perspective in these areas can be called *supporting strategies*.

The strategic perspectives of each product/market will be consolidated into an SBU strategic plan. It is quite conceivable that in some cases an SBU consists of just one product/market. In that case the product/market would represent the plan of the SBU. The strategic plans of worldwide SBUs are reviewed at the corporate level for the purpose of integration and to develop a corporatewide posture to achieve synergies and realize trade-offs. Here again, the Boston Consulting Group portfolio framework can be used. Different SBUs can be positioned in the matrix shown in Figure 19.3. Based on the matrix position, the role of each SBU can be determined and resources allocated accordingly. For example, an SBU positioned as a cash cow may be expected to generate surplus cash. No new investments would be planned for such an SBU. On the other hand, a question mark SBU may be designated for conversion into a star, which would qualify it for new investments. Simultaneous consideration of different SBUs permits the corporation to consider options globally and allocate limited resources optimally to derive maximum benefit. In the integration process, the corporation may desire revision of SBU plans. Once that is accomplished, different SBU plans are approved, and a corporatewide strategic plan is formulated, after which resources are allocated.

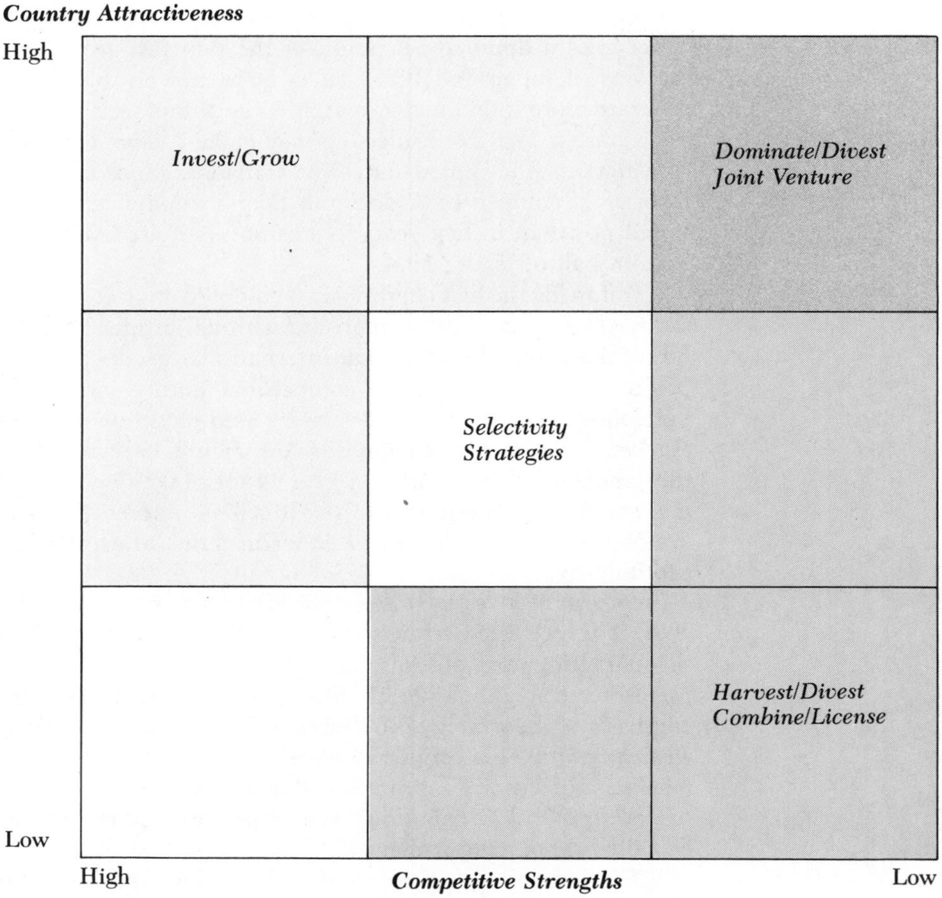

Country Attractiveness

	High		Low
High	*Invest/Grow*		*Dominate/Divest Joint Venture*
		Selectivity Strategies	
Low			*Harvest/Divest Combine/License*

High — ***Competitive Strengths*** — Low

Source: Gilbert D. Harrell and Richard O. Kiefer, "Multinational Strategic Market Portfolios," *MSU Business Topics,* Winter 1981, p. 7.

FIGURE 19.5 Matrix for Plotting Products

Figure 19.5 illustrates the Ford Motor Company's international matrix.[13] This matrix has two dimensions, "country attractiveness" and "competitive strengths," that have been based on a variety of factors. It is this multifactor characteristic that differentiates this approach from the one just discussed.

Country attractiveness was determined based on market size, market growth, government regulation, and economic and political stability. These factors were combined using a single linear scale as follows:

Country attractiveness = *market size* + 2 x *market growth* + (0.5 x *price control/regulation* + 0.25 x *homologation requirements* + 0.25 x *local content and* *compensatory export requirements)* + *(0.35* x *inflation* + *0.35* x *trade balance* + *0.3* x *political factors)*

The weights were based on Ford's strategic planning perspective. Another company may use different weights.

Competitive strength also was computed using four factors (market share, product fit, contribution margin, and market support) in the following manner:

Competitive strength = *(0.5* x *absolute market share* + *0.5 industry position)* x 2 + *product fit* + *(0.5* x *profit per unit* + *0.5* x *profit percentage of net dealer cost)* + *market support*

Figures 19.6 and 19.7 show the position of different countries on the matrix developed using the ratings that were computed based on country attractiveness and competitive strength scores. The invest/grow countries indicate where the company must make a strong commitment. The harvest/divest position refers to countries where harvesting profits or selling the business may be generally appropriate. The dominate/divest/joint venture position represents a difficult strategic choice because the firm is competitively weak but the market is appealing. The final decision demands a careful analysis of investment requirements and other available options.

Essentially, as is done with the BCG approach, the multifactor matrix approach offers guidelines for strategy formulation in international market environments. A company may position its products or country markets on the matrix to study their present standing. The future direction of different countries also can be made, assuming no changes are made in the strategy. The future perspective may be compared with the corporate mission to identify gaps between what is desired and what may be expected if no measures are taken now. Filling these gaps will require making strategic moves for different countries. Once strategic alternatives for an individual country have been identified, the final choice of a strategy will be based on the scope of the overall corporation vis-à-vis the matrix. For example, a country's prospects along the diagonal may appear good, but business in this country cannot be funded in preference to a business in the "high-high" cell.[14]

A different technique for international portfolio analysis and strategy formulation has been recommended by Wind and Douglas.[15] This technique is based on the *analytical hierarchy process approach,* which takes into account the evaluation of risk, return, and other objectives associated with alternative options in a hierarchical fashion; the ultimate decision criterion is the well-being of the host country. A portfolio of worldwide businesses is developed based on:

- Goals to be pursued (for example, optimistic versus status quo versus pessimistic scenarios)
- Set objectives (profit level, market share, sales growth, and demand on resources)

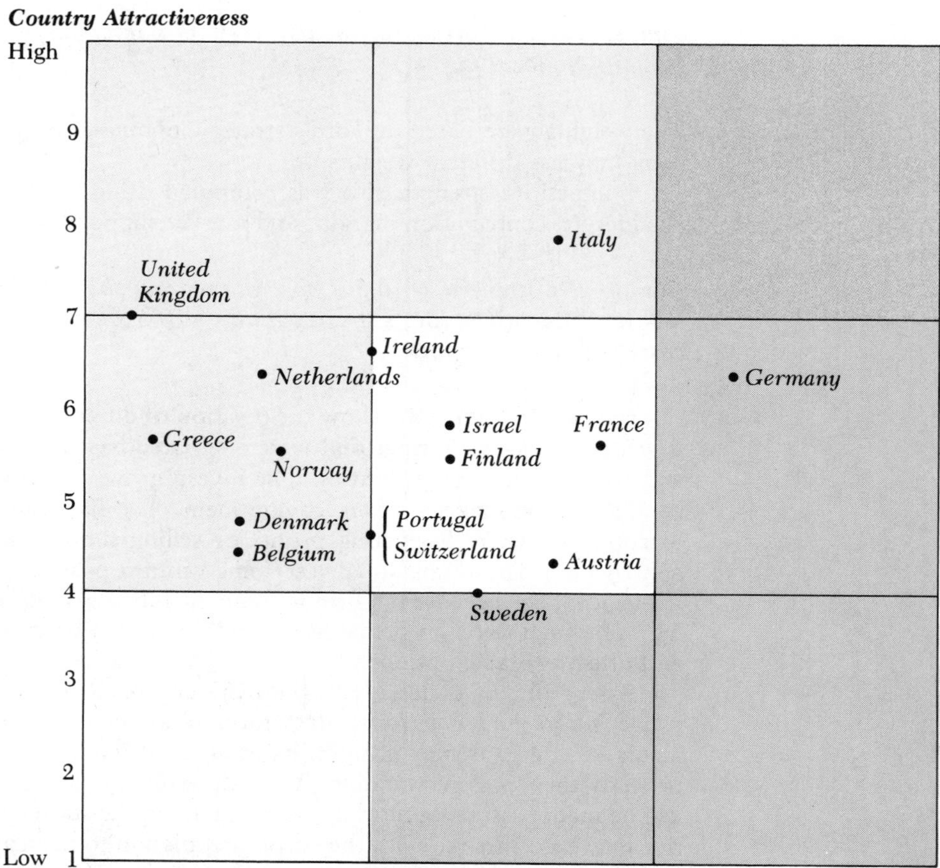

Source: Gilbert D. Harrell and Richard O. Kiefer, "Multinational Strategic Market Portfolios," *MSU Business Topics,* Winter 1981, p. 12.

FIGURE 19.6 European Matrix

- Countries considered (for example, A versus B versus C)
- Mode of entry to be sought (export, licensing, joint venture)
- Market segments to be served
- Product/technology to be positioned in each segment
- Alternative marketing strategies feasible for different products/markets

This brief mention of these various techniques is simply to make the reader aware of alternative methods. Further discussion of these techniques is available for interested readers.[16]

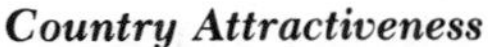

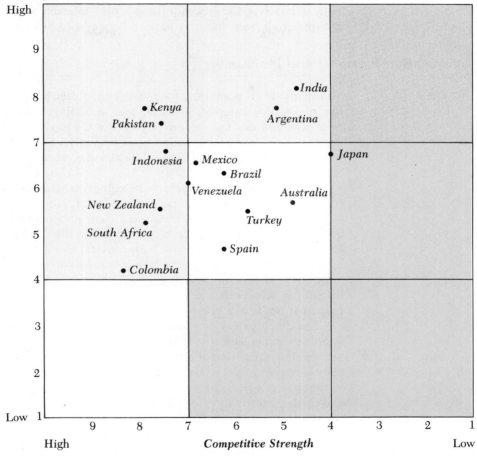

Source: Gilbert D. Harrell and Richard O. Kiefer, "Multinational Strategic Market Portfolios," *MSU Business Topics,* Winter 1981, p. 13.

FIGURE 19.7 Key Country Matrix

The strategic planning processes just discussed are equally relevant to smaller companies. For example, a small company mainly involved overseas through exporting may use the BCG framework to strategically choose markets where it should lay greater emphasis. Similarly, it may position its overseas distributors on the matrix to determine their relative importance and decide the amount of headquarters support that should be allocated to each.

A multinational corporation may have a large number of SBUs, with each SBU encompassing a number of products/markets. But a small firm may just have a few products/markets that bear a close relationship to each other. In that case, the small firm may simply locate its products/markets on the matrix and optimally allocate resources among them. The integration of products/markets into SBUs, recommended for MNCs, may not be necessary for small firms. In general, however, the procedures and tools applicable to large corporations apply to firms of all sizes, but may have to be modified as appropriate.

Information Scanning and Monitoring

Multinational corporations, today more than ever before, are profoundly sensitive to social, economic, political, and technological changes. Each company must scan and monitor relevant changes in the environment to meet these challenges. The scanned information must be analyzed for its impact on marketing strategy. Finally, the impact should be absorbed through appropriate changes in marketing strategy.

The scanning system ought to be comprehensive and include monitoring in several different areas: political, governmental, economic, social, demographic, technological, markets, and resources. Many people will be necessary for whatever monitoring system is developed, because the results must be assessed systematically. Issues considered to be most vital to a company should be followed by action plans stating what the firm is going to do in each area: nothing, gather more data, change product lines, go into new business opportunities, build a defense, or whatever. The monitoring system must be custom designed for the particular needs of a company.

The development of a system for monitoring diverse and critical areas is an important management task that requires not only the assembly of information but also the translation of information into whatever meaning it has for the company— opportunities to be grasped or threats to be averted.[17] The resultant system may simply be an organized way for a group of assigned monitors to abstract and process information in cross-disciplinary modes and define the meanings for the company; or the system may involve the use of some of the many new techniques available (for example, Delphi and cross-impact studies).

There are many organizations (for example, Business International Corporation and SRI International) and a variety of published sources with information on different areas that is pertinent to monitoring the international business scene. Some of these sources of information have been mentioned in previous chapters. For example, Chapter 10 on marketing research discussed data sources appropriate for demographic monitoring. Chapter 11 on market segmentation identified different ways of classifying market segments, a valuable tool for monitoring. Chapter 8 on political environments noted organizations active in rating countries as political risks.

Achieving Planning Effectiveness

A previous section examined the problems that hinder effective marketing planning at the subsidiary level—similar problems complicate the planning effort at the parent level. Figure 19.8 divides the problems into management-type or

Problem Locus		*Problem Type*: Management	*Problem Type*: Planning System
Problem Locus	Headquarters	*A* • *poor definition of planning roles* • *unclear expectations from planning* • *short-run perspective* • *insensitivity to foreign conditions*	*C* • *oversophistication for subsidiary* • *overformalization* • *standardized criteria for evaluation* • *insufficient data support for subsidiary*
	Foreign Subsidiary	*B* • *resistance to headquarters direction* • *cultural bias against forward planning* • *local market myopia* • *"doctoring" of data*	*D* • *scarce market data* • *unreliable or outdated information* • *inadequate information system* • *unskilled planners*

Source: William K. Brandt, James M. Hulbert, and Raimar Richers, "Pitfalls in Planning for Multinational Operations," *Long Range Planning,* December 1980, p. 26.

FIGURE 19.8 A Paradigm of Planning Problems

planning-type problems. The problem may exist either at headquarters or at the foreign subsidiary. The geneses of these problems are unwillingness to change, lack of adequate and timely information, and poor communications. While some problems must be tolerated as constraints because of complexity of planning in multinational corporations, some difficulties can be solved, or at least minimized, by streamlining the system and encouraging mutual understanding of others' roles and viewpoints. The planners at headquarters can play a unique role in smoothing the functioning of the planning activity.

Exhibit 19.1 presents a number of suggestions for improving multinational marketing planning at headquarters. While some of these suggestions are global in nature and are applicable to any planning effort, others are relevant only to marketing planning. In order for planning professionals at headquarters to play a key role in more effective planning, they should serve as agents for bringing corporate direction and subsidiary goals together. For example, the headquarters planners should provide information about techniques and factual data related to international decisions to top management. Planners should find ways of reconciling corporate needs and host country requirements.

EXHIBIT 19.1 Planner's Role in Improving International Marketing (at the headquarters level)

1. Participate in the assessment of important management attitudes that regulate the activities of the corporation and the development of plans. This way, the planner can prevent "marketing myopia" by his or her company, help it examine risk policies, make them explicit and call attention to the need for change, describe in specific terms what it means to be an enlightened corporation in today's world, and catalyze the development of a creed (a code of ethics) in a participative way, despite the far-flung nature of many corporations.
2. Participate in bringing to management's attention the multiple ways of providing opportunities for host country participation in the activities of MNCs beyond various degrees of ownership, such as licensing, management contracts, royalty agreements, production and marketing agreements, training, and technology transfer agreements.
3. Learn how to mesh corporate plans with the stated national goals and objectives of host countries in order to maximize the synergy. Learn how to live in situations where national goals have not been made explicit and when regional goals and community goals in host countries are in conflict with national goals.
4. Include in planning efforts the need to influence various diverse publics (at home, in host countries, and the world at large), especially legislative bodies, by supporting and offering planning skills to public affairs and governmental affairs officers or other organizational entities charged with institutionalizing relationships with external bodies.
5. Help corporate top management move toward new methods for assessing the performance of subsidiaries (especially those operating in nations with planned economies) beyond the usual bottom-line appraisals to measures that reflect the corporation's contribution to host country goals.
6. Use the currently published information on assessing investment opportunities in host countries to manage the initiation and maintenance of investments and disinvestments—activities that must be carefully planned.
7. Develop plans for eventual situations of nationalization and expropriation that include methods for the protection of persons and property and for continuity of relationships with the host country after such actions take place.
8. Participate in plans for periodic assessment of the corporation's impact on host countries and home country and the communication of this impact to a variety of publics.
9. Predict the next requests for information disclosure and develop the corporate plan for compliance, rate of compliance, and the plan for resistance to such requests if the situation warrants resistance.
10. Discover the range of governmental incentives (home country, host countries, and international bodies—the World Bank) that might be employed to reach mutual goals and develop a plan for taking advantage of these incentives.
11. Predict the next series of tax changes and their effect on the corporation; develop a plan for resistance in some instances by interpreting the results of the tax changes on the industry and the plan for compliance in others.
12. Assist industrial relations in the area of workforce planning by developing a plan for employing and training nationals at all levels or a plan for using older workers in the myriad opportunities related to "local content" requirements and other labor pressures.

(*continued*)

EXHIBIT 19.1 *(Continued)*

13. Develop a plan for helping the corporation prepare itself for the likely spread of the industrial democracy (codetermination) movement.
14. Develop a corporate monitoring system to monitor political, governmental, economic, social, market, demographic, technological, and resource changes. Determine how to use the results of such monitoring in alternative action plans for the corporation.
15. Catalyze the use of participative methods for generating the hierarchy of objectives whence the policies, plans, and programs emanate, the communication of these objectives, and their translation into the specific objectives required for corporate integration.
16. Use corporate plans to transmit the specific expectancies for innovation from every function of the corporation and the methodology for appraising the achievement of these expectancies.
17. Catalyze needed improvements in the internal corporate communications system between functions, product areas, and geographical locations, through the use of special meetings, task forces, different organizational structures,and other tactics; for example, the use of the planning processes as vehicles for improved communications.
18. Institute periodic reviews of the adequacy of organization structures (degrees of centralization and decentralization, approaches to matrix forms) and the planned correction of structural arrangements.
19. Fill many new roles that are required to meet the innovative needs of the corporation (the product champions, bridge persons, technological gatekeepers). The persons in the planning department must recognize the need for these roles, support their presence and their activities, and in some instances perform some of these needed activities.
20. Participate in the development and application of multiple criteria used to judge ideas, concepts, projects, and programs as they move across various developmental stages, now an important management task. Planners who must implement the results of criteria application should catalyze the development of useful criteria sets and call attention to the pitfalls of criteria application.
21. Develop the many techniques that are required for implementing these recommendations (scenario development, Delphi technique, cross-impact matrices, creative problem-solving methods). Planners should acquire an appreciation for these methods and catalyze their use in the corporation.

Conclusion

This section concludes not only this chapter but also this book, and therefore it seems appropriate to include an overview of American business and trade across national boundaries. A projection of things to come indicates many challenges for international marketers in future years.

For much of the postwar period, international trade and finance occupied only a minor role in the U.S. economy. Exports and imports were a small percentage of U.S. gross national product as compared with the significant, and sometimes dominant, role played by foreign trade in most other industrial economies. Since the driving forces behind the U.S. economy were primarily domestic, policy initiatives by governments of other countries were thought to have only a small impact on the course of this country's economic growth and prosperity.

In addition, during the same period, the U.S. trading position was believed strong, particularly in capital goods, transportation, scientific equipment, and other high-technology industries. Concern among Europeans focused on fears of a growing and perhaps permanent "technological gap" between themselves and the United States. U.S. direct investment abroad was increasing continuously and rapidly, accounting for a significant portion of the world's production and exports and giving rise to large-scale development of the world's production and distribution systems to serve world markets. The U.S. dollar was the key international reserve currency, and although the United States balance-of-payments deficits were becoming a permanent feature of the postwar period, their size generally was not thought to cause major disequilibrating problems for the world economy. Indeed, the main issue was how best to manage aid, trade, and investment without straining the absorbing capabilities of foreign economies.[18]

The United States was the dominant force in the world economy at the end of World War II and for approximately two decades thereafter. It took the lead in restructuring the world's economic and political systems and in fostering the postwar trend toward greater international economic and political integration through both its domestic and foreign policies and programs. Its active participation in the United Nations, the International Monetary Fund, the International Bank for Reconstruction and Development (World Bank), the General Agreement on Tariffs and Trade (GATT), and other postwar international organizations has shown the United States' leadership and its commitment to global cooperation. Although U.S. foreign sector activities in the past have had relatively little effect on the U.S. economy, its trade, investment, and monetary policies and programs were essential to the economic and political interests of the free world.

New International Realities

The current situation presents a marked contrast. The issues and problems confronting the world economy have grown in number, size, and complexity, with profound implications for U.S. international competitiveness. Although both the rate of economic growth and the domestic and international economic policies and programs of the United States continue to exert a strong influence on the economies of the industrialized and the developing world, U.S. economic prosperity now is inexorably linked with economic and political developments occurring in other countries.

> United States exports and imports as a percentage of GNP and as a proportion of the total output of goods rose markedly in the 1970s and early 1980s and will continue to rise in relation to greater international interdependence. For some U.S. industries, exports and imports constitute a considerable percentage of total domestic output, and for a growing number of industries, changes in merchandise trade patterns can result in a significant number of gains or losses in domestic employment opportunities. For example, in

1989, (1) one out of every six jobs in the manufacturing sector depended on exports; (2) for each of those jobs an additional one was created in a supporting industry; (3) over 7 million domestic jobs depended on U.S. exports; (4) approximately 60 percent of U.S. imports were either essential minerals (for example, chromium, manganese, cobalt, and tin) or products that could not be readily produced domestically; and (5) one out of every three dollars of U.S. corporate profits was derived from international activities.[19]

Although U.S. technological gains have been impressive, the technological accomplishments of its main trading partners—particularly Japan, the Federal Republic of Germany, and the United Kingdom—and the high-technology manufacturing capabilities of the advanced developing countries—South Korea, India, Brazil, and Taiwan—have resulted in both a consistent narrowing of the so-called technological gap and greater competition among manufacturers of high-technology products.[20]

Record-setting United States balance-of-payment deficits have led to declines in the value of the U.S. dollar, whether measured as severe in relation to key foreign currencies or as moderate on a trade-weighted basis. As a result, concern developed, both at home and abroad, that the U.S. economy would no longer be competitive in world markets and that the stability of the world monetary arrangements had been severely and perhaps permanently affected. The depreciated U.S. dollar and persistent trade deficits with certain industrialized countries showed the United States that it was no longer free to pursue economic policies with internal rather than external considerations in mind. Indeed, they were symptomatic of a need for the United States to coordinate economic policies with those of other large industrialized countries.[21]

These examples show not only that U.S. policies and programs have profound effects on other countries, but also that the United States has become more vulnerable to developments in other countries. Clearly, the world is becoming increasingly interdependent, economically and politically. An important feature of this growing economic interdependence—and a measure of it—is the degree to which economic developments in one country (particularly those of the United States) are increasingly transmitted via market forces, or spillover, into other countries. In turn, this leads to foreign trade (and other) feedback effects that have an impact on U.S. domestic economic activity (see International Marketing Highlight 19.4).

The Current and Future U.S. Role

As the foregoing discussion indicates, the United States has an enormous stake in economic and political interdependence. On the one hand, the United States is no longer insulated from international market developments with regard to terms of trade, price, availability of energy, fulfillment of raw materials requirements, and other relevant factors. On the other hand, the United States is the largest exporter and importer of goods and services, and the world's largest foreign investor. In addition, it is becoming the world's greatest host for foreign direct and portfolio investment and is a significant developer and exporter of

International Marketing Highlight 19.4

How Do You Compete with Mexican Workers?

Dario Sanchez Delgado
26, married, two children
Work: Welder at Chrysler plant in Toluca, Mexico
Seniority: 5 years
Pay: $1.75 an hour
Benefits: Mandated profit-sharing, extra vacation pay, one month's bonus at Christmas, a one-cent lunch
Education: Junior high school

Michael Schultz
36, married, one child
Work: Welder at Chrysler's Sterling Heights, Michigan, plant
Seniority: 17 years
Pay: $16 an hour
Benefits: Paid vacation, full health care, income protection for layoffs
Education: High school, working on associate degree

Source: Business Week, March 16, 1992, p. 100.

high technology. The extent of U.S. leadership in restructuring the world's international economic system is likely to be a function of its perceptions of its current and future competitive strength. The central questions are what is the current international competitive position of U.S. industries and how can U.S. competitiveness be improved through public and private policies? (See International Marketing Highlight 19.5).

U.S. corporations face a strategic challenge. Competition from Europe, Japan, and elsewhere is becoming insurmountable. As the global market adapts and evolves, competition will further intensify. To cope with worldwide competition, U.S. companies must place renewed emphasis on marketing strategy. At the same time, the U.S. government should adopt policies that enhance, not hinder, corporate efforts in their struggle against foreign competition. As Toyne et al. noted:

> The challenges confronting the textile mill products industries of all countries are indicative of a global industry undergoing fundamental change. Technological innovation is accelerating, government intervention is increasing, production is becoming more capital-intensive, and growth in demand is shifting from the developed to the developing countries. Consequently, the adjustment strategies selected and implemented by national industries, governments, and individual firms will be critical to their long-term competitiveness, even to their survival.
>
> Some industries and firms have responded competitively to these challenges; others have only reacted. It is still too early to pass judgment on the merits of the various adjustment strategies identified in this study. It does appear, however, that strategies which are internationally focused are more successful than strategies which are internally focused. The experiences of France and the United Kingdom on the one hand, and those of West Germany, Italy, Japan, the Netherlands, and Taiwan on the other, suggest that future strategies must be aimed at developing an international competitiveness, not just an internally focused domestic competitiveness. Even the U.S. industry, which is unique because of its large domestic market, is beginning to show signs of lagging behind the more internationally oriented industries in its ability to remain internationally competitive.[22]

International Marketing Highlight 19.5

Honda's Double-Edged Sword

Honda's self-contained U.S. operations are going to haunt U.S. automakers for a long time. The company established two auto plants and an engine plant in central Ohio, receiving at least $70 million in incentives from the state government. Further, in the devastated Midwest area, people don't believe in unions, and the workforce is mostly young, pensionless, and hard working.

For many years, U.S. auto companies argued that it was difficult to compete against the Japanese due to their cost advantage. After Honda started making Civic autos in 1984, skeptics still complained that these were "screwdriver operations," assembling mostly Japanese parts. They wanted greater domestic content.

Now with Honda having achieved a domestic content of 70 percent to 75 percent, its cars are more "American" than many G.M., Ford, or Chrysler models. A Japanese company is using American labor, American land, and American parts to be a low-cost, high-quality producer. Unlike the initial low-price Japanese imports, their cars will be mid-size, aimed at the heart of Detroit's profitability.

It is sobering to note that the Japanese car manufacturers are creating a world-class auto industry in the United States. It is from here that the battle for global supremacy in the auto market will be fought. What can U.S. automakers do? Among other moves, they should work effectively with states and communities to seek incentives similar to those exacted by the Japanese companies. They should also work with the United Auto Workers to achieve the same productivity the Japanese are able to get from American workers.

Source: Business Week, October 19, 1987, p. 154.

Strategic Challenges for Multinational Corporations

The following review considers some of the important factors affecting the competitive position of U.S. multinationals in world markets and suggests positive courses of action for MNCs.[23]

Management of Foreign-Dominated Liquid Assets MNCs conduct business in a number of foreign currencies. The exchange rates of these currencies are subject to great upheavals with far-reaching consequences for earnings. These changes result from disturbances in international, social, political, and economic environments. Thus, in addition to protecting their business from competitive inroads, the management of foreign funds carries impact (for example, the decision on the best currency mix to maintain on a short-term basis).

Expansion or Growth Policies Traditionally, U.S. corporations have pursued expansion or growth overseas as an important corporate objective. Growth per se, however, may be problematic. The trade deficits of many countries (both among industrialized and Third World nations) and a common desire among nations for self-sufficiency may render achievement of perpetual growth in foreign markets difficult. Even where opportunities abound, an entry should be clearly earmarked with the possibility of retrenchment and/or exit forced through economic nationalism or other political reasons. For example, it may become virtually impossible to raise capital in a host country, the traditional source of long-term funding, and that would certainly block growth.

Decentralization of the Production Process For both political and economic reasons, more and more industries may follow the strategic lead of the electronics industry and seek component specialization over product specialization. If not all components of a product can be efficiently manufactured by an MNC in one host country, the MNC may opt for specialization in a few components while depending on other sources for others. The decentralization of the production process can serve as a protection against expropriation of foreign operations by a host country. As a matter of fact, arrangements that involve more than one host country business should be attractive to host nations because local involvement in the manufacture of the product would be encouraged.

Automation of Assembly Lines In advanced countries especially, many routine tasks on the assembly line might be performed by robots. Japan is way ahead in this area. The United States will probably move in the same direction in the coming years. Such automation of assembly lines should result in substantial cost reductions and uniformity in product quality, which in turn should affect favorably the United States' competitive position in the world markets.[24]

Corporate-Labor Relationships The Third World MNCs, with the abundance of cheap labor in their factories, may emerge as a newly significant competitive force. This is likely to have a far-reaching impact on corporate-labor relationships in the United States. A new form of understanding and harmony between the traditional adversaries will become necessary for mutual survival. The change in labor-management agreements for the U.S. auto industry bears testimony to the emergence of this trend.

Globalization of Consumer Tastes Another interesting phenomenon concerns the development of a common worldwide preference for a variety of consumer goods. The global craze for designer jeans and fast foods illustrates the point.[25] But the commonality of demand does not mean that the same marketing mix strategies will be effective in every overseas market. The marketing strategies must be appropriately customized to the local customs and traditions. For example, a successful jeans ad using a female model in the U.S. market would be ineffective in an Islamic country.

The world marketplace, as the end of the century approaches, will be quite different from what it was in, say, the 1960s, the 1970s, or even the 1980s. While opportunities should abound, international marketers will need new strategic perspectives to capitalize successfully on these opportunities. The big growth and profits may not come from traditional policies and strategies. Corporations will need to develop new marketing strategies that not only enhance their competitiveness but also fit the needs of the future.

International Marketing Highlight 19.6

Enlightened Capitalism

The London-based Body Shop, with fourteen outlets in the United States, puts environmental concerns at its core and in the process finds its way to the green in customers' pockets. The skin- and hair-care stores display literature on ozone depletion next to sunscreens and fill their windows with information on issues like global warming. Every employee is assigned to spend half a day each week on activist work. Customers get discounts if they bring their old bottles back to the store for recycling. In 1988 the chain collected over a million signatures in Britain on a petition asking Brazil's president to save the rain forests. In thirteen years the Body Shop has opened 420 stores in thirty-eight countries.

Source: Fortune, February 12, 1990, p. 50.

Businesses as Citizens Environmental issues such as waste disposal and pollution are becoming ever more important. Businesses will be expected to play an important role in solving these problems (see International Marketing Highlight 19.6). In addition, improvement in the quality of education will be another significant social issue affecting the organizations. It is commonly felt that business can make a very useful contribution to basic literacy skills.[26]

People Power In the 1990s, a dramatic convergence of demographic, technological, competitive, and global forces is likely to shift power from employers to employees, from the board room to the workplace, where value is added and wealth is created. Throughout North America, Europe, and Japan, these forces will converge in a strikingly similar manner—the power of the 1990s will be people power.

Summary

Effective global marketing calls for a systematic planning effort and an explicit statement of strategy. The need for a planned perspective has never been greater than in the past few years. The world marketplace is highly competitive and changing. The favorable conditions that American business once faced are no longer descriptive of the U.S. situation. The economic turbulence during the 1970s and early 1980s shifted the balance so that the simple extension of domestic business overseas could not suffice. The future has never held promises that the past will return. Thus, adequate strategic planning is essential to business success abroad.

Planning in the area of marketing must be undertaken both at the subsidiary and the headquarters levels. An overseas subsidiary should engage in both short-term and strategic planning. Essentially, short-term planning involves reviewing past performance, making sales forecasts, and developing/revising marketing strategies to achieve the objectives. The next step is a budget, itemizing the various programs in the marketing strategy in monetary terms. The plan is then submitted to the corporation for approval. Usually the chief executive of the subsidiary presents the plan to the corporation at a meeting held in the United States. Plan approval follows after revisions recommended by the corporation have been incorporated. Often the planning activity is conducted according to systems and procedures spelled out by corporate headquarters to foster homogeneity in the planning efforts of different subsidiaries.

Strategic planning is usually an exercise in long-term projections of sales and related matters. Both parent corporation and subsidiary share the blame for poor strategic planning. While the parent may consider strategy development to be its prerogative, the subsidiary fails if it too does not take initiative in this direction. Various problems hinder effective planning at the subsidiary level, and some methods can improve a subsidiary's planning activities.

At the corporate level the major emphasis is on strategic planning. In addition, the corporation reviews and approves the plans of subsidiaries. The corporate-level strategic planning process begins with a commitment to international business. This commitment is followed by a delineation of the scope of its overseas business and the identification of strategy centers and/or strategic business units. A strategic business unit may be defined as a stand-alone business with identifiable independence from other businesses of the corporation in terms of competition, prices, substitutability of product, style/quality, and impact of product withdrawal.

Strategy development efforts center on an SBU with a review of the environment and an analysis of the business's strategic role. Objectives of the SBU are set, and appropriate marketing strategies outlined. Strategies of different SBUs are reviewed and incorporated by the corporate people. Once the SBU plans have been approved, resources are allocated and the strategic plan becomes the guideline for direction and decision making.

The concept of product portfolio was introduced to determine an appropriate role for each business and to review and integrate SBU perspectives at the corporate level.

Worldwide strategic planning development is still rudimentary. This may be attributed in part to the relatively new development of the art of strategic planning. Strategic planners, however, can play a key role in improving the planning perspectives of their corporations. Suggestions have been made for planners to strive for improvements in strategic planning.

The chapter ended with an overview of the emerging environment—a summary of the shape of things to come—as identified and examined in previous chapters. Finally, eight strategic challenges (management of foreign-dominated liquid assets, expansion or growth policies, decentralization of the production process, automation of assembly lines, reevaluation of corporate-labor relationships, globalization of consumer tastes, the role of businesses as citizens, and the shift of power from employers to employees) that multinational corporations will likely face in coming years were summarized, and their implications for marketers were examined.

Review Questions

1. What type of planning is mainly conducted by overseas subsidiaries? What input does the parent corporation supposedly provide in their planning effort?
2. Why do many foreign subsidiaries *not* undertake strategic planning? Discuss.
3. What problems hinder a good planning job at the subsidiary level?
4. Examine the reasons that make strategic planning an important activity for the multinational corporation.
5. How can a product portfolio framework apply in the international strategic planning process?
6. What role can strategic planners play in streamlining the planning activity? How?
7. Briefly list the environments/areas that multinational corporations should scan. Why is such scanning necessary?
8. Summarize the strategic challenges that multinational corporations are likely to face in the future years.

Endnotes

1. P. Doyle, J. Saunders, and V. Wong, "Japanese Marketing Strategies in the U.K.: A Comparative Study," *Journal of International Business Studies,* Spring 1986, pp. 27–46.
2. James M. Hulbert, William K. Brandt, and Raimar Richers, "Marketing Planning in Multinational Subsidiary: Practices and Problems," *Journal of Marketing,* Summer 1980, p. 8.
3. Frank P. Popoff, "Planning the Multinational's Future," *Business Horizons,* March–April 1984, p. 64.
4. Yoram Wind, Susan Douglas, and Howard V. Perlmutter, "Guidelines for Developing International Marketing Strategies," *Journal of Marketing,* April 1973, p. 17.
5. Susan P. Douglas and C. Samuel Craig, "Examining Performance of U.S. Multinationals in Foreign Markets," *Journal of International Business Studies,* Winter 1983, pp. 51–62.
6. Jagdish N. Sheth, "A Conceptual Model of Long-Range Multinational Marketing Planning," in Subhash C. Jain and Lewis R. Tucker, Jr., eds. *International Marketing: Managerial Perspectives* (Boston: CBI Publishing, 1979), pp. 424–432.
7. OECD, 1985.
8. Bronislaw J. Verhage and Eric Waarts, "Marketing Planning for Improved Performance: A Comparative Analysis," *International Marketing Review,* Summer 1988, pp. 20–30. *Also see* Martin Van Mesdag, "Winning It in Foreign Markets," *Harvard Business Review,* January–February 1987, pp. 71–74.
9. *See* Robert J. Mockler, "Strategic Planning for Multinational Operations: The Decision Making Process Involved," *Working Paper,* Business Research Institute, St. John's University, 1990.
10. Robert G. Cooper and Elko J. Kleinschmidt, "The Impact of Export Strategy on Export Sales Performance," *Journal of International Business Studies,* Spring 1985, pp. 37–56. *Also see* Leslie M. Dawson, "Multinational Strategic Planning for Third World Markets," *Journal of Global Marketing,* Spring 1988, pp. 29–50.
11. Subhash C. Jain, *Marketing Planning and Strategy,* 2nd ed. (Cincinnati, OH: South-Western Publishing Company, 1985), pp. 475–487.
12. Jean-Claude Larréché, "The International Product-Market Portfolio," in Subhash C. Jain, ed., *Research Frontiers in Marketing: Dialogues and Directions,* Educators' Conference Proceedings (Chicago: American Marketing Association, 1978), pp. 276–

281. *Also see* William L. Shanklin and John K. Ryans, Jr., "Is the International Cash Cow Really a Prize Heifer?" *Business Horizons,* March–April 1981, pp. 10–16.

13. Gilbert D. Harrell and Richard O. Kiefer, "Multinational Strategic Market Portfolios," *MSU Business Topics,* Winter 1981, pp. 5–15.
14. Susan P. Douglas and Dong Kee Rhee, "Examining Generic Competitive Strategy Types in U.S. and European Markets," *Journal of International Business Studies,* Fall 1985, pp. 437–464.
15. Yoram Wind and Susan Douglas, "International Portfolio Analysis and Strategy: The Challenge of the 80s," *Journal of International Business Studies,* Fall 1981, pp. 69–82. *Also see* Richard M. Burton, "Variety in Strategic Planning: An Alternative to the Problem Solving Approach," *Columbia Journal of World Business,* Winter 1984, pp. 92–98.; Attila Yaprak and Nizam Aydin, "Strategic Market Planning in International Marketing: Current Approaches and a New Framework," a paper presented at the 1984 National Meetings of the Academy of International Business, Cleveland, Ohio, October 1984.
16. *See* Yoram Wind and Vijay Mahajan, "Designing Product and Business Portfolio," *Harvard Business Review,* January–February 1981, pp. 155–165; Ingolf Bamberger, "Portfolio Analysis for the Small Firm," *Long Range Planning,* December 1982, pp. 49–57; Walter Kiechel III, "Oh Where, Oh Where Has My Little Dog Gone? Or My Cash Cow? Or My Star?" *Fortune,* November 2, 1981, p. 148; Derek F. Abell and John S. Hammond, *Strategic Market Planning* (Englewood Cliffs, NJ: Prentice-Hall, 1980); Michael E. Porter, *Competitive Strategy* (New York: Free Press, 1980); George S. Day, "Diagnosing the Product Portfolio," *Journal of Marketing,* April 1977, pp. 29–38; Balaji S. Chakravarthy and Howard V. Perlmutter, "Strategic Planning for a Global Business," *Columbia Journal of World Business,* Summer 1985, pp. 3–10.
17. Sumantra Ghoshal, "Environmental Scanning in Korean Firms: Organizational Isomorphism in Action," *Journal of International Business Studies,* Spring 1988, pp. 69–86.
18. Irma Adelman, "Interaction of U.S. and Foreign Economic Growth Rates and Patterns," in *U.S. Economic Growth from 1976 to 1986: Prospects, Problems, and Patterns* (Washington, D.C.: U.S. Government Printing Office, May 23, 1977), pp. 18–24. *Also see* Thomas Hout, Michael E. Porter, and Eileen Rudden, "How Global Companies Win Out," *Harvard Business Review,* September–October 1982, pp. 98–105.
19. *Business America,* April 22, 1991; and *Business America,* Special Edition 1991, p. 32.
20. Norihiko Shirouzu, "Korean Auto Makers Seeking to Tiptoe into Japan's Market," *Asian Wall Street Journal Weekly,* October 3, 1988, p. 4.
21. Peter Nulty, "How the World Will Change," *Fortune* January 15, 1990, p. 44.
22. Brian Toyne, Jeffrey S. Arpan, Andy H. Barnett, and David A. Ricks, "The International Competitiveness of U.S. Textile Mill Products Industry: Corporate Strategies for the Future," *Journal of International Business Studies,* Winter 1984, p. 160. *Also see* David A. Ricks et al., "Global Changes and Strategies for Increasing the International Competitiveness of the U.S. Man-Made Fibers Industry," *Columbia Journal of World Business,* Summer 1986, pp. 75–84.
23. *See* Raj Aggarwal, "The Strategic Challenge of the Evolving Global Economy," *Business Horizons,* July/August 1987, pp. 38–44. *Also see* Jagjit Brar, R. David Ramsey, and Peter Wright, "Six Challenges to Global Corporations," *The Collegiate Forum,* Spring 1982, p. 14.
24. Kenichi Ohmae, *Triad Power* (New York: The Free Press, 1985), Chapter 2. *Also see* Philip Kotler, Somkid Jatusripitak, and Liam Fahey, "Strategic Global Marketing: Lessons from the Japanese," *Columbia Journal of World Business,* Spring 1985, pp. 47–54.
25. Theodore Levitt, "The Globalization of Markets," *Harvard Business Review,* May–June 1983, pp. 92–102. *Also see* Hajo Riesenbeck and Anthony Freeling, "How Global Are Global Brands?" *The McKinsey Quarterly,* no. 4 (1991), pp. 3–18.
26. *See* Rosabeth Moss Kanter, "Transcending Business Boundaries: 12,000 World Managers View Change," *Harvard Business Review,* May–June 1991, pp. 151–164. *Also see* "The CEOs' View of the 1990s: Companies Must Stress Globalization and Quality," *Business International,* May 21, 1990, pp. 163–164.

PART • 6

Cases

Case 25: Standard Consumer Business Products

In 1989, Frederick C. Dixon, president of Standard Consumer Business Products of North America, was concerned about the company's ability to maintain its sales level and competitive position in the typewriter industry. The majority of Standard's past sales had been generated from Japanese-imported typewriters sold under the Standard name; Standard did not manufacture typewriters. Underlying the threat to the company's position was the new policy of Standard's parent company in Germany, Aiken-Haus, insisting that Standard source its products from Aiken-Haus. From past experience, Mr. Dixon knew that the typewriters produced by Aiken-Haus did not sell well in the United States, while sales of Standard's Japanese-sourced typewriters were extremely impressive. Mr. Dixon understood that he must comply with the parent company's wishes, but the fact remained that Aiken-Haus did not understand the U.S. consumer market as well as the Japanese did. He tried to communicate the product changes that Aiken-Haus needed to make, but his message often fell on deaf ears: a communication gap existed between the parent, Aiken-Haus, and the subsidiary, Standard Consumer Business Products.

Company History

In 1908, Standard Typewriter moved its headquarters from Brooklyn, New York, to Hartford, Connecticut. Standard manufactured typewriters in Hartford until 1973, when the cost to produce in the United States became prohibitive. Production was moved overseas to Hull, England, while Standard's headquarters remained in Hartford and later moved to Windsor, Connecticut. At this time, Standard Typewriter was a division of the billion-dollar conglomerate Tarrett Industries. Standard had expanded its product line to office electric and manual typewriters, portable typewriters, copiers, and calculators.

By 1985, Standard was no longer a division of Tarrett; it was a subsidiary of Aiken-Haus, a West German producer of office equipment (see Figure 1). Aiken-Haus was majority owned by West German Motors, a major West German auto manufacturer. In 1989, Standard was divided according to product lines: Standard Business Machines (office equipment and copiers), Standard Consumer Business Products (portable typewriters, calculators, personal copiers, small cash registers), Caster Peripherals (computer products), and Standard Type (typewriter ribbons, computer printers).

Subsidiary's Position

Standard Consumer Business Products' inability to communicate with its parent company, Aiken-Haus, was due to more than just the language barrier. Standard and Aiken-Haus served two totally different typewriter markets. Standard mainly sold to consumers, while Aiken-Haus

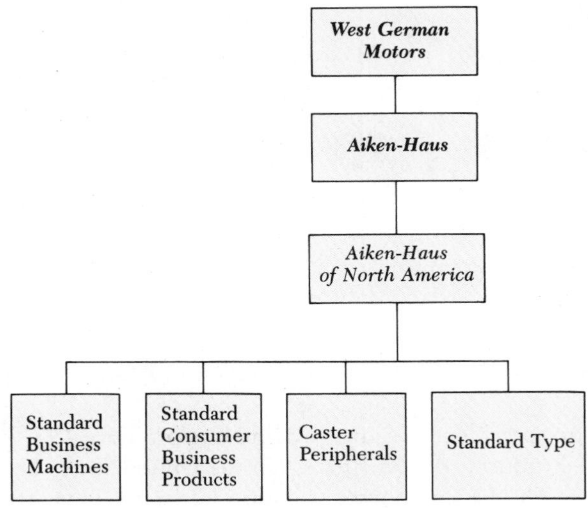

FIGURE 1 **Organizational Structure of West German Motors**

served business customers. Each understood its market thoroughly. After years of producing typewriters, Standard was aware of the needs of the U.S. consumer market. Standard, no longer capable of producing in the United States (because of costs), needed to purchase or source the product from companies with lower costs that were located outside the United States. Standard found that the Japanese-sourced typewriters were best suited for the U.S. consumer market, while those manufactured by Aiken-Haus were not satisfactory for the U.S. consumer market. The typewriters that Aiken-Haus produced best served the European office market where end-use differences dictated a different kind of product and service.

U.S. Consumer Market

The portable typewriter market in the United States was very competitive. Standard held a modest share of the market. Its competition included big names such as IBM, Olivetti, Brother, Smith-Corona, and Xerox. Because of the competitive nature of the market, low price was imperative.

From experience, Mr. Dixon realized that the U.S. consumer wanted a low-priced portable typewriter that offered just a few features. It was unnecessary, and too costly, to provide a typewriter with a vast array of features and a great degree of durability; consumers wanted a low-end electronic portable typewriter. Previously, the only electronic typewriter offered was a high-end, expensive office typewriter. In 1981, a low-end electronic portable typewriter was developed, offering features the old portable electric typewriter could not—programmability and text storage capability. It was less labor intensive and had fewer moving parts, allowing costs to remain low. Overall, the electronic typewriter industry was expected to achieve a sales growth of 19 percent in 1989.

The Japanese appeared to have the greatest advantage in this growing market. Not only did they have expertise in the electronic typewriter field, but they were also able to develop this new low-end portable electronic typewriter at a lower cost than anyone else in the industry. Since price was an important factor to the typewriter buyer, Japanese portable electronic typewriter sales skyrocketed, hurting both its U.S. and European competitors.

Perhaps the only problem the Japanese experienced was in establishing distribution channels in the United States. They used a "pull" strategy with heavy advertising. Standard, with its established channels of distribution, recognized the opportunity to source these well-made Japanese electronic typewriters and thus allowed the Japanese to use Standard's channels of distribution.

Mr. Dixon had established a good working relationship with major retailers such as Caldor and Service Merchandise. This relationship was developed over the years so that the logistics of delivery, the quantity ordered, and the price charged were now established practices. Guarantees on the product were provided, and quality testing substantially reduced the need for returns.

Aiken-Haus' Position

Aiken-Haus produced a heavy-duty, high-end office typewriter. Mr. Dixon raised the question "What would the U.S. consumer do with a heavy-duty office machine?" First, the price would be outrageous. Second, there would be too many features, and a great deal of confusion. Third, besides being overbuilt, the typewriter would also be overpacked, because these office typewriters were intended for distribution through office equipment dealers. Aiken-Haus, however, viewed its typewriters as a superior product that superseded the Japanese portable electronic typewriters in every way.

Although Aiken-Haus believed its product was superior, it served only the office equipment market of West Germany and other parts of Europe. The European portable typewriter market was served primarily by the Japanese, just as it was in the United States. This Japanese control of the portable typewriter market was of major concern to the European Community. In 1989, the EC found the Japanese guilty of dumping typewriters in Europe and generally stopped buying from these Japanese companies. Therefore, the portable typewriter market was open for Aiken-Haus to enter.

Aiken-Haus was looking to improve its financial position, as it had incurred a loss of $70 million in the past two years. Without the financial backing obtained from its parent, West German Motors, Aiken-Haus would not have survived. In addition to seeking the opportunity to enter the European consumer typewriter market, Aiken-Haus also wanted to pursue the U.S. consumer market to a greater extent. Thus, Aiken-Haus insisted that Standard purchase only Aiken-Haus typewriters. Aiken-Haus hoped to achieve the half million unit sales in the United States that Standard had reached the previous year. By insisting that Standard stop buying from the Japanese, Aiken-Haus was complying with the EC's policy to eliminate electronic typewriter purchases from the Japanese.

The Conflict

Mr. Dixon maintained his position that Aiken-Haus needed to change the product design of their typewriters in order to achieve substantial sales in the U.S. consumer market. Aiken-Haus believed, however, that what was good for West Germany was good for the rest of the world. The high-quality, well-built, multifeatured typewriter was second to none according to Aiken-Haus.

This stance created a real dilemma for Mr. Dixon. Standard was expected to buy the overbuilt Aiken-Haus typewriters. Mr. Dixon had resigned himself to the fact that Aiken-Haus would be the new supplier (out of support to the parent company); however, he still wanted Aiken-Haus to see that product changes were necessary. Aiken-Haus did little to change the product to serve the new market: Standard was receiving Aiken-Haus typewriters built to last ten times longer than the average consumer needed. Mr. Dixon wondered if there was any way to get his message across.

Barriers to Communication

The situation was delicate and could not be resolved with a few meetings. Mr. Dixon pinpointed two barriers obstructing the free flow of communication: the language barrier and the attitude barrier. These barriers had not been erected intentionally, but were a result of different cultures.

During the meetings, the Germans, knowing little English, kept their answers short, which the Americans interpreted as excessive bluntness. Mr. Dixon gave an example: when discussing ways to build a particular typewriter model for a specific cost, the German executives simply stated that it could not be done and gave no explanation. Alternative methods were presented, but the answer was firm. Mr. Dixon suspected that the Germans' inability to speak English well inhibited them from elaborating on details.

Another barrier was what Mr. Dixon referred to as the attitude barrier. The Germans believed what was good for West Germany was good for the rest of the world. This ethnocentric approach to management created major difficulties. Aiken-Haus' management, with its set policy, seldom even listened to what Standard had to say. On the occasions that Aiken-Haus did listen, nothing was done with the suggestions. Aiken-Haus regarded the Japanese portable electronic typewriters as garbage because German quality standards were high. Although Aiken-Haus was manufacturing typewriters for the office market, it saw no reason why the average consumer should not want this high-quality typewriter.

Problem Resolution

To resolve this conflict, Mr. Dixon had begun to develop his future plans. He would still pursue product changes in order to have the desired product for the U.S. market, since Standard's market share would be at stake if the product failed to satisfy the U.S. consumer. Changeover to the Aiken-Haus products could be successful as long as careful steps were taken to ensure product compatibility with the U.S. market.

Mr. Dixon appointed a liaison to establish better lines of communication. The liaison would be dedicated to firming up product specifications while interfacing with the West German executives of Aiken-Haus. The person he hired had been born and raised in Germany and had been living in the States for quite some time.

Case 26: Mubarak Dairies Limited

Mubarak—An Innovative Company

Mubarak Dairies Limited (MDL) is established in Jhang, with its head office in Lahore, Pakistan. MDL aims to become a market leader in the production and distribution of prepacked milk. MDL plans to innovate at the level of packaging and distribution. In order to test the viability of its creative ideas, a consumer market survey was commissioned. Students at Punjab University in Lahore and Quaid-e-Azam University in Islamabad carried out the field work under the direction of Mohammad Khan, a marketing executive from MDL. When the results of the

This case is printed here with the permission of the authors, Lyn S. Amine of St. Louis University and Mohammad Ishaq Khan.

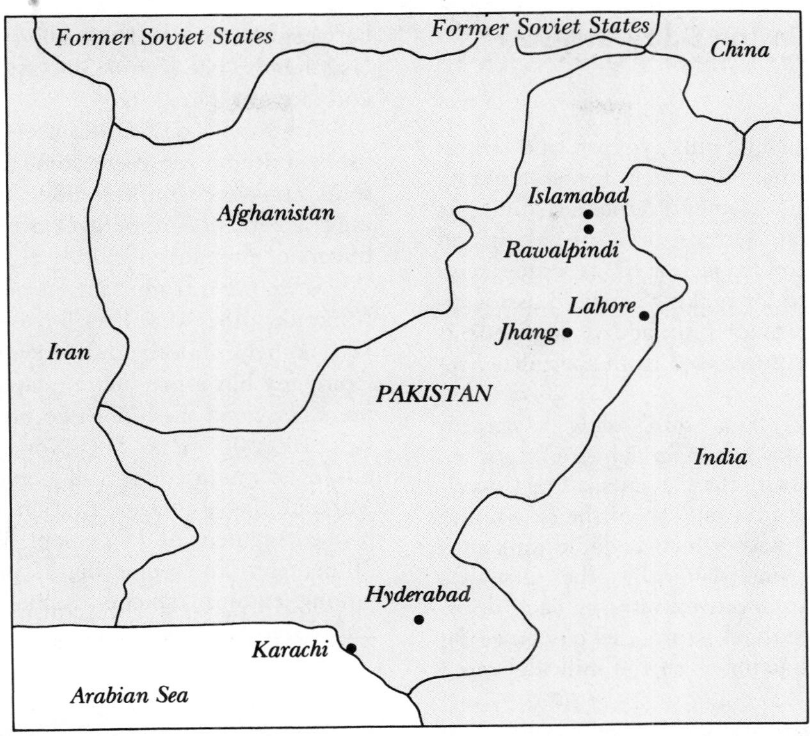

FIGURE 1

survey were presented to the chief executive officer, decisions had to be made about critical aspects of the marketing mix.

The Market Environment of Pakistan

Pakistan is the seventh-largest country in Asia. It is bounded to the west by Iran, to the north by Afghanistan and the former Soviet States, to the northeast by China, to the east and southeast by India, and to the south by the Arabian Sea (Figure 1). The population in 1985 was estimated at some 100 million inhabitants, with an annual growth rate of 2.7 percent. Forty-five percent of the population is under 15 years old. Urdu is the official language. Ninety-seven percent of the population are Muslims, and there are Christians and a small number of other minorities.

Although only 28 percent of the population is urban, the influx of rural migrants to Pakistan's few and crowded cities causes housing shortages and overburdens transportation. Islamabad, the capital, had a population in the early 1980s of 201,000; Karachi, 5.1 million; and Lahore, 2.9 million.

Pakistan has a developing mixed economy based largely on agriculture, light industries, and services. GNP totaled U.S. $35 billion in 1983, and the GNP per capita was $370. The overall literacy rate is 26 percent, but for women the rate is only 16 percent. Television is therefore the most important communications medium, and the government radio broadcasts in more than twenty languages.

Competition in the Dairy Industry

The Gawallas

Dairy products include milk, yogurt, and butter. Milk is used as a main ingredient for tea-making, and is an important element in the diet of infants and small children. Butter is used for baking and for breakfast. Yogurt is served at home with meals, and is used for making "lassi." Lassi is diluted yogurt churned with added sugar. It is made at home or purchased from specialized retail outlets.

Traditionally, fresh milk with 5 percent to 7 percent full fat has been delivered door-to-door to consumers by the Gawallas. The Gawallas bring the milk in a big can of their own and carry a measure, with which to ladle milk into each customer's jug. Typically, the Gawallas will spend five to seven minutes at each door, and will seek feedback from the customer on the level of satisfaction with the milk delivered each day.

The Gawallas are local people who own small dairy farms, ranging from a couple of cows to as many as one hundred. All their methods of production are manual, and milk is delivered by horse-drawn carts or bicycles, and just occasionally by small motorcycles or lightweight trucks. The milk provided by the Gawallas is fresh, not processed in any way, and does not contain any preservatives. It is delivered to each customer's door twice a day, between 6 and 9 A.M. and 2:30 and 6:30 P.M., in time for breakfast and evening tea preparation. The tradition of home delivery is long-established and carried on from one generation to the next.

Prepacked Milk

Prepacked milk was introduced into Pakistan by the Milkpak Company, under the brand name TetraPak some ten to fifteen years ago. Originally, it was bought from small retail stores by occasional customers who needed to buy milk between the hours of the delivery by the Gawallas, that is, between 9:30 A.M. and 1:30 P.M., and late at night.

Gradually, occasional users became regular users and now represent some 23 percent of the total consumer milk market. Of the remaining 77 percent, 74 percent are now occasional buyers of prepacked milk.

Since the introduction of prepacked milk by Milkpak, other suppliers have entered the market, namely Haleeb and Greens. The Milkpak Company has a production capacity of 150,000 liters/day, and the other two producers can provide 100,000 liters/day. None of these plants has ever operated at full capacity. Currently, Milkpak has a national market share in the prepacked segment of 35 percent while Haleeb has 30 percent. The remaining 35 percent is divided among eight producers, some of whom serve only local markets.

Finding a Niche in the Prepacked Milk Market

Mubarak Dairies Ltd. (MDL) believed that it could compete against the Gawallas and the other milk packers by emphasizing two key competitive advantages: packaging in plastic pouches and home delivery. In order to test the strength of these two features, the market survey was commissioned. Two objectives were identified: to study current buying behavior among households and to analyze potential demand for a new prepacked milk product.

On the basis of survey results, a market launch strategy would be developed.

The Consumer Survey

A consumer sample of 1,000 households and a trade sample of 200 grocers were designed, based on three major cities. Sample organization was designed as follows:

TABLE 1 Sources of Milk Purchases in Rawalpindi and Islamabad

ZONE	GAWALLAS	PREPACKED SUPPLIER (REGULAR)%	PREPACKED SUPPLIER (OCCASIONAL)%
I	97	3	69
II	88	8	72
III	80	8	87
IV	79	20	82
V	70	28	58

Note: Percentages do not total 100 due to multiple answers.

CITY	NO. OF CONSUMERS	NO. OF GROCERS	NO. OF CITY ZONES
Lahore	500	100	5
Rawalpindi	250	50	3
Islamabad	250	50	2
Total	1,000	200	10

The research budget was estimated at about 25,000 rupees (Rs) (U.S., $1.00: Rs 17.50). Key results from the consumer survey are presented in Tables 1 through 8.

Additional Results

Respondents were asked which size pack they prefer. In Rawalpindi and Islamabad, 72 percent prefer a 500 milliliter pack, 27 percent a 1 liter pack, and the rest a 250 milliliter pack. In contrast, in Lahore, preferences were 10 percent for 250 milliliter, 50 percent for 500 milliliter, and 40 percent for 1 liter.

Respondents also identified inconvenient features of present milk packages. Ninety-five percent of respondents in Rawalpindi and Islamabad and 85 percent in Lahore favor a change in packaging. The major complaint focused on the problem of storing the angular TetraPak, a reinforced paper container with four triangular sides. To open a TetraPak, typically a corner is cut off and used as a pouring spout. Spillage occurs easily if the pack is not handled carefully.

Developing a Market Plan for MDL

The management at MDL considered that the survey results indicated at least two significant findings:

1. Consumers were familiar with prepacked milk and valued its features.
2. Consumers were dissatisfied with current brand offerings of prepacked milk. The pointed TetraPak, in particular, tended to

TABLE 2 Monthly Household Income by Zone—Rawalpindi and Islamabad

ZONE	1000–2500 Rs. %	2501–4000 Rs. %	4001–5500 Rs. %	Above 5501 Rs. %
I	32	30	19	19
II	32	27	15	26
III	17	20	18	45
IV	21	48	18	13
V	2	17	17	64

Note: Percentages total 100 reading across the columns. One U.S. dollar equals 17.50 rupees.

TABLE 3 **Monthly Household Income by Zone—Lahore**

ZONE	1000–2500 Rs. %	2501–4000 Rs %	4000–5500 Rs. %	Above 5501 Rs. %
I	16	49	19	16
II	21	27	24	28
III	43	21	16	20
IV	4	26	23	47
V	7	19	25	49

Note: Percentages total 100 reading across the columns. One U.S. dollar equals 17.50 rupees.

tear plastic shopping bags during the trip home.

Therefore, the following market plan was developed.

Marketing Objective

- Market penetration

Sales Goal

- 10,000 liters/day in each of the three target cities by the end of the three months

Market Share Goal

- 10 percent of the prepacked milk market after three months

Product Policy

- Produce better-quality milk than Milkpak or Haleeb, the two largest competitors
- Use a family brand name for milk and extend this later to butter and yogurt
- Introduce the new plastic pouch for prepacked milk; emphasize the convenience features as a special advantage
- Produce three sizes of pack: 250 milliliters, 500 milliliters, and 1 liter, with emphasis on the 250 milliliter pack in order to satisfy the preferences of occasional buyers
- Develop a special milk for children

Pricing Policy

- Meet major competitors' retail prices at Rs. 6.00/liter
- Squeeze out smaller suppliers by increasing retailers' commissions to Rs. 0.80/liter from Rs. 0.50
- Sell direct to institutional buyers at Rs. 5.40/liter for a minimum order of 50 liters/day (known as "bulk sales")

TABLE 4 **Sources of Milk Purchases—Lahore**

ZONE	GAWALLAS %	RETAIL STORES %
I	75	25
II	69	31
III	70	30
IV	62	38
V	56	44

TABLE 5 Reasons Why Consumers Prefer to Buy from Gawallas

CITY/ZONE	AVAILABILITY %	LOW PRICE %	FRESHNESS %	PURITY %	CREDIT FACILITY %	HOME DELIVERY %
Rawalpindi and Islamabad						
I	25	3	28	21	6	17
II	22	1	28	20	6	23
III	25	4	26	26	8	11
IV	15	4	31	26	4	20
V	19	8	30	22	0	21
Lahore						
I	22	9	20	13	13	23
II	25	11	20	12	9	23
III	24	11	23	16	3	23
IV	24	7	19	15	7	28
V	20	8	24	13	7	28

Note: Percentages total 100 reading across the columns. Only the major reason was solicited.

Promotional Policy

- Advertising would be used at a later stage to support the new flavors of milk
- A "push" strategy as the main promotional strategy, based on increased retail commissions

Distribution Policy

- MDL prepacked milk to be home-delivered and credit facilities to be offered, as a means of competing directly with the Gawallas

TABLE 6 Reasons Why Consumers Buy Prepacked Milk

CITY/ZONE	AVAILABILITY %	LOW PRICE %	FRESHNESS %	HYGIENE* %	EASE OF STORAGE %	QUALITY %	STATUS %	OTHER %
Rawalpindi and Islamabad								
I	21	2	15	18	15	10	0	19
II	20	5	22	28	10	14	0	1
III	21	5	20	23	9	18	1	3
IV	27	1	23	26	6	12	0	5
V	12	1	22	28	14	20	1	2
Lahore								
I	28	5	18	17	13	13	1	5
II	28	0	17	11	14	17	3	10
III	27	3	18	16	8	10	1	17
IV	36	3	16	12	12	10	1	10
V	28	3	13	26	9	7	0	14

Note: Percentages total 100 reading across the columns. Only the major reason was solicited.
*Pasteurized and homogenized at 3.5% fat.

TABLE 7 Major Decision Maker for the Purchase of Prepacked Milk

CITY	MALE HEAD %	CHILDREN %	HOUSEWIFE %	SERVANT'S DISCRETION %
Rawalpindi and Islamabad	28	14	54	4
Lahore	32	15	50	3

Note: Percentage responses by city zone have been averaged.

- MDL also to be distributed to retailers such as general grocery stores and bakeries

During the research survey, it was ascertained that consumers preferred the Gawallas as a source of milk due to the facility of home delivery. MDL saw this as a major opportunity and identified a creative means of distributing the new brand of milk.

Home Delivery—A Key Competitive Weapon

School children are transported to school in vans. Primary education is free, and enrollment is about 80 percent for boys but only 30 percent for girls. Children are transported twice a day, with about thirty in each van. During the rest of the day, the drivers are unoccupied. The same is true for Friday, the day of prayer, and for vacations, which run from June to mid-August.

MDL believed that these drivers had both the knowledge of the community, the time available, and the motivation to deliver milk during their quiet times. Most drivers own their own vans. MDL believed that these drivers could use their contacts with the thirty families they each already knew to identify another forty families who would like to buy home-delivered, prepacked milk. MDL had set a goal of distributing 200 liters of milk each day to seventy families, a rate of consumption documented in the consumer survey.

MDL proposed to pay the van drivers the higher retail commission of Rs. 0.80/liter, or Rs. 160.00 daily. It was estimated that a driver would be able to sell 200 liters a day in a forty-mile radius, and expenses for gas and depreciation were estimated at Rs. 30.00 and Rs. 20.00 respectively. Total daily earnings for each driver would be, therefore, about Rs. 110.00 (Rs. 160.00 − Rs. 50.00).

Thus, home delivery promised to be a cost-effective means of distribution, as well as a way of achieving high levels of customer satisfaction.

TABLE 8 Actual Purchaser of Prepacked Milk

CITY	MALE HEAD %	CHILDREN %	HOUSEWIFE %	SERVANT %
Rawalpindi and Islamabad	39	34	10	17
Lahore	25	40	11	24

Note: Percentage responses by city zone have been averaged.

Case 27: American Express International, Inc.

In January 1984, Seoul branch executive of American Express International, Inc., Mr. Steve Lowe, was considering the marketing strategy for the American Express Card's introduction to Korea with a local advertising agency, ORI-COM. They were reviewing whether to enter the Korean market and, if so, what marketing strategy to adopt.

Company Background

American Express Company, founded in 1850, is a diversified financial and travel services company. Through its four principal operating units—American Express Travel Related Services, IDS Financial Services, Shearson Lehman Hutton, and American Express Bank—the company is one of the leaders in payment systems, travel, asset management, investment banking, international banking, etc.

American Express Travel Related Services (TRS), the largest operating unit, markets the American Express Card along with Gold Card, Corporate Card, American Express travelers checks, and American Express money orders. The company's network of over 1,400 travel offices serves millions of people around the world each year. Internationally, Japan, Brazil, Germany, Hong Kong, Italy, and Spain are expected to experience sharp gains in American Express Cards in force. Asia, Korea, India, and China are expected to be the next target markets for the cards.

Korean Operation

As an initial stage to launch the American Express Card in Korea, a branch of American Express International, Inc., was installed in Seoul in 1983. Branch director Steve Lowe, assisted by a small staff of local MBAs, was primarily responsible for the successful preparation of its introduction. As soon as the decision to enter the Korean market was made, the branch was expanded with more staff and local networks established across the country.

Product

By the end of 1983, over 20 million American Express Cards were in force worldwide; this figure was expected to reach over 30 million in 1990. The card offers a wide range of financial services to cardholders such as credit line, insurance, and online cash services.

The basic operation of the card is similar worldwide. Cardholders pay an annual fee for the American Express Card, and are supposed to pay for their purchases within a certain period of time. The card to be offered in Korea would provide the same services. Monthly balance can be paid in won (Korean currency) or U.S. dollars.

Competition

There are generally two major categories to classify various credit cards available in Korea: (1) bank cards: National, Visa, Bank Credit, long-term bank, and (2) charge cards: both American Express and Diners Club cards were expected to be available soon.

A bank card did not require any fee for card membership; if a person had an account with a bank, he or she could get the bank card without any annual fee and initial application charge. In contrast, a charge card such as the American Express or Diners Club required both application and annual fees, which could discourage some people from holding charge cards.

In addition to the competition of bank cards,

This case was prepared by Kwangsu Kim, a graduate student at the University of Connecticut, under the supervision of the author.

EXHIBIT 1 Comparative Features of Different Cards

NAME	TRANSACTION FEE	ANNUAL FEE	PURCHASE LIMIT	INTEREST RATE (YR)	CASH LOAN LIMIT	INSURANCE LIMIT
National card	$1	None	$500	19%	$300	$2000
Bank credit card	$1	None	$500	19%	$300	$2000
Visa	$5	None	$1500	19%	$500	Unlimited
Long-term bank card	$1	None	$1000	19%	$500	$2000
American Express	None	$45	No limit	12.9%	$1500	Unlimited
Diners Club	None	$45	No limit	3%/month	$1000	Unlimited

Source: Company records.

it was expected that a charge card would be introduced in Korea by Diners Club in spring 1984. If both American Express and Diners Club were to launch their cards, there should be direct competition between the two to maintain the market share.

Exhibit 1 shows the comparative features of different cards. There are relative advantages and disadvantages associated with various cards. The American Express Card would charge substantial annual fees whereas National Bank, Bank Credit, and long-term bank cards would charge nothing (while they require a transaction fee upon opening the account, the amount is minimal).

Further, the banks have branches across the country while American Express did not have a branch network in Korea, resulting in inconvenience for the cardholders. But the American Express Card has its own strengths. First, the card can provide services abroad and permits purchase of airplane tickets. Second, it provides substantially more cash loan than the bank cards.

Market

Since a department store credit card was introduced in 1969 in Korea, there have been several other department store cards issued. But the era of the credit card was initiated in 1982, when eight banks formed an association to introduce Bank Credit card. The same year Visa card was also introduced for use in foreign countries as well as in the domestic market.

Exhibits 2 and 3 show the market-related information.

In 1983, the ad agency, at the request of American Express International, Inc., conducted a study to predict the potential market for the charge card. The number of subjects sampled was 1,500. They were over 25 years old and lived in cities such as Seoul, Pusan, and Kwangjoo. In addition, their average annual incomes were above 8 million won (U.S. $13,700). The results of the study are shown in Exhibit 4.

Based on the consumer survey, the target market has a strong level of awareness of the

EXHIBIT 2 Size of the Market Provided by the Advertising Agency

Number of households in the country	7,971,147
Number of households in 6 metropolitan cities	3,409,371
Number of households whose annual income is greater than 7 million won (U.S. $12,000)	477,000
Number of cardholders	850,000

Source: Company records

EXHIBIT 3 Market Position of Select Cards

NAME	NUMBER OF CARDHOLDERS	SERVICE ESTABLISHMENTS
National	470,000	25,000
Visa	38,000	7,000
Bank Credit	300,000	16,000

Source: Company records.

charge card. It was encouraging that the awareness level of the American Express Card reached 22 percent even before its launch. According to the consumer survey, the target market should be businesspeople who travel frequently and often organize business receptions.

Marketing Strategy

The ad agency proposed the following marketing strategy:

a. *Marketing Goal*
Launch the American Express Card in won (Korean currency).
Obtain 8,000 cardholders by the end of 1984.
Obtain 2,850 service establishments who would accept the card by the end of 1984.

b. *Strategy Thrust*
Increase awareness of the card through advertising and direct marketing.

c. *Advertising Strategy*
Advertising goal: increase awareness/establish brand image as a quality card.
Primary target market: more than 35 years old; income more than U.S. $10,000; businesspeople.
Additional target market: more than 25 years old; income more than U.S. $10,000; businesspeople.

EXHIBIT 4 Highlights of Consumer Survey

Awareness of American Express Card	22%
Awareness of Diners Club Card	6%
Awareness of National Card	58%
Percent of National Bank Card members	15%
Percent of Bank Credit Card members	6%
Foreign travel in last 2 years	12% (average 2–3 times)
Purpose of foreign travel	business (84%)
Domestic travel in last 2 years	78% (average 6 times)
Purpose of domestice travel	business (57%)
Business reception* in last month	51% (4–5 times)

**Business reception refers to the occasions when business partners entertain each other to promote mutual relationship and interests.*
Source: Company records

Brand positioning: The American Express Card is a high-quality card, which can be used in foreign countries as well as domestically. It is convenient for traveling and business entertaining. In particular, it symbolizes business success.

Prelaunch advertising: in major daily newspapers to increase the expectation of the launch; to counterattack the launch of such competitive cards as Diners Club.

d. *Direct Marketing Strategy*

Direct mailings will be sent to the following:
(1) Passport holders (those who have passports evidently travel abroad).
(2) List of car owners (in Korea those who own autos are thought to be rich).
(3) Lists of golf-club memberships (high-income people).

e. *Promotion*

A trade show will be held to celebrate and promote the card's launch. At the show, application forms will be distributed.

f. *Distribution Efforts*

Application forms should be available in travel agencies, banks, service establishments, etc.

Based on the above information, the branch executive had to decide whether the American Express Card should be launched in Korea and, if so, when and how the card could be introduced. The decision to enter the market seemed obvious in that the country has been economically strong and was expected to grow constantly in the future. Further, after the Summer Olympic Games scheduled to be held in Seoul in 1984, the country was expected to experience further economic growth.

However, Mr. Lowe wondered if the proposed marketing strategy by the local agency emphasized too much advertising. He felt greater emphasis should be placed on direct marketing. For example, travel agents could be included as one of the target markets since they might persuade travelers to apply for the American Express Card.

Further, since there were anti-American demonstrations recently among the university students, he thought-that the older segments of the population should be targeted. He also believed advertising in major daily newspapers would be appropriate.

As Mr. Lowe left the office, he planned to think the problems over.

Case 28: Ulker Biscuits, Inc.

On November 4, 1983, at 10:00 A.M. Ali Korkmaz, marketing director of Ulker Biscuits, Inc., was meeting with Hasan Beyaz, manager of the company's Export Department in Istanbul. They were discussing a report on the prosperous trading relationship that was developing between Turkey and a number of her Middle Eastern neighbors. Korkmaz thought Ulker could market its biscuit and candy products in these foreign markets; but, before he made decisions, he wanted information that could help the company identify the most lucrative markets in the Middle East for these products. He also wanted Beyaz to prepare a tentative operational plan for penetrating these foreign markets. Korkmaz knew that the key to success lay in efficient distribution, which he thought could be achieved in one of two ways. On the one hand, he thought, adopting a distribution system in which the regional

This case is printed here with the permission of the author, Erdener Kaynak of Pennsylvania State University at Harrisburg.

distributors were controlled by the company and worked for the long-term benefit of the company would be the best method to achieve success. In this system, the control mechanism would be achieved by the joint ownership of the newly built automated plant by the company and its regional distributors. Beyaz realized, however, that to persuade foreign regional distributors to enter a joint venture arrangement with the company would involve a great deal of development work. On the other hand, he also considered a diversification strategy by which the company would appoint regional distributors rapidly in a number of selected foreign markets without requiring their participation in a joint venture. This would lead to much faster market penetration although the risk of lower motivation on the part of foreign distributors could be a problem. Another advantage of this strategy would be that the company could be in the most lucrative foreign markets before some of its main competitors followed it to those markets. Korkmaz and Beyaz agreed to meet on November 18 to finalize the operational plan.

Now Beyaz wondered which one of the following market entry strategy options and operating decisions would maximize their potential for success:

a. Straight extension into the three countries (Libya, Saudi Arabia, and Cyprus) to which they had exported their products in the past.
b. Forming a joint venture with a local company in one of the key countries of the region.
c. Market penetration strategy using import agents and regional distributors.
d. Other strategies

Company Background

Ulker, a family-owned business, was founded in Istanbul (the largest Turkish city) in 1948. For a long time, biscuits and other candies had been prepared with human labor in flat trays. Over the last fifteen years, however, new machinery had been brought in that essentially eliminated the manual labor component of production. There were many reasons for this development. For example, technological progress had resulted in the reduction of production costs, the national income had risen, and population was growing rapidly, necessitating modern production methods. According to Korkmaz new ways were needed to meet the increasing demand in the industry. To meet this growing demand, Ulker had opened a second automated facility in Ankara, the capital of Turkey, three years ago. Shareholders in the new plant were a number of regional distributors in addition to Ulker's owners.

These regional distributors owned the majority of the equity of the Ankara plant. Top management of the company had made this gesture to demonstrate its interest in its regional distributors and hence to help assure their aggressive promotion of Ulker products across the country.

Ulker's major competitors were other large biscuit manufacturers, Eti, Ari, and Besler, although there were smaller biscuit manufacturers in the market also. However, these did not present any imminent danger to Ulker's competitive position in its domestic market. At present, Ulker was the clear leader of the industry in terms of sales volume and profits earned. Ulker maintained a 60 percent market share, compared to Eti's and Ari's 30 percent, and 10 percent shared by Besler and the smaller manufacturers (mostly regional). Ulker had the capacity to produce between 300 to 340 tons of biscuit, biscuit combination, and candies per day. Ari and Eti could produce only 100 to 140 tons a day, which put them in second and third place in the country, respectively.

Ulker's Distribution System

The company owned approximately 30 trailers, 100 large trucks, 20 minibuses and 300 to 400 service trucks to fulfill its transportation needs.

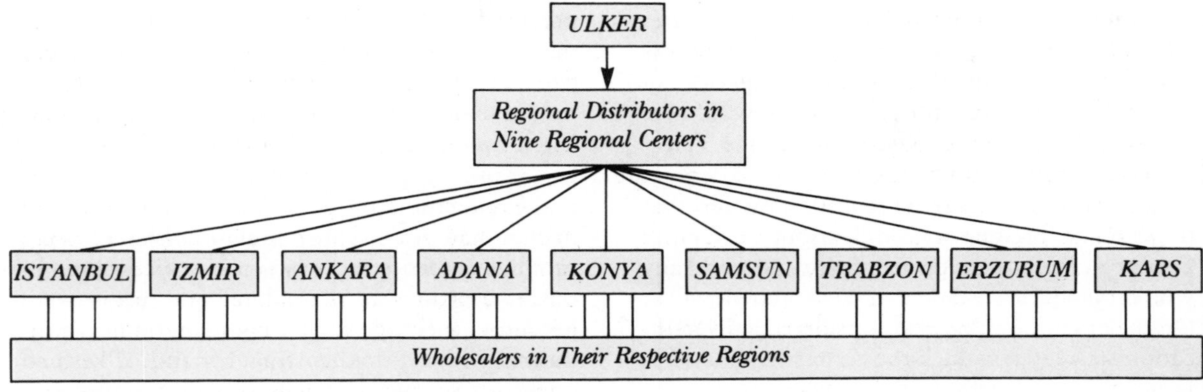

FIGURE 1

The regional distributors could either use the company's transportation vehicles or their own means to deliver the goods to their warehouses in their respective regions. Some of the bigger regional distributors had their own transportation fleets; all of the regional distributors owned their own warehouses and used their own personnel. The selling functions these regional distributors performed were the backbone of the entire distribution function of the firm. The distribution channel structure for Ulker's products is depicted in Figure 1.

The regional distributors were Ulker's exclusive dealers under contract through special agreements. They were not allowed to handle any other biscuit and/or candy lines. In return, Ulker did not deal with wholesalers and retailers directly in any region except in Istanbul and Ankara where the company's two plants were located. Outside of these two cities Ulker had agreed not to perform any selling activities without the consent of the regional distributors. So far, Ulker had never tried to bypass this agreement. The regional distributors worked on a fixed commission, which was 5 percent of sales plus bonus. Generally, the company depended exclusively on its distributors to distribute its goods throughout the country. Without these distributors, Ulker could encounter distribution difficulties.

The regional distributors carried the goods to warehouses in their respective locations with their own fleets. The distributors as well as the company did not believe in stocking more than a day's demand for the goods. They operated and stocked according to orders from their respective wholesalers and retailers. The company produced according to the orders taken from its regional distributors on a daily basis. From the regional distribution centers, the goods were distributed through the channel as shown in Figure 2. The regional distributor used his own sales agents and his own service vehicles for the distribution in two ways:

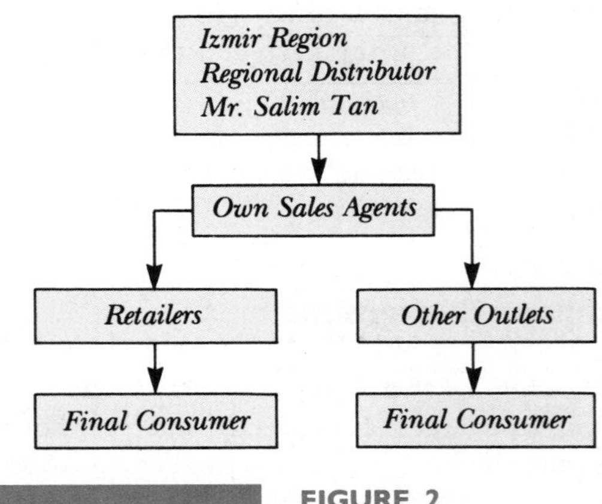

FIGURE 2

1. Sales agents were assigned to specific sales areas in the region. These agents paid visits to their respective areas covering retail grocery stores and other outlets such as canteens. They solicited orders from different retail outlets as well as institutional buyers. Sales agents came back with a list of sales orders. The distributor then sent a truck-full of the combination of goods that had been ordered.
2. Another type of sales agents, similar to drop shipper with a truck-full of goods, covered their respective areas and sold Ulker products only. These sales agents did not accept orders from retailers and other outlets. They delivered goods to their customers at least once a week.

Both types of sales agents worked for a salary plus a bonus for sales above a specified quota. These sales agents were trained by the regional distributor and they reported only to him. In most cases, their training was accomplished in a very primitive way. Salim Tan, regional distributor for Izmir, was quoted as saying, "A new sales agent will go around selling with an experienced salesman for about ten days; then he will be on his own. That is it. . . ."

As shown in Figure 3, there were also independent sales agents who owned their own service trucks and employed their own personnel to push Ulker's goods at their own expense. These independent sales agents sold only Ulker's goods for a commission from the regional distributor. In general, they were in competition with other companies' salesmen as well as with the regional distributors' own selling agents. Different types of independent agents competed with each other on the basis of service rendered and credit facilities provided. Ulker, as a company policy, promoted one price policy for everyone. The only exception to this rule was that the price could be different at the retail level where the company could not maintain standard prices because of severe price competition from other firms. At times, the regional distributors' own inspectors would go around asking retailers how much they paid for different Ulker products. That is how they controlled whether the one-price policy of Ulker was respected.

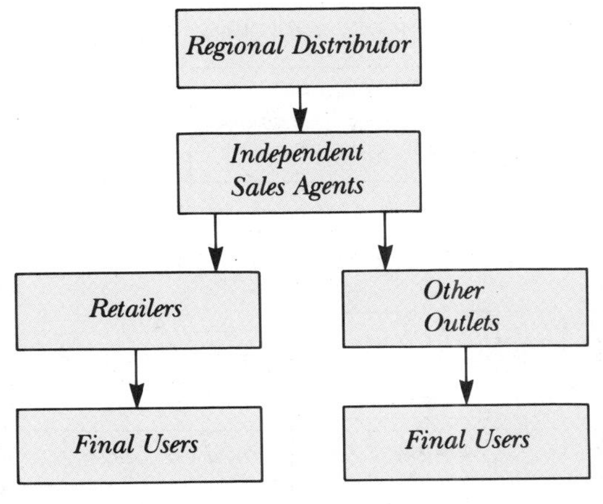

FIGURE 3

Another supplier in the distribution channel was the secondary vendor who bought only from the regional distributor, not directly from Ulker. These agencies like BAKSAN and AYKER would, in turn, sell to grocery stores, canteens, and buffets as they wished. They used their own service trucks and personnel to do the selling job. These agencies bought merchandise in larger quantities and thus obtained price discounts from the distributor. These agencies were not tied exclusively to Ulker, and therefore were not required to carry only Ulker's goods. As a result, they carried not only company products, but also other, often competing firms' products. They were completely independent agencies.

Regional distributors also dealt with wholesalers in their own regions (Figure 4). These wholesalers were more or less secondary vendors except that they were more passive participants. As such, they would order and stock a particular line of goods. They would sit back in their offices and wait for the retailers to come to them. These wholesalers were in competition with other wholesalers. Ulker's own sales agents, independent agents, or other sales agents in their own

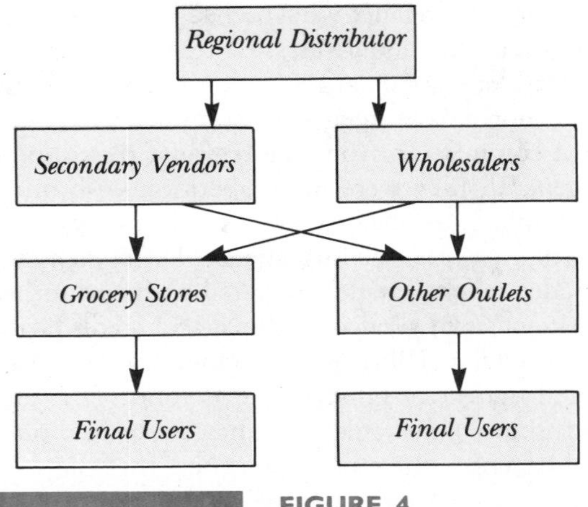

FIGURE 4

areas. When demand increased, they would call the regional distributors and order the goods that were needed. These wholesalers would get discounts when they bought in large quantities and/or in cash. They could only charge what Ulker had suggested for each type of product. They were not allowed to charge the grocer more than the suggested wholesale selling price. This form of distribution is illustrated in Figure 5.

Before the regional distributors were established in Eastern Turkey, the wholesalers played an extremely important role in the distribution of Ulker products. The wholesalers were used to buying directly from the firm as the regional distributors do today except that they did not have the same exclusive deal with the company. Ulker used its own trucks to deliver goods to that part of the country. Ulker maintained regional wholesalers in Erzurum and Kars who could sell Ulker's goods to the wholesalers. Ulker, in most cases, was unwilling to deal directly with the wholesalers because of the agreement signed between Ulker and its regional distributors. Ulker used its own sales personnel for selling its products in Ankara and Istanbul. These salesmen worked for the company, and were trained and paid by the company. They did the same type of selling and distribution as did the regional distributors' own salesmen.

Foreign Market Survey

In a recent Economic Intelligence Unit Country Survey on Turkey it was stated that the country's dealings with the Arab world and Iran presented a much more stable picture. Trade links with countries such as Jordan and Egypt, which had been somewhat tenuous in the past, had now strengthened. The relationship with Iran was particularly intriguing as that country was about as much the antithesis (under its present leadership) of Kemalist secularism as it was possible to imagine. However, it now seemed that Iran was leaning heavily on Turkey for provisions and possibly some political mediation.

In 1983, Turkey continues to expand its

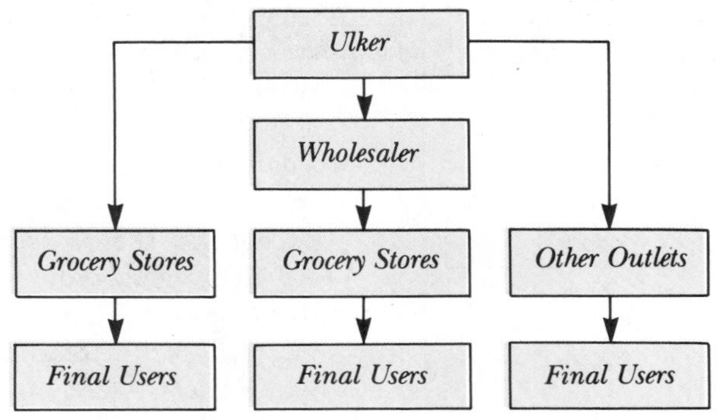

FIGURE 5

trade with both Iran and Iraq, and seems to have become Iran's major supplier. On February 19, 1983, an economic treaty was signed in Ankara that included work on a new railway bridge over the Euphrates at Habur to make railway connections possible between Turkey and Iraq, bypassing Syria. Apart from construction services, Iraq is now a major purchaser of Turkish cement, sugar, foodstuffs, vehicles, and machinery. Two years ago, it replaced West Germany as Turkey's main trading partner. However, it was removed from that position in 1982 by Iran. Turkey also signed an important economic protocol with Iran on April 21, 1983. This was the latest in a series of economic negotiations with that country. According to Kemal Canturk, Turkey's Minister of Trade, Turkey and Iran could do as much as $2.5 billion in trade in 1983. The latest trade agreement covers products like foods, wheat, sugar, barley, dairy products, machinery, ploughs, tractors, chemicals, and 600,000 tons of iron and steel. Turkey is also to expand its infrastructural links and create some joint banking services with Iran. Similar to the proposal for a Turkish-Iraqi bank, Turkey has managed to get Iran to agree that Turkish trucks will have the sole right to transport Turkish exports to Iran and will also undertake freight tasks for Iran. The strength of the agreement, coming at a time when Iran is turning its back on the U.S.S.R., is politically very interesting; but, whether Turkey would be able to hang on to its advantage if the Gulf War were to end is another question. There must also be doubts as to whether present and future supply of foods stocks in Turkey will permit exports to stay indefinitely at the present levels.

In the last few years, Ulker has exported biscuits and candy products, on a piecemeal basis, to some of the selected countries of the Middle East from its warehouses in Istanbul (see Figure 6). These were unsolicited orders from foreign import agents. Because of the socioeconomic and cultural similarities between Turkey and most of the Middle Eastern countries, Ali Korkmaz was of the opinion that there were vast market opportunities for Ulker's biscuit, candy, and combination products in these growth markets.

In reviewing all this relevant information, Korkmaz realized that he would have to prepare a very dynamic analysis of the marketing variables he and Beyaz would have to address during their next meeting. Since time was critical, he wondered what the order should be in setting down his lists of things to be done.

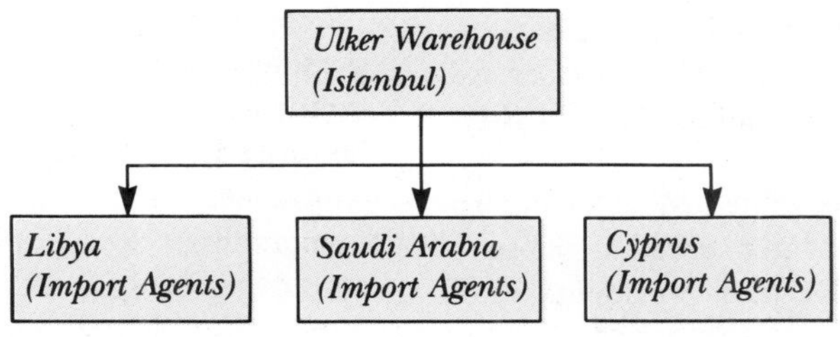

FIGURE 6

Case 29: MacDermid, Inc.

In 1990, Buzz Fanning, technical liaison for MacDermid, Inc., was sent to Korea to investigate MacDermid's loss of market share in the Korean market. MacDermid was an international specialty chemical company that supplied the metal finishing, printed circuit board, and microelectronics industries. The majority of sales in the Far East were for the printed circuit board (PC) market. In a two-year period, MacDermid had gone from a 30 percent to 50 percent market share to a 10 percent market share in the Korean PC market. Fanning was charged with regaining MacDermid's market share and its leadership position in Korea.

Background of the Company

MacDermid, Inc., was founded on February 2, 1922, in Waterbury, Connecticut, by Archie J. MacDermid, a Scottish immigrant. MacDermid's first product was Metex Metal Cleaner #1 for the metal finishing industry. Metex was an alkaline metal soak and electrolytic cleaner that was used to clean brass and other metals. The thriving brass industry in Connecticut provided a large market for MacDermid. In 1930 MacDermid moved its manufacturing facilities to a new location in Waterbury. This plant still serves as MacDermid's primary manufacturing facility in the U.S.

In 1938 Harold Leever joined MacDermid as a research chemist. Leever later served as the second of only three MacDermid presidents and subsequently as chairman of the board. It was Leever's innovative and insightful ideas that led MacDermid to be a world leader in specialty chemicals for the metal finishing, printed circuit board, and microelectronics industries.

Leever began changing the company when he developed Anodex, a reverse-current alkaline cleaner. Anodex could be used to clean steel and this opened the automotive market to MacDermid. With this, MacDermid became a national marketer.

Leever also developed the philosophy of "sales and service." This philosophy merged research and sales by requiring that research conducted in Waterbury start from and serve the customer's needs. This philosophy still works at MacDermid today.

During the 1940s and 1950s, MacDermid introduced some industry firsts. Cyanide bright copper addition agents eliminated dull finishes and the need for buffing procedures. Dry acid salt replaced the more hazardous liquid acids thus providing environmental improvements. Metal strippers allowed customers to salvage scrapped electroplated parts. Metex Acid Salt M-629 was a refinement of the original salt and provided a longer life and a better adhesion of plated metals. Chromate conversion coatings improved corrosion resistance and appearance. The 1950s also saw the construction of another MacDermid manufacturing facility located in Ferndale, Michigan. MacDermid had emerged as an innovator and market leader in the metal finishing industry. This reputation would help propel the company into new markets.

By 1954, Leever had earned the position of president of MacDermid. Archie MacDermid remained active in the company until 1959 when he retired. With $3 million in sales, seventy-five employees, and fifty products, Archie offered ownership of the company to the employees. The employees bought 29,000 of Archie's shares for $961,640. This allowed control of the company to remain with those who had helped make it successful.

Leever introduced the concept of "Complete Cycle Responsibility," which then became company policy. This policy stated that every MacDermid representative will accept responsibility for satisfactory operation of a complete processing cycle.

In the 1960s MacDermid began to develop and market chemicals for a new industry that was very significant in size—the electronics industry. Printed circuit boards are an essential component of this market. Chemicals are used to clean, coat, etch, strip, and protect printed circuit boards. MacDermid's first product in this market was alkaline etchant. This eliminated the need for hazardous chromic acids and ferric chloride and thus improved working conditions and worker safety.

In 1966 a public stock offering of 20 percent of the 510,456 outstanding shares was made. By this time, MacDermid had also begun to compete internationally, with $200,000 in overseas sales. A 50/50 joint venture with Occidental Petroleum Corporation was formed and called MOSA. MOSA was responsible for worldwide manufacturing and distribution of proprietary chemicals. This agreement was terminated in 1973.

In 1977, MacDermid had $42 million in sales, 440 employees, and 500 specialty chemicals. There were manufacturing plants in Connecticut, Michigan, California, Missouri, England, and Spain, and a research facility in Tel Aviv, Israel. There were sales and service operations throughout the world. It was in this growing environment that Arthur J. LoVetere was made the third and current president of MacDermid. LoVetere joined MacDermid when he was eighteen as a summer worker. He continued his association with MacDermid as he earned his BS in chemical engineering and his MBA. In 1963, after receiving his MBA, LoVetere began as a technical sales representative for the mid-Atlantic. By 1966, LoVetere was the company's youngest regional sales manager at age 27. In 1973 he became vice president of marketing and by 1975 he was vice president and chief operating officer. In 1977 he was made president and chief executive officer. LoVetere believed in management by participation. Although LoVetere was now responsible for daily operations, Leever remained as an active participant in the company and chairman of the board.

Under LoVetere, the company continued to expand its operations by acquisitions and entry into international markets. In 1978 MacDermid had 6,000 customers in the U.S. and Canada. Products were marketed in Europe by twenty-five sales representatives located throughout England, Germany, the Netherlands, Spain, and Switzerland. Proprietary products were manufactured and sold in Australia, Italy, and on a limited basis in Japan. MacDermid purchased the Plating Systems Division of 3M. This acquisition provided manufacturing, distribution networks, and a basis for overseas business that were extremely valuable, especially in the Far East.

In 1980, the Employee Stock Ownership Plan was instituted, continuing the tradition of employee ownership. Employee ownership was now 40 percent with retirees, friends, and families of employees constituting another 25 percent.

By 1990, MacDermid had $106 million in sales, 800 employees, 1,000 products, and served twenty-three countries. The company was still characterized as an innovator and industry leader. There was no rigid organizational chart and the "MacDermid Spirit" was evident to anyone who came in contact with a MacDermid employee. In 1986, a 2,500-square-foot manufacturing plant was built in Taiwan.

Products—PC Market

MacDermid had a full line of products to service the PC industry. Products included Metex activators, accelerators, acid cleaners and acid salts, electrocleaners, strippers, antitarnish coatings, circuit board tapes, polymer thick films, solder pastes, resists and masks, and etch resists and inks. These products are used in such applications as communication systems, television, video and sound recorders, compact discs, microwaves, radios, industrial automation and robotics, computer system electronics, navigation electronics, and medical instrumentation and monitoring devices. MacDermid was considered one of the major competitors in this market. It was the only specialty chemical company with direct operations in every major market in the world.

Competition

Shiplee Corporation of Germany was MacDermid's major competitor. Shiplee was privately owned and had a significant market share. Their claim to success was consistent quality. Shiplee competed with MacDermid in most major markets in the world.

Korean Market

MacDermid was well established in Japan, Korea, Singapore, Hong Kong, and Taiwan. MacDermid had its own manufacturing facility in Taiwan and used contract manufacturers in Japan. For thirteen years, the Korean market had been served by MacDermid out of its Japanese division. The Japanese fully controlled the market. The Korean market had become significantly large due to the government's commitment to the electronics industry. However, because of the loss of one major account, MacDermid's market share had dropped to 10 percent. There was considerable animosity between the Koreans and the Japanese. A brief history lesson highlights the fact that the Japanese invaded Korea during World War II. In addition, the cultural, political, and economic differences between the two nations further increased the friction.

The Korean market was serviced by Japanese salesmen. There was no local representation. The price charged by the Japanese division was twice that available in the U.S. This was primarily due to the strength of the yen. In 1990, the Korean sales volume was $400,000 per year.

The Korean government had recently mandated a balance of trade. Currently, there was an excess of imports from Japan and an excess of exports to the United States and Hong Kong. The Korean customers were requesting to deal directly with the U.S. division, which would result in a better balance with the United States and Japan (i.e., fewer imports from Japan and more imports from the United States). MacDermid's Japanese employees furiously fought this option. They would lose a large percentage of sales if they lost the Korean market. Buzz was challenged with finding a solution to this complicated international problem.

Case 30: Barossa Winery

Mr. George Steen, marketing manager for the Barossa Winery, had just been given an interesting assignment: to evaluate the feasibility of launching a major export drive. The Barossa Winery, an Australian producer of quality table wines, had experienced rapid growth in the early 1980s, but in 1986 and 1987 sales and profits had slowed considerably. At a strategy meeting held in early July 1988, the senior management group, which included Mr. Steen, decided that a growth opportunity existed in export markets and Mr. Steen agreed to prepare a feasibility study for the next strategy meeting.

As Mr. Steen sat in his office, Mr. Tony

This case is printed here with the permission of the author, Gordon H. G. McDougall of Wilfrid Laurier University, Canada.

Clark, the general manager, came in and they began discussing the assignment. Mr. Steen said, "There will never be a better opportunity for us to get into foreign markets in a big way. The world has now heard of Australia because of Crocodile Dundee and the Bicentennial Celebration, we've got a very favorable exchange rate, and we produce great wines." Mr. Clark replied, "I agree, it's a good opportunity for growth and we've got the capacity of doing it and making a profit. I know our wines are as good and, in some instances, better than comparable European wines, but the consumer doesn't know that." Mr. Steen replied, "That's true, but we only need a small share of any one of a number of markets to sell a large volume of wine. I think it's a matter of selecting one or two markets and going after them." Mr. Clark responded, "You are probably right, but I'm more cautious. I'll be very interested in hearing what you recommend. Our future growth may depend on your report."

The Company

The Barossa Winery, located in the Barossa Valley of South Australia, was started in the early 1960s by a winemaker, Mr. Rolf Mann, who had obtained a degree in viticulture from a well-regarded French school and emigrated to Australia. Since 1970, the firm had captured numerous awards every year at national and regional wine shows for both its red and white wines. By 1980, the company had established a solid reputation in Australia as a consistent producer of high-quality premium table wines.

The company was also known for its marketing skills. Mr. Steen, who joined the company in 1976, instituted various marketing initiatives including a series of labels that were regarded by many industry analysts as exceptional in terms of communicating the quality of the wines and "standing out" among the many competitive brands. As well, Mr. Steen established a distribution system that resulted in the prominent display of the company's products in many retail outlets. Finally, many of the advertising campaigns prepared for the Barossa Winery were judged as innovative and had contributed to the recognition and acceptance of the company's brands.

These efforts had resulted in rapid growth for the company. Between 1980 and 1985 sales increased from $17,500,000 to $33,900,000 and profits before tax from $1,600,000 to $3,100,000 (Exhibit 1).[1] However, in 1986 and 1987 sales grew more slowly and profits were unchanged. Company officials felt that recent results were due, in part, to a slowdown in the growth of both the overall market and the table wine market (Exhibit 2). As well, increased competition in the quality premium bottled table wine market had led to price discounting by some wineries. As a policy, the Barossa Winery did not engage in price discounting.

With respect to export activity up to now the company could best be described as a passive exporter. While George Steen had made one overseas trip in the past two years (the trip covered stops in the United States, Canada, and the United Kingdom) to "drum up" some business with wine importers, no explicit export strategy had been established. In fact, the company's export sales had been generated by wine importers who had approached the Barossa Winery.

The interest of those wine importers (primarily from the United Kingdom) in Barossa Winery products was due to the increasing recognition by many knowledgeable buyers of the quality of Australian and the company's wines. In the early 1980s, wine experts from the United Kingdom visited Australia and sampled numerous wines. Upon their return home, many wrote glowing reports on the quality of these wines, including Barossa Winery's products.

In 1987, the company exported 37,400 cases of wine valued at $2,094,400, an increase of 42 percent in volume and 70 percent in dollar value

[1]All figures in this case are quoted in Australian dollars, unless otherwise noted. At the time of the case, $1.00 Australian = $0.99 Canadian.

EXHIBIT 1 **Barossa Winery—Selected Company Statistics (1980 to 1987)**

	1980	1981	1982	1983	1984	1985	1986	1987
Profit and loss statement (in $000,000)								
Sales	17.5	20.6	23.6	26.8	30.5	33.9	35.3	36.8
Cost of goods sold	11.7	13.8	15.6	17.9	20.8	23.2	24.4	25.7
Gross margin	5.8	6.8	8.0	8.9	9.7	10.7	10.9	11.1
Marketing expenses	3.0	3.5	3.9	4.5	4.8	5.5	5.7	5.8
Net margin	2.8	3.3	4.1	4.4	4.9	5.2	5.2	5.3
Administration and overheads	1.2	1.5	1.7	1.8	2.0	2.1	2.2	2.2
Profit before tax	1.6	1.8	2.4	2.6	2.9	3.1	3.0	3.1
Sales by Volume								
(000 litres)	4,120	4,520	4,830	4,950	5,210	5,680	5,800	5,900
(000 cases)[a]	468	502	537	550	579	631	644	656
Average selling price per case ($)	37.40	41.00	44.00	48.70	52.70	53.70	54.80	56.10
Export statistics								
Export sales (000 litres)	84.2	122.0	115.9	158.4	187.6	215.8	237.8	336.3
Export sales (000 cases)	9.4	13.6	12.9	17.6	20.8	24.0	26.4	37.4
Average selling price/case ($)[b]	31.80	34.90	37.40	41.40	44.80	45.60	46.60	56.00
Export sales ($000)[c]	298.9	474.6	482.5	728.6	931.8	1094.4	1230.2	2094.4
Consumer Price Index	100.0	109.8	120.8	135.5	148.7	160.9	176.7	186.0

[a]One case equals 9 L (12 bottles containing 750 mL each).
[b]Up to 1987 detailed sales records on prices were not kept. Company officials estimated that between 1980 and 1986 the average selling price per case was approximately 15% less than the domestic price per case.
[c]It was estimated that marketing expenses and administration and overheads amounted to 3% of sales for export sales versus around 8% for domestic sales.
Source: Company records.

compared to 1986 (Exhibit 1). In fact, 1987 was the first year the company received the same average price for its wine in both the domestic and export markets. In prior years it was estimated (no records had been kept) that export sales generated a price per case of approximately 15 percent less than the average price received in the domestic market.

The Australian Wine Industry

In many ways, the Australian wine industry is similar to other world wine markets. The first requirement for producing good wines was to have the appropriate climate and soil conditions. Many regions of Australia had these conditions and produced wine grapes including such classics as Cabernet Sauvignon, Grenache, and Pinot Noir for red wines, and Clare, Rhine Riesling, and Traminer for white wines. Most medium- and large-sized wineries in Australia made a complete range of wines, each with their own individuality. The Barossa Winery made six different white wines with two brands, Barossa Chardonnay and Barossa Rhine Riesling, making up over 80 percent of the company's white wine sales. The company produced five different red wines and, again, two brands, Barossa Cabernet Sauvignon and Barossa Hermitage, accounted for the majority of sales. Dry white wines accounted for 85 percent of total company sales.

A second requirement for producing good wines was to have a skilled winemaker. Mr. Mann had quickly established a reputation

EXHIBIT 2 Australian Wine Market—Selected Statistics (1980 to 1987) (000 liters)

	1980	1981	1982	1983	1984	1985	1986	1987
Total wine sales	245,040	262,872	278,595	293,582	305,802	320,478	325,183	329,952
Table	160,867	179,278	197,904	216,948	227,805	245,400	253,045	258,231
Fortified[a]	45,587	45,868	45,189	43,027	42,587	38,617	36,819	36,246
Sparkling[b]	29,915	29,577	27,749	27,022	29,021	31,277	30,413	30,098
All other[c]	8,671	8,158	7,753	6,585	6,389	5,182	4,907	5,378
Table wine sales by variety								
Dry white	121,093	138,016	155,310	172,334	175,341	179,286	171,780	176,227
Sweet white	3,497	3,912	4,529	4,929	10,060	20,840	36,936	34,657
Red	27,667	29,258	30,362	31,856	34,480	37,805	37,188	40,192
Rose	8,610	8,091	7,706	7,830	7,924	7,466	7,140	7,155
Table wine sales by package								
Soft pack—white	51,148	69,525	84,680	103,585	111,486	137,675	140,788	138,787
Bottled—white	34,300	36,709	39,368	38,644	36,278	39,559	38,851	41,743
Soft pack—red	7,451	8,871	11,263	12,787	14,425	16,191	16,927	17,659
Bottled—red	11,507	12,455	12,252	12,657	14,058	16,779	16,838	19,004
All other[d]	56,461	51,718	50,341	49,275	51,558	35,196	39,641	41,038

[a]Includes sherry and dessert wines.
[b]Includes champagne and carbonated wines.
[c]Includes flavored and vermouth.
[d]Includes white, red, and rose sold in bulk and in bottles over one litre in size.
Source: Australian Wine and Brandy Corporation.

throughout Australia for producing high-quality wines on a consistent basis. He was renowned for his ability to purchase the finest grapes (the company did not own any vineyards, but instead purchased its grapes from among the over 4,000 grape growers in Australia), and he used the latest technology in producing many award-winning wines.

The third requirement was the ability to market the company's wines. Few, if any, product categories offered the consumer as wide a choice of varieties and brands as the wine category. For example, one of the large wholesalers of beer, wine, and spirits in Australia listed 577 brands of bottled table wines, including 256 red wines and 273 white wines. Most of these listed wines would be supplied by the fifty medium to large wineries in Australia.

Retail liquor outlets would not carry the complete range of wines offered by a wholesaler, but a typical outlet would handle at least 100 different brands of red and white bottled table wines. This large selection meant that marketing was critical in getting a brand known and recognized by consumers. While wine connoisseurs understood the differences between the varieties and brands of wines, these consumers constituted a very small percentage of the wine buying public. A second group, who knew a reasonable amount about wines and could identify the major and some minor brands, tended to purchase the majority of the bottled table wines.

In terms of quantity, most table wine in Australia was sold in two- or four-liter casks to consumers who were relatively price sensitive. Retail liquor outlets in Australia could advertise and offer beer, wine, and spirits at any price. A consumer could purchase a four-liter cask of average-quality Riesling for about $7.00 on sale (regular price $10.00) or a 750 mL bottle of slightly higher quality Riesling for $3.50 on sale (regular price of $6.50). As shown in Exhibit 2, soft pack or cask sales of table wine constituted about 61 percent of total table wine sales, while bottled table wines constituted about 24 percent of total table wine sales by volume.

A further indication of the price sensitivity of the market was the impact of government taxation policies on the level of wine consumption. In late 1984, a ten percent tax was placed on wines, and in 1985 the tax was increased to 20 percent. As shown in Exhibit 2, the total market growth rate, which averaged 5 percent between 1980 and 1984 declined to 1.5 percent in 1985.

On a broader scale, the consumption of wine in Australia appeared to have peaked in 1985 at twenty-one liters per capita. This compared to per capita consumption of nine liters in 1970, twelve liters in 1975, and seventeen liters in 1980.

Against this backdrop, the Barossa Winery competed in the bottled table wine markets. Its target market was the relatively sophisticated wine drinker who was somewhat knowledgeable about wines and was likely to drink wine with his or her evening meal two or more times a week. Within this target market, the Barossa Winery competed with virtually all the wineries in Australia as this was the most profitable segment. However, only a few companies, such as Wolf Blass and Leasingham had been as successful as the Barossa Winery within this segment. While no market data were available, some industry observers felt that Wolf Blass and Leasingham were increasing their share of the market at a faster rate than the Barossa Winery.

The World Wine Industry

On a worldwide basis, the wine market was dominated by the European Community (EC) and within the community, by three countries, France, Italy, and Spain. The EC vineyards accounted for approximately 27 percent of the total area of the world under vines, 38 percent of the world's grapes, and 60 percent of the world's production of wines. Because of price supports within the EC for the wine industry in the past, the EC countries typically produced more wine than could be consumed within the EC. Consequently, there was considerable pressure to export wine. Due to declining consumption within the EC countries and revised price support policies, in recent years the production of wine by EC nations had declined (Exhibit 3). However, a surplus of wine was still produced within the EC, and the countries collectively exported over four billion liters of wine annually. Exporting of wine was encouraged by governments as the EC provided export refunds and subsidies for table wine exported outside the EC.

Australian Wine Imports and Exports

Between 1980 and 1985 only a small portion (about 3 percent) of Australia's total wine production was exported. In the 1985–86 period exports increased to 11 million liters, and in 1986–87 exports rose to 21 million liters (Exhibit 4). This was due primarily to a more favorable exchange rate as the Australian dollar had fallen sharply against most foreign currencies (Exhibit 5). Two other factors also contributed to this increase. First, the Chernobyl nuclear incident (a nuclear reactor exploded in Ukraine in 1986 and nuclear waste was spread across Europe) had raised concern in a number of countries (particularly in Scandinavia) about contamination of European grapes. Second, there was a growing awareness in many countries of the quality of Australian wines.

The vast majority of Australian wine exports were table wines and most of these exports went to seven countries with the United States, the United Kingdom, and Canada being three of the largest markets. The value per liter of export sales varied considerably by country. At the lower end, Sweden purchased wine in bulk (it was shipped from Australia in large containers) at a value per liter of $1.01. The wine was bot-

EXHIBIT 3 World Wine Industry—Selected Data (000,000 liters)

	PRODUCTION			EXPORTS	IMPORTS	PER CAPITA CONSUMPTION (LITERS)	
	1983–84	1984–85	1985–86	1985	1985	1983	1985
France	6,855	6,436	7,015	1,189	701	85	80
Italy	8,228	7,090	6,258	1,803	n.a.	91	85
Spain	3,247	3,625	3,277	731	n.a.	57	48
Portugal	845	850	855	152	n.a.	89	87
West Germany	1,340	889	540	292	962	27	26
Greece	525	503	478	140	n.a.	44	43
United Kingdom	—	—	—	—	580	9	10
Total EC	21,040	19,393	18,423	4,307	2,243		
Europe—All others (incl. U.S.S.R.)	7,031	6,692	5,804	—	—	—	—
United States	1,476	1,670	1,810	—	519	8	9
Australia	396	451	480	11	8	20	21
Canada	47	50	50	—	140	9	10
Africa, Latin America, and South Africa	3,312	2,931	3,124	—	—	—	—
All others	1,002	918	981	—	—	—	—
Total	34,304	32,105	30,672	4,318	2,910		

Source: Australian Wine and Brandy Corporation.

tled and sold by the Swedish liquor control board. At the upper end, all of the wine exported to the United States was in bottle form at an average price to the exporter of $3.59 per liter.

The Export Decision

In preparing the report, Mr. Steen first considered the possible countries where the Barossa Winery could achieve significant sales. Based on a preliminary screening, he decided to limit his investigation to the three countries that he felt offered a good potential for the company's products: Canada, the United States, and the United Kingdom.

Canada

Canada was an attractive market because the domestic wine industry was not well developed and was not recognized as producing quality wines (Exhibit 6). The marketing of wine and spirits in Canada was strictly controlled by the ten provincial governments, and most sales were made through government liquor stores. In March 1988, the Australian Wine and Brandy Corporation sponsored a tour of the listing agents for the ten liquor control boards of Canada. The agents visited the major wine-growing areas and sampled many of the wines available for export. The main objective of the tour was to acquaint the agents with the quality, variety, and availability of Australian wines.

The two major drawbacks to the Canadian market were the difficulties in getting a general listing and the restrictions placed on marketing activities. Australian wines would compete against all other wine-producing countries for listings. It was estimated that up to 1,000 listing requests were received by each of the ten boards every year and a selection committee might list seventy-five new wines. Chances of acceptance

EXHIBIT 4 Australian Wine Imports and Exports, 1986–1987

	IMPORTS*			EXPORTS		
	Liters (000)	Value ($000)	Value/ Liter ($)	Liters (000)	Value ($000)	Value/ Liter ($)
Champagne	1,134	19,628	17.31	370	1,484	4.01
Table wine	4,852	17,084	3.52	18,627	37,967	2.04
All others	1,573	4,899	3.11	2,326	5,170	2.22
Total	7,559	41,611	5.50	21,323	44,621	2.09

Exports From Australia by Destination (000 Liters or $000)

	CHAMPAGNE		TABLE WINE		ALL OTHERS		TOTAL		VALUE/ LITER
	L	Value	L	Value	L	Value	L	Value	
United States	36	$ 171	2,455	$ 9,029	422	$1,255	2,913	$10,455	$3.59
United Kingdom	34	122	2,190	6,775	96	352	2,320	7,249	3.12
Sweden	—	—	5,223	5,257	—	—	5,223	5,257	1.01
New Zealand	183	611	1,054	3,397	177	540	1,414	4,548	3.22
Canada	—	—	1,228	3,017	791	1,283	2,019	4,300	2.13
Hong Kong	28	149	527	1,009	108	246	663	1,404	2.12
Fiji	14	67	230	426	72	136	316	629	1.99
All Other	75	364	5,720	9,057	660	1,358	6,455	10,779	1.67
Total	370	$1,484	18,627	$37,967	2,326	$5,170	21,323	$44,621	$2.09

*Largest imports (in 1000 L) come from Italy (2,714), France (1,981), and Portugal (777).

EXHIBIT 5 Exchange Rates (units of foreign currency per $ Australian)

JUNE	UNITED STATES DOLLAR	CANADIAN DOLLAR	U.K. POUND STERLING	WEST GERMAN MARK	FRENCH FRANC	ITALIAN LIRA	TRADE WEIGHTED INDEX*
1984	0.86	1.14	0.64	2.40	7.36	1,477.13	79.2
1985	0.67	0.91	0.51	2.03	6.19	1,294.40	65.0
1986	0.68	0.94	0.44	1.48	4.73	1,019.90	56.3
1987	0.72	0.96	0.45	1.31	4.40	955.48	56.6
1988	0.81	0.99	0.44	0.99	3.97	1,099.32	56.8

*Trade-weighted index of average value of the Australian dollars vis-à-vis currencies of Australia's trading partners. May 1970 index = 100.

Source: Reserve Bank of Australia, *Bulletin,* Publication No. NBP 4521.

EXHIBIT 6 Fact Sheet on Canada

- Canadian consumption of wine, particularly imported wine, is increasing despite severe marketing restrictions. The import and retailing of all alcoholic beverages is controlled by individual provincial monopolies, as are all aspects of product marketing (for example, advertising, sampling).
- Import licensing as such is not required. However, distribution is controlled by the provincial government liquor monopolies who will only list a brand if convinced it will achieve the required sales volume.
- Import duties are $12 Canadian per imperial gallon (one imperial gallon equals 4.546 liters). Excise taxes are $.35 Canadian per liter. Federal sales taxes are 12 percent on the landed duty and excise paid value. As of June 1988, import duties in Australian dollars would be $2.64 per liter, excise duties would be $0.35 per liter, and federal sales tax would be $1.14 per liter.
- No major difficulties in terms of certification, packaging, etc. However, with respect to labels, the label information must be in English and French.
- Canada produces less than one-half of its wine requirements and Canada's climate is not conducive to grape growing.
- Prices to the provincial monopolies should be quoted in Canadian dollars CIF (cost, insurance, freight). Each province arbitrarily sets the retail price of a product by applying a fixed markup to the landed cost (C$CIF). For example, Alberta has a markup of 55 percent; British Columbia has a markup of 50 percent on B.C.-produced table wines, 110 percent on other Canadian-produced table wines, and 110 percent on imported wines; Ontario has a markup of 58 percent on Ontario-produced table wines, 98 percent on other Canadian-produced table wines, and 123 percent on imported wines; Québec has a markup of 80 percent on Québec-produced table wines, 114 percent on other Canadian-produced table wines, and 120 percent on imported table wines.
- Distribution of all wine and spirits sold in Canada is controlled by government monopolies and/or liquor boards. Each of the ten provinces has its own liquor board. Since each province will only stock a limited range of wines out of the hundreds of different types and brands available, it establishes a price list giving the names of those wines available for sale. However, even when a wine is listed, it will probably not be available in every store.
- The majority of Canada's 26 million people reside in Ontario, Québec, British Columbia, and Alberta.

Primary source: Australian Wine and Brandy Corporation, *Export Market Grid.*

were improved by a personal visit to present the listing application. Primarily, it was felt that price (within a given quality range) was the dominant criterion in getting accepted on the list. Government restrictions placed on marketing activities (for example, no price discounting, restrictions as to the amount and type of advertising, no point-of-purchase displays) made it difficult to develop brand awareness and trial by consumers.

In preparing his report Mr. Steen obtained information on the largest Australian wine exporter's operations in Canada (Hardy's Wines). It was rumored that Hardy's held somewhat over 40 percent share of the Canadian table wine market for Australian wines. As well, Hardy's was thought to have about a 50 percent share of the "All Other" wines category. It had achieved this position by spending approximately $200,000 each year in Canada. Hardy's had two full-time employees, one in Ontario and one in Québec (total costs for both employees including salaries, office space, cars, and expenses were $100,000), and the company spent about $100,000 on all types of promotions, including visits by the Australian export manager. The two employees spent the majority of their time making regular calls on the liquor board head offices, checking stocks, and calling on individual liquor stores to ensure that the product was available. As well, the employees would have the product on hand at any wine tastings within the provinces. A further important duty was to encourage Canadian wine writers for newspapers and magazines to write about Hardy's Wines. Hardy's also employed agents in Alberta and British Columbia who received a 10 percent commission plus up to 5 percent more for expenses.

Most Australian wine producers who exported to Canada used agents to perform the marketing function. The agents worked on a commission basis (usually 10 percent of the landed cost in Canada) and their prime role was to obtain product exposure. This could be done by convincing restaurants and hotels to include the product on wine lists, by conducting tastings, and by obtaining good press for the product. Agents could be valuable because the need for personal selling was considerable in Canada. Wine consumption in Canada had been increasing and per capita consumption had risen from 6.3 liters per year in 1976 to 10 liters in 1985. Over 50 percent the wine sold in Canada was imported and over 80 percent of that came from the wine-producing countries of the EC. Some well-known European brands such as Blue Nun, Black Tower, and Mateus had substantial sales in Canada. Of the 140,000,000 liters of wine imported to Canada in 1985, 90 percent were table wines.

United States

By Australian standards, the magnitude of the U.S. market was staggering (Exhibit 7). Imports of table wine alone were about 313 million liters in 1986, most of it coming from Italy (48 percent), France (30 percent), and West Germany (11 percent). The Italian wine imports tended to be lower-priced ($1.52/liter on average), while the French imports were relatively high-priced ($4.43/liter). The German imports ($2.89/liter) were close to the average of all imports ($3.09/liter).[2] In 1986, the Australian share of the U.S. table wine market was estimated at 0.06 percent.

The top-selling import brands in the U.S. market included Riunite from Italy (8,500,000 cases), Blue Nun from Germany (1,000,000 cases), and Mateus from Portugal (800,000 cases). It was estimated that the wholesale prices per case for these brands were: Riunite $19.35 ($2.15/liter), Blue Nun $33.12 ($3.68/liter), and Mateus $21.30 ($2.37/liter). Promotion expenditures for many of the imported wines were extensive, and while total expenditures were not available it was estimated that Riunite spent over $12,000,000 in television advertising and Blue Nun spent approximately $2,400,000 in radio advertising.

With respect to markets, the top ten markets for table wine in the United States accounted for 65 percent of all sales. The New York metropolitan area had sales of 5.9 million cases of imported table wine, and Detroit (ninth-ranked) had sales of 550,000 cases in 1986.

Selection of an agent or importer was obviously an important consideration. Numerous spirit agents were available ranging from small companies that specialized in a few product lines in one area of the country to national distributors that had a vast product line and covered the entire country.

Marketing activities for wine companies, particularly in the nonmonopoly states, could be extensive and include advertising, in-store promotions, and price specials. Many United States wine producers, particularly from California, had established well-known brand names and were recognized as producing quality wines.

[2]Value at foreign export port exclusive of shipping costs and taxes.

EXHIBIT 7 Fact Sheet on the United States

- The United States consumption of wine, both domestic and imported, has been increasing and the absolute size of the market is one of the most attractive in the world. Estimated sales for 1988 are 2 billion liters.
- Import licenses may only be held by U.S. citizens.
- Import duties on table wines are $0.375 U.S. per U.S. gallon (one U.S. gallon = 3.785 liters). Excise taxes are $0.17 U.S. per U.S. gallon. As of June 1988, import duties in Australian dollars would be $0.12 per liter and excise taxes would be $0.06 per liter.
- No major difficulties in terms of certification, packaging, labeling, etc.
- Seventy-two percent of the table wine sold in the U.S. was produced in California, 24 percent was imported, and 4 percent was produced by other states in 1986.
- The U.S. market, because of its size and complexity, should be treated on a state-by-state basis. The sale of alcoholic beverages is controlled by state organizations, the degree of authority ranging from minimal licensing requirements to complete control of retail outlets. There are eighteen "monopoly" states that operate in a similar manner to Canada. Most of the larger states, including California and New York, are nonmonopoly states. The nonmonopoly states operate in a similar manner to the Australian system. In these states, the product can only enter the U.S. through a licensed importer, who, in turn, can only then sell to a wholesaler. A direct sale to the retailer or consumer level is not permitted. Importers' or agents' margins range from 10 percent to 25 percent of landed cost, wholesalers' around 15 percent to 30 percent and retailers' 30 percent to 40 percent.
- In 1968, the majority of table wines sold in the U.S. retailed in Asutralian dollars between $3.40 and $5.25 (69 percent), $5.26 and $7.10 (15 percent), and $7.11 and $9.26 (9 percent).

Primary source: Austrialian Wine and Brandy Corporation, *Export Market Grid.*

United Kingdom

The third market under consideration was the United Kingdom (Exhibit 8). In the past few years, per capita wine consumption in the United Kingdom had increased and stood at ten liters in 1985. A review of the U.K. wine market in 1986 noted that Australia had less than 2 percent of the table wine market.

The U.K. market was very competitive and extensive advertising, point-of-purchase displays, and price specials were used at the retail level to promote individual brands.

The major drawback for any exporter in developing the U.K. market was the potential threat that import regulations for wines might be changed. In the past France had engaged in certain activities that "changed the rules" resulting in a new set of regulations that disrupted the marketing activities of exporters to the EC.

Most of the larger and some of the medium-sized Australian wine producers had entered the export market by focusing first on the United Kingdom. For example, one of the largest Australian producers, Orlando Wines, had been very active in the United Kingdom. Orlando regarded the U.K. as an important market. As one executive of Orlando stated: "If you can be successful in the U.K., it will stand you in good stead in other export markets." Orlando had established its own company in the U.K. and the subsidiary performed the role of the importer. The export marketing manager visited the U.K. four times a year, spending two weeks on each visit. His main activities were to motivate the distributor of the company's brands and to discuss the brands with

EXHIBIT 8 Fact Sheet on the United Kingdom

- The U.K. consumption of wine has been increasing and all wine consumed in the U.K. is imported. The U.K. is a member of the EC.
- Import licenses can be easily obtained although there are major difficulties in complying with various EC requirements for import.
- Import duties on table wines entering the EC are £8.58 per hundred liters. It should be noted that wines entering the EC must exceed a minimum threshold price. Excise taxes in the U.K. are £0.980/liter on table wine. As well, a value added tax of 15 percent is placed on all products. As of June 1988, import duties in Australian dollars would be $0.20 per liter, excise taxes would be $2.23 per liter, and the value added tax would be $1.34 per liter.
- Considerable efforts are required to comply with EC standards with respect to certification, packaging, and labeling. In particular, an EC analysis certificate that describes the wine's characteristics including actual alcohol strength, total dry extract, total acidity, and residual sugar must be completed (the analysis can be done in Australia) and meet EC requirements.
- In 1985, the United Kingdom imported 580 million liters of wine, most of it from member countries of the EC.

Primary source: Australian Wine and Brandy Corporation, *Export Market Grid.*

wine writers, if possible. The distributor was a medium-sized wholesaler who sold to retail liquor chains, primarily in the London area. While no figures were available on Orlando's export sales it was estimated that in 1988, its sales into the U.K. market would be approximately 40,000 cases.

Orlando did some advertising in both consumer and trade magazines in the United Kingdom. In a recent issue of *Decanter* (a consumer magazine targeted at wine buffs) Orlando had a full-page ad emphasizing the quality of its brands and stated, "They [the two brands] compare beautifully with similar wines from France, yet only cost around half as much."

Another company that was actively involved in export marketing was Wolf Blass, a well-known medium-size producer of quality wines. In 1985, it set up distributorships with agents in both the United States and the United Kingdom. Wolf Blass was one of the few companies that received the same price of wine in both the domestic and export markets (in 1987, the average price received was approximately $65 per case). In selecting the distributors in both the U.S. and the U.K., Wolf Blass had decided on large agents to give them access to the markets they wanted. In 1987, Wolf Blass had sold a total of 50,000 cases in the export market, but it was not clear whether it had made any profits. Some experts felt that the money Wolf Blass invested to develop the export markets (estimated annual marketing expenditures for both major markets were $600,000) had been substantial and that no profits would be obtained for at least four years.

Preliminary Cost Data

Mr. Steen prepared some rough calculations on the costs of getting a case of wine to each of the three markets and what it might sell for at retail (Exhibit 9). With respect to costs of production, Mr. Steen had read a recent newspaper article on the costs of wine and was surprised at how close those costs were to those of the Barossa Winery. As shown in Exhibit 10, the production cost for a 750 mL bottle of good-quality Chardonnay was $3.02. By the time the consumer purchased it, the price was $11.08. While the cost of grapes

EXHIBIT 9 Estimated Retail Price of a Case of Barossa Wine in the Three Markets

	UNITED KINGDOM	UNITED STATES	CANADA
Barossa Winery price	$ 56.00	$ 56.00	$ 56.00
Transport to destination[1]	2.55	2.85	2.85
Landed cost	58.55	58.85	58.85
Import duties and excise tax[2]	21.90	1.60	26.90
Other taxes[2]	12.05	—	10.30
Landed cost with duties/taxes	92.50	60.45	96.05
Importer/agent margin[3]	27.75	9.10	9.60
Importer price	120.25	69.55	105.65
Wholesale margin[4]	—	13.90	—
Wholesale price	120.25	83.45	105.65
Retail margin[5]	60.15	29.20	64.75
Retail price	180.40	112.65	170.40
Bottle price (750 mL)	$ 15.00	$ 9.40	$ 14.20

Assumptions:

[1]It costs $347 to ship a container from the Barossa Valley to Port Adelaide. On average, a container holds 1,000 cases. One case contains 9 L or 12 bottles (750 mL). Port Adelaide to U.K. is $2,200 per container; to U.S. or Canada, approximately $2,500.

[2]Based on information in fact sheets.

[3]Importer margin in U.K. ranges from 25% to 40% of landed cost (assume 30% for estimation purposes); in U.S. range is 10% to 25% (assume 15%); in Canada agents average 10%.

[4]Wholesale margins in U.S. range from 15% to 30% (assume 20%).

[5]Retail margins in U.K. are about 50%; in U.S. from 30% to 40% (assume 35%); in Canada, range from 55% to 123% of landed cost (assume 110%).

for some of the other varieties of wines could be considerably less (for example, $600 per metric ton for Semillon), most of the price of a bottle of wine ($8.06 per the example) was made up of margins and taxes.

Mr. Steen also worked out some preliminary estimates of what it would cost to actively enter all three export markets. In terms of personnel, the cost of an export sales manager was about $60,000 and if the manager made six overseas trips a year, this expense would be about $100,000. One or two sales clerks might be required at a cost of $30,000 each. Preparation of custom requirements including documentation, obtaining label approvals, and sending samples could cost up to $30,000. Promotion costs were difficult to estimate, but they could exceed $100,000 for expenditures on wine tastings and shows for both the public and the trade, advertising expenditures for consumers and the trade, and public relations.

A portion of these expenditures could be recovered from the federal government through the Export Market Development Grant. Firms engaged in export marketing were eligible (for the first five years) to receive up to 70 percent of certain export costs including printing of special labels, preparation and printing of point-of-sale material, a portion of the cost of any personnel who were located in the export market, air travel, and a portion of accommodation expenses for managers visiting the export markets,

EXHIBIT 10 Typical Cost Structure of a Bottle/Case of Wine

	PER BOTTLE	PER CASE
Product*	$ 1.61	
Packaging	1.07	
Bottling	.22	
Transportation	.12	
Total production cost	3.02	$ 36.24
Manufacturer margin (50% of costs)	1.50	
Price to wholesaler	4.52	54.24
Wholesaler margin (25%)	1.13	
Wholesaler price before taxes	5.65	
Federal tax (20%)	1.13	
Wholesaler price after federal tax	6.78	
State tax (9%)	.61	
Wholesaler price after taxes	7.39	88.68
Retailer margin (50%)	3.69	
Retail price	11.08	132.96

*Based on premium Chardonnay fruit at a price per metric ton of $1,200. One metric ton will produce 744 bottles of 750 mL wine. A case contains 12 bottles (9 L).

samples, and expenses related to wine trade shows. While it was difficult to estimate the precise proportion of costs that would be recovered, depending on the type of expenditure, Barossa Winery could receive up to $100,000 each year.

Although the Barossa Winery had not aggressively pursued the export market, Mr. Steen was quick to capitalize on any export opportunity that was presented. For example, if a British importer expressed interest in any of the company's products, Mr. Steen, or a member of the marketing group, would provide free samples, information on the wines, and product availability. If an importer placed an order, Mr. Steen ensured that the order was shipped as quickly as possible with proper documentation. As Mr. Steen once joked to a colleague, "We may not go after the export business, but if anybody comes to us, we'll offer better service and support than any other winery in Australia."

Mr. Steen was pleased with the growth of exports in the past few years, but he was concerned about the tenuous nature of the business. While the export business had experienced steady growth, the source of sales often changed substantially on a yearly basis. For example, sales to the United Kingdom had been made through two different U.K. importers in the past three years. Between 1981 and 1984, Star Importers, a U.K. importer who specialized in Australian wines, had purchased up to 10,000 cases of Barossa Wines in a given year. In late 1984, Star Importers switched their major buying from Barossa to a competitive winery in New South Wales. In 1985, the Reid Company, another U.K. importer, began buying Barossa Wines and in 1987 purchased 18,000 cases for the U.K. market.

Similarly, the company had been approached in the past five years by six different United States importers. The Barossa Winery had conducted business with all six (sales in a given year to any one of the importers ranged from 400 to 4,500 cases) over the years and in 1987 sold a total 9,000 cases through four importers to the U.S. market. Two sales agents in Canada (who have been importing the product for about four years) had generated sales of about 800 cases in Ontario and Alberta. As well, the company had sold about 10,000 cases to the "rest of the world" through two Australian exporters. These two firms approached Australian wine producers and obtained products that they would sell to distributors at the wholesale or retail level in other countries. As far as Mr. Steen could tell the two exporters who sold Barossa Wines had most of their sales in New Zealand, Micronesia, and the Far East (for example, Japan, Taiwan, Thailand, Hong Kong).

Mr. Steen realized that the Barossa Winery did not have strong links with these importers or exporters in that no formal contracts were signed with any of them in terms of an exclusive agreement. In all cases, both parties were free to buy from or sell to anyone. Further, the company had little expertise in exporting as most of the work and all of the marketing was done by the importer or exporter. In the final analysis, Mr. Steen felt that the company's success to date had been a combination of good service, good prices, and good-quality wine.

The Decision

Having gathered the preliminary data, Mr. Steen began thinking about the report. He was not certain what he should recommend. On the one hand, export sales were growing with little effort and expense on the company's part. Possibly with a little more effort, sales could be increased without going "full speed ahead" into exporting. One the other hand, the tenuous nature of the company's relationship with its exporters and importers suggested that some action should be taken.

Mr. Steen knew that the senior management group was expecting a report that contained specific recommendations including whether the Barossa Winery should aggressively enter the export market and, if so, how many markets to enter. As well, the group would expect to receive details of the proposed strategy Mr. Steen would pursue for the next three years in the export area. With these thoughts in mind, Mr. Steen began writing the report.

Subject Index

Name and Company Index